LETTERS OF
ALDOUS HUXLEY

A [*Carcanet*] BOOK

BOOKS BY ALDOUS HUXLEY

NOVELS

Island
The Genius and the Goddess
Ape and Essence
Time Must Have a Stop
After Many a Summer Dies
  the Swan
Eyeless in Gaza
Point Counter Point
Those Barren Leaves
Antic Hay
Crome Yellow
Brave New World

ESSAYS AND
BELLES LETTRES

On Art and Artists
Collected Essays
Brave New World Revisited
Tomorrow and Tomorrow
  and Tomorrow
Heaven and Hell
The Doors of Perception
The Devils of Loudun
Themes and Variations
Ends and Means
Texts and Pretexts
The Olive Tree
Music at Night
Vulgarity in Literature
Do What You Will
Proper Studies
Jesting Pilate
Along the Road
On the Margin
Essays New and Old
The Art of Seeing
The Perennial Philosophy
Science, Liberty and Peace

SHORT STORIES

Collected Short Stories
Brief Candles
Two or Three Graces
Limbo
Little Mexican
Mortal Coils

BIOGRAPHY

Grey Eminence

POETRY

The Cicadas
Leda

TRAVEL

Beyond the Mexique Bay

DRAMA

Mortal Coils—A Play
The World of Light
The Discovery, adapted from
  Frances Sheridan

SELECTED WORKS

Rotunda
The World of Aldous Huxley
Letters of Aldous Huxley

Jay Bar

ALDOUS HUXLEY

LETTERS

OF

ALDOUS HUXLEY

EDITED BY

Grover Smith

1817

HARPER & ROW, PUBLISHERS
NEW YORK AND EVANSTON

The editor
in gratitude and admiration
dedicates this book to
JULIETTE

Contents

PREFACE

THE letters of Aldous Huxley form a kind of autobiography, like any such collection. They were written by a man of extraordinary intellect, who during his life, being constitutionally disinclined to devote himself to any single branch of art or science, acquired the mastery of many. They illustrate in profusion the analytic powers of the literary and social critic and the synthetic powers of the creative artist and idealist. If, as some psychologists have argued, intellectuality is proportionate to the ability to think analogically, the mind of Huxley was superior to a pitch beyond the average man's imagining. This trait may appear, as certain emotional hard edges in his writings have appeared to some, a little 'inhuman'. The truth is that reason and imagination only graduate man above the sub-human creation, man being the *thinking* animal. And, because by the same token he is the thinking *animal*, the qualities of gentleness which we honour as 'human' are part of the animal residuum. The virtuous emotions, equally with the savage ones, stem from the beasts. Huxley, who was a humorous man with strong physical emotions, always had a vivid sense of this connexion. His bias towards intellect, along with purely cultural habits, disposed him to rebel against the gross passions and to satirize them, but he was too affectionate to be coldly intellectual and too candid for intellectual pride. Living aware of man's duality, he made it a theme of his works; in effect it was something he enjoyed. Animal enjoyment of the human state pervades his letters. Though often tinged with a profound instinct to weep for life, it—and by no means the sadness of *lacrimae rerum*—is Huxley's hallmark. He must be recognized as one of the most human of men and letter-writers; and this was precisely because in his nature feeling was as highly developed as mind. Always in Huxley compassion and scorn, revulsion and tenderness, strove together and, as it were, through a dialectic of emotions regulated by intelligence, produced his multivalent attitude towards the world.

We cannot read Huxley's works of fiction and drama without meeting the scientific philosopher, nor his essays on men and ideas without meeting the artist. He was more interested in life than in art, and in art only as a function of life. Since the time of Coleridge, we have come to expect that the creative writer should be intensely concerned with the artistic vision. That was not Huxley's emphasis. He was first a student of man the physical and spiritual organism. In literature the element to which he attached the most importance and which he handled with the greatest skill was character. To him the supreme curiosity in the world was the individual. And he approached character as a scientist—a zoölogist, an anthropologist, a psychologist, a psychiatrist, a physician. Having specialized as none of these, he could, in contexts of art or theory, practise as all. The *casuistic* method employed in his essay on Maine de Biran and already adumbrated in *Do What You Will*—

the earlier work being a study of certain eminent individuals and their peculiarities, the later an analysis of the meaning of individuality in history —is implied in his fiction from its beginning. The dual personality in his 'Farcical History of Richard Greenow', the Baudelairean neurotic (Spandrell) in *Point Counter Point*, and the emotional parasite (Maartens) in *The Genius and the Goddess* are cases drawn from life. Elsewhere we find Huxley inventing cases to fit general hypotheses—psychological in the play 'Happy Families', technological and pharmacological in *Brave New World*, evolutionary in *After Many a Summer*, where he toys with Ludwig Bolk's foetal theory of the descent of man. His attraction to Vedanta and Buddhism was in large part that of a psychologist; and his presentations from the *Tibetan Book of the Dead* in *Time Must Have a Stop* and from the data of psychedelic research in *Heaven and Hell* were akin in their speculative origins. It must not be forgotten that Huxley was fundamentally a sceptic; from this cast of mind proceeded his satiric impulse, which never lay far beneath the surface of his approval. He was suspicious of beliefs as such, especially when they led men to extravagance of action. He lived to witness the transformation of the psychedelic movement into a dangerous enthusiasm, so that he derided and deplored it. It was a foible of his that although he never really expected the rest of mankind to be as cautious and temperate as himself, he was irked by their follies.

As an artist Huxley started with the fascinations of idiosyncrasy; as a philosopher he ended by affirming, quite undogmatically, the value of private visionary truth. Both attentions were rooted in the conviction that, finally, individual experience had to be the test of everything. He saw all men as unique and complex. In his philosophy of society he stood with Jefferson. Whatever infringed upon human uniqueness, such as an ideology, political or religious, that won allegiance at the cost of individual function and experience, or a symbolism that at like cost interpreted reality, would provoke his antipathies. So likewise would any therapy, medical or social, that ignored individual complexity and neglected to minister to the 'mind-body' at all levels. He never so concentrated on theory as to abandon his art; and though his later novels suffered from the competing pressure of other enterprises, he grew ever more brilliant as an analyst of character. Of this fact there is ample evidence in his letters on dramatic writing, for example those to Shepard Traube, Joseph Anthony, and John Whiting.

Huxley's letters collectively reveal him experiencing, thinking, and becoming, all the while marvelling at the strangeness of existence and discovering new richness in human relationships. Some men affect always to know where they are going; Huxley in his exploratory wisdom refused to be sure. As with his favourite Micawber, something would always turn up—not to rescue a life bogged down in improvidence, for such was not Huxley's, but to stimulate a life receptive to fresh motivations. His life, like his writings, was constantly improvising. Its graces were its rewards—stoical good humour, enquiring genius, and deep but uneffusive affections.

In his sixty-nine years Huxley perhaps wrote at the very least ten thousand letters. I have had the opportunity of examining more than twenty-five hundred, about half of which are business letters and minor notes. The present compilation represents therefore a choice of fewer than two-fifths of the known items. Predominating here is material selected for its biographical, literary, or philosophical qualities. There are some gaps. All but one of Huxley's letters to his brother Trevenen have disappeared, having presumably been thrown away after the latter's death. A disastrous fire which in 1961 consumed Huxley's house in Los Angeles destroyed not only his files of manuscripts but any letters to his first wife, Maria Nys Huxley. That collection was of undetermined size but was probably large; its loss must be deeply regretted. The same fate befell the earliest of his letters to his second wife, Mrs Laura Archera Huxley. A sampling, however, of his later correspondence with her has been published in her book *This Timeless Moment* (1968), and is not reprinted here. His letters to Lady Ottoline Morrell, exclusive of one item belonging to the University of Texas, have been held back by their present owner. The same is true of all of his letters to Mrs Mary Hutchinson. Fortunately a number of important collections have generously been made available. The most valuable of these, comprising the letters to Leonard Huxley, Sir Julian and Lady Huxley, Mr Matthew Huxley, Mrs Ellen Giffard, Mr Gervas Huxley, Lady Mitchison (Naomi Mitchison), Dr Humphry Osmond, Mrs Kethevan Roberts, Mrs Beth Wendel, Mme Victoria Ocampo, Robert Nichols, Lewis Gielgud, Huxley's English and American publishers, and his literary agents James B. Pinker and Sons, form the essential structure of an assemblage which contains also several minor collections and a large variety of miscellaneous pieces. The names of other correspondents here, such as D. H. Lawrence and Frieda (Ravagli), Arnold Bennett, the Honourable Dorothy Brett, Norman Douglas, Edwin Hubble, Anita Loos, Christopher Isherwood, Paul Valéry, T. S. Eliot, and Alan Watts, indicate the catholicity of the associations which may be traced through this volume.

All of the letters included have been prepared for the press personally. For the majority I have been able to work from the originals or from photographic copies. For a few I have followed carbon copies of the originals; these are identified. Three letters, including the two to Hermann Broch, have been derived solely from printed sources in the absence of manuscripts; any others previously printed, as, notably, those appearing in *Aldous Huxley: A Memorial Volume* (1965), edited by Sir Julian Huxley, have been checked against the originals. Letters 811 and 882 both result from conflation, the former being based on two slightly different versions provided by the same person, the latter on copies made by two different people. A dagger (†) placed at the head of any letter here means that I have been unable to examine the text as executed by Huxley and have had to rely on someone else's transcription.

Many of the letters, from the year 1912 onward, were typewritten; this is true of most of those to Sir Julian Huxley and it is generally true of the longest ones, though of comparatively few to Huxley's father, Leonard Huxley. Mostly, those no longer than two or three hundred words were written in rapid but clear and often beautiful longhand. Until his final illness Huxley appears to have dictated none. His punctuation was normal and was reasonably good even in his childhood; it has been kept unaltered with minor exceptions. In respect of this there are trivial differences between the typewritten and the holograph letters. In his youth, especially during his Oxford period, he commonly used dashes for commas when writing by hand; similarly he often used suspension points (. . .) in place of commas or final stops when typewriting. Both of these specialities are preserved, but suspension points are regularized in number in accordance with usual printing practice. Sometimes he would fail to insert a closing mark of parenthesis. In each instance of this kind I have repaired the omission according to the sense of the passage. Elsewhere I have occasionally added or shifted an apostrophe. Huxley's style in designating literary titles was unsystematic: he would frequently quote book titles in the Continental fashion, with lower-case instead of capital letters; he would sometimes underline and sometimes not; and sometimes he would employ inverted commas, which might be either single or double and might even be combined with underlining. All of this has been reduced to a conventional system. His careful spelling has lightened one labour. Childhood misspellings have been reproduced here; many minor slips have been silently corrected, particularly when due to hasty typewriting; other errors, as with proper names often, have been emended with insertions in brackets. The ampersand, a purely graphic device which Huxley used with abundance in handwritten letters, has not been retained. Brackets, which Huxley himself practically never used, have been brought in to show major editorial changes and all editorial insertions, such as dates for undated letters. They have also been used with dashes, thus [——], to show the editorial suppression of names, and with suspension points, thus, [. . .] or [. . . .], to show that other matter has been left out. In the majority of cases, omitted matter is simply repetitious or unimportant; in some few cases, its publication might have given offence to living people.

Some of the undated letters have been difficult to place, but where a definite date is supplied in brackets it may be regarded as correct. A great deal of external evidence has been consulted to ensure accuracy in this respect. Most of the undated early letters addressed to Leonard Huxley were at some time dated by him, probably from postmarks. A slight margin of error must be allowed for where these letters are concerned, since they need not have been posted on the day of writing. A very few letters are found to have been misdated by Huxley himself. His usual style of dating, especially in handwritten letters, took the form '20.iv.54'; but in his later typewritten letters the name of the month is ordinarily written out, always preceding the day. A uniform style has been adopted here, in the certainty that it facilitates references.

English translations have been subjoined to Huxley's letters in French. I make no literary claims for these versions, which in everything but a few minute details are of my own making, except that they convey the sense of the original. In presenting a small selection of letters by Maria Nys Huxley, I have silently modified her punctuation and, where necessary, her spelling. She often wrote on a typewriter, but otherwise in a handwriting extremely hard to decipher, with a multitude of dashes in both the right and the wrong places. Her fine sensibility would be unfairly obscured if all the merely mechanical imperfections of her letters were put on display.

GROVER SMITH

Durham, North Carolina,
16 October, 1968.

ACKNOWLEDGMENTS

I gratefully acknowledge the generosity of everyone who has provided me with material for this book. The letters included in it have come from the following sources:

Letters to *Charles Abbott*, Lockwood Memorial Library, State University of New York, Buffalo; to *Richard Aldington*, University of Texas Libraries; to *Frederick L. Allen*, Library of Congress; to *Rita Allen*, Mrs Beth Wendel; to *Joseph Anthony*, Mrs Beth Wendel; to *Jelly d'Aranyi*, Mme D'Aranyi; to *Edward C. Aswell*, Harper & Row, Inc.; to *John Atkins*, Mr Leon Drucker; to *Clifford Bax*, University of Texas Libraries; to *Sybille Bedford*, Mrs Bedford; to *Max Beerbohm*, Mrs Eva G. Reichmann; to *Clive Bell*, Mr Quentin Bell; to *Arnold Bennett*, Mr Goodwin G. Weinberg; to *Hubert Benoit*, M. Benoit; to *Leonard Bernstein*, Mr Bernstein; to *Ludwig von Bertalanffy*, Dr Von Bertalanffy; to *Simon Michael Bessie*, Harper & Row, Inc.; to *Cyril Bibby*, Mr Bibby; to *Alberto Bonnoli*, Library of Congress; to *Marian Elizabeth Bremer*, Mrs Bremer; to the *Honourable Dorothy Brett*, Yale University Library (No. 327) and University of Texas Libraries (all others); to *Hermann Broch*, Mr H. F. Broch de Rothermann and Suhrkamp Verlag, Frankfurt am Main; to *Anthony Brooke*, Lady Huxley and Mr Timothy Leary; to *B. G. Brooks*, Dr Brooks; to *György Buday*, Mr Buday; to *Joan Collier Buzzard*, Mrs Buzzard; to *Henry S. Canby*, Yale University Library; to *Cass Canfield*, Mr Canfield and Harper & Row, Inc.; to *Dorothy Carrington*, University of Texas Libraries; to *Catherine Carswell*, Mr Harry T. Moore; to *Olivia de Haulleville Cassapidis*, Mme Cassapidis; to *Hannah Closs*, Mr August Closs; to *Constance Collier*, Mr Goodwin G. Weinberg; to *Ethel Huxley Collier*, Mrs Joan Buzzard; to *Cyril Connolly*, University of Texas Libraries; to *Helen Corke*, University of Texas Libraries; to *Jeffreys Corner*, Mrs Corner; to *Robert Craft*, Mr Craft; to *Colin Craigie*, Mr Craigie; to *Allan J. Crane*, Mr Crane; to *Jo Davidson*, Library of Congress; to *C. Day Lewis*, Library of the University of California at Los Angeles; to *George B. Doran*, Mr Goodwin G. Weinberg; to *Norman Douglas*, Mr Kenneth Macpherson; to *Nathan Dubin*, Dr Dubin; to *Philippe Dumaine*, M. Dumaine; to *T. W. H. Eckersley*, Mr Eckersley; to *T. S. Eliot*, Mrs Valerie Eliot; to *Claire John Eschelbach*, Mr Eschelbach; to *George H. Estabrooks*, Colgate University Library (No. 869) and Mr Estabrooks (all others); to *Howard Fabing*, Dr Humphry Osmond; to *Roy Fenton*, Mr Fenton; to 'the Finder', Sir Julian Huxley; to *Ellen Fitch*, Mrs Fitch; to *Ossip K. Flechtheim*, Dr Flechtheim; to *E. M. Forster*, Mr Forster; to *Reid Gardner*, Mr Gardner; to *Eileen J. Garrett*, Mrs Garrett; to *Mark Gertler*, Mr Luke Gertler; to *Kate Terry Lewis Gielgud*, Mr Goodwin G. Weinberg; to *Lewis Gielgud*, Mrs Zita Gielgud Sutton and Miss Maina Gielgud; to *Douglas Glass*, Henry W. and Albert A. Berg Collection of The New York Public Library,

Astor, Lenox and Tilden Foundations; to *Roger and Alice Godel*, Mme Godel; to *Russell Green*, Mr Green; to *Sally Handley*, Major Leonard Handley; to *Jean E. Hare*, Mrs Jean Heywood; to *Allanah Harper (Statlender)*, Mrs Sybille Bedford; to *Helen Harvey*, Mrs Beth Wendel (No. 728) and Mr Matthew Huxley (No. 783); to *Rose Nys de Haulleville (Wessberg)*, Mme de Haulleville; to *Carolyn Hawley*, Mrs Hawley; to *E. S. P. Haynes*, Mr Crispin Tickell (Nos. 203, 269, 441), Mrs Renée Tickell (No. 218), and Library of the University of California at Los Angeles (No. 495); to *James Hepburn*, Mr Hepburn; to *Miss Hepworth and Mr Green*, Mr Goodwin G. Weinberg; to *Eva Herrmann*, Miss Herrmann; to *John Hersey*, Mr Hersey; to *Albert Hofmann*, Dr Hofmann; to *Camille R. Honig*, Mr Honig and Mr Goodwin G. Weinberg; to *Edwin and Grace Hubble*, Mrs Hubble and the Henry E. Huntington Library; to *Robert M. Hutchins*, Mr Hutchins; to *Gervas Huxley*, Mr Gervas Huxley; to *Henrietta Heathorn Huxley*, Mrs Rosalind Huxley; to *Sir Julian Huxley*, Sir Julian; to *Lady Huxley (Juliette Baillot)*, Lady Huxley; to *Leonard and Rosalind Huxley*, Mrs Rosalind Huxley; to *Mark Trevenen Huxley*, Mr Mark Trevenen Huxley; to *Matthew Huxley and Ellen Huxley Giffard*, Mrs Giffard (Nos. 626, 629, 652, 653, 663, 665, 674, 682, 692, 723, 726, 738, 742, 746, 757, 761, 763, 769, 791, 794, 799, 805, 806, 831, 928, 940) and Mr Matthew Huxley (all others); to *Matthew and Judith Huxley*, Mr and Mrs Matthew Huxley; to *Noel Trevenen Huxley*, Mrs Rosalind Huxley; to *Teresa Huxley*, Miss Huxley; to *Christopher Isherwood*, Mr Isherwood; to *Margaret Isherwood*, Miss Isherwood; to *Oscar Janiger*, Dr Janiger; to *C. E. M. Joad*, University of Texas Libraries; to *Lucille Kahn*, Mrs Kahn; to *E. McKnight Kauffer*, Pierpont Morgan Library; to *Nancy Kelly*, Mrs Beth Wendel; to *James G. Kennedy*, Mr Kennedy; to *Max Kester*, Mrs Laura Huxley and Mrs Beth Wendel; to *Carlyle King*, Mr King; to *William and Margaret Kiskadden*, Mrs Kiskadden; to *Herbert Klemmer*, Dr Klemmer and the Menninger Foundation; to *Scudder Klyce*, Library of Congress; to *G. Wilson Knight*, University of Houston Library; to *Krishna Kripalani*, Chatto and Windus, Ltd; to *Heinz Kusel*, Mr Kusel; to *Peggy Lamson*, Mr Roy Lamson; to *Myrick Land*, Mr Land and Berg Collection, New York Public Library; to *D. H. Lawrence*, Berg Collection, New York Public Library (No. 282) and University of Virginia Library (No. 302); to *Timothy Leary*, Mr Leary; to *Florence A. Leonard*, Mrs Leonard; to *Seymour Leslie*, Berg Collection, New York Public Library; to *Leon M. Lion*, Sir Julian Huxley (No. 487) and Mr Mark Haymon (No. 535); to *Anita Loos*, Miss Loos; to *Mabel Dodge Luhan*, Yale University Library; to *Thomas H. McCormack, Jr*, Mr and Mrs McCormack, to *Mary McEldowney*, Mrs Mary McEldowney Hupfel; to *Felix Mann*, Dr Mann; to *Klaus Mann and Thomas Mann*, Miss Erika Mann; to *Edward Marsh*, Berg Collection, New York Public Library; to *Kingsley Martin*, Sir Julian Huxley; to *H. L. Mencken*, Enoch Pratt Free Library; to *Thomas Merton*, the late Fr Merton and Sr M. Thérèse; to *Henry Miller*, Library of the University of California

7

at Los Angeles; to *Naomi Haldane Mitchison*, Lady Mitchison; to *Harold Monro*, Lockwood Memorial Library, State University of New York, Buffalo (No 170) and University of Texas Libraries (No. 172); to *Christopher Morley*, University of Texas Libraries; to *Lady Ottoline Morrell*, University of Texas Libraries; to *A. W. and Elise Murrell*, Mrs Murrell; to *John Middleton Murry*, Mrs Mary Murry and University of Texas Libraries; to *Mary Murry*, Mrs Murry; to *Howard Nelson*, Mme Sylvia Nicolas de Semprun; to *Georges and Jeanne Nys Neveux*, M. and Mme Neveux; to *Noële Neveux*, Mlle Neveux; to *Marianna Schauer Newton*, Mrs Newton; to *Robert Nichols*, Berg Collection, New York Public Library (Nos. 326, 359, 408) and University of Houston Library (all others); to *Joep and Suzanne Nys Nicolas*, M. and Mme Nicolas; to the *Vicomte de Noailles*, M. le Vicomte; to *Miss Noon*, Sir Julian Huxley; to *E. E. A. Norris*, Mr Norris and Mr Ronald W. Clark; to *Victoria Ocampo*, Mme Ocampo; to *George Orwell*, Library of University College, London; to *Fairfield Osborn*, Mr Osborn; to *Daniel T. O'Shea*, Mrs Anne W. Geller; to *Humphry Osmond*, Dr Osmond; to *Violet Paget*, Colby College Library; to *Ian Parsons*, Mr Parsons and Chatto and Windus, Ltd; to *Frances Petersen*, Mrs Frances Petersen Zuccaro (Nos. 94, 97, 98) and Berg Collection, New York Public Library (all others); to *Maria Petrie*, Mrs Petrie; to *Josephine Piercy*, Miss Piercy and Indiana University Library; to *James B. Pinker and Sons*, Berg Collection, New York Public Library (No. 434) and University of Texas Libraries (all others); to *Lawrence C. Powell*, Library of the University of California at Los Angeles; to *Swami Prabhavananda*, Swami Prabhavananda; to *C. H. C. Prentice*, Chatto and Windus, Ltd; to *J. B. Priestley*, University of Texas Libraries; to *Bertha L. Prouty*, Mrs Prouty; to *Jean Queval*, M. Queval; to *Frieda Lawrence Ravagli*, Berg Collection, New York Public Library (No. 310) and University of Texas Libraries (all others); to *Harold Raymond*, Mr Raymond and Chatto and Windus, Ltd; to *Piers Raymond*, Chatto and Windus, Ltd; to *J. B. Rhine*, Mr Rhine; to *Kethevan Roberts*, Mrs Roberts; to *G. Gidley Robinson*, University of Texas Libraries; to *Ned Rorem*, Mr Rorem; to *Ralph Rose*, University of Texas Libraries; to *Sanford Roth*, Mrs Beulah Roth; to *William Rothenstein*, Harvard College Library, Harvard University; to *Dilip Kumar Roy*, Mr K. D. Sethna; to *Naomi Royde-Smith*, University of Texas Libraries; to *Henry E. Ryland*, Mr Ryland; to the *Honourable Edward Sackville-West*, the late Baron Sackville; to *N. Sagar*, University of Texas Libraries; to *Eugene F. Saxton*, Harper & Row, Inc.; to *Martha Saxton*, Mr Mark Saxton; to *Martin Secker*, Berg Collection, New York Public Library; to *George Seldes*, Mr Seldes; to *Gordon Sewell*, Mr Sewell; to *William H. Sheldon*, Dr Sheldon; to *H. R. L. Sheppard*, Berg Collection, New York Public Library; to *Clement K. Shorter*, Mr Goodwin G. Weinberg; to *Solomon Simonson*, Mr Simonson; to *Maharaja Dr Karan Singh, of Jammu and Kashmir*, H. H. the Maharaja; to *Edith Sitwell*, Mrs Beulah Roth; to *Grover Smith*, the editor; to *J. C. Squire*, University of Texas Libraries

(No. 143) and Berg Collection, New York Public Library (No. 160); to *Edith A. Standen*, Miss Standen; to *Barry Stevens*, Mrs Stevens; to *Lytton Strachey*, the late Mr James Strachey and the editor; to *Heinrich Straumann*, Herr Straumann; to *Igor Stravinsky*, Mr Stravinsky; to *Anne Strick*, Mrs Strick; to *Flora Strousse*, Mrs Strousse; to *Ernest W. Tedlock, Jr*, Mr Tedlock; to *Renée Tickell*, Mrs Tickell; to *Edward Titus*, University of Texas Libraries; to *Shepard Traube*, Manuscript Division, New York Public Library; to *Paul Valéry*, Mme Julien Cain; to *John van Druten*, Library and Museum of the Performing Arts, New York Public Library; to *Alan Watts*, Mr Watts; to *H. G. Wells*, University of Illinois Library; to *Beth Wendel*, Mrs Wendel; to *Sigfrid Wessberg*, Mr Wessberg; to *Claire Nicolas White*, Mrs White; to *Victor F. White*, Mr White; to *John Whiting*, Mr A. D. Peters and Mrs John Whiting; to *George Wickes*, Mr Wickes; to *Charles Wilson*, Berg Collection, New York Public Library; to *Leonard Woolf*, Mr Woolf; to *Elinor Wylie*, Yale University Library; to *Philip Wylie*, Mr Wylie and Princeton University Library; to *John Yale*, Swami Prabhavananda; to *Jacob I. Zeitlin*, Library of the University of California at Los Angeles.

Letters of Maria Nys Huxley, from the collections of Mr Roy Fenton, Mrs Ellen Giffard, Harper & Row, Inc., Sir Julian and Lady Huxley, Mrs Rosalind Huxley, Miss Anita Loos, Mrs Elise Murrell, and Dr Humphry Osmond, are printed by permission of Mr Matthew Huxley. A letter of Julia Arnold Huxley is printed by permission of Sir Julian Huxley. Quotations from letters of Mrs Laura Archera Huxley, Mr Matthew Huxley, and Dr Humphry Osmond are made by permission of the writers.

I wish to thank all of those who have supplied me with information about letters in their possession, in particular Mrs Beth Wendel, Sir Julian and Lady Huxley, Mr Gervas Huxley, Mr and Mrs Matthew Huxley, Lady Mitchison, Mrs Ellen Giffard, Mrs Margaret Kiskadden, Mr Christopher Isherwood, Mrs Joan Buzzard, Dr Humphry Osmond, Miss Anita Loos, Mme Victoria Ocampo, Mrs Marianna Newton, Mme Jeanne Neveux, Mme Suzanne Nicolas, Mme Rose de Haulleville, and Mrs Kethevan Roberts. For other information or assistance I am obliged to Mrs Barbara Hiles Bagenal, Mrs Sybille Bedford, Mr Samuel N. Behrman, Miss Eileen Bowser, the Honourable Dorothy Brett, Mr John C. Broderick, Mr Richard Burkett, Sir George Clark, Mr Ronald W. Clark, Mrs Pamela Diamand, Mr Val Gielgud, the late Mr John D. Gordan, Mr Duncan Grant, Mr Russell Green, Mr L. P. Hartley, Mrs Mary M. Hirth, Mr Charles Gouverneur Hoffman, Mr Charles M. Holmes, Mr David Huxley, Mr Max Kester, Mrs Joyce Kilburn, Mr N. C. Kittermaster, Mr Seymour Leslie, Mr Carter Lodge, Dr Marjorie K. McCorquodale, Mr Allen Macduff, Mr Elgin W. Mellown, Jr, Mrs Mary Moorman, Mr Laurence Pollinger, Mr H. K. Prescot, Mrs Marian Rolland, Mr C. Richard Sanders, Mrs Alix Strachey, Mrs Zita Sutton, Mr Crispin Tickell, Mr Goodwin G. Weinberg, and Mme Sophie Welling.

In gathering material for this book, I have been assisted with research grants from the Duke University Council on Research, the American Council of Learned Societies, and the Penrose Fund of the American Philosophical Society. In the editing, I have benefited at many points from the good counsels of my wife, Barbara, and at all times from her encouragement.

CHRONOLOGY

1894   26 July: Aldous Leonard Huxley, the third son of Leonard and Julia Arnold Huxley, is born at 'new' Laleham, the house recently occupied by his parents near the Charterhouse School, Godalming, Surrey.

1899   December: birth of Margaret Arnold Huxley.

1901   The family move to Julia Huxley's school, Prior's Field, in Godalming.

1903   Along with his cousin Gervas Huxley, H. becomes a pupil at Hillside. Friendship with Lewis Gielgud.

1908   August: holiday at Chamonix, Haute-Savoie.
September: H. enters Eton, where he expects to specialize in biology.
November: death of Julia Huxley.

1909   Leonard Huxley moves to 27 Westbourne Square, W.2. His younger children spend their holidays with relatives; Aldous, mainly with his aunt Mrs Humphry Ward, at Tring.
April: H. goes on holiday to Lake Como.

1910   Autumn: H. undergoes an attack of *keratitis punctata*, causing blindness and necessitating his withdrawal from Eton. He is sent to stay with the Selwyns at Hindhead and with other relatives.

1911   H. writes his first novel, afterwards lost. He is tutored by George Clark. He partially recovers his sight after surgery.

1912   Spring: H. is at Marburg through June, studying German and music.

1913   H. attends lectures at the University of London and at Oxford.
April: H. and his brother Trev help perform Naomi Haldane's play *Saunes Bairos* in Oxford.
July-August: holiday with Lewis Gielgud at La Tronche.
October: H. enters Balliol and prepares for Pass Moderations, attending lectures of Sir Walter Raleigh.

1914   February: completion of P. Mods.
March: publication of 'A Lunndon Mountaineering Essay' in the *Climbers' Club Journal*.
August: holiday with Julian Huxley at Connel, Argyll. Suicide of Trev Huxley at Reigate.
October: H. returns to Oxford and lodges with the Haldane family at Cherwell.
December: H. passes the Examination in Holy Scripture ('Divvers'), which he has previously failed.

1915   Studies of French poetry. H. composes imitations of Mallarmé. His Byronic poem on Glastonbury fails to gain the Newdigate Prize. Composition of 'Mole'.
October: return to rooms in Balliol. Friendships with Frances Petersen, T. W. Earp, H. C. Harwood, Robert Nichols, and Russell Green.

December: visit to Philip and Lady Ottoline Morrell at Garsington Manor; meeting with Juliette Baillot and with his future wife, Maria Nys. Visits to D. H. and Frieda Lawrence in Hampstead.

1916   January: H. is classified as physically unfit for military duty.

February: publication of *The Palatine Review*, containing 'Mole'.

June: Schools Examinations; H. receives a First in English Literature. He is awarded the Stanhope Historical Essay Prize. Editor, with W. R. Childe and T. W. Earp, of *Oxford Poetry 1916*.

July: temporary teaching post at Repton.

August: three poems published in *Nation*. Summer holiday at Garsington Manor. Friendship with Dorothy Carrington.

September: *The Burning Wheel*. Beginning of eight-month stay at Garsington. Friendships with J. Middleton Murry, Katherine Mansfield, the Honourable Dorothy Brett, and Bertrand Russell. Courtship of Maria Nys.

1917   January: departure of Maria Nys for Florence. Book reviews by H. appear in the *New Statesman*.

April-July: job with the Air Board. Friendships with T. S. Eliot, the Sitwells, Raymond Mortimer, Mary Hutchinson, Clive Bell, Viola Tree, and the Honourable Evan Morgan. Nine poems accepted for *Wheels, 1917*.

September: teaching post at Eton (until February, 1919).

December: *Jonah*.

1918   February: H. writes 'Leda' (completed, Part I only, in January, 1919).

July: composition of 'Happily Ever After' in dramatic form.

August: *The Defeat of Youth*.

October: composition of 'Happy Families'.

November: composition of 'Farcical History of Richard Greenow'.

1919   March: marriage of Julian Huxley to Juliette Baillot.

April: H. visits the Baltus and Nys families at St. Trond, Belgium. On returning to London, he joins the editorial staff of the *Athenaeum*.

June: H. moves into the flat at 18 Hampstead Hill Gardens, N.W.3.

10 July: H. is married to Maria Nys at Bellem.

November: friendship with Arnold Bennett.

1920   January: holiday in Paris.

February: *Limbo*.

April: birth of Matthew Huxley. H. becomes the dramatic critic for the *Westminster Gazette*. He has completed 'Permutations among the Nightingales' and the lost play 'Red and White'.

May: *Leda*.

May-July: part-time job with the Chelsea Book Club.

October: H. begins work for Condé Nast on *House and Garden*.

December: dramatic collaboration with Lewis Gielgud during Paris visit.

1921 January-March: H. lodges with T. W. Earp and Russell Green at 36 Regent Square, W.C.1.

March-May: the Huxleys occupy a flat in Florence.

May: J. B. Pinker becomes H.'s agent and sells 'The Gioconda Smile' to the *English Review*.

May-September: summer at Forte dei Marmi, where H. writes *Crome Yellow*.

September: the Huxleys return to London and occupy the flat at 155 Westbourne Terrace, W.2. H. resumes work for Condé Nast (until the summer of 1923).

November: *Crome Yellow*.

1922 May: *Mortal Coils*.

August-September: holiday at Forte dei Marmi.

1923 January: the Huxleys occupy the flat at 44 Prince's Gardens, S.W.7.

April: holiday in Florence.

May: *On the Margin*.

June-July: summer in Siena and at Forte dei Marmi, where H. writes *Antic Hay*.

August: the Huxleys move into the house at 15 Via Santa Margherita a Montici, Florence (until June, 1925).

November: *Antic Hay*.

1924 April-October: composition of *Those Barren Leaves*.

May: *Little Mexican*.

June: *The Discovery*.

July-August: holiday at Forte dei Marmi and in Paris.

September: visit to London.

November: trip to Rome and the south of Italy.

1925 January: *Those Barren Leaves*.

March-April: holiday in Tunisia.

July-September: visits to London, Belgium, and Paris.

September: *Along the Road*.

September: round-the-world journey to India, the Straits Settlements, Java, Hong Kong, and the United States (until June, 1926). H. writes *Jesting Pilate*.

1926 May: *Two or Three Graces*. Friendship with Anita Loos.

August: the Huxleys occupy a villa at Cortina in the Dolomites.

October: *Jesting Pilate*. Friendship with D. H. Lawrence, whom H. meets in Florence.

December: *Essays New and Old*.

1927 January: *Point Counter Point* in progress.

March-May: visits to Belgium and England.

May-December: the Huxleys occupy the Villa Majetta, Forte dei Marmi.

June: visit of Lawrence to Forte.

November: *Proper Studies.*

1928   January-February: winter holiday with the Julian Huxleys and the Lawrences at Les Diablerets.

March-May: visit to London.

June-September: summer at Forte dei Marmi.

October: *Point Counter Point.*

October: the Huxleys occupy the house at 3 rue du Bac, Suresnes (until April, 1930).

1929   January: friendship with Gerald Heard.

February: motor trip to Florence.

April: visits to Spain and England.

May: *Arabia Infelix.*

June-September: summer at Forte dei Marmi. Visit by Lawrence.

July: visit to Montecatini with Pino Orioli.

October: *Do What You Will.*

October-November: motor tour of Spain.

1930   January: production in London of *This Way to Paradise.*

March: death of Lawrence at Vence.

April: the Huxleys occupy the house at La Gorguette, Sanary (until February, 1937).

May: *Brief Candles.*

September-October: visit to England and the Durham coal fields, trip to Berlin with J. W. N. Sullivan.

December: *Vulgarity in Literature.*

1931   January-March: winter in London.

March: death of Arnold Bennett. Production in London of *The World of Light.*

April: *The World of Light.*

May: *The Cicadas.*

May-August: H. writes *Brave New World.*

September: *Music at Night.*

September-December: visit to London. Friendship with Victoria Ocampo.

1932   January: return to Sanary. *Brave New World.*

May: visits to Germany and Belgium. Private dinner with the royal family of the Belgians. *T. H. Huxley as a Man of Letters.*

June: return to Sanary. *Rotunda.*

July-November: H. writes the lost play 'Now More Than Ever'.

September: *The Letters of D. H. Lawrence.*

November: *Texts and Pretexts.* H. begins *Eyeless in Gaza* (completed in March, 1936).

December: visit to London.

1933   January-May: journey to the West Indies, Venezuela, Guatemala, Mexico, and the United States. H. begins *Beyond the Mexique Bay*.
May: death of Leonard Huxley.
June: return to Sanary.
July: H. resumes work on *Eyeless in Gaza*.
December: *Retrospect*.

1934   March-April: holiday in Italy.
April: *Beyond the Mexique Bay*.
April-September: summer at Sanary.
September: winter in London (until March, 1935).
Ca. November: H. suffers from insomnia and depression, by which he is increasingly disabled for the next year.

1935   January: trip to Paris.
March: return to Sanary.
June: H. attends a writers' congress in Paris.
October: winter in London (until March, 1936). H. is treated by F. M. Alexander. Restoration to health and completion of *Eyeless in Gaza*.
H. becomes active in the pacifist movement.

1936   April: *What Are You Going to Do about It?*
March-September: spring and summer at Sanary.
July: *Eyeless in Gaza*.
September-December: visits to Belgium, Holland, and England.
December: *The Olive Tree*.

1937   February-March: the Huxleys visit Paris and London before leaving for America.
April: voyage to the United States, tour of the South and Southwest in April and May. Friendship with J. B. Rhine.
May-September: summer on Frieda Lawrence's ranch at San Cristobal, New Mexico.
July: *An Encyclopaedia of Pacifism*.
August: friendship with Jacob I. Zeitlin.
September-November: in Hollywood at 1425½ N. Crescent Heights Boulevard.
October: friendships with Edwin Hubble, Paulette Goddard, and Charles Chaplin.
November: *Ends and Means*. H. goes on a lecture tour with Gerald Heard, continuing it alone (until January, 1938) after Heard breaks his leg in Iowa.
December: friendship with W. H. Sheldon. The Huxleys spend holidays at Rhinebeck, New York.

1938   Late January: the Huxleys return to Hollywood, occupying the house at 1340 N. Laurel Avenue.

February-March: severe illness of H., followed by a relapse in May.
April: H. begins a novel, never completed.
July: summer at 710 N. Linden Drive, Beverly Hills. H. contracts to write a film script on the life of Madame Curie for Metro-Goldwyn-Mayer.
September: Matthew Huxley enters the University of Colorado. The Huxleys occupy the house at 1320 N. Crescent Heights Boulevard, Hollywood.

1939   February-July: H. writes *After Many a Summer*.
April: the Huxleys move to 701 S. Amalfi Drive, Pacific Palisades (until February, 1942).
Spring: H. begins following the Bates Method for training the eyes.
Summer: friendship with Christopher Isherwood.
August: H. works on the film script of *Pride and Prejudice* for Metro-Goldwyn-Mayer (until January, 1940).
October: *After Many a Summer*.
November: Maria's niece Sophie Moulaert comes to live with the Huxleys.

1940   February: H. collects material for a Utopian novel, never completed.
August: H. begins *Grey Eminence* (completed in May, 1941).

1941   Summer: H. works on the film script of *Jane Eyre* for Twentieth Century-Fox (until April, 1942).
October: *Grey Eminence*.
November: H. begins *Time Must Have a Stop* (completed in February, 1944).

1942   February: the Huxleys acquire and occupy a house at Llano, California.
April-July: H. writes *The Art of Seeing*.
October: *The Art of Seeing*.

1943   Summer: long visit to Trabuco College. H. suffers from a severe skin allergy.
Ca. September: the Huxleys move temporarily into the flat at 145½ S. Doheny Drive, Los Angeles (until *ca.* February, 1944).

1944   February: return to Llano.
H. collects material for *The Perennial Philosophy* (until March, 1945).
August: *Time Must Have a Stop*.

1945   September: *The Perennial Philosophy*. H. writes *Science, Liberty and Peace*.
October: discussion of plans for a film of *Brave New World*, never produced.

1946   March: *Science, Liberty and Peace*.
Spring: H. begins compiling an anthology of essays commissioned by *The Encyclopaedia Britannica*, not published.
June: acquisition of the house at Wrightwood, California.

July-October: H. works on the film script of *The Gioconda Smile* for Universal.

September: plans for an historical novel about St Catherine of Siena, never completed.

October: H. begins writing the stage version of *The Gioconda Smile*.

November: the Huxleys move to Wrightwood (until summer, 1949).

1947 July-September: filming of *The Gioconda Smile* (*A Woman's Vengeance*).

November: *The World of Aldous Huxley*.

Autumn: H. writes *Ape and Essence* (completed in February, 1948).

1948 February: *Mortal Coils* (stage version of *The Gioconda Smile*).

June: London stage production of *The Gioconda Smile*.

June-September: journey to Italy.

August: *Ape and Essence*.

November: winter at Palm Desert (until February, 1949).

December: H. works on a dramatization of *Ape and Essence*, never produced.

1949 February: Paris stage production of *The Gioconda Smile* (*Le Sourire de la Joconde*).

May: acquisition of the house at 740 N. Kings Road, Los Angeles, to which the Huxleys move gradually during the summer.

1950 April: *Themes and Variations*. Marriage of Matthew Huxley to Ellen Hovde.

May-September: visits to France, Italy, and England.

October: New York stage production of *The Gioconda Smile*. Visit to Frieda Lawrence in New Mexico.

1951 H. writes *The Devils of Loudun*.

March: H. is ill with a virus infection which affects his right eye.

July: severe attack of iritis.

October: birth of Mark Trevenen Huxley.

December: discussion of plans for a film on the life of Gandhi, for which H. would write the script; the film is never produced.

1952 January: Maria Huxley has an operation for breast cancer; the disease recurs after six months.

October: *The Devils of Loudun*.

December: H. works on the script for a film about the sun.

1953 February: death of Lewis Gielgud.

May: H. takes mescalin under the supervision of Dr Humphry Osmond.

June: holiday tour of Northwestern states.

October: birth of Teresa Huxley.

1954 February: *The Doors of Perception*.

April: the Huxleys visit Eileen Garrett and H. attends a parapsychological conference at St Paul de Vence.

May: visit to Dr Roger Godel at Ismailia.

May-August: tour in the Near East, Cyprus, Greece, Italy, France, and England.

October: lecture, 'Visionary Experience, Visionary Art and the Other World'.

November: H. begins collaborating with Beth Wendel on the play *The Genius and the Goddess*.

1955   January: H. contracts to write articles regularly for *Esquire*.

February: death of Maria Huxley.

April-May: motor trip with Rose Wessberg to New York *via* the Southern states.

May-June: H. is in New York trying to arrange for production of *The Genius and the Goddess*.

June: novel *The Genius and the Goddess*.

July-August: summer with Matthew and Ellen Huxley at Guilford, Connecticut.

August: arrangement with Rita Allen for a stage production of *The Genius and the Goddess* (terminated in February, 1956).

September: H. returns to Los Angeles and continues revising the play script.

1956   February: *Heaven and Hell*.

19 March: H. is married to Laura Archera at Yuma, Arizona.

July: the Huxleys move into the house at 3276 Deronda Drive, Los Angeles. H. works on the novel *Island* (completed in June, 1961).

August: H. writes the synopsis of a proposed film on population.

September: visit of Julian and Juliette Huxley to California.

September-December: H. writes a musical version of *Brave New World*, never produced.

October: *Adonis and the Alphabet* (*Tomorrow and Tomorrow and Tomorrow*).

1957   March: arrangement with Courtney Burr for stage production of *The Genius and the Goddess*.

April: H. revises Ralph Rose's dramatic version of *After Many a Summer*, never produced.

June: *Collected Short Stories*.

Summer: H. is in New York revising the script of *The Genius and the Goddess* and attending rehearsals (until November).

November: stage production of *The Genius and the Goddess* in New Haven and in Philadelphia, where H. leaves the company.

December: H. begins writing *Brave New World Revisited*.

1958   June: Los Angeles stage production of *The Gioconda Smile*.

July-August: the Huxleys visit Peru and Brazil.

September-October: visits to Italy and England.

October: *Brave New World Revisited*.

November: H. lectures at Turin, Milan, Rome, and Naples. Illness with influenza and bronchial complications.

December: return to Los Angeles.

1959   January: separation of Matthew and Ellen Huxley.

February-May: H. delivers his first course of lectures at the University of California, Santa Barbara, on 'The Human Situation'.

May: H. receives the Award of Merit Medal of the American Academy of Arts and Letters.

July: H. is painfully injured by a fall.

August: *Collected Essays*.

September-December: second course of lectures at Santa Barbara.

1960   March-April: visiting professorship at the Menninger Foundation, Topeka.

May: H. learns that he has cancer of the tongue; he refuses surgery.

June: radium-needle treatments for cancer.

August: *On Art and Artists*.

September: H. attends a conference at Dartmouth College on medical ethics.

September-November: visiting professorship at the Massachusetts Institute of Technology.

1961   January: visit to Hawaii.

February: conference in San Francisco on control of the mind.

March: H. collaborates with Peggy Lamson on a dramatic version of 'Voices' (until April, 1962).

April: address at M.I.T. centennial celebration.

May: the house at 3276 Deronda Drive is destroyed by fire; H's journals and manuscripts and the letters to Maria Huxley are lost.

June-September: visits to Europe and England. H. returns in June to his birthplace at Godalming.

July: parapsychological conference at Le Piol.

August: visit to Krishnamurti at Gstaad; conference on applied psychology at Copenhagen.

September: the Huxleys move to 6233 Mulholland Highway, Los Angeles.

November: flight to India for the Tagore centenary celebration, New Delhi.

1962   February-May: visiting professorship at the University of California, Berkeley. H. lives at 2533 Hillegass Avenue, Berkeley.

March: *Island*. Conference at Santa Barbara on technology in the modern world.

April: conference at Colgate University on hypnosis. H. visits Sir Julian Huxley at Portland, Oregon.

June: H. is designated a Companion of Literature. Stage production of *The Genius and the Goddess* at Oxford and in London.

July: H. has an operation for the removal of a neck gland, which is found to contain malignancy.

August–September: meeting of the World Academy of Arts and Sciences, Brussels.

November: H. lectures in the South and East.

December: *Literature and Science* in progress.

1963 March: H. attends sessions in Rome of the United Nations Food and Agriculture Organization. Audience with Pope John XXIII. Marriage of Matthew Huxley to Judith Wallet Bordage.

April: H. has radiation treatments for cancer.

August: meeting of the World Academy of Arts and Sciences, Stockholm.

August–September: H. pays his final visits to England and Italy.

September: *Literature and Science*.

October: composition of 'Shakespeare and Religion'.

22 November: H. dies at Los Angeles. His body is cremated the same day. There is no funeral, but friends in London hold a memorial service on 17 December.

I
ENGLAND
1899–1923

1: TO MISS NOON

Stocks, Tring
[Christmas, 1899 or 1900]

Dear Miss Noon,

Thank you very much for my cannon. I hope you had a very nice Christmas. We had a littla [sic] Christmas tree and six presents.

your loving
Aldous

2: TO JULIAN HUXLEY

Prior's Field, Godalming
[Summer, probably 1902]

Dear Julian,

The weather is very bad, it has been raining nearly all the week. Trev has found some green man [orchises]. I am learning to swim. We were going a picnic to St. Marthas yesterday, only it rained, so we played hide and seek indoors instead. We are going to play a match next Wednesday against the Albury club. I was in the second class last week. The building is getting on fast. They have moved the gas house, and are moving the green house into the field by the pig-stye. The swing has come back mended and painted green. The tool house has been moved away.

Your loving brother
Aldous

3: TO JULIAN HUXLEY

[Prior's Field, Godalming]
7 December, 1902

My dear Julian,

[I]t is very frosty weather: and I can stand on the pond. We have been giving crumbs to the birds; the pigeons can fly nicely now (we saw them drinking out of the pond just now). The staircase in the cottage has been put up. I and Kathleen [Fordham] found a mouse in the pig's bran and we chased it about till at last it escaped. One of the pigs has a cough. We went to church,

---

1 *This letter was written to one of the Noon sisters who kept an infants' school, attended by Huxley, at Godalming. One of them also taught drawing at the boys' preparatory school, Hillside. Stocks was the house of Julia Huxley's sister, Mrs Humphry Ward.*

2 *Orchises: the word is erased. Sir Julian Huxley suggests this as a probable reading. Trev, the second of the Huxley brothers, was two years younger than Julian, five years older than Aldous. Julian was a schoolboy at Eton.*

Emy, I, Kathleen, Miss English, and Miss Neroutsos at Puttenham and came back over the common. The others went to [C]ut[t]-[M]ill.

> *Good by, your loving brother*
> *Aldous*

4: ALDOUS AND JULIA HUXLEY TO JULIAN HUXLEY

> *Prior's Field, Godalming*
> *[June, probably* 1903]

Dear Julian,

Many happy returns of the day.

The weather is very nice here to day; I hope it is fine at Eton. We have found some ripe 'strawberries' in the garden, and a lot came yesterday from Warsash. Baby [Margaret] said to mother the other day, 'How amusingly silly you are'.

Last night I developed some photographs with Kathleen, and the lamp caught fire so we had to put it out with cups of water. The nest in the woods is a lesser white throat. We have found a chiffchaffs nest too.

> *Your loving brother*
> *Aldous*

P.S. Aldous is sending you a present.

> *Mother*

5: TO JULIAN HUXLEY

> *[Hillside, Godalming]*
> *Sun[day],* 14 *February,* 1904

Dear Julian,

Thank you very much for your letter. Answer to solution = Robin and Big Tit. Mother has got me a book with texts in which I can paint. And a picture Postcard Album and two books, *Ich lerne jetzt Deut[s]ch*! Baby wants me to tell you that 'you ar[e] *not* as good looking as a JELLYFISH'. This morning we went to P. F. not indoors, only in the kitchen. We are in the cottage nearest the gate so that we can see the boys playing on Lessington. It has not rained to day but when it rains its all lake and to see the boys splashing[.]

3 *Miss English and Miss Neroutsos: teachers at Prior's Field, Julia Huxley's school for girls. Kathleen Fordham, who became Julian Huxley's fiancée, was a pupil there; she later married W. P. Watt, the literary agent. Cutt Mill: a farmhouse and mill on a lake near Godalming, often visited for picnics.*

4 *Julian Huxley's birthday was* 22 *June. Huxley's sister, Margaret, was three and a half.*

5 *'We' refers to Huxley and his cousin Gervas. The two boys were almost exactly the same age.*

Hillside, Godalming
Sunday 17 [*November,* 1907]

My dear Julian,

Thanks for your coarse p.c. I have discovered how the nose turns blue:
I placed it on the hot pipes and it promptly turned a deep ultramarine. There
of course is nothing to say as usual except about the lectures, matches etc.
of the past weeks. I'm longing for Christmas to come: THE SECRET PARCEL!
Ha! Ha! Have you heard anything about it yet. I am going to give you a
Louis XVI bedgown for Christmas in three styles. [*Sketch of a pianist and a
gramophone.*]

As there is nil to say I will finish off with some verses out of lays of modern
Oxford. There was a great scholar of Balliol who was asked what he knew
of Gamaliel etc.

6 *Julian Huxley was in his second year at Balliol. Mr Taylor: the mathematics
master at Hillside and an amateur biologist. At Christmas,* 1907, *Aldous was asked to
write down what he liked best in the Vicar's sermon. His answer, in an improvised poem,
was* 'Mincepie'—*evidently as the pragmatic equivalent of* Peace, *good will toward
men.*

> '*Want an answer*
> *I'm a bit off it*
> *but in the words of the prophet*
> *Peace, Peace, beautiful peace*
> *in the beautiful Kingdom of Bong*
> *Peace on the whole*
> *is quite a Christmas novelty.*
> *not a music-hall rôle*
> *or a gaudy frivolity*
> *but a new conciliation*
> *of a squabble-loving nation*
> *or a village or a family or town*
> *In my mind's eye*
> *this is best done by a hot mince pie*
> *which offered with morality*
> *and excessive frugality*
> *would soothe*
> *General Boothe*
> *To return to the point,*
> *(my mind's a bit out of joint)*
> *the nicest thing to me*
> *was the conciliation of the family*
> *arguing family*
> *over the birth-day cake at tea*
> *But cease*
> *now in peace.*'

DO YOU KNOW ANY NICE catchy tunes Mr. Taylor wants to know for the PENNY READING. *ANSWER!*

> If a . . .
> meet a . . .
> going . . .
> if a . . .
> greet a . . .
> need a . . .

Farewell
Aldous

7: TO GERVAS HUXLEY

Tudor House, Lyme Regis
17th [April, 1908]

Dear Ger.,

I'm sorry I haven't written before, but I quite forgot. I [won]der how you like Poldhu? Lyme is most awfully swizzy. It is most fearfully old and mother says it has hardly altered since she saw it last 19 years ago. These lodgings are quite nice. This place is a most awful one to get hungry in. I eat about 86 times as much as I have ever eaten before. I am almost prostrated just now by an ENOURMOUS [sic] Hot cross Bun. There are quite a lot of fossils here. We found a ripping one of some flying lizard beast. We all march about with hammers now slamming bits of rock. There is a funny artificial stone harbour called the Cobb. It has existed since 1300 odd. I have not seen the ghost lady dropping coins yet but I hope to soon.

Your loving
Aldous

8: TO JULIAN HUXLEY

Prior's Field, Godalming
Thursday, 28 [May, 1908]

Dear Julian,

Thanks for your extremely pseudo-letter. Trev tells me you have of course not written to him. Ong passong I have written twice. Talking about writing I have composed a most beautiful ode for your coming of age as you asked me.

> Now let us eat the festal cake
> and munch the festal bun
> for hoary time shall shortly take
> (that nasty chap with scythe and rake)
> of J's years twenty-one.

8 *Design: a caricature of a gentleman and a lady sitting on a bench, viewed from the rear, their arms round each other.*

Since that he soon shall come of age
   take up his book of life,
and turn it over page by page
   youll find it full of wicked rage
and fratricidal strife

Proceeding on from leaf to leaf
   you find mid more confusions
of martyred brothers patient grief
   and love affairs beyond belief,
of Peggy the intrusions

And do not notice lovely A.
   nor V. nor P. unduly,
nor P. [nor] I. nor beauteous K.
   (you'll wonder what a lot are they)
nor Naughty Mouse unruly.

I can't make any more. This ode is not on Horatian lines I may tell you, its entirely my own. [*Sketch.*] This I'm sure is the style of humour you appreciate. That is a design for a comic postcard.

Saturday 13th June

Sorry not to have continued my letter. But I must be up and off—I hear a sound as of a bell to call me to my *ice* cold bath.

   Farewell.

Your loving bro.
Aldous

9: TO THE FINDER

Prior's Field, Godalming
15 *June,* 1908

Any one finding this shall know that I A. L. Huxley did inhabit this cubicle for 3 terms. Altogether he was in cubicles for the space of 4 years. In Summer 1908 he was head of the school. In Spring term 1908 he was enjoying the disease of mumps (the which he had for June weeks) and in Lower Large he concealed a treasure. The directions to the finding thereof are as follows. Go to the Eastern windows (overlooking the croquet lawn). On the left hand side of the middle of these windows you shall see a brass fixture origionaly [sic] intended for pulling up things upon unscrewing and raising this plate you shall find the treasure you shall by no means lose.

A. L. Huxley

9 *A note left presumably at Hillside when Huxley went back after his convalescence at Prior's Field.*

[*Hillside, Godalming*]
Monday 29th [*June*, 1908]

Dear Ger.,

Thanks very much for your epistle. I'm sorry your optics have pur-
pureated [sic]. It must be rotten in the sun now. I hope you got out by speech
day. We have as you so aptly put it a great many aw, ahem new *men*
dontcher know, most of whom are quite ap[p]alling. There is one Joseph
who is the most boundlessly assinine [sic] redhaired fool I've ever seen. He
is in I. B. but his standard only up to remove. There is one Wild, a small
facsimile of T. L. H. S[mith-]P[earce] in face and manner. There is one
Carruthers who is a little bounder. The little Wadham is a very decent little
kid, almost microscopic. There is a small Cursham who is a fool and a very
nice kid named Randall. The new master is a man called Vesey. He's not
half a bad chap—considerably better than Clark (pfht) at any rate. De bello
Aitchisonalio. At the beginning of the term he was raided but since has been
left quiet. He is now captain of the XI. Last Wednesday I saw your ma at
Oxford where I went up to hear Julian spout his poem (the Newdigate).
Gilps wrote to me the other day. The most deceiving letter I've ever seen
with only 2 pages written on. Old Jacko constantly asks me in his double
bass voice, 'Major written yet min*or*, (he always lays emphasis on the *or* of
minor) 'mislaid those cig: cards in hols want to know his address you know'
etc etc ad lib ult ad naus. Excuse this paper: it is sketch book stuff: I have
none left: I have exhausted all mine writing to Trev (who is in Germany).
Latest News Stop Press Strawbugs for tea Bell Ringing.

Your loving Cousin
Aldous—alias Ogre, the Jaws etc

10 *Gervas Huxley had left Hillside for Rugby at the end of the Easter term,* 1908.
*He identifies 'old Jacko' as a Mr Jacques, science master at Hillside. Of the boys
mentioned, 'the little Wadham' was J. W. Wadham, younger brother of Nicholas
Wadham, who was a particular friend of the Huxley cousins. Aitchison was probably
R. A. C. Aitchison, afterwards at Charterhouse; he was killed at Armentières,* 1914.
*'Gilps' (otherwise 'Giller') was Lewis Evelyn Gielgud, eldest son of Frank and Kate
Terry Lewis Gielgud. Gielgud, who had gone on scholarship to Eton from Hillside the
preceding year, was Aldous' closest friend, both there and later at Oxford. Newdigate:
Julian Huxley had won the Newdigate Prize for* 1908 *with his poem on the subject set,
'Holyrood'. The signature to this letter, 'Ogre', refers to the nickname 'Ogie', bestowed
on Aldous in childhood because of his large head.*

[Eton College, Windsor]
[Late November, 1908]

Dear Ger,

Yes I confirm these sad doings of Gilps it is dreadful to think that one so young should be so debauched. I notice with horror you say 'term' instead of 'half' the only and obvious expression. Poor little me has to do fagging for 3 halves however I am in the Lower Vth now: all Collegers start there, M' tutor, who is also my house tutor and my division beak, is a dear man nomine [A.W.] Whitworth. We have gone through the most awful event of the half i.e. 'Extra Books' consisting of 800 lines of Homer and about 400 lines [of] Vergil. Monday is St. Andrews day. Julian and Trev are coming I think. They are dreadful bugs now, so am I for that matter. I look so chic in tail coats mouldy collars and white ties. I suppose you wear some type of rational dress like pyjamas and bowler hats: dont you. I think the [D]oddite is most frightfully jolly especially 'Football' by Aitchison, greedy little yellow devil he is to write such a fatuous and hyperbolically idiotic thing. Have you done anything bad in the fagging line lately such as burning yr fagmasters toast or put[t]ing his tea in his bath or breaking 2 dozen eggs. I cant say I have yet: I have only been whipped twice so far (1) in a general working off of the whole of college for hiding a letter and (2) for forgetting to take VI form cheese out of Hall. When does your Half end ours is horrid late 23rd Dec. Filthy[,] sir! Loathesome! [sic] and beastly. I cannot say what an awful man Gielgud is. His Face gets more and more like a turnip every day.

Yr lov'g cousin
Aldous

12: TO JULIAN HUXLEY

[Eton College, Windsor]
[2 April, 1909]

M'dear Julian,

Thanks for letter. We go back next Thursday (8th I rather believe). Yes I did an chamber high jump but with 4-3″ not 4-8″ as Bella stated. I have not received any money yet!!! The day of Coll[ege] Sports was Woden's day not[,] Thor his day on account of the rain. The sight of the day was [E.T.N.] Grove casting the hammer. He had 4 throws and each throw instead of going—I will draw a picker—[sketch]. The first shot nearly ended in tragedy. Kissack (the photographer) his man was kneeling down to take a light-writing of the actual cast. The hammer passed within 18 ins of him

---

11 *Huxley's first term at Eton. This was written a few days before his mother's death. St Andrew's Day (30 November): the day of the annual wall game. The Doddite: a literary paper started at Hillside in 1907 by Gielgud and the Huxley cousins.*

without exaggerager. If it had come 18 ins nearer[,] Kissack his man would have been lying screaming and disembowelled on the ground. The last shot went into the river and was only fished out with great difficulty. Trials began to day. How jolly frogs their eggs must be: personally I only experiment on devils-their-fishes-their-eggs. I am very bored—we have been experimenting with quick-his-silver[,] and 2 sovereigns (Yes Sir £s in red gold) must have touched the mess, for this morning I found them demi-white and demi-red. I am having 'em cleaned at Hollyer (Jeweller)-his-shop. I have just completed today a most elaborate picture, of an ELEPHANT!! (?)—!! It is adorable. But Trev's picker of Joan I consider perfectly offensive. I would not have it were I paid BUT I'd g— Interval for unseen translation[—] give the red gold for that picture youve got of Her. VI Form, as might be supposed have been behaving themselves PRETTY offensively. Thank Heaven Maggers and [E.D.] Spring-Rice are leaving: But 'tis a pity that LRM N(apier) is leaving and also it is a grander pity that Meagens has decided to leave. Very sad—but I hope hell leave me some of his furniture. Talking about furniture there is to be an huge auction of all the appurtenances of the leaving fellahs[.] I think I'll go and waste some red gold there—eh what!!?

Goodbye

Yrs e'er

A

13: TO JULIAN HUXLEY

Villa Bonaventura,
Cadenattia, Lago di Como
Wednesday (I don't know the date)
[28 *April,* 1909]

My Dear Julian,
(This letter is for Trev as well as for you.) The lake is in storm to day as the result of the high wind and some rain in the night.

> Storm fell over the lake
> and the lake was covered with fleas
> the fleas were the ghosts of the hake
> and the hake were covered with bees
> the bees were the ghosts of the cows
> and the cows were covered [with] slugs

12 *Bella: Fräulein Ella Salkowski, of Königsberg. She was nanny to Trev, Aldous, and their sister Margaret, and in later years to Aldous' son Matthew. Joan: this was Huxley's cousin Joan Collier, for whom he had a romantic attachment. She was the daughter of the Hon. John Collier and Huxley's Aunt Ethel. Two sketches conclude this letter, the one of a house labelled 'Bedlam' with an escaping figure labelled 'You', the other depicting a man whose head protrudes from the top of a barrel, identified as 'Aristarchus in a barrel'. 'Demosthenes in a tub'. 'Aphrodite in a cast' (sic), and 'Diogenes in a hogshead'.*

and the slugs were the ghosts of the sows
and the sows were covered with bugs,
and so on ad infi-nauseam.

This country is remarkable for its geology[,] fauna, flora and smells. I will give a list. It is decided that—(1) the rocks be of limestone (2) that the strata do go about slanting ot upright but never horizontal and do therefore present little possibilities of climbing, (3) that there be no great number of fossils in this country (thereof have I seen none but I have read that they do exist in a cave which is a long distance up the mountain and the which I do not wish to explore as, according to the books about this country, there is in it a bottomless or paene-bottomless abyss down the which, it is said, a stone may be heard falling for 3 minutes and it also is said to be joined to the lake, though how this comes to pass is strange as the cave is full 1½ miles in-land.) (4) that, according to what I have heard the stone does turn into marble in places, which may often be seen by the road-side (thereof do I enclose a piece which is marble or, it may be, quartz the which I do not know) (5) that there be many caves in this country and not a few stalactites (9) [sic] that the dogs be all mongrels and mostly of a strawberry colour, (10) that the cats be mostly purple (11) that the flowers be numerous (12) that I have counted 54 sorts (13) that the [*illegible*] be numerous (14) that the smells if coloured would present quite a kaleidoscopic appearance in the villages.

Eton

Good though rather rough voyage. Am up to Mr. [A.M.] Goodhart in middle division. Cricket is pretty boring. Weather poor. Trev had better come down some time soon. Long leave on June 12th.

Yours
Aldous

14: TO JULIAN HUXLEY

New Buildings, Eton College, Windsor
14 *November*, 1909

My dear Julian,
Many thanks for your highly illegible letter parts of which I have hardly yet made out: particularly about Anaxagoras' limerick. You omitted to give your address but I gather that it is merely 'the Zoological Station' will find you. Or is it Zoological Gardens?

As I suppose you have heard The Provost [J. J. Hornby] has died and there was a very solemn funeral yesterday week in which College partook. All sorts of jolly people were there. Lord Rosebery, Lord Roberts, Lord Peel, the Rt Rev Dan Leno Lord Bishop of Oxford, Dr. [Edmond] Warre and heaps of others.

---

14 *Julian Huxley was in Naples as a research scholar at the Marine Biological Station. Dan Leno: music-hall comedian. M. D. Hill was the zoology master at Eton.*

I am about to begin remit drill on Tuesday after a long wait. Rather a bore as it will be 2 days before extra Books wh: take place next Thursday.

I received a pic from Bella today from Aden—a fortnight old. She must be nearly there now.

Mr. Piggy [M.D.] Hill accosted me the other day and asked after you and whether you had good quarters. I replied I did not know. Perhaps you might provide some first hand information on the subject. Father tells me you have discovered a HUGE INFUSORIA and are making experiments in regeneration on it. I hope your Italian is very good. The only Italian I know is 'Buona Sera' and 'Ritirata del Wagone' which help you along in an almost miraculous fashion.

Ever Your Loving Bro:
Aldous

15: TO GERVAS HUXLEY

Eton College, Windsor
14 December, 1909

Dear Ger.,

I hope I find you (by letter) well. I also hope I find the Bidger [Nicholas Wadham]—!!! Gielgud and I have been sending a steady stream of p.c's at him requesting him to write—but with no effect. Might not you with soft words or even physical persuasion compel him to write!

I suppose you are on the verge of being plunged into a heavy sea of trials (what do you call them of course I mean ex-am-i-na-ti-ons). I begin on Thursday.

By the way,—did you subscribe one of your usual mellifluous bits of composition for the *Doddite? I did!* You will of course recognize my amusing and breezy style in the best story of the number. I leave you to guess which! I got a delightful letter from H. W. M. P[arr] the other day which I answered in about a month's time.

I have, in company with Gielgud, accomplished forty recruit drills this half and am now very nearly a full fledge[d] territorial only I have now to pass a shooting test. I dont suppose I shall see much of you next holidays. The 1st fortnight I shall be at Montana then (probably) a week or so at Tring. So I shan't be long in London.

Ever thine
Aldous

15 *Parr, a master at Hillside, encouraged and oversaw* The Doddite. *Montana in Switzerland was a favourite resort for winter sports, both of the Huxleys and of their cousins the Colliers.*

New Buildings, Eton College, Windsor
15 February, 1910

My Dear Julian,

Thank you so very much for the box of lush produce that you sent. I was besieged by countless crowds of food-seeking animals. Thank you also very much for the Pompeian lamp which adorns my room. I was fourth in trials last half which hurls me forth from upper tea-room fag to captain of L[ower] T[ea] a change I think for the better. For to wield the fork is certainly a superior pastime to carrying the kettle.

This half we are all up to that ignorant creature [A.C.G.] Heygate. I have successfully proved his ignorance by making a remark in my Sunday questions about Bismarck's duel with Graf Wetterstable. I don't know whether Bismarck ever had a duel and Graf Wetterstable came from the depths of my lurid imagination. In the same way last year there was a Q. about Ophir and Solomon's mines and someone put that they were called 'umpas-weegee' (or words to that effect) = 'Houses of the Gods' by the natives. I am now in C. But when I do get into B I am afraid I shall find no more extras. They have all been abolished now in C and B and French substituted in their stead!!! Isn't it absurd.

I am just beginning to paint with Mr [S.T.G.] Evans and will probably launch into doing so tomorrow. I fear my efforts are all at present in the drawing school but I will take one and send it next week. Ria and Ted Haynes came down on Saturday and we spent the afternoon looking at the portraits in the Provost's lodge.

By the way I have written two poems one in the style of Noyes and the other Browningesque. Here goes.

> Balliol in the twilight! is J.S.H. asleep
> Grey and ghostly shadows all around him creep
> Shadows of amoebae round him bite and grope
> Waiting for their enemy who wields the microscope.
>
> Balliol in the noonday! J.S.H. is near
> (His salary en passant is £100 a year
> Rooms too are provided—room for all his snails
> And all his frogs in picklepots and all th' amoebas' tails.)
>
> Merry merry England has kiss'd the lips of June
> So has Julian—often—here, beneath the moon

16 *Julian Huxley had been appointed Lecturer in Zoology at Balliol, a post he held for two years. Ria and Ted Haynes: Ria was the daughter of Huxley's aunt Jessie Oriana Waller; her husband, E. S. P. Haynes, was a well known lawyer and writer.*

Only her name wasn't June: it happened to be[—]woa!
Personalities are absolutely barred you know.

Love is in Balliol building him an house
(A builder'd do it better had he the smallest νοῦς)
Love is in Balliol—thats really awfully nice
If he's come to put an end to the loathely rats and mice.

Julian, Julian, Julian: in the museum
Place this mouldy poem, leave it there and come
Come home from Italy come from far away
To Balliol to Balliol about the break of day.

Now for the Browningesque one

I am no naturalist who am not natural!
I have a post at Ball-i-ol that you're all
Dying to have, you miserable crew
But I, I have it and with it rooms too!!!
Give her but a least excuse to love me

(Hear! Hear!)

Hear! let her for some slight reason reprove me
—Some little thing like drinking too much beer—
She'll love me, if it to miserable weeping move me.

(Hist! said Julian
    But oh said the scout that washed the dishes
Tis but an unseen carolling man
    Wanting embarasse de richesse.)

        A flea in my coat
        A mouse in my cheese
        A wasps nest near home
        Conspire to please,

To please, aye, all to please me, for I'm drawing
One hundred sovereigns sterling every annum

(I find it hard to write these lines and scan 'em
So I will cease, for rooks around are cawing
        Th' approach of night
        When firefly
        Creeps forth to light
        The darkling sky.)

34

New Buildings, Eton College, Windsor
5 May, [1910]

My dear Julian,

Many thanks for the p.p.c. of Adam and Eve. Here am I at Eton again after my arduous holidays. For the first fortnight I was down in S. Devon with Aunt Sophy and Co. A lovely place only spoilt by bad weather. Our hotel was very small and only a few yards from the sea. In the middle of our little bay was a large arched rock,—so [*sketch*] accessible at low—but an island at high-tide. Among the rocks were lots of lovely anemones red, green, whitish. Flowers inland were lovely—primroses lined the hedges, bluebells beginning to open and garden flowers advanced enormously.

I am in B now, up to Muggins [H. V. Macnaghten] which is rather an effort. Gielgud's election are all in 1st 100 now and [C. R.] Hollway (I don't suppose you know him, but he is quite ridiculous) will be Captain of the School. Rain, rain serenely shining or rather falling has been the programme of this last week. Talking about the Follies that reminds me I saw Roger Eckersley on Tuesday: he has a lovely new two step—not gnats—also he has an offer to join the Grotesques [—] Q? [—] and also a very funny story about Gladys Go[t]ch (you remember down at Laleham). Well! it is this. One day down at Sidmouth he got into talk with a Belgian chauffeur who said his master kept 6 motors and gave him £600 a year salary. R. asked who the lucky man was. 'Mr. Go[t]ch.' 'Has he a daughter called Gladys' 'Yes'. Pressing ½ crown into his horny palm R. requested him to ask her if she remembered Roger Eckersley at Laleham. A few days later they met again. 'She only remembair one Rogair.' R. discovered her hotel and that she was departing that day. He lay in wait till she appeared. Instant recognition metaphorically flying into each others arms. Interview with pa and ma: request to come and see at 1 Belgrave Square! Roger says the address is rather too much for him!

Love
Aldous

17 *Aunt Sophy: the wife of Dr Henry Huxley and mother of Gervas Huxley. Roger Eckersley: a son of Huxley's Aunt Rachel. He and his brother Thomas had lived with Leonard Huxley's family in the early 'nineties while their father, Alfred, was in Mexico. The Gotches were family friends.*

Eton College, Windsor
[24 May, 1910]

Dear Jerry,

Many thanks for your insalubrious epistle. I could only read about half of it. Damn your bloody eyes. Many thanks for the photograph of pinkbottom. Why in the Devil's name were you allowed to go to town to see the procession. I of course down here was holding an official position in lining the route and keeping the rabble back with the butt end of my rifle. As we were reversing arms most of the time it was very hard to see anything much. The heat was simply dreadful but we were thank God allowed to sit down on the edge of the avenue, we were lining most of the time. I wrote a long letter to Joan the other day to ask forgiveness for that hideous post-card. All is now forgiven in a *gigantic* letter which arrived about 3 days ago.

From what I can see in the more unintelligible part of yr letter you mention something about Chapman. It's all off: he's been and married Giller's little friend, Malcolm.

Whole holiday to day—Victorias birthday. Cricket most of day rain—bore. [*Sketch.*] Love from Giller. Love to Stamer, Bidger and rest of your umbrose crew.

Ever thine
Aldous Leonard Huxley

19: TO LEONARD HUXLEY

Eton College, Windsor
[5 June, 1910]

Dearest Father,

Many thanks for the letter. I enclose Julian's letter even more illegible than when it reached me, as it has been in the water since then. But thereby hangs a tale. Last Friday was a whole holiday and I went with two wet-bobs up the river about 5 miles to an island where one has tea and at which one can answer 5.30 absence on certain days if one puts ones name down. Well we arrived, had tea, answered absence and sat down in our boat preparatory to pushing off. So doing someone else pushed off from us and tipped our boat over sideways and swamped us in about 4 ft of water. There we were,

18 *Procession: the funeral of King Edward VII, on 20 May. After the state procession in London, the King's body was taken to Windsor for burial at Frogmore. The Eton College Officers' Training Corps were posted to guard the route. Besides Wadham (Bidger), already mentioned in the correspondence, the boys named in this letter were D. A. J. Chapman and Pulteney Malcolm, both of Eton, and William Donovan Stamer, who was at Rugby with Gervas Huxley.*

dripping wet, with a boat full of water. We decided it wasn't worth emptying our vessel and so we were put across from the island to the main land and walked and ran straight home across country, over hedge and ditch, thro nettles and corn and mustard-fields and as we only had shorts and socks and shoes on our nether members, you can imagine we got pretty dirty and scratched. To crown all we were 5 minutes late for lock-up!

Nothing at all yesterday, and a good thing too, considering the weather wh: was *almost* as bad as last year's 4th.

I am doing sketches now out of doors and learning to paint, which is rather nice.

Well—'Hard, O hard! is the metre of Catullus' and I must see what can be done with my verses.

Yr. loving son
Aldous

20: TO LEONARD HUXLEY

Eton College, Windsor
19 June, 1910

Dearest Father,

Many thanks for your letter. I think I had better try and answer a few questions first. We come up on Friday in time for lunch: I dont suppose I shall want to watch the match *all* the time so a little tennis at 51 wd. be v. acceptable. Did Julian enjoy the earthquake? It must have been rather an experience for him.

By the by another question about camp—I expect we leave it on the 5th—possibly the 6th.

Today it has been positively too hot to do anything at all but sit and read with the curtains drawn. It has been the first really hot day we've had so far this half unless you count those sweltering thundery days. Where's Trev now. If he's at home tell him to come down here or at any rate write and answer my p.c. Well there is nought to say and I must return to my grizly Sunday questions and verses, which luckily can be put into English verse, which saves a lot of time. In fact I have all ready done a copy—a gross caricature of Shelley.

Love from your loving son
Aldous

20 51: *Dr Henry Huxley's London house at* 51 *Porchester Terrace. Leonard Huxley, after his wife's death, had moved up to London, his address being* 27 *Westbourne Square. He continued as a director of Prior's Field School, which was now run by Mrs Burton-Brown, formerly Julia Huxley's assistant.*

D Company, Eton Contingent, O.T.C. Camp,
Farnboro' Common, Hants
3 July, [1910]

Dear Gran'moo,

After making the necessary apologies for pencil and rather loathely paper, thank you very, very much for the present, which arrived with the utmost safety and punctiliousness. From my address you may observe I am in camp—at the present moment writing beneath the fitful radiance of a quarter candle-power candle. We marched to this place from Eton— 8 miles on Wednesday and 16 on Thursday, a rather boring proceeding during which I strained my Tendo Achilles.

To day a grand inspection was held by the Duke of Connaught in which we were bored to the verge of complete exstinction, while H.R.H. was considerably unpunctual. I calculated that the whole brigade together wasted 333 days, allowing each man to have wasted 2 hours and the brigade to consist of 4000 men.

To night we are going to do night operations for some hours! I shall be glad to return to civilization, hot baths and other than straw mattresses to sleep on. Forgive this loathesome letter and thank you very, very much.

Your loving grandson
Aldous

22: TO JULIAN HUXLEY

[*Windsor*]
11 *December,* 1910

Dear Julian,

I shall be delighted to receive you on Wednesday. I am invited to break my fast with P[iggy] Hill on Thursday morn: Trials begin on that day, which is rather a dim prospect. We shall have to chat with Mr. Aymer William Whitworth about specialising. I think I shd. prefer it. I have invented rather a good riddle. The name of what curious animal does a man (or woman [as the case may be]) mention when calling his cat to partake of its plate of

21 *To his grandmother. The paper is spotted with a substance labelled '? Boot Blacking'.*
22 *Huxley hoped to specialize in biology, so as to prepare for the study of medicine. Eton, as he was to recall during a television interview in 1962, kept the younger boys occupied one whole day every week—Tuesday from morning till bedtime—in the writing of Latin verses, but offered also a good programme of scientific studies, on which he was already launched. Ironically the reference to specializing, in this letter, came on the eve of his blindness, which put an end to his plans. Reginald Smith: editor of* The Cornhill *and director of the publishing firm of Smith, Elder and Company, for which Leonard Huxley worked.*

food? (For answer see next page, i.e over the leaf.) The Reginald Smiths came down yesterday week. We had an enormous beano at Fullers and they left me a hamper of battleship tonnage, containing about 727 cub[ic] in[che]s of cake, 3 kqr of jam, 2½ kabs of sardines and 4⅘ lustres of fruit; I still have about 235 cub: ins of cake. We have been more or less flooded these last few days, but now the River has sunk about a foot and the stummicks of the water fowl touch bottom as they sit in the stagnant pools. [*Labelled diagram.*] The answer to the riddle of course is 'Here's your platter puss' (platypus) you may add another creature and say Here's your platter pussy mew for it. [P]latypus emu! Ha! Ha! it made me laugh till I cried the whole of one night.

> *Yr loving bro*
> *Julian* [sic]

23: †TO JOAN COLLIER

> *Undershaw, Hindhead*
> [*July*, 1911]

Dearest Joan,

Scuse bad writing which same I cant see.

As my writing much would mean nervous breakdown for those reading I will simply say gratters awfully on your engagement.

> *Ever yours,*
> *Aldous*

23 *Written when Huxley was blind. In the Preface to* The Art of Seeing (1942), *he spoke of his 'eighteen months of near-blindness', which began when he was sixteen. But for practical purposes he was totally blind, though retaining faint light-perception in his better eye, the left one. An infection of staphylococcus aureus had produced* keratitis punctata, *the scarring being severe. The exact date of onset is unknown. According to Eton records, Huxley did not complete the Lent term of 1911. On the other hand there is no indication whether he even started that term. Letter 26 shows that he was active by mid-May, 1912, and letter 22 shows that he was not wholly blind at the time of examinations in December, 1910 (though the 'dim prospect' apparently refers to difficulty with his eyes). Probably he was not in fact disabled for quite eighteen months; indeed, if letters 24 and 25, mentioning his cycling, were written towards the end of March, 1912, the period was shorter still. But the improvement in his vision during 1912, after surgery, was very gradual. His right eye stayed nearly blind, and it was only his left eye that he was able to use with any efficiency. When he wrote the present letter, within a few weeks of his cousin Joan's marriage to Frank Anstie Buzzard, in August, 1911, he could read only Braille. During this time he conducted a correspondence with Lewis Gielgud, who of course continued at Eton and who learned Braille in order to write to him. Unfortunately those letters have vanished. Undershaw was the residence of the Reverend E. Carus Selwyn and his wife Maud, who were indirectly related to Huxley, Selwyn's first wife, Lucy, having been a sister of Julia Arnold Huxley. The house belonged to Sir Arthur Conan Doyle, formerly its occupant.*

Dormers, Bovingdon, Herts.
[Circa late March, 1912]

Dearest father,

Many thanks for your letter. The prospect of Falmouth sounds very jolly. Talking about bicycles to go with me, my poor aged one is rather incapacitated. To day the back tyre exploded with a glorious detonation just outside Berkhampsted and I had to walk home. I do not know the exact extent of the damage, but I should think that, as in the case of the *Oceana*, there is a hole large enough to drive a motor bus through. This, I should think, will almost have done for the tyre, which was on its last wheels. In which case, would it be possible to have the new bicycle of which you spoke last Wednesday?

Ever your loving son,
Aldous

25: TO LEONARD HUXLEY

Dormers
[Circa late March, 1912]

Dearest father,

The bicycle arrived on Friday and is now in the hands of the mender. He promises to have it done by Monday so that I shall be able to ride down to the station on it on Wednesday. I fear I shant have enough cash to pay for the repair and to get to town, so please can I have some more before Wednesday.

Mr Whitworth has just sent me my long delayed certificate, a beautiful parchment bearing witness to the fact that in 1910 I satisfied the examiners in no less than seven subjects. He asks me to come and stay for a week end with him whenever I can, so I think I might get over to Eton sometime on

24 *This and the following letter may belong to the winter of 1913; but 1912 is indicated by the reference to the* Oceana *shipping disaster, which had occurred on 16 March, off Beachy Head, near Eastbourne, where Huxley's grandmother lived. The mention of Falmouth implies a possible arrangement for an Easter holiday in Cornwall; Easter Day fell on 7 April. The question remains whether Huxley's eyesight would have permitted his cycling so early as March, even though he was hiking and climbing in May. On the whole this seems the best dating. These two letters are his earliest known typewritten ones, both done apparently on the same machine he used to write some of the letters from Marburg in May and June. His touch typewriting was well developed. He composed a novel on the typewriter while blind but lost the script before his vision had cleared enough to enable him to read it. The Bovingdon address was that of his uncle, Dr Frank Arnold. Mrs Buzzard recalls that when Aldous came to visit her once during his blindness, after staying at Dormers, his clothes had been so neglected that they had to be burned.*

25 *The incomplete sentence at the end is typed off the margin of the paper.*

my bicycle: I dont suppose its more [than] five and twenty miles, if that.

The frost holds here with great effect and there are three inches of ice on most of the ponds. Ther[e] is also one of the coldest winds blowing I have ever felt—almost as cold as the wind at Aldeburgh.

I am debating what to get out of the library next. Darwinism will last till next Wednesday, when I can go round in person. The catalogue is, I think, in my room and it contains that list y [. . . .]

Good bye till Wednesday.

Your loving
Aldous

26: TO LEONARD HUXLEY

Marburg
13 *May*, [1912]

Dearest father,

Many thanks for your last letter, which, I regret to say was rather too small for me to read with any comfort. In fact I was only able to take the cream off each sentence by picking out one word in every four or so. Type-writer would be all right but a lot would be rather trying, I think.

I spent all yesterday with Professor Keyser [F. H. E. Kayser] on one of his geological expeditions. We started forth at eight A.M. and in two bands of about twenty five each marched—with occasional halts where anything of geological interest appeared in view—till about half past twelve. We had lunch in a wayside inn—eggs ham sausage milk and raspberry lemonade forming the staple food, with an almost unlimited supply of coffee after-wards. After lunch we ascended one berg, whose name I have forgotten, on the northern bank of the Lahn then returned and climbed a considerably higher one—the Rimberg, on the other side. It was particularly hot and as there was thunder in the air the climb up the Rimberg was rather a job. It was like walking up the side of a baking pan in a damp oven. However it was very nice at the top—beechwoods in early leaf and a tremendous view. It is a spot of pilgrimage for holiday makers: there was a gingerbeer and other beer stall and a dancing floor where about fifty peasants in weird Hessian costume were dancing what I learnt was a Rhinelander, which looks like a mixture between a polka and a two-step. They appeared to reverse quite as much, if not more, than they went forwards, which was odd. We remained on the top for an hour or so while it persistently thundered in the middle distance, and came down in time to catch the train back to Marburg. At all the stations there were crowds of holiday makers—there must have been about 120 at our little station—and people were standing in all the carriages. We got back at a little past eight having been out the whole day. I was pleasantly tired and very hot and thirsty. To-day the temperature has fallen considerably and I dont think I shall start bathing yet, after all.

The K[a]ysers have got the most delightful dog, which appeared in the course of last week, having been in the charge of a forester, while they were away—the forester lived at the delightful address of Schafsgarten, bei Schweinsberg. He, the dog, is a beautiful Irish setter, the only one of his kind within a radius of miles, as the beast has only just been introduced into Germany.

To-day was the funeral of a professor at which all the student verbindungs turn out with banners and form an enormous cortege. The banner bearers and chief members of the verbindungs wear marvellous uniforms—usually consisting of a coat of the verbindung's colours, a sort of turbanny object or a cocked hat, also with the verbindung colours splashed about on it, white breeches and highly polished top-boots—not to mention swords. The other members wear black frock coats and everything suitable for a funeral except for their dissipated railway-porters caps of the verbindung colour—scarlet, magenta or both. Everybody who possessed a uniform was wearing it. The supernumerary boiler washers of the state railway, the Imperio-municipal sewage farmers the grand herzogian gamekeepers—all in magnificent uniforms and resplendent railway-porters caps of many colours. I felt quite lost and wished I had brought my E.C.O.T.C. private's uniform so that I could outshine the sewage farmers at least.

Your loving son,
Aldous

Love to all. I hope you are enjoying the heat wave which the papers say is devastating England. We have it pretty nearly as hot here.

27: TO NOEL TREVENEN HUXLEY

[*Marburg*]
[8 *June*, 1912]

Many thanks for yr letter. I write a p. c. because it is so cheap. You will now be accomplishing your schools, I imagine: when you have got yr B. A. you'll know nearly as much as the average German before he goes to the University—a most comforting thought. I've just got a copy of Gielgud's and [E. C.] Benthall's 4 June paper, with my story figuring very largely in the midst. A most witty work, in parts. A man might bathe here in the intervals between the thunder storms and the blasting winds, but such intervals are few: I hope to nip one in the bud to day. I have made a new philosophy, but it is too long to explain on a p. c. It is called Space and suet or organised imagination. I have almost finished my tome, and shall be quite ready to

27 *Apparently the only extant letter of Huxley to his brother Trev. Barbara Hiles, later Mrs Nicholas Bagenal, had been a pupil at Prior's Field while Huxley was still at Hillside. They often went caterpillar or butterfly hunting together on Sunday mornings in the summer, or would join Julian in orchis hunting when he was at home from Oxford.*

begin it again when I get back—or perhaps I might start my work about Australia when I return. Father appears to think that one of the places in Wales is settled—the name is too much for this machine—and he also seems to think that the Biles [i.e., Hiles] family will be on the spot. I seem to remember Harbara [i.e., Barbara] of that ilk. An interesting discovery about Ethyl Mercaptan, child of the old salt, Petre M. betrothed to Hyde Roxsyll, cousin of the scion of an old English family, A. C. Tate of Ledd and friend of the Italian noblewoman Manga Nese (contessa) di Occhside.

A. L. H.

28: TO LEONARD HUXLEY

Deutschhausstrasse 28, [Marburg]
16 *June*, 1912

Dearest Father,

I write shivering from Arctic cold: we are enjoying that peculiar sort of weather that would be quite warm if it were not so cold—you know the kind I mean, sun and a wilting wind. To-day we have even lost the sun and the wind howls more grimly than usual. I begin to be sorry that I took a season ticket at the baths as bathing is quite impossible now.

I see exciting headlines on the English papers, which one shop here keeps —Shot in Parliament, National Strike and such-like. People talk much about Haldane's Chancellorship: everyone in Germany had hoped he would come as ambassador to Berlin as a fair exchange for the new man in London, whose name I forget, but whom everyone says is the best German diplomatist going. We have been reading in the german line lately the ballads of Schiller and Charybdis—chiefly the former, owing to the paucity of the latter's balladic outpourings. There are always a great many words in the Schiller ballads, which makes them good to exercise on. In the musical line, we have just polished off the Beethoven Funeral March, having before that completed one of the variations in the sonata: I think that we are going to begin on a Chopin prelude next time—the one in F major, I think, but am not sure. The Germans insist on calling them Preludchen in ordinary speech and some carry the love of belittling things so far as to talk about Beethoven sonatinas as opposed to sonatas.

The people of Marburg have succeeded in almost completely spoiling a street by erecting the most hideous memorial I have ever set eyes on. The victim of the memorial is [W. F.] Roser—I seem to have heard the name, but what he did I dont know. (Possibly I am thinking of Salvator Rosa.) It is made of a peculiar grey stone, which looks just like that horrible papier-mâché stone of which ruined castles are made in exhibitions of Merrie England. They are also on the point of putting up a war memorial, though none of the

---

28 *Roser had been a distinguished surgeon at the University of Marburg.*

people who were in the war want it and it is now a little late in the day. They have been wrangling about it for months and months: a Hessian sculptor— said to be very good especially with animals—offered to do them a Hessian lion: but this wouldn't satisfy them: they insist on having a ramping Germania arm in arm with a blood-stained Victoria or something equally vulgar and commonplace. The German people seem to have a passion for memorials even surpassing that of other nations. There are more than 200 Bismar[c]k towers scattered up and down the country where bonfires are regularly lighted, and of course countless other Bismar[c]k memorials. They want now to make a mountain on the Rhine somewhere and cover it with memorials of him.

I really have very few opinions about the Autumn: it all so very much depends on E[rnest] Clark[e]'s remarks. I dont know if it would be good to use the one eye for doing anything much. The right does not seem to alter much, but the left is certainly progressing well.

Love to all.

Your loving son
Aldous

29: TO JULIAN HUXLEY

Deutschhausstrasse 28, [*Marburg*]
18 *June*, [1912]

Dear Julian,

Many thanks for yrs. to hand: I never can remember if your birthday is on the longest or the shortest—or rather the next longest—day of the year. I write early, to be prepared for any emergency, to wish you Happy returns, Maidenhair ferns etc.

I cannot tell you how delighted I was to-day to observe in the town advertisements of a 'Grosser Walzerabend, mit der jugendlichen Cornetopistonvirtuosin Fräulein So and So'. A more charming occupation for young ladies, I could hardly imagine. We are suffering from Midsummer Half gales and exotic rainstorms. It is far worse than England.

I have been creating and illustrating, on my walks in the neighbourhood, a series of Limericks on Explorers, from Ibn Batu[ta] to Scott (not excluding Sancho Panza and Caesar Borgia) also one or two 'Limericks of Affliction',

---

28 *Ernest Clarke was Huxley's oculist in London. It was decided that Huxley should wait another year before going up to Oxford. His sight was still greatly impaired, and he perhaps felt behindhand in his studies.*

29 *Precipitops: probably George (later Sir George) Clark, the historian. About September, 1911, while still a student, he had lived with the Huxley family for a month, tutoring Aldous in early English history. When Aldous needed books, Clark would lead him round from the Huxleys' house in Westbourne Square to the Braille lending library at Whiteley's department store.*

including that of the curate who works in this diocese afflicted by elephantiasis, etc.

> The Martyr and Saint Anastasia,
> Tho' in Heav'n, suffers still from aphasia.
> She consistently talks
> Of St. Paul as Guy Faukes,
> And gives her own name as Aspasia.

'Very laughable—complete in cardboard box 1/1½. From other dealers 1/3.'

I will explain my new Philosophy, 'Space and Suet' or 'Organised Imagination', when I get back. It really is immense and satisfies everything. It may perhaps be accused of being pessimistic, but I myself find it most comforting and elevating. I think I shall write a book about it.

We have been reading ungeheuere Massen—as Prof: K. wd say—of Schiller and Charybdis (not mine), and are now embarked on the former's vast erg, Die Glocke which is to the last degree philosophisch and ethisch and dich[t]erisch, in fact ungeheuer Kolossal.

While in the musikalisch line, I have been Funereally Marching at Beethoven's Expense. I hope to prelude Chopin in F Ma. shortly. [*Sketch of pianist*] Abersoggumber [Abersoch] o't to be good—all the way to Aberdeen to buy a Burberry gabardene [sic], as Shylock so aptly remarked. Father said something about the Harbara Biles [Barbara Hiles] family being there.

Margaret's correspondence with me has, up to date, been telepathetic—ditto with Trev, as he says she hasn't written to him and I hear she has been diphther[i]tic lately so she might have used her spare time in writing. But perhaps the letters would have been infectious—so it is all for the best.

I don't know if the Oxford termicelli has yet run its course. At any rate, if you have evaporated, the porter will know where you are.

My love to precipitops if you see him. This place would amuse him, I feel sure. I must hasten again funereally to March, so farewell.

Ever yours
A. L. H.

P.S. How good my writing is!
P.P.S. Just returned from Music Lesson with a severe attack of virtuoso's instep, from pedalling too much.

30: TO LEONARD HUXLEY

Deutschhausstrasse 28, [*Marburg*]
23 *June*, [1912]

Dearest Father,

Many thanks to you and Trev for the double-barrelled letter. Trev, I suppose, is at the moment being a soldier. If it's as hot in England as it is here, I'm sorry for him if he's at Aldershot. The weather has changed with startling abruptness and bathing, with water at 65°, is pleasant. On Midsummer's Day, the students celebrated Bismarck from 8 till 12 P.M. On the Bismarck Tower a bonfire was lighted and 1000 odd students processed from the tower to the University, down about ½ mile of winding paths, and thence all round the town. Quantities of Bands discoursing martial music enlivened the night—and altogether it was very jolly.

For the past week the K[a]ysers's beautiful red setter has been ill, refusing nourishment. We have all been trying to persuade him to feed. I think he's quite well now—only he still imagines food is bad and can only be tempted to eat when humans pretend to eat his biscuits and will only drink when his milk is poured on the floor. I dont suppose he will ever do anything different and will tend to be rather laborious.

We shall have to be beginning fairly soon to settle how and when I shall return. Next week July begins—the time flies. I think that, by skilful arrangement, the journey might be reduced in time; in getting an Express to Cöln from here I can do the journey in 3½ as opposed to 6 hours coming. But connections thence are dubious. At any rate, I'd prefer 2½ hours in Cöln than in a dull little train.

We have just started to read *Wallenstein*, rather a vast task; also, in music, Prelude in C Sharp Ma. Extraordinarily much easier than the Beethoven.

Love to all.

Yr. loving son
Aldous

31: TO JULIAN HUXLEY

[*London*]
[3 *February*, 1913]

My dear Julian,
[. . . .]
A thousand apologies for the non-existent . . . wrong there, it should be unremitted . . . examples of typography and calligraphy: for, to tell the truth, I had written three sheets on my cream laid Tudor Block (price, complete

31 *Julian Huxley was a research associate of the Rice Institute, Texas, in 1912-13, and was studying German at Heidelberg. Stammering: an allusion to the fact that their brother Trev stuttered. Aunt Marooe: Aunt Mary, Mrs Ward. The Haldanes: John Scott Haldane and his wife, Louisa, who lived in Oxford; Aldous frequently visited them at their house, Cherwell. They were the parents of J. B. S. Haldane, the biologist, and of Naomi Mitchison (Lady Mitchison) the novelist. Professor Haldane's elder brother, Viscount Haldane, had become Lord Chancellor in 1912. Cunningham: apparently Sir Henry Hardinge Cunynghame, then Assistant Under-Secretary of the Home Office; he was a barrister and an authority on various developments in technology.*

in plush-nugget box, £o:so:d3—written, indeed, but, on the other hand, never posted. You see . . . hein??

Many and great thanks for the Meistersingers, which, one says, we are to see at Covent Garden within the month. I have begun various bits of the Overture, such as befit my playing: the terrible thing about it is that it never stops . . . not a double bar thro'out at which a man can draw b-b-breath. (Dont imagine I've taken to stammering: it's only want of space, which compels me, all too reluctantly to triplicate the B.)

Well, well . . . and I had a very good vacation, or do you call it Ree-cess?, as one (female) American asked me. Trev and I rolled very merrily over the Southern Downings—rain here, rain there, and the devil and all, in fact. Trev loosened his off rear shoe and I have altogether ruined my pasterns and fetlocks: still, everything is right in this best of possible worlds. Then a while chez Aunt Marooe [Mary], who, I regret to say, suffers from a very distressing lack of memory, for, having promised to send Trev and me a belated Xmas present of MONEY to buy Books with . . . she has quite forgotten—and, what makes it worse I have bought some of the books I would have got with it and so has Trev. Such, however, is relatively speaking, life.

All my most valuable time is taken up at present by reading MacAulay, and ten chapters of him at that, for matriculatio ad absurdum. Dreadful old man to write in Latin Prose style: still, it must be.

At Oxford, where (conceive) I was (you know), I met, at the [J. S.] Haldanes' (imagine) a sort of man, called sir Beelzebub Cunningham (Kt), who had met you at Lord Haldane's (Visct)—not to mention lady Jamrachel C: he talked about efficiency, with several capitals and advised me to eat, drink, sleep, think, read, dream, admire, love etcaetera, nothing but internal combustion gas-engines for ten years, by the end of which time, provided I was not dead, withered, blighted, putrefied, dull, mad, neurotic, or ero[t]ic, I should be efficient, (capitals as before) and then I would be of some use to the EMPIRE. Of course I should.

At Oxon, I stayed with the Bodley head [Falconer Madan], and went round Bodley's subterranean book-bowels—a fine place.

When do you return from Teuton Constipation, back into the Good Old English freedom of Thought and Bowels . . . Hein?

Things happen, one must suppose, but Gott sei Dank, I dont read the papers, barring *Pu[n]ch*, *L'Illustration* and *London Opinion*, of course: hence I cannot tell you what is happening here. Ah, you have the inestimable advantage of being able to read *Lusty Leaves*, and *Simplicissimus*, and dear old *Doctor Ulk*—whereas, if I want to get them I have to go to Charlotte Street, Tottenham Court Road, where the German Quarter is, and pay twice as much for a copy of one of these inestimable papers—and so I am prohibited from buying them from purely economic causes. So much for this: more apologies for having covered quite so much space with this.

A.L.H. . . . . ½'"?⅞:³⁵⁄₈₈.()¼/ = -£%¾1234567809

48 Banbury Road, Oxford
[End of April, 1913]

Dearest Father,

Just to wish you the time of day and so forth, and to enquire whether all be well within the brass-doored house.

This city is slowly recovering from the influx of Black Slugs for Convocation and its inevitable Obscurantism. A jolly business! I am going to Sir W[alter] Raleigh's lectures and doing a good lot of reading on the period he's doing—pre-Shakspere drama—reading, amongst others, rather a good book of Jno. Addington Symonds on the subject. He is, perhaps, a shade too lush—but really very readable and interesting.

All Trev's and my spare evenings and afternoons are taken up with rehearsals of Naomi Haldane's stupendous play. When I tell you that there are 52 characters in it, that the stage is about 10 ft by 12, and that 2 periods of 9 years apiece elapse in the middle, you will realize what the thing is like and what its results, as staged by us, will be. If it were not for Lewis Gielgud's supreme talents as a stage-manager, the thing would never go through at all.

I suppose you'll be packing M[argaret] off to school pretty shortly.

How, where, why and when is Julian?

My love to the famiglia.

Your loving son
Aldous

33: TO LEONARD HUXLEY

Villa Belledonne, La Tronche
2 July, [1913]

Dearest Father,

Behold me here the whole of today, having finally decided not to stay in Paris—the connection being easily catchable. The journey was rather wearisome and I didn't sleep much. The last half hour or so was quite extraordinary. Everywhere enormous white limestone cliffs absolutely perpendicular, with broad flat valleys at the bottom. The town itself is chiefly dominated by the hill in the postcard of the villa, which is just behind. It is quite absurd to look along busy streets and see at the end of them, high above the very tall houses, vast great hills sprouting up.

---

32 *The address would seem to belong to Trev Huxley's Oxford 'digs'. Aldous had not matriculated, but was still catching up on his studies. Naomi Mitchison identifies the play as* Saunes Bairos, *presented at Lynam's School in May, 1913. The following year Aldous took part in her play* Prisoners of War *and on the latter occasion had also the rôle of Charon in the* Frogs *of Aristophanes.*

33 *Huxley was later joined at La Tronche by Lewis Gielgud.*

I had rather an awful time on arriving. I drove up to La Tronche—a longish way from the station—and found that they weren't expecting me at the villa and didn't want me at all—and packed me off to M. Lincelon who owns this pension but lives in another in the town. So I drove down there—found M. L, who is an Abbé; had breakfast, which I was badly in need of, while he explained it was all a mistake somewhere and packed me up again here, where I am finally installed.

I am going to have lessons from him—arranged this afternoon—he seems very good.

The keynote of the people staying here is Respectability—very intense and rather middle-aged—so I shall be glad when Lewis appears or some other interesting animal. More news later.

Love to everyone.

Your loving son
Aldous

34: TO LEONARD HUXLEY

Villa B., La Tronche
9 July, 1913

Dearest Father,

Just got your letter; very many thanks therefor. I haven't actually yet got the Bank's note, but I expect it'll come, and there is no pressing need.

I was just translating large hunks of E. F. Benson into French when your letter arrived. It is very hard to find equivalents—particularly as I have a dictionary about so big [*sketch of a rectangle approximately* 20 *mm.* × 30 *mm.*] which has so far told me about five words I didn't know before, one of which was perfectly wrong. Still—one can just get on without. I am reading several books lent by the abbé—some plays of De Musset's, a book on La Fontaine by Taine, which is extremely interesting, and filling it up with *Oxford Book of French Verse.* The people here are really much nicer than I thought. There is a French boy, a little older than I and, I have discovered, one of the ancienne noblesse, being a count, I think, and he is here with a lot of incredibly aristocratic relations—and appears to do nothing at all, (the only professions open to him being army and church) except talk. He is, of course, a royalist and—tho' this is not necessary to a count—an exponent of the tango and one-step; and he knows all the waltzes of years past.

We had a great evening yesterday, when he gave us an exhibition of dancing and an elderly and stout German lady sang several songs, one of which was so emotional and she so temeramentsvoll [temperamentvoll] that she had to stop in the middle, which was lucky, as it allowed the roof to settle down again after it had been lifted several inches by the high notes.

So far it's been not at all too hot: the sky is always cloudy and there is no clear view, but some grand effects in blue. The mountains behind are extraordinary—with splendid shapes and very steep. What is so absurd is that on their slopes there are copses of the homeliest trees, just like in the low valleys of Wales: one expects—what with the precipices, and rushing streams—stunted pines and birches—but one is still so very low. There are acres of vines—dirty little plants—and lots of little farms up on the hills, with countless paths going hither and thither.

Grenoble is one of those places where electricity is running like water. Trams everywhere, telephones, electric light in the smallest villages. The trams go right into the country along very fine roads, where the dust is fearfully deep.

Today there's a touch of rain and a mistral or a tramontane raising up great mountains of dust. It looks bad for going into the town for my lesson this afternoon. I have then to give a discourse on 'England as a military and naval power'—a great speech a quarter of an hour long. A little trying but good for one's French.

Your loving son
Aldous

35: TO LEONARD HUXLEY

Villa Belledonne, La Tronche
Monday, 14 July, 1913

Dearest Father,
   I dont suppose this'll go today—being the national beano—but still, I can but post it. I didn't write yesterday, being out from morn to black night on a most wonderful expedition. I went with a delightful young American couple and my young count—starting at 7.30 from here and 8.15 from the Gare of Grenoble, thronged with Sunday outing-ers, we trundled along the Valley of the Drac, Southwards. After ½ an hour we changed into a charming little electric train, with open work carriages. We then began to rise thus [*diagram*] with tunnels and hairpin turns—in 2 or 3 miles we got right up over the Drac (or one of its tributaries), which came pouring out of a gorge. A little bit further on we were on the edge of the gorge, hanging on by the skin of our teeth, with drops of 500 to 1000 feet, in places very nearly perpendicular. In places the other side of the gorge cant have been more than a hundred yards or so away. We finally left the gorge to enter a high plateau, about 3000 ft up, where our destination, La Mure was. It was an anticlimax after the journey, but was sufficiently amusing and we got a very fine view from on top of a hill. We came down towards sunset—the ravine in shadow and all the limestone crags—in the most fanatastic shapes, violet colour behind. It really is the most wonderful country. I've been finding out about the Grande Chartreuse. It appears it's only 4 hours walking from here—tho' following the road it's about 18 miles.

   The weather is still unsettled—fine yesterday but today very hot and thundery and with occasional bursts of wind and rain of a quite incredible violence—most unsafe to go out as the storms appear out of nowhere in no time. At any rate the heat is so horrible as to make walking very nasty. They threaten fireworks to-night in Grenoble—I don't think they contrive to kill quite so many here as 10 days ago in America—tho' there was a diminution there this year.

By the way, did you say you had arranged with the Bank—as they haven't said anything yet and the purchase of a pair of boots has considerably reduced my present stock.

I hope everyone flourishes, Julian in particular.

Your loving son
Aldous

36: TO MRS ETHEL COLLIER

Villa Belledonne, La Tronche, Grenoble
[30] *July,* 1913

Dear Aunt Ethel,

It really was an amazing feat to have remembered the date of my anniversary—and thank you very much for the letter, which would have arrived on the ipsissimus day, had not the French Postal System contrived to make it take 36 hours to get from Grenoble to La Tronche, a distance of 2 kilometres 17½ toises. Pretty brisk work: they manage these things better in France.

This is really a very good place—a centre of tourism and villégiature, as the indigenes tell us. The hills are very good and rise very steep-like out of a flat plain—unfortunately all the ones near the town are covered with forts to shoot at the Italians, and, of course, one isn't allowed to go in or near— tho' its not as crude as germany where one can't go five yards without meeting a man of blood with his black and white post. [*Sketch.*] The Americans here are very wonderful—they all go to the classes at the University and all speak French as one would in their native city, Pygmalionville (Kans:)— they rarely understand me when I speak their mother tongue with my English accent that one could cut with a spoon. And they say Gee, whiz, bully, my lands, my soul, By ginger, trolley (for tram), gasolene (for petrol) and all the other delightful things one reads in books. But I still await the time when I shall catch them out with YEP and NOPE—but I fear its only in Mo: Wash: Tex: and such outlandish parts that they say that.

Yours affectionately
Aldous

36 *Misdated 'July 3rd 1913'. The sketch shows a stout, baggy and heavily moustached German ('german') sentry pointing his pistol in an enquiring way from behind his post. He is accompanied by a sinuous dachshund.*

Villa B., [La Tronche]
30 July, 1913

Dearest Father,

Thanks for felicitations—a great stroke—3 letters on the day—yours, Trev's and Miss Ella's—and two days late one from Aunt Ethel. The heat has begun with a burst. Yesterday was intolerable and to-day was pretty much the same till it thundered heavily and rained in the afternoon. We attempted a longish expedition up the mountain behind—St. Eynard. We took not the wholly correct path, which landed us at the door of the fort on the summit or nearly so—a strange place, once a convent, built on a precipice, which is full of mysterious holes and cuttings:—unfortunately, one isn't allowed to get thro' it without a permit and as the rocks all round are like the sides of houses and, to make a traverse, one would have to penetrate the maquis which is thicker than anything I've ever seen before, oak, hazel, maple, wild cherry and a pine or two in the more open spaces, when one goes into it, one is liable to come out without a rag on one's back—a thing which happens to about a dozen Germans every year, who go on the difficult hill called le Casque de Néron and invariably have to be looked for by a battalion of Pompiers and Chasseur and are found stark naked and covered with scratches, perched on some impossible pinnacle in the midst of an ocean of maquis. It's curious that it's always Germans, who get lost or killed here: it's their overweening pride and proud stomach in going in places, where they are warned not to go.

We've spent two days in looking for mules—Lewis hankers to ride to the Grande Chartreuse. But on enquiries I have found that the nearest mule is at Voreppe, twenty miles off and as I should think riding a mule up hill and down dale would lack something in comfort, I've given up the idea. [*Sketch*] The great thing is to start early, we were off by 6.30 and it was delicious, tho' even then the sun is hot in full shine. Butterflies and flowers were better to-day than I've seen 'em so far, wonderful Apollos and Camberwell Beauties and fritillaries, brand new and shining like new minted coins— and in flower line, splendid companulas and lots of that little Alpine pink and the starry pink stuff which grows in low plants and is on rockeries and whose name I forget. And an immense green lizard which I accidentally kicked, getting a fearful start. Fruit is good—immense and luscious raspberries, ditto ditto peaches, do. do. greengages and large, but poor figs.

Thunder still continues—hail, rain, and artillery practice seem to accompany it.

Oh, by the by, I rather lack in the shirt line—could you ask Sarah to send the two which were at the wash when I went—also I could do with Trev's maps.

Love to all.

Aldous

37 *Sarah: the Huxleys' parlourmaid.*

Villa B., [La Tronche]
11 *August*, 1913

Dearest Father,

Many thanks for the letter—tho it's rather a shock to be wandering over Europe, as I shall. The Q is—what if Axenfeldt [Axenfeld] says he cant see me till well on in September? but that remains to be seen.

Lewis and I have planned a little two day walk to the Eastward. Some road to begin with and then a path which keeps a good 6-7000 ft level straight opposite the Grande Rousse glaciers and so down near Bourg-d'Oisans. We did an amusing scramble t'other day; having taken a path, which ended in the midst of the maquis we had to penetrate thro' several hundred feet of scrub. It is an apelike form of climbing where the slimmest and the one with tightest buttoned coat succeeds best. I can well understand how Germans, beer-laden and with rucksack and umbrella get pretty badly mauled in it, particularly in the thornier places, which were fairly rare where we were— and what makes it awkward is the number of gulleys going up the hills— dry at this time but deep and with jaggy edges and unpleasantly precipitous sides.

The weather alternates between being admirable for the ducks and the devil—the happy mean is rarely found except at night, most of the last of which I spent in trying to teach the stupidest mass of French people how to dance a Sir Roger de C.—which the Americans call a 'Virginia Reel', for wh: I very justly crushed them and especially the 'Cultured' Bawston lady, who did not know who Sir R. was. She is very wonderful with an old mother who is far more amazing and who, if you're not careful, will sit down and talk pure nonsense in the style of A. C. Benson for hours together. We discovered the daughter wrote 'poetry' and that someone had written her a sonnet calling her a second E. B. Browning and for several days we have plotted to see it: Lewis shewed her a sonnet on his native land—and thence hangs another tale of her—she produced a great quantity of verse, which almost any magazine would be willing to publish for a trifling payment—all about 'brooks that babbled' and 'streams that foamed' in 'silver loops' and quite the correct style, except for an occasional lapse into unrhythm and rhymelessness. Her great aim is to come to Oxford to learn 'versification'.

But the story about Poland is wonderful—she entered into conversation with a lady who described herself in French as a 'Polonaise': Mrs. Parker approached us in the evening and as we seem to her to be veritable mines of knowledge asked us 'what was the history of Polonesia as she could only remember its vaguest outlines'.

Well I hope Connel will be dryish. Trev sent me his maps, which are

---

38 *Dr Theodor Axenfeld was an eminent German oculist.*

very pleasing: I hope his Civil S[ervice] goes all right. And its good Julian
having at least slept once.

Love to R[osalind] and M[argaret].

Your loving son
Aldous

39: TO LEONARD HUXLEY

Balliol
Sunday, [12 October, 1913]

Dearest Father,

Behold me established in the little alcove of my room, with a fine view
of Balliol Chapel in the foreground and some bluer sky than usual in the back.

I have been settling with my Trinity tutor, [R. J. E.] Tiddy, about work.
Some of Sir Walter Raleigh's lectures seem to be indicated combined with
one or two others for the actual literary part and I see another man tomorrow,
who will deal with the Anglo-Saxon portions of my education. I shall be
doing Chaucer mostly with Tiddy himself—and for that purpose I seem to
be reading about three quarters of his works before Wednesday week—and
shall join Raleigh's classes on 17th century, where I shall have essays also.
[N.S.] Talbot is taking me twice a week in logic for P. Mods. and he seems
to want me to do some Plato therefor—*Apology* and *Meno*.

Of course, at least twenty mistakes have been made about Ger and me.
Notes go wrong: Gervas has refused a dance in my name, or rather in his
own, the invitation going wrong. People come and talk at great length to
both of us, thinking each is the other—and so forth. I hope they will live and
learn.

There are many freshmen, of whom a rather large percentage is subfusc
and many come from the Newer world.

I heard some music at the Prices' t'other night—Oliver, Alice P[rice]
and Ernest Walker performing Brahms' clarionet trio (with fiddle for
clarionet) (twice over, too) and Schumann D minor trio. The first is very
fine but I think depressing but the Schumann is great fun with some splendid
passages.

What has occurred to Trev?

Your loving son
Aldous

38 *Connel: in Argyll, where Leonard Huxley generally took his family in the
summer. Rosalind: Aldous' stepmother, Rosalind Bruce Huxley. His father had re-
married in 1912.*

39 *Huxley and his cousin Gervas both went up to Balliol in the Michaelmas term
of 1913. Tiddy, Huxley's tutor until 1915, was a Lecturer in Classics and English
Literature. The Prices: family friends of the Huxleys; they lived in the Judge's
Lodgings, St Giles, where they frequently gave musical parties. Ernest Walker:
Director of Music, Balliol.*

Balliol
[11 *November*, 1913]

Dearest father,

Many thanks for the letter, with good news of your appearing here. I have never come across the Poultons yet, but, up to a certain point, I am always quite prepared to increase my academic and North-Oxfordly acquaintance. To get too heavily ensnared in the Parks is fatal, of course, but it gives one something to do on Sunday afternoons, knowing people in the North. I have been having a good dose of one part of the north lately, in the shape of the Haldanes, who carried off their double event birthday party on Friday and Saturday. Friday was their dance . . . in honour of Jack [J. B. S. Haldane]'s twenty-firster . . . and on Saturday was the common or garden birthday party. The dance was very amusing . . . the Haldanes always contrive to know and invite very good people to their functions: however, I must get to dance better, or otherwise everyone suffers. But the Saturday party is the really wonderful affair: I came at 4.30 and left at 11.30: the first half of the time was occupied in eating tea and playing other essentially childish games, for the benefit of the hordes of infants: the H's have a most admirable device for breaking the ice. They turn the whole party . . . about forty, with the children . . . into a large and empty room, in the middle of which stands a bran pie, where bran is replaced by confetti. Everyone having dived in the pie and removed something, one proceeds to take the confetti and throw it at everyone else. After half an hour of this . . . ones hair, pockets, stomach and inmost underclothing being completely filled with confetti . . . shyness, as such, almost completely ceases to exist. One then comes out into an ante-chamber, where seven highly trained, amateur officials remove as much of the confetti from one's hair and outer garments as is humanly possible. That didn't prevent me strewing my whole room with little bits of paper, when I undressed that night. Fireworks ensue, then (children dismissed) supper and afterwards, the most magnificent Nebuchadnezzars, and finally a good form of blind-man's buff, where everyone stands round the room in a circle and the blind man walks up and prods someone, telling him at the same time to make a noise . . . such as the sound of rain falling on mu[d] —and the speaker has to be recognised by the sound of his voice.

I have been quite busy and have got very much interested in my paper for Raleigh: the history of 'Absalom and Achitophel' and the answers and counter answers is most exciting and I have found in Bodley, the most fascinating volume, in which the original satires and all the other pamphlets and poems and ballads connected with them are bound up. There is the most glorious work by Settle, one of the more serious answers, called 'Absalom

40 *Poultons: E. B. Poulton was a Fellow of Jesus and Hope Professor of Zoology.*

Senior', being about the Duke of York, with the false Achitophel turned into the brave Achitophel and all turned the other way round. And really the poem is extremely good in itself and does something more than what Dryden himself said of his work . . . that it rhymed and rattled. Then there are some excellent ballads and hundreds of other poems, which I haven't had time to look at yet, interlarded with splendid Broadside songs, with the tune and words all on one great folio sheet: the music is rather hard to read: their clefs seem to have different signs and their sharp and flat signs are quite different: I think I shall take a few down and examine them at my leisure. I'm afraid they don't provide a piano in Bodley for that purpose.

It gives one a queer new sensation, seeing all these absurd old books, as one somehow always pictures past ages as producing about ten classical works by one or two great names and nothing much else, whereas the trash must have been quite as plentiful in comparison, if not more so, than it is now.

What news of Julian? Everyone enquires whether and when he is coming down here.

Love to all concerned.

Your loving son
Aldous

41: TO LEONARD HUXLEY

Union Society, Oxford
[*25 November*, 1913]

Dearest Father,

Just a line: I've been very busy lately with this paper for Raleigh, which wd. grow indefinitely if I used all the material possible. As it is, dealing only with the more reputable and less anonymous of Dryden's enemies, there is a lot to do. And also, Bodley is so detestable. It has lost the 2 copies it's supposed to have of Shadwell's *Satires*, without which I am very much stumoured, as only small passages have been reprinted by Scott in his life of D[ryden]. I've been touting round the College libraries in the hope of finding a copy— but without success. To day I've found out about a new, signed satire wh: I'll have to read and write about—and all, with what I can make of skimpy bits of Shadwell, by Thursday. Still, it's great fun.

I'm lunching with Geoffrey Young to-day, he being in this city for a day or two. I hear there was some sort of climber's binge on Saturday, where Trev was seen by Geoffrey Madan of this College.

41 *Geoffrey Winthrop Young was the president of the Climbers' Club (see Robert Graves,* Good-bye to All That, *Chapter IX). Trevenen Huxley edited the* Climbers' Club Journal, *to which, in March, 1914, his brother Aldous contributed 'A Lunndon Mountaineering Essay', on staircase climbing. Geoffrey Madan, whom Huxley had known at Eton, was the son of Falconer Madan, the Bodley Librarian.*

Enormous numbers of absurd collections coming on now, which are rather a bore.

Love to R.

Your loving son
Aldous

42: TO LEONARD HUXLEY

Union Society, Oxford
[February, 1914]

Dearest Father,

Many thanks for your p.c. I will admit there has been some such abeyance of epistolary communication as you mention! Well, things flourish—the only fly in the ointment being P. Mods—infernally stupid exam, trod out by the feet of weeping boys from the wine-press of boredom.

The whole city is permeated with the Mission to Undergraduates—the Bp of Oxford being heard twice nightly in a knock-about sermon at St. Mary's. Of course the only people who go are those who are already saved— the busy mockers preferring to gnash their false teeth in comfort at their own firesides.

I saw the most magnificent performance of McBeth [sic] at Linham's [Lynam's] School t'other day—the whole thing taken as a roaring farce, frightfully exciting but not quite, perhaps, as old Shakebake meant it. The fights were truly brilliant. I've never seen anything so realistic—hammer and tongs at one another—swords broken by the dozen—one or two good bangs on the head—and the whole school cheering the various favourites:— even up to the last when fate had to decide the contest McB got his cheers and exhortations.

The most admirable buses ply these days in the town—something of a relief after the so-called trams—rival companies, private and municipal, a great joke. I shall be sorry however when, between them, they shake down Magdalen tower. However, the course of progress must not be stayed for an effete bit of architecture like that.

Love to all.

Aldous

43: TO LEONARD HUXLEY

Union Society, Oxford
Sunday, [22 February, 1914]

Dearest Father,

Many thanks for your letter with its news of Julian. No very great excitements in this town, except the O.U.D.S. *Acharnians*, which I saw last

42 *Lynam's School: 'Skipper' Lynam's Oxford Preparatory School, later the Dragon School. The Haldane children had been pupils there.*

night. The sole benefit conferred by P. Mods reading was that I understood all very well,—recognising with more than ordinary and almost inhuman distinctness the passages which had been set in a collection two days before. The acting was remarkably good—the leading man wonderfully fluent and at home with the language—his fault being one on the good side, in this sort of incomprehensible play, the fault of overacting. Hubert Parry's music was most delightful. An overture, which introduced 'Rule Brit[annia]', 'Hitchy-koo', 'What can the matter be' etc etc. and in the middle the most priceless 'Little pigs minuet', piccolo and double bass imitating swine at earlier and later ages. After the performance, P., who had been conducting made a speech, very ridiculous and amusing. I met Timmy Jekyll outside [the] theatre and he carried me off to partake of an enormous and luxurious supper he had prepared in the digs he was stopping the week-end. About 12 people there, including a man, who had been at Montana and recognised me, tho' I couldn't remember his name—a doctor, I think, smallish, light brown hair and short moustache.

Toggers in full swing—a row thro', so far, every night for the 1st boat, while the 2nd, bumped by Merton and Wadham, has sunk into the 3rd division, escaping being sent down yet further by Hertford and immense difficulty.

Love to everybody.

Your loving son,
Aldous

44: TO LEONARD HUXLEY

[*Balliol*]
Wednesday, [13 *May,* 1914]

Dearest Father,

A line before bed-time, after a very boring evening's reading of all the rather second-class XVIIIth century poets in quest of early changes from Augustan to romantic style and natural description. It is melancholy work ploughing thro' the 'elegancies' and the 'just thoughts' in which they all abound. How the age could bear the platitudinising of its more serious poetry is quite beyond me. It is impossible to put oneself in their point of view.

What news of Julian lately? I have heard nothing for some time. Trev's state, too, seems somewhat dim—I don't know whether he's coming down this week-end or not.

44 *Eastbourne: Henrietta Heathorn Huxley, the mother of Leonard Huxley, had died, and he was closing her house, Hodeslea, built as a residence by T. H. Huxley in 1890. Illustrations from 'A Bad-Taste Exhibition' appeared in* The Sketch *of 13 May, p. 163.*

I hope things at Eastbourne are more or less settled now—the letters sorted and burnt and the furniture packed. I gather that 27 will fairly burst with bits of objects of vertu and utility.

Talking about objects of vertu,—there were some delightful pictures in this weeks *Sketch* of an exhibition of bad taste, the crowning feature of which was a cast of the Venus of Milo, with a clock let flush into her stomach. It must have needed a really great mind to think of that particular method of combining utility and beauty.

I want to take some lessons in illustrative drawing—a form I most appreciate in modern art and the one I am best adapted to by nature. It wd be quite fun to take a course. I am told the 'Press Art Achool' is quite good.

The question of funds, however, is rather troublous. My exam fees, £12.12, combined with Union and battels have sorely reduced me. If you could advance me some cash, it wd. be a great boon and I cd. start my drawing.

Love to Rosalind.

Ever your loving son
Aldous

45: TO LEONARD HUXLEY

Hadspen House, Castle Cary, Somerset
[Summer, 1914]

Dearest Father,

Providentially cool once more—overcast since my arrival and some rain. This is a delightful house, with nice sloping gardens and traces of a complex system of avenues laid out in William IV fashion over the park in front. However, storms have carried away most of the elms that made the avenues, but there are one or two very jolly old rides left.

This is an almost Devonshire-like country, with sudden, deep valleys and cider in the foreground and cows and the like. We went to Glastonbury yesterday a delightful spot and most interesting—it being (α) Avalon, (β) (and more authentically) a home of lake-dwellers, (γ) the resting place of Joseph of Arimathea and St. Patrick, (δ) the site of a most stupendous abbey, the remains of which are very good. It is a queer flat land all round Glastonbury, once, no doubt overrun by the sea and now regularly flooded. In the middle stand out little hillocks, best of which is Glastonbury Tor, at whose base the lake dwellers villages have been dug up. [*Sketch*]

The Newdigate for next year is apparently on Glastonbury—so we have been collecting copy. Joseph of A. really appeals to me—I think I shall write a Masefieldian epic about Jolly old Joe-bags.

I gather the party breaks up on Monday so I shall return then—there is to be a large week-end gathering.

45 *Hadspen House: the seat of the Hobhouse family.*

By the way—a horrid shock—I discovered at the station I had ½ and not a whole sovereign in my purse, so could only run to a single. Could you send me a pound to escape hence. I have no cheque book with me.

Love
Aldous

46: TO LEWIS GIELGUD

27 Westbourne Square, W.
[Summer, 1914]

I'm glad to think you are mortifying the flesh in the sunshine of Lucerne —but, of course, the heat can have been nothing like what we had here last week: 'Why, it's monstrous, shameful, shocking, brave old warrior, but beware' K.T.L. The fear of death came before me one night: I should have perished had I remained at home: seizing my opera cloak and foaming at the mouth to keep myself cool, I rushed out of the house, only to find near Charing Cross that in my anguish at home I had undone my tie and collar and shirt, all of them soft: consciousness almost lost for the next hour, vague remembrances of the embankment and suicide float before me, but I picture myself more clearly at last in Gambrin[i]s, drinking iced beer and talking some foreign tongue to a strange woman: that iced beer saved me from death, my good sir—but as for the Long Acre Club . . . it was, on the whole, lucky that we did not go there the night we intended to, seeing as how the said Club has been shut almost since the beginning of last term: this fact I learned from VERY RELIABLE SOURCES. Returned from a very argumentative five days with the Hobhoi [Hobhouses], all very capital and so forth on: it is too much trouble to describe it any further: I will refer you to chapter XXIII of my Life and Letters.

I cannot think that anything of interest occurs in this land. Everything is lost except HONOUR. Who knows how long that bubble may remain unprickt?

Communications with Mrs. Parker have filled most of my time. She is too utterly intolerable: bah, let her go . . . Pismire creature, brushed lightly off the flanks of my colossal personality.

In spite of your name, dear old chap, I recognise you as an Englishman and an undergraduate. 'All who serve her are her sons (slight gesture with left hand) and besides (change of voice into mellower key) if Hermes is still the guide of the dead, he will take us, because we have not worshipped these women's gods (proudly, and with another movement of the left hand) out of Asia.' But I do not grant your likeness to the bewitching siren of Stella (special Oxford Times representative) her choice. The perfect feature was calling Robertson Tobinson, which is almost infinitely funny.

Why should I go on writing any more? It is too hot, it is too late, I am too bored, God is too bad, life is too short, everything is too much something else . . . it all goes to prove that the policy of excessivism is the only right one: the whole natural world is habitually in a state of excess. One must keep up with nature: exceed the limit—only, of course, one hasnt got enough money, everything comes down to that at last: if one had, what a magnificent ideal one would have to live up to . . . smoking too much, drinking too much, thinking too much, poking too much, walking too much, talking too much.

So to bed.

A. L. H.

47: TO LEONARD HUXLEY

Connel, [Argyll]
Saturday, [22 August, 1914]

Dearest Father,

We have just got your telegram, which is distinctly cheering: it is a great thing to have heard of Trev's being seen and to have localized the clues. We await your letter and further details.

Julian would write, were he not a little tired after a longish day out on the *Princess Louise*. We went south to the Isles of the Sea, a most lovely cruise down the Sound of Kerrera and out into the Firth of Lorne—a day of cloud and sun, with wonderful colours and shadows everywhere. I do hope this latest clue will prove the right one.

The afternoon post is to be caught. Love to Rosalind.

Your loving son
Aldous

48: TO GERVAS HUXLEY

Connel, Argyll
[Late August, 1914]

My dear Gerry,

Thank you so much for your letter.

There is—apart from the sheer grief of the loss—an added pain in the cynicism of the situation. It is just the highest and best in Trev—his ideals—which have driven him to his death—while there are thousands, who shelter

---

47 *Noel Trevenen Huxley had been missing since 15 August from the Hermitage, a nursing home near Reigate. On the 23rd it was found that he had hanged himself. He was twenty-four years old. He had become deeply depressed through a combination of circumstances: his achieving only a second instead of a first-class degree at Oxford; his failure in an examination for the Civil Service; and, quite unknown to the family until after his death, an unwise love affair with a girl whom for social reasons he could see no clear way to marry. Trev had been especially endeared to Aldous by his sensitive, gracious and upright character.*

their weakness from the same fate by a cynical, unidealistic outlook on life. Trev was not strong, but he had the courage to face life with ideals—and his ideals were too much for him.

ALH

49: TO LEONARD HUXLEY

Northfield, St. Abbs, Berwicks.
[14 September, 1914]

Dearest Father,

As you are staying on at Connel, Aunt S[ophy] has asked me to stay on a corresponding period here. Everyone but the elder members of the family goes to-day and I shall be able to do some quiet reading, in an advantageously bracing air.

What news today! It's splendid. As for the Russians—we have had more alarms, excursions and counter-excursions about them than we can count. They culminate today in a letter from a Captain Bertie Stobart, at the front in Belgium, who announces that the Russians are at the base—presumably Ostend. This is fairly circumstantial. On the whole, I doubt if any have come thro' England. Much more likely to have gone all round by sea. Frank Stobart, a N[orth] E[astern] R[ailway] director, says, for certain, that none have passed over East Coast lines. Lawrence [Laurence Collier], at the F.O., says the scheme was broached and abandoned. I'm told this weeks *Bystander* has a photo of troops landing at Ostend, who look very suspiciously Russian. On the whole, from everything, I think one can be fairly sure that the Russians have come round by sea to Belgium.

I dare say Julian told you that we actually saw the *Pathfinder* explosion— a great white cloud with its foot in the sea. The St. Abbs' lifeboat came in with the most appalling accounts of the scene. There was not a piece of wood, they said, big enough to float a man—and over acres the sea was covered with fragments—human and otherwise. They brought back a sailor's cap with half a man's head inside it. The explosion must have been frightful. It is thought to be a German submarine that did it, or, possibly, a torpedo fired from one of the refitted German trawlers, which cruise all round, painted with the British port letters and flying the British flag.

This is an extremely jolly place—a large and correspondingly hideous house, right on the cliff's edge—and very fine crags and rolling country inland. We motored to Norham t'other day—a fine place. Love to R.

Your loving son
Aldous

49 *The Stobarts were relations of Mrs Henry Huxley (Aunt Sophy). Laurence (now Sir Laurence) Collier: Huxley's cousin, the brother of Joan. H.M.S.* Pathfinder *had been sunk off St Abbs on 5 September.*

27, Westbourne Square, W.
Saturday, [probably September, 1914]

My dear Jelly

I have just got your letter and am sitting down to answer it here, in the room that Trev and I used to share together, where every book and every picture helps to keep alive the memories—which, though they bring a terrible sadness with them, are always of a past time that has been very happy.

It is of that one ought to think, of the past, and one ought to be grateful and thankful for all the years one has spent with one that was among the noblest and best of men—but Oh God, it's bitter sometimes to sit in this room reading before the fire—alone and to think of all the happy evenings we sat there together and all the hours I hoped to have again, when he was better. It's a selfish grief perhaps, but oh Jelly, you know what he was to me.

I had just been thinking, when your letter came, of you and what had happened to that dear friend of his and mine during these fearful times. Julian has started for America this very day—so much better than he was, when he came over to spend the summer with us in July. And Margaret is back at school: she is still so much of a child in some ways—and I am glad for her sake, because it has saved her from fully realising the whole tragedy—: and my father, too, is better now; he was most terribly broken for a time.

Dear Jelly, I should like so very much to see you again. Might I come and visit you? My father and step-mother arent really seeing very many people at present, or else it would have been so nice if you could have come here.

Good-bye, Jelly dear, and thank you so much for having written.

Yours affectionately
Aldous

Cherwell, Oxford
Thursday night, [autumn, 1914]

My dear Jelly,

I would have written before—only, somehow, I was always busy—to tell you how very, very much I enjoyed seeing you again. One has so few friends left to one in these days, when everyone has gone off to the wars, that those, who are left, are still more precious than they were before. One only realises, when one's friends are gone, how much their friendship meant to one.

It is nicer, I think, being here than in an empty Balliol. They are very

---

50 *Mlle Jelly d'Aranyi (then von Aranyi), the concert violinist, was a family friend of the Huxleys. Julian Huxley held an appointment as Assistant Professor of Zoology at the Rice Institute, Texas.*

nice, these people I am staying with. The mother is charming and the daughter, who is only sixteen, but who has just got engaged is quite amusing. One good thing about living out of college is that I can do much more work, not having friends coming in and talking to me all the time. Oh dear—I must go to bed—the middle of the night and my fire has gone out. One always feels so queer in the middle of the night, dreadfully melancholy, and fierce, and sentimental, and bored. Everything seems to be so grim and one feels at times like Baudelaire where he says:—

> L'ennui, fruit de la morne incuriosité,
> Prend les proportions de l'Immortalité.

Wonderful stuff French poetry—I once tried to write some myself, without much success, as you might imagine!

Write to me, do.

Yours affectionately
Aldous

52: TO LEONARD HUXLEY

Union Society, Oxford
[January, 1915]

Dearest Father,

Many thanks for sending books—which, however, I'd forgotten till too late to prevent my being fined 1/-: but they arrived on the day of the notice of the fine and there is no increased daily increment to be paid on them.

I'm taking a French conversation once a week with the Haldanes and one or two other people—our instructress being a very charming French lady [Yvette Chapelain], stranded over here since before the war. She shocked Naomi and Mrs. H., by her very French and very orthodox Catholic views about the education of la jeune fille—the Haldanes' principle being much like the French magazine *Je Sais Tout*—while the French lady was all for the becoming and pretty ignorance of the jeune fille.

Jack Haldane, we hear to-day, is starting for France on Tuesday.
Love to R.

Your loving son
Aldous

53: TO LEONARD HUXLEY

Union Society, Oxford
[Circa January, 1915]

Dearest Father,

It was the 24th, wasn't it, that you suggested coming? Mrs. Haldane remarked today that it would be nice if you cd. come to Cherwell—however, she is going to be away on the 24th. She said she was going to write.

51 *Huxley was living with Professor and Mrs Haldane. Their daughter, Naomi, was engaged to Richard Mitchison (now Baron Mitchison), to whom she was married in February, 1916.*

By the way, before I forget, could you get me some more Pogenstecker ointment at Martindale's.

Things at Balliol adjust themselves to present circs:—to such a degree that a man in my year, who, before this time, enjoyed the name of Reuben Bussweiler, has now returned as Ronald Boswell. Rather a subtile change!

I am working this term on the mediaeval creatures, Lydgate, Occleve and the like—terrible people, who never wrote anything less than an epic—unless it was an allegory in five thousand lines.

I find myself secretary this term of Raleigh's essay society, which is reading papers on XVIIIth cent: nearly all the members are Americans. I shall have to try and understand them, when they read their papers, in order to take résumés of them for the minutes.

Love to R.

Your loving son
Aldous

54: TO JULIAN HUXLEY

Balliol College, Oxford
1 *February*, [1915]

My dear Julian,

I am sending you a copy of my Glastonbury effort to look at . . . an experiment in realism, in which, for the moment, I believe quite uniquely.

'Realism in art and letters, in everything, except life' . . . that is my motto, and it seems to me to be about the ne plus ultra of human wisdom. But here's another work, which occurred to me in my bath this morning and which is worth a hundred Newdigates, by reason of its golden and pastoral simplicity;

> Lorsque tu seras toute à moi,
> Nous viverons [sic] en reine et roi:
> Nous mangerons de beaux [sic] asperges,
> Nous buverons [sic] le lait des vierges:
> Notre lit sera aussi grand
> Que ce du bon roi de Basan,
> Où, chaque nuit, et tous les jours,
> Nous goûterons nos doux amours.

How pale, compared to this, is Marlowe's effort!

Practically speaking, Sligger [F. F. Urquhart] and myself are the only two possible people left alive in Oxford; even the few possibilities of last term have now vanished, leaving only a sort of obscene riff-raff . . . [. . . .]

Quite a considerable proportion of my acquaintance, including Gervas and Jack Haldane are now out at the front; the rest anticipate going in the spring, I suppose. I suggest that the war be over in September, in order that the relics of them may come back for the Michaelmas term. But as I expect this is going to be a Thirty Years War, I regard the prospect as unlikely. This argle-bargling about who began the damned thing is most undignified. It is, of course, axiomatic that the Germans are lying about it . . . but still, it is for the historian of 2000 to settle that question, for us to extirpate the vipers.

Ive been reading miracle plays . . . a most charming form of literature, very reminiscent of the Nebuchadnezzar, tho' more blasphemous, and also very very like *The Dynasts*, which, as I suppose has percolated through to your side, has been put on the stage this Xmas by [H. Granville] Barker. The miracle play cycles were on just the same epic scale and introduced all the illustrative irrelevancies of the Hardeian work. The verse of the miracles is distinctly better than Hardy's turgid stuff, which is often amazingly well-versed in 'the art of sinking'. However, it is the thing to *have* seen, especially for the LITERARY MANNIKIN!

Well, well, when London and Oxford are both wiped out by bombs, I shall work my passage over to America and come to your academy as Professor of Obstetrics or something of the sort. Meanwhile, the quiet life of Anglo Saxon lectures amid a crowd of painful young women.

Veuillez agréer mes tendresses les plus aiguës.

A. L. H. . . .

55: TO LEONARD HUXLEY

Union Society, Oxford
[5 *February*, 1915]

Dearest Father,

Many thanks for your letter—with apologies for any lâches [sic] on my part.

A fearful blow has just fallen on me—in the fact that I am being widowed of my tutor, who is going to serve his King and country in Territorial armies at Nottingham. The result is I am to be shifted to a stranger that knows not Israel—one [Percy] Simpson, who lives—and this is quite too unthinkably awful—at 155 Iffley Road, where I am to see him after Hall to-night. It is all rather a bore.

I had the most appalling tea-party t'other day, at which a Belgian Professor and his wife were present. Mrs. H. and J[ack] and Mrs Belgian spoke French, Mr. H. speaks only German, neither the Belgian nor wife spoke English and one of the other guests spoke anything but English. So Mrs. Belgian, Mrs. H. and J. talked French on one side, Mr. Belgian and Prof. H. German on the other, while into the no man's land in the midst we each hurled words of English—or else one talked across the table in German mixed with French. Resulting strain was fearful.

I've been reading a lot of French in spare time lately, especially poetry, which is much more interesting than one supposes at first sight. The moderner men are most amusing—such as Mallarmé, the symbolist who never says what he means, whose syntax is extremely peculiar and who prints his works without any punctuation except full-stops. Under such circumstances it is no dishonour for the mere foreigner to retire, vanquished, from the field—particularly as the French themselves understand very little. I hope the day will come, when I shall be French enough to appreciate Hugo—but I don't think it ever will.

Your loving son
Aldous

56: TO LEONARD HUXLEY

Union Society, Oxford
Sunday, [*circa* 21 *February,* 1915]

Dearest Father,

Many thanks for your letter. The stye had begun to subside on its own initiative, when I had the 500,000,000 staphylococks injected—but this dose and another at a suitable interval will prevent it recurring: the real trouble was that, attacking my sound eye, the stye made it hard to see.

I heard a very jolly concert the tother night—Lady's Musical—where we had the Brahms 5tet in F minor, which is really magnificent, and one appreciates it more each time one hears it.

I'm working on old plays with my new tutor, who is one of the world's experts on Elizabethan drama—which, it must be confessed, is, in the bulk, rather tedious. The ebullitions of the critics, like J. A. Symonds and Swinburne, are rather absurd—seeing that no critic can possibly deny that—with the exception of Shakespeare's best—all Elizabethan tragedy is melodrama. All the critics pick out individual scenes which are, of course, astonishingly good, while they neglect to consider the pieces as a whole.

Sligger's nephew, Frank Tyr[r]ell, has just been killed, which is sad— and I see that a man of my year, [A. R.] Cross, has been wounded, tho I don't yet know how badly.

I must stop as I must be off to tea with the Gilbert Murrays—whom, for one reason or another, I've never yet contrived to meet. The neglect should, I feel, be remedied.

Love to R.

Your loving son
Aldous

57: †TO JELLY D'ARANYI

Cherwell, Oxford
Thursday, [*early spring,* 1915]

Now, my dear Jelly, we can't have you abusing yourself in this manner—! We will agree, if you like, to differ in our opinions about ourselves. But you must, at least, admit that you are a great dear for having written such a charming letter!

We have had a real spring day to-day. Sunshine and blue sky and birds singing: it cheers one up after these black weeks of rain and mud. But it is horrible to think that what most people are really looking forward to the spring for is that they will be able to begin to fight more fiercely than ever. But I suppose it will be really a good thing, if it finishes off the matter a little quicker.

After this war I dont think it will be the fashion to write depressing books any more—Ibsen and Galsworthy and all that nonsense will be quite démodé. We shall begin again to write cheerful books; as in the nineteenth century after the Napoleonic wars—just for a change from the horribleness of life. The depressing, sordid books come after long peace, when people have been used to seeing only the comfortable side of life—and then someone discovers that life is really rather grim and says so in a book—and all the middle-class people who have never seen anything but the pleasant side, read it and say the man is a genius—and all the silly young men and women say it's the only form of literature—just because they have never seen grimness in life and find it a pleasant novelty in a book. But the war will put a stop to it—people will have discovered only too thoroughly that there is a black side to life and in consequence, they will go to literature to see the sunny side. There will be a great change, I am sure.

What a long silly letter: it's like a sermon!

Goodbye, dear Jelly.

Yours ever
Aldous

P.S. How's the dancing? I should love to see you, because I'm sure you would look charming!

58: TO LEONARD HUXLEY

Train [en route to Oxford]
[23 April, 1915]

Dearest Father,

Not at all a nice journey—a most fearful crowd—chiefly military—and we weren't in till nearly six. *If M[argaret] is coming up alone on Monday, send her 1st or 2nd*—otherwise it may well be rather unpleasant for her.

27 in state of chaos—but my bed and a dining table at least remain above the surface—so all was comparatively well.

On Thursday night I went to D[uke] of York's to see Gaby Deslys in

58 *Bice: daughter of Mrs Burton-Brown of Prior's Field. North House: the Hon. John Collier's residence, 69 Eton Avenue, N.W. Leonard and Rosalind Huxley were staying in Dorset at the Grand Hotel, Swanage, where Aldous had passed his spring holidays.*

Barry [J. M. Barrie]'s farce-revue *Rosy Rapture*. Things began well by my finding in D4 and 5 of Dress Circle (myself being D3) no other than Mrs. B[urton]-B[rown] and Bice—while just below me were Lawrence [Laurence Collier] and [Philip] Guedalla. The thing is extremely funny by reason of its magnificent inconsequence and fatuity:—and some of the mechanical jokes —such as the cinema of the baby in the automobile pram, who runs over— Juggernaut-fashion—those who get in the way—are very good. Further the playlet which precedes it is excellent. All worth seeing—in fact Gaby Deslys quite won the heart of Mrs. B-B!

Lunched today (Fri) at N[orth] House—where all in good form—: and La[u]rence tells me that the reason why we've shilly-shallied so long at the Dardanelles is that the French wanted to get some neutrals to come in, in the neighbourhood—fatal policy.

Best love to all.

Your loving son
Aldous

59: TO LEONARD HUXLEY

Union Society, Oxford
[*26 April*, 1915]

Dearest Father,

Many thanks for your letter. The Wards' scheme for Lakes after Scotland seems good—but we must work it out in greater detail during this prospective week-end of mine—which may be almost any time even in the middle of the week—whenever most convenient. But we'll see.

K[itchener]'s Army seems to be streaming out now, which means that a great many more people I know will go.

Jack H[aldane] appears to be slightly hit in right arm and left side by portions of J. Johnson. Whereabouts unknown—but a wire from the clearing-station, brought back by one of Dr. H's assistants in France, prognosticates 3 weeks. Naomi's fiancé is just off—with a draft—cavalry, too, —so I suppose they'll be needed now.

Poor [Robert] Gibson—our don—is missing—and things look rather black—and I suppose it's John Selwyn who appears in a list as wounded about 3 days ago. I must write to Aunt Maud—meanwhile you see that Gordon and Phyllis [Selwyn] have had another infant.

This hustling of aliens is rather damnable—mob-law of a type one only expects among Apaches—and the Government taking a repressive action on the strength of it seems to me to be the last word in lack of dignity. If

---

59 *J. Johnson: a German heavy shell, especially the 5.9, was known as Jack Johnson (see Partridge,* Dictionary of Slang and Unconventional English). *The Selwyn brothers were Huxley's cousins, sons of the Rev. E. Carus Selwyn and Lucy Arnold Selwyn.*

anything of the kind was wanted it certainly was wanted 10 months ago,—
and now it betrays mere feeblemindedness to drift on the stream of popular
passion. We're losing our heads and our senses of humour—and soon we
shall be reduced to writing Hymns of Hate—then we're lost.

What news of J?

Love to R.

Your loving son
Aldous

60: TO G. GIDLEY ROBINSON

Union Society, Oxford
[*18 May,* 1915]

Dear Mr. Robinson,

It was so kind of you to write. This subject of the teaching of English
literature as a matter of fact interests me a good deal. I think it was about a
year ago that I saw—rather glimpsed little more than the title—a pamphlet
about the teaching of the subject at Rugby. I should very much like to see
the numbers of the *P*[*reparatory*] *S*[*chools*] *Review* where the question of
'back-bone' to the mere reading of literature is discussed. 'Backbone' here
at Oxford is provided, of course, by the Anglo Saxon branch of the school.
But I think that, unless it was almost miraculously taught, it would be unsuitable for the young—seeing that it is considerably more difficult than
Greek and that the literature is obscure and dull. However, I think a little
philology would be good—and—well taught—interesting.

What I have always thought would be good to combine with a more or
less systematic reading of literature—is a sort of history of culture—or
civilisation since that word is now branded. One would get the children to
read books—or compile anthologies for them—throwing light on the conditions of life:—a sort of Macaulay 'England in 1684' chapter one would make,
out of the best literature, and even from the obscurer tracts of any given age.
Further, one might tag on to literature-study a sketched history of thought—
old conceptions of medicine, development of alchemy and astrology into
scientific channels—shewing how

'by the way there doth befall
Some odoriferous thing or medicinal'

—while, possibly, one might touch on the development of religion and
philosophy—tho' that would necessarily be for the older and more advanced.

I am sure that this sort of history would be extremely interesting—
particularly as the learners would have some standard of their own to work
by—would see their own gas-light and railway trains and doctors and would

60 *G. Gidley Robinson had been the headmaster of Hillside. The verse quotation is*
from Donne, 'Love's Alchemy'.

thence more fully appreciate the development of them from a past that lacked them. Whereas, the ordinary history book is liable to convey not very much. All I carry away of that period's history learning are one or two of [C. W. C.] Oman's less felicitous phrases—'King James... that stuttering, lolling pedant' and the like—while the peace of Utrecht survives only as the woodcut of a steeple and a canal, labelled 'Utrecht', adorning [J. R.] Green's shortest history.

Of course a whole series of books would have to be written, out of an existing void, in order to make such a history possible—moreover there would have to be some development of it at universities—a school, perhaps, of the history of science and philosophy, the school of essential rather than accidental history!

I should very much like to come over some time to Newbury—some time in June I should think. But may I crystallize my present nebulousness later?

Please give my best regards to Mrs. Robinson.

Yours sincerely
Aldous Huxley

61: TO LEONARD HUXLEY

Union Society, Oxford
[8 *June*, 1915]

Dearest Father,

Many thanks for your letter. Fearful heat rages here, making one wish only to bathe—a pleasure from which I am temporarily debarred owing to a rather absurd accident. I walked into some nitric acid, which one of Dr. Haldane's assistants had put outside the lab and left in the pathway. It squirted over my foot and leg—a fact which I didn't at the time notice: and only ¾ of an hour later did I begin to feel something odd. I thought at first it was a fly of particular virulence that had bitten me and it was some time later that I discovered, on removing my sock that my heel was stained a brilliant yellow and was beginning to blister. Today walking has to be done with caution: it is all rather a bore, tho' not really bad—only a question of blisters and loss of skin.

I'm going to town next Friday to attend a dinner at the Gielguds' in honour of Lewis' 21st birthday. Term ends, I suppose on Saturday week or the following Monday. I shall have to see about getting a suitable ticket so as to stop at the Lakes on the way back—also, I must see if the Harries propose to have me any time—in which case further arrangements will have to be made. August at P. F. sounds nice. I may come up here in September to do some reading in Bodley for the Stanhope Prize, which sets as this year's

61 *The Harries: i.e., presumably, 'the Harrys'—Henry Huxley's family.*

subject: 'Development of Satire from Restoration to Revolution'—upon which I've already touched in a paper and got some quite useful material. There are of couse a great many besides Dryden—while there is a huge corpus of ribald anonymity, parts of which are often entertaining.

I trust weather will improve at Connel.

Love to R.

Your loving son
Aldous

62: TO LEONARD HUXLEY

Union Society, Oxford
[Mid-June, 1915]

Dearest Father,

Thanks for the letter and the very useful list of trains. I find that it will probably be impossible to get away before Monday—Balliol has that unpleasant habit of keeping you up over the week-end. So expect me [at Connel] Tuesday morning. I find no difficulty in getting the £3.3. ticket from here—so all will be well—and I see no reason why I should go home first.

I am still hobbling about in rather an absurd way—but the saffron skin is peeling off and leaving a healthier, if somewhat over-raw, skin below.

I went to town on Friday to celebrate Lewis' 21ster and there found Gervas—invalided home with hay fever—tho' otherwise very flourishing. We went round shopping together—and I was immensely tickled to see the huge respect and sympathy paid to my limp—while Ger—who was wearing a new uniform—was regarded merely as a specimen of K[itchener]'s nth Army! I am thinking, therefore, of keeping up my wounded hero limp for the duration of the war. It will always secure seats in buses!

Love to R.

Aldous

63: † TO JELLY D'ARANYI

Connel Ferry, Argyll
[Late June, 1915]

My dear Jelly,

It *was* nice to get your letter! I am here, enjoying a week of west-coast of Scotland summer after the stuffiness of Oxford. I know nothing more beautiful than this place, with its beautifully shaped mountains, its great lochs running in among the hills, its islands and its glimpses of broad seas— particularly at this time of year, when the sun doesn't set till half past nine

63 'Les lacs éperdus . . .': from Laforgue's 'Complainte à Notre-Dame des Soirs', slightly misquoted.

and it is twilight till nearly midnight. These evenings are so wonderfully peaceful—

> Les lacs éperdus des longs couchants défunts
> Dorlotent mon voilier dans leur plus riche rade,
> Comme un ange malade.

It all helps to mellow the thought, that one's friends are being killed, into a quiet kind of resigned sadness. One does feel tremendously, when one is in this beautiful country, that one is a part of a larger soul, which embraces everything. —But then again I myself feel equally keenly, when I get back among all the wretchedness of the town, that it is impossible to recognise this splendid unity. It looks as though the amount of good and evil were about the same in the world. I think the good will probably win in the end— though not necessarily, unless the most persistent and tremendous efforts are made. I dont think one is justified in taking a holiday, under the belief that everything is necessarily falling out for the best. But I'm not a pessimist, and I think it will be all right. I think we shall ultimately work all the disorder into a single principle, which will be an Absolute—but which at present exists only potentially and at the nature of which we can only very dimly guess.

This is rather rambling! I apologise! Meanwhile, if you're not too bored, read this sonnet; which I wrote the other day and which is called 'Senti-mentalité d'un Soir d'Été'. I am not very clear what it is about! But you know the vagueness of Schwärmerei!

> J'entends venir le vent, qui chante la nénie
> D'encore un soleil mort: les pétales du soir
> Se sont flétris: dans le beau nonchaloir
> Du ciel des yeux, dont le regard m'épie,
> Se voilent. Une voix, qu'à travers de la vie
> Le vent apporte à moi, m'a dit un 'Au revoir'.
> J'attends—et l'avenir tremble à l'horizon noir;
> Et je sens sur mon front des doigts de féerie:
> Des doigts de féerie—oui, c'est Toi! La nuit
> Fait filer la clarté des astres enchanteurs
> Avec le noir des cieux, et en fisser la frame
> Où le divin accord de la chair et de l'âme
> Figurent ta beauté—toile, qui sous les pleurs
> S' attriste, et qui, riant, sous le soleil reluit.

It is certain, I'm afraid, now that poor Bob Gibson is killed. He was as good a soldier as he was a don. He was mentioned in dispatches and on the day he was killed he had just been made a captain. I get back to London in a week or so—and then I must see you—so au revoir.

Yours
Aldous

73

27, *Westbourne Square, W.*
8*th* [*July*, 1915]

How uniformly intelligent my dear Naomi, are the suggestions of Dick [Mitchison]. Synge has all my approval.

En passant—I may say that in going to see Mestrovic's works I was somewhat alarmed on going into the room by discovering a huge portrait-head of Dick (labelled 'Frowning Hero') staring malignantly down at me. Did you notice it? The thing is the most astonishing caricature of Dick in his more sombre moods. I'll try and get a reproduction of it. 'The Annunciation' was v. jolly—but I confess I laughed heartily at some of the other bas-reliefs —as they were so irresistibly reminiscent of the best work of Caran d'Ache. But I think those heads and groups indubitably prove him a great man— and the temple is superb—the model would be so charming for a doll's house.

Gerry has been dispatched to his depôt at Hull, Hell, or Halifax etc. But I gather has ingeniously stipulated that he must periodically return to town for treatment for his hay fever.

Do you know the charming tale of the printed prayer discovered on a German prisoner—which began thus:—'O Gott, Du, Der über Seraphinen, Cherubinen und Zeppelinen im höchsten Himmel thronst . . .'. Quite pleasant.

ALH

65: † TO JELLY D'ARANYI

27, *Westbourne Square*, W.
[26 *July*, 1915]

My dear Jelly,

I gather that my father made an attempt to get you to come and help celebrate my birthday. I wish you could have. I will get my stepmother to suggest some other day before we go away.

Well, I'm twenty-one today—grown up—what a good opportunity to be sentimental about the days of my youth! I trust you have had the rest you so much required, when I saw you last.

Au revoir—when? Write and say when I can come and see you.

Yours ever
Aldous

64 Synge: *an Abbey Players production of* In the Shadow of the Glen *opened at the Coliseum on 19 July. The Mestrovic exhibition was at the Victoria and Albert Museum from 24 June.*

66: † TO JELLY D'ARANYI

Prior's Field, Godalming
Saturday, [August, 1915]

My dear Jelly,

What luck, your coming down to Godalming. We are staying just next to the Hardcastles in Margaret's school; which has been lent us. We occupy one tiny piece of the huge building. We stay till Sunday—so I shall have a chance of seeing you, which will be very nice! Tell me your address. I saw the Hardcastles the other day and their funny old uncle, Mr Judson, who is my godfather. The country round about here is looking lovely—the sad part is that they have made a big camp on one of the open heathery commons and it will never be the same again—however there are still a great many places where the soldiers are not! Our last letter from Julian is quite cheerful: he's on his holiday—riding a horse all day long like a cowboy. But I'll tell you more when I see you.

Aldous

67: TO FRANCES PETERSEN

Prior's Field, Godalming
[August, 1915]

My dear Frances,

Many thanks for the letter, with the masterly criticism of Laforgue. Admitting everything you say about him, I yet believe that he was a great man. He was limited to a morbid outlook on life, but that was because (a) he had consumption, of which he died when he was twenty seven and (b) he was reader in French to the Empress Augusta, which was possibly the greater trial; he also wore an invariable top hat. Moreover, he was typically the Greats-man, who has not had time to live down the crudely imbibed philosophies of his extreme youth; he was, I take it, a Schopenhauerian pessimist, likewise a believer in the system of one Hartmann, a Boche, whose metaphysic enthrones the Unconscious ... whatever that may be ... in the midst of all things. As the Old Song says:—

'Oh, it's the Unconscious, the Unconscious, the Unconscious
    that makes the world go round.'

Dim as the concept of the Unconscious may be, it does however lay a very desirable prominence on the non-intellectual features of humanity. . . .

66 *Mr Judson: this was John Edward Judson, who had been an assistant master and afterwards a housemaster at Charterhouse, where he knew Leonard Huxley.*
67 *Frances Petersen, a grand-daughter of P. W. Henderson, Warden of Wadham College, was a home student, 1915-1918. Laforgue: the quotations were from memory—'Complainte des Nostalgies préhistoriques', 'Complainte des Voix sous le Figuier bouddhique', 'Complainte à Notre-Dame des Soirs'.*

Laforgue was also a hearty Darwinian and liked the thought of being a developed beast . . . hence you see him all for instinct and the like, and down on consciousness and the intellect as rather supererogatory excrescences on the Unconsh. Hence, I think, the repetition of the hated 'anonyme' . . . nameless unreason; hence his definition of love and other human activities as 'actions reflexes' and mere 'tics' . . . and then that capital poem about atavism that begins, La nuit bruine sur la ville, which I think is the most excellent expression of a mood one often feels . . . all modern life in that last stanza, Se raser le masque, s'orner d'un frac deuil, dîner avec art . . . I wish I could remember it. And then, of course, he is impressionist, recorder of passing moods . . . the rapidity of whose change leads him into that strange elliptical style, that violent alternation of opposites. That he did not have any but the gloomier moods to describe is perhaps not his fault, consumption and Queen Augusta, you see: . . . but what he does do is first class, with what astonishing originality, made obscure by compression . . . that capital phrase in which he sums up the whole of Petrarch and the angel-in-the-house platonists; la femme . . . beau commis voyageur, d'une maison là-haut . . . and those queer sentimental poems, L'extase du soleil, peuh! La Nature, fade Usine de sève aux lymphatiques parfums; Mais les lacs éperdus des longs couchants défunts Dorlotent mon voilier dans leur plus riche rade, Comme un ange malade . . . the cynical pieces, like the Croque Mort knocking at the door, 'L'oubli des morts' . . . the romantic ones like the 'Roi de Thulé'. Further, his revolt against the poetic language is an excellent thing, corollary, of course, to his impressionism, which could not tolerate anything artificial standing between life and its expression. This I fear is all very heavy; pardon . . . but I do like the man and find immense pleasure in poring over his ingenuities, even his rather decadent and queer similes . . . which are almost always suggestive and remind me of the dear old quaint conceit of the seventeenth century, which, in spite of Doctor Johnson, I have the ill taste to revel in. I propose to get Laforgue's prose; note books . . . only one volume of them . . . but said to contain the most priceless gems of thought, philosophic and critical.

I intensely sympathise with your dislike of [J. E.] Flecker, a complete second rate; I dont think I have found one completely good poem in his works; people are fascinated by the names, Samarkand, Bathrolaire and the like . . . but it's all a little cheap . . . and one would like to see the kindred spirit who has come from Persia and written the 'Jacynth Journey to Bootle' . . . a name doubtless as suggestive and romantic to Perian ears as Samarkand to ours. I think I go to the H's in Sept, with my sister, a quaint child . . . au revoir, meanwhile Anglo Saxon . . . .

Aldous Huxley

Do read [Rupert] Brooke—some absolutely first class—also [Walter] de la Mare.

27 Westbourne Square, W.
[Circa September, 1915]

My dear Frances,

    Rather a good novel about the war . . . comes from appearing, as the French say. I saw it very well reviewed in the *Times Litt Supp* and went and got it. I think you'd like it; it's a little less vaporous than [Jules Romains's] *Mort de Quelqu'un*. I have read one other book of this man, *Les Transatlantiques*, quite incredibly funny . . . about Americans in Paris. I like best in this book the scenes where all the family act at once in their best parts . . . particularly the tragic child.

    It rains, the days draw in, it is all very like a scene from Maeterlinck.

FIRST PARALYTIC. Oh, oh. It rains, it is certainly damp.

SECOND PARALYTIC. But how this is dim. There are no lights. It is depressing. It is certainly most depressing.

THIRD PARALYTIC. You forgot I am also blind. I cannot see how dim it is. But I hear something. I am sure I hear something. It is a Zeppelin. Something is certainly going to happen.

ALL THREE PARALYTICS. Oh, oh. We cannot move ourselves. But how this is depressing. It is certainly most annoying. We are all irritated. Oh yes, we are irritated.

FOURTH PARALYTIC, who is also a blind deaf-mute, remains perfectly happy. The lights slowly grow dimmer. The days draw further in. The rain monotonously falls. After all, nothing has happened. It is all very depressing.

Au revoir
A. L. H.

[Oxford]
[?1915]

Velvet slashed with the gold of laughter
Covers the head . . . Daguerreotype
Or ostrich: veins throb with the not-yet-after
Of wines; and the red-smouldering pipe

Tinges the subtleties of thought and smoke.
Youth at the helm and pleasure at the prow;
Hands cool adrip, raised up, invoke
Bacchus' companion. Silence . . . now!

---

68 Heures de guerre de la Famille Valadier, *by Abel Hermant, author of* Les Transatlantiques, *was reviewed in* T.L.S. 9 *September,* 1915.

Are spasms reverberated into sound?
And does the palace rosy pale
As a sea-shell opening; profound
As the universe itself, entail

Moaning upon its heriting queens
Whene'er the boskage of its doors
Admits the conqueror? Are scenes
From Cleopatran Nilus' shores

Enacted where the parsons please
Their sleekly christian bodies in the stream.
Dear nights! Would all were such as these.
Dear God, the waking . . . and farewell the dream!. . . .

Wrote this under the influence of Hera's ban. An account . . . incoherent
and Mallarméan . . . of one of those evenings in the lap of God. Question:
Does God live anywhere but in Magdalen on the Cher? Ask [——].
His daughter blushes because she believes that God is Beauty. . . . Frances
told me she does, it's true . . . so that she has some inkling of the truth
. . . God in the phallus as well as the chalice, in the breast physical as well as
in the breast metaphorical . . . and so that is why she flushes . . . realising
that her father with his hellish doctrine of masochism and Xtian asceticism
and duty is the devil and that she herself and you and me or I or is it me? are
God and her mother, who after all paints pictures and believes in the human
form I suppose, is a bloody hermaphrodite. Does God exist? Triumphantly,
YES. Do I exist? Answer, at the moment, NO . . . but generally PERHAPS,
though not with such hard gem-like intensity as perhaps some others, whose
experience in nuptial arms and legs and among infinitely great Art, has made
them live timelessly for a longer and sublimer period . . . though you
must admit that no omphaloskeptic, nay, not Plotinus, could have so utterly
realized the Infinite as at moments one did to night. And so farewell and hail.

70: TO JULIAN HUXLEY

Balliol College, Oxford
[October, 1915]

My good Julian,
    I seem to have noted in the last six months a certain conspicuousness of
absence that characterizes all your correspondence. Accordingly I make a

70   *Warren: Sir Herbert Warren, then Professor of Poetry. The Newdigate
Prize was not awarded in* 1915. *'Mole': first published in* The Palatine Review,
January-February, 1916; *the version sent with this letter differs from the printed one
in the reading 'Unconscionable usury/To that grim Shylock life' for 'Unconscionable
usury/To unrelenting life'. Laforgue: the line quoted is from 'Complainte des Voix sous
le Figuier bouddhique'.*

78

move, provocative, as I hope, of reprisals . . . like the dear old Boches and their Zepps, which always get back bomb for bomb on their open towns. Meanwhile, in accordance with the Teutonic suggestion, I have, as a civilian, evacuated the fortress of London . . . only to establish myself in another citadel, notorious for the strength of its walls and the aggressive appearance of its castle.

Meanwhile, pray heaven our offensive continues all right. As a beginning the capture of twenty five thousand whole skinned Boches and a hundred and fifty guns is excellent . . . success is cheering; it came just at the dimmest moment; also [Alfred] Harmsworth is said to be dying, thank god, a painful and lingering death . . . nervous break down lack of sleep, decaying circulation . . . journalistic, not corporeal. Whether we shall have conscription . . . I expect so; Asquith is said merely to bury his head in his hands and weep when he is faced with the at all major problems, but as L[loyd] George and Kitch[ener] seem to favour it I expect it will arrive before long. What Labor, as you would call it, will say remains to be seen; meanwhile one introduces measures of a state socialistic kind, which will probably continue after the war and be extended to other trades beside the suppliers of war material . . . reduction of profits, fixation of wages centrally and the like. And what will the Boches do afterwards? . . . a republic I suppose . . . they can hardly tolerate Kronprinz . . . a sort of magnified Fabian society state, organized even further than at present . . . automatism as opposed to life . . . vide Bergson; we represent life; but the poet laureate [Robert Bridges] says we represent Christ, as opposed to Sheitan, the Boche; do X and life mean the same? Possibly. But what really is interesting is the very frank manicheism that is coming out now. Not that I suppose anybody ever was anything else but a Manichean dualist at heart, but in old days, when there was nothing worse than Lloyd George in the *Times* for breakfast, they vaguely and superficially believed that there was a Perfect Trine, an excellent old Absolute and the like. Against this hellish and immoral conception, which allows a perpetual week end off from all the energies of life, I have for long protested. And now, when the attempt to justify God's ways to man has culminated in worthy divines saying that if the allies do not win they will never open their bibles again, one feels that one might really just as well adopt Manicheism as a state religion as any other. The ritual and tradition are of course rather absurd, but the principle is good and the ethics are identical with Xtian ethics. Whereas the Boche is old testamentary; and like the excellent Marcion, we have come to recognize that Jahveh is the same as the devil.

I hope you have been properly edified by the quite incredibly comic statements emanating from Boche-land. What I liked best was the remark by Lasson, Berlin philosopher, to the effect that:—'We are morally and intellectually superior to all men. We are peerless'. This touches the sublime. The decadent and putrefying nations of England France and Russia quake.

79

But one has only to listen to Stravinsky and Rimsky-Korsakov and then to Strauss and Reger to discover which is the country that is fullest of life. Strauss is perhaps in his music the most typical example of modern Germanism. The brutal and the sentimental join hands; weltering sensuality, noise and violence for their own sakes; and Reger the intensely classical, not classical in the sense of expressing his ideas in the best original manner he can but in the sense that he takes the existing classical and imitates and develops a little . . . not however with any of that originality of Scriabin, who steeped in the same way in the classics, followed the old methods to logical conclusions and was not content to rest stagnantly. The Germans have remained in the nineties. Wilde is their favourite modern English author. With their brutal sentimentality they cling to the spirit of Rops and Louis Legrand in art; a mixture of the macabre, the monstrous, the huge and the slyly obscene dominates them artistically. Look at Strauss with his vulgar beastliness, his sensationalism, his big noise that goes on without check or diminution; and then such draughtsmen as Kley, Gluck, and the Munich school. The gross and the large dominate. There is that worship of sheer beastly strength which induces some women to marry niggers and prizefighters. One has but to look at their work to see it . . . the bull necked, browless figures of the Munich painters, nudes with puffy muscles and green flesh tints, stark and ugly. And then their new Leipsig memorial, immense, squat-pillared, crouching like a toad and ornamented inside with figures in colossal bas-relief . . . all in a sort of debased Egyptian manner that lays stress only on the starkness and hugeness. Set against this the slavonic music and art, sparkling with life and strong, not with the rigid automatic strength of the boche, but gracefully and vitally. Compare Mestrovic and the French Rodin with Klingel . . . or is he Klinger, the man who did the Salome and the Beethoven and all the rest . . . Klinge[r], in his Boche way, is a genius; he has made starkness and sensationalism as artistic as they can be made. Mestrovic and Rodin, starting unhampered by the Teuton ideal, make a statuary where strength is graceful and where life shews itself not necessarily in an aimless and colossal energy.

That we have much of the Boche about us is undeniable. Elgar's music, Leighton's and Tadema's pictures and in literature the relics of the Wildeian nineties. But I think there is more of the vital spirit than there is of the boche spirit. The Boche is like the Eastern American; he suffers from a hearty decay; he is immature and blatant and at the same time decadent. That, as I learn from travellers to your great nootral country, is what Eastern America is like, and that is what Germany seems to be like . . . a new growing country, swelled with its own pride, filled by its growing pains with an immense folie de grandeur and prematurely rank and rotten. All new countries get this disease of decadence and it rages more violently than it does in an old one. But they generally throw it off sooner than the Boches have done.

Well, well, never mind about them; most of them will be dead and the rest will be trying to put their bankrupt country to rights by the time they've done.

Meanwhile one anticipates that none of one's friends will be left alive. A bloody waste. . . .

You were right about my Newdigate; it did not obtain a prize. T. Herbert Warren, when questioned, remarked that 'there was one Byronic production; amused us very much, but we did not know whether it was meant to be serious' . . . as if it wasnt manifest that the thing was positively EARNEST! I am engaged at present in writing an immense didactic poem, in the manner of Donne and Dryden with a large infusion of the Romantic. It treats of Me and God and Women, together with various other phenomena in time and space. Its full title will, in the Wordsworthian manner, run something like this . . . 'An account of a walk taken in the neighbourhood of an University Town by the Author, not wholly, at intervals, unaccompanied by a young Lady in the form of a Needlecase, etc.' When this monumental work is finished . . . and there is no particular reason why it should not go on indefinitely . . . I will send it you. Meanwhile I send you a little poem on the habits of the MOLE, which pleases me quite a lot. I have discovered one of the great poets of modern times . . . not that he is either great or particularly modern; but let that pass; he is interesting and amusing and intensely young, which is all that matters . . . and that is a mannikin called Laforgue. A philosophic lyrist; he pleases me by his affinity with Donne, intense intellectuality, intense passion concealed and restrained, intense sadness. He was a disciple of Hartmann of 'Unconscious' fame and he deserves to live if only for having coined the words 'Eternullité' and 'Sangsuel' and for having summed up the whole of the Petrarchian convention in the words applied to woman:— Beau commis voyageur d'une maison là-haut . . . which is unique. How good French poetry is . . . but I cant bear Hugo . . . the other romantics are a different kettle of fish; Gautier's exquisite pedantry, his faintly sentimental yet so real human lyrics touch one as only the best of Browning can. They have probably a larger sum of good lyrics of the period than we, though there is nothing so great as Shelley or Keats or Browning.

But oh the Anglo Saxon . . . why couldnt I have inherited my poor dear grandfather [Thomas Arnold]'s affection for *Beowulf*. . . . and to think that that damned MS passed through a fire and only got singed, which merely made the reading more difficult and provided greater scope for the activity of the Boche scholar. Oh Dog, as Socrates would say, νὴ τὸν κύνα—but O Bokh as the Russians say—God is their small beer.

Кукушка, уатер клозетъ, корсетъ—the 3 words in the Russian language recognisable by an Englishman—cuckoo, watercloset and corset!

[*Oxford*]
[*Mid-October*, 1915]

Dearest Father,

I trust all goes well within the brass-doored house. How is it finally decided to connote the infant?

If you hear any news about Lewis from any quarter I wish you'd communicate it, as we've not heard anything for about a week—when he was in a very parlous condition—having developed gas-gangrene.

Oxford is very curious now. There are a good many (relatively) nice people left—most of them oddities of one kind or another—aesthetic, exotically religious and the like. However, they mostly have sense and are excellent souls—more especially in comparison with the black, yellow, brown, greenish and puce men, who, with the Americans, make up the rest of the university—particularly Queens, where there are more men up than at any other college and where the population consists of Indians, and Americans of the name of Schnitzbaum, Boschwurst, Schweinsbauch, and the like. Not a jolly place, is Queens.

I am doing a paper for Raleigh's society on Fulke Greville, Lord Brooke —an interesting creature, and really, sometimes, a great poet—tho' his intense intellectuality and his careless style render him always very obscure.

Gloomy weather, cold and windy. The elms are behaving very oddly this year—their leaves fading in definitely outlined patches, where they assume a very brilliant lemon colour. The general [effect] is one of branches of laburnum blossom suddenly sprouting in the otherwise green tree.

Love to R.

ALH

Balliol
[*October*, 1915]

Dearest Father,

I have retired abruptly into college, as Naomi developed scarlet fever at St. Thomas', where she was working, and was to be brought home today in an ambulance. In such a case discretion is the better part—so me voilà. I have quite a nice room in the new building—airy and light. At present I share Balliol with one perfectly black man, whose English is of the pigeon nature and who rather repels me at meals by his very oriental habit of shewing satisfaction with the food: Sir Toby Belch was not in it.

71 *Infant: Huxley's half-brother, David Bruce Huxley.*
72 *James Clark: nickname of George (later Sir George) Clark. Colonel F. H. Fairt-lough had lived at Godalming. Concerning Ka Cox, who married Will Arnold-Forster, a second cousin of Huxley, see Christopher Hassall,* Rupert Brooke (*London*, 1964).

I heard from Lewis two days ago, and I gather he goes on all right: his thigh was slightly fractured and they extracted from it (a) a disintegrated bullet (b) a bully-beef tin opener—the latter a little septic in its action—but he hopes to be back fairly soon.

James Clark, the All Souls porter tells me, was barely touched, patched up on the spot and returned to the trenches after a day or two—and I hear much the same from Ka[tharine] Cox.

I was very sorry to see that Colonel Fairtlough had been killed: the lists have been appalling lately—and with a new front prospectively to be opened, one fears they will be longer still.

It is rather difficult to see what game the excellent Tino [Salandra] is playing—not ours apparently.

Love to Rosalind.

Your loving son
Aldous

73: † TO JELLY D'ARANYI

Balliol College, Oxford
[October, 1915]

My dear Jelly,

Thank you so much for your letter. I am glad you have finally got the 'Rire' [Bergson, *Le Rire*]. I am sure you'll like it—particularly that fine rhetorical passage on art—which besides being very well written seems to me to be very good sense.

I wish I had been in town to see Adila's wedding. I got a note from her a day or two ago.

I have just moved into Balliol again after having been out of college for a year. It is very nice in some ways but rather sad too; for one is everywhere so constantly reminded of one's absent friends. These long casualty lists of the last weeks have been perfectly dreadful—such a lot of names I knew. This war impresses on me more than ever the fact that friendship, love, whatever you like to call it is the only reality. When one is young and one's mind is in a perpetual state of change and chaos it seems to remain as the one stable and reliable thing. It simply is truth in the highest form we can attain to. You never knew my mother—I wish you had because she was a very wonderful woman: Trev was most like her. I have just been reading again what she wrote to me just before she died. The last words of her letter were 'Dont be too critical of other people and "love much" '—and I have come to see more and more how wise that advice was. It's a warning against a rather conceited and selfish fault of my own and it's a whole philosophy of life.

73 *Adila: Jelly d'Aranyi's sister, who married Alexander Fachiri. Huxley enclosed with this letter a copy of 'August 1915: the Old Home' ('In this wood—how the hazels have grown!'), which was published in* The Burning Wheel (1916).

I'm rather ashamed of these silly little poems I'm sending you. I am in the middle now of a long one, which I'll send you when it's done.

Good bye dear Jelly.

Aldous

74: TO LEWIS GIELGUD

Balliol College, Oxford
[End of October, 1915]

My dear old Lewis,

I was relieved and pleased to get your letter. I had not written before, not knowing how much you were in a condition to read letters. These maximal horrors of war are really too unthinkably appalling; but things I trust are on the right track now for health.

We celebrated James [Street]'s birthday yesterday, James, Sandy [Andrew] Ritchie, [T. R.] Gambier-Parry and little Hoffers [C. G. Hoffman] were present. Ritchie is curiously shaken up and on edge after his bout at the front, falling into a positive passion of contradiction concerning an old MS which he and Parry were discussing. James, I think, finds him rather a tiring guest, as he declines to go to bed before two and cannot get to sleep without being partially drunk. However, all things now seem rosy to the worthy James, whose affair of the heart appears to prosper, flourish and succeed without abate or diminishment. It seems to stimulate his spiritual forces, . . . for he is always particularly amusing, positively brilliant after one of his famous Sunday afternoon tea-parties . . . not I hope in the worst sense of the word. I like little Hoffers very much. He has had his brother staying with him recently, Hegesippus Hoffers [Stoddard Hoffman] of Dakota, a wonderful being. He is a cut above the average American at present found in Oxford. They swarm. Queens, for instance, consists entirely of black men and Americans of the name of Schnitzenbaum and Fischmacher and Schnoppelganger-Fleischmann. Indeed, we proposed starting an English club, on the lines of the American club or Indian club. But the project had to be given up owing to the impossibility of getting enough members. Meanwhile, we have founded a club, chiefly for the purpose of self protection against Queen's and for the propagation of Kultur . . . the real article. More accurately defined it is a club for the spread of folly and the wasting of time, such as all Great Societies, from the Balliol Night Club downwards, have always been. We call ourselves the Thuliots, or inhabitants of Thule, ultima . . . a study of whose history is one of the purposes of the club. Altogether it is delightfully stupid. We are also looking for an Oxford Virgil, who will write a series of poems entitled the *Bucolics*, the *Georgics* and the *Cadeneid* . . . this last an epic about a hero from Keble College who basely deserts one of the Queenly waitresses of the Cadena and after a terrific campaign becomes President of the Union, finally drifting out of the story in an odour of sanctity.

Cherwell is still filled with plague, though I gather that Noo is perfectly healthy and is allowed to talk to people out of the window. I propose to go and hail her this afternoon. Which indeed I will straight-way do. So farewell.

Aldous

James sends his love—which superadd to all mine.

75: TO NAOMI HALDANE

[*Oxford*]
[*November*, 1915]

False alarm. Group-crush dont come off till Sat 27th—4.15, Co-op.

Meanwhile, on next Sat: there is to be a conciliabule at the Co-op of Patricians—or members of a non-existent St. Patrick's club: there will be tea, where you'll meet Robin Fausset, Grattan Esmonde, myself and the Inimitable Miss [Aileen] Cox—together with others—including supers such as parsons, buffoons, old ladies to act as chaperons. It will be funny, so come. You can be one of the non Irish members like myself—the joke being that the tame parson thinks it's a serious meeting for the spread of Erse and Keltic Kultur! If you come, find me in College at about 4—or, better, I'll come up and find you.

About Sunday, —I'd love to come, but must stay v. short time, as I am frightfully busy, having to write an essay and a vast literary paper by Monday and Tuesday, respectively—neither of which I've touched so far.

But—will you come to tea on Wed.—not unaccompanied by your mother, if she'd care to: I will try and secure Frances [Petersen].

ALH

76: TO LEONARD HUXLEY

[*Balliol College, Oxford*]
[*November*, 1915]

Dearest Father,

Life, despite the horrors of an Oxford November, proceeds brightly enough. People are almost restless in their desire to be doing things. They make up for the lack of the quantity of life by its violent quality—all which provides one with plenty to do and talk about.

What an odd business it was about the suppression of Lawrence's book, *The Rainbow*. It is always the serious books that get sat on—how much better to suppress Mrs. [Elinor] Glyn. At any rate, it's a silly thing to do—particularly when the book is so dull that no one would under ordinary circumstances read it. I hear it is to be privately printed and sold by sub-scription. Meanwhile I suppose Methuen's must be feeling a little foolish

---

75 *The people named were all undergraduates; Aileen Cox, afterwards Mrs Thomas Bodkin, wrote verse and contributed to* Oxford Poetry 1916.

after having bribed Lawrence away from Martin Secker—his first book to be submitted being this!

I see Aunt Mary's undergraduate novel has begun in the *Cornhill*—this makes about the tenth of the kind in the last few years. I think I shall write one of Oxford in war and peace—quite a good subject. I see the inevitable earls daughters, with the usual appendages, butlers and footmen and heavy dinners, are coming into Aunt M's book again. Why can't she resolutely keep them out? How much better this book wd. have been had she made it a study of don-life in the 80's—which she wd. be particularly competent to deal with—instead of the usual politico-Debrett clap-trap.

I successfully piloted the P[rior's] F[ield lacrosse] team round Oxford—disseminating large numbers of baseless myths concerning the place amongst them. I hadn't time to take them to Balliol to shew them Devorguila's sepulchre, which I shd. have liked to have done! It is said to have got into the American guide-books by this time as a thing to go and see.

I trust R is well and the infant Hercules.

Love,
Aldous

77: TO LEONARD HUXLEY

[*Oxford*]
[8 *December*, 1915]

Dearest Father,

Many thanks for your letter and the trans-atlantic enclosures, which were most entertaining. I am sending them back.

I see from the *Times Lit. Supp.*—in a not very good article—that you [i.e., Smith, Elder and Company] have just brought out a new and improved edition of Sidney Lee's *Life of Shaker*. If you get a copy of it you might bear in mind that 'twould make an acceptable Xmas present!

I had an amusing day on Sunday—going out to Garsington for luncheon to the Philip Morrells, who have bought the lovely Elizabethan manor there. Lady Ottoline, Philips wife, is a quite incredible creature—arty beyond the dreams of avarice and a patroness of literature and the modernities. She is intelligent, but her affectation is overwhelming. Her husband, the MP, is a conceited ass, very amiable, but quite a buffoon.

I went on to dine with the Gilbert Murrays, where I was lucky enough to see one of Gilbert's thought reading performances. He is considered one of the best telepathists going—at any rate, he was astonishing on Sunday. He

---

76 *Martin Secker: Huxley's error for Duckworth and Company*. The Cornhill *began serializing* Lady Connie, *by Mrs Humphry Ward (Aunt Mary), in its December*, 1915, *number*.

77 *It was Murray's elder daughter, Rosalind, who showed a particular rapport in his telepathic sessions. The examples given by Huxley are typical of Murray's proficiency.*

86

was best, of course, with his daughter, with whom he generally does it. With her he can describe scenes in books he has never read. He did two on Sunday —one out of Conrad's new book [*Victory*], which he got almost word for word as his daughter described it and one out of [Compton Mackenzie's] *Sinister Street*. He feels the atmosphere of the thought: thus as soon as he came into the room the time his daughter had thought of *Sinister St*—a scene of undergraduates talking together—he said 'How I hate these people'— the aesthetic young man being very hostile to him. He tried one with me, which came off extraordinarily well considering I was a stranger. I had thought of the following scene: the Master of Balliol [J. L. Strachan-David- son] listening to an essay on [Meredith's] *The Egoist*, a book he has not read. Gilbert Murray stood holding my hand about half a minute, then began to laugh and said 'Oh of course, it's the old Master of Balliol being embarrassed. I'm not very clear what about, but I think it's a conversation about a new poet'—which is close enough for a first attempt with an unfamiliar mind. He can't exactly describe the process—it seems to be a kind of smelling out of the thought, of detecting it in the atmosphere. Altogether it was most interesting. I have never seen anything like it before—it is a wonderful gift to possess.

I shall be returning I expect on Wednesday next: for tho' term ends on Sat of this week, I am going to the Morrells for the week-end and have arranged to lunch with Walter Raleigh on Tuesday, so that it will be easiest if I stay another night and come back Wed: morning.

Love to R.

Ever your loving son
Aldous

78: TO JULIAN HUXLEY

[*London*]
[*December*, 1915]

My dear Julian,

I seem to remember writing to you some months ago. I can recall no response. Meanwhile all is forgiven and forgotten if you subscribe to the *Palatine* (6 numbers 3/6. T. W. Earp 32 Beaumont St. Oxford.) . . . vide multicoloured manifest thus conceived, which you had better distribute among the Texans as symbolical of true trans-oceanic kultur. Even if the Texans fail to support as whole-heartedly and full-pursedly as they might the good and great work of the *Palatine*, I insist, positively and autocratically, that you personally shall subscribe. All the men who are running the *Palatine*, who are infused with the Palatinate group-consciousness, which is a good group-consciousness, are good men. They deserve to be supported, most especially by the arrogant trans-atlantics. It is UP TO YOU, as the Bishop of Cape Town so aptly said, to roll in the Texan subscriptions, while our agents in Boston, New York and South Dakota are doing THEIR BIT, as the late Lord Roberts used to say, to mop up other corners of the dark continent.

I have come to agree with Thomas Aquinas that individuality . . . in the animal kingdom if you like . . . is nothing more than a question of mere matter. We are potentially at least, though habit of matter has separated us, unanimous. One cannot escape mysticism; it positively thrusts itself, the only possibility, upon one.

So much for that.

What if I came next year, D[eo] V[olente] and W[eather] P[ermitting] of course, to visit your transatlantic Home . . . observe that the Americans do not pronounce the o of home diphthongally o-u, as do the English, but as nearly pure o with perhaps the smallest vanish of u . . . what of it? Furthermore, there is a good man going to Florida, one D. H. Lawrence, a novelist and poet and genius . . . whose recent work *The Rainbow* was regrettably burnt by the common hangman for obscenity, supposed by the magistrate who had not read it to be subversive to England, Home and Duty . . . well, well, this good man, who impresses me as a good man more than most, proposes, how unwisely soever it may appear, to go to the deserts of Florida there, with one Armenian, one German wife and, problematically, one young woman called Dorothy Warren, to found a sort of unanimist colony. The purposes of which are to await a sort of Pentecostal inspiration of new life, which, whether it will come is another question. But Lawrence is a great man, and as he finds the world too destructive for his taste, he must, I suppose be allowed to get out of it to some place where he can construct freely and where, by a unanimous process, the rest of his young colony, might do the same. The gist of all of which is that when, and if, I go and see you, I shall very likely go and see him also, to spend, perhaps, a little while in his eremitic colony . . . which, I am sure, would be quite particularly medicinal to my soul.

But we have wandered from the point which is THE PALATINE and nothing but. So that I expect your subscription, less mark you than one dollar, together with the remaining Texan subscriptions, within the next thirty five

78 *Lawrence, acting on a suggestion made by Lady Ottoline Morrell, had written to Huxley on 7 December and had invited him to come to Hampstead for tea. (The letter is in* The Collected Letters of D. H. Lawrence, *edited by Harry T. Moore, New York, 1962, I, 393.) The Lawrences were staying at 1 Byron Villas, Vale of Health. Huxley became acquainted with them between the 15th, when he came down from Oxford, and the 21st, when they went away. On the 22nd or thereabouts, Lawrence wrote to Lady Ottoline: 'I liked Huxley very much. He will come to Florida.' Lawrence was hoping to sail within a few weeks and was already behind schedule. Huxley, it appears from his letter, saw his own participation in the utopia as a possibility for a remoter time. For his later recollections see his Introduction to* The Letters of D. H. Lawrence, *which he edited (London, 1932), pp. xxviii-xxix. The Armenian referred to in this letter was of course Dikran Kouyoumdjian (Michael Arlen).*

days. Otherwise anathema awaits you ... for my colleague, Mr Osmond Grattan Esmonde is a chamberlain in the Papal household, and a turn of his hand will get the whole of Texas cursed ex cathedra and with bell, book and candle. So you can't be too careful.

A. L. H.

79: TO LEONARD HUXLEY

Balliol College, Oxford
[21 January, 1916]

Dearest Father,

I am moving in here today from the Haldanes. I had a very pleasant time with the Morrells. The strange creature Lytton Strachey, the writer, was staying there—a long-haired and bearded individual very like a Russian in appearance and very entertaining. Even more mysterious was Henry Bentinck, Lady O[ttoline]'s brother, who sits in Parliament as a Tory, but whose expressed opinions are more violently socialistic than those of any one I have ever heard! He was invalided back from Gallipoli with enteric. He had a rather good story of an American correspondent, who, having examined the hideously unhygienic state of the trenches, observed to his guide: 'Say, kiddo, guess you're between the Devil and the W. C.'

I got myself attested on Thursday. The wretched recruiting office had been driven almost frantic by the ceaseless orders and counter-orders that arrived on the average every 3 hours from the W. O. No wonder that it was impossible to run the thing efficiently. Just that day they had issued quite the most senseless of all the orders, to the effect that men must be attested, sworn in, assigned to the groups etc. *before* seeing the doctor. The process of filling up all the papers takes a good half hours work and of course, when a man is unfit, that is all wasted. Thus in my papers I was elaborately put down as belonging to group S4—according to which I should be already serving. However, when I went to the major who was to swear me in, he refused to do it, saying it was the most abject folly to go thro' all the farce with someone so almost certainly unfit: so I was sent to the doctor unsworn—who made me take all my clothes off, to examine my eyes, and declared me totally unfit—class I category A—so I returned and got my card signed and my armlet—tho' no 2s/9d as I had not been attested—a gross swindle!

I am doing some reading for the Stanhope in Bodley—which they keep so hideously stuffy that it is hardly possible to stop going to sleep. Many people can't work there at all: it just knocks them out after half an hour—and its a mere question of making a few more panes in the large and numerous windows to open. Very silly.

Love to R.

Yours
Aldous

Balliol College, Oxford
Saturday, [5 February, 1916]

Dearest Father,

I was sorry just to have missed you the other day—but to have waited for the next train wd. have meant too late an arrival.

Our Review [*The Palatine Review*] is just appearing—today, I hope and expect—tho' it's a week late owing partly to the eleventh hour failure of a printer, who had lost his men to the army, partly to the break-down of one of our contributors out in France—together with his contribution. But all is well now. We have got advertisements for the whole year—cheap but regular—they work out to about £1 per issue, ⅕ of total cost of each issue. Also about 30 subscribers have already paid up for the year and sales in Oxford and London and Cambridge shd. be fair. Also I hope we shall get some American subscribers—besides Julian—as we have quite an efficient ex-Rhodes scholar who is a literary man in New York and takes an interest in the thing, so that he may dispose of a few copies.

Sunday

I got a long letter from Julian to-day. He seems moderately cheerful, but still intrigued about his position—wondering whether to come back or no—an action I shall strongly advise him against—seeing that there is a huge waiting list for the better jobs on all the Govt. Depts., while for the minor clerical work there is the whole of class B among the Derby attestees.

I went to lunch with the Morrells today at Garsington, where I found Barbara Hiles, delightfully cheerful and irresponsible as ever—with her hair still close-cut and curly and gold, gipsy-like rings in her ears—a striking figure.

I am busy with Milton at present—my special subject—set off by a nauseous diet of Anglo Saxon, which appals me more and more as I continue with it.

Love to R.

Your loving son
Aldous

Balliol College, Oxford
[13 February, 1916]

Dearest Father,

I trust you're getting some rest from the Hooker—a lull after the deluge of new letters—which must have been a nasty surprise.

81 *Hooker: Leonard Huxley was working on the* Life and Letters of Sir Joseph Dalton Hooker; *the book appeared in 1918.*

I have had quite a pleasant week. Sunday to the Morrells, where was B. Hiles, as I think I told you. On Friday I went to see Naomi H. married in the Register Office. It is a pleasantly short, discreet and business-like ceremony. You get tied up almost before you know where you are. A small—but very distinguished audience attended the function and they then dashed off to somewhere down the Thames valley—where they pass their honeymoon—dampish perhaps, tho' the weather is on the whole good—too good in fact, for all the flowers and leaves are preposterously precocious, and I fear the lions of opening March may furiously devour. I was pleasantly surprised yesterday to receive a visit from James Clark, who stayed to lunch and had a long talk. He is still on light duty—so gets plenty of leave from Salisbury Plain. He is still doing his famous 'bluff-tough-gruff-rough-soldier' stunt and is miraculously well the beef-eating, beer-drinking Briton. I am going to dine with him tonight in All Souls, where I hope I shall see W. P. Ker, who usually comes down of a Sunday.

I had lunch today with the Prices, who remembered themselves to you. Their house is as full as ever of cats and pugs and Belgians. They find themselves rather starved of music, for Oxford indulges now in little but ballad concerts and military bands—'Sonorous metal blowing martial strains'— good of their kind, but perhaps a leetle trying after a time.

Love to R. and the stout David—whose name shd. be altered to Goliath if he proceeds at this rate.

Your loving son
Aldous

82: TO LEONARD HUXLEY

Balliol College, Oxford
[2 March, 1916]

Dearest Father,

Many thanks for your letter. I have at last finished my [Stanhope Prize] essay—thank heaven—tho' I feel it to have been rather a waste of time and energy as it isn't good enough. The final days of writing of it have been rather nightmarish, as I've had a lingering cold and the snow gave me neuralgia—so that I became almost totally devoid of sense—and was utterly unable to write anything but clichés. Fortunately this filthy snow has now gone, and I begin to feel less of a corpse: it is enormously reviving to see the green of the grass again and to hear the birds chirping in more vernally hopeful tones.

I went today to listen to the judgments of the Oxford tribunal, which was dealing with appeals against conscription. I shd. say that this is a better and more decent one than some—but it left one with the impression of injustice being done. All the talk about keeping the pledge to married men is very well—but why not keep the pledge to widows with sons that support them?

Presumably because they have no votes. A great many of the cases were of men supporting widowed mothers and in surprisingly few instances were they allowed more than a short temporary exemption, during which they were to make other arrangements. Conscientious objectors were not so disgustingly hectored as they seem to have been in London—but the tribunals are far from treating them with the respect to which they are entitled both by the Act and by ordinary good feeling. There was one very funny case of a friend of mine at Magdalen, a Quaker, who was before the court to day. He objected to war-work of any kind, combatant or non-. They gave him exemption from combatant only, making the statement that they had no power to give absolute exemption, which is the most complete lie. And as this man knew his Act he was able to prove they were liars, scoring heavily—at which, it was interesting to note, there was general applause among the audience—sympathy being largely with the objectors.

It's a nasty business: there's a v. good article in the *Nation* of this week called 'How to make the War unpopular', which shews that the petty tyrannies and the wholesale attempts to cheat men into the army are doing a world of harm. The cases of cheating exposed by [Sir John] Simon are monstrous. They seem to be deliberately sending the conscription notices to every one, in the hope that the weaker, less-educated and unprotected—tho' passed unfit since Aug. 16th—may be bamboozled somehow into believing their exemptions null and void and may be dragged—without medical exam —into the army. There have been some shameless cases. The whole thing enormously decreases popular sympathy with the war. It may of course lead to an earlier demand for peace, which will be good—but on the whole it seems thoroughly bad—distracting people's minds from the real ends and by domestic injustice vitiating the belief in the justice of any of our actions.

Term I think ends circa 18th March, but I may be here a few days longer. Love to R.

Your loving son
Aldous

83: TO LEONARD HUXLEY

Balliol College, Oxford
[10 *March*, 1916]

Dearest Father,

Nightmarish collections in Anglo-Saxon are at last over; it is a relief. That loathsome language is a nuisance beyond all words.

Great excitement prevails now in Oxford on account of the arrest under the Defence of the Realm Act of an undergraduate at John's, by name [J. A.] Kaye, né Kaufmann. He is a German Jew, son of a naturalized Britisher. He came before the tribunal the other day to apply for exemption on the grounds of conscientious objection to war . . . he being an international socialist. His case was not heard, because the military representative leapt up and made a Phillipic against him, bringing up the fact that his real name was Kaufmann, that he was the son of a naturalized German, that he was a Jew, that he had often been in Germany and finally . . . tho' perhaps it was a little bathetic . . . that he was a member of the Fabian Society. On the grounds of his being of alien extraction he declared that the army did not want him and that the tribunal had no powers to deal with him, a civil court meeting the case more adequately. The military man brandished a manifesto of the No-Conscription Fellowship, which Kaye had distributed and which was thought to do harm to recruiting. He was arrested yesterday and is to appear before the magistrate tomorrow, to be remanded, one supposes, for trial. The case cannot rest, I imagine, solely on the distribution of the no conscription pamphlet. It was one of the documents which had been passed by the Press Bureau and which could hardly be treated as treasonable under the circumstances. More probably he has had communication with the German socialists, in which case he is completely done in. He is a curious little creature this Kaye. He was born with a passion for intrigue, like the Earl of Shaftesbury. He used to make plots and counter-plots in every society of which he was a member, intriguing with infinite elaboration merely for intriguing sake, not because it led to anything. He was a practicer of the Pure Intrigue, like the Pure Mathematick, and despised the merely applied. He is quite an amiable creature and I am sorry for him; but he has very much brought it on himself and has made a lot of unnecessary mischief. What I fear is that we shall have a bundle of articles from the *Daily Express* and the papers of its kidney. There was a great utterance in the *Morning Post* to day about the Universities, where it was said the so called intellectuals were no more than a set of Pro-Germans . . . and so forth, ad nauseam. The popular arguments against the Germans consist merely in a series of nick-names, like Hun and so forth; and if anyone dares to suggest that there may be some way of ascertaining the truth other than by calling names that appeal merely to the passions, he is instantly stamped as a supporter of the enemy. This sentimental honeymoon of hate has gone on long enough; it is time we settled down to thinking reasonably about each other.

We had our Zeppelin scare the other night. Fortunately I had not gone to bed, or rather was just going, when the hooter sounded; so I had the pleasure of rushing round waking people up. When I had driven everybody into the I.C.R., thoroughly miserable and unhappy at being robbed of their sleep, I proceeded to go to bed, not believing for an instant that the Zepps were within fifty miles of us . . . which proved to be true. My unhappy victims, many of them, stayed up till three and four. That is what I call one of the good jokes.

Snow and sleet have come down intermittently these last days; it is all very nasty. The process of creeping across the quad to have breakfast in hall through the snow on an icy morning is too incredibly horrible; nine o'clock is the latest one can get food!

Love to R.

Your loving son
Aldous

84: TO LEONARD HUXLEY

Balliol College, Oxford
[19 *March*, 1916]

Dearest Father,

Many thanks for letter. It would be very jolly if Stocks were able to let us have the Cottage. I shall return home I think on Friday and as far as I know have no particular engagement except for the first week-end in April and perhaps a few days just before next term, when I shall probably go and stay at Cam[p]den in the Cotswolds with my friend [T.W.] Earp.

The excellent Mr Kaye has been sentenced to two months, but has appealed and is now out on bail; I am not exactly sure what is the court that one does appeal to from the police-court; assizes I suppose. I get extraordinarily irritated with some of these Internationalists, who conscientiously object; so many of them are merely half-baked, crude and without any real opinions of their own. It is all rather silly.

I am glad you like my things in the *Palatine*. I have received a very great compliment with regard to the 'Mole' poem. [H. W.] Massingham, of the *Nation*, saw a copy and seems to have been struck by it. At any rate, he wrote to me yesterday, saying how much he liked it, and would I send him some poems for him to select from for publication in the new quarterly called *Form*, which is just appearing, with the most tremendously distinguished lot of writers and artists doing work for it. I am just getting ready some things to send him. I have nothing exactly like the 'Mole'; but if he doesn't like the rest, I see no reason why he shouldn't reprint that; the *Palatine* hardly counts as previous publication. It will be very nice if he does accept something; all advertisements are useful! It is pleasant to think that one has taken in at least one person. One succeeds so rarely in doing so.

I am much relieved by the result of my Anglo-Saxon collection, which had a number of auspicious questions. Beta double plus is quite adequate for language, and if I manage to do that in the schools all is yet well. Still, it must be admitted that luck had a good deal to do with this good result. How pleasant again to take in someone!

I saw at the cinema last night the most wonderful representation of *Jane Eyre*. The plot of the novel was absolutely destroyed in the process of

84 Jane Eyre: *probably the film version of* 1915, *which was made by Biograph, like* The Birth of a Nation.

cinematising it . . . but that is of course of no importance. One pleasant feature was that it was done by an American company, somewhere obviously sub-tropical . . . California or Florida . . . so that the old English country house, surrounded as it was by palms and rococo pseudo-Japanese gardens, filled with cacti and baobabs, was not altogether so convincing as it might have been.

I want very much to see the *Birth of a Nation*, which is said to be a really great film, an epic in pictures. It is said to mark quite a new epoch in cinematographic art. In time, no doubt, we shall have cinemas being bought up by the political parties for propagandist work, in which they will soon excel even the newspapers. The effect of them in China is said to be prodigious, while Rumania is described as a Cinematocracy.

I trust that David continues his growth with all the regularity and speed he has shewn in the past. Love to R.

Your loving son,
A. L. H.

85: TO JULIAN HUXLEY

27 Westbourne Square, W.
Friday, 31 March, [1916]

My dear Julian,

I regret that for so long your letter should have remained unresponded to. Time percolates with a distressing rapidity through the coffee-machines of life, without, however, making as much or as good or as strong coffee as might be warrantably anticipated from the amount of Mocha . . . finest per 2/- lb. . . . deposited in said instruments. So you see, pom, pom, where we are? . . . as the old song says.

Life seems to continue in much the old way . . . one dines, lunches and all the rest, perhaps a shade less well, except when one is the guest of the military, who, brutal and licentious as they may be, are yet the only people who are getting any money. One talks not a little of the war . . . subject of ineffable squalor, and which one hopes may be exhausted for ever by the end of this year, provided God is good and anyone has any sense; one discusses too the collapse of English civilisation, whose rapid decay under the sinister influence of Prussianism is everywhere apparent . . . no one cares for the liberty of the subject except Sir Bill B[y]les, and even he lost his enthusiasm over the suppression of Lawrence's novel when he heard that the most objected to passage was Lesbian in tone; for when it was explained to him what the isle of Lesbos had been famed for he was terribly distrest because he thought it was Lemnos and the fear that the Gallipolitan soldiery might be

---

85 *Julian Huxley returned to England from Texas in October and took up war service. Sir William Pollard Byles: a Radical Member of Parliament, active in causes involving the liberty of the subject.*

corrupted by the descendants of Sappho led him to abandon the cause of free speech . . . so we know—pom, pom—where we are!

Nor must we forget that we have now no Habeas Corpus; that interesting Act, about which one learnt at school with so lacklustre an enthusiasm, is now one of the mossy relics of the happy or shall we say less sordid past. A lettre de cachet from a Lord Lieutenant or from almost any bureaucrat can put one snugly away in the Jail or Jug without any prospect of a trial for periods quite indefinitely coextensive with the war or even eternity. So we know—pom, pom—where we are . . . though not so well as we used to.

Meanwhile, liberty is all utterly démodé. My friend Byron would have had a little to say about things now, but he, alas, perished in one of these repulsive Balkan squabbles, so continually in the past, so insistently in the present and so inevitably in the future the cause of strife. And, talking of the Balkans, my great act of University Reform remains still unaccepted by the authorities; I propose that every don who lectures, reads addresses, writes books, pamphlets or articles upon the Balkans or upon the solution of Balkanic problems or upon so-called theories of Balkanism, shall be summarily deprived of his fellowship and of all his degrees and at the same time be turned out of the University, never more to return . . . sine ulla spe regressionis, as the statutes of Bodley say. Had this excellent statute been passed we should already have got rid of Arnold Toynbee, Gilbert Murray, J. A. R. Marriott, A. L. Smith, J. A. Smith and Grant Robertson, to mention only a few of the most flagrant offenders; a great deal of paper would have remained virgin from the defilements of folly, a great many unsuspecting minds would have retained their pristine innocence. Furthermore, I am having a silver medal struck to be distributed to all those who have refrained from writing to the papers during the war; so far as I know I am the only qualifier for it.

The people that I propose you shall read are as follows:—Blake perpetually, with a foundation of Jacob Behmen; that will keep your religion all right, the importance of which I cannot overemphasize. Laforgue for your philosophy, your sense of humour and your intellectual titillation, not to mention for the sake of his poetry (though you must read his prose *Moralités Légendaires* as well). Then the immortal Villiers de l'Isle Adam, greatest romantic, greatest symbolist, greatest satirist of the nineteenth century; next a little Romains, just to keep you in touch with the social life of the soul, its unanimistic energies. For pictures, I cannot see that you could do better than to look at Monticelli, for the sake of pure beauty; and Jugend provides the necessary flesh and bones, the necessary Will for the expression of the Spirit of Monticelli. And finally, of course, you should write a good deal of poetry: and if you do all this, I cannot see that you can go very far wrong or escape being what the *Times* would call a Right-Thinking Man.

Continued in the train on my way to Oxford to stay with Lady Ottoline Morrell at Garsington. I don't know whether you know that delightful person: I think you know her husband Philip. The Morrell household is among the most delightful I know: always interesting people there and v. good talk: I go over from Oxford often to see them. I saw the amiable Barbara Hiles there the other day—very entertaining, and gipsy-esque with short hair and gold earrings.

I cannot help thinking that it would be unwise to come home. There is very little to be done unless one means to fight: and in these days when one can't get commissions it is impossible to fight with that elegance and efficiency which in the old days, as an officer, were within one's reach. Work in munitions factories is intolerable. They are destroying the potential value of thousands of workers by systematic overworking. Government departments are sometimes interesting, but of a fearful strenuity. I thought of going into the Foreign Press dept. of the W. O. last winter, which wd. have been v. nice, but found that 12-14 hrs. per diem was normal—so that it wd. have been quite beyond my ocular abilities to stand the strain. The longer this war goes on, the more one loathes and detests it. At the beginning I shd. have liked very much to fight: but now, if I could (having seen all the results), I think I'd be a conscientious objector, or nearly so. But I shudder to think what England will be like afterwards—barely habitable.

Yrs.
ALH

86: TO LEONARD HUXLEY

Balliol College, Oxford
Monday, [1 *May,* 1916]

Dearest Father,

Thanks for sending on the wire, which was however unnecessary, as another had been sent to Balliol, which reached me in time for me to catch the afternoon train to Campden. I don't know if you are acquainted with the place, which is in itself quite as much of a 'wonder' as any historical mystery which may have taken place there. I know few things more beautiful than its long grey street of houses almost all dating from the 17th century—all built of Cotswold stone and Stonesfield slates. On Thursday we went an immense walk, about 20 miles, rather too far considering the intense heat and the fact that we were going all thro' the noonday along the most exposed and treeless Cotswold ridge, where one got full benefit of the sun. We lunched at a pleasant little village called Snow's Hill (pronounced locally 'Snozzle') and then proceeded to Ford and Temple Guiting, some four or five miles on. I was tired when I got back, but pleasantly: and as I had not brought a change of linen, attired myself in pyjamas, which with a tie and under an ordinary suit make a very respectable shirt and pants.

86 *The first paragraph refers to Huxley's holiday visit to T. W. Earp in the Cotswolds. Earlier he had been staying with Leonard Huxley at Stocks Cottage, Tring, on the Humphry Wards' estate.*

As you will have seen, they have elected A. L. Smith as Master. I wish they could have got W. P. Ker: I don't know if he was ever proposed: but I'm sure he would have made a very good master.

I am busy with revision, doing papers for my tutor under examination conditions. Three hours of strenuous writing this afternoon: it is an uncomfortable process having to put down your thoughts under pressure and without due reflection. I fear I have not the Bensonian faculty of writing 1500 words an hour—600 is about my exam rate, tho' I suppose with practice one cd. increase the amount.

Love to R.

Your loving son
Aldous

P.S. I forgot! I wonder if my white shoes cd. be sent. So sorry.

87: TO LEONARD HUXLEY

[*Oxford*]
[*Circa* 9 *May*, 1916]

Dearest Father,

Many thanks for your letter and the previous arrival of white shoes. I have at the moment staying with me in Balliol young Robert Nichols, who descended on me for a day or two yesterday. He is a curious creature . . . quite a good poet, having vastly and beyond recognition improved on anything he could do six months ago when his book came out; but at the same time he is strangely violent and lacking in finesse: so that he finds himself somewhat of a stranded fish here, where conversation is so aerial, so merely suggestive that it is comic to see him bustiously rolling in its impalpable meshes, trying to make a way through. However, he takes his revenge by talking about himself. . . .

I hear that the fantastic Gael Chavasse has been released again. He was once more arrested in Dublin for the same offence as before . . . refusing to talk English to the soldiery; but he is not a Sinn Feiner and has been let out. The whole thing is really the most horrible waste of all, this flinging away of life. It is hardly possible to believe that they could have imagined that they could achieve anything under the present circumstances. And yet, according to people who knew them, Joe Plunkett and MacDonagh and Pearse were sensible enough.

86 *A. L. Smith, the historian, was the new Master of Balliol. With W. P. Ker, the mediaevalist, Huxley had been acquainted since* 1913 (*or possibly the end of* 1912), *when he attended Ker's lectures on literary history at University College, London, while preparing for Oxford.*

87 *Nichols' book was* Invocation: War Poems and Others (*London,* 1915). *Parry family: C. H. Parry was an assistant master at Charterhouse. P. E. Matheson, of New College, was a classics don.*

I saw the Parry family the other day, who were staying at Oxford for their holidays. There is a curious dimness . . . not, however, altogether unpleasing . . . hanging about them. Mr Parry was complaining about the shortage of masters at schools, so that your suggestion about getting a temporary job as an English pedagogue is, I think, quite good; though I would not propose to adopt it permanently. Still, for a bit it might be pleasant. I shall enquire of Sligger whether he knows of any niche that is positively yawning for me anywhere.

I am going to tea to day with the Mathesons to see Rachel Russell, which will be pleasant. I might at the same time get some news of Ka Cox. Love to R.

Your loving son
Aldous

I hope David has learnt to *crawl*: I am sure it is high time he gave up his unscientific kicking.

88: TO LEONARD HUXLEY

Balliol
[*Late May*, 1916]

Dearest Father,

The heat wave has left me positively flattened, tho' a wet morning has materially improved the position of affairs. London must be rather hideous under the circumstances.

I met Violet Bonham-Carter last week at the Morrells. She is a very delightful creature. Much less alarming than one generally hears her described—tho' perhaps she is more consciously scintillating at larger assemblies. She had a very pleasant story about her father and [Horatio] Bottomley. It was at the time when the Chancellorship of the Duchy was lying vacant a few months ago. The Prime received suddenly one morning a letter to the following effect—'Dear Mr. A[squith]. After yourself I am the man with the greatest influence in the country. Much as it would harm my financial and social status, I would, thro' a stern sense of duty, accept the Chancellorship of the Duchy, as I think my services would be of use to the Nation in the cabinet. Yours Horatio B.'

The Prime was greatly touched at this self-sacrifice and at the extremely gracious statement that Bottomley was only the second most influential man in England; and wrote politely back that he really thought Bottomley cd. use his talents to better purpose for the nation as editor of *John Bull* than by demeaning himself with a sinecure in the cabinet: and so the matter ended—tho I see that *John Bull*—while expressing great personal affection for Asquith—is running him down enormously!

Oh these awful papers who demand 'STRONG MEN'! These lawyers are our salvation. We should be at war with every neutral if we had had a few

STRONG fools of the [Sir Edward] Carson type in power. The only time they tried to do anything STRONG—Lloyd George doing the dictator stunt in S. Wales—they were absolutely crumpled up and had to climb down and grovel at once. So lawyers and inefficiency are going to save Old England yet!

Love to R and David.

Your loving son
Aldous

89: TO LYTTON STRACHEY

Balliol
Monday, [5 June, 1916]

Dear Strachey,
Would you care to come to tea here either on Thursday or on Saturday?
Yours sincerely
Aldous Huxley

90: TO LEONARD HUXLEY

Balliol
Sunday, [18 June, 1916]

Dearest Father,
Many thanks for your letter and Julian's—to whom, by the way, I ordered a B.A. hood to be sent two days before the beginning of this term. If it hasn't arrived, it is no fault of mine.

I am in the middle of Schools—which I find more tiring than any labour I have ever undertaken. Not only is the mental strain great, but the physical strain on the eyes—even using a typewriter—is very considerable: and I stagger out of the papers feeling as if I had been bruised all over after an acute attack of influenza.

The papers have, as a whole, been bad. What I thought wd. be the worst—Historical Grammar—turned out to be very decent. Chaucer—which I had hoped much of—was an uninteresting paper: and contained, moreover, (this year for the first time) a number of Grammar Questions, which had to be attempted.

Shakespeare I knew I shd find hard—but this was also uninteresting. The first history of literature paper—1400-1637—was a disgrace to the University. It was, I presume, set by [C. H.] Firth—that mine of useless information, a not very good historian and a very bad littérateur, who for some reason is our chief examiner: at any rate, I think it must have been he;

89 *Huxley and Strachey did not much care for each other. Some of Huxley's opinions may be found in 'The Author of* Eminent Victorians' *(1922), reprinted in* On the Margin.

for I cannot credit Raleigh with the lack of sense to set a paper on that period without a single question on:—

   1) English or Scottish Chaucerians
   2) Elizabethan Novel
   3) ,, ,, ,, Stage
   4) Any Elizabethan poet except Spenser
   5) Donne

—merely to mention a few of the omissions. The type of question set was the purely text-book question:—such as 'the influence of Caxton's prose on contemporary style'—the sort of thing only discoverable and indeed only treated in text-books. So far as I know, it had no effect whatever—but still!

Well, well—if the other period papers—which they have twisted round and altered the dates of in an extraordinary way this year—are like that, my opinion of this University will descend enormously. They degrade themselves to the level of the third class colonial cram-book-colleges.

I finish on Tuesday, which will be a blessed relief, as I am feeling very tired.

Summer shews signs of beginning here—tho' on alternate days there are relapses, and it begins to rain and blow.

I trust I don't have to read the Stanhope at the Encaenia. It is not good, as I had to write it in such a frightful hurry because of mistaking the date. I shan't print it unless I re-write it: it might be worth doing so, if I made it much larger and comparatively comprehensive, with plenty of extracts etc— so that it might be a useful book on the subject. They give me £20 worth of books: where I shall put them Gott weiss! I am getting a lot of good modern editions of authors, such as one otherwise wdn't be able to afford—like Skeat's big Chaucer, the Clarendon Press Donne, etc. and the Cambridge Beaumont and Fletcher.

Love to R. and Sarah.

Your loving son
Aldous

91: TO LEONARD HUXLEY

Balliol
Tuesday, [27 *June,* 1916]

Dearest Father,

Many thanks for your letter.

To deal with business before I forget. I want to be in town for 3 or 4 days from Monday next. I wrote to ask Aunt Sophy if she could have me, but I hear to-day from her that Aunt Rachel will be with her, so that there will be no room in the Hotel Porchester. However, she says I may take the more important meals there, if I sleep at 27. I will write to 27 to say that I propose to sleep there, and if Rosalind would add her confirming word to my request I should be grateful. I have a lot of people that I want to see in town during those days, and at the same time I shall take the opportunity of going down to Eton to see Whitworth about possible jobs. I have already written to him. The Appointments Committee says that it will send my name round to the various head-masters. Meanwhile it has nothing particular to offer and advises me to apply to Eton and elsewhere in places where I have any personal interest.

I have my viva on Thursday, while tomorrow I have to read portions of my Essay at the Encaenia. They are holding the function in the Divinity School this year. The acoustic properties of the room are appalling. You open your mouth and speak a word and the whole space under the groined roof becomes filled with a loud continuous rumbling sound, so complicated is the reverberation from the fretted roof. I had to rehearse there this afternoon and it was really extraordinarily funny to listen to the noise even of one's own voice. I think I was the most articulate person there, but the disjointing of my words was apparent even from my rostrum; while less clear enunciators sounded like someone trundling a barrel, no single word being individually audible. Possibly it will be a little better when there is an audience, from whose thick paddedness the words will not be able to rebound so nimbly.

My hoped-for summer has not yet arrived. Instead Oxford is swathed with a malarial dampness, out of which fall large drops of warm water, alternating with very violent downpours. I cannot remember to have seen the sun for at least ten days. Altogether very beastly.

I have been having quite an amusing time with *Oxford Poetry*. I think we have massacred three men and no less than six young women already. Really the stuff that people can produce . . . and particularly the women, who contrive to combine total technical ineptitude with total lack of even the most rudimentary common-sense. However, I have discovered one poetess; really very good, I think, who has much sense and originality and very great skill in writing.

I heard such a pleasant story the other day of Curzon. He was being taken round the front. Among other things he saw a swimming-bath, in which soldiers were bathing. He was very thoughtful as he came away, and at length said: 'Interesting, very interesting! What white skins they have . . . quite like ourselves. I always thought the lower classes had very dark skins and were covered with thick brown hair'.

I cant remember whether I told you that James Clark was safely a prisoner. I had a talk with [F. W.] Pember to-day about him and learn that he is in a very pleasant camp (whose name I forget) near Osnabrück. He has

91 *Hotel Porchester: i.e.,* 51 *Porchester Terrace, W., Dr Henry Huxley's house. Aunt Rachel: Mrs Harold Shawcross, the mother of the Eckersley brothers. Pember was the Warden of All Souls.*

been treated very well, is uninjured and is now learning Russian from his fellow prisoners. All which is good.

Give my love to Rosalind and Sarah; and may you have better weather than we are suffering from.

Your loving son,
Aldous

92: TO JULIAN HUXLEY

Balliol
30 *June,* [1916]

My dear Julian,

Your hood you know was sent off . . . or at least I gave directions for it to be sent . . . about nine weeks ago; so that it ought to have arrived and if it hasnt it is no fault of mine. But to return to more congenial topics. My schools are over and my viva; I wait the results . . . a second I should say, perhaps a first. All is in the womb of futurity.

Papers were on the whole stupid, some quite particularly so; indeed they were positively a disgrace to Oxford . . . merest text-book papers, such as would be set by a Middle Western College out your way. But meanwhile, one is a little comforted, if one does do badly in schools, by the fact of having picked off the Stanhope prize . . . quite unexpectedly. For it was a shoddy piece of work, my essay; seeing that by some curious, tho' characteristic mistake, I miscalculated the date of sending in, supposing it to be March 31st. About Feb 22 I discovered that the thing had to be in by March 1 . . . and me with no word written. O God . . . the hustle; I never spent a more beastly week, and then I hadnt all the information I wanted. However, All's well that ends Wells, as the man said on reading one of H.G.W.'s articles on the future in the *Daily Chronicle* (or else, in that sublime writer's own words, let us hope that this is THE war that will END WELLS.) well, as I was saying all has proved to be well . . . the best of all possible worlds, my dear Candide, and the innocent examiners have given me the pot, which, regrettably, has to be got in books . . . one would have preferred the naked cash. Still, £20 worth of tomes is pleasing, deny it who will.

Meanwhile, I look about for ways of escaping the work-house. The solution of the HEIRESS presents itself. Memorandum: to enquire into the affairs of one's young friends.

Of the more repulsive solutions two main ones appear. (a) To disseminate mendacity on our great Modern Press.

92 *For the Stanhope Historical Essay Prize, Huxley had written on 'The Development of Political Satire in England from the Restoration to the Revolution'. Besides himself, the only student to receive a first in Schools (in English literature) was M. D. Niven of Somerville.*

(b) To disseminate mendacity in our Great Modern Public Schools to the Youth of the Nation or rather Empire. On the whole the latter alternative, with bouts of mild journalismus seems to me the better. But we shall see.

Meanwhile, I am bringing out a book of verse in the Autumn. Some of it is very good; all of it is distinguished by sense and the embellishments of taste and literary tact . . . which is more than can be said of everybody, as I have come to know from assisting to edit *Oxford Poetry 1916*. You would hardly credit your eyes if you saw some of the stuff that young women send us in the hope of its being published. It is incredible.

The *Palatine* continues bravely, though this latest number [*sc.* No. 3] is bad . . . with the notable exception of [W. R.] Childe's poem ['The Fairy Land of Shipscar'] and my own ['The Wheel'] . . . particularly Childe's. We propose to take it to London and make it larger and get other people to write for it, which will be good. Now, see here, this is a proposition. Will you do us an article . . . scrupulously unpaid . . . in from two to four thousand words on anything rather cosmic from patriotism to obstetrics . . . preferably upon one of the numerous subjects in which you are a specialist, the relation of poetry and science, etc, etc. It would be very nice of you if you would, and I can assure you your work would be read by many distinguished people. Think over this and let us have it as soon as poss:

Meanwhile, I think we shall make the *Palatine* an organ for the defence of Oxford. It is absolutely necessary that these awful old dons should not be allowed to ruin Oxford with their bloody war memorials . . . their nefarious work has, indeed, already begun, and fools like [Sir George] Frampton are being set on to make statues of khaki-clad heroes in bronze and marble to desecrate chapels. There they will stand, perfectly dead, stupid things, a perpetual eyesore. What must be done is that the young men should have the running of the memorial. They will have to do with it afterwards. Either the money collected for a war memorial should be given to the university endowment, which would be sensible enough; or else we must have some living institution, a theatre, a college, an art school—anything, provided it is not the stuffed figure of a young man carved in marble by Sir Frampton. Steps must quickly be taken, or we shall find the place full of effigies and all the money spent before we know where we are. Or perhaps we had better imitate the Germans and build a series of Carson-turms in every town in the country, all of exactly the same pattern of bull-necked hideousness.

I heard from Jelly the other day, who complains that you havent written to her. She seems rather depressed, poor dear.

We have had on the average half an inch of rain a day during the whole of this June. God! . . . !

Yrs.
A.L.H.

Just heard the results of schools—only 2 firsts—myself and a woman.
I have at last discovered a nice Belgian: wonders will never cease.

A.L.H.

93: TO LEONARD HUXLEY

Repton, Derby
[Circa 12 July, 1916]

Dearest Father,

I imagine you must be back in town by this time. I am now pretty well
settled here—teaching Latin to the Lower IV and English and History to
other low forms. My predecessor, as I gather from the masters and still more
from the boys, was both incompetent and unpleasant—a parson, ex-head-
master of a Grammar School (blacklisted by the *Assistant Masters' Journal*)
who had been taken on temporarily. I have grave suspicions that he was
positively sacked—tho' officially he has gone to take up a cure of souls. The
souls he has been curing here in the fourth form have suffered in the process:
he has made them forget everything they can ever have known. His methods
were simply ridiculous. In history, for instance, he wd. give the boys 'notes'
—which consisted in this sort of thing: Acts of Parliament in the XVIIIth
century, and then a list of names and dates. I asked the boys if they knew
what these acts were: no, he had never told them. He has done the same sort
of thing throughout: so that the boys know nil and whatever I manage to
teach will be pure gain.

I find one master here that I knew— one [Victor] Gollancz, who was at
New Coll my first year. Then there is a friend of Julian's and an older man,
Vassall, who seems to have been at Charterhouse and to have known me
when I was 'so high'.

I am in quite pleasant digs, tho' rather lonely. The job is quite interesting,
but I feel it's rather a waste of one's energies that one shd. be teaching on the
strength of P. Mods, when one has a 1st in English. I went to Eton last week
and find that I cd. probably get a job there next term—doing the same sort
of thing as here—no English being taught at all. On the whole I dont want
to go if I can help it. I shall look for a university job: it will give one scope to
use one's knowledge. I wonder if W. P. Ker wd. know of any place either in
London or elsewhere that I cd. fill.

I return to Oxford on Aug 1st, where I shall be for a few days combining
a visit with last packings. Then on to P. F.

Love to R.

Your loving son
Aldous

93 *Huxley was teaching at Repton School, the job having suddenly been offered at
the beginning of July by the Headmaster, Geoffrey Francis Fisher (later Archbishop of
Canterbury, now Baron Fisher of Lambeth).*

Repton, Derby
[*Circa* 12 *July,* 1916]

My dear Frances,

Business first ... this postal order is *not* for you ... au contraire, for me. Would you enormously mind pinching from the co-op any day you are down there, a 2 oz packet of John Cotton Medium and sending it to me. If no J. C. there is, I believe, Fryers Mixture at the co-op: so send that at a pinch. It would be very angelic of you. This village is too small to provide a decent shop and the boys evidently don't smoke enough. They are, so far as I have had to deal with them, very well behaved. But the Masters ... what a set of Calibans ..., and the Headmaster [...] today in chapel (where I attend with great pomp and piety) [...] prayed for the friendly relations between labour and capital ... urging the Almighty to restrain the covetousness of the workers and to make the masters holy and good. I could hardly restrain my derisive laughter.

The longer I live in my solitary digs here, the more convinced am I of the positive necessity for the establishment of the Palazzo Minns. It really is too utterly ... pardon my saying so ... bloody living alone: and even if one shared digs with say one or two others one might well get bored with them in time: whereas the Palazzo Minns would be a small college with plenty of variety: Grand Variety ... twice nightly.

What a wonderful week-end ... so gloriously fantastic: it gives me secret pleasure to think of it, when I have to be more than usually solemn and pedagogic in chapel or elsewhere.

I hope Aileen [Cox] has got over safely [to Ireland] and has found her house all right. Did you know Gollancz of New College: the great feminist in ancient days before the war? He's here teaching. Pleasant in his extremely Hebraic way. It was he who congratulated Agnes Murray on the 'exquisite *symbolical* meaning' of her poem in *Oxford Poetry 1915* ... to which the cold response was given by A. M. 'It is *not* symbolical'. I can't at the moment remember how much of this story I invented: I believe it is at least founded on something which might once have been called a fact ... *Walden.* ... To bed, to bed! I have to get up at 6.30! Ten thousand fiends seize the inventors of early school. ...

Yours ever,
A. L. H.

94 *Agnes Murray was the younger daughter of Professor Gilbert Murray. She died in 1922. Her poem, written while she was at Somerville, was called 'Domino Meo'.*

Repton, Derby
[Circa 12 July, 1916]

My dear Bob,

Many thanks for your letter: I'm sorry to hear of your feeling so profoundly dim—but trust all will soon be better.

As you may gather from my address I am now acting as pedagogue in one of our GREAT PUBLIC SCHOOLS—temporary job till end of term. I teach small lads Latin and History; it is really quite fun simulating the possession of knowledge: it becomes a kind of sport concealing one's ignorance from the boys. The boys behave very nicely: my fellow-ushers are a set of Calibans [....] I remain here till August 1st, when I hope to return nearer to civilisation.

I succeeded in flattening out my Schools to the tune of a First—thank God. It's a wrench leaving Oxford—so personal has it become.

I had a pleasant 5 days in town last week—saw Massingham and [Frederick] Carter, the daughtsman, and went with Earp and Surawardi [H. S. Surawardy] to visit [Adrian] Allinson and his works—some of which were pleasant. Also, if in town, don't miss an excellent show of [Anders] Zorn's etchings at Colnaghi's. Then, for lighter diversion, I took Oxford's most charming undergraduate (female) to a theatre—and on my return to Oxford found myself staying in the same house with her—which was pleasant. We all behaved like children—acting charades in the middle of Bagley Wood at dead of night; while most of the next night was spent crouched under a tarpaulin on top of a haystack—altogether very pleasant. And then on here, where I am very much alone and at times depressed.

I like your thing fairly: the romantic properties seem perhaps a little too stagey. But on the whole pleasant.

I was very prolific about a fortnight ago—but since then dried up, until suddenly in form today I felt a passionate desire to write: so I made the boys do an essay, which left me quiet to put pencil to paper.

I trust I'll see you when I get back to town. What I'm going to do—God knows (tho', mark you, I for one am no believer in God's omniscience).

Yrs.
ALH

96: TO LEONARD HUXLEY

Repton, Derby
[22 July, 1916]

Dearest Father,

How very pleasant for you to have got another week—during which I trust that the weather has been better than what we have been suffering here —our only fine day yesterday looked promising—but to-day comes a smashing thunderstorm, which however, may be a definite prelude of better things. Exams begin on Monday and already the horrors of terminal marks are upon me—very complicated, as they have an unpleasant method by which people receive bonuses above their actual marks in the subject rated according to the divisions they are in for such subjects as maths, German etc: so that when I get the marks for these subjects there is always a gymnastic feat of arithmetic to be done with each one—adding the bonus and then reducing to some proportionable total.

It is incredible what a lot of stuff is sent to one in relation to *Oxford Poetry 1916*. Young women, especially, whom one has never heard of, are apt to hurl great budgets of verse unexpectedly at one: how in the first place they come to hear of my having any connexion with the thing, I don't know: I am not the chief editor, so they can't have got the information from Blackwell, the publisher. But mysteriously, the news seems to get about—along with all that mass of gossip which drifts round Oxford—especially the female side of it: indications reach me from time to time that I am one of the mythical figures of this world: to be tall, shaggy and romantic in appearance as well as the author of a low-comic poem is enough to place one among the figures of the undergraduatess's Solar Muthos. However, to return to the point: one wd. hardly believe that so many young women wrote verse,—so badly. However, one poetess has been discovered—something at any rate.

When do you go to P. F.? I don't expect I shall be in town before the 5th, where I may perhaps want to stay a night if poss: tho' it may not be necessary or if so and it's inconvenient I can billet myself elsewhere.

I was so sorry to see Victor Horsley had died. Love to R.

Your loving son

Aldous

Later

Business first: I find cash runs out and no place in this village to change cheque into money: cd. you send me £3 as soon as poss:

I got yr. and [A. A.] David's letter simultaneously. I think I'll go there on Tuesday or Thursday, if exams are not too pressing. It sounds a good job: with excellent wages. On the whole I think I'll accept it if David definitely offers it.

97: † TO FRANCES PETERSEN

Garsington Manor, Oxford
[7 August, 1916]

My dear Frances,

Many thanks for your letter. I was a little alarmed and taken aback by the

96 *Sir Victor Horsley, an eminent brain-surgeon, died on service in Mesopotamia. He and his wife's family, the Gotches, were particular friends of Dr Henry Huxley. David: Master of Rugby School. He did not offer Huxley a post.*

97 *Artistic young woman: this must have been Dorothy Carrington, later to become a model for Mary Bracegirdle in Huxley's* Crome Yellow (1921).

address, which, for a moment, I thought to be that of my father's office . . .
15 Waterloo Place, S.W. but then happily perceived that Dublin also . . .
with a very touching patriotism had celebrated our NATIONAL VICTORY.

True . . . I have come into the neighbourhood of Oxford but have gone
to stay here . . . fulfilling an engagement interrupted by my visit to Repton.
I will not describe my adventures here: they are always peculiar, but this
time more amusing even than usual. These interludes make one forget the
hollowness of existence . . . a hollowness, which I find peculiarly reverberant
when I come to regard my future prospects. Damn them!

I don't in the least know what I'm going to do in the Autumn. I have
quarrelled with Rugby . . . somewhat to my relief, and I don't want any
of the other jobs I have been offered. I think, unless anything good turns up,
I shall go and hoe the ground somewhere. I have a belief that it would be
very good for one . . . better than school mastering at any rate.

I fear it is impossible to go to Ireland . . . much as I should like to. I've
arranged to be with my people in the country during August, and, as I've
not seen them for about 4 months I really shall have to go.

I am going there tomorrow . . . it will be rather boring but placid and I
hope to do some writing . . . boring indeed, after this place, where for most
of the time I have been hectically talking after the enforced silence of Repton
. . . talking with intelligent people . . . while of nights, I have been sleeping
out on the roof in company with an artistic young woman in short hair
and purple pyjamas . . . spending most of the night in conversation or in
singing folk-songs and rag-time to the stars . . . while early in the morning
we would be wakened by a gorgeous great peacock howling like a damned
soul or woman wailing for her demon lover, while he stalked about the tiles
showing off his plumage to the sunrise.

Give my love to Aileen.

> *Yrs.*
> *A. L. H.*

98: †TO FRANCES PETERSEN

> *Prior's Field, Godalming*
> *23 August, 1916*

My dear Frances,

The days slide away, as rapid and elusive as macaroni from the corners of
an Englishman's mouth.

Even newspapers, safest landmarks in the desert of time, do not intrude
themselves here . . . at least not until the evening, when my father brings
them back from London . . . and then the day is done with and one takes no
more interest in it, desiring neither to know its name nor to discover its
position relatively to other days. That it is still August I gather from the fact
that Their Right Reverences the Bishops of London and Chelmsford write

letters to the *Times* of a fatuity that would be unprintable in any other time but the Silly Season.

And are you, my dear Frances, proposing to be a woman messenger in the Great National Mission, and do you propose to testify your devotion to the Church of England to your fellow-Xtians? Then I warn you that you will not be permitted to do so from a) the pulpit, b) the chancel steps, c) the lectern. The above cited Bishops consider that it is a work of the Devil to suggest anything of the kind and, within their dioceses, have utterly forbidden it.

I intruded shyly into the world of actuality by going for a couple of nights to London to stay with the sinister [H. C.] Harwood, who is occupying one of Earp's mansions, a flat in Clement's Inn. My first evening was a little embarrassing—Harwood took me to see a poet called [Edward] Shanks and his wife, residing in Hampstead. We had hardly arrived, when he turned deathly pale and, rushing out of the room, proceeded to be sick—while Shanks tried, vainly, to restore him to health, Mrs Shanks and I nervously conversed about music until about midnight, when Harwood was sufficiently recovered to be borne limply home. And that is what comes of drinking absinthe before dinner in the Café R[———] . . . the incredible folly of drinking absinthe, now that the importation of it has ceased and unscrupulous innkeepers, to make their stocks last, fill up the bottle with wood-alcohol and other atrocities, enough to make any man ill, being sheer poison.

And then, the following day, I went and had lunch with the notorious E. S. P. Haynes, England's most strenuous struggler for freedom of divorce, a man of immense grossness, both of body and mind, very Bellocian in his conviviality and withal an extremely acute lawyer. We lunched for about three hours in a shop full of lobsters, consuming the said lobsters and washing them down with huge quantities of Chablis and talking of liberty and sex and the decadence of the Huns in loud resonant voices . . . and then back to Lincoln's Inn, where out of strong boxes, come all Rupert Brooke's papers with dozens of unpublished poems, which a less intoxicated man would have read with ease, but which to me seemed somehow rather hieroglyphic, though ultimately their meaning was never hidden to me . . . but it was trivial stuff, some of it rather funny, though, and all testifying to the various amours of the beautiful Brooke in all the continents of this and several of the other planets.

And then the folly, the criminal silliness of the *Nation*, which has printed three of my poems, but which has been good enough to sign them with my father's name . . . so that the first I heard of their publication was a letter from A. C. Benson to my father congratulating him on the extreme beauty of his verses and quoting Coleridge, aptly and with charm, to prove the fact. And now wherever my father goes showers of felicitations fall upon him and he lives haloed with a reputation entirely fictitious.

I feel sure that something hideous of the same kind will happen with my book, of which I have just been correcting first proofs; it will make a lamentable appearance in the world fathered on Russell Green or Rypins or [Eric] Dickinson or someone of the sort, which would be more than I could bear.

I trust you return in health from your stay with Aileen, from whom I heard the other day . . . a letter scrawled on the sort of paper you wrap bloaters in with an imperfectly licked and unsharpened pencil stump. So far as I can make out anything, she does not seem to say much.

If you are in London in September and if I am we might do something intelligent or not, as the case may be.

I do not know what I am going to do for a profession; I cannot even play the clarionette outside public houses.

Goodbye . . . .

Yours ever,
A. L. H.

P. S. Who, by the way, was the second party in the matrimonial arrangement planned for you by Mrs T[——] and about which you told me? I meant to have inquired before. You told me that you had elicited from that woman her hideous secrets.

99: TO JULIAN HUXLEY

[London]
7 September, 1916

My dear Julian,

They tell me that, for some reason best, I suppose, known to yourself and the God who is credited with making you—though mark you, I hold with the Bogomils in upholding the theory of man's Satanic origin . . . they tell me, en fin, that you are returning to the once-merry England. Or else pacifically to what the Editor of *Truth* would call THE PLAYGROUND OF EUROPE.

Were I you, I think I should do neither the one nor the other.

I dont know how you propose to function here. In any case they will almost inevitably conscribe you. The more men, I feel, that there are left in the world unconnected with this bloody affair, the better for the said world.

And as for the other affair . . . though many of my sympathies go with the idea, I fear it will not be efficient. The more peaceably inclined people here . . . and at one time or another I have met a good many of the moving spirits . . . do not seem much to believe in the value of these international businesses during hostilities. Any campaigns must originate within the various countries. None will be imposed on from without, regarding it, naturally, if not quite justly, as an unwarrantable interference of people who 'have

99 *The 'other affair', in the fourth paragraph, was the American-inspired unofficial congress for peace, at Berne.*

nothing to do with the case, tra la'. I should not be surprised if there was a good deal of movement in that direction in England in the course of this autumn. I have seen signs and heard rumours about it.

I am shortly going to Garsington, near Oxford, to work on the land during the autumn; it will be on the farm of my very dear friends the Morrells, and the experience should be pleasing. Being only a few miles from Oxford will also be an advantage; I keep permanently a little cache of friends there and, after all, friendship is the one thing that makes life supremely worth living. . . . Acquaintances and all the conventional social intercourse with people indifferent are an intolerable bore. But friends . . . how essential to one. I am utterly stranded and wretched without them, if I am long alone. Though one does enjoy one's own company from time to time; one talks so inimitably well to oneself.

My book of poems comes out in a week or so . . . a tomelet of fifty pages and on every page a deceased personality. One changes, grows with the rapidity of one of those amorphophallic tropical fungi. To look through that book . . . and oh how heartily sick I am of all but about four things in it . . . is, for me, like going through my own private Morgue where every alcove is occupied by a corpse of myself. And that's only the corpses which could be shewed in public.

Well, Oxford is over. Crowned with the artificial roses of academic distinction, I stagger, magnificently drunk with youthful conceit, into the symposium, not of philosophers, but of apes and wolves and swine . . . in short, into what the Bishop of Mombasa would call the 'Larger World', 'the Realm of Reality'. No more of the sheltered, the academic life . . . the life, which, I believe, when led by a man of high and independent spirit, is the fullest and best of lives, though one of the most bedraggled and wretched as led by the ordinary crew of bovine intellectuals. I should like to go on for ever learning. I lust for knowledge, as well theoretic as empirical. Comparing small things with great, I think I am rather like the incomparable John Donne.

But what we want is men who write prose. And we dont get them. Alas, alas, it is very difficult and discouraging work looking for prose. No young men write anything but journalism or verse. A sad fact. And that pure verbal beauty, that conscientiousness so necessary in the maker of a good style, is nowhere to be got. If you know of any young student at the R[ice] I[nstitute] who writes consummately good and unsellable prose, tell him to send it to me. Oh, but I am serious. Well, well, when we have done crying havoc and letting slip the hogs of war, I dare say there will be a few young men who will be found able to write prose. A pious hope. When we have done with what all the editors of all the influential Journals and the whole Bench of Bishops, more especially the COLONIAL BISHOPS, would call the 'Stern

99 *Huxley's forthcoming volume of poems was* The Burning Wheel.

Realities' . . . in other words finished off this nightmarish interruption of reality, of all that matters . . . then I somehow, and probably quite unjustifiably, feel that there will be a race of golden young men and crystal young women, who will give us the prose we require. Much more likely we shall have a generation of creatures incapable of thought or of action, victims of the incredible anarchy that others brought about.

Well, I have said enough. There is a time, though how few realize the fact, for silence.

It will be good to see you if you do come back. You will have to come down and visit me, where, either like G. Washington, I am cutting down trees, or like W. E. Gladstone, I am planting them . . . for it is, they seem to think, as a forester that I am going to function upon that curious and utterly unknown quantity, THE LAND. You would, I think, like the Morrells.

Yours,

A.

100: TO LEONARD HUXLEY

Garsington Manor, Oxford
[Circa 23 September, 1916]

Dearest Father,

Should a parcel containing atropine have come for me from the J[oint] A[rmy] and N[avy] S[tores], wd. you mind sending it on: and if not will you ask why not; I ordered it this day last week.

I returned yesterday from seeing my baronne. It transpires that she is not writing memoirs at all—but is a poetess, dramatist and prosateur; she has published in French—with, as she says, éclat—and now wants to do the same in English: and I am to correct her work and discuss her ideas—which she says are very strange and startling ones—and such as an astonished world has not hitherto seen. I dare say she may discover that the younger generation may be quite distressingly familiar with them! However, I think she's intelligent, tho' quite surprisingly ignorant both of English and French literature. Her husband must have been an interesting old boy: he was for 3 years a companion and secretary of Dumas and knew well all the literary men of the period. His wife has known a good many of the newer men—but all of them belonging on the whole I shd. say, to the second class. I am to begin my séances with her at the end of October. Once a week: I think I'll ask a guinea.

Lady O[ttoline] has been ill with feverish cold ever since I've been here and I expect will have to go to Harrogate when fit to travel.

I've got an early copy of my book and the review copies have been sent out and it will be on the market I think at the start of next week.

100 *Baronne: unidentified.*

I have been cutting wood and making the second crop of hay—the former a very searching process of strain on back and side muscles.

Love to R.

Ever your loving son
Aldous

101: TO LEWIS GIELGUD

The Manor House,
Garsington, Oxford
29 September, 1916

Why, my dear Lewis, do people get engaged? . . . the only reasons I can assign for it are (a) that they want to get rid of their friends, the world forgetting, by the world forgot and all that—for the process is only less disastrous and stupid than dying, (b) that they wish to provide the industrious feuilletoniste with the materials for his hideous business . . . the fact being, of course, as you will have very well divined, that, having been at one time a little in love with Aileen, I am correspondingly a little jealous. Happily, as I fall in love with every woman I meet . . . no, perhaps that is putting matters a little too strongly, but at any rate with the better women I meet . . . it isn't very serious.

How I thank God that James [Street] has escaped the clutches of HOLY MATRIMONY or even the repulsive preludes to it. I went into Magdalen twice in the hopes of seeing him, but found him on both occasions from home.

I am so nauseated with the sight of my poems that I have not yet had the strength to cut a copy of my book, but I confess that I contemplate the exterior banana with affection and pleasure. And as to my sensuality, why, after all, not? I am sensual . . . though the thing in question [? 'The Higher Sensualism'] is admittedly not much more than an exercise and almost an adaptation from the French, written in the depths of boredom at Repton, while I was supposed to be supervising the creatures at their exams. The waggon ['Two Realities'] is very vulgar. The best things in the book in my opinion are 'Mirror', the Horses sub fornice ['Quotidian Vision'], 'The Garden', Amoret ['Philoclea in the Forest'], '[The Burning] Wheel', Mucus [sic] and last, but not least, the ever-memorable and unforgettable 'Mole' . . . poem that has the power of arousing a hatred or an enthusiasm among its readers and which, I foresee, is destined to become a cause of rupture in the world, dividing it up into Guelfs and Ghibellines, Blues and Greens, Monts and Caps, Mouldiwarpians and Swat-that-Moleites.

I shall be interested to see what, if anything, the papers have to say. They cant go on commenting on the type and 'artistic' (oh so distressingly artistic) get-up of booklets . . . which was the only criticism passed on the first volumes. They will perhaps criticise these; more likely preserve that

114

dignified and impenetrable silence for which the BRITISH NATION has so justly been praised. I have just received three guineas for my outpourings in the *Nation*, which gratifies me. I think I shall write an Ode in praise of money.

The man [R. C. B.] Fellowes lies wounded in 48 Bryanston Sq. I should like to tell you of my Baroness, of the Herculean manner in which I drive wedges into great trunks of trees, of how Ottoline is sick and has gone to Harrogate, of many men so beautiful, of women more lovely still ... but my spirit swoons at the thought of it all. It is too much, too much. God is weary of it all; He shakes his elm-trees at me in a manner at once playful and menacing; He is like Herbert Spencer playing a practical joke ... terrible, appalling.

A. L. H.

102: TO LEONARD HUXLEY

Garsington Manor, Oxford
1 October, [1916]

Dearest Father,

Many thanks for seeing about the atropine, wh: has arrived safely.

The household is a little quiet and depressed since Lady O. has gone away to Harrogate. Philip is very busy stocking a new farm he has just taken over and is always going to sales, whence he returns with sheep, cows, horses, waggons, machines etc.

Do I or do I not remember your talking about [G. P.] Putnam's representative in England? I rather seem to recall your telling me about talks you've had with him. The fruit of them is that he wrote (as Blackwell told me the other day) for an advance copy of my book and then—being pleased with it—for all the other books in the series. So that you are an unconscious benefactor of a whole generation of young poets and poetesses.

Today arrived a queer creature called [Boris] Anrep, the Military Secretary of the Russian Government in England and in ordinary life a sculptor and painter. In type of countenance very German and Prussian too in mind—curiously cynical about the war, which he describes as being one of Tartars v. Huns, Russian against German—nothing else being important for him but that question of race. He is very cheerful too about atrocities—saying that of course the Russians have committed as many as the Germans, have destroyed all the libraries and churches they can in Poland and elsewhere—and he justifies it quite happily by saying 'War is War' and all we are out for is to smash and kill and destroy as much of Germany as we can and the Germans are justified in doing the same to us. Altogether strangely bloody in his ideas. Otherwise very charming and amusing and clever and talented.

What news is there of Julian? I want so much to hear. I am very hearty and well—immersed in *War and Peace*, which has claims, I think, to being

115

the greatest book—incredible, there is no other word for it. I await reviews of my book with interest.

Love to R: I trust David flourishes like a cedar of Mount Lebanon.

Your loving son
Aldous

103: TO LEONARD HUXLEY

Garsington Manor, Oxford
[Circa 13 October, 1916]

Dearest Father,

Many thanks for your letter from the lambery—(I dare say that a technically-minded agriculturist like myself wd. recognize them as really being tegs or theaves or four-toothers!). It sounds indeed a pleasant place.

The household here is yet further reduced by the going of Philip to Parliament, which keeps him in London in the middle of the week, leaving him longish week-ends here. Lady O. returns, I fancy, next week. I have been doing my usual wood-cutting—useful for a house which exclusively uses logs for fuel—and have been lopping a big branch from the huge immemorial ilex in front of the house, sawing it into lengths and splitting them with wedges and beetle into suitable billets. I went into Oxford to see the Haldanes last week. Prof. H has gone to America. Naomi was there for the night—her husband now miraculously better and with every prospect of being quite all right, despite a very badly cracked skull.

I expect I shall begin making my London visits soon, as the baronne is to come to town towards the end of Oct:, so I shall see you periodically then. I shd. like to make my deferred visit to Ernest Clarke one day when I come up: so will let you know dates in due time.

I was amused by the *Times* review of me—pleasantly offensive—tho' I am still quite at a loss to make out what they objected to in the 'eyes of cats'. To impugn my taste!—that is the last and unforgivable insult:—I whose literary tact is well-known to be as faultless as the manners of an under-taker! And in that context, too: the thing being obviously slightly ironical and—let me at once admit the plagiarism—the image stolen from as reput-able a writer as Drayton and from as admirable a work as *Nymphidia*—or at least I fancy that it comes there—that description of the Fairy Palace, whose windows were made of the eyes of cats.

By the way, I had quite forgotten my last term's battels, which I ordi-narily wd. pay at the beginning of this term. They amount I fancy to just about £53. I shall have to take my degree some time, tho' it doesn't matter

103 The Burning Wheel, *with two other books of poetry published by Blackwell in the 'Adventurers All' series, was reviewed in* T.L.S., *5 October, 1916.*

when—before, at any rate, I get an academic job, about which I've just written to Raleigh.

Love to R.

Your loving son
Aldous

104: TO LEONARD HUXLEY

The Manor House,
Garsington, Oxford
[Early December, 1916]

Dearest Father,

I have at last got an appointment out of E. Clarke. After having said he wd. see no one till the 3rd week in Jan he has relented and written that I can come Thursday 14th, 12.15—which I will do—meeting you there if you want to come, tho' there's no need for your presence if it's inconvenient.

I saw [B. L.] Richmond on Monday, who was v. polite and almost infinitely loquacious—thereby very nearly making me miss my train—and said I was to study the list of New Books in the *Litt Supp* and send him a p. c. with the names of any I wanted to do: in which case he might or might not give them to me—he cd. not be positive which.

Old [Augustine] Birrell came down here last week—very eighteenth century in appearance and manners—very entertaining and charming—professing an almost total je-m'en-ficheisme about the war and the horrors of the world, content in his library. I hope Clarke will give me goggles, I shall urge him to if he can. They wd. simplify things so much. Post imminent.

Much love from
Aldous

P.S. Heard at last from the baronne—very apologetic—she comes to town after Xmas and I shall begin to cook her goose then.

105: TO JULIAN HUXLEY

[Garsington]
[29 December, 1916]

My dear Julian,

Many thanks for the letter and the book. I fancy that a good deal of this is [E. L.] Masters' earlier work, except the *Arabella* poems, in which he seems to me just not [to] have done what T. S. Eliot has succeeded in achieving. You ought to read his things. They are all the more remarkable when one knows the man, ordinarily just an Europeanized American, overwhelmingly cultured, talking about French literature in the most uninspired fashion imaginable.

I am at present weighed down by the stupidity of a bad cold and incapable of thought or of action, which is rather trying. But thank God,

---

104 *Litt Supp: the* Times Literary Supplement. *Richmond was the editor.*

at last this vile frost has broken and the south-west comes pouring in again, warm and moist.

I wrote to [C. A.] Alington, who replied that there was no vacancy at Eton this half. So I have now applied to my venerable godfather, Juddy, to ask if he knows of anything at Charterhouse. Whether there will be a crystallisation in the Munitions, I dont know. I was sorry I missed that job . . . and by so little . . . as it seemed an interesting one. Still, it may present itself again.

I am glad the Americans have come out so creditably. I think they've put peace definitely within sight. If the Germans are recalcitrant they'll declare war on them; if we are, they'll stop our imports . . . a thing which, I gather, they are likely to do in any case, owing to their own shortage of grain. In either case the contingency is to be avoided, and I hope it will make both sides see reason. Middleton Murry, who is up in the press of the country, assures me that there will be a revolution in Russia if they stop soon without getting Constantinople . . . which makes one all the more anxious for an immediate cessation.

An amusing Xmas party here. Murry, Katherine Mansfield, Lytton Strachey, [the Hon. Dorothy] Brett and Carrington, Bertrand Russell and Maria Nys. We performed a superb play invented by Katherine, improvising as we went along. It was a huge success, with Murry as a Dostoevsky character and Lytton as an incredibly wicked old grandfather.

I lighted in to-day's *Morning Post* on a little puff of myself, apropos of *Oxford Poetry, '16*. Quite pleasing. I am contemplating bringing out another book in the summer, more serious, larger, better, more passionate, more distinguished, more modern, more sincere . . . enfin the 1917 Model 24-30 H. P.

My monocle is very grandiose, but gives me rather a Greco-Roman air of rocococity.

Yours
A.L.H.

106: TO LEWIS GIELGUD

[*Garsington*]
1 *January*, 1917
The worst, my dear Lewis, has not lost the opportunity of happening. It

105 *Alington was the Headmaster at Eton.*
106 *The suicide of Reginald Smith had occurred on 26 December. Maria was Maria Nys, undoubtedly the 'nice Belgian' of letter 92. She had been sent by her parents to England in 1915 and had lived at Garsington, where presumably she and Huxley first met, until about the time he moved there. Between October and the end of 1916 she was in London, giving French lessons. Huxley, who went down to see her as often as he could manage the journey from Garsington, fell in love with her during these months. Her departure for Florence brought about a separation lasting more than two years.*

118

rarely does. Poor Maria is being hustled out remorselessly to her ghoulish mother [Marguerite Nys] in Florence. One achieves resignation . . . incomplete and somewhat rebellious . . . but not gaiety. It is altogether painful; I dont know where the 'sweet' part of this much vaunted sorrow comes in. I find the imminence of separation briny enough and the thing itself will doubtless be worse. And then for how long? It's the indefiniteness that is so distressing. Six months, a year, three years . . . the vistas lengthen out. Wait and see is the only policy, as ever. Oh the infinite greatness of Asquith to realize that quietism is the sole possibility. It is a pity that that old man is so malodorous . . . I speak literally and physically, for he was here to-day.

Still no job. I missed one in the Munitions by about twelve hours. Eton wont have me. I dangle for Charterhouse . . . God preserve me! I see that the head of my father's firm has flung himself out of window, under the impression that his existence polluted the water supply. If only one could persuade George and Harmsworth that the same . . . and much more . . . was true of them! Their bowels might gush forth with the horror of their self-realisation. I almost begin faintly to believe that the war will be over by the end of the summer, conceivably earlier. It is too wonderful to think of peace . . . happy time when the young may come back to thank the old for their amazing Christian Fortitude in bearing their (the young's) sufferings. Prospect of peace is the one ray of comfort in an otherwise somewhat dim outlook. I hope I'll see you again soon.

Flourish, my dear Lewis.

A.L.H.

Just quietly think over these few points:—

The incomprehensibility of women and their unlikeness to anything one had expected.

The question whether passion is necessary to love, or whether it gambols like a faun round the shrine, unconnected and irresponsible.

The notion of Time as a God. Time the creator and destroyer in one, the father of truth. A good religion, it seems to me, and the only sensible and rational one.

The dangerous doctrine of purification by suffering. It encourages the old to maltreat the young.

The thesis that the soul leaves the body before death . . . at an age varying in individuals from forty to sixty.

Good bye. Did you see the review of *Oxford Poetry* in the *Morning Post*. They make me out very distinguished, dont they.

The Manor House,
Garsington, Oxford
5 January, [1917]

My dear Frances,

By a stroke of chance I shall very likely be in the metropolis on Wed-Fri next—trying to get out of England, as I've been offered a job—a poor one, but it will be fairly interesting—in an American school. It will be interesting to go—both to see the Home of LIBERTY and its denizens, and also for the sake of getting out of the war. I don't know how long I'll stay:—I trust not more than a year. But of course they mayn't let me out, and I may be con-scribed as a dock-labourer in Aden or a poisoner of stray cats in our Northern suburbs. Any how, I shall be coming to town to try and procure a permit at the beginning of next week: and if you ring up 6529 Padd[ington] on Wed or Thur you'll probably find me. I cannot guarantee my mental state: I am becoming a third class tragi-comedian these days.

When does Aileen commit her rash act? One seems always to be getting married, doesn't one?

ALH

We will come in to Bing Boy tomorrow (Sat:) aft! If in Oxford have a late tea at George and youll probably see the whole boiling.

108: TO LEONARD HUXLEY

The Manor House,
Garsington, Oxford
22 January, 1917

Dearest Father,

As yet no news at all from the Passport Office. It's nearly time they made some response. Meanwhile I am very busy finishing off three articles for Uncle Humphry's fifth vol of English poets, and reading a bundle of books to review for the *Statesman*—a varied lot, 1 Japanese, 2 Russian and 1 Belgian.

107 *Bing Boy: a popular musical comedy,* The Bing Boys Are Here. *Job: this came to nothing.*

108 *Thomas Humphry Ward's* The English Poets (1918) *contained essays by Huxley on John Davidson, Ernest Dowson, and Richard Middleton. The reviews for the* New Statesman, *which would have been commissioned by J. C. Squire, the literary editor (then acting editor), dealt with Fenollosa and Pound's 'Noh', or 'Accomplish-ment': A Study of the Classical Stage of Japan (17 February), and conjecturally, with Verhaeren's* Love Poems (20 January) *and two Russian verse collections, Pollen's* Russian Songs and Lyrics *and Livesay's* Songs of Ukraina (10 February). *Probably Huxley continued to write reviews for Squire; see letter 143.*

I've just returned from a week end at Oxford, having had a most uncomfortable walk out over roads that were sheeted with ice, owing to a combination of fine rain and hard frost. Quite impossible to walk except on the grass at the side of the road.

I expect Julian will have a lively time in Italy—plenty of shellfire and such like, if, at least, conditions with the Ambulance are as they were a year or so ago, when a friend of mine was there driving a car.

I may, of course, have to come up about my passport at short notice. I'll wire or write if I do.

Much love to all.

Your loving son
Aldous

109: TO DOROTHY CARRINGTON

The Manor House,
Garsington, Oxford
[Early March, 1917]

My dear Carrington,

The effect upon Philip, when I remarked with a gay nonchalance that we had been to the Palladium on Wednesday night, was very noticeably perturbing. 'Thursday, did you say?' 'No: *Wednesday* night.' Vain hope shattered. He remains pensive, while I retail a full account of the performance. I bemoan the fact that Brandsby Williams took Tich's place: Philip murmurs sympathetically. I describe the acrobats: Philip agrees that they must have been wonderful. I remark that you had brought your sketch book and spent most of the time in drawing pictures of types in the audience: Philip changes the conversation. Researches have proved that [——] is at present in town, where the pug bitch presented to her on leaving has just died in giving birth to a child begotten incestuously by her Borgia-esque brother, Gobbo. All fits well—and all the time Philip is suffering from a bronchitic cold, which forbids his going out at nights!

You should really go and see *Seven Days' Leave* at the Lyceum. It is sublime. There are Hun spies—hissed by the audiences—heroines in bathing costumes—submarines rising from the sea—naval battles—high comedy: and with clockwork regularity, come references to the *Lusitania* and Nurse Cavell; and the British Public cheers itself hoarse over its own patriotic feelings. Also a comic Conscientious Objector. You must go. 3/- stalls and smoking allowed.

Yours
Aldous Huxley

109 *Huxley and Carrington had been to the Palladium on Wednesday, 28 February. He stayed in London that week, working at the Food Office on a trial basis.*

Garsington
Saturday, [circa 10 March, 1917]

Dearest Father,

I hope the move has gone without hitch and that you are once more in a state of comparative tranquillity.

I have heard from the Baroness once more, to the effect that she has at last come to town and wishes to begin her séances at once—next Tuesday, so that, if its convenient I'll stay the night and have the pleasure of seeing the new house. I shall also take the opportunity of seeing John Murray at the Munitions. I am going into Oxford for the weekend to the Haldanes. Jack was wounded in Mesopotamy but has wired to say that it's very slight and he's not even in hospital.

The Dardanelles Report shows a pretty state of imbecillity: it's not pleasant to think of lives thrown away by the sheer folly of the politicians.

Love to all.

A.L.H.

111: TO LEONARD HUXLEY

Garsington
3 April, 1917

Dearest Father,

I sent you a very hurried p. c. yesterday. Let me explain. I went to town and saw an acquaintance who before I knew where I was fairly pushed me into a place in the Naval Law dept. of the Admiralty. Rather long hours—54 a week—and ill-paid—£2. I agreed to start at once, but have decided at any rate to postpone till after Easter as I have a number of other offers pouring in on me as the result of a judicious advertisement in the *Times* Agony Column. Most of them sound a good deal more interesting and lucrative than a job as 3rd class admiralty clerk; and if I settle up with one or other, I shall throw up the admiralty, which would in any case be a considerable strain, 9 hours daily at filling forms.

At the same time other and better Govt. posts may be procurable: (a) thro' Fluffy Davies [Davis], (b) thro' Violet Bonham-Carter, who seems to think some secretaryship might be got for me somewhere. I rushed into

---

110 *Move: Leonard Huxley and his family had moved to 16 Bracknell Gardens, Frognal Lane, N.W.3. Following the death of Reginald Smith, he succeeded to the editorship of* The Cornhill.

111 *'Fluffy' Davis: Henry William Carless Davis, Fellow and Tutor of Balliol, a member of the War Trade Advisory Committee. Huxley's advertisement had appeared on 31 March:* 'YOUNG MAN, 22 *(rejected), Public School and Oxford, First-class Honours, desires* LITERARY, SECRETARIAL, *or other* Work'.

the admiralty thing rather in a moment of despair and before I got the answers of my advertisement or heard of Lady B-Carter's efforts. I'll come up in any case to-morrow for a few days and see people in town who apply for me. One good person asks me to state 'my height and other relevant details'! I trust he will be impressed by my excess of inches.

Love to R. and M.

Aldous

P.S. Among others the Medici people (Lee Warner) ask me to see them.

112: TO JULIAN HUXLEY

The Manor House,
Garsington, Oxford
Easter, [8 *April,* 1917]

My dear Julian,

Many thanks for your letter. Since last I saw you I have been inundated with jobs. I went up on Monday and found myself pushed—almost william-william—into a very nasty and ill-paid job at the Admiralty [. . . .] However, I am going to lie and chuck it up for a much better thing at the Air Board, which is all settled and I go there next week—screw, they tell me, from £200 to £250[. . . .]

I go up to town on Tuesday.

Yrs.
ALH

113: TO MRS NAOMI MITCHISON

[*London*]
[*Circa May,* 1917]

My dear Naomi,

I shall be delighted to dine with you on Thursday—the only trouble is that I can't remember, whether it's that night or the next I've asked the poet [T. S.] Eliot to dine with me—but if we dine at the Isola Bella in Frith St., Soho at circa 7.17 we shall be all right—for if it *is* Thursday he's dining with me he will be there; and he's a very nice creature. I hope you don't mind the Isola Bella—it's a very charming place.

'No dress' concurred in with enthusiasm.

I trust you flourish: I do not—a kind of mouldy misery clings putre-fyingly round a core of exhausted apathy, which is ME.

I am, Gentlemen,
Your obediant
Servant

(*Signed*) *Aldous Huxley*
for Director of Aeronautical Contracts

112 *Huxley worked at the Air Board until July.*

[*London*]
May, 1917

1   2
AS/3414/1917/(CA3)
Messrs British Emaillite Co Ltd.
5 *Hythe Road*
Cumberland Park, Willesden
Gent.

Carriage charges on 11,000 *gallons of returned Dope*

With ref to your letter 1746/0 of the 1st inst, I am to inform you that the above charges will be borne by this Dept—but whether ALH can bear this Dept much longer is another question. Porco di Madonna, the people in this place—suburban business-men, with absolutely no interest in life but making money and gossiping about their hideous homes. They add to the soul-weariness with which this place overcomes one, as well as with physical fatigue. It is all too too bloody. And then the war becomes more ghastly day by day and every day it becomes most obvious that it is a folly and a crime to go on. Massingham showed me a letter from Anatole France—a terrific Rabelaisian affair—about Peace with Victory, written in reply to someone who had said that peace was not peace without victory and we must go on ad lib to get it. The letter began with a wonderful tirade about peace without victory, that it was like tripe without onions, a cat without hair, that it was a cripple, a hemorrhoidal cul-de-jatte etc etc and ending up with a very Anatolian little wink in the shape of—'Mais cela ne coûte que dix milles hommes par jour'. France is already a first class power no longer. We shall merrily go on till on a level with Hayti and Liberia. I gather that at the secret session George revealed no policy whatever, and had no thought of any kind except to get 800,000 more men to replace casualties this year.

I wish to God one could say Je m'en fiche of the whole thing—but one cant—it's too insistent. There seems to be some hope among the people who have had nothing to do with it, such as the Irish; and I fancy that the best part of political life after the war will be an unofficial Sinn Feinism all over the world. Sinn Fein itself in Ireland and in the rest of Europe I.L.P. and syndicalism acting with organized anarchy apart from the existing parties.

I hear that M[argaret] is not to go to Oxford this year after all. I think it would have been better, but still— The importance of acquiring non-war kultur seems so important at this time when it is the fashion to regard education as an expensive frippery. But if she goes to London University half the time it will be fairly all right and if the war ends, she can go abroad or something of the sort.

About your questions. I know no pocket Rabelais but one in five volumes. I have ceased to read now: it's quite impossible as I'm always too tired in the evening—and I take almost no interest in anything but my food, which is a poor subject to be interested in these days especially when one has diarrhoea. Hope to see you soon.

ALH

115: TO LEWIS GIELGUD

16 *Bracknell Gardens, N.W.*3
[*Late May*, 1917]

Your post-card to hand, as the saying is. I trust you flourish—the more so, it may be, because you have as yet had no time to see PARIS—or should it be HELEN? The quotidian gloom has been a little relieved by the fact that the result of my medical re-examination has been complete rejection, so that I am safe from these body-snatchers, kidnappers, baby killers and white slave traffickers, the Recruiters. But oh—the process of being rejected. Had I been fit to start with I should have sunk three classes by the time they looked at me. I presented myself at 10 at the Oxford recruiting office—and there I waited till 4, herded in a sort of pen with some 80 or so of the scum of the district—all of whom were additionally horrible by being hospital cases of the most painful kind—halfwits, syphilitics, hunchbacks, cul-de-jattes, hemorrhoidal and estropiated dwarfs, goitrous cretins, men with unprecedented combinations of disease, diabetic consumptives suffering from Bright's disease, rheumatic lepers and so on and so on. There, as I say, we waited—in an atmosphere that was typical of Oxford—sweltering heat impregnated with rain which dropped occasionally, scalding, from the leaden sky: no place to sit down: men swooned and vomited all about: when any one tried to repose an instant on the steps of the doctors' motors, soldiers with fixed bayonets drove them away, cursing brutally. By dint of assuring the doctors that I was one of the most important figures in the Air Board, I got them to reject me utterly, instead of putting me into C3, which might have been bloody—for they'd still have had a hold on me.

There is no particular news—the misery of life proceeds. Write some time or other. I will do the same soon.

ALH

116: TO JULIETTE BAILLOT

[*London*]
[*Circa* 14 *June*, 1917]

My dear Juliette,

Thank you very much for your letter and poem. I like the soaring of

116 *Juliette Baillot, whom Huxley had first met in* 1915 *and who was later to become the wife of his brother Julian, was employed as governess-companion to Lady Ottoline Morrell's daughter, Julian, at Garsington Manor.*

wild birds and the idea of the whole of it: but it's an idea panting and struggling for expression—and as yet hasn't got its adequate form. The thought and the feeling are still in prison, weighed down by the matter which ought to be their instrument, but is a clog. But as Tommy [Earp] says, it is simply a matter of practice. Your mind has to learn how to be master of its material: and mastership will certainly come in time.

But where is 'The Golden Key'?! I will encourage you to send it by showing you this French effort of mine on the subject of nature and art, unsophistication and subtlety—I fear it is a little obscure as well as a little flippant in tone.

> Tout en martyrisant les divines mandores
> Du mensonge sacré des mots, je songe, ô si
> Nonchalamment belle! à ta voix de colibri:
> Avec ta triste voix de colibri tu dores
> Toute imbécillité qu'exhale[nt] les landores
> Dans leurs meurtres de sens à jamais aboli.
> Inconsciente, tu perces le cœur ravi
> Où je ne puis qu'à peine ouvrir un peu les stores.
>
> Péniblement de mes bouquins moisis j'évoque
> L'esprit mystique et pais de la Sainte Alacoque,
> Mais sans verve pour moi saigne le Sacré Coeur.
> Tu parles: et ton chant de petite ingénue
> Imite un séraphin, cul nu sur une nue,
> Louant Dieu de son psaume infiniment moqueur.

After that I don't see that you can with decency refuse to show me 'The Golden Key'! I regret to say that I rarely write in French—and then only when I want to be un peu scabreux: it certainly is the best language for indecency ever invented: they have carried the technical vocabulary to a greater perfection than anyone else and they can combine grossness with grace in a way no other nation can.

We are being pestered by these German aeroplanes. Yesterday they were all round us: there was a fiendish banging of bombs eastward towards St. Pauls and the air was full of bursting shrapnel, while overhead one could hear the rattle of the machine guns in the German and English machines fighting in mid air. Today—just as I was in the middle of this letter—another alarm: distant bangs; general order to go to the basement: so we all flocked down and ate a large tea in the underground refreshment rooms till the scare was over. I expect it's a new German policy: they'll probably come every day now, and if they come in large flocks, hundreds at a time, they'll do a most unpleasant amount of slaughter.

I have been meeting a distinguished Russian poet, Goumilov [N. S. Gumilyov] (of whom I may say I had never heard—but still!) who is also editor of their paper, *Apollon*. We talked to each other with great difficulty in

French, which he speaks rather haltingly and which I always stumble and trip in most fearfully. But he seemed quite interesting and pleasant. Anrep wants to bring him to Garsington this Sunday.

Au revoir, my dear Juliette. Write and tell me about Julian [Morrell] and the events of life at G[arsington] in general. I am writing also to J.

Yours
Aldous

117: TO JULIETTE BAILLOT

[<i>London</i>]
[<i>June</i>, 1917]

My dear Juliette,

Thank you for your letter and 'The Golden Key'. I liked it, but, again, it too suffers from difficulties in expression. The statue is still within the block: your tools have only begun to cut it out. Here and there a curve or a line of the figure you mean to carve stands out clear and clean, but much is still the raw unhewn marble, still only potentially the Phoebus, the Eros or Athene you wanted to create. But go on: it is the only thing. Try using very simple words and straightforward expressions. I should be inclined to mistrust any archaic expressions or grammatical forms and to use practically only the words of everyday speech—educated speech of course, not necessarily words of one syllable—and the grammatical constructions and verbal order, as far as possible, of prose.

I have been reading Laforgue's poetry again with a very great pleasure and sympathy. I wrote a little 'Hommage' to him the other day, which might amuse you.

> Que je t'aime mon cher Laforgue,—
> Frère qui as connu les nostalgies
> Qu'engendrent les sanglots des violons:
> Et puis, dans la rue, les pâmoisons
> Crépusculaires des orgues—des orgues
> D'une par trop lointaine Barbarie—
> O ciel, tu les as senties
> Percer ton coeur de bon Breton!
>
> Tu avais la solitude dans l'âme:
> Orphelin par ton génie,
> Tu n'as jamais trouvé la femme
> Qui pourrait être l'Unique Amie.

---

117 *The 'Hommage' and the poem in letter 116 (called 'Sonnet à l'Ingénue') were both printed in Huxley's* Jonah (1917).

Parmi les parfums at les froufrous
Malgré toi ta chair a resté pure,
Et tu en as devenu presque fou:—
Tu pensais; tu étais un Hors-Nature.

Hélas, il faut que l'on vivote
Selon la nature et le père Aristote:
Si c'était un bien autre loi
Que nous suivons, toi et moi,
Vois-tu, mon pauvre Jules,
Nous nous sommes faits assez ridicules!

I hope you wont have started for the sea by the time I come next—if I do come soon.

Yours
Aldous

118: TO JULIETTE BAILLOT

16, Bracknell Gardens,
Frognal Lane, N.W.3
10 July, [1917]

My dear Juliette,

Thank you for both your letters—and apologies for not having answered the first before. I'd like to have come to Bembridge, but doubt if I can. I've practically arranged to go down to Oxford at the end of this week— and up till then I am all booked up. Furthermore you'd be almost coming back by the time I could possibly come—so that what with all this and the ridiculous expensiveness of a journey of even that distance, I think it's impossible.

Coming back to books again is a pleasure and so is not having to get to the other end of London by 9.30 in the morning.

I have been having numbers of curious adventures with Evan—he is an adventurous person, a man of action, and he is very salutary in stirring up my contemplative lethargy—with the result that we have the greatest fun.

I heard from Earp—at last! And have sent him my translation of the 'Après-midi d'un Faune' to be printed in this year's *Oxford Poetry*. I hope you'll enjoy yourselves. Love to all.

Affectionately
Aldous

118 *Evan: the Hon. Evan Morgan, later Viscount Tredegar.*

16 *Bracknell Gardens, N.W.*3
14 *July,* 1917

My dear Carrington,

Your nose for the scabrous is unerring. There was indeed a story buried between the lines of my postcard . . . a story from which Philip could make one of his noblest Homilies on Virgin Behaviour. The protagonists are Evan, myself and a young woman of eighteen exactly like Nell Gwynn; the scene a romantic little house in a forest discovered by a most peculiar series of chances. Immense cherry trees, laden with fruit, to right and left of the stage; Nell Gwynn, whose peculiarities are that she is partially Dutch and partially French, ascends ladders and throws cherries at the young men . . . there is a snake's-eye-view of ankles and calves, perhaps a shade thick. . . . And so it begins. In the heart of Nell Gwynn the most dangerous passion is kindled . . . not merely for one but for both simultaneously; it is the wildest desire mixed with an almost religious awe, as though for gods.

Scene two. In the forest at evening the mosquito[e]s bite; so do the young women. Rather disquietingly it begins to occur to us that the creature is perfectly innocent.

Then the strangest scene in our bed-room. We become perfectly convinced that she is completely virginal. Without any shame she caresses both of us with all the fire of her native sensuality. We explain that we cannot take her virginity; we are simply passers by and it would be the merest robbery. She is in tears about it, begs and implores that we should. We are inexorable; Evan sitting up in bed like a young Sicilian shepherd with no clothes on orders her back to her room with his most imperious manner; he is the descendent of Welsh princes; she obeys and creeps off to a cold and solitary couch. We sink to sleep. At about three I wake up, aware that someone is passionately kissing my neck and shoulders. I hasten to add that it was not Evan. Nell Gwynn has returned. I give her the hospitality of my bed for a few minutes and send her away; it is all a little nerve-racking. The next night she goes to Evan; the fate of virginity hangs rather in the balance, but escapes intact; this time we lock the door. On Monday we depart, and there are terrible adieus. We feel that by our self control we have probably ruined a young girl's life. However, in my case the adieu is an au revoir, for making my way from Beaconsfield to Eton on Wednesday it occurs to me that it would be more amusing to spend the night with Nell Gwynn than with my tutor at Eton. I drop in and resume my study of the character of the unsophisticated virgin . . . feeling like Maurice Barrès in the process of cultivating 'son Moi'.

But the half of it can never be told; it was all so peculiar . . . like something which must have happened in the Balkans, impossible in England.

I am too unhappy about the seraphic Phyllis [Boyd]. I go to-day into the country, to Oxford, to stay with my antique and admirable friends the Haldanes. But if you could definitely secure Phyllis some day I might rush up . . . except that travelling is so atrociously expensive. But I expect I shall be up for a few days at the end of the month or the beginning of August and then, and then—

It was a thousand pities you couldn't come to Evan's birthday party last night. An empty place waited for you. It was a tremendous affair; at least five and twenty people and the drink flowed. Marie Beerhohm and I achieved a distinct rapprochement, positively a mutual épanchement, in our cups . . . though sober we have always been rather alarmed of one another. She is a nice creature I should say—at any rate when tight. I also established a contact with Nina Hamnett, which I had never dared to do before; at one time I even distinctly remember winding a red ribbon round her legs in the form of a Malvolio garter, but that was entirely by the way. In one corner of the room Lady Constance [Stewart-Richardson] supported [Augustus] John on her bosom. A sombre group of indistinguishably vicious women—I cant remember who they were—circled about the centre of the floor, dancing. In another corner [Ambrose] McEvoy peered out through his hair like a sheep-dog with shining eyes. Then there was a curious sediment of the upper middle classes . . . two perfectly nice young men with two perfectly nasty young women . . . and they were like the people who figure in *Punch* and who enjoy that journal. They were infinitely facetious and so boring that—as by some mishap I found myself at dinner sitting in the middle of them—I had to play a little game of spillikins all by myself throughout the meal with a pile of knives and forks and spoons. But they disappeared quite soon, or at any rate one lost sight of them.

Well, au revoir my dear Carrington. Let me know what are your schemes for late July and August, what, too are the movements of the delicate, though, I take it, somewhat hyper-nubile, Phyllis. You find me at 'Cherwell, Oxford' . . . no more.

Mr Mills has asked me to go and stay with him at Pevensey, but I think it's impossible. At any rate we will see.

Devotedly,
Aldous

Give my love to Alix: I trust she recovers.

119 *Phyllis Boyd: 'smart set' friend of Carrington. Marie Beerbohm: foot-loose niece of Max Beerbohm. Nina Hamnett was a writer and painter; Augustus John once flattered her by saying that she was one of the three best English lady painters. John's friend McEvoy, a gifted portraitist, did a fine canvas of Lord Jowitt as a young man which hangs in the Tate. Lady Constance Stewart-Richardson, daughter of the second Earl of Cromartie, was the widow of Captain Sir Edward Austin Stewart-Richardson, Bt; she was a talented dancer in the style of Isadora Duncan. Alix Florence, afterwards Mrs James Strachey, shared rooms with Carrington in Soho. Mr Mills is Weymer J.*

Garsington Manor, Oxford
3 August, 1917

My dear Julian,

Much thanks for your letter, which reminds me, in its description of your surroundings [at Canterbury], of the worst passages in the *Brothers Karamazov* . . . to such a point bestial and sordid do your companions and mode of life sound. I wish you all luck with the Intelligence job, which cannot be worse than your present business and might be really pleasant.

Oxford has been jolly enough; the usual weather, overcast and sweltering heat with great warm tears of rain dropping out of the sky; infinitely enervating. Only Mrs Haldane can preserve energy in the face of Oxford, and she is really incredible. Problem: If five men can dig a garden in a fortnight, how long would it take two women, one of whom was Mrs Haldane, to accomplish the same piece of work. Answer: two days.

After the Haldanes I went for some days to stay with the Petersens on Boar's Hill, where also was Lewis. Except that it rained and that we spent the best part of two days in meeting trains supposed to be bringing Miss Marie Beerbohm from London and never did, it was most peaceful and pleasant there. Marie ultimately arrived . . . at 5.30 on Sunday afternoon, proposing to return to town at eight, from which you may judge the character of this lively young woman. I may add that I have seen her décolletage descending to within .047 mm of her navel . . . but that was an ordinary walking dress that she was wearing at lunch. Her *evening* dresses. . . .

I made friends with Will Arnold-Forster before I left London; he is a very charming creature, though indubitably a leprechaun. But my great new friend has been the inimitable Evan Morgan, poet, painter, musician, aristocrat and millionaire . . . the unique fairy prince of modern life. His fabulous wealth is a wishing-cap that gives him whatever he wants, his restless temperament carries within it the secret of perpetual motion, his charm is the Rose and Ring which wins all hearts. Add to this that he is a child for vanity and you have him complete.

I went to see Alington about Eton. What a Coxcomb, was the impression of one luncheon; but I dare say there is gold beneath the brass. I am to share a house there with the Reverendissimo [C. O.] Bevan, which will be calm, if not precisely bracing. Heaven knows what I shall teach these boys; it is all very alarming.

I am writing a certain amount. Did father tell you of how I submitted my poetical works [to] John Murray's, where I was urged to wait, polish and so forth. How trying one's elders are, to be sure. What I think I shall do is to prepare a largish book including my prose poems and try and induce someone to take it. Its mere size might be imposing; but in these times of no paper or labour it is a thankless job. I have given one or two of the little prosicles to be printed by Eliot in the horrid little paper which he has recently joined as a sub-editor, *The Egoist*, which is filled by Aldington and his fellow whatyoumay-callem-ists . . . I cannot think of their tribal name at the moment. I hope Eliot will contrive to improve it. I am also contributing to the well-known Society Anthology, *Wheels*, in company with illustrious young persons like Miss Nancy Cunard, Miss Iris Tree and the kindred spirits who figure in the gossip page of the *Daily Mirror*. This year, containing as it does, selections from me and Mr Sherard Vines, it should be quite a bright production. The folk who run it are a family called Sitwell, alias Shufflebottom, one sister and two brothers, Edith, Osbert and Sacheverell—isnt that superb—each of them larger and whiter than the other. I like Edith, but Ozzy and Sachy are still rather too large to swallow. Their great object is to REBEL, which sounds quite charming; only one finds that the steps they are prepared to take, the lengths they will go are so small as to be hardly perceptible to the naked eye. But they are so earnest and humble . . . these dear solid people who have suddenly discovered intellect and begin to get drunk on it . . . it is a charming type.

This rain proves pretty conclusively what I had long suspected . . . that God is a pro-German. As Dean Inge said early in this war, 'God is sitting on the fence and it is perfectly uncertain on which side He will come down'. It appears now to be clear.

News from Italy is good. I wonder if this bloody war will be over in time for me to get out there at Christmas or Easter.

> *Yours,*
> *A. L. H.*

121: TO MRS NAOMI MITCHISON

> *The Old Christopher,*
> *Eton College, Windsor*
> *26 September,* [1917]

My dear Naomi,

Your letter reached me here, where I have been since the eighteenth, an absurdly early beginning of term. Otherwise I should have loved to come. Week ends from here are rather difficult, if not impossible, owing to early school on Monday, though one might perhaps get away for Saturday night. I share this strange old house with the Rev C. O. Bevan . . . a placid though not very bracing companion, with whom I get on quite well and with no

120 *Huxley's one contribution to* The Egoist, *the prose piece 'Miss Zoe', was appearing in the August number.*

121 *Mrs Warre-Cornish, the wife of Francis Warre-Cornish, was the original of Mrs Cravister in Huxley's 'Farcical History of Richard Greenow'.*

friction: we discuss the staff, fruitful topic of which one only realizes the rich oddity when one becomes, as a master, initiated into its inner life; other good subjects of conversation are the boys, food and the advisability of allowing scientific housemasters to prepare their pupils for confirmation. I cannot think that I am a born schoolmaster; I dont think I teach the boys anything, but we get on moderately well, which is all that is important for a quiet life.

You had better come some day and pay me a visit, preferably when Julian is staying here, which I hope he will be doing in a fortnight or so, when he gets some leave after the completion of his intelligence course.

I have been writing a certain amount; one or two poems, good ones too, and a certain amount of prose of one kind or another; but there is, of course, not very much time here. Ah, the sad fate of the Clewer sisters. . . !

> There once were some sisters of Clewer,
> Who daily grew fewer and fewer:
>   Some went on the stage,
>   Some died of old age,
> And the last one eloped with a brewer.

How melancholy. But I went to see Mrs [Blanche Warre-] Cornish yesterday and we spent a strange afternoon in discussing French literature and Hugh Sidgwick and music with that peculiar incoherence that only belongs to conversations with that extraordinary woman; and as we talked we kept rambling into other people's houses and sitting down in their drawing rooms and then, as soon as they appeared, going away again.

I am sending you a cheque for a pound for the [Italian] lessons with Yvette [Chapelain], of which I had two besides those I had with you. I am very sorry she should be in such a hole; what a bore the necessities of life are.

Love to your mother.

Aldous

Pardon the error in the name on cheque!!

122: TO LEWIS GIELGUD

> *The Old Christopher,*
> *Eton College, Windsor*
> *30 September,* [1917]

My dear Lewis,

I dont know whether to advise you to become a pedagogue: it has its pleasant side, to be sure, but also its tediousnesses . . . for instance I have spent the morning in correcting twenty eight essays on the possibility and desirability of a League of Nations, and with such few exceptions they are all so stupid. But they are most of them very nice fellows and treat me, all being considered, wonderfully well, though I wish I could see them more penetratingly: I expect the secret of their quietness lies in the fact that they are deeply engaged in something very far removed from the sordid present, poles apart from any clap trap I may be talking about English literature or Molière's plays. Most of my creatures are immensely grown up; one division consists almost wholly of members of Pop, for whom it is very difficult not to feel awe and reverence. It is a wonderful tribute to the efficacy of their youthful taming that these superb lions refrain from rending me as they so very well might—the most they do is occasionally to shirk my school, taking advantage of the fact that I dont yet know them by sight and getting their names answered by somebody else ... but they were regrettably caught at the time just entering Tap, with, I presume, the worst consequences.

And then there is the Reverend Bevan ... a very good soul ('soul' by definition does not include mind) and we live very snugly and with no friction, talking over our meals, which are frequent and large—for Bevan is something of an epicure—about the Staff, about food, about Confirmation, about the boys, occasionally about the political outlook, but that very very rarely. Then we retire, each to his separate room and all is well, except that sometimes I feel most intolerably lonely; these ushers are so nice, but so remote, so alien. On the whole I am fairly happy, but I have decided that God never intended me to do any regular work. Just at the moment when I feel that I might write some masterpiece comes in another batch of essays, or else I have to go and stand up in face of these sinister young men and try and keep them amused. What a life ... I don't think I can stand it for very long. It would be pleasanter if there were someone jolly on the staff with whom to walk and talk: I say walk and talk, for as things are, all the beaks rush off and play foot-ball or run to Maidenhead or dig potatoes when they are not working, and the only people who take life quietly are the antiques, like Broader [Henry Broadbent] with whom I went for a constitutional along the Datchett golf course the other day, fretting and fuming at having to walk at two miles an hour and at having to wait several minutes at each artificial bunker, all of which Bent had the greatest difficulty in negotiating.

What news of this jolly old war? Are the French socialists going to make much fuss at Bordeaux? I think and hope we are all Jusquauboutistes here.

I am writing some biblical sonnets ... one on Jonah.

> A cream of phosphorescent light
> Floats on the wash that, to and fro,
> Slides round his feet—enough to show
> Many a pendulous stalactite
> Of naked mucus: whorls and wreaths
> And huge festoons of mottled tripes,
> And smaller palpitating pipes
> Wherein some yeasty liquor seethes.

122 *The poems appeared in* Jonah.

Seated upon the convex mound
Of one vast kidney, Jonah prays
And sings his canticles and hymns,
Making the hollow vault resound
God's goodness and mysterious ways,
Till the great fish spouts music as he swims.

Behemoth
His eyes are little rutilant stones
Sunk in black basalt: scale by scale
Men count the wealth of silver mail
That laps his flesh and iron bones:
And from his hollow navel, wide
As an old Cyclops' drinking-bowl,
Spring those stout nerves of twisted hide
Which are his strength and life and soul.

Basking his belly, fast asleep
He sprawls on the warm shingle bank,
And the bold Ethiops come, and creep
Along his polished heaving flank
And in his navel brew their wine
And drink vast strength and grow divine.

Some day I shall publish a large volume of religious poetry. One could do an admirable series of sonnets on the articles of the Christian faith, on the nature of angels and on the sexual hygiene of the Mosaic Law ... all beautifully polished and rich and elaborate. I see great possibilities; the book might be used while preparing boys for confirmation, all the teaching of religion in bright concise form.

I also started a poem on the Oxford Volunteers, inspired by the lamentable spectacle of them marching along as I rode through the town some few weeks ago.

The Volunteers in vomit-colour
Go forth to shoot the Lamb of God.
Their leaden faces redden to a blazing comet-colour,
    And they sweat as they plod.

Parson and poet-laureate,
Professor, grocer, don,
This one as fat as Ehud that, poor dear! would grow the more he ate
    Yet more a skeleton.

Some have piles and some have goitres,
Most of them have Bright's disease,
Uric acid has made them flaccid and one gouty hero loiters,
    Anchylosed in toes and knees.

135

I am sorry I wrote you that somewhat unhinged letter of a few weeks ago; it was the result of a passing pang of misery, due to nothing in particular, but exactly coinciding with a period of poetical constipation covering some weeks. It means, I suppose, some minor suppressed complex that has to be purged away somehow or another. As a matter of fact I think I was full of injustice then towards Maria; so pay very little attention to anything I may have said.

I was very sorry to hear of Hubert O'Connor's death. I enjoyed the few meetings I had with him. It is all too hopelessly grim. Hugh Sidgwick has just been killed. Geoffrey Young has lost a leg.

Au revoir, my dear Lewis. The Bursar bade me send you his love.

A. L. H.

123: TO LEONARD HUXLEY

The Old Christopher,
Eton College, Windsor
12 *November,* 1917

Dearest Father,

It pains me to think that I have a double—for a double it must have been if it was on Wednesday that Margaret saw her vision. I was up on Tuesday having lunch with Mlle [Juliette] Baillot—a whole holiday in honour of somebody . . . and again on Thursday to see Gervas, who urged me to come and stay the night, which I did—getting back early next morning. Altogether a quite exceptionally diversified week, ending up with a most interesting tea party on Saturday, when my bright young pupil, De La Warr, invited the Labour man, George Landsbury [Lansbury] to meet me. It is a pleasant thought . . . the editor of our most revolutionary paper, invited by a peer to the home of all that is least revolutionary, where Floreat Etona tacitly implies Floreat the economical status quo. I found Lansbury extremely interesting, very tolerant, not bitter like so many of these labour men, but extremely anxious to avoid any violent upheaval, full of constructive rather than destructive enthusiasm. I had a long talk with him alone in my room after tea and shall try and get to know him better if I can. He is a great friend, I find, of Lady Ottoline's brother, Lord Henry Bentinck; their views on most things appear to be almost identical, despite the fact that Lord H. is nominally a tory—heaven only knows why he continues to call himself one; I suppose it would pain the poor Duke [of Portland] too much if he sat in Parliament as a member of the I.L.P.

I have long discussions with De La Warr and other boys on the subject of Theosophy, which appears to have excited a number of the more serious minded and thoughtful of the boys. One has to go to work with care; it is no good being too violent. I point out Mrs [Annie] Besant's errors in science and history, which thickly encrust her books, and try to wean them from the merely superstitious side of it. Except for the bunkum about astral bodies, spiritual hierarchies, reincarnation and so forth, theosophy seems to be a good enough religion—its main principles being that all religions contain some truth and that we ought to be tolerant, which is the sort of thing to be encouraged in an Anglican stronghold like this. A little judicious theosophy seems on the whole an excellent thing.

About my poems [*The Defeat of Youth and Other Poems*]. Blackwell said that he would like to publish them, so I sent them, after revision and additions, to him; he tells me that he will begin printing them in January . . . a quite pleasant format and much more solid than the last little book. The sonnets are twenty two in number. I have written a certain number of things recently with which I am very well pleased. I find that more and more I am unsatisfied with what is merely personal in poetry. What one wants, it seems to me, is this: first to receive one's impressions of outward things, then to form one's thoughts and judgments about them, and last to re-objectify those thoughts and judgments in a new world of fancy and imagination. The intermediate subjective stage must be cut away altogether. One presents the fait accompli of fancy, as realized in the metaphor and simile; but one omits the 'as' or 'like', making the simile world exist as a real objective world in itself. That of course represents the idea carried to its extremes. I am sending you one of my last works, which may amuse you.

Give my love to Rosalind and Margaret.

Your loving son,
Aldous

124: TO MRS NAOMI MITCHISON

Eton College, Windsor
22 November, 1917

My dear Naomi,

About staying on the 30th—I fear that week end is made impossible for me by the fact that I have been summoned by the brutal and licentious soldiery to present myself for re-examination at the White City on the 1st. I am in terror lest they should pass me for sanitary duties at Aden or something equally pleasant. You, I take it, will be in town for some days. One might arrange a little lunch with Margaret or anyone else, if I can get away.

The school . . . or rather one section of it . . . is buzzing with excitement over the proposed foundation of an Eton Political Society. The moving spirit is my young friend the Earl, De La Warr, who is a passionate socialist. The society is to be radical, on the whole, in the tone, but eminently respectable and altogether cum privilegio. These boys propose to invite all the celebrities of Europe to come and speak to them, also to write in their paper [*The Eton Review*], which it is proposed to float next half. I have been discussing the paper all this evening with De La Warr and a boy who is apparently a cousin of yours, called [G. P. D.] Vessey, a strange, clever creature. I have been commissioned to find out if Asquith would come and speak on the league of nations; they long, too, to get your uncle. The whole idea amuses me very much and should be encouraged, I am sure. You had better be our Oxford Correspondent and expert on all matters concerning women's rights.

What it is to be young and full of hope and ambition, I say to myself as I look at these boys. Once I too . . . and I shake the head and drop the silent tear.

I shall be glad when this half is over; this teaching takes a tremendous lot out of one and I have not been sleeping well of late, so that I am very tired, though less so than I was a week ago.

Oxford Poetry . . . dear me. Poor Lewis, why does he ever try to be sublime . . .? The outstanding thing seems to me to be Dodd's [E. R. Dodds'] 'Measure'; the real thing. And then 'Ducklington' . . . what a work of genius! and who is Flora Fo[r]ster? I am so much épris with her poem that I shall write to her . . . passionately begging her to be my Duckling. Helen Simpson is very bright. Nichols is clap trap, Childe is Childe, Earp the parody of Earp. Eugene Parker Chase moves me quite unmentionably. But I cherish the thought of [Dorothy L.] Sayers peeping through young Mr Blackwell's door and shouting 'Ha, Reynault, ha, true Love!' Quant à moi, I am like the aged Swift looking back on the work of his youth: 'What genius I had then!' is all that I can exclaim, while I shake the head and drop the silent tear etc.

Au revoir. Give my love to your mother.

Aldous

125: TO LEONARD HUXLEY

Eton College, Windsor
9 December, [1917]

Dearest Father,

Thanks for the typewritten epistle. What a wonderful account from Mrs. Cornish: I do in fact go, if possible, next Wednesday to Mrs. [Sybil] Colefax's (whoever she may be) to read some works—not, however, in French. It will be vulgar but perhaps entertaining.

I am thankful that the end of the half approaches, as I am most fiendishly tired and not sleeping well and altogether feeling as if I had no life whatever—which is more or less how I have felt all these last two months. This climate

124 Oxford Poetry 1917 *contains Huxley's translation of* 'L'Après-midi d'un Faune'. ' "Ha, Reynault",' *etc., is the refrain of Dorothy L. Sayers' 'Fair Erembours: A Song of the Web, French, XII C'.*

125 *Sybil Colefax, the wife of Arthur (later Sir Arthur) Colefax, was a famous hostess whose salon flourished from the Edwardian period until after World War II. She and Huxley remained friends up to her death in 1950.*

gives you no chance: once you are down the Eton atmosphere weighs on you like a wet feather-bed and prevents you rising to your feet again.

Our new Political Society started with great éclat last night, when we were addressed by William Temple, the Bishop of Oxford and George Lansbury—who outlined the topics which the Society ought to discuss—altogether a great success. I made the acquaintance of the rest of the De La Warr family, who seemed very pleasant.

I had a very alluring suggestion made to me the other day by Lady Tredegar, the mother of my friend Evan Morgan, to the effect that I should accompany Evan abroad—probably to Sicily,—where he has to go for his lungs. Lady T. would stand the trip for both of us, and it wd. be for six months. However, in these days of suspicion, it seems very unlikely one would be able to get a passport; otherwise it's an opportunity too good to be missed. Lady T. is an extremely nice and interesting creature: I like her better the more I see of her.

I am sending you one or two of the other poems I have done fairly recently: I think perhaps the 'Song of Poplars' is the best—or at any rate it pleased me most at the time of writing it, which was after a long period of poetical constipation, which had made me almost as uncomfortable mentally as the grosser ailment would have done physically.

I sent M[argaret] the new *Oxford Book of Mystical Verse*, which she said she'd like for a birthday present. It contains a lot of tosh, such as this by Professor [J. S.] Blackie—

> 'Brahma's eyes look forth divining
>   From the welkin's brow:
> Full bright eyes—the same are shining
>   In the sacred cow.'

Love to the family.

> *Your loving son*
> *Aldous*

126: TO JULIETTE BAILLOT

> *The Old Christopher,*
> *Eton College, Windsor*
> 11 *December,* [1917]

My dear Juliette,

Thank you so very much for the delightful handkerchief ... almost too beautiful for the vulgar purposes of nose-blowing; one pauses before the desecration.

I trust that the children will have proved a success. They will at least temper the loneliness with a little noise; and the Ranee [of Sarawak] should be entertaining when she re-appears.

For my part, I find the grim solitudes of Eton quite insupportable, unless I take a periodical jaunt to London, where a little sympathetic company infuses life enough to carry one on for the next few days. I have been seeing a good deal of the dashing Evan Morgan recently as well as his mother, Lady Tredegar, who is a very delightful person. Carrington, too, I saw the other day; the first time for many months; in tremendous form and as enchanting as I habitually find her after an interval of not meeting her. Last Sunday I looked in on Katherine [Mansfield] in her curious little kennel in Chelsea; all very mysterious, particularly when she suddenly gave a shout in the middle of our conversation and was answered by the sleepy voice of somebody who was in bed behind a curtain and whose presence I had never realized. From there I whisked to lunch with Lady Tredegar and after that to Eliot, whom I found as haggard and ill-looking as usual; we held a council of war about a poetry reading, in which both of us are supposed to be performing to-morrow; I look forward to it with mixed feelings.

There is, happily, only a week more of this term to run, and then I hope to go to Garsington, where I look forward to having a mental and physical tonic and bracing. What amusements we had last year, in spite of the somewhat wet blanket of Bloomsbury!

I have just been reading *Elle et Lui*, which strikes me as one of the finest books; I really must read some more of George Sand—she is personally such a superb character. Beyond that, I don't think I have read anything that is of the least interest—except a rather pleasant pre-Corneille play by Pichou, called *Les Folies de Cardenio*; romantic, like an English play in the late Elizabethan manner and with very pleasant pretty pieces of poetry in it. But you probably know it quite well, together with all the other works of Pichou, besides a thousand other plays of the same style and period! I take my warning from the snub that old Clive [Bell] got, when he boasted about the author he had discovered (I cant remember his name) whose works had been known to you from the age of two. That was a terrible blow for poor Clive; so I will be careful and moderate my transports about Pichou.

Well, au revoir in the, I hope, not too distant future. Loneliness has all my sympathies; I hope it will be better soon.

Yours,
Aldous

P.S. I havent seen my sister for some time, but I see no reason to suppose that her views on you were as unsympathetic as you seem to think.

126 *Juliette Baillot was at Wimbledon, where she had gone to take charge of the household and to be governess to the children of the Ranee of Sarawak (daughter of Viscount Esher and sister of the Hon. Dorothy Brett), during the Ranee's absence abroad. Katherine Mansfield: at this time she was sharing her flat, at 141a Church Street, Chelsea, with Ida Baker, who had a bed in a little gallery curtained for privacy.*

Eton College, Windsor
13 December, [1917]

My dear Julian,

Many thanks for your very amusing letter. I may, perhaps, see you at the 1917 Club dinner, to which I hope to go—the first night of holidays, after which I proceed to Garsington for Xmas, where I shall find all that is left of poor Middleton Murry after a most hideous breakdown.

I spent a strange day yesterday in town—being a performing poet for the sake of charity or something before a large expensive audience of the BEST PEOPLE. Gosse in the chair—the bloodiest little old man I have ever seen— dear Robbie Ross stage-managing, Bob Nichols thrusting himself to the fore as the leader of us young bards (*bards* was the sort of thing Gosse called us) —then myself, Viola Tree, a girl called McLeod and troops of Shuffle- bottoms, alias Sitwells bringing up the rear: last and best, Eliot. But oh— what a performance: Eliot and I were the only people who had any dignity: Bob Nichols raved and screamed and hooted and moaned his filthy war poems like a Lyceum Villain who hasn't learnt how to act: Viola Tree declaimed in a voice so syrupy and fruity and rich, that one felt quite cloyed and sick by two lines: the Shufflebottoms were respectable but terribly nervous: the Macleod became quite intoxicated by her own verses: Gosse was like a reciter at a penny reading. The best part of the whole affair was dinner at the Sitwells' afterwards, when I got into a corner with [Montague] Shear- man and Mary Hutchinson and Mme [Lalla] Vandervelde, and we all got tight to just the right extent—horrible when I had to totter out into the cold cold night and get back to this hole.

[. . . .]

Yrs.
ALH

Eton College, Windsor
5 February, 1918

My dear Frances,

It was thoughtful of you to interview the Duckling [Flora Forster]. I am so glad she is not of the ugly variety: you must introduce me to her some time when I am at Oxford and I will lay my homage in person at her feet.

127 *Julian Huxley was now billeted at Colchester. Robbie Ross: best known as Oscar Wilde's executor. McLeod or Macleod: probably Irene Rutherford McLeod. Lalla Vandervelde and Mary Hutchinson, (Mrs St John Hutchinson) were long-time friends of Huxley; Mme Vandervelde was the wife of Emile Vandervelde, the Belgian socialist.*

I like to think of you defending my character against the detractors who think me a sinister and crooked sort of devil. It wd. interest me to hear what was said by either side in the controversy. Both were probably perfectly right!—but I'm glad you liked the poems, the fruits of what is, on the whole, my more pleasing self.

Life trickles along here in its usual style—time always occupied, nothing of real importance ever achieved. Saturday saw me in London cheering myself a little with wine and sympathetic conversation—necessary relaxations.

I write occasionally—here a word and there a word: but it amounts to nothing. Nothing amounts to anything—I am forced to this painful conclusion by the logic of circumstance.

I trust Lewis may have some leave soon: it will be pleasant to see him again after so long. And as for that chit Aileen—we never sent our ultimatum. What about the following as a rough draft:—

Declaration of war aims by the Allies
(1) Recognition by old friends
(2) Reparation for past offences in the shape of numerous letters of apology
(3) Permanence of international relations

Unless these righteous and democratic terms are agreed to within 72 hours from the time of receiving this ultimatum our governments will be compelled to break off relations and a state of aggrieved hostility will be declared to exist.

(Signed)————————.
————————.

Will you draw up the ultimatum and dispatch it to the suitable quarter, duly signed with your name and mine—and there wd. be no harm in adding Lewis' as well.

I hope Naomi is as well as may be expected. Really, the patience and courage required to have a baby are quite incredible. I am thankful that I am not called upon to display them.

Flourish and dont work too hard.

Bien à toi, mon vieux.
Aldous

129: TO JULIETTE BAILLOT

Eton College, Windsor
5 February, 1918

My dear Juliette,
I seemed to have no time the last day or two I was in London: but I must really make an attempt some Saint's day or Sunday to come and pay you a visit in the Palazzo Tilney.

I am glad that teaching makes you a child—I was about to say more of a child; I am always afraid of being made old by the continual assumption of superiority, the unceasing pretence of knowing better, of being respectable and a good example, which has to be kept up. I do my best to make my boys have no respect for me whatever. Most of my work this term consists in going over essays with a number of the elder boys. I have some fifty a week of them coming in for half an hour each to have their essays corrected and commented on. It is quite interesting at times and preferable to doing much work with large forms in school.

Our political society flourishes very vigorously: we had a meeting on Sunday at which Lord Henry Bentinck came down and spoke—very well: and the political paper is being worked into shape for not long distant publication.

I long to have the leisure to write: but as it does I cant even get a batch of reviews finished which ought to be sent in at once. All I can do is an occasional line or two of poetry—but no prose, for which one has to settle down for hours at a stretch, a thing I cant of course ever do here. I am doing a most luscious poem about Leda—the lady whom Jupiter visited in the form of a Swan and who thereupon laid two eggs, one containing Helen and Clytemnestra, the other Castor and Pollux. It is the most charming story which is susceptible of perfectly serious and perfectly ironic treatment at one and the same time. When I have finished it, Brett has undertaken to do me some illustrations, which will be pleasant.

Au revoir, dear Juliette. If I can manage a jaunt to Wimbledon I will let you know. Will you be there all the winter, or do you remove the children to more rural scenes?

Love from Aldous

130: TO FRANCES PETERSEN

Eton College, Windsor
[February, 1918]

My dear Frances,

I wish I'd seen you—but the Fates willed otherwise, which is one of their habits. You have all my sympathies about Schools: but I beg you not to let them prey on your mind. What is the good, after all, of an unconquerable soul if one is going to have it devastated by the hoofs of a few grimy Dons? There must be no compromise with these gentry, no admission—particularly on business: you mustn't permit yourself to be hustled.

I spent a moderately happy holidays alternately imbibing alcohol and reading the works of Lord Bacon. In these dismal days there seems to be almost nothing else to do. When the works of Lord Bacon are finished there will be nothing but the alcohol—unless we go dry before then. The world is really too atrocious: escape the only way of life. But one wakes up periodically to the realisation that one is a clown and without genius—a painful and restless moment—and then one makes haste to retire once more into the fastnesses of Baron Verulam's jejune philosophy or the less arid Edens of the fourth glass of Madeira—my favourite wine, owing to its traditional connexion with seed-cake and funerals. But what is all this to you? Nothing, my good Frances.

Apropos: I saw *Harwood* the other day—sombre apparition—who asked after Earp and said he hoped he hadn't married Miss Petersen!

I saw Naomi the other day, which was very pleasant. I had not seen her since the arrival of the baby: she looks so much more beautiful than she ever did. Quant à Geoff[rey]—well—he is admirable as babies go I suppose. But as I remarked to Naomi about him: 'How awful to think that you and I were like that once'.

Remember me to your mother and grandfather and the rest of the family.

Au revoir—(when? I wonder. Soon—I hope).

Aldous

131: TO JULIETTE BAILLLOT

Eton College, Windsor
25 February, 1918

My dear Juliette,
The trouble about my jaunts to London is they are so short that they leave no time to get to Wimbledon—for I can rarely get up before about 4.0 in the afternoon. However I think I shall be coming up next Saturday afternoon, March 2nd, and I wondered whether you cd. possibly come into town and meet me at the Private View of [C. R. W.] Nevinson's pictures at the Leicester Galleries in Leicester Sq., for which I have an invitation. It would be very nice if you could come: say 4.15 at the door of the Leicester Galleries, which are on the South side of the Square where it leads down towards St. Martin's Lane and Trafalgar Sq. Here is a little map. Do come if you can and let me know soon.

Yours
Aldous

130 *Naomi Mitchison's first child, Geoffrey, who died in 1927, appears as little Phil in Huxley's* Point Counter Point.

131 *The work of Nevinson as official war artist had been exhibited first in 1916; the present showing included all of his later and best work. Owing to illness, Huxley was unable to go to London on 2 March, but he and Juliette Baillot attended the Nevinson exhibition the Saturday following.*

Eton College, Windsor
3 March, 1918

My dear Julian,

Your letter of the 22nd reached me this morning. One of the reasons why I hadnt written was that I did not know your address—the exact wording etc. When I asked father he replied with about three pages of that curious literary coyness and circumlocution, talking about the things that you mightnt say and which George Trevelyan heroically did say, hoping that the censors wouldnt object if he reminded me that the town you were living in might have been the academical Alma Mater of Gervasius of Tilbury, but that it was certainly the cruel stepmother of Paschasius Radbert and Notker Balbulus, etc—without ever committing himself to those few gross naked words which I required. And even when I asked him again—twice over—he never answered my question; so that I became annoyed and was determined to take no action till I heard from the fountain head.

I am glad you flourish to the extent you do. For my part, I cannot be said to flourish at all, having dragged out a miserable existence all last week culminating in two days in bed with fluy chill and temperature—which I had had for three days before I got to bed; and now, when I am well on the road to recovery from the chill and can eat, sleep and to some extent move once more, I have been seized by a violent intercostal rheumatism, which takes the shape of a great ache all up and down my left side with a storm-centre of intense pain just over my heart. All, apparently, that there is to do is to remain quiet and warm, and hope for the best, meanwhile taking some stuff of the doctor's to deaden the pain—the effects of which only last three to four hours, so that one wakes at intervals during the night, feeling like Prometheus at the renewed activity of the vulture. However, I hope a few days indoors—avoiding the devil's own east wind—will put all to rights and I shall be soon a moderately human being again.

Lewis, who was over here last week, told me of his glimpse of you in Paris. He seems very well and happy and incredibly efficient—a state of affairs which tends to apply, I find, to almost everybody except myself. He came down here for a night, and we sat up talking very late, till the thought of what Cobby [the Rev. C. O. Bevan]'s feelings would be, if he knew that two adulterous young men were discussing their crimes above his virgin bed, put us to shame. I saw him again at the week end, when I went to stay with the Sitwells—a moderately entertaining party.

My work here this half has been on the whole quite pleasant: a great deal of going-over of essays—for all the history specialists—some of which are interesting: little in school, only a dozen hours or so a week, for which I am thankful, as I find it really quite impossible. If they dont pay me better this term than last, I shall strike for more wages; for it is obviously ridiculous for me to pass my time here at a loss.

I have been bamboozled into talking once a week about Victorian literature, which embarrasses me, as I have read almost nothing whatever of it. I somehow escaped that normal course in youth, that plowing through the Victorian Great and being reminded all the time that they are great: (What a vast number of people, nine tenths, never think of anyone being Great outside the nineteenth century). Perhaps it is lucky, for when, if ever, I do read them, I shall be able to see what claims they have, looking at them with exactly the same critical eye with which one regards writers of other periods.

The war looks daily gloomier. Lloyd George seems more securely enthroned than ever, backed stoutly by his two new colleagues, Northcliffe and Beaverbrook. However, all is compensated by the almost Providential capture of Jericho; the greatest care has been taken not to molest such sacred places as the tomb of Rahab.

Bertie Russell, did you see? has been sentenced to six months for saying the American troops were to be stationed here to put down strikes—a task to which they were so well used at home. Not a thing I'd choose to be sentenced on—it is so curiously foolish. I remember his throwing out the idea in conversation last Christmas. He is appealing, but I dont suppose that will make any difference, unless to increase his sentence.

Our political society and paper proceed well. The paper on the verge of appearance, with a signed article by Lord Haldane on Democracy. The one blow at the eleventh hour was the Vice Provost [Francis Warre-Cornish]'s refusal to allow De La Warr's article on Labour and the War to be printed, as being too revolutionary and pacifist. I have discovered another young aristocrat, Lord David Cecil, son of Ld Salisbury, who is, in point of sheer brains and imagination far beyond De La Warr, though in a literary and not a political direction. He is only sixteen, is the most brilliant conversationalist, has written one or two uncommonly good poems and, considering it is his first attempt at anything of the sort and considering how hopelessly uncritical boys are, the most remarkable article on the latest Georgian Poetry book. He is one of the people who give you the sense of being enormously thoroughbred; a wonderful character in his way.

By the way, before I forget it; if and when you go to Florence, the Nys family have changed their address, being turned out of their former house by the military—for an Air Board, I suppose. The present address is as follows:

Castel Montici,
Via Santa Margherita a Montici,

which is outside and above Florence proper, I gather. They seem to have got a very lovely villa there with a garden overlooking the city. I hope you'll go, if only to tell me what the rest of the family are like, whom I have never seen.

Farewell,
A.L.H.

Eton College, Windsor
10 *March,* 1918

Dearest Father,

I am completely recovered now, tho' I had a more unpleasant time than I anticipated [. . . .]

I heard from Julian at last; a cheerful letter. He seems to be quite enjoying himself and to be feeling fitter than he did while he was here. The air raid sounds most unpleasant: happily we get only the distant reverberations of them here. The one time they let off the guns here—whole salvoes of artillery one Sunday night—was on an occasion when, so the police afterwards informed the school authorities, no aeroplane was within forty miles of the place.

I hear that Bowyer Nichols is very ill and likely, I believe, to die—which is sad news. It may be an exaggeration as my informant was vague: and I dont know what it is that's specifically wrong.

I heard from Naomi Mitchison the other day—very happy with her baby, which, I suppose you saw, arrived a week or two ago—all parties doing very well.

[C. H.] Blakiston from this place is succeeding [E.] Gordon [Selwyn] at Radley, a very good man, very clever and also very efficient. He should do very well by the school—better than the worthy but humourless Gordo. Blakiston will be a great loss here, as he could do everything and his talents were freely employed in every direction.

I am looking forward to the end of the half on April 3rd, as my touch of flu has left me not very enthusiastic for the wearing business of teaching.

Love to the household.

Your loving son
Aldous

134: TO LEONARD HUXLEY

Eton College, Windsor
Wed., 27 *March,* [1918]

Dearest Father,

Out of the depths of examination papers . . . but thank heaven, only a week more with a respite in the shape of Good Friday.

As for plans:—return on Wednesday (or possibly Tuesday evening, but I dont think so): then to [Great] Enton for the week end 6th-9th: then to Oxford from about the 13th, which is the end of the week, for about a

133 *The Huxleys were close friends of the Nichols family—John Bowyer Nichols (who died in* 1939*), and his children Robert (the poet), Philip, and Irene.*
134 *Great Enton was Dr Henry Huxley's house at Witley, Surrey.*

fortnight, I shd. think, which ought to coincide with your Leicester visit more or less. Term begins again about May 2nd.

I got a letter from my old Baroness yesterday about some MS or other which she wants to get published. I enclose the note to see what you think of it. Meanwhile I will write as discouragingly as possible about the paper shortage etc! There might, of course, be something in it.

I have been dining this evening at Marten's to meet Sir Sidney Low and his wife. What a strange looking man—like Jekyll in his more Hydian moments; and what a power of talking! I have come away almost deaf. He sent his regards to you.

I was irritated to see myself described last Sunday by the literary gossip of the *Weekly Dispatch* as 'Mr. Aldous Hunley, whose new book is announced etc.' I am not sure one couldn't get damages these days for being called Hunley: it is libel to call a man a German. To bed: it grows late. Love to the family. One great relief: I am not invigilating in trials.

Your loving son
Aldous

135: TO LEWIS GIELGUD

Garsington Manor, Oxford
18 *April*, 1918

My dear Lewis,

It pains me to think that you are as gloomy as your letter would lead me to think you are. Not that one can offer much comfort these days; there is no superfluity of it now to pass round.

However, as far as circumstances will permit, I am enjoying my brief liberty a good deal. First a week or so in London, the first three days of which I seem to have spent with Hugh Terriss [Terres], Marie [Beerbohm] and Lady Constance Stuart [Stewart]-Richardson either in the Eiffel or on divans in Constance's flat, where we used to lie day and night eating bread and honey and indulging in desultory conversation—the whole so unreal that it is difficult to remember whether it was all a nightmare or not. Then a week end with Aunt Sapphira [Sophy], then two or three more days of London, brightened by interludes of an almost nuptial character with Marie, then down here, where it almost immediately started to snow and rain and blow. If it wasn't that one thought about the bloody war and the horrors of the situation, one would be able to do more writing; as it is, I blot a little paper every now and then and contrive to read a few heavy books for the good of my soul. I wrote my masterpiece yesterday, when bicycling into Oxford in the icy rain I composed a lyric on Middle Age of exquisite beauty.

135 *Eiffel: the Eiffel Tower restaurant, in Percy Street, later the White Tower.*
Lyric: this appeared in Oxford Poetry 1918.

Men of a certain age
Grow sad remembering
Their youth's libertinage,
Drinking and chambering.

She whom devotedly
Once they solicited
Proves all too bloatedly
Gross when revisited

Twenty years after—
Sordid years.
Ironic laughter,
And bitter tears.

When we are bald and fat, my dear Lewis, how revolting we shall be.

There is utterly no news:—a letter from Evan the other day describing the picturesque beauties of nature in Algeria, the rumoured reappearance of Harwood upon the stage of common life . . . nothing.

So much for the life of action, and as for the life of thought, it has come to a standstill. Some day I hope to be able to write more rationally.

Have you any news of the *Times* man? More important, what news of peace? O God.

Yours,
A.L.H.

136: TO JULIAN HUXLEY

Cherwell
30 [*April*], 1918

My dear Julian,

Many thanks for your note about the two men you are suggesting should come and see me. So far no sign, but I shall be prepared when they turn up.

My holidays draw painfully nearly to their close; I return, in fact, to morrow—three months more of Cobby. I had hoped to do a good deal of writing during my time of freedom—and have done some, but not quite so much as I had rosily anticipated, for I find the pleasures of social life so intoxicating and distracting after a few months of peopled solitude at Eton that it has been hard to find time to do much but whizz around, at least while in London, where one goes about mixing one's people like discordantly flavoured drinks—Eliot for luncheon, Aunt Mary for tea, Sitwells and the Icelander for dinner and afterwards the ever-increasingly sinister Mr Mills, the Viper of Chelsea. Or else one sticks to one rich vintage all day long— Marie Beerbohm, fine flavoured, but not full-bodied (for she is remarkably

136 *Misdated* '30.1.18'. *The Icelander: unidentified.*

willowy) at lunch, tea, dinner and half the night long. A very remarkable character, Marie; tremendous vitality to carry her through the arduous frivolousness of a perpetually whirling life; the marvellous niceness common to all Beerbohms, which keeps her charming and unspoiled through episodes in themselves somewhat sordid; a good mind, rather like Max's in its fantastic cleverness, which you dont discover till you know her well, and then you are startled to discover the very self-conscious analysis and penetration in a person who appears to one at first sight as a butterfly living wholly in the external life of the moment. And then one is somehow always finding oneself in the profoundly exhausting company of Lady Constance Stuart [Stewart]-Richardson, the worst dancer in the world but one of the most remarkable athletes, whose strength is as the strength of ten—not, I think, for the same reason as Galahad's, for she is something of a man-eater and has a strangely hungry look in her eyes and is moreover very much of a certain age, a rather pathetic figure, for her real friends and contemporaries, with whom she shot elephants in Africa, buffalo in the Rockies, bears in Tibet, with whom she head-hunted in Borneo and galloped after ostriches in Patagonia, Olympians like Lord Lucas, seem to have died or been killed. She is a lonely anachronism, one of those travelling English sportswomen of a by-gone era—lonely, and therefore disinclined to lose hold of anyone she may casually meet, so that one has to take a good deal of pains to avoid her; otherwise one finds oneself sitting up all night listening to her traveller's tales, and eating bread and honey at dawn in a state of complete exhaustion, while Constance gaily starts a new day; for her iron constitution requires no rest. She rarely goes to bed more than three times a week, and then it is in a blanket on a sofa or in a flea-bag on the floor, and she hardly realizes that the normal human being requires eight hours per night to keep his machinery in working order. I sometimes wish that she had not been a swimming champion and swum, as I believe was the case, from the sinking <u>Titanic</u> to the coast of America, a distance of three hundred and forty miles, arriving in time for an early breakfast before taking the train to Cody Town to see her old friend Buffalo Bill, with his two trusted lieutenants, White Beaver and Reckless Davies. However, she is a curiosity and so, I suppose, worth a sleepless night or two.

Retiring to Garsington after the restless whirl of London, I contrived to do a little writing and reading; and there saw what was perhaps the last of Bertie Russell before he goes to prison; his trial takes place to-morrow, the appeal, which wont, I imagine, do any good except perhaps to change his six months from second to first division. He read us chapters from a new book on socialism, syndicalism and anarchy—marvellously lucid and intellectual, a twentieth century Godwin. Old Birrell was there the last week end, charming as usual with his conversation of the old school, wit and wonderfully told anecdotes.

I am spending a night here before my return to Eton. Naomi and the infant flourish exceedingly. Mrs H. performs the duties of gardener, war-worker, grandmother, farmer and marraine to some thousands of soldiers with her usual fabulous energy.

You say you'd like a book of memoirs. I will send you the first volume of Casanova, which is all about Venice and North Italy of the eighteenth century, a wonderful picture enlivened by the piquancy of countless amours. One volume at a time is enough; the full six might cloy. I will see if I can find something else suitable and convenient to send.

Did you hear from Maria? She told me she had written to you, but I didn't hear whether you had replied.

I sometimes wonder whether the war is going to last three or six years more. Good bye. I will write again comparatively soon.

Love from
ALH

137: TO JULIETTE BAILLOT

The Old Christopher,
Eton College, Windsor
20 May, 1918

My dear Juliette,

I am horribly afraid I have been in debt to you for a letter for a very long time. I am one of the world's worst correspondents and always have been, and, I fear, always will be, Amen. In fact it must be at least a month ago since you wrote—and among other things I have left your letter in London and so dont know your address, so that this will have to go to Garsington. Altogether, I am thoroughly ashamed of the whole affair.

Meanwhile I hope you flourish as you should. Scotland ought to be getting lovely; in another month it will be at its best, with blue transparent days which make everything wholly unreal and ethereal and quite fabulously beautiful. Here in the south we are having the perfect moments of summer; hot clear days and the leaves still fresh and small, not yet tired by the weight of summer and its dust. I bicycle out into Windsor forest and sit under the oak trees and peruse the works of the French romantics till my soul begins to burst with emotion or till something par trop ridicule sets me roaring with laughter. To-day I even went so far as to compose a poem under a pink may-tree.

> A tramp in life, I'd like to be
> Respectable through eternity.
> Therefore, good friends, when I die,
> Put on my old Etonian tie;
> Buy me a bowler, neat but cheap
> With one of those white things that peep

137 *Juliette Baillot was at Callander, Perthshire, with the Ranee's children.*

Over the rich man's fancy vest
And see that my trousers are well pressed.
And then I'd like to have—dont spare
Any expense—a splendid pair
Of those cloth-topped boots of patent leather,
Which are both boot and spat together,
Wedded as fast as man and wife.
Thus fitted out for future life,
I shall be able without shame
To walk down Bond Street in New Jerusalem.

You must forgive any errors in the typing. I am writing in the dark, with one bright pencil of moonlight coming in from the south and the castle looking like one of those lovely German picture postcards which you hold up to the light to make the windows shine yellow. Bank holiday crowds, growing sparser now, still giggle along the streets. It is profoundly melancholy; one feels like Chatterton. Furthermore it is painfully obvious tonight that the moon is a globe in a void vast and not a comfortable memorial plaque stuck up on the wall of a great man's house. Do you remember our moon-gazings on the roof, avec ce navrant paysage transi d'une lumière d'outre-tombe? I wonder now we didnt begin to howl like dogs out of melancholy, or kiss one another for comfort's sake.

Talking about BELLS . . . I have discovered the meaning of the phrase on the post-card, 'raising the bells'. It is a term used in conducting an orchestra. When you want a good bang in the finale you raise the bells, take the muting off everything; so that the metaphor means Let us clear the atmosphere, let us make an end . . . or so at least I imagine.

There is no news, or if there was, this seems hardly the occasion to retail it. I may think of some chatty information some other day, when it is not bank holiday night.

Meanwhile I have composed one of the Hundred Best French Lyrics, which runs as follows.

Le revenant de ton mari hante
Ta tante,
Ma riante Marie-Antoinette.

The closer you come to look at it the more superb you will see that it is. It was an age before I arrived at that perfection.

I hear you have cut your hair. Foolish child; but I withhold further criticism till I see the result. You ought to have watch chains made of what you have cut off. Or bracelets, plaited, for your gentleman friends, bracelets such as the poet Donne wore and wrote poems about. You can plait me one.

Good bye, my dear Juliette. I hope you are happy.

Aldous

The Old Christopher,
Eton College, Windsor
24 May, 1918

My dear Julian,

Your letter was most welcome. I envy you your jaunt to Rome. What you say about their religion of nationalism is interesting. It was summed up in that immortal phrase used by one of their bandit politicians on the entry of Italy into the war, when he said that the principle guiding Italy's policy must be that of sacro egoismo. I have been reading our secret treaty with them recently. It really makes one gasp; one wonders which is greatest, the stupidity or the wickedness of our rulers. I think their stupidity; the ideas which inspire them are fundamentally stupid, the way in which they carry them out is criminal. Sacro egoismo is almost as frank a formulation of policy as Machiavelli's in *The Prince*, which I have just been reading. While one admires the consistency and honesty of men who so completely throw off the mask as does Machiavelli, one yet realizes with tremendous force on reading him how valuable a quality is hypocrisy. The existence of hypocrisy at least postulates a belief, dimly cherished, that good is better than evil, and the mere desire to be respectable, to appear to live up to some standard, may prevent men doing things which they certainly would do if everybody were as frank as Machiavelli. A general spread of frankness, a general dropping of the cloak of hypocritical respectability would certainly lead to the most devastating results. Only the very clever people, like Machiavelli, can be allowed to be unhypocritical. If the tendency spread among the vulgar the world would come to an end. I have been reading *The Prince* in order to compare its ideas with those of some of Machiavelli's contemporaries, the men of the English Renaissance, Colet, More, Erasmus, of whom I undertook to talk to historians at the beginnng of this half—rashly, for I knew nothing about them beyond their names. My researches into their history have filled me with the greatest respect for them. Colet was a magnificent creature and the inspiration of his two more obviously brilliant friends, More and Erasmus. The political theories of these two men, expressed in *Utopia* and Erasmus' *Christian Prince*, are extraordinarily good, the very opposite of Machiavelli. Erasmus is a really marvellous character. When I have more time I must study him more closely.

A spell of pure summer, baking hot in the midst of spring foliage and bird-song, has just come to an end in the most fearful thunderstorm I have seen since that amazing one in 1907 which blocked all the roads to the station with fallen trees just as we were all setting out on our summer holidays—do you remember? We are plunged back into an ill-disguised winter.

I saw [——] the other day at Frank Schuster's house on the river at

Bray, where my friend Bob Nichols is spending the summer. What a sinister character she is, very pretty, brilliant and so forth, but one wouldnt trust her one fifteenth of an inch. However, we fell on one another's necks with great show of mutual delight, not having seen one another since we were so high etc. She and Bob make a very good pair in self-advertisement; the conversation turned most of the time on the size of their editions, the lusciousness of their reviews, each trying to outdo the other. The only difference between them is that [———] is a good deal cleverer and less blatant than poor Bob, who cannot remain in any company of people for five minutes without telling them (a) that he is a poet, (b) that he is extremely successful in his profession and (c) that he knows everybody in England who is worth knowing—and I cordially grant that of these statements (b) is perfectly true. What a bore arrivisme is, to be sure; but I suppose it is a pity one hasnt more of it oneself.

Meanwhile I have had the first proofs of my book [*The Defeat of Youth and Other Poems*], which is satisfactory, and am engaged in writing an epic on a day in the life of a young man ['Soles Occidere et Redire Possunt'], which should be quite revoltingly delicious when it's finished.

As to what you say of Maria. I think I realize her faults clearly enough. The fundamental fact about her, I think, is that her aesthetic sensibility is very great; she has—hideous expression—the artistic temperament to an advanced degree. Aestheticism is a dangerous thing; in fact I dont believe that anyone who lives wholly on sensations is safe; it leads almost inevitably in the end to a sort of corruption and deliquescence of the character. What I have tried to persuade Maria to do is to centre her life on thought rather than on sensation, to adopt some fixed intellectual occupation, involving a certain amount of effort and mental concentration, and not merely to live on the aesthetic sensations of the moment. She is educating herself—in a rather desultory way perhaps—but the process gives her a solid foundation for her existence. When she first went out to Italy she was so completely bowled over by the wealth of beauty round her that she could hardly think of anything else; her life was a mere series of sensuous enjoyments. But she has, to judge from her letters, settled down a good deal since then. I think she will grow up all right. 'Grow up', for you mustnt forget how absurdly young she is, only nineteen. When one considers how infinitely half-baked, jejune and unhealthy one was at that age, one's surprise is, not that she shouldnt have achieved more, but that she should be as much developed as she is. I only wish I was with her, for I think I could be of help to her in growing up— not to mention the fact that she would help me out of the curiously unpleasant slough of uncertainty in which one seems to wallow so hopelessly these days. I have spared you more lyrical effusions about her, not because I dont

138 *Frank Schuster: music patron and connoisseur. He was the brother of Adela Schuster, who gave Oscar Wilde £1,000 while he was out on bail.*

feel lyrically, but because it would be so tedious for you. One's aim in leading
the life of reason should be to combine the lyrical with the critical, to be
simultaneously Shelley and the *Edinburgh Review*. I have only given you
my *Edinburgh Review* opinions about Maria; for the others see my Works
passim!

I have been sketching out an article on Alfred de Musset and George
Sand, which I hope I may persuade Squire or somebody else to publish.
Their liaison has fascinated me for months past. It throws such a vivid light
on the spirit of Romanticism. What a glorious age to have lived in, the
twenties and thirties of last century! The eighteenth century played out,
Napoleon exploded, despotism settled in the saddle once more, the inventions
beginning and wealth starting to flow—an extraordinary mixture of hopelessness and anticipation. God coming into fashion, men of genius the
modern prophets; if you were a man of genius—or even if you werent—
you kicked over the traces, did what you liked and justified yourself by
calling your whims and passions by holy names. All George's infidelities were
directly inspired by the Holy Ghost: Alfred's spiritual sadisme, his enjoyment of pain for its own sake was justified by a religious philosophy which
said that pain was the great purifier. Their happiness was intense and their
misery equally piercing. It was a great life.

Au revoir. Let me know how you fare.

Aldous

139: TO JULIAN HUXLEY

Eton College, Windsor
28 June, 1918

My dear Julian,

I have been waiting to write till I heard your address, either from you or
from father. However, as nothing has reached me I am sending this letter to
the British Mission, with very little expectation of its reaching you.

I hope your convalescence is progressing as it should and that the
Riviera is pleasant and restful. I suppose it was your old lurking enemy the
malaria which attacked you.

You ask me to keep you informed about new books and the events of the
world. I am the last person you should apply to, seeing that I almost never
read anything under a century old, and then preferably in a foreign language;
and as for the events of the world—one knows nothing about what is going
on except by conversation and of conversation I am completely deprived
here. The only modern book I have heard of at all is Lytton Strachey's
Eminent Victorians, which I have not read—except parts in MS—but which
one says is very good. In the world of poetry De la Mare has published a
volume, good in the sense that it is purest De la Mare, but it doesnt go beyond what he has done before. Then there are the usual Bob Nichols
volumes, which one hardly keeps count of; and a little book by young Sachie

Sitwell, interesting and with potentialities; but he is not yet grown up. As for the things which go on in the world. The [N. P.] Billing trial has subsided, though the after-swell of the storm in the cess-pool still heaves—such as the letter sent by Robbie Ross to the public prosecutor, calling him a bastard—which I believe he actually is—and various other things for not having dealt faithfully with Alfred Douglas:—poor Robbie, it is still the dismal idée fixe of the Wilde case, which everyone is getting so bored with. Then there have been two cases of pneumonic plague in Sussex, which is encouraging. Nothing else, that I can remember.

I am sorry that you too should have been taken in by the dashing and brilliant [——]. Desmond MacCarthy is her latest bag: the history of that hunt is entertaining. Then there is her social success, culminating in Baroness d'Erlanger and the amiable, rich, intelligent etc Prince Bibesco. (Here, if the typewriter would run to it, I should put a MARBLED PAGE in imitation of Sterne.)

I went over to Marlow the other day and saw Eliot and his wife who have taken a house there. Eliot in excellent form and his wife too; I rather like her; she is such a genuine person, vulgar, but with no attempt to conceal her vulgarity, with no snobbery of the kind that makes people say they like things, such as Bach or Cézanne, when they dont.

Last week end I spent at Garsington and in Oxford, where I hadnt been since Easter.

I have been reading a book which I think you would like—and you could read it in the original—viz, *The Life of Alfieri*, by himself. He is a wonderfully interesting character and his *Life* is thrilling, though not nearly so exciting as he might have made it if he'd been a little less reticent. Among other things he had a twenty years' liaison with the wife of Charles Edward, the countess of Albany. Besides that I have been reading, to my great pleasure, the *Epistolae Obscurorum Virorum*, which, unlike most books considered humorous in the past, remains inimitably funny to this day: and not only funny, but superlatively interesting from the historical point of view. Then I find that occasional doses of La Rochefoucauld are a very good spiritual tonic. Phrases like, Nous avons tous assez de force pour supporter les maux d'autrui, are solid enough to be well meditated, and oh, so applicable in these days of We shall not sweathe the schword etc.

I am told that Wells has published a new book [*Joan and Peter*], about war or peace or the future or something. If that sort of thing is what you want I will send it you: otherwise I should advise you to read something interesting like Alfieri!

I got your coins and pearl pendant safely. Some of the coins are delightful.

139 *Billing trial: Billing, a Member of Parliament, had written of a production of Wilde's* Salome *that it was, among other things, part of a German plot to convert Englishmen to homosexuality. He was prosecuted for libel and acquitted.*

Comparing them with a handful of coppers from my pocket I am reluctantly compelled to admit that they ordered these things better in Greece.

Au revoir and flourish rapidly. I only hope that this letter will reach you, though your loss will not be very great if it dont.

Love from Aldous

140: TO JULIAN HUXLEY

Eton College, Windsor
21 July, 1918

My dear Julian,

I was glad to get your letter, for my information with regard to you has been confined during the last four or five weeks to those curiously veiled and periphrastic allusions which constitute father's method of imparting news. I am glad the riviera was pleasant and healthy and that you are so far recovered.

I had a very delightful day with Lewis Gielgud this week who was back on three days leave from Paris. He has undertaken to try and find me a job there, which would be very entertaining if it could be wangled, though I flatter myself with no hopes on the subject. There is something very delightful about the low politico-personal intrigues by which the war appears to be run in the exalted upper regions of the inter-allied staff. Lewis' account of it all, as seen from within, is most amusing; the only fault in the system is that all these people are so happy and have so much power that they will never allow the war to stop if they can possibly help it.

I have been writing a play, but it is so wholly undramatic and the story of it is so obviously much more suitable for a long-drawn Henry Jamesian short story that I shall abandon it and reshape it. The only character in the piece who is at all realized is a representation of Cobby, who is superb. Plays are obviously the things one must pay attention to. Imprimis, they are the only literary essays out of which a lot of money can be made; and I am determined to make writing pay. Furthermore, infinitely crude as they are, they have distinct possibilities in the way of liveliness. I shall try and write a farce with a perfectly good machine-made plot—no easy task, I imagine; but it will be good practice and might, if acted, make money. After that, one can begin seriously considering some new and better stage convention by which some of the crudities of the theatre can be overcome. There is a very good play by Andreieff in which the various conflicting characteristics in the hero are actually embodied and become acting characters in the piece. There seem to me to be possibilities in that method. Then one must certainly get rid of a great deal of the realism with regard to time and place. Then one must be permitted to have hundreds of scenes like Shakespeare—the

140 *Play: this seems to have evolved into the long story 'Happily Ever After';*
Bevan was depicted as the Rev. Roger Petherton.

cinema has already given a very good example in that respect. Altogether, there are certainly possibilities. Meanwhile I am getting on with my epyll on the life of a young man during one day,—getting on, but very far from satisfied. I wrote the most lovely little song which comes into it at one point —quite Tennysonian, both in respect to its perfection of form and in its recognition, so highly acclaimed by Grand Pater [T. H. Huxley] in the late Poet Laureate, of the truths of Science.

A million million spermatozoa,
    All of them alive:
Out of their cataclysm but one poor Noah
    Dare hope to survive.

And among that billion minus one
    Might have chanced to be
Shakespeare, another Newton, a new Donne;
    But the One was Me.

Shame on you to oust your betters thus,
    Take ark leaving the rest outside!
Better for all of us, froward Homunculus,
    If you'd quietly died.

I heard the Bishop of London [A. F. W. Ingram] preach the other day; for ignorance, sincere vulgarity and complete lack of the faculty of discursive reasoning, he is second only to the great preachers in print of the *Sunday Pictorial*, headed by the Patriarch of Newgate, Bottomley. One of the most striking remarks that he made was to the effect that if we importuned [G]od sufficiently he would stretch forth his arm, clothed in white samite, mystic, wonderful, to help us—the first time I ever heard the almighty's clothes described. The more sermons I listen to, the more peculiar and incomprehensible do I find the root assumption which is at the bottom of them all— viz, that there is such a thing as a personal god who occupies himself with human politics. I suppose if you have the flair of god it is believable; but if you happen to be colour blind in that particular respect it seems curiously fantastic. Alington's sermons are generally pretty good; but, I should think, very shattering to faith; for he has a habit of putting the awkward problems, such as the triumph of evil and suffering, and then, as far as I can see, answering them wholly inadequately or not at all. He would have made me an atheist long ago, if I had been a believer to begin with. We had rather an amusing time last Sunday when the Archbish of Cantua [R. T. Davidson] came and addressed the Political society on the position of the C. of E., getting, at the end of the proceedings, a solid vote for disestablishment from the boys.

Talking about the political society reminds me of the painful fate which has overtaken the movement at Repton, the first school to begin it. Their

158

paper has been suppressed, their politics class disbanded and Gollancz, the man who was running it chiefly, summarily sacked in the middle of the term. A complete triumph for the forces of reaction. Meanwhile Gollancz and his colleague, David Somervell, have written a rather interesting little book on the Repton experiment, called [P]olitical [E]ducation at a [P]ublic [S]chool. I agree with and approve of a great deal of it, except the assumption that politics can be made the basis of education.

I return to the happy home in two days time; in London for a week; then to P. F. for a fortnight or so; thence to Bath, to my French Baroness; thence to Garsington. I should rather like to go and look at a mountain somewhere, but this bloody place pays me so atrociously and my expenses are so large that I have no money whatever. It is all very sordid and irritating; I am on the whole a moderate man, but I like to have at least the power of being extravagant on occasion. When I have paid my board and lodging and my haberdashers' bills I shall have swallowed up the whole of my screw for this half—a pleasing prospect, seeing that I receive no further wages till Christmas. It becomes more than ever necessary to write that successful vaudeville.

The copper bowl sounds delightful; thank you very much in anticipation.

Ever yours
A.L.H.

141: TO JULIAN HUXLEY

Prior's Field
12 *August*, 1918

My dear Julian,
Your letter to hand with the bad and better news of your throat. I gather you are going to Garda for a few days, which should be very pleasant. I imagine it must be a sort of super-killarney, 'heaven's refle-hex, Killerharney!'

Here all is very pleasant—after having been a very fair reflex of Africa in the rainy season for the first week. I am sorry to be leaving the place just as everything has become so jolly. But I go tomorrow to study the Home Life of a Major Poet at first hand—to stay with Bobo Nichols in the ancestral Hall. It should be quite amusing. Thence to the Baronne at Bath, where it will at least be interesting to explore the town, which I dont know. Thence, at the end of the month, to Garsington, probably. Thence, I imagine, home and then, alas, to the unloveliness of The Old Christopher and Cobby B.

I have been writing quite a lot down here, for the quiet is undisturbed, save by the cries of triumph or despair uttered by the infants. Re-shaping two old stories and evolving a new one, which should be pretty good.

141 *The Nicholses' 'ancestral Hall' was Lawford Hall, at Manningtree.*

Meanwhile I have just received the proofs of some prose poems of mine which I am printing in the Sitwells' *Wheels*, together with 'Zoo Céleste' from *Jonah*—all of which looked, I thought, very satisfactory in print and all, I flatter myself, bearing a somewhat inimitable cachet, hall-marked A.L.H. I rather like the notion of *Wheels* with its toreador attitude towards the bloody-bloodies of this world. It makes a place to print a type of work which wouldn't fit in very well elsewhere.

I went over for a couple of nights to [Great] Enton last week when Gervas was back on leave. He was, on the whole, in good form, confident the war will be over in a year because of the dwindling man power of the Boche, thinks we may win a victory even, which he dreads owing to the way we'd use it; prussianism being infectious. Whatever happens, we may be sure it will be for the worst. I dread the inevitable acceleration of American world domination which will be the ultimate result of it all. It was a thing that had got to come in time, but this will hasten its arrival by a century. We shall all be colonized; Europe will no longer be Europe; we shall all be buffeted on huge fabulous new oceans, longing all the while for the little old dark pond where a frail and wizened child launches its paper boat towards the sunset.

Frail and wizened is the last thing you could call our grandchildren. Andrew is like Gargantua and seven times in every day he drains the bursting udders of three thousand four hundred and sixty three cows, drinking eight hundred and thirty pipes, twelve hogsheads of rich milk, to say nothing of the nineteen Imperial Kilderkins of cream and the thirty two quintals of sugar and prepared foods. His face is like the rising sun of a shepherd's warning, his belly like Montgolfier's aerostat, his legs are as columns in the temple of Serapis in Thebes. As for David, he is in incessant motion for twelve hours out of every twenty four; running at the rate he does, he cannot cover less than eight hundred leagues a day.

I saw [——] at Enton for the first time for about three years. From a most irritating schoolboy he has grown up into a physically superb and mentally very powerful young Ouida guardsman—altogether very splendid, and I gather the ladies are bowled over; and I also gather that he is gathering that the female Olympians of the Upper Classes do not feel themselves bound by those deplorably cramping codes which weigh on their sisters of the middle class. A course of the passions is the best possible method of carrying out the first commandment, GNOTHI SEAUTON, and for a man with the personality and strength of intelligence of [——] it can do, I think, nothing but good: for he will not be dragged into the futility of the Upper Class existence—that deplorable living on passing impressions, passing emotions, perpetual carpe diem; he has the guts to remain himself; he will

---

141 *Grandchildren: i.e., stepbrothers, the second of whom, Andrew Fielding Huxley, had been born in 1917.*

go superbly among them, get what he wants, which is primarily knowledge of himself, and then leave them and pass on to something else—or so I take it, if my estimate of [——]'s character is correct. I do admire the Upper Classes very much in a way; but there is no doubt that that living for the moment is a danger to be most carefully avoided. For it is tremendously exciting and absorbing while it lasts, but when you wake up and look back, you find a vacuum.

I thought the Ka [Cox]-Will [Arnold-Forster] affair seemed altogether excellent; good from both sides; it will save Ka from becoming a Civil Servant and middle aged.

[. . . .]

A.L.H.

142: TO MRS NAOMI MITCHISON

Prior's Field,
Godalming, Surrey
12 *August*, 1918

My dear Naomi,

We have answered one another's absence of letters with a punctuality which is most meritorious. Let us now see whether we can manage a more positive correspondence as effectively. You, I gather through dim sources, are at present somewhere in Scotland—that country where every prospect pleases and only Man etc, a land, as Cleiveland says, 'which brings in question and suspense God's omni-presence' . . . adding that 'Had Cain been Scot, God would have changed his doom, Not forced him wander, but confined him home'. I trust it is suiting both yourself and the progeny. My grandchildren, I mean step-brothers, are doing very well. The youngest one rivals Gargantua in consuming seven times daily the milk of three thousand and sixty three cows, to say nothing of a hogshead or two of cream and the one or two firkins of sugar and prepared foods thrown in as an appetiser. The other one, aged two and a half, now eats whole sheep at a sitting, bones and all. All is very pleasant here; the garden blooms and blazes in the day and waves its thuribles of unseen incense across the night. I sit with my faithful typewriter outside, surrounded by gillyflowers and peacock butterflies, and write immortal works in prose—a short story which should, I think, be good.

[. . . .]

I saw the arbiter of the elegancies, Lewis, the other day when he was over on about half an hour's leave. He was very French—his party manners more exquisite and irritating than ever, but beneath this top dressing of artificial manure one found the same good Ukrainian black earth unchanged, and growing in it the old parthenogenetic twangum tree hung with the fruits

of unripe passion, upon whose branches sit the screaming gulls who, unfortunately, deposit the guano on the surface of the primeval steppe. You
catch my meaning? or would you prefer it expressed cartographically?
Write to me soon of this and that—of bonnie Scotland, The Kyles of Bute,
the Kyles of Bute where burning Whilcox loved and sung; of you and yours
—thee and thine, as I might even say by reason of the age-long familiarity
which, begetting, as it has done, in you contempt and in me esteem and awe,
would seem almost to justify the familiar, if somewhat obsolete, singular.
After which I can do no more.

Bien à toi.

A.L.H.

143: TO J. C. SQUIRE

The Manor House,
Garsington, Oxford
[Late August, 1918]

Dear Squire,

Here is a review of that Buddhist book. How much I disapprove of the
Wisdom of the East! Also two sketches, one about G. Sand and A. de Musset,
the other about nothing at all, which you might care to look at. Will you be
in town any time in the first half of September? If so, I wish you'd come and
have luncheon with me one day. I shall be in town from about the 6th till I
go back to Eton on the 18th.

Isn't it a fact that young [H. J.] Massingham is now at or near Oxford?
I shd. be grateful if you'd give me his address; for I'd like to see him again.
It is an age since I met him last.

You hear poor Eliot has been called up and will probably be a private in
the Kentucky Yeomanry or the Memphis, Ohio, Fusiliers in a month's time?
It's too deplorable. I hope something can be done for him.

Yours

Aldous Huxley

142 *Whilcox: presumably Ella Wheeler Wilcox.*

143 *The review of the Buddhist book seems not to have appeared in the* New
Statesman. *There may, however, have been other unsigned reviews by Huxley in 1918,
either in the* New Statesman *or in the* Nation. *His bibliographers have overlooked not
only those from 1917 (see letter 108) but two printed by the* New Statesman *in 1919
(mentioned in letter 160), the one of Selma Lagerlöf's* Göste Berling's Saga *(16
August), the other of W. H. Hudson's* A Short History of French Literature *(20
September), as well as four instalments of the 'World of Books' feature in the* Nation
*during 1919 (31 May, 2 August, 16 August, 6 December), these last signed 'A.L.H.'
He had in addition two signed articles in the* Nation *that year, probably as the result of
H. W. Massingham's interest.*

16 Bracknell Gardens, N.W.3
14 September, 1918

My dear Juliette,

I don't know why—after months of silence—you should fob me off with a letter six lines long, even tho' you do send a *Vie Parisienne* (which hasn't yet arrived, by the way). It is true I had not written to you, but my impression is that the initiative, as the military critics [say], was in your hands and that it was for you to take the offensive: in other words that I wrote last and it was your turn to send me a letter. However, I may be wrong: I generally am: it is a habit of mine.

I picture you at Callander, sitting like Wordsworth's Old and Solitary Sheep on the top of a naked fell and poring over old numbers of the *Vie Parisienne* in the vain hope of seeing what life is really like in the places where life exists. I lose no time in assuring you that life is only too little like the *Vie Parisienne*—I wish it were sometimes: oh for a galaxy of delicious Gerda Wegener girls waiting for one with open arms whenever one felt disinclined to work ... but there aren't any.

The only thing which brightens the general darkness is the Russian Ballet, which is pure beauty, like a glimpse into another world. We—Ottoline, Julian [Morrell], Brett, [Mark] Gertler and I—had a great evening of it the other day: almost everybody in London was there, and we all went round to the back afterwards to see [Lydia] Lopokova the première danseuse, who is ravishing—finding there no less a person than André Gide, who looks like a baboon with the voice, manners and education of Bloomsbury in French.

I write—immortally (or do I mean immorally? I am not quite sure) and read in between the bouts of an odious restaurant life, which always makes me feel very ill and reduces me almost to death and absolutely to tears— BUT THERE IS NO ESCAPE FROM IT! because—mark my words—one has no tolerable domestic life. I pine and long for domesticity (combined with intelligence) and all I find is domesticity so tedious as to be impossible and restaurant life so sordid as to be intolerable. We are on the HORNS OF A DILEMMA ... and where is the escape? I know so well ... but Fate is so prejudiced against one that it blocks the road.

I hear Brett is coming North fairly soon: she seems to me to have become much odder and Brettier than ever: no development, but an accentuation of eccentricities. But I thought she was painting a very good picture. She is going to do some illustrations for my 'Leda' poem. When do you remove from Callander to a more salubrious and lively climate? Write to me properly, please—to Eton, whither, alas! I return next Wednesday.

> Passent les jours et passent les semaines
> Ni temps passé
> Ni les amours reviennent. ...

Do write, my dear.   *Aldous*

Eton College, Windsor
7 October, 1918

My dear Brett,

I trust you flourish in Bonnie Scotland. I picture you stumping out in mackintosh breeks to fish and in the intervals tearing the clothes off Mademoiselle [Baillot]'s back and drawing her. At least, that's what I hope you're doing: for I am most excited to see the Swans begun and the Leda illustrations too. I have written a bit more of the poem—but hardly enough to send you yet. It is a description of Jove's visit to Venus, who is found reclining on a purple-draped couch (with folds arranged carefully à la Cézanne) attended by marvellously slender Cupids. I hope to get on to the actual outrage and the Swan himself soon.

I went down to Southend the other day for two hours—a marvellous place which I had never seen before. The journey is picturesque to a degree. To the East of London, where the town begins to decay away into the Essex flats, there are landscapes of incredible beauty. I send you a sketch I did out of the window of the train of an enormous solitary gasometer, seventy feet high, standing like a dull red Castle of St. Angelo against a lurid black and yellow sky that turned to purple on the absolutely level horizon that was fretted with a dim pattern of towers and chimneys. In the foreground a plain of sickly grass cut transversely by a ditch of water, shining like an eye in the lifeless earth. Somebody really ought to paint it. The gasometer is our only modern specimen of grim and grandiose architecture—corresponding to the Norman keeps and donjons of the 12th century.

Give my love to Mlle., and tell her I will write to her and that meanwhile I much appreciated her letter.

Yours
Aldous

146: TO JULIETTE BAILLOT

The Old Christopher,
Eton College, Windsor
10 *October,* 1918

My dear Juliette,

If you think I took what you said hardly, you are quite mistaken. For I didn't: on the contrary, I recognized it as a bit of advice which I probably often need and which has, indeed, been given me before. That I am lamentably bad at taking good advice is shown by the fact that you have given it again now.

What are you worried and miserable about—not about this, I hope, at all. It distresses me that you should be, and if I can be of any assistance I wish you'd tell me. The atmosphere of Scotland in the autumn, further chilled and dimmed by the Eshers, must indeed be enough to make the strongest spirit quail. It will be better, I hope, when and if you return to London. In fact I think you would do better to do some independent work on your own in London, or at least in a civilized country, either teaching in a school—which you may or may not find bloody (il n'y a pas d'autre mot!), or else in a Government office, censoring, propaganding or something of the kind where your languages wd. be useful. You would at any rate be seeing more people; nearer the heart of life: and at the least there wd. be the cinemas!

I saw Fredegond [Shove] the other day and she talked very affectionately about you—we both did, I may say!—tho' she said she felt most guilty in not having written: but letter writing with her is, I think, almost a physical impossibility. The nervous effort required to sit down and compose her thoughts into the requisite mould is altogether too much for her: so that she procrastinates for so long that she at last feels too much ashamed to write at all, even if she could. Curious process!

I never knew that brother Julian had gone up to see you. I did not see him after Saturday of the week before last, and he did not tell me what he was going to do in the remaining days. He has an insatiable thirst for rushing about and seeing more and more and ever different people. When he gets back to Italy, he will need a rest cure. I hope he was nice to you and you to him.

I am glad you liked my book. I find it hard to judge the thing. Much of it I feel to be rather remote from myself at present. I have done an admirable short story—so heartless and cruel that you wd. probably scream if you read it. The concentrated venom of it is quite delicious—while the subtle horror of my modern epic and the strange mixture of pure beauty and irony, found in my 'Leda', beggar description: you will have to read them to realize to the full the truth of your judgment about me—about one of my ME's: but the other is—what? a sentimentalist? a hero of romance? a bon bourgeois? I leave you to judge: and as it is very very late and I must get up rather early to-morrow, I will leave you to consider this charming problem by yourself and bid you a very good night, en vous embrassant bien affectueusement. Write to me at length and soon.

Aldous

147: TO LADY OTTOLINE MORRELL

Eton College, Windsor
20 October, 1918

Dearest Ottoline,

It was very delightful to hear from you this morning, for it is indeed a long time since we coincided in space and time—Hampton Court some four weeks ago was, I think, the last occasion. I wish I cd. have come up that Thursday for *Schéherazade's* first night, but I can manage no weekday evening except Saturday. I did, as a matter of fact, see the thing with the

Sitwells that Saturday night—and there was a great moment, as we were standing in the foyer waiting patiently for Frau Carmen Hill to stop, when the telegraphic tape-machine began to tick and letter by letter we saw the German answer to Wilson's terms. We celebrated peace at the accursed Eiffel—at Henry Mond's expense, an admirable shekel-producing machine —cheerfully but on the whole decently, with the exception, of course, of [Patrick] Dallas, whom we found there, sodden and quivering. The Sitwells now call him 'Tremblers', which is an admirable name. I really find him quite disgusting, and entirely agree with you about the unpleasantness of all this deplorable boozing.

I begin to hope that we shall have Peace by Xmas: the *Daily Mail* and the heroes of the last generation but three will be sadly disappointed.

I have just tramped over to Frank Schuster's at Bray and back, where I had a very pleasant lunch. La Grosse Lalla [Vandervelde] was there, fresh from Paris and very hopeful about peace: also old Edward Elgar, who seemed an amusing old bird, and Adrian Boult. It was a pleasure to be with comparatively human intelligent beings again, even tho' it entailed a walk of eleven miles thro' the rain.

I am reading D'Annunzio's *Forse che si, forse che no* for the sake of my Italian. It's thick rich stuff, like almond icing scented with patchouli or some such rather *canaille* perfume, but very beautiful, I think—and also very difficult. Most of the words are not in the dictionary.

I wonder if I cd. come over to G[arsington] one Saturday night in the next month? It wd. be very jolly and I think it cd. be managed, tho' I shd. have to get back on Sunday. I shd. take the opportunity to see my sister who's now at Somerville. Meanwhile it wd. be very jolly if you could come down here one day.

To turn to a somewhat *macabre* and painful subject—I wonder if you know what means Bertie Russell employed to cure his piles: for I have been slightly afflicted of late by that 'distressing but almost universal complaint'. I must really apologize for this question!

I wrote to Brett in Scotland about a fortnight ago, but have received no answer: I wonder if she ever got my letter, or why she doesn't reply. When does she return? I trust she wont be too too Esherish. I heard from Mlle. the other day that my brother had gone all the way up to Callander to see her in the last days of his leave. I knew nothing about it from him: is it a Romance? Persistent rumours to the effect that Lytton and Carrington have got secretly married go rumbling round me. I pour scorn on them: but is there any justification for them?

I heard from Maria yesterday from Rome, where the family are halting on their way to Naples. She seems pretty well and happy.

Good bye. I hope I shall see you all soon.

Yours affectionately
Aldous

The Old Christopher,
Eton College, Windsor
30 October, 1918

My dear J,

I have not, I fear, done very well in the writing line. One gets no grip
on time in this place and, what with a host of little occupations, it slips from
one before one is aware and with all one's good intentions unfulfilled in
practice. However, to-day I have, for a miracle, a free after twelve—though
it may cease to be so at any minute—and stimulated by that and the arrival
of your letter of the 24th, I have at last settled down, full of determination
before the tick machine.

What news? I really can think of none, except that on Trafalgar Day this
year Cobby made PRECISELY THE SAME REMARKS ABOUT LORD NELSON AND
LADY HAMILTON AS LAST YEAR—which I thought was really very perfect. It
always seems to me one of the greatest tragedies of human life that people
always are repeating themselves—how often one catches oneself in the process! It shows the deplorable limitations of the mind, and the fact, it seems to
me, is one to be very much insisted upon in any analysis of psychology; I
always bring it in in some form. One is a chess player with a certain quantity,
more or less according to one's intelligence, of gambits. New ones are learnt
with infinite difficulty, and beyond a certain age not at all. A certain age—
that reminds me of the charming lyric I am having printed in this year's
Oxford Poetry. [*Here follows the text of 'Men of a Certain Age'.*] And
a certain age again reminds me of the fact that I went last week end to stay
with old Roger Fry, who for a man of over fifty is far the youngest person
I have ever seen. I am not sure that he isn't really younger than one is
oneself. So susceptible to new ideas, so much interested in things, so dis-
liking the old—it is wonderful. Have you ever met him? He is an enchanting
old thing. There was staying there the red-haired and French Mrs [Andrée]
MacColl, whom you met, I believe, at Anrep's party. I thought she was very
charming, and made great friends with her. Fry asked me if I would undertake the editorship of the *Burlington Magazine*, but as (a) I know nil about
art and (b) the wages are very small, I am inclined to think I shall not.

I have not been to London much recently for fear of the influenza, which
it would be boring to catch. I was last there three or four weeks ago for the
first performance of *Scheherazade* at the Coliseum. It was the night of the first
German peace note and while we were waiting in the foyer for the preliminary
horrors to stop and the ballet to begin, the message ticked itself out on the

148 *The Cobbyesque remarks about Nelson and Lady Hamilton occur in Huxley's
story 'Happily Ever After' (III). The farce recently completed was 'Happy Families',
which shows the influence of Andreieff; see letter 140. Mrs MacColl was the wife of
D. S. MacColl, critic and painter.*

tape machine, most dramatically—and it seemed as though peace were actually on us. We concluded the evening with potations (suitably enough at the expense of [. . .] Henry Mond) at the Eiffel Tower. But peace, I fear isnt quite so close as we then thought. Wilson adds on a point at every note; it will soon be the thirty nine articles, rather than the fourteen p's— and almost as impossible to accept as those glorious protocols. However, impossible or not, it looks as though the Germans would have to accept them soon, big willy little nilly, so to speak. But I hope to [G]od we shall not let scoundrels like Roosevelt and Lodge and Taft and Northcliffe and B[eaver]brook direct our peace policy. Meanwhile the heroes of the generation before last, like Lord Wrenbury (ci-devant Judge Buckley) write to the *Times* screaming for blood, the destruction of Berlin, the systematic raping of every German woman above fourteen etc. etc.

Poor Robbie Ross, it was very sad. He died quite suddenly in his sleep of a syncope—his heart had, apparently, always been in a perilous condition. He was the most charming creature. One of the oases in the pervading gloom of London is removed by his death.

I have not yet seen the copper bowl, as I've not been to Hampstead since you were here; but I will rout it out from its place of concealment when I am next there.

I havent heard from Margaret, but hope to; for I wrote to her for her birthday asking what she'd like for a present. I hope also to see her on the 9th, when I am going (D.V.) to Garsington for a Saturday night. I mean if I can go to Oxford itself later, for I want to talk to Raleigh about prospects there. Sligger tells me there is no likelihood of anything at Balliol, for they have taken on Eccles during the war, who is a good man and whom they wouldnt want to turn out. Still, there will be other colleges in need of an English lecturer—Trinity, for instance, who have had poor Tiddy killed. Meanwhile you might talk to George [Trevelyan] as you suggested about the *Manchester Guardian*; it might be a possibility. What I want more than anything really is to get a year with nothing to do except write. I dont know if I shall be able to manage it, but I shall try. I could live for very little in the Sitwells' enormous house near Florence—the Castel Acciaiuoli, a twelfth century palace of such gigantic proportions that it was at one time used as a village, accommodating fifty-two separate families within it. I cannot write properly in the midst of the perpetual distraction here, and besides I am always much too tired. I succeeded, however, in dashing off a little symbolic farce in two or three days recently. It is not good, because I had not the time to concentrate on it properly; but it is quite amusing, and it may be printed in that advanced American paper, the *Little Review*. If it is, I will send you a copy. But to settle down to any long bit of prose, which needs concentration or preparatory study is practically impossible. No sooner has one started than nineteen or fifty boys come in and demand to have their essays looked over and my mind is switched off from the sublime to ridiculous discussions of questions such as What is History? East is East and W. is W and never the t shall m etc, which may be all very well in their way, but which certainly exhaust time and energy. However, I have really nothing to complain of; and I remember with horrible vividness that when I was about six I was presented with one of those yellow mugs to drink my evening milk out of, with the following inscription on it:

Oh isn't the world extremely flat
With nothing whatever to grumble at.

It hurt my feelings most horribly at the time and so did the mockery of the family; but it is a good remark.

Fare well.
A.L.H.

I hear you went to Callander before you returned to Italy. That was rather romantic, wasn't it?

149: TO JULIAN HUXLEY

The Old Christopher,
Eton College, Windsor
20 November, 1918

My dear Julian,

It was very good of you to offer to lend me that money. I shall accept the loan most gratefully when the time comes and if I want it. At present the situation is so obscure that I dont, so to say, see my hand more than three weeks before my face. I go to Oxford this week-end and am lunching with Walter Raleigh on Sunday, from whom I hope to find out what the prospects and possibilities are of a job at Oxford or elsewhere. If necessary I could probably stay on here till the end of the summer, though I should think it quite possible that Alington will have all his normal and permanent staff in the place by next half. Meanwhile the situation is somewhat complicated by Maria's probable movements. The family will, of course, return to Belgium as soon as they can get passports and permits. The father appears to be in Brussels. Up till recently, I gather, he has been at Courtrai, where I think is the family business or in his country house somewhere near by. I should think it quite likely that the whole family will be back early in the new year; there seems to be no reason why they shouldnt. In which case the point of starting off as soon as possible to Italy would rather have gone. In a month or two's time I shall be able, I hope, to see a little more clearly into the future.

We have got over the jollifications of the first days of peace and are beginning to examine the facts, which, I must say, have a peculiarly repulsive aspect. Bolshevism a serious possibility (and there are delightful stories, less serious perhaps, such as this: that three hundred thousand perfectly good Mills bombs are missing from munition factories on the Clyde!), the immediate prospect of the election with George's triumphant return to power, the consequent abolition of any serious kind of parliamentary government and the substitution for it of bureaucracy, private bargains with the big money interests and rule by the press—consequent exacerbation of revolutionary elements, who will find it impossible to make themselves felt by legitimate constitutional means and will therefore resort to strikes on a large scale and perhaps force: (and one has to remember that two thirds of the adult male population is highly skilled in the use of the most complicated weapons and will do the barricade business in quite professional style). It will all end by America having to go in for what Mr Roosevelt poetically calls 'Preparedness for Ever', in order to crush revolution in the rest of the world—a task which only America can perform as she is the one definitely anti-socialistic nation among the great powers.

The school has been thrown considerably out of gear by the influenza, casualties being very heavy among the ushers, which causes a lot of disorganisation. One blessed result is the complete suspension of early school for the present. So far I have been safe from the pest and hope to be able to struggle through till the end of the half.

I have been writing a little recently—a little allegorical farce, portions of my dual personality story ['Farcical History of Richard Greenow'], which tends to grow under my hands, and a few lines of verse. But I have spent most of my leisure recently in reading; chiefly novels, *Mme. Bovary* and *Bouvard et Pécuchet* of Flaubert—both admirable—you should read the latter especially; it would, I think, amuse you a lot; then Stendhal's *Lucien Leuwen*, a book which increases my already very great esteem for that author, who has, I think, claims to being the greatest novelist outside Russia; I am now reading Balzac's *Eugénie Grandet*—good in its very different way. Among the quite moderns I sip the brilliant *Ulysses* of James Joyce; it has, to be sure, a slight flavour of excrements, but is none the worse for that. For heavier reading I have been perusing an admirable book by one Arthur MacDowall [McDowall], called *Realism*—a critical study of the phenomenon of realism in art and thought; very interesting.

I saw Eliot last week in London and had a delightful literary talk with him. He has published three or four new poems in the *Little Review*, two of which are interesting, the others not. He is, I think, very remarkable. Also very charming.

How long are they likely to keep you in Italy or Austria? It would be a bore to have to act as an army of occupation for a long time after everything is done; I can imagine no dismaller waste of one's time.

I am feeling too stupid to write anything intelligent or indeed to write anything at all. Fare well. I will make an effort to let you have another line next week. Writing letters I find the most difficult process in the world; it takes me weeks to make up my mind to sit down and start; so that you must forgive me if I am a poor correspondent.

Ever yours,
A.L.H.

My dear Juliette,

Your letter was welcome, but reminded me rather painfully that I had not answered either your or Brett's last communications. No excuse, beyond the usual anaemia of the will power with which, in the matter of letter writing, I am habitually affected.

So far I have escaped influenza, tho' there are 250 cases of it in the school. I pity your plight: the whiskey bottle seems the only refuge from that post-flu depression.

I was not at Garsington on armistice day, but the day before, as I had to get back to this place on the Sunday night. My enthusiasm for peace demonstrations was a little damped by the fact that one fireman was killed outright with a hatchet while attempting to quench the bonfire in Trafalgar Square, and three policemen were thrown into the river—while the chief instigator of the outrages was that repulsive German Jew, [——].

I have just come back from a day in Oxford, where I spent some time in looking for work—with no prospect of success: the English School there seems to be too impoverished to be able to pay the men it already possesses: much less can it contemplate taking on any new ones, at any rate yet awhile. A future of poverty, hunger and dirt looms menacingly.

I saw old Earp: poor thing, very much upset by the death from flu of his Indian friend [Sharna] Rao, with whom he used always to go about on those strange expeditions to Falmouth and the Cotswolds. He was very charming, I thought.

[. . . .]

I am trying to arrange to go to Paris for the Christmas holidays: but doubt whether it will be feasible. Still I shall make a great effort, as I want very much to go.

Tell Brett that I am just approaching the crucial moment of 'Leda'. The Swan is seen approaching—but I get on very slowly: the accouchements of my Muse are few and laborious. Tell Brett also to remember to vote, and to vote Labour, our only hope.

I have been reading nothing but Flaubert and Stendhal of late: the greatest of Frenchmen. And the Goncourt *Journals*, and Casanova—all good. But there is too much to read: and it so easily becomes a mere indulgence, a vice of the mind quite as deplorable as any other bad habit. I never really feel I am performing a wholly *moral* action, except when I am writing. Then and only then one is not wasting time.

Good bye my dear.

Aldous

The Old Christopher,
Eton College, Windsor
1 *December,* 1918

My dear Brett,

Your letter heaped coals of fire—I wish they were of the kind that made one warm—upon my head, repaying my neglect to answer your last by a new and even more entertaining epistle. I have no excuse for not having written —only natural indolence and the general sense of dimness and the pressure, not very heavy, but distracting, of the daily round, the common task. So that, even though I have escaped the flu—never very bad here—I have succeeded in writing very little more of 'Leda', and have only just come to the point when the Swan approaches and does his worst. When that episode is finished, I will send you a copy of the whole thing as far as it has gone. for it will be the first part of the poem complete—the rest being concerned with the hideous problems of parentage which arise on Leda's production (do you think she cackled?) of the two eggs. I can get along at a good pace when I am in the mood, but that has not been the case of late. There is a jolly Tintoretto at Hampton Court, representing the Nine Muses lying about in a state of pleasantly ample Venetian nakedness. You will find it in this little book, page 21; it is a good study of people naked out of doors, and I like the confused mass of legs—rather like Gertler's bathers, only it seems to me to come off better than Gertler! You really must go to that place and see the Earl of Surrey and the Lady Arabella Stuart; they are too enchanting. Personally, too, I am very fond of the absurd Mabuse 'Adam and Eve' on page 56; in the original, the flesh is very light and bright and these almost too discreet leaves are very dark, giving the most gloriously artificial and unreal effect. I should like very much to get permission to see the 'Leda' of Titian (or it may be Tintoret) which is hidden in the vaults of the National Gallery for fear its rich realism should pervert the mind of the Gt Brit Pub. I think I must really wangle it somehow; I feel it would be such an inspiration.

I saw Carrington not long ago, just after the armistice, and thought her enchanting; which indeed I always do whenever I see her, losing my heart completely as long as she is on the spot, but recovering it as soon as she is no longer there. We went to see the show at the Omega, where there was what I thought an admirable Gertler and a good Duncan Grant and a rather jolly Vanessa Bell. Carrington and I had a long argument on the fruitful subject of virginity: I may say it was she who provoked it by saying that she intended to remain a vestal for the rest of her life. All expostulations on my part were vain.

I am glad you are keeping your ears pricked at your end of this strange potential romance. I know very little from my side, except that Brother J,

151 *Romance: Julian Huxley and Juliette Baillot were married in March,* 1919.

when I wrote to him saying I thought his Scottish journey romantic, did not deny the soft impeachment, but said that he had taken on Mlle as his Marraine for the war. Whether the wartime godmother-godson arrangement will blossom into any other kind of relationship in the piping days of peace remains to be seen. I know nothing.

I dont know what I shall be doing this Christmas holidays. It is conceivable I may make an effort to get to Paris, as Maria may be returning from Italy and stop there on her way to Belgium. But that is all very uncertain. I expect I shall be at Garsington some time.

Money, as you say, is the problem. It haunts me sometimes, the horror of it. I feel myself growing perceptibly poorer every minute. Whether it will ever be solved seems to me extremely doubtful.

This term ends on the 19th, thank heavens. It has not been unpleasant, only rather boring, and the humorousness of the parson sometimes palls a little. My fur gloves are almost my only joy. I think, if I were an immensely rich voluptuary, I would dress my mistresses from head to foot in squirrel's fur tights. Better than a water bottle these cold winter nights. . . .

I was in Oxford last week-end and saw old Earp, melancholy at the loss of his faithful dog-like Indian friend, but very charming—more so than I had expected after all the stories of his London orgies.

Good bye, dear Brett.

Aldous

152: TO JULIAN HUXLEY

16, *Bracknell Gardens*
5 *January*, 1919

My dear Julian,
Many thanks for the letter and the books, which I found waiting here for me on my return from Stocks on Thursday. I hope you will be back here before I return to Eton. But at any rate you will be able to come and stay with me there for a few days if you come back after the 22nd. I suppose you will be settling down to a job at Oxford pretty soon. I wish I could find anything there; Raleigh is not at all encouraging, saying that the English school is so poor that it cannot afford to pay the people it has already got, much less take on any new ones. However, he is on the look out for something for me at a provincial place. If the worst came to the worst, I might with your aid make an attempt on America, though I dont want to—except that I rather think America will be the only place where revolution will not break out; and I have no desire to find myself in the middle of a revolution; great events are both terrifying and boring, terrifying because one may be killed and boring because they interfere with the free exercise of the mind—and after all, that freedom is the only thing in the world worth having and the people who can use it properly are the only ones worthy of the least respect: the others are all madmen, pursuing shadows and prepared at any moment to commit acts of

violence. The prospects of the universe seem to me dim and dismal to a degree. But they are nothing to one's own personal prospects, which are what the Russians would go so far as to call Nevsky prospects, nay, the nevskyest of prospects. What I want to do is to marry and settle down to write. What I shall have to do is very different and so far quite uncertain. I shall go out to Belgium, if I can, at Easter to see Maria and her family. It would be a great comfort of course if she had a little money; but I dont know how far they have been ruined by the war. I gather that the father's factory, which had remained intact for four years, was more or less destroyed in our last offensive. However, it's rather depressing to ponder over these things too much, and as one doesnt in the least know what's going to happen there is not much point in it. Let us turn to pleasanter topics.

I have finished the first part of my 'Leda', culminating in the actual swan episode. It is extremely lovely and luscious, and Brett's illustrations promise to be the same. The second part, containing the laying of the eggs and the decision of the medical men of the period regarding their respective parentage, remains to be written. I am advancing too with my dual personality story and my other long poem. But the mere physical obstacles in this house to doing any work are so great; the cold is so piercing that it strikes to the very soul and numbs the faculties of the mind as well as the sinews of the body. In mere self defence, obeying the primal law of preservation, one is compelled to go out and move about to keep warm. At moments I almost long for Eton, where Cobbie has, of course, contrived to heap together great hoards of coal and we are never seriously cold at all. How the English have supported life during all these centuries with no adequate heating apparatus to counteract what is admittedly one of the worst climates, owing to its dampness, in the world, is more than I can imagine.

Here is a multi-coloured manifest of a new paper [*Art and Letters*] which will probably be rather good and to which I think you had better subscribe. I am having one or two little things in the first issue and hope to have my story—the one you saw when you were here last—in the next number. Reproductions of drawings ought to be interesting too; an admirable Picasso drawing in this number. But it really seems to me that the only hope is to have a dual personality paper, where the good and the vulgar are mixed; people will swallow the good quite eagerly if it is sufficiently tempered with the vulgar. The ideal paper then would be one where a drawing, say, by Gertler would alternate with a delicious prurience by Raphael Kirchner and a poem by myself with an outgush of la Whilcox [Ella Wheeler Wilcox]. Such a paper is, I believe, on the point of being started; and if it is I have slight hopes of becoming the editor of the good side of it.

152 *The 'ideal' paper (last paragraph) appears to have been* Coterie, *which was first published in May,* 1919. *Huxley's search for a remunerative post ended with his acceptance of an editorial job with the* Athenaeum *in April.*

Well, au revoir I trust fairly soon. You shall have your nail scissors. I must be off to lunch in Chelsea, and it's a long long way—almost as far as the proverbial Tipperary.

Yours
Aldous

153: TO LEONARD HUXLEY

Eton College, Windsor
26 February, 1919

Dearest Father,

Would you care to come here for the weekend of the 8th-10th? Our domestic crises are over and it is possible to put up people here now.

Apropos of what you say in your last letter: I dont, of course, propose to marry on nothing at all. In fact I shouldn't like to risk it under a total of £500 a year. If I hear of something before Easter I shall try and get married then: otherwise I shall just go over and see how things are and arrange about future possibilities. I go to Oxford next weekend and hope to hear something about prospects there. Meanwhile, I am poking about among editors in the hope of securing a certain amount of reviewing and literary work. One ought to be able to make an extra £100 a year by that without too much grind or the prostitution of one's pen. The money would be very useful and that amount of the work not unpleasant—tho' I should be sorry to have to depend on that for my whole living.

Whether Maria's people will be able to let her have anything, I dont know. At any rate it wont be much.

What is the position of the P[rior's] F[ield] thing at present? It would be a very great help if you could let me have a little—though I feel rather odious in asking you for any thing: for I seem already to have claimed—and as a matter of course—so much of your work and of your life. I hope I shall do something not unworthy of all you have given me.

Come on the 8th if you can.

Your loving son
Aldous

154: TO LEONARD HUXLEY

Grand' Place,
St. Trond, [Belgium]
[April, 1919]

Dearest Father,

Here I am, settled down in this rather oddly un-English life. A quite Balzacian Ville de Province, where nothing happens and where everybody

153 *Prior's Field School yielded Leonard Huxley a certain income.*

who is anybody is everybody else's relation. The old grandfather and grandmother [M. and Mme Baltus] are the patriarchs of the town and at any given moment they can easily collect twenty-five members of the family, of the first and second generation, about them. I live with Mme. [Marguerite] and M. [Norbert] Nys and the 2nd daughter [Jehanne] in another house 2 or 3 hundred yards away from the grandparents where Maria is staying. It is a queer household when we are all assembled chez grandpapa. The 2 old people—he with the appearance of a retired colonel, deaf, very kindly and human devoting his old age to reading which he never had time to do in his active days of cloth-manufacturing. The old lady is a person of rather witch-like appearance, not quite so amiable as he, I think. Then Georges Baltus, the eldest son, professor of art at Glasgow with his German wife [Sylvia], a daughter of Hildebrand, the sculptor—both very cultured and he extremely amusing. Then Mme. [Marguerite] Nys, whom I like very much—intelligent and nice, tho' rather a creature of moods (some of the moods tiresome). Much younger is their brother, Raymond, who has lived for 10 years in England and is a British subject. [. . . .] Raymond was regarded rather as the black sheep of the family, but he has returned now, wounded, with all the éclat of the Prodigal Son. It is really wonderful when we all sit down to dinner together—such an extraordinary collection of varied types.

Then there are all the other uncles and aunts—all rich commerçants living in large and hideous houses dotted about the town. Some make cloth, some sugar, some do a little of everything. A few are very cultured, the rest not at all. I think they are fairly reassured by my appearance. They had, I fancy, rather anticipated a roaring lion: they are relieved to find a sheep. We are just going on a little trip to the Nys's destroyed home in East Flanders, sightseeing in Brussels, Ghent and Bruges by the way. I wonder if you cd send me five pounds' worth of Belgian money in a registered envelope: I may not need it, but dont want to be short on my return. I WILL REPAY, saith the Lord!

I am very happy: will write again soon. I trust all goes well at home. Love to all.

Your loving son
Aldous

155: MARIA NYS TO LEONARD HUXLEY

Grand Place 19, Saint Trond
21 June, 1919

Dear Mr Huxley,

Your letter has made a deep impression on me and I thank you so much for the affection it expresses. I am so ready to love you and hope you will find in me a good wife to Aldous and a good daughter to you—and as I have no wisdom at all I shall be very much in need of the one you so kindly offer me.

I only received your letter last night as it was forwarded first to the country and then back here: which accounts for the delay of my answering such a good welcome in your home.

Will you please thank Mrs Huxley for her kind message and I may assure you of my most sincerest affection.

Maria Nys

156: TO LEONARD HUXLEY

18 *Hampstead Hill Gardens, N.W.*3
26 *June*, 1919

Dearest Father,

These wretches want your consent legalised par acte notorial. Could you possibly get that done in Oban before a Commissioner of Oaths, or some such creature. It is a nuisance, particularly as I believe the thing to be wholly unnecessary and superfluous. Could you then send it direct to Maria, 29 Rue de la Station, St. Trond, and she will send it on to the Mayor of Bellem. If all is well I shall go out quite early in July—4th or 5th—I think—and return as soon as possible.

I hope the journey was not too intolerable and that weather and other things are treating you well now you're there.

I have been very busy getting odds and ends, passports, visas and such—leading rather a hunted existence.

Great haste. Love to all the family and yourself in particular.

Your loving son
Aldous

157: TO MRS ROSALIND HUXLEY

18 *Hampstead Hill Gardens, N.W.*3
29 *June*, 1919

Dearest Rosalind,

What shop did you order the Cash's names from? They dont seem to have sent them yet, so I thought I might hurry them up a bit. I have been leading a very strenuous life, shopping, painting furniture etc. Today Brett and I painted all the woodwork in the little sitting room—a beautiful dove grey, and on Wednesday Marjorie is coming up to help me paper it. She has done some admirable paper-hanging at 51 and it is quite up to professional standards. I shall try and get some nice yellow, orange or pink paper—if it's procurable. But I'll have to hunt for it. The carpet has come and looks nice: so do the things from Heal's. I bought a marvellous instrument for heating

157 *Huxley's cousin Marjorie Huxley (afterwards Lady Harding), the daughter of Dr Henry Huxley, was helped with the paper-hanging by another cousin, Joyce Kilburn, the daughter of Marian Huxley Collier.*

water—a little bar which you fasten to the light and dip into your water: it will boil a pint in about 5 minutes—very useful for shaving and the like, also for simple cooking, such as eggs and tea: much quicker than a spirit lamp.

I trust the weather treats you well: it howls with wind here.

Much haste. Love to all.

Yours
Aldous

158: MRS MARIA HUXLEY TO LEONARD HUXLEY

18 *Hampstead Hill Gardens,*
London
16 *July,* 1919

Dear Mr Huxley,

We arrived after all our 'peripeties' quite safely in our delightful little flat. I like it so much and am sure we will be very happy.

I have been much amused in seeing A[ldous] painting and sawing and being busy in the house. I never suspected him of being so handy at all. We had a depressingly cold and wet journey but now the sun is gaily bright and warm and makes life even more happy.

A[ldous] said you were coming back early in August which is a great pleasure to me as I had not expected to see you till later.

Will you please give my love to Mrs Huxley.

Yours affectionately
Maria

159: TO LEONARD HUXLEY

18 *Hampstead Hill Gardens*
5 *August,* 1919

Dearest Father,

I had meant to write before, but have been frantically busy with hosts of books to review and odds and ends of all sorts to write. Talking about things to write, I have just signed an agreement with Constables to do a book on Balzac for their 'Makers of the XIX Century' series to be finished by the end of 1920: it will be a big task, but interesting, I think. £50 down and royalties of 15%, which seems all right. It is a good series to get into. I am rather appalled at the prospect of having to read *all* Balzac!

We go to stay at Stocks next weekend—a prospect which M[aria] regards with certain qualms of terror!

I had a letter from Julian today. Slightly more cheerful, I thought.

158 *Aldous and Maria had been married at Bellem on 10 July.*

178

Love to the family, and all my best wishes and congratulations to Marjorie B[ruce].

Your loving son
Aldous

160: TO J. C. SQUIRE

18 *Hampstead Hill Gardens, N.W.*3
7 *August,* 1919

Dear Squire,

I enclose review on Selma Lagerlöf. [Brand Whitlock's] *Belgium under German Occupation* has never reached me. I dont know where it was sent. This is my permanent address. I found the *French Literature* waiting at Garsington a week ago. I will let you have the review by the beginning of next week.

I'm so sorry I have kept you waiting. I have been getting married in Belgium and setting up house here, so have had my hands very full. I am a bit more settled now. It would be pleasant to see you again. Couldn't we meet at luncheon one day?

Would you care for a sort of comprehensive review of French books that have appeared during the last 3 months? I see most of them as they come out.

Yours
Aldous Huxley

161: TO G. GIDLEY ROBINSON

18 *Hampstead Hill Gardens, N.W.*3
9 *August,* 1919

Dear Mr. Robinson,

The salt cellars have arrived and are not only beautiful, but very useful. My wife joins with me in thanking you for your very delightful gift. It was very kind of you to think of me after all these years. The Hill Side days seem to belong to an age before the flood. I hope I shall have an opportunity of seeing you again before long. Perhaps, if you ever come to London you would visit us in our little apartment here in Hampstead, where we are surrounded by trees and grass and enjoy a quiet that is like the quiet of the country. And withal only twenty-odd minutes in a Bus from Charing Cross.

I am very busy now, working for the *Athenaeum,* reviewing a lot and doing odds and ends for the paper, while I do a fair amount of work for

---

160 *On the reviews see the footnote to letter* 143. *In November,* 1919, *Squire started the* London Mercury, *with Huxley a regular contributor, but their arrangement ended after five months. Since April, Huxley had been a member of the editorial staff of the* Athenaeum, *under the editorship of J. Middleton Murry. In April,* 1920, *he became also dramatic critic for the* Westminster Gazette.

other papers as well and try, in the somewhat rare intervals, to do things of my own. It is a crowded sort of life, but I enjoy the work, and the whole atmosphere of the *Athenaeum* is so delightfully remote, in its purely literary preoccupations, from the horrors of the present that it is in a way restful work.

My father returns in a few days' time from his holiday in Scotland. I hope it will have done him good, for he was rather tired and run down when he set out. I hope that you also flourish. Thank you again so very much.

Yours sincerely
Aldous Huxley

162: MARIA AND ALDOUS HUXLEY TO JULIAN HUXLEY

18 *Hampstead Hill Gardens, N.W.*3
12 [*August*], 1919

My dear Julian,

I hope [. . .] that you will come back well and happy. I suppose you are having as hot and fine weather as we are. I adore it . . . except on week ends though, as long as one is in the train; the last one we spent with Mrs Humphry Ward the prospect of whom simply terrified me, however I found such a nice and charming old lady that all vanished except my momentary astonishment at her being so unlike Vernon Lee. We walked round of course, but only the exquisite kitchen garden did I love with peaches growing brightly[?] looking out by the next window panes.

On Sunday by tea time an immense family party was spreading itself as far as one could see and for one moment I really thought I would give way to terror and despair—a very snooty cousin and a sporty one—young ladies and old ones and an uncle and a lady—very thin and stern poor woman suffering from rheumatism.

Now next week end it is to your Aunt Sophie we go. She of course terrifies me to extremes though I have seen her twice—always equally energetic and wanting to rule. Gervas will have the young lady down he has just got engaged to—a Miss [Lindsey] Foot.

Our flat is quite delightful and comfortable. I love it and was already studying how one might find out one more room so as to enable us to remain here all our life—though I of course long to go to Italy—and Spain and all those wonderful places.

Aldous is working very hard but is well I think and happy. It was very nice seeing your father today—they came from Scotland this morning, which did not however seem to interfere very much with the energy of those two huge and enchanting babies. The elder one quite won my heart—he went on and on asking me if I did want to water the flowers, and longing for

162 *The conclusion of the letter is missing. Misdated 'le 12 Juillet 1919'.*

us to go, I am sure, as then he would be allowed to water them. What an amount of energy one wastes as children that one would give a fortune for now.

I shall end this by sending you my best wishes for your health and very best love for both of you.

Maria

We are going to have a pug and a cat—but I suppose this leaves you very cold. Also M[——] F[——] and Mrs L[——] have become enemies and parted.

My dear J,

I snatch a moment from a mass of work to thank you for your letter and to bid you hail, flourish and farewell. I hope the Lausanne man is doing you good and that you will return full of heartiness. How important it is! I wish one could do without sleep, that the days were twice as long and that my strength were as the strength of ten so that I could do all I want to do. But the impurity of my heart and the weakness of both flesh and spirit would make the task impossible even if the Almighty would do his part with the almanack.

If you are ever in Geneva I shd advise you to [. . . .]

[Aldous]

163: TO ARNOLD BENNETT

18 *Hampstead Hill Gardens, N.W.*3
[Circa 19 *November,* 1919]

Dear Mr. Bennett,

Siegfried Sassoon told me that you wanted to see my rendering of the 'Après Midi d'un Faune'. I hope you will accept this copy of the book in which it appeared. Let me hasten to add that I am not responsible for the linoleum in which it is bound: it is just one of Blackwell's little jokes.

Yours sincerely,
Aldous Huxley

164: TO LEONARD HUXLEY

6 *Square Alboni, Paris XVIe*
21 *January,* 1920

Dearest Father,

Here I am, taking the belated tail end of last year's holiday. Paris is at its best, blue sky and sunshine and a warmth which is quite improbable. I am staying with a friend, one Pierre Drieu la Rochelle, a young poet and writer, whose acquaintance I made last year in Belgium and whom I saw a good deal

---

163 *Bennett responded to Huxley's gift of* The Defeat of Youth *with an invitation to tea; their friendship lasted until Bennett's death.*

of later on in London. He is a charming and interesting creature. His flat is near the Trocadéro, with a fine view of the Seine and the Eiffel Tower.

I have been seeing a certain number of amusing people and hope to see more before I have done. I sight-see a certain amount, but museums here, as in most other places, have an irritating habit of being wholly or partially closed.

I had a last glimpse of Lewis and Mimi and saw them off on Monday for their journey to Poland, where they arrive to-morrow—what a horror!

Life here is very dear compared with what it was in old days—tho' with the exchange at 42 francs to a pound one finds oneself getting things pretty cheap. They seem here to be quite unable to cope with the profiteers who roar and ramp quite openly.

Love to Rosalind and the infants.

Your loving son
Aldous

165: TO THE HON. EDWARD SACKVILLE-WEST

18 *Hampstead Hill Gardens, N.W.*3
4 *March,* 1920

My dear Sackville West,

I was very glad to get your letter—the more so as I felt rather guilty about our last rencontre: for I promised to communicate and then lost your address. However, I trust you didn't regard my silence as too offensive. It wasnt meant to be.

I'm glad *Limbo* has amused you: yes, the personages in 'Happy Families' are facets of a single character—an application of the doctrine of the Trinity to psychological life.

Paris shd be amusing: I was there in January and had an entertaining time among the cubists of literature. But it's all very like London, with quite as little work of real importance being done—except, of course, in painting. I refrained from going to the ballet in Paris: somehow I have got extremely bored with it and am taking a holiday from it. In a year's time one will be able to go back to it with renewed gusto. What you must go and see in Paris is the Cirque Medrano which is by far the finest circus in the world—and an enchanting audience, bourgeois-cum-Montmartre, with a dash now, alas, of smart folk: for it's become rather a snobisme to go. If Jean Cocteau's play, *Le Boeuf sur le Toit*, is on at the Femina Theatre do go and tell me what it's like. He wrote *Parade*: and this shd be something in the same style. He is

164 *Lewis Gielgud and his wife Mimi (Elise) were going to Poland, where he was attached to the Red Cross as assistant to the Commissioner.*

165 *Sackville-West (later the fifth Baron Sackville) had been a pupil of Huxley at Eton.*

employing three marvellous clowns, the 3 Fratellini, to play in it. Cocteau has also rewritten *Romeo and Juliet*—for clowns!

Do let me know if you come to town before you go to Paris. My best wishes for Responsions. And oh, if you know of a cottage or small house in the country, anywhere, in charity tell me: for I must find one.

Yours ever,
Aldous Huxley

166: TO MRS KATE TERRY LEWIS GIELGUD

18 Hampstead Hill Gardens, N.W.3
Monday, [circa 12 April, 1920]

Dear Mrs. Gielgud,

Having been away for a few days I only got your letter today. I have not seen [C. D.] Warren for about 2 or 3 weeks and don't at all know what the thing in the *Referee* can signify, unless it is that he is on somebody's track. I have an appointment with him tomorrow, Tuesday, and I will let you know at once what the state of affairs is. It will be excellent if he has been successful. I cannot think why he wanted to put anything in the paper about it. I didn't see the *Referee* of that date, or I'd have asked him what his object was.

I had a letter from Lewis not long ago: he seemed very cheerful and happy, which is excellent.

Maria is on the whole very well and joins with me in sending her love. She goes into the nursing home towards the end of this week.

Yours very sincerely,
Aldous Huxley

167: TO ARNOLD BENNETT

18 Hampstead Hill Gardens, N.W.3
23 April, 1920

Dear Bennett,

Thank you very much for your letter. I have two plays on the stocks at the moment, neither, I fear, very suitable. One is a melodrama about Bolshevism—the break up of the Armies in 1917—what one wd call a West End melodrama as opposed to a Lyceum melo. But it is hardly in the style of the Lyric. I will get the agent to send it there to be read. The other is a one act farce that wd act about half an hour to ¾ and which has been printed in the current number of *Coterie*, of which I enclose a copy. I doubt if it's actable.

166 *To the mother of Lewis Gielgud. On 28 March, the Sunday* Referee *had announced under 'Dramatic Gossip by Carados' that Charles Denier Warren, play broker, was 'handling' a Bolshevik drama by Huxley called 'Red and White'. This rumour was premature. See the next letter, and cf. letter 229 and footnote.*

My wife has just had a son and has, I am thankful to say, weathered the tempest safely and auspiciously. These works of nature really do put works of art in the shade.

I hope I shall see you not too far hence in town.

Yours
Aldous Huxley

P.S. I find I have not a copy of *Coterie* by me: I'll send you one in the next day or two.

168: † TO DR B. G. BROOKS

18 *Hampstead Hill Gardens, N.W.*3
4 *May,* 1920

Dear Mr Brooks,

There are several little periodicals in which you will find utterances of the Dadaists. The most respectable is *Littérature,* which is edited by André Breton, Louis Aragon and Philippe Soupault, of whom Aragon is considerably the ablest. *Littérature* holds parley with both sides; the three I have mentioned are almost wholly dada in style and sympathy, but the paper also includes work by [Blaise] Cendrars, [Pierre] Drieu la Rochelle and such people, who have nothing to do with dada, and even of older men such as Paul Valéry and occasionally Gide. Then there is *Proverbe,* edited by Paul Eluard, who seems to me to be a man without any talent; *Proverbe* is very definitely a Dada organ and contains much of Tristan Tzara, [Francis] Picabia and others of the movement. The enclosed copy will show you the sort of thing it is. Most of the dadaist publications issue from a press named Au Sans Pareil, 102 Rue du Cherche Midi, Paris. Among the more recent of them are Soupault's *Rose des Vents,* and *Unique Eunuque,* by Picabia, with a preface by Tzara expressing a theory of poetry.

As for any connection between Dada and the old Italian futurist movement:—the dadaists repudiate futurism for its wild romanticism. But as a matter of fact there are a good many points in common. Only Dada is much more fundamental. Futurism demanded merely that one should be allowed to talk about trams and cinemas and electric light. Dada is out to destroy literature completely. Their watchword is 'vivre sans prétension'—just live without philosophizing or thinking. It is the destruction of the subject matter of a literature at which they first aim. Love is played out; philosophy is boring and untrue; all the old subjects are utterly dead and lifeless and it is a piece of intolerable pretentiousness to talk about them. Their own poetical theory, if they have any, is that one must get an immediate impression of life, uncontaminated by processes of digestive thought. So I take it, at least.

167 *See the preceding letter. The farce was 'Permutations among the Nightingales'. The Huxleys' son, Matthew, had been born on* 19 *April.*

Personally I don't much like their theories or their practice. Their satire is healthy, but I see no point in destroying literature; and for the most part I find their little utterances rather boring. Tzara has a certain curious talent; Aragon seems to me to have a great deal; he is very young and may do something. Of the advanced men who are not Dadaists, I like Cendrars very much. His *Du Monde Entier* (Nouvelle Revue Française) and *Dix-Neuf Poèmes Elastiques* (Au Sans Pareil) have admirable things in them. Drieu la Rochelle is good on occasion—but very very French, declamatory and logical. Cocteau is a man of fabulous cleverness, but not serious. He is just a mondain, who exploits himself for social success and does it very well. His 'young' style is purely a stunt. In the first three years of the war he was publishing poems that might almost have been written by Lamartine. I have a certain number of these people's volumes which I should be very happy to lend you, if you would care to read them.

In reprisal, may I ask you a question? Didn't you write a book called *Camelot*, published by Blackwell? If so, let me tell you that I liked it very much indeed. It seemed to me one of the very few books of verse of the last year which were worth writing. I wonder if you have anything you could spare for printing in *Coterie*, a periodical of which I am supposed to be one of the editors? I am afraid I can offer no payment and only a limited amount of glory. But still, if you care to, do let me have something.

If you ever come to London, do let me know and we might arrange a meeting.

> Yours sincerely,
> *Aldous Huxley*

169: TO EDWARD MARSH

> *The Athenaeum*, 10, *Adelphi Terrace,*
> *London, W.C.*2
> *Thursday, 6 May,* 1920

Dear Marsh,

I don't know why the *Westminster [Gazette]* should have repudiated me so utterly, but your second letter reached me in safety. Thank you for all you say very much. There is a good deal in what I have written so far that now appears to me strange and undesirable—the result of pursuing the wrong method, of following a spiral inwards, instead of outwards, if I may express myself by a metaphor which is only partially comprehensible to me and probably wholly [not] so to anyone else! The Sermon, by the way, is lifted almost without alteration from a really superb tract I came upon the other day.

169 *Sermon: apparently the one in Chapter IX of* Crome Yellow (1921); *but most of the novel had not yet been written.*

I hope one of these evenings you will share a modest dinner before a first night. If I may I will suggest one—perhaps one of the [Sacha] Guitry evenings—later on.

Yours very sincerely,
Aldous Huxley

170: TO HAROLD MONRO

18 *Hampstead Hill Gardens, N.W.*3
31 *May,* 1920

Dear Monro,

After all I find Thursday impossible; so sorry. Would Friday do instead? I suggest meeting at the *Commercio* in Frith St, Soho at about 1.0 on that day.

By the way—some business. I am now working at the Chelsea Book Club; we are having a show of [Charles] Winzer, and [Arundel] del Re tells me you have some of his paintings. Cd you let us have them for the exhibition? I will telephone about it tomorrow.

Yours
A L Huxley

About Wed:—I fear I have a theatre to go to as critic that evening. Otherwise I shd have liked much to come.

171: TO LEONARD HUXLEY

18, *Hampstead Hill Gardens, N.W.*3
23 *June,* 1920

Dearest Father,

You heap coals of fire:—and at 63/- a ton too—on my head. I have never thanked you for your last letter and the book and here you write again. My only justification is that we [have] been very busy (typewriting will be easier and quicker) darting about from here to Chelsea, from Chelsea to the *Athenaeum* and so on and so forth, as physically restless as continually and changingly active in mind. I have bought a bicycle on which I now do my voyages. Very good exercise going from Hampstead to Chelsea and back; quite ten miles, I imagine, the double journey, which I take through two

---

170 *The Chelsea Book Club was a literary bookshop in Cheyne Walk, opposite Chelsea Old Church. Opened in* 1919 *by Arundel del Re, it stocked English and French* éditions de luxe *and served as a gathering place for booklovers and young writers. Huxley worked for del Re for several months, apparently only a few hours a day. Another adviser was Antonio Pastor, later a professor of Spanish. The business soon got into financial difficulties and was reorganized by Seymour Leslie. See Leslie's* The Jerome Connexion (*London,* 1964).

171 *Leonard Huxley's book of poems, published by John Murray, was called* Anniversaries.

parks, so that it is very pleasant. Also from Chelsea to the *Adelphi* and the *Athenaeum*, which I do by the long embankments.

We are well settled in now, with all our alterations duly made. Our little hole with the sink has been given gas and lined with shelves, so that it makes a really excellent little kitchen. M's room has been distempered and serves pretty comfortably as nursery. Our little maid is a great success; intelligent, full of initiative and extremely good with the infant. We hope to go down to Garsington within the next week. I shall come up and down for a bit before I take my holiday.

I liked your book very much. Some things, like the 'Unfinished Symphony' piece, are admirable. What a nest of singing birds! Though I sometimes feel that, in this hectic life of activity, I shall never find much time for warbling. There is nothing but a commercial success that can free one from this deadly hustle. I shall go on producing plays till I can get one staged and successful. It is the only thing to do. It is quite extraordinary, the badness of the ordinary play. To go to them is just like reading second or third rate novels. Curious that the playwrights shouldn't have arrived at that reasonable average of efficiency to which their colleagues the novelists have come. It oughtn't to be difficult to outdo them at their own game.

Julian comes to us for the night to-morrow and Margaret, I hope, to luncheon. It's a long time since I saw either of them. [. . . .]

I heard a pleasing tale about the effects of analysis the other day; told of D. H. Lawrence, the slightly insane novelist, who was analysed for his complexes, dark and tufty ones, tangled in his mind. The complexes were discovered, and it is said that Lawrence has now lost, along with his slight sexual mania, all his talent as a writer and produces mild little murmurings in the style of Michael Fairlees.

Well, I must be off to the theatre. Good bye and love to you all with pious hopes for the weather. Maria sends her love and so would Matthew, who waxes and grows fat, if he were capable of doing more than eat, sleep and periodically yell.

Your loving son
Aldous

172: TO HAROLD MONRO

18, *Hampstead Hill Gardens, N.W.*3
24 *June,* 1920

Dear Monro,

I enclose two short pieces, the only things I have by me. As for prose

---

172 *Two short pieces: 'Pain' and 'Summer Night'; Monro accepted the latter for the* Chapbook, *but did not print it. He had included an article by Huxley in his March,* 1920, *number; he published the poem 'Love Letter' in January,* 1921.

poems, I feel entirely incompetent to edit any collection of them, seeing that I don't know of anybody who writes them and that I can't satisfactorily formulate for myself the formula and theory of them. There are so many things that prose poems oughtn't to be, that I hardly know what they ought to be, or indeed whether they ought to exist at all.

Yours,
Aldous Huxley

173: TO LEONARD HUXLEY

The Manor House,
Garsington, Oxford
23 July, 1920

Dearest Father,

I'm sorry I forgot to answer your question about Grandpater's things. If Julian doesn't want them I think I'd like the medals best. I shall probably be up in town on Thursday and will try to look in at the office, or B[racknell] G[ardens] if you're not there, for a talk.

You will have had M's letter with photographs of the infant by now. Our history is uneventful—the weather making most outdoor occupations precarious or impossible. I rush periodically to town, where I have been very busy arranging a loan exhibition of Walter Sickert's paintings, which has been a great success.

I am slightly irritated at the attentions of the *Daily Express* which has elected to make of me and several other youthful poets its Giant Gooseberry for this year's Silly Season. A most impertinent article about us all, headed 'The Asylum School', appeared 2 or 3 days ago and they are following it up. So I suppose we shall be in for a merry August. I am preparing counter-blasts; the man who signs the article has written verse himself—and what verse! It is here that he gives himself away into an enemy's hands. I hope to make him sit up before he has done.

Love to the family.

Your loving son
Aldous

173 '*The Asylum School*' (Daily Express, 20 *July,* 1920) *was by Louis J. McQuilland, who ridiculed the verse of the Sitwells, Iris Tree, and Huxley—'the clever gibberish of Aldous Huxley'. The article was followed up with an amusing correspondence, in which the Sitwells figured largely, over the next three weeks. It all looks rather like an arranged demonstration, especially since Huxley failed to participate.*

174: †TO DR B. G. BROOKS

The Mount, Garsington, Oxford
Stations Oxford 6 Miles, Wheatley 3 Miles
30 July, 1920

Dear Brooks,

I am glad my wire reached you safely. I shall actually be staying in Oxford next week for a day or two and it will be easy to meet. But if you care to make an expedition into the country—you see the distances and the possible station, Wheatley, on the Oxford-High Wycombe line—do come out here for a talk. I am in lodgings here with my wife and we should be delighted to see you and your friend on Sunday in the afternoon (I am rather afraid lunch wd scarcely be possible in our little digs, or I wd have suggested that you shd have come earlier). If you come on Sunday I can offer as a bait the presence of T. S. Eliot, the poet, who will be staying the weekend with my friends the Morrells here. Do come if you can any time on Sunday afternoon. There are buses from Carfax as far as Cowley Village, from which it is about 2¼ miles to walk. If Sunday is impossible we cd arrange a meeting in Oxford on Wednesday or Thursday of next week.

Yours sincerely
Aldous Huxley

175: MARIA AND ALDOUS HUXLEY TO JULIAN HUXLEY

The Manor House,
Garsington, Oxford
30 July, 1920

My dear Julian,

It *is* nice of you to be so quick about Bellem and willing to do it at all. I know nothing more about it than what I wrote, and wrote to mother at once asking her to write directly to you as being the quickest and safest way to have no muddles. I am sure she will ask you all to stay when it is habitable and you will find it enchanting and well worth while such trouble and anxiety. Aldous was very pleased with his present—in fact he is writing about it now I believe. I am sending Juliette this little photo of baby and Mlle: [?] which I think adorable—we had a great photographic campaign in order to get a real good picture for enlargement proved for my grandmothers birthday and we succeeded beyond hopes. I am so glad to hear by Naomi that she is well. Have you such villainous and muggy weather too? We suffer severely from it. Going baby nurse and all to the Haldanes from Tuesday to Saturday—it will be so nice and I hope Mrs Haldane will give

174 *The party at Garsington on 1 August included the Morrells, T. S. Eliot and Vivienne Eliot, the Huxleys, Mark Gertler, J. T. Sheppard, B. G. Brooks, and Brooks's future wife.*

189

me many hints and advices—he was so ill for a few days but the woman doctor—I shall now swear by them put him right again. Well now good bye and many grateful loves—also much love to Juliette.

Maria

Thank you so much for the sox, which I shall always wear next my heart. And thanks to Naomi too, if she is still with her: and tell her that I hope to thank her personally next week, when we meet, I hope, at Cherwell. By the way, before I forget; I hear you possess a complete Balzac. Might I borrow it for a bit while I do my studies on the monster? If you wd tell me where it is and give me a note for the people in the house I cd come and fetch it while I'm in Oxford.

I am giving up the Chelsea Book Club, which is far too bankrupt to pay me anything like the salary [. . .] promised me [. . . .] I can't afford to spend time and energy for nothing. However, I have a good job in prospect to take the place of that—sordid journalism but a screw of £400 which, at the moment and in the circs, I can't refuse. Journalism is paying in the inverse ratio of the goodness of the paper, which is rather melancholy. I shd like to be rid of the whole damned thing, but there's no chance yet.

Love to you both.

Farewell
ALH

176: TO SEYMOUR LESLIE

The Chelsea Book Club,
65 Cheyne Walk, S.W.3
12 August, 1920

Dear Leslie,

Once more moderately recovered, I have come down to see what's doing.

I make no claims against the business. It has paid me £12 and I don't wish to burden it any further.

As I am excessively busy and overworked, I shall be glad if [Alex] Whitehead can be empowered as soon as possible to sign cheques. My visits here must necessarily be spasmodic and it is necessary to have someone with the power on the spot.

Whenever I can, however, I will come down and talk to Whitehead or Miss R[oss] J[ohnstone] about French books etc. to order. I see most of the better ones as they appear and are sent out for review and am generally pretty well up to date with that knowledge.

I very much regret having had to give up active co-operation in the business. But it takes one all one's time to make a living.

Yours sincerely,
Aldous Huxley

176 *Alex Whitehead was a bookshop manager appointed for the daily running of the Chelsea Book Club; Miss Ross Johnstone, the shop assistant.*

18 *Hampstead Hill Gardens, N.W.3*
1 *November,* 1920

My dear Naomi,

You haven't said where your play is to be performed—whether at Oxford or in London. If the former I don't think I can make any promises, as I am always busy and never have a holiday. If the latter it might be more feasible. In any case I'd like to see the triplets or trilogy or whatever it is. I very much liked your obscene play on seeing it again in *Coterie* in print.

I have just helped to float a marvellous paper belonging to the *Vogue* people,—*House and Garden* (run by a 'staff of experts' as the advertisement says, or otherwise by me and a young girl). It is a huge success: more than £1000 worth of advertisements in the first number, of which the first edition of 15,000 has sold out in a week; and we are reprinting. I wish I reaped more of the profits than I do; but I don't do too badly. I now see that the only possible papers are those with pictures: nothing else can hope to pay. I am hoping to get the *Vogue* people to give me a paper called the *Patrician* for my own. I cd make it marvellously amusing and it wd *pay*!

Love from both of us to you and your mother.

ALH

I see that I have written on the wrong side of this ingenious writing paper, so that I will have to put it into an envelope after all. More expense!

178: TO LEONARD HUXLEY

18 *Hampstead Hill Gardens, N.W.3*
Wednesday, [17 *November,* 1920]

Dearest Father,

You may set your mind at rest about the question of baptism. There is

177 *Naomi Mitchison's play for performance was 'Barley, Honey and Wine',
never published; it was set in her imaginary country, Marob. The 'obscene play', called
'The Furniture', had appeared in* Coterie (*Autumn,* 1920) *under the pseudonym
'Michal'.*

178 *Baptism: when confronted with the question of infant baptism for his son
Leonard in* 1861, *T. H. Huxley had decided against disappointing his wife's wishes,
though he himself found the rite meaningless; see Leonard Huxley's comments in* The
Life and Letters of Thomas Henry Huxley (*London,* 1900), *I,* 223. *Leonard, in
similar circumstances, had followed his father's example. Evan Morgan: apparently
this was one of the occasions on which Morgan was talking of assuming holy orders or
the monastic life. His Catholic spiritual advisers always managed to dissuade him.
Berkhampstead: Maria had gone to visit George and Janet Trevelyan, then living at
Berkhampstead to be near their children Humphry and Mary (afterwards Mrs
Moorman), who were at school there. Janet Trevelyan was a daughter of Mrs Humphry
Ward.*

no question of it. The tale about Evan Morgan is, so far as I am aware, a cock and bull affair. I have never seen a man less monastic than he was when I saw him 3 or 4 days ago.

Maria has got safely to Berkhampstead. I hope to get down for a long weekend.

Your loving son
Aldous

179: TO LEONARD HUXLEY

18 *Hampstead Hill Gardens*
Thur[*sday, 2 December*, 1920]

Dearest Father,

Thanks for your letter of enquiry. The patient is quite recovered. It was the heat and bad air at the Lyceum dinner which affected me, I think: added to the nervous job of having to speak they made me feel faint and afterwards extremely sick. My visceral reactions to things are always powerful! However I am perfectly all right after a day's repose on Tuesday—only resolved never to go to one of these stuffy functions again: spiritually stuffy as well as atmospherically, in this case; for the good dames of the Lyceum Club cannot be said to rival Skegness in bracing qualities.

I'm glad you liked the Everyman Juliet: I thought her excellent. There is a very good production of *King Lear* at the Old Vic, which has become amazingly effective in these last months. Certainly the best Shakespeare production one can now see in London.

Apologies for the scrawl: this is written in the tram.

Love to R.

Your loving son
Aldous

180: TO JULIAN HUXLEY

18 *Hampstead Hill Gardens, N.W.*3
23 *December*, 1920

My dear J,

Just a word to say that if you're coming to town after Xmas I shan't be

179 *Huxley's collapse at the Lyceum dinner is mentioned in T. S. Eliot's contribution to* Aldous Huxley 1894-1963: A Memorial Volume, *ed. Julian Huxley* (1965).

180 *T. W. Earp's flat, which belonged also to Russell Green, of* Coterie, *was Huxley's headquarters before he went to Italy for the summer. Roy Campbell, a guest at the same time, describes the ménage and especially the voluble and irrepressible Green in his autobiography* Light on a Dark Horse (1952). *Huxley seems to have aroused defensive feelings in Campbell, to whom he appeared 'pedantic' because he studied animals in books instead of subduing them by main force and slaughtering and cooking them. On the collaboration with Gielgud see letter 229.*

able to put you up, as I suggested last time we met. I am going to Paris for the inside of a week on the 28th and after that shall move straight into my new quarters—36 Regent Square, Bloomsbury—in Earp's flat.

Xmas for me is the blackest and bloodiest of seasons, as it means that I have to go to at least two and sometimes three theatres per diem and write about them afterwards. I am a total wreck in consequence.

In Paris I hope to stay with Lewis Gielgud and Mimi, there to write up in frantic haste a new play which we have 'begotten by despair upon improbability' [sic].

To Italy, I hope, in March. I shall be damned glad to have a little leisure and breathing space to think and write properly.

Does the infant [Anthony Huxley] flourish? I trust so. Ours does immensely. May your Xmas be merrier than mine—it cd hardly fail to be.

Yours
ALH

P.S. Now I come to think on it, there *might* be a couch at Earp's if you wanted to come up: but I can't tell till I am there.

181: TO ARNOLD BENNETT

Paris
29 December, 1920

Dear Bennett,
Thank you very much for your extremely nice and encouraging letter—which I would have answered before if I had not been busy beyond the dreams of avarice: three theatres per diem during Christmas week, not to mention ordinary work and the supererogatory business of packing up our flat.

I am not going to Italy till March and shall be in London from next week onwards; so I hope very much to see you then. I will come and pay my respects one Sunday, if I may.

My wife is staying in Belgium until she goes south; and meanwhile we are snatching a brief and restless holiday in Paris.

A bientôt, I hope.

Yours very sincerely,
Aldous Huxley

182: TO LEONARD HUXLEY

36 Regent Square, W.C.
Wednesday, [23 March, 1921]

Dearest Father,
I enclose a cheque for £15 as a first instalment. The rest will follow next month. Off tomorrow—for which relief much thanks, as I am feeling exceedingly tired and in need of a rest. I shall try and get really well while

I'm in Italy. This perpetual lack of perfect physical health is intolerable. This was brought home to me more acutely than usual today by the refusal of the London Life Association to insure me in my present condition. It is absurd and rather humiliating to be a Bad Life and I am resolved to undertake no more work of this sort until I am definitely a Good Life, which I am sure I can easily become by leading a decent existence for a few months.

Much love to you and Rosalind.

Your loving son
Aldous

183: TO LEONARD HUXLEY

Villa Minucci,
4 *Via Santa Margherita Montici, Florence*
1 *April, 1921*

Dearest Father,

Here we are, pretty finally settled into our new abode in the wing of a very pleasant villa nearly opposite the Fasolas. We have three rooms, one more than thirty feet long, which we divide into two by means of a screen, one of about twenty by twelve and the other—the kitchen, about fifteen by twelve. We eat in the kitchen, sit in one half of the long room and sleep in the other, while Bella and Baby sleep in the other room. The flat is furnished adequately, though somewhat hideously and we pay a hundred and fifty lire a month for it, which is not much as prices go here now and singularly little when one looks at the sum in terms of the English exchange. From the western windows we get a marvellous view—a valley sloping away from the house in the foreground, planted with olives and vines, with the church of San Miniato on the hill on the opposite side; to the right, looking down the valley, we see almost the whole of Florence lying in the plain, a sort of Oxford from Boar's Hill effect, only very much more so. Altogether, I dont think we could have found a pleasanter habitation, nor one that would be much more convenient. We are sufficiently far out of and above the town to have all the advantages of country air and surroundings and at the same time

183 *The Fasolas: friends of the Nys family in Florence and hosts to Maria, her mother and sisters during the war. It was their daughter Costanza Fasola, Maria's particular friend, who gave her the nick-name Coccola ('berry', a pet name), which Aldous took up. The Fasolas lived at Castel Montici, 15 Via Santa Margherita, and had a house also at Forte dei Marmi, both of these residences being occupied by the Huxleys at different times. J. B. Pinker: Huxley's transactions with this well known literary agent were brief, for Pinker died in February, 1922. With Eric S. Pinker, who managed the agency thereafter, and with Eric's brother J. Ralph Pinker, who ran the London office after Eric opened a New York branch in 1926, Huxley had regular dealings until the Pinker brothers wound up their business affairs in 1939 and 1940, respectively.*

one can be at the centre of the city in twenty minutes or so by the tram, which runs at the bottom of the hill.

I have been doing little but sleep and eat during these days—early bed and a siesta in the heat of the day after lunch. The régime is already doing me a lot of good. After two or three days of cloud and occasional rain, the weather has turned brilliantly fine: baking sun, but enough wind to make the heat delicious.

Matthew is fabulously large and healthy, the admiration of all who see him. It requires all the energy of the faithful Bella to cope with him. She is always exactly the same, the only change being that her round red face is a little wrinkled, like a ripening apple.

We calculate that we shall be able to live on between fifteen hundred and two thousand lire a month—cheap according to the exchange, but of course dear according to nominal values. How the Italians themselves exist is a mystery. The prices are fantastic—sugar at nine lire a kilo, meat at twenty, eggs, relatively cheap, at fifty-five centimes each (in Germany, Bella tells me, they cost anything up to three marks a piece). The increase over pre-war prices must be at least four hundred per cent, if not more. A fall is anticipated fairly soon, but there is as yet no sign of the break in prices which began in England in the autumn. Bread is very strictly rationed and is of pretty bad quality. For fuel we depend on charcoal which is [toler]ably efficient. Our kitchen range has two little charcoal furnaces. When one wants intense heat, one fans the charcoal with a large straw fan. For slow cooking one leaves it alone. We are unfortunately without electricity, though it is laid on all round, so we depend on oil lamps and candles.

The revolutionary excitements of a month ago have quite died down for the time being and the police are busily engaged in trying to make out that the trouble was exclusively engineered by foreigners, as though there were not amply enough revolutionary feeling among the Italians themselves to bring about any disturbance. With this laudable end in view they are arresting all the defenceless foreigners they can lay their hands on, particularly students at the university belonging to nationalities which are powerless to afford any protection, such as Hungarians, Russians and occasionally Germans. A number of these poor wretches have been flung into gaol merely on the general principle that there must be scapegoats and that foreign scapegoats are the best.

Would you mind, in your next letter, telling me what is the address of [J. B.] Pinker, the Literary Agent. I have had some slight dealings with him before and shall use him now to dispose of stuff in America for me. Meanwhile, I have mislaid his address. It is in the telephone book, I know.

Goodbye for the present. Love to you both. M will write when she has time; but she has been very busy moving into the new house.

Your loving son,
Aldous

29 *Viale Morin,*
Forte dei Marmi (Lucca)
31 *May,* 1921

Dearest Father,

You will see from the changed address that we are now established by the sea. It was beginning to get rather hot and unpleasant in Florence, the more so since there had been a long spell of scirocco with thunder perpetually in the air, so that it was a relief to get away. We have here a minute little house with four rooms, very clean, however, and well furnished, with comfortable beds and a good batterie de cuisine, with a garden behind, entirely planted out in vines. It will, I think, be perfect if we can solve the servant problem satisfactorily; for at present we are having some difficulty in securing a local maid to come in and do the work. However, I think we are on the track of what we want now.

Forte is an admirable place. You will find it on the map about twenty miles north of Pisa on the coast, the next village beyond the large and fashionable watering place of Viareggio, which is about seven or eight miles away and connected with us by an electric tram. It is, unfortunately, a growing place, which has been getting fuller and more popular during the last few years, owing to the fact that the Italians have been unable to go abroad, as they used to. Still, it is far from being overcrowded yet and so far it is entirely deserted; for we are practically the first arrivals. The beach is flat and sandy and continues flat and sandy for miles in either direction—to beyond Massa to the north and to the mouth of the Arno at least to the south. Behind the village is a flat coastal plain, about four or five miles wide and rising out of the plain are the marble mountains of the Carrara district. The view of the hills across the plain is marvellous and there are fine walks to be made among them when the weather gets cool in autumn. Marble is the most important local product. One sees slabs of it being dragged about by teams of enormous white oxen with long horns and melancholy black eyes, and there is a little town a few miles off at the foot of the hills which derives its whole subsistence by making tombstones and monumental statuary for the U.S.A.

The coastal plain provides some very agreeable rambles. It is full of streams and ditches—indeed, it must once have been a marsh, I imagine—and by reason of its dampness, very fertile. One gets entirely English landscapes in it—rich watermeadows and very green copses and level fields of corn, with every here and there beautiful plantations of poplars, which they grow for charcoal.

The day's programme here is simple and unvarying. Work in the morning till twelve or half past, then a bathe, then lunch, then a rest till four; then tea and a little more work, till about half past five or six, when one goes out for a walk till dinner time; then reading or work till bed. Later on, I suppose, one bathes twice a day and for hours at a time; but as yet it is not hot enough for that. The heat at present is equal to that of a good English summer. One has all one's meals out of doors, wears a shirt, flannel trousers and a pair of sandals and remains a long time in the water without getting cold. The sea and the mountains provide alternate breezes, one during the heat of the early afternoon and the other in the evening. Another curiously regular phenomenon is a little shower of rain in the early part of the afternoon, accompanied by distant grumbles of thunder in the mountains.

Baby flourishes very well, enjoys paddling and playing in the sand. He begins to walk quite a lot by himself. He refuses to talk, finding roaring simpler and as expressive.

Rachel Russell comes to stay with us to-day. She has been in Florence for some time and will stop here at Forte for a bit on her way home. Florence was so thronged with people of one's acquaintance or with people who wanted to make one's acquaintance that the problem was to conceal oneself. I shudder when I think of the number of awful people who passed through the town while we were there and whom we escaped only by chance or cunning. The English colony is a queer collection; a sort of decayed provincial intelligentsia. The brightest spots among the permanent inhabitants are funny old Miss Paget (Vernon Lee) and Geoffrey and Lady Sybil Scott, who live at the Villa Medici at Fiesole. But I shouldn't much like to live in Florence permanently. To begin with it is too cold in winter and too hot in summer; then there are the inhabitants and finally there is the place itself, of which one could easily get tired—not of the country, which is astonishingly beautiful, but of the town. For my taste, at least, Florence is too tre- and quattrocento. There is too much Gothic in the architecture and too much primitive art in the galleries. I am an enthusiastic post-Raphaelite. Sixteenth and seventeenth century architecture is what I enjoy and there is very little of it in Florence. One must go to Rome for the architecture and to Venice for the painting. And then of course there are masses of little towns, like Vicenza in the north and Lecce in the south, where you find the most fabulous outflowerings of baroque building. In time, I hope, I shall get to these places.

One summer you ought really try to get out here. You could start in the middle of April, take a month's sightseeing before the weather got hot and then come to the sea for five or six weeks, retiring before the July heats became excessive. Well, now I must be off to meet Rachel at Pietrasanta, our nearest station. Love to all.

Your loving son,
Aldous

P.S. I enclose another instalment of the national debt. I am keeping £1 as you said for Matthew.

29 Viale Morin
Forte dei Marmi (Lucca)
28 June, 1921

Dearest Father,

The days flit past here like pictures on a cinema film; one is hardly aware of their passing. It must be a long time since I wrote. But a happy country has no history. We lead a calm and uneventful and enjoyable life. I am working hard at my Peacockian novel, which I have pledged myself to finish by the end of July—rather an undertaking, but I hope and think I shall be able to carry it out successfully. I do about five or six hours work a day, recreating myself with bathing, always once and sometimes twice a day. After a period of frequent thunder, the weather has settled down to uninterrupted fineness; warm, but not at all unpleasantly hot. So far we have the place almost entirely to ourselves, but I imagine that, in July and August, it will get pretty crowded.

We went for a little jaunt to Lucca last week—about fifteen miles away, inland, to the south east. One passes in the train over a very curious piece of country, a part of the coastal plain at the foot of the mountains, where there is a huge shallow lake, round the borders of which the land is so dankly fertile that they grow rice. Malarious, I should imagine. Here, though there is quite a lot of water just inland, there seems to be no malaria. When one reads the account of the fever stricken districts before the days of quinine, one wonders how the Italians survived at all. In many places, of course, they didn't and there is a great deal of fertile land in the south that has been practically deserted because of the disease. However, the fighting of malaria is one of the few things the Italians have shown themselves efficient in. Lucca is a very pleasant little town—not so little, either, for it must be nearly as populous as Oxford. The old quarter, within the fortifications, is mostly sixteenth, seventeenth and eighteenth century, with islands here and there of mediaeval antiquity. There is a very fine cathedral which contains an astonishing crucifix called the Volto Santo or holy face. We could not see the thing itself, which is only produced on certain holy days, when it still performs miracles, but the photographs of it are very remarkable. It is a wooden figure, larger than life; a bearded face with eyes of crystal. The face with its shining eyes must be peculiarly arresting; hence its curious name. Its history is entirely obscure. That it was a very famous relic in the 11th century is attested by the fact that William Rufus's favorite oath was 'by the Holy Face of Lucca'. Where it came from and when, is unknown. There is a legend, of course, that it was brought from Palestine. But as the thing seems

185 Peacockian novel: Crome Yellow. Spitzbergen: Julian Huxley, regularly Senior Demonstrator in Zoology at Oxford, where he was a Fellow of New College, went as a member of the Oxford University Expedition to Spitzbergen in 1921.

to be a piece of Byzantine sculpture of the best period, this seems a little doubtful. I shall try and go to Lucca when they take the relic out and carry it in procession round the town in September. It is a very great feast, and ought to be interesting.

I had a postcard from Julian in Norway. I suppose he is at Spitzbergen by this time. I shall be interested to hear how he gets on there.

Our servant problem is now successfully solved and we have a very nice and efficient girl, who comes in for the morning and early part of the afternoon, to do the house and cook. Prices are descending here. The ubiquitous fascisti have swooped upon the village and established an arbitrary rate above which nobody is allowed to sell. One is grateful for the intention, but one would have preferred that they should have allowed the prices to come down automatically as they were doing. For, in practice, the sole result of the fixation has been that no commodities come on the market. The activities of the Fascisti in this country are quite unbelievable. One cannot imagine how the Italian population suffers an entirely irresponsible private organization to act as the fascio does—sometimes usurping powers that should belong to the state, sometimes resorting to incredible acts of violence and brutality. People look on with a sort of resignation. It is the same attitude as one sees over the whole world—blank fatalistic resignation to stupid and wicked governments, to anything or any person with power. The post-war mentality is certainly a very extraordinary thing.

I hope Rosalind and the infants flourish. Maria sends her love and so does Matthew, who is incredibly hearty and now runs about like an express train, his one passion being to get into the sea.

Farewell.

Your loving son,
Aldous

186: TO LEONARD HUXLEY

29 Viale Morin,
Forte dei Marmi (Lucca)
4 August, 1921

Dearest Father,

It's a long time, I fear, since I wrote. My only excuse is that I have been frightfully busy with my book, which is on the verge of completion. The first 30 odd thousand words have gone off to Chatto's so that they can start printing at once if they want to, and I hope to have done the rest by the end of next week. It will be a comfort, as it has been rather a strain finishing it. Practically, I have written the whole thing, some 60,000 words in the 2 months I have been here: which is pretty good going. After it's done I shall take a rest. At the end of the month we go to Rome for a week or 10 days where we have been lent a flat. It will be a good opportunity to see the place comfortably and inexpensively: and unless the weather changes, it will be by no means too oppressively hot. In early Sept we hope that Lewis Gielgud and his wife may be coming here for a bit: which will be amusing and at the end of the month or beginning of Oct, Maria and I will be coming back to cope with the housing problem, as our flat falls in and we must move our furniture by the end of Oct.

If I can possibly manage it I shall come out here again and go south to Naples for the cold months. The thought of replunging into journalism appals me; I had been living for 2 years in a perpetual state of fatigue and I don't want to go back to it if I can help it. Moreover, here in Italy—if the exchange keeps up between 70 and 80, which there is every likelihood of its doing for months to come—I can live much more comfortably for £300 a year than I can in England on £750 or £800. The question is whether I can secure that £300. I hope to have from £70 to £100 in hand in the autumn. My book, if it does as well as the last, should bring me another £100. Letting the flat furnished one ought to be able to make at least £50 a year and what with stories and another volume of collected tales in the spring I think I ought to be able to make up the rest. But it wd be better to feel more completely secure and I'd like to start off with more of the necessary cash in hand. I shall see what the prospect is like in the autumn. By the way, do you think Rosalind cd manage to put us up at any rate for a week or two at the end of Sept—beginning of Oct? We shd be most grateful if it were feasible.

Delicious and not oppressive weather is the rule here. There is always a breeze from sea or mountains to temper the sunshine and an occasional thunderstorm cools the air. The first grapes are ripe: melons, watermelons, greengages, plums abound. Figs will soon be here. It is a succession of pleasant things.

Our neighbourhood was recently the scene of an extraordinary conflict between the Fascisti and the authorities who have, now for the first time, dared to stand up against them. A band of no less than 700 Fascisti, collected from all Tuscany, had assembled some few miles higher up the coast to 'make a demonstration' in a town, inland from here, which is apparently renowned for its socialist tendencies. News of the expedition leaked out and when the Fascisti army arrived in the early morning, after having marched all night along the coast, they were met by troops. There was a scuffle and the troops fired. About a dozen were killed by the volley and some six more were slaughtered by the infuriated peasants of the district. A horrible and extraordinary episode. Now, however, the Fascisti and the Socialists have made a treaty of peace. It remains to be seen whether they will keep it.

Maria and I made a very pleasant excursion the other day. Starting at about six—for one can only make exertions at early morning or evening—we walked some 7 or 8 miles along the coast to Marina di Massa and thence inland to the main town of the district, Massa. A marvellous walk, between the sea on the one hand and the peaks of the Apuan Alps on the other and between the beach and the hills two or 3 miles of wooded and cultivated plain with lovely quiet rivers, almost Dutch in the flatness and smoothness, flowing down through it into the sea. Massa itself is an agreeable little town standing at the foot of the mountains, with an enormous and fantastic rococo palace in the middle of it, once the residence of the Prince of Massa-Carrara, one of the smallest potentates of Italy.

What news of Julian from Spitzbergen? I shall be interested to hear. Also of you, for it is a long time since I had a letter. Love to both of you from both of us.

Your loving son
Aldous

187: TO JULIAN HUXLEY

29 Viale Morin,
Forte dei Marmi (Lucca)
24 August, 1921

My dear Julian,
Your letter from Copenhagen has just reached me after a good deal of circumnavigation. It all sounds very agreeable in the septentrional regions and I shall be interested to hear more about them when I see you next— which I hope will be in October: for M and I are coming to England at least for a month or two then to find a new flat, as the lease of the old is expiring. If financial prospects are all right I mean to come back to Italy for the winter. At the present exchange one can live much more comfortably on £300 a year than in England on £800. The only bore is making the £300. However, I hope to be able to manage it all right, as I don't at all want to come back to London and stinking journalismus. It is a monstrous thing that one shouldn't have money—when one considers all the porchi di primo ordine who over-flow with it! However. . . .

Maria and I have just come back from a week in Rome, where we had been lent a flat to do some sightseeing. What a place! It inspires one at once with a kind of passion to know it utterly and inside out. We came back through Florence and the spectacle of that second rate provincial town with its repulsive Gothic architecture and its acres of Christmas card primitives made me almost sick. The only points about Florence are the country out-side it, the Michelangelo tombs, Brunelleschi's dome and a few rare pictures. The rest is simply dung when compared with Rome. The Florentine country is, of course, as good as anything in the world; but the town . . . pooh. I was astonished to find that Rome is principally and predominantly a seventeenth century town: it was practically invented by Bernini. I feel sorry for the people who come to Rome with the preconceived certitude of the badness of Bernini and the seventeenth century. They are left nothing but Michelangelo and Raphael, the Coliseum, the columns and arches and the insupportably dreary spectacle of the rubbish in the froums. One could write a whole history of 17th century Rome round that astonishing Bernini who lived from 1600 to 1680, started his artistic career at 14 and went on to the day of his death, was the intimate of eight popes, who carved statues (and among them the most astonishing and surprising works that have ever been produced), painted pictures, drew, engineered theatrical displays, built, wrote, did everything.

I have been excessively busy—up to the time when I went to Rome—finishing a Peacockian novel for publication in the autumn. It was a job to get it done: I hope it will amuse a little when it appears. It is pleasingly baroque. I have a plan to do a gigantic Peacock in an Italian scene. An incredibly large castle—like the Sitwells' at Monte Gufone [Montegufoni], the most amazing place I have ever seen in my life—divided up, as Monte Gufone was divided till recently, into scores of separate habitations, which will be occupied, for the purposes of my story, by the most improbable people of every species and nationality. Here one has the essential Peacockian datum—a houseful of oddities. The details may be left to look after themselves; but I think I shall introduce into the texture of the book a few Lives of Queer Men—a life of Caravaggio, a life of Paganini, even, perhaps, a life of the astonishing Bernini. I am giving Realismus a little holiday: these descriptions of middle class homes are really too unspeakably boring. One must try and be readable. Meanwhile I have a choice specimen of detective-story realismus in *The English Review* for August—variations on the theme of the Greenwood Case: abbastanza buffo, I flatter myself.

What I should like now more than anything is a year or two of quiet devoted simply to seeing places and things and people: to living, in fact. When one hasn't much vitality or physical energy, it is almost impossible to live and work at the same time. At least, I find it so. Life and work are always, for me, alternatives. Circumstances demand that I should work almost continuously, and I can't squeeze in enough living.

> 'Tis money alone will cure me
> And ease me of all my pain:
> 'Twill pay all my debts and ease all my lets,
> And my mistress who cannot endure me
> Will love me and love me again.

So wrote the profound [Thomas] Jordan, who was also of the opinion, if you remember, that oysters are aphrodisiacs and that 'Fish suppers will make a man hop like a Flea'. It wd be pleasant if I cd catch that £1000 scholarship for sending the deserving poor round the world. You might mention it to Jack

187 *Detective story: 'The Gioconda Smile', suggested by the case of Harold Greenwood, who was tried and acquitted at Carmarthen, in November, 1920, on the charge of poisoning his wife. Publication had been arranged by J. B. Pinker.*

[Haldane] when you see him; in any case I shall write to him soon to remind him of it.

By the way—before I forget it. In Rome I had my pocket picked, not of very much fortunately: but in the pocket book, which happened to be an old one I hadn't used for a long time there happened to be a blank cheque on Lloyds Bank, Paddington (I think) signed by you—which you gave me to pay your nuptial expenses at St. Martin's, and which, I forget why, I never used and have preserved all this time. You had better just tell your bank to look askance at any funny looking cheque of which the name and amount isn't made out in your handwriting. It is infinitely improbable that a Roman pickpocket shd try to do anything with the cheque, but in case—you had better take the precaution.

Our infant assumes almost fabulous proportions. Round and red, he looks like a replica in miniature of the faithful Bella, who is our staff, our stay our Hope for Years to Come.

Farewell. We hope to see you all in October, which isn't, alas, so far off now: summer is wearing thin.

Yours
ALH

188: TO H. L. MENCKEN

29 *Viale Morin,*
Forte dei Marmi (Lucca)
8 *September,* 1921

Dear Mencken,

I am enclosing a short story in the hope you may find it of use for the *Smart Set*. Also a little fable which might rank as one of your fifty monthly quips.

A few days and I leave this pleasant place for England, in any case for a month or two and, possibly, as I rather fear, more or less, but preferably less, permanently. It depends whether I can lay hands on any cash without having to work for it journalizing. My address will be, at least for the next month or two:

16 Bracknell Gardens.
London. N.W.3.

I have been industrious here, completing a comic novel in the manner, vaguely, of Peacock. It is an agreeable form; and besides, at the moment, I lack the courage and the patience to sit down and turn out eighty thousand words of Realismus. Life seems too short for that.

I have recently been in Rome, which I had never seen before. What a

188 *Huxley's short story 'Over the Telephone' appeared in* The Smart Set *of April,* 1923.

town! It is certainly the place where I shall come to spend my old age and if possible, large portions of the rest of my existence. Architecture, sculpture and painting give me, I find, as much pleasure as music. Rome is as good as a perpetual concert. . . . What a queer thing it is that the contemporary Italians produce so little in the way of any form of art. It seems all to have gone into engineering, while money making and sharp practice must suck up a good deal of the energy. Papini is almost the only contemporary writer one can read with much pleasure. The effects he gets out of the language are something inconceivable. Great sharpness and clarity and wit combined with melody and organ notes and the sweeping gesture. It's something which appears to be unobtainable in other languages, certainly in English and French and German.

I suppose you don't happen to know of any editor sufficiently rammollito to offer me large sums for writing articles—word pictures, I believe they call them—about Italy and art and all that sort of thing? The contadino in his podere and the bimbo on the knees of his babbo—you know the style. Flourish.

Yours,
Aldous Huxley

189: TO LEONARD HUXLEY

29 *Viale Morin,*
Forte dei Marmi
14 *September,* 1921

Dearest Father,

Many thanks for your wire. As it happens, however, we shan't need shelter for Saturday. There has been a vague influenzaish infection here which has slightly touched baby and Maria, so that we are postponing our journey for 4 or 5 days till all is completely well. We shall arrive probably on the Tuesday or Wednesday of next week. Meanwhile I have heard that we can have a room at Regent Square, where I was staying before I started for Italy; so that we shall go there direct and begin house hunting operations on the spot. I still don't quite know what will become of us. I have been offered £750 by the *Vogue—House and Garden* people, so that if I stay in London I shall be pretty comfortable. It remains to be seen. The disadvantages of England are too much work and too little superfluous time or energy. The drawbacks of Italy are the absence of libraries and the lack of informed and intelligent society. It wd be ideal to spend half one's time in each country. But that, alas, seems impossible. Goodbye, then, for another week or so.

Ever your loving son
Aldous

155 *Westbourne Terrace, W*.2
Friday, [1921]

Dear Naomi,

Thank you very much for your letter. I am delighted to hear that *Crome Yellow* amused you. It will be a privilege to meet Mary. Who is she? It all sounds suspiciously like the story of The Race with the Shadow.

I was overwhelmed to-day by praises from the lips of one of our Great Men. [John] Drinkwater went so far as to assure me of his great admiration for 'Leda', which he had recently read—as he added in a parenthesis which I could see was meant to be deeply significant—'in the wilds of Gloucestershire'. Alone with Nature. It was all so solemn that I was at a loss to know what to say.

Lalla has been heard of at the Ladies' Athenaeum. I am going to the Old Vic on Tuesday with a bouquet.

Yours,
A.L.H.

191: TO LEONARD HUXLEY

155 *Westbourne Terrace, W*.2
21 *November*, 1921

Dearest Father,

I enclose the short story about the nun I told you about ['Nuns at Luncheon']. My impression is that the (slightly comic and schematized) sexo-religious psychology of the beginning is too long and that the story wd be better remodelled so as to give only the anecdote itself, very quickly and sharply.

I am also sending another instalment of the National Debt, which I delayed paying till I had seen through the expenses of getting in here—an unknown quantity till it was all over.

About dinner on Wed, I still know nothing—nor of *Don Giovanni* on Thur—as I've not yet heard from Maria. If you go to *Don G*. remember it begins at 7.30. I will telephone or write about both these dates.

Love from
Aldous

192: TO LYTTON STRACHEY

Vogue, *Rolls House*,
Breams Buildings, London, E.C.4
26 *May*, 1922

Dear Lytton,

The indefatigable Mr. [Frank] Crowninshield wants to know if you have any old articles (I told him you didn't much want to write new) in the style of the Henri Beyle etc in your last book, which have been published here and not in America. He wd like to use any such things in *Vanity Fair* and offers £25–£30 for about 2000 words.

Yours
Aldous Huxley

193: † TO NORMAN DOUGLAS

Vogue, *Rolls House,*
*Breams Buildings, E.C.*4
26 *May,* 1922

Dear Douglas,

As a functionary in the employ of the Condé Nast publications—and what an occupation!—I have been seeing a Mr. Crowninshield, the editor of the American *Vanity Fair*. He wants very much to get you to write something for him and has written into the Italian blue to ask you if you would. Doubting if his letter reached you, he asks me to ask if you wd be prepared to write something for him—preferably little dialogues, or comments on foreigners in Italy, or indeed almost anything at all that is not erudite or technical.

I very much hope that you flourish. I moulder along in a pretty chronic state of boredom, and my dislike of work grows steadily towards a fanatical passion. I am hoping to have a few weeks in Italy—chiefly by the sea at Forte dei Marmi—this summer.

Yours
Aldous Huxley

194: TO MAX BEERBOHM

155 *Westbourne Terrace, W.*2
8 *June,* 1922

Dear Mr. Beerbohm,

I am overwhelmed, as Little Tich would say, overwhelmed with confusion. Such a charming and all too generous letter from such a tremendous swell is an honour (the M.B.E. or Max Beerbohm's Encomium) which I almost feel I ought to decline, as being too great and undeserved. But it also gave me a great deal of pleasure and encouragement, your letter. Thank you very much indeed.

The book has been, on the whole, pretty successful here, both as regards the number of copies sold and the remarks by reviewers. One or two whom I should have liked to like it didn't; and one or two liked whom I should have preferred to dislike. But that, I suppose, was inevitable.

I am hoping, if the trans-Atlantics buy a sufficient number of copies, to get away to Italy for a fairly long spell to write another on a more grandiose scale and of a slightly solider texture. *Crome* I wrote last summer at the seaside near Massa, and I found that one could work very well in that gorgeous heat: my aim is to get there again—this time for at least a year.

You ask after Robert Nichols. He has returned from Japan, pretty sick of it, and is looking for another job—which isn't easy to find nowadays—and trying to get married—which he doesn't find easy, either, as his parents-in-law elect are extremely averse to being anything more than elect—on the score, I gather, of poor Robert's bad heredity and his own touch of rather disquietingly furious *furor poeticus*.

Quant à moi, I am very securely wedded and possess a son of two years old, whom I shall train up to be an engineer or a capitalist—none of this literary business—with a view to being supported, during my declining years, in a state of cultured ease.

When I pass through Rapallo next I shall give myself the pleasure of calling at the Villino Chiaro and thanking you in person for your very precious letter.

> *Yours sincerely,*
> *Aldous Huxley*

195: TO CLEMENT K. SHORTER

> 155 *Westbourne Terrace, W*.2
> 16 *June*, 1922

Dear Mr. Shorter,

The coals of fire you pour upon my head! For I am ashamed to say how many months I have promised to write you an article and have never done so—because really I do happen to have been most horribly busy all the time, except when I was abroad, recovering from the effects of too much work. And now, with a kindness I cannot thank you enough for, you ask me to do a story for your Christmas number. I really am ashamed.

I have in my head a little comic story which might do for your Xmas number and I will get it done as soon as possible—so as to let you see it within the next month. If it is sufficiently seasonable, well and good. If not, you will have no hesitation, I hope, in returning it.

> *Yours very sincerely,*
> *Aldous Huxley*

196: TO LEONARD HUXLEY

> 155 *Westbourne Terrace, W*.2
> 30 *July*, 1922

Dearest Father,

Thank you for the letter and its birthday wishes, as well as for all the

---

195 *Clement K. Shorter was the editor of* The Sphere. *Huxley's Christmas story,* 'Good and Old-Fashioned', *which has been overlooked by his bibliographers, was published in* The Sphere *of* 23 *December. It has never been reprinted.*

news it contained. I had no idea you had been so seedy before you started for Connel and it is a relief to hear that you are better now, in spite of the bad weather—which has been just as bad here as up north.

Julian came to stay a night here before starting for Buda Pesth and he comes to us again on his return—on Tuesday, I fancy it is. We shall be interested to get information from him, as we propose to go to Salzburg on the way to Italy, to hear the musical festivals—modern Chamber music and Mozart opera. I have raised some money from the *Westminster* for it, so that it will cost us very little. It should be very amusing. I hope we may get on for a couple of days to Vienna while we are there. Julian's information will be very useful and I shall have expert assistance on the spot in the shape of Philip Nichols (Bowyer's younger son, who was at Balliol with me) who is one of the secretaries at the embassy there. We shall enter Italy via Venice, which I have never seen, and so across to Forte.

Matthew, after having flourished very well indeed, got a nasty attack of some sort of tonsilitis, which gave him a good deal of fever and weakened him. However, he seems to have got over it now and is putting on strength again. It is a great pity he should have had this set back after being so well. Fräulein Ella has had her sister staying with her for a month—a very adventurous journey for her to take, right down from Koenigsberg. The poor woman got held up by the railway strike in Munich and thought she would have to go back again; but luckily the strike fizzled out and she was able to get to Forte at last, two or three days late. We are looking forward with a good deal of alarm and anticipatory boredom to the invasion of Forte by Aunt Nettie [Roller], who has insisted on coming to stay there—not in our cottage, fortunately—while we are there. It is rather a bore, as we have never expressed the faintest desire to see her there. We were rash to have given away the name of the place and the time we would be there. Aunt Ethel [Collier] has wisely not divulged the fact that she is going to be at Como in September; otherwise Aunt N would have been sure to descend upon her there, for Como is much nearer to Varese, where she is going to be during August, than Forte. If it weren't so malicious, we would let pussy out of her reticule and suggest to Aunt Nettie that it would be much cheaper and altogether more amusing to go and stay with the Colliers at Bellagio! However, as the old Master of Balliol used to say about compulsory attendance at chapel, we all have our little cross to bear. And I hope the cross may be lightened by the presence at Forte, this year, of Madame Vandervelde, the wife of the Belgian minister, of whom we are both very fond. The only danger is that she and Aunt Nettie may quarrel with violence, as they are both masterful, formidable women—Madame Vandervelde being capable of greater rudeness towards people she doesn't like than anyone I know. However, let us hope for the best.

I have been very busy with journalism and shall be thankful to get away from London for a bit. I find the journalistic life more and more difficult to combine with intelligent writing. It is difficult to know how to arrange one's existence so as to be able to make money and, at the same time, do the necessary quiet thinking which one must do in order to write. I have been able to do practically none of my own stuff for the last six months. It is all very tiresome. What I should like to get is one of those charming jobs on a Sunday newspaper—seven or eight hundred a year and one article a week. But alas, they are few and the present occupants of them stick like limpets to the post of duty.

Good bye and love to Rosalind and the infants from both of us. Let us hope you will do better in the way of weather than we have been doing of late.

Your loving son,
Aldous

197: TO LEONARD HUXLEY

Villa Tacchella,
Forte dei Marmi (Lucca)
9 September, 1922

Dearest Father,

By this time, I suppose, you will be back from Connel—where I hope the season was favourable to your rest and amusement. We got here a fortnight or so ago, coming via Venice, where we spent a couple of nights and did some most agreeable sight-seeing, Padua, where we passed a day, and Bologna.

We found Baby splendidly well. His illness has, in a way, done him a lot of good. For the result of a long compulsory fast during the time when he had fever seems to have been that he has got rid of some toxic element in his inside; so that now he digests much better, his tongue is never white as it used so often to be, he eats much more and puts on strength and flesh at a great rate. The photograph shows how big he has grown.

The long drought broke a few days ago with a frightful storm, which assumed the proportions of a cloud burst a few miles higher up the coast, and we have had constantly recurring tempests ever since, which have rather spoiled what is generally the best moment of the summer. It does not look as though we should have really solidly settled Italian weather again before we start back, which is in about a week from now—Maria, Bella and Baby to Belgium and I to London.

I have been pretty busy, doing various articles and odds and ends which I had engaged to do, besides writing a few little divertimenti for my own pleasure; reading a fair amount and lying in the sun and bathing a lot.

Aunt Nettie is with us: but happily she is in a very calm and piano mood so that she is quite an agreeable companion. Mme Vandervelde was not able to come: a fact to be regretted in the absolute; but relatively to the presence of Aunt N perhaps it is a good thing.

Love from Maria and myself to both of you.

Your loving son
Aldous

198: TO WILLIAM ROTHENSTEIN

155 *Westbourne Terrace, W.*2
3 *October,* 1922

Dear Mr. Rothenstein,

I am delighted to think that I shall have an opportunity of renewing an acquaintance begun so long ago under Earp's auspices and so quickly ended. It will be a pleasure and an honour to sit for you.

This week my existence will be somewhat restless and uncertain—a house-hunt in the country is threatened—so that I had better put off my first visit till next. Unless I hear to the contrary, I will turn up at the R[oyal] C[ollege] of A[rt] on Thursday the 12th at about three in the afternoon.

Yours very sincerely,
Aldous Huxley

199: TO GEORGE H. DORAN

155, *Westbourne Terrace, W.*2
23 *December,* 1922

Dear Mr. Doran,

[Frank] Swinnerton has forwarded to me your letter about next Friday. I shall be delighted to come; and in any case I am looking forward to meeting you with F.S. on the Thursday.

I have just received from New York two magnificently bound copies of *Crome Yellow* and *Mortal Coils.* I am glad that I shall soon have the opportunity of thanking you in person for this delightful Christmas present.

Yours sincerely,
Aldous Huxley

198 *After various delays Huxley managed to find leisure to sit to Rothenstein for a portrait. This was finished in time for a reproduction to be included in Rothenstein's* Twenty-four Portraits, Second Series (*London,* 1923).

199 *Doran, who had issued* Limbo *in* 1920, *was Huxley's regular American publisher until* 1930. *In that year Doran left the firm of Doubleday, Doran, which had been formed by his merger with Doubleday, Page in* 1927, *and threw in his lot with William Randolph Hearst. Doubleday continued to publish Huxley until* 1933.

44 *Princes Gardens, S.W.*7
19 *January,* 1923

Dear Bennett,

In case you shd have nothing better to do tomorrow, about midnight, I send you this card, asking you to forgive me for not having sent it earlier (it didn't reach me before) and for not asking you to come and dine here first (we are hardly sufficiently settled in as yet and in the absence of the nurse Maria is too much occupied with the infant to be able to cope with much besides).

Yours
Aldous Huxley

44 *Princes Gardens, S.W.*7
9 *February,* 1923

Dearest Suzanne,

This portrait of you, executed about 3000 years ago, is very much more ressemblant than Gertler's. You and your family—in your previous incarnations—are having a great deal of publicity here.

When are you coming to stay with us again? We can offer you le confort moderne in this house: no horrors of the kind which abounded at Westbourne Terrace. Do come.

Not much of interest recently in London. Gertler's new show, just opened, is interesting and we have bought a very nice drawing. A few good concerts: but otherwise not very much.

I am very busy with journalism; but can see an end to it now, which is a blessing. After April I shall be able to write what I want.

Au revoir, chère Nefertiti.

ALH

200 *It appears from Bennett's reply, dated the 23rd, that the invitation (unspecified) included a breakfast to follow at the Cave of Harmony. He had been unable to accept, owing to an absence over the week-end.*

201 *Suzanne Nys, afterwards Mme Joep Nicolas, was the third of the Nys sisters. Maria Nys was the eldest, Jehanne (Jeanne) the second, and Rose the youngest. Gertler: Mark Gertler, the painter. Heavily disguised, he figures in* Crome Yellow *as Gombauld. 'Publicity' refers to the current excitement over the discovery and excavation of Tutankamen's tomb.*

44 Princes Gardens, S.W.7
Friday, [6 April, 1923]

Dear Bennett,

It sounds a delightful and interesting party: but, alas, I am going away tomorrow—to Florence, where Maria is already ensconced—for two or three weeks holiday, which I feel I have deserved after a lot of beastly work and an attack of influenza.

When we come back, I hope very much you will come and see us here.

Yours
Aldous Huxley

203: TO E. S. P. HAYNES

44 Princes Gardens, S.W.7
4 May, 1923

My dear Ted,

Thank you for both your letters: one of which caught me in Paris and the other here, on my return this evening: and for the script of the review, which I liked. I'm very glad you enjoyed these marginal notes of mine [*On the Margin*]. They were fun to write and they look to me, as I turn over the pages, quite good fun to read.

Italy was pleasant, tho' a little chilly. It may interest you to hear that your article in the *Sat Review*, on the decline of Liberty, was quoted with approbation in the *Corriere della Sera* a week or two ago. I cut the article out—but like an ass have lost it.

I look forward to the book when it appears and will do all I can to raise a little publicity round it. I'll try to do something in the Sat: *Westminster* on it when it appears; it depends on the Bright and Brainy one, however.

One day next week I will come and open your oyster,—and extract the pearls of wisdom and obscenity that so richly mature there between the hours of two and three-thirty.

Yours
ALH

203 *Haynes's book was* The Enemies of Liberty (*London,* 1923). *Bright and Brainy one: presumably Ramsay Muir, the editor of the* Weekly Westminster, *or one of his staff. Oyster: Haynes's fondness for shellfish was celebrated; see David Garnett,* The Flowers of the Forest (1956), *Chapter X, and cf. letter* 98. *Haynes had lunch every week-day at an oyster bar where he kept his own wine, and where he invited chosen kindred spirits to join him.*

II
ABROAD
1923–1937

Hotel Toscana, Siena
2 July, 1923

My dear Robert,

I am ashamed at my remissness in not having written to you before to thank you for the copy of *Fantastica*. It arrived just at the moment when I was leaving England in rather a hurry—Maria not having been at all well, and we deciding all of a sudden to get away out of the piercing English spring and the odious tumult of London into warmth and peace. It arrived, as I say, at a moment when I couldn't write, and ever since I have been in Italy I have been so wildly busy tapping on this machine for my living—a book to be finished by the beginning of August and hardly ten words on paper before I started—that I found it hard to write for any other motive, even friendship. However, now I am taking a brief holiday—for the Palio, that most marvellous of all festas—and as your second communication has opportunely arrived at this very moment, I profit by my leisure to answer it and to thank you for [your] book. That interested me much, especially, of course, the 'Golgotha', which I'd not seen before. You ask me what I think of the writing. My general criticism of it is this: though there are very fine and really eloquent things in plenty, the whole style, I think, ought to be cooler, at a lower temperature. For me, it is too feverish. It has that heat and violence of Milton's prose. Compare it with the coolness of Shakespeare's— in *Hamlet*, for instance, where the prince talks to Rosenkranza [sic] and G'stern (the 'nor woman neither' passage). The Miltonic, violent, feverish style—which was all too popular, I think, in the first half of last century in one form or another, not necessarily Miltonic—defeats its own end, I always feel. Like soldiers always saying bloody and bugger till the words cease to tell. Moreover—and this is highly speculative and may, for all I know, be all balls—I rather feel that that sort of Miltonic, violent style is really, inherently more suitable to comic than to serious writing. That prodigious 'biological' as opposed to spiritual energy which is the essential quality of real comedy requires a violent and exuberant and rather tormented style to express itself. (Motteux's *Rabelais*, the juiciest bits of Dickens, Aristophanes.) Take Milton himself; the passages where his style seems to me to come off most completely are precisely the comical ones—such as the admirable bit about the imprimaturs in *Areopagitica*—the friars, you remember, ducking their shaven crowns to one another. It always seems to me that Melville often defeated his own ends in *Moby Dick* by protesting too much, by trying to be Elizabethan in the wrong way—taking the decorative scroll work as the essential body of his own style. It seems to me the same in pictorial art. The best baroque sculptors were undoubtedly very sincere and passionately earnest men; but how they defeated themselves by the feverishness of their style. More coolness, it seems to me, is what your writing needs; and perhaps less consciously produced sonority. I think there are too many long words. I can't help feeling that the result of more coolness and less violence would be a real increase in power. I am not advocating any finicking dix-huitième frigidity; nor the long drawn, calm literary masturbations of an exquisite like Gide, shall we say. But the coolness of that bit in *Hamlet*—passionate and piercing as any bit of prose you like to think of.

I couldn't review *Fantastica* anywhere, as I don't do any reviewing now; and indeed I am now cutting myself off almost completely from regular journalism, which is a comfort. I am even abandoning Condé Nast, so far as his English publications are concerned, though I shall still go on writing for *Vanity Fair* in America. Meanwhile, we are proposing to settle, more or less permanently— as far as any arrangement with us is ever permanent—in Italy, and have taken a villa outside Florence from September onwards: Castel Montici, Via Santa Margherita a Montici, Florence is the precise address. There I shall settle down to grind out two yearly books of fiction for Chatto's and any other things I can manage. The life, I think, ought to be agreeable and one's money goes nearly twice as far as in London. I shall come back to civilisation a few months every year to find out what is going on.

About jobs in London, more especially with the Nast people. The position is this: they have put a new editor into *Vogue*—one Miss Todd—who is trying to ginger up the paper and turn it, from an exclusive fashion paper into a something slightly more interesting. Whether she wants anyone permanently on the spot, or whether she will rely on casual contributions, I don't quite know. But in any case there is no harm in writing to her and asking, telling her that I told you to write. The difficulty, of course, is your remoteness as Miss Todd has lived long enough in U.S.A. to be very insistent on the Personal Touch. And I think it rather unlikely that she'd make any offer firm enough for you to come back across the world on, without personally touching you and bothering you at close range. She is efficient and quite intelligent. But capricious and rather uncertain. Which would make arrangements from ten thousand miles away rather difficult to fix up. But write to her in any case.

If you don't want journalism that is literary, why not try—it's a little ghoulish, no doubt—*John of London* or the new and similar *Cassell's weekly*. You could turn them out thoughts on the Classics with professorial authority and they clamour for that; also for comments on the young. (I may add, confidentially, that a page in J of L's weekly was recently devoted to quotations from my book of essays, under the title: 'Nibbles from A. L. H.') I don't know the editors of either of these papers; but it shouldn't, I imagine, be too difficult to get into touch with them. *Nation* and *Statesman* and suchlike, besides being hard work, are really hopeless, as they pay so atrociously badly; and the sort of work one does for them—reviewing—is a vomitory.

Nor, under its new Bloomsbury management, is the *Nation* much catch, I think.

If you are really going to have a regular five to six hundred a year, with such pickings as can be made by casual stories, articles etc, why don't you live in Italy. It could be done with comfort. Or are you too much wedded to the mud and the grey days to appreciate sunshine, dust, grapes and scirocco? Not to mention the icy winters in imperfectly warmed houses?

Well, let me hear of you occasionally. I will let you know if I hear of anything that might be of interest to you when I go back at the end of this month—which will only be for a few days, however, as I go on to Belgium for a little, then to Italy.

Yours,
A.L.H.

205: TO ERIC PINKER

Castel Montici,
Via Santa Margherita a Montici, Florence
13 *August,* 1923

Dear Pinker,

I enclose a letter from Chatto's which explains itself. Will you communicate with Chappell's and see what can be done? How they propose to turn *Crome Yellow* into a play, a musical comedy or a film, I can't imagine. But if they like to try they are welcome. You will be able to find out what sort of terms they are likely to offer. Please let me know what the results of your conversation with these people is.

With regard to your letter about MSS:—unfortunately I do practically all my writing direct on to the machine. There is not much catch in typescript, I imagine.

The heat here has been fabulous, but there are signs of approaching rain —much to everybody's relief; especially mine, as I have been suffering from a sort of suppressed jaundice for the last 10 days and in this condition haven't been appreciating warm weather as much as I generally do.

Yours
Aldous Huxley

206: TO LEONARD HUXLEY

Castel Montici,
15 *Via Santa Margherita a Montici, Florence*
2 *September,* 1923

Dearest Father,

I have been owing you a letter for a long while and the debt has lain on my conscience. But meanwhile I have also been having a (mercifully slight) jaundice lying on my liver, which reduced me to a fearful state of weltschmerz and incapacity to do anything. Now I am completely recovered and very busily trying to make up for lost time.

We are settled in here—moderately comfortably, but not yet entirely to our satisfaction, as the electric pump which is supposed to send the water for baths etc up to the cistern is too feeble to do the work and we have to be content with pails laboriously carried up. At the moment we are argle-bargling with the proprietress, whose strategy consists in not answering any communication. However today we will present an ultimatum, saying that if she doesn't do something herself, we will have a new pump in and charge it up to her when the next instalment of rent has to be paid. It will be interest-ing to see what she does then! Otherwise the house is quite satisfactory: large—4 rooms including a drawingroom 25 feet square on the ground floor, with a kitchen and another vague room for storing things, and a bath-room. Upstairs, 6 bedrooms, a bathroom and finally a room in a tower which commands the most prodigious view—but being under the roof and all windows is at present too hot for habitation. In the winter it should be delicious. There is also a balcony-terrace facing S.W. that runs the whole breadth of the house—about 50 feet: also splendid for the winter. The house is ugly and has been badly done up recently; but the position is marvellous. We are about 5½ miles out of town and about 450 feet above it, with views on to Florence, up the Arno valley, on to the Apennines—almost a complete circular panorama, for we are practically on the crest of a hill.

We were all in Belgium at the beginning of August—I with the MS of my book [*Antic Hay*] finally off my hands; rather tired with having had to write the best part of 100,000 words in 2 months. It was in Belgium I began my jaundice, which made the journey and all the affairs of the next 3 weeks very depressing. From Brussels we went direct to Milan: stopped (in a heat wave of the first magnitude) for a night and started off the next evening in the car, which by dint of considerable hoarding I had saved up enough money to buy. It is a 4-seater Citroen: very good on the whole, I think. We took a chauffeur with us for the first part of the trip, as Maria didn't feel quite confident enough to drive without expert supervision. The first night we got to Modena, driving at a tremendous rate along the perfectly flat Roman roads of the great plain (in the heat one must drive early or late: the noonday hours are bad for everyone, engine and tyres included). Then up early the next morning and for about 100 miles through the mountains—up to 4500 feet—descending finally on Lucca, and from there to Forte dei Marmi, a long day's drive—our altitude permitting us to continue even at midday. The scenery in these Modenese alps is something prodigious. At Forte we spent 4 or 5 days—for me always made rather gloomy by jaundice—then on to Florence, going by Volterra (fabulous scenery again) and Siena, where we stopped to look at the great feast of the Palio—horse-racing in the piazza and a procession in mediaeval costume: the most memorable and lovely thing. There we met a number of compatriots, including a Commissioner of lunacy and Lady Diana Manners! We arrived here in a great drought and heat; this house, however, is remarkably cool, getting a lot of air—whatever there is, in fact—owing to its height. Now, fortunately, the weather has broken: we have had two tremendous storms and the days continue cool. Since then we have been getting straight, as far as it is possible to do so without the bulk of the luggage which is still on its way from England, coming by *petite vitesse* which appears to be extremely petite, especially in Italy, in which country we know it has already been more than 10 days on the way from Milan—and how much longer goodness knows.

We were expecting Margaret on the 1st, but have heard no news: and don't know whether she has changed her plans or what. We shall wire to Belgium today, to Maria's mother, to find out.

Maria is better here, I think; tho' still very thin and too light. Eating and resting ought to do her good: and this excellent air. Matthew and Bella are still at the sea, staying with the Fasola's. We shall have them back here in another week or so, I think. Until the house was ready it wd have been difficult to have Matthew: moreover the servant problem still remains to be completely settled. He enjoys the sea and it does him good, I think: and there are some very nice children—diminutive marquises and nobildonne, like almost everybody here!—living next door with whom he plays.

When the pump and the servants are properly functioning, you and R must come out and stay. Perhaps if you go to Switzerland, you cd come on here after Xmas. The journey is nothing. Think it over. Much love to all from both of us.

Your loving son
A.

207: TO H. L. MENCKEN

15 *Via Santa Margherita a Montici,*
Florence
10 *September,* 1923

Dear Mencken,

What with travelling, getting into a new house, having jaundice and doing the necessary bread and butter work, I have sadly neglected your letter. Apologies for the delay.

Your news is interesting. From what I know of serious journals in America I shd say that the USA cd do very well with something less stuffy than the *Yale* and *Atlantic* and less eclectically odd-and-endy than *Dial*.

I have little or nil on hand—except the enclosed outburst in blank verse—which I sent to the Editor of the *New Republic*, he having invited me to contribute a tuneful number, and which he returned as being too

207 *Mencken's new magazine was* The American Mercury, *which began publishing in January,* 1924.

obscene for his pages. I send it to you in hopes. It contains some good lines.

In mind I have (a) a whole bunch of Imaginary Conversations: but these might be too purely literary for you. Still, if you'd like to see them, I'd let you have one or two as they get done. When will they get done?

(b) Moderately instructive articles on Italy: which is a queer, problematic country at the moment.

(c) Several articles on subjects connected with art—subject matter in art; vitality and the problem of its transference from the artist to the work, as illustrated particularly by 17th cent Italian baroque. And so on.

Most of my time is taken up doing fiction—I am contracted to produce a certain wad of it each year. I find it more interesting and more profitable than miscellaneous journalism. It also enables me to live here: which I prefer to London, finding on the whole that the pleasingness of the prospect makes up for the vileness of Man in these regions.

As for people who might be of use in writing for your paper: a few names occur to me. Desmond MacCarthy, c/o *New Statesman*, 10 Gt. Queen Street, W.C.: he always has something interesting to say and a certain literary juiciness in his way of saying it. A queer and very able fellow is Wyndham Lewis (Lee Studio, Adam and Eve Mews, Kensington): but he's not the man for getting copy from at a definite date! J. W. N. Sullivan (6 Pond Street, N.W.3) writes well on scientific (physics and astronomy) themes. And if you want a specialist on biology, my brother, Julian, (8 Holywell, Oxford) writes lucidly on these themes. W. J. Turner can turn out a good article, especially on musical and theatrical themes: for the next month or two he is, I hope, going to stay with me here. And then what about Norman Douglas (24 Via dei Benci, Florence)? Osbert Sitwell can do very amusing things: set him on to the Georgian poets and you will have fun. His address is, 2 Carlyle Square, S.W.3.

I don't know if any of these suggestions are of any use to you. I hope so. If ever you pass this way, do let me know. I long to visit the Land of the Free: and if I cd do it gratis and without clowning out lectures I would. One must pray for cash.

> *Yours*
> *Aldous Huxley*

208: TO LEONARD HUXLEY

> 15 *Via Santa Margherita a Montici,*
> *Florence*
> 12 *October,* 1923

Dearest Father,
Your letter and a letter from the Banca Commerciale arrived together

---

208 *Julian's book:* Essays of a Biologist. *Aunt Fan: Frances Arnold, Huxley's great aunt, the youngest daughter of Dr Arnold of Rugby.*

to-day. Thank you for both. . . . My momentary shortage was due to big expenses like insurance coming on top of moving and journey. These things have a way of coming all at once. Food is certainly quite as expensive here as in London. We calculate about eighteen shillings per head per week. The other ten shillings of Margaret's pension covered washing, which is fairly dear—disproportionately, considering the general cheapness of unskilled labour—and jaunts in town, which in tourist-infested Florence are always expensive. The cheapness in Italy consists, as you say, in rent—though that's relatively high in Florence (two or three times more than the corresponding prices in a little provincial town) absence of taxes and service; one pays no servant more than eighteen pounds a year. Certain articles of clothing are also cheaper. Or at any rate, you get better value for money; the best hand-made shoes, for example, cost what moderately decent machine-made ones would do in England.

Life proceeds very calmly here and I manage to get a good deal of work done, together with a certain amount of reading. How whole-heartedly I agree with Dr Johnson in his contempt for authors who write more than they read. Unfortunately one doesn't always have the time or energy to do both. I envy those herculean creatures like Balzac who could keep up eighteen hours a day for months at a stretch. (But it must be admitted that he died at fifty, completely worn out.) I find that eight hours of writing is my extreme limit.

I have just got Julian's book, which I have not yet finished. I like it, on the whole, very much; though the writing is, at times, rather loose for my taste. But then I have an excessive affection for tightness. It was only quite by the way, in the note he sent me with his book, that I heard of Aunt Fan's death. I rarely see the English papers and the news hadn't penetrated to the Italian ones. It is a sad breaking of a link with the past; but I suppose, after the poor old lady's stroke, death came as rather a merciful relief.

I saw recently Sir George Sitwell, who spoke of Gordon Wordsworth, whom he knew, apparently, at Oxford. He described him as 'extremely frivolous'. Sir George, who has spent his whole life in riding the most expensive and fantastic hobby horses, would call himself very serious, I suppose.

Florence is filled with English people; but our distance out of town permits us to avoid those we don't want to see; which is a great comfort. Moreover, it's so pleasant up on our hill, that one rarely feels tempted to venture into the town, even for the sake of seeing pleasant people. So that I still owe several calls—on Miss Paget (Vernon Lee) in particular and Geoffrey and Lady Sybil Scott, who live at the marvellous Villa Medici at Fiesole.

Poor Signora Fasola—you remember Maria's friend, Costanza—is incurably ill of cancer in the stomach. It is a question of only a few months at the outside, I should imagine. Fortunately she suffers little or no pain. But it's a dreadful business.

That's the end of my typewriter ribbon which has gone on marking wonderfully to the very last: but now it's worn right through with the tapping of the type. I'll finish this by hand.

Matthew is very flourishing and so for that matter are all of us. Maria has put on about 2 kilos since she came here; which is good.

Love from all.

Your loving son
Aldous

209: TO JULIAN HUXLEY

15 *Via S. Margherita a Montici,*
Florence
12 *November,* 1923

My dear J,

All these weeks and weeks without writing to thank you for your book. I suffer sometimes, like Margaret, from the letter complex. It is the result, in my case, of having to write so much professionally—hours a day. The thought of writing becomes extremely forbidding.

I hope the book is doing well. Personally I liked it very much and thought the substance of it very sound. My only complaint is that the writing is sometimes rather loose, as though it had been dictated. In your next book I think you ought to write from a scientific point of view about the immediate problems of the next few years. I try to disinterest myself from politics; but really, when things are in the state they are, one can't help feeling a little concerned about them. These monsters will end up by making such a mess that we shall all suffer. The deplorable thing is that so long as we go on saying that in no circumstances will we go to war, so long will France and the rest of Europe continue to treat us as a third rate power. One determined Poincaré can defeat and make life impossible for ten philosopher-kings. And when in place of philosopher kings we have Baldwins—then it's all up. It would be interesting to discuss, as a biologist and psychologist, the question of leadership in the modern state. Is it any longer possible in communities as large and as complicated as the modern state for one man to be able to lead successfully? Is it possible for him to combine those qualities of what, for lack of a better word, one must call animal magnetism—necessary for anyone who is going to make men obey him and impress people with confidence—with the degree of intelligence, sensitiveness to the lessons of experience and vast knowledge required in the leader of a modern state? A good leader must be something of a charlatan and an actor; he must have courage and determination and charm. It seems to me that the chances of finding an active charlatan who is also a philosopher and man of science—and to lead a modern state one must be those too—are almost infinitely small. Mussolini, I suppose, comes as near as anyone to fulfilling the conditions.

A little more pure reason and he would be the philosopher king. But think of the other creatures. And the difficulty of finding suitable leaders will become progressively greater as society grows more complex and communities larger. Society, moreover, can less and less afford to be governed by imbeciles or even by charlatans of genius. The dilemma seems to me serious.

Summer, with occasional spells of rain, lingers and lingers deliciously here. The beauty of this country is really fabulous. Motoring to Rome the other day was really a revelation. We went by Arezzo and Cortona—grim Etruscan town on an immense mountain with a view over Trasimene—stopping the first night at Chiusi. Then on to Orvieto, where I had never been before; lunch at Montefiascone, famous for its wine, which must be drunk on the spot to be fully appreciated—and what a town! Two thousand feet up, a hill crowned by an immense Renaissance cupola looking over the perfectly circular bright blue lake of Bolsena. Thence to Viterbo; over the volcanic hills past the incredible Lago di Vico and then on, through the Campagna, where the roads are of fabulous badness, to Rome. We had a tiny flat there, which was very agreeable, and with the car we did the surrounding country—Tivoli (for me a first visit), Frascati and from there through Albano to Nemi; but the country there is so crowded now. The road is like the road from Kingston to Surbiton—so many villas all the way, such a lot of people. I suppose one has to keep right off the roads and walk through the woods to find anything wild in the Alban hills now. And the Campagna too is getting overrun. They have a Città Giardino just outside to the north and the number of horrible little villini, factories, aeroplane sheds and the like that are springing up everywhere in the plain, is extraordinary. What their occupants do and how they manage to survive the summer in open Campagna is more than I can imagine. However, the Appian Way is still unbuilt-over, which is something. We also went to Ostia—really marvellous and second, I suppose, only to Pompeii, which of course I've never seen. We came back along the Tiber valley for the first thirty miles or so, then over a range of perfectly enormous mountains—hugely high and quite barren—to Terni. It is, apparently, a way which no knowing motorist ever takes, owing to the terrible climbing—we must have gone up to three thousand feet at least and the road dips and climbs for twenty miles—and the complete absence of any assistance if you break down. Luckily our little Citroen did the whole thing without turning a hair. From Terni we went over the Somma pass—very high again and thoroughly Alpine—to Spoleto, where we stayed the first night. Thence through the plain of Clitumnus, which looks like the Chinese willow pattern come to life and is charming, past Trevi, to Assisi. Saw the Giottos—and my word, aren't they astonishing?—and went on to Perugia, where we spent another night, coming home by Trasimene and Arezzo the next day.

We're firmly settled here once more and very busy, at least I speak for myself. Occasional descents into Florence to see Norman Douglas or

Geoffrey Scott. John Mavrogordato and his wife have been here lately and an occasional Colefax or so drifts through from time to time. When I've finished my present book, I may come to England for a little to work in libraries on that bloody book on Balzac which, in an insane moment years ago, I pledged myself to write. Williams and Constables seem to take my contract seriously; so I suppose I shall have to. But I loathe the thought of doing the book and am bored stiff with Balzac. Quelle vie! It would be pleasant if you could come out here at Christmas, perhaps, though the weather wouldn't be particularly tempting then. If not, it will have to be the spring.

Love from all of us to all of you.

Yours,
A.L.H.

210: TO LEONARD HUXLEY

15 *Via S. Margherita a Montici,*
Florence
26 *November,* 1923

Dearest Father,

I am sorry you should have found my book so distasteful. Like you, I have no desire to enter into argument about it: argument, indeed, would be useless, as we should start from entirely different premises. I will only point out that it is a book written by a member of what I may call the war-generation for others of his kind; and that it is intended to reflect—fantastic-ally, of course, but none the less faithfully—the life and opinions of an age which has seen the violent disruption of almost all the standards, conventions and values current in the previous epoch.

The book is, I may say without fatuity, a good book. It is also a very serious book. Artistically, too, it has a certain novelty, being a work in which all the ordinarily separated categories—tragic, comic, fantastic, realistic—are combined so to say chemically into a single entity, whose unfamiliar character makes it appear at first sight rather repulsive.

I can't say that I expected you would enjoy the book. But on the other hand I expected that my contemporaries would; and so far as I know by what people have written to me, they have.

And there, I think, I had better leave it, only pausing long enough to express my surprise that you should accuse me, when I speak of a young man's tender recollections of his dead mother, of botanizing on my mother's grave.

The book from Doran's may safely be left to look after itself. I have no time to read superfluities.

All flourish here.

Your loving son
Aldous

210 *His book was of course* Antic Hay.

15 *Via S. Margherita a Montici,*
Florence
7 *January,* 1924

Dear Pinker,

Thank you for your letter and the excellent news it contains. As soon as I have got my present quota of stuff done for Chatto's—which I hope to send you in three or four weeks time—I will do some things for *Harper's.* I have one or two excellent ideas, I think, that would do for short stories and articles for them. By the way, I hope it will be all right if 'Little Mexican' is published in my next volume, as I mean it to be. I imagine they will have got it out serially before it comes out in book form in America. But if there's any doubt, it might be worth finding out for certain.

I wonder, by the way, if you ever got a letter of mine which I sent off about Christmas. I presume you did not, as you do not mention it; and I fear it may have suffered the fate of a good many letters that perished in the Christmas rush. What I asked you in it was for advice on the following point. Four years ago, being at that time very young, very foolish and poor, I contracted with Constable's to write a book on Balzac for their series, the 'Makers of the Nineteenth Century'. I did a good deal of work on it in the first year, but have really found it completely impossible to get the time to do more since; so that there only exists of this monumental work a certain number of notes. Constable's now want the book—for which I don't blame them, as it is years overdue. But the thought of getting down to it fills me with horror. What I wondered is whether (a) I can decently get out of the engagement altogether—which I imagine would be rather difficult; or (b) if Constables could be persuaded to take another book in lieu of this horrible Balzac. I have stupidly not got the contract with me here; it is stored with my chattels in London. But it was the usual sort of thing; fifty pounds down on receipt of the MS as advanced royalties, and fifteen per cent, I think, of the published price. I have, of course, received nothing in advance. I have often cursed my folly in making this contract and it would be a vast relief

---

211 *Constable had reminded Huxley on* 17 *December that the Balzac manuscript was promised for delivery by the end of* 1920. *Huxley wrote to Pinker on* 21 *December. Acting on Huxley's two letters, Pinker took the matter up with Constable; and on* 16 *January Michael Sadleir replied that the firm would prefer of possible substitutes for the Balzac book a critical biography of some other writer, perhaps an eighteenth-century writer of 'contes galants'; but that they would find quite acceptable a collection of imaginary conversations of the quality of the Ninon de Lenclos dialogue, which Huxley had contributed to* Coterie *in* 1919. *Huxley favoured the latter suggestion; but subsequent correspondence shows that it was not carried out owing to an objection from his regular publishers, Chatto and Windus, and Pinker arranged for cancellation of the agreement.*

for me to know if I can get out of it in any way decently, either scot free or by doing some more congenial book. As a substitute I could give them either a collection of essays, or perhaps one longish critical study of the Comic in art and literature, which I have been contemplating for some time. I shall be most grateful to hear what you have to say about this and if you think that something can be arranged.

I am so sorry to bother you. Let me end up by repeating the best wishes for 1924 which I included in my last, lost letter; and by adding my very grateful thanks for the great things you have done and are doing with my work.

Yours ever,
Aldous Huxley

212: TO LEONARD HUXLEY

15 Via S. Margherita a Montici,
Florence
25 January, 1924

Dearest Father,

Your letter heaped coals of fire on my head; for I had not written to thank you for the Smith Elder book, which I read with much interest. These marginal comments on history are often as interesting as the history itself, which they permit one to look at from another angle.

I have been most desperately busy the last two months and shall continue to be so for another fortnight or more, until I have got the book of short stories on which I am working at present entirely off my chest. Even then I shan't be able to be so very idle, as I have my next novel to think of and a collection of Imaginary historical Conversations, which I am doing for Constable's in lieu of a portentous tome on Balzac which I madly promised to do for them years ago—without realizing that a book about an author of that fecundity requires at least a year to itself, without the intervention of any other preoccupations. Moreover, I must confess, the more familiar I became with Balzac, the less, on the whole, I thought of him. He is a sort of gigantic film-scenario writer—marvellous in his energy, his power of rapidly and effectively creating, his picturesqueness; but so astonishingly remote from life—at any rate from interior life; for the exterior life he hits off very vividly in general—and so remarkably lacking in subtlety. I always enjoy his books; but there are very few of them I think particularly good. What an immense difference between him and a really great novelist, like Dostoevsky or Tolstoy. And what a difference, in his own sphere of fantastic creation, between him and the incredibly much more fertile and juicy Dickens. Well,

212 *Smith Elder book: Leonard Huxley's* The House of Smith Elder (*London,* 1923).

I am now free of him; which is a great comfort to me and am doing these dialogues instead. They ought to be quite interesting to write.

We have been having the worst winter since Dante wrote the *Inferno*: but thank goodness, that isn't quite so bad as a bad English winter, and we do have, every now and then, miraculous days when the sun is so hot that one cannot sit in it for long without feeling positively dizzy with the warmth. The earlier part of the winter was terribly rainy—floods all over the country; now we are having finer days, but with a great deal of frost. There is good ski-ing this year in Vallombrosa and at Abetone, I hope you will be finding it as satisfactory at Morgins.

We have staying with us now a most interesting man, J. W. N. Sullivan (whom I think you have met, by the way, in connection with articles about the Einstein theory for *Cornhill*). He has a very clear, hard and acute intelligence and a very considerable knowledge, not merely on his own subjects— mathematics, physics and astronomy—but on literature and particularly music. A stimulating companion. He was brought up at Maynooth under the Jesuits; they intended him to be a controversial apologist and seeing the bent of his mind, trained him on Thomas Aquinas—a good basis for a mathematician. But after he had been with them for a year or two they turned him out—though at that time he was still a firm believer—telling him that they could see that with his mind he would inevitably become a sceptic. Which he did—three years later! Fairly acute psychological insight on the part of the reverend fathers—for whose intelligence, indeed, he retains the highest respect.

Well, I must get back to my labours. The best of holidays.

Your loving son,
Aldous

213: TO ERIC PINKER

15 *Via S. Margherita a Montici,*
Florence
25 *February,* 1924

Dear Pinker,
Your two letters came on consecutive days. With regard to the first and the rather gloomy news about Constable's: the Tunisia book, if Chattos don't want it, would suit me best. My plans about it have slightly changed and enlarged and what I propose doing now is to start in the early autumn— as I shan't have time now—and motor not merely through Tunisia but along the whole of North Africa, Tunisia, Algeria and Morocco. I think that would be rather an interesting subject.

I hope you received the main part of my MS [*Little Mexican*], which I sent last week. I am just copying out the last fifteen thousand words and hope to get it off the day after to-morrow.

Do let me know precisely when you are going to the south of France and where you will be. My wife and I had, as a matter of fact, thought vaguely of going there for a day or two this spring and it would be very pleasant if we could arrange our trip, if we make it, so as to coincide with yours.

Yours,

Aldous Huxley

P.S. I find I have omitted to mention the most important item in your last letter—the *Discovery*. I have no copy of this; but [C. H. C.] Prentice can get one either from Nigel Playfair or from Mrs Geoffrey Whitworth. My suggestion is that he should get hold of it, read it and see if it is worth publishing. It's such a long time since I did the thing that I can't remember anything about it. If, after reading, he still likes the idea of it, then certainly I see no reason why it shouldn't be published. The best form, I think, would be something small, cheap and pretty. Covers of Italian paper or something of the kind. People wouldn't pay more than a certain pretty small sum for it, I should think.

214: TO LEONARD HUXLEY

15 *Via S. Margherita a Montici,*
Florence
29 *April,* 1924

Dearest Father,

Many thanks for your letter, which was rather a coal of fire. I have been very busy on a new book—or most of the time on the false starts for a new book; for it is horribly difficult to find the right way of saying what one wants to say. My volume of stories, among which 'Little Mexican' is included, is coming out some time in May. It consists of six stories, the first of considerable length, about thirty thousand words, and has some quite good stuff in it, I think. What I am working on now is a novel [*Those Barren Leaves*], which is to be, as much as anything, a discussion and fictional illustration of different views of life. The mere business of telling a story interests me less and less. I find it very difficult to understand the mentality of a man like Bennett who can sit down and spin out an immense realistic affair about life in Clerkenwell (his latest, *Riceyman Steps* is that.) When it was first done that sort of thing had a certain interest; I suppose it was Balzac who first exploited the curious subject. But it is a purely factitious interest. The only really and permanently absorbing things are attitudes towards life and the relation of man to the world.

213 *Huxley's adaptation of Frances Sheridan's play* The Discovery *was issued in both a regular and a special binding. Charles Prentice and his partner Harold Raymond, of Chatto and Windus, are missing as correspondents of Huxley before 1926, partly at least because the Pinker agency served as intermediary in ordinary business matters.*

Here too we have had a bad winter—though in comparison with yours I should imagine it would seem marvellous. In March, when we were crossing the Apennines in the car, we got held up by snow and had to stay the night in a horrible little village about 3000 feet up in the hills. In the end we had to take another circuitous route to get through. We made a rather pleasant trip then—it was a little relaxation after getting my book finished. Went first to Bologna, then up the perfectly straight, perfectly flat Roman Via Emilia to Parma, via Modena, Reggio etc. From Parma, which is a superb town, fairly plastered with Correggio's paintings, we went across country to Mantua, pausing on the way at a little village called Sabbioneta, where one of the sixteenth century Gonzaga created a brilliant little court, leaving two or three palaces, a Palladian theatre with fixed scene and various other delights. From Mantua we went to Padua, thence to Venice for a couple of days and back, through Ferrara, to Ravenna and from Ravenna to Bologna and so home. Motoring like that gives one some idea of the size of the north-Italian plain. It is like a billiard board for literally hundreds of miles at a stretch, and all of it incredibly fertile and cultivated to the highest degree.

We have begun to have some warmth, real warmth, now. But the season is by no means well established and the weather instead of being set fair as it ought to be is still variable. Still, we are having sweet peas and roses in the garden; the tulips have been over weeks ago and the wistaria is in full bloom.

I shall be curious to see how my adaptation of Mrs Sheridan will do on the stage. Reading it through again in proof—they are bringing out a little edition—it seems quite amusing; and Playfair, who is producing it for the 300 club performance, seems to think that it will make a very good entertainment and has some hopes of getting it put on for a run. Let us hope for the best.

Maria has just come back from Belgium, where she has been for a fortnight, seeing her sister Suzanne married. She has chosen well, I think—a very pleasant young Dutchman [Joep Nicolas], trained as an advocate, but who prefers to be a painter—a trade at which he actually earns quite a lot of money, getting big commissions for frescoing catholic churches in Holland. They will live near Amsterdam. Meanwhile, for their honeymoon, they are in Italy, and after a week or so in Venice—hardly avoidable if one is honeymooning —will come here for a bit.

The number of foreigners this year is enormous. Every hotel in every at all well known Italian town is quite full. What is remarkable is the immense quantity of Germans—rich schiebers, who have grown fat on the collapse of the currency. (An industrialist could borrow from the Reichsbank and repay, not in gold value, but in paper; so that one might take out say a thousand million marks, worth last August, about £1000 and pay the sum back in November, when they were worth two pence—plus a halfpenny, being 100 per cent interest for three months. The thousand pounds was, of course, at once invested in dollars—in which currency, or sterling, all the Germans here pay.) Meanwhile, poor professors etc can hardly live and cannot hope to take a holiday abroad, because of the 500 gold marks which, by the new law, have to be deposited before one can leave the country. To the schieber this is nothing; to the rest it means a lot.

We are celebrating Matthew's fourth birthday to-day, though it actually occurred on the 19th, when, however, Maria was in Belgium. He is very large and lively, though still fearfully difficult about food, declining absolutely to eat either meat or fish—partly because he is very sensitive to smells and the smell of both disgusts him, partly for sentimental reasons, as he realizes that meat is dead animals and partly out of sheer nervous cussedness; having once refused he must always refuse; the disgust has become ingrained. However, he gets on all right on a vegetarian diet. I sometimes wonder, though, whether a course of mild hypnotism and suggestion mightn't do good; but I don't know how young that sort of thing can be begun. He knows his letters, but is too lazy to read, resolutely refusing to take the trouble. We don't worry him, however; a too early passion for reading detracts from the powers of observation and it is more important for the child to notice vividly what is going on outside him than to make a precocious acquaintance with the inside of books.

Byron's centenary, I confess, leaves me remarkably unmoved. There is a certain charm about the man; he was so candid and transparent in his egotism. But he had a fearful streak of vulgarity in him, which comes out with a vengeance both in his life and works. And how little substance there is for us, nowadays, in almost everything he wrote. More and more I find that I can only read poets who have something to say, not those who make beauty in the void. It has always puzzled me that a man like Wordsworth should so much have admired Spenser, the perfect poetical example of vox et praeterea nihil.

Love to the family from all of us.

Your loving son,
Aldous

215: † TO DR B. G. BROOKS

Villa Fasola, Forte dei Marmi (Lucca)
9 August, 1924

Dear Brooks,

It was most kind of you to send me another copy of your book. I should have written to thank you before this, but I have been most desperately busy—and still am, tho' nearly at the end of my task, thank God!—that I have had no time to do anything.

My principal criticism of your *Exile* is that it partakes too much of a volume of personal notes. The technical achievement is remarkable through-out: the vers libre is genuinely musical and is not—as with most practitioners of the form—mere chopped prose. But it seems to me that you have been too often content with just finding the right, poetical expression for some personal experience—emotional or merely sensational—with putting Samuel Butler's notebooks into excellent vers libre. Those billiard players, for instance—they're excellent; the lights from the hanging lamps on the table couldn't have been captured more successfully. But I feel that it's not enough. Standing alone, such a note is not sufficiently significant. It may be mere folie de grandeur and pompier prejudice on my part—but I feel that a note like that becomes significant only when it's attached to something more generalized and important than itself, something that, for lack of a better word, one has to call philosophical. Not that 'Great thoughts' make great poetry. Far from it: the people who have deliberately set out to put great thoughts into verse have generally been the worst poets on record. But, per contra, the best poets have generally implied or directly expressed great thoughts, a philosophy of some kind or other. I cannot help feeling that you are wasting your obvious talent on the meticulous recapture of passing emotions and sensations which in themselves are too insubstantial to be the stuff of lasting poetry.

I hope you are having an agreeable holiday. Belgium's a curious country. Not that I know much of it: but what I do know is odd. But Italy is the real place. The more one goes into it, the more one is astonished by its richness. All that these creatures poured out in the past—and *cui bono*? What has become of all their thought and passion? It seems to have had no particular effect on anything. The fossilized remains are still here—miraculous: the tourists look at them—and that's all.

Yours
Aldous Huxley

216: TO MRS ETHEL COLLIER

25 bis Rue Decamps, Paris XVIe.
29 August, 1924

Dear Aunt Ethel,

I got your letter only this morning—which is due to the fact that for the last fortnight or so we have been floating, without much of an address, between here and Italy. We left the seaside near Pisa on the 11th, meaning to stop in the mountains, on our way across the Alps, for a few days so that I could finish the book I had to get done in time for this autumn. But when we got on top of the Mont Cenis the temperature fell to 2° centigrade and the rain fell in torrents; so that we were driven down into the plain—only to find that every hotel we came to was completely full. After sleeping one night in a kitchen we at last found rooms at an absurd little place called Ambérieu, where we stayed 10 days. When I got my work done, we drove on and got here yesterday, where we are staying for a couple of nights with Lewis Gielgud, before going on to London. This means, I'm afraid, that we shall just miss you, if you're going to Como, on the 1st. And by the time you're back, we shall probably be off again. It's sad; for we should have liked very much to stay at North House. As it is, we're going to be in some rooms in Chelsea. Uncle Jack's portrait must remain, alas, for the time being in a state of potentiality. I hope he'll let me sit some other time. The process will, I am sure, be less painful than sitting for Rothenstein, who insists on treating his victims rather as tho' they were pieces of architecture—demanding a stone-like rigidity and taking constant measurements with plumb lines, theodolites, compasses and other instruments of the same sort.

Maria is well and sends her love. She drives our little Citroen with great vigour and skill and has taken us across the Alps and through France in a most dashing fashion. Matthew we have left at the sea side, where—thank the Lord and unberufen—he has at last begun to eat properly—owing to the presence of half a dozen other children in the house, who have roused a spirit of emulation in him at meal-times; so that he now puts away beefsteaks and fish like a hero. The result has been a marked improvement in his digestion—no more dirty tongue etc. Let's hope it will last. Love from both of us to you and Uncle Jack. I hope Bellagio will be pleasant—tho' I see in the papers that it's been very wet là-bas.

Yours
Aldous

217: TO T. S. ELIOT

*258 King's Road, Chelsea, S.W.*3
24 September, 1924

Dear Tom,

I was most sorry to have missed you last Thursday. I had to go to an insurance office in the same street and was kept just two minutes too long; so that when I got to your office, it was to find that you and [J. W. N.] Sullivan had just gone out. Would lunch either on Wednesday or Thursday be a possibility for you? I hope so.

Meanwhile I have to make very belated apologies for having failed to produce the article I pledged myself to write last summer for the *Criterion*. The truth is that, deep in other work, I kept putting off and putting off the the writing of it, until finally there wasn't time to do the thing adequately. And I still feel that it couldn't be done adequately without a lot of special reading. And special reading, as I dare say you know only too well, tends to get postponed in a most horrible way ad infinitum and to be jostled out of the way by innumerable thronging affairs. One of my reasons for coming to England was to do some reading at the libraries; but I haven't managed to

217 *Vivien: Vivienne Haigh Haigh-Wood Eliot, Eliot's first wife, who was an ether drinker. While in London the Huxleys were occupying a flat lent to them by an old friend, Rachel Russell.*

do very much. I did not write before because I always hoped to get the article finally done, to my satisfaction. But it looks to me as though the day of its completion were still very remote.

I hope Vivien is better than when I was here last.

Yours,
Aldous Huxley

218: † TO E. S. P. HAYNES

[*London*]
29 *September*, 1924

Dear Ted,

These few lines to tell you how much I enjoyed *Fritto Misto*. My only complaint is that some [*sic*] are too short. You start such delightful hares and haven't the leisure to pursue; you drop exciting hints and resume whole branches of learning in single sentences. One wants to hear more. Some day, I hope, you will give it us. The personalities are particularly good, I think. Little sketches like that of old Forbes at Balliol are quite admirable. Altogether a very pleasant book—and Philip Sainsbury's printing added a peculiar charm.

Knowing your interest in Arnold Ward, I must tell you this delightful story which I had from Osbert Sitwell a day or two since. Osbert was in the St. James's Club one night when A. W. reeled in, very drunk and entered into conversation with him. Osbert, to make talk said, 'I believe that a great friend of mine, Aldous Huxley, is a relation of yours'. To which A. W. replied in a very dignified and outraged tone 'Yes; and if I were to meet him now in Piccadilly I should bloody well take his trousers off and leave him there'. 'Dear me', said Osbert 'and why, may I ask?' 'Because', A. W. replies 'because I consider (hiccough) that he's disgraced his ancestors.' (My offence was writing *Antic Hay*.)

I hope your holiday has been a success and that the S. of France has been a little warmer than London, where rainstorms have alternated with half gales every day since you left.

Yours,
A.L.H.

219: TO ROBERT NICHOLS

[25 *bis Rue Decamps, Paris XVIe*]
As from: 15 *Via S. Margherita a Montici,*
Florence
5 *October*, 1924

My dear Robert,

I am in debt to you for two letters—a debt I would have acquitted earlier,

218 *Arnold Ward: Huxley's cousin, the son of Mrs Humphry Ward.*

233

but for the fact that I have been strenuously doing boring business in London and after, strenuously sight-seeing in Holland and Belgium. Arrived in Paris, I have a few moments quiet in which to answer them.

Let me talk of practical things first. About life in Italy: it can be done all right on about £600 a year. I can indicate the main items of budget. Rent —you can get a 10 or 15-roomed furnished house in the neighbourhood of Florence (or, if you're wise, elsewhere) for, at the outside, £100 a year. You oughtn't to spend more than £70 or £80. Service—a good maid can be got for 30/- a month, £18 per annum. Food works out at from 15/- to £1 per week per head. There are no taxes, unless you own your house or make it apparent that you are a permanent inhabitant. Fuel and light oughtn't to cost more than £30 or £40 a year. Personally, I find that money goes just about twice as far as in London. On the same income on which I just kept alive, uncomfortably, in London, I live in a large house, with 2 servants and nurse, keep a small car, travel quite a lot and save money to boot. I am also far healthier, put on weight. I think I shall certainly stay in Italy (tho' not in Florence, whose English population is a bit too frightful to be lived among) until it is time for Matthew to be educated. Then, I suppose, London or Oxford. Chi sa?

I saw your father the other day (he very kindly put us up for a night on our way to Harwich); he seemed to hope you'd stay là-bas in the hope of something agreeable turning up. I don't know America: but I shd imagine your father was rather optimistic. I, at any rate, shall stick to southern Europe for the present.

The musical fragment you send looks full of promise. I don't think I know the thing it comes from and here I have no music to consult. How I wish I could play the piano. But I can't: and the time required to learn to strum with facility at sight seems beyond my powers to make, at present. This last year I have been incessantly busy, writing: and shall be next, I suppose. And meanwhile, all the things one wants to do and learn! It's really desperate. The really prodigious creatures managed to make the time. They had a capacity for working long and rapidly which one can only envy. I just get tired out when I try to do all I want to do: and there's an end of it.

I was looking at 'Golgotha and Co' the other day and liked it more than I did before. You throw your net very wide and you catch a lot. I still think the form and manner not quite satisfactory—tho' I can't offer any alternatives. What are you doing now?

I have just finished a novel which is to appear in January. It comes off fairly well, I think. The main theme of it is the undercutting of everything by a sort of despairing scepticism and then the undercutting of that by mysticism.

Have you ever read the *Life of Clerk Maxwell* [by Lewis Campbell]? An astonishing book—not the life, which is stupid and in a snuffling style— but the letters and essays of Maxwell's contained in it. They're marvellous.

234

I don't think I ever read things that made me so profoundly admire and respect the writer. A huge intelligence that played justly over the whole range of ideas; and then, in the teeth of the Victorian materialism which surrounded him, this clear, calm mysticism. Talk of undercutting all under-cuttings—his life and work cut down under everything. One of the greatest men of science: not a specialist with one luminous spot, like Newton, but universally judicious and intelligent; takes everything into account and finishes up in a state of *avahat-ship*. Very astonishing. You should read it, if you don't know it already. Remember me to your wife. And if you do elect to come to Italy, let me know.

Yours
ALH

220: TO EUGENE F. SAXTON

15 *Via S. Margherita a Montici,*
Florence
28 October, 1924

Dear Saxton,

I was very glad to have your letter and to hear that you liked *Those Barren Leaves*. It cuts more ice, I think, than the others and is more explicit and to the point. The characters too, are better, I think.

Our friend at the Eiffel Tower is a bit of a liar, I'm afraid. For I've not been near his place for upwards of a year—a brief visit to London this September being the only occasion I've been in England since about May 1923. However, I hope you enjoyed the wine and I thank you very much for drinking my health in it, not to mention that of the Holy Ghost or, as the Japanese call him, 'the honourable Bird'.

I find that I feel so much better in Italy than in London—and the same applies to my wife and child—that I shall stay here for the next few years—until such time as my small boy has to go to school, when I suppose we shall have to settle in England again. But that is still fairly remote. When you're next in Europe you must come to Italy. It is one of the few habitable parts of the continent.

220 *This letter is the earliest preserved of Huxley's long correspondence with Saxton, which ended with the latter's death in 1943. Saxton, who had formerly been a journalist and had edited* The Bookman, *worked for George H. Doran, Huxley's American publisher, until 1925, when he became the head of the editorial department of Harper & Brothers. His personal friendship with Huxley, maintained during the suspension of their editor-author relationship, was intensified after Harper became Huxley's publisher in 1933 with the publication of* Texts and Pretexts. *Saxton was for years Huxley's closest friend in the United States, and his presence helped appreciably to create the climate of welcome to which Huxley was attracted from his home in France in the late 1930's.*

I am at work on a volume of essays, the central theme of which is travel (but the variations on the theme are numerous) to be called something like *Along the Road* or *At the Road's Edge*—a title which wd indicate the subject of the book and serve at the same time to connect it with *On the Margin*. I hope to have the MS ready by Xmas, so that you might, if you want it, publish in the spring, between *Those Barren Leaves* and the next fiction book, which shd be ready for autumn publication. That will consist either of 3 or 4 long short stories or a novel. It depends how the ideas I have for the last mature in the next few months.

With best wishes,

Yours very sincerely
Aldous Huxley

221: TO LEONARD HUXLEY

15 *Via S. Margherita a Montici,*
Florence
[3 *December,* 1924]

Dearest Father,

I have been meaning to write these weeks past; but business combined with laziness has hindered me, and time passes, when one is fully occupied, with such an incredible rapidity, that it is only every month or so that one wakes from the trance of life to realize that it's a long while since last one took stock.

Our journey back was entirely successful. Holland was a revelation, especially the country, which is the place for Last Rides Together: one longs to drive on and on across the unbroken plain. But my word, how cold! And the prices! Though it must be admitted they give you more for your money than anyone else. A table d'hôte luncheon in Holland contains enough nourishment to supply two ordinary English gluttons for forty-eight hours. It rained most of the time we were in Belgium, so that we did not see the Meuse valley, as we went south, at its best. But it is marvellously lovely, and exactly like those strangely improbable little landscapes of Patinir (there is one, at least, in the National) which I always thought mere fancies before driving from Namur to the French frontier.

Reims was a sad spectacle of desolation. But superb, even as a skeleton. And the country round is wonderfully beautiful. But the best time began after Paris, when the weather settled into the most perfect autumn serenity. We went south rather deviously, through Chartres, Orléans, Bourges, Moulins, Lyons. Chartres fine, but Bourges unbelievably magnificent. Its interior by far the most splendid piece of Gothic architecture I have ever seen. The country, too, is lovely in a placid way; rolling plains, with forests periodically, the whole extraordinarily thinly populated. Indeed, a motor journey through France is politically most instructive; for one realizes how

236

few people there are in this enormous country. I have never been in a flat and fertile country where there were so few villages or signs of life. In Italy, wherever one goes, even in the mountains, one sees new houses being built, towns growing, villages multiplying themselves. In France, I don't remember to have seen a single new house under construction, except in the devastated areas. No wonder they're frightened of the Germans. The solution will be a sort of peaceful penetration; colonies of Italians in the south, Belgians in the north, Germans in the east. Already they import, temporarily, upwards of a million labourers every year; and enormous numbers of foreigners are permanently settled.

After Lyons (over roads of an indescribable badness, very tightly rolled macadam with very deep holes and this for fifty, sixty, seventy miles at a stretch, so that it completely disheartened one) we went through Provence, to Orange and Avignon. Fine; but one should have seen them before Italy, not after. Thence to Marseilles, very lively and southern, and from there, by the inland road, about the worst we met on the whole journey, which is saying a good deal, to Fréjus; through the forest of Esterel to Cannes and along the coast to Nice. Thence along the French and Italian riviera to Genoa—a rather tiresome drive; for that riviera landscape—mountains tumbling into the sea, becomes very tedious after a little. I prefer incomparably the landscape further south, by Massa, where you have a plain between the sea and the mountains. Everything shows there to much better advantage and you have more variety.

The car went through its ordeals in a marvellous fashion, the only weakness being, at a given moment, a leak of oil into the clutch, which made the engine race without turning the wheels as it ought. However, that was remedied by suitable ablutions of petrol before the most serious mountain climbing—between Chiavari and Spezia—had to be done; so all was well. Between London and Florence we did about three thousand kilometres.

Since then I have been busy on a book of essays, mostly arising out of the incidents and sights of travel. I hope to have the MS ready by the new year. I mean to send you one or two of the essays to see if you would like them for the *Cornhill*.

Matthew has been very well, and is eating much better than he did; but at present has a bit of a cold. The doctor tells us that his heart is not too strong, so that we must be careful not to make him overdo it, unless we want him laid up on his back for a period of months later on.

We have been having a horrible spell of cold weather—icy nights with fogs in the valleys. However, we are high enough to get plenty of sun at mid day; and at the moment I am sitting out on the terrace, in my shirtsleeves. But the sun is not entirely welcome; for there has been a long drought and we are most horribly short of water. Baths have been out of the question for the last three weeks. The water problem and the great difficulty of heating the house in winter have made us anxious for some time past to find something better. Moreover, Florence is not ideal, either climatically or socially. There is too much fog in the valleys and too little water on the hills, too many bores to be avoided and too many casual tourists. We have just returned from a four days trip to look at what, I hope, will be the ideal place. It is Monte Circeo. You will see it on the map about seventy miles south of Rome, near Terracina. It is an isolated fragment of the Apennines once, no doubt, an island, but now rising out of the flat plain of the Pomptine marshes. It has the climate of Capri, without the disadvantages of that island—remoteness and the presence of the most intolerable foreigners. It is incredibly beautiful. A great limestone mountain, five miles long and eighteen hundred feet high at its highest peak, falling on one side into the sea and on the other into the almost Dutch plain of the Pomptine marshes, on the further side of which rise the Volscian hills. From the summit one can see, in clear weather, both the dome of St Peter's and Vesuvius.

The mountain is covered with woods of cork trees and a kind of macchia or bush of fragrant shrubs and tall white heather. On its lower slopes are vineyards producing some of the best muscat grapes in Italy. The coast is partly rocky and partly sandy. In the plain, which has mostly been reclaimed from malaria—all the part near Circeo is now cultivated—are wild tracts full of birds of every kind, from ducks to quail; and huge herds of half wild grey buffaloes graze there, tended by cowboys on horseback; so that one has a further element of Wild West to add variety. At the western end of the mountain are the ruins of a Roman town, with Lucullus's villa and fishponds, where fish are still bred. We found on Circeo, just below the modern village, on the shore, a charming little house, very well and comfortably furnished and belonging to a pleasant retired business man from Rome, who lives in an adjoining house and runs a little estate. The rent is a hundred a year and I think we shall take it; for it is getting more and more difficult and expensive to get anything at the sea further north. The summer climate is made temperate by sea and mountain breezes. We find that the sea does Matthew so much good that we want to try the effect of a good many months at a stretch in a place where he can get all the advantages of sun and sea air at every season —with occasional changes, of course, to other airs. We got there from Rome in about three and a half hours. But with balloon tyres—which we should certainly have fitted, if we lived there—we should probably get it down to three. For it is only the bad surface of the Via Appia—particularly the cobbled part of it, from Rome as far as Velletri—that prevents one from going as fast as the engine can take one. The road itself is mostly quite straight, broad and with only a short spell of hill. Balloons will also make it easier to get to Naples, if ever we want to. The south is not remarkable for its good roads.

We came back from Rome by the most fearfully twisty and mountainous route: from Viterbo to the west of Monte Amiata and so to Siena. One is constantly running up to eight or nine hundred metres and down again. Beautiful country, like the best part of Sussex, but much more so—higher hills, deeper valleys, larger woods, But not for motoring, at any rate if one is in a hurry. In that case the best way to Rome from Florence is Arezzo, Perugia, Todi, Narni, Civita Castellana and so on, across the campagna. By that route one avoids the worst climbs. I doubt if there is anything up to two thousand feet. And the major part of the way is remarkably flat. But it is long—three hundred and fifty kilometres. Siena and Radicofani save fifty, but the country is much more up and down all the way, there is one pass of three thousand and one of two thousand five hundred and the last forty miles into Rome are over a road that can only be compared for badness with the French roads at their worst. Still, the French take the prize.

Love to the family, which I hope flourishes.

Your loving son,
Aldous

P.S. Just got your letter as I was preparing to put this into its envelope. The news seems good. I'm glad Margaret has found things satisfactory in Africa. Let's hope she will do her share to keep them satisfactory. I envy you the new Morris. If we get a new car, which won't be yet awhile, it will be Italian and more powerful than the Citroen, in order to deal with these hills. Possibly the new Lancia, or even, if it's not too dear, the new 6 cylinder Itala, which is said to have all the qualities of the Alfa Romeo, which won the Grand Prix this year, together with better material and greater durability.

222: † TO NORMAN DOUGLAS

15 *Via S. Margherita a Montici,*
Florence
6 December, 1924

Dear Douglas,

I'm most sorry to hear you've been ill. From Orioli I had gloomy accounts of an abscess in the cheek, but I hope very much this is better.

If I called for you at your house on Wednesday or Thursday morning next, could you come and lunch with me in some eating hell in town? Living here is like being at the north pole; it is quite incredibly difficult to meet people if one wants to (tho' it has the advantage of making it very easy to avoid those one doesn't want to meet). Hence this long-sighted plotting— which I hope will be successful, as I shd like very much to see you after all these ages.

Yours
Aldous Huxley

221 *Margaret: Huxley's sister had gone out to South Africa to teach.*
222 *Orioli: Giuseppi (Pino) Orioli, publisher and antiquarian, friend of Norman Douglas.*

15 *Via S. Margherita a Montici,*
Florence
25 *January,* 1925

My dear J,

Your letter was most welcome, the more so as it has broken that spell of silence which seems to have prevented us for so long from communicating. To me, when I am working, the writing of letters is a positive nightmare; and as it is seldom that I'm not working, I rarely write any letters. At the moment I am taking a few days off, having just finished a collection of essays [*Along the Road*], which took me longer to do than I bargained for.

Here life goes on as quietly and pleasantly as usual. The greatest luxury of this existence is the feeling and being well—unberufen. I think we should all have been in the grave by this time if we had stayed on in London. That is what chiefly persuades me to stay on here for the present. Not, however, in Florence, which has various disadvantages, the worst of which are the people and the water supply. I am inclined to think we shall move southwards in the spring or early summer to Monte Circeo, half way between Rome and Naples, a place that has all the climatic and picturesque advantages of Capri without its intolerable disadvantages; it is on the mainland and it is not inhabited by Sodomites. Also it has those miraculously beautiful Pontine Marshes behind it and is quite close, by car, to Rome; which is, after all, the only town. We are in treaty for a very nice house, which I hope we shall get. If we do, I think you ought to come and stay there in the summer. It would be very restful and healthy—much more so than a bicycle tour in France which, I gather from Juliette's letter to Maria, is the alternative you have in mind. Considering the state of the French roads, of which we had only too much experience this summer, I should think a bicycle tour in hell would be preferable. Where they are not cobbled, the roads are full of shell holes—sometimes for a hundred miles at a time. They can only be negotiated with balloon tyres. The Italian roads are better, on the whole—not so good as the best bits of the French, but not nearly so bad as the worst. It seems to me that what is indicated is sea bathing, sunshine and the wine-and-macaroni cure.

You suggest lectures for lucre in the U.S.A.:—I have had several offers from various lecture agencies, but have always declined to have anything to do with them. The fatigue and the boredom of a lecture tour frighten me too much. When I hear accounts from my literary friends who have trodden that dreary path, I make up my mind that I won't go to the U.S.A. till I can afford to go there on my own. The prospect of lecturing to women's clubs and being entertained to preliminary luncheon by each—with a few well chosen words about what one thinks of America or the sex problem to finish up the repast—is altogether too repulsive. Nor, I gather, are these tours always so profitable as one is led to suppose. Frank Swinnerton, who has an enormous reputation over there, was actually out of pocket, I fancy, at the end of his tour. How unchanging national characteristics are! I have been re-reading *Martin Chuzzlewit* and the letters from America printed in the *Life of Dickens*; the people—at any rate to judge from the specimens one meets here and from what they write—are just the same; the same interminable canting balderdash about high moral principles and ideals, couched in the same verbose, pseudo-philosophic, sham-scientific, meaningless language, the same pretentiousness then as now. One thing, however, which they didn't seem to have invented in Dickens's day is that awful chivalry—that spoiling of women by the men—which makes most of the American women one meets so intolerably importunate for attention, so cock-sure that you are going to be interested in their 'poysonalities'. And, oh dear, how little interest one does take!

I have put myself up to the Vice-Chancellor as a candidate for the Kahn travelling fellowship. The election takes place in February. I fear I have very little chance of getting the swag, which they will dole out, very properly, to some learned and meritorious sociologist who will return from his travels in a position to write some perfectly unreadable book about something completely unimportant. The V-C asked me what I proposed to study on my travels if I should be awarded the fellowship. Rather a stumper! I could only say Art—the last refuge of the ignorant—with particular reference (and this I thought rather a stroke of genius) to the American and Asiatic developments of European renaissance architectural styles! Considering the complete futility of this subject—an ideal thesis for a doctorate—I have some faint, faint hopes that they may give me a thousand pounds to permit me to visit the Jesuit missions in Mexico and Goa. But it would be too good to be true.

I have just been reading Benjamin Kidd's *Principles of Western Civilization*; which, under its hideous verbiage, is full of interesting ideas. What an extraordinary contrast when you compare it with the corresponding book of fifty years earlier—Buckle's *History of Civilization*. That half century knocked a lot of complacency out of the world and pricked a great many very pleasant bubbles.

What about [Jules] Romains? Is there anything in eyeless sight? My last news with regard to it was, if I remember, an unfavourable verdict from the Institute, or whatever does give unfavourable verdicts on scientific hypotheses in France. Not that this is conclusive, I imagine, by any means. (You remember the unanimously favourable verdict in favour of N rays?) Does he eliminate all possibilities of thought transference from the sighted spectator who can read with his eyes what the blind man is trying to read with his stomach?

Talking about thought transference reminds me of an uncommonly interesting French book—I forget the exact title—by a Dr Osty about supernormal states and faculties. He gives some most extraordinary cases—the oddest, I think, about the use of specially talented mediums for medical

241

diagnosis; and the people who have an 'autoscopic' faculty and can plainly see all the details of their own internal anatomy. What a pity that all these issues are so frightfully confused by these Conan Doyles and post-mortem interviews with Lord Northcliffe!

[. . . .]

Love from both of us to both of you.

Yours,
Aldous

224: TO MRS NAOMI MITCHISON

15 Via S. Margherita a Montici,
Florence
25 February, 1925

My dear Naomi,

Thank you for your very friendly and pleasing letter of a couple of weeks ago. I'm glad you liked the *Leaves*. They are all right, certainly; tremendously accomplished, but in a queer way, I now feel, jejune and shallow and off the point. All I've written so far has been off the point. And I've taken such enormous pains to get off it; that's the stupidity. All this fuss in the intellectual void; and meanwhile the other things go on in a quiet domestic way, quite undisturbed. I wish I could afford to stop writing for a bit.

No, I don't read much ethics, if only because it is perfectly obvious to me that ethics are transcendental and that any attempt to rationalize them is hopeless. Benjamin Kidd is quite interesting in his attempt to find a biological theory of the transcendental authority of ethics. But of course all these delightfully simple theories based on the idea of natural selection have got to be taken with considerable caution. Before they can be swallowed we have got to find out if, and how, natural selection selects. You Mendelians have made all that extremely uplifting and stimulating evolutionary philosophy look a bit dubious. Still, I think there's a good deal in Kidd's theories of religion and morals. But of course the discovery of the origins of a thing constitutes no explanation of the thing. You can discover the biological function of ethics, you can establish a connection between religion and intestinal stasis or sexual desires. But your discoveries will not in the least affect the value of the ethical and religious experiences of the individual. The theory of those individual experiences must be worked out separately. On this subject Lao Tsz[u] is most remarkable. His little book on the Tao is a sort of philosophical explanation of the ethics of Christianity. It gives the reasons why it is necessary to lose one's life in order to gain it: because it is impossible to have a real and absolute self, so long as the superficial self is allowed to control things. It is the sacrifice of one egoism for the sake of realizing another and much profounder egoism. It is the same idea as lies at the bottom of the Yogi system. The same, of course, as in Christianity; but more explicitly and more intellectually stated.

Your deplorable taste for the countries of the barbarians seems to keep you away from Italy. Which is a pity. If you bring with you a northern soul, northern friends and northern books, it is the perfect country. For you possess, indoors, the speciality of the north—the soul—and you have out of doors the speciality of the Mediterranean—beauty. In the north you have to be content with souls only.

Yours,
Aldous

225: TO JOHN MIDDLETON MURRY

15 *Via S. Margherita a Montici,*
Florence
5 *March,* 1925

Dear Murry,

Thanks for your letter. The article in question is in the hands of Pinker and I am not sure whether he has sold it in England. I have written to him to tell him to send it you, if it hasn't already appeared. You could ring him up and find out.

The question of the pseudo-sciences is a most interesting one. Fundamentally, the mistake of all of the modern ones is, I think, this: they suppose that they have explained a thing when they have traced its origins. For example, the psychos imagine that they have shed some light on art by affirming that the origin of art is an infantile coprophily. Even if that were the origin of art—which it pretty obviously is not—it would not enlighten us in the slightest degree about Giotto or Michelangelo. You might as well try to 'explain' sight by insisting that eyes are derived from spots of pigment. Obviously, the origins have an interest, are worth trying to discover; but the study of them must be kept quite distinct from the study of actual, contemporary developments.

I shall be most interested to see how you set about building up a system of comparative psychology. I suppose there would have to be a large historical section showing how differently organized societies have affected the individual—who must have remained practically unchanged, on the average, during historical time—bringing out or masking one or other of his potentialities. And then the alarming results in present days of the collapse, for an ever widening circle of individuals, of the social system—the uncomfortable results of an utter scepticism about society in its present form. The individual left to himself, with nothing to support him; consequently finding the virtues of love, humility and faith more than ever difficult to

225 *Article: 'Our Contemporary Hocus-Pocus', which had appeared in the March number of* Forum. *Murry reprinted it in the May number of* The Adelphi.

practise. Moreover, habituated to the practice of self analysis on a scale never before attempted—self analysis, which always has the terrible effect of making the analyser conscious of the evil opposites of everything good that he analyses. Analysing love for a fellow being, he discovers hatred; analysing purity, he discovers impurity. That is the penalty we pay for excessive self-consciousness.

Yours,
Aldous Huxley

226: TO JOSEPHINE PIERCY

15 *Via S. Margherita a Montici,*
Florence, Italy
11 *March,* 1925

Dear Miss Piercy,

Your letter of February 10th has reached me, after considerable delay, just as I am on the point of leaving for North Africa. I can do no more at the present than acknowledge the receipt of it and assure you that I will think of what you have asked me during my absence. If I can think of anything that might be of use to your pupils, I will let you have it on my return. But having had some experience of teaching myself, I know the great difficulty of imparting notions of good writing to those not naturally gifted with a certain sense of words and a certain interest in words as such. To be quite honest, I really haven't the faintest idea how good writing, apart from merely grammatical writing, can be taught. My own ambition in teaching English has never risen higher than this; to teach my pupils to write grammar and sense in the fewest and least pretentious words. The great danger now is the journalistic habit of using long, pretentious, abstract words, lumped together in formless, doughy sentences. May I suggest to you an excellent example which you could give your students of good and bad writing on rather similar themes? Take Benjamin Kidd's *Principles of Western Civilization* and select from it at random almost any passage—the whole book is almost uniformly bad as writing, though its ideas are often good—and place it in juxtaposition with a passage from Burke's writings on the French Revolution, say the extremely noble passage on the indissolubility of the social contract. Kidd is about as bad as modern journalistic writing can be; he is a perfect example of how not to express abstract ideas. Burke, on the other hand, is about as good as anything in that kind could be.

Please forgive this rather incoherent letter, which is written in great haste.

Yours very truly,
Aldous Huxley

226 *Josephine Piercy, now retired from the faculty of Indiana University, was a teacher of English.*

15 *Via S. Margherita a Montici,*
Florence
10 *April,* 1925

My dear Robert,

Thank you for your long, friendly and interesting letter of March 2nd, which I found waiting for me here on my return from a brief jaunt in Tunisia. I entirely agree with most of your criticisms. My references [in 'Our Contemporary Hocus-Pocus'] to Dr Ernest Jones's lyrical remarks about art and anuses were only intended to make fun [. . . .] I quite agree with you in what you say about roots and fruits. The fundamental error of all the modern pseudo-sciences consists in supposing that they have explained a thing when they have dug up its origins, or at least what they suppose to be its origins.

I must certainly read Goethe, of whom, as you point out to me, I am lamentably ignorant. Pascal, on the other hand, is a tried companion. I have dipped into Hulme. A bit too slap dash, I thought; but stimulating. Don't call Wittgenstein a mere rationalist. He uses his rationalism to take away, stone by stone, the whole fabric of reason under him. At the end of that extraordinary little book you find yourself in empty spiritual space—and if you don't sprout a pair of angel's wings, you fall. Gentile I have not read. Is it possible that Mussolini's ex-minister of education can really have something good to say? It is, by the way, a remarkable fact: that since philosophers have directed the educational policy of Italy—Croce and Gentile —the grants in favour of scientific research have been reduced almost to zero. Vaihinger, I foresee, I shall have to read.

But for me the most vital problem is not the mental so much as the ethical and emotional. The fundamental problem is love and humility, which are the same thing. The enormous difficulty of love and humility—a difficulty greater now, I feel, than ever; because men are more solitary now than they were; all authority has gone; the tribe has disappeared and every at all conscious man stands alone, surrounded by other solitary individuals and fragments of the old tribe, for which he feels no respect. Obviously, the only thing to be done is to go right through with the process; to realize individuality to the full, the real individuality, Lao-Tsz[u]'s individuality, the Yogis' individuality, and with it the oneness of everything. Obviously! But the difficulty is huge. And meanwhile the world is peopled with miserable beings who are neither one thing nor the other; who are solitary and yet not complete individuals; conscious only of the worst part of themselves (that deplorable and characteristic self-consciousness of the present time that examines all that is good and beautiful until it discovers its opposite); and devilishly proud of what they regard as their marvellous independence and their acuteness of spirit. For them love and humility are impossible. And hence everything else of any value is also impossible of achievement. What's to be done about it? That's the great question. Some day I may find some sort of an answer. And then I may write a good book, or at any rate a mature book, not a queer sophisticatedly jejune book, like this last affair, like all the blooming lot, in fact.

You say nothing of your activities, my dear Robert. Or rather you say something, but only in pencil at the end of your letter—in such dim pencil that I can't make out anything beyond the words 'two acts of a play'. Tell me, I beg—but in ink. And when are you coming to Europe? I cannot believe that 622345678 Glen Av, Hollywood is really a very salubrious address. We are moving to Rome, if we can find a house there, this autumn. And then, if I have money, I'd like to go travelling, somewhere remote and luscious. But all this is vague in the extreme. Your sister Irene comes to stay with us tomorrow for a few days. Good bye.

Yours,
Aldous H.

228: TO JULIAN HUXLEY

15 *Via S. Margherita a Montici,*
Florence
21 *April,* 1925

My dear J,
About plans: the house at Monte Circeo has fallen through, so I fear we shan't be able to put you up as we hoped. On the other hand, I think it quite possible that we may be in Switzerland for a little this summer. What part of the country are you going to? We might at least choose the same canton. We shall probably be in the Rhone valley off and on during the summer, as we are going to try the effect of Dr [Auguste] Rollier's sun-cure kindergarten at Leysin on Matthew, who, though well on the whole, has been curiously languid and easily-tired of late. The doctors here seem to think that Leysin can do nothing but good. And I think that in any case the mountain air may be tonic as a change from the sea of previous summers. Also, the other children will be good for him. Circeo having failed us, we shall probably look for something in Rome this autumn. After a third-rate provincial town, colonized by English sodomites and middle-aged Lesbians, which is, after all, what Florence is, a genuine metropolis will be lively. Not to mention the fact that it is incomparably the most lovely place in the world.

We enjoyed Tunisia very much, especially the great Saharan oases in the south—Gabes, Tozeur and, above all, Nefta. The beauty of Nefta is really unimaginable until one has seen it—a dense forest of 400,000 palm trees clustering in the middle of the desert; water flowing in little streams and

228 *Dohrns: Anton Dohrn founded the Marine Biological Station at Naples;*
Julian Huxley had been a research scholar there in 1909-10.

canals everywhere; fruit trees of every sort growing thickly under the palms; here and there little white domed marabouts; the hotel overlooking the market place, so that you can watch the habits of the aborigines at leisure. The perfect place to spend a winter holiday. It never rains, I fancy; it is warm enough to grow bananas, pepper and castor oil. It is cheap and comfortable. An occasional dust storm is the chief affliction. Moreover, next winter there will even be a line of motor buses plying across the desert, 200 kilometres, to Touggourt and Biskra. All the conveniences.

We lunched with the Dohrns at Naples—very nice and friendly. But their house is being spoilt; for the land in front is being covered with immense tenements, which will soon regorge with the usual Neapolitan stink, children, dirt, lice and cutthroats. What a beastly town it is! Far dirtier than any Arab village. And for beauty it doesn't compare with Palermo in the same sort of style.

Busy as usual, pegging away. I am trying to arrange for syndication of articles in America. Golden lures. I have a sad feeling that it's all too good to be true and that I shall never make the money out of these devils that other people contrive to make. It's most distressing to think that there, on the other side of the water, are one hundred and five million beings whose sole function—if you look at their lives sub specie aeternitatis—is to provide people like us with money, and that yet we remain poor.

Well, I must go to my mill again. I wish it were as easy to write a book as it is to read it. The amount of sheer ass's labour in the process is very distasteful. And yet if there weren't that ass's labour, what could one do? For being three parts ass oneself one is obviously only fit to do ass's work for three quarters of one's time.

Love to the family.

Aldous

229: TO ERIC PINKER

15 *Via S. Margherita a Montici,*
Florence
14 *May,* 1925

Dear Pinker,

This is to recommend to your attention a novel by my friend, Mr. Lewis Gielgud. It deals with an exciting phase of recent history—the beginnings of the Russian Revolution; deals with it without political bias, but very dramatically.

229 *Gielgud's novel* Red Soil *was published by Heinemann in January,* 1926. *Since it resembled in theme a play which Huxley had helped do (and indeed had begun apparently without Gielgud's collaboration—see letters* 166 *and* 167 *as well as letter* 180), *his* démarche *to Pinker was not a disinterested one. Also, before the novel was published Huxley and Gielgud themselves composed a film scenario adapted from their earlier experiments. That seems not to have been sold.*

As you will see, the story is written so as to lend itself to serial publication. And I am sure that you will also notice its eminent suitability to serve as a basis for a film. In this last respect it seems to me to offer great possibilities.

Yours
Aldous Huxley

230: TO VIOLET PAGET

15 *Via S. Margherita a Montici,*
Firenze
26 *May,* 1925

Dear Miss Paget,

I have been savouring the *Golden Keys*—if one can be said to savour a key—at leisure and with the keenest enjoyment. I tend to like best the papers about the places I know myself—Bologna and that beautiful Bologna road (where we were once held up for a night, in arctic cold, by the snow) and that exquisite Villa Gori at Siena (which it was only the lack of drains and water that prevented us once from actually living in). They recall old delights and make me observe significant details which I had not noticed or insufficiently appreciated.

From the known I proceed with confidence to the unknown, feeling sure that, when I come to visit Vezelay and Semur and Wolframsdorf, I shall find that I know them already—know the essential and artistically important things about them—from your book.

How much I like, too, your generalizations about the Genius Loci! One may be born a worshipper of more spectacular deities—from Jehovah to D. H. Lawrence's Dark God, from Dionysus to the object of Boehme's ecstasies—one may be born but it is useless to try to make oneself, consciously, a worshipper at such shrines. For most of us, I fancy, Wordsworth's Natural Pieties are the most decent and satisfactory thing. Of the theory and practice of the Natural Pieties your books are a most delicate and beautiful exposition.

I am looking forward with faith, hope and patience to the end of this abominable weather. When it comes, I shall venture to propose myself again one afternoon. And if it doesn't come—which seems, after all, likely enough—well, I shall do the same.

Yours very sincerely,
Aldous Huxley

231: TO LEONARD HUXLEY

15 *Via S. Margherita a Montici,*
Florence
21 *June,* 1925

Dearest Father,

I have fears that you may already be halfway to the North Pole by the time we reach the southern shores of the British isles. We hope to be in England about the middle of July for a short time. Will you be in Scotland? I hope not, but I am rather afraid you will be.

We propose to leave Florence about the 1st of July and shall go, possibly in the car, to Belgium, leaving Matthew with his grandmother at St. Trond, while we come on to England. I hope that, if we decide to take the car, we shall have more propitious weather than we had last year, when we were half frozen on the Mont Cenis, and more than half drowned all the way from Chambéry to Paris.

We had a curious taste of fascist methods the other day, when our house was suddenly invaded by four of the most sinister looking gallows' birds you ever saw—they gave themselves out to be commissaries of police, and indeed I am sure they really were—who demanded to search it, in order to find either the person of, or documents belonging to, a certain Professor [Gaetano] Salvemini of the University of Florence, who was wanted for having written against the government. As a matter of fact we had never even met Salvemini; but he was the friend of friends of ours, which was, I suppose, the reason why they associated him with us. I made a great fuss, demanded to see their warrant, which they hadn't got, swore I'd complain to my ambassador etc. They ended up by being rather ashamed of themselves. But it was a tiresome and unpleasant business. Meanwhile Salvemini—who is one of the most distinguished of Italian historians—is in prison. Curious country! And this latest project, which has just been passed through the lower house, for 'reforming' the bureaucracy, (which includes the magistrature), by turning out all civil servants who are not fascist in sympathy —it's really too fantastic, wd be comic if it weren't tragic.

Love to all of you from all of us. Matthew is flourishing.

Your loving son,

Aldous

232: TO JULIAN HUXLEY

15 *Via S. Margherita a Montici,*
Florence
21 *June,* 1925

My dear Julian,

We expect to be in England about the middle of July. Will you be there then? I hope so. If not we must combine to meet somewhere else.

Maria went with Matthew to Leysin, but found that the little school-kindergarten which seemed indicated for him, tho' admirable, was too old for him, the youngest child being seven. Hence it wd have been too tiring for him. So she brought him back, and he has been very well and flourishing since. We go to Belgium from here, probably by car, on the 1st of July; shall leave Matthew with his grandmother at St. Trond and come for a bit to England.

We are living in the midst of considerable confusion, packing up in preparation to leave this house: a confusion increased by the size of our household, for we have Maria's sister Jehanne, her husband [René Moulaert] and child [Sophie] staying with us. Work is rather difficult to get done in the circumstances. However I am tolerably well up on my engagements.

Jack Hutchinson and Earp were here recently and we accompanied them on a little tour through Emilia and Lombardy—lovely places which I was happy to see again. Their news of London made me quite glad not to be living there.

Some pleasant American acquaintances of yours came to see us not long ago, Mr. and Mrs. Glaser. I thought she was very nice. He seemed to me a bit of a bore, talking in that loose pretentious meaningless American way— a sort of scientific Jefferson Brick. But I may misjudge.

Another pleasing American scientific man who wrote to me out of the blue and came to see me—first last year and again this—was one Dr. Kopeloff, an expert on lunatics. Most agreeable. He spends his spare time saving the lives of sufferers from general paralysis of the insane by inoculating them with malaria and so raising their temperatures to 104°. G. P. is cured: but he was taciturn when I asked him how soon they died of enlarged spleen and the other consequences of malaria. But in any case, it's a triumph of science!

Meanwhile I hope your science triumphs. I wish you'd tell me what's a good book on the effect of modern genetic discoveries on the Darwinian theory. How do organisms ever get out of that hereditary predestination exhibited by mendelism?

Love to all from all of us.

A.

233: † TO NORMAN DOUGLAS

15 *Via S. Margherita a Montici,*
Florence
26 *June,* 1925

Dear Douglas,

I feel very guilty for having kept you and your son hanging aimlessly about, that day when we were starting for Tunisia. The fact is that we had, in the end, to lunch hurriedly at home, owing to various delays at the last minute. Hence our failure to appear—and your very justifiable violation of the request one sees on church doors: not to swear. I apologize profoundly.

Tunisia was very good fun: especially Nefta, which is really a miracle of beauty. One winter, I shall certainly go and spend some months there, about the time of the date harvest—tho' I have no doubt that the sight of the Arabs picking and packing the dates wd be enough to make one's gorge turn every time one set eyes on that fruit for the rest of one's life. How tremendously

European one feels when one has seen these devils in their native muck! And to think that we are busily teaching them all the mechanical arts of peace and war which gave us, in the past, our superiority over their numbers! In fifty years time, it seems to me, Europe can't fail to be wiped out by these monsters. *Intanto. . . .*

No news of Florence, at least that I know of. For I seem to have been remote from that city, during the last months, even [more] than usual. No contact. A glimpse once or twice of Geoffrey Scott—whose *Portrait of 'Zélide'* I read, but found too literary for my taste. It is full of that kind of exquisitely good writing that is, one feels instinctively, only another kind of bad writing. Santayana is the most perfect specimen of the type. Otherwise, I've seen practically nobody belonging to the town.

We leave this house in two days' time, for good. Plans a bit vague: but I prefer them so. I mean, if possible, to go to India this autumn, to have a look at those devils there. Nothing like knowing what one is up against. After that, who knows?

How is Tanganyika? Paradisiacal? or infernal? or just like everywhere else? I hope you will treat us to an *Old Calabria* on the subject.

The address which always finds me, sooner or later, is the Athenaeum, Pall Mall, S.W.1—a club, by the way, which has more smutty books in its library than any other. (You shd see the bishops, how they gloat over that familiar item in the 'curious' section of the booksellers' catalogues, 'Rev: Cooper's *History of the Rod*'. It does one good to look at.)

Yours
Aldous Huxley

234: TO LEONARD HUXLEY

The Athenaeum, Pall Mall, S.W.1
24 July, 1925

Dearest Father,

We start for Belgium on Sunday or Monday; so there won't, I fear, be any hope of seeing you this year. Vague plans for remoter travelling this autumn have become concrete in the last few days and I have settled definitely to go to India this autumn, to take a look round. Seeing that one practises a profession that does not tie one down, I feel that one ought to see as much of this planet as one can. We shall start from Naples in the middle of September so as to be in India by the beginning of October, proceeding straight to Kashmir (which becomes untenable with cold and rain later in the autumn) where we shall stay in a houseboat belonging to an Indian I knew at Oxford and whom I have met again here. After that we shall probably stay with him at Lahore for a bit and thence wander about. If finances run to it—which depends on articles: I hope to fix up something with the editor of *The Times*, whom I go to see tomorrow,—we shall push onwards and come back by the other side, through America. But all that remains to be seen. Matthew, meanwhile, will be with his grandmother.

London has been strenuous and, though my stay has been very enjoyable, I shall be glad to get away to work again. I find complete holidays from work bad for my health in the long run. One requires steady occupation to preserve one's mental and physical harmony.

Julian seems to have failed in his house hunt. I suppose he will have to stay on in Oxford for another six months and come up from there to King's Coll[ege], while they search at leisure. Much love to you all.

Your loving son

Aldous

235: TO LEONARD HUXLEY

S.S. Genova, Naples

16 September, 1925

Dearest Father,

Here we are, embarked, on a quite comfortable ship, the sea flat (so far!), the weather fine, the food copious and not bad, the company mixed—but with good streaks in it. We started from Genoa yesterday and are here for the inside of a day, before setting out for Suez. I have been frantically busy, finishing a book of short stories—not quite finished even now—and doing some articles against time for America. Not to mention making preparations for the voyage. I hope to do some quiet reading and a little writing on the ship. Let's hope it won't be intolerably hot in the Red Sea or intolerably stormy in the Indian Ocean. We go almost directly on arrival to Kashmir for a month. Address there, I don't yet know. But till mid-November the following will always find me:—

> c/o Chaman Lall,
> Race View,
> Golf Road,
> Lahore.

(An address like that makes one realize why the English are a great and conquering race! Who else would have thought of calling the houses and streets of an ancient oriental city after the names of the national sports? Their great secret is behaving in exotic lands in exactly the same way as in their own—allowing no romantic imaginative sympathy to alter their fundamental national characteristics. Race View, Golf Road, Lahore—it is magnificent!)

235 *Huxley had finished all but one of his stories for* Two or Three Graces *before his departure. The travel articles making up his book* Jesting Pilate *would be serialized in* The Nation (*London*) *and* The Bookman (*New York*) *under the title* 'Diary of an Eastward Journey'.

I look forward to seeing much that is curious and interesting, particularly as we shall be looking at things mostly from the Indian side of the fence. It will be curious seeing the political business. My knowledge of Indians in Europe—very small, it must be admitted—makes me very sceptical of their capacity to govern themselves. I shall be interested to see what conclusions a closer acquaintance will bring one to.

I shall be writing a certain number of articles for America and *The Times* has offered to take periodical outpourings. I don't quite know yet whether I shall take advantage of their offer. I shall feel freer to move about among the Indians if I'm not writing my impressions as I go along. However, I shall see how things pan out when I get there. I am doing the same with regard to all arrangements. It is no good making definite plans about the unknown; what we shall do after Kashmir depends on conditions of travelling and climate—how tiring, how hot etc—and expenses. Also our homeward route.

I have told the publishers to send you a copy of my volume of essays '*Along the Road*' which is appearing, I think, tomorrow—rather early in view of the threatened strike of packers on October 1st. I think it's a readable and pleasant enough collection.

Have been reading a most interesting book—Burtt's *Metaphysical Foundations of Modern Science*, which shows historically just how, why and when the assumptions at the bottom of modern science came into existence. One realizes what a curiously arbitrary set of assumptions they are. Science has chosen to regard as 'real' only those aspects of the world that can be treated mathematically. Quite gratuitously, it has gone on to assume that all aspects of the world that can't be treated mathematically are illusory. Burtt shows the history of the growth of these assumptions and points out the insoluble difficulties they involve. Well worth reading—and for the work of an American professor, not badly written—in a language bearing quite an appreciable resemblance to English.

Goodbye. I will keep you posted with regard to our movements. Much love from both of us to all the family.

> *Your loving son,*
> *Aldous*

236: TO JULIAN HUXLEY

> *Taj Mahal Hotel, Bombay*
> *4 October, 1925*

My dear J,

Here we are, at last, after an excellent voyage over perfectly flat seas. We have been two days in Bombay and have met most of the local intelligentsia—journalists, politicians etc. The majority of them are frail little men, very gentle and underfed-looking. In comparison with them I feel myself a prizefighter. No wonder the British rule, if these are typical. The only real He-Man among them is a woman—a Mrs. [Sarojini] Naidu, who seems to be one of the most important political leaders in the country, after Gandhi and Nehru. A charming woman and really alive, radiating energy. She has a daughter at Lady Margaret, whose principal claim to fame is that when Miss [Emily] Penrose—she was dining at Somerville—asked her to give her her arm, she replied: 'All right, old fish'. If she's like her mother, she must be charming and intelligent. And at any rate she knows most of the interesting people in India such as Gandhi. Do ask her to tea one day.

Bombay is hideously expensive. At this hotel one pays the same sort of prices as at the Carlton. However, we leave tomorrow for Lahore and Kashmir. I hope we may arrive in Kashmir in time to see the ceremonies of Sir Hari Singh's (Mr. A's) enthronement as Maharajah—the old man having just died. In December we are to attend an All India Congress, where we shall meet everybody from Gandhi downwards. It is not merely political: there are also women's congresses, congresses for the protection of cows, a poets' congress and I don't know what beside. After that to Delhi for the meeting of the Legislative Assembly—which shd be curious, for the Indians are said to be most eloquent . . . in bad English. Several of our friends here make speeches the whole time. There is one who is always talking about the inconsistency of the English in teaching Indians about liberty and not granting it in practice. 'Burke and Bacon, Milton and Macaulay (gesture)— I tell you, we have drunk from dat fountain.' And this in casual conversation. We heard him, also, lecturing a fellow journalist because the English in his newspaper was so bad. 'Your contributor may be a most profound tinker, *but* his grammar is jolly rotten (they adore slang); de style of de man is not chaste.'

Later

This afternoon we went to a politico-social function—the presentation of an address to Patel, the new speaker of the Legislative Assembly, by members of his caste or community in Bombay. He comes of an agricultural caste in Gujarat and has climbed out of it higher than any of its members have ever climbed before. A charming old man, like a minor prophet—very impassive and inscrutable, with a slightly ironic twinkle about him; yet immensely courageous and prepared to suffer for his convictions: has been in jail even, I fancy. It was a curious performance—reminding me, in its incongruities and lack of suitable solemnity, of an Italian function. Children sang a chorus, but the band played and everybody talked; somebody recited a poem in Gujarati, chanting lugubriously, but the band went on playing—'Why did you kiss that girl?' People made speeches; but the noise of the crows and jackdaws going to bed in the trees outside was so deafening (there are more birds here, from vultures to sparrows, than I have ever seen before; crows sit on the roof of the hotel and kites fly along the main streets)

236 *The Indian liberal appears as Mr Sita Ram in Chapter VI of* Point Counter Point.

that no word was audible. In the end, garlands of flowers, incredibly fragrant, were produced and hung round the necks of all the distinguished people present, including ourselves. After which we went out into the garden and ate a strange meal of ice cream, hot dumplings stuffed with curried mince, chocolates and spice-flavoured mineral water. Altogether most curious and amusing. These people—Patel and the others with him on the platform—impress me more favourably than the journalists. They have life and guts.

Do ask Miss Naidu to tea. Her mother has been so very nice to us that I'd like to do something vicariously for the daughter. Perhaps she'd get on with Naomi Mitchison too. If you think so, put her on to Naomi's track. She spends her vacations in London.

Love to you both from both of us.

Yours
A.

237: TO LEONARD HUXLEY

Srinagar
12 October, 1925

Dearest Father,

Here we are, at the end of the first stage of our journey. We arrived in Kashmir yesterday and have so far seen very little of it, having been chiefly busied setting our house in some kind of order. I write at once, however, in order to be sure of catching the mail; for though this will be posted on Tuesday, it is such a devilish long way to Bombay that it will have to hurry if it is to leave India by Saturday's ship. We have seen little; but enough, in any case, to discover that the place is very lovely. Our bungalow looks out across the valley, which is full of beautiful poplar trees, to the blue foothills, ten or fifteen miles away and, beyond them, the snowy peaks. The Dai lake, which is the prime beauty spot of the town, we have not yet seen. Of it later. The weather meanwhile is heavenly. Brilliantly clear and sunny all day, the air at this height of five thousand feet very bracing and invigorating. Cool, even cold at nights.

We have lived strenuously since our arrival in Bombay on the second—seen many people and things and travelled sixteen hundred miles. Bombay was hot, muggy and expensive.

[. . . .]

After Bombay straight through, in two nights and a day, to Lahore. Travelling, in spite of the heat, is comfortable. One can reserve coupé compartments for two, thus ensuring privacy, the lack of which is the chief horror in ordinary railway travelling. This permits one to wear as little as one likes. There are good fans and the seats turn into very tolerable couches, on which one spreads one's own bedding. The worst is the dust, which comes through everything, even plate glass. At Lahore we stayed with my friend

Chaman Lall, whom I knew at Oxford. He is a young barrister and politician, has an English wife and belongs to a very influential family, the head of which is his father, a fabulously wealthy old land-owner and barrister of Rawalpindi. They are very classy Brahmins and have a hereditary title—Diwan. We spent a couple of days at Lahore, looking at a few of the Moghul monuments, which are in a style of architecture that I really don't like at all, and meeting a number of people, the pleasantest of whom was the Director of Industries under the Punjab government, a very able and energetic Indian called Rawlley, who took us round and showed us various of the local industrial developments. The Civil Lines in Lahore are in the midst of delightful lawns and gardens, full of trees, among which the parrots fly in screaming flocks. The heat was considerable during the day, but the evenings were deliciously cool.

From Lahore we went on to Rawalpindi by train. A desolate, beastly sort of a place—no proper town, merely an excuse for the soldiers, who swarm in vast quantities; to protect India from whom, I don't quite know. Pindi is the nearest railway station to Srinagar—a hundred and ninety seven miles! After crossing a pass of about seven thousand feet, one descends into the Jhelum valley, which one follows all the rest of the way—fine but rather monotonous and the road, though beautifully kept, slightly nerve-racking, owing to the corners, the precipices and the prodigious quantity of traffic. We spent a night on the way, having started pretty late from Pindi and came on here in the early afternoon. Our home is a bungalow belonging to Chaman Lall, which he has lent us. It is only two or three doors off the palace of 'Mr A', who has just come to the throne, the old Maharaja having died a fortnight ago. He leaves in a day or two for his other capital, Jammu, in the plains, so we shall probably not see him. We shall be here about a month and I hope to get some work done in the delicious quiet. After that, back to Lahore, same address: Race View, Golf Road.

In haste, for the post must be caught. Love from us both.

Ever your loving son,
Aldous

238: TO LEONARD HUXLEY

Srinagar, Kashmir
2 November, 1925

Dearest Father,

I hope you got my first letter from Kashmir, which I posted a fortnight ago. Since then we have seen much, both of things and of people, from ruined temples to the gaol and the lunatic asylum, from the English Resident to the

238 *The Guillemards: Sir Laurence Nunns Guillemard was the Governor of the Straits Settlements.*

Kashmiri Governor of the Province, from the local missionary to the Minister of Agriculture. Once one has a little start, in this part of the world, one goes automatically a long way. It's the first step that counts and our introductions from Lahore enabled us to make it at once.

First for the country. It is fine, certainly, but, I must confess, not quite so fine as people make out. Indians, from the Great Moguls downwards, have always described Kashmir as the earthly paradise—and so it is, of course, in comparison with the Panjab in summer. But the Panjab in summer, according to all accounts, is the earthly hell—115 to 120 degrees in the shade, total aridity till the arrival of the rains, and after their arrival, malaria, fish insects, cobras in the back garden, mildew and so forth. To us, accustomed to happier climates, Kashmir is something quite familiar—a sort of Swiss valley with a kind of Italian lake in the middle of it. Everything is on rather a large scale, of course; but you don't notice it and the twenty-thousand foot peaks in the far distance don't look any more remarkable than the twelve thousand footers at home. The lake is lovely—but Como is a great deal lovelier, both as regards [sic] to the scenery and vegetation surrounding it and to the architectural embellishments. The Mogul gardens and pleasure houses which surround the lake are very inferior to anything Italian in the same line. The cascades, fountains and terraces of the Nishat Bagh are nothing in comparison with those of the Villa d'Este at Tivoli, the famous Shalimar gardens are simply a kind of park, set off with a tank, fountains and a black marble summer house of poor design. The palaces are small, gimcrack and rustically inelegant. There is very little invention anywhere. The plan of the gardens is rigidly formal and of a very obvious formality at that. The best feature of all these gardens is their trees, which are mostly magnificent chenars—a kind of plane, which grows to a gigantic size (forty, fifty and even sixty feet round the bole) and whose leaves, at this season, turn a wonderful orange-vermilion colour, most lovely against their white trunks and the blue sky beyond—when there is blue sky, let me add! The poplars too are very fine now. The immense avenues of them, which go for miles and miles across the plain of the valley, are now bright yellow. Beautiful, too, at this season are the fields of saffron, which is largely cultivated here. I had always imagined, I must confess, that the saffron flower was saffron coloured; but it isn't. It is a purple crocus, with long trailing red-gold stamens, which hang down between the petals. It is from these that the saffron is made, by a process of boiling, straining and drying, I fancy. The product of the first boiling is immensely valuable and fetches its weight in gold—in paper, I dare say. The Indians use it as a medicine. Whether it has any medicinal qualities, I don't know; but they pay for it, which is the main point. The second and third qualities make the colouring matter which one sees in cakes etc.

We have done a fair amount of motoring with different people. One day we went east towards the head of the valley, visiting the lovely Mogul gardens of Achibal and the source of the river Jhelum, which is a deep pool at the foot of the mountains, fed by springs from beneath, and enclosed by Shah Jahan so as to form an octagonal tank, which is surrounded by an arcade. Yesterday we went in the other direction up into the mountains, to a place called Gulmarg, the great summer resort for Europeans from the plains, but totally deserted at this time of year. It is a high Alpine shelf of meadow land standing at about eight thousand five hundred feet, looking down from one side on to the valley and across it, far away, to Nanga Parbat, 26,000 feet, and dominated on the other by mountains of fourteen or fifteen thousand feet. The snow was down to within a few hundred feet of the place and the air was pretty nipping. But it was very lovely, particularly the ride up through the deodar forests from the place where the car had to be left. It is too cold now to do it in comfort, otherwise the thing to have done would have been to go up into Ladakh—fifteen days march from Srinagar—where the inhabitants are Tibetans and Buddhists, and follow all the customs of their brothers in the secret land. One sees a lot of them here; for they come down in the winter to work in the plains—strange yellow men, dressed in furs. We saw still queerer men, the other day, at the Central Asian Caravanserai, where all the traders coming down from Chinese Turkestan stop on their way through to India. We went with the Kashmiri head of the Customs —a very nice and intelligent man—and so had opportunities of seeing everything in the best possible circumstances—all the traders being anxious, naturally, to keep in the good graces of the great man. These traders come from Yarkhand and are mostly yellow Tartars. It takes them six weeks to walk to Srinagar and, I suppose, another month or so to get to Bombay, where most of them finally go. They bring furs, carpets, jade, Chinese silk, hand-woven and printed materials. And they take back with them cotton piece goods, velvets, spices and otter skins. They can only make one journey a year, coming down, for the most part, between the middle of September and the beginning of November, when the passes are clear of snow and the rivers are not too much swollen by the summer's melting, and returning in March and April, when the winter snow has begun to go. They make their profits mainly, it seems, on the goods they bring back to Turkestan, contenting themselves with selling what they bring (which consists mostly of things which India itself produces) almost at cost price, so as to compete with the Indian products. We bought two fur coats—one of sheepskin for me and one of a beautiful Russian fur, an arctic hare, I think—two carpets and twelve yards of hand woven material for something under six pounds. The furs are already coming in useful; for it is uncommonly cold here—almost or quite freezing nights and days which, when sunless, are icy. Even in the Panjab, I gather, we shall find the nights very chilly.

From my various official and semi-official acquaintances here I have heard a good deal about the workings of the state. What a queer anachronism, this 17th century absolute monarchy, with its courtiers flattering the ruler and intriguing for advantage over one another. The administration seems to be exceedingly corrupt—indeed, it is notoriously so, even among Indian native states—and the corruption, I regret to hear, is not confined to Indian officials. Some of the English in the maharajah's service appear to become a great deal richer than they ought. I gather that corruption is the great curse everywhere in India and that it is very difficult to get anything done without first oiling somebody's palm. On the railways, for example, it appears to be quite impossible to get one's goods transported without paying bribes on top of the weight freight rates. It is common for station masters earning a hundred and fifteen rupees a month to retire with fortunes of five or ten lakhs. It seems to be much the same as it was and, I suppose, still is in Russia.

The Resident very civilly asked us to tea the other day. He is a man called Sir John Wood, once Political Secretary to the Government of India, and some three or four years ago [. . . .] relegated from that very important position to this second-rate Residentship. [. . . .] he is obviously a most astute and intelligent man; but exceedingly deep. I got a few good stories, but very little information on any of the subjects I should like to have heard about.

We went with the Chief Medical Officer of the state, a pleasant old Hindu, who studied in Edinburgh, to see the prison, of which he is the governor. A model institution and the cleanest place in Srinagar—far cleaner than the maharajah's palaces, I should guess. There was a plentiful supply of murderers in the gaol; for they only hang the most outrageous assassins—and, generally, the killers of cows. For, though the bulk of the people is Mohammedan, the rulers are orthodox Hindus and the life of a cow is held more sacred than that of a man. They wander everywhere in the streets, small sacred bulls, belonging to nobody in particular—wander very majestically and slowly, being perfectly aware that they are sacred and that no motorist will dare to run over them. Throughout Kashmir they are the bane of motorists. If you have the bad luck to run over one, the only thing to do is to jam on the accelerator and run for it; several years imprisonment is the least one would get for the offence. The law against cow killing is so strict that one may not introduce Bovril into the country and I heard of a European woman who was turned back at the frontier because she had some corned beef among her provisions. The odd thing is that, though these people have infinite scruples about taking away a cow's life, they have none about making that life a hell on earth. They treat their draught animals very badly and systematically underfeed them. It is difficult to catch their point of view.

The dirt and poverty of these wretched Kashmiris is deplorable. Srinagar fairly festers. The people are dressed in ancient rags, suffer agonies from cold and work for so little, that it is cheaper to have a cart drawn by men than by horses or oxen. They are much smellier than the people in the plains, because they wear more clothes. For a half naked man may sweat and smell very little; it is the accumulated sweat of days, not to mention the other, nameless dirts with which garments are impregnated, that smell. An English crowd is far more odoriferous than a crowd of Indians in the plains.

We stay here for another ten days or so, then go down to Lahore again. Thence for a tour through Rajputana. I am trying to collect introductions. They make all the difference. Talking of introductions, I gather that the Guillemards are still at Singapore. As we may very likely be going on there from Burma, I'd like to exploit them a little! I suppose Lady G would know who I am if I wrote to her—though it must be fifteen years since I've seen her (no; on second thoughts, I remember going over to see her at Bowl-head Green from Enton with Aunt Sophy—which can't have been more than five years ago). If by any chance you should ever be writing in that direction, you might drop a hint of the possibility of our arrival in those parts.

Maria sends all apologies for having omitted to enclose the photograph in her letter. She is having another copy printed here and will send it by the next mail. Meanwhile, I hope all goes well with you. Our news of Matthew is good and we ourselves are very well. This mountain air is healthy and we do justice to the admirable cooking of our servant—a man who, we have just discovered, went to Tibet in 1903 with Younghusband's expedition. He is a great treasure. I wish one could find the likes of him in Europe. The only contretemps, to date, has been the attack made upon me a few days ago by a gigantic hornet, which stung me in the leg. The sting did not produce much swelling locally, but about half an hour later enormous white spots and blisters began to appear all over my body—a sort of violent nettle rash. After which I felt very cold and shaky, as though I had developed influenza, and was sick. However, the evil effects passed off after a few hours and I was left with nothing but a rather puffy leg. What it must be like to fall into a hornets' nest, I do not like to think. I should imagine that you might die if you were stung by enough of them.

Best love to all of you,

Your loving son,
Aldous

239: TO LEWIS GIELGUD

[*As from*] *Race View, Golf Road, Lahore*
17 December, 1925

My dear Lewis,

Your letter of last mail has been more or less replied to by my previous letter [of 1 December] about Matthew's conditions of health. Since writing that letter we have had news from Belgium to say that he is getting on so much better that they are postponing sending him to Switzerland—rather unwisely, I think, if the doctor has advised it. But it is difficult to judge without being on the spot. In any case, however, I think it would probably be a bad thing to choose this particular moment to move into a town. Switzerland may not be vitally necessary: but in any case, I think the country and an open air life will be essential for the next year or two. It looks, I am afraid, as though Paris will have to be postponed for a bit.

We have been strenuously doing Rajputana, hobnobbing with Maharajas, prime ministers, Chief Justices, feudal lords in Jaipur, Bikaner and Jodhpur and are going to continue the process, I think, in Udaipur and Indore. An interesting and picturesque country, but unfortunately traversed by railways on which the trains never average more than fourteen miles an hour. Hence, travelling is rather a trial to the patience. It is a very orthodox part of India, so that one sees everywhere innumerable phallic symbols, in shrines by the way side, on an enormous scale in the temples, for sale in the shops. To our eyes a pleasing and comic spectacle; but to the blackamoors, of course, neither more nor less comic than would be a cross or a statue of the virgin chez nous. The symbols are comprehensive, consisting of male emblems sprouting out of female ones. We saw enormous numbers of them to-day at Pushkar, the most sacred bathing place in India, close to Ajmer. Here, however, there is a little peculiarity which is rather pleasing. The phalli are always shown in conjunction with a sacred cow in marble or sandstone, which kneels before the emblem and gazes at it with a fixed and rapturous expression of love, admiration, longing, mystical bliss.

The sort of Englishman one meets here in trains, station restaurants and Dak bungalows is beyond all words repulsive. Stupid, uncultured, underbred, the complete and perfect cad. In their company, one understands the Indians' nationalistic aspirations. As a matter of fact, I understand them even when I am in the presence of the nice Englishmen. We really have no business here. And there is no doubt whatever that we are steadily making the country poorer and poorer. The statistics make the fact manifest. On the other hand, if we were to lose the Indian market, we should go half way into bankruptcy. It's altogether a cheerful look out.

We are going eastward in the early spring—Burma, Malaya etc. Conceivably, since it's not more than seven or eight hundred miles out of the way, to Siam. If you happen to know any useful people in Siam—Red Cross officials or what not, you might give me their names. And perhaps you or Mimi might conceivably know somebody in the French colonies next door, Cambodia or Cochin.

I hope the fall of the franc is enriching you. What are they going to do about it? It looks as though the worst might quite easily happen.

Love to you both from both of us.

Yours,
A.L.H.

Guest House, Udaipur, Mewar
21 December, 1925

Dearest Father,

Here we are, staying—with some splendour, as state guests—at Udaipur, which we leave, alas, today for Indore. Udaipur certainly lives up to its reputation as the most beautiful place in Rajputana. The lakes, the mountains, the white palaces, the gardens, the jungle that covers the surrounding country —all are very fine. The artistic details are not so good as at Jaipur; but as a whole the place is lovelier. Chitor, too, which lies in Udaipur Territory and has a famous fort which, before its capture by Akbar, was the capital of Mewar, is magnificent. A superb position and very fine, though rather ruinous, architecture. Bikaner was interesting, set in the midst of its desert and in-habited—strangely enough—by a community which counts more million-aires to the thousand than any other population in India, perhaps in the world. These are the Mewari merchants, the Jews of India, who come back to their native desert, when they have grown rich in Bombay or Calcutta and build the most fantastic carved palaces in the city, with bungalows in the suburban desert—of fabulous expense and inconceivable bad taste. Very odd. We saw the Maharajah—amiable and intelligent and a good ruler, one is told.

At Jodhpur we met a very interesting Indian scholar, now the chief judge of the state, and had much talk. It is a fine town with a great fort-palace on a precipitous hill in the middle of it and a deserted city in the environs.

Ajmer is also beautiful. Hilly, with an artificial lake—half dry after the bad monsoon—and a few miles away the most sacred waters of India, Pushkar, where every selfrespecting Hindu must come and bathe—even at the risk of being eaten by the crocodiles which abound in it and which may not be killed, owing to the holiness of the place. It is full of temples and innumerable phallic symbols, which stand for Siva—who is mostly wor-shipped under that particular aspect.

As the mail doesn't go for another day or two, I will interrupt this now and continue from Indore [. . . .]

Later. Indore.

[. . .] the state seems well governed and prosperous. And the people are said to be so lightly taxed that there is a continual immigration into Indore from British India. We have not seen the Maharaja, who is living in camp out of town in a state of great melancholy, poor man, owing to the fact that the only daughter of his second and favourite wife has recently been burnt to death while playing with fireworks. However, we have interviewed the Prime Minister and been taken about by the Private Secretary of the Prince, who was at Oxford (before my time, however) at the House. A nice and able fellow. He took us to see the new palace which is now building, a very sumptuous affair purely in European style, with a profusion of Carrara marble and ornaments copied from Versailles, and Adam rooms, and Empire boudoirs and what not. The whole designed by an English architect who has been out in these parts for the last 25 years building for the Indian Princes of this neighbourhood—Ratlam, Bhopal, Indore etc. A pleasant man—though not a conspicuously good architect—and a very ingenious inventor of gadgets, labour saving devices, new methods of construction. The kitchens at the New Palace here are a miracle of ingenuity and common sense.

We start this evening for Cawnpore—a long and horrible journey, involving a change at 4 AM at Bhopal. Gandhi regards trains and railways as the inventions of the devil. One need only come to India and travel on the smaller lines to see that he is probably right!

Our latest news regarding Matthew is that his Swiss stay has been postponed, at any rate for the present. M's mother is afraid that the effect on his *morale* of going alone to a school there wd do more harm than the effect of the air would do good. She may be right. If there is no urgency, I think the best wd be if he were to stay in Belgium—at the sea if possible—till our return, when we will make our headquarters in some suitable mountain place either in France, Switzerland or Italy—perhaps Cortina in the Italian Dolomites which is, from all accounts, a lovely and salubrious place. The doctors say that it is of essential importance that he should develop his lungs (Cortina is high enough up, I think, to force the breathing sufficiently), otherwise he may grow up into a definitely tubercular condition. We have wired to suggest this solution—Belgium for the moment and the mountains with us when we come back—and if there is no immediate urgency, I think that will be the best. We have not had time to get an answer to our suggestion.

Well, goodbye. May the New Year bring all healths and happinesses. Love to all.

Your loving Son
Aldous

241: TO JULIAN HUXLEY

Benares
6 January, 1926

My dear J,

Your letter was welcome. Many thanks for it. I reply only very briefly, as the mail goes in an hour or two; but will do better later on.

We have been having a very strenuous month of it, touring through the native states of Rajputana, where, by a slight error in the original introduction which made us state guests at the various capitals, I was always received and honoured as 'Professor Huxley'. All protests on my part were quite vain. In the end I accepted my professorship. In that part of the world they respect the learned man much more than the artist—it is the same as in Europe up to three centuries ago. Udaipur, Chitor, Jodhpur and Jaipur were all fine. After

Rajputana we went to Cawnpore for the session of the All India Congress—rather an impressive performance and one which all strenuous imperialists should certainly attend. We sat, or rather squatted, on the platform with the big wigs; one day we were next to Gandhi, who does the holy ascetic in a loin cloth—hence his influence over the people, who are still stupid enough in this country to believe in flesh-mortifying sanctity—and who, at the moment, is looked after by a young woman called Miss Slade, who is a niece of Carr Saunders and, I think, has met you. A rather tiresome, dully earnest woman, who sits there worshipping Gandhi like a dog—handing him his spectacles, adjusting his loin cloth, giving him his food when it is brought and so on. He just treats her as though she weren't there, or were at least only a dumb waiter. Mrs Naidu assured us that he professes not to know who looks after him and that when she reproaches him for having these adoring females round him he looks up in astonishment and says: What, *are* they women? More sympathetic to me, at any rate, were the Swarajist leaders—Pandit Motilal Nehru and his son, Jawaharlal, who was at Harrow and Cambridge, where he took no interest in politics, returned to India, was outraged by the treatment of the country, threw himself into the Non-cooperation movement and was lodged in gaol for six months: the Ali brothers: Lala Lajpat Rai and the rest. They are mostly prodigiously aristocratic—as only high-caste Indians can be aristocratic in these later days—are, or have been, rich (for most of them have given up their sources of income) and certainly impress one with their intelligence and capacity. Whenever you see among the politicians a face that is conspicuous for its intelligence, sensitiveness or power you are sure, on enquiry, to discover that the owner of it has been to gaol for political offences. One certainly comes to feel, very strongly, that we have no business to be here, ruling the country. But how the Indians are going to manage themselves, how they're going to settle the Hindu-Moslem business and the relation between the autocratic native states and a presumably democratic ex-British India, I really cannot see. Anyway, it's their look out, not mine. I am profoundly thankful that I have nothing to do officially with this country and no sort of responsibility for it. If I had, it would drive me out of my mind. Meanwhile the British Government plays off Hindus against Moslems and the Princes against the nationalist, who are also democratic, extremists, for all it is worth. If they are clever, the British have got a long lease of imperial life before them in India. Judicious manipulation of the balancing powers can keep this place in a state of equilibrium almost indefinitely, I should think.

We are resting and working here for a fortnight. A disappointing place. Very bad architecture and art. But the pilgrims are curious of course, and there is a certain charm about the neat little bonfires where they burn the corpses. People sit round gossiping and doing their business, children gambol around and, practically, roast chestnuts in the fire. It's all very jolly. After that we go to Delhi for the opening of the Legislative Assembly. Thence

Calcutta and Burma. After that to Singapore. Between the end of January and Feb 5th write to us care of Thos Cook and Sons, Rangoon, Burma. Between Feb 5th and March 5th write care of Thos Cook and Sons, Singapore, Straits Settlements. After that, who knows? I don't, at present. I think we shall proceed to San Francisco, thence to New York and so home. If you know anyone we should see at either of those places, let me have the names at Singapore or, if you can send the letter in time, Rangoon.

I've not yet heard from the Ranee, but gather from Juliette that she was travelling in India when we sent our letter for Juliette to forward to her. I thing I had better write again to Sarawak. If Juliette is writing there she might mention that we shall be in the neighbourhood—Cooks at Singapore —during April.

Love to all the family. Tell father when you see him that I will write later and meanwhile thank him from me for his letter.

Yours,

A.

Please thank Juliette for both of us for having taken all that trouble about our furniture. I am afraid it's been a great burden and bother.

242: TO ELINOR WYLIE

Benares

6 January, 1926

Dear Elinor Wylie,

It is from a somewhat Extreme Orient—and therefore with a special gratitude—that I write to thank you for the gift of your delightfully Western book. It was not till I set foot in India that I knew how good a European I was. Now I realize my passionate spiritual patriotism. In this alien world, where the old is so old that it has nothing to do with our problems and the new is only a bad imitation of the West—old-fashioned at that, for modernity in the East is still wearing bustles and leg-of-mutton sleeves—your *Venetian Glass Nephew* has been to me as a friend from home. Thank you for sending him.

I hope some time in spring or early summer to have the opportunity of thanking you in person. For if money can be made to go so far—six thousand miles at least!—my wife and I propose to enter America by the Pacific back door, cross it and go out by the front. If at that time you should be inhabiting some part of your enormous continent not too many hundred miles from San Francisco or New York I wish you would drop me a line c/o Thomas Cook and Sons, Singapore, Straits Settlements, to say if there would be any prospect of seeing you.

I am writing to you care of Doran and hoping for the best.

Yours sincerely,

Aldous Huxley

Calcutta
3 February, 1926

My dear Robert,

Are you in America or Europe? I am writing speculatively to Hollywood to find out if you will be there in May or June, when we shall be arriving (DV and WP) at S. Francisco. Let me know c/o Thomas Cook and Son, Manila, Philippines.

This is a queer country—a nightmare, out of which I am really rather glad to escape. The whole situation is so hopeless. Nothing can possibly get the English out—short of a miracle. The miracle was very nearly achieved by Gandhi 5 years ago. But as he was only a saint and not a politician, he missed his chance and achieved nothing. Perhaps the miracle may recur: but I doubt it. The English can always play one religion against the other, one type of civilization and polity against the other. In extremity, they can always provoke another Afghan war and prove themselves indispensable by repulsing the enemy. The relations of the races are the source of an extraordinary comedy. But it is a painful and tragical farce. I am only thankful I have no connection with the place.

Later

Just been to Cook's office and found among my mail your letter of December 6th, incredibly delayed. It must have waited for some time in London before following us here. A good subject to talk about, cinematography. But is it a good medium to work in? I say no, because you can't do it by yourself. You depend on Jews with money, on 'art directors', on little bitches with curly hair and teeth, on young men who recommend skin foods in the advertisements, on photographers. Without their cooperation your ideas can't become actual. You are at their mercy. What a disgust and a humiliation! It seems one worse, if possible, than the theatre. I shall stick to an art in which I can do all the work by myself, sitting alone, without having to entrust my soul to a crowd of swindlers, vulgarians and mountebanks. If one cd make films oneself, I'd be all for the movies. But as it is—no. Surely Hollywood must have made you feel the same.

Yours
Aldous

244: TO JULIAN HUXLEY

S. S. Erinpura
6 February, 1926

My dear J,

The enclosed cheque is to pay for the freight and insurance of two packages containing warm coats and bedding which I am sending home, as we shan't need them (let us hope) in the tropics. Will you be kind enough to give them lodgment till we return. I have sent them carriage forward in order to stimulate the zeal of Thomas Cook, who is apt to be remiss if paid in advance.

Here we are on the high seas between Calcutta and Burma. Pleasant weather—a hot sun and a cool breeze, with practically no movement of the sea. We had an amusing fortnight at Delhi, in the midst of politics, which we had an opportunity of looking at from both sides—the government's and the opposition's. As people, I must say I preferred the opposition. Most of the Englishmen are of the export variety one rarely meets at home—at any rate in one's own monde: rich vulgar jute manufacturers, representing the European community in the Legislative Assembly, and then the officials—decent fellows, but terribly insect-like, as Civil Servants generally are. The Swarajists are more entertaining and various. There is Pandit Motilal Nehru —a superb old man of the world, positively dix huitième in polish and aristocracy: there are the Mohammedans, the Ali Brothers and Kidwai—wild passionate creatures: there is young Goswami, the treasurer of the party, a millionaire with an income of £80,000 a year; and all the rest, a most varied assemblage. But what a farce the Assembly is. The statistics show that less than one per cent of the resolutions passed by the Assembly are given effect to by the government. Such are the Reforms. One isn't surprised to find that the Indians are rather depressed. The government holds all the trump cards and shows no sign—naturally enough—of surrendering them.

We spent 3 days in Calcutta, and went one afternoon to Sir J. C. Bose's institute. He showed us round for 3 hours and we saw all the experiments in full blast—the heart beats of plants, plants being drugged and recording their symptoms automatically in a graph, and so forth. Really astonishing. I had been sceptical—such is the force of ancient prejudice—I thought there must be something fishy about the results. But when you *see* the plants making records of their own sensations—well, you've got to believe. And I suppose one's also got to believe Bose's earlier results on the fatigue of metals and the effects of drugs on them. The results were published in 1900. Why haven't they been more used than they have? Is it that people don't believe—or what? If they're sound, it does seem to be an experimental proof of what, by deduction, one had supposed to be true—that life is implicit in all 'inanimate' matter. Bose is just about to start for Europe. I expect you'll see him and his experiments—if he brings his apparatus.

Love to you all from both of us.

A.

P.S. Maria asks if Juliette will kindly open the packages when they arrive and send the fur coats and (if she thinks it necessary) the blue greatcoat to be cleaned, so as to make sure of eliminating any moths. *Beware when opening, as the box is full of pepper and formalin.*

Government House, Singapore
4 March, 1926

My dear J,

Just received your letter with the enclosed introductions: for which much thanks. I doubt whether we shall be able to use more than a few of them, as we shall be going pretty straight to N. Y. from Frisco (where we arrive, I hope, on May 5th) so as to be there before people go away for the summer—which they do early, I gather. Besides, I don't want to spend unnecessarily on traipsing round the continent. We shall have had enough of travelling by then, I expect.

We are staying here with the Guillemards, in very great splendour. It is rather like staying at Buckingham Palace—soldiers on guard, innumerable footmen, everybody standing up when His or Her Excellency enter the room etc. But they are very pleasant and kind, and the place is delightful. The house stands in a sort of super-park—equatorial England—the town is a great Chinese metropolis, the island abounds in panoramas. We came down from Penang by train—through hundreds of miles of jungle and hundreds more miles of neat but scraggy rubber plantations. The whole place breathes prosperity: everyone seems to have enough to eat and not too much to do—a great relief after the deserts of upper India and their starved and hopeless inhabitants.

We go to Java tomorrow, scamper through the islands, come back here and take a ship that goes up along the coast of Borneo to a place called Zamboanga in the southern Philippines, whence (with luck) we shall get another ship to take us to Manila in time to catch the liner leaving for Frisco on April 7th. It ought to be very pleasant, I think.

The heat, so far, is not bad. Singapore is the Palm House at Kew with a breeze. Java, I gather, has no breeze: palm house untempered.

Love to all.

Yours
A.

246: TO ROBERT NICHOLS

The Train, near Chicago
13 *May,* [1926]

A day's march nearer home, my dear Robert, and not such an uncomfortable one as I had feared. Indeed, the journey has been admirably good. Given the privacy of these compartments and their comforts, one wouldn't mind going on for days.

The Grand Canyon was quite up to specifications and only man was vile.

246 Misdated '13.v.25'.

(But then, poor devil, he can hardly fail to be when he is as closely concentrated as he necessarily must be round the point where the railway touches the canyon.) One trundles in motor buses along the brink of the chasm. Or if one has more time or, being a woman, likes the shape of one's haunches in breeches, one mounts a mule and goes off with a movie cowboy down into the gulf. The breeches, I must say, added something to the charms of the scene.

How delightful it was to see you again, my dear Bob, after all these years —and how still more delightful to think that you will soon be returning to civilization. Hollywood is altogether too antipodean to be lived in; it gives you no chance of escape. Italy seems to me clearly indicated. And after all it's in the grand poetic tradition. Every good English poet, with the exception of Shakespeare, has been to Italy for a more or less lengthy period. It is an indispensable phase in the poetic life—also, in these days of high taxation and high prices, of the purely prosaic life!

I hope 'Don Juan' prospers. I like what I heard of him very much. He ought to be a bit of a monument by the time he's done. He should flourish, I am sure, in an Italian scene.

Farewell, dear Robert. If I don't thank you in set terms for having made my day in Joy City so truly joyful, it isn't because I'm not grateful—I am, exceedingly—but because I don't want to write you the usual Collins. Take thanks as richly implied, if not actually uttered. Both our loves to both of you.

Yours,
Aldous

247: TO ANITA LOOS

Congress Hotel and Annex, Chicago
(As from: c/o *G. H. Doran Co.,*
244 *Madison Avenue, New York City*)
14 *May,* 1926

Dear Miss Anita Loos,

I have no excuse for writing to you—no excuse, except that I was enraptured by the book, have just hugely enjoyed the play, and am to be in America so short a time that I have no leisure to do things in the polite and tortuous way. My wife and I are to be in New York for about a fortnight from Monday 17th onwards, and it would be a very great pleasure—for us at any rate—if we could arrange a meeting with you during that time. Please forgive

247 *Book:* Gentlemen Prefer Blondes. *The meeting in New York took place and led to a lifelong friendship between Huxley and Anita Loos. From New York the Huxleys went to London, where Aldous remained until August, at first with his brother and then with his Aunt Ethel, whose husband, the Hon. John Collier, began to paint a portrait of him. Maria meanwhile rejoined her relations in Belgium.*

my impertinence and accept the sincere admiration which is its cause and justification.

Yours very sincerely,
Aldous Huxley

248: TO ELINOR WYLIE

*The Athenaeum, Pall Mall, S.W.*1
7 July, 1926

Dear Elinor Wylie,

This is to confirm our arrangement for Monday. I rang up Virginia and Leonard Woolf and they have very kindly insisted that we should dine with them at their house in Tavistock Square—*not* dressing. So I will call for you a few minutes before 7.30 on Monday at the Dysart Hotel.

I'm afraid that I was a little reticent on the telephone this morning about my Aunt—but the fact is that the telephone is in a very public part of this house and as I am staying here with another Aunt—I have a whole Swarm of Termites, or Great White Aunts—I could not embark on an audible discussion of her sister—the more so as there have been enormous family quarrels and there are still certain smouldering coolnesses. The Aunt you saw is all right—but in homoeopathic doses, as you wd no doubt discover for yourself if you saw her more often. She's a little formidable, both in her affection and her hatred. I am suffering at the moment from her affection.

Looking forward to Monday, I am

Yours
Aldous Huxley

249: TO ANITA LOOS

The Athenaeum, Pall Mall,
*London, S.W.*1
21 July, 1926

Dear Anita Loos,

How well I understand your reluctance to come to London while it is still inhabited. Particularly if you aren't in ebullient health—and I am most sorry to hear that you and your husband have not been as well as you should have been. Lady Colefax's double set of glands have been functioning with unparalleled activity; she reduced poor Doug[las Fairbanks] and Mary [Pickford] to the verge of the tomb. I had 3 letters, 2 telegrams and 2 notes

248 *This letter was written on paper with the printed heading 'North House, 69 Eton Avenue, N.W.', which Huxley crossed off; the address was that of his aunt Ethel Collier. The aunt that Elinor Wylie had met was his Aunt Nettie, Mrs Roller, whose nephews and nieces enjoyed her whimsical favour by turns: they liked to characterize the favourite of the moment as 'It'.*

by special messenger in the course of 5 days a little while ago. Since when I have retired to the country.

I shall have left London before the 12th. But on the other hand I shall be in Paris—probably from the 8th onwards. Please let me know your address in Paris during the days 9th-12th August. I am hoping that the franc will not have fallen to 2 or 3 million by then. If it has, the Parisians probably won't like us very much. 'Ces sales Anglo-Saxons.' Do let us be sure of colliding in Paris, since London is out of the question.

Yours very sincerely
Aldous Huxley

250: TO JULIAN HUXLEY

19 Grand' Place, St Trond,
Belgium
10 August, 1926

My Dear J,

This is just to tell you of a rather gloomy account of travelling on the lower Danube, which I have just had from someone who has done it. It appears that vermin are numerous and that you are apt, even in first class carriages, to see bugs pullulating like ants. Also, the typhoid is said to be very bad, especially in early autumn, which is always the worst time for typhoid anywhere, owing to the ground being dry, cracking and letting the surface filth run down, unfiltered, into the subterranean springs. This being so, it would be as well to be fore-armed and take a lot of Keatings and something to disinfect all water or raw fruit and vegetables. In India we always used a stuff called chlorogen, which is much recommended by doctors there. It is, I believe, simply neat hydrochloric acid. You carry it in little phials, which have stoppers fitted with glass rods. The rods take up a drop of the acid when withdrawn from the phial and you dip them into your tumbler of water. The drop is sufficient to sterilize it. There is a faint taste of chlorine, almost imperceptible, unless you put more than a drop in. Otherwise you can take permanganate of potash. It turns the water a bit pink, but does no harm when drunk and doesn't taste bad. It might even be worth having anti-typhoid injections. They make you feel rather ill at the time—a few hours fever after each injection—but they give one confidence afterwards. All this may sound a little Rosalindish; but in these matters, I think it is best to take plenty of precautions. There is such a lot of typhoid even in France. How much more in the Balkans, where, I should imagine, hardly any towns have adequate sewage arrangements or uncontaminable water supply.

I found Matthew very well and in uproarious spirits. He eats copiously and makes himself a great nuisance—healthy signs. We leave for Cortina on Sunday, halting at Basel and Innsbruck en route, so as not to sleep in the train.

I had a very pleasant evening on Friday last with Anita Loos, who is ravishing. One would like to keep her as a pet. She is the doyenne of Hollywood, having started to write for the movies when she was seven. Now, at the age of, I suppose, about twenty-eight, she feels that she can retire with a good conscience, to live in cultured ease on the fruits of her labours. What she really likes doing, it appears, is plain sewing; spends all her holidays in making underclothes which nobody can wear.

I hope the British Ass[ociation] has been amusing and not too fatiguing, and that the movies of the birds were a success. I read and much enjoyed your article on the 'Biological Meaning of Individuality'. It is curious, when one comes to think of it, how one human being can be a constituent part of several social individuals seemingly of the most diverse and hostile character —as Faraday, who was at once a Sandemanian and a Fellow of the Royal Society, or as a man who is simultaneously a soldier, a Christian and a sodomite.

I will let you know as soon as we are settled at Cortina what our plans are. I am inclined to doubt whether we shall be able to get away for the whole trip. In any case, however, I look forward to seeing you when you get back to Italy. I so much enjoyed being with you at Highgate and only wish its mountains were a thousand metres higher, so that we could enjoy the benefits of the Dolomites with those of London and your company.

Love from us all.

A.

251: TO LEONARD HUXLEY

Villa Ino Colli, Ronco,
Cortina d'Ampezzo (Belluno), Italy
9 September, 1926

Dearest Father,

After considerable troubles here we are, settled in—though not yet completely—into a rather nice little house. We had first thought of staying in the hotel all through the winter. But it was so cramped and we heard such gloomy stories of the reluctance of hotel keepers to give one adequate heating during the off-season months, when there are few people in the inns, that we thought it best to find a house, which was not so easy as it should have been, considering that Cortina pullulates with furnished houses. Most of them are so badly built that they get no sun, lack bathrooms and central heating and are absurdly dear. But at last we hit on this, which has a perfect aspect, teems with terraces and balconies on which it is possible to get every ray of sunlight that falls on Cortina between dawn and evening, has baths, a garage and central heating, is simply but very comfortably and sensibly furnished and

251 *Matthew's governess was a Mademoiselle LaPorte, called 'Zezelle'.*

272

costs something less than nine pounds a month. We are not entirely installed yet, as there are still summer-season visitors staying in the lowest floor and servants are not obtainable before the middle of September. M and I sleep here and take our meals at the hotel, where Matthew and his governess are still occupying their rooms.

Cortina seems already to have done Matthew a great deal of good. He is perceptibly more robust than he was, has a fine colour and eats well. Our governess is a great treasure—young, intelligent and very highly trained, having taught at the famous Decroly school in Brussels and at that big co-ed school, St Christopher's, at Letchworth, not to mention the fact that she has gone through the prescribed courses of pedagogy and so forth at the Belgian Ecole Normale. She also has a good working knowledge of gymnastics. Matthew likes her and learns well. So that is a great comfort.

Cortina is a wide saucer shaped valley surrounded by enormous limestone crags, like the Mappin Terraces at the Zoo on a large scale. There is a lot of sun and the air is extraordinarily keen and stimulating. So far it has been almost uninterruptedly fine and warm. The bad time is November, I believe, when it rains a great deal. After that it remains very fine, with occasional snow storms, all through the winter. The meteorological reports show an average of sixty-five completely cloudless days out of every hundred during the winter months—which isn't bad.

The summer season is just ending, which is rather a relief, as there were too many people and, above all, too many motors. The great Dolomite road which goes up hill and down dale between this point and Bolzano was almost like the Brighton road on a Saturday afternoon when we drove along it about a fortnight ago. Incredibly dangerous, as the road is narrow, tortuous, very steep and flanked most of the way by precipices, while the number of enormous charabancs is appalling. We witnessed one all-but disaster, when the driver of a charabanc passing the car we were in misjudged his turning and took his machine right into the loose stones and the posts at the edge of the road. One wheel of the car was actually over the edge of the precipice by the time it was at a standstill. If it had been going a mile or two faster, it would have gone over two or three hundred feet, with twenty or thirty people on board.

We went down to Florence last week to get our car, which we found in perfect order; but had great difficulties in getting permission to drive it, as all driving licence holders have been compelled by a recent law to undergo a second examination. Before you can enter for the examination, you have got to produce documents showing that you have never been in prison and so forth—a process which takes weeks. Luckily fascism has not lessened the corruptibility of the officials and by a judicious distribution of largesse we got a temporary licence to drive, while the documents are being collected. But M will have to go back in a few weeks time and do her examination —and probably distribute a little more in the process. It's no doubt a very good thing that the authorities should insist on a high standard of driving among motorists—they really ought to institute an examination system in England —but it is a bore when one finds oneself enmeshed in spiders' webs of red tape.

We are expecting to see Julian and Juliette on their way back from the Balkans some time towards the twentieth of this month. I should have liked to accompany them; but had no time, as I have much to do. This place promises to be a good place to work in.

How has Scotland been this year? Fine, I hope. And the family? May it flourish. Much love from us all. I will get Matthew to write you a letter. He does it very well now.

> *Your loving son,*
> *Aldous*

252: TO LEONARD HUXLEY

> *Florence*
> 21 *October,* 1926

Dearest Father,

Enclosed is a letter which the porter of the Athenaeum has mistakenly forwarded to me. I hope it contains nothing of urgent importance; for the news will be rather stale by the time it reaches you.

We are here for a few days—mostly for the sake of dentists who do not flourish in the high altitudes of Cortina. I have a tiresome tooth which needs prolonged disinfection and cannot be filled too soon owing to tendencies to form abscesses in the roots. However I hope we shall get away by the middle of next week. Matthew meanwhile flourishes at Cortina and is putting on weight well—900 grammes the first month and the second (in spite of a tummy upset which held him back) 250, with a centimetre of growth. We are ever more delighted with our charming governess, who teaches him very well, so that he already writes very creditably and can calculate in a manner quite remarkable, considering his descent from one whose mathematics had a way, as Miss Noon put it, of remaining *in statu quo.*

Florence is (or rather was until it began to rain yesterday) marvellously beautiful and I regret having to go up again into the mountains, where I shall miss the delicate colouring of the Tuscan landscape, the soft yet grandly noble forms of the hills, the white villas with their gardens, the patiently elaborated terraces on the slopes with their grey olives, their vines and strips of ploughland, and here and there the black cypresses and the clumps of ilex and bay trees.

I am very busy preparing for and doing bits of an ambitious novel, the aim of which will be to show a piece of life, not only from a good many

252 *The 'ambitious novel' was to be* Point Counter Point.

individual points of view, but also under its various aspects such as scientific, emotional, economic, political, aesthetic etc. The same person is simultaneously a mass of atoms, a physiology, a mind, an object with a shape that can be painted, a cog in the economic machine, a voter, a lover etc etc. I shall try to imply at any rate the existence of the other categories of existence behind the ordinary categories employed in judging everyday emotional life. It will be difficult, but interesting.

I hope the family flourishes. Give both our loves to all and accept them for yourself.

Your loving son
Aldous

253: TO THE HON. EDWARD SACKVILLE-WEST

Villa Ino Colli,
Cortina d'Ampezzo (Belluno), Italy
2 November, 1926

My dear Eddy,

Thank you for your very friendly letter. I am greatly pleased you like *Jesting Pilate*, which I also like. I look forward to seeing your review.

I am sorry you should have been *embêté* about your last book. I hope that at least it has not—like one of mine—been burnt by the Library of Alexandria (which, I had always been taught, was burnt down in its entirety two thousand years ago, but seems now to have arisen Phoenix-like for the express purpose of indulging in a little private conflagration at my expense).

Lady Colefax's accounts are a little exaggerated. Cortina is not exactly paradisiacal—especially now, when it is raining with an unremitting violence, day in day out. But we exist in tolerable contentment. I work hard at an inordinately large and complicated novel.

In Florence, where we spent a fortnight, I passed some very delightful hours with D. H. Lawrence, whom I like so much. Also with old Vernon Lee, the most astonishing and brilliant of talkers when she is at her best.

Do you do winter sports? I don't really expect you do—but if you should feel like them, why not practise them here at Cortina.

Yours
Aldous H.
P.S. Next Page.

P.S. This letter has failed to get itself posted; so I take the opportunity to add a few words. I have given a letter of introduction, addressed to you, to Luigino Franchetti, who is over in England for a month or two. A very nice

253 *Huxley's friendship with Lawrence, whom in* 1915 *he had met only once or twice briefly, begins now; on its genesis see his Introduction to* The Letters of D. H. Lawrence, *pp. xxix-xxx.*

fellow and a beautiful pianist. One of the few artists I know who has the traditional 'artistic temperament' of the 19th century romantic epoch—quite natural and spontaneous in him. [. . . .]

254: TO ROBERT NICHOLS

Villa Ino Colli,
Cortina d'Ampezzo (Belluno), Italy
14 November, 1926

My dear Robert,

I was very glad to get your long letter, though sorry that it contained such a gloomy account of your health. However, I hope that the treatment by the poetry-loving physician is doing you good and that you will soon be entirely restored. In a way I am glad you have not come to Italy this winter; for we shouldn't have seen you if you had, this place (though now, since the war, a part of Italy) being merely Tyrolean and having about as much connection with real Italy as the Rocky Mountains. Next year, if all goes well and our little boy is thoroughly solid (the climate of this gloomy place is doing him a vast amount of good) we may return, for part of the year at least, to Florence which is after all, as I rediscovered when we went down there recently for a week or two, the only place—not so much the town itself, as the miraculous country all round. Perhaps you will come out to Italy then.

At the moment, we are plunged in what seems a permanent cold foggy drizzle. We live in a cloud; the air is like iced blotting paper. But it will be sunny again some time—at least I piously hope so—and when the sun does make its appearance it shines positively with ferocity. Meanwhile, I work away on a long and complicated novel, which I want to make a picture of life in its different aspects, the synchronous portrait of the different things an individual simultaneously is—atoms, physiology, mystic, cog in the economic machine, lover, etc. Very difficult, and I doubt if I shall succeed in doing what I want to. But it is interesting to tinker away at the idea. In the intervals I read—MacDougall's [William McDougall's] *Outline of Abnormal Psychology*, very interesting and, except in parts, I should say very sound and true. Then a vast book by the Italian Sociologist Vilfredo Pareto, very good as far as I have got; he really does take the lid off and show you the works, at some length, unfortunately; for there are three thick volumes, in Italian, which makes it a slight additional fatigue to read; then Burtt's *Metaphysical Foundations of Modern Science*, which I am rereading, more thoroughly than before; an interesting and important book, which if you haven't already read you should. Not to mention odds and ends of many kinds; for example, a translation (small Latin, alas, and less Greek) of the *Mimes* of Herodas, very entertaining; and they cast a bright and rather unpleasantly revealing light on middle class Greek life. The way the slaves are treated makes one rather uncomfortable. There is one very indecent

276

dialogue between two ladies who discuss the virtues of a dildo made of red Morocco leather which they have had made for them by the cobbler. Curious in every sense, and good.

How is England? My trouble is that there never seem to be any new people when I return periodically. The same old set, slowly putrefying in their own juice. But I suppose there are young people; only one doesn't see them. Or do you see them? I agree with you about the incomprehensibleness of some of our contemporaries; it seems to me the fruit of a profound stupidity. Einstein is incomprehensible because he is too intelligent; dogs are incomprehensible because they are too stupid. These smart young French and imitation French who want to abolish psychology, abolish reason, abolish speculation, analysis, everything beyond immediate sensation, the more violent the better, and mere animal action are just stupid, like dogs, non-human—there is no more to be said. Or perhaps the truth is that they belong to a different species from us—the species that is just content to live, to whom the end of life is feeling and action, not thought, who are so sociable that the mere presence of other human animals makes them happy, and so easily amused that they can pass their time between the cradle and the grave playing games. The more I see of human beings, the more I am convinced of the specific, almost generic, differences between them. One species can scarcely communicate with the other. It is, perhaps, unfortunate that they can breed together. No, on second thoughts, it is probably a good thing; otherwise the speculative species would eat itself up with contemplation and the others would become too stupid to compete successfully with the animals. It is the mules who get things done in the world I suppose.

I am glad you liked the book; I too. It seems to me at any rate the right sort of book, various, containing a bit of everything, a sort of chaos, but an elegant chaos.

Our loves to both of you. Get and keep well.

Yours,
Aldous H.

255: TO ELINOR WYLIE

Villa Ino Colli,
Cortina d'Ampezzo (Belluno), Italy
Christmas Day, 1926

Dear Elinor

How kind it was of you to send me your angelic orphan! I read the book, when at last I got it away from Maria, with very great pleasure, enjoying very much a certain glassy and translucent beauty which pervades it all. It has something of the quality of Shelley's own poems. Being by nature

255 *Orphan:* The Orphan Angel, *a novel.*

extremely malicious, I think I would have liked you to treat Shiloh a little less handsomely than you do. If I had written the book, I would have let him (it sounds fiendish, I know) grow old, just for the diabolic fun of seeing what would have happened to a man who achieved complete maturity at about twenty, to remain thereafter almost unmalleable by experience. I would have let him live far enough into the Victorian era to witness the complete over-throw of the tyrannies he hated, priesthood and privileged aristocracy, and the consequent millenium of industrial wickedness. I would have made him survive into the Pecksniffian epoch, so that he could indulge in his ardently romantic platonisms (and non-platonisms, for after all his passions were not invariably ethereal) in the appalling gloom and stuffiness of the mid-nineteenth century environment. But then, I repeat, I am malicious. You have chosen what is perhaps the better course of keeping him young and completely angelic. Certainly it was the more difficult course to pursue successfully; for nothing is harder than to make a really good, crystalline character interesting. Anyone can draw devils; but angels are another matter. I congratulate you on the way in which you have made your orphan angel live.

I hope you flourish, and also your husband. We sit perched on an icy solitude, which would be intolerable if it didn't do us all, especially the little boy and Maria, so much good. Best wishes from both of us for the new year.

Ever yours,
Aldous Huxley

256: TO LEONARD HUXLEY

Cortina d'Ampezzo
31 December, 1926

Dearest Father,

Just a word to say how very pleased I was to have the photographs of Mother as a little girl. They are particularly charming and touching little pictures and I have always wanted a copy of them.

Cortina seems to be about the only place on the Continent of Europe which isn't cold. I see that Lisbon has had snow; we, meanwhile, are as dry as a bone with only a degree or two of frost each night. Whatever snow there was, and there was never more than an inch or so, has disappeared; and even at six or seven thousand feet there is very little in the neighbourhood. A few days ago there was actually a shower of rain. The hotelkeepers tear their hair and the tourists depart as soon as they arrive.

We spent a few days in Venice and Padua doing Christmas shopping

256 *The Belgian child, who was called Minet, was the son of a Dr Weil, of Brussels, a former employer of Matthew's governess, Mademoiselle LaPorte. Essays:* Essays New and Old.

last week and found them much colder than Cortina—Venice wrapped in an icy white fog might have been some place on the North Sea in February. We came up with Maria's sister [Rose Nys] and a young friend, who arrived at Padua, bringing with them a little Belgian boy, who is going to stay, I hope, several months. He is a nice child, the son of a doctor, or rather of two doctors—for both mother and father practise the art—rather delicate and overgrown; his parents who are very busy have no time to take him to the mountains and are glad of the opportunity of sending him. So here he is, a great success with Matthew. They get on very well together.

We are expecting an American family of our acquaintance in the next few days and, later on in January, no less a personage than the great Arnold Bennett, who is always very good company.

I am glad you liked the essays and the travel book. The latter has done very well, considering the extremely high price—sixteen shillings—which they put on it. The best part of three thousand copies have been sold since it was published in the middle of October, which seems to me very good, considering the slumpy state of the book trade and of all other trades during the last months.

Much love to all. I hope the children's Tunisian dates will arrive fairly soon. We have heard that they were sent off on December 14th; but the Lord knows when they will reach their destination.

Your loving son,
Aldous

257: MARIA HUXLEY TO EUGENE F. SAXTON

Villa Ino Colli,
Cortina d'Ampezzo (Belluno)
2 January, 1927

Dear Saxton,

How nice of you to wish us happiness for this year and for Xmas; thank you so much and please do not think it too late to accept our wishes in return. The very best for all that is best in this world, and, selfishly, that includes a visit to Europe and to your friends, doesn't it?

We were expecting your family to-day and much looking forward to it but Mrs Saxton seems not to have received some of my letters and therefore the arrival is postponed till the 7th. I pray there may be snow by then for they would be too disappointed and I feel too guilty for having dragged them up this place to find only a deliciously warm sun, an atmosphere of spring and desolated tourists who curse the heaven for its serenity—but they would also find devoted friends, and that might make up for the climate.

Cortina I have hated for so long so intensely that now I quite like it; perhaps there is no hate left or it is that the place doing me so much good has found favour with us, but most probably it is that the sun warms us since the last month. But we shall go away soon; and that is the best part of the beginning of this year. We start for London sometime toward the end of February, Aldous's work be praised for that necessity, and we shall travel slowly through Florence, the riviera (which I hate but is the only way into France, or rather out of Italy, in the winter), Paris, and London for a long time. Will you be there? Surely you will—on business?

We went down to the plains to fetch my little sister and a friend, a little boy friend of Baby's, before Xmas, and you would have laughed to see our car: though it is now a much larger one it was as full as it could be with seven human beings and about as many large toy animals: and not a short drive as the one you took home with us; from ten in the morning till four, with an interval however for a copious Italian lunch. I love my new car, it is very fast and whizzes up the hills never minding corners or hair-pin bends; but in the little Citroen one got much more excitement out of less speed than in these real cars; that one made such a rattling noise and menaced to jump off the road at 50 miles an hour and one got all the excitement without the horror of the scenic railway, whereas this one shows speed only on the speedo-meter.

On New Year's eve we took my little sister and her friend, both very young and straight from the convent, to their first public ball in the smartest hotel. It was very funny to be and feel a chaperon and looking after those two ravishing creatures in white frills and pink flowers who missed not a single dance and got very gay on almost no champagne. Aldous and I looked pompous and spent most of our time playing at games and though winning many silly prizes losing much money, however I am sure that first luck of the year will bring us some all the year round.

What a pity that you have to take your holidays in turns; we are so much looking forward to the arrival of Mrs Saxton and the children and how much more if you were with them. Baby is in bed with a bad cold which has gone round the family and was brought from Venice where we went to amuse ourselves a few days but suffered so intensely from the cold of dense fogs that we thought with melancholy of Cortina and the sun.

Aldous is working very hard at a novel now, and did you hear that one of your compatriots arranged *Antic Hay* for the stage? She came here with it and for a fortnight travelled with us while Aldous corrected the play. I have not read it in the final version, they were in such a hurry to let her go off with it, but it is supposed to be very funny. I cannot help thinking it is too indecent, and unless it made us very very rich would as soon it remained where it is; the novel is quite enough of it. But this is a very very private opinion.

I suppose we will hear about you much next week but do also write and tell us how you are and whether you have any London plans. And you must give our love to Mr. Parmentier. I liked him so much. A rather formidable friend [Lalla Vandervelde], not really so formidable as she thinks herself to

257 *The dramatic version of* Antic Hay *was made by a Miss Werner.*

be, is going to America and we have given her a letter for you. I believe you will like her for she is very entertaining.

With much love from both of us.

Maria Huxley

258: TO ROBERT NICHOLS

Villa Ino Colli,
Cortina d'Ampezzo (Belluno), Italy
18 January, 1927

My dear Robert,

I should have answered your long and delightful letter before; but, suffering as I do from a slight letter-complex, I have been putting off the duty, which is also a pleasure (a complex opposes itself even to a pleasure), from day to day, for weeks.

Your account of the dinner party with Wells was amusing. I am not astonished that he has not read *The Idiot.* It would surprise me more to hear that he had read anything by Dostoievsky. I don't know him at all well; but he has always struck me as a rather horrid, vulgar little man. And what about his books? *The Outline of History* seemed to me very good. But the other day I thought I would re-read, after how many years? one of those novels that seemed so very good when one was a boy, before the War. I tried *Tono Bungay*—and found it thin, shoddy, uninteresting and written in that dreadful swill-tub style, which I had thought was, perhaps, a recent development, but now perceive to have been H.G.'s native woodnote.

[Julien] Benda is always interesting. *Belphégor* and *Eleuthère* have excellent things in them—though they're by no means great. Exceedingly intelligent, rather. *L'Ordination* seems to me good in parts. The first half is excellent as an analysis of a decaying passion, as a statement of the inevitably impossible relationship between men and women. But the second half, where he gives up having ideas for the sake of his scrofulous daughter, strikes me as very mechanical and unreal. People are not interested in ideas by choice (not in the way and to the extent, at any rate, which Benda describes), but by temperament. They are predestined to ideas as they are predestined to a Roman nose. And little daughters, however scrofulous, cannot change them from idea-lovers to domestic pussy cats. Temporarily they may give up ideas; but after a little their nature will reassert itself, they will spring back into their normal position. I am left entirely unconvinced by the second half of *L'Ordination.*

Gide, as you say, is disappointing. He has a faculty for always touching on interesting subjects and never really getting hold of them. He attacks great moral problems and then, before the campaign has well started, beats an elegant, literary and genteel retreat. The only good book he has written is the last, *Les Faux Monnayeurs,* which is very interesting and in its way

281

very good. It is good, I think, because it is the first book in which Gide has ventured to talk about the one thing in the world that really interests him—sentimental sodomy. Now that Proust has given the world his guide-book to the cities of the plain, the other sodomites feel that they can follow suit without scandal, sheltering themselves behind his precedent. Hitherto Gide could never harness the springs of his instinctive energy to the doing of literary work; his books were all apart from the main current of his life. Now, circumstances have permitted him to use that current; for the first time the literary mill wheel really turns. The result is admirable.

Have you read [François] Porché's recently published *Vie de Baudelaire?* It's well done and, if you haven't read a good life of B. before (which I hadn't) very interesting. What a hellish life—inwardly predestined to hellishness by the man's own character. I have been reading a number of biographies recently. Liszt (by Pourtalès, bad), Nietzsche (by Mügge), Rimbaud, Mme de Guyon. I even tried to read Renan's *Vie de Jésus*, but had to stop after a hundred pages—it was so profoundly disgusting; one felt that it had been written by an old man in a chronic state of slight erection. His favourite epithets for Jesus are *charmant* and *délicieux*, as though he were a mixture of a cocotte, a child and a strawberry ice. The other lives I got through more successfully. How odd they are, and how little they obey any rule! In some cases the man's work is the compensation for his life, in others it is the expression of it. *Zarathustra* was written by a dyspeptic professor who could never refrain from over-eating when his mother sent him a hamper of sweet things, and was always punctually sick in consequence. But Rimbaud's life and poetry are the same. Mme de Guyon became a mystic because her mother-in-law was odious and her husband disgusted her and gave her no physical pleasure. But Liszt was as brilliantly romantic as his own music.

We hope to come to England in March and that you will still be there. Good bye till then, dear Robert. I trust your health improves. I will let you know nearer the time the date of our arrival. Love to Norah.

Yours,
Aldous H.

259: TO LEONARD HUXLEY

Villa Ino Colli,
Cortina d'Ampezzo (Belluno), Italy
14 February, 1927

Dearest Father,

Time slips by at a great rate here, and I am afraid that my last letter must have been sent off many days ago. That is the trouble of living in a place where there are no events of any particular significance. One loses count of the days, and every fresh glance at the calendar brings a shock.

The chief amusement of the last weeks has consisted in Arnold Bennett, whom we have seen every day and who has been in excellent form. Another old friend turned up surprisingly and quite unexpectedly in the shape of Lulu Selwyn, whom I had not seen for I don't know how many years. I think she has improved with age. At any rate we found her a very nice intelligent self-possessed girl. She left last week and Bennett departs to-morrow. Nor shall we be here very long; for we hope to come to London quite soon for some weeks, as I have to collect some materials for my book which I cannot evolve out of my inner consciousness. We hope to come by car, via the Riviera—the only road open at this time of year—arriving some time early in March. Matthew and his little friend will stay here with the governess till we return.

Cortina may not be very interesting as a centre of European culture; but I must say that as a place to get well in, it is unrivalled. Matthew flourishes in an unprecedented manner and so does the little friend, and so for that matter do we all. The sun has been shining violently every day for a month—so violently, indeed, that the snow is already beginning to disappear very rapidly and, unless there is a new fall soon, the season will be over unusually early. As it began exceptionally late, the inhabitants of Cortina will not be best pleased. We had an international ski jumping competition here last week—a most stupendous performance, for me at any rate, who had never seen any good jumping before. The winners did fifty-four metres, which is about as much as can be done on this particular jump, though the world's record, at Pontresina, is over sixty, I believe. The spectacle of those men hurtling through the air above the level of one's head is really astounding.

I have done fifty or sixty thousand words of a novel, but have stopped, as the thing was getting too formidable for me to proceed with without further thinking over and ruminative living with. In the mean time I am working at some essays and perhaps shall go on to do some stories before continuing the novel; it depends partly on the heavenly muse and partly, alas, on finance!

Love to the family from all of us.

Your loving son,
Aldous

260: TO JULIAN HUXLEY

1 *Via S. Margherita a Montici,*
Florence
25 *February,* 1927

My dear J,
Your letter of the 20th was forwarded here to-day and gave me much pleasure. I had meant to write before to say we were coming over to England; but the instant I got to Florence, I went down with flu, which I have been having ever since, to-day being the second day of convalescence. Really, it

283

is time that something was done about these preposterous microbes; they have no right to interfere with one's life in this way. In a week of fever I have squandered the small fortune of health accumulated during the months at Cortina; but hope to pick up again soon. We shall leave here by car, if all goes well, on the third of March and make our way across France by easy stages, possibly stopping a day or two on the riviera for a little health giving sunshine. In any case, we should be in London soon after the tenth. I will let you know at once. We have our little studio again—this time with an extra bed and some conveniences.

The news about the H. G. [Wells] book [*The Science of Life*] is very exciting. My advice is: Of course stop teaching. If the majority of people were worth teaching, there might be some inducement to go on at it. But they so manifestly aren't that it seems unnecessary for a man of talent to waste his powers doing no good to fools when he might be using them valuably on something else.

By my word! what sums these literary nabobs can command. Arnold Bennett who, as you know, was up at Cortina for three weeks, revealed a few of the secrets. He himself never writes for less than two shillings per word, like an Atlantic cable! And even I am beginning to profit by prestige. In the course of the last six months I have sold two articles in America for a thousand dollars apiece! Crazy—and it probably won't be repeated. So on the strength of it we have gone and bought a really rather tremendous car— an Itala six cylinder two-litres. What a machine! We have so far done only sixty-five m.p.h. in it—with vastly less trepidation than the Citroen doing thirty five—but it will do over seventy. On hills it is incredible; one's speed is only limited by the corners. Altogether, we're extremely pleased, so far.

I am glad you think like that about [A. N.] Whitehead's new book [*Science and the Modern World*]. I told Sullivan so in a letter, who replied as though I'd committed the sin against the Holy Ghost. I can't see that there's anything to distinguish his rationalizings of religious emotions from those of anyone else. Metaphysical entities, Absolute Goods and so forth are as completely unobservable as gods and goddesses. Regarded as truth, in the scientific sense of the word, there's nothing to choose between Good inherent in the Universe and devils inherent in the Gadarene swine. These things may exist, or they may not. We have, up to date, no methods for discovering. And why should the sense of values be the only complex of feelings to have the privilege of being hypostasized into absoluteness? Why not hypostasize the sexual feelings—which are just as fundamental, universal and biologically important. In point of fact, this has been done. Millions of people have and still do believe in deities of love, principles of reproduction etc. Even an eminent philosopher, Lucretius, made Venus a first principle. And there is just as much and just as little reason to supposing that Lucretius was right as for supposing that Whitehead is right.

I am writing some essays on religion and other sociological subjects, which I hope will appear this autumn, as I shan't be able to get my novel out by then—it grows under my hands and becomes increasingly difficult, though increasingly interesting. I need to see a lot more people and things before I can go on with it. Hence this visit to England.

How nice to have found a cottage at Cutt Mill. But won't the shopping be a bit of a problem? But I suppose Selfridge's and Harrod's deliver at your doorstep—I had forgotten that England was a civilized country and was thinking of Italy.

Melancholy about poor Uncle Frank. I had not seen him for at least five or six years. He was one of the Arnolds in whom the intelligence had taken the wrong turning and become fantastic, absorbing itself in futilities also, like puzzles and acrostics. I shall never forget one occasion when I was staying there—poor Uncle Frank's extraordinary indignation because he had got one word wrong in some dreadful newspaper conundrum, which he felt he ought to have been right about. The clue was in rhyme, I remember:

> Seldom said, though true,
> Say, of Jabiru.

By consulting encyclopaedias about jabirus, he had discovered that the characteristic feature of these animals is to be, let us say, dolichoduodenal. But the puzzle editor had hit on some feature of much more superficial significance, as its pentorchism, for example. It was not only bad science, it was bad faith—and in a liberal paper too. Poor Uncle Frank.

I enjoyed your essays very much. The substance interesting; the manner eminently lucid. I find the desire for lucidity grows in me. Not simplification, but clean dissection and clear exposition of as much of the immeasurable complexity of things as one can dig into.

Love from both of us. A bientôt.

A.

261: TO H. G. WELLS

*The Athenaeum, Pall Mall, S.W.*1
24 *March*, 1927

Dear Wells,

Thank you for writing the wholly excellent article in the *Sunday Express*. I was saying, 'Them's my sentiments' all the time as I read it. But I wish I'd seen it before meeting you on the boat last Saturday; for then I'd have asked you about the one point which seemed to me obscure in your exposition—

261 *A miscellaneous series of articles by H. G. Wells had been appearing bi-weekly in the* Sunday Express *since January. Huxley was referring to the article of 20 March,* 'Is Parliament Doomed?—The Farce of Our Elections: New Experiments in Government'.

about the possible remedy to present chaos in a form of proportional representation. How are you going to make a strong working government from a body of people elected on a great variety of different tickets and not bound together by party ties? It would be easy enough if men were rational beings. But since they are what they are. . . . I wish you'd give me an opportunity of asking you one evening, next week, if you're in town. Could you have dinner with me here, say Wednesday next, or Thursday?

Yours very sincerely
Aldous Huxley

262: TO LEWIS GIELGUD

19 *Grand' Place, St Trond*
17 *May,* 1927

My dear Lewis,

Maria's grandfather has just died, which means, I am afraid, that all our plans will have to be altered. We shall have to attend the funeral, of course; and it will be impossible to get out of staying several days after it, as M's grandmother very much desires it and finds M's presence particularly comforting. In the circumstances we cannot refuse to stay. The result of this will be that we must, alas, give Paris a miss; for we are compelled, in any circumstances, to be back in Cortina by the end of the month and as we shan't be able to leave St Trond till the 25th or 26th, we shall have to go direct without any halt longer than a night on the way. A sad, bad business. But on the other hand M's sister and infant won't be coming to Forte after all; so that we shall be able to put you up in the house whenever you like to come. The rooms, I gather, are not enormous; but if you and Mimi don't go in too much for swinging cats, I hope and think you will be comfortable. Let us have an idea of when we may expect you.

All this is, as you can imagine, at once lugubrious and farcical—the real Balzacian comedy of a funeral in a little town; friends and relations in crape; lettres de faire part; prodigal sons turning up to be reconciled and pinching the cigars and a thousand francs for a black overcoat; the poor old man's body in full evening dress; monks and sisters of charity padding about; preparations for a colossal funeral banquet—all very fantastic and everything happening to the strains of the steam organs and electric pianos of the inevitable Flemish kermesse just round the corner in the parish of St Gangulphus.

Maria sends her love to you both, as do I, and asks Mimi to forgive her for not writing, as she is terribly busy.

Farewell, then, till Forte.

Yours,
Aldous

19 *Grand' Place, St Trond,*
Belgium
23 *May,* 1927

Dear Brooks,

How good of you to send me your volume of poems! I read them with pleasure but without, I confess, entire comprehension. For my mind is not one of those that easily 'gets' an incantation. Voici le temps de la magie—alas, I am old-fashioned and only really at home with the most unmagical kind of direct statement. My chief criticism—so far as I can criticize—is that some of the magic is too private and individual, a record of particular experiences which it is difficult to interpret except in the light of your memory of those experiences—themselves of a tenuous and rarefied order. Another point—there are, for my taste at least, too many epithets. This is made inevitable by your extreme brevity, a part of the magical technique which I, as a non-magician, object to—preferring length and a gradual and easy statement of experiences without this desperate research of le mot juste and infinite treasure in a little room, which leads to the undue insistence on adjectives. I wish, for example, that you had expanded your 'Dostoievsky', (which I liked). It would have lost nothing of its point and gained by length, becoming more massive and solid. However, this probably seems all nonsense to you and beside the point, like a deaf man's criticism of music.

I am glad to hear you are getting married. Marriage is, after all, the only practical solution of most of the problems of living. Let me wish you all happiness.

We are moving southward in a day or two to spend the summer by the Mediterranean—the only possible sea for those who, like myself, are not so well covered with blubber that they can stand the icy waters of the north. I am very busy with various literary works—a volume of essays on sociological subjects, a long and complicated novel. Verse I find almost unwriteable these days. My only recent effort was a thing called 'Arabia Infelix' which appeared in an anthological volume with the ironical title of *The Best Poems of 1926.* It seemed to me not bad. I will send you a copy, if I [can] find one in Italy, or, failing that, can remember who the publisher is. I doubt if I shall be in England till the winter—perhaps not till spring. It depends on work. I'll let you know when the moment comes.

Best wishes.

Yours
Aldous Huxley

263 *The title of Brooks's book* Interludes and Incantations *and its epigraph* '*Voici le temps de la magie*' (*Behold the time of magic*)—(*from a poem by Apollinaire*) *explain the references in the early part of this letter.*

Villa Majetta,
Forte dei Marmi (Lucca), Italy
[July, 1927]

Dearest Father,

This has been, I fear, a very long silence. My only excuse is the violence of recent labours. They are now, thank goodness, finished and the MS [of *Proper Studies*] has gone off to the publishers. A great relief. I can do a little reading and basking in the sun with a good conscience. The heat is considerable; but we all flourish so far, and I trust shall continue to do so. Matthew has put on nine hundred grammes in the last six weeks—pretty good, considering the sun and the sea bathing. We went to Florence the other day to see our poor friend D. H. Lawrence, the novelist, who was down with a nasty attack of haemorrhage from the lungs—long standing tuberculosis, which has suddenly taken a turn for the worse. This is decidedly not a temperature to be ill in, and the poor wretch is not strong enough, nor secure enough from fresh bleedings, to move away from Florence into the cool of the mountains. He was with us at Forte, some three or four weeks ago, and I am afraid that bathing did him no good. The first attack came on shortly after he had left us. He is a very extraordinary man, for whom I have a great admiration and liking—but difficult to get on with, passionate, queer, violent. However, age is improving him and now his illness has cured him of his violences and left him touchingly gentle. I hope profoundly he'll get over this business. The doctor seemed to think he'd be all right; but with these haemorrhages one can never be quite certain. A particularly violent bout of bleeding can happen, even when the patient seems to be getting much better, and the end can be quite sudden and unexpected.

We have been fortunate this summer in our neighbours, among whom was Léner, of the Léner string quartet, who was staying with some rich Americans, the [Charles] Loesers, who have a house in Florence and a fine collection of pictures. Mrs Loeser is a professional pianist and plays with the Léners when they do quintets. There was also a first-rate Italian cellist staying and we had some delightful musical evenings—Beethoven trios. Nor was that the only music. For my friend Luigino Franchetti has also been here—a first-rate pianist. However, they have both departed now, leaving us only the gramophone as consolation.

August will be a lively month, as we are expecting Lewis Gielgud and his wife to stay, and there will probably be friends of theirs in the background. As the house is rather small, we shall probably send Matthew with Maria's

264 *Maria's uncle: Georges Baltus, an artist. He and his wife, formerly Sylvia von Hildebrand, lived with their child, Ado, in a villa at Forte which had belonged to the sculptor Hildebrand.*

sister to stay in the mountains, with M's uncle and his little boy, who will be there in August. Their mountain place is only a few miles away—though only accessible on mules—among the marble crags of Massa and Carrara. (Such wonderfully beautiful mountains they are, both in themselves and for the astounding panoramas of coast, sea, islands which they command.) I think the high air and the coolness may be good for the child in the August heats; for the place is pretty high—three thousand feet or more.

Italy under the new régime is becoming, not only very expensive, but also very irritating. In their enthusiasm for law and order, the fascist authorities are multiplying petty regulations and instituting a kind of police persecution. In these parts, for example, it is hardly possible to go out in a car without being fined, however slowly one may drive. And the scandal is that the police don't measure your speed between two points and don't even stop you. What happens is simply this; a single policeman sits at the side of the road—often in a pub, with a glass of wine—watching the cars which pass and taking down their numbers. When he has collected enough, he takes the list back to headquarters. Headquarters make the necessary enquiries and a few days later an official comes round with a paper, telling you that you owe the state so many lire. The thing is pure brigandage—the more so as the police themselves get a third of every fine they impose. The constables of Forte openly boast of the villas they have built for themselves out of the fines levied on car owners during the season. The only consolation is that the thing is becoming such an enormous scandal that the higher authorities have been forced to take some notice. Fining people who have not been stopped has been made illegal during the last few days in the next parish and I hope will soon be illegal here. But meanwhile we have already had to pay four fines. And I know other people who have paid literally dozens. The latest piece of police ingenuity in Florence is a regulation prescribing the circumstances in which you may leave you car standing at the curb of the principal street. On the odd days of the month you have to leave it on the left side, looking from the river; on the even days on the right. Twenty-five lire fine if you mistake the day. If they go on at this rate Italy will cease to be habitable.

I suppose you have moved, or are on the point of moving, up to Connel. May your weather be as good as ours. Best love from us all.

Your loving son,
Aldous

265: TO JULIAN HUXLEY

Villa Majetta,
Forte dei Marmi (Lucca), Italy
5 September, 1927

My dear J,

It would be delightful if you all came to Cortina this winter. With regard to details, it is impossible for us to be definite as yet. For we do not know—and shall not probably for some weeks—whether our last year's house is let or not. If the man can let it from before Christmas, he will obviously have no interest to give it to us, who come after Christmas. So that until we hear whether he has let, we can't say what accommodation we shall have. If he lets to someone else, I don't know whether we shall look out for another house or apartment, or go to a hotel. We shall probably hear in the course of this month what's happening. Meanwhile, I'm sorry I can't be any more specific. But I don't imagine you're in any clamorous hurry to make arrangements.

Ischia might be a good idea next summer. We had also thought of exploring the coast of France, west of Marseilles, quite close to the Spanish border. It appears that there are some very lovely places there. They would have the merit of being less remote than Ischia and not being islands— against which I have a certain prejudice (which ought to mean, according to Freud, that I have secret homosexual tastes; for islands, it is well known, are symbols of the female genitals . . .). But of this we can talk later. Meanwhile, it seems to me quite likely that we may want to come back to Forte, which remains incredibly lovely, in spite of everything.

I have thought of various further recommendations for the *Encyclopaedia*. Do insist that there must be a full bibliography to every article. Even in the new volumes there are plenty of quite important articles without any bibliography—which makes them perfectly useless for the serious student. Also, I notice a certain tendency to make the articles a little too chattily untechnical. I think this is rather dangerous. Two specific instances in the old volumes: Swinburne's article on Victor Hugo cannot be allowed to be reprinted. Read it; it's really extraordinary. He speaks of old man Hugo as though he were rather better than a combination of Shakespeare, Aeschylus, Pindar, Homer rolled into one. Such extravagances have no place in what should be a serious and dispassionate work of reference. Unwary readers might take them seriously, Similarly, I deplore for the same reasons Robert Lynd's lyrical article about Barrie in the new vols. It's a bit premature to start talking about his greatness and genius in the *Britannica*, I feel. But Lynd was always a fool.

> The chief defects of Robert Lynd
> Were cracking jokes and breaking wind,

as the poet has said. Another marvellous thing in the old vols is the article about Bronzino, which I quote in full. 'Bronzino, Il, the name given to Angelo Allori (1502–1572) the Florentine painter. He became the favourite pupil of J. da Pontormo. He painted the portraits of some of the most famous men of his day, such as Dante, Petrarch and Boccac[c]io. (*Sic.*) Most of his best works are in Florence, but examples are in the National Gallery, London, and elsewhere.' A remarkable article, that.

I hope your conferences have been amusing. The Italian press has been very violent about the birth controllers at Geneva. I see that Musso wants twenty million new Italians in twenty-five years. Presumably to fight France with; one can't imagine any other reason for their existence. Meanwhile, he has made illegal the sale of all contraceptive devices.

I work away at my novel, getting more and more deeply involved in its difficulties. I wish I could afford, like Flaubert, to spend four or five years over a book. There might be a chance then of making it rather good.

Our loves to all of you.

Yours,
A.

P.S. About Mme Guyon. It was during her fourth *grossesse* that the ecstasies became more marked—about the 4th month. Pierre Janet mentions many cases of hysterics who forget all their obsessions at the 4th month and are transfigured with happiness. 'Il y a même des familles où ce fait singulier amène les femmes à rechercher ardemment les grossesses fréquentes.' (See Leuba, *Religious Mysticism*.) I send this to England to make sure of catching you.

266: TO LEONARD HUXLEY

Florence (as from Villa Majetta)
Forte dei Marmi
8 October, 1927

Dearest Father,
Time rushes past as though it were trying to win the Schneider Cup, and goodness knows when I wrote to you last or heard from you. *Of* you I heard from Julian yesterday, and was glad to learn that you all flourished. What bad luck about poor little Francis's glands! Let's hope an Alpine winter will bring the mump down. I trust we shall be able to get the same house at Cortina as we had last year, in which case we shd be able to put up the child and his governess. All of us flourish, dieu merci. We have come to Florence for a few days to do various businesses and are regretting, in the icy north wind of this bleak Apennine town, the balmy warmth of Forte, where I sit working on the beach with nothing on but a pair of bathing drawers and where we regularly bathe. Matthew is very well and is busy at the three R's with his governess. I have been working away as usual and reading much in the intervals. I have a volume of essays coming out early in November and am hoping to get my novel ready in time for publication in the spring— but don't know if I shall succeed. Except for this trip to Florence we haven't stirred from Forte since July—save for a half day at Lucca to look at the festa of a very astonishing Byzantine crucifix called the Holy Face, which is only exhibited 3 times a year and then in the midst of great popular excitement and very fine processions. We are staying here with the Franchettis.

He is a professional pianist, and I tell Maria that she can be thankful that I play on no instrument louder than the typewriter. I cannot believe that six hours daily practising is the food of love! But the little Baronessa [Yvonne Franchetti] seems not to be particularly disturbed. Her nerves must be robust. I don't think I could stand it, however fond I was of the practiser. At the moment it is Liszt—prodigious technical difficulties enclosing a vacuum. However, when one can get Franchetti to play, it makes up for the practising—nearly, at any rate!

I've just had a notice from Doran's my American publishers, to say that they are amalgamating with Doubleday—which means Heinemann over in Europe. What an immense concern! I don't know whether one's interests are better looked after by an individual or a Ford factory. There are pros and cons on both sides.

Much love from both of us to you all.

Your loving son
Aldous

267: TO JULIAN HUXLEY

Villa Majetta
Forte dei Marmi (Lucca)
17 November, 1927

My dear J,

Your letter arrived this morning. During these last days, as it happens, I have myself been feeling more and more dubious and uncomfortable about the Cortina plan, as I have realized with increasing certainty that my novel can't be finished, as I hoped, by the beginning of January and that I shall need at least an extra month's work to get it done. As I want, if possible, to get it out next spring or early summer, I shall have to go on working at it all through January—seven or eight hours a day, which would make rather nonsense of a joint holiday. So that I think, all things considered, it would be wisest if I abandoned the idea of joining the party and dug myself in somewhere with Maria for a few more weeks of solitary work. This is a great disappointment, for I had looked forward so much to having a free time of leisure with you in the mountains. However, as we expect to be in England all spring and summer, I hope we shall be able to make up for this later on. *Intanto*, if you're going to be in full strength, either housed or hotelled, somewhere in Switzerland, may Matthew and Mademoiselle join you? It would be great fun for the children to be together; and if you had thought of leaving Francis and his Mlle after your return, ours could keep them company, until we move northwards in force in Feb or March, first to Belgium and then England. Let me know if this is feasible. For if it is, M will rush up to Cortina to collect the winter things which we unfortunately left there last year (a slight bore, as Cortina is 400 km away from Forte). I have a pair of excellent skis which can come along with the rest of the luggage if Matthew and Mlle join you. It is sad that all our plans should have gone so groggy. But I really must get this bloody book off my hands and I know that I should find the task almost impossibly difficult in the midst of a friendly party. I can only work satisfactorily when I am silently stewing in my own juice. We must try to arrange something for Easter in England.

After mature consideration we have come to the conclusion that the best solution for the settlement-in-England problem will be to build a house (cheaper than buying and you can get what you want) in the country within easy reach of London. I had thought of Frensham, as it will be near Matthew's school, is a lovely place and near enough to the metropolis to enable one to go when one likes, but far enough from it to prevent casual social life from invading and engulfing one. If you stick to Cutt Mill, that will be all the better. I look forward to getting a place to deposit things in and return to; also to being more in England. If only the sun shone! The fact that it doesn't makes it essential to build a house in which the most modern and efficient heating system will guarantee at least the domestic weather.

Love to you all from all of us.

> *Yours*
> *ALH*

P.S. Let us know soon whether you can take Matthew and Mlle.

268: TO JULIAN HUXLEY

> *[Forte dei Marmi (Lucca)]*
> *18 November, 1927*

My dear J,

Thinking it over again—after all I could get my work done all right, particularly if we were in a house; and it would be very nice to be together. We shall come as far as possible by car (for shall need it going on afterwards). If it's Diablerets, as Juliette suggests in her letter, shall see if we can put it on the train through the Simplon and come down the Rhone Valley, parking it somewhere at the bottom of the hill. I presume the valley road is always feasible. What are Juliette's views about this? And I suppose one can drive out again the other side. At any rate, hope for the best.

> *Love*
> *ALH*

269: TO E. S. P. HAYNES

> *1 Via S. Margherita a Montici,*
> *Florence*
> *24 December, 1927*

My dear Ted,

Thank you for your letter and the pleasant things you say about the book, which I'm glad you liked. I have been much confirmed in my leanings towards aristrocracy by the reading of a very interesting book on life, art and thought in modern Russia, called *The Mind and Face of Bolshevism*, by a German called [René] Fülöp-Miller. Do read it if you haven't already done so. It's really humiliating that human beings can be so stupid as these Russians seem to be. They really are the devil. Europeans must join together to resist all the enemies of our civilization—Russians, Americans, orientals— each in their own way a hideous menace. There are limits to toleration and they all overstep those limits!

We have been vegetating by the seaside all the autumn and are here over Christmas, whence we proceed to Switzerland to rejoin Julian and family (Chalet des Aroles, Les Diablerets); there I shall try to finish a novel I have in hand and be winter-sportive in the intervals. After that to England, where we shall fix ourselves a little more permanently than in the past, as Matthew has to go to school. Give our love and seasonable auguries to the family: I hope it flourishes. Also to yourself.

> *Yours*
> *Aldous H.*

270: TO C. H. C. PRENTICE

> *Chalet des Aroles,*
> *Les Diablerets (Vaud), Switzerland*
> *23 January, 1928*

Dear Prentice,

I feel very apologetic; but this wretched book refuses, in spite of incessant labours, to get finished. I might perhaps contrive to scramble through the final additions and alterations in the course of another month; but I'd much prefer to take more time and produce for the autumn something which I hope would be better. I hope this won't be a great inconvenience; but I do want to get this thing thoroughly ship-shape.

Meanwhile, I am bothered by the thought that this delay of mine may involve you in financial loss; and since I haven't fulfilled my side of the contract, I think it would be only fair if the next two quarters' instalments were at least reduced. I'm writing to Pinker to this effect.

We are a very large party here, ourselves, the Julians, and various relations, making up ten souls including three children in this fortunately capacious chalet; with D. H. Lawrence and his wife two minutes away across the snow in another wooden hut. So that leisure moments are amusingly filled.

Best wishes to yourself and Raymond and please forgive the delay.

> *Yours,*
> *Aldous Huxley*

Chalet des Aroles,
Les Diablerets (Vaud), Suisse
20 February, 1928

My dear Lewis,

Forgive me for not having answered your letter before. I am up to the eyes in my bloody novel, which I had hoped to have finished at the beginning of this month and which I foresee I shan't get done till the end of next— such are the difficulties of fiction, especially to one who, like myself, isn't really a born novelist but has large aspirations. How thankful I shall be to have this burden off my hands!

We have been here since early January, rather a poor sort of specimen even of a mountain resort, which is a ghastly species. However, after much bad weather, the sun is now marvellous. We share a chalet with Julian and family—the family peculiarly obstreperous. J. has now departed and so has Maria, who has left for Florence. I labour on, and propose to join her in France on 1st March. May we spend a night or two (without the child, who stays here) with you about 5th March? We shall go for a couple of days to M's sister [Jehanne Moulaert] in the suburbs, at Le Raincy, and then, if we may, descend on you. Very briefly this time—but may we come again for a longer stretch later on in the season, say mid-May? That wd suit us very well and wd be a pleasanter season for Paris. We have to be over in London early in March, as I must arrange various things about publishing, typing MSS and we have to inspect some schools. So if you could take us in on our way out of England, we'd be grateful indeed. Plans most vague. May go to Forte in the summer; don't quite know what after: it depends very much on how Matthew gets on at school. We are thinking perhaps next year of going for 6 months to live on D. H. Lawrence's ranch in New Mexico. It sounds very agreeable there and would be a good place for writing, if in the meantime I collect good store of matter. But all this is dim.

Give my love to Mimi. Hope you both flourish.

Yours

A.

3 Onslow Mews East, S.W.7
Tuesday [1 May, 1928]

Dear Prentice,

Matthew's arrival and his imminent departure for school mean such an enormous amount of shopping, zoo-visiting and calling on relations that there really is not a moment we can call our own. May we, therefore, post-pone our lunch with you till after we return from the country, whither we go for some days next week? I'm sorry to be putting you off in this way; but there are moments when parenthood is really a whole time job.

I am expecting to receive the end of typescript on Thursday, in which case you'll have the whole by the beginning of next week. Would it be very serious if I changed the title? *Point Counter Point* doesn't really get all I want to express; I have found in a poem (quoted in 'How the Days Draw In' in *On the Margin*) the very thing I want.

> O wearisome condition of humanity!
> Born under one law, to another bound;
> Vainly begot and yet forbidden vanity;
> Created sick, commanded to be sound.
> What meaneth Nature by these *diverse laws?*
> Passion and reason, self-division's cause.

Diverse Laws is just what I want: and I'll quote the stanza on the title page. Or possibly *These Diverse Laws?* But I think that's too close to *Those Barren Leaves* and also less pleasing on the whole than *Diverse Laws tout court*. I hope you approve.

Mr. Crosby Gaige of New York was lunching here today and broached a notion about a preliminary limited edition of the book before the ordinary one. He threatens to come and talk to you about it.

Yours

A H

273: TO ROBERT NICHOLS

*3 Onslow Mews East, S.W.*7
23 May, 1928

My dear Robert,

A word on *Twenty Below*, which we saw on Monday night with a pleasure tempered, alas, by irritation with these abominable actors. How they ruin the first act, the devils! That conversation round the fire, which requires a most sensitive and understanding interpretation to bring out the dramatic counterpoint, is reduced by the idiots almost to unintelligibility at times. However, the arrival of the girl brings life, and the whole of the second act, thanks to her, goes admirably. How good she is! She gives the play a chance to exist. The others do their best to suffocate it. In the third act I thought the scene of the death—which is extremely moving—might have been improved by the excision of a few of her words after the Yegg is dead. It

---

272 *The title* Point Counter Point—*meaning 'note against note' as Huxley remarked in a letter to Harold Raymond—was preferred by the American publisher and was retained.*

273 Nichols's *play* Twenty Below, *written in collaboration with J. Tully, had opened on 16 May at the Gate Theatre Studio, London.*

seemed to me that those phrases addressed to the dead man about the spiritual gift he has made to her might with advantage have been left unspoken. The scene, the acting, her behaviour sufficiently imply them; and I felt that the actual utterance of the sentiments had a slightly unnatural and stagey ring. I would have left a silence between her last words to the living man and the entirely appropriate and admirable address to the dead man when she takes the money out of his shoe. All the rest, or almost all, could be expressed by the acting and has been implied by what went before. So, at least, it seems to me.

I talked to my medical uncle [Dr Henry Huxley], whom I saw on Monday; and he says that he has known TB of the intestine greatly benefited by heliotherapy, either in natural or in artificial sunlight (when properly administered by experienced people). Of its effect on the kidneys he knew less, but thought it could certainly do no harm and might do good, particularly if the treatment benefited the rest of the organism. My advice would certainly be to talk to your doctor about it and suggest the taking of a treatment of artificial sunlight, since you wouldn't want to take the natural sun in a regular heliotherapy clinic abroad. I should think you could certainly find some hospital or individual doctor at Hastings who could give the treatment 2 or 3 times a week, if you didn't want to go to London. It's a question of the apparatus and the skilled medical electrician. Anyhow, when (and if) the weather becomes warm, I'd do a little lying out with my belly exhibitionistically exposed to the natural sun. My uncle spoke of one of his patients who had spent some months sunning her tummy at Broadstairs and got completely cured of intestinal TB in consequence.

Hope we'll see you and Norah in Paris. C/o Gielgud, 25 bis Rue Decamps, Paris XVIe is our address. Give Norah my love and tell her and yourself how much I enjoyed my weekend—*really*, and damn Mr. Collins! Good bye, Robert and do your damnedest to get and keep well. Take care of the body and the soul will take care of itself. Sound bowels are better than coronets. Etc.

Yours
Aldous

274: TO LEWIS GIELGUD

Il Canneto, Forte dei Marmi (Lucca)
2 July, 1928

My dear Lewis,

A word to remind you that if your walking should take you in this direction there will always be a platter of spaghetti and a flask of wine at your disposal—with a bed somewhere, tho' probably not in this house which is minute (but very pleasant, standing back from the road in the middle of the pines, not noisy or dusty or overlooked by neighbours).

How was Poland? It was sad you should have had to fly off so soon.

But I hope the voyage was pleasant. Mimi will have told you of our doings in your absence—poor Beltran's rage at being given a rival to the favours of Mme Depage. (And by the way how is he?): Mrs. [Mona] Henryson Caird's invasions, followed by an immediate scuttle to safety of all concerned— M and I to our room, Brodrick to the kitchen and the company of Flora, while the dear lady warbled interminably in the salon.

Your little man in Touraine hardly seems to have come up to scratch. The table he sent was a real horror. Not antique but merely very second-hand. I suppose one must be on the spot personally: otherwise one gets done in. Love to Mimi from us both, and to yourself and many many thanks. I look forward to getting into the *Cottage* at Suresnes. (Tho' I wonder if we shall ever be there. We have already planned to visit Germany, Spain and Khartum in the course of the next year! But then, what are plans for unless to be unmade?)

Yours

A.

275: TO JULIAN HUXLEY

Il Canneto, Forte dei Marmi (Lucca)
2 July, 1928

My dear J,

Thanks for your letter. I'm glad to hear that the monstrous opus is getting on so well. I can't at the moment think of any picture of people with skulls—except various St. Jeromes. But St. Jerome was hardly a biologist—except in so far as he kept a tame lion. What about Rembrandt's 'Anatomy Lesson'? A little macabre, but highly scientific. Or one of Leonardo's anatomical drawings? Or Dürer's rhinoceros?! But, I must say, the Old Masters seem to have been remarkably unbiological in their preoccupations. I seem to remember some rather ridiculous primitive of animals being created. But where or what? My mind's dim. Anyhow, they were much fonder of last judgments than creations. Couldn't you give M. Angelo's Adam his cache-sexe and have done with it?

We arrived here 3 days since having come from Paris via Switzerland— into which country, by the way, never take a motor car. We were fined 30 francs for going at 20 m.p.h. in a deserted village and then the policeman who nabbed us accompanied us to the next town on his motor-bike, so that we cd change some money to pay him, and proceeded to do 25 m.p.h. (in spite of the notice saying he must do 12) through the crowded street: and when we, who had been following him in the car, pointed it out, he merely

---

274 *Beltran and Mme Depage: unidentified; possibly cats. Mrs Henryson Caird: late–Victorian novelist and writer on social questions. Brodrick: the rival to Mme Depage's favours?*

laughed. Such are the Swiss, as you may tell Juliette. Found Lawrence surprisingly well, all things considered. Staying at Chexbres above the L of Geneva in a very pleasant and cheap hotel, if ever you are in need of such a thing. (Grand Hotel, Chexbres, Vaud.) We entered Italy by the Simplon— a fine pass—and came down to Milan from Lago Maggiore by the new autostrada, reserved for cars only and avoiding all towns, where you can go any speed you like. Without ever doing more than 50 we averaged 47 all the way.

We have a very nice little house here among the pines—back from the road and consequently dustless; also noiseless, but for the nightly frogs in the middle distance. Weather flawless, tremendous sun, sea at 70°. Very good. I hope Brittany will be pleasant. I've never been there. But they say it's most agreeable. Our little house at Suresnes is getting gradually into shape and will end, I think, by being very nice. The surroundings are really delightful—a tiny provincial town, enlivened by Sunday boating, with the river at the door and the Bois—where one can walk on weekdays for an hour and hardly see a soul—3 minutes away; and the whole a quarter of an hour by car from the Rue de la Paix. Really quite pleasant.

Our love to you both.

Yours
ALH

276: TO C. H. C. PRENTICE

Il Canneto, Forte dei Marmi (Lucca)
10 *July*, 1928

Dear Prentice,

I enclose all the outstanding proofs, together with the returned batches of printers' queries. The lost section turned up and I sent it back corrected about a week ago; so you must have it by now.

Aren't they marble, those gates? I always piously imagined so. I think they'd have gone blacker if they'd been Portland stone. I think in any case we may make a practical application of Vaihinger's *Philosophy of As If* and treat them as marble for the occasion!

I've not done much here so far, except read these beastly proofs, write one or two little essays and take notes for the biographies. I am going into the question of Pascal at present—a most extraordinary character very difficult of comprehension. I'd be extremely grateful if you could find out for me if H. F. Stewart's book on Pascal is still in print. I know nothing about it except that the title of the French translation is *La Sainteté de Pascal* and that the author is or was a fellow of Trinity, Cambridge, and

276 *Gates: presumably 'the marble gateways of Hyde Park Corner', in Chapter XXXII of* Point Counter Point. *Biographies: for the collection which became* Do What You Will.

that it's said to be very good. If it's available could you order it for me, to be sent here, and let me know the damage?

Yours
ALH

277: TO C. H. C. PRENTICE

Il Canneto,
Forte dei Marmi (Lucca), Italy
17 July, 1928

Dear Prentice,

If it's not already too late I'd be very glad if the accompanying corrections could be incorporated. The first is the most important and entails the addition of about half a dozen lines of new matter—not very difficult in the circumstances, as there is a chapter ending on the next page and plenty of room for new stuff to be taken up in the available space. The additions make the character of Philip Quarles a little clearer. As I had written it, he is too impossibly inhuman. The other corrections are less important. But if they can still go in, well and good.

With all apologies for this last-minute alteration and in haste,

Yours,
ALH

278: TO LEONARD HUXLEY

Il Canneto, Forte dei Marmi (Lucca)
19 July, 1928

Dearest Father,

I had been uneasily thinking that it was a very long time since I'd written, when your letter came and reminded me yet more urgently of the fact. Well, here at last is a budget of our news or rather of our absence of news; for our existence has been placidly without any remarkable incident since last I saw you. We spent some 3 weeks in Paris superintending the alterations to the little house at Suresnes—which I think ought to be most agreeable when it's in good order—and in the intervals seeing a number of people, more or less amusing. Thence we motored south via Switzerland, where we spent 3 days at Chexbres above Vevey with the D H Lawrences in a pleasant and cheap hotel with a very handsome Turneresque view of the lake below us. Thence over the Simplon—the G[ran]d St. Bernard being still closed—to Milan (the last 40 miles along the marvellous auto-strada, where you pay a toll and are guaranteed a perfect surface, no cross roads, no towns and no traffic except fast moving cars. Without ever taking the car above 50 m.p.h. we averaged 47 along the whole stretch.) From Milan we came on to Forte, across the Lombard plain which was blisteringly hot, over the Apennines by the road from Parma to Sarzana, 60 miles of hills.

very lovely. Here we have a very tiny but charming little house back from the road and the sea in the pine woods. Very quiet, very green, no dust and being 400 yds from the sea about 1/3 of the price of the houses on the front. The weather has been perfect—exceedingly hot (about 94 in the shade for the last 10 days) but healthily so, with no scirocco and a good wind from the west, with cool breezes from the mountains at night. As one wears nothing but a pair of shorts and a pair of sandals heat doesn't matter. Also we have invested in an electric fan, which makes it possible to work, if one wants to, even in the worst hours after lunch. The difference between still and moving air is really incredible.

There are a few friends here and some acquaintances—among whom one or two rather boring ones, from whom it is hard to escape. And in the intervals of bathing and basking I do some writing and reading—the last with a view to some biographical studies I want to do, illustrating various departures from the harmoniously human norm—as the pervert of ascetic spirituality, the pervert of intellectuality, the pervert of too rigid principle, the pervert of passionless Don-Juanism, the pervert of business and money-making. I'm busy now on Pascal—really one of the strangest and most interesting of men, and certainly, I think, the subtlest and profoundest intellect France ever produced—and have already collected my materials on Baudelaire and to some extent on Burns, whom I shall take [as] an example of a man who wasn't a pervert but developed (at any rate until near the end of his life) as a complete and harmonious human being. Really, what a staggeringly great poet! I'd always been put off by that difficult Scottish language. But how well worth taking a little trouble, as with Chaucer, to master the philology for the sake of the poetry underneath.

Thank goodness, my proofs are now corrected for the novel, which will appear some time in the autumn. It has been selected in advance by a thing called The Literary Guild in the U.S.A. as their book of the month, which means a considerable sale over and above the ordinary figures and a corresponding quantity of filthy lucre. Which is agreeable.

Fare well. I hope Connel will treat you handsomely in the way of weather this summer. Our loves to you all, and thank you for the anticipated birthday wishes.

Your loving son
Aldous

279: TO ROBERT NICHOLS

3 Rue du Bac, Suresnes (Seine)
8 October, 1928

My dear Robert,

Arrived yesterday in the car to find your very friendly and for me satisfying letter awaiting me—the first reaction, outside Maria's, to the book; and I'm glad you like it. Thank you for all the pleasant things you say of it.

I heard of you briefly from Julian who said he'd been to stay with you and enjoyed himself very much. What good news about the health! I hope the gain will be permanent and progressive. Meanwhile, how is 'Don Juan'?

The house is in a state of chaos—painters and paperers still at work, furniture huddled here and there. Hideous! But in a couple of weeks it ought to be fairly habitable. When are you coming to Paris again? We'll have no room, I fear, to put you up—but there will be food and drink.

Summer in Italy was phenomenally hot and lovely and there were still remains of it on the Riviera when we motored through four days ago. You ought to take a little house at one of the small French places one winter—very cheap, and lovely. Eight pounds a month will get you 5 rooms with central heating on the coast between Hyères and Ste. Maxime and there are magnificent woods and plenty of solitude—with enormous palms and colossal cacti to testify to the tropicality of the climate (for the vegetable, like the camera, cannot lie: or at least, so one fondly believes).

What about Mr. [——] and the play? (What a horrible squelchy sort of bugger that was!)

Maria sends her love to you both, as do I.

Yours
ALH

280: TO JULIAN HUXLEY

3 *rue du Bac, Suresnes (Seine)*
25 *October,* 1928

My dear Julian,

Thank you so much for your letter and for the cheque which I'm returning—for the furniture, such as it was (and it wasn't anything that really could be called *furniture*), was a present, a rather mangy one at that, I fear. But if it's of any use, do stick to it.

We are now actually living in our house, or rather camping; for it's only very sparsely furnished as yet and still rather in confusion. But the main work is done—heating installed with a guarantee of 20° centigrade indoors, if we want it, when it's — 5° outside: so I think we ought at least to be warm: carpets laid; all painting and papering done. It will be very nice, I think, when it's all ship-shape.

If we're here in January we'd love to see you, of course: but I fear we shan't be, as we have arranged to go and be braced by the North Sea in

280 The Realist: *a new intellectual review in which Julian Huxley was interested. Aldous' essay 'Pascal' appeared there. The magazine ceased publication after a few numbers. Its editor, Gerald Heard, who was introduced to Aldous by Raymond Mortimer in January,* 1929, *became a lifelong friend. He accompanied the Huxleys to America in* 1937 *and settled near them in California. The early Huxley-Heard correspondence has been lost or destroyed.*

Holland with Maria's sister Suzanne, who lives on the dunes north of Alkmaer. Perhaps there may even be skating on the canals, which must be very romantic. I don't yet know what we'll be doing before that. One or both of us may be coming to London at the beginning of November, or perhaps in December. But it's a little uncertain.

I'm glad you like the book. I think it comes off all right. I had a very nice note from H. G. Wells about it today, and I gather from the various letters I've had about it that it has pleased. There is a man here, [Gabriel] Marcel, a critic on the *Nouvelle Revue Française* who is most anxious to have it translated at once.

About the *Realist*—yes, by all means; I'll be a member of the committee so long as it doesn't entail any work beyond occasionally contributing; for I'm afraid I'm not sufficiently preoccupied about the future of the human race to be prepared to read manuscripts or do anything of that sort! I am meditating some biographico-critical essays which might be suitable for the paper—on Pascal, on Baudelaire, on St. Francis and others. All as realistic as I can make them.

We are just back from a melancholy stay in Belgium where Maria's grandmother has just died and been buried with that peculiar funereal pomp which only survives in small Belgian towns—dress clothes at 11 A.M, with black studs and links, top hat with crape up to the crown, black kid gloves etc.

Give my love to the family.

Ever yours
ALH

281: TO MRS FLORA STROUSSE

*The Athenaeum, Pall Mall, S.W.*1
9 November, 1928

Dear Mr. or Miss Floyd Starkey,

Thank you for two letters. I remember the one you wrote when I was in India. If I failed to answer the second it was not because you were she not he, but because I have a slightly maniacal objection to writing anything except books and only answer letters when I absolutely have to—once every few months. You are fortunate that today happens to be a letter-writing day. Otherwise yours would have remained unreplied to till goodness knows when, perhaps for ever.

About detachment—I find it rather disastrous and wd like to have more of the qualities you deplore. But heredity and circumstances dictate and one must obey. But I suppose your medical surroundings must certainly be a little too human. Anyhow nobody can give any valid advice to someone else about the problems of living—nobody, unless perhaps the late Dr. Frank Crane.

281 *Floyd Starkey is the pseudonym under which some of Mrs Strousse's writings have been published.*

Goodbye and excuse me for being a brief bad correspondent. When my epistolophobia becomes too acute I will apply to you for professional aid. In the interval I shall always be glad to know that you do not suffer from the same neurosis. Thank you for all the friendly things you say about my books. I have at last written rather a good, but also rather a frightful, novel, which perhaps you had better not read if you feel like that about things.

Yours sincerely
Aldous Huxley

282: TO D. H. LAWRENCE

3 <i>Rue du Bac, Suresnes (Seine)</i>
12 <i>December</i>, 1928

Dear Lawrence,

What an intolerable business about the pirating of *Lady C.*! M. has seen a copy of the spurious edition, for which they ask 5000 francs. Wdn't it be worth while for Orioli to come to Paris, interview the booksellers and get rid of his remaining stock at some reasonable rate between the original 2 guineas and the 5000 frcs asked by the pirates? He would undersell the devils and at the same time turn an honest penny. Also he'd be able to get rid of the paper bound copies at the same time. I feel that Paris is a good centre owing to absence of censor-nonsense and presence of large numbers of English and Americans. If you want to multiply your own edition remember that the photographic process is simple and (as far as I remember what my publishers once told me about it) cheap. It's much used now in producing cheap editions of books that have gone out of print. The type is photoed on to sheets of jelly, I believe; and printed from the jelly, which is good for several thousand copies. (I think this is correct.) If you can't get it done in Italy you cd certainly find some firm who'd do it in Paris. That's why I think Orioli wd be well advised to come here and explore the ground. I think there's much to be done—and it needs doing quickly if the pirates are not to get away with the loot. I don't know anybody in the bookselling trade here, or else I'd suggest. Is Sylvia Beach reliable? I have a prejudice against her, probably quite unfounded. But she might be useful.

282 *Lawrence, at Bandol, had written Huxley and his wife a letter dated 'Monday'* (sc. 10 December), *asking them to find out whether the pirated* Lady Chatterley's Lover *was being sold in Paris. After hearing from Huxley, Lawrence wrote again on* 15 December. (*The order of the two letters was transposed in Huxley's edition,* The Letters of D. H. Lawrence, London, 1932, pp. 765-67.) *Lawrence rejected the idea of having Orioli act for him in Paris and sent Huxley a letter to forward to Sylvia Beach, of Shakespeare and Company; Huxley called on her, but nothing came of his attempt to interest her in publishing the book. In March, Lawrence went to Paris to pursue enquiries, and an edition was published there in May by Edward Titus. The Brewsters: Lawrence's admirers Earl and Achsah Brewster.*

The house now begins to look like a house, which is a good thing as, outside, the weather doesn't look at all like weather, but rather a damp cold hell. Not more than an hour of sunlight in the last month. It makes one want to write to *The Times* about it.

Have read nothing of interest recently. A tiresome book by Virginia Woolf—*Orlando*—which is so terribly literary and *fantaisiste* that nothing is left in it at all. It's almost the most highly exhausted vacuum I've ever known. Then there's Lytton Strachey on Queen Elizabeth—which I've not yet had time to do more than look at. Henry Williamson's *The Pathway* seemed not half bad, as far as I got with it. *Intanto* have been re-reading *Our Mutual Friend* which contains some grand things in the way of Veneerings etc. So painfully true to life.

The funniest feature of this town is the people who try to be wicked in supposed haunts of sin. The spectacle, occasionally, is really comic. Also the sins. We went to a night-bar the other day devoted to Lesbians. Part of the entertainment was a wrestling match between two gigantic female athletes. The whole thing was ghoulishly funny. It was just the place for the Brewsters! Love to Frieda.

> *Yours*
> *ALH*

283: TO C. H. C. PRENTICE

> *3 Rue du Bac, Suresnes (Seine)*
> *18 December, 1928*

My dear Prentice,

May I ask your advice as a typographical expert? The problem is this: D. H. Lawrence's *Lady Chatterley* has been pirated and one or possibly 2 clandestine editions photographically reproduced from the original are being sold to booksellers. DHL wants to reply by producing another edition of his own and underselling the pirates (whom it wd be very difficult to get at by legal methods). I suggested that he should have his first Florence edition photographed and published fairly cheaply, preferably here in Paris. Can you tell me about this photographic process?

(a) is it quick?

(b) does it cost less than setting up in the ordinary way? (DHL's original type is distributed.)

(c) can you print many copies from the plates?

(d) do most printers undertake the job? or if not who are the people who do the photography?

(e) what is the technical name of the process, if any? and is it probable that one cd get it done over here?

I'm sorry to bother you with all these questions; but I am anxious to get all the information I can to help Lawrence in his campaign against the pirates, and as I know your good nature and your knowledgeableness of the subject I make bold to exploit you.

I was very much pleased to hear that the book had got past the 10,000 mark. Considering the price of the volume it seems remarkably good.

All seasonable wishes to yourself and Raymond.

Yours
ALH

[*Postscript on envelope*] Will you answer to: 19 Grand' Place, St. Trond, Belgium.

ALH

284: TO MRS FLORA STROUSSE

*The Athenaeum, London, S.W.*1
7 January, 1929

My dear Starkey,

On the contrary, I have almost no ideas about myself and don't like having them—avoid having them—on principle even—and only improvise them, when somebody like you asks to know them. For 'know thyself' was probably one of the stupidest pieces of advice ever given—that is to say, if it meant turning the self inside out by introspection. If one spent one's time knowing oneself in that way, one wouldn't have any self to know— for the self only exists in relation to circumstances outside itself and intro- spection which distracts one from the outside world is a kind of suicide. An artist is bound in any case to detach himself from actual life in favour of the fictitious existence of his creations—is bound to, unless he happens to possess, which I don't, the exuberant vitality and power which suffices for two simultaneous lives: he is therefore the last person who can afford to go about cultivating ideas of himself. Perhaps that's one of the reasons of my epistolophobia? For it's difficult to write letters other than those of the 'Yours of the nth inst to hand' variety without going in for ideas about one- self. And anyhow when one's profession is to commit hara-kari every publishing season and wreathe one's entrails in elegant festoons—le style c'est l'homme—all over the bookstalls . . . well, really in those circumstances having ideas about oneself in letters or conversation becomes, it seems to me, rather a work of supererogation. Jehovah's attitude towards psycho-analysis has always seemed to me entirely satisfying. 'I am that I am'—what could be truer? what more profoundly wise?

But Starkey who has no professional outlet for ideas about himself— is professionally, indeed, a receptacle for other and demented people's ideas about *them*selves—Starkey, I perceive, is a Socratic, believes in γνῶθι σεαυτόν, with the result that he (or she), so far from being what he is, like Jehovah, tends distractedly to be what she isn't and not to be what she is. Am I right?

306

This has been, for me, a very long letter. God forgive you for causing me to write it.

Yours sincerely
Aldous Huxley

285: TO JULIAN HUXLEY

3 *rue du Bac, Suresnes* (*Seine*)
22 *February*, 1929

My dear J,

Thank you for your letter, which I found here on my return from Florence. The City of Flowers was deep under snow when we left it, the thermometer at —10°, the Arno frozen from shore to shore etc etc. So that our fortnight in the South wasn't very agreeable. Also it was the worst possible moment for selling a car. Nobody could try the machine—and the mere idea of driving was enough to make one feel sick. So we've left the car there for the garage man to sell when the weather improves. Our journey to Florence was disagreeable. First Bandol was dreadfully icy and I got a liver disease, partly from cold and partly from the revolting food cooked in monkey-nut oil at the hotel. When at last we could set out again, it was through a howling wind, in a frost. At Albenga on the Italian riviera, our magneto suddenly gave out. Short circuit, something fused. Had to send it to the makers in Genoa to be put right. This meant 48 hours in an inn where there was not one single fire-place and where the only mode of heating was by hot bricks—which are all very well to put cats on to make them hop, but inadequate as a substitute for fires. Arriving then at Chiavari, we found that the road had been wiped out by a landslide. So the car had to be put on a train and carried as far as Sestri—which meant several more hours in the tramontana. However, we did arrive at last; and the hotel was warm and comfortable. Also cheap. (Let me recommend it if ever you go to Florence. Hotel Moderno: almost next door to central P.O. Hotel meublé. No restaurant and no nonsense about having to take 1/2 pension with your room. An excellent restaurant immediately opposite. You get a room with 2 beds and bathroom attached for 45 lire a day—and the water's hot, the radiators work. Very reasonable.)

On second thoughts I've declined Beaverbrook's offer. I didn't need the money: it wd have been pure avarice if I'd taken it. And the bother involved wasn't worth it. Writing against time once a week and——worse—having to read contemporary literature. Also the certainty, if I'd been really honest, of quarrelling with almost all my literary colleagues. For after all at least 99.8% of the literary production of this age—as of all other ages, for that matter—is the purest cat-piss. But one isn't popular if one says so frankly—and it seems hardly worth while to be unfrank, which one really must be, if one isn't some sort of Grand Old Man *genre* A[rnold] B[ennett] or H. G. [Wells.] At my age I shd be accused of being merely jealous if I said what I

307

thought. So I'm not having any and feeling greatly relieved at the thought that I can go my own way without disturbance.

I hope all the family flourishes in spite of this diabolic winter. Really, the evilness of Nature on these occasions! Unspeakable.

Love to you all from both of us.

Yours
ALH

286: † TO PAUL VALÉRY

3 rue du Bac, Suresnes (Seine)
11 *March*, 1929

Cher Monsieur,
Je viens de lire, très tardivement mais avec quel plaisir et quel profit!

286 TRANSLATION:—'*I have just read, very belatedly but with how much pleasure and profit! your fine introduction to the* Fleurs du Mal. *I shall not bore you with the expression of my admiration, which has been profound. But I cannot prevent myself from making a few remarks concerning what you say of Edgar Allan Poe, hoping that they will not be wholly devoid of interest for you.*

'*You say that it is only in America and in England that Poe's reputation as a poet is in dispute. And this is true. But allow me to say that, if the French appreciate Poe more than those do who speak his language, it is for the same reasons that the English (as you have said in your preface) do not appreciate La Fontaine and Racine. To foreigners all the nuances are imperceptible—vulgar ones just as much as fine and lofty ones. It is only among foreigners, endowed in this case with a fortunate deafness and blindness, that Poe can enjoy a reputation as a truly great poet. For the rest of us (to whom acquaintance with his language is, I should say, instinctive and not only a possession of conscious intelligence) there is in almost all of his poems—"[To] Helen" and "The City in the Sea" are perhaps the only perfect ones—a certain vulgarity, very subtle but none the less shocking, a vulgarity in the choice of words, in the verbal harmony and especially in the rhythms, a great many of which have for us almost the quality of the popular waltz or the polka.*

'*In translating "The Raven", Mallarmé transfigured it much as Beethoven in his great variations transfigured Diabelli's waltz. The rhythms of the original, the rather painfully popular harmonies (for, strangely, great aristocrat though he was, Poe would often express a Mozartian or Chopinesque subject with the melodies of a street organ), were made over, and the great stillborn English poem became the French masterpiece. The other poems are like "The Raven"—stillborn masterpieces which only await the talented translator to become perfect. Meanwhile, this almost imperceptible curtain of verbal and rhythmic vulgarity covers them and, to English eyes, disfigures them.*

'*I shall not conclude a letter which has become, I think, wearisomely long, without expressing the hope that you will give me the occasion to renew the acquaintance we made, already so long ago, at Madame Muhlfeld's. My wife and I are for the moment settled in Paris, or rather on the outskirts. If your walks in the Bois sometimes take you as far as Suresnes, we should be delighted to receive you . . . .'*

Valéry's introduction to the Fleurs du Mal *had appeared in 1926. Madame Jeanne Muhlfeld had an élite salon and was a friend of Valéry.*

votre belle introduction aux *Fleurs du Mal*. Je ne vous ennuierai pas avec l'expression de mon admiration, qui a été profonde. Mais je ne puis m'empêcher de faire quelques remarques sur ce que vous dites de Edgar Allan Poe, en espérant qu'elles ne seront pas tout à fait dénuées d'interêt pour vous.

Vous dites que c'est seulement en Amérique et en Angleterre que la réputation de Poe comme poète est en dispute. Et c'est vrai. Mais permettez-moi de vous dire que, si les Français apprécient Poe plus que ne font ceux qui parlent sa langue, c'est pour les mêmes raisons que les anglais (comme vous l'avez dit dans votre préface) n'apprécient pas La Fontaine et Racine. Pour les étrangers toutes les nuances sont imperceptibles—celles de vulgarité tout aussi bien que celles de noblesse raffinée. C'est seulement parmi des étrangers, doués en ce cas d'une surdité et d'un aveuglement heureux, que Poe puisse jouir de la réputation d'un vraiment grand poète. Pour nous autres (pour qui la connaissance de sa langue est, je dirais, instinctive et non seulement une possession de l'intelligence consciente) il y a dans presque toutes ses poésies— ['To] Helen' et 'The City in the Sea' sont peut-être les seules parfaites—une certaine vulgarité très subtile mais quand même choquante, une vulgarité dans le choix des mots, dans l'harmonie verbale et surtout dans les rhythmes, dont beaucoup ont pour nous une qualité presque de valse populaire ou de polka.

En le traduisant Mallarmé a transfiguré 'The Raven' à peu près comme Beethoven a transfiguré dans ses grandes variations la valse de Diabelli. Les rhythmes de l'original, les harmonies assez péniblement populaires (car, c'est étrange, ce grand aristocrate qu'était Poe a souvent exprimé une matière Mozartienne ou Chopinesque par des mélodies d'orgue de Barbarie) ont été refaits, et le grand poème manqué anglais est devenu le chef d'œuvre français. Les autres poèmes sont comme 'The Raven'—des chefs d'œuvre manqués qui n'attendent que le traducteur génial pour devenir parfaits. En attendant, cette [ce] voile presque imperceptible de la vulgarité verbale et rhythmique les couvre et, pour des yeux anglais, les défigurent.

Je ne terminerai pas une lettre devenue, je crois, ennuyeusement longue, sans exprimer l'espoir que vous me donnerez l'occasion de renouveler la connaissance que nous avons faite, il y a déjà si longtemps, chez Madame Mulphed [Muhlfeld]. Ma femme et moi, nous sommes pour le moment établis à Paris, ou plutôt dans la banlieue. Si vos promenades dans le Bois vous amènent quelquefois jusqu'à Suresnes, nous serions enchantés de vous recevoir.

Croyez, Monsieur, à l'expression de mes sentiments les plus distingués.

Aldous Huxley

3 *Rue du Bac, Suresnes (Seine)*
19 *March,* 1929

Dearest Father,

I'm most distressed to hear of Andrew's appendicitis. What a horrible thing it is! But how fortunate—relatively so—that the horror should have come on when it did. I hope all goes well. Let us have a p.c with his news.

Matthew has got off with a cold or two, nothing worse—which is satisfactory considering the season. We expect him back in a week's time, when the problem of holiday occupations will arise. We hope to have his little Belgian friend here for a few days, which will be a source of amusement, and perhaps he will go to Belgium in return for a little. Then, if the weather holds, there will be nice expeditions into the forests round Paris—if our car is ready; for the coach-builders are already a month late, the wretches! Still they've promised it by Easter—binding themselves with Stygian oaths. Our old machine we have left in Florence to be sold—it wasn't worth importing it into France and paying 65% ad valorem. So after much trying and testing and on the recommendation of the A.A. engineers in London we have fixed on the new touring model of the Bugatti; which has a most extraordinary performance and, according to the AA, is a very sound piece of engineering and building.

Our journey to Florence was somewhat frightful. I had an unpleasant chill on the liver—on the verge of becoming jaundice—en route; which didn't improve my spirits or quicken my energies, as you may imagine. Then on the Riviera near Genoa, our magneto fused internally and we had to send it into Genoa to the makers to be repaired, which meant 48 hours in a hotel with absolutely no means of heating with −10° centigrade and a northerly hurricane outside. After Genoa we ran into a landslide that had blocked the road and had to waste hours putting the car on to the train and taking it off again. And when at last we did get to Florence the cold was unbelievable—the Arno solidly frozen, deep snow in the roads (and this had been going on for more than a month when we arrived) and the miserable population, quite without proper clothes or houses for such a season, dying in thousands. Out of 225,000 inhabitants 65,000 were ill. And Florence was balmy compared with Trieste and the Adriatic ports, where the sea froze and the trains were blown off the rails by the wind. We stayed a fortnight and then crept back here, where our central heating does allow us to deal with situations like those. Now it is so stuffy that we have to think of buying a refrigerator for our food.

I'm busy and not exuberantly well—this quasi-jaundice has left me a little dubious physically. I shall take the opportunity, when we go to Forte dei Marmi this summer, to go and have a regular cure at the neighbouring spa of Montecatini, the Italian Carlsbad, which is said to do wonders for the liver.

The Charles Morgan of whom you speak must be, I think, the dramatic

critic of *The Times*, whom I've met at North House—a nice fellow. I've
not read the book, but will remember its name for when I have leisure. Of
late I've read little but history, biography and philosophy.

Our friend Valerie Barker has been making herself famous, hasn't she?
What a fantastic story! And how very mysterious!

Give our loves to Rosalind and the boys, especially the poor invalid.
And let us have a card from time to time to say how he gets on.

Your loving son
Aldous

288: TO MRS FLORA STROUSSE

3 *Rue du Bac, Suresnes (Seine)*
9 *May,* 1929

Dear Starkie,

Having at last finished the extremely difficult and mind consuming job
of work [*Do What You Will*] on which I have been busy now for months, I
can write a letter. It will be a poor return for all yours, because I am not one
of nature's letter-writers. Self-contained and placid misanthropists are bad
correspondents. How bad you will realize from the fact that the paper on
which I am writing is stamped with an address which has not been mine for
at least five years [*i.e.*, 44, Princes Gardens, S.W.7].

Your story is quite good—but a little brief and anecdotic. Also it wd
have been more interesting, because more cruel, if it had been about a less
extreme case—not a madman but somebody like B. R. Haydon, sane, but
with an infinite faith in himself completely unjustified by forty years of
passionate and industrious self-expression. The fact that faith *can't* move
mountains is one of the corner-stones of tragedy—also of comedy. I wish
you joy of Liverpool—an odious town, so far as I know anything of it,
which isn't much, thank goodness. Its chief merit is that you can get away
from it fairly easily to very fine country—N. Wales, the Roman Wall and
(if you happen to enjoy *gemütlich* sublimities) the Lake District. I have just
returned from England and feel, as usual, very gloomy about my native
land and very glad I don't have to spend all my time in it. I have reached a
point where I value sunshine more than people, culture, arts, conversation.
So I'm off to Italy for the Summer. (Incidentally it's full of people, culture
etc, as well as sunlight.) I believe and rather hope that the day of the Nordics
and their beastly northern countries is nearly over. Civilization will return
to the warm and luminous places where it was born. The Mediterranean is
the centre of the world. Everything of which human beings can feel proud
has come out of the Mediterranean—the arts of life, the fine arts, politics,

---

287 *Valerie Barker: a former pupil at Prior's Field. She was also known as Victor
Barker, and in April she was sentenced to a term of imprisonment for having entered
into a marriage (in church) with another woman.*

law, philosophy. All that's beastly in human life comes from the North or West or the East—horrible religions, asinine moralities, sordid money-grubbing, lack of proportion, over-emphasis, protesting too much, asceticism, Don Juanism etc etc. So *viva il Mediterraneo*! and down with Liverpool.

Yours
Aldous Huxley

288a: TO HENRY S. CANBY

3 rue du Bac, Suresnes (Seine)
9 May, 1929

Dear Canby,

In very belated reply to your letter and the enclosed article, I'd like to say that the novel form is preferable to the treatise because the fictionally embodied idea is different from, and much more alive than, the 'same' idea in the abstract. My book contains both abstract and (more or less effectively) embodied ideas. It would have been less effective if the embodied ones had been omitted.

Yours in haste
Aldous Huxley

289: † TO NORMAN DOUGLAS

3 Rue du Bac, Suresnes (Seine)
11 May, 1929

Dear Douglas,

Thank you very much for *Nerinda* which I found awaiting me after a considerable absence first in Spain (what an extraordinary country!) and then in poor old England, which seemed sadly mouldy and dim—even mouldier and dimmer than when I was there last. I enjoyed the story and only wished we could have had a more detailed account of your madman hacking the old man into a form nearer to his heart's desire. It seemed to me that the treatment of that episode remained too idyllic, I might almost say vegetarian. You spared the reader too much, at any rate for my Roast-beef-of-old-England tastes.

I hope we may see you in Florence in June, when we hope to be there—with a little less of Yoi, if that man be, in the background.

Maria asks me to send you her thanks and good wishes.

Yours
Aldous Huxley

288a *Canby, editor of the* Saturday Review of Literature, *had evidently sent Huxley a review of* Point Counter Point. *Earlier he had questioned Huxley about this novel, eliciting the reply (17 January): 'Models? All the characters have several models, some historical'.*

289 *Yoi: unidentified.*

Il Canneto, Forte dei Marmi (Lucca)
13 July, 1929

My dear J,

I was very glad to have your letter and hear all your news. Of the type-writer business we had already heard—rather indignantly, at first—from Mme Nys, who reproached us for giving to another the gift we had made to her. Complete incomprehension on our part, as we couldn't imagine how you even knew she had an old typewriter of mine! However, all's well that ends well, and I hope the topi will fit. I found it most comfortable—really one of the pleasantest forms of hat.

Your trip [to Uganda] sounds as if it were going to be very interesting. The only danger may be the temptation to do too much—your time being limited—in the tropical circumstances.

Lawrence was here a few days and is gone again. If you knew the struggles we had had with him about his health—but quite in vain. When he was in Paris, before he went to Majorca, we actually got him to agree to undertake a treatment, alone, *minus* Frieda, and we also actually got him to go to a doctor in Paris. He was to go back to the Dr. to be X-rayed. (Mean-while, however, the Dr. told M that, from just sounding him he could hear that one lung was practically gone and the other affected. He doubted whether very much cd be done.) Then Frieda, who had been in London, returned. L felt himself reinforced. He refused to go back to the Dr., refused to think of the treatment and set off with Frieda (of whom he had bitterly complained when he was alone with us) to Majorca. So that's that. It's no good. He doesn't *want* to know how ill he is: that, I believe, is the funda-mental reason why he won't go to Doctors and homes. He only went in Paris because he was feeling iller than usual and was even more frightened of dying at once than of hearing how ill he was. He rationalizes the fear in all kinds of ways which are, of course, quite irrelevant. And meantime he just wanders about, very tired and at bottom wretched, from one place to another, imagining that the next place will make him feel better and, when he gets [to] the next place, regretting the one before and looking back on it as a paradise. But of course no place will make him feel any better than any other now that he's as ill as he is. He's a great deal worse than he was when you saw him at Diablerets—coughs more, breathes very quickly and shallowly, has no energy. (It's pathetic to see the way he just sits and does nothing. He hasn't written a line or painted a stroke for the last 3 months. Just lack of vital strength.) He still talks a good deal and can get amused and excited into the semblance of health for an hour or two at a time. But it is only a semblance, I'm afraid. I think he's even worse than he was in Paris in March (when he had a touch of flu to complicate matters). The Doctor told M that he might drag on for quite a little time like this, unless he got a cold which turned into bronchitis or pneumonia, when he'd simply be asphyxiated. He has gone to Germany now—or is just going: for he has been in Florence these last days—of all places in this weather! We have given up trying to persuade him to be reasonable. He doesn't want to be and no one can persuade him to be—except possibly Frieda. But Frieda is worse than he is. We've told her that she's a fool and a criminal; but it has no more effect than telling an elephant. So it's hopeless. Short of handcuffing him and taking him to a sanatorium by force, there's nothing to be done.

Forte has been windy and changeable so far, with the result that I've had a slight chill on the tummy, which doesn't improve one's cheerfulness. Reading [Bronislaw] Malinowski's *Sexual Life of Savages*, which has inspired me with a desire to write a companion treatise on the *Sexual Life of Gentlemen and Ladies*. There'd be much odder customs to record than among those extraordinarily rational Trobrianders.

Give our best loves to Juliette and the children—I hope they're all well.

Yours

ALH

291: TO LEONARD HUXLEY

Il Canneto
Forte dei Marmi (Lucca), Italy
16 July, 1929

Dearest Father,

We were disappointed in our hopes of seeing you in these parts round Whitsuntide. Perhaps another year. We ourselves were only briefly in Florence on our way through to Rome, where we spent 10 days or so, in the town itself and outside, when the June heat-wave came on, in the Alban Hills at Rocca di Papa and on Monte Cavo (the highest point, where the Temple of Jupiter Latialis was and up which the magnificently paved Roman road still winds—the Via Triumphalis, on which generals who were refused their triumph by the Senate came and had one on their own). The latter is a marvellous spot with the most extraordinary view I've ever seen—lakes Nemi and Albano, surrounded by wooded hills in the foreground, and beyond the expanse of the Campagna, at this season golden with ripening corn as far as the eye can reach with the sea on one side and dim mountains shutting in the plain on the other. An ex-convent on the top is turned into a very nice little inn and at that height—1000 metres—the air is delicious even in the hottest weather. Also it has the merit of being less than 3/4 of an hour by car from the centre of Rome. We also went to see some of the Etruscan sites we'd not seen before, particularly Cerveteri, where there is an enormous necropolis of magnificent tombs, shaped like small versions of the Mole of Hadrian (Castel S. Angelo), in Rome—a circular drum of masonry topped by a high conical mound of earth. Inside, a series of chambers cut out of the tufa, few of them painted, as at Tarquinia, but very handsomely proportioned and architecturally decorated in a style that's sometimes quite Egyptian.

We drove up here along the Maremma, a beautiful road, which has now lost all its terrors, as the once malarial region has now been drained and is intensively cultivated all the way along. There are still some very wild forests off the main routes—full of wild boars even now. But mostly it's been tamed and civilized.

We are established here in the same little house as we had last year—a little back from the sea—in the midst of vineyards and trees. Up till a day or two since the weather has been uncertain—windy and cloudy, with occasional storms—with the result that I got a chill on my insides which kept me rather melancholy for a week or so. Now, however, I'm recovered and so has the weather, which is incredibly serene and looks as tho' it were set fair for quite a time. We have made an amusing acquisition this year in the shape of a rubber boat (used as collapsible life-boat in aeroplanes etc), in which one can row very efficiently in quite a rough sea—but whose charm is that one can lie in superlative air-cushion comfort and take sun baths, rocked in the cradle of the deep. Deflated, it folds up into a small hand-bag and one can take it out to explore small streams, isolated lakes etc. A most entertaining toy.

We expect Matthew in a few days now, with Maria's sister Rose, who brings him South. If the season is a hot one, I think we'll go up to the mountains somewhere for a week or so in mid-August to break the heat for him and give his system a bracing fillip. Either in the Carrara mountains just behind us here, or else at some place in the Apennine like Vallombrosa.

I hope all goes well with all of you. I heard from Julian the other day, who gave a most exciting account of his prospective trip. I only hope he won't try to do too much in the tropical surroundings. Those climates are apt to be so very malevolent. Love to Rosalind and the children and yourself from us both.

Your loving son,
Aldous

292: TO ROBERT NICHOLS

Il Canneto, Forte dei Marmi (Lucca)
2 August, 1929

My dear Robert,
I was very glad to have your news and that it was on the whole so good. Here I do Paterfamilias at the seaside, write a little and do some water-colour sketching—a pastime for which I have developed a slight passion. D. H. Lawrence was here for a little—rather worse than when I saw him last in the spring. How horrible this gradually approaching dissolution is— and in this case specially horrible, because so unnecessary, the result simply of the man's strange obstinacy against professional medicine.

A curious experience in July was a visit to Montecatini, the Carlsbad of Italy, where a touch of jaundice this spring made it advisable for me to go and drink the waters. Have you ever been to a spa? If not, go. It's the most grotesque vision imaginable—all the obese, the bilious, the gluttonous, the constipated, the red-nosed, the yellow-eyed, standing about in a pump-room, that looks like ancient Rome through the eyes of Alma Tadema, and drinking, to classical music and at 8.0 A.M. glass after glass of salt water. Really fascinating.

Have been reading a very queer book on Philip IV of Spain, by one M[artin] Hume. Quite good. And what an astonishing history! We're thinking of going to Spain this autumn for a bit. It's obviously a place one ought to know. Most mysterious.

I enclose a snapshot of myself as the Dweller in the Inmost,—the Inmost being, in this case, an inflatable rubber boat, a most divine toy for the seaside. It might amuse poor Henry Head. Have you noticed, by the way, that Love, in Watts's 'Love and Death' at the Nat. Gal., has no genital organs—only a sort of mist where they should be? What a world!

Love to you both from both of us.

Yours
ALH

293: TO LEONARD HUXLEY

Il Canneto,
Forte dei Marmi (Lucca), Italy
26 August, 1929

Dearest Father,

Thank you—rather tardily, I fear—for your letter and birthday gift, which reached me on my return here after a week at Montecatini, the Italian Carlsbad, where I had gone for a week of water drinking, rendered advisable by an attack on the liver this spring which was almost a jaundice. What a comic thing a spa is! I'd never been to one before. Montecatini has an enormous clientèle—it owns 750 hotels and pensions—and draws to its purgative fountains all the obese, the bilious, the gluttons from every corner of the peninsula. The most fantastic collection of human specimens, containing a high percentage of priests, who flock thither in black swarms to drink off the effects of the proverbial clerical overeating. I was there with a pleasant little Italian antiquary from Florence, an old friend—so the cure

---

292 *Huxley had been at Montecatini with Pino Orioli. Richard Aldington records in* Pinorman (*London,* 1954), *p.* 68, *Orioli's summary of Huxley's conversation there:* ' "*Aldous he sit and make remark*".' *This sounds like a case of Orioli's knowing whom not to confide in. Henry Head: a celebrated neurologist, friend of Nichols. He later shot himself after developing a brain tumour.*

was not too boring, tho' somewhat exhausting. Drinking daily a quart or two of salt and aperient water in a temperature which, at that time, was steadily at blood-heat in the shade, is not the most invigorating occupation. I felt very blotting-papery afterwards; but soon picked up, especially in the mountains to which we retired for a week in early August, and am now, I think, the better for my drinking. These mountains—the so-called Apuan Alps, from which the marble of Carrara is drawn—are conveniently close. Twenty minutes by car to the end of the road and then three hours on foot through the woods and across the grass slopes under the limestone precipices, and one is at 3500 feet in a rather primitive but quite possible little hotel, from which one can go for any sort of expedition from a mild walk to a perfectly perpendicular rock climb. The highest peaks are about 6000 feet and even the lesser heights command immense views up and down the coast, over the Gulf of Spezia on the one hand and down beyond Leghorn, with Lucca and Pisa in the middle distance on the other. Elba to the South and to the S.W. if the day is clear, Corsica. On the other side the huge rolling expanse of the main Apennine chain at an average height of 5000 feet or so —big lumpy hills very different in character from the limestone crags, streaked with white marble, of the Apuan Alps themselves. Altogether very fine and remarkably un-overrun owing to the absence of any roads but mule tracks up to the higher altitudes, except in one place where one of the big marble quarries at about 4000 feet has made the construction of a road, which passes through a tunnel a kilometre long at one point, commercially worth while. Since the 14th we've been back here, where the weather, after being a bit uncertain for a time, seems to have settled down to a calm warmth. Matthew has now learned to swim quite well and strikes out confidently in the open sea. We are also improving his French reading—hitherto not as good as it might have been—by means of the excellent Jules Verne, whose *Mathias Sandorf* and *Enfants du Capitaine Grant* act as carrots before the donkey's nose, luring him on to read even the pompous phraseology and scientific words of which the worthy Verne's style is compounded. (His description of the crater of Etna as 'ignivome' is characteristic!) M. was very much pleased with your letter, which I trust he will answer some time. But these summer days somehow leave very little time!

Maria and I were very sorry to hear of Rosalind's bad time this summer. I hope she's entirely re-established now. Connel sounds a bit damp. Let's hope the season is behaving itself better now for her and all your sakes.

Love to all the family from us all.

Your loving son,
ALH

3 *Rue du Bac, Suresnes (Seine)*
12 *October*, 1929

My dear J,

I was glad to have your letter. Hope you're already having fun with the gorillas. We also did the Red Sea in Sept—but it was seldom much over 100° in the shade and nothing compared with Bombay at the end of the month: that was like having one's head dried by hot air after a shampoo at the barber's—really appalling. How awful Nature is when she really lets herself go!

We are off to Spain tomorrow, to a Congress for Intellectual Cooperation at Barcelona (which I doubt, however, if we shall have the courage to attend, as it apparently consists exclusively of Jews from every corner of the globe), and then onwards through the country for a few weeks.

The summer at Forte was quiet and pleasant; but Paris is really rather frightful; the traffic seems to have doubled in the last year and for noise, stink, and danger it really rivals with New York. Towns are really uninhabitable.

We saw Wells and [——] the other night, when they came here to dine. [——] seemed a bit of a monster, I thought, in the screaming exhibitionist style. Still, I don't have to go to bed with her and if H. G. likes that sort of thing, that is, obviously, the sort of thing he likes.

I've been reading little recently except the Great Authors and have come to the conclusion that it's really rather a waste of time to read anything else. The *Odyssey*, for example—what a marvel! I'd no idea it was so incredibly good—and such a lot to be learnt from it about Life: Shakespeare, and recently the *Paradiso* of Dante, which is really staggering and, like everything by a sufficiently big man, quite dateless, completely actual and to the point.

Otherwise, have read mostly history—Lea's *Hist. of the Inquisition*, a v. fine book: Dill's *Roman Society in the Last Century of the Empire*; and various works on Spain, whose history is the strangest and most terrifying reading I've ever undertaken. I read and enjoyed Malinowski and have recently been interested by [William] McDougall's little book on *Modern Materialism*, very able and very difficult to answer or circumvent, I should fancy. Have also been keeping up with the *S[cience] of Life*, which has been excellent throughout all the recent numbers, I think—very clear and informative and well presented.

My book of essays has just come out; but I won't send it you till you're back in places where an extra book won't be a nuisance. Love to Juliette, if she's with you, and to yourself from both of us.

Yours

A.

294 The Science of Life *by H. G. Wells, Julian Huxley, and G. P. Wells.*

3 Rue du Bac, Suresnes (Seine)
24 November, 1929

Dear Starky,

On the contrary, I'm delighted that you should disagree with me about my sweeping generalizations. I disagree with most of them myself—as one must—because generalizations can't in the nature of things be true. But they must be made, even if they're glaringly untrue, just to simplify things (arbitrarily—but all our intellectual and artistic activity is purely arbitrary), just to clear the ground. Besides I am a completely irresponsible, non-social and nihilistic person, so that everything ˙I say is automatically untrue for the responsible and the sociable, the actively and affirmatively constructive.

How kind of you to send me [E. E. Cummings'] *The Enormous Room.* I read it long since and thought it very remarkable, though a little too long. He seems to me decidedly a writer—and how rare a phenomenon *that* is, as you can see by reading almost any book you care to pick up. But it doesn't matter much so far as the world at large is concerned, as not more than about three people in every hundred appear to be capable of distinguishing between something which is artistically good and something which is artistically bad. It's as though, in daily life, they couldn't tell the difference between a geranium and a frying pan. And of course there's no means of enlightening them—for the difference between geranium and frying-pan is quite arbitrary and if you don't know the language by which the objects are connoted, or if you're blind and can't see the objects, or if you happen to be born with other sense-organs than eyes, then obviously you can't know the difference. So far as all the more important and fundamental activities of life are concerned, it's impossible to explain anything to anybody. You've got to depend on luck. If you happen to find people constituted like yourself, tant mieux. If you find them differently constituted, tant pis. But as for imagining one can change their constitutions. . . .

I am just back from Spain where I have been motoring for some weeks with my wife. Really, the strangest country in Europe, at any rate that I've yet seen, one of the oddest in the world even. Half very sympathetic, half very repulsive. But always odd and full of the most extraordinary things, natural and artificial. The El Grecos, for example, which I admire much more (tho' hating them in a way) than when I saw them last—much more now than the Velasquez pictures which bowled me over at a first seeing, but turn out on a longer acquaintance to be rather incomplete as pictures, rather undercomposed except occasionally, by accident, when they completely come off and are sublime. But that's rare.

Yours
Aldous Huxley

319

3 Rue du Bac, Suresnes (Seine)
Sunday, 1 December, 1929

Dearest Father,

I was most grieved to get your letter on our return from Spain and hear you'd been so ill. I hope you're thoroughly on your feet again. One or other of us may very likely be over for a few days before Xmas to fetch Matthew, when there will be a chance of getting your news 'straight from the horse's mouth'. We're all well, I'm happy to say, tho' I rather strained my back having to start the car by hand owing to a battery trouble during the last 2 days of our journey—a rather tiring *torticolis* in the loins.

The journey passed off very well. Beginning with a week in Barcelona, where I attended—or rather mostly played truant, for it was all so utterly silly and boring—a conference of Intellectual Co-operators, we went on to Tarragona (lovely) and thence through some wonderful country along and near the coast, alternatively utterly sterile and lusciously fertile, to Valencia. There is a long stretch of coast which for picturesqueness takes the prize. A whole series of minor Gibraltars sticks out, one after another, into the sea, the most savage and fantastic rocks you ever saw. From Valencia, the surroundings of which are dull—a flat juicy plane—we went on through Alicante to Murcia, which lies in a depression among bare hills surrounded by what is simply a Saharan oasis—hundreds of thousands of date palms laden with fruit and under them every plant you can think of, quite amazing and the town very sympathetic. Thence across some wonderful bare country with every 10 miles or so a queer mountain village of which half the inhabitants are troglodytes, living in cave dwellings scooped out of the side of the hill, to Almeria of dessert-grape fame, incredibly sterile, but with the best winter climate in Europe, I fancy; and from there across the Sierra Nevada to Granada, which was very lovely with its acropolis, its gardens, its great churches. From there we made our way, (tortuously, for we lost ourselves and wandered for some time in the most astonishing mountain byways of Andalusia) to Ronda, which is a most enchanting place, staggeringly picturesque in position—a gulf separating the two parts of the town which are joined by a devil's bridge with a 2 or 300 foot drop from the parapet—and full of exquisite 18th century Andalusian houses, built in what is really the most enchanting style of domestic architecture that exists. From there downwards to the Andalusian plain to Jerez and then through S. Fernando, the Spanish Greenwich, to Cadiz on its strange promontory between the open sea and the huge bay, on the marshy fringes of which they make salt which is piled up in pyramids so that the landscape looks like a sort of fantastic white-washed Egypt. Then back through Jerez—what sherry, by the way! Not even at All Souls does one drink anything half so good as what one gets for eightpence a glass in the hotels and cafés in those parts—to Seville, where we stayed some days for the sake of the Exhibition, which is even more interesting than that of Barcelona, masses of extraordinary things from Spanish and Portuguese art treasures to Peruvian antiquities. After that to Cordoba, which is lovely, with its extraordinarily impressive great Mosque built from the 9th to 12th centuries at the best period of Arab civilization. From there straight to Madrid through the desert plateau of La Mancha and Castile. One isn't surprised at Don Quixote going mad in a country like that—hundreds of miles of rolling plain 2500 ft above the sea, Saharan in summer, Siberian in winter, quite empty for the most part, with a bleak little town every twenty miles or so. Terrifying. We were pleased to see that the windmills still functioned in La Mancha. Madrid was very cold—frightful winds and squalls of rain. And as for the Escorial, it was really hellish. We left out Avila and Segovia on account of the iciness —Avila is at 4000 ft!—and drove straight to Burgos with such a wind that the mud was lifted in sheets from the road and hurled against our windows and windscreen. Every few miles we had to stop and scrape little holes in the muck to see through. It was a comfort to get down to Atlantic softness at S. Sebastian (a lovely place) and to find Languedoc a sort of warmer Cornwall, very green and lovely. Even Paris was much warmer than Madrid. The time for Spain is obviously the spring—not merely for the climate and foliage but also for the people of whom you have the impression that they almost hibernate during the cold months. Roads on the whole very good—full of very unexpected twists and sharp ups and downs, as most of them haven't been re-engineered since coaching times—but for the most part in very good condition. From Seville to Madrid, for example, the road's as good as a French highway. And even the secondary roads were tolerable —tho' after heavy rain (and on the Mediterranean coast it *can* be heavy: Alicante had 8 inches in a day a few years since!) they must be very doubtfully passable, even the big ones, as you get torrents that have to go over them, no normal culvert, I take it, being big enough to contain the water.

Altogether a most interesting journey, which tempts one to go and have another look, not only at the country and art but the very queer (and not entirely sympathetic) people.

Had a p.c from Julian, but so old with travelling that I don't know where he is now. I gather they'll be back about the New Year?

Love to Rosalind and the children and to yourself from us both.

Your loving son,
ALH

3 *Rue du Bac, Suresnes (Seine)*
14 *December,* 1929

My dear Robert,

Work and rheumatism have kept me for a long time incapable of doing any of the things I wanted to do. Now, however, I've got temporarily rid of both, so snatch the opportunity to write to you.

I solved the Evan [Morgan] problem by congratulating on the staggering lines—and they really are extraordinary, I think—which occur here and there, by accident, I suppose, in his poems. He was over here for last week end and we passed a pleasant evening with him—the only defect being the swarms of parasitic pederasts, from Egyptian princes to retired sea-captains, who hovered round unescapably. He still remains one of my favourite characters in fiction.

I've not ventured yet to attack [Gerald] Heard's book. It seemed to be written in such a frightful way—to judge by a rapid glance. And anyhow does one—or ought one—to believe in these great generalizations? I make so many myself that I have a personal and intimate reason for mistrusting them! No, I've confined myself of late, in the very brief leisures I've had for reading, chiefly to the *Odyssey* and the *Paradiso*. The *Odyssey* is really the best book—(I think I shall suggest to that little mosquito-man, Canby, that he should select it as a book of the month. It would do everyone endless good!) All we've perversely gone back on since Homer's day! All the beastly things from tragedy and spirituality to disgust and ennui that we've invented! Plato's at the bottom of it all, I suppose. I think it's he who definitely shunted us on to the wrong track. And the extraordinary difficulty of getting back again. I think Maillol is the only artist of modern times— since Chaucer and Boccaccio anyhow—to recapture the pre-Platonic quality of feeling. His sculpture springs quite genuinely from the same roots as the best archaic Greek or (better) Etruscan—the Apollo of Veii, for example, at Rome.

Taken in alternate sips with the *Odyssey*, the *Paradiso* gains in intensity of flavour. What a *poet*—quite apart from the things he says. He's the man, I believe, that every budding versifier should be apprenticed to. The art of producing infinite effects with the minimum of obviously visible means has never been carried to such a height. And then what extraordinary things he says. He's the only man, I suppose, who's ever succeeded in making unmitigated goodness seem interesting.

What are your plans? We shall be here for at least another month, while our boy has his holidays. After that, who knows? London for a bit, perhaps?

297 *Evan Morgan's book* Canals, and Other Poems *had recently appeared. Heard's book: this was* The Ascent of Humanity: An Essay on the Evolution of Civilization from Group Consciousness through Individuality to Super-Consciousness.

or Paris? or the South. Spain was very odd and interesting; I recommend it if you're aiming Southwards. Love to Norah.

Yours
Aldous H.

298: † TO PAUL VALÉRY

3 rue du Bac, Suresnes (Seine)
4 January, 1930

Cher Monsieur,

Je vous remercie infiniment de votre *Léonard*. Je l'ai trouvé plein de beautés et de vérités—ou plutôt de beautés–vérités; car ce livre est un bel exemple de la véritable oeuvre philosophique, qui est une oeuvre d'art.

Ce que vous avez dit de la peinture–philosophie de Léonard m'a vivement intéressé. J'ai moi-même beaucoup médité sur la philosophie-musique, surtout chez Beethoven. La Messe en Ré, le Quatuor en La mineur, la Sonate Opus 111, sont des oeuvres philosophiques profondes,

298 TRANSLATION:—*'Thank you very much for your* Leonardo. *I have found it full of beauties and truths—or rather of beauty-truths; for the book is a fine example of the true work of philosophy which is a work of art.*

'What you say of Leonardo's painting-philosophy has interested me keenly. I myself have much meditated on philosophy-music, especially that of Beethoven. The Mass in D, the Quartet in A minor, the Sonata Opus 111, are profound philosophic works, subtle and by all the evidence true. But in what does this truth consist? One does not know how to put it. It is in trying to define it verbally that "musicologists"—and I am thinking especially of our friend Sullivan, who has written a book on Beethoven that is very intelligent but in the last analysis not very satisfactory—are led astray.

'Except by uncouth and ridiculous metamorphoses, musical philosophy is expressed only by music and by the composer's music alone. Its truth is a flower which survives no transplantation and whose perfume cannot be distilled. One sees this in the case of Beethoven himself. In speaking, in writing, this great philosopher—the most profound, for me, the most complete of all philosophers—shows himself to be almost clownish and of a remarkable silliness. Leonardo was an exceptional case in the sense that he could express the "same" philosophy under different forms. One saw, I suppose, a similar universality among the Greek tragedians who made philosophy in counterpoint—as poets, composers, choreographers and actors. Of all this counterpoint there remains to us only one melody; but it must be believed that the others, though vanished, expressed simultaneously the same "truths" quite as well as the written poetry expressed (and still expresses) them. Nevertheless these cases of multiple gifts do not impair the rule: beauty-truths remain untransposable. Universal geniuses are teams of specialists among whom a harmonious understanding miraculously reigns. But there is no absolute equivalence. Between William Blake's philosophy-painting-poetry, for example, and his philosophy-painting, one feels rather profound differences.

'Pardon me for chattering away for so long. Once more, please accept all my thanks for your book. I hope very much that you will allow us a great pleasure by stopping one day when passing through Suresnes. Yours truly. . . .'

Valéry's Léonard et les philosophes *was published in 1929.*

323

subtiles et de toute évidence *vraies*. Mais en quoi consiste cette vérité? On ne sait pas le dire. C'est en essayant de la définir verbalement que les 'musicologues'—et je pense spécialement à notre ami Sullivan qui a écrit un livre très intelligent mais en fin de compte très peu satisfaisant sur Beethoven—se perdent.

Sauf par des métamorphoses grossières et ridicules, la philosophie musicale ne s'exprime que par la musique et par la musique seule du compositeur. Sa vérité est une fleur qui ne souffre aucune transplantation et dont on ne réussit pas à distiller le parfum. On le voit dans le cas de Beethoven lui-même. Quand il parle, quand il écrit, ce grand philosophe—le plus profond, pour moi, le plus complet de tous les philosophes—se montre presque grotesque et d'une bêtise remarquable. Léonard a été un cas exceptionnel en ce sens qu'il a pu exprimer la 'même' philosophie sous des formes différentes. On a vu, je suppose, une semblable universalité chez les tragédiens grecs qui faisaient de la philosophie en contrepoint—comme poètes, compositeurs, chorégraphes et acteurs. De tout ce contrepoint il ne nous reste qu'une mélodie; mais il faut croire que les autres, disparues, exprimaient simultanément les mêmes 'vérités' aussi bien que les exprimait (et les exprime encore) la poésie écrite. Pourtant ces cas de dons multiples n'infirment pas la règle: les beautés–vérités restent intransposables. Les génies universels sont des équipes de spécialistes entre lesquels règne miraculeusement une entente harmonieuse. Mais il n'y a pas d'équivalence absolue. Entre la philosophie–peinture–poésie de William Blake, par exemple, et sa philosophie–peinture on sent des différences assez profondes.

Je m'excuse d'un bavardage si long et vous prie encore une fois d'accepter tous mes remerciements de votre livre. J'espère beaucoup que vous nous ferez le grand plaisir de vous arrêter un jour en passant par Suresnes. . . .

Véritablement vôtre
Aldous Huxley

299: TO SCUDDER KLYCE

3 rue du Bac,
Suresnes (Seine), France
6 January, 1930

Dear Mr Klyce,

Herewith I return, with sincere apologies for having kept it so long, the typescript of your very interesting essay on the one-many problem. You make your statement logically watertight, it seems to me—a feat I have never been able to achieve and one which the literary quality of what I write (such as it is—that quality!) renders less vitally necessary. For after all the most perfect statements and human solutions of the great metaphysical problems are all artistic, especially, it seems to me, musical. Beethoven's

299 *Klyce's book on Dewey, which was privately printed, is called* Dewey's Suppressed Psychology (*Winchester, Massachusetts,* 1928).

'Missa Solemnis', for example, and his posthumous quartets, Bach's 'Art of the Fugue' have always struck me as the subtlest, profoundest and completest metaphysical works ever composed. Though of course what they 'say' cannot be rendered in words—just as the final mystery, the continuous Whole, cannot be rendered in words. Such pieces of music, and certain passages in Dante and Shakespeare, certain paintings, certain architectural monuments get closer to the essential fact than any professional philosopher's discourse. I say this without any desire to disparage the important and absolutely necessary work undertaken by logicians such as yourself. It is good that attempts should constantly be made to get the unutterable on to paper, even though the attempts are in the last resort vain, as are even the attempts of the greatest artists. I do not illude myself with the belief that I am a great artist; but I at least possess a certain literary talent, the use of which serves in some measure to take the place of a sadly deficient logic!

About these scientists—it really is amazing the way they go on imagining that they are telling the truth, the whole truth and nothing but the truth. Their lack of realism is quite astonishing. Quite apart from the existence of a One made up of the relationship of the Many, why can't they see that the many are divided up into a whole series of orders or categories? As a matter of everyday experience, we find that what makes sense in one of these orders makes nonsense in another. Thus electrons, waves, quanta make absolutely no sense in the category inhabited by the painter of pictures and his creations. (That these orders are ultimately reconcilable I do not of course deny. But the fact of their final fusion in the One is, for most practical purposes, negligible.) The habit of the scientists was and still is to assert that the theories which work in the particular category of phenomena which they have chosen, arbitrarily, to consider, must work in *all* categories and conversely that the phenomenal categories in which these theories don't, as a matter of observed fact, work are for that reason illusory, non-existent. Hence the science-religion dispute, hence all the stoical despair of such professional scientific despairers as Bertrand Russell. I can only find it all rather comic—though also tiresome. Being an unmetaphysically-minded person preoccupied with phenomenal appearances, not ultimate reality, I think mostly of the diverse Many and not much of the final One. My essay, with those which accompany it in a recently published volume, *Do What You Will*, is a statement of the observable facts of diversity so stupidly overlooked by contemporary science and also contemporary religion. Any tentative solutions of the problems raised are never, except incidentally, metaphysical solutions, only practical, ethical, sociological and psychological solutions.

You are most kind to offer me a copy of your Dewey book. I should be very glad indeed to read it. Thank you very much indeed. If you are ever in the neighbourhood of Paris, I hope you will drop me a line.

Yours sincerely,
Aldous Huxley

3 *Rue du Bac, Suresnes (Seine)*
7 *January,* 1930

Dear Douglas,

How kind of you to send me *What [i.e. How] About Europe.* I have just finished reading it and my feelings are a mixture of pleasure and depression —depression that it should be necessary to write such books and pleasure in the excellence of the writing. And the really dismal thing is that the work could be extended to fifty volumes with ease. What a world! Did you read Malinowski's *Sexual Life of Savages?* An interesting and instructive book —very depressing inasmuch as it demonstrates the incomparable superiority, intelligence and decency, of the neolithic inhabitants of the Trobriand Islands to the English. A *Sexual Life of Ladies and Gentlemen* ought to be written as a pendant volume.

At Barcelona—whence we have recently returned—I saw a very instructive spectacle in the shape of the Missionary Pavilion at the Exhibition. The good fathers had been rash enough to arrange their show on the Before and After principle—before the coming of Xtianity and after the conversion. I never saw anything more blood-curdling than the way every trace of beauty, originality, charm, nobility, existing in the various indigenous arts and crafts—from Papuan and Melanesian to Chinese and Indian—had been utterly stamped out and replaced by a standardized Catholic beastliness. In every case something precious and lovely had been taken away and replaced by a mound of shit. It was really enough to make one cry. And the worst was that the public walked round, thinking that it was all splendid and admiring the March of Progress. Écrasez l'infâme, but the infâme is not only the priests, it's also the machines, which are almost worse. What about America? Words fail one. (I am venturing to send you a volume of essays of mine, which are essentially concerned with the same subject as your book. I hope you'll excuse the American edition. I have no English copies by me at the moment.) Maria joins me in sending best *auguri.*

Yours
Aldous Huxley

301: TO MRS FLORA STROUSSE

*The Athenaeum, Pall Mall, S.W.*1
28 *January,* 1930

Dear Starky,

Thank you for your two letters. There was no need for the second, as the first required no apologizing for. I'm sorry about it all. What is there more to say? Nothing, as far as I can see. For when you come down to bed-rock you find that you can't really say anything to anybody—say anything, that is, with the hope of establishing communication and being understood.

Solitude seems to be the one absolute and unvarying fact, which we contrive to disguise from ourselves most of the time by all kinds of means—making a noise, getting into a crowd, talking, making love etc etc—but which emerges again, the same old fact, the moment we voluntarily or involuntarily drop the disguising activities. So that's that, as Mr. [Clarence] Hatry remarked two days ago when he had just been sentenced to fourteen years penal servitude. Still, one can be very happy all the same. And in spite of the appalling possibilities of unhappiness and the appalling frequency with which the possibilities are realized, I think on the whole it's most decidedly worth while—not for any good reason, of course; but for some mysterious good unreason. All I can do is to hope you'll go on finding this unreason sufficiently strong in spite of everything.

I am suffering agonies at the moment over the rehearsals of a stage version of *Point Counter Point* which has been concocted by an ingenious young man and which is to be produced the day after tomorrow—God help us! I'm afraid the beastly thing won't even justify itself by making money and that the horror will be quite unmitigated.

I'm glad you liked those poems of Lawrence. I thought them admirable, as is also the pamphlet he has just published on obscenity and pornography. I heard from him today. He has actually consented to see a doctor and, still more extraordinary, talks of following his advice and going into a sanatorium for a bit. It's a bad sign in one way; for it means he must be feeling very ill indeed: otherwise he wd never have consented to such a thing. Let's hope the sanatorium may do him some good and that it's not too late—as I rather fear—to do anything very effective.

I wish you very well, dear Starky.

Yours
ALH

302: TO D. H. LAWRENCE

3 rue du Bac, Suresnes (Seine)
11 February, 1930

Dear Lawrence,

We were very glad to have your postcard and to know that you weren't too unhappy in the sanatorium. I'm sure that the systematic dulness and dreary regularity of the nursing home life is very good for one—if only because it's so boring that one is driven to recover in mere self-defence. I am despatching a box of the invaluable *Coréine*. It is not specifically for the liver and only cleared up mine because I was being poisoned by a spot in

301 *Campbell Dixon's adaptation of* Point Counter Point, *called* This Way to Paradise, *was produced by Leon M. Lion at Daly's Theatre, London. It closed on* 1 *March. See Lion,* The Surprise of My Life *(London, 1948), pp. 109-110.*

327

the intestine and the poison was making trouble in the liver. All that it is is mucilage—which is practically speaking vegetable gum. You swallow it: it swells up in your inside, mixes itself with the food and passes out absorbing on the way all undue moisture (which means in practice all accumulations of toxins) and mechanically pushing along any stagnating matter. In fact, it sweeps and garnishes one's guts, but in a mechanical, not pharmaceutical way—so doesn't have any of the bad effects of a purge, yet does what the purge does and also other excellent things beside. It may not act on the liver in all cases, for the good reason that the liver may be going wrong on its own account and not because of the intestine. But it can't do any harm to try it: and if there's any tendency to auto-intoxication it can only do good. Old [V. E.] Sorapure, who recommended it to me, is a great believer in it and prescribes it to all his patients, with good results.

It's pleasant to be back again in one's own house—tho' London was amusing, and the play business, tho' rather awful, very instructive. The first night was a little painful, as the actors were so nervous that they forgot most of their lines and ranted all those they could remember. Which was a pity, as the dress rehearsals had really been rather good—the whole performance miraculously coming to life, when I'd completely despaired of everything. They got much better again after the first night and the play goes on, doing moderate and (surprisingly) slightly improving business. It may run only three weeks, unless the improvement continues. If it had been produced in a small theatre with a fairly cheap cast of stock actors it might have done quite well. But it's being given in one of the largest theatres in London with very expensive actors—so that it can only survive by doing very good business. Some of the scenes turned out finally very well indeed, particularly the last where they play the Beethoven A minor quartet, while the audience waits in a long-drawn anticipation for the man to be killed. The effect was exceedingly good, theatrically, and the music created an extraordinary atmosphere of mystical tranquillity in the midst of the prevailing horror. It showed me what very astonishing things can be done on the stage by somebody with a little imagination and the necessary minimum of technique. If I could have gone over the last scene, rewriting the whole thing, I could have made it quite prodigious, I believe. Even as it was—a kind of patch-work made up of fragments of the book more or less ingeniously stitched together and not in any sense an organic whole—even as it was it went remarkably well and held the audiences—even the popular Saturday night audience—absolutely spell-bound. The only thing that deters one from experimenting much with the theatre is the theatrical world. The instruments one must use are so hopelessly unsatisfactory. Have you ever had anything to do with actors and producers? It's an eye-opener! All the same I'm tentatively writing a play at the moment. There are a few good producers in the world and I'm sure if one could see one's own dramatic ideas well realized by one of them the thrill would be enormous.

328

We have been having great fun taking 'North Sea' all round the house and seeing where it goes best. We have decided for M's little blue sitting room, which it suits by its size and its pale colouring, which is lovely in the sunshine (and actually we are having sunshine at the moment), which comes pouring in during the morning and early afternoon.

I hope we may be seeing you fairly soon. Love to you both from both of us.

Yours
ALH

303: TO ROBERT NICHOLS

3 Rue du Bac, Suresnes (Seine)
17 February, 1930

Dear Robert,

Your letter was a coal of fire. I've been meaning to write for so long; but I have such frightful difficulties in starting letters, particularly if I'm busy writing other things. Anyhow, here goes at last. We may very likely be in your parts quite soon, as we want to go South (a) to look for a house (b) to see poor D. H. Lawrence, who's in a sanatorium not far from Grasse and from all accounts is in a very bad way indeed. So will let you know when we're in the neighbourhood. It might be the beginning of next week.

The play was a curious performance. Lots of things in it that made me rather shudder—but then as I hadn't touched the dramatic version I couldn't expect it to be just as I wanted. The production was of course bad and there were many too few rehearsals—the time being so short that it wasn't possible to make the smallest change as we went along. On the first night the principal actor forgot almost all his lines in the murder scene—which didn't improve the performance. I thought all was done for; but, amazingly, the last scene, with the A Minor 4tet punctuating the dialogue at the rate of 5 minutes at a time absolutely held the audience—and continued to do so even with a popular Saturday night public. I must say the effect of the music was prodigious and quite confirmed what that man Wilson Knight wrote not long ago about Shakespeare's use of music whenever he wanted to produce or emphasize some mystical effect. My feeling about the play as a whole is that, touched up and well produced, it would be really pretty good. It moulders on at Daly's—of all curious theatres!—but I doubt if it will run much more than 3 weeks. I am writing a play of my own now; which is quite fun. But God! what a horror to have to depend on other people for your creation—not to be personally responsible for the whole, but be compelled to use instruments. And what instruments! It's like playing Bach's concerto for 2 violins on fiddles made out of packing-cases and string. Tho', my word, it must be pretty exciting if you have the luck to be interpreted by one of the human Stradivariuses which do occasionally turn up in the world of the theatre. Unhappily, as there are only about 3 of them in each generation, it's not very likely that you will have the luck!

I hope you're well and working successfully. Have you read a novel called *The Man Within* by Graham Greene? I think it's most remarkable. You can get it in Tauchnitz. Much better (between ourselves, for it's a frightful heresy!) than Virginia's *To the Lighthouse* which I'm now rather belatedly reading. It's the difference between something full and something empty; between a writer who has a close physical contact with reality and one who is a thousand miles away and only has a telescope to look, remotely, at the world. Love to Norah from us both, not to mention to yourself.

Aldous

304: TO JULIAN HUXLEY

3 *rue du Bac, Suresnes (Seine)*
23 *February*, 1930

I am sending a letter to Stark Young care of you, as I've forgotten his address. Would you mind re-addressing it? We are just off to the Midi to see Lawrence, who sounds as tho' he were in a very bad way, and to look round for a possible house. The latest is that *Lady C* is being proceeded against by the French police! Don't mention it to L. if you're writing as it wd upset him and if the affair can be arranged—I have been ringing up all the influential literary men I know—he need never know. There is no point in giving him unnecessary shocks in his present state. He takes it all so much to heart.

Love to you all from us both.

In haste
ALH

305: TO JULIAN HUXLEY

Vence
3 *March*, 1930

My dear J,

As you will have seen by the papers, DHL died yesterday. We had just got back from Villefranche, where we had been seeing the Nicholses over the weekend, and found him very weak and suffering much pain and strangely *égaré*, feeling that he wasn't there—that he was two people at once. We got the doctor up at nine, who stuck some morphia into him, and he settled off to sleep—to die quietly at 10.15. The heart had begun to go and the intestines were badly affected—general intoxication, I suppose—and he seemed to have hardly any lungs left to breathe with. It had been most distressing, the two or three times we saw him during the past week—he was such a miser-

330

able wreck of himself and suffering so much pain. Moreover the illness had reduced him to an appalling state of emaciation. So that it was a great comfort really that he went when he did—and went so quietly at the last. The funeral takes place tomorrow at Vence.

After it's over we shall go back to Cannes and thence along the coast to Toulon and Marseilles to see if we can find a nice house. On this part of the Riviera there is nothing—the whole thing is one vast and sordid suburb, the suburb of all Europe, from Mentone to Cannes—indescribably ugly and mingy and very expensive. This is a nice place and if we can find nothing by the sea, it may be we'll come back to Vence.

Frieda bears up well. She proposes to live with her daughter now. I hope she won't be too lost.

I hope all goes well with you. Love from us both to you all.

Aldous

306: TO EDWARD TITUS

Hotel Beaurivage, Bandol (Var)
8 March, 1930

Dear Mr. Titus,

I have discussed the question of a biography with Mrs. Lawrence and we have come to the conclusion that it is still too early to write a life of DHL as it shd be written—quite truthfully. However, Mrs. Lawrence wd like to see an edition of his letters published and I suggested to her the following idea—that we should intersperse the letters with personal recollections of Lawrence by various people who have known him at different epochs of his career. E.g. an account of his childhood by his sister; early manhood by a schoolmaster friend, and, for a later period, by Ezra Pound; shortly after his marriage an account by David Garnett, who accompanied DHL and Frieda on their first journey to the Continent; war-time by Middleton Murry (perhaps) and also Lady Cynthia Asquith and Lady Ottoline Morrell; perhaps a page by Bertrand Russell who knew DHL at that time; also Richard Aldington; and Norman Douglas; for the Australian time his collaborator in *The Boy in the Bush*, Miss [M. L.] Skinner; for the American period, Mabel Dodge; for the last 2 or 3 years in Italy and France, perhaps myself. I wd propose to print these recollections among the letters, as nearly as possible in chronological order, adding where necessary a bald statement of dates and doings. In this way one would produce, it seems to me, a very

306 *The idea of a memorial volume interspersed with letters was abandoned. William Heinemann Ltd. undertook to publish the letters, which Huxley edited without compensation or royalties for himself. That the other project was pursued at least a little way is indicated by a letter of Huxley to Garnett (evidently to David, not to his father Edward) asking him if he would write his reminiscences of Lawrence; this was dated 19 April.*

331

living book—DHL in his own words and as reflected by the people (mostly interesting personalities) he knew. If we can get people to let us have their letters and if the letters are not too intensely personal to make great omissions necessary, I think there wd be material for two volumes. (But this, of course, remains to be seen.) Mrs. Lawrence would like you to undertake the publication of the limited edition. With regard to subsequent unlimited trade editions, I imagine you wouldn't have the organization to undertake them for England and America. In which case one would come to some arrangement with publishers on the spot—Doubleday Doran, for example, in U.S.A. and Chatto and Windus in England. But that would have to be gone into in detail later, after we have seen exactly what D.H.L's contract with Knopf engages him to. (There would, of course, be no particular objection to Knopf and Secker doing the book, as they have also done most of his recent novels etc.)

I shall be in Paris in the course of a few days. Will you write to me at Suresnes (3 rue du Bac) and tell me your views on this subject. We will have a discussion later about details.

I would undertake whatever work the editing entailed gratuitously—that goes without saying. Only if there were much secretarial work required I'd ask you and the other publishers to provide clerical assistance.

The memoir of which you speak must be by a man who wrote a letter to Mrs. L two or three days before L's death, saying that he was doing a study of L and that he would like L himself to see it before publication. He'd better go ahead with it on his own hook. It won't harm or help our project.

Yours sincerely,
Aldous Huxley

307: TO EUGENE F. SAXTON

Grand Hotel Beau Rivage, Bandol
8 March, 1930

My dear Saxton,

Your cable and the book reached me very deviously and after a long time. Hence the inexcusable delay in thanking you for them. It was indeed good to have these reminders of your friendship. I would have written earlier if these last two weeks had not been so fully and painfully occupied with the illness and death of our poor friend D. H. Lawrence. We came down to see him a fortnight ago and found him even worse than we had expected to find him, and terribly changed from what he was—and he was already a very sick man even then—when we last saw him in the Summer. He gave one the impression that he was living by sheer force of will and by nothing else. But the dissolution of the body was breaking down the will. The end came on Sunday night. He was really, I think, the most extraordinary and impressive human being I have ever known.

Now that the funeral is over we are looking for a house on the coast here —and think we may perhaps have found one at Bandol, not far from Toulon. If we get it I hope you'll come and stay. It's a nice place and the climate, if not good, is at least less awful than most climates within reasonable distance of the centres of civilization. For the time being, however, our address is 3 rue du Bac, Suresnes, (Seine). Is there any prospect of your being in Europe this spring? It would be very pleasant to see you. How is your wife, and how are the children? Matthew has grown into a most schoolboyish schoolboy of almost ten. His letters are all about football matches and the like. All as it should be, no doubt!

We send our love to you all.

Ever yours
Aldous Huxley

308: † TO T. S. ELIOT

3 rue du Bac, Suresnes (Seine)
22 March, 1930

My dear Tom,

I should have answered your letter before, but have been living in a whirl of spirit-expending activity during the past weeks—poor Lawrence's death, then house-hunting in the midi, then a rush to London for three days, owing to the idiocy of an American publisher who wanted sheets signed for a special edition and only sent them at the very last moment. Things have settled down a little now, though I have a lot of work on hand, and I snatch the opportunity of thanking you for your letter. The suggestion you make is a very interesting one. My only objection is that it's so interesting that it would involve me in an enormous amount of reading and writing— more than I could permit myself with all that I have to do and want to do and have embarked on doing at the moment. I have the idea in my head of an essay (I don't know yet how long), which is to serve as introduction or postscript to a play I am now writing—an essay developing, more or less, the theme of R[udolf] Otto in his *Idea of the Holy*. If this goes well, I'd like to let you have a look at it for the *Criterion*—though I'm afraid it couldn't be used as a pamphlet subsequently.

I had such a brief, exasperating and frenzied time in London that I made no sign in your direction. I hope to be over again in May and to have the opportunity of establishing a leisured contact. If you want to amuse yourself with a very lively, intelligent and malicious pamphlet, read Em[m]anuel Berl's *Mort de la Morale Bourgeoise*, which has just appeared; also his *Mort de la Pensée Bourgeoise*, which came out last year, if you haven't already read it. He is an excellent toreador and gives some superb performances of

308 *Special edition: of* Brief Candles, *published by the Fountain Press in New York.*

dart-sticking. His baiting of the egregious [Charles] Du Bos made me laugh a great deal.

I hope Vivienne is better. Please give her our love.

Ever yours,
Aldous H.

309: TO T. S. ELIOT

La Gorguette, Sanary (Var)
24 April, 1930

My dear Tom,

I'm sorry to be always saying no to your suggestions; but there are several reasons why I couldn't write the book you suggest on Lawrence as a poet—chief among which is that I am bound by contract exclusively to Chatto's in England and Doran's in America and that, tho' I might have got leave to do something as short as a pamphlet elsewhere, I certainly wouldn't be allowed to do a book of even the size of your *Dante*—which you gave me and which I very much liked for being so much to the point and saying such a lot in so small a compass—with another publisher. In the second place I don't really like a great deal of DHL's poetry, which seems to me insufficiently organized artistically—rather the raw material of poetry (the most astonishing raw material very often) than poetry itself.

Here, on this Coast of Azure, the wind as usual howls and the rain pours down: but a certain vegetable tradition that the climate was once good still lingers on in the visible forms of olives, cypresses and the like, making the landscape classically lovely. So it's pleasant all the same—and at any rate the weather's no worse than it is anywhere else. I hope to see you in May.

Yours
Aldous H.

310: TO MRS FRIEDA LAWRENCE

La Gorguette, Sanary (Var)
27 April, 1930

Dear Frieda,

Alas, I shan't be able to get over to Vence before going to London. There were various impediments—weather and then the arrival of Mary Hutchinson to stay and then the fact that it was the last tail-end of the boy's holiday, so that we didn't want to leave him. I go to England with him tomorrow. Maria stays here and will proceed to Italy in a few days: she will

309 *The Huxleys had just finished moving into their new house at Sanary, which remained their home for the next seven years.*

310 *Play:* The World of Light. *Extracts from a correspondence between Huxley and Leon M. Lion during the writing and production of this play have been printed in Lion's* The Surprise of My Life, *pp.* 111-14. *American friend: unidentified. Barby was Barbara Weekley, Frieda Lawrence's younger daughter.*

call in on you either going or returning, but will give you warning of her arrival. I'll let you know from London how I get on with the letters.

I've been busy with my play of which I've done about three quarters now. Quite amusing and interesting to do. I hope it will be actable. I shall have to try it on the experts in London.

About the money—there is no hurry, of course. It's at your convenience. The amount is 3700 [francs] for the rent, plus 300 for the nurse, plus the 3000 in cash borrowed from our American friend in Antibes for immediate expenses, and which I repaid her. Total 7000. But don't bother about it till it's convenient. I hope Barby's better. Shall we see you later on in these parts? Will keep you posted about London.

Love from us both.

Yours
Aldous

311: TO ROBERT NICHOLS

*The Athenaeum, Pall Mall, S.W.*1
[4 *May*, 1930]

My dear Robert,

Is there any chance of seeing you in the course of the next few weeks? I shall be in London till the end of the week, then to Oxford for I don't quite know how long, then, I suppose, London again. I'm hunting up Lawrence letters. So if you know anyone who's likely to have any, do let me know. What a queer devil he was! The queerer, the more I think of him and know about him. So many charming and beautiful things in him, such a lot too that wasn't sympathetic. I gather from your letters that you got Frieda a bit on the nerves. Well, I'm not surprised—I like her in a way; but being with her makes me believe that Buddha was right when he numbered stupidity among the deadly sins.

So glad to hear you're better—in spite of Villefranche! We've got a charming little house at Bandol, exactly like Bouvard et Pécuchet's house. A museum piece—it seems almost a crime to alter or refurnish it.

Love to Norah.

Yours
Aldous H.

312: TO HELEN CORKE

*The Athenaeum, Pall Mall, S.W.*1
7 *May*, 1930

Dear Miss Corke,

Thank you for the extracts from DHL's letters. I wholly understand

312 *Helen Corke: an early friend of Lawrence and author of the manuscript on which his novel* The Trespasser *was based. Huxley included portions of Lawrence's letters to her in the edition, identifying her by initials only.*

your attitude about the others. The rather indecent display of personalities which has become so unpleasantly common now is something which, if I have any say in the matter, shall be avoided in Lawrence's case. All that I am doing now is to collect as many letters as I can find—before they are scattered and lost—in view of a publication which I hope may be delayed for many years. With regard to anything like the immediate future, I am still rather uncertain. A selection may be published—but only of the more impersonal letters.

Yours sincerely
Aldous Huxley

313: TO MRS JULIETTE HUXLEY

La Gorguette, Sanary (Var)
31 *May*, 1930

My dear Juliette,

Will you be very kind and give hospitality to a box which I am asking Paul Hamann to send to Hillway to await an opportunity of being taken to France. It ought not to be large, so will not, I hope, be a great nuisance. It contains—this may be of interest to you—some casts of a life-mask which Hamann (who is a rather bad sculptor, but an ingenious workman) did of me. I've not seen it yet: but the masks he did of other people were incredibly good—like very good portrait heads. If you or Julian feel like having yourselves done, he will be in London for about a fortnight longer at 2 Alma Studios, Stratford Road, Kensington W 8; he's having a show at D[orothy] Warren's gallery, also. He's not dear—not more than one of these beastly photographers—10 guineas for the mould and one cast and 2 guineas for the next two casts, 35/- for each cast after that up till six, when he has to make another gelatine mould from the original matrix. The process is very curious and rather amusing. So that if you want yourselves recorded three-dimensionally, get into touch with him. Meanwhile, please be an angel and keep the box for me.

Here all is exquisitely lovely. Sun, roses, fruit, warmth. We bathe and bask. Best love to you all.

Yours
A.

314: TO RICHARD ALDINGTON

La Gorguette, Sanary (Var)
1 *June*, 1930

Dear Mr. Aldington,

Thank you for your letter and the cheque, which I am returning to you, because I think it would be best if you sent it direct to Percy Robinson,

314 *Huxley was only slightly acquainted with Aldington at this time.*

15 Gt. Marlborough Street, London W 1, the solicitor in charge of Lawrence's estate. As L. died intestate there are no executors—only administrators (whatever the difference may be), who are Frieda and L's brother George. The best thing wd be, I think, to make the cheque payable to Robinson or to the Estate.

I am not a literary executor—nobody is: there is only to be a kind of unofficial little committee to advise the administrators, if any literary problems should arise. I have been asked, however, to collect the letters with a view to publishing a selection in the nearish future and to having the whole lot ready if, much later, it's desired to publish them all. My own view is that the selection should be as far as possible impersonal. I don't like the bodysnatching business. There will be a lot in L's letters (of which several hundreds have already been got together) which can be published—and beautiful stuff, it is—without any offensive display of intimacies or any posthumous libel of third parties. If you have any letters, would you allow me to have copies made of them? I'd let you know, when the time came, what it was proposed to publish. The rest would remain in the general reservoir of letters for the remoter future to decide on. If you are willing, will you send your letters to Mrs. [Enid] Hilton, 44 Mecklenburg Square, London W C 1, who is doing the typing and filing. (She is a nice woman, an old friend of L's, and very reliable.) She will take copies and return as soon as possible.

I was only in Paris a few hours, so had no opportunity to accept your very friendly invitation. But I expect to be there again some time in July and if you're still there, will do so then. Meanwhile, if you're in the neighbourhood of Marseille or Toulon, do remember this address—30 m. from Marseille, 10 from Toulon.

Yours sincerely
Aldous Huxley

315: TO MRS FLORA STROUSSE

La Gorguette,
Sanary (Var), France
14 June, 1930

Dear Starky,

I have been so desperately cluttered up with business of late—partly my own work, but more a lot of correspondence in connection with the letters of D. H. Lawrence, which I am collecting and ultimately editing— that I haven't been able to think of letter writing. However, here's a momentary lull; so I snatch the opportunity to thank you for your letters. I'm glad you liked those *Candles*. Such English reviews of it as I have seen— only two or three, for I do my best not to see reviews—have been rather snorty and high-souled about the book. English literary criticism for the moment is all for being nice and gentlemanly and public-schooly, with a touch of whimsical Dickensism or rather (for one mustn't insult Dickens, who was a very great man) a smear of Barrieism to relieve the gentlemanly tedium. Books have got to be as though Mr [——] had written them. In a word, to quote the fashion experts, literature is being worn rather short this year—so short, indeed, that you wouldn't notice it was literature at all. However, it doesn't much matter, I suppose. Poor Fanning! I thought he was rather a charming character. The story ['After the Fireworks'] is an elaboration and emendation of an incident recorded in the letters of Chateaubriand. When he was sixty, a very young girl at a watering place came and threw herself at his head. He wrote her a most exquisite letter, which is extant. And there the matter ended, even though she did invade his house one evening. With my usual sadism, I thought it would be amusing to give it the cruel ending. And as one couldn't use Chateaubriand himself— that monstrous pride and loneliness and, underneath the burning imagination, that emotional aridity would have been impracticable to handle—I made the hero one of those people (they have always fascinated me and provoked a certain envy) who know how to shirk natural consequences and get something for nothing, give Nemesis the slip.

I have just written a play, which was quite amusing work, and am hoping and praying that someone will take it and that it will make some money, as I've just bought a little house down here on the Mediterranean, between Marseille and Toulon and am finding the necessary alterations very expensive. It's a lovely place, though, hot and sunny, and the provençal people are very decent. Paris got rather trying, partly because it was a big town and I hate living in big towns—only like visiting them from time to time— and also because French literary society is really a bit too literary and, owing to stringent economic conditions in the intellectual world, terribly Darwinian. If you want to see nature red in tooth and claw go to a French literary salon. The only more Darwinian spectacle is a collection of French women. However, they're a marvellous people all the same and I owe them enormous debts.
Farewell.

Yours,
Aldous Huxley

316: TO THE HON. DOROTHY BRETT

Cap de la Gorguette, Sanary (Var)
23 June, 1930

My dear Brett,
I have been asked by Frieda and George Lawrence, as joint administrators of Lawrence's estate, to collect his letters. The point at the moment is to

---

316 *The original of this letter is torn. Missing words are supplied from the letter written by Huxley on the same day to Mrs Mabel Dodge Luhan, which is very similar but has a different closing paragraph:'Please excuse this long letter from a stranger and believe me Yours very sincerely. . . .'*

get together copies of as many of the letters as possible without delay, so that they shall not be dispersed. The question of publication will arise later. Nobody is anxious that personalities about other people or the still more private personalities should be published now. What happens many years hence is the affair of posterity. There will, if I am successful, be a complete collection of letters for posterity to work on. If a volume is published in anything like the immediate future, it will be a volume of, as far as possible, impersonal letters. Will you let me take copies of any letters from Lawrence which you may have? Letters are being typed and filed by Mrs Hilton, 44 Mecklenburg Square, London W.C.1. We have already got together several hundred. Would you send yours? Mrs H is most reliable and the letters will be returned, registered, as soon as they have been copied. Alternativ[ely,] if you have someone who can make reliable [and] accurate copies, will you have them done over there and send two typescripts? On t[he] whole, it would be better if you would tr[ust] the originals to Mrs Hilton, as it is goo[d that] one person should make all the copies, so [that] the idiosyncrasies of L's punctuation, e[tc] can be reproduced by th[e] same typographical conventions through[out].

I am writing also to Mrs Luhan. Will yo[u be] kind enough to give me names and address[es of] any people whom you know to possess Lawre[nce] letters. I am sending a letter to the Am[erican] press on the subject. But I should also [like] to write personally to as many people as [poss]ible.

We are just moving into a little house here on the sea, not far from Toulon. A l[ovely] place. If you ever condescend to revisit [the] Old World, remember our address. Maria wo[uld] certainly send her love if she were here but at the moment she's away in Paris.

Yours,
Aldous H.

317: TO MRS FLORA STROUSSE

La Gorguette, Sanary (Var)
[Circa July, 1930]

Dear Starkey,
You seem to be getting very close to this place. I hope you will drop off if you pass. We can offer a meal, but not accommodation, as we are living in the midst of workmen, who are demolishing and re-putting-up the house. Toulon is 10 miles off: all expresses stop there and there are buses from Toulon (a really lovely town, incidentally) to Sanary.

Have I 'done' Lawrence? No. Kingham [in *Two or Three Graces*] was concocted before I knew him—at least I'd only seen him once, during the

317 *Of the sketch of himself in* Point Counter Point, *Lawrence had written to Huxley, '. . . your Rampion is the most boring character in the book—a gas-bag'.* (The Letters of D. H. Lawrence, *ed. Huxley, p. 758.)

War. Rampion is just some of Lawrence's notions on legs. The actual character of the man was incomparably queerer and more complex than that.

Cannes is dreadful. All that coast is just the suburb of Europe—a sort of California for retired business men of all nationalities. It's still fairly clean here, the coast—and inland it's virgin.

Yours
Aldous Huxley

318: TO MRS MABEL DODGE LUHAN

Cap de la Gorguette, Sanary (Var)
22 July, 1930

Dear Mrs. Luhan,

Thank you for your letter. I understand your unwillingness to send personal letters. With regard to the question of publishing personalities— I quite agree with you that L. was 'the most personal creature in the world'; and it is precisely for that reason that I am averse from publishing personalities by him or about him. I have seldom met anyone who was less of a public man than Lawrence, more essentially a man of the private life. It seems to me, therefore, that the most rudimentary loyalty to his memory demands that one should refrain, when he is dead, from exposing those privacies, about which he felt during his lifetime, that the public had no business to know anything more than what he chose to reveal indirectly in his books. I am not particularly anxious that any letters should be published yet awhile; but if it should be decided to publish any, I shall do my best to insist on the exclusion of those personalities which Lawrence would have hated to have published. He always regarded public curiosity about his affairs as a 'damned impertinence' (that was how he put it to me), and I see no reason why we should not respect his fastidiousness until the passage of time has rendered this curiosity practically impersonal.

Yours sincerely,
Aldous Huxley

319: TO CHARLES WILSON

The Athenaeum, Pall Mall, S.W.1
20 September, 1930

Dear Mr. Wilson,

I have rather unexpectedly had to come to London and as I shall have

318 *Mrs Luhan supplied no letters of Lawrence for Huxley's edition, saving them for her own book,* Lorenzo in Taos.

319 *Wilson, recipient of three poems by Lawrence as a 'New Year's Greeting to the Willington Men, for 1929', conducted classes for coal miners at Willington, near Durham. Huxley went up on 10 October, gave a talk, and toured the neighbourhood. Reflections on his visit appeared in his article 'Abroad in England',* Nash's Pall Mall Magazine, *May, 1931.*

to go up into the Northern Midlands some time in October, I thought I might proceed a step further and pass your way. I am an infinitely bad lecturer—never do it if I can help it—but if you think it wd be of interest to your students I could read them something say on the subject of poetry and its relation to science—an important theme. What date wd suit you? Some time before October 12, shall we say, and after Oct. 3—but these dates cd be modified. Does one go to Durham and change for Willington? Or what?

What you say about conditions near you is very depressing. But then what isn't depressing now? And one really doesn't see any very obvious way out of the difficulty. Shortage of gold, overproduction, closing of the largest Eastern markets by political disturbance, development of autonomous industries in places that used to depend on English goods—the only conceivable remedy is a rational policy of all the world in agreement. But as the world seems incapable of agreeing. . . .

Well, well.

Yours very truly
Aldous Huxley

320: TO JO DAVIDSON

The Athenaeum, Pall Mall, S.W.1
25 September, 1930

Dear Davidson,

Your letter has followed me here, somewhat circuitously. I shall probably be in London towards the middle of October: so will you drop me a line at this address when you come? If we don't coincide then, there will be good prospects of a meeting in Paris some time in the late autumn.

I hope all goes well with you. Please give my kindest regards to your wife. Maria is not with me: otherwise she would join me in this message.

Yours
Aldous Huxley

P.S. Our new address in France is:—

La Gorguette
Sanary
(Var)

—which is about 10 miles West of Toulon, on the sea. I hope you'll remember the address when you pass that way.

ALH

320 *Davidson had been commissioned by George H. Doran to execute a bust of Huxley for a gallery to include representations of twelve authors published by Doran's firm. Huxley sat to Davidson early in the year. Davidson wrote on 16 September that the bust was now in wax and that he wanted Huxley to give him another sitting before it was put into bronze. Apparently Huxley did so in December or later.*

Nottingham.
As from:—*The Athenaeum Club, Pall Mall, S.W.*1
15 *October,* 1930

Dear Mrs. Roberts,

I have been out of London and so got your letter after some delay. A rather disquieting letter—for it's no joke being at the end of one's resources in London.

(a) About Italian books. I don't know much about modern Italian literature; but you might think of a novel by Giovanni Verga. D. H. Lawrence translated *Maestro Don Gesualdo* and *Cavalleria Rusticana*: this means that his name is known here, so that people might be interested in the other Sicilian novel, *I Malavoglia.* Alternatively there are the novels of Grazia Deledda (the woman who got the Nobel Prize), of which only one, so far as I know, has been done into English. I could find out the names of other likely books from Italian friends—but am ignorant myself: at any rate can't think of any I've read recently (except perhaps those of Borgese) which seemed interesting enough to translate.

[b] If you do French books, get hold of Malraux's new book *Route Royale* (I think is the title) appearing in the *Revue de Paris* and shortly to be issued by Nouvelle Revue Française. Or his earlier novel, *Les Conquérants* his previous novel [*sic*] (if the rights haven't already been disposed of). I shall be leaving England in a few days; but should be glad to meet you before I go. Would you care to dine with me on Saturday? If so it wd perhaps be simplest if you called for me at the Club (corner of Pall Mall and Lower Regent St, entrance in Lower Regent St) or if you prefer I would call at your rooms. Let me know at the Athenaeum.

Yours very truly,
Aldous Huxley

322: TO ROBERT NICHOLS

[London]
Saturday evening [18 *October,* 1930]

My dear Robert,

I have had a most agitated stay in England this time—so agitated,

---

321 *In a note dated Thursday* (16th), *Huxley added:* 'Gli Indifferenti *was one of the books I tried to think of—but couldn't remember its name. I've not read it—tho' I met the author* [Moravia] *in Paris not long ago: but I have heard it very well spoken of by competent critics. It is said to present a very disagreeable picture of Italian family life—hence the attack upon it made by Arnaldo Mussolini*'.

Mrs Roberts had met Huxley in London apparently the previous winter after corresponding with him from Poland, where she had read Point Counter Point. *They exchanged letters intermittently for the next twenty-five years or more.*

322 *Novel: never completed—unless this was a forecast of* Eyeless in Gaza (1936).

indeed, that for a good deal of the time I wasn't in England at all, but making a tour of Great Men in Berlin and Paris with old Sullivan (a most entertaining piece of sight seeing) and since then I have had to go up to Durham to lecture (and incidentally look at mining villages—than which nothing can be much more frightful) and to Nottingham to see DHL's relations. So that I've really had very little time to call my own, and as I return on Monday—urgent need to do a little work—I fear I shall altogether miss seeing you. Which I greatly regret, as there's much I'd have liked arguing about with you—quite apart from the fact that it wd have been very pleasant to walk and talk, think and drink, eat and, even, excrete under the same roof for a friendly day or two. Let's hope for better luck next time. Meanwhile, is there any prospect of your coming our way? It's lovely country there—much less suburban and overrun than where you were at Villefranche. And tho' the Mistral does blow rather hellishly at times, the sun is bright and, in sheltered spots, warm. We have spare rooms now.

I am projecting a kind of picaresque novel of the intellect and emotions —a mixture between *Gil Blas*, *Bouvard et Pécuchet* and *Le Rouge et le Noir*. I think it is quite impossible to do—but it will be fun to try and something may come out of the attempt—something none the worse perhaps for being quite different from what it was meant to be.

> *Yours*
> *Aldous H.*

So remember our address

> La Gorguette
> Sanary
> (Var)

Give my love to Norah and to yourself. How is the 'Don'? Going strong, I hope. [*Sketch*.]

323: † TO MRS KETHEVAN ROBERTS

Cap de la Gorguette, Sanary (Var)
28 November, 1930

Dear Mrs. Roberts,

Forgive me for having been so long in answering your letter. I was away for some little time and have been very busy since. What you say of *Gli Indifferenti* interests me: I must read it. (How many thousand things there are that one *must* read: 'La chair est triste, hélas, et j'ai lu tous les livres'— perhaps it is no less 'triste' when one has not read them all.) The books I mentioned were, I think, *To the Lighthouse* by V. Woolf: *A Passage to India* by E. M. Forster: *Sexual Life of Savages* by Malinowski: (and at the same time it might be of interest to read *Growing up in New Guinea* by (I *think*) Margaret Mead—an account of savages more puritanical than New

England Calvinists in the 17th century!) *Parallelen der Liebe* is the German title of *Those Barren Leaves*—idiotic: I told them to use the sub-title of one of the sections of that book which is 'The Loves of the Parallels'—a reference among other things to Canning's parody of Darwin, *The Loves of the Triangles*, incidentally an excellent description of the loves of these particular characters—perhaps of *most* love, in so far as all love is between entities which obey Euclid rather than Lobatchevsky and 'never meet'. Well, the imbeciles went and put *Parallelen der Liebe* instead of *Die Liebe der Parallelen*. One just gives up hope and takes to resignation, when that sort of thing happens. One might as well be dealing with cows.

Your description of Russian life before the Flood sounds very agreeable. Domestic life in Dostoevsky is of course purely nightmarish; nobody can even eat in the normal way, much less sit or sleep. And the horrors of the overcrowding which he describes make one's hair stand on end. I sometimes wonder, though, whether it isn't perhaps rather bad for one to have been born and brought up a bourgeois in tolerably easy circumstances—with baths, fresh air, plenty of space, privacy and the other luxuries of bourgeois existence. The result is that any diminution of that treasure of space and time which money can buy—leisure and room to be alone in—seems an appalling hardship: and the actual physical contact with members of one's own species fills one with dismay and horror. The Marxian philosophy of life is not exclusively true: but, my word, it goes a good way, and covers a devil of a lot of ground.

I hope you have found some moderately congenial job—it would be too optimistic to hope for anything more than moderately congenial.

Yours sincerely,
Aldous Huxley

324: TO CLIVE BELL

La Gorguette, Sanary (Var)
5 *January,* 1931

My dear Clive,

I was so very much distressed to hear from Jean Cocteau, whom we saw chez Noailles at Hyères, that you were having trouble with your eyes. Knowing something about it at first hand, I can sympathize particularly deeply. I do hope that your treatment in Switzerland will be successful; but I suppose, like most treatments, it will be a long job.

My advice to those who are going to be deprived even only temporarily and briefly of the power of reading is always to learn Braille. It takes a very short time—I think I was only 3 or 4 weeks before I could read with reason-

---

324 *The Vicomte de Noailles and his wife, Marie Laure, were often hosts to the Huxleys and also to Edith Wharton, who lived at Hyères.*

able facility and speed—and makes an astonishing difference. The Braille lending library (at any rate in London) is excellent, all things considered— plenty of solid books and even modern novels. Even if you're merely ordered to restrict your reading by the oculist I think it wd be worth your while to learn—to save your eyes and yet not be left to blank inactivity. Everything has its compensations, and I remember with pleasure the volupté of reading Braille in bed, in the dark and with one's book and hands snugly under the bed-clothes.

We are going to England for a bit in a week or so's time. Do let me know if there is any prospect of seeing you there or, later, in these parts.

Yours
Aldous H.

325: TO MRS FLORA STROUSSE

La Gorguette, Sanary (Var)
6 January, [1931]

My dear Starky,

Please forgive me for being so atrocious a correspondent. Time seems to have been oiled this autumn, like an Indian thief, for the express purpose of slipping between fingers—and he has got away with weeks and months of booty, leaving how little, so far as I'm concerned, in return—some essays, a few poems, some on the whole rather melancholy reflections, a certain number of drawings and paintings in oils—my first experiments in the medium and a great thrill—for me, at least.

What a world we live in. The human race fills me with a steadily growing dismay. I was staying in the Durham coal-field this autumn, in the heart of English unemployment, and it was awful. If only one cd believe that the remedies proposed for the awfulness (Communism etc.) weren't even worse than the disease—in fact weren't the disease itself in another form, with superficially different symptoms. The sad and humiliating conclusion is forced on one that the only thing to do is to flee and hide. Nothing one can do is any good and the doing is liable to infect one with the disease one is trying to treat. So there's nothing for it but to make one's escape while one can, as long as one can.

If you want to read a *good* book, get *The Castle* by Kafka, translated by Edwin Muir: it makes the other German novelists, even Mann, look pretty thin and insubstantial. For me it's one of the most important books of this time. Then I re-read with the most intense pleasure Stendhal's *Le Rouge et le Noir*. What a masterpiece! Farewell and may 1931 be propitious.

Yours
Aldous Huxley

325 *Misdated* '6.i.30'.

*The Athenaeum, Pall Mall, S.W.*1
18 January, 1931

My dear Robert,

Your letter followed me here, so I wont reply at length as I hope I'll soon see you. Is there any prospect of your being in London next week? Maria arrives Tuesday or Wednesday and we shall stay for the time being at least at the Regent Palace—what a place! I am there now, fascinated with horror: but it's 2 yards from Piccadilly Circus, the bedrooms are quiet and price only 9/6 for bed and breakfast.

I have been writing some verse of late—what a labour! it absolutely knocks me out. I can't imagine how you go on with your 'Don'—and hope to publish a 'slim volume' with the enclosed *plus* what came out in limited edition form in *Arabia Infelix*. If you have time will you glance at these and tell me what you think of them when we meet. Some, I think, are all right. But I don't really know and rely on your judgment.

A bad business about Heseltine—tho' I confess that when I saw him this spring he rather gave me the goose-flesh.

Love to Norah.

Yours
Aldous H.

327: TO THE HON. DOROTHY BRETT

La Gorguette,
Sanary (Var), France
10 March, 1931

My dear Brett,

Thank you so much for your note and the DHL letters; which I have made a very interesting choice from. There are a tremendous lot, with more possibilities in the offing. The early ones are particularly interesting and delightful—such high spirits: which he lost as he grew older and iller. The horror of that creeping disease! Its progress is painfully visible between the lines of the letters when one sees them all in the mass. I am cutting out feeling-hurting passages, uninteresting bits and things which are repeated in several letters to different people. (Often there's one obviously best version of the same thought written down about the same time to different correspondents

---

326 *Huxley and his wife remained in England until the end of March, staying at Dalmeny Court, Duke Street, S.W.*1. *Philip Heseltine ('Peter Warlock' the composer) had committed suicide in December. He was the original of Halliday in Lawrence's* Women in Love *and of Coleman in Huxley's* Antic Hay.

—tho' it's often worth keeping repetitions because of the subtle variations introduced by L in varying his mood to different correspondents.)

I'm glad you've finally got rid of the [——]. I thought she was without any exception the most awful human being I'd ever seen. The agonies which poor L suffered when she came! He used to flee from the hotel immediately after breakfast and come and hide in our house the whole day, so as to escape her terrible presence.

We may perhaps be in USA this autumn—who knows? Don't expect to get any definite answer about anything out of Frieda. Definite answers don't grow in her brain. She's been rather ill and down, poor F, lately. Barby is better, thank God. A bientôt, perhaps. Love from M.

Yours
Aldous H.

328: TO HEINRICH STRAUMANN

La Gorguette, Sanary (Var)
[Circa April, 1931]

Dear Mr. *Straumann,*

Thank you for your very interesting letter and for the cutting from the Zurich paper. Your book sounds most interesting. There is a good treatment of the subject of survival in C. [D.] Broad's *Place of Mind in Nature*: also in René Sudré's *Traité de Métapsychie*: while Gerald Heard says some interesting things—in his queer enigmatic way—in the *Ascent of Humanity*. For the broad historical outlines Leuba's *Belief in God and Immortality* is quite good. And I imagine (tho' I've not yet read the book) that there wd be matter of interest in Denis Saurat's *L'Occultisme et la Tradition Littéraire*, or some such title. But evidently you have dealt with the recent development much more thoroughly than anyone. The question seems to me important both philosophically and sociologically—the more so as spiritualism appears to be one of the expanding religions of the epoch. I was struck, when paying some visits in small Midland mining towns lately, to see the number of Spiritualist Chapels recently built or in course of building. The day-dreaming of the masses has two alternative outlets—in Communism and spiritualism, earthly paradise in future time or heavenly paradise in posthumous eternity. Earth is more popular at the moment: but heaven still has an important clientèle.

I wish you had introduced yourself at the Royalty. I left England at once after the performance and expect to remain abroad for some time. If you are likely to remain for long in London we might meet later on and discuss our

328 *Straumann, the author of* Justinus Kerner und der Okkultismus in der deutschen Romantik, *had helped introduce the work of Huxley to the German-speaking public with an article in the* Neue Zürcher Zeitung (2 *June,* 1929). *Royalty:* The World of Light *had opened at the Royalty Theatre on* 30 *March.*

subject—or rather *your* subject, since you have made yourself master of it, while I am a mere dilettante fluttering outside on the periphery.

Yours
Aldous Huxley

329: TO MRS KETHEVAN ROBERTS

La Gorguette, Sanary (Var)
18 *May,* 1931

Dear Mrs. Roberts,

I have been incapable of writing any letters for months past—being bothered with the composition of a book and finding correspondence distracting to the point of impossibility. Please forgive my rudeness in leaving your letters unanswered. Your castle sounds gloomy.

Desmond MacCarthy's article on *The World of Light* seemed to me to be justified in demanding a more definite solution to the play's problem. For even tho' there would not in fact have been such a solution in life, it is perhaps one of the functions of art to provide definite solutions—to consummate wish-fulfilments, in the language of psycho-analysis. The difficulty was (a) finding any plausible solution at all and (b) finding one that could be got into the terribly limited space at a playwright's disposal. A difficulty so great that, after many attempts, I stuck to mere verisimilitude and left the situation hanging in the void. Certainly the lack of solution, (coupled with the spiritualistic theme) has prevented the public from liking the play—which has made less money than any play since the *Agamemnon* of Aeschylus.

I am writing a novel about the future [*Brave New World*]—on the horror of the Wellsian Utopia and a revolt against it. Very difficult. I have hardly enough imagination to deal with such a subject. But it is none the less interesting work.

The sun shines feebly in spite of our latitude—and as a gesture towards disarmament the French military authorities are preparing to make a battery of 14-inch guns almost in our garden. How awful people are!

Yours
Aldous Huxley

330: TO JULIAN HUXLEY

La Gorguette, Sanary (Var)
27 *May,* 1931

My dear Julian,

Thanks for the letter. The projects sound more and more exciting. But since writing last I have been overwhelmed by a literary catastrophe—the

330 *Huxley had previously accepted an invitation from his brother to join him in a Russian trip under the auspices of the S.C.R. The Huxley lecture: one of a series of memorial lectures on T. H. Huxley at the Imperial College of Science and Technology.*

discovery that all I've been writing during the last month won't do and that I must re-write in quite another way. This throws me right back in my work and as I must, if humanly possible, get my book done before the autumn I see no alternative but to renounce the Russian scheme altogether. Which is sad —but there! I'm afraid there's no alternative. I feel less depressed as it seems, from the literature sent by [the] S[ociety for] C[ultural] R[elations], that one can do the trip quite fairly easily and without inordinate expense on one's own. Perhaps, having tasted blood, you'll come back—in June, I shd suppose, is the perfect time, when the nights are white and the weather not too hot. *Intanto, buon viaggio.* I am sick about this; but it must be.

I've written to say I'll do the Huxley Lecture. I think it should be interesting. There will be things to say about science and literature in general and the style of men of science and philosophers.

I'm so glad you have better news of Francis. Our best love to you both.

ALH

331: TO VICTORIA OCAMPO

La Gorguette, Sanary (Var)
19 July, 1931

Chère Madame,
    Je vous remercie de votre aimable lettre et des exemplaires de *Sur*, qui viennent d'arriver.

331 TRANSLATION:—'*Thank you for your kind letter and for the copies of* Sur, *which have just got here.*

'*I read Spanish—though badly and in a horribly illiterate manner—well enough in any case to have already found, in leafing through the magazine, things which please me.*

'*What you say in your article on* Lady Chatterley's Lover *has interested me very much. It is a book of which one could make an entire study with very interesting results. This very curious fact, for example, that Lawrence never says anything about the feelings and sensations of Mellors—that he only talks about the woman. And then this method he proposes for transcending the individual and the concerns of personality, by going not towards a light, towards the open spaces of the mind, but towards a visceral, sub-personal night, like a Jonah in his whale. I enormously admire Lawrence's books and I greatly loved him personally—but in reading him I often suffer from a kind of claustrophobia, I have the impression of having been swallowed up like the unfortunate prophet. What a relief to get out of a whale-book like* Lady Chatterley *and to be able to stroll about, for example, in the vast spaces of the* Paradiso!

'*Thank you once more. Please believe me yours sincerely . . . .*

'*P.S. I have had to ask my agent, Pinker, about the translation rights to* Point Counter Point—*everything is in his hands, and I never know precisely what he has done or is doing. He writes me that he has cabled you direct.*'

Victoria Ocampo, the editor of the literary review Sur, *in Buenos Aires, was printing Huxley's 'Pygmalion versus Galatea', which he had agreed to send her at the request of Pierre Drieu la Rochelle.*

Je lis, quoique mal et d'une manière horriblement illettrée, l'espagnol—assez bien en tout cas pour avoir déjà trouvé, en feuilletant la revue, des choses qui me plaisent.

Ce que vous dites dans votre article de *Lady Chatterley's Lover* m'a beaucoup intéressé. C'est un livre sur lequel on pourrait faire toute une étude très intéressante. Ce fait si curieux, par exemple, que Lawrence ne dit rien sur les sentiments et les sensations de Mellors—qu'il parle seulement de la femme. . . . Et puis cette méthode qu'il propose de dépasser l'individu, les intérêts personnels, en allant non vers une lumière, vers des espaces libres de l'esprit, mais vers une nuit viscérale, sous-personnelle, comme un Jonas dans sa baleine. . . . J'admire énormément les livres de Lawrence et je l'ai beaucoup aimé personnellement—mais je souffre souvent en le lisant d'une espèce de claustrophobie, j'ai l'impression d'avoir été avalé comme le malheureux prophète. Quel soulagement de sortir d'une livre-baleine comme *Lady Chatterley* et de pouvoir se promener, par exemple, dans les immenses espaces du *Paradiso*!

En vous remerciant encore une fois je vous prie de me croire sincèrement vôtre.

Aldous Huxley

P.S. J'ai dû demander à mon agent, Pinker, à propos des droits de traduction de *Contrepoint*—car il a tout en main, et je ne sais jamais trop bien ce qu'il a fait ou est en train de faire. Il m'écrit qu'il vous a télégraphié directement.

332: TO E. MCKNIGHT KAUFFER

La Gorguette, Sanary (Var)
6 August, 1931

Dear Kauffer,

Thank you so much for your letter. What you say about the play gives me great pleasure: I am so glad you liked it.

This is written in haste as a complement to Jack's letter to you about Cassis. I think you'd find the house singularly depressing: it's a spring and autumn house—not a summer one, being shadeless, two miles from the sea (and from a very squalid sea at that) and having its only large room, the studio, under the roof, so that the heat is something incredible. (It felt about 90° at 7 P M when we were there.) Also the price is far above the current market rate. For a small house like that without light and so far from the sea 500 francs a month is normal. Small houses near the sea, at this season, should be about 1500 a month—perhaps less in September. I advise you not to commit yourself to the Cassis place. Why not come for a few days and stay

---

332 *Kauffer, with Marion V. Dorn, stayed at Cassis and paid a visit to the Huxleys in September.*

with us here? You can look round at leisure. There are lots of pleasant places and there will be something to be had in the nature of a house. Anyhow don't pay for 6 weeks in advance at Cassis. I think that would be very rash— the more so as there are much more interesting painting places on the coast— e.g. La Ciotat or Toulon harbour, which combine the Mediterranean and industrialism in a fascinating way. There are bits of Toulon harbour—ship-building and ship-breaking yards, against a back-ground of blue sea and mountains which I have always longed to paint. Cassis is just a rather Italianly picturesque fishing port with intolerably Wagnerian precipices all round it. Too spectacular and too limited. In any case don't hesitate to make use of us. We should love to have you.

Yours
Aldous Huxley

333: TO LEONARD HUXLEY

La Gorguette, Sanary (Var)
24 *August,* 1931

Dearest Father,

I have been a shockingly long time without thanking you for your birth-day letter. My only excuse is that I have been harried with work—which I have at last, thank heaven, got rid of:—a comic, or at least satirical, novel about the Future, showing the appallingness (at any rate by our standards) of Utopia and adumbrating the effects on thought and feeling of such quite possible biological inventions as the production of children in bottles, (with consequent abolition of the family and all the Freudian 'complexes' for which family relationships are responsible), the prolongation of youth, the devising of some harmless but effective substitute for alcohol, cocaine, opium etc:— and also the effects of such sociological reforms as Pavlovian conditioning of all children from birth and before birth, universal peace, security and stability. It has been a job writing the book and I'm glad it's done. I'm taking a holiday from writing in painting in oils—an occupation I find so fascinating and which I follow with such ardour that I foresee that I shall soon have to take a holiday from my holiday!

I hope the heart has been behaving as it should, and that it permits you to indulge at any rate in some of the Connel amusements. Newspaper accounts of English weather are blood-curdling. I hope you're not suffering the full horror. We have had a cool and very windy Summer, but a very dry one. Even the vines are suffering from lack of moisture—a very rare occur-rence.

Maria was rather ill in July and got very much run down. But she is much better now thanks to a treatment of dried stomach tissue which I made her take. Stomach tissue is apparently one better than liver as a specific

351

against anaemia, and as M has always been anaemic and as her anaemia has resisted everything that any doctor ever prescribed, I decided on the strength of the accounts I read in a medical paper, to get the stomach. The results of this mystic cannibalism have been excellent: she has put on weight, got a good colour, no longer suffers from head-aches. If you know anybody who suffers from the same sort of run-downness I think you can confidently recommend it. I gather that the only precaution required with stomach-tissue is that you must take enough. Too little has no effect at all. There seem to be no contra-indications.

We had J. W. N. Sullivan staying with us for some weeks, which was pleasant: also [. . .] the second Mrs. Arnold Bennett [. . . .] We were so sorry for her at the time of poor Bennett's death [. . . .] Matthew is exceedingly flourishing, I am glad to say. We are reading *Monte Cristo* aloud. What a book! I had never read it before: it is a kind of Niagara! I have heard nothing from Julian but a letter written while he was still on the Baltic. I hope all has gone well. The accounts of travelling in Russia which I received the other day from a Soviet enthusiast, Lady Cynthia Moseley [Mosley], were distinctly depressing. My own courage would quail before the dirt she described. Did you read [P. S.] Romanov's novel: *Three Pairs of Silk Stockings?* If not, do so. It's much the most real and convincing account of life in Russia— particularly life for the intellectual class—I have ever read. His other book of short stories *Without Cherry Blossom* is also good. Hideously gloomy! Nevertheless I do feel more and more certain that unless the rest of the world adopts something on the lines of the Five Year Plan, it will break down. Modern industry is too huge and complicated to be left to individualistic enterprise. Now that the beastly thing exists, the only thing is to reduce it to order—as was done, after all, during the War.

Much love to you all from us all.

Ever your loving son
Aldous

334: TO MRS FLORA STROUSSE

La Gorguette, Sanary (Var)
8 September, 1931

Dear Starky,

[. . . .] There is plenty of room for more to be written about Lawrence. He is large enough to accommodate a lot of interpreters. [J. M.] Murry's vindictive hagiography was pretty slimy—the slug's-eye view of poor L: and if you knew the intimate history of his relations with L and Mrs. L, you'd really shudder. One day it really ought to be published. Some of the

333 *Arnold Bennett had died on 27 March of a relapse from typhoid fever.*
334 *Murry's* Son of Woman *had appeared in April.*

details are quite fantastically ghoulish and foul. The letters will come out, I suppose, in 6 months or 1 year from now. They will contain a mass of most important material. There are some really astonishing letters among them. I think it would be foolish to do more than begin a study of Lawrence until they have appeared.

[. . . .]

Ever yours
Aldous Huxley

335: TO G. WILSON KNIGHT

La Gorguette, Sanary (Var)
15 *September,* 1931

Dear Mr. Knight,

You must forgive me for not having written before: I have been very much preoccupied with a difficult piece of work—a Swiftian novel about the Future, showing the horrors of Utopia and the strange and appalling effects on feeling, 'instinct' and general *weltanschauung* of the application of psychological, physiological and mechanical knowledge to the fundamentals of human life. It is a comic book—but seriously comic.

I am glad you liked *The World of Light*. I tried to get something of the subtlety of a novel's psychological analysis into a play—with partial success: but it's difficult. And the public doesn't seem to want it, being used to plays by dramatists who are fundamentally not *serious*—but treat characters as puppets and conversation as waggery-contests and rant.

About this philosophy business—I agree that the Life business isn't enough. Too much insistence on it makes Lawrence's books oppressively *visceral*. Reading, one feels like Jonah in the whale's belly. One longs for the open air of intellectual abstraction and pure spirituality—if only for a change of climate. L. himself admits this theoretically—but doesn't practise it in his writing. How he managed to stand that whale-belly atmosphere so uninterruptedly I can't really conceive. But perhaps he got enough relief in his perceptions of the non-human impersonal beauty of nature: he couldn't have got it in the impersonal dark ecstasy of the senses—for that is merely going further into the belly. The real defect of Murry's book seems to me that it is fundamentally malignant—a malignant and vindictive hagiography. Most repulsive. Tho' of course it is able and in parts very true—only truth told by Murry about Lawrence subtly becomes something else.

Did you read Gerald Heard's book—*The Social Substance of Religion?* Very curious and interesting—but again, a bit visceral: a getting back to the snugness of contact and co-consciousness. But perhaps one must get back to that, perhaps the solitary life of individuals is impracticable, psychologically and socially. Goodness knows.

353

I have been reading the *Journal Intime* of Maine de Biran—2nd volume, recently published. Most interesting. The only psychologist-philosopher who has really gone to the trouble of carefully observing the relation of soul to body.

I see to my dismay that I have delayed so long that your address will no longer be Cheltenham. Still, I send in the hope of its being forwarded. I hope you'll like Toronto. I expect to be in New York this autumn, from about October 20th. My address there is:—

c/o J B Pinker & Sons
9 East 46th St.
New York, N.Y.

Do give me your Toronto address and I will send you a copy of the volume of essays [*Music at Night*] in one of which I mention your work on Shakespeare and music.

Yours sincerely
Aldous Huxley

336: TO EUGENE F. SAXTON

*The Athenaeum, Pall Mall, S.W.*1
24 September, 1931

My dear Gene,

This startling out-falling of the bottom of old England has made me change my autumn plans—and I have decided that we shan't be coming to New York after all: partly for reasons of expense and partly because I want very much to be on the spot while the crisis is being solved—or not solved! —during the next few weeks and months. One develops a strong sense of patriotism when the moment comes, and I feel I don't at all want to be out of London at this time. And even if I did want, my pounds wouldn't take me very far. So I must beg you to forgive me for having troubled you so much and to no purpose. I do hope I haven't put you to great inconvenience. Thank you so much for all you have done: I hope to take advantage of your kindness at some future date, when events are less painfully exciting.

Meanwhile, how goes it with you and the family? Well, I hope. Maria is not yet in London—otherwise she wd send her love along with mine. All good wishes and all apologies and best thanks.

Yours
Aldous H.

336 *The 'out-falling' refers to the fall of sterling, which marked the end of the nineteen-twenties prosperity for foreigners living in France.*

*The Athenaeum, Pall Mall, S.W.*1
Friday [25 *September*, 1931]

Dear Mrs. Carswell,

I have just come over and got your letter at once. I am glad you are doing something about Murry's book: it is one of the most odious and also one of the most extraordinary things I have ever read—a vindictive hagiography, malice expressed in terms of worship. And that horribly snuffling Stiggins tone! Horrible. But it's done with great ability, of course. And the master stroke of ignoring the fact that L. was an artist! I am making notes for a short study of L. to serve as introduction to the letters—and tho' this cannot be specifically a retort to Murry it will in effect try to undo some of the mischief that that slug has undoubtedly done. (Another sign of his cleverness was the exploiting of the psycho-analytical rigmarole, which will fetch 100's of earnest imbeciles.)

About the quotations so far as I'm concerned there is no objection. (Not that I have any authority to do anything.) The line that is being taken by Heinemann as publisher of the letters (I saw Frere Reeves yesterday) is to get the Estate to stop the publication of any collection of letters likely to be prejudicial to the sale of the big work. Thus they have put the lid on Mabel Luhan (to whom Frieda has, of course, given permission to publish her memoirs and complete letters) and the Brewsters, who have also got out [?] a memoir and complete set of letters. This I think is reasonable enough, as anything that would prejudice the sale of the big collection *wd* be to the detriment of the Estate, and there is no reason why these books *shdn't* come out after. Your memoir seems to belong to quite a different category, for it doesn't incorporate anything like a complete correspondence but contains only illustrative quotations from letters. Tho' Reeves has no authority, he is in a position to advise the Estate (i.e. George) and to get his advice accepted and acted on. This being so, I think it might be best for you to send him a note saying what you are doing and explaining that there wd be no valid reason for his advising George to refuse permission as your memoir wd not interfere with the sale of the *Letters*, but wd tend on the whole to stimulate interest rather than, by anticipating the publication of a complete correspondence, to diminish it. I am going out of town for tonight, but expect to be back tomorrow evening—am staying at Dalmeny Court, Duke St (under that name in the phone book). Perhaps we cd meet and have a talk—it wd be pleasant and also, in the Murryish circumstances, useful!

Yours sincerely
Aldous Huxley

337 *Text from a handwritten copy. It has been necessary to expand abbreviations of a few words. Mrs Luhan's* Lorenzo in Taos *was published in* 1933; *the Brewsters'* D. H. Lawrence: Reminiscences and Correspondence *in* 1934. *Mrs Carswell's* The Savage Pilgrimage *was nearly completed and it appeared in June,* 1932.

*The Athenaeum, Pall Mall, S.W.*1
10 *October,* 1931

Dear Mrs. Roberts,

I am sending a copy of *Music at Night,* and have asked Chattos to send a copy of *The Cicadas.* Return the latter if you like, but please keep the former. I shd like you to have it.

Your castle sounds very gloomy still. I am sorry. It's a bad world; at the moment worse than usual. One has the impression of being in a lunatic asylum —at the mercy of drivelling imbeciles and dangerous madmen in a state of frenzy—the politicians.

Poor H. G. does squeak—but I think he's right in supposing that, given a little intelligence now, the world cd really be made quite decent, materially (*too* decent perhaps? chi lo sa?), also right in fearing that the necessary intelligence will not be applied, but that stupidity, coupled with cupidity, will prevail, as of old, and plunge us deeper in the mire.

Yours sincerely
Aldous Huxley

La Gorguette, Sanary (Var)
15 *February,* 1932

My dear Eddy,

I was glad to get your long letter. Luckily the *affaire Aragon* has not yet come my way personally—tho' I have read of it in the papers and heard it gossiped about. It certainly isn't the affair of foreigners to interfere. The man has a great deal of talent—*Libertinage* had astonishing things in it, and there were one or two poems in *La Grande Gaîté* quite amazingly good. I have not seen him for 10 years I should think. [. . . .]

I'm glad to hear you're doing a book on Kafka. I have only read *The Castle* and some of the short stories in German. Can't face *The Trial* in German, so am waiting for the translation. Do you know when it's coming out? Kierkegaard is very queer, I think. I read some selections in German last year and a French translation of that episode in the huge novel *Eltern Eller* called *Le Journal du Séducteur,* a very odd and good book. You might persuade an English publisher to do a few selections from him. There is apparently one such book published in America by some minor University Press. I've not seen it.

I am busy compiling a sort of anthology interlarded with comments of my own—a mixture between an *Oxford Book* (tho' not very Oxonian in choice of selections) and a book of essays. It's a pleasant thing to do and should be quite agreeable, I think, to read. But what an appalling amount of bad stuff has been written even by the best authors. It's unbelievable what 80% of even Shelley is like. And as for Wordsworth, Browning, Spenser (whom I find almost totally unreadable)—it's like extracting radium from pitchblende, one gramme in 200 tons.

Raymond [Mortimer] was here for a fortnight, a charming guest; but we are now alone. I work hard and in the intervals amuse myself even harder by painting, a most exhausting process, I find, but extraordinarily pleasure-giving. Give my love to all such friends as you may meet. Maria sends you hers.

Yours
Aldous H.

340: TO MRS FLORA STROUSSE

La Gorguette, Sanary (Var)
19 *February,* 1932

Dear Starkey,

Thank you for your letter. I'm sorry about the collapse of the relationship with B. It really is very awful, the way something can almost suddenly become nothing—like a mummy that looks perfectly intact and sound when the archaeologists unbury it and crumbles to dust at a touch—nothing left. I share with you a fear of the responsibilities of relationships—have only one that really counts at all, with my wife—nothing else that commits me in any serious way. It's awful to be committed—but at the same time, if one isn't one gets very little in return: and if one is, and the other party doesn't feel committed. . . . The endless possibilities of misery and the few of happiness!

I am compiling an anthology of poetry, interlarded with comments of my own—a book of essays combined with a Golden Treasury—only the metal is of a somewhat different kind from Mr. Palgrave's. There's a great deal of queer, good, interesting stuff in English poetry that never gets into most anthologies. I am putting a little of it into this one of mine. It's interesting and pleasant work. Also am re-reading my grandfather's works and *Life*, as I have to deliver a lecture on T. H. Huxley as a literary man. He was really a very impressive figure. Do you know the *Life and Letters* by my father? It's a good book. And the essays are first class and really astonishingly up-to-date. People try to make out that he was a dogmatical-materialistic old ass, who couldn't understand the finer shades. But it's not in the least true. He was quite as much aware of things as any of the Jeans-Eddington people. And how well he wrote! and what a heroic figure of a man! This century doesn't seem to breed them as the last did. But enough ancestor-worship!

Lawrence's letters are selected and I have to think of doing an introduction to them—a big job: and what makes everything worse, from the point of

357

view of the job-doer, is that I have developed a passion for painting and that, if I didn't keep it in check, I shd spend the whole of every day at it. If only one didn't have to sleep!

I'm glad you liked *Brave New World*. I gather that it's been rather badly received by the critics on your side. Which is a pity from the business point of view. In England, surprisingly, they have chirped up most laudatorily and the book is selling hard. I had feared an outcry, because of those Zippers—the symbol of the New World, its crest. Thank heaven I was wrong.

Farewell. I hope things will go more happily with you.

Yours
Aldous Huxley

341: TO DOUGLAS GLASS

La Gorguette, Sanary (Var), France
9 March, 1932

Dear Sir,

I have not seen the Potocki case mentioned, as I read very few English papers when abroad. But I take your word for it that it is a case of injustice and I enclose a small contribution towards the defence fund.

Yours truly
Aldous Huxley

342: TO HAROLD RAYMOND

La Gorguette, Sanary (Var)
19 March, 1932

Dear Harold,

I'm so sorry not to have answered your letter before—I'd got very tired, and we went away to Cannes for a few days—and also that I have made you send another proof of *Rotunda*. I think the book looks very nice, in spite of its massiveness. (Thank heaven I don't have to read proofs!)

We look forward to seeing the boys: I hope they'll be able to amuse themselves. I'm glad the book still does so well. In Cannes, we saw H. G. Wells

341 *Count Geoffrey Wladisla Potocki de Montalk had been found guilty in London on 8 February of uttering and publishing an obscene libel, having attempted to arrange for the publication of a volume of poems containing, among other matter, passages translated from Rabelais. He was arrested on the complaint of a printer, was tried and was sentenced to six months' imprisonment.*

342 *According to Gerald Heard, Wells wrote Huxley 'an angry letter' about his supposed treason to science in* Brave New World. *No trace of a reply has been found. Certainly there is no evidence of a quarrel, and Huxley's later notes to Wells, including a greeting on his seventieth birthday, are amicable enough.*

who, I fear, wasn't best pleased with it. On the contrary (surprisingly enough) Edith Wharton is enthusiastic!

I hope all goes well with you both.

Yours
ALH

343: TO MRS KETHEVAN ROBERTS

La Gorguette, Sanary (Var)
[Summer, 1932]

Thank you for your letter, which I will answer later. Meanwhile, I have been looking up the Medici family. The only Giulianos I can find are the brother of Il Magnifico and a brother of Pope Leo, who was Duke of Nemours. There was a Cardinal Giulio who became Pope Clement VII and a Cardinal Ippolito, natural son of Giuliano, Duke of Nemours, who died at 25—poisoned by Alessandro. I can't find a trace of a Cardinal Giuliano. Which of all these, I wonder, was the author of the sonnet? If, as you say you can, you will find out from Italy who it was, I will be most grateful. *Affanno* might be rendered *distress*, which connotes both physical and mental pain. Yes, you are obviously right about *manco*. But that first *affanno* is difficult. 'Cowardly is he who *senza affanno* thinks to have less suffering in life.' I suppose *senza affanno* is an elliptical way of reinforcing *travagliar manco*—to suffer less and be without distress. It is difficult.

Yours
AH

344: TO LEONARD HUXLEY

La Gorguette, Sanary (Var)
22 July, 1932

Dearest Father,

I heard of you indirectly from Matthew, who told us that he had had a splendid time going out with you 'in the new car'—'which goes really quite fast'. I hope the machinery of life at no. 16 goes as smoothly as that of the Austin. Here we pursue our usual course. I have, thank goodness, finished my anthology-with-commentaries, on which I had been working these last months, and am now engaged mainly in working off arrears of reading. (Have just finished, among others, an excellent book on the present economic situation—*The Economic Consequences of Power Production*, by Fred Henderson (Allen and Unwin)—a most excellently clear analysis, which I greatly recommend you to read if you have the chance. I am sure he has got hold of the essential inwardness of the situation. But, alas, it takes a fearful long time

343 *Sonnet: by Giuliano de' Medici. It had been sent to Huxley by Mrs Roberts; he used it in* Texts and Pretexts.

for such books to make any effect on governments. 'In politics, everything is as stupid as it seems.' Bagehot, I think—and painfully true!)

We had an interesting time in Germany—but rather depressing: the smaller towns were very gloomy. Of the little old cities, like Bamberg, Ansbach and the like, one feels that they have been all but killed by the economic depression. Berlin was at least gayer: and the looking after the unemployed seems to be pretty efficient: at any rate, one saw no very obvious external signs of misery even in the poorer quarters. What is going to happen now, I wonder? Goodness knows.

Our dinner with the King and Queen of the Belgians went off very pleasantly. She is a really charming woman—a typical cultured idealistic Bavarian of the late 19th century generation, reminding me very much of Maria's aunts-by-marriage, the daughters of the sculptor Hildebrand. He is also sympathetic—a very thorough, rather ponderous mind, grinding exceeding small and rather slowly. Curiously enough, speaking French with that typically royal German accent which distinguished royal English up to the time of Edward VII! We dined *en intimité;* only Maria's Uncle, Georges Baltus, ourselves, Willie de Grunne, (who was at Balliol with Julian and Trev and is now the Queen's chamberlain) and a lady in waiting and A.D.C. The palace, like all palaces, was a bit mouldy in its splendour: actually moths flew out of the sofas when one sat down! A great difficulty was talking in the third person, which etiquette demands and which is distinctly cramping to conversation when one isn't used to it. The old King, Leopold, used always, it appears, to speak of himself in the 3rd person, like a baby. When he was annoyed, he could be heard rushing round the palace shouting, 'Le Roi est hors de lui!' At table, it was: 'Le potage du Roi est trop chaud'.

I suppose you will be starting for Connel quite soon. Let's hope the weather will be propitious. Here we have had a lot of storms—now sunshine, but wind. Love to all from us both.

Your loving son
Aldous

345: † TO LEONARD HUXLEY

La Gorguette, Sanary
12 September, 1932

Dearest Father,

From a Post-card which Maria received to-day from Rosalind I gathered by implication—for R. said you were better—that you had been ill. I am so very sorry to hear this and do hope that you are now well over your troubles. [. . . .]

We are all tolerably flourishing. Matthew is at present afflicted by one of his periodical outbreaks of boils and sties (styes? who knows?)—which are tiresome, but we seem to be combatting pretty successfully this time with a staphylococcus vaccine that is taken through the mouth, and accompanied by doses of sulphur—the favourite medical theory at the moment being that the bugs congregate in the intestines, and should be attacked at head-quarters. We have had a tutor for him during the last 3 or 4 weeks, who has, I think, been good for him. Mentally he is the image of M's family—quick, with a remarkable intuitive power for grasping the essentials of a situation, a natural gift for living; but with a quite unusual incapacity to grasp and apply general principles—which is rather deplorable if he wants to embrace any of the more learned professions. He is just the opposite of me; for he knows how to deal with people, but not with abstract ideas: whereas I know how to deal with abstract ideas but not with people.

I have been going on with my painting,—with continued enjoyment—using *gouache* or tempera, a most delightful medium that combines many of the advantages of oils with many of the advantages of water-colours. It dries quickly, but you can correct mistakes by painting over. You paint with water, but you can produce a moderate impasto. Painting is obviously the most delightful of the arts to practise. There is the intellectual pleasure of composing your picture, and the semi-physical pleasure of using your hands skilfully. Furthermore the problems (if you dont paint elaborate subject-pieces) are purely internal to the work of art—problems of relations within the picture and of relations to the object represented. You dont have to bother yourself, as in literature, with ethics, politics, sociology, psychology and all the rest. It's a small closed universe with its own private laws. Most agreeable, particularly at moments like the present, when the great world is like one vast lunatic asylum.

We all send our loves, as also to Rosalind and the boys.

Ever your loving son,
Aldous

346: TO MRS NAOMI MITCHISON

La Gorguette, Sanary (Var)
[Circa September, 1932]

Dear Naomi,

Thank you for your letter. I hope something will be done about this hideous Scottsboro' business. Your friend writes to me that there is now a blockade of silence in the entire American press. It's terrifying what can be done by people who have a monopoly of means of propaganda—private money-grubbers in the U.S.A., Musso and Co in Italy, Communist Party in U.R.R.S. [*i.e.*, U.S.S.R.].

Yes, I perfectly believe that a lot of people are happy in Russia—because,

346 *The Scottsboro case came before the Supreme Court of the United States in October, 1932, after months of public controversy during which extensive reports appeared in the American press.*

361

as I said in my letter, happiness is a by-product of something else and they've got a Cause, the working for which gives them happiness. But various questions arise: when they've attained their ideal and filled Russia with machines, what then? Causes die of two diseases (a) failure (b) success. They're effective for the few years while their fate's in the balance and while people aren't bored with them. Europe in the years immediately after the Franciscan preaching must have been full of the same sort of happiness as there is now in Russia. It lasted about 20 years—the enthusiasm. In Russia, where propaganda is more efficient, it may last a bit longer—: but in no circumstances beyond the time when the plan succeeds. The danger of the 5-year-plan ideal is that it is realizable. The donkey gets its carrot and then ceases to run—or is annoyed because the carrot is only a carrot. Have you ever met people who have achieved their ambition and come up in the world? They don't spend their time comparing their present prosperity with the miseries of the past. They spend it complaining of the evils of their present lot (and relatively to general comfort, quite a small discomfort is a real evil) and trying to better it—trying with ever diminishing success as old age creeps on them. And this is why, it seems to me, any dispassionate consideration of individual destiny must be pessimistic. Because the moment the individual becomes conscious he cannot remain contented with his lot. He is aware (a) of what he believes to be a better lot beyond his reach (b) of his own steadily declining powers to achieve the better lot and (c) of death as the end. The only remedies are (a) working for a good cause, (the by-product of such work being happiness). This is excellent so far as it goes: but it is always, as history demonstrates, in the nature of a temporary intoxication. Causes tend to lose their glamour after a few years and a new one or a new version of an old one has to be supplied. The Russians are trying to supply a new cause—another dose of intoxicant—every 5 years. How long will they succeed in putting it over? (b) The next remedy is love, for an individual or for one's neighbours in general. This is the most powerful antidote against the misery of individual existence. If one has luck one may find an individual to be true to: and if one is born with the right temperament and undergoes a suitable training one may be able to love one's neighbours in general. For people with temperaments and endowments that are in any way exceptional, the trouble is that they have so few real neighbours. See Lawrence's *Last Poems* for some very good remarks on this subject.

Well, well—it is all very obscure and distressing. I wish I could even see clear into the economic problem. This system is bad and, on a large scale, seems not even to work. But at the same time without some private property, what is to become of individual liberty? Private property is the only guarantee possessed by individuals against the tyranny of the State (and let us remember that the State is not an abstraction, but just Jones and Brown invested with power). Proudhon insisted on a limited amount of private property—and I think he was quite right. The difficulty arises in determining where the

362

limits are to be placed. What a world! I'm sorry you shd be feeling so gloomy. I am rereading *War and Peace*—which, I find, is a great consolation and tonic. In the intervals I try to write a play—which is interesting and difficult. Love from us both.

Yours
Aldous

347: TO MRS KETHEVAN ROBERTS

La Gorguette, Sanary (Var)
1 *October,* 1932

Dear Mrs. Roberts

Thank you so much for the information. I'm glad it *was* Giuliano after all, as I had put it down as by him in my book—and there wd probably have been no time to change it if the author had been somebody else.

We are just back from a brief visit to Italy to see various friends who have been ill and having babies and what not—a fearful trip through incessant rain of quite unbelievable violence. (One night we ran into a kind of water spout between Florence and Lucca; the water got into the electric apparatus of the car and we were left standing for 2 hours under a rain that was like the Niagara falls. And not only the elements were against us—humanity also. Thieves broke into the garage of the hotel at San Remo and cut huge holes in the back and sides of the hood—*per dispetto*, chiefly: for owing to the general *miseria* there is a lot of dislike of motors and motorists.)

At Forte de' Marmi I met (once more) Moravia and liked him much better than last time—thought him very nice in fact, and extremely intelligent. Also [Enrico] Pea, whose novel *Il Servitore del Diavolo* I have just started to read, together with the painters, Carrà and Magnelli—a very pleasant and intelligent company.

Am rereading *War and Peace*—what a most astonishing book! The old man makes most other writers look pretty silly, I must say. And what an excellent commentary on Mussolini his remarks about Napoleon are! All that stupid unreal rhetoric of fascism—the *incrollabile volontà* and the *fede ardente*—it's beautifully ticked off, in its earlier and different manifestation, by Tolstoy. I think people are getting a bit tired of the nonsense in Italy. Certainly there's more criticism of the government openly expressed, and more ironical scepticism displayed by the public at the *manifestazioni* and speeches of fascism. But perhaps the fact that the government allows these comments to be made is merely a sign that it feels itself to be immovably secure.

I'm sorry you missed your Bermuda job. Richmond will be a poorish substitute—but better than Scotland, no doubt.

Thank you again so much.

Yours
Aldous Huxley

La Gorguette, Sanary (Var)
15 October, 1932

Dear Starky,

Thank you for your letter. I am very glad you liked the introduction to L's letters. I think it makes several important points about L—points that needed making and emphasizing.

The book seems to be doing very well, which I'm glad of for Frieda Lawrence's sake: tho' the stupid woman is embarking on enormously expensive legal proceedings against L's brother now—quite unnecessarily in my opinion: but she rushes in where angels fear to tread. Her diplomatic methods consist in calling everyone a liar, a swine and a lousy swindler, and then in the next letter being charming—and then she's surprised that people don't succumb to the charm. Since L is no longer there to keep her in order, she plunges about in the most hopeless way. I like her very much; but she's in many ways quite impossible. She was only possible for someone who happened to be in love with her and married to her—and not only in love and married but, as Lawrence was, in some strange way dependent on her presence, physically dependent, as one is dependent on the liver in one's belly, or one's spinal marrow. I have seen him on two occasions rise from what I thought was his death bed, when Frieda, who had been away, came back after a short absence. The mysteries of human relationships are impenetrably obscure.

I have just finished a play. Let's hope a few members of the theatre going public may find it as interesting as I do. They didn't go near my other play.

I hope you flourish in mind and body.

Yours
Aldous Huxley

349: TO MARTIN SECKER

La Gorguette, Sanary (Var)
21 October, 1932

Dear Mr. Secker,

I have just finished the *Sleepwalkers* of Hermann Broch, which you so kindly sent me. I read the trilogy with steadily increasing admiration. It is the work of a mind of extraordinary power and depth, and at the same time of extraordinary subtlety and sensibility—of a philosopher who is also an

348 *In a note to J. Ralph Pinker dated 24 July, Huxley had written: 'I am working out the scenario of what may be, I think, rather a good play—with a Kreuger-like figure as the central character—linking the story up with general economic ideas, wh[ich] might be timely, as everyone is bothered about these things'. The play, 'Now More Than Ever', was never produced or published. The suicide of the Swedish financier Ivar Kreuger had occurred the previous spring.*

artist of exceptional refinement and purity. It is a difficult book that makes great demands on the reader—nothing less than his whole mind at the highest pitch of attention. Not at all a book for tired business men! But I hope, all the same, that it will be widely read; for it is manifestly a work of first-rate importance.

Thank you once more for having sent it.

Yours very truly
Aldous Huxley

350: TO THE VICOMTE DE NOAILLES

La Gorguette, Sanary (Var)
5 November, 1932

Dear Noailles,

Thank you so much for your note. I am so glad you liked my preface to the Lawrence letters. I think it makes some important points about L and his way of looking at the world. What is needed now, I feel, is an acceptable philosophical system which will permit ordinary human beings to give due value both to Lawrence's aspect of reality and to that other aspect, which he refused to admit the validity of—the scientific, rational aspect.

We have remained quietly here all autumn, except for a brief excursion into Italy, where it rained torrentially and without ceasing all the time. We had intended to go for a little journey—but it was so comfortable to stay at home, that we stuck tight; and we have had Maria's sister [Suzanne] and her husband, who is a Dutch painter—rather a brilliant one, I think—staying with us. Sanary is full of the usual Lesbian baronesses—all of them in a flutter of excitement to know Mr. [William] Seabrook, because the rumour has gone round the village that he beats his lady friend. One is reminded of the hysterical excitement of cows when they see a bull in the next field coupling with another cow! We look forward to seeing you in December.

Yours
Aldous Huxley

351: TO EUGENE F. SAXTON

La Gorguette, Sanary (Var)
9 November, 1932

My dear Gene,

I was glad to get your letter and to know that you liked my little anthology. I think it makes a pleasant and interesting book. I have amused myself this summer with writing a play, just finished; and am now meditating a novel—feeling rather incapable of getting it under way, as usual in these

350 *On Seabrook see Marjorie Worthington,* The Strange World of Willie Seabrook (1966). *That book contains a letter of Huxley (10 August, 1934) on the sociology of Vilfredo Pareto.*

circumstances, but hoping that the thing will begin to flow one day. If it does start flowing, it might well be finished by the end of next summer. But this is all very uncertain and I shdn't be able to say anything definite for another few months. If it didn't come satisfactorily, I shd ask Harper's to suspend all payments until such time as I was able to cope with the thing— abandoning myself to journalism while the novel ripened: for I know by bitter experience that I can't force myself to write anything that isn't ripe. I hope this won't happen: but if it should, well, then I'll ask Pinkers to make the necessary business arrangements to suit the situation. Meanwhile, I am just accumulating notes and writing experimental pages.

We expect to be in London from the 2nd half of January onwards: it wd be pleasant to see you then if you came over. If only this blasted world would become a little less like a lunatic asylum! What a misery it is!

It's astonishing to think of Mark at Harvard. I hope he'll like it and find it profitable. Matthew has just moved to a new school, a very remarkable experiment which may, I think, turn out to be something very remarkable. Anyhow he seems to be happy and well; which is a good beginning.

Give our loves to the family.

Yours
Aldous H.

352: TO C. H. C. PRENTICE

*The Athenaeum, Pall Mall, S.W.*1
[Circa 27 December, 1932]

My dear Prentice,

Thank you for your letter. I didn't think you'd be able to do much with our Singhalese friend—tho' he's a very intelligent little man in his way. I always feel very sorry for these people who stand on the frontier of two worlds and can't get a real footing in either. It seems unfair—but the fact remains that, whatever may be their personal merits, circumstances conspire to keep them out of any comfortable resting place. The moral of it all being: Don't on any account be born simultaneously intelligent and Singhalese!

We have been hanging suspended here waiting for Matthew's temperature and cough to subside—not quite all here, so to speak, so that it was impossible to do anything. Today, however, the doctor gives him a clean bill of health and I start for Paris this afternoon, as I have to be interviewed about the forthcoming French version of *Brave New World*. (The publishers there seem to have a charming system of squaring the more important critics

351 *Novel:* Eyeless in Gaza. *Matthew's new school was Dartington, at Totnes, Devon. In September*, 1935, *his father transferred him to the Institut Gabriel Rauch, at Lausanne.*

352 *The Huxleys had arrived in London on* 1 *December, planning to return to Sanary after the school holidays began, but they were delayed by Matthew's influenza.*

in advance! They have arranged for me to meet two of them.) Maria and Matthew follow tomorrow and we go straight through to the South, where I hope to get some useful preliminary work done on the projected novel. Then back in January—when I look forward to seeing you. Meanwhile, all the seasonable wishes.

Yours
ALH

353: TO LEONARD HUXLEY

Dalmeny Court, Duke Street,
Piccadilly, S.W.1
26 January, 1933

Dearest Father,

Events have moved rather rapidly in the last day or so, and we are now booked to sail on the *Britannic*, which leaves on Saturday for a West Indian cruise and which we shall leave at Kingston, Jamaica. This means a bit of a rush; but the advantage is that the ship is very large and steady. We shall be very hard at work all tomorrow, and I am afraid shall be unable to get up to see you. So I send this line to bid farewell. I was so sorry to hear from Juliette this afternoon that Rosalind was finding it difficult to throw off her flu. What a miserable business it is! I do hope she will get over her troubles soon. Please give her best love from us both, as also to the boys.

Ever your loving son,
Aldous

354: TO LEONARD HUXLEY

Palace Hotel, Guatemala, C.A.
24 March, 1933

Dearest Father,

I fear I have not written for some time: but we have been engaged so strenuously in exploring this country—one of the most delightful and most interesting I have ever seen—that there seems to have been no time for letters. We arrived a month ago at Port Barrios on the Atlantic Coast—after a call at Belize in Brit Honduras, a place that is definitely the end of the world—and went up to Quirigua, where the United Fruit Company has its hospital run by a most charming and saint-like old Scotsman called Dr. MacPhail, with whom we stayed for two days, with the banana plantations, the jungle and the ruins of the Maya City to amuse us. The last—the ruins—are very fine. Huge sculptured stelae standing up in the jungle, in a kind of square forum, surrounded by artificial mounds, on which the temples stood—still stand, indeed, in fragments.

Thence we went up to Guatemala City which stands at about 5000 ft and has a most agreeable climate, tho' it's a bit dusty at this dry season. Rather a one-horse town, of course: but odd to look at. After a few days we set out on our travels, going first to Antigua, the old capital abandoned after an earthquake in 1773, and full of really magnificent Spanish ruins—palaces, churches, convents—and quite a number of unruined specimens of 16th, 17th and 18th century architecture. Most interesting and beautiful, and in a rich valley dominated by three huge volcanoes, two of which are still active. Then after a day or two on a coffee plantation at 2500 ft, near the Pacific Coast (a paradise, at this season) up into the highlands by the most astonishingly bad, twisting and precipitous roads. Our first stop was Lake Atitlan, almost twice or three times Windermere at 6500 ft, bristling with volcanoes and surrounded by very interesting Indian villages. From there to Chichicastenango, which is the centre of the native life of the Quiché Indians, who thickly inhabit the plateaus—about 7000 ft up—which lie among the mountains. A small hotel has just been opened there; but the Indian life is still untouched. They wear their old costumes, entirely hand woven on the most primitive looms, and practise an extraordinary religion compounded of their old preconquest worship mixed with Catholicism. Thus one sees them all day long in the Church burning candles all along the floor of the nave, praying, then ritually scattering flowers round the candles and pouring libations of aguardiente, the local vodka. More curious still, if one walks out into the country one finds altars in the woods, regularly used by the Indians who burn copal incense before old Maya idols *and* crosses, at the same altar! At one place there were groups of several hundred altars, and there are many secret ones far off in the woods and ravines, where they still sacrifice animals. At the same time they have the greatest respect for such priests as the anti-clerical government allows them to have, giving them service, food and offerings of money. But if a too zealous bishop interferes with their customs, he is liable to find himself chased away with clubs and machetes! We spent 10 days at Chichicastenango, making periodical expeditions all about. All the country round is dotted with old pre-conquest tombs and ruins, and a great deal of fine pottery and jade-ite carvings has been found there. It is a country where one wd like to spend a long time, studying the endlessly queer interactions of paganism and Catholicism, looking at the dances, attending the really amazingly picturesque markets, and looking for antiquities—to say nothing of enjoying the amazing beauty of the mountain landscape. We came down with regret and are now waiting to go by ship to a little Port (Port Angel) on the Pacific Coast of Mexico, near which we have been invited to stay on a coffee plantation, whence—on mules for two days, and afterwards by car and train—we propose to go to Oaxaca and so up to Mexico City. Yesterday we joined a party of Americans in chartering an aeroplane to fly to Copan in Honduras, to see the great Maya ruins there. All went well and we saw the ruins, which are very impressive. But, when it came to departing, we found the plane surrounded by Honduranean police armed with ancient muskets. We had got all the necessary permits for landing: but the authorities at the capital had not warned those at Copan: so we had to spend four hours under guard while frantic telegrams went out in all directions. Finally they let us go—very reluctantly: for they wd have loved to keep us there for a day or two. Annoying foreigners and especially white Gringoes is a national sport in Honduras: besides the plane, (the second ever to land in Copan!) and ourselves provided wonderful free amusement for the inhabitants who came in hundreds, bringing their picnic baskets with them, to look at us. People who know the country tell us we were lucky to get away without spending at least a night in gaol!

I hope all goes well with you and the family. I wish the world at large were in a better state. One reads of the turmoil in the local papers. But it all seems infinitely remote and irrelevant here. I have never been in a country which *felt* so far away. Best love to you all from us both.

Your loving son
Aldous

P.S. Please tell Aunt Rachel [Shawcross] that we have met here a charming old American, Captain Grace of the Texas Rangers, who knew her in Mexico. 'A very good horsewoman!'

355: TO LEONARD HUXLEY

On Board S.S. Siboney
29 April, 1933

Dearest Father,

Here we are en route from Mexico to New York, and glad to be on the homeward road. Mexico was unpleasant, but very curious. Such a strange Neapolitan ice, with its layers of Indian, mestizo, white—of Neolithic, Aztec-Spanish, Spanish-French and Yankee culture. We saw a fair amount of the country—tho' little in comparison with its enormous size—as we came in on the Pacific Coast of the State of Oaxaca, rode across the Sierra to Oaxaca city, saw the archaeological remains of Mitla and Monte Alban (very remarkable), then went to Puebla (a lovely colonial town) and thence to Mexico City, whence we did excursions to the neighbouring ruins and pyramids, which are most impressive, and to various small towns in Morelos and Guerrero. In the City we met a lot of literary gents—some charming and most intelligent—one or two politicians and sprinklings of diplomats and foreign business people.

One most curious incident was the visit of a Mexican gentleman called Señor Eduardo Huxley, who wanted to know if he were a relation. His

---

355 Leonard Huxley died on 3 May, before this letter was delivered. Though Dr Edward Huxley was not a brother of T. H. Huxley, whose 'doctor brother' was Dr James Edmund Huxley, born in 1821, he may have been otherwise related in view of the Ealing connection. T. H. Huxley was born at Ealing; his father, George Huxley, was the Senior Assistant Master of Great Ealing School.

Grandfather, whose photo he showed me (taken in Ealing, a man with a large square beard and a nose which seemed to me rather of the family type) was called Dr. Edward Huxley and he was born, according to an old *Shakespeare Birthday Book* in his grandson's possession, in 1825. His son, George Spooner Huxley, came to Mexico, married a Mexican, produced a family and died young. My Eduardo appears to be his only surviving child. One brother, whose name I saw in the birthday book, was called Jesus Huxley! (Grand Pater wd have liked that, I think.) But he died young.

Is this Dr. Edward Huxley any relation? I knew there was a doctor brother of Grandpater's—but cd not recall the Christian name: also it seemed to me unlikely a brother shd have been born in the same year. I promised to let the man know if I could throw any light on his ancestry. So can you drop me a p.c

> c/o Eric Pinker
> 9 East 46th St.
> New York

and I will forward the information.

I hope the family flourishes. There was very little news in the letters we found in Mexico City and I am hoping we may find a bit more in New York. Meanwhile, this carries our best loves to you all.

> *Ever your loving son*
> *Aldous*

356: TO EUGENE F. SAXTON

> *S.S. Statendam*
> *Wednesday* [24 *May*, 1933]

My dear Gene,

I do apologize about the typewriter! But what luck that you found it! I will communicate with Harpers as soon as I get to London and find out when they expect it. The elements are co-operating with you to make this voyage exceedingly comfortable. Sea like a millpond, and the cabin, as you know, palatial. So we're in clover. (The only fly in the ointment is Dr. Hay, who doesn't allow us to eat as much of the excellent Dutch food as we feel tempted to do!)

I have been reading the [Edna] Millay poems with very great pleasure. Thank you for sending them, and thank you also, dear Gene, for all the other kindnesses with which you loaded us during our stay in New York. You were quite extraordinarily nice to us and I wish I could tell you adequately how grateful we both feel for everything.

Thanks to the smoothness of the sea, I have been able to do a bit of work

356 Ann Vickers, Glories of Venus, Family Reunion: *novels by Sinclair Lewis, Susan C. Smith, and Janet C. Owen.*

—rather refreshing after the whirligig leisure of New York. I find there is nothing like work to counteract the effects of a strenuous holiday! In the intervals have read *Ann Vickers*—a bit dull and superficial, I thought, but commendable; also the *Glories of Venus*, a good book in its way, it seemed to me, with a lot of quality about it—a lot of the thing that Sinclair Lewis, however admirable and conscientious, so deplorably lacks. *Family Reunion* seemed to me pretty interesting, too. Very penetrating as a presentation of characters. The thing that lacks in it, it seems to me, is some sort of philosophy of life in the background, some standard of values posited, explicitly or implicitly, against which the behaviour of the people would take on some more general significance. But then I probably have an entirely erroneous view about fiction. For I feel about fiction as Nurse Cavell felt about patriotism: that it is not enough. Whereas the 'born story teller' obviously feels that it is enough. So let's leave it at that and say good bye and I'll add once more, thank you.

Yours
Aldous H.

357: MARIA HUXLEY TO ROY FENTON

La Gorguette, Sanary (Var), France
1 *July*, 1933

My dear Roy,

I found your letter waiting here for me and I do hope that tired waiting for my answer you wont have sent someone else that superb crocodile skin which I long for. This is our permanent address and en plus—I hope it will be our address for a long time. It is such a joy to be home at last. Mexico City we still enjoyed but New York was a great comedown—financially and because we had to rush off as Aldous's father died suddenly while we were there and we had to return via England which we had not intended to do and then again I was delayed a long time in Paris as my sister was ill. But all feels better since we are home with my lamb impertinently looking up from the tiled floor and a hot sun and a very very blue sea. But Europe *is* in a mess. German Jew authors—and non jewish too—have chosen Bandol and Sanary as a retreat so we cannot escape from th[at] Barbarous German news. The dollar goes down the price of life goes up. I am not sure that on the whole the wilds of Mexican coffee plantations are not the best to live in at the moment where other problems are more vital than politics. Aldous is working feverishly on a novel—the travel book which we both long for was not

357 *Roy Fenton had entertained the Huxleys on his coffee plantation and had accompanied them on their journey by mule-back between Pochutla and the Oaxaca road, in southern Mexico. Publication problems with the travel book,* Beyond the Mexique Bay, *were settled early in the summer, and Huxley finished the manuscript in November.*

inviting to the publishers!—publishing had no good news for us I am afraid —and hope coffee is doing better. I drink a lot and think of the dark bushes the shade trees and the ravines—how lovely it all was—but very much a dream! I loved your letter and—dont mind—I laughed at you and your dip since you were not drowned or devoured, and we both hope you will write us again—life here seems so dull in comparison of yours. My chief occupation is watering jacaranda trees which are about 5 inches high and grown from seed which I sent from Guatemala—and also a stone of a ahuacate [aguacate] which I brought from New York but which seems very stubborn. You might enclose a few ahuacate stones if they are in season— stuff the crocodile with it—they might be a little more willing than the U.S.—I should not wonder. I hated New York and those Americans unable to pick themselves up and try and help the 'crisis'—as low in 1933 as they were bumptious in 1927—and Paris was tiring—smelly and hot while here it is divine and I hope that one day you will come and stay and agree. This goes with all our wishes and much love and I hope my crocodile is still for me.

Yours
Maria

358: TO MRS NAOMI MITCHISON

La Gorguette, Sanary (Var)
13 *August,* 1933

My dear Naomi,

Yes, you may say by all means that I am not becoming a carthlick. How much carth would a carthlick lick if a carthlick could lick carth? Answer: an almost infinite quantity. I have never more passionately felt the need of using reason jusqu'au bout. I was re-reading Wordsworth's account of his visit to France during the Revolution. Damned good; and topical.

> The land all swarmed with passion, like a plain
> Devoured by locusts.

Which is exactly Europe in '33—the awful sense of invisible vermin of hate, envy, anger crawling about looking for blood to suck. And reason in the midst, like Bishop Hatto, waiting to be devoured, not by rats, but bugs. The only possible comment is the one made by Frederick the Great to his Inspector of Education, who had said that human beings were 'naturally' good. 'Ach, lieber Sulzer, er kennt nicht diese verdammte Rasse.' And yet, of course, Sulzer was also right.

Do you think I am kind and unpossessive? Quien sabe? Perhaps I am only a person of rather delicate constitution who likes a quiet life. How senseless psychological and moral judgments really are apart from physiologi-

---

358 *Naomi Mitchison's book:* We Have Been Warned (*London,* 1935). *There was a pre-publication controversy over certain passages.*

cal judgments! And of course I am also to a considerable extent a function of defective eyesight. Keratitis punctata shaped and shapes me; and I in my turn made and make use of it.

I am sorry about your book. But, given the existing laws, it's hard to see what should be done. It's a nice question whether a trial with the accompanying torrents of [. . .] from James Douglas and Hannen Swaffer in the daily papers may not be more harmful to the good cause than surreptitious publication and boot-leg sale. One of the great dangers is vulgarity, lowering of quality. One must be careful not to give the [. . .] too many opportunities to [. . . .] God knows, they have enough already. Vulgarity is probably the price that has to be paid for mental freedom from strict traditions. Primitives are never vulgar, only stupid—stupid, however, with a certain style. Problem: can congenitally rather stupid masses be stupid stylishly when the constraints of tradition have been removed and they are free to respond to the most effective propaganda that happens to be going about? Perhaps a free society *must* be vulgar. I suspect the best that can be hoped for is something à la H. G. Wells—enlargements and proliferations, with a row of dots after them. . . . But not much in the way of intensifications and refinements. Consequently, I fear, a trifle boring.

I am writing about our travels—that is, about everything from politics (undoubtedly best studied in Central America) to art. Tell Dick to study the history of the five Central American republics. They illustrate very clearly the modern fallacy of supposing economics to be at the bottom of everything. In C A there were no economics, only evil passions. And the same is at least 50% true of Europe. Once more, the locusts, the crawling bugs.

Yours
Aldous

359: TO ROBERT NICHOLS

La Gorguette, Sanary (Var)
9 October, 1933

My dear Robert,

I was so glad to hear from Norah that you were going on as well as cd be expected. It will be a weary business for a bit, no doubt—sitting still and being a vegetable.

No news here: I go on with my travel book, which I think will turn out rather interesting, and in the intervals paint like mad. Really, it is the ideal art—involving one in nothing outside itself and having a technique which it is a pleasure to employ (when one thinks of the horror of using a pen or a typewriter!). I long, when I have reached a certain level of competence, to launch out on something more ambitious. It is deplorable that only bad painters shd now undertake important and intrinsically significant subjects and that good ones should live in terror of all that is obviously beautiful, or dramatic, or sublime. The Zeitgeist is a most dismal animal and I wish to heaven one cd escape from its clutches. There wd be more chance of doing so, I think, in an art which wasn't really one's own, an art one practised *en amateur* and for fun. When one is a professional, one begins to get a bit neurasthenic about technical problems; begins to fear doing things in the obvious way—to hanker for new methods—to grow inexpressibly bored with the old familiar devices. Rushing in where angels fear to tread, one has no such inhibitions: I feel that, if I had the necessary technical resources, I shd really enjoy painting a Last Judgment, an Apotheosis of President Roosevelt, the Circumcision of George V or any other scene of similar scale and sublimity. Whereas I shd have the greatest reluctance to undertake the same job in terms of literature.

Well, dear Robert, à bientôt, I hope; for we mean to try to get to England after Xmas. Flourish as best you can. (Did you know, by the way, (I didn't till the other day when I discovered it by chance) that the etymology of kidney is parallel to that of Cockney? Cockney=cock's egg and kidney= cod's egg; cod being the cod of peascod and meaning belly in this context.) Our love to you and to Norah.

Yours

A H

360: TO JULIAN HUXLEY

La Gorguette, Sanary (Var)
14 *October, 1933*

My dear Julian,

I was so sorry to hear of Anthony's accident. But what luck it wasn't worse. There are always such hideous potentialities for disaster in an event like that.

We have had a quiet summer—very busy with work on my travel book and painting for me and domesticities for M. We are at present engaged in making alterations in the house in the interest of economy of running— making the kitchen into a dining room and the veranda in front of it into a kitchen. Have also installed a geyser in the bathroom, worked by *butane*, which you buy in cylinders each of which provides you with a month of baths or cooking. An excellent invention: and I hope that the net result of all the changes will be that we can run the house more cheaply. At the present rate of exchange it costs a lot: but I hope that the French will find themselves forced off their perch of gold within the next few months. They have got to reduce real wages somehow, and, short of imposing reduction by force, devaluating their money is the only method.

Gerald was here for 10 days, very nice and more encyclopaedic than ever

360 *Anthony: the elder son of Julian and Juliette Huxley. He was born in* 1920; *his brother, Francis, in* 1923.

—also more pessimistic than ever, advising us all to clear out to some safe spot in South America or the Pacific islands before it is too late. He enjoys his glooms: but the fact does not necessarily mean that the glooms are unfounded. The German spectacle is really too frightening. Talking of that, we have had all the literary exiles here this summer—Thomas Mann, Heinrich Mann, [Julius] Meier-Graefe, and a rich selection of Jews such as [Lion] Feuchtwanger and Arnold Zweig. Rather a dismal crew, already showing the disastrous effects of exile. Let us hope we shall not have to scuttle when Tom [Sir Oswald] Mosley gets into power. I am leaving tonight for Paris to take part in a Congress under the presidency of Valéry—intellectuals discussing what if anything can be done to safeguard the intellect in the present state of affairs. It will probably be a futile affair, but there may be curious people there—particularly French politicians, whom I shd like to have a peep at. Besides we are to be received by the President at the Elysée; which shd provide at least one good laugh.

I hope to finish my book, which I think will be interesting, in about 6 weeks. Then shall take a brief holiday, if practicable, and come to England perhaps after Xmas. I'm so sorry Juliette is no better and that [——] manners—always atrocious!—are getting on her nerves. Perhaps he will succeed in spite of them: I do hope so. Send me a p.c. to say when you are speaking on the wireless—dates and times. I hear London Regional and National very well.

Love to you all from us both.

Yours

A.

361: TO MRS KETHEVAN ROBERTS

La Gorguette, Sanary (Var)
22 December, 1933

Dear Mrs. Roberts,

For some mysterious reasons parcels, in this country, are not delivered: so yours remained several days at the station before I cd go and fetch it. Hence this delay in thanking you for the record—which I thought extremely moving, not so much because the music itself is sublime, (because I don't think it's more than just ordinarily good), but because of the quality of the voices—so rich, with such depth. No other voices have it. I remember the first time I heard *Boris Godounov* with Chaliapine and a complete Russian company and choruses—the extraordinary impression the quality of the voices made on me. I can't think what it is due to: for after all Russian vocal cords must be very much the same as other people's vocal cords. *Mystère.* Anyhow, thank you very much indeed. I shall often listen to the record for that strange vocal quality of depth and religious passion. For me, the *music* that possesses that quality is the Beethoven 'Missa Solemnis' and bits of Mozart's 'Requiem' and his marvellous motet, 'Ave Verum Corpus'. The

Bach 'passions' are lovely and splendid beyond words—but lack this agonized, poignant quality.

It seems to me knowledge is not far enough advanced for any attempt at a cosmology to be more than an exercise of imagination. The different 'universes of discourse'—physical, biological, aesthetic etc—exist, each in its own right; but the connections which presumably exist between them are as yet undiscoverable. Their only unity consists in the fact that we can think in terms of all of them—and think effectively. One gets back to the Kantian notion of categories. We can't help selecting these aspects of reality, because that is how we happen to be made. So far as I can understand these matters—which is not very far!—the latest discoveries in physics leave the other universes of discourse exactly where they were before: they do not make values more valuable or less valuable. And the 19th-century supposition that 'iron laws of nature' and atoms like billiard balls somehow devalued values seems also to have been an irrelevance. Values exist in their own right in a universe of discourse of their own. Physics may talk of billiard balls or energy-quanta; but it's talk on the moon, whereas values inhabit Mars.

I have been looking again at that astonishing old monster, Vilfredo Pareto. What a prodigious monument that *Sociologia* is! Better than anything else of its kind, I think. But how depressing!

My book on Central America is finished and shd appear in April. I think it is quite interesting. I am thinking now about a novel. The theme, fundamentally, is liberty. What happens to someone who becomes really very free—materially first (for after all liberty must depend very largely on property) and then mentally and emotionally. The rather awful vacuum that such freedom turns out to be. But I haven't yet worked out the whole of the fable—only the first part.

I liked very much what you said of the *World of Light*. The imbecility of critics is really rather astonishing—their refusal to accept *real* characters and their insistence on attributing reality only to well-worn stage puppets. Almost equally few people are going to see it this time as last—the odd thing being that quite a lot of people have always gone whenever the play was done in the provinces—at Edinburgh, Liverpool, Brighton even. I believe it has something obscurely to do with the size of the towns. In a huge town people inevitably become suburban—London is just one vast suburb, except for a tiny intellectual nucleus. Whereas in smaller towns people as a whole are more *urban*, because they can feel themselves citizens of the place, can participate to some extent in the corporate life. But perhaps—probably!—this is all nonsense. Thank you once more.

Yours
Aldous Huxley

361 The World of Light *had opened for an advertised run of three weeks at the Playhouse, London, on 4 December.*

362: † TO HENRY E. RYLAND

La Gorguette, Sanary (Var)
[1933]

Dear Mr. Ryland

Thank you for your poems, which I return. I think "Away from my Woman" is the best as it is furthest away from the Laforgueian preciosities of the others—verbal ingenuities which I used to love and imitate, but which I now like a great deal less than I did. (Re-reading Laforgue the other day, I found I no longer admired the greater part of him at all—only the later plainer stuff and some of the prose.) The reason for using the Laforgueian devices is intrinsically commendable—a desire for brevity, for focussed and concentrated significance: but the particular nature of the device gives to the brevity something rather tinny, something (in an undesirable sense) artificial. I want my brevities to be achieved in some other way—my contrasts between fact and fancy, horror and the romantic, the weltanschauung of 1933 and that of tradition, to be made in different, less flashy terms. Not easy— but worth trying; particularly for one who obviously has, as you have, a certain genuine talent. This criticism of your stuff is also a criticism of my own.

Yours,
Aldous Huxley

363: TO THE HON. EDWARD SACKVILLE-WEST

La Gorguette, Sanary (Var)
5 March, 1934

My dear Eddy,

I wonder so much how you are getting on and how long you will be immobilized by your wretched accident. What miserable bad luck! I heard from Raymond the other day—a cheerful letter:—he seems to be well on the way to recovery. But I gather your damage was much more serious.

Maria has been away for a time—returns today, I am glad to say. But I had Sybille [von Schönebeck] to look after me, as she was *en disponibilité*, Eva [Herrmann] being absent skiing in Austria. Life trickles along very quietly here and it is from a great distance that one contemplates, with astonishment and horror, a world that, with Stavisky and the murder of M. Prince, grows more and more like Edgar Wallace and Bulldog Drummond

363 *Eva Herrmann and Sybille von Schönebeck, later Mrs Bedford, lived at Sanary. Stavisky: a notorious swindler who had died on 8 January in avoiding arrest, this incident being followed, on 21 February, by the gang murder of Albert Prince, a Paris judge.*

every day. The only exciting local news is that we are to have a bordel in La Gorguette—installed at the house occupied by Feuchtwanger, which is to be re-christened 'La Case à Papa'. So when you next come, you will know where to spend the tedious hours when inspiration flags and books seem to have lost their appeal.

The Germans are evaporating. [René] Schickele goes to Nice, the Manns have decided definitely on Florence—only Feuchtwanger seems determined to settle here. Fortunately he cannot find a house to suit him and, whenever I see him, I tell him about the really splendid villas one can find at Saint-Raphael and Agay.

We think of going to Italy for Easter, as we want to show Matthew Rome and I feel in need of a change of scene, being stickily entangled in a novel I can't quite find a satisfactory machinery for. Besides one must take a last glance at Rome before Musso definitely destroys it all. So far he has only destroyed about two thirds of it. I dread the spectacle of so much new devastation. It was bad enough when we were there last in 29 or 30: but he has knocked down whole quarters of the city since then—and what's worse put them up again in the form of fascist-baroque ferro-concrete buildings clustered round the holes in the ground where the new excavations are. It's all a fruit of political megalomania: acting the part of the Noblest Roman of Them All, he has to destroy everything that isn't imperial, genuine antique. The whole of the middle ages and baroque is doomed, as it doesn't lend itself to verbiage about *incrollabile volontà* and the imperial destinies of the race. What a weary imbecility it all is!

Meanwhile, *bonne santé*.

Ever yours
Aldous

364: TO T. S. ELIOT

La Gorguette, Sanary (Var)
[Circa 18 March, 1934]

My dear Tom,

Yes, I will certainly sign—do sign in fact, and return the letter herewith. Douglas may be wrong—tho' I can't detect the error in a good exposition of his theory, such as Marshall Hattersley's *This Age of Plenty*—but anyhow he—and Joddy—are obviously talking about something very important which ought to be looked into. The trouble is—who by? A royal commission wd be composed of and wd get evidence from experts—i.e. bankers and other financiers committed in advance to another theory. Still, I am all for trying

364 *Letter: a communication urging 'a thorough and public examination of some scheme of national credit'. This appeared in* The Times *of 5 April and was signed by Lascelles Abercrombie, Bonamy Dobrée, Eliot, Huxley, Hewlett Johnson, Edwin Muir, Hamish Miles, Herbert Read, and I. A. Richards.*

to get the thing considered seriously. I'm glad the young conservatives are also waking up to it. There seemed to be a lot of sense in Harold Macmillan's contentions.

We are off to Rome in a week's time, which I shall be glad to cast one last look at before Mussolini definitely destroys it all in order to dig up more rubbish heaps of imperial glory. Archaeology directed by politics is a very bad business indeed.

Yours
Aldous H.

365: TO MRS ROSALIND HUXLEY

La Gorguette, Sanary (Var)
24 March, 1934

My dear Rosalind,
Thank you for your letter and the cheque. So long as the boys are still being educated, I had rather not draw any money that may come from Prior's Field, which I regard as a family thing rather than a personal one. I am therefore returning you the cheque and the receipt: it seems a less complicated method than arranging legally for the interest to be paid to you. Dear Rosalind, I hope that, if the present crisis in Prior's Field affairs continues and the problem of the boys' education becomes more difficult, you will not hesitate to let me know; for I should like to be able to do anything within my power for David and Andrew.

We go tomorrow to Italy over Easter, and hope to be in England in May, when I look forward to seeing you.

Love from us both.

Ever your affectionate,
Aldous

366: TO T. S. ELIOT

La Gorguette, Sanary (Var)
28 April, 1934

My Dear Tom,
I returned yesterday from Italy, to find your letter of the twentieth. With regard to [Vilfredo] Pareto—yes, I will willingly look at a few specimen pages. They can be selected at random; for, as the book is in numbered sections, it is easy to find the place. The Italian is not difficult—fortunately; for it's a very hard language to read the moment it becomes at all rarefied— and I don't think any translator could go far wrong with it. I will also willingly

366 *Pareto:* The Mind and Society, *translated by Arthur Livingston. Huxley reviewed the book as 'Pareto's Museum of Human Stupidity',* New York Herald Tribune Books, *9 June, 1935.*

write an introduction, if you think it would do the book any good. Only wouldn't it be more suitable to have some sociological* pontiff do the job—seeing that it's definitely a scientific work, not at all an affair of belles lettres? Still, if you like and think fit, I shall enjoy saying something about the old man, because I like and admire the book so much. I had some fascinating details about him as an individual from old Carlo Placci, that astonishing professional friend of all the Great in every field of human activity. His character was exactly what it ought to have been, what the treatise would make you suppose it had been—with marvellous little touches such as, one would suppose, only a very good novelist could have invented.

As for selling the book .... All I can say is that, in both Italy and France it has gone into a second edition (of how many copies per edition, I don't know). The publishers, it is true, got it into fewer volumes. The Italian edition was three volumes of text and one of appendices and index. The French, I believe, has got itself into two volumes. But it may be that this edition is slightly abridged; I don't know. I think the psychological moment might be fairly auspicious; for it is obvious that Wellsian Progress doesn't cut much ice any more. Pareto is a prodigious debunker; but, at the same time, (which most debunkers are not) a realist, one who takes into account all the facts. Moreover, he doesn't, like these 'deep' and muddy Germans, invent gratuitous metaphysical entities to do the work which should be done by honest working hypotheses. The book is strictly scientific; and the old boy is perfectly aware of the limitations of the scientific method, also perfectly aware of its rights. He neither trespasses on other domains, nor allows other people to trespass on his. If there is a public anxious to see a bit clearly through the welter—and I think there is—then, I think, Pareto is their man. But whether this public has the money to buy five volumes is another question.

It rained without stopping all the time we were in Italy; and the strutting of the fascists, the cringing hypocritical acceptance of fascism by the masses were most depressing. We entered the country on the day of the election. Horrible, but interesting; for it was all an organized attempt at apotheosis—as for Caesar or Augustus. I happened to be reading Edwyn Bevan's *Later Greek Religion*, and his chapter on the deification of kings from Alexandrian times onwards was fantastically topical. One understands, in Italy and, I suppose, in Germany too, why the Jews and early Christians were so much concerned about idolatry. Indeed the whole world at present is given up to idolatry—state-worship, nation-worship, man-worship, organization-worship.

Yours,
Aldous H

*Note: Pareto was also an expert on mathematical economics—Pure Economy—and something shd be said about that. I cd only take that side of him on trust.

La Gorguette, Sanary (Var)
23 June, 1934

Cher ami,

De retour de Londres, j'ai trouvé hier votre lettre. En ce qui concerne [Lion] Feuchtwanger, je suis dans une situation un peu difficile: car je n'ai jamais lu un de ses livres. Donc, je ne puis en parler. Mais je suis naturellement tout prêt à me joindre aux autres en le félicitant personnellement sur son cinquantième anniversaire et en lui souhaitant toute espèce de bonnes choses. Je crois que le moyen le plus simple serait de le faire télégraphiquement comme si je l'avais félicité par fil. *'Congratulations and best wishes. Aldous Huxley.'* Je regrette que je ne peux pas faire mieux!

Je me sens un peu coupable envers vous et *Die Sammlung* pour ne vous avoir jamais écrit à propos de la revue. Mais le fait est que je lis très difficilement l'allemand et que, à cause de ma demi-cécité, je dois me rationner—me 'contingenter'—très strictement pour la lecture: donc il m'est matériellement presque impossible de me tenir au courant de ce qui paraît dans la *Sammlung*. Je le regrette beaucoup—mais le fait est là; et je suis heureux de prendre cette occasion pour vous assurer que, si j'ai tant négligé la *Sammlung*, c'est à cause, non d'une mauvaise volonté, mais d'une faiblesse physique, l'incapacité dans laquelle je me trouve de faire plus que je ne fais actuellement avec des yeux qui ne peuvent fournir qu'une quantité de travail strictement limitée.

367 TRANSLATION:—*'On returning from London, I found your letter yesterday. With regard to [Lion] Feuchtwanger, I am in a slightly difficult situation: for I have never read any of his books. Hence I cannot speak of them. But I am naturally quite ready to join the others in congratulating him personally on his fiftieth birthday and in wishing him good things of every kind. I think that the simplest means would be to do it in telegraphese as if I had been congratulating him by wire.* "Congratulations and best wishes. Aldous Huxley." *I am sorry I cannot do better!*

'I feel a little guilty towards you and Die Sammlung *for never having written to you about the review. But the fact is that I read German with great difficulty and, owing to my semi-blindness, I must ration myself—"quota" myself—very strictly as to reading: hence in terms of volume it is almost impossible for me to keep abreast of what appears in the* Sammlung. *I regret it very much—but such are the facts; and I am happy to take this occasion to assure you that, if I have so much neglected the* Sammlung, *it is owing not to unwillingness but to a physical weakness, the incapacity I find in myself to do more than I am currently doing with eyes which can afford only a strictly limited amount of work.*

'Meanwhile, I wish you all possible success. I hope that we shall have your father at Sanary this summer; but I have an idea that he has abandoned us for Italy. He is wrong: for Italy at present is one of the saddest countries in the world. At Easter, when we spent several weeks there, it was painfully brought home to me . Best wishes. . . .'

Mann's literary review, Die Sammlung, *published in Holland, was an organ of German writers in exile.*

En attendant, je vous souhaite tout le succès possible. J'espère que nous aurons votre père à Sanary cet été; mais j'ai l'idée qu'il nous a abandonnés pour l'Italie. Il a tort: car l'Italie actuellement est un des pays les plus tristes du monde. A Pâques, quand nous y avons passé quelques semaines, j'en étais péniblement impressioné.

Bien à vous
Aldous Huxley

368: TO JULIAN HUXLEY

La Gorguette, Sanary (Var)
22 *July,* 1934

My dear J,

What good news about the Zoo! I don't know what the disadvantages of the job are—but it seems to me to have a lot of advantages, from financial security to a house that, if my memory of its exterior does not fail me, compares not too unfavourably with that of the gorillas! When do you take possession?

Am pretty busy, as usual, scrabbling away at a novel, painting and doing some miscellaneous sociological and historical reading. Have also read rather an interesting book published this spring by Oxford University Press— *Yoga and Western Psychology*, by a woman called [Geraldine] Coster— containing what seems an excellent summary and analysis of Patanjali's teaching and a comparison between it and the recent developments of psychoanalysis. I've always felt that it was vitally necessary for people to have some efficient technique for personal development—for obviously sociological and mechanical improvements can't produce their best effects on people who are mentally and spiritually undeveloped and barbarous. It seems to me quite possible that some modification of this yoga technique may provide what's needed—the more so, as the author of this book points out, since it is as entirely independent of religion, in the current sense of the word, as Freudism —many Indian yogis being in fact atheists. Do read the book: it's quite short, and I think you'll find it full of interesting stuff.

Thank you for asking Matthew. We'd hesitated to ask you to put him up, because of the distance: it seems so far to hoick him up to Highgate from Paddington and hoick him down again to Victoria. I'm not absolutely sure if he's staying in London or going on by the late train to Paris the same day. If he stays, the arrangement is that he goes to Raymond Mortimer's. He leaves Dartington either on the Friday or the Saturday of next week—this week, rather, as today is Sunday. His time on Lundy seems to have been a great success. At any rate, he seems to have enjoyed himself: how good a

368 *Julian Huxley had been appointed Secretary of the Zoological Society of London.*

bird watcher he is I don't know! Our love to you both and to the children.
I hope Switzerland will be a success.

Yours
A.

P.S. The official description of Goebbels is:—nachgedunkelte Schrumpf-
Germane—an after-darkened shrink-German. I have tried to find out where
it was made, but without success: still, my German friends here swear it's
genuine.

369: TO N. SAGAR

La Gorguette, Sanary (Var)
12 September, 1934

Dear Mr. Sagar,

Thank you for your letter of Sept 7th. I expect to be in England from the
21st of this month onwards, so could discuss the subject of the article with the
Editor of *Nash's*. Meanwhile I make the following tentative suggestions:—

(1) An article on the subject of psychical research, dealing not so much
with the question of survival as with the evidence for and significance of
supernormal states of consciousness such as telepathy, and linking this up
with the wider problem of the training and development of consciousness—
'personal planning' as a necessary counterpart of social planning.

(2) An article on Propaganda—the new instrument of government of
which increasing use is being made in all countries, especially dictatorial
ones. Discuss its present limitations and its possibilities, both for good and
evil, in the light of history and recent scientific developments.

Yours truly
Aldous Huxley

P.S. I expect to be leaving this address on the 19th. The Athenaeum, Pall
Mall, S.W.1, will find me on my arrival in London: but in any case I shall
ring up the office.

370: TO RUSSELL GREEN

The Athenaeum, Pall Mall, S.W.1
1 October, 1934

My dear Russell,

Sorry not to have written before; but I was exceedingly busy and have
only just had time to finish *Prophet Without Honour*. If I were reviewing the
book, I should say of it that it fell between two stools—the stool of the
novel of a developing personality and the stool of the novel of social history.

369 *Sagar was a member of Pinker's London staff.*
370 *Green has written several semi-autobiographical* romans à clef *as well as an*
unpublished memoir.

The book, it seems to me, is neither the story of its hero's mental and emotional unfolding, nor yet the story of an industrial town in the middle of the 19th century. It is a bit of both, but not quite either. The form of the hero is constantly being veiled, as it were, by the form of the town; but the town hardly gets its full share of the limelight because of the hero, whose social position in the world happens to be such that his individual life has no perceptible influence on the life of the town and is not particularly illustrative of social history. I don't see, as a matter of technique, that it's possible to write a novel that shall be at once personal and social unless one at least of the principal characters is in some sort a social symbol, a paradigm of the whole life of the community. Your tallyman is not a paradigm—rather an exception to the industrial rule of his time and place; the result is that your evocations of the history of the town, excellent as they are, have a certain irrelevance to the main theme—an irrelevance, it seems to me, that makes you afraid to go on with them too long, so that you break off just when the reader is getting thoroughly interested in your social history. The total effect, I found, is one of indeterminacy. There is a certain vagueness in the central structure of the book, a vagueness that robs its excellent details and decorations of a great deal of their charm and value.

I am afraid you will feel that this criticism is captious and unjust; but it is what a careful reading of the book suggests to me, and I have too much respect for you personally and as a judge of letters not to tell you what I think, as a literary critic, about *Prophet Without Honour*. I will sum up my criticism by saying that I regard the book as a novel of parts (in all senses of the word!), but hardly a whole. If you still feel after all this that you'd like to, I hope you'll come and lunch with me one day—say Monday or Tuesday of next week, here, at about 1.15.

Yours ever
Aldous H.

371: TO MRS FLORA STROUSSE

*The Athenaeum, Pall Mall, S.W.*1
13 *October,* 1934

Dear Starkey,

I have been unforgivably long without writing. A sort of horror at any kind of personal contact with people, other than those in the immediate neighbourhood—and even with those!—has kept me sealed in a shell for months. A mania, really—though having an excuse in a self-preservative husbanding of my small resources of physical and therefore psychological

371 *The Huxleys, after stopping temporarily at Dalmeny Court, had moved to* 18 *St Alban's Place, S.W.*1; *but in mid-December they moved again, to E*2 *Albany, Piccadilly, while Maria Huxley was still recovering from an illness which had required a stay in hospital.*

energy. Probably a mistaken notion, this husbanding. For it may well be that it's by pouring energy out that one renews the stores of it. One's ideal, I dare say, should be, not the snail, but the slug—naked, not armoured. Unless one is vulnerable, one probably never learns to be strong; and spending, more spending, is perhaps the cure of the personal, psychological slump just as it seems to be the cure of the social and economic one.

We are in London for the winter—having found a studio flat, miraculously large, cheap and quiet, within 200 yards of this club and 200 of Piccadilly Circus, at the very navel of metropolitan life. I work at a difficult novel about the problem of freedom, do a bit of painting when I have the time, read a little, see a certain number of people. London is cheerful on the whole. The English have convinced themselves that they are well off at the moment and are acting accordingly—which appears to have the same result as *being* well off.

How are you? Well, I hope. Forgive me my intolerably bad manners.

Yours
Aldous Huxley

372: † TO NORMAN DOUGLAS

18 *St. Alban's Place, S.W.*1
13 *October,* 1934

Dear Norman,

I have heard of Guyon's book—*De la Légitimité des Actes Sexuelles,* I think it is called in French—but have not read. Shall do so, however—with a great interest after your recommendation. A book about this subject which you pronounce a *revelation* must, I feel, be remarkable! I didn't imagine there were any revelations any more! Certainly Dr. Norman Haire's *Encyclopaedia of Sexual Knowledge,* which I have been asked to review, contains nothing new. The same set of odd anecdotes from Havelock Ellis and Kraf[f]t-Ebing, with a few similar ones added from more recent experience. But always the old depressing picture of people like automata going through their absurd actions under psychological compulsion—chewing guardsmen's dirty socks, masturbating over boots, etc. Comic, but also, I find, rather depressing. One feels that Homo Sapiens might think of something rather better.

We are here for the winter in a studio flat—2 bedrooms, large studio, kitchen and bath—within 150 yards of Piccadilly Circus, at £5 a week—altogether a miracle. It is very quiet and I manage to do a certain amount of work and even some painting in the afternoons.

I hope you flourish. Did you see the excellent [David] Low cartoon of Musso drilling an army of babies in black diapers armed with bayoneted rifles? Very good.

Maria sends her love. Tante cose from us both to Pino.

Yours
Aldous

373: TO J. RALPH PINKER

The Athenaeum, Pall Mall, S.W.1
25 October, 1934

Dear Ralph,

Here are the letters, duly signed.

I was seeing poor old J. W. N. Sullivan yesterday, who was in a state of some distress about a debt he had incurred to you—I gather in connexion with some contract with the Viking Press. I don't know what the circumstances are—except that Sullivan is always extremely dilatory and unreliable. At the moment, however, he has some justification for his dilatoriness; for he has entered the first stages of an incurable paralysis, and this has naturally upset him a great deal and interfered with his work. However, he's resigned himself rather heroically to the situation and, as he's still well enough to work, is actually working pretty hard, I think. So that he should be able to repay you fairly soon. Meanwhile, I shall ask you to let me guarantee the debt— or rather to pay it provisionally out of any monies which may come in to my account with you. As Sullivan's earnings come in, you can pay them back into my account to the amount of the debt. I shouldn't want you to mention this arrangement to Sullivan, of course. Merely tell him that the debt can be repaid in instalments as he earns it. In this way he won't be worried—which incidentally will help him to work better and earn more effectively!—and at the same time you won't be out of pocket in regard to a debt which, though not, I am convinced, a bad debt, may take a bit of time to liquefy itself. Sullivan is a very old friend of mine, and I am glad to have this opportunity to spare him even this small worry during the exceedingly bad time he is going through and will have to go through in the future.

Yours
Aldous H.

374: TO H. G. WELLS

The Athenaeum, Pall Mall, S.W.1
11 November, 1934

Dear H. G.,

I don't know whether you have heard of the disaster which has overtaken poor J. W. N. Sullivan. He has developed creeping paralysis—of some kind which the doctors don't appear to be able to diagnose, much less cure— which has already affected his legs and is destined to attack the arms next and then the trunk, finally the speech and mental faculties. He can still work— and is doing so; but I don't know how long he will be able to keep it up, the more so as, quite apart from the paralytic symptoms, he looks very ill and run down. Various of his friends are now getting together—without Sullivan's knowledge, of course—to get up a little fund to be used for his maintenance when it should become necessary—enough to tide over at

386

least the first period of his incapacity, until some sort of permanent arrangement for his support can be made. [Sydney] Waterlow, Sydney Schiff (I hope), Milne of the British Museum, Koteliansky and I hope to put up about £200 between us; and if you felt you could add something to the fund, I should be more than grateful. I'm sorry to worry you with this; but the disastrous nature of the case must serve as sufficient excuse.

Yours
Aldous H.

375: TO H. G. WELLS

The Athenaeum, Pall Mall, S.W.1
[November, 1934]

Dear H. G.,

That really was nice of you to send me the autobiography! Thank you very much indeed. I had read part of the earlier sections, with much pleasure and profit, and now look forward to going on to the rest.

Thank you once more.

Yours
Aldous H.

376: TO MRS SALLY HANDLEY

The Athenaeum, Pall Mall, S.W.1
9 December, 1934

My dear Sally,

I have been a monster not to write before and thank you for your charming letter and for the present. But you know how it is—one damned thing after another, so that there's no time or place for the undamned things, the pleasant, human, friendly things, like writing to you.

I suppose you have been in a turmoil of preparations and packings—interspersed, no doubt, with the usual Sallyesque motor accidents, attempted murders by charwomen, missed trains, mislaid cars and infuriated friends to be pacified by means of those magnificent fictions over the telephone. Here I do a fair amount of work—articles, bits of my novel—and have had to make another discourse for charity, a full length lecture, this time, in the drawing room (like Lyons' Corner House at its gaudiest) of Sir Philip Sassoon's house in Park Lane. In the intervals, we dash out and try to find furniture, cheap, for the new flat—into which we move, God willing (which

375 Wells's Experiment in Autobiography *appeared as two volumes in October and November.*
376 Sally Handley *and her husband, Major Leonard Handley, were an Anglo-Indian couple whom the Huxleys had first met at Sanary in 1930. Mrs Handley lectured at the Victoria League.*

it seems likely He won't do) next Saturday. If we don't succeed, we shall have to sleep on the Embankment, as we seem to have succeeded in letting our present abode from that date. Such is life in the great West. I hope it will be better in the great East. Tho', frankly, I doubt it! Much love to you, dear Sally, from us both, as also to Len.

Ever your affectionate
Aldous

377: † TO PAUL VALÉRY

Hôtel Perez, Paris VIIIe
7 January, 1935

Cher Valéry,

Me voici, ayant accepté—sans me rendre compte, comme je le constate actuellement, de tout le travail que l'acceptation comportait—de faire une série d'articles pour *Paris-Soir* sur la situation en France au début de 1935, vue par un étranger naturellement. La seule personne à *Paris-Soir* qui soit au courant de la chose est absente jusqu'à mercredi, et j'ai dû me débrouiller de mon mieux pour arranger des entretiens avec des hommes représentatifs. J'espère être reçu en audience par M. Mallarmé (ne pas confondre) et de pouvoir ensuite jeter un regard sur la machine éducatrice française. Mais si, de votre côté, vous pouviez me donner un mot pour quelque savant—avec la possibilité peut-être de visiter les installations scientifiques, laboratoires, etc—je vous serais très reconnaissant.

En attendant j'espère que j'aurai le plaisir de vous voir. Peut-être déjeunez-vous quelquefois en ville? En tout cas je voudrais venir une après-midi présenter mes hommages à Madame Valéry.

Bien sincèrement vôtre
Aldous Huxley

377 TRANSLATION:—'*Here I am, having agreed—without realising, as I do now, the amount of work the undertaking involves—to do a series of articles for* Paris-Soir *on the situation in France at the outset of 1935, naturally from a foreigner's point of view. The only person at* Paris-Soir *who is in touch with the thing is away till Wednesday, and I have had to cut through red-tape as well as I could in order to arrange interviews with representative men. I hope to be received in audience by M. Mallarmé (not to be confused with . . .) and then to be able to take a look at the French educational machine. But if, for your part, you could write me a word to some scientist—with the possibility that I might visit scientific installations, laboratories, etc.—I should be most grateful to you.*

'*Meanwhile I hope to have the pleasure of seeing you. Perhaps you sometimes have lunch in town? In any case I should like to come one afternoon to pay my respects to Madame Valéry. Yours very sincerely. . . .*'

Huxley *frequently closed his letters in French with* 'Bien sincèrement vôtre' *having noticed that Gide did so. M. Mallarmé was André Mallarmé, the Minister of National Education.*

E2 *Albany, Piccadilly, W.*1
13 *January,* 1935

My dear Robert,

Your letter has been a long time reaching me. It went first to Sanary, then here—but we were away in the country after Christmas, and from the country I went direct to Paris to do a bit of journalistic work for a French paper on 'la France au seuil de l'année 1935', which meant scurrying about seeing countless people from Communist mayors of Parisian suburbs to schoolmasters and cabinet ministers—till I was in such a state of exhaustion that I returned here for a respite and found your letter waiting. I'm sorry to hear about the persistent insomnia. I had a spell of it recently and found I could do something to help the drugs by means of breathing exercises of the Yoga sort with accompanying mental concentration and finally attempted elimination of irrelevant thoughts and feelings—the latter a very difficult process which I don't pretend ever to have succeeded in mastering. The bore of this Yoga mind control is that it's so frightfully difficult and takes so long— also that it probably demands a pretty careful regulation of diet and sexual habits. But even tho' one mayn't have the energy to go through with the process, I think quite a lot can be done in the way of securing a certain serenity by means of breathing. Gerald Heard has often spoken to me of the work of a man called Dr. E[dmund] Jacobson on relaxation; but I have never read it and can only speak by hearsay of his methods which I believe are very good. Anyhow, I have a considerable belief in such psycho-physical methods of mind and body control. Do you think it will be wise, in your present state—with insomnia hanging over you—to re-embark at once on the 'Don'? Nothing is more inclined to keep me awake than word-hunting and the wrestling with difficult technical problems. I should have thought you wd do better to try for a bit the effect of some other and quite different kind of job—e.g. in the movies or even as a lecturer. Something not requiring the fearful mental tension of versification and poetic invention, but at the same time moderately interesting and involving contact with a number of new people. It is a good thing, I think, when one has been knocked out of one's balance by circumstances to have some external job or duty to hang on to. Writing has the merits—which in certain circumstances [are] the defects— of being an entirely individual job, offering no support but what one can supply from within. Whereas when one's ill or unhappy, one needs something outside oneself to hold one up. It's like the famous Consolations of Philosophy which console only those who are strong. I am afraid that you may find the writing of poetry, not a distraction and a support, but an *in*traction—a drawing in on yourself—and a drain on your strength.

378 *The Huxleys had spent a few days after Christmas visiting Sir William Jowitt at Wittersham, Kent.*

I liked Phisbo [*Fisbo*] very much indeed. There are really magnificent passages in it. The only bits I felt any doubts about were the conversational passages. For I really don't believe that verse is a satisfactory medium for rendering the idiosyncrasies of talk—that is unless it's verse in dramatic form that can be broken up *ad libitum*. I never feel comfortable with Browning's most completely *talked* poems, and found something of the same malaise in certain passages of Phisbo. But this may be merely a personal idiosyncrasy and not valid criticism.

I am sending this to your London address in case you have moved away from Munich. We expect to be here for a bit longer—tho' I may have to go to France again for a day or two for these beastly articles I have so stupidly engaged myself to do. M. sends her love, as do I, dear Robert.

Yours
Aldous H.

379: TO MRS KETHEVAN ROBERTS

*The Athenaeum, Pall Mall, S.W.*1
13 *January*, [1935]

Dear Mrs. Roberts,

The description of your hellish town makes me feel ashamed of being here, leading my 'godlike life', as you call it. I sometimes have the disquieting sense that I am being somehow punished by so much good fortune—that it is a scheme to lead me deeper into my besetting sin, the dread and avoidance of emotion, the escape from personal responsibility, the substitution of aesthetic and intellectual values for moral values—of art and thought for sanctity.

I have been in France for a few days [. . . .]

I have been working a fair amount, but with not much results, as I am in chronic trouble with my book and have been sleeping rather badly. In the intervals have read bits of [Léon] Brunschvicg's book on the *Progress of Consciousness*; some Groddeck on *Psycho-Analysis*—interesting but alarming: for if the human psyche is as profoundly anti-rational as he makes out, then really it's a bad look out. Also Kretschmer on *Physique and Character* —very interesting and, to judge by one's own casual experience, full of truth. Bertrand Russell's book on 19th century history, tho' not good as a whole, was excellent if regarded as a series of essays on different aspects of the time— Marxism, Philosophical Radicalism and so forth. Have seen only one play, *Hamlet*, acted by John Gielgud—very well, I thought. And what a play it is! Everything else seems so empty beside it. I think it is the work of art with the greatest amount of substance ever put into words. I really don't know why one goes on writing when one sees what writing can be—and what one's own writing is not.

379 *Misdated* '13.i.34'.

Goodbye. I hope your nightmare will become a little less nightmarish as time goes on: or that some escape will be possible.

Yours
AH

380: † TO E. M. FORSTER

*The Athenaeum, Pall Mall, S.W.*1
17 February, 1935

Dear Forster,

I'm so sorry not to have answered your letter before. I have been in France for about ten days—to collect material for some articles I agreed to write, as a foreigner, on *La France au seuil de* 1935, and which I've finally declined to write, not having sufficient effrontery to pour out my opinions on a subject of which, the more I look into it, the less I find I know. The main result is that I'm sadly out of date with my correspondence.

About the London Library—I feel about Italian Literature even more strongly and for yet better reasons than I feel about *La France au seuil* etc. I really don't know anything about it—have read very few recent Italian books (and thought most of those I read pretty bad). So if it's as an expert on Italian that I'm wanted, I'm afraid it's no good at all my coming in. Surely Orlo Williams is the man: he has read every inch of spaghetti that has ever emerged from the Italian presses.

We have taken a flat in Albany, Piccadilly (number E2)—and I hope so much you'll come and see us when you're in town. Telephone is Regent 2870. It would be very nice indeed to see you.

I share your gloom about the period, and add to it a considerable gloom about myself. Bertie Russell, whom I've just been lunching with, says one oughtn't to mind about the superficial things like ideas, manners, politics, even wars—that the really important things, conditioned by scientific technique, go steadily on and up (like the eternal feminine, I suppose) in a straight, un-undulating trajectory. It's nice to think so; but meanwhile there the superficial undulations are, and one lives superficially: and who knows if that straight trajectory isn't aiming directly for some fantastic denial of humanity? Anyhow, I do hope you'll let us know when you're next in town.

Yours
Aldous Huxley

381: TO HAROLD RAYMOND

Merton Hall, Cambridge
25 February, 1935

My dear Harold,

I ought to have thanked you before for your very kind and generous letter—but this sleeplessness leaves one in a sorry state of incapacity to do

391

anything. If, as I hope, I get over the state fairly soon, I trust to have the
book finished by next autumn. Otherwise—God knows. Meanwhile, I
don't want to let my indebtedness to Chatto's pile up; and, seeing that I can
live on my own resources for a time, I think it will be best if you suspend
payments till I get properly under weigh again.

Meanwhile, I thank you again very much. Give my love to Vera.

Yours
Aldous H.

382: TO THOMAS MANN

[La Gorguette, Sanary (Var)]
April, 1935

From one who is still a citizen of Sanary to one who, alas, has migrated
elsewhere, birthday greetings and cordial good wishes for happiness and
health! I am looking forward to the time when Mario the Magician shall
change his name to Marius and settle, at least for the duration of a short
story or even (would it be too much to hope?) for that of a whole novel,
nearer his native Marseille and this village, where I hope I may soon have
the pleasure of seeing you, dear Thomas Mann, once again.

Yours
Aldous Huxley

383: MARIA HUXLEY TO ROY FENTON

La Gorguette, Sanary (Var), France
4 May, 1935

My dear Roy,

I was so glad to get your long letter addressed here though you don't
seem to have received mine sent from London; with *my* account of our
evening at your mothers and with the story attached to the importation of
the longed-for Quetzal; nor either my gloomy account of that winter, as
grey as it was gloomy. But I shall not go back to that because now we are in
the summer, in a bright country even if the season is bad and we are cheerful.
Aldous has suffered for more than six months from insomnia and all that
therefrom necessarily follows in the way of gloom, irritation, lack of work
and so on. But he is cured, definitely cured, it seems since about a month.
Work goes well and everything goes well.

Work goes madly as a matter of fact. He is finishing a novel already born
when we were out to you so you see what it means: the strain was terrific.
I am typing it out; some of it already, and that is always a sign that it nears

*382 Written for a collection of tributes to Mann on his sixtieth birthday. The
curious reference to 'Mario and the Magician' suggests that Huxley may not have
been familiar with the story. His acquaintance with Mann was to be renewed in
California.*

completion. Apart from that we lead the peasant's life with painting in the afternoon and a lot of reading [so] the days are as much too short as they are in your full-crop days.

[. . . .]

As for literary gossip there is none I know of. We have been reading chiefly easy or more difficult scientific books of interest to Aldous and which I read with great gusto. We sit about in our garden as we would sit on a Liner: deck-chairs, rugs and all and laugh at ourselves for it is inconceivable that we should not already be wearing shorts and bathing and complaining of the heat.

I have done a lot of 'good-housekeeping' lately, I say with rather a sigh, for I do not get to like it and prefer weeding the garden, or mending fuses. We have had such an abundance of cherries that not with the help of all the friends and servants and neighbours have we been able to eat them, so they have been preserved in all ways possible. Bottled, made into jams, made into queso, like membrillo, under alcohol, and into syrop. This is all the harder work because my cook cannot read and the maid has a baby which she must go to always just at the most critical moment so that I am often left with a boiling syrop literally in my hands. Last night we sat in the kitchen, I on a stool above the gas-range turning a lovely bubbling red juice in a copper saucepan reading aloud to Aldous who was sitting far below, a book on the history of philosophy . . . and the jam was not burnt. We finished at eleven thirty and it is now only sad to think that except the children and a few guests no one eats jam in this house. . . .

But what is more comic still is that Aldous has decided to take violent exercise for the sake of his health and that that exercise is the most concisely found in the form of gardening. So he digs every spare inch of the ground and causes havoc all round him to the despair of the gardener who is very good this year. My despair is compensated by the fact that I believe it to be good for him. We put in a lot of soya beans to be 'à la page' but don't know how we shall eat them when they are ready, or even what will be the moment they are ready. Now there is nothing left to do but dig a well and find no water ever, so that will be a good long task. What a pity we cannot replace all that with some good riding in the cafetales.

[. . . .]

Maria

384: TO E. MCKNIGHT KAUFFER

La Gorguette, Sanary (Var)
[Circa May, 1935]

My dear Ted,

I'm so glad to hear Spain's a success, and hope your painting is ditto. Are you oiling or water-colouring or gouaching? I've been so busy with my bloody book that I've hardly painted at all—for I find the strain as great as that of writing, if not greater: and that I can't manage hard writing and painting at the same time.

Which way do you go to Seville? It's worth spending an hour at Cadiz—for the sake of its strange position and for the lovely 18th century Andalusian architecture of San Fernando on the neck of the long peninsula leading out to it. At Jerez don't get too drunk in the sherry cellars—at any rate not so drunk that you can't go out 2 miles to the Cartuja, where in the old monastery is a collection of stallions for the army remount department—mostly Arab and Andalusians, the most beautiful animals you ever saw.

At Toledo stay at least a night. It's a marvellous town to walk in after dark—specially if, as is practically certain, you lose your way. Drive to the other side of the river to look at the town from the point where Greco painted his picture of it. The main Grecos are easily visible—at his house and in S. Vincente. Then there is 'Count Orgaz'—wh. I never thought one of his best. And don't fail to go out to the hospital—I forget its name—where there is a very late baptism—most instructive to compare with the earlier, middle-period picture of the same theme in Madrid. The greatest knockout is the 'Assumption' at S. Vincente, where there are also some small pictures of absolutely staggering beauty—I remember specially one of a child Saint walking with a very tall man. At Madrid, the Savoy is a good hotel, immediately opposite the Prado. Going North it may be worth making a slight detour to look at Avila or Segovia: Roman aqueduct at the latter, fine churches, mediaeval walls and St. Teresa at the latter [*i.e.*, the former]—also a most extraordinary position and a market that looks like Mexico when the peasants come in—incredibly poor and remote and non-European.

I have collected stuff on dreams. But there really isn't much point in making an elaborate theoretical discourse. Everything depends on what we can do in practice. The theory will largely have to adapt itself to the photography. I think the most illustratable common dreams—for it's clear we must stick to common dreams—are flying dreams; dreams of terror (with ferocious animals or what not); dreams of paralysis; dreams of being naked in public. Whether it's possible or worth while to illustrate a psychological conflict finding expression in dreams and having its symbols interpreted, I very much doubt.

Our love to you both.

Yours
Aldous

385: TO JULIAN HUXLEY

La Gorguette, Sanary (Var)
17 *May*, 1935

My dear J,

I was glad to hear from you and that the installation in the Zoo was taking place without too exorbitant a strain. I suppose you will soon be inhabiting the flat.

I have been dithering along with various downs as well as ups. At the moment, thank heaven, have an up in progress and am sleeping quite well with the aid of a wholly non-toxic mixture of calcium and magnesium, which, for some extraordinary reason, acts as a nervous sedative and mild hypnotic. I recommend it if ever you get too much badgered by existence: it's called *Calsédine* (made in France), does no harm, produces (so my doctor swears) no habituation, and leaves one perfectly fresh and cheerful in the morning. With its aid, I do a fair amount of work—and about time too, as I have earned very little for a long time past. Have also taken to digging in the garden—like Tolstoy—as a sleep-producing exercise. How grateful one can be to Providence for making one an intellectual!

If you see [Alexander] Korda, casually mention *Brave New World* by all means and see what his reactions are. I saw him several times this winter and he was very amiable. It is more or less arranged that Ted Kauffer and I shall do some shorts for him—on psychological themes such as Dreams (a bit of fun there, what with Freudian interpretations and trick photography); Hand-reading and graphology, and hands in general; survival of superstitions in modern times (have just come across a charming advertisement in the French equivalent of *Radio Times*—an ad for a brochure that will explain 'la divination par T.S.F.'). I wanted very much to do a short on Physique and Character and have indeed prepared it: but that requires a lot of people to act the different types of schizothymes and pyknics, or a great deal of field work; so for the moment that's being left aside. If Korda hasn't changed his mind, we shd start on the scheme this autumn. Meanwhile, I hope to get my book done by the end of the summer, if this beastly insomnia gives me the chance. It has been cold here and rainy, but pleasant none the less. Mme de Béhague and the Noailles have gone—a relief, au fond: for, tho' nice, they have the rich persons' inability to conceive that other people have anything better to do than eat lunches and teas in their houses. Poor Edith Wharton has had a slight stroke and is still here—indeed we are just off to see her; so I must stop. Our love to you both.

Yours

A.

386: TO JULIAN HUXLEY

La Gorguette, Sanary, Var
5 June, 1935

My dear J,

Old Henri Barbusse is trying to organize a mammoth congress in favour of peace, for the armistice day of this year. His hobby is congresses and he has already organized one peace demonstration—at Amsterdam in 32, I think. But this first congress was predominantly left; and there is a natural tendency for the public to mistrust peace when associated with communists. So he wants to have a really representative anti-war congress this time. His own left organizations in France will of course be on tap; he can also get the Catholic organizations; he has the adhesion of various individual scientists, including Langevin and the Jol[i]ot-Curies, and is going to try to get professional bodies—scientific, technical, legal, etc—to send representatives to the Committee. This last scheme I very strongly urged him to go for with all his might; for if these congresses are any good at all they will only be good, (because impressive) if they represent large numbers of respectable organizations. A peace demonstration would look serious if it were supported by the trade unions of doctors, engineers, lawyers, scientists and so forth in different countries. Individual eminences are all right; but their importance, in this context, is greatly magnified if they represent professional organizations. I am writing therefore to ask you whether you think there'd be any hope of getting official representation from some important scientific body in England. If there's such a chance, I would tell old man Barbusse to write direct to it in the name of his committee. He's a dear old thing, indefatigable in verbiage and good works, and exactly like a clergyman of the old, pre-jocular-Christian school, droning interminably not, as his prototype would have done, about Conscience and Heaven, but about the Social Consciousness and Russia—ignoring all facts and merely stating, again and again, what ought to be. But as he enjoys organizing things and writing, as he boasts, two thousand letters a month, he's the perfect man for the job; and he will have more distinguished Frenchmen round him, as well as Swiss, Dutch etc. This being so, I think he's deserving; and if there are to be peace congresses, it is obviously desirable that they should be as effective as possible. So let me know what you think.

Talking of Congresses, I have been blackmailed into promising to attend an international writers' congress in favour of free speech in Paris, on the 21st of this month. It will be an intolerable bore, but I think it's a duty to *faire acte de présence*. It is possible that after that I may come for a day or two to London, as I have various things to do and to look up in libraries.

Am sleeping rather better now, with a minimum of dope, and that of a purely non-toxic nature—a concoction of magnesium and calcium phosphate, so can do a fair amount of work, which is a comfort. Weather here has been atrocious, heavy rain until the last few days, occasioning a positively biblical plague of snails. Hope you're by now installed in the new flat.

Love from us both to you and Juliette.

Yours,

A.

387: TO VICTORIA OCAMPO

Sanary
[June, 1935]

Dear Victoria,

On second thoughts I'm not sending you the speech I made at the literary

Congress. I want to do some more work on it before it is published—and at the moment have absolutely no time to look at it.* The Congress was, of course, a great disappointment. I had hoped for serious, technical discussion between writers—but in fact the thing simply turned out to be a series of public meetings organized by the French Communist writers for their own glorification and by the Russians as a piece of Soviet propaganda. Amusing to observe, as a rather discreditable episode in the Comédie Humaine; but it made one angry when one thought of what might have been done and wasn't, when one saw the cynical indifference of the Communist organizers to the wretched little delegates from the Balkans etc, who had come hoping for some serious effort on the part of other writers to understand their problems, and who found no opportunity of discussing them but only endless Communist demagogy in front of an audience of 2000 people. One finds on these occasions all the worst aspects of religion—the refusal of some to use their intelligence, because they need the consolation of faith; and the cynical ambition of others, who don't believe anything but are anxious to rise in the Communist hierarchy. And everywhere a complete indifference to truth and the common decencies of civilized existence.

Drieu is here in the neighbourhood, for the summer—not very well; but cheerful when we saw him. I am better, but still horribly busy. So is Maria—for we have had various guests staying. En attendant, we send our love.

Yours
Aldous

*I am sending instead an article I did recently for the *N.Y Herald Tribune* on Pareto. If you don't mind its having appeared in English and if it interests you, make what use of it you like.

388: TO ROBERT NICHOLS

La Gorguette, Sanary, Var
20 September, 1935

My dear Robert,
    [. . . .]
I'm sure you're wise in wanting to prepare yourself for further stage writing by learning all about the theatre. If only theatrical people weren't almost invariably so awful! Why is it that when one enters that world, one always finds oneself with crooks, imbeciles, narcissus complexes, grotesquely inflated egotisms of every variety? Partly no doubt it's a historical accident that these creatures should be where they are; but I suspect also that, in the nature of things, the actor has got to be vain, inflated, unstable and stupid. One must just accept and make the best of the messy and unpalatable medium.

Here I'm hard at work on a novel that won't get finished. Expect to be in England in another month or so—unless of course we're plunged in war by then. In which case we shall probably all be dead. I wish I could see any remedy for the horrors of human beings except religion or could see any religion that we could all believe in.

Yours,
Aldous

389: TO VICTORIA OCAMPO

E2 Albany, London, W.1
19 November, 1935

My dear Victoria,

Thank you so much for the trouble you have taken in making arrangements for lectures. I accept your suggestions for 3 lectures with the Amigos and one before the Jockey Club with pleasure. You must tell me what sort of things they want to be lectured about.

We are here in London again—settling down after a most disturbed few weeks. First we had to go to Belgium for the marriage of Maria's youngest sister [Rose]: then we had endless trouble about poor [——] who was on the point of being deported from England. It's an epic story which I will tell you *viva voce*. I am working at my book and in the interval talking over ways and means, with Gerald, for getting an adequate pacifist movement onto its feet. The thing finally resolves itself into a religious problem—an uncomfortable fact which one must be prepared to face and which I have come during the last year to find it easier to face. Meanwhile what an appalling situation we've all got ourselves into! Musso attacking Abyssinia: we using sanctions and so forcing the Italians to rally round Musso: the dictator's *amour propre* so septically inflamed—like a boil on his face—that he can't admit any kind of defeat or make any compromise; and if he is forced into a corner he will act like Samson and pull the whole building down on his head —if he has got to go, then let the whole of Europe go too! It's the sort of behaviour one saw going on at one's preparatory school—and the whole world is threatened by it. The only hope lies in the pacifists being better disciplined than the militarists and prepared to put up with as great hardships and dangers with a courage equal to theirs. Not easy. But I suppose nothing of any value is easy. Maria sends her love, as do I.

A bientôt, I hope. When are you coming over?

Yours
Aldous

389 *Rose Nys was married to Baron Eric de Haulleville.*

390: TO THE REV. H. R. L. SHEPPARD

Tredegar Park, Newport,
Monmouthshire
19 January, 1936

Dear Sheppard,

I was so sorry you cd not come the other day and still more sorry when I learned the reason. I hope so much that you will soon be over your troubles.

I enclose L[aurence] Housman's letter, which I read with interest. It seems to me that the point at issue is only one of terminology. Humanism, as he defines it, is not the same as humanism, according to Marxians, which was the humanism I was talking about. I accept his humanism, but not the other. It is all a matter of defining one's terms before using them. I made the mistake in my talk of not doing so—an intellectual offence which I will try not to repeat in the future.

Yours
Aldous Huxley

391: TO DOUGLAS GLASS

E2 Albany, W.1
30 January, 1936

Dear Mr. Glass,

I understand from Potocki that the report of his trial is with your papers abroad and that it is difficult for you to get at it. If it is a matter of getting someone on the spot to look it out and send it, I will gladly meet any reasonable expenses involved; for I consider it very important, as you know, that Potocki shd if possible get this book done, for his own sake first of all and also because I think that the book will be of value at the present time, when the police and Attorney General seem to be embarking on a new campaign against freedom of expression.

Yours
Aldous Huxley

392: MARIA HUXLEY TO EUGENE F. SAXTON

E2 Albany, W.1
[21 February, 1936]

Dear Gene,

How nice to know that we shall see you soon as we shall certainly be in England when you come. So hurry along. Aldous really thinks he is going to answer your letter but I know better and that is why I am doing it and trying to give you a few answers. They will be vaguer than if Aldous gave

390 The Rev. H. R. L. Sheppard was active in the Peace Pledge Union and maintained an information centre at Walton-on-Thames. Huxley had so far overcome his dread of the lecture platform as to give talks advocating pacifism. The heading of this letter, Tredegar Park, shows that Huxley had paid a visit to Evan Morgan.

them to you but I hope they will be better than nothing; and anyhow *correct*.

We believe that certainly the manuscript will go to Chatto's in the first week in March.

No the old enemy of insomnia is checked and by the man [F. M.] Alexander but more of that later as I am trying to answer your letter point by point as an efficient secretary should, I believe, do.

Aldous does not wish to see the proof.

Not only does Aldous know about Alexander but goes to him each day since the autumn. He believes he has made a very important, in fact essential, discovery. He certainly has made a new and unrecognizable person of Aldous, not physically only but mentally and therefore morally. Or rather, he has brought out, actively, all we, Aldous's best friends, know never came out either in the novels or with strangers.

A propos of [Alexis] Carrell's book, who in fact asks for a solution of Alexander's kind without knowing that Alexander exists, Aldous is willing to do an article later on about Carrell and Alexander. Thank you for sending the book. I have been reading it as it was lent to me. But Aldous has not and it is a book which will be delightful to possess. I hope all this will be good news to you. I am also very well as I go to Alexander and we cannot wait patiently till the summer because then we shall send Matthew and Sophy. So there. Probably you will think we have gone cracky, so did I think of Aldous until I saw the results and particularly since I went myself. It comes in the novel too. Oh, how I hate that novel. Except that now that it is finished I really don't care any more; but I did hate it. Not meaning that it is not very good. When I say I hate it it is for very different and personal reasons. The misery it has caused us and so on.

Well, I hope you are all as well as we are. I send you our love and to Martha and to my friend Sandy. What is he up to? It will be so nice to have your news soon. The Frere Reeves are returning tonight I believe; and then you will arrive soon. Is Martha coming too? I suppose not as you don't say. A bientôt, and with our love and our wishes.

Maria

393: † TO LEONARD WOOLF

E2 *Albany*, *W*.1
2 *March*, 1936

Dear Leonard,

Thank you for the pamphlet. I think you mis-state the pacifist position.

392 *F. M. Alexander: therapist, author of* Man's Supreme Inheritance (1910), Constructive Control of the Individual (1923), The Use of the Self (1932), *and* The Universal Constant in Living (1942). *He was a model for the character Miller in Huxley's* Eyeless in Gaza.

393 *Woolf's pamphlet was called* The League and Abyssinia.

The pacifist doesn't behave like an ostrich and say he will 'have nothing to do with evil'. He examines the evil and asks what is the best way of dealing with it. To this question experience gives a clear answer: the worst way of dealing with one evil is to do another evil, or to threaten another evil. Making threats of war doesn't prevent people from making aggressions—merely stimulates them to build up their own armaments. And the results of war are always identical, however good the intentions of the war makers and however 'collective' their actions: people are slaughtered and a passionate sense of wrong and desire for vengeance are created in the survivors—feelings which make yet further wars inevitable. What you say of albatrosses is profoundly true. All evil acts have their consequences. Acts of generous reparation can neutralize the effects of evil acts—witness our policy in S. Africa after the Boer War. What the pacifist suggests is the eminently reasonable course of using intelligent generosity to begin with—rather than waiting to use it till the evil act has been committed. In the present circumstances this policy expresses itself in the pacifist proposal to call a conference at which the dissatisfied powers wd be asked to express their grievances. An honest attempt on the part of the satisfied to find out how many of these grievances cd be met and in what way might have a chance of securing peace. Banding together in military alliances for protective security will certainly not achieve this end. The other, pacifist way may not succeed; but on the other hand it might. And if it succeeded only partially, the international atmosphere wd be cleared and a chance given for the reconstruction of the League on a more satisfactory basis.

Yours
Aldous H.

P.S. I am quoting a line of your pamphlet in *Time and Tide* this week.

394: TO VICTORIA OCAMPO

E2 Albany, W.1
18 *March*, 1936

Dear Victoria,

All my plans have been changed in the last few days, as my doctor insists that I shall renew the treatment he has been giving me recently, this summer —so won't hear of my going so far afield as Buenos Ayres. If the man weren't doing me so much good, I wd ignore what he says; but the fact that he seems to be delivering me from the miseries that have oppressed me during the last year or so makes me very attentive to his advice. He says he can make a complete job of the thing if I have another treatment this summer. So I really have no alternative but to do what he tells me; for I have no intention of relapsing into the condition I was in last year, if I can possibly help it. I regret this very much as it will prevent our seeing you this year. Also I feel rather guiltily that it may put you to inconvenience with regard to the lectures. I am so very sorry.

For the moment I have mislaid [Antonio] Aíta's address, so will ask you to forward the enclosed letter to him.

No news here, except that I've been desperately busy trying to finish off my book—a very slow job till recently, as I've been so unwell. However, I've been able to work under normal pressure during the last month or so, thanks to the efforts of my doctor, and the task is almost at an end.

Maria sends her best love, as do I. In haste,

Yours
Aldous

395: TO E. MCKNIGHT KAUFFER

*E2 Albany, W.*1
19 *March,* 1936

My dear Ted,

How very sweet of you to send me these flowers! I feel I've been given them on rather false pretences; for I emerged today from bed, having cut short what promised to be a really horrible bout of flu in 48 hours. However, one can enjoy flowers better when one's well than when one's ill; and I thank you for them all the more heartily.

May Voss was telling us that you'd not been at all well—not sleeping, overtired, blood pressure too low etc. This is so exactly like what was happening to me last year that I feel I must tell you how I have got out of this horrible condition. In my case—which is typical and like millions of others—these were all symptoms of chronic intestinal intoxication. With the washing out of the intestine (by a course of colonic lavage) and the receiving of two injections of a vaccine prepared from the pathogenic organisms found in the faeces, the whole business has cleared up. Insomnia has gone. The feeling of fatigue has gone; (I used to feel utterly exhausted after 4 hours work; now I can do 8 or more). Blood pressure has returned to normal. So has the blood picture. Symptoms of asthenia—nervousness, indecision, phobias etc—have disappeared. Two patches of eczema, which I'd had for years, have quite cleared up. Skin of face, extremely sallow in the past, has returned to a more normal colour. Nasal catarrh, which was more or less chronic, has gone. The treatment is one which can do no harm and has such potentialities for good that I wd recommend anyone to try it. Its great merit is that it aims at the root cause of ill health, not at the symptoms. These may seem to be quite unrelated phenomena. E.g. there seems to be no obvious connexion between eczema, insomnia and catarrh—but (as my own experience shows) they are intimately related and disappear with the disappearance of the focus of

394 *Aíta was the president of the Argentine branch of the PEN Club.*

intoxication. Whereas the ordinary medical treatment aims at each symptom separately—ointments for eczema, drugs for insomnia, sprays and operations for catarrh, etc.

All our love.

Yours
Aldous

396: TO HAROLD RAYMOND

E2 Albany, W.1
Saturday, 21 March, 1936

Dear Harold,

I am enclosing corrected proof copies of the pamphlet (complete and correct, except that the price—3d.—is to be printed on the inner side of the front cover.) Eric Gregory of Percy Lund Humphries says that the printing shd be done in about a fortnight: meanwhile, perhaps your travellers cd get down to work with these copies. (If more are needed, perhaps you cd communicate with the printers, either in London or at the works, 'The Country Press', Bradford.)

Hope to let you have the last of the novel by the end of next week.

Yours
Aldous

397: TO T. S. ELIOT

La Gorguette, Sanary (Var)
30 May, 1936

My dear Tom,

How nice of you to suggest coming to stay with us! The end of July wd suit us very well indeed—rather better than early August, tho' that wd be quite feasible. The nearest station is Bandol and the night train leaving Paris at (I think) 9.20 P.M. stops there: with most other trains you must change at Marseille. You can now get 3rd class sleepers, the price of which is within 10/- of the ordinary 2nd class fare. They're strongly to be recommended—but you must book well in advance, as there's apt to be a run on them.

About the short stories—the trouble is that I am so deeply ignorant on the subject and that, in order to cope with it, I shd have to undertake a great

---

396 *Huxley's pamphlet,* What Are You Going To Do About It? The Case for Constructive Peace, *was projected at the suggestion of a member of the Chatto firm, apparently Harold Raymond; it was intended for the benefit of Sheppard's Peace Pledge group. Huxley also wrote an essay, 'Pacifism and Philosophy', which was included in a collection called* The New Pacifism, *and he edited for the Peace Pledge Union* An Encyclopaedia of Pacifism (1937).

amount of reading for which I have no time. This being so, I had better say no. But thank you very much for asking me.

Let us know exactly when you mean to come, as soon as you have made your arrangements. Maria sends her love.

Yours
Aldous

398: TO C. E. M. JOAD

La Gorguette, Sanary (Var)
7 June, 1936

Dear Joad,

Thank you for your p.c—too late, alas, for any effective step to be taken. What an ass I am! I've not been by rail to the Lake District—only by car—for twenty years and had quite forgotten the details of railway geography—but imagined, like a fool, that I knew them. It is a lesson.

I'm very glad to know that you think the book's all right. I had lost all sense of what it was like—wd have liked, if it had been possible, to put it aside and look at it again after two or three years. Wolves at doors imposed immediate publication and I let it go, feeling uncomfortably in the dark about [the] thing.

Yours
Aldous Huxley

398a: TO GYÖRGY BUDAY

La Gorguette, Sanary (Var)
3 July, 1936

Dear Mr. Buday,

Your letter and the books have been forwarded to me here. Thank you very much for them indeed. Your request has caused me a certain embarrassment; for it so happens that the woodcut is a form of art which has never appealed to me, even at its best—and your engravings are certainly very fine examples of the art. I like painting and I like drawing; but I have never been able to find full satisfaction in the violently contrasted blacks and whites of the woodcut. Another barrier separating me from your work is

398 *Joad had been provided with proofs of* Eyeless in Gaza *so that he might discuss the novel in a long article surveying the career of Huxley; this appeared, as a review of Alexander Henderson's* Aldous Huxley, *in* The Outline, *supplement to* John O'London's Weekly (25 *July,* 1936). *The error he discovered was evidently Huxley's reference in Chapter XXXVI to 'the platform at Ambleside', where there is no railway station.*

398a *György Buday, at that time a lecturer on graphic arts at the Royal Hungarian University, Szeged, was planning a portfolio edition of his woodcut illustrations to* The Tragedy of Man. *He had asked Huxley to consider writing a brief introduction to be published with the work.*

the fact that I feel little interest in folk-art in any of its forms, plastic or musical. (Your illustrations to [Emeric Madach's] *The Tragedy of Man* are the furthest removed from works of folk-art and are in consequence those which appeal to me most of all your engravings.) These obtusenesses of sensibility make me peculiarly unfit to write of your work. I can see that it is good; but at the same time my lack of appreciation of the medium and of the folk-art which has been your inspiration cuts me off from any intense enjoyment of its merits. You are the citizen of a country where folk-art is still a living reality, where it still possesses vital significances transcending its aesthetic value. In England there has been no such thing as folk-art for at least a century and the modern attempts to revive it had been wholly artificial and sophisticated, and therefore foredoomed to failure. My aesthetic world has always been the world of self-conscious, professional art; and I therefore find it very hard to derive satisfaction from folk-art. If I were to write an introduction to your engravings, it would have to consist of an explanation why, in spite of the power and skill of their creator, I am unable to appreciate them as they deserve. There must be people much better qualified than I am to introduce your work—better qualified by their aesthetic sensibilities and feeling for the significance and value of folk-art.

Please forgive this letter; but I thought it best to explain exactly what my position was.

Yours sincerely,
Aldous Huxley

399: TO T. S. ELIOT

La Gorguette, Sanary (Var)
8 July, 1936

My dear Tom,

Maria and I are much disappointed that you can't come; we had looked forward so much to seeing you. I suppose there is no chance of your taking the boat from Marseille. There are, I believe, quite decent ships of the American Merchant Line, or one of those large cargo lines, which take a few passengers in very comfortable circumstances, quite cheap, leaving from Marseille. If there were a suitable sailing, it would not increase expense appreciably; and of course you would be able to do work very quietly here, if you wanted to finish off the *Criterion.*

I quite agree with you that meditation requires a metaphysical or theological background. Even in the pamphlet, there is a faint hint at such a background; but as I had to get a great deal into thirty-two pages, there really didn't seem to be any possibility of enlarging on the subject. Meditation itself is just a method of training, comparable to that, on the physical plane, of the athlete. You can train to climb Everest or to become a first-class murderer. Similarly with meditation. It can be used for strengthening the powers at the disposal of pride and ambition, or of lust, or of mediumship, just as effectively as it can be used for strengthening the powers at the disposal of the desire for perfection. And of course the teachers of meditation, such as Patanjali, solemnly warn the postulant against using it in the wrong way. It is significant that Japanese naval cadets were until recently and perhaps still are sent to a Zen Buddhist monastery to take a course in meditation, to train them in impassibility, courage and patriotic devotion. In the hands of an intelligent dictator, it might become a most fearful instrument. For it is, I believe, effective—even when practised, as I do it, rather unsystematically and with difficulty. True, the difficulty grows less, I find, as one persists; one is able to keep the mind directed, focussed, one-pointed more easily, after a few months, than at the beginning. For those who think in such terms, visual images must be a great distraction and obstacle. I think very little in images, so my interruptions are mainly verbal. Presumably each individual should select a method of meditation adapted to his mental type. There is a very well informed and interesting book by a Catholic priest, Fr Bede Frost, called *The Art of Mental Prayer*—do you know it?—which summarizes the very numerous techniques of meditation evolved at different times during the last five centuries. There are also a number of distinct techniques among the Indians, Chinese and Tibetans. A great deal could be done, I believe, to make this immensely valuable spiritual training more easily available by someone who would systematically investigate which techniques were suitable to which individuals. But of course, as you say, one also needs a metaphysic. A man who has a mastery over means without knowing what ends to use them for, or who knows only bad ends, may be a most dangerous character. And conversely a man who knows which are the best ends, but lacks the means to realize them, to put his good intentions into practice, isn't much use to himself or anyone else.

Do try to come, if you can.

Yours,
Aldous

400: TO JULIAN HUXLEY

La Gorguette, Sanary (Var)
[Circa end of July, 1936]

My dear J,
Thank you for your letter. I am enclosing £2 to cover your gift to the

399 *In a letter to Mrs Kethevan Roberts on 30 July, Huxley said of techniques of meditation or mental prayer: 'Their effect will be modified to some extent by the nature of the underlying metaphysic, which may regard the substratum of the universe as personal or impersonal. It seems to me (a) truer and (b) more useful to regard the substratum as impersonal. Moreover it w[oul]d be possible to produce effects without having any metaphysic whatever, but concentrating, as the Pali Canon of Buddhism prescribes, solely on the technique'.*

char. Who she is neither M nor I quite know. Certainly not anyone who came to us regularly. Let's hope the case was at least deserving—tho' I confess I shd be sorry if I were always to be judged on my deserts!

Nothing much has been happening here, except for a motor accident involving a French friend [Jean Coutrot] and a friend of his, a woman. The latter, I fear, is done for; the other is getting better. He's an interesting man— an engineer and industrial psychologist, who has written two valuable books called *De Quoi Vivre* and *L'Humanisme Economique*, containing an alternative programme to Marxism. He and his friends, who have made an organization called the Centre Polytechnique (they are all ex-pupils of the Ecole Polytechnique) des Etudes Economiques seem to be becoming unofficially the brain trust of the Blum government. I met a number of them at Pontigny a few weeks ago—extremely able and placed in strategic positions for influencing policy. They were moderately optimistic about the possibility of getting large-scale changes through without violence. This problem of the means to desirable ends is always and everywhere the most urgent. Is large-scale planning, rapidly carried out, compatible with democratic methods? If not and if one is forced to use anti-democratic methods what are your prospects of achieving the good ends proposed? Do not the anti-democratic methods change the whole situation in such a way that the ends, when achieved, are not the same as the ends proposed? It is the same with war. Can a democracy defend itself—which means, since (as [C.A.] Lindbergh remarked at Berlin) there is now no such thing as defensive war: can it attack and be attacked with thermite, high explosives and vesicants—and remain a democracy? Is it likely that the means will permit of the desired end—the preservation of democracy—being achieved? In the war industries technological progress is being made at the rate of about ten per cent per annum. In these circumstances can we possibly afford to go on using war-like means to preserve peace? It is unfortunate that we still go on using the old, abstract words such [as] war, force etc in spite of the fact that their connotations in concrete terms have completely changed. I am always appalled when I hear people prattling away of 'force in the hands of the League', 'police action by League forces' and the like, when in fact they mean thermite, high explosives and vesicants on open cities.

Meanwhile the prospects look to me worse than ever. The Russian and German press campaigns and army increases are very bad symptoms. And meanwhile everyone goes on like Mr. Micawber, waiting for something to turn up—waiting until it is too late. What an appalling illustration of the truth behind the legend of the Sybilline books post-war history has been! Less and less for a higher and higher price—till very soon there will be nothing and the price will be almost infinite!

I hope you had a pleasant and fairly restful holiday. I expect to be in London with Matthew in about 10 days time. M is superficially flourishing, but is still subject to his profound fatigues which make him fade out altogether. We are going to put him into the hands of our thaumaturges this autumn—[J.E.R.] McDonagh and old man Alexander. He is monstrously badly co-ordinated and I am sure that Alexander can do him a lot of good in that direction, while McD will, I hope, get rid of the tendency to intoxicate himself thro' his intestines which he has had since childhood.

Love to all.

Yours
A.

401: TO VICTORIA OCAMPO

La Gorguette, Sanary (Var)
[July, 1936]

Dear Victoria,

I am very glad you liked *Eyeless in Gaza*. I still don't quite know what I think about it. All I'm certain of is that I shd have liked another year to work at it. But I couldn't afford to give the time—and perhaps anyhow it wouldn't have been any good: the book might have gone stale and dead on my hands if I'd gone on.

We are on the verge of leaving for the North. Matthew has to prepare for an examination and to take treatment from the doctor in London—so we can't prolong our stay here. I shall probably try to collaborate with Gerald Heard this winter to produce a kind of synthesis, starting from a metaphysical basis and building up through individual and group psychology to politics and economics. There is a great mass of useful material lying about in fragments here and there; but it needs to be brought together and correlated in a coherent whole, embracing theory and practice, the individual and society, religion and economics. Obviously we shan't succeed in doing the job perfectly; but I think we may produce something that will at least be useful as a pointer. H. G. Wells ought to have achieved it; but somehow didn't succeed. There is something deeply unsatisfactory about even his best attempts at synthesis. And meanwhile the need for a synthesis—a synthesis for free human beings, not a synthesis à la mode de Berlin, Rome or Moscow—is becoming more and more urgent.

There will also, I expect, be work in connection with the peace business. And then 'bothering about people'! A thing I find very difficult to do in such a way that I don't bother them and myself in the process. But like so many other kinds of incapacity, it's a matter of the will rather than of a native lack of power. We're generally stupid because for some reason we want to be—because it suits us to be stupid. A painful constatation—but ultimately consoling, since it reveals the possibility of change.

Love to you from us both.

Yours
Aldous

Mount Royal [*London*]
30 *November*, 1936

My dear Rosalind,

This has no relevance to your state of mind, I'm afraid, but I would like, in illustration of what I was doing, to set forth the history of the composition of the characters in my book. In the case of Mr. Beavis, the primary nucleus of the character came from an autobiographical poem by Coventry Patmore called 'Tired Memory'. This is a most striking psychological document about bereavement and remarriage and the whole of the episodes of the dreams etc is an elaboration of the matter in that poem. I wrote it originally as a short story; then adapted it to the purposes of the longer book. Following a principle which I have always used—that the only way of rendering simultaneously the subjective feeling of a person and the objective judgment of other people upon that person is to mingle tragedy with a certain element of extravagance—I introduced the element of philology. This was based upon descriptions given by Frieda Lawrence of her first husband [Ernest Weekley], who was a philologist. Treated in a different manner, the character yet has a strong resemblance to the parson in D. H. Lawrence's *Virgin and the Gypsy*, a figure who was actually derived from the same source. After that it became necessary to fix the personage in time, as the inhabitant of a certain epoch. And here, I am afraid quite unjustifiably, I made use of mannerisms and phrases some of which were recognizably father's. I had not thought that they would prove recognizable to others and I am most distressed to find that they should have been.

In the case of the other character I started with the story of the betrayal by the friend, which was based upon a case of which I had heard. The character was, of course, definitely Trev's. If I preserved the stammer and insisted on the ascetic obsession, it was for this reason: that it is, artistically speaking, (and perhaps there are also profounder, ethical and psychological reasons as well) all but impossible to represent an entirely good character that is without weakness. There are no completely healthy or completely grown-up good characters in imaginative literature. The Duke in *Measure for Measure* is a symbol. Dostoevsky's Idiot is an epileptic. Dickens's good characters are all infantile. Gorky's Hermit is extravagantly eccentric. To represent a completely adult, healthy good man one must be adultly good oneself. And nobody who was not himself adultly good would understand what was being talked about if such a character were truthfully rendered. That is why all deeply good characters in imaginative literature have to be, as it were, diluted with weakness or eccentricity; for only on such conditions are they comprehensible by readers and expressible by writers. Hence the ascetic obsession attributed to the Brian of the book and that stammer—which you find in bad taste, but which I cannot regret, since it was reproduced entirely in love and in an attempt to understand a character which I profoundly admired.

Yours
Aldous

403: TO EUGENE F. SAXTON

La Gorguette, Sanary, Var
24 December, 1936

My dear Gene,

After a touch of flu all round, Maria and I have got to Sanary, while Matthew has gone off to Switzerland to do winter sports. It's a great comfort to be out of London. The more I see of capital cities, the less I like them; one increasingly has the feeling that one is living in a madhouse.

Thank you for the further information about colleges. At this distance it is obviously impossible to come to any definite decision; but when we get across the Atlantic, I will have a good discussion and a look round. Meanwhile. I should be very grateful if you would do something for me. If Matthew is to have his educational visa and if, as seems likely, we ourselves stay for more than six months in America, it is necessary that the Consular authorities in London should have some kind of proof of my ability to support Matthew and myself while in the USA. This being so, I think it would be best if Harpers were to write an official letter to me stating that such and such sums were due to me, or that I should be in receipt of such and such an average income over the next two or three years and that my prospects were such that it is not immediately probable that Matthew or Maria or myself should become a burden on the American taxpayer in the immediate future. If you can do this within the next month, I shall be most grateful. I shall need the document in February, as I expect that we shall be coming over in March.

We came back here to find a mass of Harper publicity for *Eyeless*. I must say that you have done me proud and I'm most grateful to you and the firm for what has been done for the book. Where has it got to now?

The sun blazes away in unbroken splendour here and, by a miracle, there is no wind; so I am sorely tempted away from all the work I ought to do. Our Christmas season promises to be very quiet, as all our neighbours, with the exception of Edith Wharton, are away. Meanwhile I hope you and the family have been having a good time and that you're getting through the

403 *Correspondence between Gerald Heard and J. B. Rhine, the parapsychologist, indicates that the Huxleys' journey to the United States was being planned in October. Heard expected to go over later, about midsummer of 1937. Huxley contemplated enrolling his son, Matthew, as a pre-medical student at Duke University (which the Parapsychology Laboratory there had put on the map). Maria Huxley wrote to Roy Fenton on 24 December that they should remain in America for about nine months or a year. Matthew was finally entered at the University of Colorado, chosen mainly for geographical reasons, upon his finishing another year of preparation.*

horrors of winter in the city without too many of the inevitable colds and grippes. Our love to Martha and the boys, as well as to yourself.

Yours,
Aldous H.

404: TO C. DAY LEWIS

La Gorguette, Sanary (Var)
[Circa 6 January, 1937]

Dear Mr. Day Lewis,

I have just read your pamphlet in reply to the one I wrote last year. With one or two of your criticisms I am in agreement; for there are places where the case is inadequately argued in my pamphlet. But the case as a whole still seems to me absolutely unanswerable and, so far as your pamphlet and other anti-pacifist writings are concerned, unanswered. Bertrand Russell's *Which Way to Peace?* and Barthélemy de Ligt's *Pour Vaincre sans Violence* present the case most fully, I think.

You accuse me of using too many abstractions. But may I say that you fall into the same snare.* 'Collective Security' sounds fine: but in reality what is it? In the contemporary circumstances it is two opposing groups of military alliances only distinguishable from those existing before 1914 by the fact that the weapons at their disposal are much more destructive. 'Defending democracy' also sounds fine; but to defend democracy by military means, one must be militarily efficient, and one cannot become militarily efficient without centralizing power, setting up a tyranny, imposing some form of conscription or slavery to the state. In other words the military defence of democracy in contemporary circumstances entails the abolition of democracy even before war starts. When it is over and there is social chaos and material ruin, democracy will have even less chance of flourishing. (I had forgotten to add that the preparation for war involves a particularly horrible form of education for children. See Russell on this subject in *Which Way to Peace?*) Your vague abstractions are utterly deceptive. Use words which express the facts of contemporary reality. When such words are used, they make nonsense of the collective-security, L[eague]-of-N[ations]-war-to-end-war, military-defence-of-democracy argument. There are many other points; but I am up to the eyes in work and time is lacking.

Yours sincerely
Aldous Huxley

*And what about analogies? You can't compare nations to gangsters. The police capture one definite gangster: an army (even a L. of N army or an

404 *Written about 6 January; the Sanary postmark is illegible, but a London forwarding postmark reads 8 January. Day Lewis's pamplet was called* We're Not Going to Do Nothing: A Reply to Mr. Aldous Huxley's Pamphlet 'What Are You Going to Do About It?' (*London:* Left Review, 1936).

411

army defending socialism) destroys indiscriminately—or rather tends to discriminate in favour of the guilty governments and ruling classes, who get out of the way, and to exterminate the masses of perfectly innocent people.

405: TO MARK GERTLER

La Gorguette, Sanary (Var)
24 January, 1937

My dear Mark,

Yes, I will gladly write a preface to your show. We expect to be in London towards the end of February and if it's not too late, I wd have a look at your pictures and write the thing then. I could do it without seeing these particular pictures, as I should make the thing a sort of generalized appreciation of your work.

I hope all goes well with you and the family. We flourish tolerably well here. I have read recently a very good book on art by the German critic, Wölfflin, translated into English with the title (as far as I remember) *Principles of Art Criticism.* It is really very well worth reading. It appeared several years ago. I got it out of the Times Book Club.

Our love to you both.

Yours
Aldous H.

406: TO EUGENE F. SAXTON

La Gorguette, Sanary (Var)
7 February, 1937

My dear Gene,

Hamish Hamilton wrote to me the other day saying that you were going to publish Gerald Heard's books in America and asking for a few lines of blurb about them. I am writing something on a separate sheet of paper. Meanwhile, I am writing to tell you that Gerald Heard himself will be crossing with us, and we expect to be travelling with him in the USA. He is the trustee for a big estate out West and has to wind up the affair, and we shall make our way by easy stages with him across the continent and probably find some place in the mountains of Montana to stay at during the summer while he does his business in the neighbourhood. Gerald is a very dear friend of ours and a most remarkable man; I hope very much you will be able to do something with his books. While we're in NY you must meet him; I'm sure you'll like him and that you will find him interesting.

This leads me on to practical details. We shall probably reach NY about April 12th. We don't want, on this occasion, to stay more than a week or so,

405 *Huxley wrote the preface and sent it to Gertler on 1 April. Gertler's show was held at the Reid and Lefevre galleries, King Street, St James's, 9-30 April.*

412

as we have to go southwards for Matthew's affairs and then a very long way north westwards for Gerald's—and incidentally for our own pleasure and instruction; for I am greatly looking forward, as are all of us, to exploring the country. We'd be most grateful if you could find us accommodation for our stay—a couple of single rooms for Matthew and Gerald Heard, and a bedroom and sitting room with kitchenette, if possible, for Maria and myself. The position needn't of course be elegant, so long as it's fairly quiet. Then there's another point; we shall do our travelling by easy stages in a car and I'd be glad of a little advice, when I arrive, on this subject—whether it's better to get, say, a new Ford or a second-hand specimen of some larger and more majestic vehicle. I expect we shall need a small trailer for luggage. Hints on this subject will be most welcome. Forgive me for importuning you in this way; that's the reward of your previous kindnesses—to be asked to be kind yet again!

Our love to you and Martha and the boys.

Yours,
Aldous H.

407: † TO MARY MCELDOWNEY

[La Gorguette, Sanary (Var)]
16 February, 1937

Dear Miss McEldowney,

Your letter of October last has remained long unacknowledged—for which I must ask your pardon. I found it most interesting. I quite agree with you that a complete change in the system of ownership is necessary—but I don't think such a change will do much good unless accompanied by decentralization, a reduction of the power of the state, self-government in every activity—in a word, anarchism in the sense in which Kropotkin uses the word. Only in this way are we likely seriously to modify society and individuals for the better.

'Transitional dictatorship' imposed by violence is not much good—because it will require another revolution to get rid of it. I am convinced that desirable changes can only be achieved by attacking all along the line simultaneously: on the economic, the political, the educational, the psychological fronts. (Take the case of education: what's the use of economic changes if you establish a system of education which, as Bertrand Russell has pointed out in his last book, *Which Way to Peace?*, is calculated to turn individuals into militarists, at once bullying and obsequious? And such education is necessary in a country which wishes to be efficient militarily. The change which has overtaken Russian education in recent years may

407 *The correspondent (afterwards Mrs Hupfel) was a young woman in New York who had written to Huxley about the philosophical implications of* Eyeless in Gaza, John Strachey's The Coming Struggle for Power, *and other matters.*

have been considered necessary in view of the military situation, but it remains none the less true that it must do much to postpone the emergence of a satisfactory society for another generation.) I don't see that you can hope to achieve what you want to achieve except by using the means which are strictly appropriate. To use one appropriate means while still employing other means which are wholly inappropriate is to condemn yourself in advance to frustration.

Yours sincerely,
Aldous Huxley

408: TO ROBERT NICHOLS

La Gorguette, Sanary (Var)
16 *February,* 1937

My dear Robert,

I ought to have written long since to thank you for your Sunrise Poem, about which I felt strongly that them was my sentiments. I find that, on the whole, natural beauty means more to me than it did—perhaps because I look at it with a painter's eye, with a greater appreciation of forms and colours—which means a greater appreciation of the glory of God. One of the great facts about the glory of God is that one can enjoy it without monopolizing it, without depriving anyone else of it or claiming exclusive proprietary rights. There is a fine passage in Dante's *Purgatorio*—XIV.82— which ends up with the question addressed to the human race: Why do you place your heart there where sharing is impossible? And there's an almost equally fine piece of prose in Malebranche, 'Deux hommes ne peuvent pas se nourrir d'un même fruit, embrasser le même corps. Toutes les créatures sont des êtres particuliers, qui ne peuvent être un bien général et commun. Ceux qui possèdent ces biens particuliers en privent les autres et en font des ennemis. Mais la Raison (and he might have added la Beauté) est un bien commun qui unit d'une amité parfaite et durable ceux qui la possèdent. Etc.' It is always slightly irritating to find that what the philosophers say is perfectly true; but there it is. One may be, as Spinoza says, excusable for one's weakness in succumbing to passion; but the fact remains that one will pay for one's weakness by being extremely unhappy and 'irretrievably lost', as he puts it. One is up against the brute facts of experience which can no more be changed than the facts of gravitation. But luckily, as you point out in your Sunrise poem, there is the glory of God and the whole gamut of thoughts

---

408 *The passage from Malebranche may be translated: 'Two men cannot be fed with the same piece of fruit, embrace the same body. All created things are particular beings, which cannot be a general and common possession. Those who own these particular possessions deprive others of them and in consequence make enemies. But Reason is a common possession which unites in perfect and enduring friendship those who possess it'.*

and feelings associated with it—thoughts and feelings that one should, I am sure, deliberately cultivate in the hope that in time they may fill the universe of one's mind in its entirety.

I hope you've been getting through the winter without too much discomfort. A bientôt, I expect.

Yours
Aldous H.

P.S. I find that I've got no record of your London address and M is away, having taken her address book. So I send this to Lawford [Hall] in the hope it will be forwarded.

409: TO J. B. RHINE

La Gorguette, Sanary (Var)
17 *February*, 1937

Dear Professor Rhine,

I should have written before to thank you for the reprint of your interesting article. The problem now is, having established the facts (and there can really be no doubt about them), to formulate a satisfactory hypothesis as to the nature and *modus operandi* of the faculty. [C. D.] Broad's presidential address to the SPR is interesting in this context.

It strikes me that an interesting experiment might be made by getting a number of subjects to work simultaneously. It would be interesting to see whether they helped or hindered one another—whether the telepathy between them would cause all the choices to be the same—whether the scores of each wd be better or worse than when the tests were being made on each individually.

If all goes well, I expect to be in your neighbourhood by the end of April or beginning of May, with my wife and son, and Gerald Heard. I hope you will be at Duke at that time and that I shall have the pleasure of meeting you.

Yours sincerely
Aldous Huxley

410: TO JULIAN HUXLEY

25 *bis rue Decamps,*
Paris 16ᵐᵉ
25 *February*, 1937

My dear Julian,

I shd have written before to thank you for your postcards from the snow. I hope you enjoyed yourselves and that the holiday did you good. Quant à moi, I was in the pink until about a week ago when an undeveloped wisdom tooth began to give trouble, brought me extremely low with

---

409 *Huxley visited Rhine in Durham, North Carolina, at about the end of April.*

continuous pain and lack of sleep and has now produced an inflammation of the sinus. I go into hospital tomorrow or the day after to have the thing hacked out. It is all a very great bore and has delayed our return to London, where, but for this, we shd have been yesterday.

Have seen very few people in Paris beyond dentists and doctors. Mimi is well: poor Lewis, whom I have not yet seen, is seeking a new divorce [. . . .] He has cut himself off from all his old acquaintances, refusing even to talk to most of them. It is all very unfortunate, the more so as he seems to be thoroughly ill, very hard up (since he has to pension Lily) and increasingly unpopular at his office. It is slightly exasperating to find that all the philosophers are perfectly right and that there is no way of escaping from what Spinoza calls Human Bondage except by delivering oneself from the passions. With incorrigible optimism one goes on thinking that one can have genuine liberty *and* passions; but, alas, the facts are against one. One has to choose. [. . . .]

I have been collecting notes for a small book on the means that must be used—and used simultaneously—if we are ever to realize the ends which everyone desires, i.e. justice, peace, etc. This mania for oversimplification, for wanting to explain everything in terms of one causative principle is the undoing of everything. It has as its corollary the insane belief that you can concentrate on one sort of reform and neglect all the other sorts, thus undoing with one hand all that you do with the other—e.g. the belief that you can have democracy simultaneously with extreme centralization, peace simultaneously with authoritarian education (not to mention armaments, centralization, etc). And so on.

A recrudescence of neuralgic pain makes me want to stop writing—so I send our love to you both.

Yours
Aldous

411: TO HAROLD RAYMOND

*Mount Royal, W.*1
30 *March,* 1937

Dear Harold,

Excellent news. I have talked to the secretary of the PPU and he agrees that it will be best to go ahead with the 6d. edition in paper—20,000 copies. So will you set that in motion at once.

410 *Lewis Gielgud was three times married and three times divorced. His third marriage, to Zita Gordon, took place in* 1937.

411 *The opening paragraph concerns* An Encyclopaedia of Pacifism. Brave New World *had originally been banned in Australia before an official book censorship committee was appointed. Such a committee had since been formed with powers of review, and it recommended that the government now lift the ban placed on* Brave New World *and, with it,* A Farewell to Arms.

I saw the note in *The Times* yesterday about the raising of the ban on *Brave New World*, but didn't anticipate so prompt or profitable a reaction on the part of the Antipodeans. It certainly has given the book an immense amount of gratuitous advertising.

I had a rather dismal Easter, owing to a recrudescence of trouble in the jaw—a lot of pain culminating in the extraction of four more teeth. All has gone quite well: but it hasn't been exactly a bracing holiday and I am still a bit limp.

About plans:—I am hoping to finish by the middle of the summer a short philosophico-psychologico-sociological book on the various means which must be employed if desirable social changes are to be realized—pointing out the folly of the idea that there is a single cause to our troubles and therefore a single panacea, and enumerating the more important of the many fronts along which the problem of reform must be attacked simultaneously. I shall keep the book pretty short (a) because I want to get it out quickly, as I have just heard that old Herbert Samuel is projecting an enormous work on a somewhat similar theme. (This will be pretty dull, no doubt, as he is a dullish man; but it wd be as well to stake out an earlier claim.) (b) because it's obviously impossible to make such a large synthesis with anything like complete thoroughness; a sketch and a set of suggestions will be in a certain sense more stimulating and valuable than an attempted, but inadequate, text book. I have about 10,000 words of this already done and shall aim at a total length of 50,000 or 60,000. If I can finish this by the end of July, which I hope—so much the better.

Yours
Aldous H.

III
AMERICA
1937–1952

412: TO JULIAN HUXLEY

[Del Rio, Texas]
[7 May, 1937]

Spent the night at your ex-home-town, Houston, yesterday, and are now at Del Rio, on the Mexican frontier, in a tourist cabin, waiting for the temperature to go down. We have had a very pleasant and interesting trip so far. Have seen various seats of learning, from Charlottesville (mouldy) to Black Mountain (interesting), from Duke (a remarkable phenomenon) to Dillard, the negro coll[ege] at N[ew] Orleans (rather depressing). Saw [A. E.] Morgan at Knoxville. Hope tomorrow to visit world's largest cavern—complete with elevator service (702 ft) and cafeteria. Love.

Aldous

413: TO JULIAN HUXLEY

San Cristobal, New Mexico
3 June, 1937

Dearest J,

I don't know how fast or slow the posts are from this place, but trust this may arrive round about your birthday, with all best wishes for the occasion and its happy returns. I trust all goes well with you and the family.

The above is our summer address. We have a log cabin—to which a bathroom is in process of being added—on Frieda Lawrence's ranch in the mountains here. A very extraordinary place—more than 8000 feet up in a clearing in the woods, which are composed of pine, aspen, birch and oak-scrub. Below in the plain—which lies at about 7000 feet—is the sage-brush desert, pale whitey-green and tawny, with the canyon of the Rio Grande running through the midst and blue mountains beyond. The sky is full of enormous dramas of cloud and sunshine—with periodical thunderstorms of incredible violence. Boiling hot sunshine alternates with cold shade and icy nights. There are whirlwinds of dust in the desert below us and, after rain, the roads are impassable. Nearest town (20 miles off) is Taos—2000 inhabitants, with an Indian Pueblo just outside, inhabited by men in pigtails

412 *Postmarked El Paso, 8 May, 8.30 A.M., indicating an all-night drive from Del Rio. Morgan was the chairman of the Tennessee Valley Authority. The Huxleys, with Gerald Heard, had sailed on the* Normandie *in early April and had driven south from New York with the object first of visiting Duke University and then of proceeding west, they and Heard by different routes, to New Mexico. Once there, they decided, at Frieda Lawrence's invitation, to spend the summer on her ranch while Huxley finished his current book,* Ends and Means.

and top-knots, swathed in blankets, women equally swathed, in white moccasins. The rest consist of about 85% Mexicans and 15% whites, of whom an uncomfortably large sprinkling are artists. Our nearest railway is Santa Fe, 70 miles away, and our metropole is Denver at 350 miles. So you see we are well away from civilization. The country is most astonishing and beautiful—but I don't know if one cd stand it very long. I've never been in any place, except parts of Mexico, which gave such an impression of being alien, even hostile, to man. Humans crawl about in this savage, empty vastness like irrelevant ticks—just not counting. (I see by my map that New Mexico is twice as large as England and has a population of 400,000—about 3½ per square mile, which must have been the density in England at the time of the arrival of Julius Caesar! In western Texas, which we crossed in the midst of a premature heatwave (dust-spouts in a temperature of 105° in the shade—tho' of course there is no shade) the density of population is somewhat under 2 per sq. mile.) It's a rummy country, this. Just how rummy one can't tell until one has driven about it in a Ford.

Frieda is well, cheerful and a great deal calmer than she used to be. Later middle age is suiting her. The Capitano turns out to be a very decent sort of middle-class Italian—rather naif, at the same time intelligent and active. As far as one can judge he doesn't exploit Frieda: on the contrary, manages her affairs very efficiently.

We saw Brett—who has not been on speaking terms with F since she (Brett) and Mabel Luhan made a plot, 2 years ago, to steal Lawrence's ashes out of the little chapel that F. has built for them. Deafer and odder than ever, in a Mexican 10-gallon hat, with a turkey's feather stuck in it, sky-blue breeks, top boots and a strong American accent. I tremble to think what the late Lord E[sher] wd have thought of her if he cd have seen her in her present guise.

No further news, beyond the fact that we're all well. I've settled down to work and hope to be able to get a lot done this summer. Gerald arrives from his tour of inspection of the Plunkett estates in Neb[raska] and Wy[oming] next Saturday. They (the estates) must have presented a cheerful spectacle amid the dust and the erosion. Our love to you all.

Yours

A.

413 *The Capitano: Angelo Ravagli. Brett: the Hon. Dorothy Brett relates that, abetted by Mabel Luhan, she and four other people plotted (though not seriously) to take Lawrence's ashes from the little cement chapel built by Ravagli and to scatter them over the ranch in accordance with Lawrence's wishes. Brett, who was painting the round window of the chapel, would remove them; the others would join in scattering them. She does not know who informed Frieda, whose rage she considers out of proportion: earlier, Frieda had lost the ashes once and once had forgotten them at the house of a friend in Taos.*

[? *San Cristobal, New Mexico*]
[*Circa June*, 1937]

My sympathies are, of course, with the Government side, especially the Anarchists; for Anarchism seems to me much more likely to lead to desirable social change than highly centralized, dictatorial Communism. As for 'taking sides'—the choice, it seems to me, is no longer between two users of violence, two systems of dictatorship. Violence and dictatorship cannot produce peace and liberty; they can only produce the results of violence and dictatorship, results with which history has made us only too sickeningly familiar.

The choice now is between militarism and pacifism. To me, the necessity of pacifism seems absolutely clear.

415: TO JACOB I. ZEITLIN

San Cristobal, New Mexico
12 *July*, 1937

Dear Mr Zeitlin,

With regard to the handling of my work, I am prepared to authorize you to take up the matter with film studios for the remainder of the present year.

The most promising books and stories for film purposes are, I should say, the following.

Antic Hay. There is good comic material here and the character of the shy young man who disguises himself in order to act the part of Don Juan is a part full of amusing possibilities for an actor.

The short story, 'The Gioconda Smile', from the volume, *Mortal Coils*, is a good study in the psychology of crime and has a dramatic plot. The end would probably have to be changed.

Point Counter Point contains a great deal of material that might be used and so does my last book, *Eyeless in Gaza*. Both are probably a bit long and complicated to be used in their entirety.

The long short-story, 'After the Fireworks', is another possibility.

I should also recommend you to consider carefully my play, *The World of Light*, which is a psychological comedy capable of expansion for the film (which could include scenes of the young men's life on their West Indian

414 *An answer to the question, circulated among a number of British and Irish writers:* 'Are you for, or against, the legal Government and the People of Republican Spain? Are you for, or against, Franco and Fascism?' *Published in* Authors Take Sides on the Spanish War (*London:* Left Review, 1937).

415 *Zeitlin, a Los Angeles bookseller and manuscript dealer, had approached Huxley through Frieda Lawrence. After receiving this letter he visited San Cristobal in August and urged Huxley to go to Hollywood. During the autumn, Huxley drafted a scenario entitled 'Success'; this, however, was not sold.*

island, scenes that are only mentioned in the play). It also has the merit of being written in dialogue form—very good dialogue, if I may say so!—which would make the task of preparing a talking film version considerably easier.

As I told you in my previous letter, the rights in *Brave New World* are already sold, though the purchasers seem to have no intention of making a film of the book.

About the possibility of my working in Hollywood—it is probable that I shall be staying in California for a time after the New Year. (Before that date, I expect to be lecturing up and down the country.) I might perhaps make that stay an occasion for doing work for the films, if something satisfactory could be found. Will you, as you suggest, make tactful enquiries, without, please, in any way committing me definitely? I hope we may see you here in the course of the summer.

Yours sincerely,
Aldous Huxley

416: TO CHARLES ABBOTT

San Cristobal, New Mexico
28 August, 1937

Dear Mr. Abbott,

Your letter has reached me here. I have few MSS either in this place or anywhere else; for they tend to get thrown away.

I send you, however, these two pages on which are scribblings in pen, and tappings with a machine, having reference to a still unpublished poem about driving in a car at night and the symbolic significance of the narrow universe created by the headlights. The final form of the poem, if it ever achieves one, will probably be along the lines of the second hand-written fragment on page two.

Yours sincerely
Aldous Huxley

417: MARIA HUXLEY TO ROY FENTON

1425½ *N. Crescent Heights Boulevard,*
Hollywood West, Los Angeles
13 October, 1937

Dearest Roy,
    [. . . .]
Well, we arrived in New York on the *Normandie* with Gerald Heard

416 *Charles Abbott was the director of the Lockwood Memorial Library at the University of Buffalo. Huxley's poem is briefly discussed by Rudolf Arnheim in a book for which Abbott wrote the Introduction,* Poets at Work (*New York*, 1948), *pp.* 144-46.
    417 *Matthew Huxley's school: Fountain Valley, in Colorado. Sister: Jehanne Nys (ex-Moulaert); Maria included her New York address in the heading of the letter. Professor Hubble: Edwin Hubble, the astronomer. The Huxleys had been in Los Angeles since the first week of September.*

and Christopher Wood, the whole family in fact and in New York we only stayed a very short while; time to buy a Ford car and see our friends the William Seabrooks. Then we started out in the car, Aldous Matthew Gerald and me and we saw a great deal of America Southward. We saw people and places and the beauty of the country enchanted us. The grandeur of the dams thrilled us and for Morgan (of the T.V.A.) we felt sorry.

But soon, as we reached through the tobacco country and the cotton country with blacks sweating over the land and miserable white trash in huts, to the fringes of Florida the many heat-waves began. When, in Europe one travels for one's curiosity there is not only the curiosity of looking at the countryside, there are towns with monuments, there are museums and ravishing quarters and then, when one is tired, there are terraces outside the cafés on which one can sit and rest; but in this country there is nothing but the earth and its population and nowhere to rest and sit when one is tired of that. So we got on pretty fast, through the swamps of New Orléans which were covered in delicate blue water-lilies. Then we began crossing Texas; at leisure first when the country was rolling and scrubby and alive with animals and tortoises crossing the roads. But soon the desert grew more desertic, the roads dustier and the sun more and more vicious till we became almost hysterical and drove from air-cooled cinemas to air-cooled hotel bed-rooms. And what an oasis they are. There is no doubt that this discovery will transform life in the tropics and probably give the fiendish coloniser even more energy to exploit the natives who will never have enough means to install these sources of revitalisation.

After about six thousand miles we arrived in New Mexico where our friend Frieda Lawrence, the widow of D.H., has a ranch near Taos and there she offered us a little house next to her own. It was neat and tidy and comfortable. It stood on the edge of a rushing brook. It stood under large trees and was surrounded by green grass and there were animals and there was quietness and there was peace and above all that there was Frieda whom we had always been very fond of and we liked her Italian friend the captain. So we stayed. But I had no maid because there were none. And so I learned a great many things and the most amusing was to make bread. But it took us a long while to get used to the altitude and therefore we first got thinner and thinner. Then soon we got fatter and fatter. Aldous started writing a book and finished it and I typed it and now it is to come out in November and of course you always come at the head of the list to the publisher for sending the volumes off. But Gerald and Chris were in Hollywood. So, suddenly as soon as the book was finished in the beginning of September, we became impatient and the family crowded itself once more with an infinite amount of luggage in the stolid little Ford and we drove through all the view places and the petrified forests and the grand-canyons and sure enough we arrived here with another heat wave.

I do not remember whether you know Hollywood. It is like a permanent

International Exhibition. The buildings are ravishing, fantastic and flimsy. They are all surrounded by green lawns and huge palmtrees and flowering hibiscus and to finish it off the population wear fancy-dress costume, or rather, in the hot weather, fancy-undress costume and everyone looks happy and cheerful. But it is also immense and of course we see many many people.

For the first two weeks we lay low as Aldous had to correct the proofs for both countries and do a little work and we also wanted to bathe in these monstrous pacific rollers but it was cool on the beach (only 30 minutes driving away) and we saw the sights and then Matthew departed for his school. Matthew is now a very world-wise young man. Nearly eighteen and in full favour of America. Well, so now are we, I think. After finding the barbarousness of this living with no cheap labour very unpleasant and uncivilized, we have now got used to it and seen that it does not really matter, that it is merely different and not worse. After meeting here so many very interesting and so many very nice people; after getting used to the terribly dry climate and the low altitude we think there are many worse countries in the world, particularly in Europe (I cannot tell you how' oppressive the place was before we left it) and we would not mind staying here for a while. Matthew is probably going to Duke University in North Carolina next year so I shall not want to go back to Europe all the time. My sister, as you see by my address, has just arrived in New York where she will take a job and that is another reason to keep me here. But anyhow we cannot leave till after Xmas even for Mexico because Aldous is giving a lecture tour. He has succumbed at last. Not to the financial aspect which unfortunately is not what it was, but Gerald convinced him, quite rightly perhaps, that this was the moment or never to say what they had to say. And they are doing it together. A sort of Mutt and Jeff on war and peace and religion and so on. But all this was settled and signed in April and since then Aldous wrote the book on the same subject and I can see how bored he is with the eternal repetitions of the same thing. They are giving their first lecture here on Monday and I have heard them repeat once or twice. I wonder how it will go. While they give their lectures I may drive them about or I may go and stay in N.Y. with my sister for she is rather lonely and not too pleased with certain aspects of american life which was completely unknown to her. And so they were to me until I lived here, and lived in the heart of the country and surrounded by ranchers. For our ranch was at nine thousand feet, up a mud road of four miles, unpassable in bad weather and we had no electricity. But we were comfortably installed whereas some of our neighbours were desperately primitive. Not even a bath-room or electric light which suddenly drooped and failed like at Progreso. [. . . .]

We have met here all the very eminent world of The Technical Institute of Pasadena, gone up Mount Wilson and looked at the sky with professor Hubble, we visited in country and prosperous ranches, we have met scholars on Bacon and novelists and sociologists and on the same day we have met

Gary Cooper or Anita Loos or Charlie and the whole pattern becomes fantastic and improbable but makes one realize what could become of America if it went on a definite track. In fact we have seen so much, including the only Chinchilla farm in the World and the largest hogs, and the making of the Mickey mouse films and the working on orchids with mineral salts (because orchids are the cheapest flowers to work on as they can be well sold!) and oil drilling and hideous pictures shows and the best and largest private collection of French Modern pictures in the house of a nice mad-man. In fact we now want to have a rest. Because if only one could do all that without talking; but it is this incessant burbling unnecessary words that sometimes drives me crazy. Yesterday we had a very *intellectual* dinner with Charlie Chaplin. Paulette Goddard a very good and very handsome hostess and Upton Sinclair one of the guests. Charlie we have always loved and admired. He did, yesterday, a mimic of Mussolini making a speech which was admirable; and the Indians of Bali singing and dancing. But he is a sad little man and looks ill now. [. . . .]

I am sure you will be very interested in the new book. It is far the best thing Aldous has done. Non-fiction of course and it is a philosophical, sociological manual in a way. But difficult to explain. It ought to arrive in about two months. But I just remember that I told London to send it. Perhaps it would be as well to tell New York too. I will ask Aldous.

I would have many hours more to tell you and not come to the end of all we think and do. But it is time to take Aldous to the dentist as there are no busses or trams and distances so enormous taxis would ruin us. But my chauffeur hours are not so bad as I get through a good deal of reading. The only misery can be the heat if I have to park in the sun. Do you know it is still as much as 92 and 3 here. Too much to live a town life and keep tidy and polite. But as it is now fall the women have all gone in their dark woollen clothes, apparently to show that they have money to buy them, and the men have stored their cotton suits and everyone is sweltering!

[. . . .]

Yours
Maria

418: TO JULIAN HUXLEY

Manufacturers and Bankers Club
of Philadelphia
6 December, 1937

Dearest J,

This improbable address is where they have put me while lecturing here at Philadelphia. A sort of mouldier version of a really solid, old-fashioned English club—dismal to a degree. This lecture tour has been disagreeably eventful; for poor Gerald Heard, with whom I was giving a series of discussions, fell in the snow in Iowa and broke an arm. He remained in hospital at Cedar Rapids (home of Quaker Oats), while I had to continue single-handed. Very unpleasant for him—as he had a bad fracture just beneath the shoulder—and very boring for me, as I find this process of lecturing extremely tedious. It was more tolerable when we were two and could throw the ball back and forth in a lively discussion. I got back to Cedar Rapids after 10 days and managed to transport Gerald, still strapped up and in considerable pain, to the house of a very remarkable doctor in Indiana where he is now staying till the arm is better, while I have come on East. So that's that. I expect to go on with the lecturing after a break for Christmas, through January; then hope to get back to Europe, unless anything turns up in relation to possible cinema versions of my stuff. Improbable, but possible. The best they cd do in Hollywood was to ask me to adapt *The Forsyte Saga* for the screen: but even the lure of enormous lucre cd not reconcile me to remaining closeted for months with the ghost of the late poor John Galsworthy. I couldn't face it! However, there is just a chance that they may take an interest in something of mine: in which case I might go back to the West Coast for a short time to see what was happening.

I met in Chicago a very remarkable man called [W. H.] Sheldon, a psychologist, who has been working for 10 years in the field that Kretschmer worked in and who has evolved, I believe, a genuinely scientific conception of psychological types—or rather of the typological factors present in varying amounts in different individuals. He seems to me to have evolved a genuine algebra in terms of which to discuss the problem, so that it now becomes possible to talk concretely, quantitatively and scientifically on a subject about which one cd only speculate in a vaguely intuitive, personal way. His book will be out in a few months and I suspect it will prove to be of first-rate importance.

How do things go with you all? Well, I trust, as they do with us—tho' I find myself often a bit overwhelmed by the curious rigidity and opacity of most human beings. There's something dismally fixed, stony, sclerotic about most of them—a lack of sensibility and awareness and flexibility, which is most depressing. There seems to be nothing much to be done, beyond, of course, doing one's best to prevent the oncoming of mental sclerosis in oneself, to keep the mind open to the world and to that which transcends the world and gives it sense and value. Such seems to be the only genuine contribution that one can make to the betterment of the concern—making oneself into a little window through which at least some light can be admitted; keeping oneself alive and aware so that at least some point in the vast stony structure shall be in a position to grow and respond. There is something, I think, very suggestive about the myth of the Bodhisattvas in Mahayana Buddhism—and how wholesome is the Mahayana inculcation of infinite patience! Love to you all and a Merry Christmas.

Your affectionate

A.

Dairy Cottage, Foxhollow Farm,
Rhinebeck, N.Y.
15 December, 1937

My dear Harold,

[. . . .] For the moment I have a respite; but after the new year shall have to set off on my travels again, going to Washington, Philadelphia, Toronto and perhaps other places. (Pardon this diminuendo, due to my not noticing that the ribbon had to change its direction!) After that I expect we shall be heading for Europe, unless in the interval I get any news about a scenario I wrote while out in Hollywood. If there was a prospect of somebody wanting to do something with it, I might go back there for a bit to try to prevent them from doing absolutely the worst.

This is a most beautiful piece of country here—up the Hudson river, which flows majestically between wooded bluffs about half a mile from the house. This last is an appendage on one of the numerous vast estates of what are called 'The River Families', who have been living here in a feudal sort of way, in some cases, for two or more centuries. Most of them now are either bankrupt or dotty or both. Which adds a certain charm to the neighbourhood. Weather is cold, but brilliant, with very bright sun and blue skies.

Give our best love and sympathy to Vera. I know what a misery boils can be and hope she'll soon be rid of the beastly things. All best Christmas greetings.

Yours,
Aldous H.

P.S. Have noted a misprint on p 210 line 20, 'unquestionably' shd read 'unquestioningly'.

420: TO J. B. PRIESTLEY

Dairy Cottage, Foxhollow Farm,
Rhinebeck, N.Y.
17 December, 1937

Dear Priestley,

Thank you for your very interesting and friendly letter.

419 *The Huxleys were staying on the old Dows estate, the property of J. J. Astor, in order to have a* pied à terre *for the winter months near their friends William Seabrook and his wife (formerly Marjorie Worthington), who lived at Rhinebeck. Maria had joined her husband by driving alone from California, with a brief stop to call on Frieda Lawrence at San Cristobal. They kept the cottage on Foxhollow Farm until the beginning of February. The scenario Huxley was hoping for news of was presumably* 'Success'.

In view of the kind of book I was trying to write, it seemed to me best to stick to the historical and impersonal, descriptive approach to mysticism. In another kind of book it would be better, I quite agree, to approach it from a personal, autobiographical angle, even though (which would be true in my case) one's own experiences were of a fragmentary and rudimentary nature.

About the sexual business—the significant thing here is the fact, brought out by [J. D.] Unwin in his heavily documented book [*Sex and Culture*], that there does seem to exist a correlation between social energy and a degree of restraint, of which the most obvious symptoms are pre-marital continence and monogamy. My own suspicion is that the important element is not the physical one (though this may be significant in adolescence); it is rather the emotional and conative element. In other words, what matters, so far as civilization is concerned, is not the amount of copulation, but the quantity of attention given by men and women to the subject of sex, the importance conventionally attached to it by social tradition. Where it is 'done' to attach a great deal of importance to the achievement of promiscuous satisfaction and where that promiscuity is felt to be absorbingly thrilling and an end in itself, there, it seems to me, will the amount of attention given to other matters decline and along with it the intensity of the emotions connected with other matters. In a monogamous society—even a monogamous society mitigated by a lot of prostitution—the amount of attention given to copulation and the intensity of the emotions connected with it will not be very great, even though the actual amount of copulation performed may be as considerable [as] in a society devoted to promiscuity, regarded as a worthy end in itself. Thus, the French aristocrat at the end of the *ancien régime* was not, perhaps, copulating more than the respectable bourgeois in a lower stratum of society; but the tradition of gallantry was such that he was undoubtedly giving much more attention to this matter than was the bourgeois. Consequently, since the amount of attention that can be given by any individual seems to be a limited quantity, he was unable to give adequate attention to other aspects of life. This is not in Unwin's book, which is concerned with establishing the fact that some sort of correlation exists; it is my interpretation of the facts.

As to pre-marital continence, there is a great deal of evidence that this is important if there is to be higher education. Gandhi, in his auto-biography, points out how incompatible early marriage in India is with higher education, and there are plenty of other Indian educators who have harped on the same point—which is also frequently made by educators in Africa and other parts of the world where indiscriminate sexual experience starts very young. In his book, *Psychology and the Promethean Will*, Dr Wm Sheldon of Chicago has some interesting things to say on precocious sexuality in this country and the bad effects it has, There can, I think, be little doubt that the deflection of attention

430

on to sexuality in adolescence makes it very hard for young people to think about other matters.

Perhaps I have been unjust to the theatre. My excuse is that there is an incredible amount of tosh talked, in this country especially, about the theatre and the other arts. People chatter about these things as though an education consisting of acting plays or daubing canvas were a complete training for a human being. This seems to me absolutely false—the real truth being that people who accept any kind of art, theatrical or otherwise, as the basis for a life are done for. Art won't stand the strain, was never meant to stand it. The sooner people can be induced to stop talking nonsense about 'creative' activities in the field of the theatrical and other arts, the better, it seems to me, it will be for education.

I expect to be at this address over Christmas. In January I have to go out and do a few lectures, but shall return here in the intervals. If you ever have a free day and would like a pleasant drive of a hundred miles into very beautiful country, do propose yourself for a meal. Accommodation would be rather more difficult, but might be achieved, if my son hasn't got a friend staying. Anyhow, this village has a charming hotel—famed as being the oldest in America.

Please remember me to your wife and believe me, with all best Christmas wishes,

Yours very sincerely,
Aldous Huxley

421: TO GORDON SEWELL

Rhinebeck, N.Y.
31 December, 1937

Dear Mr. Sewell,

Thank you for your interesting letter and the cutting referring to Bailey's adventures in Tibet—which reads curiously like some of the adventures of the Chinese pilgrim, Hiuan Tsiang, in the 7th century.

So far as I am aware, the exercise which consists of demonstrating to oneself the imaginary nature of the gods is common in Northern Buddhism. There are descriptions of these exercises in one of Evans Wentz's translations from the Tibetan (published by the Oxford University Press)—I think the second volume, on Yoga. (Can't remember title: but it's the volume that isn't either *The Book of the Dead* or *Milarepa*.) However, this exercise in demonstrating the imaginary nature of the gods is designed to clear the mind for an understanding of the reality of the 'Buddha nature' immanent in all beings. Or so at least I understand it.

About the 'Dark Night'—there wd seem to be several varieties of this. One due to the loss of a sense of the personality of the godhead, as described by St John of the Cross: another due to the sense of unworthiness: another to 'dryness' or the inability to transcend personality and perhaps another due to a kind of temporary psycho-physical disintegration.

Yours sincerely
Aldous Huxley

422: TO JACOB I. ZEITLIN

Rhinebeck, N.Y.
10 *January,* 1938

Dear Jake,

Will you forward the enclosed to Mr Lissauer, whose address I seem to have mislaid?

About the MSS—I think I shall have to talk the matter over with Frieda. She has left these manuscripts to us in her will. But it is quite on the cards that she may desire or find it necessary to change her testamentary dispositions and resume possession of the manuscripts. This being so, I don't feel I have a right, without her express permission, to take over possession now. Anyhow, there's no hurry.

Our plans have crystallized more or less as follows. After my last lecture, which is at the beginning of next week, we expect to spend a day or two in New York, then to pack up here and set out by easy stages for the West. We shall probably see Frieda en route and certainly, I think, go to Colorado Springs for a day or so to see Matthew at school. (His address, incidentally, is Fountain Valley School, Colorado Springs, Colo:.) After that we shall aim at Los Angeles. Whether the stay there is to be short or long depends partly on the fate of the scenario, partly on other matters, not yet fully decided. I want anyhow to see how Gerald Heard is getting on; he is out there now. If all goes well, we should be seeing you at no very distant date. The most hopeful addresses en route will be Frieda's and Matthew's. (Better enclose any letters in notes explaining they are to be held till arrival.) However don't place too much reliance on any communications reaching us. They probably will; but they possibly may not, for it often happens that one covers the ground more rapidly or more slowly than one expected, or that one changes one's course.

I hope you're well and that business has not been too bad. Here we sit in the snow, with the mercury, these last days, at twenty below—but keep tolerably well. I am ruminating a novel, which threatens, if I am not careful, to turn into the *Comédie Humaine.* Let's hope to God it can be restrained before it's too late!

Maria sends her love.

Yours,
Aldous H.

1340 N. Laurel Avenue,
Hollywood, Calif.
15 March, 1938

Dear Mrs. Roberts,

I was glad to hear from you from Buda Pest. I have been lecturing in this country, after which I was sick for some time with a relatively benign form of pneumonia and am now beginning to creep about again like a blue-bottle fly, aroused from sleep by the sun.

The world makes one despair; but I suppose that's foolish. As the Chinese ambassador said to Goncourt after the siege of Paris, when the latter had apologized for the unfavourable view of France that the envoy had had: 'But when one belongs to an old civilization like mine, one knows that such things are normal. They occur from time to time'. We are silly, I suppose, to imagine that they will stop occurring. Life in what the Christians wd call a 'fallen world' entails the siege of Paris etc, just as it entails the simple pleasures of sensuous, instinctive and emotional satisfaction. You doubtless can't have the one without the other. The only alternative is Reality, the Kingdom of Heaven, Nirvana etc. You mention *Genji*—enchanting book! But one must remember that within about 40 years of its writing Japan was plunged in the chaotic barbarism of feudal civil wars. One never gets anything for nothing.

In this country I have associated—by an odd series of accidents— mainly with doctors and astronomers. Very nice professions, both of them; for the doctors can feel they're doing good, while the astronomers can be fairly sure that they're not doing much harm. There are not many other people who can feel the same. And then the mere fun of those trades! The experimental work on a new cancer cure which I saw being done—fascinating and exciting. And here in southern California, the endless amusement which is being derived from the new 200-inch telescope, which poses problems in every domain of science and technology, from optics and pure mathematics to metallurgy and chemistry and engineering.

All good wishes.

Yours
Aldous Huxley

423 *The Huxleys, after buying a new Ford car, had returned to California by way of Colorado and New Mexico. They arrived at Los Angeles on Friday, 11 February, and moved into a rented house two days later. Huxley had felt ill at Tucson, during the last stage of the journey, and by the following Monday he was suffering from respiratory inflammation and severe urticaria, with a moderate fever. He was in bed for the next four weeks, part of the time in hospital. He relapsed in May and was still suffering after-effects as late as the autumn.*

1340 *N. Laurel Avenue,*
Hollywood, Calif.
12 *April,* 1938

My dear J,

I was very sorry to hear of your troubles and that you might have to have an operation. I do hope it won't pull you down too much and that, above all, it will keep you well in the future. Curiously enough, we saw not long ago the doctor who looked after you in an earlier sinus trouble—Dr. Gerald Webb of Colorado Springs, who spoke very affectionately of you and went into great details about your sinus, even telling us that you were an interesting case inasmuch as you had no frontal sinus. I thought him a most remarkable old man, and they all say he's one of the *sommités* in the matter of TB.

My own troubles began shortly after seeing him and consisted of a subacute pneumonia that never got really bad, but refused to get well, and so kept me in bed for some weeks. I'm out and about again, but still going cautiously as there appears to be some slight bronchial thickening even now.

News that they might take a scenario I wrote last autumn brought me back here. But nothing has happened up to date; for the whole picture industry is in a state of neurasthenia and panic, and it's impossible for anyone to make any decision, at any rate for the moment.

Meanwhile I'm working on a novel and collecting whatever information I can pick up in regard to the technique for giving a viable economic and social basis to philosophic anarchism—it being more and more clear that the present system of production necessarily involves centralization and dictatorship, whatever the political context—communist, fascist or merely plutocratic. I was much interested, out East, in seeing Ralph Borsodi, whose work you probably know and who has set up what he calls a 'School of Living' for giving practical effect to his ideas about decentralization and small-scale production. One of the interesting things he has discovered, as a result of very careful investigation of the subject from the point of view of a cost accountant (which was his profession) is that in 2/3 of the field of economics decentralized production in the home and the small workshop, using small power units and machines, is from 20% to 35% cheaper than centralized mass production. So that quite apart from any question of social and political desirability, decentralized production is in a large number of cases demonstrably more efficient, in contemporary circumstances, than mass production. Meanwhile, unfortunately, people are so much obsessed with the

---

424 *The novel in progress, on which Huxley worked intermittently from 1938 to 1940, was never completed. Ralph Borsodi: in* After Many a Summer, *written in 1939, Borsodi's theories were shown in practical application through a character called Mr Propter. The School of Living was at Suffern, New York.*

old idea that mass production is the only possible method, that economists and legislators go on working out more and more elaborate (and consequently more and more dictatorial) plans for the purpose of making a centralized mass-producing industry work. It's a bad and depressing business —like everything else.

The cancer-man [Beaumont Cornell], about whom I wrote you, never went to England; but his work, both at Lambeth and over here, where it is being taken up by various institutions and individuals, is giving very remarkable results. It looks as tho' he had hit on something very fundamental.

There's a remarkable little man here called [R. R.] Mellon, from the Mellon Institute at Pittsburgh, who has done some very queer work on bacteria—getting one form to transform itself into another, e.g. pneumococcus into diphtheria bacillus. Nobody wd believe him at first, because it was too revolutionary. But it seems that now the Rockefeller Institution has grudgingly taken it up—after nearly 15 years of stubborn resistance! It confirms old McDonagh's odd theories of bacteria being mutations from one form.

Our best love to you both and special wishes for yourself in regard to this beastly sinus.

Ever your affectionate
A.

P.S. I was so very glad to hear of the FRS.

425: TO JULIAN HUXLEY

710 *N. Linden Dr.,*
Beverly Hills, Calif.
22 *July,* 1938

My dear J,

Thank you for forwarding Emma Goldman's letter and for your own. I was sorry to have the continued unsatisfactory news about your health. What a curse it must be to have such a chronic brake on activity I can guess by my own experience with the aftermaths of this spring's pneumonia. For tho' I'm quite well, I still get much too easily fatigued and go down like an express elevator if I put forth too much energy at a given moment. So I am going slowly and trying to combine the slowness with compensatory steadiness. After about 3 months or more of indecision, the film people seem at last to have made up their minds to ask me to do the life of Mme Curie for the screen. The contract is not yet signed; but is going to be in all probability, within the next week. (It is still of course on the cards that they may change

425 *The Metro-Goldwyn-Mayer film of* Madame Curie, *produced by Sidney Franklin, was delayed by problems of casting, and by the time it was released, in* 1943, *Mervyn Le Roy had replaced Cukor as director and Huxley's script had been superseded. According to a letter of Maria Huxley to the Vicomte de Noailles, Huxley received about* $15,000 *for his version.*

their minds—which seem to have the characteristics of the minds of chim-panzees, agitated and infinitely distractable.) I shall enjoy doing the job—if they leave me reasonably in peace—and it also has the merit of being so enormously overpaid that I hope to be able to save enough in a few weeks to keep me a year without having to bother about anything else. Garbo will do Mme Curie and there is to be an intelligent director, George Kukor [Cukor]. [. . . .]

Meanwhile, I have been at work on a novel which is at the same time a sort of philosophical Summa in anecdotal form. Interesting to write, if only, as seems quite possible, it is [not] strictly unwriteable.

Have you read [Alfred] Korzybski's *Science and Sanity*? If not, I think you shd—in spite of the fact that the author is maddening and his book 800 pp long. For he does seem to have said things about 'Semantics'—the relation of words to things and events—which are of the highest importance. And incidentally he seems to have read practically everything.

Our best love to you all. I do hope you'll be rid of your troubles soon.

Ever your affectionate
Aldous

426: TO CHRISTOPHER MORLEY

710 N. Linden Drive,
Beverly Hills, Calif.
4 August, 1938

Dear Mr. Morley,

Jake Zeitlin has shown me the letter you sent him recently. I did dis-cover your *Trojan Horse* shortly after it appeared and enjoyed it very much, as a genuinely Chaucerian work. It made me realize, yet again, how useful, artistically and philosophically, it is to have a known and accepted mythology at one's disposal. Each generation can re-tell and re-interpret the stories in its own way. There is even a lot to be said for sacred books; for the interpre-tation and allegorizing of such works as Genesis or the Song of Songs has evoked, in the course of ages, a great volume of important philosophical and psychological speculation. The disappearance of the Bible from the contemporary consciousness threatens a serious loss to culture.

The only thing I missed from your *Horse* was a touch, not of Chaucer, but of Matthew Arnold—the Arnold of the mystical tradition who wrote of the Palladium:

> 'And Hector was in Ilium there below,
> And fought, and saw it not, but there it stood . . .
> So, in its lovely moonlight, lives the soul. . . .'

And so on. It is a psychologically and philosophically legitimate addition to the Trojan myth.

Yours very sincerely
Aldous Huxley

1320 *N. Crescent Heights Blvd.,*
L. A., Cal.
18 *November,* 1938

My dear J,

Your accident must have been a very near shave, indeed. I'm thankful you all got off as lightly as you did. I hope that Juliette has got over the psychological shock of the thing. There's something very deadly in these violent blows below the conscious water-line, so to speak.

Not much news here. The tiresome bronchiectasis which has remained as a hang-over from the pneumonia I had this spring has continued to get me down at intervals below par, and the doctors have consequently put me on to a regimen of 12 hours rest per day—10 hours at night, 2 in the afternoon—with the threat of winter in the desert unless the lungs clear up—which I think they're doing all right, as the rest seems to have done me a lot of good already. I shall keep on with it and stick to a warm climate for the time being.

In the intervals of resting I've done a fair amount of work: a 'treatment', as they call it in the jargon of the films, of the life of Mme Curie for Garbo. Rather an amusing job—tho' I shdn't like too many of the kind, since this telling a story in purely pictorial terms doesn't allow of any of the experimentation with words in their relation to things, events and ideas, which is *au fond* my business. They gave me 8 weeks to do the job and I turned in what is, I think, quite a good script in which the scientific processes used by the Curies and the trains of reasoning they pursued are rendered in pictorial terms (all within the space of about 5 minutes, which is about all the public will tolerate of this kind of thing!). It now remains to be seen whether the studio will preserve anything of what I've done. They have followed their usual procedure and handed my treatment over to several other people to make a screen-play out of. By the time they are ready to shoot it may have been through twenty pairs of hands. What will be left? One shudders to think. Meanwhile they have paid me a lot of money and I find myself able to go on for a year, I should think, without further worry about finance. Always a pleasant state of affairs. Since finishing Curie, I've been at work on a kind of novel which is, at the same time as a story of people, an analysis of narratives in general, of the nature of individuality, of the relationship between words and things—the whole culminating, I hope, in some kind of general theory of the world. Goodness knows what it will be like when it's done—if it ever gets done! Meanwhile, it interests me a lot and has set me reading along a number of interesting lines—Carnap, Neurath, Morris and

427 *At the end of September the Huxleys had moved back to Hollywood from Beverly Hills, taking a house for a six-month term.*

Korzybski on the problems of semiosis; the Abbé Brémond on the history of religious psychology—a most fascinating book incidentally and one which makes one all the more regretful that Catholicism shd have got itself tied up with those preposterous dogmas and that in many ways dreadful Hebrew book. One sees that theology is mainly an obstacle race; one covers the course with intellectual hedges, chevaux-de-frise, pitfalls, booby-traps; having done which one spends enormous ingenuity and subtlety in circumventing these obstacles. In the intervals the theologians make the most remarkable psychological discoveries, record astonishing insights. One sees the immense good fortune of Buddhists in not being cursed with a sacred book or an impossible dogma. True, they invented a lot of dogmas and paid idolatrous respect to a number of texts as they went along; but there was happily never such an orthodoxy as in Christianity and never a Bible. The modern psychologist has no obstacle; but on the whole how shallow and how incomplete he is! To find a psychology covering the whole range of human potentiality, not merely the range known to the *homme moyen sensuel*, one must study the religious philosophers.

All this, of course, seems rather like fiddling while Rome burns, in view of what's happening in the world. But, then, what is happening in the world is happening, among other reasons, because people have neglected that side of the psychological problem discussed (with so many unfortunately irrelevant absurdities) by the best theologians. Rome burns because it has not been sufficiently fiddled over. I think there is definitely an important job to be done in the restatement in contemporary terms of these psychological facts. Meanwhile, God knows what the world is in for. Every day one is more and more appalled by what is happening—and what is likely to happen, seeing that Gresham's Law holds good in every field and that bad politics tends to drive out good politics just as bad money drives out good money. The progressive deterioration of the remaining islands and oases of decency is to be expected—has already begun, of course. One of the most alarming features in the situation is that, technologically, governments are so much better equipped to be tyrannical than in the past. Being able to tyrannize, they will exert tyranny, because tyranny is agreeable to tyrants. Bertie Russell's new book on Power brings out the psychological mechanism of tyranny very clearly. Opportunity makes the tyrant as well as the thief; and tyrants have never had such opportunities as they have today, with planes, tanks, wireless and all the rest at their disposal. These things are not yet exploited to the full in democratic countries, because there is still, in Burke's phrase, a 'crust of custom' favourable to liberty. Under the stress of events the crust is rapidly dissolving.

Our love to you all.

Ever your affectionate

A.

1320 N. Crescent Heights Blvd., L. A.
19 November, 1938

Dear Jake,

After having thought over the suggestion you made last night, I have decided that I had better say no. I used at one time to do a lot of writing letters to the papers and signing statements; but recently have been coming to the conclusion that it is better not to do these things, unless there is some specific and concrete piece of good to be gained by doing so—as there was, for example, in the case of the Spanish children, where my preface might serve to raise a little extra money. Expressions of generalized opinions, outbursts of indignation and the like don't seem to me to fulfill any very useful purpose. One is reminded, when one reads them, of the anecdote about President Coolidge who was asked what the sermon he had been listening to was about. 'About sin', he answered. 'What was the line taken by the preacher?' 'He was against it.' We are all against sin; but it doesn't seem to be much good to record the fact unless either one can do something to mitigate the results of sin in some particular case or, alternatively, elaborate a general theory accounting for sin, accompanied by a theory as to the best way of creating circumstances in which the commission of sins shall be less frequent. If one confines oneself to denouncing or expressing horror, one is merely indulging and permitting others to indulge in the pleasures (very considerable, admittedly) of using intemperate language. It took me about three hundred pages to elaborate the kind of theory I have been talking about; and I see now that there are considerable additions and modifications that ought to be made.

This being so, I don't see that any good would be done by my writing even two or three thousand words on the subject. The persecution of the Jews in Germany is horrible in the extreme; but it is not by proclaiming the fact in a loud voice that this particular persecution will be stopped or that human beings will discontinue the habit of persecution, which is immensely old and which is bound up with habits of thought, feeling, action and belief, with traditional methods of social and economic organization such that, if the latter persist, the former must inevitably manifest itself. It is useless to treat small-pox by cutting out the individual pustules and stitching up the wounds.

Yours,
Aldous Huxley

1320 N. Crescent Heights Blvd.,
L.A., Calif.
19 February, 1939

My dear Harold,

Thanks for your letter of Jan 17. The idea of a library edition makes me feel most horribly posthumous, and at the same time a bit self-important, as though attaching an excessive value to the published books. I say this all the more frankly because I feel certain doubts in regard to the soundness of the project as a publishing venture. Do people buy sets? My chief knowledge of the subject is derived from the catalogues of second-hand booksellers, where remainders of sumptuous library editions of standard authors tend to figure rather largely, at sacrifice prices. I can't help feeling that the modest three and sixpenny is at bottom the sounder proposition, and that if any new project is to be undertaken, it should be along the lines of in some way gingering up the three and sixpenny editions as they exist already—either by some fancy quirk of binding or title-paging, or perhaps by some judicious use of illustrations by some competent artist. This last, I think, mightn't be a bad plan. If each volume in the three and sixpenny edition had one or more really good drawings by a sound hand, this would be an added incentive for getting the whole lot, or at any rate, more than one. The chief question is one of expense. I merely throw out the suggestion as a possible alternative to the library edition idea, about which, I confess, I don't feel entirely happy.

Did I tell you that I had put aside the long, elaborate novel for the time being and am hard at work on a short phantasy [*After Many a Summer*], in the manner, more or less, of *Brave New World*? It seems to be going pretty well, and I hope to have it finished in time for early autumn publication. The book, as I hope it will be, is a phantasy, but built up of solidly realistic psychological elements; a wild extravaganza, but with the quality of a most serious parable. I hope it will get itself written fairly smoothly and expeditiously. After that, I shall write the eight lectures on religion which I have to deliver this year in Calcutta for a thing appropriately called the Gosh Foundation. These will make, I hope, quite an interesting volume. Our love to Vera and yourself.

Yours,

A.

429 *This letter was one of the first to be typewritten on Huxley's new machine, with oversize type, the capital letters being five millimetres high and the others large in proportion. He stopped using it after a few months.*

1320 N. Crescent Heights Blvd.,
Los Angeles, Calif.
11 March, 1939

Dearest Joan,

Thank you for your letter with its good news about the children's approaching arrival and their American affidavits. This last is very good, as I hadn't been making much progress in the matter from this end.

Use the cheque for any purpose connected with the children, of course. Further to my last letter, as they say—I think I can manage about £100 a year for the next two years: more if I get another overpaid film job! (But that's still hypothetical.)

Bless you all.

Your affectionate
Aldous

431: TO JULIAN HUXLEY

701 S. Amalfi Drive,
Pacific Palisades, Cal.
30 July, 1939

My dear Julian,

It's a long time since I last wrote, I'm afraid. Extreme busy-ness must serve as my excuse. Now, thank goodness, I am momentarily free, having finished the book I have been working on for these past months. It is a kind of fantasy, at once comic and cautionary, farcical, blood-curdling and reflective.

In the intervals of writing, I have been working on my eyes, taking lessons in seeing from an admirable teacher here who was trained by the late Dr. [W. H.] Bates of New York, the deviser of the method which bears his name. Optometrists loathe the method, because it endangers a hundred-and-fifty-million-dollar-a-year spectacle industry. Most doctors oppose it, because Bates's experimental work established unquestionably, it seems to me after reading his papers—that the Helmholtz theory regarding accommodation

430 *A German woman who, along with Huxley's cousin Joan Collier (Mrs Buzzard), had been a pupil of his mother at Prior's Field during his childhood was preparing to send her two children out of Germany, where they were in danger because of Jewish ancestry. The original plan of having them join relations in America was abandoned after they reached England; General Buzzard and his wife took them in as foster children, and Huxley made large regular contributions towards their education.*

431 *Huxley, who was later to write* The Art of Seeing, *was taught the Bates method by Margaret D. Corbett, the author of* How to Improve Your Eyes *(1938). Bates had described his techniques in* Perfect Sight Without Glasses *(1920).*

and refractive error is wrong. Still, the more liberal doctors have now got to the point of saying that it can't do any harm. Meanwhile there are the empirical facts, which are these in my own case. After having worn bi-focals, first of six and-a-half and eight diopters of magnification, then of eight and ten diopters, plus special reading glasses of fifteen diopters, I am now wearing no glasses, seeing much better at a distance, reading, and all without strain and with a general improvement in health and nervous condition. I have just done the whole of the revision of my typescript (a very trying job, as you doubtless know) without glasses and, except for a slight discomfort the first day (corrected by taking the proper precautions) without fatigue. Meanwhile, the vision of the right eye has increased in the last three months, so that, from seeing the big 200-foot letter on the chart at three feet, I can now read the 70-foot line at six feet and large nursery print at the near point. The scar tissue is quite definitely clearing up, and I have good hopes that, if I persist, I may get back as much vision in the bad eye as I had in the good eye and that the good eye may be pushed on from fifty per cent of normal vision (where it is now, having been raised from about fifteen per cent) to something considerably nearer normal. Meanwhile, I have seen other cases responding in the same way. Constance Collier, the actress, took the treatment for a cataract which had reduced one eye to a mere perception of light and darkness. After four months, she can now read normal print with this eye. Incipient cataracts clear up completely in as little as a month. Glaucoma is relieved very rapidly. I have seen several cases of children with squint completely cured. Pigmented retina recovers normal vision and even partially detached retinas come back to normal. And all through a perfectly rational and simple series of practices designed, first, to relax the eye and increase its circulation of blood and lymph; second, to train the mind to interpret what the eye sends it and not to interfere with the functioning of the eye by straining or staring. The deplorable thing is that the number of efficient teachers of the Bates method is at present ludicrously small. There are one or two here, one or two in New York—*et praeterea nihil*, except, apparently, in Germany, where, I hear, a modified form of the method is being taken up intensively. In London there are a few teachers, but none of them, apparently, is really good. It's really a great shame, considering what remarkable results can be achieved by anyone who knows the technique and can get co-operation from the patient.

News here is unexciting. We live very quietly, see a minimum of people. I think a good deal about the lectures I am supposed to give in the course of the winter at Calcutta and shall soon have to start writing the things—wishing, meanwhile, that I had more time, as there is so much I don't know enough about; for example, language—so immeasurably important in religion as in every other activity, so little studied or understood, probably

431 *Huxley's lecture engagement in Calcutta was cancelled. The Huxleys had moved to Pacific Palisades about 1 April.*

because people have a real emotional horror of analysing the medium in which they do most of their living. Indeed, the more one reads about language, the more obvious it is that there is a real taboo in relation to it. The science of linguistics is more than a century old; but it has entered into the curricula of schools and universities to a lesser extent than any other science. Only a few specialists touch it. The rest remain perfectly ignorant of its findings. And not only ignorant—actually misinformed. For what little is taught about language happens to be mainly wrong—for it consists of the traditional grammar, as taught by the Greeks and Romans, a most inadequate affair. There is obviously no hope of thinking or acting rationally about any of the major issues of life until we learn to understand the instrument we use to think about them. The fact that there is this powerful taboo against the analysis of language makes one suspect, (what every person of deep religious insight has always insisted to be true) that most people don't want to think correctly about the world because they get such a lot of short-range fun (which outweighs for them the long-range miseries that always follow) from thinking incorrectly and acting stupidly. When men and women are faced with Spinoza's choice between human bondage and human freedom, they choose bondage, because it seems more amusing and to promise a 'better time'.

I hope all goes well with you and the family. We are all in good shape. Matthew seems to have taken a definite step towards consolidating his health and strength. His basal metabolism, which was extremely low, is up close to normal, thanks to a combination of a judicious endocrine treatment with the stimulus provided by the high altitude of Colorado.

Our best love to you all.

Ever your affectionate,
Aldous

432: † TO KINGSLEY MARTIN

701 *S. Amalfi Drive,*
Pacific Palisades, Calif.
30 *July,* 1939

Dear Kingsley Martin,

Many thanks for your letter, and apologies for not having answered it before—a delay due to pressure of work.

I don't know where you got your information about Gerald and myself being about to start a community; it doesn't happen to be true. I can't speak for Gerald; but certainly I don't know nearly enough about many things to be able to embark on such a venture with any prospect of success. This

432 *Community: Heard did start a community, Trabuco College, in* 1942, *for which Huxley helped write the prospectus and at which he spent considerable time.*

doesn't diminish my interest in such ventures; for I become more and more firmly convinced that it is completely pointless to work in the field of politics, in the ordinary sense of the word—first, because one can't achieve anything unless one is in a key position, and, second, because, even if one were in a key position, all one could achieve would be, at the best, a deflection of evil into slightly different channels. The existing system seems to be even less viable than previous social systems (because more efficient and therefore capable of achieving greater evil in a shorter space of time than previous systems). One is forced to the conclusion that the men of religious insight were right in insisting that society at large and men and women as they are on the average, in the 'unregenerate' state, are doomed to perpetual self-frustration and self-destruction. Every great religious leader has been profoundly pessimistic about society at large and men and women as they are. (Generation of vipers. Many are called, few chosen. The needle's eye. From those that have not shall be taken away even that which they have. Unless your righteousness exceed that of the Scribes and Pharisees. Maya. Fallen World. Etc. etc.) On the other hand, they have been profoundly optimistic about the potentialities of individuals and very small associations of such individuals. (The kingdom of heaven. Nirvana. Non-attachment. Sub specie aeternitatis. Dying to the ordinary life of personality to be reborn. Etc etc.) Nineteenth-century humanists (who were members of the more prosperous classes in the more go-ahead countries of the West) reversed the traditional attitude and were optimistic about society at large and men and women as they are (social reform, compulsory education, Utopia, evolution. Etc. etc.) At the same time they were so pessimistic about the things that every religious teacher had been optimistic about that they were simply unaware of the possibility that human beings could ever transcend their miserable little egos. This attitude is becoming less and less acceptable, even in the West and even among the prosperous. It is obvious now that the religious teachers were right and that nothing can be achieved on the exclusively political plane except palliation and the deflection of evils. So long as the majority of human beings choose to live like the *homme moyen sensuel*, in an 'unregenerate' state, society at large cannot do anything except stagger along from catastrophe to catastrophe. Religious people who think that they can go into politics and transform the world always end by going into politics and being transformed by the world. (E.g. the Jesuits, Père Joseph, the Oxford Group.) Religion can have no politics except the creation of small-scale societies of chosen individuals outside and on the margin of the essentially unviable large-scale societies, whose nature dooms them to self-frustration and suicide.

It seems a dismal conclusion; but it is the one that every religious teacher has always insisted on as unescapable.

Yours
Aldous Huxley

444

701 *Amalfi Drive,*
Pacific Palisades, Calif.
1 *August,* 1939

Dearest Eva,

How sweet of you and Sybille to remember my birthday. It was a more than ordinarily cheerful day this year, as it coincided with the completion of the novel I have been working on for the last months—a novel, incidentally, the whole of which was written and revised without spectacles; for I have been taking a course of eye training by what is called the Bates Method [. . . .] All this, as you can imagine, has been extremely interesting and exciting and, incidentally, encouraging; for it shows that there are some things about which one is justified in feeling hopeful and optimistic in this hideous world. Society at large is obviously for ever doomed to a continual process of self-frustration; but for individuals there remain enormous potentialities, both physical and psychological—potentialities which, in the ordinary course of events, remain completely unrealized, but which, if one knows how and is prepared to take the trouble, one can realize. It looks as though the overwhelming majority of people were content to live at about twenty per cent of their potential capacities. The discovery of methods for realizing the full hundred per cent—this seems to be about the only sensible and constructive thing that one can do in this lunatic asylum we've got into.

I hope the painting goes well. I have not been able to do any for more than a year now and am almost scared of beginning again, for fear of getting too much involved in it, to the exclusion of everything else. It's a pity one can't do more than, say, three whole-time jobs at one moment! It is really quite extraordinary how bad most of the painting in this country is! Not that it is much better anywhere else, at the present time; for there were certainly no new people in Paris when I left, and Pierre Roy, who was here recently, assured me that the dealers were still searching for new talent, in vain. But meanwhile the stuff they turn out here seems to be even worse than in Europe. [Georgia] O'Keefe was here not long ago and spoke of you. Those urini-genital flowers of hers continue to blossom with success. The most remarkable paintings I have seen recently were by a child—a deaf and dumb Spanish boy of fifteen, now a refugee in Mexico, who seems to be in painting what Mozart was in music, with a wealth of invention, a sureness of touch, a brilliancy of execution, a faultlessness of taste, which are perfectly incredible. It remains to be seen whether he will carry his gifts into maturity.

Let us know the news of Sanary. [. . . .]
Much love from

Your affectionate,
Aldous

701 *S. Amalfi Drive,*
Pacific Palisades, Calif.
8 *August,* 1939

Dear Ralph,

I have just received the half yearly statement from my bank, and I find that you paid into my account in May a sum of seventeen hundred pounds. The account sent me from your office in April showed a credit of £2564. In my last letter, written many weeks ago, I asked you to place the whole of the sum due to me in my bank; it is therefore with great surprise and annoyance that I find that this has not been done, and that my account is at present insufficient to cover the amounts which I have drawn upon it in recent cheques. Please place these sums immediately and in their entirety to my account in the Westminster Bank, West End branch. I am at a loss to understand why money which was paid to you on my behalf as much (in some cases) as a year ago should still be withheld from me, and in future I must insist that accountings shall be made quarterly and that the sums due shall be paid into my bank at the time the accountings are made. Meanwhile, I shall be obliged if you will pay the residue of the sum owed me into my bank at once, so that the cheques I have drawn recently can be met.

Yours,
Aldous H.

435: TO HAROLD RAYMOND

701 *S. Amalfi Dr.,*
Pacific Palisades, Calif.
20 *August,* 1939

Dear Harold,

Thank you for your letter. I am very glad you like the book [*After Many a Summer*]. Proof reading will be difficult to manage in time; so I am sending you on a separate page a series of corrections relating mainly to the finer shades of the American language, on which I have been taking expert opinion [from Anita Loos]. The name Dowlas, I am afraid, has got to be changed, owing to its fortuitous resemblance to that of a notorious lady in this neighbourhood [Marion Davies]. I think that Maunciple should prove a sufficiently euphonious and safe substitute. Please have a careful eye kept on the proofs to see that every mention of the name is corrected.

Yours in haste,
Aldous H.

P.S. Wd you kindly send a copy of the galleys, when they're ready, to my sister-in-law, Madame Nys, 82 rue Bonaparte, Paris, VI.

PPS What about a design of *carp* on the dust cover?

434 *The 'last letter', referred to here, had been written on* 15 *June. See letters* 448 *and* 450.

701 *S. Amalfi Drive,*
Pacific Palisades, Cal.
2 *November,* 1939

My dear Gene,

Many thanks for your letter of the 26th. With regard to the commission question, I don't see any particular reason why Pinker should get a percentage on this. So will you tell the office to pay the check into my account at the Fifth Avenue Branch of the Guaranty Trust?

No special news here. I work away at the adaptation of *Pride and Prejudice* for the moment—an odd, cross-word puzzle job. One tries to do one's best for Jane Austen; but actually the very fact of transforming the book into a picture must necessarily alter its whole quality in a profound way. In any picture or play, the story is essential and primary. In Jane Austen's books, it is a matter of secondary importance (every dramatic event in *Pride and Prejudice* is recorded in a couple of lines, generally in a letter) and serves merely as a receptacle for the dilute irony in which the characters are bathed. Any other kind of receptacle would have served the purpose equally well; and the insistence upon the story as opposed to the diffuse irony which the story is designed to contain, is a major falsification of Miss Austen.

In the intervals I make notes for a book along the lines of the lectures which I should have given at Calcutta this winter. Essentially, the book will consist of an examination, in the light of modern analysis of language and in terms of a Bridgmanesque operational philosophy, of the more important words and concepts of religion. But all this will be for the time when *Pride and Prejudice* is done with—which should be, I hope, by the New Year.

Please give my love to Martha and tell her that, since Europe is cut off, we hope she and you may make California an alternative. Thank you both so much for looking after Sophie.

Yours,
Aldous H.

437: † TO JULIAN HUXLEY

701 *S. Amalfi Drive,*
Pacific Palisades, Cal.
18 *November,* 1939

My dear Julian,

What an unexpected piece of good news! If present plans hold, we shall

436 *Sophie Moulaert was travelling from France to live with the Huxleys. Since August, Huxley had been working on the script for a film of Jane Austen's* Pride and Prejudice, *which was being produced by Hunt Stromberg for Metro-Goldwyn-Mayer. The film, written partly by Jane Murfin, was directed by Robert Z. Leonard and was released in* 1940.

be here all the winter and shall be very happy to see you whenever you like, before Christmas, at Christmas, or after Christmas. If you come during the Christmas holidays you will have to share a bathroom with Matthew, who will be back from college.

I am working at present on the screen adaptation of *Pride and Prejudice*, which should, if all goes well, pay expenses for a year and permit of helping a few people caught in the nightmare on the other side of the Atlantic. I hope and even anticipate, in so far as any rational anticipation is justifiable in this lunatic industry, that the job will be finished by the time you come, so that I shall be fairly free while you are here.

Your criticism of Gerald's book [*Pain, Sex and Time*] was very interesting. I have always thought it unfortunate that Gerald should have consistently chosen to employ historical and pre-historical terms for the discussion of psychological and philosophical problems. The result is a quite unnecessary confusion of issues and the casting of a haze of dubiety over matters of plain psychological fact. What the subject of mystical religion needs above all is, first, an analysis of the language used to describe and interpret it and, second, a systematization of the materials by means of something like Bridgman's operational philosophy. Incidentally, I am hoping to attempt something of the kind when I am finished with my movie work.

If your wanderings across the country take you near Denver, do get into touch with Matthew (Men's Dormitory 312) at the University of Colorado, Boulder, Colo. He will be delighted to have a glimpse of you. I hear by roundabout ways that Gervas and his wife are in the country and are coming out here. I hope this is so.

Our best love to you; and don't take liberties with this damned climate as you cross. Let us know dates as soon as you know them yourself.

Your affectionate
A.

438: TO GERVAS HUXLEY

701 *S. Amalfi Drive,*
Pacific Palisades, Calif.
5 *January,* 1940

My dear Gerry,

I had meant to write before to tell you how very much I enjoyed seeing you—all too briefly, alas. Pride, Prejudice, Christmas and Julian's visit have conspired to keep me from carrying out my intention until Friday. I hope there may be a chance of catching another glimpse of you in the not too distant future—with Elspeth next time, I trust. Perhaps it will be in Kenya—and I think you're so wise to plan to settle there in a world you

438 *Elspeth Huxley's book was* Death of an Aryan, *published in October.*

will be a little freer to remake according to the heart's desire than obsessed, hallucinated Europe can ever be.

Tell Elspeth that we've just finished reading her book aloud. I thought it really very good. As a technician, I venture to offer a criticism of a point that was particularly in evidence during reading-aloud—which is that she has a tendency to let her descriptions fall into blank verse. But that's a small matter and easy to remedy. Otherwise it struck me as an admirable job.

Well, bless you both. Give our loves to the love-worthy. Hasta la vista.

Ever yours
Aldous

439: TO GORDON SEWELL

[701 *S. Amalfi Drive,*
Pacific Palisades, Calif.]
12 *January*, 1940

Dear Mr Sewell,

Thank you for your letter of December 11th. From what I have read about the doctrine of the Void, in Suzuki and La Vallée Poussin, I should say it corresponded very closely with the Taulerian conception.

With regard to your other point—there is a very interesting analogy between that sort of infallibility which seems to characterize the enlightened individual (for 'guidance', as every mystic has always insisted, comes only at the end of a life of religious self-training and not, as the Oxford Groupers and the innumerable similar sects that have preceded them assert, at the beginning) and the instincts of the lower animals and the sub-conscious psycho-physiological processes going on within the human body. It looks as though there were a kind of spiral development, from unconscious animal, through conscious human up to a what for lack of better words may be called super-conscious spiritual, which last exhibits the characteristics of the animal plane, but transfigured and on a higher level. Santayana uses the phrase 'animal faith' to describe our commonsense confidence in the existence of an external world. The phrase 'animal grace' might similarly be used to connote the unbelievably perfect workings of what Driesch calls the Entelechy in our bodies and nervous systems. Analogous but superior, on the corresponding point of the circumference of the spiral, but on a higher level, is spiritual grace. On the opposite side of the circumference, on the conscious human level, is 'human grace', represented in the individual by inspiration from and self-sacrifice to strictly human 'ideals', 'causes' and so forth. Human grace is an *ersatz* for spiritual grace—an *ersatz* ultimately destructive; for acceptance of human grace as the real thing (a) prevents the individual from achieving, or even knowing anything about, spiritual grace, (b) tends to interfere with animal grace; (it has been found empirically that the people under the greatest and most destructive nervous tension are those most passionately interested in, and devoted to, political causes); (c) results

449

in wars, revolutions and other large-scale lunacies which end by destroying all the human values to which the individual originally devoted himself.

Yours sincerely,
Aldous Huxley

440: † TO JULIAN HUXLEY

701 *S. Amalfi,*
Pacific Palisades, Cal.
14 *January,* 1940

Dearest Julian,

I was so glad to have your letter and to know that *malgré tout* you were still surviving, if a bit worse for wear. I do hope the lectures won't prove too exhausting.

No news here. Pee and Pee (as Jane Austen's masterpiece is called at M.G.M.) drags on—not through any fault of writers and director, but because we cannot get to see our producer without whom nothing further can be done. If he does get round to seeing us, it will all be finished in a few days: if not, God knows.

Yesterday for the first time I succeeded, for short stretches, in getting a single fixed image from both eyes together—a thing I never have had. This is a very encouraging advance; for anything that can be got momentarily like this can be built up by proper exercise into a permanent acquisition. The achievement of a fixed image—which means the realignment of the two eyes (the right having slipped out from lack of use, with a resultant tendency to outward squint in the left, good eye)—will tend to accelerate improvement in vision.

I have now found the reference to toads and cancer. It is in *The Magazine Digest* for December '39, in an article reprinted from *Je sais tout*, which cites work done by Albert Peyson at the Pasteur Institute on cancer incidence in different types of animals, and more recent work with toad venom by Robert Cornillean. It is stated that among 1800 frogs examined for this purpose, dozens of growths were found; whereas in 3000 toads no single case of cancer was observed. It sounds as tho' it were worth looking into.

I wish you had been able to stay longer here; but it was good to have had even that crowded and abbreviated glimpse. Give our best love to Juliette and the children—and keep well.

Ever your affectionate
A.

441: TO E. S. P. HAYNES

701 *S. Amalfi Drive,*
Pacific Palisades, Calif:
19 *March,* 1940

My dear Ted,

I was very glad to get your letter yesterday—I don't know what can have happened to the other, of which you write,—and to know that you are as well as can be expected in the hideous circumstances of contemporary London. The accounts I get of London now have a strange similarity to those which Homer gives of Hades—a place of diminished life, of vagueness and uncertainty and sub-acute despair. One wonders apprehensively what is to happen, when taxation and professional unemployment have destroyed the existing structure of the middle classes in Western Europe—quite apart, of course, from any other, more catastrophic modes of destruction. The precedents of Russia and Germany, where the middle classes were wiped out respectively by massacre and inflation, are not encouraging. It certainly looks as though an age of tyranny were before us; and indeed, quite apart from war, it seems that existing industrial techniques and financial organizations must inevitably impose such tyranny—inasmuch as such large-scale organization produces problems too complex to solve except by bureaucratic 'planning', which always leads to more 'planning', (because any given plan is invariably inadequate to a highly complex problem), which means more and more tyranny on the part of the planners (however good their original intentions), more and more repression and regimentation in the desperate effort to simplify the problem and make the plan work. All large-scale plans are beds of Procrustes, to fit which the people must be stretched or surgically abbreviated. I see no hope except in a reversal of existing trends and a deliberate return to a more decentralized form of society with a wider distribution of land and other property. But the probability of such reversal taking place seems almost infinitely small.

Here, the most encouraging thing I have to report is the eye-training which is slowly but surely giving me back my sight. [. . . .]

Other family news is good. Maria is pretty well and so is Matthew, who is reading medicine. We had a glimpse of Julian at Christmas—rather exhausted, but fairly well. Our love to Ria and the family.

Ever yours
Aldous H.

442: TO HAROLD RAYMOND

701 *S. Amalfi Drive,*
Pacific Palisades, Calif.
19 *March,* 1940

My dear Harold,

May I trouble you to forward the enclosed cheque to the Royal Literary Fund, whose address I do not know. The sum represents £25 given me by a woman here to hand on to a deserving charity in England, plus £5 on my own account, which is what I generally send them each year. I shall be grateful if you will send it on for me.

The new book seems to expand in scope as I consider it, and is now threatening to become a sort of *Summa* dealing with everything. The fable

451

will be that of a man who offers himself as a *corpus vile* for a prolonged experiment in the hibernation treatment which they are now using for cancer and heart disease—and who is kept on ice for a couple of centuries, when he is woken up, and finds himself in a different and better kind of world. The book will take the form of a record of his experiences in both worlds, the present and the future, and of his reflections upon them. Endless potentialities, demanding a great deal of thought for even the most partial actualization of them. I will keep you posted with regard to the progress I make. Meanwhile, give our love to Vera and the boys.

Ever yours
Aldous H.

443: † TO JULIAN HUXLEY

701 S. Amalfi Drive,
Pacific Palisades, Calif.
24 April, 1940

Dearest J,

I was sorry to hear the not too good news in your last letter and I hope that, by the time you get this, Zoo storms will have quite blown over and Juliette's hurt will be mended. Meanwhile, my own physiological affairs have not been entirely satisfactory; for I have been having successive attacks of oedematous swellings all over the body, alternated or accompanied by intestinal upsets and bronchial flare-ups. There seems to be some kind of long-standing low-grade infection at work, which is responsible for all these manifestations; and I am trying to deal with the beastly thing intensively, before it gets worse and deals with me. Meanwhile, Maria, I'm glad to say, has been pretty well, in spite of an immense amount to do; while news from Matthew is good.

Thank you for your suggestions about money. I am waiting to hear from Pinkers (who seem incidentally to have become frightfully slow, disorganized and inefficient) about the sums they have received during the last six months on my behalf; and when I know where I stand, I will write again about the matter.

I am finished, thank heaven, with movie work, and have been reading and making notes for a kind of novel, which I hope to make into a philosophical Summa, couched in fictional form. My reading and reflections have mostly been on Semantics, of whose importance I become more and more profoundly convinced. We live in language as fish in water; but all languages embody fossilized neolithic metaphysics, and unless we learn what are the true relations between words, things and thoughts, and unless we learn how to prevent ourselves from being deceived by the neolithic prejudgments implicit in the language we use to think in and communicate with, we must inevitably continue to behave as insanely as we are doing now and have done in the past. In the sphere of education, semantics is the only discipline which can unify the various fields of specialization—moreover, it is the only discipline which shows the smallest likelihood of teaching men how to carry over the scientific attitude from the laboratory to the affairs of ordinary life. The attempt to 'change human nature' by political and economic reforms, unaccompanied by reforms in the educational system, seems doomed to failure. The best that can be hoped for along these lines is the diversion of the world's criminal lunacy from one set of channels into another set of channels. Any genuine diminution of the criminal lunacy can be accomplished only by teaching people to realize that the languages they use condemn them to think in an entirely false-to-facts way about contemporary reality. Such false-to-facts ways of thinking are disastrous; but, alas, yield high psychological dividends in the way of excitement, thrills, 'kicks' etc. (The doctrines of Nazism, Communism, nationalism, etc. are manifestly idiotic; but those who believe in them get an enormous amount of heart-warming excitement from their beliefs; and this immediate excitement makes them forget the long-range disasters which such beliefs inevitably lead to.) This means that there must be a training of the will and the emotions as well as of the intellect. The techniques of applied semantics must be supplemented by the techniques of applied religion, if the 'change in human nature' is to be effective. Any system of planning which ignores these two disciplines of the intellect and the will seems foredoomed to failure. It is rather unfortunate that none of the three most systematic works on the subject should be satisfactory. Stuart Chase's popularization, *The Tyranny of Words*, is all right as far as it goes—but it goes such a little way, in certain directions, as to be childishly inadequate to the psychological facts. Alfred Korzybski's *Science and Sanity*, contains a mountain of material, together with very significant educational applications for the teaching of semantic awareness; but unhappily the book is immensely much too long, too repetitive, too wandering to have much general appeal. Finally there is *The Meaning of Meaning* by Ogden and Richards, which is excellent in its way, but which lacks the philosophic generality of Korzybski, as well as his practical, educational applications. Apart from these, I don't know of anyone who deals even tolerably adequately with the subject. The linguists, like Bloomfield and Jespersen, are philological, not philosophical or psychological. The logicians, like Carnap and Charles Morris, are concerned only with the special language of science. If I had the necessary equipment of knowledge, I might attempt the job myself; but I haven't, and the best I can do is to attempt, as I intend to, a kind of fictional hint, adumbration and prolegomenon to the desired and necessary systematization and synthesis. I don't know whether there is any solution to human problems; it seems doubtful. But if there is, it lies, I am convinced, in applied semantics and applied religion.

Only when these have been satisfactorily dealt with will there be any hope for political and economic planning.

I delivered your letter to Bertie Russell, who came to dine here the other day. His case seems pretty dismal, all the more so as anti-foreign sentiment is growing increasingly stronger in America as the war continues. His case is going to be taken through the New York courts of appeal and, if necessary, to the U.S. Supreme Court—which may take years. Meanwhile, he seems a bit uncertain of how he's going to make a living. I hope and think academic circles will keep him going if only in a makeshift, temporary way, for the next months or, if necessary, years.

Hubble, whom we saw yesterday, is very happy as he has just discovered the answer to a problem which has defeated the astronomers up to date—which way the nebulae are revolving!

Our best love to you all.

Ever your affectionate,
Aldous

444: † TO JULIAN HUXLEY

701 S. Amalfi,
Pacific Palisades, Calif.
7 July, 1940

Dearest J,

The news of your health was most distressing. Do try to arrange to have the operation done as soon as possible. Delay, I imagine, can only be bad in these cases. I have money in my London bank and also some which Pinker has had paid to him and which, in spite of repeated instructions, he has not yet paid to my account. I shall therefore cable advising him to pay you directly if he still holds the money; if, on the contrary, he should previously have paid it into my account, he will cable back and I will send a cheque.

I can sympathize physically with your account of yourself, since I am still under the weather with this wretched low infection which has been giving mild trouble for years past and which in recent months has been manifesting itself in a number of tiresome symptoms, ranging from a kind of giant urticaria to myocardial weakness. Treatment seems, however, gradually to be making headway. Meanwhile, I have been unable to do any work—an inability enhanced by the situation of the world, which is singularly unpropitious to the production of works of art and whose extreme precariousness and mutability make all political or social speculation look silly and irrelevant before the ink is dry on the paper. However, I seem at last to have something significant crystallizing in my mind—something which may permit itself to be written. I hope I may soon be well enough to begin. Meanwhile, I wish one could see much hope even in the event of the best possible outcome of the war—that the future will be anything but a descending spiral. Highly complex industrial societies cannot work without plans; but at the same time no human planners can be intelligent enough to plan for such societies in their full complexity; therefore planners must always simplify their problem—which is done in practice by means of regimentation, so that the bewildering variability of individuals is reduced by force and propaganda to a semblance of uniformity. Moreover, the technological changes proceed at an accelerating rate. Technological changes produce social changes; but societies and individuals have an inertia that is resistant to change; this inertia must be overcome by the planners, who again have to resort to regimentation. Our inventions in technology and organization have created a destiny which is pushing us willy nilly towards tyranny. And of course so long as the threat of war persists, there is a second destiny pushing behind the first.

No news here. Maria got very tired after an extremely strenuous winter, but is much better after a week in New Mexico with Frieda Lawrence. Sophie (Jehanne's child) got through her baccalaureat with success—though what good it will do her now, I don't quite know! Matthew has got through his second year of pre-medical quite well, is stronger and calmer than he was and at present hard at work on a summer course in chemistry. Meanwhile our main anxiety is for Maria's mother and sisters. Her mother and Rose, with baby daughter [Olivia], got out of Brussels and, after frightful days on the road, got to Bordeaux. Jehanne was out of Paris during the occupation. We heard from them briefly; all seemed reasonably well and we were making arrangements to get money through, when the curtain drops again. Goodness knows where they are now—whether still in France or repatriated to Belgium—and goodness knows how or when any communication is to be established with them. For the moment no money can be sent; and if it were possible to send it, who would receive it? And, of course, if the war goes on, there will be famine conditions in Belgium by the winter.

Give our love to Juliette and the boys, and bless you all.

Your affectionate,
A.

445: TO MRS FRIEDA LAWRENCE

701 *S. Amalfi Drive,*
Pacific Palisades, Calif.
14 *August,* 1940

My dear Frieda,

Your reaction to the play [*Lady Chatterley's Lover*] was to be expected; for, in its present form, it is merely the anecdote of a woman married to a cripple, who finds that it's fun to go to bed with a man who is sexually potent. All the poetry of the book had gone, and all the cosmic quality—the thing that made one feel that the story was the record of the clash of more than personal, human forces. The problem is: how to get the poetry and the cosmic quality into the play? In the book, Lawrence achieved his purpose by means of descriptions and dialogue. In the play it has to be done by dialogue and dramatic situations. [Melchior] Lengyel has, we all think, done

455

a pretty good job in the matter of carpentering. The main lines of construction are sound. But what he has failed to do is to give to the play those elements which Lawrence gave to the book by means of his astonishing descriptions. It is because of the absence of any equivalent of the descriptions that even Lawrence's own dialogue fails, in the play, to produce the effect it did in the book. For the play's purposes there is need of a good deal of new, specially written *dramatic* dialogue, which shall embody some of those poetical elements rendered in the book by descriptions. What will also be necessary is the introduction of some new situations within the existing general framework—situations which shall somehow give that sense of a cosmic conflict which the play completely lacks. To give a few examples; in the first scene it will be necessary to stress the 'heartbreak house' quality of the futile intellectualism and diabolic industrialism much more than has been done in the play. New dialogue will be needed, embodying remarks about the mining village, the by-products works and so forth—remarks which at present are merely in the stage directions. Then some sort of visible, symbolic contrast between the refinements of Chatterley's circle and the horrors of the pit must be invented. Then, to give dramatic emphasis to Connie's position, she will probably have to be made to associate herself more explicitly than she does at present with Clifford's way of life, even to the point of hotly defending the purely intellectual marriage against the jibes of the other men. Similar re-shapings will have to be done throughout the play.

Perhaps the greatest problem of all is Mellors. He is more completely lost and diminished than any other character. This is due in large measure to the unavoidable omission of the 'pornographic' episodes, in which his strange, cosmic quality comes out, and also to the minimizing of the characteristic, so immensely significant in the book, of passing from dialect to King's English. (The two types of language symbolize the two forces in conflict.) How this large-scale cosmic quality can be imparted to Mellors without the 'pornography' and perhaps without the dialect (for it is not at all certain that an American audience will have the faintest idea of the significance of that change [in] speech) is the most difficult problem of the play.

In any case, the job will be an enormous one; for, except for the general construction, which is reasonably sound, everything has to be done again and done by somebody with a profound sense and knowledge of the theatre. My own position is that I simply haven't got time to undertake such a job and, even if I had, I probably shouldn't be able to do it properly; for my own mind is entirely non-dramatic. However, I think we have the right man on the spot in the person of Christopher Isherwood, who would probably collaborate with W. H. Auden, the poet; Isherwood and Auden have had considerable experience of the stage and have written successful plays. They are interested in the problem and would like to attempt it. The idea is that, as soon as Isherwood has finished his present stint of movie work and as soon as Lengyel has finished cutting and revising the script along the lines we have suggested to date, he (Isherwood) should get down to the job, with assistance from Auden, who is in New York, and of myself. (I would stick in patches of dialogue of a kind I am best fitted to produce e.g. in the first scene.) The result will be, of course, that there will be no chance of a production this autumn. For, even if Lengyel's revised script were ready, which it isn't, the job will take several months and a great deal of discussion. Meanwhile, I don't think there's any point in your getting [Samuel] Beckett to come and work on it. Lengyel cannot be got out of the picture anyhow; and his general construction work is mainly sound and can be used. Also, Beckett's experience of the films will be of no use to him in doing a play, which is a totally different medium, requiring a special talent and special experience. The present arrangement seems to me as hopeful as any that can be contrived in the circumstances. Isherwood is an intelligent writer with a good sense of the theatre and good taste; Auden is a good poet and theatre man. I don't know much about the theatre; but I can throw up suggestions and put in bits of dialogue here and there. Between us we ought to be able to produce something—though the problem is immensely much more difficult than I had any idea of when the subject of turning the book into a play was first broached. These arrangements have been discussed with [William] Goetz, who is quite satisfied by them. I also discussed your letter with him yesterday, thinking it was best he should know the nature of your reactions—which incidentally, are only an intenser version of his own reactions; for he doesn't regard the play as at all satisfactory in its present form. He also sees no point in bringing Beckett in and is emphatic on the impossibility of getting rid of Lengyel. So I think the best thing is for you to leave Isherwood, Auden and me to see what can be done in the way of producing a dramatic equivalent to the novel. I hope something satisfactory will come of it.

Our love to you both.

Ever your affectionate,
Aldous

446: TO MRS FRIEDA LAWRENCE

701 S. Amalfi Drive,
Pacific Palisades, Calif.
7 October, 1940

My dear Frieda,

Thanks for your letter. I don't quite know what Lengyel means by saying that I am holding up work on *Lady C.* He has known for a long time that I was not prepared to undertake a complete job of dramatic composition—for that is what the re-hashing of his version would have to be, if the play is to be transformed from a distasteful anecdote about a woman married to an impotent cripple into something like the equivalent of Lawrence's cosmic drama—and that I couldn't (not being a dramatist and not having even a technical interest in the problems of dramatic form) take on more than what I had originally supposed the task would be: the polishing up of dialogue. Work was held up because Isherwood, who had undertaken to do the re-composition, was tied up at Metro-Goldwyn-Mayer. I saw Isherwood yesterday, for the first time in several weeks, and it seems they are keeping him on for another month or two at Metro and are then lending him (he being under contract to them) to Twentieth Century Fox. This means, I'm afraid, that his collaboration is ruled out. Meanwhile there is absolutely no news of Auden, who has changed his address in New York and has not written to anyone here since he came to California in August. Another disappointment has been that John van Druten has declined to take on the job. He is a very experienced playwright, who is an expert at re-furbishing unsatisfactory plays; but his comment was that, though the construction was sound, the job of turning the play into anything remotely like the book, in regard to its quality and spirit, was so enormous that he wasn't prepared to undertake it. This leaves us for the moment high and dry. I have told [William] Goetz that the only hope seems to be to find some good and experienced dramatist who is prepared to try his hand at the job. I hope he will be able to find someone satisfactory. I ought, no doubt, to have foreseen these difficulties when the matter was first broached. Unfortunately my ignorance of the theatre and of Lengyel's gifts and limitations made me unduly optimistic. It is fatally hard for a novelist to forget his own wonderfully flexible, all-embracing medium and to think in terms of the rigid, poverty-stricken medium of the theatre—a medium so frightfully limited that, as a matter of brute historical fact, only the most towering geniuses have ever been able to do anything satisfactory with it; whereas in the novel any amount of satisfactory work has been done by men and women of secondary talents, to whom the medium gave adequate opportunity for expressing themselves. Meanwhile I wish, for your sake, that things were going better and that I were able to make them go better; but this I am really incompetent to do. The job of taking Lengyel's construction and filling in the framework with a great poetical drama, equivalent to Lawrence's novel, is utterly beyond me. If I were to try, it would mean a long-drawn anguish for me and a final result which I know would be unsatisfactory. All this quite apart from the fact that I have commitments to my publisher and that the prolongation of my work at MGM, followed by a summer when I was constantly feeling under the weather, have left me, now that I am fit to work again, eight or nine months behind my schedule.

There is no news here. Matthew has gone back to Colorado. Sophie is hard at work and happy at the Reinhardt school. Maria is kept busy driving us about, and I am trying to make up for lost time with my typewriter. We see nobody, I am thankful to say. Our only sallying forth for months was a visit last week to Charlie Chaplin's studio, where we saw a private showing of his film [*The Great Dictator*] about Hitler and Mussolini, which is really a major contribution to the cause of decency and sanity—immensely funny and very moving. However, one is compelled by present circumstances to doubt whether human beings any longer want decency or sanity.

Our love to you both.

Yours affectionately,
Aldous H.

447: TO LEWIS GIELGUD

701 S. Amalfi Dr.,
Pacific Palisades, Calif:
9 October, 1940

My dear Lewis,

I was glad indeed to have news of you and to know that you were safely out of Paris. Your letter arrived by the same post with one from Happy which announced that they had just heard of poor Bill [William Wright]'s death on Sept 19, from kidney disease and complications following an operation. Unhappily they were without any news of Mimi. And of course the trouble is that, if she's in Paris, news will be very hard to get: for there is practically no communication between occupied France and the U S A— albeit I have heard recently of one or two people who have had letters from occupied France: still, the communications seem to be most irregular and precarious. Maria's mother, Jehanne and Rose, with husband and small child, got out of Belgium and Paris respectively and are at the moment in Sanary, unless they have been repatriated to Brussels, as a recent cable seemed to indicate the possibility for M's mother and Rose, while Jehanne and her new husband [Georges Neveux] (she married again [. . .]) may have returned to Paris in search of work—God help them: but maybe they can pick up a living there more effectively than in Sanary. We cabled a considerable sum of money via Switzerland recently, but have not yet heard whether they received it. Heaven knows what sort of winter is in store for them all. M's other sister and family left Holland last winter and are in N.Y, while Sophie, Jehanne's child, is with us.

As for the future—*quien sabe?* The one enormous lesson of it all—a lesson nobody ever has or apparently ever will learn—is that unless things are done in time, the most ghastly events will occur. There is a tide in the affairs of men—which no politicians ever take. There were 15 years after 1918 during which something cd have been done, either along purely Machiavellian lines or else along lines of genuine co-operation. Nothing was done, and the world drifted into the state of a man with a neglected cancer, who will die if he is left alone and will die under the knife if operated. The fable of the Sibylline books is appallingly apposite—less and less at a higher and higher price, until finally the price is practically infinite and the return practically infinitesimal. Well, well. . . . Meanwhile I hope that in spite of everything you and

Zita are all right. Here, we are tolerably well—tho' I have had a long siege from an obscure kind of low infection, from which I seem gradually to be recovering, thank goodness. For the rest one tries to alleviate, however infinitesimally, some tiny fragment of the general misery; one writes (I am engaged at the moment on a strangely apposite study of Père Joseph, collaborator of Richelieu, the most astounding case of a power politician who was also a religious mystic); one tries to understand a little of this extraordinary universe—for of course this sort of horror will go on for exactly as long as the majority of humans persist in misunderstanding it. Our love to you both and to such of your family as you see. Bless you, dear Lewis.

Yours
Aldous

448: TO HAROLD RAYMOND

701 S. Amalfi,
Pacific Palisades, Calif.
14 October, 1940

My dear Harold,

I was very sorry to learn from Julian's cable that there had been this trouble with Pinker. I have had no answer from him to any of my recent letters and was just considering the advisability of putting the matter in the hands of my lawyer, when this wire brought it all to a head. What a misery it all is [. . . .] I hope Vera and you and the boys are well, in spite of everything. We think much of our friends here, with a rather helpless concern that doesn't know what practical expression to find. Maria's news from France has been pretty good up till now; but there have been no letters for two or three weeks now, which is a little disquieting, as there had been talk earlier of M's mother being repatriated to Brussels and of her sister and the sister's new husband returning to Paris in search of work. Entry into occupied territory will make communication much harder; and the transfer of money which has been merely problematic (we don't yet know whether what we send via Switzerland gets there) quite impossible. These facts and the food shortage make the outlook for the winter very bad, I'm afraid.

I can't remember whether I told you in my last letter that I had changed my literary plans. Perhaps I hadn't changed them when I wrote. Anyhow, I've abandoned the Utopian plan for the time being—it didn't work out satisfactorily, for some reason—and have turned instead to a kind of speculative and philosophical biography of a most extraordinary person, Father Joseph, 'l'Eminence Grise', who was the collaborator and inspirer, so far as foreign policy went, of Cardinal Richelieu. He is particularly interesting as being a

448 *Ralph Pinker's agency was going into liquidation. Large sums had been owed to Huxley ever since April and May, the total being £548-8-0.*

power politician of the purest water and at the same time a practising mystic, who had evidently got quite well started on the way of illumination. The whole story has an obliquely topical interest; for Joseph was as much responsible as anyone for prolonging the Thirty Years War, which is on the direct line of ancestry to the present disasters. And he brings to focus in the most dramatic way the whole problem of the relations between politics and religious insight. I have written about a quarter of the book to date and hope to get the whole thing done within the next four months or so—perhaps six months. Meanwhile I am having trouble getting books. By hook or by crook I shall be able, I think, to secure recent French publications on Father J. But there are old books which I can't get hold of even in the Library of Congress here. If it isn't an intolerable nuisance, could you communicate with the British Museum and find out if they are still doing the photographic service they used to do.

If so, I would like very much to have the following. There is a book by Father Joseph's master, an Englishman named William Fitch, known in religion as Father Bénoit de Canf[i]eld (I don't know how he will be catalogued in the B.M.). This book is called *Règle de Perfection réduite au seul point de la volonté divine* and there are several 17th-century editions, beginning around 1610. I would like to have if possible a full sized photograph (not photostat, which is much less delicate) of the engraved frontispiece which apparently occurs in the early editions and also micro-photographs suitable for reading by means of a reading machine (all the big libraries make these micro-films now) of Part III of this book. (This is the last section and, I imagine, comprises about a hundred pages.) I enclose a cheque which ought to cover the cost of photography and carriage. I hope this will not be a terrible nuisance. But if the thing is feasible, I shall be most grateful.

Our love to you both.

Yours,
Aldous H.

449: † TO MRS KETHEVAN ROBERTS

701 *S. Amalfi Drive,*
Pacific Palisades, Calif.
26 *November,* 1940

Dear Mrs. Roberts,

Your letter of October 26th reached me here today, which is good going in the world as it is now. I was glad to hear that you were still there and well, and that you are living in a place where circumstances permit the mind a little more liberty than the bombardments allowed in Europe. Not, of course, that most of us ever used the liberty granted in peace time for any sensible purpose. But there was always the chance of such a use being made; and it is because they provide such chances that peace and democracy are valuable. The nature of the purpose which peace and democracy give people the chance to accomplish is only secondarily humanistic and cultural: primarily it is spiritual and mystical. On the humanistic and cultural level, the problem of life is, as you say, wholly insoluble. It is always a question of seeking first the kingdom of heaven, so that all the rest shall be added—not, as the Utopians, liberal, fascist, marxist, all imagine, a question of seeking first all the rest in the hope that the kingdom of heaven will be added. Brute experience and the records of history make it sufficiently clear that the Utopian way leads to hell; and since the great majority of human beings cherish the utopian idea in one form or another, it follows that the world will remain as hellish as it is and has been in the past. I have come to be profoundly pessimistic about great masses of human beings, but profoundly optimistic about individuals and groups of individuals existing upon the margins of society. And there is good reason to believe that their existence there does something to mitigate the horrors which the society forever prepares for itself. One is accused, if one takes this point of view—which, incidentally, is that of all the men to whom humanity looks up as the founders of religions—of practising escapism. One might as well accuse of escapism the mathematician who does not continually spend his talents and energies on the problem of squaring the circle. In so far as we are political and social beings, we have got ourselves into a situation (owing to the fatal human habit of never doing the proper thing in time), where we are confronted by two alternatives, each of which is as terrible as the other. Between the horns of this dilemma we cannot pass except as spiritual beings and in so far as we can become aware of ultimate reality.

I have written very little in periodicals of late, but am busy on a biography of that strange figure, Father Joseph, the Eminence Grise of Cardinal Richelieu's days. He is interesting as being the only power politician of note who started life as a mystic and continued to the very end to make a desperate effort to make the best of both worlds—needless to say without success, as he himself realized at the last. He illustrates in the most striking way the relation between public and private morality, between religion and politics, between ends envisaged, means employed and results achieved. I hope to have the book finished in a few months from now.

For the rest, there is little news. My wife is well and so is my boy, who is beginning the study of medicine. I have found someone who is teaching me to see again—by a method of training in the art of using the eyes in a state of relaxation. [. . . .] Needless to say, the doctors and optometrists are doing everything in their power to get her suppressed. But then such is life on the common human level—a matter of ignorance resulting in malice and of malice darkening the mind so that there is more ignorance.

With all good wishes for Christmas, though that seems a bit ironical in the present context, and for your health and well being I am,

Yours very sincerely,
Aldous Huxley

701 *S. Amalfi Drive,*
Pacific Palisades, Calif.
15 *December,* 1940

Dearest Julian,

Your clipper letter of November 2nd reached me only three or four days ago—which seems really unnecessarily slow. The Pinker situation sounds fantastically worse than one could have imagined. I suppose the poor imbecile started speculating to offset an overdraft and didn't stop till he'd reached minus thirty-six thousand. It is difficult to see how else he could have spent so much, seeing that he has always made an excellent income out of his business. I am sending with this a separate sheet on which I shall write an order empowering Ted [Haynes] to resume possession of all my contracts etc. There seems to be no point in waiting, in the hope that the firm will somehow be reorganized, when it pretty obviously won't be. With regard to a new agent, I shall for the moment do nothing. Translation business is at a standstill; I dislike writing articles and do as few as I can possibly get away with; Chatto's can be dealt with directly. So, until any special need should arise, I can dispense with a London agent altogether. As for America, I have for some time been doing without any agent, except in regard to movies, where I have a man belonging to one of the biggest agencies, who deals with people here and can, if I need it, deal with all matters of serialization, dramatic rights and the rest. Leland Hayward was suggested to me after Eric P. went west; and I had a brief and not very reassuring experience with [——]. But seeing that I'm not writing articles or short stories, they are quite useless, and I am better without.

I was interested by the passage in your letter about the new Ideal Man. I have long been interested in the history of such ideal men. The Renaissance all-round Greek-through-rose-coloured-spectacles. The 17th century *honnête homme.* The 18th century *philosophe.* The 19th century respectable man—(and 'highly respectable', as Surtees remarked of Mr Jorrocks, really meant 'very rich'). For the 20th century the ideal of the Social Man seems, as you say, to be imposing itself. The danger attaching to such an ideal is that it so easily has, as its corollary, the ideal of the divine state. I have now come to feel that all these ideals are disastrous, because incomplete; and that no society can hope to keep itself up even to the levels hitherto achieved unless there is something corresponding to a Brahmin class whose ideal is that of the Theocentric Man, not primarily concerned with human values at all, but merely with the business of knowing and making actual in themselves the ultimate reality of the world. (Incidentally, of course, their efficacy in dealing with human problems will be greatly increased when they have achieved this realization.)

As for the organization of society in general—there are to my mind only two satisfactory alternatives, either voluntary international and intranational co-operation, or balance of power. The unsatisfactory alternative to these is complete state control which, even if benevolent in intention, is always bad. Of the two satisfactory alternatives, the first, and better, is not likely, given contemporary habits of thought and feeling, to be realized. The second may still be realizable internationally—though possibly not, owing to modern technological developments. Within any given nation it can only be realized by the distribution to the largest possible number of individuals of private property in land, together with the instruments and skills requisite to make them, as individuals or members of co-operative groups, largely self-supporting. Thanks to modern technology, it is possible to reproduce the conditions which made Jeffersonian democracy possible—and to reproduce them without any appreciable fall in the standard of living and with enhanced security for all. It is just conceivable that the wholesale destruction of urban centres and industrial concentrations in Europe may impel people to make a change in this direction.

Our best love to you both, and to the boys.

Your affectionate
Aldous

451: TO JULIAN HUXLEY

> 701 *S. Amalfi Drive,*
> *Pacific Palisades, Calif.*
> 13 *March,* 1941

Dearest J,

I have been remiss about writing, I am afraid; but have been working very hard trying to finish off my book, which seems now to have entered the last lap, thank goodness—for I shall be glad to be done with it, though I have developed a great feeling of compassion for my poor Father Joseph, who started out to become a saint, then imagined that there was a short cut to the kingdom of heaven through politics, and got more and more deeply involved in more and more frightful power policies, which resulted in the destruction of a third of the population of Central Europe, guaranteed the rise of Prussia as the head of the German confederation and paved the way for Louis XIV, the Revolution, Napoleon and all the rest. Plain utilitarian considerations demonstrate that anyone who has any desire for sanctity, any gift for the knowledge of ultimate reality, can do far more good by sticking to his curious activities on the margin of society than by going to the centre and trying to improve matters there. Instead of raising politics to his level, he will always be pulled down to the level of politics. Whereas, if he remains on the periphery, he can do something to mitigate the consequences of what the politicians do at the centre. One sees, in the light of history, how enormously wise George Fox was, when he absolutely refused to be drawn into Cromwell's orbit—would not even dine at the Protector's table, for fear of being in any way compromised. If he had accepted Cromwell's offer and entered official life in any capacity, with the purpose and in the hope of improving the quality of government, there would have been no Quakers, and the world would have been deprived of an enormous sum of good, the loss of which would not in any way have been compensated by the little that, in the best possible circumstances, Fox could have achieved in public life. Poor Joseph is an awful warning of what happens when people who might have been saints choose instead to become politicians. Saints would appear to be the only antidote to statesmen.

We were very happy to hear from Juliette that you were all tolerably well. Our own news is quite good, and the little we hear from France is not too bad. One startling piece of information just received, is that Jehanne has suddenly gone and had a baby [Noële Neveux], only informing us of the fact after the event. Let's hope to goodness that the poor little creature can survive present conditions in France without carrying the stigmata of these months into later life.

Los Angeles is now ringed with boom towns, on account of the concentration of aircraft industries here. Meanwhile, of course, agriculture is in the doldrums, with no export trade and machines and erosion driving migrants on to the roads at the rate, as I was told the other day by a man from the Department of Agriculture in Washington, of a hundred and fifty thousand a year. Less spectacularly, but more catastrophically, the insane farming practices in the south are steadily reducing the fertility per acre, which has fallen, in spite of machines and artificial fertilizers, forty per cent in the last seventy years. In another forty years, they expect it to be at zero over large areas—just at the time when the South's high birthrate will have doubled the existing population. Meanwhile, the Rust cotton picking machine threatens to make eighty per cent of all farm hands unnecessary there and in the new irrigated cotton areas in Arizona; and behind Rust is Du Pont with talk of a new synthetic fibre better and cheaper than cotton, which will eliminate one hundred per cent of the farm hands. And the human inertia is so enormous that it seems very unlikely that they can persuade the people to change their traditional habits in time. In spite of intensive propaganda, most of the southern farmers still prefer corn mush, salt pork and pellagra to vegetables and health. And the alternative to ineffective propaganda is naked force. Where time is short—and progress in technology speeds up all social processes to the most fantastic extent, so that changes which were comfortably accomplished in a century or two, now have to be accomplished in five years—this factor of human inertia becomes all important. It looks as though, with the best will in the world, inertia cannot be overcome by general consent except in a long period of more than a human life time. Where circumstances demand that it shall be overcome quickly, there seems to be no alternative to universal bullying at the hands of an active minority. Anyhow, my friend from the Department of Agriculture was not at all optimistic.

Our best love to you all.

Ever your affectionate,
Aldous

452: TO HAROLD RAYMOND

701 *S. Amalfi Drive,*
Pacific Palisades, Calif.
27 *May,* 1941

My dear Harold,

Thank you for your letter of April 25th and the enclosed contract, which got here yesterday. I was sorry to hear of Tony's transfer into the unknown and can only hope and pray that you will continue to get good news of him, as well as of Piers. Please give Vera our very best love and tell her that we often think most affectionately of her.

I am enclosing the contract, duly signed. If, owing to the circumstances of the time, any of the clauses of this contract should become unduly onerous for Chattos, I hope you will let me know, so that we can arrange some *ad hoc* temporary agreement to cover the contingencies of the moment. With regard to future books, I am not yet certain what I shall embark on next. The Utopian idea still haunts me, and I have a new notion as to its treatment. An immense amount of rather tiresome time-machineish or sleeper-wakeish machinery can be eliminated by the simple device of putting the whole thing into the past and making the narrator a grandson of Lemuel Gulliver, voyaging during the eighteenth century. Furthermore, the eighteenth-century setting allows one to make use of an extremely succinct style of narration. I had even thought of making the Utopian episode the last of, say, three such adventures, the first comic, the second macabre and the third extremely serious. This has not got beyond the embryonic condition and will take a while to mature, Meanwhile, Father Joseph has gone off. If he doesn't arrive reasonably soon, let me know. I have no other typescript, beyond the one at Harpers, but will arrange for the sending of galley proofs as soon as they strike them off. With regard to the illustrations—I am very glad you think of putting some in. The engraving by Michel Lasne (the one in Fagniez) should serve as frontispiece. Then we might have the triple portrait of Richelieu by P. de Champagne, in the Nat Gallery. Then perhaps the frontispiece to Benet Fitch, which is fully described in the text and is a kind of diagrammatic representation of Joseph's own views about the relationship between politics and religion. Finally we might reproduce two of Callot's prints (which are also very fully described in the text). I would suggest the print of the man being broken on the wheel and another, near the end of the series, showing a band of soldiers waylaid by infuriated peasantry and done to death. In the centre is a peasant with a flail, threshing the dead body of a soldier, while another peasant pulls off his boots. I have written at some length about this Man with the Flail, who is a kind of symbol of the impotent revels of the suffering masses against the interminable military oppression. If you have anything on the dust wrapper—which I imagine you won't, owing to the expense—use either the portrait of Father Joseph (perhaps the face alone, magnified up), or else a montage made of the various illustrations in the book: Joseph praying against the background of Callot horrors: the Cardinal's face breaking through Benet Fitch's schematic representation of the contemplative and active lives in their relation to the deity. If this were well done, it would be most effective, and would symbolically sum up the main theme of the book.

Yours
Aldous

453: TO MRS JOAN BUZZARD

701 *S. Amalfi Drive,*
Pacific Palisades, Cal.
9 *June,* 1941

Dearest Joan,

Your letter, with its sad news, has just come to hand. Dear Dragon—one thinks of her as the embodiment of life in a peculiarly rare and delightful form, at once strong and gay, noble and humorous, undeviatingly purposive and yet light-hearted. The letter she wrote us last autumn about her harrowing experiences with the X-ray treatment and the blitz was a summary and a symbol of her whole life—an expression of the highest courage with the minimum of fuss and grandiloquence and the maximum of humour. At its best, humour is the modern equivalent of the supreme Christian virtue of humility; if one can make a joke even about oneself, one runs no risk of being puffed up and pretentious—as, I am afraid, so many even of the noblest Stoics undoubtedly were. The Dragon was a stoic who could take herself lightly and who thereby went beyond stoicism into something else, something better and more humane, for which nobody has yet invented a name. Perhaps we might call it Dragonism in memory of one of its great exponents.

Maria sends her best love. I think you know how very fond she was of Aunt Ethel. Bless you, dearest Joan.

Your affectionate
Aldous

454: TO EUGENE F. SAXTON

701 *S. Amalfi Drive,*
Pacific Palisades, Calif.
26 *June,* 1941

My dear Gene,

I hope to send the reproductions in another day or two; there has been a delay in the making of the photographs. My friend who offered to help in

467

the matter of finding illustrative material is Mr José Weissberger, a very learned art connoisseur and collector, who is now living at the Hotel Peter Stuyvesant, Central Park West and 86th St. I will write to him, asking him to get in touch with you.

About previous biographies of Father Joseph in English—I remember having seen in some American book of reference (I believe the *Encyclopaedia Americana*) some mention of a biography published about forty years ago. I forget the author, and anyhow had never heard of his name; also, I have never found any reference to it in any other bibliography, so don't imagine that it can have been anything of much significance. No library in this town possessed a copy, for I looked into the matter at the time of first seeing the reference. Neither Dedouvres nor Brémond had written at the date of its publication, and consequently a great deal of the significant material was not available to the author. It might be as well to check up on this, before making any definite statement on the matter.

I am sorry not to have let you know anything definite about the results of your kindness in sending us the affidavits. The reason was that we don't yet know anything very definite ourselves. Shortly after the papers went off, via the State Department, who forwarded them to the Consul in Nice, we heard from M's mother and sister that, for various reasons (partly personal, partly, I think, connected with administrative obstacles in France), they had finally decided to change their minds and not undertake the migration. But it always remains possible that, when the papers and tickets actually appear, and if circumstances over there have changed, M's mother, at least, may come after all. The odd thing, meanwhile, is that the papers have not yet turned up at the Consul's— or hadn't when they last wrote. I will let you know of any further developments in this matter, as soon as we hear of them.

Our love to you both.

Yours,
Aldous

455: TO EUGENE F. SAXTON

701 S. Amalfi,
Pacific Palisades, Calif.
2 October, 1941

My dear Gene,

I got my copies of *Grey Eminence* on Tuesday, and thought the book looked very nice indeed. One small point: as a grateful and greatly benefited exponent of the Bates Method of eye training, I'm sorry you used on the dust wrapper that old photograph with glasses—objects which I haven't worn for two years now, and to the abandonment of which I owe in great measure the improvement in my sight. So please, for any future publicity or the like let's drop the old photographs as a tribute to Bates's memory, and use only the recent photographs without spectacles. Meanwhile I find I shall need a few more copies; so would you ask the appropriate person to send me five more. I had a statement from the accounting department yesterday for the books already received and sent off. Please have these others added to the list, and have them charge the total against my earnings. I shall be interested to hear how the book goes; for I have no idea whether there will be widespread interest in the subject or not. All those who have read it to date seem to like it. Let's hope that this is symptomatic.

I am pretty near the end of my job here, and shall be glad to get down to my own work again. I haven't yet decided what I shall start on; for there seem to be a number of possibilities. Perhaps I shall begin on several things and then see which works out most satisfactorily. It is impossible to tell in advance how a subject will develop. One just has to sit down at the type-writer and find out.

I should have thanked you before for the copy of the *Imitation* in its original translation. I had been waiting until I should have had time to read it through; but the leisure has been lacking, and I have been able only to glance at the book, dipping into it here and there. This has been enough, however, to permit me to appreciate the strength and nobility of the language. Style is something one always has to be on one's guard against in this sense that splendid writing can make intrinsically unimportant or equivocal notions seem valuable and sincere; while on the contrary important and sincere thoughts may be made to seem dull, or trivial, or merely rhetorical, through being expressed by somebody who doesn't happen to have the gift of the gab. We have to consider ourselves fortunate when a book like the *Imitation*, which (though not perhaps the finest or most desirable product of mediaeval devotion) is still a very noble work, finds a form of expression that is, aesthetically, comparable in quality to the subject matter.

Our love to you both.

Ever yours,
Aldous H.

456: TO MRS FLORA STROUSSE

701 *S. Amalfi Drive,*
Pacific Palisades, Calif.
17 *November,* 1941

Dear Starky,

Thank you for your letter, which I have left too long without an answer, I fear. The application of pacifist methods to international politics always

455 *The 'job' Huxley mentions was the writing of a script for a new film version of Charlotte Brontë's* Jane Eyre, *in collaboration (at least eventually) with Robert Stevenson, who directed the picture, and with John Houseman. The film was produced by William Goetz for Twentieth Century-Fox and was released in 1944. This letter, which is on the film company's letter-paper, was probably written at the studio.*

seems to me to bear a close analogy to the application of curative treatments to cancer. If you deal with a cancer early enough, by operation and a proper regimen, there is a good chance of being able to get rid of it altogether, or for a long period at least. The longer it is neglected, the more drastic and dangerous does the treatment have to become, and the smaller the chance of success. Finally, a point is reached when, whatever may be done, disaster is certain. The patient will die on the table if operated—off the table, if not operated. It is the same with international politics. In times of peace, when there is only the potentiality of serious trouble, it is relatively easy to avert future war by making arrangements reasonably satisfactory to all concerned. The longer the delay in solving the problem, the higher the price to be paid for a solution (the price is paid in material sacrifices and losses of prestige)— and the more unlikely, therefore, that any nation will be prepared to attempt the solution. Finally comes war; and when war is waged on a large scale and for a long time between evenly matched powers, all attempts at a solution of the problems involved become equally disastrous. Thus, it is clear that to make peace now with the Germans on their terms will lead to catastrophic results. And to go on fighting until the Nazi regime is overthrown and the German armies are annihilated will lead, in all probability, to results hardly if at all less catastrophic. We live under the illusion that all problems are at all times susceptible of a reasonably satisfactory solution. They are not. In certain circumstances, some problems cannot be solved to the satisfaction of anyone. If they are permitted to become sufficiently acute, they can only work themselves out through confusion into destruction and chaos. But where complicated societies are involved, large-scale destruction and chaos cannot be remedied except by means which are bound sooner or later to create new problems of the same kind as the old. In war time, it would seem, psychological conditions are such that the application of pacifism to politics is for all practical purposes impossible. There can only be the personal pacifism of individuals. That the existence of such personal pacifists cannot produce any large-scale amelioration of social conditions is obvious. Nevertheless, they fulfil a real social function, particularly when their pacifism is based upon 'theocentric' religious experience. The world would be even more horrible than it actually is, if it were not for the existence of a small theocentric minority working along quite other lines than the anthropocentric majority. It is immensely to the credit of the English and American governments that they should have recognized the existence of personal pacifists, and provided for their functioning as integral parts of the democratic society. No democratic society can exist without an opposition—the ordinary political opposition, and an infinitesimal opposition of men and women who are simply not concerned with the things that preoccupy the great mass of human beings. A completely united society must be, in practice, a society headed towards tyranny and barbarism. England and America owe an incalculable debt to the Quakers for the way in which they have educated successive generations of rulers to realize that a theocentric opposition is a thing of enormous value to the society containing it, even when the overwhelming majority of the members of that society disagree fundamentally with the opposition's views of life and scale of values.

Not much news. I have recently published a book on a very strange man, Father Joseph, and have since been working at the adaptation of a story for the movies—tiresome work, but unavoidable, since books at the moment don't keep wolves very far from doors, and the movie work is on the whole preferable to the continual shallow improvising of articles and stories, which is the practical alternative to it.

I am glad your children are doing well. Our boy is at college, and we have a Belgian niece of eighteen with us for the duration, going through all the travail of being young.

Yours,
Aldous Huxley

457: TO JULIAN HUXLEY

701 S. Amalfi Drive,
Pacific Palisades, Calif.
27 November, 1941

My dear Julian,

Thank you so much for the little Balbus book on reconstruction, which I have now passed on to Edwin Hubble, as he expressed a desire to read it. I thought it a most interesting production and the most realistic of the many programmes I have seen or heard sketched out. Everything depends, of course, on the manner in which the provisions are executed. What James Burnham calls 'the managerial revolution' is already in progress and is bound to come to consummation within a very short space of time. One's hope is that the new ruling class—the heads of government bureaus, the heads of industrial production and distribution, together with such other professional men as may constitute the élite of 'managers'—will behave better than the ruling class now on its way out—the manipulators of finance. Burnham, whose book I presume you have read, anticipates in the not distant future 'managerial wars', as opposed to 'capitalist wars', waged between the three great super-states which, for practical purposes, will take the place of the existing system of nations—the super-states based on the three centres of heavy industry and advanced technology—Europe, North America and East Asia. Such wars, he thinks, would be for the control of the rest of the world and its markets and raw materials. But of course all this is a matter of speculation. What is actually to happen will depend, not merely upon the will of the governing class in the various parts of the world, but also upon

---

457 *Balbus book: Julian Huxley's* Needs and Opportunities (1941)—(*American title* Reconstruction and Peace), *a pamphlet published under the pseudonym Balbus.*

the circumstances affecting or determining that will—the nature and intensity of local feeling, the amount of destruction perpetrated and the amount of military and other equipment available in given areas, the rise of new technological processes. These last may make nonsense of every calculation. And even if nothing immensely revolutionary should turn up in the near future, this technological progress must necessarily be a most important and disturbing element in the whole situation. Constantly changing external conditions are disturbing to the human mind, which has evolved to meet the demands of an environment relatively stable and unchanging. At the same time ever increasing governmental control will be required to keep society properly adapted to the constant changes brought about by technological progress. This brings us back again to the character of the 'managers'. If it is good, then, in spite of ubiquitous governmental control, we shall have a new kind of non-Jeffersonian democracy. If it is bad, we shall have a benevolent or even a non-benevolent totalitarianism.

There is not much news with us, Maria's mother and youngest sister have their visas for the U S and are now trying to cut through French and Portuguese red tape—which may take a long time. They have all been pretty well up till now in the south of France, though Rose sounds as if she were in a rather disturbing pre-tubercular condition. The food situation there is not at all good and seems to tell especially on schoolchildren and adolescents, according to the report we received from a man who had recently returned from distributing milk and meals to children on behalf of the Quakers. I presume that even these small distributions will now be stopped, on account of the new French orientation in regard to Weygand and the colonies. We get occasional letters from Belgium, where things seem to be a good deal worse than in unoccupied France. From occupied France there are only indirect reports, mainly from French people who have succeeded in getting over in recent months. Paul Valéry, it seems, had a very bad breakdown in 1940 and was in a home for nerve cases; however, he seems to be better now and is said to have some kind of post in the education ministry. My old friend Drieu La Rochelle has, alas, carried his pre-war infatuation with [Jacques] Doriot to its logical conclusion and become, as the new editor of the *Nouvelle Revue Française*, an ardent advocate of collaboration. He is an outstanding example of the strange things that happen when a naturally weak man, whose talents are entirely literary, conceives a romantic desire for action and a romantic ambition for political power and position. Rushing in where angels fear to tread, he does the most insensate things. It is the greatest pity; for there was something very nice about Drieu and I had a real affection for him. We occasionally hear from Charles de Noailles, when he gets leave to pass into unoccupied territory. The family camps in a few rooms of their huge house in Paris. [. . . .] It all sounds pretty gloomy. Mme de Behague is dead, and so is Robert Norton. Of Mimi we once had indirect word about a year ago, but since then nothing.

For ourselves, we are pretty well. I have started preliminary work on a new book, a kind of novel [*Time Must Have a Stop*]. Maria is busy as usual with a thousand things. Sophie has deserted acting for a secretarial school. Matthew never writes; but we interpret no news as good news. I hope the winter isn't stirring up your sinus trouble again and that Juliette will have no recurrence of her infection. Our best love to you all and a Christmas as happy as circumstances will permit.

Ever your affectionate,
Aldous

458: TO MISS HEPWORTH AND MR GREEN

701 *S. Amalfi Drive,*
Pacific Palisades, Calif.
[1942]

Dear Miss Hepworth and Mr. Green,

I find it hard to answer your request for autobiographical information. My life has been uneventful, and I can speak only in terms of being and becoming, not of doing and happening. I am an intellectual with a certain gift for literary art, physically delicate, without very strong emotions, not much interested in practical activity and impatient of routine. I am not very sociable and am always glad to return to solitude and the freedom that goes with solitude. This desire for freedom and solitude has led not only to a consistent effort to avoid situations in which I would be under the control of other people, but also to an indifference to the satisfactions of power and position, things which impose a servitude of business and responsibility.

As a boy I went almost blind for nearly two years and have remained since then with very imperfect vision. This greatly affected my life inasmuch as the disability tended to reinforce my natural tendency towards solitude and away from practical matters. Three years ago, I accidentally stumbled upon an educational method (that of Dr. W. H. Bates of New York, now dead, but survived by a number of excellent pupils), by the aid of which I am gradually learning to see again, while the damaged organs of vision get better in proportion as the visual function is improved. The practice of the Bates method, as also of the method for mastering the primary control of the organism devised by F. M. Alexander, has been profoundly important to me. These two techniques have demonstrated the possibility, on the physiological plane, of a complete reconditioning, analogous to that which takes place through the techniques of mysticism on the psychological and spiritual planes. Given mysticism and such psycho-physical techniques as the Bates method and the Alexander method, it is possible to conceive of a totally

458 *The correspondents are unidentified.*

new kind of education starting at the level of bodily function and going up to the heights of the spirit. Existing systems of education are about ten per cent efficient in the matter of teaching pupils to conform to ideal standards of health, morals and religion. The new type of education has a chance of being a hundred per cent efficient and might have an over-all efficiency at least equal to that of the internal combustion engine! It would be an education in the art of conforming to the nature of things, to 'Tao' in all its aspects— an education in the art of seeking first the kingdom of God and thereby having all the other things added, from health and virtue to heightened awareness and liberation.

As a young man, I cared supremely for knowledge for its own sake, for the play of ideas, for the arts of literature, painting and music. But for some years now I have felt a certain dissatisfaction with these things, have felt that even the greatest masterpieces were somehow inadequate. Recently I have begun to know something about the reality in relation to which such things as art and general knowledge can be appraised. Inadequate in and for themselves, these activities of the mind can be seen in their true perspective when looked at from the vantage point of mysticism. 'Those barren leaves of science and of art' are barren only when regarded as ultimate ends. The secret here, as the fields of morals and politics, lies in the indirect approach. Beauty, truth, goodness and happiness cannot be achieved (except at a price which sooner or later stultifies the achievement) by aiming directly at these ends, but only by aiming primarily at something else. In a world that is busily engaged in destroying itself, because people insist on taking the direct approach to what seems to them good, the only thing to do is to go on harping on the necessity of that ultimate indirection, by which alone the desired goods can be achieved.

Yours sincerely
Aldous Huxley

459: TO CHRISTOPHER ISHERWOOD

701 S. Amalfi Drive,
Pacific Palisades, Calif.
7 February, 1942

My dear Christopher,

I have been meaning to write for a long time, but have been in one of those states where it seems difficult to get the things done that one wants to do—a state partly due to my having slightly strained my heart at the ranch, with resultant chronic fatigue, partly to having reached an impasse in my writing, where I don't know whether I can achieve what I want to achieve,

459 Isherwood was doing work with the Quakers at a hostel near Haverford, Pennsylvania.

or how exactly to do it. I would like to do something else altogether for a little; but my physical condition makes it difficult for me to do anything but the usual sedentary work. So there we are. Meanwhile, I wish you were here, and shall be very happy to see you when you come. I heard from my brother, Julian, that he had seen you at the [Bertrand] Russells', and that you had got on well together. He whirls indefatigably about the country lecturing and having talks with innumerable people about the blue prints of a future society, whose adumbrations, in his essays and letters, fill me, I must confess, with a good deal of gloom. However, I suppose it's the sort of society that people want; and the adumbrations are probably a good deal better than anything they in fact will get.

We went to visit Gerald the other day, and drove over to see the site of his new monastery [Trabuco College], which is now a-building. It is a huge estate of three hundred and sixty acres, in a very beautiful, rather English country-side behind Laguna. Pretty muggy, I should imagine, in hot weather, but with many compensatory attractions. The plans for the monastery have been drawn up and are very ambitious; I don't imagine, however, that it will be possible to put the whole scheme into effect at this time. During the rubber shortage, one rather serious problem will be communication with the outside world. The nearest store is about twenty miles away, so that, with tires at a premium, it won't be possible to do very frequent marketings. However, with careful planning, it should be possible to manage for the next two years or so. After which, Lord knows what may happen.

Our own building in the desert goes forward apace. The old house should be finished in a few days, and Maria expects to go down and live there at the end of next week, while I shall remain in town, not here, but staying at various friendly houses, until the two new rooms are finished. I hope you will come and stay with us when you come out West again. There will always be some place available. We had a great deal of trouble at the beginning, owing to the fact that we hired an old English caretaker, who would persist in imagining himself to be a country gentleman and was so lordlily indifferent to practical matters that, by his negligence, he completely demolished the pump, which has had to be replaced at great expense. He is now out of the picture, and we have found, to take his place, a real treasure, full of activity and resourcefulness.

Have you been reading anything of interest? My own more serious reading has been Eckhart, in the new Blakney translation, and the *Theologia Germanica*, to which I always return with great satisfaction. Also Poulain, who is a real Mrs Beeton for thoroughness and precision. Three vast tomes have recently come, too, from Pondichéry—Aruobindo's [Aurobindo Ghose's] last work. It looks good, as I glance through it, but is intolerably too long and verbose. Better than books have been some recent conversations with Krishnamurti, who has spoken to me of some of his experiences in a most interesting and illuminating way.

475

If you are ever in New York, it might be worth your while to get in touch with a man, with whom I have exchanged one or two letters of late—a Catholic called Thomas Merton, whose address is St. Bonaventura, New York. (I presume it is some sort of school or college.) He wrote very interestingly from a Catholic viewpoint about *Grey Eminence*, and described what sounds like a remarkable venture in saintliness functioning in Harlem among the poorest negroes. It is called Friendship House, 34 W 135th St, and is run by a woman called Catherine de Heuck, a Russian Catholic.

Do let us hear of your doings and when we may hope to see you. Love from us both.

Yours,
Aldous

460: TO MRS SYBILLE BEDFORD

701 *S. Amalfi,*
Pacific Palisades, Calif.
10 *February,* 1942

My dear Sybille,

I have just read your article on *Grey Eminence* in *Decision*, and am writing to tell you how good I think it is. Painfully good, at times, so far as I am concerned; for you have said many true and searching things in it. I was born wandering between two worlds, one dead, the other powerless to be born, and have made, in a curious way, the worst of both. For each requires that one should be whole-heartedly *there*, at the moment—with Micawber, as he is and for his own sake, while he is drinking his punch: with the Clear Light of the Void as it is and for its own sake, in an analogous way. Whereas I have always tended to be somewhere else, in a world of analysis, unfavourable equally to Micawberish living, Tolstoyan art and contemplative spirituality. The title of my first book of stories, *Limbo*, was, I now see, oddly prophetic!

We move out of this house tomorrow. Maria goes to the desert and will live in the old house which is now refurbished, and I hope to follow later when the new rooms are complete. Meanwhile I shall be staying for a bit with Eva [Herrmann]. I hope all goes well with you and Allanah [Harper]. Maria joins with me in sending love.

Your affectionate
Aldous

460 '*Wandering between two worlds, one dead, the other powerless to be born*' is quoted from Matthew Arnold's '*Stanzas from the Grande Chartreuse*'. Allanah Harper (*Mme Statlender*): founder and editor of the Paris quarterly Echanges. *Her memoir* All Trivial Fond Records *was published in* 1948.

Llano, Calif.
23 April, 1942

My dear Gene,

Many thanks for your last letter. [. . . .]

I have been doing some work on a movie of *Jane Eyre*, but am now through with it, except perhaps for a few days of revision later on. My novel and other ideas on a large scale are still simmering, and in the interval I have started work on a little book of pure utility, about the Bates Method of visual education. I am anxious to get this out pretty quickly; for the optometrists are lobbying their hardest, in this and other states, to get it legislated out of existence, nominally because the teachers of the method are 'unqualified', actually because theirs (the optometrists') is an overcrowded profession and they fear the inroads of rivals who may cause a diminution in the sale of optical glass. A little book by a reasonably sane and responsible person might help to keep this unquestionably very valuable technique alive and contribute towards its official recognition as a recognized branch of education. Incidentally, I think that if I can make it brief, clear and practical, it might have a good and enduring sale among the many millions who suffer from eye defects and do not get complete relief from artificial lenses. I hope, if all goes well, to get this done by the end of the summer. The title I have chosen is *The Art of Seeing*. When I finish that, I hope to be able to get down in real earnest to the novel.

I hope the news of Martha and yourself, and of the boys, remains good. Maria joins me in sending love and good wishes.

Yours ever
Aldous H.

462: TO MRS BERTHA L. PROUTY

Llano, Calif:
21 May, 1942

Dear Mrs. Prouty,

Thank you for your very friendly letter of May 8th. It was a great pleasure to receive it.

Your question is a very hard one to answer, for it becomes increasingly difficult to know what men and women of good will can do within the field of politics. Indeed, it may be that, aside from using their vote in issues that seem reasonably clear-cut, the best thing they can do is to work outside the

461 *Huxley's hopes for the popularity of* The Art of Seeing *were fully realized: the book enjoyed remarkable sales, especially in Britain.*
462 *Replying to a question about matters in* Ends and Means.

political field, concentrating on the personal and small-scale-social problems within their reach, in the hope that a sufficient number of good solutions of such problems may produce a cumulative effect on the large-scale world with which the politicians deal. It seems clear, when one observes the behaviour of people at the present time, that there is such a thing as too much preoccupation with politics—with problems beyond the individual's range and beyond his power to alter for good or evil. Such preoccupation results in a lot of emotional disturbance, divorced from emotion's proper outlet—appropriate action. Hence much neurosis, hysteria and impaired personal and social relationships. 'Sufficient unto the day is the evil thereof' is a piece of the deepest wisdom; and the saying may be supplemented, in many cases, by another: 'Sufficient unto the place is the evil thereof'. Too much of what is called 'an intelligent interest in politics' is just the working up of harmful and futile emotional attitudes about evils remote in time and place, about which the excited person is physically unable to do anything at all. As the result of this excitement, immediate tasks are left undone and near-by opportunities for doing small, but concrete, goods are neglected. The press and radio are responsible for working up this agitation about remote evils, and I believe that it is often necessary to subject oneself to strict rationing in regard to reading and listening in. To refrain from excessive indulgence in papers and radios may be one of the most salutary—as it is also one of the most painful, for many people—of necessary mortifications.

With all good wishes for the health and happiness of yourself and your family, I remain

Yours sincerely
Aldous Huxley

463: TO JACOB I. ZEITLIN

Llano, Calif:
2 June, 1942

My dear Jake,

Thank you for your letter. *Jonah* was printed in an edition of 50 or 60, I forget which, to send out as a Christmas Card, in 1916, I believe [i.e., in 1917]. A young woman artist, called Carrington, who afterwards devoted her life to Lytton Strachey, as his housekeeper and secretary, and committed suicide after his death, made a very good drawing of Jonah seated on the whale's kidney—but I lacked the funds to have it reproduced.

All goes well here, as I hope it does with you and Josephine. If ever I get to town, I will try to look in on you—with a few pea-nuts, if any ever come up, which I doubt.

Yours
Aldous H.

Llano, Calif:
5 July, 1942

Dearest Joan,

Thank you for your letter of May 30th, which crossed one of mine, bringing a contribution to the children's education. I'm afraid you must have had a very difficult time with the boy and the mother, and am glad that there is now a prospect of your having your burden lightened. I was sorry to read the account of your health. What a misery one's body can be! Something vaguely similar to your trouble has been afflicting me:—at any rate, my excellent Austrian doctor here attributes everything ultimately to a hereditary condition of the vegetative nervous system, which shows up in a number of tiresome symptoms—one of the minor ones being the inability to keep a proper nail on one of my fingers, owing to some defect in spinal nerve fibre, which keeps that particular finger under-nourished with circulation and, in general, insufficiently alive. This seems like a small-scale version of your trouble. I suppose we inherit it from common ancestors.

Maria's youngest sister has suddenly turned up in America, having married again and, by some miracle of which we haven't yet heard the details, managed to get on to the S.S. *Drottingholm* with her husband and baby. They are now in New York. Another piece of good news was a cable from M's mother, saying that she expected to get to Lisbon this month—after 18 months of wrestling with visas etc., and more than a year after we had aeroplane tickets for her passage. I hope she will get a place on a plane fairly soon. With bad luck, people get stuck in Lisbon almost indefinitely. I'm glad there is a prospect of her getting out. Conditions in France had been getting very bad, and the lot of the elderly there is particularly hard. One looks forward with dread to the next big flu epidemic: it will kill off these under-nourished people like flies. Indeed, disease is likely to play a very big part in the drama before the curtain is rung down. Medical circles here are very apprehensive of what may happen owing to the movement of large numbers of men from temperate zone to tropics, and to the general speeding up of communications between different parts of the world. Blackwater fever, which came by plane from Africa to Brazil, is spreading rapidly in its new home and might easily obtain a foothold in N. America. They now find that yellow fever can be carried by many kinds of mosquito, and that jungle animals can act as intermediate hosts—so that the optimistic belief, 20 years ago, that it was a thing of the past seems to be unfounded. Meanwhile the highway from the USA to S. America is being pushed rapidly ahead—and the doctors are wondering what infections will travel northwards

464 *Rose Nys de Haulleville's first husband, Eric, had died in* 1941. *She was now married to William Wessberg.*

with the traffic. It's a pity that the march of Progress should always be also a march of Regress. Love to the family.

Your aff [*ectionate*]

[*Aldous*]

465: TO HAROLD RAYMOND

Llano, Calif.

12 *July,* 1942

Dear Harold,

Many thanks for your letter and the enclosed accounts, which strike me as very satisfactory in view of the current situation.

The script of my little book on *The Art of Seeing* is now being typed, and I hope to send it off within the next three days. [. . . .]

When I am finished with this and one or two small jobs which I have to do, I hope to get down to my long delayed novel, which seems to be shaping up better than in the past. I hope to goodness it will go all right now. After that, if all goes well, I might try my hand, as you suggest, at another bio-graphico-historical subject. I have in mind one of the most fantastically strange stories in all French history—the story of the demoniac possession of the nuns of Loudun, which begins with fraud, hysteria, malicious plotting; goes on with the commission of a monstrous judicial crime, the burning of Urbain Grandier, as the supposed author of the possession; continues posthumously with more diabolic manifestations and the bringing on to the scene of Father Surin, one of the most saintly ecclesiastics of his age, who tries to exorcise the Abbess of the convent, responsible finally for all the mischief and thoroughly enjoying the enormous publicity which the posses-sion had given her; in the course of his exorcisms, which take the form of trying to teach the woman a form of direct mystical approach to the divine, Surin, by a kind of psychological infection, himself succumbs to possession and becomes half mad, but with perfectly lucid intervals, in which he realizes the full extent of his misfortune. Surin remains in this state for nearly twenty years, but finally emerges into a serene old age of something like perfected sanctity, during which he writes some of the most important spiritual works of his period. Meanwhile, the Abbess consoles herself for having ceased to be the fashion by assuming the airs of a kind of bogus mystical spirituality—acting the part of a contemplative saint with the most horrible skill. In the end, however, she develops cancer and, during the long slow illness, has as her constant companion a genuinely saintly lay woman, who pays no attention to her play-acting and finally brings the poor woman to a state of genuine devotion, in which condition she dies. The details of the possessions, the exorcisms, the trial of Grandier, the public reactions, the sceptical enquiries are of enormous picturesqueness; while the characters of the Abbess and Surin are absorbingly interesting. My only trouble is that I haven't got an adequate supply of documents, and that the obtaining of books from libraries outside Los Angeles is a tiresome process and an unsatisfactory one, since one can't keep the books for more than ten days. I should, therefore, be immensely grateful if you would get some good bookseller to look out for some of the necessary volumes, buy whatever you can on my behalf and ship them out to me.

[. . . .]

My efforts to pick up any of these here have so far proved fruitless; but there should be a much better chance in London.

We had a nice letter from Piers a few days after I got yours—written from India in March, I believe it was. I hope your news of Tony is still good, in spite of the Libyan situation. Presumably, you only hear very briefly and fitfully from him.

Maria's mother cabled a week or two ago saying that she hoped to be in Lisbon early in July, in which case she ought to be able to use the transportation we have waiting for her there. This will be a great comfort to M., for life for a Belgian refugee in France was getting very hard. Our love to you both.

Yours,
Aldous H

466: TO ALAN WATTS

Llano, Calif:
3 August, 1942

Dear Mr. Watts,

Thank you for your very interesting letter of July 15th. I look forward very much to seeing your new translation of Dionysius. There is something peculiarly strange and interesting about mysticism in the Western tradition; for, as Abbot Chapman remarks in one of his spiritual letters, it is extremely hard to reconcile Christianity with mysticism. He quotes Abbot Marmion as saying that St John of the Cross is a sponge filled with Christianity. You can squeeze out all the Christianity and the full mystical doctrine and praxis remain. I wish very much that Chapman—who was a man of remarkable ability, as well as a man of prayer,—might have lived to undertake a full-length discussion of the whole problem. The attitude of the Church—alternately, or even simultaneously, persecuting mystics and canonizing them—indicates how very thorny it is.

Yours very sincerely
Aldous Huxley

467: TO JULIAN HUXLEY

Llano, Calif.
23 November, 1942

Dearest Julian,

I was so glad to get your letter, though sorry indeed for its bad news of

481

your health and the Zoo. I do hope you'll find a satisfactory alternative for the latter, and some way to improve the former. How strange it is that there seems as yet no satisfactory treatment for sinus. I suspect the reason to be that the predisposition to sinus trouble is due to some fundamental trouble in the autonomic nervous system—an inadequacy of the innervation in those delicate areas, with consequent low resistance to infection. Hence no local treatment can do much good; and, as all doctors admit, there is nothing so difficult to deal with as the autonomic nervous system. My own troubles seem to have been of this origin—the trouble in the nervous apparatus betraying itself in such diverse symptoms as heart irregularity, intestinal spasm, hives, bronchitis and the continuous falling off of one of my finger-nails, which was evidently insufficiently innervated and so inadequately supplied with blood. Now, thanks to my rather crazy but very good Viennese doctor, the heart is going pretty well again, the spasm is diminishing and the nail, after three years of hopeless struggling, at last shows signs of growing back to normal. He has achieved this by a long-range course of medication, designed to stimulate mildly and so strengthen the nervous apparatus, and by a very stringent diet—meatless, milkless, saltless, so that the minimum of strain may be thrown on the eliminatory processes, and the minimum of such substances as cadaverine and indican produced within the body. Beans and other legumes are now my main source of proteins—a bit boring, especially without salt; but one gets used to anything, and the treatment is doing me a lot of good. Maybe, something along similar lines would be of help in your case. What a nuisance the body of this death really is!

Matthew suddenly went down with appendicitis a few weeks ago, and had to be operated on in a great hurry. They got the thing out just in time. A few hours more, it seems, and it would have ruptured. Luckily he was in town at the moment it happened, so they were able to dig into him without delay. He is out of hospital now, and taking things quietly while the tissues are being firmly consolidated. He will probably be called up, when he gets better, as in other respects he seems to be in a much stronger condition than he was even this summer, and incomparably better than last winter. I didn't know Francis was going to sea. It must be a very anxious-making thing for Juliette and you.

My little book on *The Art of Seeing* has recently come out here, and should appear in England fairly soon—though there has been some delay, owing to corrected proofs from Harpers having failed to reach Chattos; so they must now do the correcting from the book. It is really astonishing what results Mrs Corbett and her teachers are getting with young men who have been turned down for the navy and air force, but are obstinately determined to have another try. They are so anxious to normalize their vision that they are ready to take a lesson every day and to practise intensively for hours at a stretch. The result is that scores of them get through their tests after only a few weeks, sometimes even a few days, of training. The doctors still oppose the whole method on *a priori* grounds; but a number of air force and navy officers responsible for recruitment are now actually recommending young men who can't pass the tests, but whom they would like to have, to go and get themselves normalized by Mrs Corbett. In another twenty or thirty years, even medical orthodoxy may come round to it.

I am working on a kind of novel now and hope, when that is done, to get down to some more or less philosophical writing, on the subject of non-dogmatic religious mysticism—the only common element, at once theoretical and practical, speculative and devotional, in the various religions of the world. Christianity as such can never hope to become the religion of this new technologically and perhaps militaristically unified world we are moving into— it can never hope to become the world religion, because it has become associated, in the eyes of all non-European peoples, with the beastlinesses of our political and economic imperialism. But there is in all the religions of any degree of development this highest common factor of mysticism, on which everybody can agree, because it is empirical and does not depend on revelation or history. Mysticism also has the enormous merit of being concerned with the eternal present, and not, as humanism is, with the future. The moment you get a religion which thinks primarily about the bigger and better future—as do all the political religions from Communism and Nazism up to the, at present, harmless, because unorganized and powerless, forms of Humanism and Utopianism—it runs the risk of becoming ruthless, of liquidating the people it happens to find inconvenient now for the sake of the people who are going, hypothetically, to be so much better and happier and more intelligent in the year 2000, of sacrificing the present to a future, about which the one thing that can certainly be said is that we are totally incapable of foreseeing it accurately. I think that is one of the reasons why, as Sorokin has made so clear by his accumulated statistics, an age whose chief settled concern is with transcendental religion is so much less fertile in wars and revolutions than an age whose settled and primary concern is with humanism and the future.

Not much further news. We are on the brink of gasoline rationing, and everybody in this country of immense distances and wholly inadequate public transportation is getting a bit nervous. But doubtless it will settle itself somehow. For ourselves it means staying put rather more than before —and anyhow it has been very difficult to move about much; for though there has been fuel, the necessity of conserving tyres has reduced all motion to a minimum.

Our love to you both.

Ever your affectionate

A.

Llano, Calif.
30 December, 1942

Dear Dr Rhine,

Herewith the script which was forwarded to me by Gerald Heard. Thank you so much for having given me the opportunity for seeing it. On the practical side I have no comments to make. The method you have adopted is obviously right for the purposes of laboratory use and for statistical testing. Outside the laboratory one can only rely on what you have called anecdotal evidence. To me, the great interest and importance of your work is that it will finally compel those who suffer from 'voluntary ignorance' to reconsider the anecdotal evidence and to accept a good deal of it as valid—with fascinating consequences for philosophy and religion. It will be necessary to revive some form of the Buddhist and Hindu doctrines in regard to a 'psychic' world of mental forces, either completely immaterial or else making use of forms of energy akin to those observable in the ordinary space-time world, but more subtle. Under suitable conditions, the mental activities of individuals and groups release forces sufficiently powerful, if not to move mountains, certainly to cure serious lesions and even perhaps to multiply food. (The 'miracles' of the nineteenth-century Curé d'Ars in this matter are borne out by a lot of testimony.) Another point, strongly stressed by the oriental theologians, but unfortunately neglected by those of the West, is that certain types of mental activity by individuals or groups may result in the creation within the psychic world of more or less permanent vortices of force. This means that any religion, if intensely enough believed in, creates the objects of its worship—gods, defunct saints and the like. These objectifications or projections may become centres of energy reinforcing the energies of individual prayers, desires and imaginations, and thus may assist the worshipper in getting the results he desires. Oriental philosophers have always been perfectly clear about the nature of these objectifications. Thus, in a Mahayana Buddhist scripture *The Tibetan Book of the Dead* (translated by Evans Wentz and published by the Oxford University Press) are to be found the most categorical statements to the effect that the tutelary deities of the worshipper and even the High Buddhas themselves are objectifications projected by human minds and ultimately unreal. The finally independent reality is the Clear Light of the Void, the undifferentiated, timeless consciousness which is the self-subsistent principle of all things, and which the mystic discovers progressively in pure contemplation. Christian mystics have said nearly the same thing; but have never been able to carry their argument (which is based on direct experience, as the arguments of the physical scientists are based on direct sense impressions) to its logical conclusion, owing to the fact that orthodox Christianity has persisted in regarding its 'tutelary deities' and its 'High Buddhas', not as projections of the minds of generations of worshippers, but as independent, self-subsistent entities. In the light of the anecdotal and now the statistical evidence that has piled up in regard to the powers of the mind, I feel that the orthodox Christian view is untenable. Moreover, it is not in accord with the direct experience of the mystics, who have been unanimous in warning aspirants to the knowledge of God to have nothing to do with the psychic powers which they are likely to develop while pursuing the path of contemplation; for such powers and the 'miracles' which they allow their owners to perform have no more to do with divine Reality than the more familiar kinds of psycho-physical phenomena and, if attended to with too much interest, as though they were ends in themselves, are fatal obstacles in the way of the apprehension of Reality. Philosophers like Reiser, who conceive of a revival of religion based upon ESP and kindred 'psychic' phenomena completely neglect these warnings. Such an attitude, it seems to me, is fatal; for all that it can result in is the strengthening and extension of such religions as Christian Science, Theosophy, New Thought, 'I Am', in which the stress is wholly on powers, personal advantages and future time and not where all the great spiritual leaders have insisted that it should be placed, on eternity, abandonment to the will of God and humility. All of which has taken us rather far from throwing dice; but the relation between craps and Reality is a real one, and will have to be faced by the professional philosophers. Meanwhile, as an extremely unprofessional one, I raise my little chirrup.

All good wishes for yourself and the work during 1943.

Yours very sincerely,
Aldous Huxley

469: TO SWAMI PRABHAVANANDA

Llano, Calif:
4 February, 1943

Dear Swami,

I had hoped to be able to get to town for the opening of the monastery on Saturday; but I am afraid it is not going to be practicable, and I must therefore confine myself to sending these few words of good wishes. May the new undertaking prosper and prove spiritually fruitful.

Yours very sincerely
Aldous Huxley

468 *The dice-throwing tests devised at Rhine's Parapsychology Laboratory were being used to measure the ability of selected subjects to predict throws correctly. Repeated successes beyond the range of statistical probability were taken as possible evidence of extra-sensory perception (ESP) or of a related power, telekinesis.*

469 *Monastery: founded under the auspices of the Vedanta Society of Southern California.*

Llano, Calif:
4 *March*, 1943

Dearest J,

I hope all goes well with yourself and the family and that you've all got through the worst of the winter without sickness. Here things have been satisfactory. Matthew got over his operation quickly and is now in so much better condition than he was a year ago, when the doctors insisted on his leaving college for rest and treatment, that he has just been drafted into the Medical Corps and has gone off for training to Abilene, Texas. So far he seems to be quite cheerful and enjoying the experience. Meanwhile Maria and I have been well—tho' M has been kept very busy these last two months as we have had Rose's little girl of four [Olivia de Haulleville] staying here, while Rose herself was expecting and successfully giving birth to a son [Sigfrid Wessberg] by her new American husband. It seems a rather dismal moment of history to bring children into the world; but let's hope the optimism may be justified.

War is beginning to produce dislocations even here. The food situation is startlingly much worse than anybody suspected it could be, largely owing to indiscriminate conscription of farm labour, but also to transportation difficulties and shipment of food abroad on a greater scale than even this land of plenty can afford. Also there seems to have been a lot of mismanagement combined with wishful thinking. The Sec: of Agriculture has been saying for several months that 1943 production would be 8% above 1942. And now suddenly a questionnaire issued to the agricultural inspectors on the ground elicits the forecast that, in nine tenths of the counties in all the States, there will be a decline, in 1943, of 30%.

Other curious and rather ominous consequences of war are the increased anti-Semitism which one meets with in all classes, particularly the common people, and the strong recrudescence of anti-negro passions in the South. The first is due to the age-old dislike of a monied, influential and pushing minority, coupled with a special grudge against the Jews as being chiefly instrumental, in popular opinion, in getting America into the war. The second is due to the negroes' position being improved and to white resentment of the fact (there are no more coloured servants to be had in the South), coupled with general Southern dislike of racial equality as a war aim. The result is a strong Southern-Democratic reaction in Congress and out of it against the administration and the New Deal. Meanwhile intelligent negroes with whom I've talked are very gloomy about the prospects of their people in the immediate future.

I have been reading lately Dr. Wm. Sheldon's new book, *The Varieties of Temperament*, a sequel to his *Varieties of Physique*, based on ten years of systematic research. It's by far the best thing of its kind ever produced, going far beyond Kretschmer and Viola in accuracy and in quantification. If you have not read it, please do; for it is obviously very important. Some of his findings raise once more, in a much clearer and more definite form, the problems discussed by Wm. James in his *Moral Equivalent of War*. There exists, as Sheldon makes clear, a certain percentage of people—he calls them 'Somatotonics'—who are constitutionally aggressive, who love risk and adventure for their own sake, who lust for power and dominance, who are psychologically callous and have no squeamishness about killing, who are insensitive to pain and tirelessly energetic. How can these be prevented from wrecking the world? Christianity tried to keep them down by means of a 'Cerebrotonic' system of ethical restraints. But there has been a revolt against cerebrotonic religion and ethics during the last 25 years and the somatotonics are in the saddle, not only physically, but also intellectually and philosophically. No amount of economic or political rearrangement can change their constitutional tendencies. A revival of cerebrotonic philosophy in some generally acceptable form, with a practical system of sublimational outlets, seems to be the only hope for keeping the constitutional barbarians to some extent harmless and usefully, not destructively, employed. Sheldon himself admits that, as a psychiatrist, he is often baffled by the problem of individual somatotonics living in a society that has thrown off the restraints of a cerebrotonic ethic and religion. It is certainly a subject that needs thinking about.

I've been working away at a novel, which I hope to get finished by the summer. After which I have a number of possible alternatives—but then so has the world at large! So I don't make any plans.

Give our best love to Juliette. I hope she still has good news of her mother —tho' I imagine life in Switzerland must be getting pretty difficult these days. Our last news from M's sister Jehanne dates from November. They were all well at that time and planning to go to Paris for a time. An odd symptom of undernourishment—she and almost all her friends and neighbours have been tormented by boils which have gone on multiplying for months.

Keep well.

Ever your affectionate

A.

471: TO JULIAN HUXLEY

Llano, Calif.
7 *May*, 1943

Dearest J.,

Your *Evolution* came to me from Harpers a few days ago, and I want to write and thank you for it. I have had no time to do more than turn the pages and read occasional passages—but it has been enough to make me realize the enormous scope of the book and also its masterly lucidity of exposition. You must feel pleased to have set up such a massive and at the same time elegant monument. I'm glad the critical response in England has been so good. I have not seen any reviews here—but then I don't read any of the papers in which such reviews are liable to appear.

Talking of papers, I wonder if you know a very curious publication which I have recently subscribed to—*Main Currents in Modern Thought?* It is a sort of glorified digest of the latest in scientific philosophy, with leading articles by a man called [F. L.] Kunz, who seems to be almost too clever and well informed by half. The whole performance is interesting and stimulating—though there runs through it all that touching naïveté of extremely clever people, which consists in believing that the multiplication of information and the spread of a sound philosophy will automatically result in the improvement of human behaviour. It's a pity it doesn't happen to be true; for then the way to the millennium would be short indeed. But how odd it is that such men don't realize that most people can say of themselves

> video meliora, proboque;
> deteriora sequor,

and that the crucial problem is always that of the will to act upon the increased information and in accordance with the principles of the improved philosophy. The mere fact of knowing about the law of gravitation is not sufficient to prevent people from dropping bombs on one another's heads. And the same is true in regard to the moral and spiritual laws. They might be demonstrated mathematically and in terms of a flawless logic; but people would continue to violate them so long as the immediate kick to be obtained from the violation were sufficient to outweigh the consideration of the ultimate consequences. The stories of the people who sold their souls to the devil, even though they were convinced that the mundane good time would have to be paid for by eternal damnation, are psychologically true, and demonstrate the fallacy of the belief that more information and correcter philosophies are enough. All the same, *Main Currents* is worth looking at each month.

My own work goes ahead slowly, but I hope surely. I am fairly near the end of a long kind of novel, and have a number of essays on philosophical and religious topics ready to be worked up when that is done. Meanwhile, my little book on *Seeing* goes ahead very nicely here, while in England Raymond tells me, the first edition of ten thousand went in a few days. Which is most extraordinary. There was some interesting stuff in *Nature* last autumn, by a group of Russians who had been working on the favourable and unfavourable conditions of seeing and other sense processes. Some of the stuff was what any person with bad sight and a certain awareness of his psycho-physical processes could have told them without any laboratory experimentation. But there were also new and interesting findings. And anyhow it is always a good thing when men of science laboriously discover the obvious; for then other men of science may be persuaded that the obvious is true. Otherwise, if it doesn't happen to be a piece of obviousness within their own world of specialization, they can't believe in it.

Our news of Matthew is not too good at the moment. He was transferred from Texas to Denver, where he started training as a laboratory technician and was liking the work very well, when he went down with measles, was let out of hospital after a fortnight, only to return three days later with some obscure kind of nose and throat infection, which is still keeping him in bed. Measles is a horribly treacherous disease because of its aftermaths; and I hope very much that this may not prove to be something unpleasant with long-range consequences. Meanwhile one can only wait and see—and pray that the army doctors aren't merely pumping him full of toxic sulfanilamide for lack of knowing any other treatment—which is what so many medicos do nowadays, since the sulfa drugs became fashionable. They even give sulfa pills to six months-old babies for a cold in the head. The cold is short-circuited, of course; but so is the baby, who generally takes months to recover from the effects of his cure. One day I should like to write a little book on fashions in medicine. The history would be as extravagantly farcical as that of the fashions in women's clothes. But fortunately no animal species possesses anything approaching the toughness of man.

I hope your news of Francis is still good, and that the rest of the family is well. Summer should help your sinus trouble, unless too much work counteracts the effects of the weather. Best love to you both from both of us.

Ever your affectionate,
Aldous

472: TO J. B. RHINE

Llano, Calif.
11 *May,* 1943

Dear Dr Rhine,

Thank you for your letter and the outline of the plan for research into survival. I think your idea of a sequel to *New Frontiers* is excellent. I would venture to suggest, however, the inclusion of an additional chapter in which existing theories of the incorporeal world should be discussed. [C. D.] Broad's theory of the psychic factor and his and [Hereward] Carrington's speculations regarding precognition could be mentioned. And I would like very much to see an account of oriental thought upon the subject—the Buddhist notion of skandhas, or psychic crystallizations; the Hindu 'subtle body' and its relations to the gross body on the one hand and to atman and Brahma on the other.* It seems to me that a serious and well-informed discussion of such hypotheses would arouse a great deal of public interest, and would give people a notion of the lines along which some explanation of the, to us, odder and less familiar sides of experience might be formulated. People who might help with the oriental side are Dr [A. K.] Coomaraswamy of the Boston Museum of Fine Arts, and perhaps also Kunz, the editor of *Main Currents in Modern Thought*, who seems to have a wide knowledge of, and interest in, Indian thought, which he views very sympathetically from the point of view of an advanced mathematician and philosophy-of-science man. I have been interested to note that he finds in certain Hindu doctrines, (such as that of logical atomism, which seemed entirely silly and arbitrary to nineteenth-century Sanskrit scholars), bold generalizations in full accord with the findings of modern mathematical physics. This being so, it seems quite possible that he might have valuable and stimulating things to say about the Indian view of the incorporeal world and its relevance to the views of post-Einsteinian Western thinkers. It is by such means, I believe, that one might hope to establish some sort of bridge between contemporary scientific thought and practice on the one hand and ancient oriental thought, based upon centuries of accumulated experience as well as on direct intuition by exceptional minds.

With all good wishes for the book and the new research, as well as for yourself, I am

Yours very sincerely
Aldous Huxley

*And cp the mediaeval concept of the *scintilla animae*, the synteresis or *apex mentis*, lying beyond the ordinary everyday psyche, and capable of direct contact with God.

473: TO JULIAN HUXLEY

Llano, Calif.
26 June, 1943

Dearest J.,

I was delighted to get your letters of a month ago, which came pretty quickly for a change—for mails, both airy and watery, have been much slower of late. News of the family seems pretty good, though I'm sorry to hear of your flu, and hope you will be well over it by the time you get this.

Matthew is now back with us, having been discharged from the army about a week ago as the result of a long, severe and undiagnosed illness which he got while training at Denver. He started with a bout of German measles, was let out after ten days; but three days later was back with temperature and inflamed throat. Fever continued and pains in the joints appeared, making the doctors think at one time that it might be rheumatic fever. But it wasn't. And after about seven weeks of it they still didn't know what had been the matter. But the upshot is that he has lost forty pounds and is in a very low condition. He hasn't yet seen his doctor here; so I don't know what his state really is. Indications are that the lungs are all right, though kidneys, which were the chief point of trouble eighteen months ago, when he left college, are not quite satisfactory. It is all very unfortunate; and I hope to goodness it isn't going to have lasting bad consequences. For the moment what he needs is complete rest.

Yes, I agree with you about the interestingness and importance of the Ogden-Richards work on language. Basic English is a miracle of ingenuity. Whether Chinese and blackamoors will make a universal language of it is another question. But meanwhile it furnishes an excellent scholastic discipline. Nothing is better for clarifying muddled ideas than having to translate a passage, say, of Carlyle, or St Paul, or Plato into Basic. I presume you have read Korzybski's *Science and Sanity*—an absolutely maddening book, owing to its repetitiousness and its wanderings, but necessary, I am afraid, if one wants to grasp the significance of semantics to all fields of human activity. Good too is *Language Habits and Human Affairs* by Irving J. Lee. And then there are the more technical aspects of the matter, dealt with by Morris and Woodger in a relatively comprehensible fashion in fascicules of the Chicago University Press's *Encyclopaedia of Unified Science*. Bertie Russell's last book on the subject—*The Nature of Truth*, or some such title—I haven't read, but I suppose it ought to be read. On language in general I have got more, I think, from Bloomfield's *Language* than from any other book. Jespers[e]n is good too.

A very strange fact, as Bloomfield, I think, points out is that the modern analysis of language has been going on for more than a century now (the beginning came with the translation of the Sanskrit grammar by the Hindu grammarian Panini, which, though written some time B.C., remains apparently the most 'modern' and scientific treatment of a language ever undertaken), its results are made available to only a tiny handful of specialists. No attempt has been made to incorporate them into primary, secondary or even higher education. Language is studied in terms of the grammatical rules formulated by the Alexandrian scholars, and no one is ever taught to consider the real relation of words to things—so that the vast majority of people continue to think and act as though things were the signs of words, not words of things. Sometimes I think that the reason for this strange state of affairs must be a kind of instinctive self-protective instinct on the part of existing society. For of course the effects of broadcasting a knowledge of semantics, of teaching all men the habit of analysing the language they not only use, but actually swim in, like fishes in the sea, would be profoundly revolutionary. So much so that it may be doubted whether any of the most sacred institutions and ideas would remain unaffected by the educational reform. So we go on teaching our children gender rhymes—'common are sacerdos, dux, vates, parens, et conjux'—which never put any disturbing ideas into anybody's head! Still, the subject remains a fascinating one, about which one can speculate interminably. For example, at present no language spoken in the ordinary way by ordinary people is capable of expressing the fact, which is the keystone of modern science, that the universe is a continuum; that there is no such thing as simple location, in Whitehead's phrase; that nothing is separate and independent, but that everything exists in a field and is bound up with everything else. Continuity can be talked about only by means of the calculus. Will everyday language ever conform itself to the facts of the universe? Or will mankind for ever be condemned to do his talking and non-mathematical thinking in terms of an instrument which cannot in the nature of things express the truth?

Things jog along here, with a great deal of complaining over the food situation, which seems to have been scandalously mismanaged from Washington. Anyhow, the result of cutting the supply of farm machinery by seventy per cent and simultaneously drafting farm labour has been to reduce production this year by about twenty per cent. And meanwhile the Almighty, who is, I suspect, determined to teach us all a good lesson by staging a world famine, probably accompanied by a world pestilence, has stepped in with the worst floods in a century, which have completely devastated about four million acres of the best land in the Middle West, and have destroyed vast quantities of live-stock. The race trouble, which I think I mentioned in an earlier letter, is flaring up again, with anti-Mexican riots in Los Angeles and really frightful anti-negro disturbances in Detroit. It looks as though one of the results of trying to implement the Atlantic Charter elsewhere will be a heightening of race prejudice in America. But these are the things, I suppose, one has to expect.

Love from us both to Juliette, yourself and the boys,

Your affectionate
A.

474: TO MRS MARTHA SAXTON

Trabuco Ranch,
Trabuco Canyon P.O., Calif:
6 July, 1943

My dear Martha,

I have been away from home, and the news about Gene reached me only today. As I think about him now, I realize with surprise how few in all these years were the occasions on which I was with him, and how brief—and yet I always thought of him as one among the best of my friends. It was as though he possessed some quality stronger than absence and distance—an essential lovableness and reliability and warmth that continued to affect one in spite of the obstacles interposed by space and time. In a curious, hardly analysable way Gene was, for me, a living proof of the triumph of character over matter —physically almost always absent, and yet firmly present in my mind as a trusted friend, to whom I knew I could turn in any crisis without fear of disappointment.

And to you, dear Martha, what can I possibly say? There are no consola-

474 *Eugene F. Saxton had died on 26 June.*

tions that can be administered from without—only the mitigations of grief that come with time, and perhaps one's own tentative answers to the agonizing questions of life and death.

Ever yours affectionately,
Aldous H.

475: TO MATTHEW HUXLEY

Trabuco Ranch,
Trabuco Canyon P.O., Calif.
13 August, 1943

Dearest M.,

Coccola writes that you haven't been quite so well this last week or so. I hope you were able to get in touch with [Dr. Joseph] Kolisch on the phone. But if not, do remember what he said about the need to help yourself. Don't take risks—as I very rashly did the other day, by walking in rough grass too soon. This is a matter about which you'll have to be particularly careful when you're in town and tempted to sit up too late and eat the wrong things. Also don't relapse into bottle feeding, but make an effort to keep on a good mixed diet with plenty of vegetables, as well as your milk. Vegetables and fruit are particularly important, as they provide the cellulose bulk which keeps the internal functionings normal, and also because they furnish a wide variety of minerals and vitamins. Also, I would go periodically to old man Gaylor for a twisting and pummelling, which gives you in concentrated form the equivalents of the exercise you aren't at present allowed to take. And also, remember: Head forward and up—not Belly forward and down, which is what lanky ectomorphs of our kind tend all too naturally to do.

I expect to be up on Monday the twenty-third. Hope to see Chambers that afternoon and Mrs Corbett the following morning or early P.M. So that we should be able to drive back to the desert some time towards evening on Tuesday. Meanwhile I hope [———]'s visit and your trip to town will be a success and that you'll be feeling better again by the time you get this. Best love to Coccola and yourself.

Ever your affectionate,
Aldous

476: TO HAROLD RAYMOND

Llano, Calif.
6 September, 1943

Dear Harold,

Herewith the contract for the Swedish rights. I believe I signed and returned one earlier in the summer, but am sending this to make sure. News of *The Art of Seeing* seems very good. It is doing well here now, having got to about twenty-three thousand, I think.

Not much news here. Matthew is getting better, but is still subject to considerable downs as well as ups. The doctor wants him to find some light manual job for some months, before embarking on anything more complicated. Meanwhile it seems pretty clear that the undiagnosed illness he had while in the army was produced by the massive immunization shots for tetanus, typhoid, smallpox and various other items—shots which don't do one much harm if one is strong, but which, if there is a constitutional weakness, often play havoc, since they act as an unspecific protein shock to the system. The last straw was the treatment by sulphanilamide, which they gave him while he was having his fever; this produced a considerable degree of anaemia. So, as you see, it's another splendid case of the Triumphs of Science! Meanwhile I have been wrestling all summer with a very tiresome plant allergy, brought on by handling a particularly malevolent kind of burr weed while gardening this spring. This has kept me itching for several months, during which I have had to be away from home most of the time, since the inflammation flares up whenever I go back. I am hoping, however, to get the thing quieted down now by a new treatment. But it has been an awful nuisance and most unconducive to work.

The best news I have seen regarding the food situation appeared a few weeks ago. Perhaps you have seen it? It concerns the development of new strains of yeast, which are extremely palatable, some of them tasting like beef steaks, some like nuts, some like celery. As yeast multiplies its bulk sixteen times every twenty-four hours, when grown in a suitable sugar solution, and as it contains twice as much protein as does beef steak and heaven knows how many times more vitamins, there seems to be a real hope of getting adequate nourishment to starving areas in sufficient quantities and in a short time. Some of the big brewery companies here are already producing the stuff in bulk for Lend Lease and the army.

I hope you still have good news of the boys. Presumably Tony is in Sicily now—or in Italy perhaps?

Our love to Vera and yourself.

Ever yours,
Aldous.

477: TO VICTORIA OCAMPO

[*Trabuco Ranch,*
Trabuco Canyon, California]
[*September,* 1943]

My dear Victoria,

By this time, I hope you have recovered from New York and American literature and your strained knee. I wish you hadn't stayed in California under such unpropitious conditions and for so short a time. The renewal of a friendship requires more calm and leisure than we had during your visit. Still, I'm very glad you came even as fleetingly and as hurriedly as you did. One is grateful for one's friends even in the smallest doses.

What you ask about the rôle of the heart in mystical religion can be answered very simply. The heart cannot be commanded—but the will can. In other words it is in our power to exercise the rational and voluntary love of God, because our will is free and we can always make the choice of serving and honouring God rather than the contrary choice of serving and honouring ourselves. This rational voluntary love may or may not be accompanied by a movement of the heart. If so, it is good. But the right choice is none the less right for being unaccompanied by affective emotion—and there is no use in trying to force oneself to *feel* the love of God, if the feeling does not arise spontaneously. St. Teresa records how she used to try to compel herself to feel love as well as to act it out in a series of deliberate choices. She was quite unable to command her emotions and came to realize that voluntary and rational love was just as truly love as that which was accompanied by emotion. When it was so accompanied, she was glad; but when it wasn't, she did not feel depressed.

Talking of St. Teresa, a big new biography of the saint by an American Catholic historian called [William T.] Walsh has just come out, and we are reading it aloud. It is very interesting, despite the fact that Mr. Walsh thinks he writes rather better than he actually does, and is therefore fond of inserting passages of eloquence which are rather distressing. But he seems to know his subject—which is the main thing. We are also reading the most charming book—Pierre Camus's *Esprit de St François de Sales*, a sort of Boswellian record of conversation during 14 years of intimate friendship. The picture of St François that emerges is profoundly impressive. I don't know of anybody whom I wd more have liked to know.

We are staying for a few days with Gerald Heard at his 'monastery', which is very pleasant and profitable. After that we hope at last to be able to return to the desert. I am getting fairly near the end of my book and am eager to have done with it.

Our love to you, dear Victoria. Be well and happy, and let us all pray that the end of Europe's worst miseries is near.

Ever yours affectionately
Aldous

478: TO LAWRENCE C. POWELL

Llano, Calif.
18 *September,* 1943

Dear Mr Powell,

If it isn't too much bother, I wish you'd pass on the enclosed information to the proper quarters at UCLA. The matter concerns visual training and archery, which I know is practised in a fairly big way at the university. There is a young man at one of the army camps in the middle West, who is an

478 *Lawrence Clark Powell was the librarian of the University of California at Los Angeles.*

instructor in archery for commando troops and flyers. He has found—and his experience is confirmed by the commander of the camp and the camp optometrist—that startling improvements in vision can be secured by the practice of archery, particularly when combined with certain simple practices designed to keep the eyes systematically shifting their focus from near to far. He has written a long letter on the subject to Mrs Corbett, whose book on the improvement of vision he had previously read. In view of the fact that he seems to get remarkable results among the men at his camp, and of the further fact that there are very many boys at the university who wish to improve their vision so as to be able to pass air force and navy tests, it seems to me that the authorities in charge of archery would do well to look into the matter. The best thing would be for the archery expert to get in touch directly with Mrs Corbett, who has the young man's communications on the subject, and who would probably be able to furnish valuable suggestions based upon her own long and unique experience with visual education. Alternatively, if the authorities don't wish to involve themselves in optometrical unorthodoxy, I could probably arrange for copies of the letters to be made and sent to them. The thing I would like to see happen is this: to get a few of the fundamental principles of visual education incorporated into an accredited sport, so that boys and girls could learn the art of seeing while at play and without the necessity of doing a lot of tiresome exercises, which they would always be tempted to neglect. This would have the further advantage of completely by-passing the oculists and optometrists, who could not have anything to say on the matter.

I am staying for a few days at

1227 North Horn Ave.
West Hollywood, Calif.
Crestview 1-8523

With all good wishes, I am

Yours very sincerely,
Aldous Huxley

479: TO MATTHEW HUXLEY

1227 North Horn,
West Hollywood, Calif.
21 September, 1943

Dearest M,

I have just heard from Coccola that Rosalind [Rajagopal] might take you at Ojai. I am inclined to think this would be a very good plan, and shall talk of it to Kolisch, when I see him tomorrow. The scheme is all the better, since K's plans are still extremely indefinite; he has only got as far as thinking

478 *The North Horn address belonged to Rose and William Wessberg.*
479 *Rosalind Rajagopal is the director of the Happy Valley Foundation at Ojai, California.*

of going one of these days to look at his horses, which are still at grass at the ranch on the San Jacinto mountains where he was this summer.

If you go to Ojai, I feel very strongly that you should make the event an occasion for reorganizing your existence altogether. That the complete *désoeuvrement* of the desert has been good for you on the whole, I am sure. But for the last month or two it has been less good and from this time forth might be actually harmful. It is essential for you now to be a bit more directed, less disintegrated and drifting. And this applies not merely to physical and mental activities; it applies also and fundamentally to general attitude, to ethical behaviour in the widest sense of the word. You are extremely critical of other people's shortcomings in the matter of self-indulgence and inconsiderateness and slackness—critical often to the point of intolerance. But you are not critical, you are all too tolerant, of the same shortcomings in yourself. Letting things slide, forgetting what ought to be remembered, not bothering to do things because you don't happen to feel like doing them, permitting an immediate distraction, such as the purposeless reading of an intrinsically worthless magazine article, to get in the way of doing a present duty or thinking rationally about the future—these are things about which, in yourself, you are altogether too indulgent, at any rate when you are at home. For I think you permit yourself many things at home which you would not dream of doing when with other people. You earned no bad marks while you were in the army; but I'm afraid you would have earned a good many while at home—though why Coccola should be less deserving of consideration than other people, particularly as she does much more for you than other people, is a question which it is hard to answer rationally. Of course, this quirk is not confined to you alone. Most young people tend to permit themselves worse manners and less considerate behaviour at home than with other people. But it is a sign of adulthood to realize that even one's closest relations deserve as much thought and as many small, boring self-sacrifices as do strangers. But meanwhile it is a good thing to be delivered from temptation by being on one's own with people who don't belong to one's family and with whom one feels compelled by what the Greeks called *aidos*, the sense of shame, to be on one's best behaviour. So I feel very confident that, if you go to Ojai, or anywhere else, you'll make a success of it from your own point of view and leave an excellent impression on others. And this will be made easier for you if, as I hope, you have definite chores to do in a routine that has to be strictly observed. But there is also the intellectual side. Kolisch doesn't want you to do much of that; but do try to see that what little you undertake is purposeful and systematic. Promiscuous reading can become a really pernicious addiction, like oversmoking or drinking. It is far better, both intellectually and morally, to read less, but with a purpose, and always with a deliberate effort to understand clearly and fully to remember what you read. If you're going back to college, read the books that will help you in your English course, take regular notes on them, exercise yourself in accurately remembering what they contain and in critically judging their substance and style. This is, of course, best done by actually writing out précis and critiques. And do the same with such magazine articles as you read and find interesting. You like general information; but make the effort to co-ordinate what you learn and to make it accurate by jotting down the important points in your miscellaneous reading. I myself have not done this as much as I should; but I find myself constantly grateful for having done it only a little—and the little I have done now mounts up to a collection of a good many hundred cards in a card index.

And then finally there is the need to be systematic and purposeful in regard to health, as Kolisch has so constantly insisted—to take the medicines regularly, not to put off an injection to some later time because you don't feel like taking it now and because you subconsciously hope that, when the later time comes, you will have forgotten all about it and so have a completely valid excuse for not taking it at all. This again is just self-indulgence—preferring the pleasure of the moment (which is not even a pleasure, but the mere negative satisfaction of not having to take trouble) to the substantial future good of getting well.

And of course you know all this as well as I do. But it is necessary that it should be said again, because one is apt to pay very little attention to one's own knowledge of one's own weaknesses and defects. So read this carefully and see what you can do in the way of reorganizing, both at home, when you are there, and away from home, if you go to Ojai or elsewhere.

Much love from

Your affectionate

A.

480: TO CASS CANFIELD

(*Temporarily at*) 145½ *So. Doheny,*
Los Angeles, Calif:
7 *December,* 1943

Dear Canfield,

Your letter went to Llano, where I was not and from which there was nobody, until the last few days, to forward it. Hence this long delay, for which I apologize.

The book is nearly done. I have about 40 more pages to write, I should guess, and then shall have to go through the whole MS. All being well, I think I ought to be able to let you have the fair-copied script by the end of February. Meanwhile, however, I will have a part of it typed and send it you in advance.

The book may be described as a piece of the *Comédie Humaine* that

480 *The title chosen for the novel was of course* Time Must Have a Stop. *After the death of Saxton, Harper correspondence with Huxley was conducted by Cass Canfield.*

modulates into a version of the *Divina Commedia*. About half way through the story, which I have deliberately kept light, with events on a small scale minutely described, the principal comic character dies, and all that follows takes place against the background of his posthumous experience, which is, of course, wholly and disquietingly incompatible with the life he was leading and which goes on among those who survive him. The other principal character is a very precocious and talented boy of only 17 during the main story—whose date is 1929—and whom we meet again in an epilogue, of present date, as a young man, maimed in the war, and concerned with the problem of the relationship between art (for he is a poet) and religion, the aesthetic and the spiritual life. Altogether it is an odd sort of book; but I hope it has come off.

The title is still a matter of uncertainty. I had thought of
(1) 'Glassy Essence', from *Measure for Measure*

> but man, proud man . . .
> Most ignorant of what he is most assured,
> His glassy essence, like an angry ape
> Plays such fantastic tricks etc.

Unfortunately 'Glassy Essence' is a bit sibilant, don't you think?
(2) 'Time's Fool' from Hotspur's dying speech:

> But thought's the slave of life, and life's time's fool,
> And time, which takes survey of all the world,
> Must have a stop.

(3) Or I might call it 'The Barnacks' after the name of the family about whom the story is written.

And of course something else may turn up. But meanwhile do let me know what you think of these first suggestions.

Ever yours
Aldous Huxley

P.S What news, I wonder, of *The Art of Seeing*?

481: TO JULIAN HUXLEY

[145½ *S. Doheny Drive,*
Los Angeles, Calif.]
[31 *December,* 1943]

Dearest J,

Matthew will have given you our news, and this is no more than a

---

481 *Matthew wrote to Julian and Juliette Huxley on* 31 *December, reporting that his father was in cheerful spirits and was working hard on his novel, though still tormented by his skin trouble. He described an exercising board which his parents had set up in their temporary flat in town: 'Consists of rotating top on a solid foundation. Method is to wriggle vigorously. Every hour or so Aldous appears and solemnly imitates a whirling Dervish in the middle of the drawing room'.*

scribble to wish you and Juliette and the boys best things for 1944. Let's
hope it may see the end of the horror in Europe—and at not too frightful a
cost, either in lives or property damage—for the latter is the guarantee (along
with political and economic anarchy) of totalitarian centralization, since
when people have no possessions left they become completely dependent
for even clothing and shelter on government authority; their life is barrack
life and the very possibility of personal independence, unorthodox views
and behaviour, is completely ruled out. More and more it seems to me clear
that Jefferson was right and that democratic institutions cannot exist where
there is not a wide distribution of private property in land, utilizable goods
and means of production. Over most of Europe, if the destruction is too
much prolonged and intensified, there will be practically no private property
any more, therefore no possibility of anybody's disagreeing with a central
authority that provides all the means of existence, therefore no possibility
of democracy—only of passive obedience or, as its alternative, despairing
revolutionary violence.

I hope the African expedition will turn out to be pleasant and useful. It
sounds a most interesting assignment.

Here I am very busy, in the last stages of a book, which I shall be glad
to get off my hands. Love to you all.

Ever your affectionate
A.

482: TO MRS FRIEDA LAWRENCE

Llano, Calif.
24 February, 1944

My dear Frieda,

I have just finished my book, thank goodness, so have a breathing space
to thank you for the charming swan, by which you have reminded me of an
earlier indiscretion.

Tee hee, tee hee, oh sweet delight!
He tickles this age who can
Call Tullia's ape a marmosite
And Leda's goose a swan.

And, who knows? perhaps Europa's bull was an ox and Ganymede's eagle
a buzzard—but that's better than an aeroplane.

I hope your news is still good, and pray that it may remain so, especially
for Angelino's children. Will Rome be totally obliterated? I wonder? And
Florence, Pisa, Bologna, Venice and all the rest? Presumably Europe will
be rebuilt in holes, two hundred feet underground. But then they'll drop
poison gas that's heavier than air and the population will be in the position

482 The verse quotation in the first paragraph occurs in Texts and Pretexts.

of ground squirrels, when the exterminator comes round with his cyanide gun.

Julian has gone to West Africa on a Royal Commission that is going to decide what sort of higher education to give to the blackamoors. I wish *they'd* send a Royal Commission to Europe to work out a system of lower education for what remains of the next generation of pale-faces. Meanwhile, one of J's boys [Francis] is on a destroyer—which isn't a very healthy place to be, I'm afraid. Poor Juliette must be very anxious. [. . . .]

Other letters from England all breathe an enormous fatigue—the result of continuous overwork and anxiety. Last time the breaking point was reached after four and a half years; but now there seems to be a greater toughness. Due, I suspect, to better understanding of diet, more intelligent use of such food as there is. Maybe they will be able to prolong the agony for another year or so, before the collapse comes. But of course one never knows; the thing may go suddenly, with a bang.

Give my love to Angelino. When I get back to the desert—we are in town for a few days—I will return him his two anthologies of jokes and proverbs.

Ever your affectionate,
Aldous

483: TO CASS CANFIELD

Llano, Calif.
Easter Day [*9 April*], 1944

Dear Canfield,

Thank you for your wire and now the letter and enclosure. I wouldn't have bothered you about the MS, except that I wanted to be absolutely certain of its arrival before sending off my only other fair copy to England. I don't know yet when Chattos will publish; but I expect they would like a copy of the corrected proofs when these come through. However, there is probably plenty of time to decide about this, since I don't imagine they will want or be able to publish much before you do.

I think the description of the book is excellent. There is only one point in which I think it might be supplemented and clarified, and this is in regard to the chapters dealing with Eustace's posthumous experience. As the thing is worded now, a casual reader might not realize from this description that such material was included in the book. I think it would be best to bring this out a little more specifically. I would suggest something like this, introduced after the first sentence of the second paragraph (the one ending 'future'). 'The story is treated contrapuntally. A theme from the Human Comedy is in process of development, when suddenly and startlingly a new theme is introduced—a theme from the Divine Comedy of man's eternal destiny. And thenceforward the two themes run parallel, the after-death experience throwing light on what is going on in the material world, the events in time taking on a new significance against the background of eternity. Here is an interweaving of many different modes of existence—the unregenerately human and the spiritual, the intellectual and the psychic, the timeless and the temporal. Here too is humour and pathos. . .' the rest of the sentence as in the original draft. This, or something like this, it seems to me, is needed to bring out clearly what at present is plain only to people who have already read the book.

I am very glad to hear the good news of *The Art of Seeing*. The book has all the appearance of a hardy perennial.

After getting rid of one or two necessary chores, I hope to be able to get down to a project which I have had in mind for some time, which is an anthology with comments, along the lines of *Texts and Pretexts*, but devoted to what has been called the Perennial Philosophy—the Highest Common Factor underlying all the great religious and metaphysical systems of the world. It would bring together, under a series of headings, quotations from Western and Oriental sources of every period, set in a connecting matrix of commentary. Seeing that it is perfectly obvious that we shall never have more than a temporary truce until most men accept a common *weltan-schauung*, it would seem to be useful and timely to produce such a book, showing precisely what the best and most intelligent human beings have in fact agreed upon during the last three thousand years or so.

Ever yours,
Aldous Huxley

484: TO MRS FRIEDA LAWRENCE

Llano, Calif.
10 *April,* 1944

My dear Frieda,

How sweet of you to send us the *First Lady C*! I have not had time to read more than the first two chapters of the book; but it looks as if it were going to be very good, with a kind of ease and freshness such as only Lawrence at his best possesses. And I loved your preface; it was so touching and even beautiful. And you find the most wonderful phrases sometimes. That one about the asparagus tips is a classic and should go into an anthology.

Life goes on here much as usual. I have got the MS of my book off to the publishers. Harpers expect to bring it out at the end of August, and I don't imagine that Chattos, in England, will want or be able to publish much before then. Paper and binding present the most frightful problems over there, and even here they are beginning to raise difficulties. At the present I am working with Christopher Isherwood on an original story for the movies. I hope we shall be able to sell it, as it will solve a lot of economic problems and will make it unnecessary to go into temporary slavery at one of the studios.

Maria is busy as usual with the house, but has been pretty well on the whole. Her sister Rose has now had to come down to the desert, as her husband has been taken for the army and she can't afford to live in the house they were renting in town. So she and her two children are occupying a little house in the neighbouring village which we bought two or three months ago because it was such a bargain—it being not only quite a nice house, with trees round it, water laid on from a good supply, electricity installed, but fully furnished and equipped down to an electric washing machine. So now it has turned out a real godsend for Rose.

Matthew is in town, looking for a job on the technical side of the movies. So far unsuccessfully—for the two or three apparently definite offers he has had have all fallen through. Such jobs are hard to get at the moment, since they are making fewer films than usual and so need a smaller supply of technicians. However, I think and hope he'll find something before long. The main point is that he is very well again—much better than he was before going into the army last year and before he was almost killed by the doctors giving him all those immunization shots and then treating the resulting sickness with sulfanilamide. His three months in hospital were a triumphant demonstration of what modern science can do.

Not much news from England, and what comes is unutterably drab and weary. People are tired and bored to the extreme limit. Julian is in West Africa, Juliette sounds sad and exhausted, Anthony has a baby, Francis is on a battleship. Meanwhile, I hear from a man who has just come back from an eight months investigation of conditions in England on behalf of the Quakers that things have changed in the strangest way. Dishonesty is everywhere rampant, as it used to be in southern Italy. Luggage is stolen at the station if you leave it unguarded for a minute; every parcel has to be registered, or else it won't arrive: people swipe the electric light bulbs out of railway carriages by the hundreds of thousands—and not only that, they wantonly break windows, slash upholstery, demolish furnishings. Then the sex life is like Sodom and Gomorrah. Government tyranny is complete. There is no Habeas Corpus and people can be, and are, sent to prison indefinitely without trial— or even *after* trial and acquittal, by government fiat. Parliament has no power whatever, and MP's feel this so much that they don't even bother to turn up at debates. Last summer at a full dress debate on Indian policy, eighteen members out of more than six hundred were present. And this winter, at the debate on the terrible Bengal famine, thirty-five members turned up. So there isn't much nonsense about democratic institutions any more. And peace is going to bring economic problems so frightfully insoluble that there will probably be no relaxation of control, but a continued totalitarianism. Incidentally, the only people with any liberal ideas left are the conservatives.

484 *Story for the movies: 'Jacob's Hands', the story of a healer; it was never filmed but was later adapted and broadcast as a radio play. The description in this letter of the state of things in England was grossly exaggerative in the social aspect and wildly inaccurate in the political.*

The Left-wing Intellectuals and the Labour Party are eager Totalitarians—because they're convinced that they can Do Good, that fatal illusion which justifies every form of wickedness, oppression and tyranny.

Our love to Angelino and yourself, dear Frieda.

Ever your affectionate,
Aldous

485: TO ALAN WATTS

Llano, Calif:
25 April, 1944

Dear Mr. Watts,

Thank you so much for the copy of your translation of the *Mystical Theology.* I liked the introduction very much. It said what needed saying in the clearest possible way.

I am sending under separate cover a micro-photographic reproduction of Fitch's *Regula Perfectionis,* which I got the British Museum to make for me from their copy. If there is a reading machine in your local library, you will be able to get at the heart of the mystery without much difficulty. Harvard has a copy of the Italian translation of the book. I didn't hear of any other copies in this country when I was looking out for it. Brémond is a bit inaccurate about Fitch, and I have the impression that he read him very hastily. [Evelyn] Underhill copies Brémond and adds a mistake of her own about dates—making him out to be over eighty when he entered the Capuchin order, when so far as can be discovered from available information, he was in his thirties!

I have recently been reading William Law—with the greatest pleasure and profit. What a really wonderful writer, when he is at his best! It is sadly typical of our education that we are all made to read the second-rate amiabilities of Addison and Steele—but that one of the great masters of devotion and of philosophical theology is passed over almost in silence, so that even well-read people have never done more than glance at the *Serious Call* and know nothing of Law's later works.

Yours sincerely
Aldous Huxley

486: TO MRS GRACE HUBBLE

[Llano, Calif.]
[10 May, 1944]

My dear Grace,

This is to announce that the moment has come for me to exploit your kindness, and that the first seventy or so galleys of *Time Must Have a Stop* are going off to you by ordinary mail. The rest will follow, I hope, in two or three days. Professional proof reading has now reached a pitch of ineptitude undreamed of in happier times and my own talents in this direction have not improved correspondingly; so I am afraid that you may find a good many slips to correct. Harpers have written that they would like the proofs back as soon after the first of June as possible. Should you have anything you want to say to them, write direct to Cass Canfield, the president of the company, who now deals with my affairs since the death of Gene Saxton. The address is 49 East 33rd St, New York City. Meanwhile, I hope you won't find the labour too tiresome.

I suppose your winter is over at last, and that you are poised in a brief halcyon period between the cold and the suffocating heats to come. Here we have had an unusually cold season with a lot of rain, which has brought out a fine harvest of flowers—now almost over—and a great deal of grass, so that the desert has become California's best grazing range and is covered with cattle. In a platonic way we participate in the beef bonanza; for our caretaker is running thirty head of cattle of his own and the ranch is agreeably lively with calves, cows, steers, horses, not to mention the inevitable dogs and cats that always pullulate in the country. Maria, meanwhile, has been well, and so have I, with my allergic itch pretty well under control up to the present. Matthew has quite recovered from the nameless diseases induced in him by the army's inoculations, followed up by sulfa drugs. It took him a long time —for he was in a bad state. But now he seems very well and is working as a reader, making synopses of books for Warner Brothers—a job he seems to like quite well, except when he has to read the *Lad[ie]s' Home Journal* and *True Confessions* in search of dramatic nuggets which are never there.

In the intervals of proof reading I have been at work on an article on W. H. Sheldon's work. Have you read his two books, by the way? If not do. *The Varieties of Human Physique* and *The Varieties of Temperament* are not only absorbingly interesting and well written; they also, I believe, constitute a major contribution to a genuine science of man. For the first time the old insights and intuitions about the different kinds of human beings have been clarified and put on a firmly objective and measurable basis. The books provide a new and extremely efficient instrument for thinking about human affairs in all their multifarious variety. [. . . .]

Are you both well? I hope so, and that we may soon be seeing you again; for that will mean that the present horror will be over—at least the acute phase of it; for it looks as though the sub-acute and chronic conditions might last for years after the fighting is finished, with political and economic confusion; proletarianization of the bourgeoisie on an unprecedented scale and the consequent creation of thousands of well-educated and able potential fascists, communists or other revolutionaries; half the population of Europe living in barracks in absolute dependence on absolute governments; casualties in some areas so heavy as to disrupt family life completely and to impose on women, children and the old a great part of the burden of carrying on industry and agriculture. And all the rest, almost ad infinitum. One comes

back to the Buddha's 'I show you sorrow and the ending of sorrow'—with
its corollary that the ending of sorrow is a very difficult and enacting process
and that many are called but few are chosen, because few choose to be chosen,
preferring to run after the satisfactions that result in the sorrows which they
dread, but can't bring themselves to put an end to in the only way they can
be put an end to.

Maria joins me in sending best love to you both.

Ever yours affectionately,

Aldous

487: †TO LEON M. LION

Llano, Calif.
24 *May,* 1944

My dear Leon,

I received your letter about two months ago and within a few days sent
an answer, of which unfortunately I did not keep a copy. I am very sorry
that this should have failed to turn up. It is a long time since a letter disappeared like this. One regrets it all the more because the loss probably means
that there was a sinking in the Atlantic. (Incidentally, I see that your current
letter carries an address of the Savage Club which seems to me different
from that to which I sent my answer two months ago. Is this possible? And,
if the address has changed, might the letter have gone astray in London?)

By all means make use of my old letters to you. But please cut out
anything libellous that they may possibly contain. I don't want to be uncharitable about even the lowest of God's creatures—even about dramatic
critics! I am also enclosing a few lines in which I have tried to reproduce
the little note which accompanied my previous letter.

Meanwhile, I hope your health is keeping up. Here, all of us are doing
pretty well—though Matthew had a very bad time last year being invalided
out of the army because of an undiagnosed disease, which was quite evidently
brought on by a plethora of immunization shots and aggravated by sulpha
drugs used in trying to alleviate the symptoms. He came out three stone
lighter than he went in and with a bad case of anaemia; but is now, I'm glad
to say, quite well again and working. Altogether it was one of those Triumphs
of Science, of which our unhappy world is now getting such an overdose.

487 *A curious composite letter, incorporating phrases from this but based on
another letter of Huxley to Lion (28 March) was published in Lion's* The Surprise of
My Life, *pp.* 110-11. *The editor has not seen the original of either letter. A copy of
the earlier exists in the files of Chatto and Windus; the text of the present one is from
a copy belonging to Sir Julian Huxley. Both appear to have been typed by the same
person, probably when Lion was assembling material for his book. The 'Prefatory Note'
published there (p.* 103) *seems to be the earlier of Huxley's two versions; the other is
unpublished.*

I have written no more plays since last I saw you; but have dabbled a little in the making of screen plays—a most laborious, niggling type of work, requiring the learning of a technique that is entirely different from that of the dramatist.

Maria joins with me in sending kindest regards and all good wishes,

Ever yours,
Aldous Huxley

488: TO HAROLD RAYMOND

Llano, Calif.
9 July, 1944

Dear Harold,

Thank you so much for taking all that trouble with the Bank; it is really most kind of you. Your advice with regard to income tax returns is probably very sound, and I will get my tax accountant here to fill them up in that neat epigrammatic style, which I never seem to be able to achieve in this particular branch of literature. With regard to investments, I have been making enquiries recently about the possibilities of buying life insurance with at least a part of what I have in hand—one of those policies which can either mature into an annuity payable from, say, the age of sixty, or else, if one should die before that age or have no need for the annuity when it is reached, accumulate to a sum payable to one's heirs. The enormous scale of life insurance, which in this country, at any rate, is practically coextensive with the electorate, makes it unlikely that governments will ever permit inflation to the extent of wiping out the values of outstanding policies. So it's probably the safest, as it is certainly the simplest and least bothersome, of investments.

I hope these horrible robot bombs haven't done you any damage or robbed you of too much well-earned rest. In their present state of development I imagine they cannot play a decisive part in war. But the possibilities they open up for the future are really blood-curdling. One can be safe in betting that, within ten years, there will be rockets, or jet-propelled flying bombs, carrying several tons of phosphorus or explosives, capable of flying any distance up to five thousand miles, and travelling along a radio beam precisely to their destination. Five thousand launching stations, firing off twenty robots apiece—and that would be the end of any metropolis in the world. And of course the logic of technology and the inner necessities of power politics are such that that is what governments will think it right and reasonable to prepare for. They may talk about leagues and security; but meanwhile they will be engaged in intensive research on, and manufacture of, these long-range robot bombs. And the whole history of war is there to show that the possession of large stocks of efficient armament constitutes an almost compulsive temptation to use them; while all the history of politics

507

is there to show that power is of its very nature aggressive, either actively aggressive, or else negatively so, by the mere act of holding on to the fruits of previous active aggression.

Meanwhile, let's hope that the current campaigns on east and west may bring at least the European misery to a quick conclusion. There seems at last to be a real probability that it may end fairly soon.

Our love to Vera and yourself.

Ever yours,
Aldous

489: TO FREDERICK L. ALLEN

Llano, Calif.
19 *July,* 1944

Dear Mr Allen,

Many thanks for your letter. I am very glad you liked the article.

With regard to illustrations—I think the idea is excellent. Moreover, I see no reason why the drawings should not be both amusing and substantially accurate. In Sheldon's *Varieties of Human Physique* (which is published by Harpers) the frontispiece shows the three extreme types, and there are also scores of other photographs illustrating the intermediate types of male physique, with a series of line drawings at the end of the book devoted to the female form divine. From these a good draughtsman could turn out true representations of the various somatotypes—the fat, endomorphic family man, for example, giving his brood an airing in the baby carriage; the football team entirely composed of big-boned, large-faced mesomorphs, the thin, small-faced, but large-headed ectomorph averting his gaze in an agony of shyness from the sumptuous young female whom he desires with the almost frantic sexuality characteristic of his kind. Or the massive mixtures of endomorphy and mesomorphy who sing at the opera. Or the ectomorph and his endomorphic wife in the museum, looking at the mesomorphic ideal of Greek sculpture. There are any number of possibilities. But I think that it might in any case be a good thing to get Sheldon's own views on the subject. He is a very intelligent man with a keen sense of humour, and I don't think would have any objection to the drawings being amusing; but he is also an ardent man of science and would probably like them to be accurate. At the moment I don't know his address, since he has just been discharged from the army [. . . .] I fancy he has gone back to the University of Chicago, but am not sure. Meanwhile, I think you will be able to get his address from Denver Lindley, The Appleton Company, 35 West 32nd, NYC. By this same mail I am writing to Lindley myself, enclosing a letter for him to for-

489 *Huxley's article 'Who Are You?' appeared in* Harper's Magazine, *November,* 1944, *with illustrations by James Thurber.*

ward to Sheldon, in which I shall speak about illustrations along the lines discussed in this letter.

Yours sincerely,
Aldous Huxley

[. . . .]

490: TO MATTHEW HUXLEY

Llano, Calif.
22 *July*, 1944

Dearest Matthew,

Anticipating a little on my birthday, I opened the Corelli records last night and played them. The music has a beautifully pure, delicate quality—not powerful, but very fine; and there is a curious quality of pungency in the combination of organ and strings, which is rather strange and very pleasing. Thank you very much for them. I know I shall often enjoy playing them.

Talking of records—the gramophone will need a little of your attention when you are here next, as the whole turntable seems to be unduly loose and to have dropped a fraction of an inch, so that it touches the brake lever, making a loud maddening tick. We temporarily and partially cured the defect by pulling out a little cork—with the result that the brake doesn't brake any more. Which doesn't greatly matter.

The great news is that Hubert has hitched the house to the windmill water supply and we are getting, for the first time, genuinely clean water. Pressure is low, of course, but quite adequate—even for a shower. To celebrate the occasion the wind has been blowing like mad. Rather nerve-racking, since it is very warm and dry, as well as violent. If you think of it send Hubert a post-card, congratulating him on the achievement—not serious, but light in tone. It will give him pleasure.

No other news, except that Billy [Wessberg] is apparently in hospital again, this time with some kind of water on the elbow and inflammation of the sheath of the tendons. If it's bad enough, I suppose it may mean discharge or noncombatant duty; for obviously a man with a game arm is no good for strenuous work.

I had a new and I think good idea about possible films on art, which is this—to illustrate the technique of the various arts as well as the actual works as they have appeared in the course of history. Thus one might start with etching and show some competent master of the craft preparing the plate, drawing on the wax, putting the plate in acid and taking the impressions on paper, all with a running commentary. Then he could take out of a portfolio a number of prints illustrating the history of etching from the Italian engravers, through Rembrandt, Callot, Goya, Méryon, Whistler, etc down to the present. Steve Wright (the son of Mimi's Bill) who lives at Pasadena and is a competent, though undistinguished, etcher would probably be delighted to act the star part in the proceeding. Then one could do

509

the same with oil painting and sculpture—having a painter discuss his palette, comment on the way he lays on colours etc, while the sculptor talks about clay and stone or wood. All this could be livened up and made pictorially exciting and censorable by having the painter or sculptor at work on a nude, with the model in the background. This approach would interest people more than the merely historical or aesthetic discussion of painting; for everybody likes to know how a thing is done. I believe it would be worth your while to write out a page or two on, say, the etching and the painting or sculpture idea—going if necessary to the Encyclopaedia for a few technical points to put into the script—and registering the notion. After which you would be in a position to start talking about production. The painting movie should be shot, I think, in an art school. The master going his rounds from pupil to pupil would then have a justification for touching on the various phases of technique. Also the pictorial opportunities for camera work would be excellent in an art school.

Best love from us both.

Ever your affectionate,
Aldous

491: TO CHRISTOPHER ISHERWOOD

Llano, Calif.
28 July, 1944

My dear Christopher,

From Donald Hyde at Wm Morris I have just had a rather gloomy account of our story. It appears that the reason for the hitherto universal rejection of it is fear of the doctors. (The story of Sister Kenny is having a very difficult time at present, it would seem, owing to Fishbein objections to unorthodox methods.) I have written at length to Hyde exposing all the reasons why the doctors have no grounds for complaint—the healer's biggest medical success is a moral failure, his biggest moral success a medical failure, he retires from all but veterinary business because he feels he can't use his gift rightly. Also, the fact of what Charles Fort calls 'wild talents' is admitted by all open-minded people and our story merely accepts this fact and from the premiss builds up a drama where only the moral and psychological consequences of healing are involved, never the medical modus operandi. Moreover, the orthodox point of view, that it is all suggestion, is stated by the doctor after Earl's first meeting with Jacob. So everything is safeguarded. As for the crookedness of Dr Waldo—that is considerably less than the real-life crookedness of more than a thousand New York doctors, who are in trouble with the law at this moment for being involved in a hugely profitable racket for swindling insurance companies and the state. (Details in this week's

491 Gita: *the translation by Isherwood and Swami Prabhavananda.* Tat Tvam Asi: *'That Art Thou', the doctrine of the unity of Atman and Brahman.*

Time.) You might pass on to your agent these simple talking points, with which to allay the studios' fears of the medical Klu Klux Klan.

I hope all goes well with the printing of the *Gita*. No news here, except that we are still enjoying a deliciously unseasonable coolness. I am getting ahead with my anthology. Talking of which, I wish you would ask the Swami to indicate which is the clearest and most fully developed statement of the *Tat tvam Asi* doctrine in the *Upanishads*, or in Samkara, or elsewhere. I have some rather brief and sketchy quotations from the *Bhagavatam* and the *Gita*, but would like something a bit longer and more systematic, if it exists.

Love from us both.

Ever yours,
Aldous

492: TO HAROLD RAYMOND

Llano, Calif.
31 *October*, 1944

My dear Harold,

Thank you for letter, contract and telegram. I will return the contract by ordinary mail. Meanwhile this goes by air.

The Verlaine quotation is correct, as you can see by looking into the *Poèmes Saturniens*. I have always imagined that oarystis must be a variety of flowers, along the line of myosotis and clematis. But the word is not listed even in quite big French dictionaries. I have not consulted the very largest *Littré*, as I have not had an opportunity of going to the University library. It is possible, of course, that Verlaine invented the word because it sounded so nice and conveyed such a wonderful impression of remote, nostalgically remembered beauty.

[. . . .]

Time Must have a Stop has done very well here, the last figures dating from two or three weeks back being well over forty thousand, with sales still good. This is much better than I ever expected.

The presidential election is now in its final stages of ebullition. To an outsider it seems largely a choice between evils. [. . . .] A party composed of an incompatible mixture of liberals (with Bonapartist tendencies towards tyranny by plebiscite), southern conservatives with slave-holding mentalities, and corrupt city bosses. And against it a party in which the dominating power is in the hands of the big capitalists and money manipulators. I presume that Roosevelt will win—though nobody seems to know for sure. I doubt whether either candidate will be able to do very much to shape foreign policy, which will depend on circumstances—first, on what Russia wants to do with Europe (a matter on which, it is now obvious, nobody but Stalin is going to be allowed to have much say); second, on the extent and intensity of the reaction of the great masses of Americans and their representatives in Congress towards a disgusted isolationism or a purely national imperalism, making use of the most colossal naval, air and military forces ever brought together in history.

Give our love to Vera. And congratulate Tony on being now able to look Blimp in the eye from the same official level. I hope you have good news of Piers.

Ever yours,
Aldous H.

492a: TO COLIN CRAIGIE

Llano, Calif., U.S.A.
25 December, 1944

Dear Mr. Craigie,

Your brother, Captain Craigie, has written me a note, saying that, since you read my books, you might be glad to have a word from their author. So here goes!

I am always a bit embarrassed and apprehensive when I hear of people who seem to attach a great deal of importance to what I write. Enjoying to a unique degree the privilege of my own acquaintance, I feel certain doubts about the value of my productions, have a certain sense of putting something across under false pretenses. This being so, I feel rather better about my current work—which is in the nature of an anthology with comments: selections from exponents of what has been called the Perennial Philosophy, at all times and in all parts of the world, embedded in a setting of exposition and elucidation. This has been very interesting and instructive to compile and write, and I hope will be the same to read—if only because so much of the book will be by people in whom I feel much more confidence than in myself.

All good wishes for the New Year—above all the wish that this hideous business may end very soon.

Yours sincerely,
Aldous Huxley

493: TO MRS FLORA STROUSSE

Llano, Calif.
21 January, 1945

Dear Starky,

Many thanks for your letter. I'm sorry to hear that your son is in the

492a *The recipient of this letter was a young man of twenty-one, serving with the forces in Normandy.*
493 Generation of Vipers: *by Philip Wylie* (1942).

Philippines. Whether the horror is actually more awful there in the tropics than it is in Europe and against European enemies, I don't know; but for some reason it seems more ghastly. I do hope he'll be all right. And meanwhile the whole dreadful business grinds on, producing precisely the kind of political, economic and moral results that were anticipated. Sausage machines produce sausages, calculating machines produce calculations and war machines produce what *they* were made to produce, namely misery, chaos and more war.

Yes, I looked at *Generation of Vipers*, but felt that the violence of the tone and a certain lowness in the aesthetic quality of the style in some sort nullified the effectiveness of the truth which it unquestionably contained. It's perfectly true that Jesus made use of the phrase, 'generation of vipers'; but it wasn't his *only* phrase. He also spoke the parable of the Prodigal Son and the Sermon on the Mount. And, of course, the negative is always enormously much easier to express than the positive. Any fool can see motes in other people's eyes, even when his own are full of beams. But it takes a genius to describe, convincingly and interestingly, a character who is mote-free and a saint to describe, at first hand, the nature of Light as it is when there are no motes or beams to interfere with its radiance and modify its quality.

If you don't know Sheldon's books, you should read them. The first, *Psychology and the Promethean Will*, is excellent in its way; and the other two, *Varieties of Human Physique* and *Varieties of Temperament* are of the greatest importance. My article, owing to its brevity, had to be over-simplified. But Sheldon's great merit is that he never succumbs to that temptation. Also he writes extremely well. Some of the full-length descriptions of characters are quite admirable. The medical aspects of the work are also interesting. A first beginning on the subject has been made by Draper and Dupertuis, who use his classification system and have recently published the results of long years of observation on the influence of constitution upon disease. Incidentally, Sheldon's classification throws much light on certain religious problems. Thus, the three types of religion enumerated in the *Bhagavad Gita*, (karma marga, the way of works or action; Bhakti marga, the way of devotion; and jnana marga, the way of knowledge) correspond precisely to the three extremes of somatotonic, viscerotonic and cerebrotonic temperament. And in reference to a point you make—though Sheldon insists that the fundamental patterns cannot be changed, he points out that certain diets can prevent distressing manifestations of certain temperamental characteristics. Thus, the hypersensitiveness of neurotic cerebrotonics can often be cured (i.e masked) by the simple procedure of feeding them a diet rich in cream and bananas, and so making them put on three or four pounds of weight. A good deal cheaper than going for three years, twice a week, to a psycho-analyst!

I am near the end of what I think may be a useful and interesting book—

an anthology of passages, drawn from the most various sources, Western and Oriental, illustrating the 'Perennial Philosophy', which is the highest common factor of all the higher religions, the whole arranged under different headings and embedded in an explanatory commentary of my own. The greatest merit of the book is that about forty per cent of it is not by me, but by a lot of saints, many of whom were also men of genius.

All good wishes for you and yours. We are all pretty well, I'm glad to say. Our boy, who was invalided out of the army last year, very sick indeed, is now quite well and has a job as a Reader at one of the big movie studios in Hollywood.

Yours very sincerely,
Aldous Huxley

494: TO SOLOMON SIMONSON

Llano, Calif.
30 January, 1945

Dear Dr Simonson,

Being wholly without legal knowledge and training, I don't feel at all qualified to criticize the technical side of your article. But the whole crux of the problem seems to me to lie in the problem of acceptance. For example, is it likely that a country like Russia which (leaving out of account the territories which it will certainly annex in the course of the current war) will have grown, according to the population experts, who have proved themselves in the past to be very good prophets, to a nation of two hundred and fifty millions by 1975—is it likely to be content to have the same number of votes in an international assembly as a nation of eight millions, like Belgium—or for that matter, a nation like England which, by 1975, will probably have declined to under forty millions, one quarter of whom will be drawing old age pensions, whereas the majority of Russians, with their bounding birth rate will be in the younger age brackets? Russia's refusal at Dumbarton Oaks to permit herself in any circumstances to be called an aggressor seems to provide a sufficient answer. And if the voting is on the basis of population, then where goes national sovereignty? Or if a mixed form of representation is adopted, as in this country, with a house of representatives elected on a basis of population, and a senate with equal representation from each sovereign state, regardless of size, power and numbers—then we may expect chronic deadlocks, resolved by the force of the stronger party. It is obviously of the highest importance to have an efficiently planned legal framework in which international affairs may be conducted. But, given the existing *weltanschauung* of a world whose real religions are a series of idolatries of

494 *Simonson, then of Northwestern University, now of Yeshiva University, had invited Huxley's comments on a plan for international law and order.*

nation, state and political boss, I don't myself see any likelihood of anyone (except members of small nations, like the Swiss, whose very existence depends on the respect of law) wholeheartedly accepting even the best legal machinery or seriously desiring to make it work. And here one should consider the very serious fact that the standard of decency in law and international relations has gravely declined in recent generations. The eighteenth century saw a great many wars; but in no circumstances did any country wish to destroy its enemies. War between France and England, for example, was never total and never prevented cultural relations continuing between the two nations. Sterne's *Sentimental Journey* was undertaken while England and France were at war. Moreover the actual fighting was done under a code of chivalry. Marlborough always gave two days warning before he bombarded a town. The first change for the worse began under Napoleon, when universal conscription was adopted, thus breaking with the traditional idea of war as a vocation for a caste of kshatriyas or born warriors. Napoleon outraged world opinion by interning the English tourists, who had flocked abroad after the peace of Amiens; his methods in Spain were unutterably barbarous; and his aim was the destruction of the enemy as a national entity. During the Crimean war there was a return to eighteenth-century decency. Thus, Lord Raglan rejected with indignation the idea that he should send balloons over Sebastopol to drop sulphur upon its defenders. The two great wars of the present century have been conducted with a growing disregard for any kind of decency. The present war has been total and without limits. The Germans have tortured and slaughtered the inhabitants of occupied countries; the allies have inflicted well over a million civilian deaths by the bombardment of German cities. The evaluation of human life, as intrinsically precious and to be respected, has declined sharply under all totalitarian regimes, whether left or right, and will probably decline elsewhere, as the 'managerial revolution' goes forward and the ideal of liberty is replaced by that of efficiency. And meanwhile technological advances are being made so rapidly and are of so revolutionary a nature, that their application tends to make nonsense, within a few years, of any administrative blue-print for a better world, however ingeniously and painstakingly drawn up. And so long as there is no widespread and radical change in the world's philosophy of life, I see no reason to suppose that, when led into the temptations offered so invitingly by political power, (due to population and industrialization) or by technological advance in the making of military gadgets, peoples will not gleefully succumb to them, in precisely the same way as they are doing now.

Yours sincerely,
Aldous Huxley

Llano, Calif.
25 *March*, 1945

My dear Ted,

Thank you very much for your wire, which gave me great pleasure.
I am very glad you liked the book. I liked it pretty well myself—though I
remain sadly aware that I am not a born novelist, but some other kind of man
of letters, possessing enough ingenuity to be able to simulate a novelist's
behaviour not too unconvincingly. To put the matter physiologically, I am
the wrong shape for a story teller and sympathetic delineator of character
within a broad social canvas. The fertile inventors and narrators and genre
painters have all been rather burly genial fellows. Scott looked like a farmer.
Balzac and Dumas were florid to the point of fatness. Dickens was athletic
and had a passion for amateur theatricals. Tolstoy was an intellectual moujik.
Dostoevsky was physically tough enough to come through imprisonment in
Siberia. Conan Doyle was a barrel, Wells is a tub. Dear old Arnold Bennett
was a chamber pot on spindly legs and Marcel Proust was the wreck of congenital sleekness. So what chance has an emaciated fellow on stilts? And of
course this is no joke. There is a real correlation between shape and mind.
If you want to see the matter systematically studied, and at the same time to
read a very interesting and well-written book, get hold of Dr William H.
Sheldon's *Varieties of Temperament* and its companion volume, *The Varieties
of Human Physique.* They contain the first serious advance in the science of
man since the days of Aristotle. All other psychologists are merely psychological, and talk as though the mind were unrelated to its muscles, intestines
and bones. Sheldon considers human beings as they really are—psycho-
physical wholes or mind-bodies. Take one concrete example of the absurdity
of mere psychologism. The gut of a round fat man, like G. K. Chesterton,
may be as much as forty feet long. The gut of a thin man, like myself, may be
as little as eighteen feet long and weigh less than half what the Chestertonian
intestine weighs. It would obviously be miraculous if this physical difference
were not correlated with a mental difference. And yet these asinine psychiatrists and sociologists continue to talk of minds and characters as though they
existed in a vacuum.

I hope all goes well with you and Ria and the family. It looks as though at
least the European misery might be over pretty soon, and then, let us hope,
things may be slightly better in England and on the continent—though how
long it will take to put Humpty Dumpty together again, or whether he will
ever be put together in anything but a nightmarishly totalitarian and pauper-
ized form is another question. Even the minor problems seem to be quite
insoluble. For example, the statisticians say that, when this is over, there
will be at least fifteen million more women than men in Europe. What
will be the effect of this on family life and sexual morality? Echo answers,

What—or perhaps the word is also of four letters and even more Anglo Saxon.

Have you seen Julian lately? Juliette's last letter, some weeks ago, pronounced him better; but I am still very much worried about him.

Here, I'm glad to say, all goes well with us. Matthew got very ill while in the army with an undiagnosed fever due, I feel pretty sure, to his reacting badly to all that horse serum they pump into recruits, by way of immunizing them. The doctors treated this disease, which they had artificially produced, by means of sulpha drugs—with the result that he became extremely anaemic. After that they discharged him in a thoroughly wrecked condition. However he is now re-established in reasonably good health and is working as a reader and book reviewer for one of the film studios. Maria and I have both been pretty well, and M's mother and youngest sister, whom we got over here two years ago from France—after a trek on foot from Brussels, during the invasion—are also flourishing. One of M's sisters remains in France and writes that she and her young child are all right—though life seems to be unutterably difficult. However, they have a roof over their heads, which is more than a great many unhappy people have nowadays.

Thank you again, dear Ted.

Ever yours,
Aldous Huxley

496: TO VICTORIA OCAMPO

Llano, Calif.
2 April, 1945

My dear Victoria,

Your letter brought us the first news of poor Drieu [la Rochelle]'s death. There was a mention of his name about six or eight weeks ago in *Time*, saying that he had been imprisoned—the only French author, besides Maurras, to have been so treated for collaboration. When I read of this, I thought of the possibility of escape by suicide. And now it has happened. I had known him and been fond of him since 1919, and these last tragic chapters of his life, with their violent ending, make me feel very sad as I think of them.

You are quite right in finding the secret of his misfortune in what he once wrote about loving what was unlike himself. In Jules de Gaultier's language, he was the victim of bovarysme—the desire of a born intellectual and man of books, a born private citizen and specialist in personal relationships, to be the thing he was not—a man of action, an incarnate will to power, a public character, a leader of humanity in the mass. To use Sheldon's system of classification, there was just enough of the somatotonic in his predominantly cerebrotonic make-up to make him regret his cerebrotonia and wish to become entirely somatotonic. The result was disastrous; for of course it was impossible for him to be, except in imagination and on paper, the strong man he congenitally was not. And also it was impossible for him not to be bored and disgusted and profoundly disquieted by the strong men with whom his bovarysme made him associate and for whom he employed his talents. At heart he cannot have been anything but horrified by Doriot; and when the Germans were actually there, in power, his native sensibility and intelligence must have been constantly shocked by the coarseness, stupidity, squalor and ugliness of practically everything they did or thought or spoke or felt. And yet he forced himself to write about 'fascist socialism' and the new order, in the name of what the bovarystically fabricated, ersatz somatotonic within him regarded as 'political realism'—whereas the sensitive cerebrotonic who was, in the main, his real self knew quite well, with the nerves, the heart and the sub-conscious, that the only real realism is that the meek shall inherit the earth and that those who take the sword shall perish by the sword. In many respects, I think, Drieu was very like Benjamin Constant. Constant's was a more extreme case, of course. Drieu did not display Constant's extraordinary eccentricity—the infant-prodigyism, the passion for gambling, the fantastic mingling of *philosophe* and romantic, which made him rush into every kind of adventure and made him at the same time analyse his every thought and pass judgment on his every act, so that the most wildly romantic adventures all turned into dust and ashes and boredom, even while he was undertaking them. But there was something of this in Drieu too; and how essentially similar to Drieu's efforts in the same line were Constant's excursions into politics. He wanted to bovaryze himself into a Plutarchian tribune of the people, and though Napoleon cut short his first efforts, he actually succeeded, later on, in becoming (for others, at least, if not for himself) the great liberal leader he had bovarycally tried to be. Tragically, Drieu chose the role antithetical to tribune of the people—or perhaps it would be truer to say that he was pushed into it by circumstances, by the fact that the status quo was not a tyrant, but a corrupt democratic-capitalist machine.

The moral of the whole distressing story is that, as H. G. Wells once remarked, the mind of the Universe is able to count above two, that the dilemmas of the artist-intellectual and of the political theorist have more than two horns. Between ivory-towerism and art for art's sake on the one hand and direct political action on the other lies the alternative of spirituality. And between totalitarian fascism and totalitarian socialism lies the alternative of decentralism and co-operative enterprise—which constitutes the economico-political system most natural to spirituality. The majority of intellectuals at the present time recognize only two alternatives in their situation, and opt for one or the other, with results that are always bad, even if they happen to choose the victorious side.

Are you well, dear Victoria? I hope so. The papers speak of the terrible drought which has been ravaging Argentina, along with the rest of the

Southern hemisphere, and I suppose that this has led to a great deal of suffering in the country. Here we are all pretty well. Matthew is quite recovered and is working as a reader and book reviewer for one of the movie studios. The work is rather boring—like most work, alas!—but he busies himself with trade union politics, which he enjoys; and meanwhile the fact of having a job and of finding that he can do it efficiently has given him the poise and self-confidence which his delicate health, ever since he was a child, has tended to shake. When travel becomes possible again, I am sure he will want to take a look at the Southern Cross.

I have just finished a book which I am calling *The Perennial Philosophy* —an anthology of what is the Highest Common Factor in the World religions, the extracts drawn from a great variety of sources, western and eastern, and the whole embedded in an explanatory commentary of my own, amounting to about sixty or seventy per cent of the book. It has been very interesting for me to do, and people who have seen parts of the MS find the result interesting to read.

Maria sends her best love, as do I.

Ever yours affectionately,
Aldous

497: †TO HERMANN BROCH

Llano, California
10 *April*, 1945

Dear Mr. Broch,

I was asked to review your book for the *NY Herald Tribune*, and I enclose herewith a copy of what I have sent them. They only allowed me 700 words—which I have exceeded anyhow—and it was therefore very hard to say anything much about a work so full of substance as your *Virgil*. I hope you will not think me unjust in what I have written regarding the two sections—near the beginning and at the end—where the lyrical-philosophical material is used for many pages without contrasting passages of narrative. My own feeling is that quantity destroys quality and that though intrinsically, the sentences of which these sections are composed are rich with beauty and meaning, the very number of them—because of their intensity and their stylistic strangeness—imposes a strain upon the reader's mind and makes him, in the long run, incapable of reacting adequately to them. What Edgar Allan Poe said about the permissible length of the lyric is sound psychology. In literature one-pointedness is better achieved, it

497 *This and letter* 500 *are reprinted from Hermann Broch*, Briefe (*Zürich: Rhein-Verlag*, 1957), *where they accompany Broch's letters to Huxley. Huxley's review of* The Death of Virgil, '*Why Virgil Offered a Sacrifice*', *appeared in the* New York Herald Tribune Weekly Book Review, 8 *July*, 1945.

seems to me, by variety (such as you have in the narrative passages of *Virgil*) than by a uniform insistence on the theme which is being pointed at.

As a matter of history, I kept wondering, as I read the admirable conversations between Virgil and his friends, whether Plotius, Varius and Augustus—successful and self-satisfied members of the ruling class of an imperial nation as they were—would have found Virgil's viewpoint as odd and as incomprehensible as, for the purpose of art, you represent them as doing. They were all well educated men and must have known about, even if they did not approve of, the Orphic mysteries, Pythagoreanism and even Hermeticism, whose origins, according to authorities such as Flinders Petrie, go back to a century and a half before Virgil's birth. All of these cults are simply developments of the theme, 'Blessed are the pure in heart, for they shall see God', which was the theme of all those higher aspects of Indian religion from which they had their origins. Even the Jews, whose tradition made them peculiarly impervious to mysticism, took over the Orphic and Pythagorean doctrines in their wisdom literature and in the Hebrew mystery cult, which found its philosophical expression in Philo. So, in historical fact, I imagine Augustus and the rest would have known immediately what Virgil was talking about, and the discussion would have been carried on in the terminology of the already ancient and hallowed Greek mysteries.

Another point is doctrinal. Virgil's posthumous experience ends in the highest form of enlightenment, in which eternity is perceived within the things of time and nirvana and samsara are apprehended as ultimately the same. But every exponent of spiritual religion has always insisted that the mere act of dying is not a passport to enlightenment, that there is gnosis or jnana after death only for those who have chosen to pay the price (purity of heart, death to self in charity) of gnosis during life. Virgil's *metanoia* was in the nature of a death-bed repentance, and there is no indication in your book that it amounted to full enlightenment; consequently there would be no reason for supposing that he could have come to full enlightenment merely by dying. For the Tathagata there is no going anywhere after death, for he is there already in the full, unwavering perception of Suchness. But Virgil was not a Tathagata—merely a man of letters who wished, too late, that he had spent his life being something better. In this connection, thank you very much for the true and subtle things you say about beauty and laughter. I wish there had been space in my review to quote you at length on these subjects. But, alas, I had to 'make it snappy'.

With all good wishes for yourself and *Virgil*, I am,

Yours very sincerely,
Aldous Huxley

Llano, Calif: U.S.A.
23 April, 1945

Monsieur,

Je vous remercie de votre lettre et du poème qui l'accompagne—poème puissant, mais qui aurait, je crois, encore plus de force si l'idée du dernier quatrain s'exprimait plus objectivement, par une image concrète et extérieure à la personnalité du poète—comme ces 'million d'oiseaux d'or, ô future vigueur' de Rimbaud.

Quant au livre qui vous a frappé et dont vous dites des choses si généreuses, je l'ai écrit il y a douze ou quinze ans. Aujourd'hui je ne l'écrirais pas tel qu'il est. C'est peut-être une question d'âge; car chaque âge a sa propre *weltanschauung*, sa pensée appropriée. Les Hindous comptent quatre âges—celui de l'écolier; de l'homme marié vivant dans le monde; de l'homme mûr qui se retire dans la forêt et tâche de comprendre la nature, des choses et sa propre essence; de l'homme âgé qui se détache complètement du désir et, quoique vivant corporellement, habite l'éternité qu'il perçoit dans les choses mêmes du temps. Quant à moi, je commence à pénétrer dans la forêt.

Je vous prie, Monsieur, de me croire bien sincèrement vôtre,

Aldous Huxley

Llano, Calif:
7 May, 1945

Dearest J,

The last news of you from Juliette was encouraging, and I hope very

498 TRANSLATION:—'*Thank you for your letter and for the poem accompanying it—a powerful poem, but one which, I believe, would have even more impact if the idea in the last quatrain were expressed more objectively, by a concrete image external to the personality of the poet—like those "million golden birds, O vigour to come", of Rimbaud.*

'*As for the book you found striking, and about which you say such generous things, I wrote it twelve or fifteen years ago. Today I would not write it in that way. This is perhaps a question of age; for every age has its proper* Weltanschauung, *its appropriate thought. The Hindus reckon four ages—that of the schoolboy; that of the married man living in the world; that of the mature man who withdraws into the forest and tries to understand nature, things and his own essence; that of the aged man who detaches himself completely from desire and, though living bodily, dwells in the eternity which he perceives even in temporal things. As for myself, I begin to penetrate the forest.*

'*Please believe me very sincerely yours. . . .*'

The book about which Dumaine had written to Huxley was Do What You Will; *it had appeared in French under the title* L'Ange et la Bête. *The line of Rimbaud is from* 'Le Bateau Ivre'.

much that things have continued to go well with you and that you are now 'back to normalcy with Harding'. Let us have a word, if you ever get the time, as to how you are and what you are doing. Meanwhile I hope and suppose that the end of organized fighting in Europe will have lifted many burdens and loosened many strains in England—for the time, at least; for no doubt the Peace will bring all kinds of new strains and burdens, there as everywhere else; but less severe, let's hope, than on the Continent, where the physical destruction, killings and enslavements would seem to make the problem practically insoluble in any near future. All the king's horses and all the king's men cannot put Humpty Dumpty together again—and when they [have] succeeded, more or less, his name will be Humpsky Dumpsky and his address, poste restante Moscow. One can only hope that the Pax Sovietica may last as long as the Pax Romana, and that the Russian Empire will not be plagued by those endless fights over the control of the centralized power, which made the Pax Romana such a very uneasy peace. Personal liberty, presumably, will be gone from Continental Europe for at least a generation; for obviously the existing chaos cannot be controlled except by an iron tyranny—while the physical destruction, which has made almost the entire population dependent for everything—food, shelter, jobs, clothes, transportation—on the government positively guarantees the perpetuation of personal and bureaucratic rule by a tiny minority. No amount of eloquence about four or more freedoms can make the smallest difference; the concrete facts of the situation will decide what happens.

News from M's relatives is on the whole very good. Jehanne, her husband and small child are all well and we are beginning to be able to send parcels to relieve the acute shortage of clothes and shoes. (The child has had to go barefoot for several months as there were no shoes to be had even at a thousand francs the pair, which seems to be the price for such things.) Georges Baltus, now over 70, is well in Brussels, still painting [. . . .] His son and grandchild are all right. The only bad news concerns some of the Dutch relatives, who have completely vanished from Roermond, where they lived, and were probably deported to Germany.

Here all goes well. M. and I have been in pretty good health. Matthew, who has a job as a reader at a film studio, seems to be getting on well and hopes to proceed to the technical side of the cinema, beginning with cutting, as soon as such jobs are available. We lead an agricultural life with 40 head of cattle on the place—not ours, but our caretaker's, so that we have the pleasures of the Wild West without its troubles, which are considerable, ranging all the way from disease and sudden death by trucks on the highway to theft by gangsters supplying stolen meat to the flourishing black market.

Our best love to you both.

Ever your affectionate
Aldous

Llano, California
14 May, 1945

Dear Mr. Broch,

Thank you for your long and very interesting letter. The great difficulty in writing my review of *Virgil* was the fact that they gave me only 700 words to do it in. With four or five times as much I might have embarked upon a serious discussion of the metaphysical problem with which it deals. As it was, I could only mention the fact that you were concerned with the world of timeless reality as well as with the first century B.C., and come to a stop.

I agree with you that there can be altogether too much intellectualism and analysis, and that our world suffers from having a great deal of knowledge *about* things, but very little knowledge *of* or direct acquaintance with them. But what I feel to be a mistake in the statement you make in your letter is this—that you distinguish only two alternatives, intellectualism and metaphysical experience. But in fact there is a third, which is direct experience on the plane of the senses. There is the given material world, and there is the given spiritual world, the first apprehended by the senses, the second by super-intellectual intuition (pure intellect, as the scholastics call it), by the *scintilla animae*, which is a spark of the immanent Godhead, by the [*atman*] which is identical with Brahman and which can be known, as the result of dying to self, by immediate intuition. Between these two given realities is the human non-reality of notions and ideas about given reality. When I said, in my review, that I thought some of the passages devoted to the exploration of the experience of metaphysical reality were too long and should, in order to clarify them for the reader, have been alternated with passages of 'straight' narrative, I was not at all thinking of intellectual commentary—I was thinking of passages describing and expressing the immediate experience of the given, material world, that world which is the product of the Divine, that world whose every particle and event is the *locus*, so to speak, of an intersection between creative emanation through the Logos and a ray of the pure Godhead. Scotus Erigena distinguishes between the two forms of God's giving—the *datum* and the *donum*. The *datum* is the physical world apprehended by the senses; the *donum* the spiritual world apprehended by the spirit, when it has been made capable, through mortification, of collaboration with grace. What I would have liked to see was more of the *datum*, [to] balance, explain and throw light upon your account of the *donum*—an account necessarily difficult to follow, because it deals with matters which are strictly ineffable. As for intellectual analysis—that homemade, all too human product of the busy mind—there was no need of any more of that; for, obviously, the work of art you were composing was concerned with reality and not with our distorting commentaries on any substitutes for reality.

You call the historical Virgil a pre-Christian, but I would rather be inclined to say that he was a pre-mystic, just as most Christians are and have always been pre-mystics, content with notions about God, feelings about these notions and rites attuned to these notions and feelings, not prepared to go on, through self-naughting, to 'perfection' in contemplation. (There are few contemplatives, says the author of the *Imitation*, because there are few who are perfectly humble.) Knowledge is a function of being. Only the pure in heart can see God. And they can see Him, of course, at any moment of history, if they so desire. Virgil wanted to see God, but, to judge by his writings, didn't want it quite strongly enough. If he had, he would have subjected himself to the purificatory discipline of one of the mystery religions—the Greek versions of that not merely theoretical, but practical *Philosophia Perennis*, which is the central core of Christianity and the religions of the Orient. The conclusions to which your book—mine also, for that matter—points can be summed up in those wonderful words by Cardinal [Bérulle], when he says of man that he is 'a nothing surrounded by God, indigent of God, capable of God, filled with God if he so desires'. The means for becoming filled have been known from time immemorial. The Prophets and Incarnations of the Divine appear at intervals to remind us of what is always in our power to discover. In some historical epochs it may be a little easier to make the efforts which are necessary if individuals are to cooperate with grace. But I don't think history makes very much difference. One has only to read an account of the mediaeval 'age of faith' to see that most people were just as far from being filled with the God of whom they were capable as were Augustus and Varius. Virgil is certainly a precursor—but a precursor, not of something in history, rather of that everlastingly possible psychological condition, which is the individual's *metanoia*, or change of mind, out of the temporal into the eternal order. And to my mind there is not the faintest prospect of any enduring improvement in human affairs until a larger minority than at present, or in the past, decides that it is worth while to bring about this change of mind within itself. The most one can hope to do by means of social reform and rearrangement of economic and political and educational patterns is to remove some of the standing temptations towards remaining with mind unchanged. We pray to be delivered from temptation, because experience shows that, if we are tempted often and strongly enough, we almost inevitably fall. A social rearrangement which shall remove some of the current temptations towards power-lust, covetousness, emotional incontinence, mental distraction, uncharitableness and pride will make it a little easier for the individual man and woman to achieve their final end. The social function of the artist or intellectual, as I see it, is to suggest means for mitigating the strength of the temptations which, now and in the past, the social order has forced upon the individual, luring him away from his true end towards other, necessarily self-stultifying and destructive goals. Your *Virgil* is valuable socially, inasmuch as it indicates the true end and points to the profound dangers of that aesthetic temptation, to which the more sensitive and intelligent among our contemporaries so enthusiastically succumb.

Yours very sincerely,
Aldous Huxley

501: TO EDWARD C. ASWELL

Llano, Calif.
21 May, 1945

Dear Mr Aswell,

Your secretary sent me a draft of the 'blurb' for the dust cover of *The Perennial Philosophy*. I have ventured to re-write it altogether in a less personal key, explaining in the briefest possible compass what the book is about and why it may be of value. This is not only more truthful than affirming that I am a 'great philosopher' and a 'great novelist'—when in fact I am some sort of essayist sufficiently ingenious to get away with writing a very limited kind of fiction and sufficiently cautious to avoid long-drawn metaphysical disquisitions and logical arguments, in which I should inevitably break down—: it is also, I believe, a better sales talk for the book. Incidentally, the line about not wanting to found a new religion is important, as it may take the wind out of the sails of some of the ecclesiastical critics who will want to say that I am another Mrs Eddy. The whole book makes this statement implicitly. But as I have neglected to make it explicitly within the covers, I had better do so in no uncertain terms *on* the cover.

As for a line on the front of the cover—do we really need one? I prefer the idea of the plain unvarnished title.

Yours sincerely,
Aldous Huxley

502: TO JULIAN HUXLEY

Llano, Calif.
27 May, 1945

Dearest Julian,
  [. . . .]
There is, as you say, something peculiarly frightful about nervous breakdown—due, no doubt, to the fact that the mind is so much closer to the essential Self than the body. Bodily ills can be objectified to some extent and regarded as happening to something not oneself. Inability to cope with them seems somehow natural. But inability to cope with mental ills seems profoundly unnatural and much more threatening. I remember feeling this during the time when I came nearest to having a breakdown— a long spell of insomnia. I was pulled out of it by the combined efforts of old F. M. Alexander and that odd fish, J. E. R. McDonough [McDonagh]—

the first by teaching me a measure of conscious control of bodily activities, especially in regard to that correct posture which alone permits of organs and the autonomous nervous system functioning in the way they were intended to function, the second by de-toxicating my insides and putting me on to a better diet. I was sent the other day the MS of a new translation of the book on Psychoneuroses by the famous Swiss psychiatrist, who died some ten years ago—Dr Vittoz. It interested me very much because his method—which was apparently remarkably successful—combines a form of psycho-analysis with a form of what Alexander calls 'conscious creative control' of the body. On the physical side his methods are not as good as Alexander's, since he did not understand the fundamental importance of correct posture and the importance, in establishing correct posture, of securing a proper relationship between head, neck and trunk. But what Vittoz's methods do bring out very clearly is the great importance of doing physical actions consciously and voluntarily, not permitting them to be done hugger-mugger and automatically, in a blind, thoughtless process of 'end-gaining' that totally ignores the 'means-whereby'. The re-establishment of conscious and voluntary control over small physical activities results, according to Vittoz, in a general tonifying and strengthening of the mental processes and of the power of willing, often more or less completely lost in neurasthenia. It would be very interesting to get hold of a group of intelligent, adequately educated and open-minded doctors—not a common type, alas!—who had the time and the desire to study Alexander, Vittoz, Bates and Jacobson (the man who wrote on *Progressive Relaxation*) and who would co-ordinate their work in clinical practice. And it would be still better if they knew, not merely theoretically but by first-hand experience, something about 'spiritual exercises'. For it is remarkable how the empirical findings of these various therapists confirm the findings of those who, in the East and West, have been concerned with the achievement of personal integration, self-transcendence and immediate awareness of God, Suchness, Tao, Atman-Brahman or whatever else you choose to call the primordial, immanent-transcendent reality substantial to phenomena. Buddhist and Hindu Yoga insist continually on the necessity of becoming conscious of what one is doing. With that remorseless thoroughness which characterizes his discourses, the Buddha of the Pali scriptures demands that his followers shall be mindful of everything they do—including, at the end of a long list, the act of excretion. The correct posture, with special emphasis on the relation of head to spine, is much insisted upon by Hindu Yoga. In later, Mahayana Buddhism much is said about the dangers of fixed, strained, rigid concentration of the attention (such as was practised by the Hinayanists, who thereby got themselves side-tracked into 'false samadhi') and the necessity of being passively alert and open and empty. Similar warnings are given by Alexander and Bates and Jacobson—who point out that tension and wrong use of the organism as a whole and of the seeing apparatus in particular are induced by improper ways of attending to things and by using consciousness, not to let go and open up, but to tighten the grasp upon personal prejudices and bad habits. The whole gamut of therapeutic and spiritual procedures can best be thought about, I find, in terms of the Chinese conception of Tao—the Way, the Norm, the immanent and transcendent Suchness with which man, being a self-conscious creature enjoying freedom of will, may co-operate or not, as he chooses. If he doesn't co-operate, if he regards himself as autonomous, if his primary concern is with his self-conscious ego, then everything goes wrong on every plane from the physiological to the spiritual. He interferes with the normal functioning of his own body and worries or strains himself into stomach ulcers, bad vision, high blood pressure and all the countless diseases which even conservative doctors are now having to correlate with wrong states of mind. At the same time he cuts himself off, not merely from the 'animal grace' of normal and natural functioning, but from mental and spiritual graces—the grace of aesthetic experience, for example, which depends, in Roger Fry's words, on being in a state of 'alert passivity' as opposed to self-assertion, and the grace of mystical experience, which can only come when alert passivity is carried further, to the point of complete humility and selflessness. ('There are few contemplatives', says the *Imitation*, 'because there are few truly humble people.') Vittoz, Bates, Alexander, Jacobson— these and others like them are concerned, in various ways, with getting people into a sufficiently selfless condition to receive the grace of Tao on the physiological and mental planes. Spiritual exercises and mortification (which need not, of course, entail severe bodily austerities) aim at making people capable of Tao, not merely on the two lower levels, but also on the level of spirit, pneuma, atman—capable of knowing Tao as it is in itself and not *quoad nos*, which is possible, in spite of Kant, for those who are totally selfless and therefore have no *nos* for Tao to be *quoad*. In Hindu phrase, they reach a point where thinker, thinking and thought are one, where samsara and nirvana are perceived to be one and the same. And that, as Buddha says, is the ending of sorrow—and for anybody who remains short of that consummation there can, in the nature of things, be only sorrow, mixed of course with pleasures and distractions, which themselves are the cause of more sorrow. And the more one sees of the world, the more certain does it seem that this diagnosis—which is the diagnosis of all the masters of the spiritual life—is substantially correct. And the only sensible thing to do seems to try, however feebly and with however many failures and back-slidings, to regulate one's life in conformity with the diagnosis and the empirical findings associated with it.

What you say about the general hopelessness of the world at large and the insolubility of its problems is painfully true. 'The wicked are punished,' as somebody remarked, 'but the situation does not improve.' On the contrary, it tends to become worse in proportion to the severity of the punishment—and it is obvious that now, even if the Allies desired to treat Germany non-punitively and in a reformatory spirit, it will be impossible for anything but the *lex talionis* to function. The consequences of the bombing will of themselves constitute a long-drawn revenge on the entire German people. And the chief political result of that is likely to be the turning of the Germans towards Russia, as being, in their eyes, the most humane of the victor nations, inasmuch as the only one that did not use saturation bombing. Moreover, after the harvest of 1946, Russia will probably be the only power (being in control of Rumania and Hungary) to offer the Germans bread— which will be given, out of the conquered wheatlands, in exchange for political and economic collaboration. And when that happens the balance of power in Europe will be more completely gone than it is even at present. Let's hope that the Western nations may have the sense to accept the inevitable and come to terms with those whom population, birth-rate, resources and territory predestine to be the masters of Asia and Europe. They had better 'agree with thine enemy while thou art in the way with him', and not run the risk of being knocked to pieces by a power that is now of positively cosmic proportions. If you are still able to laugh in the midst of the present calamities, I recommend an article which appeared in the April 18th issue of *The Christian Century*, in which the author describes what has happened since Stalin did the Constantine act and made the Greek Orthodox Church officially a partner in the new Russian imperial scheme. The Patriarch has given him the following titles: Defender of the Faith, Father of All Slavs, Saviour of Europe, Deliverer of Colonial Peoples— the last a gentle hint to Britain! And, better still, the Exarch of Bulgaria recently remarked that, to a discriminating mind, there was really nothing to choose between Saint Mark and Karl Marx. So now, among other things, Uncle Jo is the Spiritual Head of a hundred and fifty million Christians whose church is a close second to the Pope's. The trouble about being a satirical writer nowadays is that plain facts outdo anything an ironist could concoct out of his head.

All goes well with us here. Matthew is away at the moment on his holiday, but will be back again soon. The work of reading and reviewing bores him a bit, and he is anxious to get into the technical side of the business. But there has been a long-drawn jurisdictional strike going on in the studios and this is a very bad moment for attempting a change. And meanwhile he thinks of finding some relief job in Europe, if the Quakers or some other agency will make use of him—though at present they can't do much, owing to military restrictions. I think it would be a very good thing for him if he could get such a job—though his health is still not very robust and the rigours of Europe in the coming months might be a bit severe for him. Still, the risk would be worth taking. Meanwhile I hope your news of Francis remains good. It seems possible that the Asiatic War may come to an end suddenly with the Japanese deciding the game isn't worth the candle. But on the other hand they may decide to go on until everyone is killed or has committed suicide. Evidently the martyr-making power of Shintoism is beyond anything we can imagine in Europe. And the staggering thing is that, in its modern form, Shintoism is only eighty years old and a synthetic product, deliberately and cynically manufactured by astute politicians. It makes one see why the Old Testament made such a fuss about idolatry.

Love from us both to both of you.

Ever your affectionate,
Aldous

503: TO HENRY MILLER

Llano, Calif.
5 July, 1945

Dear Henry Miller,

The reading of your article on Haniel Long in *Circle* has jogged me into doing what I should have done some time ago—that is, writing to thank you for the copy of *Murder the Murderers*. I liked both the pamphlet and the article very much and I hope soon to be able to thank you for them more adequately by sending you a copy of a book which is to appear some time this autumn, a book which I think will be of interest to you. I call it *The Perennial Philosophy*, and it consists of an anthology of passages drawn from Oriental and Western writers, illustrating that *philosophia perennis* which lies at the core and constitutes the highest common factor of all the great world religions, the whole embedded in an illustrative commentary of my own. The book was very interesting to compile and write and will, I think, be valuable as setting forth in the most unequivocal and explicit terms the doctrine taught by every master of the spiritual life for the last three thousand years—a doctrine of which the modern world has chosen to be ignorant, preferring radios and four-motored bombers and salvation-through-organization, with the catastrophic consequences that we see all about us.

Your Cabeza de Vaca article raises an interesting point in regard to miracles. The rationalist, who believes only in matter, attaches immense importance to miracles, because their occurrence would upset his favourite theories; that is why he is so anxious to affirm that they never take place. But the masters of the spiritual life take a different view; experience has taught them that, on the way to man's final end in the unitive knowledge of the Godhead, an individual frequently finds himself capable of performing miracles (and observation has shown them that the power to do miracles may be inborn in some individuals, or may be acquired by undertaking bodily austerities, and this without any thought of God or man's final end). They therefore freely admit that miracles occur, but they add that, from their point of view and for their purely spiritual purposes, they are not at all important. Indeed, they go further and say that the ability to perform miracles may, if indulged in, prove an obstacle on the path to man's final end. The

Indians constantly warn against using 'siddhis', or supernormal powers; and the Christian mystics are almost equally emphatic on the subject. Even orthodox scholastic theology lays down that 'gratuitous graces' (the powers to heal, raise the dead and do other supernormal feats) may be given to persons in a state of mortal sin and are neither necessary nor sufficient to salvation. This corresponds exactly to the Hindu attitude and to the views of the Buddha, as expressed in the Pali scriptures. One must therefore, I think, be very cautious in equating the discovery of psychic powers, such as Cabeza de Vaca had, with the achievement of a genuinely spiritual insight into reality. All the evidence points to the fact that, in many primitives, the power to perform certain supernormal feats is fairly widely distributed. But though there may be many primitive psychics, there are probably very few primitive spirituals—as few as there are among civilized peoples. ('There are few contemplatives', says the *Imitation*, 'because few are truly humble.') Many ethnologists would probably deny that primitives ever attain to genuine spirituality. But Paul Radin brought together evidence in his *Primitive Man as Philosopher*, which shows that there are contemporary savages, whose esoteric doctrines closely resemble the mystical theology which is the essence of the higher religions. And where such doctrines exist, it is to be presumed that at least a few individuals will take the trouble to act upon them in such a way as to realize by immediate experience the truths talked about in doctrinal theory. And it should be remembered that it is not only among primitives that supernormal powers are found. There are genuine mediums and healers in civilized societies. But certainly none of those whom I have met showed any signs of being spiritually advanced, in the sense of having a greater direct acquaintance with the divine Ground of all being than ordinary people. They were accomplished psychics; but spiritually they were as blind and impervious to Reality as any President of any Junior Chamber of Commerce. This does not mean, of course, that Cabeza de Vaca may not have passed through psychism into genuine spirituality. But it does mean, I believe, that one has no right to generalize in regard to the necessary connection between the demi-monde of psychic phenomena and the higher, timeless world of the spirit. It seems to me quite likely that, in the future, men of science may live down their current prejudice against psychic phenomena and, realizing the practical advantages to be gained by acquiring 'gratuitous graces', may adopt and stream-line some of the psychological, physiological and even mortificatory methods of yoga and Christian asceticism for the purpose of developing 'siddhis'. And of course their last state will be much worse than the first. For psychic powers without humility and without the guiding insights of spirituality will lead astray even more fatally than material powers, similarly unguided, are doing at present.

With all good wishes, I am

Yours very sincerely,
Aldous Huxley

Llano, Calif.
8 August, 1945

Dear Harold,

Thanks for your letter and the enclosures [. . . .]

The election results were certainly rather startling. I hope a few years will elapse before Chattos are nationalized. But then perhaps you will be compensated for that by being made Minister of Imperial Culture, or at the very least Under-Secretary for Publication. But seriously I wish one could feel entirely happy about state socialism. Obviously in a country like England, where people have been brought up under democratic conditions and with a respect for personal liberty, the first generation of bureaucratic managers will not be much tempted to abuse their powers. But when these die and are replaced by men and women who have been brought up under Statism and who have been taught to believe that the State is more important than the individual—what then? Certainly the records of history give one no comfort; for what they make more abundantly clear than anything else is that no person or class or institution can possess undisputed power for any length of time without being corrupted by it. Personally I come more and more to believe in decentralization and small-scale ownership of land and means of production. The trouble is that, in an over-populated country like Britain, this is only partially feasible. Mass production, coupled with mass regimentation, for export in exchange for food seems to be the ineluctable destiny of those who have made Malthus's nightmare come true. Besides a country with a decentralized (which is a humane) economy could not compete as a military power with countries having a top-heavy capital goods industry and a highly regimented, rootless and mobile labour force. And since, clearly, there is not the faintest intention of giving up war as an instrument of policy, the prospects of decentralization are nowhere bright. But the alternative is a steadily increasing tyranny of the state and the quasi-certainty of more wars with worse weapons.

Our love to Vera.

Ever yours,
Aldous

Llano, Calif.
10 *August,* 1945

My dear Victoria,

It was kind of you to ask me to write something on Valéry. (I did not realize, incidentally, that he was so old as his obituaries declared him to be —would have supposed him nearer to sixty-five than his actual seventy-three years.) I had to say no to your suggestion, since I could not write about him without re-reading him, and I have none of his books here—and very little time to go through them even if they were available. I was very fond of him personally and always derived much pleasure and profit from that almost incomprehensibly rapid and elliptic conversation. But I have never been unequivocally enthusiastic about his work. The best of his poetry was very beautiful. But much of it had a certain quality of forced imagination and *voulue* phantasy, resulting in tropes and images that used to remind me, curiously enough, of the Abbé Delille and the brilliant artificiality of his poem on Gardens. Again, the best of the essays were excellent; but there was always a tendency in Valéry to pretend to a philosophico-mathematical profundity and precision of thought which in many cases he did not have. The result was a curious incongruity between form and substance—dense and inspissated sentences expressing light, rapid generalizations and airy thoughts more fitted for the conversation he loved and was, being a méridional, in a sense born to.

I hope all goes well with you, as it does, I am glad to say, with us. Thank God we are to have peace very soon. But I confess that I find a peace with atomic bombs hanging overhead a rather disquieting prospect. National states armed by science with superhuman military power always remind me of Swift's description of Gulliver being carried up to the roof of the King of Brobdingnag's palace by a gigantic monkey: reason, human decency and spirituality, which are strictly individual matters, find themselves in the clutches of the collective will, which has the mentality of a delinquent boy of fourteen in conjunction with the physical power of a god.

Maria sends her love, as do I.

Ever yours,
Aldous

506: TO JOHN VAN DRUTEN

Wrightwood, Calif.
27 August, 1945

My dear Van Druten,

Thank you for your kind and friendly letter. Alas, publishers will be publishers—even when they are no longer boys, but hoary old centenarians like Harpers. Blurb-making and blurb-hunting are among their least engaging tricks. I always try to discourage it and have succeeded (at least I hope I have and that they won't double-cross me at the last moment) in getting a lot of sickly nonsense off the dust-cover of this latest volume. The only outside blurbs of which I have been informed were those of Rufus Jones and [W. E] Hocking—and I can see some faint point in sending a book by an

506 *Van Druten (whom Huxley had known since soon after coming to California) had been invited by Harper and Brothers to comment on* The Perennial Philosophy *in advance of publication.*

amateur to two veteran professional scholars (though even in this case, I don't know why the book should have to come out with preliminary imprimaturs). Meanwhile I am very glad you liked the book. It was certainly very interesting to compile and write, and it is good to know that it should seem interesting to read.

I hope we may meet next time you are on this side of the continent. For the moment we are up in the mountains, but later on I expect we shall be mainly in the desert, with occasional brief interludes in town.

Yours very sincerely,
Aldous Huxley

507: TO PHILIPPE DUMAINE

Llano, Calif.
3 September, 1945

Dear Mr Dumaine,

My typewriter being without accents, I must write in English to thank you for your letter and the copy of your poems [*Cortèges*], which I have read with interest and admiration. They have a kind of Baudelairean weightiness and force, which too many contemporary poems (with their allusions, their inconclusiveness, their inchoate and fragmentary forms) conspicuously lack—a weightiness and a force which contemporary circumstances seem to require, if they are to be expressed with any degree of adequacy.

Thank you also for inviting me to contribute to your review. For the present I am working on a kind of pamphlet which has to be finished by a certain date, so that it is impossible for me to interrupt myself in order to do anything else. As it happens, I have dealt rather fully with the subject that interests you in a book that is to appear towards the end of the present month. The title of this book is *The Perennial Philosophy* and it consists (to about one third of its length) of passages taken from oriental and western authors embedded in a commentary of my own, the whole arranged in a series of chapters, each dealing with one particular aspect of the doctrine and praxis which constitute the highest common factor present in the great world religions. The chapter which will, I think, be of most interest to you is the one I have entitled 'God in the World', in which I have collected and commented upon a number of passages that show what 'the pure in heart' of all ages and places have regarded as the necessary conditions that must be fulfilled, if men were to become completely at home in [the] world. Many of these passages are derived from Taoist and Zen Buddhist sources; for it was especially in the Far East and under Mahayana Buddhism that salvation was primarily conceived as a reconciliation of time and eternity, a realization (which of course had to be earned) that Nirvana and Samsara (the world of becoming) are ultimately one. There are, of course, similar utterances to be found among the writers in other religious traditions. (Particularly beautiful examples may be found in *The Centuries of Meditation* of the seventeenth-century Anglican writer, Thomas Traherne.) But it is among the Zen masters that this doctrine is most clearly and most poetically set forth. D. T. Suzuki's *Manual of Zen Buddhism* contains translations of the most interesting writings of these Chinese and Japanese mystics— mystics who made use of world-denying self-discipline for the purpose of being able and worthy to become world-accepting on that higher level where a man can say, with Augustine, *Ama et fac quod vis*. If you would care to reprint all or part of this chapter in your review, you are very welcome to do so, and I will send you a copy of the book. It contains what I (and, more important, what those who are my spiritual betters) have to say upon the subject expressed with a fulness which I could not reproduce in another article, even if I had the time to write such an article, which I have not at the moment and probably shall not have even when I have finished my present work—since I have a number of ideas germinating in my mind which will soon, I suspect, urgently require systematic development.

Once more, thank you for your gift. With all good wishes, I am,

Yours very sincerely,
Aldous Huxley

508: TO ANITA LOOS

145½ *South Doheny, L A 36, Cal.*
13 *October,* 1945

Dearest Anita,

Thank you so much for your good letter and the enclosed comments on the book, which I greatly liked. I haven't heard from Harpers since its publication; but the advance sales were good for a work of its kind—about twelve thousand.

In regard to *Brave New World*, I have had no very revolutionary ideas, except the notion that it will probably be necessary, for film purposes, to write the scenes of the future in the form of cut-forwards from a contemporary starting point. My feeling is that audiences may be confused and worried, if we plunge straight into the twenty-seventh century A.D. as is done in the book. Also, if we do this, there will have to be a certain amount of retrospective explanation of historical events during the preceding centuries. It is essential, I think, to anchor the brave-new-worldian events very firmly to the present, so as to show that even the most extravagant pieces of satiric phantasy stem inevitably and logically from present-day seeds and are the natural end-product of present-day tendencies. This will give the picture a strong topical interest and will give a specific point to its satire. Something about the atom bomb will of course have to be brought in. But the point of the original story must be kept—namely, that the really revolutionary changes will come about from advances in biology and psychology, not from advances in physics. The adumbrations of future possibilities are to be seen in the practices of contemporary dictatorships—artificial insemination of women with the semen of racially pure sires, selective breeding, use of scopolamine and other drugs to extract confessions and make people more susceptible to propaganda, special training of future leaders with a view to eliminating all the normal human decencies, and so forth. The nature of the contemporary spring-board will have to be discussed in detail. I had thought vaguely of the possibility of making it revolve around the person of a very clever but physically unattractive scientist, desperately trying to make a gorgeous blonde, who is repelled by his pimples but fascinated by the intelligence of his conversation, as he steers her round his laboratory, showing her artificially impregnated rabbits, newts with tails grafted on to the stumps of legs, dogs that salivate at the sound of a bell, and the other objects of interest usually found in such places. He holds forth about the possibilities of applied biology—babies in bottles etc—and we cut forward to the story, from which, at intervals, we cut back to his contemporary comments, which serve as a kind of Greek Chorus to the drama of the future. In the end, he screws his courage to the sticking point, makes violent passes at the blonde, gets his face slapped and is left disconsolate among the white mice and the rabbit ova—an emblem of personal frustration who is yet the most revolutionary and subversive force in the modern world. One practical point worries me: what will the Hays Office say about babies in bottles? We must have them, since no other symbol of the triumph of science over nature is anything like as effective as this. But will they allow it? This and other problems will need a lot of discussion later on, when Paulette [Goddard] and [Burgess] Meredith get back, and I hope you will be there too with that dramatist's-eye view of things, which I don't have.

Meanwhile, as Donald Hyde has probably told you, I am about to sign up with Disney for the script of an *Alice in Wonderland*, which is to be a cartoon version of Tenniel's drawings and Carroll's story, embedded in a flesh-and-blood episode of the life of the Rev. Charles Dodgson. I think something rather nice might be made out of this—the unutterably odd, repressed and ridiculous Oxford lecturer on logic and mathematics, seeking refuge in the company of little girls and in his own phantasy. There is plenty of comic material in Dodgson's life, and I think it will be legitimate to invent some such absurd climax as a visit of Queen Victoria to Oxford and her insistence on having the author of *Alice* presented to her, in preference to all the big wigs—the scene dissolving, in Carroll's fancy, to the end of *Alice*: 'They're nothing but a pack of cards'—and the Queen and her retinue become ridiculous cartoon figures and are scattered to the four winds.

508 *Hays Office: the board of motion-picture censors supported by the American film industry; later the Johnson Office. Donald Hyde: a representative of the William Morris Agency in Beverly Hills. Picket line: at the Warner Brothers studios. Matthew Huxley went to Berkeley, specialized in Latin American studies, and took the degree with Honours in 1947.*

Matthew was fortunately absent when the violence broke out on the picket line, but he got arrested and spent some hours in jail on the following day. He is going north to Berkeley in another week or so, to take some courses at the U of C, with a view to getting into some kind of administrative work later on. The reading job is a dead end, and there is no prospect of his being able to get into the technical side of the movies now that the ex-cutters are being demobilized. So I think he is very wise to take a bit of specialist training with a view to embarking on another line.

Our best love to you both.

Ever your affectionate,
Aldous

509: TO VICTORIA OCAMPO

Llano, Calif.
24 *November,* 1945

My dear Victoria,

I should have written long since to thank you for the truly beautiful volume of pictures of the Indians of the Andes, and for your letter about poor Drieu's death. I often find myself thinking of him and of the tragic fate of all those who aspire to exercise influence and power (generally with the best intentions) within one or other of the alternative political systems which are, at the present, going concerns. Either you choose, like Drieu, to be a totalitarian fascist, aiming at 'le socialisme fasciste'—and you find yourself immediately involved in the most atrocious military tyranny. Or you choose socialism or communism, call the resulting totalitarianism by the name of 'democracy' and end up, if you are sensitive and honest, by finding yourself horribly disillusioned. Or finally you cling to democratic capitalism and find yourself forced, by the logic of advancing technology, to embrace some form of totalitarianism. There is no way out along any of these lines. The only issue, as far as I can see, is in the direction of decentralism and distributism—the dispersion of property in land and means of production among the greatest possible number of individuals and the encouragement of free co-operative enterprise and self-government. But this is not a going concern, except on the smallest scale; and it is highly distasteful to those who have a vested interest in the concentration of political and economic power, as well as to those who think in terms of war and the domination of one nation over the others. And meanwhile we have the atom bomb and the idolatry of nationalism—an idolatry which shows no signs of abating and which absolutely guarantees that, sooner or later, somebody will use the atom bomb on a really large and heroic scale.

Not much news here. Maria and I have been pretty well, and Matthew, after having been deeply involved in the strike which dragged on all summer in the movie studios, has given up his job there and gone back for a year to the university of California at Berkeley, where he is studying Latin

American history, geography and government, with a view to getting some kind of administrative or public-relations job in connection with Good Neighbourliness. So perhaps you may see him one of these days in the Southern Hemisphere.

There are possibilities that my book *Brave New World* may be turned into a film—it is dreadfully topical at the moment and shows every sign (unless we are all blown to bits in the interval) of coming literally true within the next two or three generations. If the negotiations with the present owners of the rights go through, I shall probably do the screen play. It will be interesting to see how much can be said in that medium—and how much one will be allowed to say. The fact that films cannot pay their expenses unless they are seen by twenty or thirty million people, imposes the most enormous intellectual and conventional limitations. There can be no change in the present situation until arrangements are made for exhibiting special films to a limited public, as is done with plays and with books. But this can't be done unless the cost of making films is enormously reduced.

Meanwhile I have been asked by Disney to help in the production of *Alice in Wonderland*. The phantasy will be embedded in real-life episodes of the life of Charles Dodgson, the Oxford don who wrote under the name of Lewis Carroll. Dodgson is a fascinating mid-Victorian eccentric, and I had hoped to be able to bring in something of the old, unreformed Oxford of the eighteen-sixties—but, as usual, it turns out to be impossible to make any of the documentary points which it would be so amusing (at any rate for me) to elaborate. My mother was brought up there as a child—and incidentally Dodgson, who was a passionate amateur photographer, made a number of delightful pictures of her, some of which are reproduced in the volume of Dodgson's letters to his child friends. Also my aunt, Mrs Humphry Ward, lived there as a young married woman and has left a very lively account of the place in her *Recollections of a Writer*. It would be nice to be able to reconstruct the university of the period, with its long-drawn struggles between tory High Churchmen and liberal Modernists, under Jowett and Pattison. But, alas, there is no time in an hour of film—and even if there were time, how few of the millions who see the film would take the smallest interest in the reconstruction of this odd fragment of the forgotten past! So I have to be content with bringing out as many of the oddities of Dodgson as possible, and with preventing producer and director from putting in too many anachronisms and impossibilities for the sake of the story.

I have been reading recently a book which I certainly ought to have read many years ago, but which for some reason I never did read—namely, Walt Whitman's prose *Specimen Days in America*. The little essays in the middle portion of the book, with their delicately precise descriptions of nature and their curiously Taoist philosophy, are really wonderful—preferable, in some ways, to much of Whitman's verse, which tends to be too eloquent and declamatory; whereas these little notes and jottings make no pretensions to anything but a simple fidelity to experience and are, in consequence, much more moving than many of the pieces which he wrote with the intention of being moving. Do re-read them, if you haven't looked at them lately.

Maria sends her best love, as do I.

Ever yours affectionately,
Aldous

510: †TO JEAN E. HARE

Llano, Calif.
30 December, 1945

I don't think there was any special significance of the kind you speak of, in the structure of *Point Counter Point* and the others. They represent experiments in the technique of narrative and of the exploration of the mind carried on by one who is not congenitally a novelist and therefore is compelled to resort to devices which the born novelist would never think of using—being perfectly capable of covering the necessary ground without departing from straightforward techniques.

The conclusion of *Point Counter Point* is the concentrated expression of that kind of aesthetic mysticism which runs through the book and which is the analogue on another plane (perhaps even, to some extent, it is the homologue) of the ultimate, spiritual mysticism. Anyhow, it was through the aesthetic that I came to the spiritual—having begun by rejecting the spiritual in favour of the aesthetic and by identifying it with the aesthetic, making the part include the whole. The sense that even the highest art was not good enough, that if this was all it was a pretty poor thing to be man's final end—this was, at bottom, the impelling motive.

Yours sincerely,
Aldous Huxley

511: TO JULIAN HUXLEY

Llano, Calif.
18 March, 1946

Dearest J,

What interesting news about your new job! Some are born UNOs, but some make themselves UNOs for the kingdom of heaven's sake. I hope you belong to the second category, and that, if not actually the kingdom of heaven, at least something a little less like the kingdom of hell than the world we are actually living in may result from your activities. My only experience of a congress at the old institute for intellectual co-operation

510 *The correspondent was a graduate student at the University of Toronto, who had enquired about a connection between form and ideas in* Point Counter Point.
511 *New job: as Executive Secretary of Unesco.*

538

showed me that the two major obstacles in the way of intellectuals doing anything in groups and as groups were (a) egotism, first personal and then national and professional and (b) the mind's infinite capacity for irrelevance. People either wanted to talk about themselves, their job and their country; or else they couldn't stick to the point at issue, but wandered off into interstellar space. Because of these two all too human failings, absolutely nothing whatever was achieved by a congress which lasted for days and must have cost the League of Nations a tidy penny. The truth is, I suspect, that you can't have a successful congress unless the subject under discussion is concrete and strictly limited and unless there is at least professional solidarity between the delegates. To discuss Culture, as we did at the intellectual co-op, is absolutely fatal; for the subject is too big and the cultivated belong to too many varieties.

Brave New World's filming has had to be put off, more or less indefinitely owing to the [. . .] tactics of a gentleman [. . .], who was given dramatic rights in the story, many years ago. Although he has no rights in the movie [. . .] the producers and their financial backers won't embark on the thing until he signs a release. Meanwhile the situation has been made more complex by the fact that the Pinker brothers, [. . .] were inexcusably inefficient— so much so that no trace of the original contract with Mr [——] can be discovered. So there we are, in the midst of a first-class mess. Which is a pity, since the book has taken on a fearful topicality. For it looks as though, if we don't get blown up within the next few years, the Brave New World is only a couple of generations away, with really scientific dictatorships using all the resources of applied psychology and biology to make their subjects like the slavery to which they have been reduced, instead of, as now, ineptly and unsuccessfully trying to bludgeon and liquidate them into acquiescence. But perhaps [——] may relent one day. Only by that time Burgess Meredith will [. . .] be busy with something else [. . . .] In the mean time I am busy on an anthology of essays and criticism which I have undertaken, rather rashly as I now find, to do for the *Encyclopaedia Britannica* people. It is quite interesting and educative; but involves a lot of work.

[. . . .]

Our news from France is only fairly good, Jeanne's husband has developed phlebitis, which is a horrid thing, and an insufficient diet and the general anxiety induced by mounting inflation seems to be getting everybody down. It looks as though the inflation would soon amount to a total collapse of the franc. In which case the results might be very bad for the rest of Western Europe. For the time being Belgium seems, by sheer good management, to be pretty well off, and Maria's relations there are all in tolerable health and reasonably prosperous.

Give Juliette our best love.

Ever your affectionate,
Aldous

Llano, Calif.
20 March, 1946

My dear Joep,

   A few days ago Mère expressed a wish to repay, in its entirety or in part, the money I have given her during the last five years. Though I am fortunately not pressed for funds at the moment, I like the idea, since it would permit the setting aside of a considerable sum for future contingencies. But meanwhile the problem is to get Mère's available capital over from Europe. (Incidentally, this seems to me desirable quite apart from any personal considerations, since it is probable that the French franc will collapse in the not too distant future, with serious repercussions on the currency of France's neighbours.) I understand from her that a sum of money which she had in Holland is being paid back in small monthly instalments, in dollars. In view of the precariousness of the European situation, it would obviously be a good thing if the rate of payment could be speeded up and if, at the same time, arrangements could be made to get her liquid assets in Belgium converted into dollars and brought over here. This can be achieved, so far as I know, only by finding someone who has need of florins or Belgian francs in Europe and who is ready to pay the equivalent here in dollars. I know of various English people who have made such arrangements for the transfer of pounds; but unfortunately I am not acquainted with anyone needing Dutch or Belgian currency. Nor is Los Angeles a very good place to find such people. It occurred to me that you, who live in New York and who must certainly have many Dutch and some Belgian acquaintances and business connections there, might be able without too much difficulty to discover someone who would be glad to purchase some or all of Mère's assets in florins and francs for a sum of dollars payable to her in this country. I should be most grateful if you could look out for such a person. If you could arrange it, you would be doing us all a good turn. And the quicker it is done, the better; for almost anything may happen to the financial structure of Western Europe during the coming months, and it would be deplorable and idiotic if Mère's assets, which still have a considerable value, were to be allowed to evaporate into the thin air of inflation.

   I have been seeing some of your children's drawings and writings recently. They certainly have remarkable talents. One feels that almost anything might happen when they come to maturity. Meanwhile I hope all goes well with you and your work. Our best love to you both.

Ever yours,
Aldous

P.S. Don't bother to answer this. But if you shd hear of a possibility of getting the money across, let Mère know directly, so that she can at once make the necessary arrangements.

Llano, Calif.
28 March, 1946

My dear Victoria,

Thank you for your letter. I hope you will like my little pamphlet [*Science, Liberty and Peace*]. I think it says some things that need saying—absurdly simple things such as 'the Sabbath was made for man, not man for the Sabbath', things which men of science like to forget because it is such enormous fun enquiring into the processes of nature and designing bigger and better gadgets that they do not wish to realize that human beings are being sacrificed to applied science, being stretched and truncated to fit its Procrustean bed, and that the pious talk about science serving mankind is (as things are at present) pure nonsense and hypocrisy, meant only to justify the scientists in continuing to have their fun and to justify the capitalists and centralized governments in continuing to exercise ever-increasing power over the masses. I have said all this as drily and unemphatically as possible, since nothing is gained in this sort of case by rhetoric. If you decide to publish the book in Spanish, the Fellowship of Reconciliation, for whom I originally wrote the pamphlet and to whom I have assigned any royalties accruing from its sale, will have to be consulted, so as to make quite sure that they have made no previous arrangements for translation. Incidentally the book is full of printer's errors [. . . .]

Yes, how remote it seems, the time of our first meeting, and what a stupid, unsatisfactory kind of existence I was leading! And what a strange Decline-and-Fall world it was we were living in! What Europe must be like now, after the Fall, is hard to imagine. And of course it must get much worse, politically, socially and personally, as the hunger grows more intense in the coming months. I was sent a number of French books recently—all rather horrifying, I thought. Novels about the Resistance—half heroism, half unutterable moral squalor; essays by existentialists, which are just Kierkegaard without God and also without genius. I hope, and I presume, that there must be something better—indeed I have seen something better in the shape of some poems by Patrice de la Tour du Pin in *Les Vivants*. And meanwhile a rather touching young Frenchman came to see us the other day, an industrialist with liberal ideas, who came with an introduction from Hyacinthe Dubreuil and, under a certain absurdity of manner, and in spite of that kind of Ecole Normale eloquence, full of clichés, which French intellectuals of the second order love to indulge in, was really very nice and even gave one a sense of reassurance about the future of France.

Perhaps you will see my brother in London—his address is 31 Pond Street, London NW3; but he may, of course, be on his travels, since he has recently been made the head of the United Nations commission on science, culture, education and a few other things of the same kind, and will have to fly about the planet, collecting information and trying to persuade people to behave a little better next time. It is the old Institute of Intellectual Cooperation brought up to date and under new management.

Love from us both.

Ever yours,
Aldous

514: TO OSSIP K. FLECHTHEIM

Llano, Calif.
29 March, 1946

Dear Mr Flechtheim,

Thank you for your letter of January 30th and the interesting enclosure on 'Teaching the Future'. I think that 'futurology' might be a very good thing, provided the teaching of it were accompanied by a teaching of what I might call 'eternitology'. It is not much use knowing what is likely, given present tendencies, to happen, unless one has clear ideas about man's Final End, in the light of which those tendencies and their probable outcome can be evaluated. Thomas Traherne complained that in the Oxford of the Cromwellian period there was no 'tutor of felicity'—by which he meant that there was nobody to tell the students what was the purpose of individual consciousness and how that purpose might be achieved. The statement of that purpose and hints on the way he achieved it are set forth in Traherne's *Centuries of Meditation,* which speak of the unitive knowledge of God in the soul and in the world and the purity of heart which is the condition of 'seeing God'. The same account of the end and the means has been given by all who are qualified to know, from Lao Tzu and Buddha onwards; but in recent years the knowledge has been either dismissed as ignorance or, more often, politely ignored. A completely valid judgment on a given social environment, whether past, present or future, can only be arrived at in the light of the Final End of the individual. Does this social environment help or hinder individuals in their attempt to achieve the Final End of life and consciousness? This higher utilitarianism permits of sounder judgments than the Benthamite principle. For example, let us suppose that future dictatorships become genuinely scientific (the postulate of my *Brave New World,* which to-day seems much closer to us, if we don't blow ourselves to bits, than it did only fifteen years ago); suppose the new dictatorship applies the findings of biologists and psychologists so as to make the overwhelming majority of the people love the slavery to which they have been reduced. According to the greatest happiness of the greatest number theory, such scientific dictatorship would produce a perfect social environment. It is only when we use the principles of the higher utilitarianism and ask how such a social environment would affect the realization of the individual's

514 *Dr Flechtheim is Professor at the Otto Suhr Institut of the Free Berlin University.*

Final End that we see how entirely evil such a society would be, even though it employed very little violence (only systematic lying) and even though it guaranteed prosperity and happiness to everybody. So please, if you teach young people futurology, slip in a course of eternitology to enable them to judge present trends and coming probabilities so that, having judged, they may have a motive to change those trends and the necessary knowledge to change them in the right way.

Yours sincerely,
Aldous Huxley

515: TO VICTORIA OCAMPO

Llano, Calif.
Easter Day [21 *April*], 1946

My dear Victoria,

We were in town for a few days, returning only last night. Consequently I have only just read your letter of the fourteenth and am afraid that this note may not reach you before the *Queen Mary* sails. It brings you all good wishes for your journey and the hope that we may see you on your way back. We expect to be up in the mountains, during July, at a little place, some twenty miles from here,* where we have a little house at about six thousand feet altitude in a landscape that is half Swiss, half Western desert—pine forests alternating with sage brush. The air is very good and the climate very agreeable and one can take the car to over eight thousand feet and go for spectacular walks. Our house is too small to put you up; but by the time you get here, we may have a second chalet in which, if you don't mind a certain primitiveness, you can stay. (There is running water, electric light and bottled gas, so that the fundamentals are all right; but the furniture, which we get with the house, is ugly and probably not excessively comfortable. If you have your maid with you, there would be room for her.)

I have read Camus' novel [*L'Etranger*] in French. It is rather good, but a bit pointless. I also have his book on suicide, which I have only glanced at, but which seems interesting.

Bon voyage et bon retour.

Yours affectionately,
Aldous

* The address there is: Wrightwood, Cal.
P.S. Poor Drieu's uneasy spirit—how strange and moving that he should suddenly speak again!

516: TO E. MCKNIGHT KAUFFER

Llano, Calif.
14 *May,* 1946

My dear Ted,

Harpers have just sent me the rough sketches for the jacket of *BNW*.

My feeling is that the sketch I have marked A is the better of the two as regards proportion of colours and lettering. But I am wondering whether it would not be possible to incorporate into it the embryo motif of sketch B. Instead of the sphere and scroll of sketch A, might we not have an egg or, better, a bottle on its side, occupying the same amount of space, with the hint of an embryo appearing, as it does from the upright egg in sketch B? I envisage the bottle as a kind of gourd-shaped, or whirling-spray-shaped, or conventionalized womb-shaped object, with perhaps the suggestion of tubing and stop-cocks at one end, and the embryo (or embryos) either in the middle of it, or emergent. I enclose a series of suggestions—but don't know how to convey the right sense of embryologico-mechanical obscenity.

Meanwhile let us have a line to know how you both are, and what your address is. Are you coming out West again, I wonder? All goes well here. Matthew is at Berkeley and we have been pretty solidly in the desert for the past months, but expect to go up into the mountains as summer warms up.

Maria sends love, as do I.

Ever yours,
Aldous

517: TO JOHN MIDDLETON MURRY

Llano, Calif.
26 May, 1946

Dear Murry,

Thank you for your very friendly letter. I am glad you liked the pamphlet and glad too to have this opportunity for saying that I admire very much what you have done and for telling you that I am sorry for some of the things I have done. That wonderful Chinese allegory, *Monkey*, which [Arthur] Waley translated a few years back, gives a very forceful account of that blessing and curse of cleverness, with which the Fairy Godmother, who is also the Wicked Fairy, endowed me, and with which, as a young man, I was in considerable measure identified. However, there is, let us hope, Evolution and a Descent of Man; and I have tried to drop the old tail and tricks, or at least to make use of them for better and less malicious purposes than in the past.

I am sending by ordinary mail the script of a preface to a new edition of *Brave New World*, which is to be issued in New York late this summer. It

517 *Huxley had lost patience with Murry many years before—possibly in working for him on the* Athenaeum, *certainly in absorbing Lawrence's exasperation. The result was the caricature of Murry as Burlap in* Point Counter Point. *Then, after Lawrence's death, came Murry's 'malignant and vindictive hagiography',* Son of Woman, *which deepened Huxley's dislike into contempt. Fifteen years after that Huxley was disposed to be charitable, but he had not sacrificed his judgment. See letters 833 and 889.*

is written deliberately with a certain brio, but contains, I think, some interesting and useful things, and you may find it suitable for the *Adelphi*.

And meanwhile what *is* going to happen to the world? The desire for even physiological salvation seems to be merely superficial; the deep and enduring will (to judge by the actions of those in authority) is a will to self-destruction. The situation is such that one comes to wonder whether there may not, after all, be some truth in the notion of diabolic possession.

Yours,
Aldous Huxley

518: †TO THOMAS H. MCCORMACK, JR

Llano, Calif.
9 *June,* 1946

Dear Mr McCormack,

Thank you for your letter. In regard to the Curé d'Ars, it seems to be perfectly possible for a man to move up and down from one level of spirituality to another, or from spirituality to occultism—just as he moves from ecstatic spirituality back to normal life, which he may live, at moments, in a largely non-spiritual way. The Curé d'Ars undoubtedly achieved a high state of union; but he was also a Catholic, with a strong belief in purgatory and in the possibility of getting out of purgatory by preliminary austerities on earth; also with a belief in the desirability of miracles for philanthropic purposes. (And perhaps they may be desirable in relation to someone like the Curé d'Ars or the recently canonized Dom Bosco.) Similarly Ramakrishna was constantly moving about from emotional bhakti to jnana (which he evidently enjoyed less), and from visions to the contemplation of God without form, and from a super-normal 'discernment of spirits' and second-sight to 'simple regard' and 'the spiritual marriage'.

As for the discursive reasoning having to give place on the highest levels to pure intuition, in which knowledge, knower and known are one, this is surely adumbrated in Plato and made specific in Plotinus and the later neo-Platonists down to Dionysius the Areopagite, by whom the scholastics and the whole western tradition has been profoundly influenced. Aristotle was most certainly not a mystic; nor was Seneca, that multi-millionaire who spent his life preaching the charms of poverty, and who inculcated compassion while being involved with his pupil, Nero, in the murder of the latter's mother. No mystic in his senses has any objection to discursive reason within the field of relative knowledge, where we *must* make use of it under penalty of becoming victims to prejudice, emotion and ignorance. But, just as the objects of sense cannot be apprehended by discursive reason, but only by a direct intuition, so with God, who can only be known about by means of discourse, but cannot be known-by-immediate-acquaintance except in an act of unifying intuition, to which different mystics have given a variety of names. One can sum up by saying that discursive reason deals with the relations between given facts; but that these facts are not given to discursive reason, but to non-rational intuition of a sensuous nature on the lower levels and of a 'psychic' or spiritual nature on the higher levels.

Yours sincerely,
Aldous Huxley

519: TO JOHN MIDDLETON MURRY

Wrightwood, Calif.
19 *June,* 1946

Dear Murry,

Thank you for your letter and the articles on *Science, Liberty and Peace.* I have just finished writing some rather random reflections on nationalism, which I will send you as soon as they get themselves revised and fair-copied. They don't arrive at any very helpful or concrete conclusion, because I simply don't know how the intensity of nationalistic idolatry is to be mitigated in any span of future time short enough to be of very much service to the contemporary world. But the article may be of some interest as touching on a number of different facets of the subject.

About a German translation of the pamphlet—the situation is as follows. I wrote the book at the request of Nevin Sayre of the F[ellowship] o[f] R[econciliation] and have made over all royalties on it to the FOR, telling them that they can arrange for translation and publication wherever they see fit, but also telling them to arrange this through Chatto and Windus, who handle my translation business and so are in a position to know what commitments have been previously made, or what options given. I am sure the FOR would like to have the pamphlet translated into German, and I therefore suggest that your correspondent should get in touch with FOR headquarters in London, find out if Nevin Sayre made any arrangements with them about the book while he was in England recently, and if necessary get in touch with FOR in New York (2929 Broadway). Then having found out if they are agreeable to his making the translation, FOR in London should talk to Chatto and Windus and find out from them what publisher (probably in Switzerland) has proved most efficient in handling German translations. Or alternatively if they know of somebody in Germany who might do the job better, they could discuss this with Chatto. In this dreadfully unsettled state of things in middle Europe, one must pick the distributor who seems, at the moment, to be best equipped to handle the particular job in question, not attempt to stick to any one publisher on a priori grounds.

As for Possession by forces of evil—I think that what may happen is this. Given such phenomena as telepathy (and I think they have to be accepted as actually occurring), we must postulate as C. D. Broad does, a kind of psychic medium in which all personal minds bathe, like fish in water. What individuals and groups of individuals think and above all strongly feel and will, may create, as it were, vortices in this medium; and these vortices may become enduring entities, leading a more or less independent life of their own, and endowed with a kind of second-hand objectivity, so that they exist 'out there' and not merely in individual minds. Hence I believe, that sense we get of a numinous presence in certain churches, hence the ability of certain intensely worshipped relics, images and so forth to 'work miracles' and hence the decline of that power, as the fashions in devotion change. And hence also hauntings, which are vortices created, in general, by intensely painful or evil feelings. What men have been feeling, willing, doing and suffering for the last seven years, and indeed for much longer than that time, may very well have established enduring and independent vortices in the psychic medium—vortices powerful enough to affect all minds that are not actively preoccupied with good, or that have not deliberately laid themselves open to the action of the Spirit, which is transcendent to and immanent in the space-time universe and its psychic extensions. Whether there are powers of evil other than our own home-made devils is an open question. But in order to account for the seemingly possessed and demoniac behaviour of our rulers at the present time, I don't think we need go beyond the products of our own past behaviour.

Yours,
Aldous Huxley

520: TO VICTORIA OCAMPO

Wrightwood, Calif.
3 September, 1946

My dear Victoria,

It was good to get your letter and to learn that we may soon be seeing you. As for the article on T. E. Lawrence—I will do my best; but it will take a little time, since I shall have to find out something about him. I read about a quarter of the *Seven Pillars* some fifteen years ago, and since then have not had a copy of the book in my hands. The truth is that I don't read very much in the way of general literature. My eyes make it impossible for me to 'keep up' with what is being published; and at the same time my primary preoccupation is the achievement of some kind of over-all understanding of the world, directly and, at one remove, through the building up of some hypothesis that accounts for the facts and 'saves the appearances'. Most of the limited reading I am able to do is aimed at the refinement and clarification of the guiding hypothesis. In regard to belles lettres—outside the few stupendous things, whose periodical re-perusal throws ever fresh light on the central problem—I read what chance brings to hand, paying attention only to what contributes in one way or another to the furthering of my underlying purpose.

If I have not read T. E. Lawrence, it is because I have not gone out of my way to get his books and because fate has not brought them my way; and also because what little of his writings I have read did not seem to promise to contribute very much to the achievement of my purpose. But it may well be that I was wrong in this and that a re-reading may reveal significances which I did not previously suspect. And the same may perhaps be true of Valéry—though, knowing his work much more fully than I know Lawrence's, I doubt it. For admirably intelligent as Valéry was, his insight generally stopped short of the ultimate nature of things; and gifted artist as he was, the beauty of the formal relationships within his prose and poetry was not of that highest order of beauty, which constitutes a genuine revelation of the supreme reality. That was why, my physical capacities being what they are, I had not re-read any of his writings for a long time and was therefore not in a position to write about him, when you asked me to last winter.

A bientôt, I hope.

Ever yours affectionately,
Aldous

521: TO CASS CANFIELD

Wrightwood, Calif:
14 *September*, 1946

Dear Cass,

Many thanks for your letter. It is good news that *The Art of Seeing* shd still be moving. I have been busy with a screen version of my short story 'The Gioconda Smile', which is now about finished and shd make quite an interesting picture. I may even make a version for the stage, using much of the screen play dialogue, provided suitable arrangements for production can be made. Meanwhile I am working on preparations for a short historical novel—for I think I shall drop a more ambitious scheme I had for combining historical and contemporary material to concentrate solely on the historical —about 14th-century Italy. The story will be based on a very strange episode in which St Catherine of Siena became involved. It is a fascinating period—for St Catherine is contemporary with Boccaccio, Chaucer, Froissart, Wyclif, Petrarch and the Black Death—so that the world's usual anomalies and mutual irrelevances are at the highest pitch of picturesque contrast.

[. . . .]

All good wishes.

Yours
Aldous H.

521 *Huxley had written to Harold Raymond on* 12 *September that he might possibly use the St. Catherine episode for a* 'contemporary novel having this story, and the writing of it, as a continuing leit-motiv'. *Neither this* 'more ambitious scheme' *nor the plan for an historical novel was carried to completion.*

145½ South Doheny Drive,
Los Angeles 36, California
4 October, 1946

Dearest Anita,

We are all in a state of confusion about the date of your Boston opening. The date I always had in mind was the fifth; but Halley, whom I rang up this morning, says it took place yesterday, and we have failed up till now to get hold of Mary to confirm or deny. So if it was yesterday, I hope you won't think that the absence of a wire of good wishes meant that we weren't thinking of you and the play and wishing you and Helen every possible success with it. Meanwhile I hope rehearsals have gone off well and that you are getting the kind of acting you want. Also that you aren't too much exhausted by the campaign.

If your opening was yesterday, it coincided with ours—the opening of Maria's sister [Suzanne]'s show of sculpture at the Taylor Galleries. It was a good show, with some really excellent things in it, and we rounded up quite a good collection of people. Let's hope to goodness they will do some buying and ordering of portraits. Grace and Edwin were there, just back from the Rockies—and just off to the East for a brief trip, in the course of which you may perhaps see them. They seemed well and cheerful. Constance has been a great help and stand-by during the preparations for the show, and gets on very well with Maria's sister and with her two daughters [Claire and Sylvia Nicolas], who are very sweet, amusing and talented girls—the elder, who writes and has commissions to do articles for *Harper's Bazaar*, being a charmingly vague, wraith-like being, and the younger, who draws extremely well, having her feet firmly planted on the ground and knowing her way around in the most decided way—the two together forming a most amusing contrast. They have been a great success with everyone who has seen them.

I have finished my screen play of 'The Gioconda Smile', and I think it should make a very lively movie. It is still uncertain whether it will be done here or in England. If here, it will be produced either by Wanger or Einfeld of Enterprise. If in England, by Alex Korda. In either case the producers would be prepared to delay the release of the film and to provide the necessary backing so that a dramatic version of the story could be produced on the stage. So I am at present working on this stage adaptation. It raises some rather tough problems. But I think they can be satisfactorily solved. I wish you were here, so that I could talk to you about them and get the benefit of your experience. Working on the script with Zoltan Korda was very pleasant. He is a nice, intelligent fellow and we were able to co-ordinate

522 *Boston opening: of* Happy Birthday, *a play by Miss Loos, which starred* Helen Hayes. *Halley Jenkins was Anita Loos's cook; Mary Anita Sale, Miss Loos's niece.*

our respective specialities of writer and director without the interference of a producer. Consequently the work was done quickly and efficiently, without being held up by retired button-manufacturers using the Divine Right of Money to obstruct the activities of those who do the actual work.

In the intervals of all this I am collecting materials for a historical novel I want to write on fourteenth-century Italy. I have dug up some really delightful things. E.g. the mediaeval equivalent of chemical warfare, which was this: when you besieged a town or castle you would charge the catapults, which were ordinarily used for throwing rocks against the walls, with the putrefied carcases of animals, which you then tossed into the besieged place, in the hope that the stink and infection would produce disease. And when you wanted to add psychological to chemical warfare, you bombarded the place with the carcases exclusively of donkeys. This last insult drove the people of Siena almost out of their minds when it was inflicted on them by the besieging Florentines.

Maria sends her best love, as do I.

Ever yours affectionately,

Sorry, Something seems to have gone wrong. Anyhow it drove the Sienese out of their minds when the insult was inflicted on them by the besieging Florentines. And we both send you our best love.

Ever yours affectionately
Aldous

523: TO J. B. RHINE

Llano, Cal.
26 October, 1946

Dear Dr Rhine,

I was greatly interested in your article on the difficulties in the way of parapsychological research, published in the latest issue of the *Journal*. This whole business of attention defeating its own object when too rigidly concentrated is one which had interested me in other fields, particularly in that [of] the training of defective eyesight along the lines laid down by the late Dr W. H. Bates. I have no copy by me here; otherwise I would send you a little book I wrote on the subject three or four years ago—*The Art of Seeing*. In the opening part of this there is a discussion of the problem of attention in relation to seeing. Ribot had pointed out long ago that fixed concentration of any sense organ upon its object tended to produce insensitivity to that object, and that attention, to be effective, must be shifting. This is basic in the Bates method—one of whose principal aims is to break the vision-impairing habit of staring and to encourage constant shifting of the eyes and their mind. The difficulty you mention seems to be a special case of a general law—

522 *Huxley's typewriter ribbon became hung as he was writing about the people of Siena, with the result that the next few lines were almost illegible.*

namely that too much concentration defeats its own end, and that effective concentration has to work by a process of decentration. In yogic practices there is a form of intense concentration which induces 'false samadhi', or self-hypnosis. This is discussed in many Mahayana Buddhist texts, where it is pointed out that this way of the 'sravakas and pratyekabuddhas' is a blind alley and that, to the Bodhisattva, the condition of annihilation produced by their methods seems, not bliss, but hell.

The anecdotal evidence seems to indicate that it is possible for people to become aware of when they are right in their extra-sensory perceptions of certain classes of phenomena. There seems to be no doubt that many saintly persons have had what is called 'the discernment of spirits' and have known with astonishing accuracy, not only the general state of the soul of those who came in contact with them, but also the particular matters with which they were at the moment preoccupied. Perhaps this ability to know when the paranormal perception is correct occurs only in cases where that which is known is of high intrinsic interest. Discernment of spirits is of intenser concern to more aspects of the personality than is the discernment of dice.

Yours sincerely,
Aldous Huxley

524: TO JULIAN HUXLEY

Llano, Cal.
27 October, 1946

Dearest J,

I was delighted to get your good letter and to learn that all goes well with you and the infant Unesco. I certainly hope they don't choose Biddle for the permanent Director, or even Wallace [. . .], and that you will have a chance of continuing the work you have begun.

I shall be interested to see your remarks on progress when they appear. It is a subject about which I have been thinking quite a lot of late. You are certainly right in saying that it is not a subjective phenomenon (and yet it seems to me that some of the conditions you lay down for progress are of a purely subjective nature—mainly a matter of individual volition rather than of the effects upon individuals of economic, political and social arrangements). Indeed, the chief reason I have for feeling rather dubious about the whole idea of progress, in its nineteenth- and twentieth-century expressions, at any rate, is that, in the very nature of man, progress can never be consciously experienced by the individuals who are supposedly progressing. There are several good reasons for this. First, every human life consists of a rise to maturity and plenitude of faculties, followed by a decline through old age to death. Old people are weak, sickly, lonely, ignored by their younger contemporaries. They cannot experience the progress going on in the world, because they personally are not progressing, but falling into decline. They tend to feel that the good old days, when they were young and personally progressing, were better than the present, even though the present may be a time to which future historians will give the name of a progressive age.

Second, human beings have an almost infinite capacity for taking things for granted. The new gadget, the new organization, the new amenities and privileges give positive satisfaction for only a few months or days, and are then accepted as part of the order of things. When we come into the possession of a refrigerator, we do not spend our time gratefully comparing the present with the ice-boxless past; we take the convenience for granted and start to curse when the mechanism goes wrong. And what is true of refrigerators is true, mutatis mutandis, of increases in salary, improved social services, finer public buildings and more sensible political arrangements. Every ceiling, when reached, becomes a floor, upon which one walks as a matter of course and prescriptive right. This means that no progress is ever experienced as progress by those taking part in, or subjected to, the process.

Third, for the vast majority of men and women private life is the only thing which has significance and value. The unchanging essence of existence consists, in Rozanov's words, in 'picking one's nose and looking at the sunset'. Most of the social, political, artistic and scientific developments, which are ordinarily classified as symptoms of progress, have little influence on the physiological and lower mental processes, which, for the vast majority, constitute the real substance of life. Given an adequate amount of food and shelter and not too much interference from the ruling minority, the masses can pick their noses and look at the sunset just as well at one period of history as at another. People like ourselves, who are interested in other things besides a strictly private life, have always been in a minority. And it is not certain, as Tolstoy is never tired of pointing out in *War and Peace* and elsewhere, that those who take the largest views, those who are most intensely preoccupied with 'doing good to humanity', are either the morally best or socially most useful individuals. Talking with nice, ordinary, simple people, I am always amazed at their quiet and mainly voluntary ignorance of the larger issues of the time. Their life is entirely identified with family relationships, the business of earning a living, the goings-on of the neighbours. Art, science, philosophy and politics simply do not interest them. To them, progress is largely an irrelevance. In confirmation of this one may note the interesting fact that the people who actually lived through periods which we now regard as having achieved progress, have often been wholly unconscious of being progressive. The thirteenth century, for example, was one of the great flowering times of history. But as Coulton (who has read all the documents) points out, those who, in that century, wrote about their own period were uniformly of opinion that it was an age of decadence. And anyhow what kind of relationship exists between an efflorescence of art, technology and philosophical thinking on the one hand and the happiness and morality of the masses on the other? The fact that Aquinas and Dante made their appearance at a certain time casts singularly little light on the lives of their contemporaries.

Again, the characteristic art of Machiavelli's world (a world remarkably like our own, but in miniature) was that of Perugino. But I challenge the most ingenious Marxist to infer the necessary existence of Perugino from what is written in the *Prince* and the *Discourses*. The truth is, I believe, that people have enormously exaggerated the role of art, philosophy, pure science, and the other indices of progress, as expressions of the general life of their period. Artists and thinkers are not, as a rule, deeply preoccupied with the 'main currents' of their age. Some, the more lyrical, are concerned with picking their noses and looking at the sunset, and are valued precisely because the majority of mankind are interested in nose-picking and sunset-gazing. Others are impelled by their originality, their unlikeness to those around them, to go exploring in unfamiliar fields of thought and feeling. That is why all the dictators, fascist and communist alike, have to use threats, bribes and brute force to compel their artists to be 'social-minded'. (See the recent accounts of Russian purges of insufficiently patriotic and Marxist writers and even musicians.) So where and how precisely is progress related to the actual life of the majority of individuals at any given moment? I don't know and have never read an answer that seemed to me entirely satisfying. Actually, objective progress seems to be something recorded by later historians (who also have to record periods of regress and stagnation). It may and apparently very often does have little or no significance for the masses existing at the time during which, according to the historians, the progress was taking place.

Fourth, we never get something for nothing. Gains in one field are paid for by losses in another. E.g. the advantages of mass production methods have entailed the decay of craftsmanship (with all the subjective satisfactions arising from it) and the destruction of the basic, popular arts. And who is qualified to decide whether the gain, in any given instance, outweighs the loss? Who is in a position to tell us, for example, whether an advance in the effectiveness of analytical thinking is a progress, if this entails (as it often seems to do) a regression in what may be called integral, intuitive thinking? Recently I heard a lecture by a Chinaman who, comparing his country with the West, summed up the basic difference by saying: 'We understand more than we know; you know more than you understand'. Is the increase in knowledge at the expense of 'understanding' a progress? I don't know, and I see no reason to suppose that anyone else does either. The ideal would seem to be some kind of balance. But it may be that a society consisting in the main of perfectly balanced, all-round individuals is one which doesn't make much progress of the objective kind recorded by historians. *Quien sabe?*

Meanwhile one must obviously attempt objective improvements—preferably with a short-range objective. For it seems to be a fact that when people think of far-off communist Utopias or Thousand-Year Reichs, they are so much dazzled by the beauty of what they see (by how prodigious an act of faith!) in the unknowable future, that they are ready to commit any atrocity in the present and to sacrifice millions of contemporary victims for the sake of the glorious time that will be had by all two or three hundred years from now. Incidentally I have never said that concrete improvements should be disregarded. On the contrary, they are indispensable means to the subjective end—provided always that we make the kind of improvements that seem likely to subserve the subjective end and do not, as is the case today, sacrifice man to the sabbath, individuals to the state, human beings to gadgets and efficient organizations. Genuine improvements, I come to feel more and more strongly, can only be achieved on a small, a human scale—by decentralization of power, production and population, through self-governing co-operative groups working for themselves and not manipulated by government managers and experts.

As for the Final End—that can, of course, be expressed in purely operational terms, as is done in many Buddhist texts, where the psychological (or should one say, 'autological') expression 'Nirvana' is used in place of the ontological expressions 'experience of God', 'union with Atman-Brahman' and so forth. I would have no objection to using these operational terms. But the book was primarily an anthology, and most of the writers on the subject have preferred to use ontological expressions. And I would say that, just as there seems to be justification for passing from purely operational descriptions of physical phenomena as observed in experiments to ontological descriptions in terms of atoms and the rest, so there seems to be justification for passing from operational expressions such as 'Nirvana' to ontological expressions such as 'Mind', 'Brahman' and so forth. The trouble begins when theologians start to get completely away from their operational base, or start with a base which is not experimental but 'revealed', in the sense of being arbitrary and fantastic.

I have been very busy all this spring and summer—first with the compilation of an anthology of essays and criticism for the *Encyclopaedia Britannica* people, a job much bigger than I anticipated; and then on the script for a film version of my old short story, 'The Gioconda Smile'. This last was quite enjoyable and interesting, as I was working only with the director—Zoltan Korda, brother of Alexander, and a very nice and much-gifted man—undisturbed by Producers, representing the money interest, and always concerned to affirm the Divine Right of Money by interfering with those who do the real work. This script is now finished, and I am engaged in seeing if I can make a stage play out of the same material. After that I expect to get to work on a novel—a historical one, by way of experiment, on fourteenth-century Italy, a time and place where the anomalies and contrasts always present in human society were particularly intense, odd and picturesque.

Perhaps next year we might come to Europe, though I confess I don't feel very strongly drawn to leave the sunshine and the blessed emptiness of this desert. Unlike Dr Johnson, I prefer climate to conversation. And, over and above climate, the enormous merit of this country is the fact that it contains so few people. How wonderful, for example, that Nevada should only have a hundred and fifty thousand inhabitants in a hundred thousand square miles of territory! And of course this business of population is the one thing these bloody politicians should be thinking about at this time. Barring catastrophes in the interval, the population of the planet will pass from two thousand to three thousand millions within a short life-time. Poverty in the midst of plenty is largely bosh. There is poverty in the midst of poverty—we just can't feed all the existing two thousand millions with existing resources. What happens when there are three thousand millions to feed? All this criminal haggling as to who shall bully whom, which is all the peace conferences can think about, seems pretty silly, to say the least. Just gangsterizing while the world starves. Did I send you a little pamphlet I wrote this spring, largely on this topic, called *Science, Liberty and Peace?*

You say nothing of the boys. I hope they flourish. Matthew is at Berkeley, taking courses in Latin American history, economics and languages. A good idea, I think, as he wants to travel and there are sure to be plenty of openings available for anyone who really knows his stuff.

Our best love to you both.

Ever your affectionate,
Aldous

P.S. We have just heard from Sophie (Jeanne's daughter) that she seems to be on the verge of a job in Unesco—as a stenotypist and secretary. (We have just sent her stenotype machine over.) She was trained here to be very efficient with it. If you can, do give her a helping hand. She did very well when she worked here.

525: TO CYRIL CONNOLLY

Wrightwood, Calif.
5 November, 1946

Dear Cyril,

Thank you for your note and the invitation to contribute to *Horizon,* which I certainly will do when I have anything to contribute. But at the moment everything I do seems to run to unserializable length.

I liked Palinurus. There is a very distinctive flavour about its weltanschauung—a flavour which might easily become contagious, so that, just as we now note something we can describe as Wertherism, say, or Byronism, future historians of literature may discover lingering strains of palinuremia.

Did you ever read Sheldon's *Varieties of Temperament* in the original? If not, do. He has case histories of various extreme types which are real masterpieces in the Theophrastian genre of the Character. His account of a Rumano-Jewish somatotonic, belonging to a philoprogenitive family in

525 *Palinurus: Connolly's* The Unquiet Grave, a Word Cycle, by Palinurus (1944). *Huxley's witticism alludes to Connolly's remarks on the etymology of* Palinurus.

which there were over one hundred first cousins, is one of the most hair-raising things in all literature.

                                                             Yours,
                                                             Aldous H.

526: TO JOHN MIDDLETON MURRY

                                                Wrightwood, Calif.
                                                5 November, 1946

Dear John Murry,

Forgive me for not having answered your letter before this. The article on nationalism seemed a bit unsatisfactory on a re-reading and I am thinking of embodying the relevant features of it in a longer study of modern Idolatry. Few things are more striking than the general retreat from monotheism which has taken place in recent times. Idolatrous worship of that which is less than God has always existed; but it has existed as a heresy, as a phenomenon for which there could be no theological or philosophical justification. Today the nationalists and political ideologists preach what they practise, building up elaborate systems of thought by which to justify the practice of idolatrous polytheism. And whereas the old polytheism was tolerant, so that the gods of one city could be incorporated into the pantheon of another city, the modern variety has all the ferocious exclusiveness of the old-fashioned revealed religion. And yet vast numbers of people seem to prefer suicidal nonsense to beneficent sense.

At the moment I am too deeply involved in a large-scale project to be able to do any other writing. But after the new year I hope, if all goes well, to have a breathing spell, when I should like to do a few short pieces. One of these, which may suit the *Adelphi*, would be on the curious anomaly that progress can be noted and estimated by historians after the event but cannot, it would seem, be actually experienced by the individuals composing the society regarded as progressive. When I get this written, I will send it you.

I spoke to Gerald Heard the other day, and he said that, when he had something, he would send it you.

                                                             Yours,
                                                             Aldous Huxley

527: TO JULIAN HUXLEY

                                                   Llano, Calif.
                                                   9 December, 1946

Dearest J,

I was so delighted to hear that you had been elected to the permanent secretaryship of Unesco. I had not seen the news in the paper; but heard of it yesterday from the Edwin Hubbles, who were as much pleased about it as Maria and I, and who sent their good wishes and greetings. I suppose it will mean that you and Juliette will now spend the bulk of your time in Paris—

which in certain respects, I suppose, is somewhat livelier than London, owing to the more flourishing black market and the less efficient rationing for the rich.

I wonder if there is any hope, through Unesco, of persuading the technologists, when they apply the results of pure science to industry, to remember that the sabbath was made for man and not vice versa; that human beings with certain physical and psychological needs come first and that applied science should serve those needs and those human beings and should not compel the human beings to be the slaves of applied science and its capitalistic or governmental owners and managers. The ideal would be if technologists and pure scientists could meet, consider the human situation, evaluate human needs in the way of food, clothing, shelter, peace, individual liberty, group self-government etc; and then frame a policy of research designed to fulfil those needs. E.g. it is perfectly obvious that atomic energy, being generated from uranium, which is a natural monopoly, is a power-source no less politically unsatisfactory than petroleum. Like petroleum, uranium may occur within the territories of powerful nations—in which case it increases their power and their tendency to bully others; or it may be found within the borders of weak nations—in which case it invites aggression and international chicanery, as is now the case with the oil of the Middle East. If they chose, technologists could by-pass the whole difficulty by concentrating on the development of a source of power which is not a natural monopoly—and which, also, is not a wasting asset, like uranium, or petroleum, or even coal. The most obvious power source hitherto inadequately exploited is wind. I gather that the experimental wind turbine which has been producing fifteen hundred kilowatts in Maine has proved entirely satisfactory. If scientists genuinely want to contribute to peace and well being, they can collectively and intensively consider the yet more efficient development of such wind turbines and thereby end natural monopolies and remove one of the standing temptations to aggression, war and foreign burrowing from within. But they prefer to concentrate on atomic power, which creates unparalleled temptations in the political sphere. And yet the only thing that large-scale social, political and economic arrangements can hope to achieve in the way of human betterment is the diminution of temptations to evil. 'Lead us not into temptation.' Why? Because all experience proves that, when we are tempted sufficiently strongly, we almost invariably succumb. So it would seem mere common sense to concentrate on technological applications of scientific discoveries that shall make for individual welfare without creating collective temptations, which the bosses in power will certainly be unable to resist. But I suppose there is not the faintest hope that such perfectly obvious considerations will be heeded.

Our best love and Christmas greetings to you both.

Ever your affectionate,

Aldous

Llano, Cal.
12 *December,* 1946

My dear Victoria,

I gather from your telegram that you will not be coming this way before proceeding là-bas. Our own immediate plans are contingent on circumstances not within my control. I have been making a screen play out of an old short story of mine, which was bought by a director last year. The script is more or less finished; but it is certain that, when a company actually undertakes the shooting, I will have to be on hand for last-minute changes and also to prevent, if possible, any irreparable damage being done to the story, which I should be sorry to see destroyed. Moreover I have also made a stage version of the original story, and this may perhaps be produced some time in the earlier part of next year. If this happens, I might have to be on the spot during rehearsals—indeed, would probably have to be on the spot; for it is only at rehearsals that the final improvements in a play can be made, and it is also at rehearsals that one learns something about the art of writing for the theatre—an art which has now begun to interest me and which I might perhaps attempt to practise, if I am granted the necessary life, opportunity and inspiration. This present essay is of no great importance—though it deals with one or two interesting and significant problems. But it may be that, if I get a bit more accustomed to the medium, I may be able to tackle something more considerable. All this adds up in practice to the conclusion that we shall not be able to launch out immediately for the southern hemisphere. But perhaps later in the year—quien sabe? We have also to see what Matthew is going to do, when he gets out of College in February. He is working very hard at his courses in Latin American history, economics etc—has written an original research paper on the Argentine labour movement, and is doing another monograph on some phase, I think, of Chilean history. All of which he seems to enjoy very much. I hope some satisfactory opportunity for making use of his knowledge will present itself.

We had a busy but pleasant summer, as Maria's sister, Suzanne Nicolas, who is quite a good sculptor, was here with her two daughters, of eighteen and twenty-one. We had not seen them for many years, but became very fond of them all. Suzanne has a consuming passion for her work, and the two girls, while very [diffe]rent in character, are equally gifted and charming, and equally unaffected and unspoiled. They are on their way back to New York now—having already had one miraculous escape, when their station wagon overturned—and I hope will make the rest of the journey without untoward incident. Get Pepe [José Weissberger] to bring you together; I think you would like Suzanne and would certainly be charmed and amused by the children, one of whom has a real gift for writing, while the other promises to be a good draughtsman.

My experience with T. E. Lawrence has not been very happy, I am afraid.

To tell you the truth, I greatly prefer your little book about him to the *Seven Pillars*, which I found as hard to read now as I found it in the past. The reason is to be found in the fact that, even in this writing, Lawrence was a man of the conscious will. He *wanted* to write well, and he wrote about as well as a conscious will can make one write. But the consciously willed style always, it seems to me, stops short of the best, the genuinely good. It is always what the other Lawrence calls 'would-be'. A consciously willed style is necessarily artificial; but not all artificial styles are of the 'would-be' variety. To some people it comes natural to write artificially; they are artificial with freshness and unction—like Milton, for example. Nothing could be more artificial than 'Lycidas', but nothing could be more deeply spontaneous, less of the surface. 'Lycidas' is as much a product of the Tao as are the 'wood-notes wild' of more natural poets. But with T. E. Lawrence I never feel any freshness or spontaneity. His descriptions of nature have an aridity about them that contrasts most painfully, for me at least, with the descriptions of such unwilled stylists as Ruskin, or D. H. Lawrence or (to take another and much smaller writer who has described the Arabian scene) even Kinglake. T. E. makes me think of Alfieri—to some extent as a man, but more as a writer; for Alfieri willed to be a great tragic poet and came as near to being one as will can make anyone. Freshness, the free-working of the Tao, the something not ourselves that makes for beauty and significance—these are the things I find myself valuing more and more in style. And these are the things I don't find in the *Seven Pillars*, which I read with admiration for the man, but without pleasure in the writing and, except intellectually, without profit. As a character, I find Lawrence extremely interesting; and I think you have said almost everything there is to be said on the subject. He was a Charles de Foucauld, whose tragedy it was to be incapable of opening himself to that which lies beyond the will—to the Inner Light, to Suchness, to Sat Chit Ananda. Hence, one divines, a really appalling unhappiness and sense of frustration. If one wants a demonstration of the basic *misère de l'homme*, one could hardly choose better than Lawrence; for he had everything that the human individual, as an individual, can possess—talent, courage, indomitable will, intelligence, everything, and though his gifts permitted him to do extraordinary, hardly credible things, they availed him nothing in relation to 'enlightenment', 'salvation', 'liberation'. Nothing burns in hell except self-will, says the author of the *Theologia Germanica*. Lawrence had a self-will of heroic, even of Titanic, proportions; and one has the impression that he lived for the most part in one of the more painful corners of the inferno. He is one of those great men for whom one feels intensely sorry, because he was nothing but a great man.

Maria sends her best love and all good Christmas wishes, as do I, dear Victoria.

Ever yours affectionately,
Aldous

Llano, Calif.
14 *December,* 1946

Dear van Druten,

Thank you for your helpful letter. I think you are certainly right about the necessity of developing Janet as a pre-murder personality—it was a thing I had been concerned about myself—and probably right about the division into short scenes. I think I see a trick for developing continuity by means of a framework, out of which the scenes will emerge and into which they will return. It is just a trick, of course; but all writing is a game of catch-as-catch-can; and if any trick is effective, it is legitimate. Also I expect you are right about the nurse, the general and the committee. I put them in with the purpose of suggesting the great and terrible truth that, whatever may be happening to *us*, other people's lives go on unchanged by our joys and sufferings, other people continue to ride their hobby horses around and across our fields of tragedy without even noticing that anything out of the ordinary is happening. But this is something which cannot, perhaps, ever be rendered in drama. A play can tell the truth and nothing but the truth; but it can never (or at any rate has never up till now) told, or rather implied—for it can never be fully told—the whole truth. That is why, I think, I have never cared profoundly for the theatre. Even Shakespeare is compelled by the nature of the medium he is working in to stop short of telling the whole truth. And if he accepted the aesthetic and, in some sort, the moral limitations of the medium, then it is doubtless presumptuously silly to attempt to transcend them by putting in scenes that stress the basic irrelevance to our sufferings of other people's lives, and even of our own lives, on the physiological level. Still, I should dearly like to be artist enough to incorporate the irrelevant relevantly into a drama and, by that incorporation, to intensify the dramatic quality of the main theme.

I expect to be in town next week, and will ring you up to see if we can arrange a meeting. Meanwhile would you please hold the script for me.

Yours very sincerely,
Aldous Huxley

529 *Van Druten's criticisms of the play* The Gioconda Smile *in its early draft led to his collaborating with Huxley in revising it, his part being kept secret at his insistence. According to Beth Wendel, Huxley was quite unable to visualize creatively. In his fiction he always 'saw' his characters and settings from memory. In order to imagine the projection of a play on to the stage, he needed to have it described by someone else. An important task of the collaborator was to supply all the descriptions of sets, action, entrances and exits.*

Llano, Cal.
16 December, 1946

Dear Dr Rhine,

By all means make use of the letter, if you think it worth printing.

The real trouble is, as you say, that there is no single key that will open the doors of the problem, which is so complex and whose existence is in a world still so obscure, that we have to feel our way along many avenues of approach simultaneously, in the hope that the resultant failures and successes may provide indications of what exactly it is we are dealing with.

Our current model of the mind—a sub-conscious basement, a conscious ground floor and a watertight roof—is inadequate to the facts. The Indians have a more complicated model, with several additional floors above ground level and no roof—no ultimate obstacle between atman and Brahman, or even between the spiritual space contained in the lower storeys and the spiritual space outside. And on top of everything there is the problem of time—how it can be made to fit the facts of prevision. In this context the last chapter of Schroedinger's *What is Life?* was interesting, I thought. Meanwhile I admire you for not going mad under the strain of devising scientific experiments in a field where there is no really satisfactory working hypothesis!

Yours sincerely,
Aldous Huxley

531: †TO MRS HANNAH CLOSS

Llano Cal.,
7 January, 1947

Dear Mrs Closs,

Your letter of August last got put away in a place, in which ordinarily I never put letters requiring an answer, and only came to the surface again today. Please forgive me for the long delay in acknowledging it. I shall certainly read your book on the Albigenses, if I can lay my hands on it. They have always interested me, and I would like to learn more about them. Also I would like to see how you handle religious matters in fictional form—a problem to which I am thinking of addressing myself in a novel on fourteenth-century Italy, which I have been thinking vaguely of writing some day. My book would have, in the background of the story, the extraordinary figure of St Catherine of Siena—or perhaps, if too much historicity seemed undesirable, a figure based upon St Catherine. These real saints are so much more improbable than anything one can possibly invent, that I don't quite know how to deal with the problem; so shall be curious to see how you manage the perfect ones among the Albigenses—whether you venture to endow them with

531 *Mrs Closs was the author of* The Albigensian Triology.

poltergeists, supernormal powers, capacity to subsist on little or no food etc; in a word, all the truth-is-stranger-than-fiction attributes which distinguished not only St Catherine, but so many others—Philip Neri, the Curé d'Ars, John Bosco, to mention only a few. One hardly dares to touch these matters; and yet if one wants to tell the truth, one has to face the fact that *siddhis* do seem to accompany high states of contemplative prayer and, above all, of devotional prayer. It is all very embarrassing for the poor novelist who has to preserve an appearance of verisimilitude!

Yours sincerely,
Aldous Huxley

532: TO GERVAS HUXLEY

Llano, Cal.
8 January, 1947

My dear Gervas,

I have an awful suspicion that I never acknowledged your letter of last June and the charming photograph of young Charles, which accompanied it. He seems to be very much of the family—more conspicuously so, I should say, than Julian's boys, or Matthew ever seemed—though I remember Michael's Tom as a very Huxleian type.

I hope all goes well with you all, *malgré tout.* (And what a lot of *tout* there is to *malgré,* nowadays!) I read some extracts from some very interesting articles by Elspeth on East Africa—where, as in the rest of the continent, everything seems to be going about as badly as can be expected and only a little less badly than it is going in most of the other portions of the world. Of Kit [Christopher Huxley] I heard at second hand from my friend Edwin Hubble, the astronomer, who met him this summer at some fishing resort in the Rockies and struck up quite a friendship. My news of Michael is confined to reports from Maria's nieces in New York, who used to see the children during the war. And meanwhile what about Tea? The stuff they sell under that name hereabouts is pretty forbidding, and I confess that we have taken to drinking maté, to which a smoky flavour as of Lapsang Soochong has been imparted by its purveyor, an ancient tea-importer of Boston, called Mark Wendell, who puts this out because he can't get any of the genuine article from China. I suppose nothing much is coming out of Java now what with the civil war and the disrupted Dutch commerce. (And incidentally what dismal accounts one gets from Holland these days—the richest country on the continent doomed to become the poorest, if it loses its colonial trade. Holland's plight makes one realize how much of Western Europe's century of prosperity was due to, and at the expense of, its coloured subjects. The rest of the prosperity was due, in large measure, to the existence of raw-material countries in need of machines and manufactured goods; now these countries have their own industries. So both of these sources of prosperity have been removed—just at the time when Malthus's nightmare has come true in the natural course of events, and is being aggravated by the cutting off of all Europe east of the Oder and the dumping of displaced Germans into a foodless territory which they used to supply, but where they are now merely extra mouths.) When you make your next missionary journey to these parts, do let us know.

[. . . .]

Our love to you both and to any other member of the family who may be within range.

Ever yours affectionately,
Aldous

533: TO PHILIPPE DUMAINE

Wrightwood, Calif.
19 January, 1947

Dear Mr Dumaine,

Thank you for your letter and the accompanying questionnaire. I have written a few paragraphs on the subject with which it deals, and am enclosing them herewith.

With all good wishes for the success of your venture, I remain
Yours very sincerely,
Aldous Huxley

533 The questionnaire posed the question: 'Les moyens sont-ils subordonnés à la fin ou la fin vaut-elle seulement par ce que valent les moyens?' (Are the means subordinate to the end, or is the end valuable only because the means are?) Dumaine translated Huxley's reply for Les Cahiers de Paris—Les Vivants. Huxley had written:

'In art and science, in industry, agriculture and medicine, the end we achieve is always conditioned by the means we use. A man may have the intention of raising abundant harvests, of curing the sick or of making labour-saving machinery; but if he is a bad farmer, he will succeed only in ruining the soil; if he is a bad doctor, his patients will die; if he is a bad engineer, his machines will not work. Hell is paved with good intentions: in all the fields of technology this is a self-evident truth, which nobody ever dreams of questioning.

'In the fields of personal relations and of politics, the case is different; for here self-interest and the passions are directly involved. The fact that ends are conditioned by the means employed is no longer self-evident, for the good reason that we do not wish it to be self-evident. We desire very strongly to achieve an end which, though in some cases it may seem to be idealistic, is in reality bound up with the satisfaction of some passion such as resentment, vanity, avarice or the lust for power. And because these passions and their related interests are involved, we choose to close our eyes to a whole class of facts which, in the strictly technological field, would have seemed to us of the first importance. To achieve what we regard as a good we are ready to commit evils, sometimes petty, sometimes monstrous and terrible—and we are then surprised, hurt and disillusioned because, instead of achieving the good at which we so idealistically aimed, we achieve only the deplorable results of our bad means.

[*Continued overleaf*

Wrightwood, Cal.
19 January, 1947

My dear Ted,

I was so glad to get your letter and to hear that your news was as good as can be expected in these current circumstances. We saw [S. J.] Perelman at lunch at the Town and Country Market, where he appeared with a heavily bearded companion, whose name I have now forgotten, but who didn't talk much. I thought him a very nice fellow, extremely bright in the head. I don't know where they propose to go in the Orient—he and the bearded one—since all the interesting and romantic places, from Bali to India and Burma are precisely those where the inhabitants shoot white men at sight and only enquire afterwards whether they are American subjects. And by the time they get to Africa, I should guess that much the same situation will prevail there. He seemed a little disturbed by the prospect. Let's hope all will go off without mishap.

The English invasion is less marked hereabouts. [——] comprised the greater part of it, so far as we were concerned. He seemed a sadder, if not a wiser, man than when we used to see him at Sanary, living in a state of

---

'*A philosophy which denies the facts of everyday experience does not change those facts; it merely blinds its adherents, justifies their passions by a show of reason and causes them to live in a state of chronic ignorance and self-deception. In many respects we are to-day less realistic in our approach to life than were our ancestors. Thus, the Greeks believed that* hubris, *whether towards man or Nature, was always followed by* nemesis. *We imagine that we can coerce Nature and use our fellow men as our tools and instruments, and not merely escape condign punishment, but actually achieve an increase in happiness and virtue. Again, the Hindus and the Buddhists were never tired of insisting on the law of* karma—*the law that "God is not mocked, but as a man sows, so shall he reap". Naively, we assume that we can sow atomic bombs, concentration camps, mass deportation and wholesale slaughter and enslavement—can sow these atrocities and still, after another two or three wars to end war, after five or six more revolutions and thirty or forty more Five Year Plans, reap physical well being and moral perfection in a new Age of Gold. Though they may not often have practised what they preached, the Christians of an earlier day believed that if they "first sought the Kingdom of God and His righteousness, all the rest would be added to them". Our modern notion is that, if we first seek all the rest, including massacres and coercion, the Kingdom of God will be added to us, at a conservative estimate, about the middle of the twenty-second century. And whereas our forefathers believed that the Sabbath was made for man and prayed that they might not be led into temptation, we are of opinion that man was made for his own arbitrary creations, such as Applied Science and the State, and that the best political system is one in which a small ruling oligarchy is tempted to abuse its absolute power, while the subordinate masses are tempted to indulge in irresponsibility and unintelligent obedience.*'

hardly imaginable squalor with his wife and a large number of ferrets. The whole picture of London life continuing exactly as before, except that the material basis of comfort and abundance has been taken away, never to return, I imagine, seemed unutterably depressing. As for the news one gets from other parts of Europe, that seems to be even worse.

I have been busy for some months on, first, a screen version and, second, a theatrical version of my old short story, 'The Gioconda Smile', which was bought last year by Zoltan Korda, the brother of Sir Alexander, who is much nicer than his brother and a good director. There will still be revisions to do on the screen play, and I am now near the end of the second version of the drama. It is rather maddening work, resembling jig saw puzzles rather than literature. But having embarked upon it, I feel I had better finish the damned thing as well as I can—even though it probably won't be much good, as I am far from a born playwright. After that I am thinking of doing a historical novel—not about Pascal, though that would be a fascinating subject, if one knew enough about it, but on fourteenth-century Italy, with Catherine of Siena in the background.

We are in process of getting out of our ranch at Llano—very sadly, but feeling that it is the sensible thing to do, in view of the difficulties and troubles it involves. We shall move to a more convenient spot up in the mountains, where our address will be, Wrightwood, Cal. Perhaps some day you may get out here again to see us.

It is very sweet of you to offer to give me your 'Poe', which I saw not long since at somebody's house and thought exceedingly good. I would like very much to have it and will, if you'd care for it, send you in return, when it appears, a portfolio of reproductions of Piranesi's *Prisons*, for which I have written an introduction. What strange things they are, incidentally, those *Prisons*! The nearest approach, in the realm of pictorial art, to the spirit of Kafka.

Maria sends her best love to you both, as do I.

Ever yours affectionately,
Aldous

PS I'm glad Tom Eliot was well, when you saw him. He is a man for whom I have always had a great affection, (though I have never been very intimate with him, in spite of nearly thirty years of acquaintance) as well as a profound admiration.

535: TO LEON M. LION

145½ South Doheny Drive,
Los Angeles 36, California
14 February, 1947

My dear Leon,

I have just heard in a circuitous way that you have been and indeed still are ill—which I am very sorry to hear, all the more so as I had gathered from your last letter of more than a year ago that you had emerged from sickness into a brighter region. There is an art of being ill, a making the best of the unhappy circumstances, which I always greatly admire whenever I see it being practised; and knowing how courageously and even gaily you have always made the best of the downs as well as the ups of the theatrical life, I would guess that you are probably one of those artists in illness. That you may recover to become once again an artist in another and less painful medium is my best wish and hope. But meanwhile I am afraid that the winter and the fuel crisis are not making things any easier for you. If there is anything I can send from here, do let me know and I shall be so very happy to see that you get it.

Not much news here, except that I have been working on a play—and also a movie script—based upon my old short story, 'The Gioconda Smile'. It has been quite interesting as a literary problem—this translation and development of an old theme into and through two different media. But I am glad that the jobs are nearly finished; for I have grown tired of the endless jig-saw puzzle and carpentry work that has to go into a play and, still more, into a scenario. Also, I find, one gets tired in a play of having to express everything in terms of dialogue. This would be all right if one were Shakespeare and could make of every exchange, every casual reflection, something astonishingly poetical. But not being Shakespeare, and working in the realistic medium of the modern play, one has to stick to conversational verisimilitude and to be, therefore, even less poetical than one is capable of being in narrative, where the medium permits of a greater freedom in the manipulation of words and a greater variety in the kinds of writing that it is possible to use. I have only just finished the second version of the play and have not yet heard the opinion on it of anyone directly concerned with theatrical production. It seems to me tolerably well constructed, and the story has been developed in such a way that the man who is falsely condemned for his wife's murder (I don't know if you ever read or recall the original short story, which was based on the Greenwood case of 192[0]) finds an internal solution by the acceptance of his fate, while the woman who actually did commit the murder and who seems to have successfully got away with it, refuses to accept the real state of things and thus breaks down into madness. By dividing the stage in the last act, I contrive to show, without interruption, alternating pictures of the one character on what, in spite of his circumstances, is the up grade, the other on a descending spiral. It remains to be seen whether the idea is better than the execution, or the one is as bad as the other.

I expect to sit down to a novel when play and movie are, for better or worse, completely off my hands. But it may be that, later on, I shall take your advice after all and try my hand again at the dramatic form. I feel I have learnt a good deal by the current experiment and that, in future, I should not make as many obvious mistakes as I made in my first essays. Meanwhile, in the intervals of jig-saw puzzlement and stage carpentry, I am reading and taking notes for the novel I have in mind—a historical affair about fourteenth-century Italy, a most fascinating period, in which all the colours of life are almost praeternaturally vivid, all the contrasts between light and shade intensified to the extreme limit. It is the age of the *Decameron* and Catherine of Siena, of Petrarch and the condottieri, of the Black Death and Sienese painting. All that remains is to combine the various elements into a good book!

Good bye, dear Leon, and God bless you.

Ever yours
Aldous H.

536: TO ANITA LOOS

145½ *S. Doheny,*
Los Angeles 36, Cal.
9 *March,* 1947

My dear Anita,

I read *She Stoops to Conquer* yesterday. The basic trouble is that an excellent comic idea based upon character is allowed to tail off at the end into the feeblest kind of comedy of situation. A man like Marlow, frigid with respectable women, but a dog with females of the lower classes, could never undergo the kind of conversion that Goldsmith makes him undergo. The discovery that the barmaid is Miss Hardcastle would freeze him, and he would only thaw out if she re-assumed the low-class character for the purposes of love making.

So far as I can see, the only way of making the play an acceptable offering for any audience more sophisticated than that which assembles for the end-of-term theatricals at a Junior High School would be to re-write it, developing to the full the mainly latent comedy of Goldsmith's basic character situation. I think it would have to be done along the lines of *Fanny's First Play*. It would begin with an introductory scene showing a group of young people—members of a Little Theatre Group or of some college dramatic class—discussing what they are going to put on, and agreeing to perform a revision of *She Stoops to Conquer* by one of their number. We then go into the play itself. Marlow is one of those classical cases, so dear to psychoanalysts, with a fixation on his mother, about which he feels sub-consciously guilty, so that he can't associate sex with respectability, but has to take it all out on tarts or housemaids. A parallel Freudian relationship exists between Mrs Hardcastle and Tony Lumpkin—the old lady having a kind of incestuous passion for her son, who responds with aversion—perhaps because he is a homosexual? (His big Bess Bouncer might become little Ben Bouncer.) Hastings and Miss

536 *Anita Loos had an idea for a new version of Goldsmith's play, to be written in collaboration with Huxley. The project was never carried out.*

Neville remain a bit of a problem. Perhaps the only thing to do with them is to make them even more conventional and normal than they are in Goldsmith. Old Mr Hardcastle would have to be made much more eccentric than he is. I visualize him as a kind of philosophical recluse, who comments upon all that is happening from the vantage ground of eternity, and acts as a kind of Greek chorus. The last scene between Marlow and Miss Hardcastle would show him reduced to paralysis and impotence by the discovery of her identity; but she would bring him to amorous life again by re-assuming her cockney accent and low-class brazen manner, going very nearly to the point of murmuring four-letter words into his ear. Meanwhile there would be at least one scene somewhere in the course of the play, showing the actors playing their modern selves, as in the introduction. Some sort of amusing story of their real-life, as opposed to their stage, relationships would have to be invented for them. These scenes would occupy the time taken in Goldsmith by the abyssmally un-funny scenes with the servants etc.

That anything satisfactory can be done with the piece, short of this kind of radical re-writing, seems to me doubtful. The points to be considered are these: is this idea, or another along the same kind of lines, good enough to warrant the work involved? and are audiences sufficiently well acquainted with the original Goldsmith to see the point of what is being done? This last is rather important; and I think that it would be advisable in any case to have one of the characters in the introductory scene read out a synopsis of the original play. This would be commented on, as being intolerably dull and silly, but as possessing great possibilities which might be realized if the character situations were properly developed.

Our original idea of having a Freudian comment upon Goldsmith's play as it proceeded doesn't seem to me to be radical enough. Goldsmith's *dénouement*, with its relapse into mere situation-comedy, its disregard of psychological verisimilitude, could only be talked about by the people in the wings, not corrected. The end would remain uninteresting and improbable, ruining what went before. Hence nothing less than a re-writing can serve our purpose. And yet the public must know what has been accomplished in the re-writing. Hence the need of the synopsis of Goldsmith in the first scene.

If you feel that something can be done along these lines and that it would be worth doing, we might think in greater detail about the modern frame and about a stream-lined construction for the revised Goldsmith.

All goes well here. We expect to be in town till the end of this week and then, if everything works out according to plan, we shall return to Wrightwood.

Ever yours affectionately,
Aldous

P.S In view of the O'Neill-like nature of Marlow, we might call the new version 'She Stoopeth to Conquer'.

Wrightwood, Cal.
26 March, 1947

Dearest Anita,

I think you're right as to postponing any further thinking about *She Stoops to Conquer*. It is an idea which might be worth keeping in mind, in case any particularly favourable combination of circumstances in the shape of ideal actors and producers should happen to arise. But unless the circumstances arose, it wouldn't be worth taking the very considerable trouble that would be involved.

[. . . .]

Not much news here. I potter around with the beginnings of a historical novel—only to wonder whether I know enough about the period to do it as I should like to do it. Going to the other extreme, I think perhaps I may write something about the future instead—about, among other things, a post-atomic-war society in which the chief effect of the gamma radiations had been to produce a race of men and women who don't make love all the year round, but have a brief mating season. The effect of this on politics, religion, ethics etc would be something very interesting and amusing to work out.

Maria sends her love, as do I.

Ever your affectionate,
Aldous

538: TO CLAIRE NICOLAS

[Wrightwood, Calif.]
[Spring, 1947]

My dear Claire,

Here is the article with suggested emendations. Krishnamurti is not a Vedantist, nor is Gerald Heard—tho' both have affinities with Vedanta. I have omitted Prabhavananda's name, because the significant fact is not that he personally is in S. Calif, but that the Vedanta Society has branches all

538 *Article: the draft of Claire Nicolas' 'Aldous Huxley', afterwards published in* Vogue (*New York*), *1 August, 1947. Huxley rewrote the paragraph on Vedanta, adding this note: 'The rest of the article can stand, except for the sentence beginning "His political writings . . ." and ending "his opinion", which I do not understand. No book is any more than the expression of the author's opinion, and in* Ends and Means *at least there are specific statements of my opinion as to political and economic reform—the whole point of the book being that the problem is too complex to be solved in terms of political reform alone or personal reform alone, but must be attacked simultaneously on all fronts. I would suggest the omission of this sentence altogether, or the substitution of another. E.g. "In his political writings he insists that politics are never enough and that the human problem is insoluble unless it be attacked simultaneously on all its fronts—the personal front as well as the political, the religious and philosophical as well as the economic".'*

over the USA, in S. America and in many European countries and that monks are trained in India to run these various branches.

I hope all goes well with you and the family and that you will get the *Vogue* job, which sounds as if it might be very interesting. We have often missed you all. Coccola and Matthew join me in sending best love.

Ever yours affectionately,
Aldous

P.S. The film is *not* being made by Selznick. Better not mention anyone in connection with it, as negotiations are in progress now.

539: TO IGOR STRAVINSKY

Wrightwood, Cal.
9 April, 1947

Dear Mr. Stravinsky,

I have unfortunately mislaid your address and am writing this note to my memory of it. Would you please send me a postcard to say if it is correct, and I will return your book by registered mail. (I did not like to risk it in the post without being certain of the address.)

I have greatly enjoyed and profited by the reading of your lectures—only regretting that some (particularly the one on time) are not longer. How profoundly I agree with you about Wagner. I heard a bit of the *Parsifal* Good Friday music at Easter time on the radio, and it made me feel even more 'sick to my stomach', as the Americans say, than in the past. Wagner's idea of spirituality was a kind of *onanisme prolongé à l'infini*. I look forward to seeing you at the market when we are next in town and to talking at leisure about some of the many interesting points contained in your book. Meanwhile, I am most grateful to you for having given me this opportunity of reading it.

My wife joins me in sending kindest regards to Madame Stravinsky and yourself.

Yours very sincerely
Aldous Huxley

540: TO MATTHEW HUXLEY

Doheny Drive,
17 *June,* [1947]

Dearest M.,

This letter must begin as a slight stinker. We have just seen Stravinsky, who tells us that he has received a letter from Claire, telling him that you had

540 *Claire Nicolas' article on Stravinsky had been published in the magazine* Junior Bazaar. *It was Claire Nicolas and her sister Sylvia who first introduced Huxley to Stravinsky, while lunching in the Los Angeles Town and Country Market. Huxley's problems with the film of* The Gioconda Smile *were gradually solved. The picture was made under the direction of Zoltan Korda and was released in* 1948 *under the title* A Woman's Vengeance.

told her that he didn't like her article, because she hadn't mentioned the books in his library etc. Whether Claire was wise in sending him the letter is neither here nor there.

The point is that you shouldn't—especially almost on the day of your arrival—have made a disobliging criticism of Claire's work, which must (to judge by the way Stravinsky described the letter) have upset her. And you shouldn't have made remarks about Stravinsky in a quarter from which they might so easily return to him. We did our best to soothe Stravinsky's obviously ruffled feelings, excusing you on the ground (which, to judge by your letter, is probably the true one) that you were tired by the journey, felt in a bad mood, had been in some way irritated by Claire and had put her in her place by telling her something that would depress her about her article. The net result is that he probably won't be too cordial when he sees you again, as he seems to have something of the elephant's memory for real or fancied slights. So for heaven's sake be careful in the future. Don't let physical fatigue or other bodily discomforts influence your mood to the point of saying unwise or uncharitable things. (This will be particularly important for you to remember in the semi-diplomatic career you mean to embark on.) And don't feel impelled to put people in their places, except for the most urgent and important reasons, or to disparage what they have done or what belongs to them, except for even weightier reasons. It does them no good and may do you a great deal of harm by stirring up bad feeling in all concerned.

I expect to have to be in town for a few days, patching up the script after its mangling by the censors. The Johnson office will not permit divorce to be mentioned on the screen, draws a line at pregnancy among the unmarried and won't allow anyone who has committed adultery to be represented as being anything but unhappy after the event. However, I don't think any serious harm has been done; and the scenes that have had to be taken out were not essential and integral parts of the main story line. Their removal permits the essential scenes to be treated with greater fulness—so the censors may prove, after all, to have been a blessing in disguise. Meanwhile [Claude] Raines doesn't want to play the doctor's part any more, because some of his scenes have been taken out to give more scope to [Charles] Boyer [. . . .]. It is wonderful how well actors always live up to character.

The house goes forward quite rapidly. The roof is on already, and it looks as though the final effect would be very pleasant, both from outside and in.

I hope you are having a nice time in New York and seeing pleasant people. Let us have a letter from time to time. Love from us both.

Your affectionate,
Aldous

P.S Don't pass the buck to Claire—which will only make matters worse. But just remember, for the future, and be thankful that, after all, this isn't of any real importance—merely a salutary lesson.

Wrightwood, Calif.
4 July, 1947

My dear Anita,

It was good to get your letter and to know that you are bearing up under the heat and all your theatrical projects. I hope these last mature satisfactorily.

I am glad you liked the script. Since the version Matthew showed you, a new one has come out. The censors demanded the cutting of various scenes —fortunately not essential ones; and the information they were meant to convey (about the young girl's pre-marital pregnancy) can be put across, not by honest statement, but by 'becks and nods and wreathed smiles', the principle of the Johnson Office's morality being that nothing may be said in a decent way but that all may be suggested indecently. The cutting has permitted a certain expansion of the vital scenes, to the advantage of character development, I think. The tag which you like will probably have to go, as the censors cannot permit anyone who has ever committed adultery to be shown as being happy! This is something which even Tartuffe and Pecksniff could never have imagined. I expect to go to town to-morrow for a few days to sit in at rehearsals. I saw some tests of Jessica Tandy, the English actress who is playing Janet; and she struck me as quite excellent. And the young girl who is playing Doris—Ann Blyth—is an excellent little actress. We failed to get Raines, as he wanted a salary raise and the Studio casting manager was adamant. 'In this Studio', he told Korda, 'not even Jesus Christ could get a raise in salary.' (It would make a splendid subject for a religious painting—the Saviour before Mannix, Katz and Mayer, pleading for a hike in his wages, and being turned down cold.) In consequence, we shall probably have Cedric Hardwicke as Libbard. I shall be very curious to see how the thing works out. Meanwhile there is talk of the Korda brothers, Alex and Zoltan, doing *Point Counter Point*, if I make the script. Which I wouldn't mind doing under the same conditions as I have done this one— that is, with no interference from producers, only consultation with the director.

Did you, I wonder, get the wood block of your letter head, which Maria sent by registered mail some weeks ago? If by any chance it didn't reach you, we ought to start an investigation.

Best love from us both.

Ever yours affectionately,
Aldous

541 *Huxley used the remark about a salary rise in* Ape and Essence, *Chapter I.*

Wrightwood, Calif.
27 July, 1947

My dear Anita,

How sweet of you to remember my birthday and to send me the volume of Augustus John, which has a more than aesthetic interest for me inasmuch as it contains portraits of several old friends, some dead, some still alive. Thank you very much indeed.

We are up here for a week or so, as there doesn't seem to be any urgent necessity, for the moment, for me to be near the studio. We had some trouble last week, when [——] began throwing his temperament around, saying that he could only be photographed so as to show the right side of his face (because the left was less beautiful!) and calling for modifications of some of his scenes. Korda finally persuaded him to let the left side appear at least occasionally, and I have made a few changes which strengthen one or two of his scenes without altering their import. When I left all seemed to be going pretty well. Meanwhile the scenes already filmed between Jessica Tandy and Hardwicke are quite admirable. She is a first-rate actress and seems to be likely to turn in a performance which will make most of the more celebrated Hollywood stars look merely silly. I shall go back again to town next week to see how things are going and talk over some of Boyer's worries about the final tag scene, which will be shot, but is certain to be cut out by the censors, because it shows an adulterer living in happiness.

The ticklish situation on the set made it impossible to come to New York for Claire's wedding. But we hope and intend to make the trip after the picture is finished, in September. It will be good to see you then. Meanwhile I hope all goes well with you.

Maria sends her love, as do I.

Yours affectionately,
Aldous

543: TO SWAMI PRABHAVANANDA

Wrightwood, Cal.
1 *August,* 1947

Dear Swami,

Thank you for your letter. The news of Dr. Kolisch's disaster is very sad. One can only be thankful that nobody was hurt. There have been several fires here, owing to the dry, hot weather—small ones, but still terrible. And to think that, during the war years, men deliberately caused fires on the most enormous scale!

I was very glad to have the *Crest Jewel* in its new dress and with your

542 *Wedding: Claire Nicolas was married to Robert Winthrop White, an artist.*

kindest dedication. It is a book that I often turn back to, and as I cannot read it in the original, it is very helpful to have it in a different translation from that with which I am familiar.

I will send you an article within the next two weeks. Indeed I will probably send you two articles—one a note on William Law which I wrote for a new edition of [Stephen] Hobhouse's selections from his writings, and the other a note on a volume of material issued by the newly founded Zen Institute of America.

Yours very sincerely
Aldous Huxley

544: †TO JEANNE AND GEORGES NEVEUX

Wrightwood, California
2 September, 1947

Chère Jeanne et cher Georges,

Je suis très heureux d'apprendre que la traduction de la pièce s'avance et, en même temps, très reconnaissant, cher Georges, que vous ayez donné à *Mortal Coils* le temps dont vous auriez pu faire usage pour votre propre travail.

Je viens de lire les épreuves de la pièce et je me rends compte (à un an de distance de sa composition et à la lumière de l'expérience gagnée en

544 TRANSLATION:—'*I am very happy to learn that the translation of the play goes forward and, at the same time, very grateful, dear Georges, that you have given to* Mortal Coils *the time you would have been able to use for your own work.*

'*I have just read proofs of the play and I notice (at a year's distance from its composition and in the light of the experience gained in getting the film ready and seeing it shot) that there are in the text some long-drawn-out passages which call for the surgeon. Already announced, the book is in the press, and it is impossible for me to undertake the necessary operations before its publication. But I should be even more grateful if, in translating and adapting, you could make the cuts you deem necessary with a view to a performance in a French theatre. Your trained eye will at once see the places where cutting is needed to quicken the tempo and strengthen the dramatic effect.*

'*The film is not yet finished; but so far it has all been admirably acted, and I hope the whole thing will be as good as the first two-thirds.*

'*I have written to the William Morris Agency, and you will receive a letter soon, either from America or from their European representative. Morris will make the formal contracts with you and with the eventual producer. Meanwhile this letter will do as a provisional contract between the author and the translator-adapters of the play.*

'*About the fifteenth of September we are thinking of leaving for New York, where our address will be at Suzanne's in Islip. Affectionately. . . .*'

Huxley's sister-in-law, Jeanne, and her husband, Georges Neveux, undertook the translation and adaptation of his play The Gioconda Smile *for the French stage. Neveux's works include* Plainte contre Inconnu *and* Zamore. *He also made a French dramatic adaptation of Anne Frank's* Diary of a Young Girl.

préparant et en voyant exécuter le film) qu'il y a dans le texte des longueurs qui appellent le chirurgien. Déjà annoncé, le livre est en impression, et il m'est impossible d'entreprendre avant sa publication les opérations nécessaires. Mais je serais encore plus reconnaissant si vous pouviez, en traduisant et adaptant, faire les coupures que vous jugerez nécessaires en vue d'une représentation dans un théâtre français. Votre oeil exercé verra de suite les endroits où il faut couper pour accélérer le tempo et pour fortifier l'effet dramatique.

Le film n'est pas encore achevé; mais jusqu'à présent tout a été admirablement bien joué, et j'espère que le tout sera aussi bon que les premiers deux tiers.

J'ai écrit à l'agence William Morris, et vous recevrez bientôt une lettre, ou d'Amérique, ou de leur représentant européen. C'est Morris qui fera avec vous et avec le metteur en scène éventuel les contrats formels. En attendant cette lettre servira de contrat provisoire entre l'auteur et les traducteurs-adapteurs de la pièce.

Vers le quinze septembre nous pensons partir pour New York, où notre adresse sera chez Suzanne à Islip.

Affectueusement,
Aldous

545: TO GERVAS HUXLEY

[*Little Rock, Arkansas*],
as from Wrightwood, Cal.
14 *November, 1947*

My dear Gervas,

From the Blue Bird Motel in Little Rock, Ark, where we have been held up by torrential rains, I take this opportunity of telling you how grateful we all are for your wonderfully timely and almost providential intervention on behalf of Matthew. Before leaving NY, we were able to see him settled quite comfortably into an, all things considered, very nice apartment in the West seventies, which he managed to secure by putting on all his charm for the elderly spinster who owned the building. He starts under very favourable auspices, and I hope and think that all will go well with him in his new life.

We saw Julian and Juliette on their way through to Mexico, and on the whole I found Julian better and more relaxed than I had expected he would be under the strain of his job. I gather that the Mexican conference is being rather stormy, and hope he will pull through without mishap. He was cheerful on the surface, though basically very pessimistic, in the sense of not seeing how it was going to be possible, within the current nationalistic frames of

545 *Matthew Huxley was just entering upon his new job with the Elmo Roper organization, in public-opinion analysis.*

reference, to achieve any real unity—and further being unable to see how, with the Russians resisting every attempt to mitigate national sovereignty, there could be any change in the patterns which condition all our collective thinking, feeling and action.

We saw the finally cut version of the 'Gioconda Smile' movie before leaving —very satisfactory, I think, except for the fact that the all-powerful Jewish gentlemen in charge of distribution have elected to call the thing *A Woman's Vengeance*, and there is nothing to be done about it. The consolation is that the title is seen for only thirty seconds and that the picture, thanks to the untiring resourcefulness of Zoltan Korda, came through the cutting rooms without losing anything from any of the essential scenes.

Meanwhile it is raining harder and harder and Little Rock feels every minute more and more remote from anywhere. However, the Blue Bird is clean and comfortable; so let us be thankful for small mercies.

Our love to your both.

Ever yours affectionately,
Aldous

546: †TO GEORGES NEVEUX

[145½ *S. Doheny Drive,*
Los Angeles, Calif.]
15 *December,* 1947

Cher Georges,

Je vous envoie le 2me acte, qui marche, je crois, très bien. Comme vous verrez, j'ai indiqué plusieurs coupures considérables. Je les ai faites à la

546 TRANSLATION:—'*I am sending you the 2nd act, which goes along, I think, very well. As you will see, I have indicated several considerable cuts. I have made them in the light of the experience gained in seeing the film shot. The Doris-Libbard scene (after the suicide) has succeeded well in the film, and I have tried to assimilate the play to the film, as much as possible, in this passage. In the film, the little actress, Ann Blyth, who is only 19 years old, is extremely touching. She weeps softly from the start— with tears due, one feels, as much to the physical shock that she has undergone as to all the rest; this reinforces the retort of Libbard about women who weep sensually and about the need for being strong and calm. When he gives Doris the napkin to dry her face, and when she uses it with a childishly heroic effort to control herself, the effect is very fine.*

'*For the same reason I have changed the scene between Doris and Hutton (p. 49). In the film this new version goes very well. One sees that Hutton suddenly notices Doris' devotion—the fact that she is fully a person in her own right and not simply the instrument of his own pleasures. Boyer knew how to create an atmosphere of tenderness, very simple and without any sentimentality, and I believe that we shall do well to provide the actor in the play with the chance to do the same thing with the same means.*

'*Nobody has approached me on playing* The World of Light—*but I will not give permission to play it before the birth of the other. Very affectionately to you both. . . .*'

Libbard: in the screen production this rôle was taken by Sir Cedric Hardwicke.

576

lumière de l'expérience gagnée en voyant exécuter le film. La scène Doris-Libbard (après le suicide) est très réussie dans le film, et j'ai tâché d'assimiler la pièce au film, autant que possible, dans ce passage. Dans le film, la petite actrice, Ann Blyth, qui n'a que 19 ans est extrêmement touchante. Elle pleure doucement depuis le début—avec des larmes dûes, on le sent, autant au choc physique qu'elle a subi qu'à tout le reste, ceci renforce la réplique de Libbard sur les femmes qui pleurent par sensualité et sur la nécessité d'être forte et calme. Quand il donne à Doris la serviette pour s'essuyer le visage, et quand elle l'emploie avec un effort enfantinement héroique de se contrôler, l'effet est très beau.

Pour la même raison j'ai changé la scène entre Doris et Hutton (p. 49). Dans le film cette nouvelle version va très bien. On voit que Hutton subitement se rend compte du dévouement de Doris—du fait qu'elle est pleinement une personne en son propre droit et non simplement l'instrument de ses plaisirs à lui. Boyer a su créer une atmosphère de tendresse très simple et sans aucune sentimentalité, et je crois que nous ferons bien de fournir à l'acteur de la pièce l'occasion de faire la même chose avec les mêmes moyens.

Personne ne m'a proposé de jouer le *Monde de la Lumière*—mais je ne donnerai pas la permission de le jouer avant la par[turi]tion de l'autre.

> *Bien affectueusement à vous deux,*
> *Aldous*

547: †TO GEORGES NEVEUX

Wrightwood, California
30 December, 1947

Cher Georges,

Merci pour le 2me acte. Je vous le renvoie avec les quelques suggestions que j'ai marquées. Dans la version française de l'Ancien Testament est-ce bien 'votre vengeance est mienne' qui traduit le 'vengeance is mine, saith the Lord' du verset 35 du 32me chapitre de Deuteronomie? Dieu sait ce que signifie la phrase en hébreu; mais en anglais elle veut dire que la vengeance est au Seigneur et non pas aux hommes—que justice, malgré tout, sera faite. Pour le reste je trouve que tout marche très bien et je vous remercie encore

547 TRANSLATION:—'*Thank you for the 2nd act. I am sending it back to you with the few suggestions which I have marked. In the French version of the Old Testament, is it really "your vengeance is mine" which translates the "vengeance is mine, saith the Lord" of verse 35 of the 32nd chapter of Deuteronomy? God knows what the phrase signifies in Hebrew; but in English it means that vengeance is to the Lord and not to men —that justice, in spite of all, shall be done. For the rest I find that everything proceeds very well and I thank you once more for all that you have done for the play. I have the impression, as I read it, of having miraculously learnt to write French.*

'*Happy new year and love to all. Affectionately. . . .*'

Vengeance: the passage Huxley was thinking of is Romans 12:19.

une fois de tout ce que vous avez fait pour la pièce. J'ai l'impression, [pendant] que je la lis, d'avoir miraculeusement appris à écrire en français.

Bonne année et love à tous,

Affectueusement,
Aldous

548: TO FAIRFIELD OSBORN

Wrightwood, Cal.
16 *January,* 1948

Dear Mr Osborn,

I have to thank you for having given me the opportunity of reading your very interesting book [*Our Plundered Planet*]. I airmailed a few words to Little, Brown last Tuesday, and hope that they will have got them in time. The great question now is: will the public and those in authority pay any attention to what you say, or will the politicians go on with their lunatic game of power politics, ignoring the fact that the world they are squabbling over will very shortly cease to exist in its old familiar form, but will be transformed, unless they mobilize all available intelligence and all available good will, into one huge dust bowl inhabited by creatures whom progressive hunger will make more and more sub-human? I have been trying to put this question to the general and specialized publics for the last year or two—even succeeding in planting it in the *Bulletin of the Atomic Scientists* this summer, pointing out that, while mankind could do very well without atomic energy, it cannot dispense with bread. But hitherto I have had no audible response from any quarter. I hope very much that you, with your scientific authority and your beautifully organized collection of facts, will be able to make some impression in influential quarters. But, alas, in view of what politicians and the voting public are like, hope must always be mingled with a great deal of doubt.

My own interests in recent years have turned increasingly in the direction of philosophy and mystical religion, and I see this problem of man's relation to Nature as not only an immediate practical problem, but also as a problem in ethics and religion. It is significant that neither Christianity nor Judaism has ever thought of Nature as having rights in relation to man, or as being in some way intrinsically divine. You will find orthodox Catholic moralists asserting (on the basis of those extremely unfortunate remarks in Genesis) that animals may be treated as things. (As though things didn't deserve to be treated ethically!) The vulgar boast of the modern technologist to the effect that man has conquered Nature has roots in the Western religious tradition, which affirms that God installed man as the boss, to whom Nature was to bring tribute. The Greeks knew better than the Jews and Christians. They knew that hubris towards Nature was as much of a sin as hubris towards fellow men. Xerxes is punished, not only for having attacked the Greeks, by also for having outraged Nature in the affair of bridging the Hellespont.

But for an ethical system that includes animate and inanimate Nature as well as man, one must go to Chinese Taoism, with its concept of an Order of Things, whose state of wu-wei, or balance, must be preserved; of an indwelling Lagos or Tao, which is immanent on every level of existence from the physical, through the physiological, up to the mental and the spiritual. In many passages, particularly of the *Specimen Days in America*, Whitman comes very close to the Taoist position. And because of Whitman and Wordsworth and the other 'Nature mystics' of the West, I feel that it might not be too difficult for modern Europeans and Americans to accept some kind of Taoist philosophy of life, with an ethical system comprehensive enough to take in Nature as well as man. People have got to understand that the commandment, 'Do unto others as you would that they should do unto you' applies to animals, plants and things, as well as to people; and that if it is regarded as applying only to people (as it has been in the Christian West), then the animals, plants and things will, in one way or another, do as badly by man as man has done by them. It seems to me that, if we are to have a better policy towards Nature, we must also have a better philosophy.

Yours very sincerely,
Aldous Huxley

549: TO LEWIS GIELGUD

Wrightwood, Cal.
25 January, 1948

My dear Lewis,

I was quite delighted to get the photograph of your offspring. She looks a most determined young lady, as well as a most charming and humorous one. And meanwhile how are things going with you? And how is Brussels? One gets mixed accounts—half of prosperity, half of the horrors of black market and high prices. Maria's uncle, Georges Baltus, who is now over 75 and has recently married again, groans a good deal over the latter: but then he is a rentier, living on an unelastic income.

I met your brother Jack in the street this autumn—in New York. He looked, I thought, romantically battered—perhaps as the result of playing opposite Miss Judith Anderson as Medea. Another unexpected meeting in N Y was with Gervas—on tea business, as usual; considerably strained, but nicer than ever. His is one of those vintages that improve with age. Julian also was there, en route to Mexico and the yearly conference of Unesco. The job is a pretty harassing one; but he seemed better in health and spirits than I had expected. Meanwhile I wish one cd feel much optimism about Unesco, or about any other international organization, for that matter. It's the old story: nobody wants war, but everybody wants all the things that make for war. And nobody pays any attention to the basic situation—which

549 *Offspring: Lewis and Zita Gielgud's daughter, Maina. Jack is John Gielgud.*

is that population is rushing up and soil fertility rushing down, so that in a couple of generations most of the planet will be a dust bowl inhabited by the starving and ruled (since democracy is incompatible with hunger) by tyrants.

I am working at present on a phantasy about the future and hope after that to make a screen adaptation of one of my old short stories, 'The Rest Cure'. I turned another short story, 'The Gioconda Smile', into a film last year, and as I had only the director to deal with—Zoltan Korda, brother of Alexander Korda—and as the director was intelligent and nice, the job was interesting and the result, I think, quite good. The thing is to be released next month. I also did a stage version of the same story, which (according to latest reports) is to be put on in London this spring and perhaps also (in a translation by Jeanne's husband, Georges Neveux) in Paris. In New York the production fell through, as producers are very shy of doing anything of which the film rights are already sold—costs being so high that they depend on their share of movie sales to make ends meet.

Our love to you both.

Ever yours affectionately
Aldous

550: TO HAROLD RAYMOND

Wrightwood, Cal.
2 February, 1948

My dear Harold,
Your letter of the 29th came in today. I will send a blurb about the new book in a day or two; but meanwhile a word about the play title. This is in a state of hideous confusion. The film *was* called *Mortal Coils*, as nobody was supposed to know who the Gioconda was. Then suddenly it was announced as a fait accompli (and with no redress or possibility of change) that it was to be called *A Woman's Vengeance*—shades of Mrs. Henry Wood! Meanwhile the play was originally called *Mortal Coils* to conform with the film. Then, foreseeing the difficulty you might have with the volume of short stories still in print, I changed it back on the script I sent you to *Gioconda*. But I have an awful suspicion that the script which Mr. Jack De Leon, the producer, is using is titled 'Mortal Coils'—and the U S edition comes out under that title (without the alterations I sent you). So it is all in rather a muddle. If you think the printed play shd have the same title as the acted (shd it be produced, which I assume it will) perhaps it wd be as well if you asked De Leon to adopt *Gioconda*. Sorry for this comedy of errors.

In haste
Aldous

550 *The play was produced in London, and later in New York, under the title* The Gioconda Smile, *which was also used for the London editions. The same title was afterwards adopted for the New York edition, though this first appeared as* Mortal Coils.

Wrightwood, Cal.
24 February, 1948

My dear Cass,

Thank you for yours of the sixteenth. I am sorry the anthology [*The World of Aldous Huxley*] has not done better; let us hope it will go on quietly selling. In regard to the payments on it—wouldn't it be best for Harpers to pay me what I have actually earned on current sales up to, let us say, the spring of 1949, when the whole situation can be re-examined in the light of what has happened in the interval?

I have just finished my book and propose to go into Los Angeles to-morrow to get it typed. It runs to about fifty thousand words. Because of its brevity, and above all because of the character of the story, I think it might not be a bad idea to consider the possibility of illustrations. The problem is, Whose illustrations? It would be wonderful if one could get Tchelichev. Alternatively there is Covarrubias, who might be very good on the more savage and satirical aspects of the book. Or there is my brother-in-law, Joep Nicolas, who did some charming illustrations for an edition of *Tristan and Iseult*—but the trouble with him is that he might tend to be too decorative for the subject matter. When you read the script, you will be able to judge for yourself if you think the idea of illustrations is a good one and, if good, who should be the illustrator.

I am choosing a Shakespearean title, as one can't go far wrong with the Bard—from *Measure for Measure*

> Man, proud man,
> Drest in a little brief authority—
> Most ignorant of what he is most assured,
> His glassy essence—like an angry ape,
> Plays such fantastic tricks before high heaven
> As make the angels weep.

The title will be *Ape and Essence*. If all goes well the script should be ready within about a week, and I will send you a copy immediately.

Meanwhile would you please have three copies of *The Perennial Philosophy* sent to me and charged to my account? I seem to have run out of the book completely.

Ever yours,
Aldous

551 The World of Aldous Huxley *had sold* 5,000 *copies instead of the expected* 15,000.

Wrightwood, Cal.
3 June, 1948

Dearest J,

I was delighted to get your long and interesting letter about the middle east, though sorry to hear of the dysenteric consequences of the journey. In the last few months I have heard of so many people returning from Mexico, North Africa and the like, with amoebae in their inwards—sometimes with most unpleasant long-range results. So I do hope you will have yourself promptly and thoroughly disinfected.

Our plans have almost suddenly materialized. We are going to Italy where I shall write the screen play for an up-to-date version of my old short story, 'The Rest Cure', for the Korda organization—they paying me for the story rights by financing our trip out of blocked currencies. Cunard has promised us passages some time between June seventeenth and twenty-fifth and we shall be in New York from the fifteenth onwards. (Actually I shall be there a few days earlier, for some kind of a conference on modern art, which Henry Luce of *Life* and *Time* is calling—I don't quite know why; but that is his affair.) Hotel St Regis will be our address, in case you want to or have time to write. We should be in France before the end of the month, as we shall go direct to Cherbourg. Length of stay in Paris will depend on your whereabouts. We might either stay for a week or two when we arrive, or, if it works out more conveniently for you, in September, on the way back from Italy.

I will bring with me the article I did on population last year ['The Double Crisis']. It is rather long, but I think covers a lot of ground. One can put the problem dramatically by telling people that world population increases about fifty-five thousand a day, while erosion knocks out about an equal number of fertile acres per day. In such a context every piece of medical good news—as, for example, the hope that DDT combined with new quinine substitutes may largely diminish the death toll from malaria—is a piece of bad news; for all it means is that people will be preserved from one kind of death in order to increase their own and everyone else's prospects of dying from some other kind of death. And meanwhile the whole problem is complicated by the differential birth-rate as between nations—Russia increasing by 75 millions during the next 25 years, France and England each declining by 4 millions, while the number of the aged among the survivors doubles—and as between classes—the more intelligent members of society not reproducing themselves, so that Cecil [i.e., Sir Cyril] Burt sees a drop in the average intelligence of the British population (and of other Western populations) of 5 IQ points before the end of the present century. And meanwhile we have to consider whether a sudden falling off of the birth-rate may not be a very serious biological symptom. Raymond Pearl seems to think so, and there are interesting remarks on the subject in that excellent book of James Halliday's, *Psycho-Social Medicine*, which came out here this spring, but may have come out earlier in England. (If you haven't read this, do. It is very interesting and very intelligent.) I noticed in *Nature* the other day that the British Government called a conference on the subject of the increasing neurosis and psycho-somatic disease rate as a factor militating against production. It appears that neurosis now causes as much loss of man-hours as the common cold and influenza. And it's on the up-grade. The more we advance technologically, the dottier we become. And the dottier the parents, the super-dottier are the children. So that the advance is by geometrical progression.

I read a review the other day of a book which might be very significant in your projected scientific and cultural history of mankind—a work by a Swiss historian on the history of machinery and mechanization of work. It seems to be a vast and learned work, profusely illustrated, and sounds absolutely fascinating.

I will cable you as soon as I know when we sail—which won't be, in all probability, till after the fifteenth of the month. Meanwhile I have taken the liberty of having my letters forwarded to you care of Unesco, Avenue Kléber. Would you please ask your secretary to keep them until I call for them?

Our best love to you both.

Ever your affectionate,
Aldous

553: TO VICTORIA OCAMPO

Wrightwood, Cal.
6 June, 1948

Chere Victoria,

Votre gentille lettre m'a trouvé au lit (virus pneumonia) et c'est avec un grand retard que je vous en remercie. Je suis très content que vous ayez

553 TRANSLATION:—'*Your kind letter found me in bed (virus pneumonia) and I am a good deal behindhand in thanking you for it. I am very happy that you liked the film. Korda and I are preparing another one, based on another story which I wrote a long time ago, which will be made in Italy. So as to bring the story up to date, giving it a "post-war" setting, we are going to Italy this summer. (We hope to be able to depart from New York on the 17th or the 24th of this month.) I will drop you a line from over there.*

'*Meanwhile I have talked with [——] on the subject of a film about T. E. Lawrence. [——] is a nice boy, but very ill—he suffers from cardiac asthma—and of a vague, incoherent, and spasmodic temperament. Furthermore he has the tendency to live above his intellectual means. He is a good actor, but he also wants to be a great director, a great*

[Continued overleaf

583

aimé le film. Korda et moi nous en préparons un autre, basé sur une autre nouvelle que j'ai écrite il y a longtemps, et qui sera fait en Italie. C'est pour mettre l'histoire à la page en lui donnant un 'post-war setting', que nous allons en Italie cet été. (Nous espérons pouvoir partir de New York le 17 ou 24 de ce mois courant.) Je vous écrirai un mot de là-bas.

En attendant j'ai parlé avec [———] au sujet du film sur T. E. L[awrence]. [———] est un gentil garçon, mais trés malade—il souffre d'un asthme cardiaque—et de tempérament vague, décousu et spasmodique. En autre il a la tendance de vivre au-delà de ses moyens intellectuels. Il est bon acteur, mais il veut être aussi un grand directeur, un grand écrivain, un grand innovateur artistique. Tout ceci est assez dangereux; car le cinéma est une entreprise co-opérative qui demande la collaboration de beaucoup de compétences speciales et souvent psychologiquement incompatibles, dans le sens qu'elles ne peuvent pas coexister dans une seule personne.

Quant au film considéré en soi et en dehors de [———], je ne vois pas très clairement comment on pourrait le faire. Un personnage riche et en conflit avec lui-même est très difficile à représenter à l'écran, qui ne tolère aucun soliloque, peu d'explications verbales et guère de références aux intérêts supérieurs—artistiques, philosophiques, religieux etc—d'un esprit supérieur. Dans les années mouvementées de guerre nous nous trouvons en face d'un embarras de richesse—trop de personnages, une intrigue trés compliquée. D'ailleurs les Arabes sont les héros—et tout le monde en Amérique les déteste—et les Turcs, qui sont maintenant des 'défenseurs de The American Way of Life', sont l'Ennemi. Je crois que la seule possibilité serait d'isoler un bref épisode—peut-être à la fin de la vie, et de le présenter (avec des 'flashbacks') dans la forme d'un drame bien serré et solidement bâti. En tout cas c'est un problème très dur à résoudre. J'ai devant moi deux films pour Korda et mon roman historique qui demanderont plusieurs

---

writer, a great artistic innovator. All this is pretty dangerous; for the movies are a co-operative enterprise which calls for the collaboration of many special talents, often psychologically incompatible in the sense that they cannot coexist in one person alone.

'As to the film, considered in itself and apart from [———], I don't very clearly see how it could be done. A complex character in conflict with himself is very difficult to portray on the screen, which tolerates no soliloquy, few verbal explanations and hardly any references to the superior interests—artistic, philosophical, religious etc.—of a superior mind. In the turmoil of wartime we are confronted with an embarras de richesse—too many characters, a very tangled plot. Besides, the Arabs are the heroes— and in America everybody detests them—and the Turks, who are now "defenders of The American Way of Life", are the enemy. I believe that the only possibility would be to isolate a brief episode—perhaps at the end of the life, and to present it (with flash-backs) in the form of a well knit, solidly built drama. In any case it is a very hard problem to solve. I have ahead of me two films for Korda and my historical novel which will require several years of work. Thus it will not be possible for me to busy myself with it. Love from us both. Affectionately. . . .'

années de travail. Donc il ne me sera pas possible de m'en occuper. Love
de nous deux.

Affectueusement
Aldous

554: † TO DILIP KUMAR ROY

Hotel St. Regis, New York
16 June, 1948

Dear Mr. Dilip Kumar Roy,

Thanks for your letter. I have been a bad correspondent, I fear. I think
I wrote to you about your *Among the Great*, saying how much I liked the
section on Sri Aurobindo and how helpful I found it.

Sri Aurobindo's poem 'Savitri' I have not yet read but if I see Blum
or Gide in France—and I expect to be in that country for a short time this
summer—I will find out what is being done about the Nobel Prize recommendation and add a word of my own, if they think that would be of any
avail, in favour of Sri Aurobindo's *Life Divine*, which I regard as a book
not merely of the highest importance as regards its content, but remarkably
fine as a piece of philosophic and religious literature.

I expect to be travelling for several months and it will not be until the
autumn that I shall be able to listen to the phonograph records you are so
kindly sending me.

I am asking my publishers to send you a copy of my book *The Perennial
Philosophy*—in the hope that you may be interested in this new treatment of
a very ancient theme.

Yours very sincerely,
Aldous Huxley

555: TO HAROLD RAYMOND

Palazzo Ravizza,
Pian dei Mantinelli, Siena
20 July, 1948

My dear Harold,

Thank you for your letter, with its interesting information about the
possibilities of paper allocations and the word about the play. The reviews
I saw were mixed—poor in the *New Statesman* and *Times*, good in the
Spectator, Daily Mail, Standard and elsewhere. The favourable on the whole
dominating. So I suppose they were able to get all the blurbs they wanted.
I shall be curious to see it and to compare Pamela Brown's performance
with that of Jessica Tandy in the movie, and the play's doctor (I forget his
name) with the quite admirable playing of Cedric Hardwicke. In Paris I
briefly talked with the actress who is to put it on there this autumn. She has
great charm and is said to be first-rate in her business. My brother-in-law,
Georges Neveux, knows the whole French theatre intimately and will be
able, I am sure, to see that it gets a good start.

Meanwhile here we are in Siena, which has been more agitatedly communist, since the attack on Togliatti, than any other town in Italy. Maria walked into the disturbance last Sunday, when Communists fired on the funeral procession of two policemen killed (and apparently tortured) by communist miners on Monte Amiata. She had to take refuge in a near-by house, where she found herself with a number of the local bigwigs, who had been in the procession. One of them had to make his escape by ladders over the wall of the garden. There has been a great show of governmental strength these last few days, including an entire regiment of tanks and armoured cars, and all is now quiet. The bulk of the Communists are simply peasants who work on the fifty-fifty share system with the land-owners, and who want a higher percentage, or else outright expropriation of land in their favour. The moment they get what they want, they will become staunch conservatives. Their discontents are ably organized by the few convinced and indoctrinated party members in the city. There is also a mass of unemployed persons to work on—miners, quarrymen, workers in small industries. Meanwhile the landed proprietors, with some of whom I have talked, are quite frankly for some kind of revived fascism to keep the lower classes in order. It is an ugly business and there is finally no solution, since the basic problem is too many people on too little land, with too few resources.

We stay here till August 8th (I think), when we go to Rome. The address there will be care of London Film Productions, 309 Via Nomentana, Rome. After Rome, we shall go to Sanary for a little, then to Paris. Will let you know details in due course.

I enclose one of these mysterious Swedish documents, such as I have forwarded to you in the past. I believe you send the thing to the Stockholm publishers to be dealt with.

Love to you both.

Ever yours,
Aldous

556: TO ALBERTO BONNOLI

Hotel de la Ville, Rome
18 August, 1948

Dear Dr Bonnoli,
Thank you for your kind letter and the very interesting pamphlet on the relation of man to the earth. The subject is one which has come to interest me more and more in recent years, and I have written about it in a little book, *Science, Liberty and Peace*, and in more detail in an essay which will be published, I hope, under the auspices of UNESCO. At the present

556 *Alberto Bonnoli was the author of* Lo Spazio terrestre come Elemento vitale (*Siena*, 1947).

moment our rulers are acting like the legendary Nero, who fiddled while Rome burned. They play power politics and prepare for new wars (spending as much as a third of their national revenues on armaments), while the population of the world increases at the rate of 55,000 a day and while erosion destroys every day an equal or perhaps greater number of acres of fertile land. Sir John Orr, who recently retired as Secretary General of the Food and Agricultural Organization of the UN, recently stated that 'we have a fifty-fifty chance' of solving the food problem *if* we get together, stop playing power politics and use all our intelligence and good will to find a way out. If we go on as we are going now, it is absolutely certain that we shall have a long-drawn catastrophe—a period during which Nature will achieve the balance between population and resources by killing off hundreds of millions of human beings through disease and starvation. My own view is that the food problem presents the only hope in the modern world of international co-operation. All men are agreed on only one thing—the desirability of having enough to eat. The problem of producing more food and of preventing the ruin of the soil is a technical problem, and men do not kill one another over technical problems, only over problems connected with religious or social ideologies. We know how to produce wheat without ruining the soil; but we do not know what is the best form of government or religion. In the first case we can use reason and accumulated knowledge, in the second we must rely on acts of faith and violence. How are we to persuade our rulers to think primarily of food and only secondarily of power? That is the question. We may perhaps be able to solve the problem of food; we can never solve the problem of power. Therefore we must turn our attention away from the certainly insoluble to the possibly soluble. But how? I do not know. All that can be done is, as you are doing, to tell people the truth and to hope that some day they may act in accordance with the facts.

I notice that in this section at least of your work you do not speak much of erosion and the loss of existing fertility. These facts have been stressed in two recent American publications, Fairfield Osborn's *Our Plundered Planet* and a book by William Vogt, of which I have only read a section published in the June issue of *Harpers Magazine*. Both men point out that, in many parts of the world, (e.g. South America and Central America) fertility is disappearing at a very rapid rate owing to bad agricultural methods. Most of Mexico will be a desert within fifty or sixty years, and the same is true of all the mountainous parts of South America. And meanwhile population rises at accelerating speeds.

A disturbing point is the following. Even if, per impossibile, all human beings could be persuaded to adopt birth control, and if the world's birth rate could be reduced to-morrow by twenty per cent, the number of persons in the reproductive age groups is now so great that world population must in any event (barring catastrophe) pass from 2.2 milliards to-day to well over 3 milliards at the end of the present century. But there is no prospect of governments renouncing their propaganda in favour of cannon fodder and no way of getting the majority of humans to adopt birth control. Therefore the period of intense population pressure is likely to last, not one hundred years, which would be the case if we had a twenty per cent reduction in the birth rate immediately, but at least two or three centuries.

Further problems arise because of the fact that the birth-rate is not uniform as between nations and, within certain nations, as between classes. Thus, twenty-five years from now, England and France will each have lost about four millions and will have populations in which there will be a high percentage of old people; Russia will have gained seventy-five millions and the population will be predominantly youthful. If nationalism remains the prevailing religion of the world and if war is still used [as] an instrument of policy, this fact will be of the gravest significance. Moreover, in the highly industrialized countries, there is a tendency for the less gifted members of society to have more children than the more gifted. As a result (according to an eminent English authority, Sir Cyril Burt), there will be at the end of this century twice as many feeble-minded children in the schools as there are now and half as many children of outstanding ability. Moreover the average intelligence of the community will have declined by 5 IQ points on the Binet scale. The question arises: can one have a democratic way of life in a population which is, biologically speaking, degenerating?

In every direction one is left with a question mark or a problem of the utmost difficulty. How the questions will be answered and the problems solved I do not know. For the time being one can only point to them and beg people to take notice of their presence.

Yours truly,
Aldous Huxley

557: TO HAROLD RAYMOND

La Rustique, Sanary (Var)
17 September, 1948

My dear Harold,

At last we know exact dates. I have finished the movie work—for the moment, at least—and have only some business here to attend to, in connection with the property we still have at Sanary, and in Paris and Brussels, where there are family matters to be discussed. We expect to come to London on October 2nd and are being put up at Claridge's. We look forward very much to seeing Vera and you in the very near future. From the twentieth of this month until the second of October our address will be

care of Mme de Gielgud
67 Boulevard Lannes
Paris 16.

Ever yours,
Aldous

Sage and Sun,
Palm Desert, Cal.
9 January, 1949

My dear Victoria,

We were very happy to get your letter, though saddened by much of its contents. What a world! We who were born near the end of one of history's rare Golden Ages, have a criterion by which to judge it. The young who have never known anything else, cannot compare the present with a better past and so (let us hope) find it a little more tolerable. The miseries you describe in Argentina are all the more odious since they are gratuitous. The country didn't go through a devastating war and so didn't have tyranny forced upon it by circumstances, as in so many parts of Europe and Asia.

We are still here in this desert, surrounded by sand and date palms, very glad to be out of the rains, snows, frosts and tempests which have prevailed in the rest of California and, much more so, in other parts of the country. It is quiet and one works well. I have just finished a dramatization of my phantasy about the future, *Ape and Essence.* So far as I can judge, it seems to 'work' pretty well and might be very effective on the stage. But one never knows about plays, even if one has had an enormous experience of writing and producing them. And I am a mere amateur. Did I tell you, by the way, that the stage version of *The Gioconda Smile* has done very well in London and is still playing after about nine months? It is a most surprising and gratifying thing.

After the play is polished off, I hope to get down to a volume of essays— polishing up a number of old ones and writing some new ones. I have just finished a long essay on 'Death and the Baroque', which is coming out in *Harpers Magazine* here and in *Horizon* in England. It seems to me quite good, and perhaps you might like to look at it for *Sur.* I have no copy of it here, but will send you one when I can lay my hands on it—or else send you a proof, when one comes in from London or New York. One of the essays I am planning is a study of Maine de Biran, who has always interested me, and whose *Journal Intime* I found again this summer among my books at Sanary, much annotated from reading fifteen years [ago. I have in mind(?)] another on the letters and poems of Sidonius Apollinaris, who is in so many ways analogous to ourselves—a highly cultured aristocrat living in the midst of barbarians, who don't understand and take no interest in any of the things with which he is concerned, and by whom he is constantly men- aced with liquidation. The personage could be made the centre of a very amusing play, I think—a very topical play, with the disintegrating Roman empire standing for the Europe of our youth and the Hairy Gothic savages standing for communists, militarists, technologists and all the other varieties of barbarians by whom the world is now afflicted. And the thing could be given the necessary serious and philosophic touch through emphasis on the fact that Sidonius was, as well as a cultured Roman, a pious Christian.

Maria sends her love and joins me in expressing the hope that we may soon be seeing you in the West.

Ever yours,
Aldous

559: TO MATTHEW HUXLEY

Sage and Sun,
Palm Desert, Cal.
[25] January, 1949

Dearest M,

I got your letter last night. Coccola is still in town, but should be able to get back without difficulty in spite of the continuation of the preposterous weather. Snow keeps falling every other day on the mountains and foothills. Rose's last letter told of deep snow all over the Mojave and icicles hanging from the eaves. I imagine the house at Wrightwood must simply have disappeared from view under a drift. Well, we are lucky not to be inside.

I've been thinking much, since you left, about your problems and own your letter has crystallized these thoughts round some definite points. The long-range need is obviously to find a job in which there is continuity and the possibility of going forward to positions of increasing authority and interest. Frequent changes tend, as a rule, to entail new beginnings at apprentice levels of subordination and routine work. So the wisest course, unless one is a highly equipped specialist with a rare commodity of know-how to sell, would seem to be to choose something in which one can stay and go forward. But then comes the short-range prospect of being condemned, in the great majority of jobs, to a period of donkey work. The degree of donkeyishness varies from job to job but it can be high even in such apparently lively work as literary journalism. I remember the burdensomeness of the asininity of doing 'shorter notices' of bad books on *The Athenaeum*. But the donkey work has got to get done and, in the nature of things and of social and economic organizations, it will be the new boy, the apprentice who has to do it. For this reason I should, if I were you, certainly not be too much in a hurry to turn down the research job in the Conservation concern. It won't be too interesting and it won't offer much scope for your gifts; but if there is a fair prospect of the job leading on to something of greater interest and authority in the future, I am sure you would be well advised to accept it. It is not pleasant to have to resign oneself

559 *Conservation concern: the Conservation Foundation, in New York; for which Matthew Huxley worked from 1949 to 1952. Peggy: Margaret Kiskadden, the wife of Dr William Kiskadden, well-known plastic surgeon. She and her husband were close friends of the Huxleys.*

to the conditions of apprenticeship; but if it is only through apprenticeship, with the dreariness that apprenticeship involves, that one can advance to better things, then for the sake of the long-range goal one must accept present boredom with the prospect of future satisfactions.

Meanwhile, if you are looking for second strings, what about getting in touch with Peggy's friend, Esther Lape? I have never met her, but understand she is very nice and also potentially very useful, as she is connected with all kinds of organizations, making surveys in the health and medical field, and is acquainted with all manner of important people and institutions. I don't know if Peggy ever gave you a letter to her. If not, why not write and ask her to do so? Miss Lape lives in Connecticut somewhere.

Keep us informed of your doings and your prospects. Much love.

Ever your affectionate,
Aldous

560: TO JULIAN HUXLEY

[*Palm Desert*],
as from Wrightwood, Cal.
26 *February*, 1949

Dearest J,

Where and how are you? And what are your plans for the future and your present activities? The last I heard of you was from Harold Raymond, who reported that you were just setting off for Ischia, where I hope you daily grew friskier and friskier.

Not much news here. We spent some weeks in New York, where I made the acquaintance of an interesting man called Dr Gustav Erlanger, a German-Jewish eye specialist who also did experimental physiology at the Kaiser Wilhelm Institute and in London, was turned out by the Nazis and now practises in NY. He has developed a method for treating the eyes by iontophoresis and gets remarkable results in many cases generally regarded as hopeless. I took some treatments with him and think that they did result in a slight clearing up of the old opacities. Unfortunately I developed bronchitis and had to come away; but I hope to try some more treatment later. Combined with the Bates training in proper functioning, I think they may prove very helpful.

The bronchitis has proved very tiresome and we have been, on medical advice, in the desert for the last three months, seeing what a dry and warm climate would do to clear up the condition. We have had the coldest winter on record, with snow even in the Colorado desert. However, it was better here than elsewhere, and I am very well with only a trace of bronchitis remaining. In another few weeks I expect we shall go back to Wrightwood, which has had five feet of snow this winter. Meanwhile there have been vast losses in citrus and vegetable crops, and yet vaster losses in the Rockies, where thousands of sheep and cattle have been frozen to death.

Matthew is leaving his job at Roper's and going to work with Fairfield Osborn on the latter's Conservation Foundation, which I think should be interesting and will certainly be socially useful. He comes out here to-morrow to stay for a few weeks before shifting to his new job.

We met last week a very interesting man, Edmund Jaeger, who is, I suppose, the greatest living expert on the fauna and flora of the California and Nevada deserts. He told me something that reminded me of an incident at Stocks, more than forty years ago. Do you remember that we found a nightjar at the foot of a tree, between the roots, in a state of coma, but not dead? I think we thought the bird was sick; but perhaps it was hibernating. Jaeger has observed the same poor-will, a species of nightjar common in the desert here, for two successive years hibernating in the same crevice among the rocks. He took the bird's temperature, which was only 67 F, weighed it, counted heart beats etc. It departed in the spring, but came back the following winter to hibernate in the same spot. The third winter it was missing and had no doubt gone the way of all nightjars. Jaeger says there is nothing in the American literature about hibernating poor-wills and I told him I would write to you to ask if you remembered the Stocks incident and if you knew anything about the hibernation of European nightjars. It seems that the local Indian name for the poor-will means 'the sleeper', and when Jaeger asked one of the Indians what became of the birds in winter, he was told: they go to the rocks. So presumably the natives know about this strange habit—almost worthy of Dr Johnson's swallows which, if you remember, conglobulate themselves into a spherical mass and plunge into rivers, where they pass the winter embedded in the mud.

I wish world affairs were a little less dismal. The prospects of reconciliation between East and West seem to be about on a par with the prospects of reconciliation between Christendom and Islam in the twelfth century. The best that can be hoped now is what happened then—a state of hostile symbiosis based on a series of local agreements whereby the irreconcilable antagonists bound themselves, as a matter of practical utility, to respect one another's spheres of influence. Man's life span being as long as it is, I suppose one cannot expect any major change in thought-patterns and behaviour-patterns to take place in under one or two centuries. It took that amount of time before people stopped thinking and behaving feudalistically and began thinking and behaving capitalistically; and I suppose it will take as long to pass from nationalistic thinking and behaving to genuine internationalism, or non-nationalism.

Our best love to you both.

Ever your affectionate,
Aldous

PS. Hubble came to see us the other day and showed us the first pictures taken by the 200 inch telescope. Two entirely new types of nebula have already been detected and, on the random sample selected, the nebulae went on with uniform density to a billion lightyears. If the nebula population is the same all over the heavens, there are probably about five hundred millions of them within range of the 200 inch. Crikey!

561: TO MATTHEW HUXLEY

L.A.
6 March, 1949

Dearest M,

We laughed over your very entertaining letter. Poor old Dorothy Thompson! I have never met her, but have always heard of her disease of talking—it is what St Paul calls glossolalia, tongue-wagging for tongue-wagging's sake. I met another of the Female Great out here a few days ago, [——], whom I remember when she was working on *Vanity Fair* as one of the most beautiful and toughest young creatures I have ever seen. She has mellowed a bit since then, but still has a pretty sharp tongue. She used it to describe a visit to [W. R.] Hearst and Marion Davies—the old man, who is dying, emaciated almost to the vanishing point, but desperately clinging to life; (he won't lie down, for fear of not being able to get up again, but spends all his time sitting bolt upright); Marion Davies permanently drunk, dressed only in a dressing gown which constantly flies open at the front, expressing a genuine adoration for Hearst, but meanwhile sleeping with the young Jewish [. . .] and announcing to all the world that she does so and saying what a stinker he is, both in bed and out; in the next breath confiding triumphantly to fellow-Catholic [——] that she has persuaded the old man to leave two million dollars to the convents of Southern California. The reality sounds infinitely more gruesome, and also more improbable, than the fictions of *After Many a Summer*.

We dined yesterday with Constance [Collier], where was [Alfred] Hitchcock, who was very interesting about his new techniques of movie making. He now shoots continuously a whole reel at a time, doing everything without cutting, getting the necessary close-ups and inserts and changes of distance by camera movements and movements of the actors. The proceeding requires long rehearsal and a team of technicians trained to concert pitch. But apparently the results are remarkable. [——] was also there, looking suddenly an old man and rambling away about politics and economics more incoherently than ever.

Under separate cover C is sending a copy of the script of my phantasy. I hope you will like it. As soon as you have read it, will you please deliver it to Robert Coughlan of *Life*, who wants to see it with a view to possible serialization.* I rather doubt whether this will come to pass; but there is no harm in his seeing the MS. Ring up his office and have them call for the

---

* Get it to him within the next few days, if possible.

script, or else take it over yourself—he is in the Rockefeller Centre, next door to you. He seems quite a pleasant young man—a friend, I think, of Ted's and Marion's—and might prove an agreeable acquaintance.

I'm interested to hear of your project about the Assassins. About the country in which they lived you might consult, for local colour, a travel book by an English woman called Freya Stark, who was a friend of Juliette's and did a number of extraordinary journeys, alone, among the wildest bedouins. She writes well and this book, which I haven't read—though I read her other book—might have useful historical information as well as good topographical descriptions. [Arnold] Toynbee might perhaps have something to say on the subject. He has vast learning on all kinds of odd subjects, and perhaps he has treated the Assassins fairly fully, as he has treated the Janissaries. I suppose you would tell your story from the point of view of a young man who is taken into the service of the Old Man of the Mountains, goes through the hashish treatment and the paradisal experience with the houris, acquires blind faith thereby and goes out on the Old Man's secret missions. For dramatic effect you would have to show him developing doubts about the rightness of the method—presumably, since this is a romance, because he falls in love with somebody connected with one of the victims he is to murder. It would be interesting to have him being influenced, perhaps, by some saintly Sufi. Read Jalalluddin Rumi to get the flavour of the lyrical poetry and intense mystical devotion of these people. Also the *Confessions of Al Ghazali* for a sense of how a learned philosopher reacted to the Sufis. Then I remember a study by a woman called Jones (I think) [*actually*, Margaret Smith] about a rather curious woman saint, called Rabia —who might easily be made the prototype of an interesting background character. Let me know how you get on with this plan, for I think it might turn out to be very interesting.

All our love.

Ever your affectionate,
Aldous

PS I am enclosing an Easter egg.

562: TO LEWIS GIELGUD

Wrightwood, Cal.
6 April, 1949

My dear Lewis,

I was so glad to have your letter with its good account of yourself and its note on the play [*Le Sourire de la Joconde*]. I wish it were easier to slip across land and water to see it. Jeanne writes that, although it got a good

561 *Assassins: Matthew Huxley was planning a novel on the Assassin cult.*
562 *Dryden: quoted from the paraphrase of Horace,* Odes, *III.29.*

reception from critics and public, it is not doing too well financially, as there is a general crisis of the theatre in Paris. So I don't know what its fate will be.

I should have written to you long since about your translations. I like some of them very much indeed. For example, your rendering of Intermissa, Venus, diu is really admirable. And there are things in Sic te diva potens which have the force and clarity of very good seventeenth-century writing. E.g. 'In seasoned oak and triple steel His heart was cased who, first of all Men mortal, launched his tiny keel. . . .' This has the same sort of quality as Dryden's Horatian 'Fortune, that with malicious joy Does man, her slave, oppress. Proud of her office to destroy, Is seldom pleased to bless; Still various and inconstant still, But with an inclination to be ill etc.' The *Pervigilium* is very skilful; but I don't get as much satisfaction from it as from the Horace. Perhaps the thing is basically untranslatable—in this sense, that any equivalent in English becomes automatically Swinburnian, that is to say rich without the weight and the concentration which Latin imposes even upon the most voluptuously lyrical or florid utterance. In its original Latin, the *Pervigilium* is the equivalent of a combination of Swinburne with the Milton of *Paradise Lost*. But in English such a combination seems to be impossible, and you get only the complex richness without the accompanying weight and definitiveness and finality. One can reproduce these qualities in ten- or eight-syllable quatrains and longer stanzas, such as were used by Marvell and Dryden. But they seem to vanish, in English, as soon as one writes in dactyls and anapests.

I hope for your sake that the Paris job may materialize. Keep us posted of your movements.

Ever yours,
Aldous

563: TO MATTHEW HUXLEY

145½ *S. Doheny Drive,*
Los Angeles 36, Cal.
6 April, 1949

Dearest M,

Coccola tells me you want the address of the Bates man in New York. [. . . .]

Now that we are on medical themes, let me pass on a piece of advice which was given me by my Uncle Henry Huxley, who was a very shrewd general practitioner. It refers to haemorrhoids, which used to bother me as I believe they still plague you. His advice was to wash carefully with soap and water after every defecation. I have done it ever since and never again been bothered by what used to be a really annoying tendency to piles. Only when I neglect this extremely simple precaution is there a tendency for the condition to return—and it does so almost instantly. If you are still troubled by these things, why not try this very simple treatment?

We went up to Ojai for the week end, and found Rosalind [Rajagopal] in a sea of dogs, cats, goats and school children—harassed, but very well and cheerful.

I hope things are working out satisfactorily in the new job and that Suzanne's car is behaving itself.

Much love from us both.

Ever your affectionate,
Aldous

564: †TO E. E. A. NORRIS

Wrightwood, Cal.
28 April, 1949

Dear Mr. Norris,

Thank you for your letter. It was indeed kind of you to write and tell me about poor old Ted [Haynes]'s death. I had not heard of it before, none of my correspondents in London had mentioned it.

The last time I saw him, in October, he remarked that he expected that he would die in the following spring. He was a good prophet. Modern circumstances are such that we shall not look upon his like again; for he belonged to that curious and very delightful species of the English Eccentrics —and there is no place for the Eccentric under a system of Fabian Socialism. Our world is too tidy to admit of marvellous disorder, the Dickensian leisureliness of an office such as Ted's. His death marks the passing not only of a friend, but also of an epoch of history and, one might almost say, a character in fiction.

Yours sincerely,
Aldous Huxley

565: TO HAROLD RAYMOND

Wrightwood, Cal.
8 May, 1949

Dear Harold,

Thank you for your letters and the accounts. These last seem very satisfactory. About [*a certain country*]—I have had some curious letters from there recently. One especially so, from a student who was doing some kind of a thesis on my books, and who confided that he would be compelled, in his thesis, to condemn me on dialectical-materialist grounds, though personally he felt quite differently. The letter ended with a passage saying how awful it was to live under a police state and urging everyone else to be vigilant and aware of the danger of being enslaved.

The article in *Horizon* ['Death and the Baroque'] will appear in the volume of essays and there is no reason why Herlitschka should not trans-

564 *Norris, a London bookseller, had been a friend of Haynes.*

late it now. I am still collecting material for the Maine de Biran essay, which
has involved a lot of work, partly on Biran himself and partly on related
psychological and philosophical fields which I want to touch on in relation
to Biran. I am still a bit uncertain how the thing will turn out; but shall
doubtless discover when I get down to the actual writing. I hope to let you
have the complete MS by the end of the summer.

Our love to you both.

Ever yours,
Aldous

PS. I have just had a letter from Dr. D. T. Suzuki, the well-known Japanese
scholar who is the leading authority in the field of Mahayana Buddhism. He
writes that he has a friend who wd like to translate *The Perennial Philosophy*
and who is competent to do so adequately. He adds that he does not think
it wd be possible to pay any rights on the translation. I have answered suggesting that the would-be translator shd get in touch with you, adding that
I don't know what arrangements you may have made. If none have been
made, I think Suzuki's friend might have the preference, if his competence
is vouched for by such an authority. About money—I don't imagine that it
cd ever amount to anything appreciable. So what about letting it go gratis
in the hope of getting a good translation? Dr. Suzuki's address, for your
information, is

> Shoden-An
> Engakuji
> Kamakura, Japan.

566: TO MATTHEW HUXLEY

Wrightwood, Cal.
11 *May,* 1949

Dearest M,

So we are all embarking on real estate! Coccola will have told you of
our plunge in LA. The house—large, commodious—the garden—with big
trees and plenty of space and privacy—and the location—in that curious
country lane between Santa Monica and Melrose, full of huge estates and
enormous trees—all seem ideal. And the price—ten thousand down with
thirteen thousand to pay in ten years, at $135 a month, is considered reason-
able by all the sensible people with whom we have talked. So there we are.
I hope we shall be able to dispose of Wrightwood this summer. Nice as it is,
it imposes too much of a strain, and we shall be better without it. Moreover
it is now possible to rent houses, if one wants to come up to the mountains.

And now about your projects. So far as I can judge, you can't go far
wrong on the deal, and I think your idea of paying the money back regularly
by paycheck deductions is excellent. If you pay interest and principal in
five years the total amounts, at four per cent, to $4480 or thereabouts—a
little less if one calculates month by month diminutions of principal instead

of year by year. I think it would be very unwise to try to pay back two thousand in the first year—particularly at the price of having a room mate, which you won't like. So either arrange to pay in five equal instalments of $896, or else five instalments of $800 and a sixth representing the interest. The only trouble is that, with the carrying charges, this will represent a yearly housing bill of fourteen or fifteen hundred dollars for five years. Isn't this unduly high? If so, you can arrange with the bank to repay over a longer period—say seven years. Make whatever arrangements will suit you best. Meanwhile I wish you'd do something for me: find out from Arnold Weissberger or any other official of the company what, if any, value the shares of General Panel now have. On Pepe's advice, as you know, we invested four thousand dollars in the concern. If any of this money can now be recovered, I would sell out. But perhaps Weissberger is not the man to approach on the subject? Find out what would be the most tactful way of sounding out the company's present position and future prospects. In view of all our real estate investments, I would like to get rid of this paper.

About furnishing. Klepa tells us that the thing to do is to attend the auctions to which the second hand dealers go for their wares. There, if one has patience and a good eye, one can pick up extraordinary bargains. In any case don't rush in too rapidly and don't get carried away by the thought that the place is your own, into doing anything too ambitious. It is better to adapt oneself to circumstances than to try to force circumstances into the shape of one's dream.

By a great stroke of luck my Mr Schwartz was able to find a copy of *Le Grand Maître des Assassins*—which is apparently very rare—and it came here the other day, along with the biography of Maine de Biran, for which I had been searching for a long time past. Coccola has already sent, or is about to send the *Assassin* volume to you.

Much love.

Ever your affectionate,
Aldous

567: †TO GEORGES NEVEUX

Wrightwood, California
2 June, 1949

Cher Georges,
Je vous remercie de votre lettre et je réjouis de la pensée que vous deviendrez encore une fois mon collaborateur. Si vous pensez que des

567 TRANSLATION:—'*Thank you for your letter; I take pleasure in the thought that you are once again to become my collaborator. If you think that changes (other than cuts) are necessary, please indicate them for me. [Jack] De Leon, who has written to me several times within a few weeks, wants me at all costs to add scenes "with human interest"—that is, scenes in which Poole and Loola's romance would be treated with much greater unction and other scenes in which the incentives for their elopement would*

changements (autre que des coupures) sont nécessaires, je vous prie de me les indiquer. [Jack] De Leon, qui m'a écrit plusieurs fois depuis quelques semaines, désire à tout prix que j'ajoute des scènes 'd'intérêt humain'—c'est à dire, des scènes où les amours de Poole et de Loola seraient traitées avec une plus grande onction et d'autres scènes où les motifs de leur fuite deviendraient plus 'idéalistes'. En un mot, De Leon veut que je souligne le côté 'positif' de la pièce, que je proclame plus clairement son message spiritualiste etc. Je lui ai répondu que j'hésite de suivre son conseil, car je trouve qu'une plus grande dose 'd'intérêt humain' pourrait ruiner la plausibilité de la fantaisie dans sa totalité—qu'en voulant trop rassurer le public, on risque de gâcher la pièce. D'un autre côté peut-être a-t-il raison de vouloir mitiger un peu ce que vous appelez l'impression de bombe atomique que donne la pièce. Mais je crois que cette mitigation peut se produire au moyen de coupures judicieuses et de l'introduction du spectacle et de la musique. Dites-moi très franchement ce que vous pensez de cette question de 'l'intérêt humain' et du côté 'positif' et 'spiritualiste'. S'il vous semble qu'il faut appuyer un peu sur l'amour de Poole et de Loola, appuyez sans hésitation en ajoutant ce qui vous paraît bon. Ne sachant pas trop bien ce que j'ai écrit, je n'y suis pas attaché et je puis envisager avec beaucoup de sang-froid n'importe quelle intervention chirurgicale.

La nouvelle du film est très intéressante. Les droits sont libres; l'idée de l'introduction par [C. F.] Ramuz me semble plutôt bonne—car la nature du cinéma est telle qu'il serait très dangereux de trop prolonger le cauchemar.

---

become more "idealistic". In a word, De Leon wants me to underscore the "positive" side of the play, to proclaim more clearly its spiritual message etc. I have replied to him that I hesitate to take his advice, for I am finding that a bigger dose of "human interest" could destroy the plausibility of the phantasy as a whole—that in trying too hard to reassure the public, one risks spoiling the play. On the other hand maybe he is right in wishing to mitigate a little what you call the atomic-bomb impression that the play gives. But I believe that this mitigation can be produced by means of judicious cuts and the introduction of the spectacle and music. Tell me very frankly what you think of this question of "human interest" and the "positive" and "spiritual" side. If it seems to you necessary to bear down a little on the love affair of Poole and Loola, bear down without hesitation by adding what seems good to you. Not knowing very well what I've written, I am not attached to it and I can envisage no matter what surgical intervention with complete sang froid.

'The news of the film is very interesting. The rights are clear; the idea of the introduction by [C. F.] Ramuz seems to me rather good—for the nature of the cinema is such that it would be very dangerous to prolong the nightmare too far. An introduction is necessary. A stay in Rome next year, especially if it would be for the sake of collaborating with you, is very tempting. I hope that the scheme will materialize.

'Love to Jeanne and Noële—also to Mère, if she is still staying with you. With friendly wishes. . . .'

Plans for a French dramatic Ape and Essence *were dropped.*

Une introduction est nécessaire. Un séjour à Rome l'année prochaine, surtout si ce sera pour collaborer avec vous, est très tentant. J'espère que le projet se réalisera.

Love à Jeanne et à Noële—aussi à Mère, si elle est encore chez vous.

Bien amicalement,
Aldous

568: TO PHILIP WYLIE

Wrightwood, Cal.
9 June, 1949

Dear Mr Wylie,

Thank you for your letter and *Opus 21*, which my wife has just finished reading aloud to me in the course of three or four evenings. I liked very much the fable about the clouds and the novae. How one wishes that the Universe really would express its opinion of us in these beautifully lucid and unmistakeable terms! You are probably right in what you say about the form of *Ape and Essence.* And yet there was no other form that would do. I tried at first to write it 'straight'; but the material simply wouldn't suffer itself to be expressed at length and in realistic, verisimilitudinous terms. The thing had to be short and fantastic, or else it could not be at all. So I chose the scenario form as that which best fulfilled the requirements. There seems to be a possibility that the thing may actually be turned into a film in France. If well done, it might be rather astonishing.

To come back to your book—I thought it was full of good things, but was not entirely satisfied by it as a whole. You suffer, as I have always done, from the difficulty, the all but impossibility, of combining ideas with narrative. There are two ways in which this can be done satisfactorily—one is by writing a perfectly enormous book, like the *Brothers Karamaʒov*, in which the ideas, though copious, are not too conspicuous. The other is to turn away from reality, in the narrative, and indulge in phantasy, either huge and inordinate, as in *Pantagruel,* or else small and ironical, as in the novels of Peacock. In order to write *Pantagruel* or *Karamaʒov* one has to be a major genius. And in order to write *Nightmare Abbey* one must be prepared to omit most of what is really interesting in life. The kind of book which can be written by those of us who are on the intermediate level is not vast enough to absorb ideas with ease, nor schematic and stylized enough to be a mere puppet show in which ideas are in fact the leading characters. We fall between two stools and find it horribly difficult to make a satisfactory marriage between ideas and a middle-sized, non geniusish novel. It may be that the problem is not completely soluble and that we have to be content with making a collection of good things rather than an artistically good whole.

Yours sincerely,
Aldous Huxley

Wrightwood, Cal.
30 July, 1949

My dear Edwin,

The news of your mishap was forwarded to us by Anita from New York. I do hope that by this time the enforced rest will have given the *vis medicatrix naturae* a chance to get busy and that you will soon be up again and about. Meanwhile do let us know if there is anything in the way of books you would like—for I don't imagine that Grand Junction is precisely the Athens of the West. Oddly enough I was talking of Grand Junction only the day before the news of your being there reached us. Gerald Heard was describing his trip to Aspen [Colorado] to see [Albert] Schweitzer and celebrate Goethe—and spoke of Grand Junction as a place he had stayed en route. Gerald gave a very amusing description of that strange performance in the mountains—a huge circus tent, interminable speeches about the great man (of whom Schweitzer privately remarked, 'After all, he isn't as great as all *that!*'), concerts by Rubinstein and the Minneapolis orchestra, with Hutchins brooding upon the waters like the Holy Spirit of it all. I confess I agree with Schweitzer, and have never been able to work up any great enthusiasm for Goethe, except as the author of some wonderful lyric poetry. *Faust* seems to me a mess and intolerably literary and Wardour-Streetish. *Wilhelm Meister* strikes me as the most monstrous monument to a serene and self-satisfied egotism in the whole of literature. *Werther* and the *Elective Affinities* one can't take seriously. Perhaps the supreme greatness appears in all the other things, which I have never read.

There is not much news here. We are moving into the new house—740 N. Kings Road, LA 46 is the address, Webster 3 0455 the phone number—in the intervals of being up here, where I am working on a long study of Maine de Biran—a study which is turning into a consideration of life in general as exemplified by what a particular man and thinker did, felt and thought, and also by what he didn't do or feel and think—for what is left undone is often as significant in a biography as what is done. If the thing could be done well enough—and I don't know whether I can do it well enough—it might indicate a new and more satisfactory method of philosophical exposition—philosophy through the particular existent, abstractions in terms of a concrete experience. I have become fascinated by the problems of the individual's relations with history and culture—the extent to which a man is in history and out of it, like an iceberg in water. And why on earth are certain problems simply not touched, certain classes of facts, perfectly well known, not incorporated into systems of thought? Biran, for example, was concerned all his life with the problems of psychology in relation to those of metaphysics. He had an acquaintance with the history of animal magnetism, was personally associated with some of the most reliable and honest magnetists of the generation after Mesmer, believed in the reality of reported cases of thought transference and even of pre-vision—and yet never thought of incorporating the data of magnetism into his theory of human nature and the universe. And yet one would have thought, on the face of it, that these magnetic phenomena cast a good deal of fresh light on psychology and, if telepathy and prevision be accepted, on the nature of the universe. Another very odd lacuna. Biran was a close friend of Ampère, with whom he interminably talked and corresponded about psychological problems. But Ampère was one of the two calculating boys (the other was Gauss) who developed into a man of genius in later life. And yet neither Biran nor Ampère ever discuss this fact of the latter's personal experience. Again one would have thought that the existence of calculating children was pretty significant in the construction of a psycho-logical system. Herschel at the same date perceived this—for in writing about his own gift of seeing elaborate geometrical figures with the mind's eye, he remarks that the seeing is evidently done not by what he would ordinarily call himself, but by somebody not 'himself' inhabiting his mind-body at a lower level than the conscious. One cannot help feeling that in Biran's case, as well as in the cases of many other philosophers, there is a certain reluctance to consider the full implications of facts which seem to lessen the importance of the conscious ego in the total psychic organization.

Our love to Grace and to you, dear Edwin, all best wishes for a speedy resurgence.

Ever yours,
Aldous

570: TO LUDWIG VON BERTALANFFY

740 North Kings Road,
Los Angeles 46, California
3 October, 1949

Dear Dr. von Bertalanffy,

Please excuse this long delay in thanking you for the gift of your book and for the very kind things you say in your letter and dedication. I delayed my answer hoping that I shd be able to read the book before replying; but work on a long essay, not exactly *on*, but around the French philosopher Maine de Biran took so much more time than I anticipated that I was unable to do more than glance at it; and since I do not wish to appear rude, I must delay this letter no longer, thanking you retrospectively for your kindness and in anticipation only for the profit which I am sure I shall derive from your book.

You are one of those strategically placed thinkers whose knowledge in many fields permits them to strike at the joints between the various academic

570 *Book: von Bertalanffy's* Das biologische Weltbild (*Bern,* 1949), *later translated as* Problems of Life (*London,* 1952).

disciplines—biology, philosophy, literature and the like—and so to penetrate to the quick of the living reality in a way which the specialist, however learned and gifted, can never do. If I had been able to go through with the biological and medical education, which was interrupted in my youth by a period of near blindness, this is what I shd have liked to become—a fully qualified striker at the joints between the separate armour-plates of organized knowledge. But fate decreed otherwise, and I have had to be content to be an essayist, disguised from time to time as a novelist.

I did not know that you had written on Nicholas of Cusa—a man who interests me very much, though I have read only a few of his writings and only two studies, English and French, of his thought.

Thank you once again for your greatly appreciated gift and letter.

Yours very sincerely,
Aldous Huxley

571: TO HUBERT BENOIT

740 *North Kings Road,*
Los Angeles 46, California
11 *October,* 1949

Monsieur,
J'ai lu avec le plus vif intérêt le livre que vous m'avez envoyé et dont je vous remercie—avec un retard que je vous prie d'excuser; car il était dû, non pas à une manque de reconnaissance ou d'intérêt, mais à un travail préoccupant qui m'a rendu très paresseux envers mes autres devoirs.

Un livre comme le vôtre fait pressentir l'avènement, enfin, d'une vraie science psychologique. Jusqu'à présent nous n'avons eu que des aperçus partiels. Des hommes comme Eckhart, Ruysbroeck, Suso ont connu par expérience, et reconnu théoriquement, la base éternelle de la personne

571 TRANSLATION:—'*I have read with the keenest interest the book which you sent me, and for which I thank you—with a delay which I beg you to excuse; for it was due, not to a lack of gratitude or interest, but to an absorbing task that has made me very lazy with regard to my other duties.*

'*A book like yours foreshadows the arrival, at last, of a true science of psychology. Until now we have had only partial glimpses. Men like Eckhart, Ruysbroeck, Suso knew by experience, and recognized in theory, the eternal basis of the temporal self—but they dealt with the psychology of the self as logicians rather than biographers, as Aristotelians rather than existentialists. On the other hand, in our time, when the psychologists have finally learned to consider the self biographically, life has been completely stripped of the Primordial Fact of eternity. Your merit is to have re-united the elements which historical accidents have separated, and to proclaim a psychology which will relate the temporal facts to their timeless ground.*

'*Thank you once more for your gift. Please believe me yours sincerely....*'

Book: Benoit's Métaphysique et psychanalyse: essais sur le problème de la réalisation de l'homme (1949).

603

temporelle—mais ils ont traité la psychologie de la personne en logiciens plutôt qu'en biographes, en aristotéliens plutôt qu'en existentialistes. Par contre, en nos jours, où les psychologues ont appris enfin à penser biographiquement de la personne, on a complètement perdu de vie le Fait Primordial de l'éternité. Votre mérite est d'avoir réuni les éléments que des accidents historiques ont séparés, et d'annoncer une psychologie qui rapportera les faits temporels à leur fond hors du temps.

En vous remerciant encore une fois de votre don, je vous prie de me croire

Sincèrement vôtre,
Aldous Huxley

572: TO GEORGE ORWELL (E. H. BLAIR)

Wrightwood, Cal.
21 *October*, 1949

Dear Mr. Orwell,

It was very kind of you to tell your publishers to send me a copy of your book. It arrived as I was in the midst of a piece of work that required much reading and consulting of references; and since poor sight makes it necessary for me to ration my reading, I had to wait a long time before being able to embark on *Nineteen Eighty-Four*. Agreeing with all that the critics have written of it, I need not tell you, yet once more, how fine and how profoundly important the book is. May I speak instead of the thing with which the book deals—the ultimate revolution? The first hints of a philosophy of the ultimate revolution—the revolution which lies beyond politics and economics, and which aims at the total subversion of the individual's psychology and physiology—are to be found in the Marquis de Sade, who regarded himself as the continuator, the consummator, of Robespierre and Babeuf. The philosophy of the ruling minority in *Nineteen Eighty-Four* is a sadism which has been carried to its logical conclusion by going beyond sex and denying it. Whether in actual fact the policy of the boot-on-the-face can go on indefinitely seems doubtful. My own belief is that the ruling oligarchy will find less arduous and wasteful ways of governing and of satisfying its lust for power, and that these ways will resemble those which I described in *Brave New World*. I have had occasion recently to look into the history of animal magnetism and hypnotism, and have been greatly struck by the way in which, for a hundred and fifty years, the world has refused to take serious cognizance of the discoveries of Mesmer, Braid, Esdaile and the rest. Partly because of the prevailing materialism and partly because of prevailing respectability, nineteenth-century philosophers and men of science were not willing to investigate the odder facts of psychology. Consequently there was no pure science of psychology for practical men, such as politicians, soldiers and policemen, to apply in the field of government. Thanks to the voluntary ignorance of our fathers, the advent of the ultimate revolution was delayed for five or six generations. Another lucky accident was Freud's inability to hypnotize successfully and his consequent disparagement of hypnotism. This delayed the general application of hypnotism to psychiatry for at least forty years. But now psycho-analysis is being combined with hypnosis; and hypnosis has been made easy and indefinitely extensible through the use of barbiturates, which induce a hypnoid and suggestible state in even the most recalcitrant subjects. Within the next generation I believe that the world's rulers will discover that infant conditioning and narco-hypnosis are more efficient, as instruments of government, than clubs and prisons, and that the lust for power can be just as completely satisfied by suggesting people into loving their servitude as by flogging and kicking them into obedience. In other words, I feel that the nightmare of *Nineteen Eighty-Four* is destined to modulate into the nightmare of a world having more resemblance to that which I imagined in *Brave New World*. The change will be brought about as a result of a felt need for increased efficiency. Meanwhile, of course, there may be a large-scale biological and atomic war—in which case we shall have nightmares of other and scarcely imaginable kinds.

Thank you once again for the book.

Yours sincerely,
Aldous Huxley

573: TO MATTHEW HUXLEY

740 North Kings Road,
Los Angeles 46, California
23 October, [1949]

Dearest M,

It was good to get news of you—though we were sorry to hear of the bad cold. I hope you will contrive to keep the enemy at bay during the winter.

Not much news here, except that we are pretty definitely moved in now and that I have at last finished my essay book. Coccola is pretty well, though she still gets these periodical flare-ups of temperature. [Dr. Leland] Hawkins is trying to eliminate the infection; but I don't yet feel too sure that he is on the right track. However, he may be. We must wait and see. I wrote to Erlanger saying that it was not much good coming to him, so long as the general infection persisted, with its obviously deleterious effects on the eyes. So I presume we shall be here through the winter—by which time, let us hope, the infection will have been stamped out. Meanwhile a new development of the Bates technique, taught us by one of the teachers who have seceded from Mrs [——], seems to be helping. This secession, incidentally, is a sad business; but poor Mrs [——]'s attitude of combined fearfulness and authoritarianism made it inevitable. She is a great teacher,

573 *Misdated '23.x.40'.*

but seems to be falling a victim to the disease which so easily afflicts the leaders of unpopular causes. It is all very unfortunate. Meanwhile the head of the new, seceding body turns out to be a very capable woman, with good contacts in the medical and educational world and an open mind towards anything that promises to help people to better vision. She has just gone to New York, where she intends to establish a centre for training new teachers.

I am not doing much at the moment—merely thinking about the possibility of doing the historical novel which I have vaguely had in mind for some time, reading sporadically and discussing with Christopher Isherwood and a Jewish screen writer called Lesser Samuel a scheme for an original to be sold to the movies. If we don't succeed, I suppose I shall have to take a job in some studio; for the devaluation of the pound will make a considerable difference, I fear. I see, incidentally, that the pound is not too steady even at its new price and that, if left to itself, without U S support, it might sink below two-eighty. I must say, the situation seems to be rather dismal, and one doesn't see how England can escape a considerable lowering in its present standard of living. And any remedial schemes, such as the development of Africa, must necessarily take a long time; while any substantial emigration to the dominions cannot be accomplished without enormous capital—and who is to provide it? I suppose you saw Sir John Russell's address to the British Association printed in the September 3rd issue of *Nature*. It is an excellent statement of the food and population situation, with suggestions for remedying it. The whole problem is whether the work can be done fast enough and on a big enough scale to catch up with breeding. Unhappily it is a great deal easier, and pleasanter, to beget a child than to clear the two acres of tropical jungle or irrigate the two acres of desert required for the support of the new addition to the human family. Did the UN conference on resources come to any specific conclusions? I never saw anything about it after the announcement of its inception. I hope it didn't wind up in the usual way with a string of pious resolutions and no concerted plan of action.

We saw the Hubbles yesterday. Edwin is sufficiently recovered now to be able to spend a little time in his office and to walk as much as a mile or so. He confidently hopes to be allowed to go up to Palomar as soon as the mirror is in place again after its re-grinding and re-silvering, which has kept it grounded for the last few months. He told me a sad and odd thing, which is that the party line has begun to get into Russian astronomy—that there is an orthodox doctrine regarding the origin of the solar system and that those who deviate from it are abused. They will soon, no doubt, suffer the fate of the bourgeois-idealist Mendelo-Morganists in the field of genetics. Did you, by the way, read Julian's two articles on Russian genetics in *Nature* this summer? If not, do so. They are extremely interesting and contain a vast array of facts. The picture he draws is extremely depressing. One of the significant facts is that Russian geneticists no longer use the word 'hypothesis', but always refer to 'doctrines', exactly as the Schoolmen did in the thirteenth century. I suppose they will end up in the same sterility as the Schoolmen ended in. But of course it will take some time for the effects of the new scientific policy to manifest themselves in a serious falling off in the quality of the work done.

All our love.

Ever your affectionate,
Aldous

574: TO HUBERT BENOIT

740 North Kings Road,
Los Angeles 46, California
5 November, 1949

Monsieur,

Je vous remercie de votre lettre du 23 octobre. Si vous jugez que cela puisse être utile, je vous prie de faire usage de ce que j'ai écrit dans ma lettre.

574 TRANSLATION:—'*Thank you for your letter of October 23rd. If you think that this could be useful, please avail yourself of what I wrote in my letter. I am not too sure of the French language; and if I have made any grammatical mistakes please correct them!*

'*As to publication in America—alas, I see few possibilities. Manufacturing a book has become horribly expensive, and editors mistrust any book that will not sell itself. (To pay its way now it has to sell 4000 copies.) But I wonder whether the subject could not be treated—still very seriously—in a manner which would more forcibly attract the attention of the critics and the public. It is a matter of setting forth principles and arguments through concrete examples—in the framework of a life (or of several individual lives), and of personal experiences. I have always found that a moral treatise was not only less interesting but also less rich in instruction than a volume of casuistry or of "spiritual letters". It is through the particular that the general is most clearly explained and understood. Extreme abstractness—as practised by Valéry, for instance—tends to weary and even baffle the reader. Quasi-algebraic formulas cannot be adequate to a complex and multicoloured reality. I myself, during these last months, have had an experience which—though not completely successful—has convinced me of the methodological value of a philosophical exposition in the framework of a life; for I have just brought to a conclusion a long essay, not on, but around Maine de Biran—an essay in which political, metaphysical and mystical problems are dealt with in the light of a particular life and teaching. What I advise—it is always so easy to give advice—is that you do your book over in the framework of one or of several experiences: do it over, not abstractly, but casuistically, biographically, giving an account of a temperament X who has had experiences a, b, c . . ., who at last feels the desire to realize Being, and who does certain things p, q, r, s . . . with a view to this realization. In this manner you will strike the imagination of the reader (even of the "scientific" reader with preconceived ideas) and at the same time you will see yourself driven to pass from the purely intellectual level to the personal level where in effect the drama of the realization is acted out.*

[Continued overleaf

607

Je ne suis pas trop sûr de la langue française; et si j'ai commis des fautes de grammaire je vous prie de les corriger!

Quant à une publication en Amérique—hélas, je vois peu de possibilités. La fabrication d'un livre est devenue horriblement coûteuse, et les éditeurs se méfient de tout livre qui ne se vendra pas. (Pour trouver ses frais il faut maintenant vendre 4000 exemplaires.) Mais je me demande si le sujet ne pourrait être traité—toujours très sérieusement—d'une façon qui appellerait plus fortement l'attention de la critique et du public. Il s'agit d'une exposition de principes et d'arguments à travers les cas concrets—dans le cadre d'une vie (ou de plusieurs vies) individuelles, d'expériences personnelles. J'ai toujours trouvé qu'un traité de morale était non seulement moins intéressant mais aussi moins riche d'enseignements qu'un volume de casuistique ou de 'lettres spirituelles'. C'est à travers le particulier que le général s'explique et se comprend le plus clairement. L'extrême abstraction—comme l'a pratiquée Valéry, par exemple—tend à fatiguer et même à tromper le lecteur. Les formules quasi-algébriques ne peuvent pas être adéquates à une réalité complexé et nuancée. J'ai fait moi-même, pendant ces derniers mois, une expérience qui—quoique non complètement réussie—n'a convaincu de la valeur méthodologique d'une exposition philosophique dans le cadre d'une vie; car je viens de terminer un long essai, non pas *sur*, mais *autour* de Maine de Biran—un essai où des problèmes politiques, métaphysiques et mystiques sont traités à la lumière d'une vie et d'une doctrine particulières. Ce que je vous conseille—c'est toujours si facile de donner des conseils!—c'est de refaire votre livre dans le cadre d'une ou de plusieurs expériences: de le refaire, non abstraitement, mais casuistiquement, biographiquement, à travers le compte rendu d'un tempérament X qui a eu des expériences a, b, c . . ., qui sent enfin le désir de réaliser l'Etre, et qui fait certaines choses p, q, r, s . . . en vue de cette réalisation. De cette façon vous frapperez l'imagination du lecteur (même du lecteur 'scientifique' aux idées préconçues) et en même temps vous vous verrez forcé de passer du plan purement intellectuel au plan personnel où le drame de la réalisation effectivement se joue.

'*I should like very much to learn the outcome of your practical enquiries into the way of liberation. At one time I followed the somewhat mechanical methods taught by the Swamis of the Ramakrishna Mission; but now I find more profitable those of Krishnamurti which are much closer to Zen methods. Old Suzuki wrote to me recently, announcing his next visit to the United States. I hope very much to see him. Yours sincerely. . . .*'

The new book by Benoit referred to here and in letters 581 and 583 was De l'Amour: psychologie de la vie affective et sexuelle (1952), *translated as* The Many Faces of Love: The Psychology of the Emotional and Sexual Life (*New York*, 1955). *Of the essay on Maine de Biran, Huxley had written to Harold Raymond on 12 September:* '*If the thing comes off as I hope, it will be an example of what I think is a new literary form, in which philosophical discussion is enlivened and given reality by the fact of its being particularized within a biography*'. *See letter* 569.

J'aimerais beaucoup apprendre les résultats de vos recherches pratiques de la voie libératrice. Pendant un certain temps j'ai suivi les méthodes un peu mécaniques qu'enseignent les Swamis de la Mission Ramakrishna; mais je trouve maintenant plus fructueuses celles de Krishnamurti qui sont beaucoup plus proches aux méthodes Zen. Le vieux Suzuki m'a écrit récemment, annonçant sa prochaine visite aux Etats Unis. J'espère beaucoup le voir.

Sincèrement vôtre,
Aldous Huxley

575: TO CASS CANFIELD

740 *North Kings Road,*
Los Angeles 46, California
7 *November,* 1949

My dear Cass,

Thank you for your two letters. The description of the book of essays [*Themes and Variations*] seems to me excellent and does not, I think, need any additions or subtractions.

About the volume of Spiritual Letters—the first thing to be determined is this. A history and anthology of spiritual letters exist in French. I have seen the title, but have never been able to get hold of the book; nor can I remember the name of the author, or editor. But it should not be difficult to track it down. The next thing is to find out whether it has been translated. I think it possible that it may have been, and that it may have been published by one of the Catholic publishers, such as Sheed and Ward or Burns and Oates. If it hasn't been translated, it should be looked at with a view to seeing whether it would be worth translating, or whether it would be better for a new book to be put together out of the materials there collected. As for the editing of such a book—I should hesitate to undertake the task, since it would entail more reading and checking of references than I could manage with any degree of comfort. But I do hope that the job will be undertaken; for the result will be something very delightful and valuable. Meanwhile, if Harpers are looking

575 *Huxley wrote in a paragraph used to advertise the recordings: 'For me, these records possess a certain historical, as well as a merely personal interest. For, unless my ear and memory greatly deceive me, the way I speak is practically identical with the way my mother and her brothers and sisters spoke. Language is perpetually changing; the cultivated English I listened to as a child is not the same as the cultivated English spoken by young men and women to-day. But within the general flux there are islands of linguistic conservatism; and when I listen to myself objectively, from the outside, I perceive that I am one of these islands. In the Oxford of Jowett and Lewis Carroll, the Oxford in which my mother was brought up, how did people speak the Queen's English? I can answer with a considerable degree of confidence that they spoke almost exactly as I do. These recordings of 1950 [sic] are at the same time documents from the seventies and eighties of last century.'*

for new items to reprint, why don't you think of the two small volumes of Fénelon's letters (*Letters to Men* and *Letters to Women*), which were put out in translation about sixty years ago. The translator was Lear (not the Nonsense Lear, but some other [i.e., H. S. Lear]) and the publisher, I believe, was Longmans. So far as I know these are now hopelessly out of print, both here and in England. And yet they are full of good things. Another delightful book which needs reprinting is *The Spirit of St Francis de Sales*, by Camus—a collection of first-hand accounts of conversations with the saint by a younger, Boswellizing admirer. This is also unavailable and was also, I think, published by Longman.

A stranger wrote me the other day about problems of vision and concluded her letter with a postscript, which I enclose. I don't know whether this is an expression of mere cantankerousness, or whether she had got hold of a faulty copy of the *Art of Seeing*. Anyhow, I pass it on to you for your information.

I hope all goes well with you and the family. Here we have been sweltering in a prolonged Indian summer, which has yet further aggravated the effect of five years drought and has resulted in the outbreak of many very serious forest fires. The weather seems to have gone wrong everywhere. We hear from friends in France and Spain of the ravages of drought there. And even England seems to have gone dry.

Yours,
Aldous

(P.T.O.)
PS. I forgot to tell you that I made some recordings this summer for two enterprising young sound technicians, who have turned themselves into a company called Sound Portraits. They do the job very well and I think that the finished product will be excellent. I read a long passage from *Time Must Have a Stop* (Eustace's posthumous experiences), together with the story of the dwarfs from *Crome Yellow*, a poem and the essay, 'Sermons in Cats'. They will be published in December on two long playing records. I have told the young people (Mr and Mrs Barron [. . .]) that they should mention that the books from which the selections were made are published by Harpers. I don't know whether your publicity department may have ideas as to the possibility of using the records for advertizing purposes. In case it should, you can get in touch with the Barrons and find out what their plans are.

576: TO MATTHEW HUXLEY

740 *N. Kings Rd, LA 46, Cal.*
9 *December*, 1949

Dearest Matthew,

Your letter arrived this morning and gave us the greatest happiness, both on account of the news it brought and on account of the way you conveyed it. After thirty years of it, I can say I am definitely for matrimony, and I am sure that, if Ellen is all that Suzanne tells us she is, you too will be of the same opinion in 1980. Keep us posted on what's happening and on what you plan. Meanwhile this brings the paternal blessing and every best wish for the happiest possible Christmas.

Your loving
Aldous

577: TO JULIAN HUXLEY

740 *N. Kings Rd.,*
Los Angeles 46, Cal.
9 *December,* 1949

Dearest J,

This brings you both all our good wishes for Christmas and the New Year. I hope all goes well with you and the family. Our own news is tolerably good. Maria, who has been suffering for a long time from an obscure low infection, seems definitely to have taken a turn for the better. Matthew writes that he is thoroughly enjoying his work with Osborn's Conservation Foundation. I keep well and, having completed this autumn a volume of essays (including a very long one centred on Maine de Biran), am doing some reading with a view to embarking, perhaps, on a historical novel of fourteenth-century Italy. How curiously the period reproduces, on a small scale, our present situation! Thus every intelligent person in the fourteenth century knew that there had to be a united Italy, just as everyone now knows that there has to be a united Europe and, ultimately, world. But vested interests in sovereignty were such that it was impossible to have what was obviously useful and reasonable. From the time of Dante to that of the final unification of Italy—a period of more than five and a half centuries. The historical precedent is not too encouraging! And then how closely the efforts of the Inquisition to impose uniformity of thought correspond to those of the Communist Party to-day! The chief difference is one of efficiency. The Inquisition was mercifully pretty inefficient. I wish we could say the same of modern police states equipped with the latest in radio, recording machines, card indices, narco-hypnotic techniques and all the rest. The spirit of tyranny was always willing; but, happily, the flesh of organization and technology used to be very weak. To-day both are equally robust. And, talking of the Inquisition, I have been reading your Lysenko book with the greatest interest. What a dismal picture emerges! And apparently the trend is not confined to genetics. Edwin Hubble tells me that there is now a party line in astronomy—one

576 *Ellen: Ellen Hovde. She and Matthew Huxley were married the following spring.*

577 *Lysenko book: Julian Huxley's* Soviet Genetics and World Science: Lysenko and the Meaning of Heredity (*London,* 1949); *the American title was* Heredity, East and West: Lysenko and World Science.

theory of the origin of the solar system being orthodox and all the rest not. He complains, too, that the actual work done by Russian astronomers is highly inaccurate, as regards t[he] routine observations. Incidentally, poor Edwin suffered a frightful heart attack while fishing in the mountains this summer. He got through by the skin of his teeth and is only now beginning to be up and around. Whether he will be able to go on observing at high altitudes is still uncertain. It will be a great blow to him if he can't make use of the two-hundred inch telescope, which is finally in perfect working order. But of course it's a pretty strenuous business, observing stars. The dome is unheated, the temperature at six thousand feet is often arctic, sleeping habits are badly interfered with. It may be that now that his dream of twenty years has actually come true, poor Edwin will not be allowed to profit by the new opportunities.

I have exchanged several letters recently with a man who wrote to me out of the blue from Canada—von Bertalannfy [Ludwig von Bertalanffy]. He even sent me his book on the philosophy of biology; but as it is in highly technical German, I haven't yet had the courage to embark on it. Is he a good biologist? At least he seems to be a man of many accomplishments and wide learning; for I find that he has written a monograph on that curious fifteenth-century philosopher, Nicholas of Cusa. Much of his work seems to be in the field which you have worked in—growth. So I suppose you are well up in him, and perhaps have known him personally. I understand that he is now re-organizing the biology department at the University of Ottawa.

Let me hear how you are and what you plan to do in the immediate future. All our love to you both.

Ever your affectionate,
Aldous

578: TO HUBERT BENOIT

740 *N. Kings Rd.,*
Los Angeles, Cal.
10 *December,* 1949

Monsieur,

J'ai lu avec le plus grand intérêt les trois papiers que vous m'avez envoyés. La technique que vous y décrivez est presque identique à celle qu'enseigne

578 TRANSLATION:—'*I have read with the greatest interest the three papers you sent me. The technique which you describe is almost identical with that taught by Krishnamurti—but formulated more explicitly and with a more rigorous explanatory analysis. In the* Intimate Journal *of Maine de Biran are found many passages in which the philosopher discusses with himself this problem:—how to find the Unknown God, God as he is in himself; and how to avoid the discovery of a home-made God, a God fabricated or at least deformed by the imagination? He did not find the solution to this problem; for he believed that the introspective analysis of the ego would lead him to the*

Krishnamurti—mais formulée plus explicitement et avec une analyse explicative plus rigoureuse. Dans le *Journal Intime* de Maine de Biran on trouve beaucoup de passages où le philosophe discute avec lui-même ce problème:— comment trouver le Dieu Inconnu, Dieu comme il est en lui-même; et comment éviter la découverte d'un Dieu de ménage, un Dieu fabriqué ou au moins déformé par l'imagination? Il n'a pas trouvé la solution de ce problème; car il a cru que l'analyse introspective du moi le mènerait a la rèalisation du divin non-égo; et quand, inévitablement, il s'est trouvé en échec, il a accepté *in extremis* la foi catholique. Dans des textes anciens, comme cet anonyme *Cloud of Unknowing* du 14me siècle, on trouve la description d'une technique qui vise à l'exploitation des distractions par l'acceptation.

Je n'ai jamais eu l'occasion de discuter la technique du *koan* avec un pratiquant du Zen moderne; mais il m'a semblé (après la lecture de Suzuki) que cette technique vise à l'épuisement de l'égo par l'effort prolongé. L'étude du *koan* l'éreinte, le pulvérise, et la raison divine prend, à un certain moment, sa place. Mais le Zen a existé avant la technique du *koan*; et même dans les temps modernes certains maîtres du Zen out rejeté la technique du *koan*. Et

---

realization of the divine non-ego; and when, inevitably, he found himself in check, he accepted, in extremis, *the Catholic faith. In ancient texts, such as that anonymous* Cloud of Unknowing *of the 14th century, is found the description of a technique which aims at the exploitation of distractions by acceptance.*

'*I have never had the occasion to discuss the* koan *technique with a practiser of modern Zen; but it seemed to me (after reading Suzuki) that this technique aims at the exhaustion of the ego by prolonged effort. The study of the* koan *wears it out, pulverizes it, and the divine reason takes, at a certain moment, its place. But Zen existed before the* koan *technique; and even in modern times certain Zen masters have rejected the* koan *technique. And a technique which employs uninterrupted tension is intrinsically anti-natural. For the secret of life, in all its manifestations, consists in a conjunction of grace and will—in an action whose goal is the divine passion (passion for the ego, since it is the action of the divine reason.* Cogito ergo non sum. Cogitor ergo sum. *But first I must think in such a way that I can be thought—must think to the point of the thinker's exhaustion, as in the* koan *technique, or, better, must accept what I think, without tension or effort, in order to find, as one of the Zen masters said, "the non-thought which resides in thought".*)

'*A practical question. There is published here a little review,* Vedanta and the West. *I should quite like to put before the readers of this review a translation of one or all of your papers. Tell me very frankly if the idea pleases you.*

'*Meanwhile thank you once again for having given me the occasion to read these three essays. They have been very profitable to me, and I know that I shall often return to this penetrating analysis of psychological facts.*

'*Please believe me, my dear Sir, yours sincerely....*'

Huxley translated an article by Benoit as 'Notes in Regard to a Technique of Timeless Realization' for Vedanta and the West *(March-April,* 1950), *and wrote a foreword to the English edition of his book* The Supreme Doctrine, Psychological Studies in Zen Thought (1955).

une technique qui emploie la tension ininterrompue est intrinsiquement anti-
naturelle. Car le secret de la vie, dans toutes ses manifestations, consiste dans
une conjonction de grâce et de volonté—dans une action dont le but est la
passion divine (passion pour l'égo, puisque c'est l'action de la raison divine.
Cogito ergo non sum. Cogitor ergo sum. Mais d'abord je dois penser de façon
que je puisse être pensé—penser jusqu'à l'épuisement du penseur, comme
dans la technique du *koan*, ou, mieux, accepter ce que je pense, sans tension
ni effort, afin de trouver, comme a dit un des maîtres Zen, 'la non-pensée
qui réside dans la pensée'.)

Une question pratique. On publie ici une petite revue, *Vedanta and the
West.* J'aimerais bien présenter aux lecteurs de cette revue une traduction d'un
ou de tous vos papiers. Dites-moi très franchement si l'idée vous plaît.

En attendant je vous remercie encore une fois de m'avoir donné
l'occasion de lire ces trois essais. Ils m'ont été très profitables, et je sais que je
reviendrai souvent à cette analyse si pénétrante des faits psychologiques.

Je vous prie, cher Monsieur, de me croire

Sincèrement vôtre,
Aldous Huxley

579: TO ANITA LOOS

740 *N. Kings Rd.,*
Los Angeles 46, Cal.
27 *December,* 1949

Dearest Anita,

I should have written before to thank you for the charming transparent
wallet, which came some days ago. It gives one an X-ray view of one's wealth
which is almost embarrassingly frank, at certain moments. I hope you got
the two records of me reading from my Complete Works, which I requested
the young sound technicians who made them to send you. As they seem to be
pretty inefficient in these matters, I'd be glad if you will let me know if the
records have not yet turned up. (Mine have not, so far.) In that case, I will
bawl them out.

We had a pleasant Christmas—going down to the desert on Sunday to
be with Rose and her family; then giving a tea party on Monday, to which
came, among others, Clifford (looking remarkably well) and the Hubbles
(their first trip beyond the frontiers of Pasadena since Edwin's illness).
Edwin seems much better; but we are a bit worried about Grace, who gives
the impression of being very frail. But don't write to her about these impressions of ours; for it upsets her to be told of her friends' concern; and anyhow
she is, I gather, in the hands of a good doctor.

I am so happy about *Blondes* and the prospects of a long run. The concatenation of them and the Sistine Chapel in *Life* was really remarkable. The

579 *Clifford: Dr Clifford Loos, Miss Loos's brother.*

nudity of the chorus girls was almost equal to that of Adam and Eve and the Damned in the 'Last Judgment'.

The news of Matthew's engagement sounds very satisfactory. Everyone agrees that the girl is nice, sensible and eminently suited to Matthew. And the two young people are evidently wildly in love with one another, without at the same time being unduly silly about it. So the prospects look very good.

I am doing a lot of reading at the moment in view of a possible historical novel, which I begin to envisage a little more clearly than I did. How fascinating the Middle Ages are! I was reading some early fifteenth century sermons the other day, one of which was directed against the feminine habit of painting the face and dyeing the hair. One of the reasons given for condemning these practices was that painting tends to disgust husbands and so drives them to sodomy, which is an infinitely worse offence than fornication or adultery. In another sermon San Bernardino advises his women hearers not to send their male children on errands through the town, as they are sure to be molested by sodomites. Rather send the little girls; for either they won't be touched, or if they are, it's a less serious sin for all concerned than what would happen with the boys. Incidentally, all theologians are agreed that, while the devils are frightfully lustful in the natural way (as succubi and incubi), they retain enough of their original angelic nature to be horrified by unnatural vice, and so are never lesbians or pansies.

Best love from us both and all good things for the coming year.

Yours affectionately
Aldous

PS Maria asks me to tell you how very sweet Clifford is and how very well he seemed.

580: TO SHEPARD TRAUBE

740 *N. Kings Rd.,*
Los Angeles 46, Cal.
30 *January,* 1950

Dear Mr Traube,

Thank you for your kind letter. Yes, the Morris people had told me of your intention to produce *The Gioconda Smile* in New York and I hope very much that the play may go as well there as it did in London and, later, in Paris. (Incidentally I hear news of it from the most unexpected quarters, from Finland to Brazil.)

About the title—I would, of course, prefer to stick to the original *Gioconda.* But if you think that Universal might be tempted to re-issue the film, if the play were successful, and if you think that the re-issued film might adversely affect the play, I will try to find a new one. Nothing occurs to me at the moment, except the *Mortal Coils*, which was the title of the volume in which the short story originally appeared—the title under which it was published, as a play, by Harpers. (But this too might be used by Universal, since there was a question at one time of their giving this name to the film.) I will meditate on the matter and do my best to produce something satisfactory before we meet in New York.

Incidentally we do not expect to be in New York before the end of March or the beginning of April, and plan to be there until May 9th, when we hope to sail for Europe. There will be time, during those five or six weeks, for us to work out any changes in the script you may think desirable.

With regard to casting—I think your idea of [Ralph] Richardson and [Wendy] Hiller is excellent. We should be most fortunate if we could get such skilful performers. I know too little about the New York theatre to be able to make other suggestions. All I will say is that it is very important to find a very young girl for Doris. [. . . .] The French production (which I did not see, but only heard about from competent critics, who told me that it was better than the English) had a Doris whose youthfulness produced exactly the poignant effect that the part calls for. In the movie Ann Blyth did an excellent job as Doris—precisely because, as well as a competent actress, she was only twenty or thereabouts. I would say, therefore, that you would do better with an unknown youthful actress (provided she was talented enough to respond to good direction) than with a better known, more experienced, but older woman.

I don't know if you ever saw the film. With its wonderful title in the manner of Mrs Henry Wood, it was not precisely tempting, and very few people ever seem to have seen it. But there were some interesting performances in it—Jessica Tandy as Miss Spence was admirable; Hardwicke as the doctor could hardly have been better; and the nurse was also excellent. Unfortunately I have forgotten the latter's name—can only remember that she was a very competent character actress on the New York stage. It might be worth while to locate her and find out if she would do the part in the play. In any case, I think you would be interested to see the movie, if you have not already done so, if only for the sake of Tandy, who at certain moments was quite extraordinary, and of Cedric Hardwicke, whose playing of the doctor, as he told me, was a tribute to his own father, who was a doctor and was greatly loved and respected by the son.

With all good wishes, I remain

Yours sincerely,
Aldous Huxley

580 *Huxley proposed two new alternative titles for* The Gioconda Smile—*in May,* Ripeness is All, *and in June,* Comes the Blind Fury (*an allegory, perhaps, in this); but fortunately neither was elected. The rôle of Doris in the London production was played by Brenda Bruce; in the French production, by Danièle Delorme. The nurse in* A Woman's Vengeance *was Mildred Natwick.*

740 *North Kings Road, Los Angeles 46, Cal.*
3 *February,* 1950

Dear Dr Benoit,

My typewriter cannot write accents, so this letter comes to you in English. I am delighted to hear that the manuscript of your new book is on its way, and I look forward very much to reading it. As soon as I have done so I will write to you again. Meanwhile here are a few comments on your previous letter, in which you describe the technique of visualization, aimed at inducing the mind to preserve its contact with given reality. This seems to me an excellent idea; and I would also suggest the advisability in some cases of undertaking accurate drawings of such objects as flowers, leaves etc. My feeling is that modern psychologists have gone too far in encouraging their patients to 'express themselves' in more or less symbolic drawings. This may be useful at times as a catharsis. But it seems to me that this indulgence of the fantasy should be balanced by a disciplining of the fantasy in the form of accurate, objective representations of external reality. Representational art is now out of fashion; but I feel that there is a great deal to be said for it from a therapeutic point of view and also from the point of view of liberation and the realization of Reality.

Visualization and drawing are not the only ways of disciplining a mind to become aware of reality. Vittoz, the Swiss psychiatrist, obtained good results in many cases of light neurosis by making his patients fix their attention upon the performance of some simple physical act, such as raising the hand. The hyper-organic had to become conscious of the organic and was therefore no longer free to indulge in day-dreaming and wishful thinking. Still better than Vittoz's techniques were those developed in England by F. M. Alexander, whose books (*Creative Conscious Control, Man's Supreme Inheritance, The Universal Constant of Living*) are well worth reading. Alexander discovered empirically, in experimentation on himself, that there is a correct or 'natural' relationship between the neck and the trunk and that normal functioning of the total organism cannot take place except when the neck and trunk are in this right relationship. His findings have been confirmed theoretically by various physiologists and, in practice, in the persons of the numerous pupils he has taught during the last forty-five years. (I myself am one of his pupils.) For some obscure reason the great majority of those who have come in contact with urbanized, industrial civilization tend to lose the innate capacity for preserving the correct relation between neck and trunk, and consequently never enjoy completely normal organic functioning. Alexander and the teachers he has trained re-establish the correct relationship and teach their pupils to preserve it consciously. This, as I know by experience, is an exceedingly valuable technique. For not only does one have to become aware of the data of organic reality (to the exclusion of the insane

617

life of phantasy); one also, in the process of practising this awareness, makes it possible for the physical organism to function as it ought to function, thus improving the general state of physical and mental health. (Incidentally, the 'straight-spine' position so much insisted upon by the teachers of yoga is precisely the posture advocated by Alexander. The merit of Alexander consists in having analysed the essential factors in this posture and having developed a technique for teaching the correct relation of neck and trunk to those who have lost it.)

I have just finished reading the latest volume by Dr Suzuki to be translated into English—*The Zen Doctrine of No-Mind*, published last year in London, by Ryder and Co. It is a commentary on the Sutra of the Sixth Patriarch and contains a great deal of interesting material from Chinese sources hitherto inaccessible to European readers. If you have not already read the book, I recommend it to you.

My wife and I hope to be in France this summer, and I hope very much that we may have the pleasure of making your acquaintance.

> *Yours sincerely*
> *Aldous Huxley*

582: TO SHEPARD TRAUBE

> *740 N. Kings Rd.,*
> *Los Angeles 46, Cal.*
> *16 February, 1950*

Dear Mr Traube,

This letter goes in duplicate to Ridgefield [New Jersey] and to Claridge's, so that it should catch you somewhere.

I have not yet had time to read the script, but will do so during the next few days. Meanwhile let me say how glad I am that you have put back some of the things that were cut out. Being sadly ignorant of the theatre and a very unprofessional playwright, I never feel too certain of what constitutes an intolerable *longueur* and what is a legitimate speech. So when a producer tells me that a favourite passage has to go, I generally believe him.

As for the clock business—if you think that the audience will realize what has been done, well and good. Zoltan Korda and I discussed it at some length while doing the film and came to the conclusion that it was better, for the sake of comprehensibility, to show the hands being turned back. I didn't feel, in either the play or film, that the tampering with the clock adversely affected the suspense. The fact that both Hutton and Janet are convinced that the execution is going to take place as arranged is the important and moving element in the situation, and I don't think that the tension of the emotion is relaxed, so far as the audience is concerned, by a knowledge of Libbard's strategem. It remains, until the very end, a mere trick which may or may not come off. My fear is that, if you don't show the hands being put back, the putting forward will not be immediately comprehensible and the audience

618

will feel bewildered. The thing can be tried out both ways in rehearsal; but my belief is that you will find the present one the more satisfactory. I think, too, it emphasizes the fact of Libbard's concern to get at the truth and his resourcefulness in doing so.

I think you are right in saying that Janet's guilt should be more definitely established from the first. In regard to a different opening, I would have to discuss this with you. The present one has the advantage of providing a simple and rapid means of obtaining an insight into the characters of Janet, Hutton and the Nurse. At the moment I cannot visualize the mechanics of an alternative scene, in which the coffee, Nurse's relation to patient and Nurse's departure could so easily and simply be arranged. Besides, we have to plant the business of the currants, so that we are forced to show them lunching. And if they are lunching how can we arrange matters so that they get separate entrances?

If you see Peggy Ashcroft, give her my love. Her husband, Jeremy Hutchinson, is the son of one of our oldest friends. For the rest, I know practically nobody in the theatrical world and can only wish you the very best of luck in your search for actors.

Yours very sincerely,
Aldous Huxley

583: TO HUBERT BENOIT

740 *North Kings Road,*
Los Angeles 46, California
16 *March,* 1950

Dear Dr Benoit,

I have just finished the typescript of your book, which I found extremely interesting. The criticisms I have to offer mainly concern the form of the presentation and the emphasis placed on the matters which are treated. To begin with a purely practical consideration—the book is very long and there are very few publishers in this country, or in England, who would wish to publish a book of five hundred pages or more by a hitherto unknown author. Production costs are extravagantly high in America and a book of this length would probably have to be priced at five or six dollars, with very little prospect, even at this price, of a profit to the publisher. And the same is true of England. This being so, I think I can say almost with certainty that no New York or London publishers will accept the book in its present form. Nor must we ignore the effect of this great length upon potential readers. Your analytical treatment of the subject makes considerable demands upon the reader, who is required to pay a very close and unrelaxing attention to every paragraph. Many persons, I am afraid, will be unwilling to give this kind of attention for the necessary length of time.

I do not pretend to know what the best way of shortening the book would be. Some chapters might perhaps be omitted altogether—their contents being summarized in footnotes or appendices. Other chapters might be 'streamlined'. The whole proceeding, of course, must depend upon your judgment of what is more and what is less essential.

Another point. My own feeling—and it was shared by my wife, who read the typescript aloud to me—is that the metaphysical background, in relation to which the facts of love and sexuality are analysed, was not described at sufficient length or with sufficient emphasis. You deal with the subject, of course, and you refer to it frequently, but always very succinctly and as though the average reader were already acquainted with the metaphysical system, as though he took for granted the existence of a timeless reality and the desirability of 'returning to where he has always been'. But the average reader takes nothing of the kind for granted and is plunged not merely in Ignorance, in the sense of *avidya*, but also in a more specific ignorance of Vedanta and Mahayana thought. For this reason I feel that you should lay a much stronger emphasis upon the metaphysical background of your subject.

In this context I may remark that, for very many persons, sex is important above all as a kind of samadhi, a liberation from the 'I'. If they rationalize their feeling, they assert the identity of the sex act and the 'transformation of ice into water'. In sexual love they transcend the all too human ego and this transcendence gives them momentarily a blessed sense of release. But the transcendence is 'downwards' into Nature and Animal Eternity, not 'upwards' into Grace and Spiritual Eternity. The error of D. H. Lawrence, for example, was to equate the two eternities; whereas in fact they merely occupy analogous positions on the ascending spiral of life—the spiral which passes from the animal-instinctive, through the all too human realm of the ego, to a position immediately 'above' that occupied by the instinctive animal. Lawrence was, of course, perfectly right in rejecting the claim of what he called 'love in the head', and what you call *l'amour adorant*, to be the final and most 'spiritual' consummation of love. But he was wrong in supposing that human beings could find the fulfilment of their own divine nature in 'the blood', 'the flow of life', 'the dark gods'. What they actually find there, if they plunge too persistently, is what Mallarmé speaks of in 'Tristesse d'Eté'.

> Mais ta chevelure est une rivière tiède,
> Où noyer sans frissons l'âme qui nous obsède
> Et trouver ce Néant que tu ne connais pas.

There is an interesting passage at the beginning of Maine de Biran's *Nouveaux Essais d'Anthropologie*, where he describes the soul's capacity to transcend itself either upwards into timeless realization or downwards into subpersonality.

Finally there is the question of constitutional differences between individual men and women. On several occasions you say specifically that you do not propose to consider this question in the present work. This is legitimate, no doubt; and yet I wonder if one can ignore it and still deal adequately with love and sexuality—or for that matter with any other human problem. We are fortunate to-day in possessing, at long last, a genuinely scientific method for describing physique, temperament and their interrelations in terms of continuous and measurable variations within a tri-polar system—endomorphy, mesomorphy and ectomorphy for physique, and viscerotonia, somatotonia and cerebrotonia for temperament. Among other things the Unconscious in any given individual is his body, along with the body's psychological expression in temperament. The great error of modern psychology has been to ignore this fact and to speak of the Unconscious as though it were some kind of unknowable, and of the sub-conscious as though it were determined almost exclusively by psychological reactions to the environment. But insofar as the Unconscious is the body, and insofar as the body determines temperament, the Unconscious can be known and studied, both behaviouristically and introspectively. And insofar as it is Spirit or timeless Principle, the Unconscious can be studied and finally realized in an act of unitive knowledge. The great merit of your book consists in the fact that it sets love and sexuality against the background of the Unconscious-as-Spirit. For your particular purposes you were probably justified in leaving out of account the background of the Unconscious-as-body-and-temperament. Nevertheless, I feel that a completely adequate account of this, or indeed any, psychological problem would have to take account of the Unconscious in both its aspects, bodily and spiritual.

As I wrote in my last letter, my wife and I hope to be in Paris by the middle of May.* (Aux soins de Mme Georges Neveux, 82 rue Bonaparte, Paris VI.) Exactly what we shall do then I do not know; but I expect we shall be in the Midi some time during the summer or early autumn and look forward to the pleasure of making your acquaintance then. Meanwhile I think it would probably be best not to show your typescript to my New York publishers. Their fear of length is intense and, in present economic circumstances, not unjustified; and I am afraid that they might take fright at the sight of a typescript of 516 pages and refuse even to look at it.

Yours very sincerely,
Aldous Huxley

*In New York at the Hotel Warwick after April 3rd, 65 West 54th Street

584: TO CHRISTOPHER ISHERWOOD

The Warwick, 65 West 54th Street,
New York 19, N.Y.
10 April, 1950

My dear Christopher,
How are things going? I hope very well—tho' I feel a bit guilty for leaving

584 *The story which Huxley and Isherwood were writing for the films was eventually called 'Below the Equator'. It was never sold.*

you to carry all the burden. Nothing very good in the way of a title has yet suggested itself. The only at all satisfactory one is the following, which wd do if we stress the ends-and-means side of our political situation. It involves a quotation from the *Tao-Teh-King*: 'Heaven arms with pity those whom it wd. not see destroyed'. So the title wd be 'Armed with Pity'—and the whole quotation cd be used by Tarn in talking with Pablo at the mine, and referred to again at the end, when Pablo is persuaded to give up the arms. This is the best I have been able to do to date. It may not be the perfect title yet; but it has some merits of sound and meaning.

New York is a whirl, of course. But with compensations—the meeting with Matthew's fiancée, who is the most charming girl; finding Gerald here; discovering that the producer of my play is quite nice.

Love from us both.

Yours
Aldous

585: TO SHEPARD TRAUBE

[*New York, N.Y.*]
[18 *April*, 1950]

[*Memorandum*]

The more I consider the proposed new opening of the play, the less I like it. Let us consider the reasons for and against it.

Reason for. If the audience knows from the beginning that Janet is guilty, the reaction to her later speeches and behaviour will be stronger.

Reasons against. If we give the whole show away in the first five minutes, there is an end of any kind of suspense. As Constance Collier remarked, when I discussed the change with her, 'you might as well ring down the curtain at once'.

Moreover, in real life it is very unlikely that we should discover the truth so early. Rather it would, in all likelihood, reveal itself gradually, being inferred by the onlookers from the unfolding events. My own instinct in writing the short story, the movie and the play was to leave the question of

585 *A revealing memorandum by Traube in the collection of the New York Public Library shows that after further consultation Huxley agreed to write a new opening scene. In it, Janet would only be thinking about committing the crime, not making preparations for it. Traube wanted the moral guilt for the crime to be shifted from Janet, the actual murderer, to Hutton, who has excited her passion by flirting with her. The new scene, by suggesting that Janet has a certain nobility of motive, would make the assignment of moral guilt an issue, thus compromising with the slick, ironic interpretation urged by Traube. In the original play there is no such muddying of the facts: Janet is guilty of murder, Hutton of wantonness only, and the two offences are properly distinguished in gravity.*

guilt entirely open, until such time as the circumstances make the correct answer obvious to the reader or spectator. What I am now doing is to analyze the reasons for what I did by instinct.

Another, to me, very important point. I deliberately wrote the first scene of the play in such a way that it would look like a drawing-room comedy, touched at the end by a breath almost of French farce. If the first scene is like this, the dramatic power of the other two acts is heightened by contrast. Furthermore, such a treatment brings out a point which is very important in relation to Hutton—namely that trivial acts of selfishness and wantonness may release, as though by a kind of trigger action, a huge avalanche of tragic destiny. It is essential that our first scene should make it quite clear that our main characters are 'nice people' in a thoroughly gentlemanly and cultivated environment. If we establish Janet's guilt in the first minute of the play, we lose this atmosphere of niceness and lose the ironic contrast between drawing room comedy and the later tragedy. We also ruin the character of Janet. For the whole point of Janet is to be, first, a 'mysterious Gioconda' and second, a thoroughly sympathetic woman, in the contexts of normal life—but a thoroughly sympathetic woman who has been driven, as we discover in due course, by Hutton's wanton tampering with her emotions into the commission of a monstrous (but carefully rationalized) crime. If we show her from the first as a poisoner, we lose both the mystery and the quality of being sympathetic. Both Valerie Taylor and Rathbone know their business and can be relied on to give the right impression to the audience—in Janet's case, the impression of being a wonderful daughter and friend, but also a dark horse; in Hutton's, the impression of being selfish and wanton, but at the same time utterly incapable (as Libbard recognizes) of the crime for which he is condemned.

My own conclusion, after mature thought and long discussion with Constance Collier (whose judgment in these matters I greatly respect) is as follows. Open as at present. Give no inkling of Janet's guilt, but let her merely tinkle about among the coffee cups with her back to the audience. Cut out the episode of the nurse's finding the can of weed killer, so that there is no suspicion of future foul play to mar the atmosphere of drawing room comedy. Reference to the weed killer can be introduced in the scene when Hutton returns from the inquest. The fact that his greenhouse is full of the poisonous stuff constitutes an important part of the circumstantial evidence on which he is finally condemned.

586: TO JULIAN HUXLEY

82 *rue Bonaparte, Paris VI*
21 *May,* 1950

Dearest J,

It is sad that we shd have so nicely calculated our movements as to miss one another by the margin of a day; but such is life. I'm sorry to hear such poor news of both your healths. I can sympathize, since I got a touch of flu on the boat and still remain considerably below par, with a persistent discharge in the right sinus.

As for plans—it looks as if we should miss each other again in Italy. For our scheme is to be at Siena, via air to Rome, on the tenth of June, when you will just have departed for the North. At Siena I hope to finish off the documentation for the historical novel I have been ruminating for some time. We return to France in July, when Matthew and his bride will be here. They honeymoon first at Sanary and in solitude, then move northward to stay with us and Jeanne at a house in the Limousin, which the Neveux have taken for the summer. Then go to Paris, and from there to Luxembourg, which is the spot from which their remarkably cheap plane takes off for New York. After their departure we expect to go back to the Limousin and from there strike out to various places which I want to see in connection with a study I would like some day to undertake on the devils of Loudun and the after life of the two surviving protagonists of that extraordinary drama, Soeur Jeanne des Anges and Surin. If the thing could be done well, it would be a fascinating book, exhibiting the entire gamut of the religious life from the bestial to the sublime. I have to collect some more documentation than I now have and also to take a look at the physical background of the drama. This means, in practice, that we shall probably not meet until you come to stay with [Jo] Davidson in August. We had thought of going to Spain for a couple of weeks in late August; but I now rather doubt if we shall do this on account of the fatigue and the enormous expense of travelling. We shall come to England in September, and I hope you will be there at that time. Our original plan had been to sail for NY on October 4th; but *The Gioconda Smile* is being produced on Broadway on the third, so we shall take an earlier boat, if the passages can be exchanged, leaving on September 22nd.

Our love to you both.

Ever your affectionate,
Aldous

PS. I stupidly forgot to put your memorandum in my pocket when we went to Mimi's, but will pick it up tomorrow or the day after and read it.

587: MARIA HUXLEY TO MRS JULIETTE HUXLEY

Siena
21 *June,* 1950

Dear Juliette,

I have not *quite* given up hope of our meeting: i.e. yours and mine. For instance what are you doing just after Jo Davidson? Could you spare a few

587 *Maria Huxley had her wish; the Julian Huxleys visited Sanary in August. She and Aldous afterwards spent a fortnight with Georges and Jeanne Neveux at Juillac (Corrèze), and another fortnight with Mimi Gielgud in Paris.*

days with us in Sanary—or in the Corrèze (near Limoges); it seems a shame to miss this. There is so much those two brothers wont even think of talking about. Write tentatively in Paris where we shall be from July first. I hope it suited you to have Julian ask Aldous from 11 July to 21st. If not you can always revise. Our plans always change whether it suits us or not. So we are easy to suit.

Meanwhile, herewith, I want to ask you to do 2 things I would appreciate very much:

(1) Order shirts for Aldous to find on arrival at your house. I presume and hope you can do this by telephone. In the past one could get these almost anywhere. We would like the lightest weight Airtex Cellular white cotton as in America one can only get very poor imitation of them. Aldous has no shirts except Nylon which are wonderful as long as he has his laundry-girl with him but considering he is dispensing with her services. . . . 6 Airtex Cellular white cotton to be worn with a tie, size 16-35 = sixteen collar 35 sleeves ready at arrival.

(2) Would you kindly telephone to his ex-tailor Studd and Millington and ask them whether they could make him a suit in that time (finished suit delivered on boat 22 September) and whether they can send at once samples of material to Paris.

(3) As Aldous has good taste but does not know what is practical or not, he has just bought a suit of *the* most spot and crease revealing possibilities. I would like a whipcord or speckled suit—what I believe is called a business suit—*not blue* but nice browny greys or grey or black and white [or] brown and white or *beige whipcord. Not a tweed* type but a hard woven type—middle weight—this would be really very very useful and most appreciated.

When you order shirts please ask whether they have an Airtex blue with sport collar, long sleeves; that is a collar which at will is worn with or without tie (unfortunately not good enough for London or New York or I would have the white ones like that) *of course all of them* with button at sleeve *not* links. I hope you excuse all these exact details; it is meant to help you in knowing 'what precisely do you mean, Mrs Huxley. . .' a thing I almost never know myself.

I am sure you will keep an eye on A's dirtiness and send his things to be pressed or cleaned as he never knows and is so untidy. Thank you my dear, and let me know whether we see you. We shall also be in Paris 10 to 22 September—at Mimi's. I wish you could come—could she put us all up? We would not mind a hotel at all, but feel we must go so as not to hurt her feelings. I hope you found your mother as well as possible. Please give her many affectionate messages from me. And a kiss to yourself. Julian looked very well in Rome.

M.

(P.T.O.)
Studd and Millington have 2 branches, one near Piccadilly Circus: it is that one.

Hotel Paris Dinard,
29 rue Cassette, Paris VI
3 July, 1950

Dearest J,

Thank you for your good letter, just received. I am looking forward very much to my stay with you and Juliette and shall certainly come over on the tenth, as you suggest, rather than the eleventh. I shall take a plane, since the train and boat journey is always so tiresome. When I have my tickets, I will let you know the hour of my arrival. As I remember, the bus brings one from the airport to South Kensington; and from there I will take a taxi to the house. As for the length of my stay, I can easily prolong it for a little, if you can have me. Maria is going to stay with Jeanne in the Limousin, while I am in London, and from there she will go to Sanary, where we shall meet. If it is possible, I will fly direct from London to Marseille; for the trains will be horrible at the height of the holiday season. Times can be arranged when I am in London.

I know a fair amount about [Wilhelm] Luftig, having read his book and talked with people who have been treated by him. He uses light therapy, plus homoeopathy, plus (in certain cases) very stringent diets, which are excellent for overweight people with high blood pressure and a tendency to auto-intoxication. I think I may go down to Brighton for a day to see him. There is also another unorthodox eye man, called Brooks Simpkins, who has written a very good book on the mechanics of vision and who often gets very good results by his methods of re-education. He lives at Eastbourne. And perhaps I can look in on him too. And talking of unorthodoxies, I am asking a curious and interesting Danish acquaintance of mine, Dr Christian Volf, who is an expert on hearing, to send me, care of you, one of the special recordings he has made for the relief of sinus trouble. One listens through ear-phones to a record of synthetic sounds in the lowest musical octave and the effect is to give an intense internal massage, vibrating the bones of the skull, stimulating nerve activity and circulation and resulting, in cases of congestion, in immediate discharge. I have heard of many people who keep sinusitis at bay simply by listening to the record every morning before breakfast. I am hoping that the thing may give you some relief from your miseries in this field. If, as I hope, Volf comes to London this July, we will have a talk with him. He is obviously a kind of genius in the field of invention and has done enormous research on hearing. (He has made other records for re-educating the deaf, which, in certain types of deafness, seem to work very well.) We had a lovely time in Italy, marred only by a heat wave in Rome. Our best love to you both.

Your affectionate,
Aldous

31 *Pond Street, Hampstead, N.W.*3
19 *July,* 1950

My dear Christopher,

Maria wrote a letter which reached me last night, saying that you had cabled about the MS. I am so sorry about this. I wrote you a letter from Paris and gave it to the porter to mail—but suppose he just kept the stamp money. I think the story has turned out very nicely. You must have put an enormous amount of work into it—which makes me feel rather guilty. It occurred to me that it might be an improvement if Charlie, after making his escape, were arrested in the town by police or soldiers. He and the audience think that he is being taken off to Ortiz's dungeons—but in fact he is taken to de Oliva, where he actually sees Ortiz in captivity. This wd give more suspense and excitement and remove some of the impression that problems are being solved too easily. Also I think there ought actually to be some shooting on the part of the insurgents when Oliva's forces approach the bridge. There might be a good many trucks, so that it looks like an attack. And Tarn and Moira might run through fire. There is a danger, otherwise, of the story seeming to end like a musical comedy.

As for title—what? I can't think of anything appropriate. Meanwhile has there been any reaction from the studios?

I have been here about ten days and expect to return to France next week (Villa La Rustique, Sanary, (Var) until August 18th or so). England is much more cheerful than it was 2 years ago. Some old friends are out of town; but I have seen [Stephen] Spender several times, and Edith Sitwell, and expect to see Tom Eliot tonight and [Cyril] Connolly tomorrow. Poor Osbert [Sitwell] has got Parkinson's disease and has started to tremble. It is a very depressing look-out. Things go on *als ob* there wasn't going to be another World War. And perhaps there isn't. What a world!

Give my love to Gerald and Peggy if you see them.

Ever yours
Aldous

590: TO SHEPARD TRAUBE

31 *Pond St., London, N.W.*3
21 *July,* [1950]

Dear Shepard,

Thank you for your letter. I will try to write something along the lines you mention in the course of the next two weeks, when I get down to the south of France. One of the most obvious reasons for the difference between short story and play is the question of length. An anecdote cannot fill an evening.

Meanwhile I have just talked with Valerie Taylor, who made two points, both of which were quite good. One was this:—that when she acted with Clive Brook, she never felt that Hutton had sufficiently aroused in Janet the blind physical passion which alone would have driven her to the murder. (The stuff about the talented children is, of course, a rationalization after the passional event.) To render the fact that Hutton has been flirting with Janet, deliberately rousing in her a kind of spirit of scientific-experimental wantonness, is mainly a matter of acting. But to make the matter a little clearer, I have written a few extra lines to be inserted at the top of 1.1.8—a flirtation scene, immediately preceding the poisoning of the coffee.

Another point which Valerie Taylor made referred to the finding by the nurse of the weed killer. This has always been rather painfully on the nose; and to mitigate the obviousness, I have followed her suggestion that the weed killer should merely be one of several objects left by the gardener. The new scene may help to take some of the curse off the situation.

I return to France on Monday—address

> Villa la Rustique
> Sanary
> (Var)

and shall be there till about August 16th, after which

> Maison de Joyet
> Juillac
> (Corrèze)

will find us. But I will write again before then. Love to the family.

> *Yours,*
> *Aldous*

591: TO MRS MARGARET KISKADDEN

> *La Rustique, Sanary* (Var)
> 6 *August,* 1950

Dearest Peggy,

Thank you for your letter. My bank is Bank of America, Laurel and Sunset branch—and if you will send the check there for deposit, I shall be most grateful.

I hope all goes well with everyone and that you have found or are close to finding the ideal house. My advice on this subject is: don't be tempted by the hills, by solitude, by picturesqueness. In the plain you and the child can walk abroad without having to take the car and without being fatigued by a pull up. Propinquity will make the problems of shopping and of help much more easily soluble. Solitude can be obtained by walls or judicious planting and need not depend on distance. And of course an old house with obvious disadvantages is to be preferred to a new one, built specially for you and having other disadvantages, which will become apparent only when you are living in it.

Not much news here. I spent two weeks in London, staying with my brother and seeing many old friends. He gave a family party, at which twenty-seven relatives were present—and in spite of a certain Proustian atmosphere —middle aged spreads instead of adolescent figures, bald old men instead of striplings, fathers and mothers of families instead of children—it was a pleasant and touching experience. England is much more cheerful than it was two years ago and life is easier. For how long? The horrible question mark hangs over everything. Diabolic possession seems to be the only plausible explanation of contemporary history.

Life here is a bit uneasy, as we are trying to sell the house, trying to decide what to take out of it, trying to cope with day-to-day living in the midst of labour-creating devices and an insufficiency of labour. Added to which we had an enormous heat wave during the first ten days of our stay. The weather is more tolerable now, thank goodness.

All our love to you and Bill and Bull, and to Gerald if you see him, and to Christopher.

Yours affectionately,
Aldous

592: TO CHRISTOPHER ISHERWOOD

La Rustique, Sanary (Var)
11 *August,* 1950

My dear Christopher,

Thank you for your letter. I'm sorry to hear that things are going so unsatisfactorily, and that [James] Geller hasn't yet succeeded in placing your earlier story. As for me, I live merely in hope of what the play may bring in the autumn—and of course the autumn may bring either a flop or the atomic bomb or the evacuation of New York. Other work is at a standstill, and I can't yet find the right device for my historical novel, or for anything else, for that matter. But I suppose it will turn out all right in the end.

I was in England for two weeks, staying with Julian. The atmosphere is much more cheerful than two years ago and life is easier. Nobody seemed to be much afraid of a general war. Saw Stephen Spender several times—white-haired and wonderfully distinguished looking. Cyril Connolly, [. . .] one likes him, *malgré tout*. The Sitwells—Edith a monument and Osbert suddenly rather old and tired. Sybil Colefax, bent double with her broken back, but indomitably receiving guests and going out. The Jowitts—occupying an amazing Victorian-Gothic apartment in the House of Lords, reserved for Lord Chancellors. All very much *Le Temps Retrouvé*. 'I show you sorrow and the ending of sorrow'—with no ending in sight, of course, for any of us.

We have not seen Jung and I doubt if we shall go to Switzerland, as we are busy here, trying to sell this house and pack up books. The South of France is normal again, and village life goes on as ever, like a film by Pagnol, acted by Raimu and Fernandel. How amazingly tough the French way of life has proved itself!

Thinking about our story, it suddenly strikes me that the following might be an improvement. When Charlie escaped from the General's house, we follow him through his adventures almost to the door of the ministry, but he is jumped on by a patrol of soldiers and dragged away struggling. Here we leave him, under the impression that he has been caught by the general's party. And in the last scenes we see the troops approaching from Pablo's point of view, and there is actually some shooting, in spite of a flag of truce raised by the troops. Pablo thinks this is a ruse and goes on shooting. The Tarns rush down towards the bearers of the white flag, and it is only then that we discover that the troops are led by Oliva. This removes what may be a weakness in the existing version—which is that we know too far in advance that all is well, so that all the subsequent excitements lose their poignancy. In this revised version we believe to the last moment that the General's plot has succeeded.

Love from us both.

Ever yours,
Aldous

593: TO HAROLD RAYMOND

740 North Kings Road,
Los Angeles 46, California
30 October, 1950

My dear Harold,

Herewith the contracts. As for the MSS of *Crome Yellow* and *Proper Studies,* I will see what, if anything, of these survive, among old papers. (Incidentally why did anyone choose *Proper Studies*? I would myself much prefer to be represented by *Jesting Pilate,* or *Music at Night,* or *Beyond the Mexique Bay,* or *Themes and Variations.*)

We had to leave rather earlier than we originally intended, in order that I might be in New York for the last week of rehearsals of *The Gioconda Smile.* I found everything in the most frightful mess—the actors at daggers drawn with the producer-director, the rendering of the play unsatisfactory in the extreme [. . .] I managed to restore a certain amount of harmony and to assist the director in improving the performances. But unfortunately the defects of [——] and Basil Rathbone as Hutton were built-in and constitutional, so could not be remedied. Rathbone is excellent in certain roles; but is quite unable to render the easy charm and the relaxed sense of superiority which are the essence of Hutton's character. Instead, he gets tense and becomes theatrical. However, we have very fine performances by

Valerie Taylor and George Relph. The play is still in a rather precarious condition; but has a fair chance of picking up enough to survive. We shall see.

Maria and I drove back across the continent, stopping en route at Taos, New Mexico, to see Frieda Lawrence, who was remarkably well and spry in spite of her age. (She is over seventy now.)

We got here two days ago and are now up to the neck in unpacking, answering accumulated letters and all the other horrors that follow long absence. I shall be glad when the decks are all cleared and I can get down to work.

Ever yours,
Aldous

594: TO ANITA LOOS

740 *N. Kings Rd.,*
Los Angeles 46, Cal.
15 *November,* 1950

Dearest Anita,

Forgive me for not having written before about your book. I have been meaning to for a long time past; but what with pressures from one side and another, I have only succeeded in paving hell with my good intentions.

My feeling about the story is that you have got hold of something big, but have not yet milked it for all it is worth. First of all, there is the macabre fact, revealed only in the last paragraph, that this unhappy emblem of sex appeal is condemned to death. I feel that this revelation should have been made much earlier in the story; for then the whole affair would take on the quality of one of those fifteenth-century Dances of Death, in which kings and beggars, buffoons and prelates go jigging along at the heels of a skeleton. If you can do this for Hollywood, you will have written a twentieth-century, American Morality Play. But the problem immediately arises of *how* the revelation is to be made at an earlier point. And this raises the question of narrative in the first person. It may be that, to get the fullest value from the theme, you will have to alternate a first-person diary and autobiography with a third-person narrative by someone other than the heroine—someone who can see her simultaneously from the publicity man's point of view and from the point of view of the intimate who knows that the Bust doesn't enjoy the pleasures of sex and regards the eroticism which she evokes, and on which she lives, with the disapproval of an instinctive and physiological puritanism. This means, in practice, that the second narrative would have to be the work of her ex-husband, the camera-man; for he knows and sees through the picture business; he also knows (biblically and otherwise) the Bust and has seen through her; but he is a sympathetic guy who likes and

594 *Book:* A Mouse Is Born.

is genuinely sorry for the girl. Such a double narrative will permit you to say more about Hollywood. (Incidentally, some of the things put into the Bust's mouth are too searching to be strictly in character. They could not, in reality, be uttered or even thought by her.) At the same time we should get a more comprehensive and compassionate and yet funnier view of the woman's character. Added to which, we should also be able to see her whole career as a dance of death and (which is very important) we should avoid the danger of monotony—a danger which is very real, when one is writing in the style of the uneducated. Such narratives cannot afford to be anything but short; and if one wants to develop the theme, it becomes almost imperative to find a device for slipping into another and more normal kind of language. My own feeling is that the autobiography, mingled with diary jottings, should be by the Bust, while the comments on Hollywood, now contained in the opening chapters of the book, should be by the second narrator, who will also record, from *his* point of view, the day-by-day goings-on which are recorded by the Bust from *hers*.

All this entails, I am afraid, some very radical alterations—or rather additions; for not much need be altered in the Bust's narrative, which would mainly require shortening under the new scheme, leaving quite a bit of the present material to the other narrator. However I believe the changes are worth making, if you can postpone publication; for it seems to me that it is only in this, or some similar, way that the theme can be adequately worked out. By confining yourself exclusively to the first-person narrative you make it impossible (given the character and situation of the narrator) to say all that can and should be said about your subject.

I suppose you have seen that the *Gioconda* is dead. The move from the Lyceum to the Fulton, coinciding as it did with the universally bad business during election week, brought the receipts for the final week down to about seven thousand dollars, and the advance bookings for the following week were too slim to risk continuance. So Traube decided to shut up shop. It is a pity; for the play had showed a small profit for all the preceding weeks and looked as though it might have been nursed through to health. Now it is dead, it is dead, I suppose, for keeps. At any rate so far as America is concerned [. . . .] The initial bad casting and not very competent directing created a constitutional weakness which made it impossible for the piece to survive the bad criticisms in the *Times* and *Herald Tribune*. It is a bore; for I would have enjoyed making some easy money. Now I must settle down to some honest work—and perhaps some dishonest work in the movies, if I can find it, which isn't so easy nowadays.

Are you coming out West? I hope so, though I know you don't. Best love from us both.

Ever yours affectionately,
Aldous

595: TO DR ROGER GODEL

740 *North Kings Road,*
Los Angeles 46, Cal.
10 *December,* 1950

My dear Roger,

This typewriter has no accents, so I will write in English to wish you both a merry Christmas and a new year as happy as Messrs MacArthur, Mao and Stalin will permit anyone to have. For I suppose this unhappy planet is to be sacrificed yet once more on the altar of the old ideological idols. As a child I could never understand why such a fuss was made, in the Old Testament, about idolatry. Now, it has become only too obvious. For every finite and home-made object of reverence, set up as God and worshipped as if it were the Absolute, inevitably turns into a Moloch (however noble it may superficially seem) and devours its adorers. Besides being so tragic and so horrible, this repetition of the old theme of human history is unutterably *boring*. Can't we have something genuinely new, for a change, something interesting, something which makes possible the development of man's latent potentialities? The answer given by our leaders is a loud, decided, No.

There is not much news to report. We had a strenuous time in New York, where I found the play in a state of chaos and had to work very hard at the final rehearsals. Not to much purpose, unfortunately; for the thing died after five weeks. Julian was in New York and reported making good progress with his plans. I have not heard from him since his return to England, so don't know what is happening at the moment. I also saw my friend Dr W. H. Sheldon, who is doing research at his Clinic of Constitutional Medicine and at the same time is compiling an enormous Atlas of somatotypes, to put his work on a firm, fully documented foundation. We drove back to California by car, stopping en route at the University of Ohio [Ohio State University], to see a man called [Dwight] Sherman who has devised a very interesting new technique for the training of beginning art students along the lines of gestalt psychology. Students work in a darkened room. Magic lantern slides of patterns of abstract forms are flashed for one tenth of a second on a screen and the students record their impression with crayons, on large sheets of paper, in the dark. This teaches 'unitary perception' of complex situations— in other words a sense of composition, so far as art is concerned. The results are remarkable.

Here I have been very busy working on the materials for a study of psychology and spirituality within the concrete framework of the case of the diabolic possessions of Loudun and their sequel, the case of Jean Joseph Surin. The story is fantastic in itself, and the opportunities for trying to formulate a coherent picture of the mind should be great.

595 *Godel, chief physician of the hospital of the Suez Canal Company and writer on philosophy and mysticism, had met Huxley about the end of August.*

Meanwhile we have been looking into dianetics. A psycho-therapist of our acquaintance is using it and gets good results. Basically it seems to be a procedure by which one obtains age regression without putting the patient into deep hypnosis. The aim is to get at the words and phrases, heard by the patient at moments of lowered consciousness, and accepted by him as obsessive commands, like post-hypnotic suggestions. The sub-conscious seems to take these verbal commands literally and unreasoningly, without regard to their context. The result can be disastrous, both mentally and physically. (If this is really the case, we may have here the rationale of magic spells, curses, anathemas and the like.) I will write you further on this topic when I have learned more. Meanwhile Maria joins me in sending affectionate good wishes to you both.

Yours
Aldous H

596: TO J. B. RHINE

740 N. Kings Rd.,
Los Angeles 46, Cal.
25 March, 1951

Dear Dr. Rhine,

I have to thank you and the staff of the *Journal of Parapsychology* for sending me the review as it comes out. It interests me very greatly and I look forward to each successive number very eagerly.

Have you ever thought of doing something in the field of publishing, which might be of great importance—I mean the reprinting in an anthological volume, of some of the older (and quite inaccessible) texts referring to Parapsychology before and immediately after the foundation of the SPR. E.g selections from Puységur, from Deleuze, from Elliotson and the 'Zoist', from Esdaile and Harriet Martineau and Braid and Fahnenstock [Fahnestock] (if it seemed desirable to include material on mesmeric therapy); from Gurney, F. W. H. Myers and other early SPR workers. Much of this material is intrinsically interesting; it is virtually unknown today and the problems with which it deals are sadly neglected by 20th-century practitioners of hypnosis. A volume containing reprints of the most interesting experimental material, together with some philosophical background material (e.g Myers's hypotheses on mental structure and mind's relation to the cosmos, as developed in that remarkable and scandalously neglected book *Human Personality and its Survival of Bodily Death*) would be exceedingly valuable. Wd it not be possible for some candidate for a Ph.D to undertake the work, under your supervision, and get it published by a University Press? I wish you would think of this; for I'm sure it wd be worth doing.

Hoping that we may meet again before too long, I am

Yours very sincerely
Aldous Huxley

740 North Kings Road,
Los Angeles 46, California
9 June, 1951

Dearest J,

Alas, I have been very remiss in writing. There is no excuse, except that I have been more than ordinarily busy against more than ordinary obstacles, caused by recurrent eye-inflammations which came on in March with an attack of the unusually malignant flu which has reigned here. The trouble seems to be wearing off at last, but has been a nuisance and a handicap to my work on the historical book I am now doing.

And meanwhile what news of you? Have you been well? How is Juliette? What of Francis in his jungle? And of Anthony, the paterfamilias? And what about your projects? Has M. [Antonin] Besse come up to scratch? Have you got any satisfaction from the various American Foundations? I wish I cd have come East to see you, but time and cash were lacking. For this reason,—and also because it wd have been so appallingly hot—we declined an invitation by the Godels to go with them to India, to visit holy places in the Himalayas with their friend Krishna Menon. I am hoping that his book will soon come out. I thought it very interesting when I read the MS. One welcomes any serious contribution to the study and discussion of human personality in its full range. Everything seems to point to the fact that, as one goes down through the subliminal, one passes through a layer (with which psycho-analysts commonly deal) predominantly evil and making for evil—a layer of Original Sin, if one likes to call it so—into a deeper layer of 'Original Virtue', which is one of peace, illumination and insight, which seems to be on the fringes of the Pure Ego or Atman. I have recently been seeing and working with an interesting man, who was used, as a youth, as a hypnotic subject by a systematic investigator and goes down, under passes and suggestion, to very great depths of trance—depths which are most uncommonly met with in ordinary hypnotic practice. The reports from these depths are most curious. And they confirm a very curious thing told me by a retired psychiatrist here who has specialized in automatic writing as a therapeutic method: namely that practically all automatists sooner or later produce spontaneously scripts of a philosophical nature, always of the same kind and always of a Vedantic or Neo-platonic strain, affirming the existence of a Pure Ego, Pneuma, Atman underlying the phenomenal self—and this despite the fact that, consciously, the automatist may entirely disagree with such a notion.

597 Francis Huxley was doing anthropological research in Brazil. His book Affable Savages: An Anthropologist among the Urubu Indians *appeared in* 1956. *The retired psychiatrist appears to have been Dr Anita Muhl; see letter* 633.

Whatever may be the metaphysical value of these utterances, they seem to throw a light on deep psychological structure.

Love from us both.

Yours
Aldous

598: TO DR WILLIAM H. SHELDON

740 *North Kings Road,*
Los Angeles 46, California
15 *July,* 1951

Dear Bill,

I was so happy to read in *Life* that the Rockefeller people had given you a grant for the furtherance of the good work. In Oregon you will be a little nearer to us than in New York, and I hope very much you will have an opportunity to drop in on us here, or that we may have occasion to go north.

Not much news since last we met. I have been very busy on a long historical study, which is still only half finished. Matthew and Ellen expect to make grandparents of us in September or October. Gerald flourishes and seems to be writing at least five books at once. And meanwhile the world at large slides further down into the abyss either of immediate war or of long-range overpopulation, starvation and universal unrest. So there we are.

Ever yours,
Aldous

599: TO IGOR STRAVINSKY

740 *North Kings Road,*
Los Angeles 46, California
[18] *July,* 1951

Cher ami,

Que vous êtes gentil! Je vous remercie mille fois et de tout mon coeur.

---

598 *Grandparents: of Mark Trevenen Huxley, who was born on 20 October.*

599 TRANSLATION:—'*How kind you are! A thousand thanks with all my heart.*
'*You do me too much honour in calling me the* Rake's *godfather. At most I am only the go-between who happily contrived the meeting of those two eminent Lesbians, Music and Poetry, who, for these past thirty centuries, have stuck together so notoriously. Yours very cordially. . . .*'
Dated 19 *July but postmarked the* 18th. *The* Rake *was of course* The Rake's Progress. *Stravinsky had seen Hogarth's* The Rake's Progress *on exhibition in Chicago and had immediately conceived the idea of an operatic development based on the succession of scenes. Afterwards Huxley had suggested to him that he ask W. H. Auden to write the libretto, which Auden did in collaboration with Chester Kallman.*

636

Vous me faites trop d'honneur en m'appelant le parrain du *Rake*. Je ne suis au plus que l'entremetteur qui a combiné heureusement le rencontre de ces deux éminentes lesbiennes, Musique et Poésie, dont le collage, depuis trente siècles, est si notoire.

Bien cordialement vôtre,
Aldous Huxley

600: TO CASS CANFIELD

740 *North Kings Road,*
Los Angeles 46, California
22 *July,* 1951

Dear Cass,

Thank you for your letter and the good news about the sales of *The Art of Seeing*. I wish some of the other and, from the literary point of view, more deserving titles could do as well.

I am hard at work on my historical book, which promises to turn into something very substantial and, I hope, very interesting. In the intervals of the research and writing I have taken a couple of weeks to revise the dialogue of what seems to me a very ingenious and effective stage adaptation of *After Many a Summer*, made by a young radio writer called Ralph Rose. The book was adapted for radio and performed twice, apparently with great success. (I didn't hear either performance, but understand that both went very well.) This being so, I hope there may be an opening for the stage version. We shall see.

I forget whether I mentioned it at the time; but in forty-seven, I think it was forty-seven [*actually in* 1946], I made for the *Encyclopaedia Britannica* people an anthology of essays, with introductory remarks to most of the authors by myself—remarks amounting, I should think, to thirty thousand words or more, in the aggregate. Since then the *Britannica* seems to have shelved the series in which the volume was to come out. A man called Wallace Brockway was in charge of the project at the time. Since then he has moved on to one of the other publishers. I have written to the *Britannica* to ask what is happening, but have received no answer. It seems to me rather a shame that this anthology-with-comments, which cost me a lot of work and was rather good, should remain indefinitely in cold storage. I don't know whether, if the *Britannica* would let it go, Harpers would care to publish it—or if not Harpers, someone else with an interest in this kind of book. In any case I would be most grateful if you could get in touch with *Britannica* and try to find out (a) if they ever intend to publish the book, (b) if they would permit it to be published elsewhere. They don't answer my letters; but they might answer yours!

Yours,
Aldous Huxley

740 *North Kings Road,*
Los Angeles 46, Cal.
4 *November,* 1951

Dear Mrs Murrell,

Thank you for your letters and the collection of writings. And please forgive this long delay in acknowledging them. I am trying to finish a long laborious job requiring a lot of research, and have had no energy left over for letter writing. As you see, I am in the thick of the forest—your vision of me made me laugh, albeit a little ruefully. Winding in and out among the trees like a snake, and emerging at last, after an enormous crawl, into an opening where the head enjoys a perfect view of its own tail! But I do try to find time for other things than getting lost in the wood. And anyhow God is even there. God is even in one's own posterior when at last one has crawled full circle and seen it revealed in its full glory. The infinite is totally present at every point of space and time, even the most trivial and preposterous. It is simply a matter of seeing it—or, to be more accurate, of getting out of the way so that it can see itself. Zen literature seems so puzzling because it is concerned, not with God as something other than the world, to be known and worshipped by human selves apart from the world and in contra-distinction to it, but with God as including the world (for obviously the infinite includes the finite), God as the Knower within individual knowers—the Knower who, if we can get out of the way, with all our home-made illusions, can know things as they are in themselves (in other words, as they are in the Knower) and can communicate this knowledge to the individual knower. Christianity has been so fiercely on its guard against nature-worship and pantheism, that it has rather neglected the God who includes the finite and knows finite things through the finite, if the finite will permit him, in an infinite and world-tranfiguring way. The kingdom of God is within, and it can come on earth as in heaven, on condition that, at any given moment, here and now, we permit our kingdom of cravings, abhorrences and illusions, to go. And that is Zen.

I am hoping to see Dr Suzuki one of these days. He is lecturing somewhere in this neighbourhood. He is a little old Japanese of more than eighty, with the tiniest hands I have ever seen on any human being, and with an extraordinary charm and gentleness. I saw him once a year ago, and was greatly taken by him, would like very much to talk with him again. There is a very curious book by a man called R. H. Blyth, called *Zen in English Literature.* Blyth is a professor at some Japanese university and has lived in that country for many years. The book deals with the relation between

---

601 *Elise Murrell corresponded with Huxley on visionary experience and mysti-cism. She has extra-sensory gifts.*

moment-by-moment experience of Things-as they-Are [and] Poetry. It is a bit perverse sometimes, but very illuminating at others.

My wife and I have just become grandparents. I wish the baby might have been born into a less dismal kind of a world; but perhaps it is no more dismal, after all, than it has always been. And in spite of all our efforts, we shall never succeed in making it un-divine.

God bless you.

Yours very sincerely
Aldous Huxley

602: TO DR ROGER GODEL

740 N. Kings Rd.,
Los Angeles 46, Cal.
23 December, 1951

Dear Roger,

This brings all best wishes from us both to both of you. May 1952 be as happy a year as Messrs Stalin, Truman, Mao et Cie, will permit it to be for any individual. We have thought of you often and hoped that the present troubles on the Canal are not affecting you too seriously. Meanwhile how are you both and what are you doing?

Not much news here. I have nearly finished the study on the Devils of Loudun and Father Surin, about whom I spoke to you 18 months ago. It has been a long, laborious job—and I was interrupted this summer by an attack of iritis, which fortunately affected only my half-blind eye, leaving the other undamaged. But while it lasted it was painful and incapacitating and I live in fear of a recurrence—tho' hope for the best.

Has your book come out yet? All I have seen in this field is Dr. Benoit's new book on Zen. Good in its queer way—but written in the crabbed, abstract style which made his first book so hard to read. I saw dear old Dr. Suzuki the other day and had a very pleasant and instructive talk with him. I find the whole Zen approach, together with Chinese and Japanese Zen literature, peculiarly satisfying. There is a curious book by an Englishman now living in Japan (Blyth is his name) called *Zen in English Literature* [which is] well worth reading, tho' sometimes a little exasperating. I don't know what our plans will be for 1952. I may collaborate on a film about Gandhi—here to begin with, perhaps in India later—but feel a little hesitant, in view of the precarious condition of my eyes, to go so far. *Nous verrons.* I will keep you informed. Isn't there a medical congress you could attend in this part of the world?

Yours
Aldous Huxley

602 *Godel's book:* Essais sur l'expérience libératrice (*Paris*, 1952), *which Huxley had read in manuscript.*

603: TO EDITH SITWELL

740 *North Kings Road,*
Los Angeles 46, California
28 February, 1952

My dear Edith,

This is to introduce our friend Sanford Roth, who is a most excellent photographer and would like to continue in London the series of admirable portraits which he has done in France and the USA—of Stravinsky, of Utrillo, of Chagall, of Vlaminck. It wd be a great honour if you would sit for him—and I am sure that you will like the result.

Ever yours,
Aldous

604: TO GROVER SMITH

740 *North Kings Road,*
Los Angeles 46, California
3 March, 1952

Dear Mr Smith,

Thank you for your letter. I used to see a good deal of T. S. Eliot during and just after the first World War. Whether he did me the honour of reading anything I wrote, I don't know. And anyhow Sesostris-Sosostris is an intrinsically occult name, made, as it is, of whispers and a snake's hiss. The good king who, in Herodotus, conquered all Asia and reigned almost as long as Queen Victoria is irrelevant. The real point is the sound of the name, with the suggestion, perhaps, of a male in fortune teller's clothing—and in *Crome Yellow,* of course, the incident was borrowed, with modifications, from the fortune telling scene in *Jane Eyre.*

Sincerely,
Aldous Huxley

605: TO VICTORIA OCAMPO

740 *North Kings Road,*
Los Angeles 46, California
8 March, 1952

My dear Victoria,

I hope this will catch you before you leave. Your letter was a long time reaching us; for you had left out the final zero of the address, and the Post Office, in one of those terrifying accesses of misplaced zeal which are worse

603 *Huxley wrote in similar terms, on the same day, to Cyril Connolly, T. S. Eliot, Mary Hutchinson, Julian Huxley, Sir Osbert Sitwell, and Lauro Venturi.*

604 *Prompted by a comment on a passage adapted from* Crome Yellow *in Eliot's* The Waste Land.

605 *Maria's operation was a mastectomy. In the summer of 1952 cancer reappeared at the site, and another operation was performed.*

even than bureaucratic inertia, forwarded the letter to our old address, from which it was retrieved only with difficulty and after much delay. I am sorry indeed that we are not to see you, and wish that your home-coming promised to be more joyous than you expect it to be. What a world! And who knows if, ten or twenty years from now, the survivors may not be looking back at 1952 nostalgically, as to a lost Golden Age?

Our personal news is tolerably good. Maria, as you will have heard, went through a rather serious operation in January, but is getting on very well—though she still gets very easily tired. I had an unpleasant scare last summer, with a bad attack of iritis that was very painful while it lasted and completely incapacitating; for I had to live in a dark room, being unable to tolerate the light. However, I got over it quite well—thanks, I think, to the healthy state of the eyes, owing to practice in the Bates Method—and am hoping and praying that there will be no recurrence.

I have recently finished a long historical study on the *Devils of Loudun*. The early phases of this episode are described, very inaccurately, in Michelet's *La Sorcière*. I have covered the whole story—from the first signs of the possession and Grandier's execution, to the possession of Father Surin, which lasted twenty years after his original diabolic infection, while treating the Prioress. There is a rich documentation—procès verbaux, letters, narratives, the Prioress's autobiography and the autobiography of Surin—both psychological documents of a quite extraordinary nature. And the subject leads naturally into all kinds of problems, historical, philosophical and psychological which call for treatment on the way. The MS has gone to the publishers and I hope that the book will be out by early autumn.

Now I am about to begin on a film about Gandhi—horribly difficult to do, but eminently worth doing, if it can be done well. The man who owns the rights is Gabriel Pascal, the producer of Shaw's plays—a Hungarian adventurer and Baron Munchausen, but nice in his way and capable, in spite of enormous muddling and confusion, of making good films. The work has not yet started; but I expect to begin in a week or two, after M and I have returned from a brief trip to the desert, which we have planned. The writing will be done here; but perhaps it may be necessary to go to India in the autumn for the shooting of the picture. We shall see.

We have been reading Heinrich Zimmer's books on Indian thought— *Philosophies of India* and *Myths and Symbols in Indian Religion and Culture*, both published by Pantheon. Do you know them? If not, do read them. They are excellent. Begin with the second, which is fascinating and quite short. The first is much longer and more comprehensive, but lively and full of interest.

Have you been writing anything? And, if so, what? Let us hear your news at greater length.

Love from us both.

Yours affectionately,
Aldous

740 N. Kings Rd.,
Los Angeles 46, Cal.
22 March, 1952

Dear Mrs Murrell,

Thank you for your letter. Please forgive me for my long silence—due not in the least to anything you said, (for I always enjoy your letters and find that they do me good), but to the fact that I am a bad correspondent, who finds it hard, because of native inefficiency and defective vision, to get everything done which has to be done and at the same time to write letters; and also to the fact that the last months have been filled with a more than ordinary amount of work, together with the troubles and anxieties attendant on an operation which my wife had to undergo in January. She has made an excellent recovery, thank heaven, and is getting back all her strength, little by little. We have just returned from a brief holiday in the Arizona desert—particularly wonderful at this time of year, with snow on the higher mountains, forests of giant cactus on the lower slopes and, in the warm plains, an immense profusion of wild flowers, which come rushing out after the spring rains (profuse this year) and carpet the desert for a few weeks with square miles of colour—purple of verbena, blue of lupines and phaselia, yellow of daisies, sunflowers and coreopsis, white and cream of evening primroses, pink and white of dwarf phlox, red of pen[t]stemons, apricot-colour of mallows. And here and there, in the most arid and naked plains, spring the desert lilies, which are like small madonna lilies, with grey green leaves and a pyramid of perfumed blossoms, snowy white with green veins on the outside of each petal. It is an unforgettable spectacle—the good will of life, the tenacity of it in the face of the most adverse circumstances, the patience of it (the lilies will lie dormant for as much as ten or fifteen years, if there is a drought, and then come bursting through the sand at the first moisture), the profusion, the beauty. And the yearly miracle takes place in an enormous, luminous silence. Huge spaces completely empty of human activity, flooded with light and enclosed in an immense crystal of silence, to which any sound—the song of a bird, the noise of a passing car or plane—is completely irrelevant. It remains unflawed in spite of the sound. One understands why St Anthony and the other hermits used to go out into the desert. For the desert is the most completely adequate symbol of one of the aspects of God—God unmanifested, God before and beyond creation, God in the 'Ground of the soul', where the person goes beyond personality and the mind is aware of the ultimate source of awareness. Of course it is not the only aspect of God, and therefore it is inadvisable for people to spend all their time within the symbol of this aspect. The desert has to give place to the town and the cultivated countryside. But as a change, as a means to purifying insight into the divine otherness, there is nothing to compare with that silence.

I am just about to start work on the script of a film on Gandhi. Very difficult to do properly, but worth attempting; for it might stimulate people to think about some of the fundamentals. God bless you. I enjoyed your letter. Write to me again.

Yours very sincerely,
Aldous Huxley

607: MARIA HUXLEY TO MRS ELISE MURRELL

[Los Angeles, California]
13 *May,* 1952

Dear Mrs Murrell,

Now I have taken my husband's habits of being slow at answering letters. Please excuse me. There seems so much to be done always, and so little time for the real interests. Thank you for answering my question about prayer. I suppose I know all the answers in my head, but I only understand them when I know them in my heart; but that is all right too. Lately I am much more settled in my answers, and more believing in them. Just sometimes experiences are unbelievable because oneself is the experiencer when it seems others would be much more suitable—and deserving. But even to that now I have an answer to my satisfaction. I keep your letter under my pillow so I should not forget the novena. Curiously the shape of the Madonna of Guadalupe in her medal had turned up consistently in my—visions is what I call it; but now it has become much more intense than just the seeing visions, and now I understand when you say you wanted to shout for joy from the housetops, but as well I have been choked with tears, at the same time, of gratitude. But nothing ever for others of any E.S.P.; perhaps I cannot feel enough interest, when I am in that other world, for this one—it may be uncharitable, I receiving such infinite charity—but not holding it either, as it makes me entirely transparent and as if disintegrated, yet enough there for some purpose. Is that what you would experience—a lasting, lasting joy, but a sad joyousness or a joyous sadness, very quiet, and also a nearness to death or rather a timelessness in which death would be always just there, not importantly but just there? And then such a feeling

---

607 *Maria referred to her visionary experiences again in a letter written to Mrs Murrell the following July: 'By the way the Madonna [medal] is the Spanish one for the Guadalupe shrine. I am pleased you wear it and like it. It was not Aldous who saw her in Gold. . . . It was myself in a Vision. Very large and when you mentioned it I know that was what you meant, the Vision I had with the streaming light which made it look gold. I have two lights. One very white and intense and so diffuse as well as permeating that one does not exactly see it but know it; then there is the other, the golden, which is always like a sheath, I mean solid ray, and which comes directly to and through one; it can be at the same time as the white light. They are different to look at and in result and mean something different too.'*

that this great, immense gift is for a purpose, for a need to come—no reason or dates given.

I would like to have written it all down. It happened slowly and probably since ever [apparently for ever]; now just more and more rapidly and always at first unrecognizably. But now I understand more each day, almost hour and minute, but it is impossible to write it down well and it could be done only with much time. I have so little and I dare not take time out from sleep. I get very tired still and physically empty with doing so much.

Francis Huxley—son of Julian, nephew of Aldous. One grandchild 6 months, Trevenen Mark Huxley [sic]. The photographs will arrive, in time. How sweet of you to ask. I hope you will like the one I chose of my husband. Of me there is only one here. We all like it, but I don't photograph as well as he does. I am 54.

I am sending you some chocolates. I hope you don't think it childish. All English friends like them.

Maria

608: TO JULIAN HUXLEY

740 *N. Kings Road,*
Los Angeles 46, Cal.
20 *May,* 1952

Dearest J,

Our respective silences are becoming almost too golden, and I think it is time we got back to a paper currency. So here goes. You must both be very happy to have Francis back, and I only hope that they won't send him to study for his doctorate among yet other cannibals in yet remoter jungles. And what of you? Are you feeling better than you were when you last wrote? I do hope so. And Juliette? And Juliette's mother?

Things go on quietly here with no specially striking incidents. Maria got over her operation very satisfactorily and is well. I have had no return of my iritis and, thanks to the newly invented pressure-breathing treatment, which I take at home with an oxygen tank and a special attachment, have practically eliminated the slight chronic bronchitis which has been a source, over many years, of general under-parness and various troubles of an acuter nature. My book on the *Devils of Loudun* is finished, and I have just corrected the galleys—a long wearisome job which I am glad to have put behind me. At present I am doing a few odds and ends and waiting to see if my agents can get a satisfactory contract out of Gabriel Pascal in regard to the Gandhi film. There is something *simpatico* about Pascal—he is a kind of Central European Baron Munchausen, boastful in an altogether childish way, mildly

608 *Pressure-breathing treatment: administered with a device called a Bennett valve, designed for cases of oxygen insufficiency. The Lorenz book was* King Solomon's Ring (1952).

paranoiac, but well-meaning and honest, I believe, with those he likes, and when he can afford it. But he has the Bohemian's horror of being pinned down in black and white, of having to commit himself definitely to anything. Hence the difficulty of writing a satisfactory contract—particularly one which calls for conditional payments out of future earnings. The haggling has been going on since February and is as far from a conclusion as the Korean armistice negotiations. So Lord knows what will finally happen. Meanwhile I think we may go for a little trip into the Pacific Northwest, which we have never visited and which, according to all accounts, is marvellously beautiful.

I went the other day to visit the Naval Research station in the desert, about 200 miles from here. A thousand square miles of testing grounds. Sentries and FBI men to check everybody going in or out. Huge areas and many buildings tightly closed to all but those with the magic talisman. But I saw the main building called the Michelson Laboratory—nine and a half acres of floor space, foundries and machine shops which permit the manufacture of anything from an electron microscope to a tank. Mysterious testing gadgets of every kind. And a town of twelve thousand inhabitants, mostly Ph.D's, entirely air conditioned, in the middle of the most howling of wildernesses. The whole directed exclusively to the production of bigger and better rockets. It was the most frightening exhibition of scientific and highly organized insanity I have ever seen. One vaguely thought that the human race was determined to destroy itself. After visiting the China Lake Research station, one feels quite certain of it. And the whole world is fairly crawling with physicists in barbed wire compounds working three shifts a day *ad majorem Diaboli gloriam*. What a relief to turn to the book by [Konrad] Lorenz, for which you wrote an introduction! Consider the wolves and the jackdaws. . . .

Our love to you all.

Ever your affectionate,
Aldous

609: TO SANFORD H. ROTH

740 N. Kings Rd.,
Los Angeles 46, Cal.
15 July, 1952

Dear Sandy,

Thank you for your two letters and for the excellent news contained in the second. I hope very much that you will be able to clinch the deal before you start. As for business arrangements—I am very happy to go for a partnership arrangement as you suggest. The actual drawing up of agreements

609 *Concerning plans for Huxley and Roth's* The French of Paris. *Canfield wrote to Huxley on* 17 *July that the publication date of* The Devils of Loudun *had been fixed for* 1 *October.*

645

is beyond my competence. If it is best for Chêne to draw up separate agreements with each of us, well and good. But equally well and good if you find that, for reasons of bookkeeping etc, it is better for them to draw up a single agreement, which you can sign on my behalf. (If they need my signature, the agreement can be airmailed to me here and I will airmail it back; but meanwhile it is understood that they can go ahead with the production.) In regard to the publication in the U S—I suppose we shall make a separate agreement with Harpers, who will buy the sheets and distribute. This, of course, can wait until your return. In the mean time let us wish ourselves all possible success.

I am sorry about the [——] business. I presume that, in these big foundations, favouritism and *pistonage* play a very large part. Moreover many of the world's artistic and cultural organizations are infiltrated by homosexuals, with the result that nobody who is vulgar enough to like women stands a chance. Whether this applies to [——] I don't know. But in the world as at present constituted it is a possibility—almost a probability.

I have no news as to the publication date in *Vogue*. Meanwhile will write to Canfield about your prospects. He too is very stingy with news, and I have not yet heard when they plan to issue my book on the *Devils of Loudun*.

All best wishes to you both.

Yours
Aldous

610: TO ——

740 *N. Kings Rd.,*
Los Angeles 46, Cal.
[?20] *July,* 1952

[. . . .]

And now for what you say about yourself—I wish the news were better and hope that it may soon become so. Meanwhile let me tell you a little of the experience which both Maria and I have had in the realm of psychotherapy, in the widest sense of the word. It began three or four years ago when M, who had been brought rather low by a long-standing and long undetected intestinal infection, and was in a state of serious nervous exhaustion, went to see a man who has since become a good friend—a psychotherapist specializing in hypnosis, which he uses partly as an adjunct and adjuvant of analysis, partly to give suggestion therapy, and partly as a means for non-directional therapy of a kind which I shall describe later on. After the first treatment M got an enormous sense of psycho-physical relief-of-tension. Since that time I have become a rather good hypnotic operator, and I was able, after M's very serious operation early this year, to help her very greatly, with the result that, despite the shock involved in the removal of the tumour, she has been in strikingly good psychological shape, with a serenity and cheerfulness which have undoubtedly contributed to her excellent recovery.

I myself am not a particularly good hypnotic subject, but can go at least into a light trance. When I had my bout of iritis last year I went two or three times to a man who is head of the Psychology Department at the University of California at Los Angeles, and these brief hypnotic treatments undoubtedly helped me to sleep and to deal with the pain. Moreover, by means of auto-hypnosis (which is an art not too hard to acquire if one has a good hypnotist as a teacher) and by treatments from Maria and our friend [Leslie] LeCron, the psycho-therapist, I was enabled to get over the very considerable apprehension which accompanied and followed the iritis—apprehension that the good eye might be involved and lose much of its vision, and apprehension of a relapse, which is not uncommon in these conditions.

In all these instances the benefits due to hypnosis are due fundamentally to the fact that it is accompanied by a high degree of relaxation, mental and physical. The ego is able to let go, to get out of the way, to stop interfering with the beneficent action of the 'entelechy', which is at once the physiological sub-conscious that sees to the proper functioning of the body, and the higher, non-personal sub-conscious—the thing that, in contradistinction to the personal sub-conscious where the Freudian rats and black-beetles are active, gives one 'inspirations', 'intuitions', 'good thoughts' which are as genuinely real facts as are the fears and compulsions, aggressions and despairs generated in the Freudian basement. (The chapters in F. W. H. Myers' *Human Personality*, dealing with Genius, Sleep and Hypnosis, and Poincaré's essay on mathematical inspiration, are very instructive in regard to this higher Not-Self within and beyond the self. Freud's greatest error, it seems to me, was not to have paid sufficient attention to this more than personal not-self with which we are all so blessedly associated, and to have concentrated the therapist's and the patient's attention on the self and its rats and black beetles in the personal sub-conscious.)

On the basis of what I myself have experienced, of what I have seen in the case of Maria, of what I have been able to accomplish in the case of several friends, of what I have seen done by LeCron and, more recently, by a man who is probably the greatest living virtuoso in the field of hypnosis, Dr [——], I would advise you very strongly to try hypnosis. Since success depends on a satisfactory relation between the hypnotized person and the operator, you must be prepared to 'shop around' until you find someone sympathetic as well as skilful. And I would be inclined to concentrate at first on the simply going fairly deep, and having yourself taught (by means of post-hypnotic suggestion) to hypnotize yourself if the occasion should require. Merely the letting go, the release of tension, the getting the interfering and health-destroying ego out of the way, is of enormous value. Suggestions should be kept to a minimum—to such suggestions, for example, as the ability to recapture the experience of the peace experienced under hypnosis during the hours of daily living, through the closing of the eyes for a moment and the repetition of some word like Peace. Therapeutic procedures should not be directive, but should rather be suggested by the deeper self, which can generally be relied on to come up with something of use to the organism, if it is politely asked to do so—e.g. some memory which requires to be talked out several times until there is no further emotional reaction to it, or else some symbolic image which may not seem significant at the moment, but will often turn out to make sense later on. This method of approach is, I believe, much better than any course of suggestions pushed in by the operator, or than a too busy probing of analysis. There is a part of the sub-conscious not-self which is much less stupid than the self and the personal sub-conscious, and can be relied upon to provide help if asked. In this context I am sending you under separate cover a pamphlet written by a [. . .] man [A. L. Kitselman] whom I first met some years ago when he was working on translations of Hinayana Buddhist texts from the Pali Canon and who has turned up again recently with something which, to judge by the results I have seen, is of considerable value. Essentially the procedure is a technique whereby the results of Buddhist meditation, as described in such books as the *Visuddhi Magga*, are sought and obtained by methods, not of solitary contemplation, but a collaboration between the person, who is trying to get out of the way as a self and establish contact with the bene-ficent non-self, and an observer who asks questions and otherwise provides help. [. . . .] So do read the pamphlet; it is blessedly short and explicit. Its findings are based in part on the author's findings as a practising psychologist, in part on his very considerable knowledge of the Pali texts, which suggested some of his procedures and described phenomena which subsequently dis-played themselves in practice. The booklet does not mention hypnosis; but actually most of the phenomena occur in a state of relaxed reverie, which is in fact a light hypnotic trance. Deeper trances may be useful where the conscious self is too tense and beknotted to permit the not-self to respond to the appeal made by the non-directive therapist.

This has been a very long letter; but I hope that you may find something in it that will be of some help. Heaven knows, all of us need help, and I have set forth some of the ways in which, as I know by personal experience and by observation of others, some people at least can get help, and get it even when they are in extremely tight corners.

    [. . . .]

Aldous

PS. About insomnia. On the rare occasions when I get a touch of it now I find one or other of the following procedures to be very helpful. Lie on the back and relax (often the relaxation is better if one has first stretched and tensed all the muscles of limbs and trunk—arching the whole body on the heels and shoulders as supports, so as to give a thorough tensing to the back and thigh muscles.) When in the relaxed state imagine or remember (or both at once) an occasion on which you took violent exercise. (I imagine-remember running along a beach, then walking into the sea, feeling the impact of the cold water as it rises up the legs and body, then swimming, and finally riding the waves on a surf-board and running out again, with the waves breaking against my body, and repeating the ride several times. Then one imagines drying, sun-bathing and going into the house for a nap. After which one can turn over into one's normal sleeping position.) This re-living physical activity in a state of relaxation helps many people to go to sleep—why, I don't know; but the fact remains. The other sleep-producing procedure which is often effective consists in getting relaxed and remembering the events of the day in all the detail that comes to mind. One runs through the day's history from morning till night several times in succession —the first time rather slowly, then more rapidly as one becomes familiar with the process and the memories. This bringing of the events of the day into consciousness and 'running them off' several times in succession— half a dozen times or more, if there should be any difficult or disagreeable episodes in the course of the day—seems to get rid of the tensions accumulated during the day. It is a cathartic and mildly abreactive bringing up into awareness of material which might be, which indeed *is* (if only slightly), disturbing on the lower levels of the mind. Add to this the fact, which I can't fully explain, but which must be recognized, that the process of remembering, in a relaxed, impersonal, scientific-observerish way, is intrinsically relaxing. In the Bates Method of visual re-education the act of remembering is used as a device for achieving relaxation of mind and eye muscles. Moreover memory of pleasant events can be and has been used as a method for inducing hypnosis, particularly in subjects who react badly to direct suggestions and commands. The first record of this in the literature is contained in a book mentioned by F. W. H. Myers, *Statuvolism* (God knows what the word means) by Dr Fahnestock of Chicago, published in the seventies. He was a most successful hypno-therapist who relied exclusively on the process of getting his patients to remember pleasant scenes and episodes out of their past for getting them into a trance, in which their symptoms could be dealt with. Dr [———] often uses similar techniques. (Incidentally, he can induce hypnosis in otherwise unhypnotizable people simply by talking about the weather or anything else, including the fact that they are resistant to hypnosis.) And I myself have found that I could induce a high degree first of relaxation, then of trance, by taking a subject on a walk through familiar country. (It will work even if the scenes described are not familiar to the subject, but merely evoke analogous scenes out of his own past.) In recalling scenes out of the past, you have been making use of an effective relaxation technique. To make it fully effective, it would probably be necessary to be put into a light hypnoid state and be given the post-hypnotic suggestion that this process of remembering will induce a complete detensioning. But even without this suggestion from without, this kind of

649

remembering is undoubtedly relaxing, while the systematic nightly 'running off' of the day's history is often specific against sleeplessness.

My friend LeCron, who has been editing a big symposium on hypnosis by men in this field all over the world, has given me several addresses of people with whom he has been in correspondence [. . . .]

611: TO ROGER AND ALICE GODEL

740 *North Kings Rd.,*
Los Angeles 46, Cal.
14 *August,* 1952

Dear Roger and Alice,

Many thanks for your letter and for the book, which did not reach us until several days later. We have begun reading it aloud and I will write again when we have finished it. Meanwhile this brings our best thanks and the latest news.

First as to health. Maria has got over her operation very satisfactorily and is on the whole remarkably well. She has been much helped, I think, by a modified form of the 'E Therapy' described in the booklet we sent you. The value of this technique consists in the fact that it is a non-directive therapy, addressed to the central, axial consciousness with a request for help and enlightenment, which is very often forthcoming either in the form of some kind of intuitive answer to whatever may happen to be the most urgent problem of the moment, or sometimes in the form of symbolic imagery (a Rêve Eveillé expressive of the primordial Fact), or in the shape of repressed memories which it has become important to recall, or again in some physical release of tension. The procedure is actually a form of meditation, in which the meditator does not work alone, but is helped by the questions of an auditor. Why these questions should be helpful I do not exactly know. But the fact remains that they seem to assist the mind in its task of standing aside from the ego and its preoccupations, and laying itself open to the central consciousness. In a number of cases which I have seen the results have led to a remarkable increase in insight and improvement in behaviour.

The little pamphlet was written by a young man whom I first knew twelve years ago, when he had just left the university. We met him again last winter and found him a good deal more mature. He has a considerable knowledge of the Pali texts of Hinayana Buddhism and has permitted his psychological experimentation to be directed, to a great extent, by the elaborate analysis of conscious states contained in those texts. He himself is not a born artist in the psychological field, and the method has shown more striking results in other hands. But something can be got from it by most people. It is, essentially, an application, in a rather novel way, of the Gospel injunction—'Ask and it shall be given'. The problem has always been: How and whom shall we ask?

My book on the *Devils of Loudun* is appearing at the beginning of

October in this country and perhaps (though I have not yet heard any definite announcement) a little earlier in England. I have included a long chapter on the psychological theories of the period, with discussions about the kind of picture of the human consciousness which a realistic acceptance of all the facts compels us to form. Incidentally there are passages in Surin's autobiography which are remarkably illuminating on the subject of the central consciousness, which persists even at the height of severe mental derangement. And do you know that extraordinary analysis of the central state and its surrounding 'field' given by Armelle Nicolas—the Breton servant girl who achieved the highest mystical experience while scrubbing the floors and cooking the dinner, and who came to be revered by her contemporaries as a saint? There is a book about her by de Couvelho (I think that is how the name is spelt) [*i.e.*, Le Gouvello] and long extracts from the original documents are given by Brémond in, I think, the fourth [*i.e.*, the fifth] volume of his *Histoire du Sentiment Religieux*. It is an amazingly lucid and precise account—all the more extraordinary since it was dictated by an ignorant peasant woman who did not know how to read or write. (And perhaps she was lucky in her ignorance. For consider what her descendants use their literacy to read! When one looks at the newspapers, magazines and cheap books which are now consumed by the tens of millions, one is appalled.)

I am working now on a book of essays about and around this strange and fascinating country, the American West—from the forests and mountains of Washington to the deserts and date palms of southern California. It will not be exactly a travel book—rather a series of soliloquies having Far Western places as their source and excuse. As for plans—who knows? Perhaps next year will be propitious for another European excursion. If so, we shall most certainly take advantage of your kind invitation. Our love to you both.

Yours
Aldous

612: TO LAWRENCE C. POWELL

740 N. Kings Rd.,
L A 46, Cal.
17 September, 1952

Dear Larry,

Thank you for your letter and invitation. Alas, I feel wholly unqualified to talk about Shaw, whom I don't know at all well—perhaps because I have never found him very interesting. Did he, after all, ever know anything about human beings?

Next time I come into the library I hope to see you.

Yours
Aldous

740 *N. Kings Rd.,*
Los Angeles 46, Cal.
29 September, 1952

Dearest Matthew and Ellen,

We got your long letter today, and I am sending this off at once to keep you posted of the situation here. At the moment this is rather bad on account of Bonne Maman. As C probably told you in her last letter, BM contrived to sprain her arthritic shoulder ten days ago, giving herself a great deal of pain. The acute phase quieted down very quickly, and she is back more or less where she started—with a chronic condition which she forgets about when she is amused and which, when she is bored and lonely, she feels to be a chronic martyrdom. That she has discomfort and sometimes pain is certain. It is also certain that, when she is enjoying herself, she can forget about it. At the moment she is making use of her trouble to get as much attention and service out of both Rose and Coccola as she possibly can. Rose had to rush in from the desert over the weekend—to find that there wasn't anything very much wrong; and C is kept on the hop all the time, fetching, carrying, shopping etc. This wouldn't be so bad, if it weren't for the continual stream of emphatic and self-contradictory talk by which it is accompanied, and for the elaborate and preposterous schemes and plots which BM has only too much leisure to hatch. Coccola has never had a wide margin of reserve strength to draw upon, and since her operations this margin has shrunk to a point where her mother (who, for all her age and her rheumatism, has far more physical energy than her daughters) can easily push her over the edge. The problem is a difficult and many-sided one. There is first of all the psychological problem of an old woman who has consistently refused to be anything in life but a tourist, looking on from the outside. BM resolutely declines to do anything useful, to co-operate in any way which would entail her making compromises and suiting her own convenience to that of others. She has never consented to take the trouble to do things which would be really useful to herself, such as learning lip-reading. In her touristy way she talks with enthusiasm about one of her aunts, who learned lip reading unassisted; but has never bothered to do anything of the kind herself. Because she reads the *Figaro Littéraire,* she feels herself immeasurably superior to the general run of her neighbours, and won't associate with them. She has quarrelled with the local Catholic church and so cut herself off from the social and benevolent organizations which it sponsors and in which she could certainly have found something interesting and useful to do. Age and disability make the full life of the tourist impossible for her; and she now spends her energies brooding and making life intolerable for Coccola

613 *Bonne Maman: Mme Marguerite Nys was in her mid-seventies, having been born in* 1876. *She died in* 1966.

and Rose. What can be done I don't know. Sooner or later she will have to consent to sharing her apartment (which is very expensive in relation to her present resources) with somebody who will help her, in exchange for board and lodging. The other alternative will be some sort of a sanitarium, which she will hate. In no circumstances would I think of installing her in this house. She would drive Coccola to death or madness in a few months, would make it impossible for me to do any work and, when we are away, which we may be for several months at a stretch, would be as much dependent on outside help as at present. Suzanne may consider herself extremely lucky to be three thousand miles away from this very difficult and very painful problem. I hope we may have found some kind of an interim solution by the time you arrive.

I wish those damned personnel boys would hurry up. Would you think of coming before they make up their minds? Or is your idea to hang on until you get a definite decision and then come?

I am still negotiating for the trio of short stories for cinema and TV, to be played by [Laurence] Olivier and [Vivien] Leigh. Contracts are not yet signed, but I hope they will be either within the next few days or when the producer has returned from a forthcoming trip to talk with Olivier in London.

About agents—the excitement was caused by one of Gerald's rather fanciful outpourings on the score of twenty-five cent reprints. For myself, I don't think there is very much in the whole thing. Pulp publishers won't be induced to buy more of my books [simply] because of an agent; nor, so far as I can see, can the author do much better, because of an agent, with the original publisher—with whom the contract is always made by the pulp-man. The standard rate is fifty-fifty between author and original publisher; and I don't see much prospect of doing any better. Cass wrote some weeks ago to say that he was negotiating for a pulp reprint of *Brave New World*.

In regard to agency work outside the pulp field—I now make use mainly of Chambrun, on the advice of Anita [. . . .] My own impression is that he is just a literary agent, like all the rest. I may, perhaps, try the literary agency which is embedded in the Wm Morris office in New York, to see what they can do with two essays I have recently written. Chambrun at least has sold two brief travel articles to the *Ford Times*, a trade paper which pays quite well because it can take it off the income tax as advertising. Probably there is little to choose between agencies. It is always a case of out of the frying pan into the fire—or should one say out of the bed pan into the mire.

Love to you both and to the young Hercules. George Kent rang us up the other day and was full of enthusiasm and promises of many coloured snapshots.

Ever your affectionate,
Aldous

PS. Further to Robert Hutchins—he expressed himself as highly interested in you, inasmuch as Ford is now beginning to take an interest in conservation;

told us to make sure you came to see him as soon as you got out to California and said something about himself contacting New York to see if anything could be done there. Since you have not heard from Ford in NY, I presume he failed to do anything; but I think that, if UN doesn't materialise, you would do well to see Hutchins personally out here. We have not seen him since our dinner party; but he seemed very friendly and genuinely interested. The Foundation is being forced by the Int[ernal] Revenue Dept to treat its accumulated revenue as current revenue, and so must get rid of 120 million dollars in a hurry. But as H remarks, they have millions of dollars and no ideas. But conservation is definitely to be one of the ideas.

614: TO LUDWIG VON BERTALANFFY

740 North Kings Road,
Los Angeles 46, Cal.
10 October, 1952

Dear Professor von Bertalanffy,

I owe you two [—] a double debt of gratitude, first for your kindness in sending me your *Problems of Life* and, second, for having written such an altogether admirable book. I have just finished reading it—with what a constantly sustained interest and pleasure, how much intellectual profit! It is a masterpiece of concentration and clarity. You have managed to say an enormous amount, in relatively few pages, with a lucidity of expression that sacrifices neither subtlety nor completeness. I can hardly wait for the appearance of the second volume! For I hope and think it will throw some much needed light on a matter in which, theoretically and practically, I have come to be increasingly interested—the relation of the self-conscious ego with the psycho-somatic organism as a whole. One can't accept Driesch's dear old Entelechy; and yet, viewing one's experience from the inside, it is always *as if* the self were associated with (besides the personal sub-conscious) a Not-Self, which manifests itself under two aspects—the physiological intelligence in control of the automatic functions of the body, and the spirit, pure ego, atman, in which the opposites are harmonized, the dualism transcended, not in a One, but in an advaita, a not-two consciousness of the identity of samsara and nirvana. Meanwhile, the self can stand in the way of the Not-Self, interfering with the free flow of spiritual grace, thus maintaining the self in a state of blindness, and also with the flow of animal grace, which leads to the impairment of natural functions and, in the long run, of the slower processes called structure. For each individual human being, the main practical problems are these: How can I prevent my ego from causing psychosomatic disorders? How can I prevent my ego from eclipsing the inner light, synteresis, scintilla animae, and so perpetuating the state of unregenerate illusion and blindness? And these practical problems remain unchanged, even if we abandon the notions of an entelechy or physiological intelligence, of an atman or pneuma and think, instead, in terms systems—which is what I hope you will teach us to do in your second volume. I shall be immensely interested to learn in what terms you describe the ego's powers of interfering, by means of craving, fear, hatred and the misuse of language, with the organism's capacity to maintain itself in an optimum steady state *vis à vis* the physical environment and *vis à vis* the trans-psychological or spiritual environment—though this latter, I suppose, lies beyond the sphere where any statement of a scientifically valid nature can be made.

I sent you a few days ago my recently published historical study, *The Devils of Loudun*—a very strange story made particularly interesting by reason of the wealth of first-hand documents dealing with it. I have discussed the psychological and, to a lesser extent, the physiological theories current at the time of the possession and shown how, given such theories, there were only two alternatives: either to admit the odd facts and explain them in terms of diabolic possession, or, like Descartes and those who came after him, to deny both devils and all such facts as could not be fitted into a very inadequate psychological theory. Both pre-Cartesian and post-Cartesian psychological theories were inadequate; but in some respects the post-Cartesian was the more inadequate and unrealistic of the two, in spite of having got rid of the devils.

Thank you again for a book which I know I shall often re-read and ruminate. You sent it me several years ago in its German form but then I read only a part of it. My eyesight is bad and reading in a foreign language with which I am not very familiar—I lived in Germany when I was nearly blind, learned to speak the language quite well, but not to read it and, lacking opportunity to go on speaking it, have sadly forgotten what I used to know—is *physically* fatiguing. So I lent it to an astronomer friend who has better eyes and a better knowledge of scientific German, and heard about your book only at second hand.

Very sincerely yours,
Aldous Huxley

PS. Two small points. In the last chapter you speak of J. B. S. Haldane; but from the context I think this should have been J. S. Haldane, the father of J. B. S. and a very great physiologist in the field above all of respiration, but fundamentally a vitalist. Also I notice that in your references to constitutional differences and human types (the wrong word, since variation is continuous within the race) you mention Kretschmer, but not the far more thorough and better-documented work of W. H. Sheldon—who is still, I am happy to say, going strong with a Rockefeller grant, half the year at Columbia and half at Portland in the medical school of the University of Oregon.

P.S [*on envelope*] If you have not read it, I recommend a very remarkable article by B. L. Whorf in the spring 1952 issue of *Etc* the journal of the General Semantics Institute.

740 *N. Kings Rd.,*
Los Angeles 46, Cal.
12 *October,* 1952

Dear Alan,

It is curious, indeed, that there should be so few scientific studies of the basic fact of inspiration from some deeper layer of mind than the personal—or perhaps not so curious, seeing that it is hard to make experiments in this field, and that the approach must be that of the observer, the naturalist, the collector and describer of phenomena. Outside the books you mention, I would recommend a study of the chapters in F. W. H. Myers's *Human Personality* devoted to Genius, Sleep and Hypnosis. They are richly documented and may list some useful sources. Offhand, I remember an interesting quotation from Sir John Herschel.

Some relevant work has been done in regard to the teaching of art. I have a book, which I have looked at but have not yet had time to read, entitled *The Artist in Each of Us,* by a woman, now dead, called Florence Cane. It was published about eighteen months ago by Pantheon, and describes methods for teaching children to relax and let the Other Fellow do the trick. Then there is the extremely interesting work in this field which is being done at the University of Ohio [Ohio State University] by Dwight Sherman and Samuel Renshaw. Sherman is professor of art and has devised methods of art teaching which are described in his *Drawing through Seeing.* In his school a very ingenious and, I believe, extraordinarily effective technique has been developed for getting the superficial self out of the way and leaving the seeing of the object to be drawn and the execution of the drawing to the more or less infallible Not-Self. Part of this technique was borrowed from Dr Renshaw, of the same university's psychology department, who trained very large numbers of soldiers during the war to recognize airplanes, and distinguish friendly from hostile models, by projecting slides of the various types upon a magic lantern screen for times ranging from a hundredth of a second down to a two thousandth. At first all protested that it was impossible for them to distinguish one type from another; and this was, of course, quite true for the superficial self. But the Not-Self had seen quite clearly, and when they learned to get out of the way and 'let George do it', they all acquired the art of seeing anything in a hundredth of a second, while some could do the trick at a much faster rate. Incidentally, many myopes came out of the training without myopia. This work has been applied in the kindergarten training of children in Chicago, I believe; but I have never seen any full description of this, only a passing reference. Renshaw also trained groups of miscellaneous students to develop taste discrimination to the pitch of professional tea tasters, and memory to the level of the prodigies who give performances on the music hall stage. I

met Sherman last year at Columbus; but have never seen Renshaw [. . . .]
But the work is obviously of major importance and you should get hold of as
many of his original papers as possible and examine them in the light of our
basic ideas.

Then I think it would be well to mention the therapeutic value of letting
go with the conscious self so that the entelechy or (as we should now call
it, in the language of the later organismic theory of biology) the hierarchy of
dynamic patterns constituting an organism, may maintain themselves in a
steady state at the optimum level of functioning. Dr [Edmund] Jacobson's
book *Progressive Relaxation* is significant here. And so is the more popular
work by Dr [D. H.] Fink *Release from Nervous Tension*. However, these
books are not fully adequate, inasmuch as they teach only relaxation in utter
repose and not the living paradox of relaxation-in-action, of not-doing on
the personal level so as to permit it to be done from the deeper levels. There
is a striking phrase by [Franz] von Baader, the German philosopher of the
Romantic Era, who emended Descartes' Cogito ergo sum to cogitor ergo
sum—we think only in so far as we permit ourselves to be thought by the
immanent and transcendent X.

Now for the second question raised in your letter. On the whole I think
it would be a good thing to approach Ford with a bigger proposition, of
which our project would be a part. Let it be a post-graduate school for the
study of synthesis and its methods of practical application to the educational
process on all its levels. In a letter I wrote to Hutchins some weeks ago
apropos of the lectures he gave in Sweden about Education and Democracy,
I wrote that there are only two factors common to all the innumerable
pigeon-holed items in the curriculum of a modern university. The only
things which connect, say, palaeobotany and psychology, nuclear physics
and anthropology, are (1) the fact that all these subjects are taught and
studied by human beings and (2) the fact that they are all taught and studied
in terms of language. Synthesis, therefore, can only be accomplished by a
study of the two fundamental questions: Who in heaven's name am I?
and What on earth is this system of words and syntax through which I
express myself, and by means of which my thoughts, and the ways I look at
the world, are determined—determined in profoundly different ways according to whether I speak Chinese, Maori, Hopi, or English. Our project would
lie astride of the two fields—which, in fact of course, are not separable. We
would propose to examine the ways in which persons brought up within a
given linguistic system (in other words, a given thought and feeling system)
can best be helped to establish contact with that part of the Mind which lies
beyond language and is, among other things, responsible for the original
creation of these incredibly subtle systems known as languages—systems
which, as personal selves, we are far too dumb to be able to invent or even
fully understand, except by a prodigy of analysis such as is made by professional semanticists, logical positivists, mathematicians. In each main field of

human activity—in the fields of learning, art, acquisition of physical skill, intra-personal and inter-personal behaviour—what are the best techniques for getting out of one's own light and collaborating with the Not-Self? Meanwhile the Eastern and Western thinkers can pool their theoretical resources, work out a realistic world-picture and contribute *en passant* a lot of useful ideas to the practical experimenters and teachers. The thing should start in a small way, but with adequate equipment, no strings and no red tape.

Yours
Aldous

616: TO ALAN WATTS

740 *N. Kings Rd.,*
L A 46, Cal.
17 *October,* 1952

Dear Alan,

Thanks for the memorandum, which I think is excellent as far as it goes. In my previous letter, before seeing the memorandum, I suggested some things which should, I think, be incorporated—art teaching and therapy through relaxation, both relaxation-in-rest and dynamic relaxation or relaxation-in-activity. Another book of good psychological standing is Professor Charles Baudouin's *Suggestion and Autosuggestion*. In this there are very valuable things about the relation between imagination and will, and his chapter on the Law of Reversed Effort is particularly valuable. Incidentally your use of the term is exactly opposite to the use made of it by Baudouin and, since the time of the publication of his book, generally accepted. For him, it means 'the harder you try, the less you succeed'—if, as is so often the case, your will is working in opposition to your imagination, as conditioned by some previous suggestion or auto-suggestion (of which one is generally unconscious). To this conflict between will and imagination—in which imagination always wins, since its force is 'in direct ratio to the square of the will'—must be added the automatic process of 'cortical induction', discussed by N. E. Ischlondsky M.D. in his *Brain and Behaviour*: any stimulus tends to produce its opposite, not merely on the level of sensation (optical induction) and muscular action (spinal induction, as studied by Sherrington), but on the higher levels of mind. Good techniques of education and suggestion are those which circumvent the mechanism (necessary to us in order to keep ourselves from being swayed by all the innumerable suggestions to which we are subjected) of cortical induction, in those cases where the negative of the suggestion is undesirable. There is a fairly full

616 *The typewritten portion of this letter ends at the parentheses in the last paragraph; the rest is in longhand.*

discussion of the whole problem of training in basic psycho-physical skills, with references to the literature on Attention, in the introductory chapters of my little book *The Art of Seeing*.

In regard to research, I think we should make it quite clear that there is no intention of undertaking any micro-physiological investigations of nerves, electric potentials etc, and that what we are interested in is the 'molar' phenomena of the human organism as a whole.

Among people who should be asked to help in the formulation of a policy, I would strongly suggest Ludwig von Bertalanffy, the Austrian biologist now at the University of Ottawa. He is a first-class practical biologist and also an important philosopher of biology. His recently translated and recently published book, *Problems of Life* (London 1952) is the best thing of its kind I know; and from correspondence with him (I haven't yet personally met him) I should think him exceptionally open, intelligent, well-informed. (As well as a biologist, he is a scholar in the field of religious mysticism and has written a book, which I have not read, on Nicolas of Cusa. So if we can get him, we shall be very lucky indeed!)

To come back to the memorandum. Might it not be as well to mention contemporary studies in psychosomatic medicine, with their insistence on the personal ego's capacity for interfering with the beneficent action of the automatic not-self? And I would also suggest a reference to a very remarkable book published about four years ago by the Scottish psychiatrist Dr James Halliday, *Psycho-Social Medicine*. Here he points out that there is definite evidence that urbanization and industrialization have created a tendency towards increased neurosis—i.e. towards increased interference by a fearful, or greedy, or resentful ego with the workings of the controlling not-self. (Collapse of typewriter!) This book emphasizes the medical and social urgency of finding out ways in which we can all be prevented from destroying ourselves and society, and from stultifying whatever creative capacities we may have.

Yours
Aldous

617: TO CAMILLE R. HONIG

740 N. Kings Road,
Los Angeles 46, Cal.
(Webster 30455)
[Circa 1952]

Dear Dr. Honig,

Thank you for your kind letter and the enclosed clipping. My silence in regard to Jewish mysticism has a painfully simple explanation—ignorance. Scholem's *Major Trends in Jewish Mysticism* has only recently come into my hands—too recently for me to have had time (since I am compelled by a visual handicap to ration my reading) to read it. Before that I had looked at the *Kabbalah* and quailed before its bulk and complexity. I am not a scholar and can lay no claim to exhaustiveness or accuracy, thinking it best to write of what I happen to know a little about [rather] than to wait until I had made my knowledge a little more (but always how little more!) adequate to the all but infinite subject.

If you ever come into town, why don't you give me a ring? I am available most afternoons, except Tuesdays. We might go for a stroll if you like walking, or sit here if you don't. This house is just north of Melrose, 4 blocks east of La Cienega.

Sincerely
Aldous Huxley

IV
AUN APRENDO
1953-1963

740 *N. Kings Road,*
Los Angeles 46, Cal.
25 *January,* 1953

Dearest J,

Forgive the long delay in answering your last letter. There has been rather more than the usual quota of work—a script for a 1 hour popular science film on the Sun, which requires a great deal of reading (one must read 100% in order to be able to leave out 99%, as has to be done in this medium and for a TV audience) as well as a great deal of thought in regard to the ways in which information may be conveyed in terms of photographic and animated-cartoon images. On top of work there have been a virus infection, with fever, bronchitis and a long period of under-parness, plus the arrival of Matthew, Ellen and the baby. These latter have been with us a month, and seem to be thriving—tho' poor Matthew is getting very nervous and depressed owing to the interminable delays in the materialization of his UN job. [David] Owen, I understand, or his lieutenants assured him last summer that the job wd be there in October. Then it was November. Then it was to be after the voting of the 1953 budget. And now it is still completely indefinite. I suppose these international organizations have to be like this— but it is very hard on the hapless individual who is waiting. M. returns to NY in February and, if prospects don't look more concretely promising than at present, will start hunting intensively for some alternative. It's a tiresome, dismal business, which is getting the poor boy down.

I have been seeing quite a lot recently of Bob Hutchins of the Ford Foundation. And what a strange situation there, too! He keeps asking for ideas on which to spend the accumulating dollars. One gives him some. He likes them—but then sadly discovers that his Department of [. . .] or his Dept. of [. . .], or whatever it may be, is too stuffily academic to be willing to consider them. Hutchins and [P. G.] Hoffman seem to be the prisoners of their own organization. I imagine they must have started with a dozen injudicious appointments of dreary people—with the result that dreariness has increased, not arithmetically, but by geometrical leaps and bounds, until now the whole affair is one vast fossil coprolite, in which the nominal heads of the foundation find themselves enclosed, like flies in amber.

I hope your health has been better, and that Juliette is bearing up. Age, I find, has its compensations—but also a great deal which has to be compensated for. The poem on the subject by our Uncle Matt is painfully to the point. 'Old, Master Shallow, old! She cannot choose but be old.' Nor can we, alas. All one can hope is to make the best of it. Maria is well, so long as she doesn't overdo it. Her margin of reserve strength is small, since last year's operation. It is a question of rationing and husbanding the available resources.

Our love to Anthony and, when you write next, to Francis—and to you both.

Affectionately,
Aldous

619: TO HAROLD RAYMOND

740 *N. Kings Rd.,*
L A 46, Cal.
2 *February,* 1953

Dear Harold,

Thank you for your letter and the accounts, which are very satisfactory. I only wish our rulers would permit us to keep a little more of what we earn. How odd it is that all governments should favour the successful speculator and penalize the steady worker! If you make a 'capital gain', you either pay nothing or only a little. But if you are on salary or in a profession, you belong to that lower order which must be squeezed to the limit. Incidentally, zero hour for tax-payments is approaching. How much has been paid into my account? I need to know the precise figure for the latest payment (I have the figure, of course, on the October payment), so as to transfer the necessary funds before March 15th.

I have been listening with horror to accounts of the storm in Europe. I hope none of you were seriously involved in the catastrophe.

Yours
Aldous

620: TO JULIAN HUXLEY

740 *North Kings Road,*
Los Angeles 46, Cal.
15 *February,* 1953

Dearest J,

Many thanks for the book on *Evolution in Action,* which has just arrived. I have had time, so far, only to glance here and there, but have seen enough to make me know that I shall read the whole with pleasure and much profit.

Did I tell you, in my last letter, that we had had a visit from von Bertalanffy? We both liked him very much and found him most interesting and stimulating. I also enjoyed his book, the *Problems of Life,* and only wish I knew some mathematics and chemistry, so as to be able to think more concretely about the hierarchy of organizations constituting the living world. How paradoxical it is that, when life develops organizations complex enough to be capable of thought, the emergent mind should revert, in its always oversimplified abstractions and generalizations, to patterns of symbols comparable in their subtlety and complexity only to organizations in the inorganic world, not to those in the living universe. Our thought-patterns are on the level, more or less, of crystallography; whereas the patterns of our physiology, the patterns of the relations between our physiology, our thought-patterns and the living and inorganic world, are of an immensely higher order of complexity. Hence, of course, the mess in which we find ourselves. Even with the best will in the world—and the will is generally rather bad—we *cannot* think completely realistically about ourselves and our situation.

Not much news here. Matthew and Ellen are still with us and still without any news of jobs. If you should be writing to Owen, I wish you would tactfully enquire whether there is any solid prospect for M in the UN. He, Matthew, has not been able to elicit any direct reply to this question, and I suppose that Owen does not wish to commit himself definitely either way to him. But he might give you, a third party, a provisional answer—which would be helpful in shaping Matthew's course when he gets back to New York and starts job-hunting. If their prospects were good or fair, he would aim at a temporary billet; if poor, a permanent alternative.

I hope your news of Francis is good. Love to Juliette and yourself from us all.

> *Your affectionate,*
> *Aldous*

621: TO MRS JULIETTE HUXLEY

> 740 *N. Kings Rd.,*
> *Los Angeles 46, Cal.*
> 10 *March,* 1953

Dearest Juliette,

I was happy to get your letter and to have good news of you both, as well as of Francis *là-bas*, among the savages. The Australian trip sounds as though it might be very interesting. As for our plans, I don't know what we may decide to do. It depends on a variety of factors—from Matthew's job situation and Maria's mother's health to my work on the series of lectures on art which I have to give next spring at the National Gallery in Washington.

Lewis's death came as a great shock. We had been friends for half a century, and he was a part of the order of things. I fear that his going may have serious effects on Mimi who sounds, from accounts given us by a young Belgian conductor who came to see us recently, and who had been in touch with Mimi in Spain, as if she were sinking deeper into neurosis.

And now for the Kot business. To start with, how could Viking have stopped him publishing the letters, if he had Frieda's permission? Other people published collections of DHL letters, which were not included in

621 *Lewis Gielgud had died on 25 February.*

665

the volume I edited, and the publishers raised no objections. So why he didn't go ahead, I can't imagine. If he had done so then, he would have got much more out of the letters than he is likely to do now, when the interest in Lawrence is, temporarily perhaps, but obviously, much less than it was in the years immediately following his death. Kot's hope that *Time, Life* or *Fortune* might pay largely for the serial rights of the letters seems to me wholly illusory. Perhaps *Harpers* or the *Atlantic* might take some; but certainly no magazine of mass circulation.

As for my own participation in the project—this, I fear, is out of the question. Poring over typescripts and photostats is something which, because of my eyes, I find horribly tiring. The editing of the original volume was a tremendous task, which I got through only with the help of that woman, whose name I now forget—the daughter of L's old teacher and first encourager in Nottinghamshire. These lectures I am now preparing require a great deal of reading, and I cannot take on more of the same sort of thing —but worse, from the optical point of view. In practice, moreover, I don't see the necessity for my editorship. It can easily be done by Kot himself, with the help of any competent secretary. And anyhow he would *have* to do most of the work of annotation, regardless of who was nominally the editor; for he alone knows the circumstances in which the letters were written and the facts to which they refer. I am very sorry to have to refuse and hope poor Kot won't be upset. But actually it would make so much more sense if he could do the work himself. As for an introduction—would it not be much better to have it written by somebody young, somebody to whom Lawrence has come as a fresh experience, now, than to have it done by somebody old, whose impressions of Lawrence are those made upon him a generation ago?

Maria sends her love, as do I, to you both. Good bye, dearest Juliette.

Your affectionate,
Aldous

622: TO MRS NAOMI MITCHISON

740 *N. Kings Rd.,*
Los Angeles 46, Cal.
5 *April,* [1953]

My dear Naomi,
Thank you for your letter and the little note on dear Lewis. His going seems curiously hard to take in, to realize as a fact. He had been part of my

621 *Kot: S. S. Koteliansky. He did not edit his Lawrence letters but willed them to the British Museum. Huxley's assistant for* The Letters of D. H. Lawrence, *Enid Hilton, was the daughter of Lawrence's old friends William and Sallie Hopkin.*
622 *Misdated through a typewriting error, 'April 5th 1952'.*

Order of Things for almost fifty years, ever since we first met as newboys at our preparatory school in the autumn of 1903. He was a gentle man as well as a gentleman, with all the qualities of humaneness connoted by both expressions. The obscure neurotic streak in his character came out only in his relations with the women with whom he was sexually attached. I saw it only, so to speak, from the outside—as when we travelled together in Spain after the tragic collapse of his passion for that little Siamese woman. If one wasn't involved in that kind of relationship with him, Lewis was not only one of the best, but also one of the sanest of human beings.

Please forgive me for not having written before about the [Authors' World] Peace Appeal. Various impediments have been at work for the last three months—an arduous bread-and-butter job of writing the scenario for a scientific movie on the Sun (which will probably, of course, never be produced), coupled with a long visit from Matthew, Ellen and their little boy, Trev, who at fifteen months exhibits some of the rare quality of his namesake, and the rather disturbing fact that Matthew is out of a job and finds it hard to get a new one of a satisfactory nature. He was more or less promised a billet in the Technical Bureau of the United Nations and, on the strength of it, got out of his job at the Conservation Foundation. Now thanks to red tape, uncertainty, budgetary restrictions and the usual internecine struggles that go on within any and every large organization, he finds himself in the air, with no definite prospects, merely the assurance that some day —but God knows when—he will get in. So he has had to look for alternatives, and as he was educated only in the humanities and has no technological speciality, the search is a hard one. He is back in New York and we haven't heard for a couple of weeks about the progress of his campaign.

In regard to the appeal, I think it best to have my name taken off the stationery. When you first wrote to me about the thing, I thought it was a question merely of an *ad hoc* appeal at that moment and did not envisage a continuing organization with which, for geographical reasons, I could not have anything practical to do. And there are other than geographical reasons. It is not merely that I don't like belonging to organizations in the making of whose policies I can have no say; it is also that I don't like belonging to any organizations, and have systematically kept out of them for many years. So I would rather retire from this one, in which I find myself by a misunderstanding.

I can see only one thing which writers can do collectively, as opposed to individually. Their concern is with language, and it is manifest that much of the frantic ideological fanaticism in the world is a product of intemperate and improperly used language. I can envisage a useful meeting, under international auspices, of professional language-users. The representatives from either side would have to know one another's idiom *à fond*, would have to possess a good knowledge of modern linguistics and what Benjamin Whorf called Metalinguistics, should be well trained in semantics and possess a good knowledge of the history and techniques of propaganda. Such a group would discuss the role of language in international relations and domestic policy; would consider the most obvious and disastrous [cases] of the misuse of words by politicians, clergymen, advertisers etc; would catalogue and analyse the meanings attached in different parts of the world to key words, such as 'freedom', 'justice', 'democracy', 'happiness'; and, in general, do everything possible to clean up and render more efficient the system of symbols which express and at the same time mould and condition our thinking. I have been trying in recent months to persuade various educators and some of the directors of the Ford Foundation to pay some attention to the part played by language in the current situation. But, needless to say, nobody will touch the idea with a barge pole. The reason is pretty obvious, I fear. Analysis of language is universally subversive. If words were used as they ought to be used, there would be an end of advertizing, political oratory, ideological fanaticism of every kind. To analyse language would be un-American, un-English, un-Russian, un-Chinese, un-Honduranean, un-everything. Hence its enormous and cardinal importance. Whether authors in their professional and organizational capacity can ever contrive to bootleg a little linguistic analysis into a world committed to the systematic misuse of words, the organized obfuscation of meaning, seems, I fear, doubtful. But it might be worth while to try in a small way. Meanwhile I shall go on trying to induce someone in a position of educational authority to think about the problem.

Yours affectionately,
Aldous

623: TO DR HUMPHRY OSMOND

740 N. Kings Rd.,
Los Angeles 46, Cal.
10 April, 1953

Dear Dr Osmond,

Thank you for your very interesting letter and accompanying article, and for the very kind and understanding things you say of my *Devils*. It looks as though the most satisfactory working hypothesis about the human mind must follow, to some extent, the Bergsonian model, in which the brain with its associated normal self, acts as a utilitarian device for limiting, and making selections from, the enormous possible world of consciousness, and for canalizing experience into biologically profitable channels. Disease, mescaline, emotional shock, aesthetic experience and mystical enlightenment have the power, each in its different way and in varying degrees, to inhibit the functions of the normal self and its ordinary brain activity, thus permitting the 'other world' to rise into consciousness. The basic problem of education is, How to make the best of both worlds—the world of biological utility and common sense, and the world of unlimited experience underlying it. I suspect that the complete solution of the problem can come only to those who have learned to establish themselves in the third and ultimate world of 'the spirit', the world which subtends and interpenetrates both of the other worlds. But short of this ultimate solution, there may be partial solutions, by means of which the growing child may be taught to preserve his 'intimations of immortality' into adult life. Under the current dispensation the vast majority of individuals lose, in the course of education, all the openness to inspiration, all the capacity to be aware of other things than those enumerated in the Sears-Roebuck catalogue which constitutes the conventionally 'real' world. That this is not the necessary and inevitable price extorted for biological survival and civilized efficiency is demonstrated by the existence of the few men and women who retain their contact with the other world, even while going about their business in this. Is it too much to hope that a system of education may some day be devised, which shall give results, in terms of human development, commensurate with the time, money, energy and devotion expended? In such a system of education it may be that mescaline or some other chemical substance may play a part by making it possible for young people to 'taste and see' what they have learned about at second hand, or directly but at a lower level of intensity, in the writings of the religious, or the works of poets, painters and musicians.

I hope very much that there may be a chance of seeing you in these parts during the Psychiatric Congress in May. One of the oddest fish you will meet at the congress will be a friend of ours, Dr [——], who is perhaps the greatest living virtuoso in hypnosis. (Incidentally, for some people at least, deep hypnotic trance is a way that leads into the other world—a less dramatic way than that of mescaline inasmuch as the experiences are entirely inward and do not associate themselves with sensory perceptions and the character of things and people 'out there', but still very definitely a way.) If you are coming alone to the meeting, we can provide a bed and bath—but unfortunately the accommodation is too small for more than one. You will be free to come and go as it suits you, and there will always be something to eat—though it may be a bit sketchy on the days when we don't have a cook. In any case I look forward to seeing you and to the opportunity of discussing at greater length some of the problems raised in your letter and the articles by Dr Smythies and yourself.

> *Yours sincerely,*
> *Aldous Huxley*

623 *Dr Smythies: John Smythies, then associated with Osmond and with Dr Abram Hoffer in schizophrenia research at the Saskatchewan Hospital, in Weyburn. Osmond accepted Huxley's invitation, with the results described in* The Doors of Perception.

624: TO DR HUMPHRY OSMOND

740 *N. Kings Rd.,*
L A 46, Cal.
19 *April,* 1953

Dear Dr. Osmond,

Good! We shall expect you on the third. May I suggest that you take the air line bus to the Hollywood Roosevelt Hotel, from which we can come and retrieve you—or from which it is easy to take a cab. Going to meet planes at the air port has become such a nightmare, with the increase of traffic, that my wife, who drives the car, begs everyone to come as far as the Roosevelt —which is quicker for the traveller as well as easier for the meeter.

Hoffmann La Roche has told my young doctor friend that they must send to Switzerland for a supply of mescaline—so it may be weeks before it gets here. Meanwhile do you have any of the stuff on hand? If so I hope you can bring a little; for I am eager to make the experiment and would feel particularly happy to do so under the supervision of an experienced investigator like yourself.

Yours very sincerely,
Aldous Huxley

625: TO MRS RENÉE TICKELL

740 *N. Kings Rd.,*
Los Angeles 46, Cal.
16 *May,* 1953

Dear Renee,

Thank you for your letter and the enclosure. And please forgive me for not having acknowledged and thanked you for the book you so kindly sent me. I meant to read it before answering, but other things kept thrusting themselves in and, as I can't accomplish more than a certain quota of reading, *God and the Unconscious* remained on the shelf—where it still is. But I hope soon to be able to free myself enough to tackle it.

I hope all goes well with you and the family. Give my love to your mother.

Yours
Aldous H

626: TO MATTHEW AND ELLEN HUXLEY

Jackson, Wyoming
[*Circa* 4 *June,* 1953]

Dearest Matthew and Ellen,

We are grounded here by a heavy snowfall in the Tetons and Yellow-

625 *Renée Tickell: a cousin of Huxley; daughter of E. S. P. Haynes.*
626 *A picture postcard of* 5 *June, depicting the Tetons, adds:* 'These are the *Grandest Tetons east of Marilyn Monroe'.*

stone. Hope it will be clear enough tomorrow to proceed. We had a splendid day yesterday and explored the Teton park as thoroughly as one can do in a car. Adaptation to the altitude has not gone far enough to permit of much hiking; but we did enough to see bison, elks, moose, marmots and a certain number of flowers—most of the flora is not yet out; for the season is very late. It is a bore to be stuck here; but at least we have good cabins and it is possible to do some work and some reading.

That there was no definite report on the job situation, when we talked the other day on the phone, is rather disquieting, and I have been thinking over the problem during those last days as we drove through the wilderness. I imagine that one of the problems, perhaps the main problem, is financial— namely that a newcomer to any salary-paying organization is apt to be started at a rate lower than what you need for your support. In view of this, ought we to envisage the possibility of taking some job which seems promising, if poorly paid at first—with the difference between the salary received and the amount needed for reasonable living being made up by me? I think I could manage a thousand or 1500 dollars a year for a few years; and it would be well worth it, if that subsidy would mean that you could take a job with prospects for the future, though not immediately well paying. If you had consulted me before making the decision to leave the [Conservation] Foundation, I would have proposed such a subsidy, during such time as would have been needed to find an alternative job, or to take degrees opening up possibilities in fields as yet unexplored. So please keep me posted in regard to prospects and don't repeat what I can only, in the light of experience, re-gard as the mistake which was made in leaving the Foundation, for financial reasons, without discussing with me the desirability of a temporary subsidy as a means to better things later. The temporary subsidy may be the cheapest as well as the psychologically and socially most satisfactory course to pursue.

In regard to degrees in particular and the acquisition of new skills in general, I do hope very much, Matthew, that you have gone ahead with the plans you formulated before leaving California? Perfecting your Spanish either at night school or by means of phonograph records and reading seemed an excellent short-range plan. And the long-range plan, involving the course at NYU, with the preliminary reading it involved, seemed to me even more important. Time is our only capital, and we don't, as one realizes with ad-vancing years, have too much of that. So for strictly utilitarian reasons, as well as for the sake of your own development, make the best of the time you have and don't waste any, as I am afraid you are too apt to do, in trivi-alities or unnecessary concerns. Don't let the educational projects slide, even if you should get a job. The necessary time and energy for them can be found and I am convinced that the effort will be worth making.

Love to all three of you.

Your affectionate,
Aldous

Grand Teton National Park,
Wyoming*
4 June, 1953

Cher Georges,

Votre pièce est arrivée juste avant notre départ en auto pour ce Nord-Ouest sauvage, plein d'ours, de castors, de martres, de mooses, d'énormes marmottes et de bisons. Nous avons eu le temps de la lire—avec quel

627 TRANSLATION:—'*Your play arrived just before we set out by car for the wild Northwest, full of bears, beavers, martens, moose, enormous marmots [woodchucks] and bison. We have had time to read it, with great pleasure, but the leisure to write to you was lacking. Here we are finally among the Tetons of this improbable spot, with some spare hours before leaving for Yellowstone.*

'*In* Zamore *I very much admired the extreme elegance of the composition. The line is perfect—with a perfection which must make itself strongly felt when a play is put on in the theatre. And the story is very fine. The only thing I regretted was the locale: too rural to afford a radio or television station. The idea of a crew of technicians and television interviewers flocking in strength, like vultures, around the corpse has haunted me ever since I read* Zamore. *What a subject for a film or novel! But a little too grotesque perhaps for a stage play—especially one as delicate as yours.*

'*I hope that the good omens of the opening days are materializing into a substantial success.*

'*Little news here. We are going to continue our tour of National Parks, then get back to the Pacific coast in the State of Washington. All this enormous country that we have crossed—Nevada, Utah, Idaho, Wyoming—is practically uninhabited. (Nevada for instance numbers 150,000 population in a territory of about 170,000 square kilometres. And the greater part of these people subsist on roulette (gambling being legal in Nevada) and have gambling machines in all the grocery stores, croupiers and crap-shooters in all the hotels, bars and restaurants.) Vast elevated plateaux—from 1,000 to 1,500 metres above sea-level—mainly barren, but with some oases, including one as large as Belgium oddly resembling a piece of Flanders, right up to fields of beetroot and potatoes—all tilled almost without human hands, by means of huge machines. And then chains of mountains like these Tetons, 13,000 feet high. And cowboys on horseback—or in Cadillacs or even in airplanes, for the ranches are very big. And at intervals, in the open desert, some installation of the Atomic Energy Commission, where they are manufacturing God knows what apocalyptic devices in the most absolute secrecy. Ours is an age when facts are becoming less and less probable. Affectionately. . . .*

'*P.S. Kisses to Jeanne and Noële from us both.*

* '*The "Grand Tetons" are mountains shaped like a brassière for Diana of the Ephesians.*'

Neveux's play Zamore *had been first produced at the* Thèatre de l'Atelier, *in March, 1953.*

plaisir!—mais le loisir de vous écrire manquait. Enfin nous voilà parmi les Tétons de cet endroit invraisemblable, avec quelques heures de disponibles avant le départ pour Yellowstone.

J'ai beaucoup admiré dans *Zamore* l'élégance extrême de la facture. La ligne est parfaite—avec une perfection qui doit s'imposer avec force quand on joue une pièce au théâtre. Et la fable est bien belle. La seule chose que j'aie regrettée c'est le lieu de l'action: trop rustique pour se payer une poste d'émission de radio ou de télévision. L'idée d'une équipe de techniciens et d'intervieweurs pour télévision, qui s'empressent, comme des vautours, autours du cadavre en puissance, me hante depuis la lecture de *Zamore*. Quel sujet pour un film ou une nouvelle! Mais un peu trop grotesque peut-être, pour une pièce de théâtre—surtout une pièce aussi délicate que la vôtre.

J'espère que les bons présages des premiers jours si réalisent en un succès solide.

Peu de nouvelles ici. Nous allons continuer notre tournée de National Parks, puis regagner le littoral du Pacifique dans l'état de Washington. Tout cet énorme pays que nous avons traversé—Nevada, Utah, Idaho, Wyoming —est presque inhabité. (Le Nevada, par exemple, compte 150,000 habitants dans un territoire d'à peu près 170,000 km carrés. Et la plupart de ces habitants vivent de la roulette—(car le jeu est autorisé en Nevada) et ont des machines à jouer dans toutes les épiceries, des croupiers et des jetteurs de dés dans tous les hôtels, bars, cafés.) Vastes plateaux élevés—de 1,000 à 1,500 mètres au-dessus du niveau de la mer—stériles pour la plupart, mais avec quelques oasis, dont une aussi grande que la Belgique et qui ressemble singulièrement [à un pan] de Flandre, jusqu'aux champs de betteraves et de pommes de terre—tous cultivés presque sans hommes, avec d'immenses machines. Puis des chaînes de montagnes comme ces Tétons de 13,000 pieds. Et des cowboys à cheval—ou en Cadillac, ou même en avion, car les *ranches* sont très grands. Et de temps à autre, en plein désert, quelque succursale de la Commission pour l'Energie Atomique, où on fabrique Dieu sait quoi d'apocalyptique sous le secret le plus absolu. La nôtre est une époque où les faits deviennent de moins en moins probables.

Affectueusement,
Aldous

P.S. Tendresses à Jeanne et à Noële de nous deux.

    * Les 'Grands Tétons' sont des montagnes en formes de soutien-gorge pour Diane d'Ephèse.

Coeur d'Alene, Idaho
[9 June, 1953]

There was a young lady of Butte
Who was so indescribably cute
That, each time she came out,
All the boys gave a shout,
With the Lesbians hot in pursuit.

Love
Aldous

What can one add!!

M.

629: TO MATTHEW AND ELLEN HUXLEY

Spokane, Wash.
11 June, 1953

Dearest Matthew and Ellen,

We got your great news here. It came as no surprise to Coccola, who had been hearing all about it from the [clairvoyant] for months! I think it might be a very good idea if, as she suggests, you were to send Trev to stay with us for a while, during the time when the young lady (for that is what Miss [Elsa] Hall says she will be) requires the maximum of attention. Meanwhile I wouldn't, if I were you, retire to a shack—unless, of course, you have an opportunity of doing so under exceptionally favourable circumstances. The commuting will be a great burden, and there is no point in Ellen undergoing avoidable fatigues and discomforts at this time.

I am delighted to hear of the courses at NYU, and only hope that they may lead to new and hitherto unavailable openings. Meanwhile we found a letter waiting for us here from Eileen Garrett, who said she had been trying to get in touch with you, but had failed. She has been in Florida, but is returning about now to New York where she will be until she leaves for Europe about June 20th. Why not get in touch with her? She is an interesting person, and it is possible that, through her immense circle of acquaintance, she might have some good practical suggestions to offer. There might even be something of an editorial nature in her own organization, which includes the revived version of *Tomorrow*—which could do with some very much better editing and writing than it now commands. So see

629 *News: that Ellen Huxley expected a child. This was Teresa Huxley, born 21 October. The clairvoyant Elsa Hall was a good friend of Maria Huxley.*

what can be found there—and in any case get to know her better; for she is well worth knowing.

We are just off to Grand Coulee. All our love.

Your affectionate,

Aldous

P.S. E. Garrett's address is Parapsychology Foundation, 11 East 44th St. NYC.

630: TO MATTHEW AND ELLEN HUXLEY

740 *North Kings Road,*

Los Angeles 46, California

21 *June,* 1953

Dearest Matthew and Ellen,

We got back last night, after five thousand miles of remarkably interesting travel, to find your joint letter. Its news sounded, I must say, much more promising than any that has come through in a long while. I myself would be inclined—and Coccola agrees with me—to make a push for the medical insurance prospect, with its chance of being sent to Harvard for an MA in Public Health. It seems to me that, whatever the temporary expense, this would be well worth having; for it would surely be helpful in all manner of fields—e.g. the UN if you wanted to enter it later, or any other of the international agencies, or Point Four. The sick, like the poor, will always be with us; and those who know how to deal with the poor wretches, whether medically or administratively, will always be sure of employment—and employment in a growing field—since health services are being multiplied and extended—and a field where co-workers are likely to be interesting and in which there will be some chance of seeing concrete and satisfying results. So, as I say, make a push in that direction.

Our trip ended with a couple of radiant days at Tahoe, which is quite incredibly beautiful and still, at this time of year, uncrowded. Later, in full holiday season, it must be almost unbearable, as there is only one road on which all the thousands of vacationists can move. But they are mostly gone by September, which all the old hands declare to be the best month of all. We returned via the Carson River valley, then over a huge 8000 ft pass to Mono Lake—unutterably desolate because of the chemicals which deter fish and fishermen, then up again into the barrens of the east slope of the sierras—almost no trees even at eight to ten thousand feet, just bald slopes and then the snow; and finally down, past the huge Crowley Lake where Los Angeles stores the water of the Owens River, to Bishop, whose valley, as you look down at it from above, is remarkably like the vale of Kashmir. We spent the night there, then drove on next morning for lunch [with Rose] at Pearblossom. Bonne Maman and children in very good form [. . . .]

---

630 *Matthew Huxley applied for and received a scholarship enabling him to start work on the M.Sc. degree at the Harvard School of Public Health.*

Meanwhile it is good to be home, even though the accumulations of mail are truly appalling. I shall get down, as soon as the necessary bits of business have been polished off, to my volume of essays. Your suggestion as to articles for *Holiday* came at the same time as a letter from Chambrun, saying that *Holiday* had asked him to ask me to do an article. So maybe I shall undertake one. I think a good subject would be Water—accounts of the LA aqueducts, remarks on Grand Coulee, Shasta, the new projects on the Snake River etc. It's an interesting subject and one, moreover, that lends itself to effective illustration.

Love from us both to all of you, including Mme X.

Your affectionate,
Aldous

631: TO DR HUMPHRY OSMOND

740 North Kings Road,
Los Angeles 46, California
21 June, 1953

Dear Humphry,

Our trip ended only yesterday. Hence the long delay in acknowledging your letter. I will certainly talk to Hutchins about your project when I have a good opportunity. Meanwhile I think it might be a good thing if you were to set forth in a couple of typewritten pages the nature of your project. Touch on the potential importance of mescalin studies from a purely medical point of view,* and then go on to their importance in the more generalized fields of psychology, philosophy, theory of knowledge. Point out that the available material is still ridiculously small, that greater numbers of cases are needed to determine how people of different physiques and temperaments react to the drug. E.g. do Galtonian visualizers react in a different way from non-visualizers. (I am sure they must. I am a non-visualizer, and got very little in the way of imagery. And yet visions are reported by many of those who have taken the stuff.) Again, is there any marked difference between the average reactions of extreme cerebrotonics, viscerotonics and somatotonics? Do people with a pronounced musical gift get auditory counterparts of the visions and transfigurations of the external world experienced by others? How are pure mathematicians and professional philosophers affected? (It wd be interesting to try it out on a logical positivist. Would he, like Thomas Aquinas towards the end of his life, when he had been vouchsafed an experience of 'infused contemplation', say that all his philosophy was as straw and chaff, and refuse to go on with his intellectualizing?) Armed with

631 *Project: the recording of mescalin interviews with fifty to a hundred people of outstanding abilities in various fields. This was outlined by Osmond and his colleague Dr Abram Hoffer together with a project, already under way, of strictly pharmacological research into mind-affecting drugs.*

this summary of a project, and also with my own essay on the subject [*The Doors of Perception*] (which promises to turn into quite a long-drawn affair, owing to the number of questions it raises, and the different kinds of light it sheds, within so many fields), I will go to Hutchins and try to arouse his interest. I think it quite likely he might want to take the stuff himself; and as there are a number of people of diverse idiosyncrasies who have expressed, or will certainly express, a wish to try the experiment, might it not be possible to arrange for you or John Smythies to come here, later on, for a few days in order to conduct the investigation? Interested parties could put up travelling expenses, and accommodation could be found with us, or if it were necessary to go to Pasadena to try it on Ford Foundationeers or Caltoch physicists, with Hutchins or someone else. If you think this idea feasible, let me know and I will start preparing the ground. Meanwhile let me have your summary. When my essay is done I will send it you.

Maria joins me in sending all good wishes to yourself and the family.

Yours,
Aldous H.

* Ford doesn't touch medicine, but is interested in the humanities and wd finance the project as a contribution to applied philosophy. Still, it is good to mention the medical angle—make them feel they are killing two birds with one stone.

632: TO HAROLD RAYMOND

740 *North Kings Rd.,*
Los Angeles 46, Cal.
21 *June,* 1953

My dear Harold,

We returned yesterday from a three weeks' tour through the Northwest to find your letter about Penguin. I am inclined to agree with you that this is a desirable move; so let us decide to go ahead with it.

The volume of essays on which I have been working sporadically for some time is getting on pretty well, and I hope to have the whole collection ready by the autumn. I am working at the moment on what promises to be a very long essay on an experience with mescalin, which I had this May, when an extremely able young English psychiatrist now working in Canada, with a group of equally enterprising young doctors and bio-chemists, on the

632 *Huxley's claim for the non-toxicity of mescalin was of course non-professional and it applied only to the kind of controlled dosage with which he was familiar. He knew from Osmond's correspondence that, for example, people with liver damage were intolerant of mescalin. Later experiments with this drug and with lysergic acid (LSD, a chemically different preparation synthesized in 1943 by Dr Albert Hofmann) have proved that both are capable of producing serious personality disturbances, at least in certain subjects, who apparently cannot be identified in advance.*

problem of schizophrenia, came to stay with us. You have probably read accounts of the mescaline experience—by Havelock Ellis, for example, by Weir Mitchell; and there have been many others. It is without any question the most extraordinary and significant experience available to human beings this side of the Beatific Vision; and it opens up a host of philosophical problems, throws intense light and raises all manner of questions in the fields of aesthetics, religion, theory of knowledge. The most extraordinary fact about mescaline—the active principle in the peyotl cactus used by the North American Indians in their religious ceremonies, and now synthesized—is that it is almost completely non-toxic. No unpleasant physical results, except a faint seasickish feeling at the beginning, no lowering of intellectual capacity, and absolutely no hangover—just a transformation of consciousness so that one knows exactly what Blake meant when he said, 'If the doors of perception were cleansed, everything would appear as it is, infinite and holy'. The schizophrenic gets this kind of consciousness sometimes; but since he starts with fear and since the fact of not knowing when and how he is to emerge from this condition of changed consciousness tends to increase that fear, his commonest experiences are of an Other World, not heavenly but infernal and purgatorial. What these young men in Canada are on the track of is immensely important—a bio-chemical element in the causation of schizophrenia. Mescalin and the newly isolated drug, lysergic acid, which has the same effect, are very close, chemically speaking, to adrenalin. And one of the breakdown products of adrenalin, adrenochrome, which can occur within the body, can produce, when isolated, experiences closely akin to those produced by mescalin. So perhaps they may be getting close to a cure or preventive of this great modern plague. Who knows?

Our love to you both.

Yours,
Aldous

633: TO J. B. RHINE

740 North Kings Road,
Los Angeles 46, California
19 July, 1953

Dear Dr Rhine,

I have been asked by *Life* magazine to do an article on recent developments in parapsychology, using your forthcoming book as the peg on which to hang my remarks, the news event of its publication as the moment for their appearance. Your publishers told me some time ago that they would send me proofs as soon as they became available. I have heard nothing from them for some weeks and, as I have mislaid their address, don't know how to

633 *Rhine's book was* New World of the Mind. *Hardy's article: "Biology and Psychical Research"*, Proceedings of the Society for Physical Research, *L (May, 1953), 96-134.*

678

communicate with them directly. Would you be kind enough to give them a little nudge? I would like to have the material as soon as possible.

I have just read Professor [A. C.] Hardy's article in the last issue of the *SPR* journal—a very interesting one, I thought. He mentions, briefly and cryptically, some work by Spencer Jones [*i.e.*, Spencer Brown] offering an alternative explanation for clairvoyance, PK etc. Can you tell me if any account of this work has been published, whether you yourself are acquainted with it, and if you think the matter worth discussing in an article for general circulation?

My own ventures into the parapsychological field have been in connection with deep hypnosis and the worlds which certain persons (not myself, unfortunately) enter in that state. There are worlds in which some very deep layer of the mind seems to be concerned to convey symbolically, or even by some kind of direct apprehension, the sort of knowledge which has been formulated in the Tat Tvam Asi doctrine, or the doctrine of the Inner Light. The late Dr Anita Muhl, whom I think you knew, told me that a great many automatists sooner or later produce a script, in which similar ideas are stated in words. And you will find references to the same phenomenon in Deleuze's old treatise on *Animal Magnetism*. These are very significant facts, and it seems to me that it would be worth while to collect a large number of cases.

Early this summer I took mescalin, under the supervision of Dr. Humphry Osmond, the young English psychiatrist at present working in Canada on the problems of schizophrenia. I have just finished an account of the experience, with reflections on its philosophical, aesthetic and religious implications, which I will send you as soon as it is printed. Incidentally, Osmond wants to get funds from some Foundation to carry out an investigation of the effects of mescalin upon a select group of persons with special gifts and high abilities. He thinks, and so do I, that this might throw a great deal of light on the nature of the mind and its relation with brain and nervous system.

With all good wishes to Mrs Rhine and yourself, and for the continued success of the work, I am

Yours very sincerely,
Aldous Huxley

634: TO CAMILLE R. HONIG

740 *North Kings Road,*
Los Angeles 46, California
21 *July,* 1953

Dear Dr Honig,

Thank you for your kind letter and the very generous offer to help me secretarially and research-wise. If the occasion should come I will most gladly take advantage of your offer. At the moment, however, I have nothing

679

on hand that involves any considerable research. And, I must confess, even when there is research to be done, I find it very hard to make use of other people's findings. For example, when I was working on the script of a popular science film on the sun, I had at my disposal a mass of research and a most able worker. Nevertheless I found that I had to go back to the original sources from which the material had been abstracted. For it was only when I went back to them that I found the kind of material—often on the face of it unimportant—which would give life and interest to the finished product. If I were a scholar, writing scholarly books, I could use other people's research. But in fact I am an essayist, and my research consists in reading scholarly books, being reminded by passages in them of something written by someone else, or made a note of by myself—which takes me then to other books or my own card indexes, and leads finally to another card, or something dictated on the audograph, or a fully worked out page of writing —sometimes on the theme I have been trying to elucidate, sometimes on something quite different but related, in some subterranean way, to that theme through the trains of association within my own mind, or the inspirations (to use a big word) which something in the research may have evoked. This being my method of working, I could never tell a secretary what to do. For what he or she might be doing at any given moment, though logical and sensible in the light of the 'subject' of the work in hand, could easily be irrelevant so far as I, at that moment, was concerned, and even positively obstructive. There is, in the long run (at least I hope so), some kind of method in my madness; but in the short run, on any given day of labour, the madness may be quite unamenable to any method which could be applied by anybody except the lunatic in person.

Thank you again for your kindness.

Yours very sincerely,
Aldous Huxley

635: TO J. B. RHINE

740 North Kings Road,
Los Angeles 46, California
27 July, 1953

Dear Dr Rhine,

Thank you for your letter. What you say of Spencer Brown inclines me to ignore altogether what he is doing—which is in a field, I imagine, which I am quite unqualified to talk about, probability theory. Hardy I think I shall mention on account of what he says about the possible relevance of ESP to biology.

I fear there is little prospect of my coming East in the near future and I shall have to postpone a talk with you until some later date. My article, of course, will have to be of a very general nature. I thought of beginning with a consideration of the reasons why most men of science choose to ignore ESP, then proceed to consider the factual evidence set forth in your book, and wind up with reflections about the sort of world-picture made necessary by ESP. It has been done before, of course; but it needs doing again, every year or so.

What interests me in the visionary experiences which some people get under hypnosis is above all the fact of their existence (for the mere fact that the mind can create or discover a completely coherent world of quasi-sense impressions is most extraordinary) and their apparent reference, in so many cases, to the fundamental doctrines of mysticism, East and West. My friend Dr Roger Godel (whose *Essais sur l'Expérience Libératrice* you may have read) uses Dessoile's technique of Le Rêve Eveillé (a technique for getting visionary experiences under light hypnosis) and tells me that he has found that the visions are in many cases symbolic of the Tat Tvam Asi doctrine, and that making the visionary conscious of this fact is often of great therapeutic effect in cases of anxiety and of somatic conditions, especially cardiac conditions, connected with anxiety. I have not aimed and (not being a trained researcher) would not know how to aim at ESP under hypnosis. An odd incident, however, turned up the other day. My wife was going through a visionary experience under hypnosis and saw a book in which there was a peculiar kind of writing. (Her subsequent drawings of individual letters looked like Hebrew.) When asked what the book was about she said she didn't exactly know, but that it might be alchemy. She also added that it couldn't be an ordinary book as the pages were numbered in Roman numerals, not Arabic. The following day we went to see some paintings by a young surrealist artist, who showed us a large book by Manley Hall, the writer on occultism. It was about alchemy, it contained illustrations of diagrams with Hebrew lettering and, oddest of all, its pages were numbered (by a special affectation) in Roman, not Arabic numerals. This looks like a rather good case of spontaneous prevision under hypnosis.

Sincerely,
Aldous Huxley

636: TO SIGFRID WESSBERG

740 *North Kings Road,*
Los Angeles 46, California
27 July, 1953

Dear Siggy,

Thank you for your beautiful guillotine. Everybody who has seen it admires it very much. Here is a little un-birthday present with which you can buy more materials for making new and still better models.

Love
Aldous

636 *Siggy: Maria Huxley's nephew, aged ten, who had constructed a model of a guillotine and had given it to Huxley for his birthday.*

637: †TO NED ROREM

740 *North Kings Road,*
Los Angeles 46, California
9 *August,* 1953

Dear Mr Rorem,

Thank you for your letter. There seems to be a possibility at the moment that I may collaborate with someone to write a play about the *Devils.* If and when this gets done, the problem of an opera libretto might be considered. It is, as you know better than I, a most difficult form, in which there have been very few successes. I can think of three only really good librettos— Da Ponte's for *Don Giovanni,* Boito's for *Falstaff* and Berg's for *Wozzeck.* How one could boil down the *Devils* to five or six thousand words of a libretto, make it dramatic and at the same time explain to some extent what is happening, I cannot at this time see. Perhaps it will become a little clearer after a dramatic version gets written. Meanwhile thank you for your interest. I will bear the problem in mind.

Music for such a theme should be, I imagine, dodecatonal [dodecaphonic]. *Wozzeck* screwed up to a higher pitch of excruciation. The little I know of Dallapiccola makes me think that he could produce music of the required intensity. Unfortunately I am not familiar with your music. But I will keep my ears open.

I see you are staying with the Noailles. Give my love, if you please, to Marie Laure, and, if he is there, Charles. And thank Marie Laure for her kind letter and the fascinating clipping about receiving sets grafted into the tissues of animals, so as to make them robots responsive to the radioed will of their masters. How the divine Marquis would have loved this! Girls with built in receivers. The Marquis shouts *Couche!* into his microphone, and hey presto, there they all are, on their backs.

Sincerely,
Aldous Huxley

638: TO DR HUMPHRY OSMOND

740 *North Kings Road,*
Los Angeles 46, California
17 *August,* 1953

Dear Humphry,

First a little business. Did you ever send me a brief list of the scientific papers relating to mescalin and the schizophrenia problem, by Smythies, Hoffer and yourself? If so, I can't find it and will ask you to send it me again, as I want to print it in a footnote. Can you do this, please, with the least possible delay? I ask this, because the essay is to appear in a separate volume

---

637 *The reference to the 'divine Marquis' was prompted by the fact that the Marquis de Sade was an ancestor of Madame de Noailles.*

on its own, both in the USA and, I think, in England. And the quicker all the material is in the printer's hands, the better. In the interval it is to appear serially—of all places—in Esquire—which is at present engaged in serving God and Mammon, Petty Girls and moderately serious literature, with what I understand to be a remarkable success. The P.G's pay for the S. Lit. and both ends of the central nervous system, the cerebral and the sacral, receive their appropriate stimulation—to the satisfaction of everyone concerned. Owing to the length of the piece I never dared to hope that any magazine would print it, and I am very much pleased that it is to receive this wide circulation. D. H. Lawrence used to say, about the habits of homosexuals, 'The Higher the Brow, the Lower the Bottom'—and evidently we must extend the scope of this Natural Law to modern journalism and trace a direct relationship between height of brow and volume of bosom.

Meanwhile I have had to make some small changes in the article owing to the discovery of a long monograph on 'Menomini Peyotism' (the Menomini are Indians in a reservation in Wisconsin) by Professor [J. S.] Slotkin— put a pennikin in the slotkin—published in the transactions of the American Philosophical Society in December 1952. This gives much fuller details than anything I had been able to find before on Peyote-eating within a Christian frame of reference. The various Christian-Peyote churches are all, it seems, branches of a Native American Church, founded some time back to give the Indians who take peyote for religious reasons a respectable status. Incidentally, the drug is not listed as a narcotic and its use is not forbidden by the Federal Government—although certain states have regulations restricting its use. Slotkin (the only white man who is a member of the Native American Church) says categorically that there is no increased tolerance, no need for larger doses, and no craving (habitual users often go for a month or more between rites) even among people who have been peyotists for forty or fifty years. So peyote really does seem to be, as the Indians firmly believe, God's special gift and peculiar revelation to the Red Man.

We read Chas Williams on the Grail and greatly enjoyed it—though it is rather uneven, the ending, I think, being much less good than the beginning. We hope to get on to the other books soon. Meanwhile, we have been reading a curious and interesting book by a man whom you, as a medical gent, will have to regard as a quack—L. E. Eeman, with whom I have corresponded at long intervals during more than twenty years, but have never met. The book, called Co-operative Healing is published by the author at 24 Baker Street and contains a great deal of exceedingly interesting material. If you have a chance, do look at it. Meanwhile have you made any experiments with treating the mentally sick with consoling and encouraging

638 Charles Williams: his novel on the Grail is War in Heaven (1930). L. E. Eeman described and taught a therapy based on the development of good muscular control. Huxley met him in London in August, 1954, and took several lessons from him.

statements and suggestions during sleep? I have a strong feeling that this might be very efficacious for certain lost souls.

Maria sends her love to you and the family, as do I.

Yours,
Aldous H.

639: TO DR HUMPHRY OSMOND

740 North Kings Road,
Los Angeles 46, California
25 September, 1953

Dear Humphry,

I am afraid there is nothing good to report. The mesozoic reptiles of the Ford Foundation are being as mesozoic as ever. Hutchins, whom I saw two weeks ago when my brother Julian was here on his way to Australia and Hutchins came to dinner, reports that he has received no word from [————]—nor any word from the head of the education department to whom, on my recommendation, he had recommended the work of Samuel Renshaw, of the Univ. of Ohio, in the field of training the special senses and the memory. It looks, I am afraid, as though the FF were finished. The Trustees are so frightened of doing anything unconventional—for whenever the Foundation gets any adverse publicity, people go to the nearest Ford dealer and tell him that henceforward they will buy Chevvies—that the one overriding purpose is now to do nothing at all. The ideal programme for the Foundation will be to give every professor in the country ten thousand dollars, on condition that he goes on doing exactly what he is doing now [. . . .] My brother Julian, who has been trying to get the FF to back a grandiose scheme for producing some generally acceptable weltanschauung, a little more realistic than orthodox physicalism, found everything completely blocked by [————]. So the outlook for our research in mescalin doesn't seem to be too good in this quarter. However Hutchins has recently flown to New York and has promised to do what he can with the saurians. I only hope he may prove successful.

The *Esquire* publication of the essay is off, since they could not bring it out until the August issue of 1954, and I don't want to wait so long. The thing will appear in book form, here and in England, next February.

Maria has been very busy trying to help a man we met twenty years ago in France—a Lebanese doctor who learned all the tricks of the dervishes and has made a living all these years by giving demonstrations of being buried alive, running skewers through his flesh, stopping and starting bleeding, healing himself without scars in a matter of minutes, doing telepathy etc. He spent some time in England where he worked with that strange creature Sir Alexander Cannon—on [————], among others, whom he treated for stammering by oriental methods of hypnosis, which are non-suggestive and purely physiological—finding 'hypnogenic nerves' and pressing on them till the patient falls into a state of hibernation, which may last for one or more days. A charming man—but unfortunately he contrived to spend more than two years in London without learning one word of English. This somewhat cramps his style when giving demonstrations here. He had been swindled right and left [. . .] in New York, Boston etc. Here, after two swindles, he is finally in the hands of some Armenians, who suck him dry, but at least can pay the little they promise—for they are pork manufacturers, with a farm where five thousand sows work overtime eating the garbage of the city of Long Beach and producing fifty thousand piglets per annum. At least they can talk with our poor friend [Dr —], who was brought up in Armenian—but he despises them as *marchands de cochons* and won't accept them as interpreters. So his performances are a chaos of incomprehensibility. The quicker he gets back to Lebanon, the better. He has a house there and a clinic for the mentally ill (whom he puts into lethargy for two or three days at a time, leaving Nature to do the trick of making them well—which she often does; and when that isn't enough he presses on their carotid arteries and pushes their tongues down their throats, which transforms the hibernation, with its slowed heart beat, metabolism etc, into a rampaging speed-up of all the vegetative activities—this last is generally infallible!)

Love to the family from us both, and to yourself.

Yours
Aldous

640: MARIA HUXLEY TO MRS ELISE MURRELL

[Los Angeles, California]
18 October, 1953

Dear Mrs Murrell,

I hope all is well with you both, and with Joan and her family, and I hope you are still in the country because I could see you going for walks and taking the beauty into your heart with every breathing. It is funny how I can see you, with always shoes so heavy that I laugh. I always wear, too, walking shoes which are enormous and enormously heavy. I know it is a disgracefully long time since I wrote. I even forget when, but it was when the country was fresh. Now it is golden. Did anything happen about the book? Did any friend go to see you? I fear not, because you would have written. It is a long time too since I heard from you, and suddenly I want to know. So, please write.

Mrs Hubble, our friend from California, wrote to you when she was in England. Now her husband, Dr Hubble, is dead. We try to help her. He died instantaneously in their car in their driveway. She was there. For 6 years he had recovered from a very severe heart attack and gone back to work. It was

640 *Edwin Hubble had died on 28 September.*

all right for him. She is shattered, though feeling it was wonderfully charitable the way it happened—for him. She is small and lonely and lost, but she is going to be all right. She asks much about survival. Last time I was there I just knew her husband was sitting at the tea table with us as usual. I even thought how rude of Aldous not to pay attention: he turned his back to him. Do you think I am mad? He was there, but when I looked he was there less than when I did not turn and scrutinize his chair!

Now we have news—we shall be in Europe this year, and always Aldous goes to England. This time I will go if you really want us to meet. No other reason or person would induce me to; I have no link with England, nor in fact many links at all. So much happens to me, inside, I cannot keep pace; and life is so busy, hectic, in America. Any minute now a new baby for my children; I think a little girl, but who knows. Aldous has been remarkably well, worked hard, no holiday. I am well too, but suddenly again X-ray treatments come to shatter the wellness. I think in Europe I will escape them and doctors too—probably wiser. Perhaps I will hear from you even before this reaches you. Anyway we send you both many friendly messages.

M.

641: TO CONSTANCE COLLIER

740 *North Kings Road,*
Los Angeles 46, California
18 *October,* 1953

Dearest Constance,
We think of you so often and with so much affection, so many good wishes for future health and happiness and vision. In relation to this last— to vision—I am making some experiments with a new form of visual education developed by a well-known psychologist at Ohio State University, Dr. Renshaw. If it does anything to help one to make better use of such visual resources as one has, I will let you know. Meanwhile this brings you all my love.

Your affectionate,
Aldous

642: TO DR HUMPHRY OSMOND

740 *North Kings Road,*
Los Angeles 46, California
31 *October,* 1953

Dear Humphry,
[. . . .]
Thank you for the copy of *Macleans*. The article was most interesting. Does lysergic acid always produce these terrifying results? Or did you give

642 *Article: by Sidney Katz in* Maclean's Magazine.

your guinea pig an extra large dose? Or, alternatively, did he start with a mild neurosis which was exaggerated out of all recognition? Whatever the answer, the inexplicable fact remains the nature of the visions. Who invents these astounding things? And why should the not-I who does the inventing hit on precisely this kind of thing? The jewels and architectures seem to be almost specific—a regular symptom of the mescalin experience. Does this, I wonder, have anything to do with the phantasies of the Arabian Nights and other fairy stories? The jewelled palaces are partly, no doubt, wish fulfilments—the opposite of everyday experience. But they may also be actual *choses vues*—items in the ordinary landscape of certain kinds of people. It would be interesting to know whether something of the kind would be seen by children who know nothing about jewels, or by primitives, to whom diamonds, rubies etc mean nothing.

When you go to Boston, do get in touch with Matthew. His address is 21 Francis St, Brookline, Mass. Telephone Hazel 11816—this is the number of the lodging house in which he has rooms.

Also, if you are in NY, do get in touch with Eileen Garrett at the Parapsychology Foundation, 11 East 44th, New York 17. She might prove to be useful in getting research started. The Foundation has some money. But what might prove more important is that Eileen has fingers in many pies and tentacles out in many directions. The Round Table Foundation at Glen Cove, Maine might be another useful contact.

Maria sends her love, as do I.

Yours,
Aldous

643: ALDOUS AND MARIA HUXLEY TO DR HUMPHRY OSMOND

740 North Kings Road,
Los Angeles 46, California
16 November, 1953

Dear Humphry,

Thank you for your letter and the paper, which we read aloud last night. It seems to me very good—clear, comprehensive, well arranged and presented—and I don't see the need for any changes, and don't know what you can add. I wish we understood anything about the nature of the world we get into, through dreams, visions, schizophrenia. All one can say is that it is objectively out there, that it has nothing to do, over large parts of its area, with the interests of the ego or the biological necessities of the animal. It is just One of those Things, which we have to make the best of.

643 *Paper: 'Inspiration and Method in Schizophrenic Research', which Osmond read at Montreal in December. Duck poems: songs by Osmond's daughter Helen.*

About [——]—I don't think you have to be much concerned with him. He approached me two or three months ago, saying that he was a friend and pupil of [——]. I thought he was a doctor, but it turned out when I saw him that he was a retired business man, living beyond his intellectual income—curiously empty and without any real understanding of the problems he is concerned with. He is also a bit of a snob—a getter-into-contact with everybody with any kind of a name. If I can find his address, I will forward your letter to him. But actually the only address I know is the one in [. . .], which he must now have left. So don't feel too much concern if your letter never reaches him.

I had a talk the other day with a man called Dr Maison, the head of a pharmaceutical house here—an Ethical Drug concern, attached financially to the World's Biggest Drug Store, which we visited on the day of my mescalin excursion. Maison is an able man, who has done a lot of medical and pharmacological research, knows a certain amount about consciousness-changing drugs, but can't as a business man concern himself with anything for which there is no obvious market. He gave me, however, the name of a man who might be of use to you, inasmuch as he is interested in the subject and has the ear of Foundations. He is

> Dr William Malamud
> Boston University School of Medicine
> 80 East Concord St
> Boston 18 Mass.

So perhaps it would be as well to see him when you go to Harvard next month.

Another possibility is Dr Henry Puharich of the Round Table Foundation, Glen Cove, Maine—the place where Eileen Garrett did some very interesting research on the relationship between electronics and ESP. I don't know Puharich, but have corresponded with him, mentioned the mescalin in my last letter, and have received a letter expressing much interest in the matter in return. He is for the moment with the Army, 2171 ASU, USA Dispensary, Army Chemical Center, Maryland. Probably he is a man worth exchanging ideas with, as he, like you, is working on a frontier between the partially known and the very much unknown—a different frontier, but in some way related to yours.

It has just occurred to me that perhaps man's obsessive preoccupation with precious stones—one of the most senseless of his concerns, by rational and utilitarian standards—may be due to the fact that these glittering objects are familiar to him from within. He is merely trying, when covering himself with jewels, to reproduce the marvels with which his visions have made him familiar.

I like the duck poems, and hope there may be more of them—a whole sonnet sequence. 'Shall I compare thee to a summer duck?' 'The expense of spirit in a waste of shame, Are Ducks in action and, till action, ducks . . .' etc.

Yours,
Aldous

P.S. *The Doors of P.* are being published by Harpers in New York, Chattos in London.

I also send much more affectionate messages than appear in consideration of the rare words that carry them.

M

644: TO HAROLD RAYMOND

(*As from*) 740 *N. Kings Rd.*,
Los Angeles 46, Cal.
8 *December,* 1953

My dear Harold,

Thank you for your two letters, which reached me at a halt on our way back from an expedition into the San Francisco area, where I was lecturing at a woman's college and to a group concerned with mental health—a somewhat strenuous experience, as there is a lot of social activity involved and, in the case of the college, a sitting in at philosophy and literature classes, where one is like Daniel in a lionesses' den, a prey to innumerable questions about all that is knowable and a good deal that is not. However the weather was fine and the country amazingly beautiful—vast rolling hills, plains covered with apricot, plum and almond trees, with immense fields of artichokes, lettuces and celery cultivated mechanically, by mass production methods. (Incidentally, these mechanical methods are so successful in regard to the rice cultivation, which goes on in the swampy areas around the lower reaches of the Sacramento River, that Californian producers are able to undersell their oriental competitors in their own markets. Here the rice is sown by aeroplane, manured by helicopter, reaped by a combine which threshes, sifts and packs in a single process—with the result that it is cheaper than what can be produced by coolies and child labour. Further north, in the state of Washington, where we were this summer, industrial agriculture is having a field day in the million acres of barren plain now irrigated by water pumped out of the Columbia River, impounded behind the Grand Coulee dam. Here one sees fields of peas, a mile square, with no human habitation in sight. People come out with machines three or four times a season, to sow, weed, fertilize and finally reap—the final procedure involving the association of appropriate combines with mobile refrigerating units, so that the product is deep-frozen the moment it leaves the pod. None of the

---

644 *Postmarked Pacific Palisades, Calif.,* 10 *December. Huxley had lectured at Mills College and in Palo Alto on 'Education in the Non-Verbal Humanities'.*

concepts which used to apply to agriculture has any relevance in the new circumstances. What effect all this will have on the human race remains to be seen. Meanwhile it is a fascinating spectacle.)

About your questions. I will stir up Chambrun, who has been acting as my agent—supposedly a good one; but I [. . .] may try someone else in future. As for the mystery story—alas, I have never written one, and am afraid couldn't do so if I tried. As for future work—I am at present in a state of uncertainty. I might try to do some more short stories and novelettes, or I might try my hand on a book on human beings and what, if anything, to do about them. I have written one chapter of it and have others in my mind. Or finally I might finally sit down to something I have had in my head for a long time—a novel extending from the mid nineteenth century to the present. I find it hard to decide, and will have to wait, like Mr Micawber, for Something to Turn Up.

> *Yours,*
> *Aldous*

645: TO DR HUMPHRY OSMOND

> 740 *North Kings Road,*
> *Los Angeles 46, California*
> 17 *December,* 1953

Dear Humphry,

A Merry Christmas to you all. And in the meanwhile would you send the suggestions you so kindly volunteered to supply to Maria's doctor, in regard to radiation reactions, to

> Dr William Kiskadden MD
> 1136 West Sixth St
> Los Angeles, Cal.

Kiskadden is not M's surgeon or family doctor (he is a great virtuoso in the plastic field, especially in regard to burns); but he is an old, good friend and in close touch with the other men with whom M deals professionally, acting as a kind of interpreter when they keep her in the dark, which American doctors have a way of doing, more, I think, than is necessary. We were away in the northern part of the state for a few weeks, while I lectured at Mills College and at Palo Alto, and the country was incredibly beautiful. But now we are back and poor M has to have another dose of X-rays. It is rather disquieting that they have to go on so constantly with the treatment. The malignancy was caught at a very early stage; nevertheless there are suspicious symptoms—swelling of glands in the neck etc—which make it seem as though there might be metastases trying to take hold. Presumably X-rays are the only appropriate treatment at this stage of our knowledge of the subject. But I wish the damned things didn't affect her so badly. She gets horribly nervous with them—feeling as if she were on the brink, or even over the brink, of madness. Vitamins and hypnosis help. But she is evidently one of those who can't take X rays in their stride. The effects wear off after two or three weeks, but are very horrible while they persist.

Ever yours
Aldous

646: TO FAIRFIELD OSBORN

740 North Kings Road,
Los Angeles 46, California
21 December, 1953

Dear Fairfield,

I have just finished your *Limits*, which is an excellent book. Thank you so much for sending it me. How on earth can the people who control our destinies be persuaded to stop paying attention to the insoluble and wholly gratuitous problems of power politics and ideologies, and to turn their gaze instead on the real, enduring ecological problem, which cannot fail to destroy us all unless we direct *all* our energy, knowledge, good will and money to doing something about it? I don't know what the answer to this question is. Politicians read such books as yours (if they do read them) and then go back to fiddling while Rome burns—shouting slogans and making H-bombs while the human race annually produces 30 million new candidates for starvation. All one can say is that 'those whom the gods wish to destroy, they first make mad'.

All good wishes.

Yours
Aldous H.

647: TO MRS EILEEN J. GARRETT

740 North Kings Road,
Los Angeles 46, California
21 December, 1953

My dear Eileen,

A Merry Christmas to you and the happiest of New Years! But meanwhile a Little Bird (in the sari-clad form of [——]) tells us that you are working much too hard and getting much too tired. If I knew anyone who was going to New York, I wd say, like the mother of a young family, 'Go and see what Eileen is doing and tell her not to'. And on the positive side,

646 Limits: *i.e.*, The Limits of the Earth (*Boston*, 1953).

647 *With Eileen J. Garrett, the President of the Parapsychology Foundation, both Huxley and his wife were on close, affectionate terms. Papers: the Huxleys wished to become American citizens, but as conscientious objectors to war, were unable to subscribe to the usual oath to defend the Constitution. Relief afforded to objectors with religious scruples was apparently not available to them because their scruples were not religious. Huxley finally let the applications lapse. He and his wife were technically never 'refused' American citizenship.*

do go for a bit of the pressure breathing treatment. It is really the only thing for chronic bronchitis and its long array of tiresome consequences. I feel confident that it will do you much more good than Florida or Jamaica—at considerably less expense!

No special news here. Morris Ernst has been very helpful in regard to our papers and I hope these may come through without undue delay. Poor M has had to take a series of X-ray treatments, which she finds tiring and nervously trying. Vitamins and hypnosis help; but it is a bit of an ordeal.

Humphry Osmond sent me a copy of the article on my mescalin essay, which he has written for *Tomorrow*. I have taken the liberty of forwarding it to Cass Canfield of Harpers, who may like to quote from it in his publicity. I have asked him to get in touch with *Tomorrow*, if he wants to quote.

Our best love to you.

Affectionately
Aldous

648: TO JEAN QUEVAL

740 North Kings Road,
Los Angeles 46, Cal.
3 January, 1954

Dear Mr Queval,

I have been away for several weeks and consequently could not look at the books sent me by the Editions du Seuil, nor answer your letter of December 3rd. You mention the Malraux book as being the one you would like most closely to follow. But, alas, I have no such photographic documentation as appears in that volume. I don't keep pictures or other memorials of the past—partly because such things are a physical encumbrance, but mainly out of a certain distaste for autobiography. This last makes me, I confess, view the whole project—now that I know exactly what the project is—in a new light. I have never felt the least desire to write about myself— nor to collaborate with another writer in the same task. When I answered your first letter, suggesting a meeting next spring, I envisaged only a casual conversation on the margin of your critique. But now that I have read the Malraux book and the letter in which you speak of possible alterations at my suggestion and additional notes of my own composition, I see that I was mistaken, and that the project involves a measure of active collaboration on my part. But active collaboration in this personal field would be, as I have said, extremely distasteful to me. I am sorry I did not make this clear in my first letter. My excuse is that I did not, at the time of writing, know what precisely was involved.

Sincerely yours,
Aldous Huxley

648 *The proposed book on Huxley was intended for the 'Ecrivains de Toujours' series of the Editions du Seuil; the Malraux book had been done by Gaétan Picon.*

692

740 *North Kings Road,*
Los Angeles 46, *California*
17 *January,* 1954

Dear Dr Rhine,

Thank you for your kind letter. Well, the article has appeared, and I hope it may do some good by persuading people to wonder whether there may not be a rational alternative to physicalism on the one hand and fundamentalism on the other. The final form of an extraordinary hypothesis of Mind and Nature is still, of course, unforeseeable. But we do at least know enough to feel sure that neither of the extreme explanations is adequate. For current purposes of scientific thought, a satisfactory working philosophy has been set forth by von Bertalannfy [Bertalanffy], the organismic biologist, in the November issue of the *Scientific Monthly*. He calls it 'Perspectivism', and points out that the unity of science is to be sought, until further notice, in the isomorphy of explanatory laws in the different fields and disciplines of science. The fact that extremely diversified phenomena are explained in terms of laws having the same form or pattern gives us information primarily about the mind which is the creator of all sciences and secondarily about the structure of the various levels of reality with which the mind deals; for presumably the pattern of a hypothesis must have some correspondence, if it works, with the pattern of the phenomena which it explains.

I am sending you a set of the page proofs of a forthcoming essay on the mescalin experience. The subject of what may be called the fauna and flora of the deeper subconscious is one that fascinates me. For it would seem that, beyond the personal subconscious (concerned with the problems of our private history) and beyond Jung's collective subconscious, with its Archetypes which are symbolic of the immemorial problems of the species, lies a world which has little or nothing to do with our personal or collective human interests—the world from which poets and prophets have derived their descriptions of hell and heaven and the other, remoter areas of the Other World. What turns up under mescalin and in schizophrenia is diverse; but the diversity exhibits many common features, and these common features crop up in descriptions of Christian, Moslem and Buddhist paradises and, when the experience has taken a negative turn, in descriptions of hell. There are many items in Dante which are very close to what schizophrenics and mescalin takers experience and describe. Why we should carry about with us this vast non-human universe, one simply cannot imagine. It is just 'one of those things'—like marsupials in Australia, like giraffes in Africa, only of course much much odder. For at least marsupials and giraffes are adapted

649 *Huxley's article 'A Case for ESP, PK and PSI' had appeared in* Life *on* 11 *January.*

to conditions on our planet; whereas these heaven and hell phenomena of the deep subconscious seem to be completely irrelevant to our private experience or to the experience of the race.

I may be in the East for a short time this spring, and I shall try, if it is at all feasible, to get down to Durham for a glimpse of you and the laboratory. The time, if the thing materializes, would be in the second half of March or earliest April. I will let you know later, when I myself know more about what is going to happen.

Meanwhile this brings you and Mrs Rhine all good wishes for the still moderately new year.

Yours very sincerely,
Aldous Huxley

650: TO LUDWIG VON BERTALANFFY

740 *North Kings Road,*
Los Angeles 46, California
18 *January,* 1954

Dear Dr von Bertalanffy,

Thank you for your most interesting letter and the enclosure on education. My suggestion is that you send this last along with your article to Hutchins, together with a covering letter detailing some of the points mentioned in your letter to me. The fact that other learned and above all *respectable* persons and institutions (an isolated writer is, of course, *not* respectable, academically speaking) are taking an interest in this matter is a much more cogent recommendation to a Foundation than any I could make, if I were to forward it. What the Ford people should feel is that they are on the point of missing the last bus, but that you are offering them a chance of a ride, if they jump on quickly! It might be still better if your own covering letter were supplemented by another covering letter from someone representing one of the organizations you mention. In this way the whole project would become more 'official' and carry a great academic weight. I know enough, by this time, of the ways of Foundations to realize that this is the only way of making any impression on them. Hutchins personally may be keenly interested; but his interest will not of itself carry the organization with it. The project has to go to the heads of several departments, all of whom are academic personages of much importance, upon whom nothing but academic backing will make any impression. So if you want them to sit up and take notice, prepare your way with a barrage of heavy guns from respectable institutions. If you know anyone who has had intimate (and preferably successful) dealings with a Foundation, consult him. To learn the proper strategy for a campaign against such an institution is indispensable; otherwise you are certain to be defeated in the first skirmish! I have learned this the hard way; for all the ideas I have passed on to Hutchins (some of which might have borne good fruit) were turned down by the heads of the various departments concerned. (And Hutchins is not in a position to override their decisions—a fact which I should have mentioned in my earlier letter.) But I think you will be in a sound position if you can mobilize, at the outset of the campaign, a sufficient amount of academic artillery to soften up any initial reluctance on the part of the department heads to pay attention to anything, to which they have not been accustomed.

In haste, but with all good wishes.

Yours very sincerely
Aldous Huxley

651: TO DR HUMPHRY OSMOND

740 *North Kings Road,*
Los Angeles 46, California
25 *January,* 1954

Dear Humphry,

Thank you for your letter. Let us deal with practical matters first. I will try to do a review of the epilepsy book, if I get a copy of it. I have been trying to procure the book at local stores, but without success, and so shall be glad to have an opportunity of reading it. If I can manage it, I will do a review quickly but I can't guarantee this, as there seems to be daily less and less time for more and more work, resulting in less and less accomplishment. I suppose this phenomenon is one of the symptoms of oncoming old age.

Next there is the question of speaking at the Toronto Conference. It looks at present as if we shall be in Europe next summer, if all goes well. So that rules out my attendance at Toronto. Moreover I'm not sure that I could contribute anything substantial to the psychiatrists—except perhaps along the lines of a lecture I gave recently at Mills College, on the training of the psycho-physical instrument as the basis (at present almost totally neglected) of education. I talked in the lecture about such empirically developed procedures as the F. M. Alexander technique, the Bates Method, the Renshaw techniques for training the special senses, the Bonpensiere technique in piano playing, the Zen art of archery (described by [Eugen] Herrigel in an excellent little book), with references to oriental methods for gaining control of the secondary nervous system and finally to 'spiritual exercises'—the whole assemblage of facts being shown in a frame of reference where the coordinates are the conscious self and the various not-selves, personal subconscious, entelechy, collective subconscious, superconscious and Atman-Brahman. The lecture, which I have given twice, aroused considerable interest, and I am thinking of developing the theme more fully for a book. That is, if I can find time before time finds me.

651 *Epilepsy book:* A Ray of Darkness *by Margiad Evans (P. E. A. Williams).* *Huxley did not publish a review of the book. Bonpensiere technique: developed by Luigi Bonpensiere.*

I hope the visit of the Rockefeller representative will bear some fruit. I have given up all hope of these bloody Ford people. They are obviously dedicated whole-heartedly to doing nothing that might look in any way novel or unorthodox.

I don't envy your sixty degrees of frost. Here, at last, we have some rain. We had had only four inches of precipitation in a twelve month period, and the situation was getting very bad. In the last ten days we have had two good storms—the first which brought 2.5 inches and the second which is still in progress.

I hope we may see you in New York in early April. As for summer visits to the prairie, I am afraid there was a misunderstanding. Maria said 'next summer', meaning the summer of next year.

Love to you all from us both.

Yours,
Aldous

652: TO MATTHEW HUXLEY

740 *North Kings Road,*
Los Angeles 46, California
29 January, 1954

Dearest M.

We have just had the photographs of the children, and I must say that, between you, Ellen and you have done us proud. What really beautiful little human beings! 'Heaven lies around us in our infancy'—and one can go a step further than Wordsworth and say that heaven sometimes seems to appear in us and through us. They really look like angels—though I suppose both of them have their share of original sin. And how good it was, too, to see, in the snapshots, Ellen looking so well and happy.

I hope, meanwhile, that you are keeping up your health and spirits at your end of the Boston-New York axis. How goes the work? Still interesting? Or is there a lot of drudgery? And now that February is approaching, what is the financial situation? Let me know what you need.

Our citizenship still remains in the air. We have the best naturalization lawyer in town on the job; but the department takes its bureaucratic time, and whether we shall get our papers and our passports before our sailing date remains to be seen. It is all very tiresome, all the more so as we have got into this imbroglio quite gratuitously and of our own volition.

Not much local news. I am appearing on TV on Sunday to answer questions about my new book—and on radio on Saturday to discuss ESP and my *Life* article with Dr Gustaf Stromberg of the Mount Wilson Observatory, a nice old Swedish astrophysicist who has written some very interesting stuff regarding the possible *modus operandi* of the interaction of mind and body. Meanwhile the *Readers Digest* is reprinting the *Life* article— so it will have a quite stupendous circulation before it has done.

C has just had a tooth out—a difficult extraction which has left her a bit miserable. She tells me to tell you that she doesn't write much directly to you, but concentrates on Ellen, because that is where the main life of the family is going on and because she knows that the news, such as there is, will be relayed to you.

All our love.

Ever your affectionate,
Aldous

653: TO MATTHEW HUXLEY

740 *North Kings Road,*
Los Angeles 46, California
17 *February,* 1954

Dearest M.,

Thank you for your letter, which has now been supplemented by one from Ellen. What an intolerable thing this FBI investigation is! I suppose the only reassuring feature of the situation is that things were nearly as bad during the early years of the Bolshevik scare after the first War, and later calmed down. Let's hope the same thing will happen this time. If, as seems probable, the international tension eases (for the Russians obviously don't want war and, in spite of the China Lobby, a lot of American businessmen do want trade with Mao) and if the recession doesn't go so far that the world's rulers find it necessary to resort once more to rearmament on the biggest scale (rearmament was the only thing that reduced unemployment in Europe and, even after years of New Deal, over here), then we can expect a gradual retreat of the current madness. But meanwhile the situation is very unpleasant.

No news as yet of our affairs. If the papers come through, well and good; if they don't, well and good also. Still I wish we hadn't let ourselves in for this bother and confusion.

I enclose a check for six hundred dollars, and hope it will tide you over. Let me know if anything unexpected turns up and you need more.

Much love from us both.

Ever your affectionate,
Aldous

654: TO J. B. RHINE

740 *North Kings Road,*
Los Angeles 46, California
23 *February,* 1954

Dear Dr. Rhine,

I am delighted that you shd think it worth while to use offprints of my *Life* article or the digest thereof. Please go ahead with the plan as it best suits your needs. I have not seen the *Readers Digest* condensation—nor indeed heard a word from them beyond the original telegram. They generally do a pretty good job on these things—better than the author cd do, in most cases; for digesting is a job for experienced technicians.

I think we shall be in New York from about March 17th to April 7th, and I will let you know definitely later.

Yours very sincerely
Aldous Huxley

655: TO DR HUMPHRY OSMOND

740 *North Kings Road,*
Los Angeles 46, California
2 *March,* 1954

Dear Humphry,

Thank you for your letter. Our address in New York will be Hotel Warwick, New York. Our children's address is 186 Sullivan St, and they are in the NY phone book under Matthew Huxley.

Three interesting things have turned up recently. My old friend Naomi Mitchison writes from Scotland, after reading the *Doors*, that she had an almost identical experience of the transfiguration of the outer world during her various pregnancies. Could this be due to a temporary upset in the sugar supply to the brain? (Also, a strange woman writes that she has had a mescalin-like experience during attacks of hypoglycaemia.)

A stranger writes from Seattle that he has produced extraordinary changes of consciousness—which he doesn't describe—by fasting and going without sleep over a weekend. This, of course, is what so many mystics, East and West, have done. Asceticism is only partially motivated by a sense of sin and a desire for expiation, and only partly, on the subconscious level, by masochism. It is also motivated by the desire to get in touch with the Other World, and the knowledge, personal or vicarious, that 'mortification' leads through the door in the wall.

Another stranger writes from Los Angeles. He is an ex-alcoholic, who had ecstatic experiences in his early days of alcoholism and insists, in spite of what the Freudians may say, that the longing for ecstasy is a very strong motive in many alcoholics. He is also a friend of Indians, knows some who have taken peyote but had a terrifying experience, and hints at knowing or being able to find out a good deal about the relationship between peyotism and alcoholism among Indians. I haven't seen this man, and doubt if we shall have time to do so before our departure. But (I hope you don't mind!) I have asked him to put down his information on paper and to send it to you. I think it might be of considerable value. He suggests that it might be very interesting to try the effect of mescalin on alcoholics, past and present. And I think that, if your research project gets started (or even if it doesn't), this might be a fruitful thing to do.

I also have an amiable, able [. . .] friend [A. L. Kitselman], who has evolved, out of the texts of Early Buddhism (texts which he can study in the original Pali) a form of psycho-therapy which he calls E Therapy. (E being equivalent to the Entelechy, the Bodhi.) He himself has taken peyote and proposes to launch out into mescalin, under doctor's supervision. Meanwhile he has made a few experiments with ololiuqu[i], has found that in some cases it seems to increase suggestibility, to give release from long-standing tensions, and to help the taker to obtain insights into his or her true nature. At the same time it seems to make it easier for those who are near the taker to enter into some kind of telepathic rapport with him—or should one say a sub-telegraphic rapport, inasmuch as the experiences shared are not thoughts but pains and discomforts, which the assistants feel vicariously (as has happened under deep hypnosis) and which in some way they 'discharge', to the benefit of the taker, who feels much better afterwards. Ololiuqu[i] is used by the Mexican and Cuban witch doctors to increase ESP faculties and relieve disease; so it may be that there is something psychologic-ally objective about all this. When we took it nothing much happened to Leslie LeCron and myself, except euphoria and relaxation. Maria got some very amusing and coherent visions—different in quality from those she ordinarily gets under hypnosis, and more obviously meaningful in a symbolic way. One of them was like a supplementary chapter to *Monkey*—the won-derful Chinese allegory translated by Arthur Waley. It was a vision of Monkey trying to climb to heaven up his own tail—a really admirable comment on the pretensions of the discursive intellect.

Have you ever tried the effects of mescalin on a congenitally blind man or woman? This would surely be of interest.

Love from us both to you and the family.

> *Yours,*
> *Aldous*

656: TO DR HUMPHRY OSMOND

> 740 *North Kings Road,*
> *Los Angeles 46, California*
> 7 *March,* 1954

Dear Humphry,

Thank you for your letter. I shall be glad to hear from your friend, but can't as yet give any very definite account of where we shall be, when. As things now stand, it looks as though we might, after the Conference in the South of France, fly to Egypt for a little, to stay with our friends Dr and Mme Godel (he is the Médecin Chef of the Suez Canal Co's Hospital at Ismailia)—a very remarkable man—a heart specialist who makes extensive use of psychological methods, a doctor who is an eminent Hellenist, respected by other Greek scholars, and finally a Western scientist who is interested in Enlightenment and has written some interesting essays on 'L'Expérience

Libératrice'). After that I don't know at all, except that C. G. Jung has asked us to go and visit him. The doctors here don't want M to stay away too long; but, after all, if she needs X-ray therapy, there are excellent men in Europe as well as here. We shall see. In any case I don't suppose we shall go to England before the end of the summer.

I met yesterday an interesting man, Dr Ladislao Reti, an Italian chemist living in the Argentine, who is, I believe, the greatest living expert on cactus alkaloids, including of course mescalin. He knows the subject from the chemical, not the psychological end. I gave him your address and you may hear from him before too long. He might be of assistance. Have you read his little monograph, *Cactus Alkaloids and some related Compounds*, published (1950) by Springer Verlag, Wien, in 'Fortschritte der Chemie organischer Naturstoffe'—but happily in English? He tells me he has also contributed a chapter to a symposium on Alkaloids edited by some Canadian chemist—Manskt (?) (but I can't remember the name). Also that there is a man at Detroit doing good work on cactus chemicals. His address, for your files, is Dr Ladislao Reti, A. M. Aguado 2889, Buenos Aires, Argentina. A very able man, he runs a chemical industrial plant, and does research on the side—also is an expert on Leonardo as chemist. (It appears that no chemist, before himself, ever studied the notebooks. Leonardo, needless to say, was a first-rate practical chemist—produced acetone, which he used as a solvent for his paints, invented protein plastics, like the casein stuff they now make wool from. Etc etc.)

We leave here Tuesday 16th and shall be staying at the Warwick Hotel, New York. I go down to Duke in North Carolina to see J. B. Rhine on the 21st for a couple of days; then shall be somewhere on Long Island for a meeting on the 25th and 26th. Some time we shall also go to Boston to see Matthew. But from the beginning of April until the 7th we expect to be in New York.

Maria sends her love.

Yours
Aldous

657: TO HAROLD RAYMOND

740 N. Kings Rd.,
Los Angeles 46, Cal.
8 March, 1954

Dear Harold,

Thank you for your letter and the good news about the sales of the book [*The Doors of Perception*]—excellent, I should say, for an essay. I saw Young's review—which I liked very much, and which pleased my friend Dr Osmond, the psychiatrist under whose supervision I took the stuff. Osmond himself is writing a review of the book in *Tomorrow* and his young colleague, Dr Smythies, is doing a piece, on mescalin in general, in the same magazine. Incidentally, I am amazed what a lot of work is being done on mescalin. Things keep cropping up—work at Boston, work at Chicago, work in Buenos Aires. In connection with the last, a very able Argentinian-Italian suddenly swam into my ken a day or two ago. It turns out that he is the greatest authority on the chemistry of the cactus alkaloids, including, of course, mescalin.

What Steedman said about the drug sometimes having terrifying results is, of course, perfectly true. (I mentioned the fact in the essay.) A very good account of the terror is given by a Canadian journalist called Katz in the (I think) October number of *Macleans Magazine* (a Canadian publication). He took the drug under Osmond's supervision, and his article is a blow by blow account, based on recordings and shorthand notes, of his experiences— which were perfectly appalling. How odd it is that writers like Belloc and Chesterton may sing the praises of alcohol (which is responsible for about two thirds of the car accidents and three quarters of the crimes of violence) and be regarded as good Christians and noble fellows, whereas anyone who ventures to suggest that there may be other and less harmful short cuts to self-transcendence is treated as a dangerous drug fiend and wicked perverter of weak-minded humanity!

If all goes well, we hope to be in France for a philosophical conference on April 20th. After that we might go for a little to stay with our friends, the Godels, in Egypt—where he is the head of the Suez Canal Co's hospital. Plans thereafter are vague; but I don't imagine we shall get to England till the late summer. Meanwhile I hope you have a very pleasant journey.

Our love to Vera.

Yours
Aldous

658: ALDOUS AND MARIA HUXLEY TO DR HUMPHRY OSMOND

The Warwick, New York, N.Y.
25 March, 1954

Dear Humphry,

The little piece about schizophrenia seems to me excellent. Perhaps you might develop a little further what you say about man's potentialities— point out that everything is in the universe of mind, heaven and hell, genius and subhuman imbecility, sanctity and diabolism; and that the schizophrenic gets a little of the good and a great deal of the bad. Making the matter more explicit will bring your point home more effectively, I think.

658 *Maria Huxley added the last phrase of her husband's letter as well as her own postscript. Schizophrenia: the 'little piece' was a talk for a broadcast to be called 'Prison of Madness'.*

I flew down to Duke [. . .], but developed laryngitis and bronchitis and had to return discomfited to bed. However things seem to be going pretty well and I hope to be clothed and in my right mind by the end of the week.

I have also seen Puharich, the man of the Round Table Foundation, who is doing odd adventurous work on the borderline of psychology and physics. [. . . .] Excuse typing. This is a new machine and I am still fingering it as though it were the old one. We are looking forward to seeing you soon, and Jane also.

Yours,
Aldous

Keep your fingers crossed so that Aldous recovers quickly and thoroughly. We are very sad because we thought the old enemy was conquered—but now I know we can only keep him at bay. And how un-cautious he remains —he takes none of the 'warning cues' his (?) gives him.

[Maria]

659: TO RALPH ROSE

The Warwick, New York City
5 April, 1954

Dear Ralph,

The enclosed speaks for itself. It is disappointing. Maybe there is something in what [Jack] de Leon says about the fact that Propter's philosophy makes no difference to anyone in the play. Would it be possible to bring Pete back? Maybe we wd get certain values by his reintroduction into the story—e.g. the contrast between his kind of love for Virginia and Obispo's, *plus* the chance for Propter to develop his point of view. I think this is something to consider. Maybe a new Pete will add the quality of 'humaneness' and 'sympathy', which some critics of the script have missed.

I wish I cd discuss this with you face to face. But we leave on Wednesday, and I shall be wandering in the void for some time. Meanwhile I have told de Leon that I can't work with him—(a) because this is your play and (b) because I have no time. I also told him to write you direct. If you decide to do any changes, I wd like to see the revised script. You may, on the contrary, feel that it's best to stay with what we have and hope for a producer. However it strikes me that de L. may be right and that we need Pete again—for the various reasons outlined above.

[. . . .]

Yours
Aldous

659 *This letter concerns efforts to find a producer for the stage adaptation of* After Many a Summer, *written by Rose in* 1951.

R.M.S. Queen Elizabeth
10 *April*, 1954

Dear Mr. Bax,

Thank you indeed for your very kind letter. It makes me happy to know that you have read my little book and know what it is about. (Some excellent persons seem to think it is a piece of propaganda for dope taking—while most seem to be quite incapable of grasping the fact that the human mind is anything more than, or different from, the every day self and its attached personal subconscious.) In New York, before sailing, I saw my young psychiatrist friend, Dr. Osmond, who is working on schizophrenia in Canada, and who hopes to get one of the Foundations to finance a general psychological research, with the aid of such tools as mescalin, into the remoter areas of mind. Needless to say, several Foundations have turned him down; but we have not yet lost hope. Someone may see the importance of the project and put up funds—trivially small by comparison with what is spent in other fields—for exploring systematically those Other Worlds which we all carry about with us.

I am headed for a conference at which philosophers from various countries will discuss the relevance of parapsychology to philosophy—which should be interesting. After that we may go to the Eastern Mediterranean for a while. But when I get to London later in the summer, I look forward to meeting you.

Meanwhile let me thank you once more for the pleasure your letter has given me.

Yours very sincerely,
Aldous Huxley

Le Piol, St. Paul de Vence (A.M.),
France
20 *April*, 1954

Dear Ralph,

Thank you for your letter which I found on my arrival yesterday. I agree wholeheartedly that we don't have to sacrifice existing values for the sake of a production at any cost. De Leon is by no means infallible and his ideas, if he has any concrete ideas, may not work out. So let us proceed with caution. For myself I like the mechanism of the Earl's voice (which may be one of the things he objects to as cinematographic); so let's stick firmly to that.

Propter's function as a Greek Chorus speaking from a higher region might be a little more emphasized—but without embarking into excessive speechifying.

As for Pete—what a headache! He gives something inasmuch as he serves as a contrast to Stoyte's and Obispo's attitude towards Virginia. But, as you say, he may take away from the central theme. An idea occurred to me in bed last night. Could we introduce this value in some other way, not involving the introduction of a new character with all the extra scenes required for his development? Could we, for example, make Jeremy Pordage develop a sentimental middle-aged passion for Virginia? He thinks she is Stoyte's niece. (It is as such that she is introduced.) And he goes on believing that her relations with Stoyte (in spite of all the evidence to the contrary) are pure. He falls in love with her as only aging scholars, who have never sown their wild oats, can fall in love—behaving as an adoring worshipper, writing her little poems and love-letters. Maybe he never finds out the truth, but is killed at the moment when he is about to make his declaration in form. Meanwhile, of course, Virginia, in conversation with Obispo, has been laughing at him behind his back—but at the same time she is, at moments, genuinely touched by this kind of passionately platonic devotion, of which she has had no previous experience. She finds it very wonderful to be treated, not as a tart, but as Dante's Beatrice. But at the same time she finds it all extremely ridiculous. Given this new twist to Jeremy's character, we can get some of the humanity which critics have missed and at the same time add a note of high comedy. Pete needn't be introduced, and Propter will have opportunities for being a Greek chorus. I hope this may be a feasible gimmick.

Yours,
Aldous

[Address] after May 2nd c/o Dr. R. Godel, Hôpital de la Compagnie du Canal de Suez, Ismailia, Egypt—until at least May 15.

662: ALDOUS AND MARIA HUXLEY TO DR HUMPHRY OSMOND

Le Piol, St. Paul de Vence (A.M.),
France
[End of April, 1954]

My dear Humphry,

It took two days of intensive work to decipher your last letter (you will really *have* to learn to type!); but now we have its contents reasonably clearly defined in our minds, and I am writing quickly, before we set out for the next leg of our flight, to tell you what we both think.

(1) You unquestionably *are* the man to act as liaison officer between pure science and the rest of the world in this matter of the nature of the Mind. [———] could not possibly do it. He is able and he is likeable; but he has not yet reached affective and intellectual maturity. He is obsessed by his ideas—rides them like hobby-horses and is ridden by them, so that there is in him a certain lack of flexibility, a certain one-trackedness which wd be an insurmountable obstacle in performing the necessary task. I hope, and think, he

---

662 *For the parapsychological congress at Le Piol, Huxley read a paper entitled* 'The Far Continents of the Mind'.

will not always be like this; but at the moment the handicap is there, and it rules him out. He will continue, undoubtedly, to supply fruitful suggestions; but you are the one who will have to put them into effect. And you will do it, I believe, with as much non-attachment as the task demands—more (I also believe) than most men are capable of.

[2] As for the results of the research being used for polemical purposes— I feel that this is something we don't have to worry about. Anything can be misused. The Sermon on the Mount is treated as an instrument of Western nationalism and a rallying cry against Russian nationalism—nevertheless it remains a good thing. In point of fact I doubt whether the results will be so very desirable in the Cold War context; for they are likely to take some of the specifically supernatural shine out of religion as well as the plausibility out of materialism.

The conferences are now over. There were no conclusions, of any kind, of course; but a lot of interesting things were said and there were occasions to greet very remarkable people. I liked especially Price, Ducasse, Marcel and Mundle among the philosophers; and, among the psychologists and doctors, Bender of Freiburg, Martiny and Assailly of Paris. Bender has a case of demonic possession on his hands, which exceeds in horror and in duration anything met with at Loudun—13 years of blasphemy, split personality, stigmatization (with the forms of snakes appearing on the skin, of letters on the forehead), self-mutilation—and still no end in sight, despite repeated exorcisms and incessant medical treatment.

We leave for Egypt on Monday [. . . .] Thereafter we shall be wandering, with a little stay in Rome (c/o S[anford] Roth, 13 via Villa Ruffo, Roma) then to Paris (c/o Neveux, 82 rue Bonaparte, Paris 6)— the last address will always find us. Maria sends her love to you both, as do I.

Yours
Aldous

My love to you and to Jane. We think of you and talk of you and hope we meet again soon. We are pretty hectic just now.

[*Maria*]

663: ALDOUS AND MARIA HUXLEY TO MATTHEW HUXLEY

Ismailia, Egypt
9 May, 1954

Dearest M,

We have been here nearly a week—a very extraordinary place in company with a very extraordinary man. The house stands on the edge of the canal (it was built originally for the Empress Eugénie at the time of the canal's inauguration), and the ships pass practically through one's bedroom— enormous tankers going to or coming from the Persian Gulf, liners, aircraft carriers, cargo boats of every shape and size. The town is an Egyptian town with a French quarter of elegant houses for the officials of the company. Here, at the hospital, we are 3 miles out—with irrigated parks, woods, gardens and then the naked desert.

I go with Dr. Godel every day to the hospital—disguised as a visiting doctor in a white gown. It is a liberal education to accompany him through the wards with his interns and the young doctors who come from France or Lebanon or Greece to be his pupils. He succeeds in being what [——] wanted to be, sometimes was and was finally too mad to be—a physician who is also a philosopher and psychologist. Where patients are responsible for their own illness—and how many of them, here as elsewhere, are psycho-somatics!—he treats them physically with all the resources of modern medicine, but tries at the same time to get them to recognize and, in so doing, to get rid of the underlying causes—to make them understand their own basic nature and to adapt themselves to the givenness of mental facts. He does it by Socratic questioning—often through an interpreter, for the poorer patients speak only Arabic—and it is wonderful to hear him patiently eliciting—exactly like the Socrates of the Platonic dialogues—fundamental answers about soul and body, about appearance and reality. And the thing works; for he gets amazing cures and enjoys a prodigious reputation. In himself he is a quiet gentle man—with an immense knowledge not only in medicine but also in Greek literature, especially Plato, and in philosophy. And all his knowledge is applied in the most intelligent and humane way, for the service of his patients. He takes foreign pupils—mostly doctors, but some laymen—young men who live near by and go the rounds with him and learn by listening, answering questions and doing. It would, I believe, be a wonderful thing if you cd come here for a few months and work with him. Perhaps your Foundation wd extend your scholarship so that you cd come and study this very successful Public Health set-up in a very poor and semi-tropical country. There wd be much to be learned on this score —and of course much more by association with Godel in his work. Even if you cd not get a scholarship it wd, I believe, be worth thinking of coming here independently, as an educational investment. The hospital has a villa where visiting pupils can stay where it wd be possible to find room in it for you and the family. The winter months are delightful from the point of view of climate and I imagine that one cd find congenial spirits among the personnel of the company, mainly French, but with English and other nationalities interspersed. Anyhow the project is something which you shd consider seriously; for I am sure that you wd learn a great deal, both in the Public Health field and in many other, wider fields, by coming here. The Godels wd be delighted if the plan were to materialize—and so would we;

for Coccola is as enthusiastic about the idea as I am. So ruminate and digest and make enquiries. Godel leaves for Europe in 2 weeks and returns to Ismailia on Sept 15th. We expect to meet them again in Athens in early June, and shall be in touch with them wherever we and they may be during the summer.

We leave for Cairo the day after tomorrow, shall see the sights there, then proceed to Beirut, Damascus and Istambul—short hops by air—then Athens. Then Rome where we shall stay a couple of weeks. [. . .]
Love to you both and to the children.

Ever your affectionate,
Aldous

P.S [*at head of letter*] What about the dough situation? Let me know at Rome (c/o Roth, 13 via Villa Ruffo) about this and the project outlined below.

Darlings,

This is a dream which I feel will materialize. Ellen will find a friend and helper. It is Madame Godel who at once said you must all come. Her grandchildren are in Paris. Somehow I feel it will be, and will be enjoyable and valuable—and treasured. Perhaps we may even return for some weeks next year to visit you all. I have not known a place and people so congenial at the same time. The beauty of the place passes belief, also the gentle climate, and, as it is all run by the Co. of the canal, healthy efficient modern. And by air very near really, I lose you all so nearby. From business point of view may be valuable, this hospital's pupils are snatched up before they are through. What with M's U.S. lucky event and Godel's reputation all over France and the East, he may get instant and important jobs; but, should you be interested and darlings please be, the investigations are no doubt possible on your side. 30th Sept to 1st June will be ideal. I suggest that though it will not be necessary Ellen and I sell (not even pawn) our jewelry and Aldous his typewriter and the car and everything—because this seems the best idea for us all.

Yours
Coccola

Beirut
18 *May,* 1954

I have delayed sending this until we were out of Egypt as the new government spasmodically censors letters and there are apt to be enormous delays. We had a wonderful time in Cairo. One can really form no idea of Egyptian art until one sees it in the mass and at its best—the museum is fabulous, the pyramids (in the light of a full moon) beyond description, Memphis and

Sakkara [Saqqara], with its carved and painted tombs, immensely impressive. And then there is the Coptic stuff and the Arab city with its mosques and bazaars. We were shown around by an eminent French Egyptologist and orientalist, Charles Kuentz, who could talk of things from the depths of a vast mine of knowledge.

And now to return to the Ismailia scheme. I had a long talk with Godel about it before we left, and he seems to be keener than ever on the idea. What he advises, if you are interested, is this. Go and see M. Claude Boillot, the NY representative of the Suez Canal Co., whose address is Room 3701, 30 Broad St., NYC 4 (Whitehall 23758). Tell him that Godel is our friend and suggested your going to see him to ask his advice. Godel thinks that the Canal Co. might be very pleased to have an American public health man come and look at their achievement—might even put up some money, or anyhow support a request to some Foundation. In any case it wd be wise to go and see Boillot, who is apparently a very nice and intelligent man. You cd go primarily to study the problems of public health in a backward country. But at the same time you cd collect materials for a doctoral thesis. Talking with Godel about the children who come to the hospital suffering from malnutrition and about the psychological effects of malnutrition on adults, I had an idea that you cd do a really valuable thesis on the subject: 'Malnutrition and its political consequences'. E.g. the effect of alternating apathy and frenzy upon the politics of a country whose rulers can use the most up-to-date methods of propaganda. Empty stomachs do not lead directly to Communism; but indirectly, through the psychological results of vitamin and mineral shortages, they may contribute hugely to the success of dictators. (For the psych. effects see *Nutritional Disorders of the Nervous System* by John D. Spillane MD, Edinburgh 1947.) And for crowd behaviour in general see *Foules en Délire* by Philippe de Félice (about 1948). Your last letter says that the HIP people don't want you until Sept. If you decided to try the Egyptian experiment the autumn, winter and early spring wd be the right time. So this will need some arranging. However I have the feeling that it will be worth it. All our love.

Your affectionate
Aldous

664: TO MRS EILEEN J. GARRETT

Athénée Palace Hotel, Athens
5 June, 1954

Dearest Eileen,

How are you. We have been incessantly on the go since leaving Le Piol. Egypt, Lebanon, Jerusalem, Cyprus, Greece and today we are leaving for Rome. It has been a very wonderful journey through space and time— wonderful but very depressing; for I have never had such a sense of the tragic nature of the human situation, the horror of a history in which the great works of art, the philosophies and the religions, are no more than islands in an endless stream of war, poverty, frustration, squalor and disease. One sees the misery of the Egyptians huddled about the pyramids, the hopelessness of the inhabitants of Jerusalem for whom the holiest of cities is a prison of chronic despair, punctuated by occasional panic when the handgrenades start flying. And it must always have been like this—little islands of splendour in a sea of darkness,—and then, during the times of trouble, darkness unmitigated for a few centuries. The Near East is one huge illustration of the primal tenet of the Buddha: 'I show you sorrow and the ending of sorrow'. The trouble is that so few people have ever been interested enough in the ending of sorrow to take the necessary trouble. They have preferred to go on wallowing in old misery and creating new miseries, in the hope of getting out of the old. All our love.

Aldous

665: TO MATTHEW HUXLEY

Rome
16 June, 1954

Dearest M,

Your letter reached us today. Business first: I enclose a cheque to tide you over the summer. Let me know if you need more, when you need it.

I'm sorry that the Suez plan doesn't fit into your programme, but understand very well why it doesn't. Godel is a *physician*—a very special one—and has nothing to do with the administration of the Canal Co's health insurance plan (which is simply an old-fashioned HIP affair which happens (a) to be working (in a western oasis) in a backward country and (b) to be able to function regardless of cost, since the Company is infinitely rich and wd have the money taken away by the Egyptian government.) Godel has been in charge at Ismailia for nearly 25 years and is largely responsible for the present status of the hospital. His connections in Beirut are with the French University and the Lebanese (he has a house there and knows or has treated everyone not with the Am. University). A stay at Ismailia wd have been a valuable experience, I am sure; but for the purposes of your specialization (and you *have* to start by being a specialist!) it wouldn't contribute anything concrete. So the idea will have to be given up. Which is a pity. But then so are most of the things that happen in this Vale of Tears!

Rome is still lovely to look at (at least in its central part), but absolutely infernal to listen to. The motor scooters, motor bikes, buses, trucks—all function with *scappamento aperto*, and the result in these narrow mediaeval streets is that you can't hear yourself speak, not to mention the fact that you are continually in danger of death owing to absence of sidewalks, total disregard of traffic rules, no cops and no stop signs. Walking in Rome used to be one of the great pleasures of life; it is now one of the pains.

We went to Florence for the weekend and found Costanza [Petterich, *née* Fasola] better than we had expected, but still, after her lung operation and a subsequent relapse with bronchial fistula, in a very precarious state. Yesterday we drove to see the Etruscan tombs at Tarquinia—wandering through the ripening wheat, and popping down into the rock-hewn chambers with their still gay paintings of hunting, wrestling, dancing, even copulation and sodomy. Today we went to Ciné Città, where *Helen of Troy* is being filmed, complete with wooden horse, 1200 extras, Bacchanalian orgies and Mr. Jack Warner.

On Saturday we fly to Paris and expect to go down into the Drôme, to stay at the house Jeanne has rented for the summer, early in July. In the meanwhile 82 rue Bonaparte finds us. Love to Ellen and the children.

Ever your affectionate,

A.

666: TO MME ALLANAH STATLENDER

La Combe, Dieulefit (Drome)
26 July, 1954

Dear Allanah,

Thank you for your very kind letter, and the accompanying book and magazine. Unfortunately I have such arrears of unfinished work to make up that I cannot with a good conscience accept your most tempting invitation. I hope there will be a more propitious set of circumstances on some future visit to France, and that I may have the pleasure of meeting your Egyptologist friends then.

Meanwhile I have read the article and most of the book—read them with much interest and a feeling that they have probably got hold of something highly significant. But please don't let us imagine that it is some kind of Secret Knowledge capable of making a vital difference to anyone's life. So far as man's Final End is concerned, there is no secret knowledge—there is only the Philosophia Perennis, expressible (always inadequately) in verbal, pictorial or architectural symbols, the truth which can be summed up in a couple of phrases: 'Tat tvam asi' and 'Samsara and Nirvana are one'. Nothing that the Egyptians have to say can possibly go beyond this statement of primordial fact. But the statement, whether verbal or pictorial, is valueless in itself. 'The pointing finger is not the moon which is pointed at.' 'The Buddha never preached enlightenment'—for the simple reason that enlightenment is something for every individual to experience for himself. As for cosmogony (and much of this Egyptian symbolism appears to be cosmogonical in character)—it is, so far as enlightenment is concerned, neither here nor there, irrelevant and beside the point. It may even, as the Buddha

666 *At Dieulefit the Huxleys and the Neveux were staying in the house of René Gillouin.*

710

was never tired of reminding his listeners, be a hindrance to enlightenment, an obstacle in the way of liberation—inasmuch as paying too much attention to such questions as 'How did the universe come into existence?' may be a distraction no less dangerous than the less solemn and more discreditable dissipations of the 'life of pleasure'. To know what were the cosmogonical notions of the ancients is interesting; but it is not more enlightening than the knowledge of any other historical fact, any other philosophical or scientific theory.

Excuse the length of this letter. Give our best love to Sybille [Bedford]. It was a real joy to see her again and to find her so happy, so physically and spiritually well.

Yours,
Aldous

667: TO MRS JULIETTE HUXLEY

R.M.S. Mauretania
23 *August,* 1954

Dearest Juliette,

You know, I think, without my telling you how very happy I was to be with you and Julian. *Il pleuvait dans la ville*—but, unlike Verlaine, I never felt that it was raining in my heart. On the contrary, it was always *beau fixe.* Thank you for all your sweetness and goodness.

We are eagerly looking forward to Julian's visit and to the trip into Oregon. I wish you were going to be there too.

Much love to you, my dear, and much to Julian.

Your affectionate,
Aldous

668: TO DR HUMPHRY OSMOND

740 *North Kings Road,*
Los Angeles 46, California
16 *September,* 1954

My dear Humphry,

Your letter announcing the change of plans arrived today. I am sorry your holiday will have to be postponed so long; but better late than never, and we shall be very happy to see you on November the tenth or whenever it suits you to come.

Your idea of a psychiatric text book sounds like a potential gold mine. I have always wished I could write something for students or a professional audience. Once you have broken through the academic barriers and got yourself accepted, you live in clover on a public which is *compelled* to buy you. It is the author's idea of heaven. Meanwhile, lacking the ability to write a text book, I have to plug on at these other, more precarious forms of literature—wishing to heaven, sometimes, that I could hit some dramatic or cinematographic jackpot. But these golden showers don't seem to fall on my garden. Perhaps we could write a play together one day and make enough to finance your research and our second childhood? It might be a good idea.

I can't remember if I showed you the first version of my paper on visionary experience and the account of the Other World in the various religious traditions. I have greatly enlarged the thing now, and have taken in the field of visionary art—which will be my excuse for delivering the thing as a lecture to the Institute of Modern Art at Washington at the beginning of next month. Incidentally I was delighted to find that my theory about the cult of precious stones—men spend all that time, energy and money on coloured pebbles, because these things are the nearest equivalents in the objective world to the self-luminous jewels seen in visions—was anticipated by Socrates. In the *Phaedo* he talks of the Other Earth, or Ideal World. Here all the stones are like our jewels, and in fact our jewels are simply tiny fragments of *their* rocks, gravel and boulders. Also I have brought up the odd fact that one of the standard ways of producing hypnosis is to make the patient look intently at a shiny object. There may be purely physiological reasons for this, as well as ordinary psychological reasons (induction of dissociation by concentration on a single perception). But there may also be a kind of visionary element. Shiny objects remind the subconscious of what is there, at the mind's Antipodes, and, being so reminded, the subconscious turns away from the ordinary world towards the visionary world, falling into trance in the process. But we will talk about all these things when you come. And I hope also that we may make some interesting experiments with mescalin.

The lady who wrote to you from San Francisco is a stranger to me. She wrote out of the blue saying that she wd like to give some money for research into the subject. So I wrote back giving your name and saying that the best research would be likely to go on in your vicinity.

Our love to you both.

Yours,
Aldous

669: TO J. B. RHINE

740 *North Kings Road,*
Los Angeles 46, Cal.
16 *September,* 1954

Dear Dr Rhine,

Thank you for your letter of the thirteenth. I will keep the fourth and fifth of October for Durham, as you suggest. I don't know what arrangements of an extra-curricular nature my hosts in Washington have made; but I imagine there will be goings-on over the weekend. This being so, I presume

669 *Huxley had arranged to lecture at the Institute of Modern Art in Washington on* 1 *October. There and at Durham his topic was 'Visionary Experience, Visionary Art and the Other World', forming the groundwork of his book* Heaven and Hell.

I shall fly down to Durham on the Monday, October 4th. Will write, wire, or phone the exact time later. On the whole I think it would be better if I had a room on the campus, especially if there will be lunches and meetings with people there. The inn was pleasantly quiet; but too remote to be retreated to in a hurry, for brief respites. Besides the chore of transportation devolved on you or Mrs Rhine. I look forward to seeing you soon and to hearing what is going on on the ESP front.

Sincerely yours,
Aldous Huxley

670: TO DR HUMPHRY OSMOND

740 N. Kings Rd.,
L A 46, Cal.
16 October, 1954

My dear Humphry,

Thanks for your letter and the ololiuqui paper, which I read with great interest. I wish it had been possible to try some ESP experiments while under its influence—for it is said to be used by medicine men for heightening their powers.

My brother read the paper and found it very interesting—tho' he thought it too long for the *B[ritish] M[edical] Journal* and advised complete publication elsewhere and a digested version for the *B M J*.

I got back from the East last week. Frightful heat in Washington and at Duke—97° with 96% humidity. But there were nice people in both places. I learned incidentally that the National Institute for Mental Health is experimenting with lysergic acid—to what end I cd not discover as I had no time to accept an invitation to go and see. But I pass this on for your information.

At Duke I saw much of J B Rhine and a young MD who is interested to combine ESP work with pharmacological experiments. He has worked so far only with benzedrine and barbiturates.

In New York I was happy to see my old friend W. H. Sheldon again. He has just published an *Atlas of Men* (5000 photos of naked gents) and is preparing an *Atlas of Women* which will, I fear, totally disillusion the young male about the Female Form Divine. A 6-5-1 female in her 50's is a real portent! Sheldon is most interested in your present work and future plans. So do get in touch with him when you are next in N.Y. He is at the Columbia-Presbyterian Medical Center at 168th St and Broadway. Ring him up and say I asked you to get in touch with him. You will find him pleasant and *very* able, with a fund of knowledge which may be very helpful to you in drawing up a plan for a general psycho-pharmacological research.

We are looking forward very much to seeing you.

Love from us both to both of you—and to the unknown poetess.

Yours
Aldous

671: TO DR HUMPHRY OSMOND

740 *N. Kings Rd.,*
Los Angeles 46, Cal.
25 *October,* [1954]

My dear Humphry,

Just received your letter announcing your arrival around the fifteenth to seventeenth of November. I hope you will stay here as long as you can. If you feel the need of greater quiet, we could go out into the desert somewhere for a few days, or on to the coast, or maybe for a little trip combining both, which is very feasible in these parts.

We gave most of our mescalin to our friend Dr Godel in Egypt, who knew a little about the subject but wanted to find out more. This being so, please come supplied; for you know how hard it is to get hold of anything here. I cant remember if I told you about Dr Puharich's use of lysergic acid in ESP experiments—finding that there was a period of heightened ability near the beginning, a long spell of no ability, and then another lucid period near the end. He was going to try to cut down the dose in such a way as to keep the subject in the lucid zone all the time, without being carried out of bounds into the totally Other World. Obviously we have to think of the mind in terms of a stratified Neapolitan ice, with a peculiar flavour of consciousness at each level. Pharmacology may permit us to go precisely to the level we want and no further.

Did you, by the way, ever send the plays?

Our love to you all.

Yours,
Aldous

672: TO DR HUMPHRY OSMOND

740 *N. Kings Rd.,*
L A 46, Cal.
7 *November,* 1954

Dear Humphry,

Can you please give me a little information. Where is [D. O.] Hebb's work on the effects of restricted environment published? Or, better still can you tell me in a line or two what was the nature of the experiences induced by being shut up in silence, in the dark? Were these visions of a mescalin-like kind? I want at least to mention the work in the essay on 'Visionary Experience, Vis. Art and the Other World,' which I am now enlarging.

Looking forward to seeing you soon.

Yours
Aldous

671 *Misdated through a typing error '25.x.46', the postal zone number being given as '35'.*

714

740 N. Kings Rd.,
Los Angeles 46, Cal.
30 November, 1954

Dear Ian,

Thank you for your letter. I am glad you like the story, which seems to me to come off pretty well, with a good easy flow—the easiness, I may say, was horribly difficult to get, and I have been writing and rewriting the thing for months, before, during and after our trip in the Near East.

About the title. Yes, change to 'telescope' if it seems better. I shall have to alter one of the references to opera glasses in the text, so that it shall fit the title. The first one had better remain as it is, for it refers to the act of looking at *Romeo and Juliet*, which one would hardly do through a telescope. But the later repetitions of the phrase can be changed without impropriety. Incidentally I had a lot of trouble with the title. The one I chose was the most obvious; but I recognized that it was unconscionably long, and tried to find something briefer. The only possible alternative that came to me was a Shakespearean phrase, 'The Past is Prelude'. If you prefer this, I am agreeable. Or if you can think of something better, please make a few suggestions.

I am adding two or three new essays to the collection, as well as enlarging some of the previously written ones. The whole ought to be in order by the end of the year.

Did you see the review of the *Doors of Perception* in *Pravda*? I have just been shown it by my friend Dr Osmond, who is mentioned in it. It is like a parody of Dialectical-Materialist denunciation written, not by Orwell, but by someone a good deal less clever, less capable of giving the devil his due. Heavily funny—but how extremely depressing! For there is not the slightest evidence of any wish to discover what the other fellow is trying to say—merely a wish to repeat the good old doctrine through thick and thin.

Yours,
Aldous

673 *The title* The Genius and the Goddess, *finally adopted for the new novel, was suggested early in December by a member of the Harper editorial staff. Neither Canfield nor Parsons cared much for* Through the Wrong End of the Telescope (*originally* Through the Wrong End of the Opera Glasses); *Parsons, while suggesting* The Telescope of Time, *favoured Huxley's alternative title,* The Past is Prelude. *Huxley wrote to him on 18 December: 'In some ways I prefer* The Past is Prelude; *but have no positive objection to* The Genius and the Goddess, *which is straightforward, appealing and has good precedents, like* The Virgin and the Gypsy. *Meanwhile which do you like best? The title doesn't have to be the same in the two editions. So if you prefer* The P is P *to* The G *and the G stick to it'. It is not clear why Huxley substituted 'prelude' for 'prologue' in the quotation from* The Tempest.

740 *N. Kings Rd.,*
Los Angeles 46, Cal.
5 *December,* 1954

Dearest Matthew and Ellen,

Thank you for your joint letter. I am very glad you liked the story; it took me a long time to write, but I think it comes off pretty well. Chattos talk of publishing it next spring, and I hope that Harpers can do the same. Meanwhile I am busy completing a volume of essays, which I hope to have ready by Christmas. After which, I really don't know. Whether to plunge into a long novel, or to embark on a kind of phantasy—it is hard to decide.

The subject suggested by [Francis] Thompson's film is certainly very interesting—also very difficult to write about. One would like to find out, first of all, why, as a matter of historical fact, so many cubists and other abstractionists used forms which are identical with those obtained by photographing reflections in curved surfaces. Did the suggestion actually come from hub caps and the backs of spoons? Or is there a tendency in certain minds to perform the imaginative equivalent of projection on a curved surface? Then there is the question of duration, of change in time. Can a merely static art of distortion ever convey anything like the rich significance of a dynamic art in time? The question, oddly enough, hardly arises in relation to representational art. One would never think of complaining because the Piero 'Nativity', or Rembrandt's 'Polish Rider', is not a movie. And they wouldn't be improved if they became movies. Whereas, after seeing Thompson's film, one feels very definitely that lots of Picassos, Juan Grises and the like would be greatly improved if they were animated and had a development according to the laws of the optics of curved surfaces. These are psychological facts which can only record without being able to explain. Perhaps the reason for the difference lies in this; in representational art we are shown a reality about which we can predict very little—for nobody knows what Nature, particularly living and moving Nature, will do next. Whereas in the non-representational art of reflections in a curved surface there is (given the laws of optics) a foreseeable element. Whatever may happen in the given world, its curved reflections will comport themselves in certain logically connected ways. Can this inherent logicalness of reflection-distortions, as opposed to the inherent non-foreseeability of the facts reflected, be the reason why the non-representational movie seems more satisfactory than the non-representational picture? Whereas the same is by no means true of the representational movie and picture.

Humphry Osmond has left for Canada—much to our regret; for he is a very remarkable young man, whom it is both a pleasure and a stimulus to have around. Both of us were in too precarious a state to take mescalin while

674 *Thompson's film was called* NY, NY. *Huxley discussed it in* Heaven and Hell.

he was here—Coccola because she was having X-rays* and I because I was having shingles. But Osmond made experiments on Gerald and George Hoynigen Huene, the photographer—both of them very interesting, albeit in rather different ways. Huene's reactions were wholly aesthetic; Gerald's mainly verbal and mediumistic—with other personalities talking through him from a variety of mental levels. Both agreed, however, in finding the experience uniquely significant and important.

Before he left Osmond gave a piece of advice to be passed on to you— advice in relation to small children and based on his colleagues' research and his experience with his own little girl. It is particularly apposite at the present season, when there are apt to be parties and similar jollifications. First of all, small children are unequipped, psychologically, to deal with large numbers of people. Hence large parties are intrinsically undesirable. It is like the phrase in the gospel, 'Where three or four are gathered together, there am I in the midst of them.' But when twelve or twenty small creatures are gathered together, the devil is apt to be in the midst of them, because they simply cannot cope with the experience of a crowd.

In the second place, bright intelligent nervous children tend to work themselves up into a frenzy of anticipation, with disastrous bio-chemical and metabolic results. So parties should be sprung on them at the last moment, not announced in advance.

Thirdly, the excitement of a party releases a lot of adrenalin, which tends to slow up digestive processes. This makes it very hard for the child to digest fats. The reason why so many children become diabolic half way through a party is that they have been fed with milk and ice cream and fatty cakes, but have too much adrenalin in the system to be able to digest them. Osmond advises therefore as follows. If you give a party, don't give the children milk or ice cream or creamy cakes. Let them have sugared drinks, or fruit juice with glucose, and let the cakes be plain with lots of icing—no cream fillings. When the child is to go out to a party, give him a sugary or glucose drink before he goes, or some barley sugar if he prefers; this will give him the energy needed to cope with the situation, it will be easily digestible, it will cut his appetite for fatty foods, if they are offered. A child tanked up with sugar or glucose is likely to get through a party without untoward incidents. A child stoked with fats will find it hard, because of adrenalin, to digest and will probably go into a bad psychological tailspin in consequence. Milk and fats can be digested very well in the calm of home surroundings, and the deprivation of them during a party will do no harm in relation to the overall dietary picture, and will do nothing but good in the party situation. All this sounds to me very sensible, and I suggest that you try it out over the Christmas ordeal.

Much love from your affectionate

Aldous

* *and* had taken B complex which is an antidote to mesc. [*Marginal note by Maria Huxley.*]

740 *N. Kings Road, Los Angeles 46, Cal.*
12 *December,* 1954

Dear J. B. (I think its about time—isn't it?—that we stopped Mistering and Doctoring one another!)

Your recent letter heaped coals of fire on my head. I kept postponing my answer to the first letter for a variety of reasons—preoccupation with literary work, which always makes me pathologically neglectful of my correspondence; then a long siege of herpes which intensified the consequences of too much work; then a visit from our young friend Dr Osmond, which added yet further to the effects of shingles and literature; and finally an uncertainty about plans for next year—an uncertainty for which I am not solely responsible; since much will hinge on a decision (which I thought would be made before Christmas, and which in fact won't be made until late January or early February) in regard to some TV talks which, if they come off, will have to be prepared and then recorded on film in the course of the spring. The definite news that the TV decision would not be made until after the production of a pilot film in late January came to me only yesterday; and in the light of it I can now say definitely that it would be a mistake for me to commit myself to a definite engagement in May—for I don't know what might or might not be happening in regard to these broadcast talks. So please tell the Unitarians, with all my apologies and all my thanks, that, all things considered, I had better say no.

Dr Osmond did some interesting mescalin experiments while he was here and plans, if time and funds permit, to do much more work in the psychopharmacological field, using known substances and, if he can get hold of them, many of the still very imperfectly known ones from South America and Africa. Each of them, it is clear, creates a different 'model psychosis' and opens up a different area of the mind; and he aims in this way at exploring a wide area of poorly mapped mental territory, keeping a weather eye open to ESP possibilities. Osmond is a very able, imaginative and energetic man, with a wide-angle intellectual lens capable of taking in, at one time, much more than the majority of medical or academic psychologists can do. I have great hopes that he may do work of fundamental importance.

California, as you know, is full of oddities. I saw one of them, the other day, in the shape of two aircraft engineers who have been experimenting with deep hypnosis and have come up, in one case, with a gift of tongues. I listened to the tape recording and the foreign language certainly doesn't sound like the gibberish of ordinary glossolalia. Indian students at the university say they recognize it as the dialect of Orissa. The engineers are now

675 *Unitarians: the Unitarian Layman's League, which projected a colloquium on the nature of man, to be held in Boston in May,* 1955.

engaged in trying to find a scholar who is thoroughly familiar with this brand of Bengali, and who will tell them if this is really an utterance in a language with which the speaker, in his normal state, has had no acquaintance or contact. It probably isn't anything. But if it were, how exceedingly odd it would be.

Meanwhile I am appalled by the superstitious passion for marvels displayed even by intelligent and well-educated men. I am thinking of a doctor friend of ours who, through a medium, consults his defunct professors and obtains from them, naturally enough, a complete confirmation of his own views about medicine and treatment! And I know of others who have just gone off, on a tip given by the spirits, to look for buried treasure in Arizona —in the teeth of the statement, in every serious history of the Southwest, that the aborigines did no mining and the early Jesuits and Franciscans either none or very little. Needless to say no appeal to facts or reason is of any avail. What may be called the Baconian-pyramidological-cryptographic-spiritualist-theosophical syndrome afflicts a large percentage of the human race, who get so much fun out of their mental derangement that they don't want, at any cost, to be cured.

Yours,
Aldous

676: TO ROGER AND ALICE GODEL

740 North Kings Road,
Los Angeles 46, Cal.
10 January, 1955

My dear Roger and Alice,

We were so happy to receive your New Year's letter and to learn that you were both well. I am sorry, for our sake, that the American journey has been put off, but rejoice, for yours, that you will be making this other journey through Greece and Ionia, and wish that we might be making it with you. I think so often of our enchanting excursion to Delphi and, of course, of our stay in that magical house beside the canal, of my visits with you, Roger, to the hospital—what a liberal education in psycho-somatic medicine, applied philosophy and humanity!—and of our long talks, while the ships glided silently past the windows and the dwarfs in their white nightgowns trotted along the terraces or through the rooms.

Here *le sheikh et la sheikha* have been well—but not exuberantly so. Maria had to have a long series of X-ray treatments, which achieved the desired results. She is due to be looked at once more by the surgeon and X-ray man in the course of this month, and I hope that she will not have to take another course. However, this last time they did not tire her so much as

676 *Dialogues: Godel's* Un Compagnon de Socrate: dialogues sur l'expérience libératrice (*Paris*, 1956).

previously, as she was taking very large doses of nicotinic acid, which kept the physical and psychological reactions at a minimum. Recently she has been having recurrent and very painful lumbago—which now seems to be yielding to treatment with ultrasonic vibration (greatly superior to diathermy). However, in spite of everything we are happy. I have done a great deal of work—having finished a short novel, which is to come out next April or May, and a volume of essays, including the one on visionary experience and the Other World, which you saw last spring, and which has now been greatly enlarged so as to include a discussion of visionary art.

And, talking of visions, I took mescalin yesterday, for the second time. This experience was no less remarkable than the first—but entirely different; for since I was in a group, with three other people, the experience had a human content, which the earlier, solitary experience, with its Other Worldly quality and its intensification of aesthetic experience, did not possess. For five hours I was given a series of luminous illustrations of the Christian saying, 'Judge not that ye be not judged', and the Buddhist saying, 'To set up what you like against what you dislike, this is the disease of the mind'. Incidentally some remarkable developments are now taking place in the field of mescalin. A group of psychologists and social workers in Vancouver and Seattle have developed techniques for using mescalin therapeutically. It acts in the opposite way to narcosynthesis. When psychological treatment is done under barbiturates, the ego is made drowsy and it becomes possible to get at some of the contents of the personal subconscious. But with mescalin consciousness is not narrowed, it is enormously enlarged, and the whole gamut of the psyche, up to the highest superconscious levels, is opened up. The first treatment is negative in its nature, the second positive. And the results in the cases hitherto treated (they are still rather few) have been spectacular. Delinquent boys have been totally transformed in a single sitting, and the *metanoia* has persisted. Meanwhile a considerable number of academic persons and of professional and business men have taken the stuff— and all, without exception, have declared it to be the most significant experience of their lives and have found, particularly when it is taken in groups, that mescalin brings about a profound and lasting change of outlook. There is some prospect of a mixed commission—doctors, psychologists, philosophers, social workers—being created to consider the whole subject. As the man whose book was largely responsible for the great increase of interest in mescalin, I hope to participate in the work of this commission.

Have the dialogues yet appeared? And what are you working on now? (as though your hospital work were not real work!) And how is Alice's family? And the Hellous?

I hope that 1955 will be a fruitful year for both of you and a very happy one.

Ever yours, dear Alice, and ever yours too, dear Roger,
Aldous

740 *N. Kings Rd.,*
Los Angeles 46, Cal.
11 *January,* 1955

My dear Betty,

The outline went off on Sunday night and I hope you have received it safely. I think I now have the solution for the ending. The woman Maartens marries after Katy's death is not Katy's sister, but the female musicologist at whose house he got drunk when Katy's back was turned. We will show her in the first act, entering near the end of the scene between Rivers and Ruth, after Maartens and Katy have gone out. I visualize one of those gushing, arty ladies, with a great deal of costume jewelry, beads, swinging earrings, highly coloured non-fashionable garments, and a line of talk about the soul, covering a yearning for men. Her technique is the most fulsome flattery combined with the assumption of the part of the misunderstood woman, the poor little girl who has been made to suffer. (She is about fifty, with hennaed hair and a record of two divorces.) She butters up Maartens, who falls for her flattery and would like to cultivate her acquaintance. Katy, however, keeps the woman at bay. In the first act we cannot, unfortunately, show her with Maartens; but she plays her Siren stunt with young Rivers and talks in such a way about Maartens that we understand what she is up to. When Katy returns, she refuses the woman's invitation and gets her out of the house as soon as possible, after which she tells Rivers about her and comments on the incomprehensible vanity of men—Maartens being ready to put up with this monster of affectation and ruthless femaleness, for the sake of hearing himself flattered. In the second scene, when Maartens announces that he has accepted her invitation to cocktails, Katy is very angry; but can do nothing about it, because she has to start for Chicago. After the accident, in the last scene, we see Rivers broken and Maartens in a state of psycho-somatic collapse. The musicologist pushes her way in, in spite of Beulah's protests, and we see Maartens permitting himself to be consoled by her. This makes a good ending—though the problem of reconciling this comedy with the tragedy of the accident remains ticklish.

I hope you are having a good time. Love from us both.

Yours,
Aldous

677 *Beth Wendel collaborated with Huxley in the dramatic adaptation of* The Genius and the Goddess *and suffered with him through the American stage production.*

721

740 *North Kings Rd.,*
Los Angeles 46, Cal.
12 *January,* 1955

Dear Humphry,

It was good to hear your voice so clearly across the intervening spaces. Your nice Captain tried a new experiment—group mescalinization. It worked very well for Gerald and myself, hardly at all for [——], who was given a small dose (200 mgs to our 300) and who had a subconscious resistance of tremendous power, and rather poorly for Hubbard, who tried to run the group in the way he had run other groups in Vancouver, where the drug has worked as a device for raising buried guilts and traumas and permitting people to get on to better terms with themselves. Gerald and I evaded him and went somewhere else—but not to the remote Other Worlds of the previous experiments. In both cases, albeit in different ways, it was a transcendental experience within *this* world and with human references. I hope to write something about my experience and will send you a copy in due course. Meanwhile I am hopeful that the good Captain, whose connections with Uranium seem to serve as a passport into the most exalted spheres of government, business and ecclesiastical polity, is about to take off for New York, where I hope he will storm the United Nations, take Nelson Rockefeller for a ride to Heaven and return with millions of dollars. What Babes in the Wood we literary gents and professional men are! The great World occasionally requires your services, is mildly amused by mine; but its full attention and deference are paid to Uranium and Big Business. So what extraordinary luck that this representative of both these Higher Powers should (a) have become so passionately interested in mescalin and (b) be such a very nice man.

I am enclosing a letter from France, which I mislaid and have just recovered from the depths of a coat pocket. I have asked this pharmacological lady to send you a copy of her thesis direct. It might be of some interest.

Poor Maria still has the lumbago. We have begun an ultrasonic treatment of the back under Dr Lutz, who recently acquired one of the new German machines, and I hope very much that this may do the trick.

Our love to you both.

Yours,
Aldous

678 *Huxley had telephoned Osmond apparently to get his approval before participating in the experiment. Maria Huxley, on a postal card of 11 January, told Osmond: 'Probably I ought to know that they know who is the boss—or High Priest[—] as you like. But I was very relieved to hear they had telephoned to you'. Captain Albert M. Hubbard maintained a drug-research centre in Vancouver. The 'pharmacological lady' was Madame Steiner, of Paris.*

740 *North Kings Road,*
Los Angeles 46, Cal.
16 *January,* 1955

My dear Humphry,

Thank you for your letter and the script of the talk, which I like very much indeed. All I can suggest by way of change is an addition of a line or two, indicating a little more specifically than you do what may be expected from systematic research with mescalin and similar substances. One would expect, for example, that new light might be shed on the workings of artistic and scientific insight, and perhaps some control gained over the otherwise random and gratuitous process of inspiration. One would also expect light to be shed on the problems of parapsychology. Also on those of philosophy and religion.

Gerald and I had another day with Al Hubbard, down at Long Beach. He has provided us both with a stock of carbon dioxide and oxygen mixture. I have tried this stuff before, without much effect. But I suspect it was not administered properly, and maybe there will, after all, be something to be learned by means of this simple and harmless procedure. Hubbard himself swears by it.

Maria has just left for a couple of days at the hospital, where the doctors want to run a series of tests to see why, as well as this long drawn lumbago, she has been running temperatures every evening. I suppose it is some infection in the intestine or kidney, and hope they will be able to put their finger on it and get rid of it; for she has had much too long a siege of pain and below-parness. I will let you know when I hear what the results of the tests are. Meanwhile, fare well and don't work too hard. A live grasshopper is better than a dead ant.

Yours,
Aldous

679a: TO CARLYLE KING

740 *North Kings Road,*
Los Angeles 46, Cal.
16 *January,* 1955

Dear Professor King,

Thank you for your kind letter and for the very interesting and generous

679 *Script: a talk called* 'One May Morning in Hollywood', *concerning* The Doors of Perception. *This was taped by Osmond and broadcast by the Canadian Broadcasting Company on 6 February.*

679a *King, a friend of Humphry Osmond, had published an article on Huxley in* Queen's Quarterly (*Spring,* 1954), *and had sent it to Huxley at Osmond's suggestion. The 'tunnelling' metaphor is from the early poem* 'Mole'.

article. It is always very difficult for a writer—especially for one who is advancing in years—to see himself as the critics of his already considerable output see him. To start with, he is under the enormous disadvantage of not having read any of his books since they were written—which may be more than a generation ago. In many cases he simply doesn't know, or knows only rather dimly, what it's all about. In the second place, his concern at any given moment is with the problems of that moment—technical problems, problems of expression, problems related to new ideas which have to take their place among earlier ideas, modifying and being modified by them, problems connected with novel facts of experience. The author, if he is still working, does not feel posthumously about himself, does not look back over his productions and watch them, like Pope's Alexandrine, 'drag like a wounded snake their weary length along'. He feels himself (possibly mistakenly!) as still alive, still tunnelling on, through the hard rock of literature, into the future and, at the same time, into timelessness. His attitude towards what he was is summed up by, 'Let the dead bury their dead'—or as Belloc once said, *de mortuis cui bono?* or, combining another pair of tags, *de mortuis non disputandum est.* Nevertheless thank you for disputing about my dead selves and on behalf of what I feel to be me living.

Yours very sincerely,
Aldous Huxley

680: TO IAN PARSONS

740 *North Kings Road,*
Los Angeles 46, Cal.
21 *January,* 1955

Dear Ian,

Your cable to hand. I have looked at *Crome Yellow*—which I hadn't read since the time I wrote it—and find that, in effect, there is a repetition. Evidently two versions of the same description, one of which should have been scratched out, but wasn't. I think the first of these is the better. So end the paragraph at 'a universe in themselves'. Continue with the next paragraph beginning 'The picture was more than half. . . .'

[. . . .]

I have recently accepted a most surprising offer—to send a monthly essay on anything I like to *Esquire*, that curious magazine which combines naked girls, men's fashions and a certain amount of literature. It is the only periodical, outside the most poverty stricken highbrow class, which will print an essay. Two of the essays which will appear in the new volume will be

---

680 *The two versions of the description (of Caravaggio's 'Conversion of St Paul') had occurred in Chapter XII of* Crome Yellow, *where the picture is supposed to be the work of the artist Gombauld.*

serialized in *Esquire* this summer. Another came out eighteen months ago in the same magazine. Thanks to the nude ladies, they can pay very well.

Yours,
Aldous

681: TO DR HUMPHRY OSMOND

740 *North Kings Rd.,*
Los Angeles 46, Cal.
22 *January,* 1955

My dear Humphry,

Thank you for your letter. First as to Maria—she returns from hospital today. The brace with which she has been fitted seems already to have made a great difference to her general state. For by taking the strain off the damaged area, it prevents a constant leak of vitality from taking place and at the same time permits the nerves issuing from that area to carry their charge, unimpeded, to the viscera. Some liver trouble was found; but the doctor seems to think that much of this will clear up spontaneously as the result of helping the back. I think he is also embarking on a treatment of some kind. So I hope all will be well within a short time. Meanwhile she has had, and is to have more, X-ray treatments on the back, which are often very helpful in these vaguely arthritic conditions.

Now for what you say about crowds and groups. This whole subject has been well discussed, with copious documentation from past and current history, by Philippe de Félice in his *Foules en Délire, Ecstases Collectives,* which is a most valuable book. He draws the distinction between crowd psychology and group psychology—comparing the downward self-transcendence of crowd consciousness to a kind of collective psychological cancer, and the horizontal or upward self-transcendence of group agape and solidarity to the growth of a healthy organ. And, in effect, democratic civilization is based on voluntary group activities; dictatorship, on mob emotions and non-voluntary groupings, where the aim is above all to indoctrinate the members with the ideology, in terms of which the mob-ecstasy is rationalized, and to promote habits of obedience and mutual espionage. The frenzies induced by mob ecstasy are beyond imagination. What fiction writer could have invented, for example, the self-castrations during the Adonis rites? or the collective flagellations of the great whipping crusades of 1259 and 1347? or the orgy of destruction described by Ortega y Gasset, when an entire Spanish city was devastated by a crowd which, so far as I remember, was simply celebrating some kind of a national holiday. It seems possible that there are physiological factors involved as well as merely psychological ones—that the mob produces an electrical, chemical, thermal field, in which the nervous system of its individual members bathes as in a poisonous bath. If mescalin can be used to raise the horizontal self-transcendence which goes on within purposive groups—professional, religious, therapeutic, artistic—

so that it becomes an upward self-transcendence, partaking in some measure of the mystical experience, then something remarkable will have been accomplished.

I received yesterday a letter from a Swiss literary critic, who had reviewed the *Doors* in a Zurich paper, and, along with the letter, a pamphlet, *Meskalin und LSD Rausch* by Laszlo Mátéfi. The pamphlet was sent to the critic by Prof. F. Georgi. I haven't read it yet—and hesitate to begin, since it is always such a sweat to read German. Do you know this document? And, if not, would you like it?

Love from us both to both of you.

Yours,
Aldous

682: TO MATTHEW AND ELLEN HUXLEY

740 *N. Kings Rd.,*
Los Angeles 46, *Cal.*
30 *January,* 1955

Dearest Matthew and Ellen,

We had a letter from you yesterday and also news of an indirect nature from Betty Wendel. I am sorry about the colds and hope that you will all bear up against the horrors of the cold wave, about which we hear on the radio. (Here the temperature has been in the high seventies and it has been almost uncomfortably hot to walk on the sunny side of the street.)

Coccola, as you know, I think, went back again to hospital, after coming out last week rather prematurely, and will remain there probably till next Tuesday, when they will have finished the course of X-ray treatments on the spine. These are horribly exhausting and cause nausea, so that the labour of going down every day to the hospital was too great. And meanwhile she was running a fever every evening, indicating some kind of infection. I had a long talk with Dr [Leland] Hawkins yesterday, who says that they can't find out exactly where the infection lies and that they don't want to give antibiotics while the X-ray treatments are going on. Meanwhile they have been giving some less radical anti-infection drugs and the nightly temperature[s] have gone down from 101 to 99, and we may hope that they will disappear entirely soon. Her mood is good; but she is liable to go down into enormous fatigues, almost without transition, from a plateau of reasonable well being. This may be due in part to the X-rays, in part to the infection. The X-rays are pretty massive; for their function is not only to relieve pain, but to guard against the possibility of malignancy in the bone. I hope that, when they are over, next week, she will really start to get better. It has been a bad time for her, and she has been brought, especially since Christmas, very low by the combination of troubles. In her letters, I imagine, Coccola minimizes her condition; and in writing to her, you had better reflect her attitude.

For myself, I have been kept very busy, what with cutting the first instalment of my story for *Harper's* serialization and working on the dramatic version of it with an eye to production and, let us fervently hope, some Real Dough! In relation to this dramatization, will you please do something for me? I believe you have a mathematician friend. Will you ask him to provide me with material on the following. I want to have a scene where Timmy, the little boy, comes to his father and asks for help in solving a problem. The problem is this. Suppose two men fifteen miles apart riding towards one another on bicycles at twelve miles an hour, and suppose a bee flying at forty-two miles an hour from the nose of one man to the nose of the other, and back again: how soon will the bee be crushed by the meeting of the two noses? The answer, of course, has nothing to do with the speed of the bee's flight, and is, in fact, one hour and fifteen minutes,* the time it takes two objects moving at twelve miles an hour to cover fifteen miles. But I am told that whenever this problem is propounded to a higher mathematician, he immediately starts to work it out as a problem of a series tending towards a limit, using all the resources of the calculus of series. Now, what I want is an indication, with the appropriate mathematical symbols (these have to be written on a blackboard), of how the genius would tackle this problem in terms of the calculus of series. He must write the symbols, and at the same time explain what he is doing. I want this to be accurate; or otherwise it won't be funny. The point of the scene is the contrast between the child asking for help in a problem requiring the use of common sense, the genius making use of the heaviest mathematical artillery to find the solution, and the young assistant, Rivers, who comes in, gives the solution in terms of simple arithmetic at the same moment as Maartens finds it, after covering the blackboard with symbols, by means of his calculus. If your friend can do this for me—or if he can suggest a better gag of the same nature (an immensely simple problem which Maartens sets out to solve by the most complex means), I shall be very grateful.

Love to you all.

Your affectionate,
Aldous

* No, I've got it wrong! *Both* are moving at 12 mph. So the time is $37\frac{1}{2}$ minutes.

683: TO MRS EILEEN J. GARRETT

740 *North Kings Rd.,*
Los Angeles 46, Cal.
31 *January,* 1955

My dear Eileen,
    Herewith the corrected galleys [for *Tomorrow*]. I shall be grateful if you can have two more sets of galleys sent me, after my corrections have

been made, as my typescripts of the article ['Visionary Experience, Visionary Art and the Other World'] are very messy and I need clean copies for Harpers and Chattos. My plans for book publication are to include this article in a volume of essays to be published towards the end of the year, or early next year. But what you say about a whole book with illustrations makes me wonder whether it might not be a good thing to reserve this article, enlarge it a bit and publish it by itself with, say, forty or fifty pages of illustrations of visionary works of art. If you will get the corrected galleys back to me, I will send them to Harpers and to Chatto and Windus in London and get their reactions on the idea. If the illustrations were well chosen and well reproduced, the book might be a beautiful and fascinating thing. Thank you for having suggested what may be a most excellent idea. As you say, I'm afraid the book can't be published by Creative Age, as I am contracted to Harpers.

Now for our news, which hasn't, I'm sorry to say, been too good of late. Maria's back went on for so long being painful that, after taking some more X-ray photographs and deciding that one of the vertebrae might be cracked, the doctors have taken her into hospital for a series of X-ray treatments. These are designed to relieve the pain and also to guard against the possibility of malignancy taking root in the bone. She is feeling better and will, I hope, be home again after the last of her treatments on Wednesday. But she still slips almost without transition from a state of well being into deep fatigue and also runs temperatures at night; this must be due to some infection or other, but the doctors hitherto have not been able exactly to locate it, though they have made many tests. Also her liver seems to be a bit congested —owing, I suppose, to the back condition interfering with the nerves supply-ing the viscera of the digestive tract and related organs. Given her recent medical history, one is bound to feel apprehensive at any long-standing manifestation of not obviously explainable trouble. So please, dear Eileen, pray and think for the best outcome.

Meanwhile I have been very busy—have finished a short novel of some thirty thousand words, which is being serialized in *Harpers Magazine* from March to May and will be published here in September—and in England, probably, this spring. I have also finished a volume of essays—the volume which was to have included the 'Visionary Experience', but for which I shall have to write some substitutes if that becomes a book on its own. At the moment I am at work on a dramatic version of the short novel. So there is no lack of things to be done.

As for plans—we would like to come east some time in the spring, when the weather is reasonably good, not too cold and not yet too hot. But dates are still completely vague. It will depend on several things—Maria's health, first of all, then a possible commitment to do a series of TV talks, to be recorded and filmed. This last is still an uncertainty; but I expect to be hearing definitely within the next few weeks.

Keep well and don't go gallivanting about too much in the cold, on lecture trips. I am glad you are seeing Gardner Murphy regularly; for he has an excellent, fertile and open mind. Some new developments may be taking place quite soon in the mescalin field, owing to the appearance on Osmond's, Gerald's and my horizon of a remarkable personage called Captain Hubbard —a millionaire business man-physicist, scientific director of the Uranium Corporation, who took mescalin last year, was completely bowled over by it and is now drumming up support among his influential friends—(if you have anything to do with uranium, all doors, from the Joint Chiefs of Staff's to the Pope's, are open to you)—for a commission to work on the problems of pharmaco-psychology in relation to religion, philosophy, ESP, artistic and scientific invention etc. Hubbard is a terrific man of action, and results of his efforts may begin appearing quite soon.

Yours affectionately,

Aldous

684: TO DR HUMPHRY OSMOND

740 N. Kings Rd.,
Los Angeles 46, Cal.
3 February, 1955

Dear Humphry,

Thank you for your letter. What exciting news about the new toxin! It really looks as though you were almost on the point of putting salt on the monster's tail. I am glad, too, that this new stuff is proving to be somewhat unlike mescalin; for it will give that elixir a bad name if it continues to be associated, in the public mind, with schizophrenia symptoms. People will think they are going mad, when in fact they are beginning, when they take it, to go sane—or at least to understand what going sane must be like.

[——] sent me a copy of the letter he sent you, along with another full of his new hobby, cultural anthropology. He seems now to have allowed the culture-boys to convince him that the desire for self-transcendence is a wholly environmental phenomenon and that we are all wrong in thinking that it is a personal appetite. And yet he continues to talk of the possibility of transcendental experiences, and regards the mescalin experience as being one of them. But how illogical and unrealistic to suppose that a man capable of transcendental experience must wait for cultural influences to make him crave for self-transcendence! His letters confirm the impression I had of him at Le Piol—of a very able man hampered by temperament and his private history, which conspire to prevent him from establishing a total relationship

684 New toxin: a partially identifying factor in the blood of schizophrenics, occurring also in their urine as a plant-growth inhibiting factor.

729

with events and persons and so make it impossible to use his intellectual powers to the best advantage. There is a mediaeval proverb, The heart makes the theologian. When the heart doesn't function at the full, you get monstrous heresies, like that of Calvin, or blind spots and eccentricities and naive pedantries, as in the case of [——]. I have written to him begging him to read Dr Hubert Benoit's books (*La Doctrine Suprême* and *Métaphysique et Psychanalyse*), which set forth what a very able psychiatrist, who has taken to Zen, thinks about the relationship between ego, transcendent not-self and environment.

Meanwhile the news here is discouraging. Maria is not getting better, but has recently begun showing symptoms of a liver upset—very slight jaundice and nausea. This was certainly aggravated by the X-rays on the spine (which were given partly to relieve pain, partly to guard against the spread of malignancy to that area). But she has not responded to anti-jaundice treatment in the way she should have, now that the X-ray is over. I asked Dr Hawkins this morning whether there was a possibility that there might be malignancy in the liver, and he told me he and the surgeon, Dr [Lawrence] Chaffin, have naturally considered the possibility, but that at present there is no means of pronouncing definitely one way or the other. But he added that he was discouraged by the way things were going—even though he thinks the back is now out of danger. The result of it all is that Maria is very weak and low. As soon as she can get out of hospital, I shall bring her back here and try to get hold of some sympathetic practical nurse (Hawkins doesn't think she will need a full blown registered one) to live in and take care of her, preventing her from doing more than she ought. Then I think it would be worth trying something in collaboration with Leslie LeCron, something which was done by Wetterstrand in Sweden and a few others, at the turn of the century—namely to keep the patient under hypnosis over a long period, several days and nights. Wetterstrand often got remarkable results from this—presumably by freeing the vis medicatrix naturae from all tensions caused by the interference of the ego. The process corresponds, without the toxicity, to the prolonged barbiturate sedation now used in hypertension etc. But hypnotic sedation seems to be far better, as you don't load the organism with poison and can give healing and encouraging suggestions, which may bring about functional and even organic improvement and will almost certainly improve the state of mind.

Our plans, as you may imagine, are vague in the extreme. If Maria is well enough, we want to go East in spring. If not, then we shall stay here. I wish you weren't such a hell of a long way away, my dear Humphry!

Yours,
Aldous

740 *N. Kings Rd.,*
L A 46, *Cal.*
5 *February,* 1955

My dear Peggy,

Welcome to the Western hemisphere! But I am afraid you will find things in a bad state here. Maria is very ill and, though she is to leave hospital on Monday, her condition remains a source of great anxiety. The back was treated with X rays—partly to relieve the pain, partly to guard against suspected malignancy. The X-rays brought her very low and triggered a long-smouldering liver trouble into activity, so that she has hardly been able to eat, without vomiting, for days. Hawkins gave her intravenous sugar today and she was a little less weak than yesterday. Hormone treatment is now being given and Leland says it shd show some beneficial effect in a week or ten days. I hope and pray it may. When she gets home, I shall give her a lot of hypnosis in the hope of producing deep restorative sleep and of controlling the nausea (which in these liver cases often yields to hypnosis when nothing else avails). Rose is staying in the house and Leland meanwhile will look for a good practical nurse, or undergraduate nurse, who can look after Maria when Rose has to go.

So hope and pray for the best.

Affectionately,
Aldous

686: TO PIERS RAYMOND

740 *N. Kings Rd.,*
L A 46, *Cal.*
6 *February,* 1955

Dear Piers,

I wrote a letter to Mrs Sullivan 2 or 3 days ago in response to a letter (not a cable) of hers, asking for permission to reprint my letters to J W N Sullivan, if and when she writes a book about him. I said yes—conditionally; I wd have to see copies of the letters first in order to eliminate any passages which might give offence. [. . . .]

685 *Huxley wrote to his son and daughter-in-law the same day that the malignancy was spreading 'almost explosively': 'I try not to cry when I see her, but it is difficult—after thirty-six years'. The outcome of Maria's illness had been certain since the summer of* 1952, *but emotionally Aldous had rejected the prognosis. Maria, several times, had said to the Kiskaddens: 'Aldous doesn't know; he doesn't want to know'.*

686 *Chatto and Windus had forwarded a letter and afterwards a telegram from Mrs Sullivan to Huxley. The letters to Sullivan remained unpublished in Huxley's lifetime, when his conditional permission was effective, and their present whereabouts is unknown.*

I hope Harold is better. I owe him a letter; but Maria has been, and is, very ill and it has been hard for me to write.

Yours
Aldous

P.S. I intend to send you shortly a galley of my long essay on 'Visionary Experience, Visionary Art and the Other World'—the idea being that it might be better not to include this with the other essays in a volume, but to enlarge the text and print it with illustrations as a book on its own.

687: TO DR HUMPHRY OSMOND

740 *North Kings Rd.,*
Los Angeles 46, Cal.
[10] *February,* 1955

Dear Humphry,

Thank you for your letters to Maria and myself and thank Jane for her offer to come here and help in the nursing—an offer I would accept, if it were not already too late. The old malignancy, for which M was operated in fifty-one [*i.e.*, 1952], has now attacked the liver and is advancing so rapidly that it looks as though the end must come within a matter of days. She has the nurse [Helen Halsberg] who looked after her in fifty-one [1952], a good, gentle, devoted woman who is very fond of her and for whom M has a real affection. Since yesterday we also have a nurse for the night. She came back from the hospital on Monday and though she is happier at home, though by dint of hypnotic suggestion I have stopped the nausea which made it impossible for her to keep down any food and made intravenous feeding necessary in the hospital, she has gone down a long way in these three days. Matthew flew out from New York yesterday and she got a great deal of pleasure from seeing him. Today she hardly recognizes anyone. I keep up the suggestions, however, trying to maintain her physical comfort (she has had no severe pain, thank God) and keeping her reminded of that visionary world and the

687 *Misdated 'Feb 8th* 1955*' with the marginal note, 'Thursday—I think my dates must be wrong'. In a letter of* 14 *February, Osmond replied: 'I am sure that because she could not respond to you does not mean that she did not know what was happening and appreciate its value. Maria in particular having passed the threshold before would have had few of those fears which distort the passage of those who are ignorant, and would be without those worldly attachments which make it so hard for many. So it must have been a great help to reduce the spasm and nausea so that she could sink slowly from us, into that other way.—I don't think I have ever told you a curious happening in my* 1953 *visit. The last night I was with you Maria and I had a few words. She knew that she would not be very long here. I recognised then, that I was leaving someone, a friend whose like I would not find again. I was filled with grief and wept for nearly half an hour. It seemed so hopeless. However since then I have gradually become persuaded that hopelessness was in me and not in the situation. Maria played a large part in altering my outlook. I am and always shall be most indebted to her.'*

732

Light beyond it, of which she has had experience in the past. It is hard to tell if she hears me; but I hope and think that something goes through the intervening barrier of physical disintegration and mental confusion. The *Bardo Thodol* maintains that something penetrates even after death; and of course we know that something penetrates during sleep. Think of her with love; it is the only thing we can do. I think you know how deep was her affection for you. She always regretted that she had not had the opportunity of getting to know Jane better.

Aldous

688: TO ANITA LOOS

740 *N. Kings Rd.,*
Los Angeles 46, Cal.
12 *February,* 1955

Dearest Anita,

The end came this morning after a mercifully short illness and with mercifully little pain. How mysterious this disease is! Sometimes so slow, sometimes arrestable—but sometimes explosive, headlong.

Matthew is being a great help, and so are Rose and Suzanne, and life will have to go on again, somehow.

How good of you to offer help financially! But fortunately I have a good liquid reserve and can cope with the situation satisfactorily.

Perhaps I shall be seeing you in the spring; for I hope to come East when the weather gets warmer.

Meanwhile this brings you my love and an enormous sadness.

Affectionately
Aldous

689: TO MRS FRIEDA LAWRENCE RAVAGLI

740 *N. Kings Rd.*
Los Angeles 46, Cal.
21 *February,* 1955

Dearest Frieda,

Thank you for your letter, which moved me very deeply. I thought very often of that spring night in Vence twenty-five years ago, while I was sitting beside Maria's bed. I am sending you a few pages about those last days, which I wrote last week. When you have read them, wd you return them—for I don't have spare copies. It is so difficult to know what one can do for someone who is dying—what one can do, incidentally, for oneself. What I did seemed to be of some help for her, as well as for me. The men of the middle

689 *'Few pages': see text following the next letter to Osmond. Writing to John Middleton Murry on* 15 *April, Frieda spoke of the piece as 'very moving and strange'. Frieda Lawrence,* The Memoirs and Correspondence (*New York,* 1964), *p.* 395.

ages used to talk of the Ars Moriendi—the art of dying. And perhaps we too shd think of it and reformulate it in our own terms.

Thank you for asking me to come and stay. Some other year I wd like it; but now I think I will stay here and get on with the work I have to do—a play based on a short novel which is coming out serially in *Harpers*, beginning in March, and in book form in England in April; also some essays and the sketches for a phantasy I have long wanted to write. Also there is business of various kinds. I expect to go East in late April or May and stay with Ellen and the children somewhere in New England during the hot months. Maybe there will be a chance of seeing you at Taos *en route*.

My love to Angie—and my thanks for his good letter.

Affectionately
Aldous

690: TO DR HUMPHRY OSMOND

740 North Kings Road,
Los Angeles 46, Cal.
21 February, [1955]

My dear Humphry,

Thank you for your letters, Jane's and your own. Matthew is still here, but returns to New York on Thursday. The mechanics of life are pretty well settled. Marie [LePut] will come [to cook] five days a week and Onnie [Wesley], the dear kind coloured woman who was with us at the time of your first visit, will come once or twice a week. Gerald's friend Michael will drive me wherever I want to go three afternoons a week, and one of Matthew's old schoolfellows from Dartington, a pleasant and extremely efficient young woman [Marianna Schauer], can come in the other afternoons and in the evenings, if I should need secretarial help or someone to read aloud. It is good of you to ask me to come and stay with you; some day it would be nice. But for the moment I think I will stay here with my work. I have much to do —a play which I am adapting from the short novel you read while you were

690 *Misdated 1954 by a typing error. Osmond had new typescript copies made of the essay and sent two of them to Huxley along with the original. The text here printed is from one Osmond kept.*

'*M was in hospital for two periods of about two weeks each, with an interval of a week between them. During these two periods she underwent a long series of tests and was given twelve X-ray treatments to relieve the pain in the lower spine and to guard against the spread, in that area, of what was suspected to be malignancy. These treatments were tolerated at first fairly well; but the last of them produced distressing symptoms of radiation sickness. These symptoms were aggravated, a few days later, by the appearance of jaundice, due, as it turned out, to cancer of the liver. During the last few days in hospital M was unable to keep any food or liquid on the stomach and had to be fed intravenously.*

'*She was brought home in an ambulance on Monday, February 7th, and installed*

in her own room. The nurse who had taken care of her after her operation, four [i.e. three]
years before, was waiting for her when she arrived. M had a real affection for this good,
deeply compassionate woman, and the affection was warmly reciprocated. Three days
later a second nurse was called in for night duty.

'*On the Monday afternoon her old friend L, the psychotherapist, came in for half an*
hour, put her into hypnosis and gave her suggestions to the effect that the nausea, which
had made her life miserable during the preceding days, would disappear, and that she
would be able to keep down whatever food was given her. Later that evening I repeated
these suggestions, and from that time forward there was no more nausea and it was
possible for her to take liquid nourishment and a sufficiency of water for the body's needs.
No further intravenous feeding was necessary.

'*The progress of the disease was extraordinarily rapid. She was still able to find a*
great and fully conscious happiness in seeing her son, who had flown in from New York
on Tuesday morning. But by Wednesday, when her sister S[uzanne] arrived, her
response was only just conscious. She recognized S and said a few words to her; but after
that there was very little communication. M could hear still; but it was becoming
harder and harder for her to speak, and the words, when they came, were wandering
words, whose relevance was to the inner life of illness, not to the external world.

'*I spent a good many hours of each day sitting with her, sometimes saying nothing,*
sometimes speaking. When I spoke, it was always, first of all, to give suggestions about
her physical well being. I would go through the ordinary procedure of hypnotic induction,
beginning by suggestions of muscular relaxation, then counting to five or ten, with the
suggestion that each count would send her deeper into hypnosis. I would generally
accompany the counting with passes of the hand, which I drew slowly down from the
head towards the feet. After the induction period was over, I would suggest that she was
feeling, and would continue to feel, comfortable, free from pain and nausea, desirous of
taking water and liquid nourishment whenever they should be offered. These suggestions
were, I think, effective; at any rate there was little pain and it was only during the last
thirty-six hours that sedation (with Demarol) became necessary.

'*These suggestions for physical comfort were in every case followed by a much longer*
series of suggestions addressed to the deeper levels of the mind. Under hypnosis M had
had, in the past, many remarkable visionary experiences of a kind which theologians
would call "pre-mystical". She had also had, especially while we were living in the
Mojave Desert, during the war, a number of genuinely mystical experiences, had lived
with an abiding sense of divine immanence, of Reality totally present, moment by
moment in every object, person and event. This was the reason for her passionate love of
the desert. For her, it was not merely a geographical region; it was also a state of mind,
a metaphysical reality, an unequivocal manifestation of God.

'*In the desert and, later, under hypnosis, all M's visionary and mystical experiences*
had been associated with light. (In this she was in no way exceptional. Almost all
mystics and visionaries have experienced Reality in terms of light—either of light in its
naked purity, or of light infusing and radiating out of things and persons seen with the
inner eye or in the external world.) Light had been the element in which her spirit had
lived, and it was therefore to light that all my words referred. I would begin by reminding
her of the desert she had loved so much, of the vast crystalline silence, of the overarching
sky, of the snow-covered mountains at whose feet we had lived. I would ask her to open
the eyes of memory to the desert sky and to think of it as the blue light of Peace, soft and
yet intense, gentle and yet irresistible in its tranquillizing power. And now, I would say,

it was evening in the desert, and the sun was setting. Overhead the sky was more deeply blue than ever. But in the West there was a great golden illumination deepening to red; and this was the golden light of Joy, the rosy light of Love. And to the South rose the mountains, covered with snow and glowing with the white light of pure Being—the white light which is the source of the coloured lights, the absolute Being of which love, joy and peace are manifestations and in which all the dualisms of our experience, all the pairs of opposites—positive and negative, good and evil, pleasure and pain, health and sickness, life and death—are reconciled and made one. And I would ask her to look at these lights of her beloved desert and to realize that they were not merely symbols, but actual expressions of the divine nature—an expression of pure Being; an expression of the peace that passeth all understanding; an expression of the divine joy; an expression of the love which is at the heart of things, at the core, along with peace and joy and being, of every human mind. And having reminded her of these truths—truths which we all know in the unconscious depths of our being, which some know consciously but only theoretically and which a few (M was one of them) have known directly, albeit briefly and by snatches—I would urge her to advance into those lights, to open herself up to joy, peace, love and being, to permit herself to be irradiated by them and to become one with them. I urged her to become what in fact she had always been, what all of us have always been, a part of the divine substance, a manifestation of love, joy and peace, a being identical with the One Reality. And I kept on repeating this, urging her to go deeper and deeper into the light, ever deeper and deeper.

'*So the days passed and, as her body weakened, her surface mind drifted further and further out of contact, so that she no longer recognized us or paid attention. And yet she must still have heard and understood what was said; for she would respond by appropriate action, when the nurse asked her to open her mouth or to swallow. Under anaesthesia, the sense of hearing remains awake long after the other senses have been eliminated. And even in deep sleep suggestions will be accepted and complicated sentences can be memorized. Addressing the deep mind which never sleeps, I went on suggesting that there should be relaxation on the physical level, and an absence of pain and nausea; and I continued to remind her of who she really was—a manifestation in time of the eternal, a part for ever unseparated from the whole, of the divine reality; I went on urging her to go forward into the light.*

'*At a little before three on Saturday morning the night nurse came and told us that the pulse was failing. I went and sat by M's bed and, from time to time, leaned over and spoke into her ear. I told her that I was with her and would always be with her in that light which was the central reality of our beings. I told her that she was surrounded by human love and that this love was the manifestation of a greater love, by which she was enveloped and sustained. I told her to let go, to forget the body, to leave it lying here like a bundle of old clothes, and to allow herself to be carried, as a child is carried, into the heart of the rosy light of love. She knew what love was, had been capable of love as few human beings are capable. Now she must go forward into love, must permit herself to be carried into love, deeper and deeper into it, so that at last she would be capable of loving as God loves—of loving everything, infinitely, without judging, without condemning, without either craving or abhorring. And then there was peace. How passionately, from the depth of a fatigue which illness and a frail constitution had often intensified to the point of being hardly bearable, she had longed for peace! And now she would have peace. And where there was peace and love, there too there would be joy and the river of the coloured lights was carrying her towards the white light of pure being,* here—it is being serialized, incidentally, in *Harpers*, from March to May, will be published in book form here in the autumn and in London probably in April. Then there are various essays which I want to do and—if I have time—sketches for a kind of Utopian phantasy which has been haunting the fringes of my mind for some time past. In late April or May I think I shall go East, stay in New York for a bit and then perhaps find some place on the New England coast where I could stay for the hot months with Ellen and the children, while Matthew toils at a job—which, it seems probable, will be ready for him in New Haven, when he has taken his degree. Let me know your own times and seasons, and I will try to make my presence in New York coincide with yours.

I am sending herewith a short account of Maria's last days. Gerald has read it and thinks that it might be a good thing to write something about the whole problem of death and what can be done by those who survive to help the dying—and incidentally themselves. What do you think? If I wrote it, I would do so anonymously and after consultation with people who have had a wide experience. The subject is enormously important, and it is hard to know how it ought to be treated so as to be helpful for contemporary readers who have to face the problem here and now, in the mental climate of today.

I am glad the iachinochrome work goes forward so hopefully. Let me know of any new development.

Give my love to Jane.

Affectionately,
Aldous

P.S I wd like the typescript back when you have read it as I shall have no copies after sending one to M's sister in France.

---

which is the source of all things and the reconciliation of all opposites in unity. And she was to forget, not only her poor body, but the time in which that body had lived. Let her forget the past, leave her old memories behind. Regrets, nostalgias, remorses, apprehensions—all these were barriers between her and the light. Let her forget them, forget them completely, and stand here, transparent, in the presence of the light—absorbing it, allowing herself to be made one with it in the timeless now of the present instant. "Peace now", I kept repeating. "Peace, love, joy now. Being now."

'For the last hour I sat or stood with my left hand on her head and the right on the solar plexus. Between two right-handed persons this contact seems to create a kind of vital circuit. For a restless child, for a sick or tired adult, there seems to be something soothing and refreshing about being in such a circuit. And so it proved even in this extremity. The breathing became quieter, and I had the impression that there was some kind of release. I went on with my suggestions and reminders, reducing them to their simplest form and repeating them close to her ear. "Let go, let go. Forget the body, leave it lying here; it is of no importance now. Go forward into the light. Let yourself be carried into the light. No memories, no regrets, no looking backwards, no apprehensive thoughts about your own or anyone else's future. Only the light. Only this pure being, this love, this joy. Above all this peace. Peace in this timeless moment, peace now, peace now." When the breathing ceased, at about six, it was without any struggle.'

740 *N. Kings Rd.,*
L A 46, Cal.
18 *March,* 1955

My dear Humphry,

A word, first of all, as to plans, times, seasons. I expect to drive to NY with Rose about April, arriving about May 1st. Then I have been invited to attend the mescalin evening of the Am[erican] Psych[iatric] Ass[ociatio]n meeting at Atlantic City, and to talk for 5 minutes. The invitation stated that you wd be on the panel that day. Is this true? I hope so. After that expect to be in NYC until mid-June, when I am to be lent a pent-house on Park Avenue with two retainers—very much above my station in life!

Dr. Puharich was here for a few days last week, with Alice Bouverie, and we had long talks about his latest preoccupation—amanita muscaria, which he thinks will open the doors of ESP in a big way, (provided always it doesn't first open the doors of an untimely grave). Puharich is a lively bird, and I look forward to seeing what he does when he gets out of the army.

How goes the research? Not to mention the family? For myself, I work hard at the play and seem to have interested a producer even at this early stage of the proceedings—Alfred de Liagre, who has produced most of van Druten's plays, is pleasant and a gentleman, and has a record of successes. So let us hope the project will materialize. Health is pretty good; but the house is full of the presence of an absence. My love to you both.

Affectionately
Aldous

692: TO MATTHEW HUXLEY

740 *N. Kings Rd.,*
Los Angeles 46, Cal.
25 *March,* 1955

Dearest M,

Thank you for your letter. I am enclosing a check for seven hundred dollars—the extra hundred to be used, if necessary, for house hunting. For it is clear that action will have to be taken promptly and that it will be better if either you or Ellen or both can get away for a day or two and see for yourselves. On general principles I think sea is preferable to lake—unless there is something stupendously good in the way of a lake near New Haven, which seems to me unlikely. Lakes are apt to have more mosquitoes and less breeze.

691 *Osmond did not attend the meeting of the American Psychiatric Association but saw Huxley in New York late in May.*

692 *House hunting: Matthew was about to move with his family to a place near New Haven, where he had a job with the American Public Health Association.*

My ignorance of geography makes it impossible for me to suggest a place. I don't know where Wood's Hole lies. But it has a marine laboratory, which is a certain attraction. Or what about Bar Harbour? And are the places on Cape Cod too far from New Haven? It would certainly be nice if you could commute daily, and I suppose the upper end of the Sound is sufficiently near the open sea to be cool in summer.

My plan would be to do a certain amount of work and, perhaps, seeing that we shall have the car, to do one or two trips. Possibly also to go up into Maine, where I have never been, and stay a few days near Puharich's Round Table Foundation outfit and see what he is up to there. But this, of course, would be quite a journey, to be undertaken, presumably, by plane or train. So let me suggest that one or both of you should sally forth and look around. On second thoughts, I am making the check for a thousand dollars, so that you can pay an advance on the house, if that is necessary to reserve it. I don't know what summer rentals run to; but if we have to pay a fairly stiff price, let us not hesitate. My *Esquire* articles will make that easy.

In haste but with love.

Aldous

693: TO IAN PARSONS

740 *N. Kings Rd.,*
Los Angeles 46, Cal.
25 *March,* 1955

Dear Ian,

Somebody has just pointed out that I make Henry Maartens marry a 'red-head called Alicia' (at the end of the story) and that the last Countess Russell but one was called Alicia (I always knew her as Peter) and was red-headed. So if possible please change red-head to blonde and Alicia to Virginia.

In haste
Aldous

694: TO MRS ROSE WESSBERG

740 *N. Kings Rd.,*
Los Angeles 46, Cal.
4 *April,* 1955

My dear Rose,

Thank you for your letters. Yes, by all means let us take a picnic basket so that we can be independent of restaurants when we want to be. Next, about the land. I talked to my lawyer about it, and he advises me to hold on to it indefinitely [. . . .] So it will be best if you do nothing further, just leave the whole matter where it now stands.

Frieda will be in Texas until the middle of May. This being so, I am

---

693 *There is a muddle here; the Countess' name was Patricia.*

wondering whether it might not be fun to go by the extreme southern route. It is, of course, much longer. But if we take enough time—and I really don't have to be in New York by any specific date—it might be nice to go first to Port Isabel (near Brownsville on the Gulf, the most southerly point in the country) and then go up via Houston, Baton Rouge or New Orleans, Mobile, Savannah, Charleston etc. It might mean not getting to New York for at least two weeks. Qu'en penses-tu?

Love,
Aldous

695: TO MRS CLAIRE WHITE

740 N. Kings Rd.,
Los Angeles 46, Cal.
17 April, 1955

My dear Claire,

Your poem about Maria moved me very much. She was more capable of love and understanding than almost anyone I have ever known, and in so far as I have learned to be human—and I had a great capacity for not being human—it is thanks to her. I was greatly struck, in reading this new life of my grandfather by Professor Irvine, to find that my grandmother played the same part in his development as Maria played, and plays still, as I hope, in mine—the part of interpreter and communicator, of explainer, of deepener of experience.

Perhaps I may see you and Bobby and the family this summer; for I expect to be in the East, in N Y and on the New England coast, until the early autumn.

Affectionately,
Aldous

696: TO MATTHEW AND ELLEN HUXLEY

[Port Isabel, Texas]
[25 April, 1955]

Crossed this unspeakable state in a dust storm with temperatures of 100° up. Here it is relatively cool, but damp. We start north today—New Orleans, Savannah, Charleston, Washington—don't know when we shall reach NY. Love.

Aldous

695 *Poem: a lyric elegy, unpublished. Life by Professor William Irvine:* Apes, Angels, and Victorians: the Story of Darwin, Huxley, and Evolution (*New York,* 1955).

696 *Huxley and Rose Wessberg stopped at Port Isabel for a brief visit with Frieda and Angelo Ravagli. They were in Tallahassee on the 28th and from there drove to Savannah.*

Dillon, S.C.
30 April, 1955

My dear Marianna,
I hope all goes well with you both and that the house has not yet been burned, flooded, burgled or blown down. Next time you go to it, would you mind checking on some addresses and phone numbers which I may need, for one reason or another, but don't seem to have with me.

Kiskadden—phone and address.

Gerald Heard—phone and address. (You may have to ring up to get the address, which is not in the flip-up phone book.)

Kent—phone (the new one, a Granite number).

Archera—phone.

LeCron—phone.

Betty Wendel—phone and address.

We had a pleasant two days, seeing Savannah and Charleston—charming towns, like English provincial towns with a kind of sub-tropical twist. Now we have got as far as the North Carolina border. I dont know how many thousand miles we have covered—at least four.

Love from Rose and myself.

Yours
Aldous

Washington, D. C.
3 May, 1955

Dearest M and E,
Here we are at last, after 4000 miles. Had a busy day yesterday—lunch at the Indian embassy, galleries, tea with the [R. W.] Blisses of Dumbarton Oaks. And today I go to the Nat[ional] Inst[itute] of Mental Health to see the psychiatrist who asked me to attend the Psych[iatric] Ass[ociatio]n meeting at Atlantic City next week. Another busy day tomorrow seeing Huntington Cairns, Duncan Phillips and Michael Straight—then to NY on Thursday. I shall wire to the French couple at [George] Kaufman's flat, and have written Constance [Collier] to ask her to phone them. Perhaps it wd be a good thing if you checked with Constance. I can always be located here at Robert Richman's house (we are in a motel at Alexandria). His address is 3104 Que St N.W., Wash[ington] D.C, and his phone is Hudson 3-6181. Rose plans to go directly to Islip, but has still to talk to Suzanne on the phone.

Love
Aldous

697 *Mis-headed 'Dillon, N. C.' Kent: Alma Kent (Mrs Atwater Kent), who had been a close friend of Maria. Archera: Laura Archera, whom Huxley later married.*

c/o George Kaufman,
1035 Park Ave., N Y C
7 May, 1955

My dear Betty,

We got here, finally, on Thursday evening after 4500 miles, with 2 days at Port Isabel with Frieda, and 3 in Washington seeing old friends and the sights. Here I live in a style to which I am not accustomed—pent house with terraces overlooking the City, French butler and wife (admirable cook), Siamese cat and an enormous library of plays, mutely urging me on to work —which I am doing now, like mad, for I cd do nothing en route. Have revised the first act and am now doing the second. There will be another interruption next week, when I go to Atlantic City to attend the American Psychiatrists' Assn. meeting—which may be fun, for they always fight like cats and dogs, and may also be instructive.

I saw Anita [Loos] yesterday, who was very sensible about producers, directors, actors etc. I shall arrange to meet the Boys on my return from the nut–doctors.

Thinking over the penultimate scene, I am inclined to have the children's return and discovery of Ruth's make-up merely spoken about (we have had all the fun we want with the make-up earlier) and to place the scene several days after the return, on the day of departure for the farm. We then show Ruth in her negative malignant state, as fully developed. She has a scene of sulky, silent menace with Katy—then reads her poem (which I have written) to John and Henry (who doesn't listen). Details will emerge as I write. I hope all goes well with you both, and with the second and third generation.

It was sad indeed about Constance. One comfort is that she died almost instantly, in the midst of a period of cheerfulness and good health.

Yours
Aldous

700: TO DR HUMPHRY OSMOND

Marlborough-Blenheim Hotel,
Atlantic City, N. J.
[11 May, 1955]

Dear Humphry,

Here I am in this Dome of Pleasure, floating midway on the waves, where is heard the mingled measure of the Electric Shock Boys, the Chlorpromaziners and the 57 Varieties of Psychotherapists. What a place— the luxury of early Edwardian days, massive, spacious, indescribably hideous and, under a livid sky, indescribably sinister!

699 *'The Boys': Morton Gottlieb and Albert Seldon, dramatic producers. Constance Collier had died on 25 April.*

I am under the protective wing of a bright young researcher from the Nat. Institute of Mental Health called Louis Cholden, and his wife. They steer me through the tumult and introduce me to the Grand Panjandrums, who mainly speak with German accents and whose names and faces I can never remember for more than five minutes.

I talked with Carl Meninger [Karl Menninger] yesterday, who spoke in the friendliest way of you. I fancy that, if you want to go to Topeka, he will welcome you on your own terms. If you can get the kind of peripatetic research job you envisage, it wd be a fine thing both for you and psychology and psychiatry.

I also had a chat with Abram Hoffer—who evidently hopes you will stay in Sask, very comprehensibly so far as he is concerned. Another familiar face was Dr. [——]'s who is here exhibiting his walky-talkies, or rather his sleepy-squeakies. (The trouble with his instruments, as I have found, is that they are so badly made that they are never in working order. Consequently I have not, after two years, been able to use mine once.)

Tomorrow we have an evening party with speeches about mescalin and LSD, at which I am supposed to hold forth for 10 minutes. On Friday I return to New York. I am staying

c/o George Kaufman
1035 Park Avenue.

I'm afraid I can't invite you there, as the only other bedroom is Mrs. K's and I have a strong feeling that they don't want it to be lived in by strangers. However there are hotels pretty near and, if you like, I will reserve a room for whatever date you specify. Or else at the Warwick, if you prefer.

My love to Jane and the poetess.

Yours
Aldous

701: TO DR HUMPHRY OSMOND

c/o Kaufman,
1035 *Park Avenue, N Y C.*
17 *May,* 1955

My dear Humphry,

Thank you for your letter. I hope to see you on the afternoon of the 24th. Unhappily I am booked for dinner that night and don't see how I can get out of it. But I will keep the rest of the week open. Might even go down to Princeton for a day, to see Professor [W. T.] Stace—a very nice English philosopher, to whom you might also like to talk. Incidentally, what are you doing at Princeton—lecturing?

I will look out for a room today.

In haste but affectionately,
Aldous

Care of Kaufman,
1035 *Park Avenue, New York City*
17 *May,* 1955

Dear Betty,

Thank you for your letter and the good news from the two-dollar prophetess. Here, alas, the five-cent writer is still vulgarly working. I have finished the revision of Act II and Act III, scene one, and am now on scene ii, following your outline, which is a more specific and detailed version of what I had only vaguely envisaged, as I had not yet got down to brass tacks. I have made a change at the beginning, inasmuch as I have Ruth enter, while Henry is by himself, and try to arouse his suspicions about Katy and John. The telephone rings before she can get under way; but enough is said to indicate to the audience what she is up to. This gives added point to her actions later on in the scene.

I will send you the scene when it is finished and typed.

Today I lunch with the Boys. I also had a letter from [Alfred] de Liagre this morning, and shall see him in the course of the next few days. Stanley Young, whom I met yesterday (he is the husband of Nancy Ross, the novelist, is a publisher and has written plays, of which I was embarrassingly ignorant), told me that the most strategically located producer is Roger Stevens (or is it Stevenson?), who not only puts plays on, but also owns numerous theatres. This thing is becoming a judgment of Paris. To whom shall we present the apple? That is, if any of them want the apple, when they finally see the damned thing. I foresee that I shall have to consult a fortune teller on the subject— or else leave it all to William Morris.

Yours
Aldous

1035 *Park Avenue,*
New York City
23 *May,* 1955

My dear Betty,

Thank you for your letter. We will split the hypothetical royalties as you suggest—twenty-five and seventy-five. I hope they will be *very* large.

Act III scene ii is at the typist's and should be back tomorrow or Wednesday. I will send you a copy. In writing it, I found that it could be streamlined considerably. For example, we don't need in the play anything about the letter

702 *William Morris: the Morris Agency in New York, which handled arrangements for the production of the play.*
703 *Mrs Hackenschmidt: in the play, the adventuress who marries Henry Maartens after the death of Katy. Ruth's poem: the text follows, from the unpublished script of*

recalling John to his mother, which was necessary in the book because the revelation of Ruth's poem came a week before the final picnic. This permits the scene to flow without any unnecessary mechanical complications. I end it on the poem and a brief violent outburst by Ruth immediately after the poem.

---

the play. As read by Ruth to her parents, Timmy, and John Rivers, the poem is broken after the third stanza by an interruption from Timmy, with dialogue by Ruth and Katy.

  ' "*Before the judgment seat of God*
      Two guilty lovers stand,
  With brazen looks and lustful lips,
      Hand in adulterous hand.

  ' "*The woman is a matron ripe,*
      A mother and a wife;
  Her bust and eke her hips are large,
      Advanced in middle life.

  ' "*Beside her stands a handsome youth,*
      With face both frank and free.
  And she hath caught him in her clutch.
      Oh God, can such things be!

  ' "*And they have shamefully betrayed*
      The holiest of vows;
  For he was plighted to a maid,
      And she did have a spouse.

  ' "*Seeing no judge upon the throne,*
      Those traitors did rejoice.
  '*Where's God?' they said. 'He must be dead.*'
      But then they heard a Voice.

  ' " '*Confess, confess', the Voice doth cry;*
      But they deny their crimes.
  '*Confess, confess.' But still they lie,*
      They lie a thousand times.

  ' " '*Then let the hideous Truth be seen',*
      The Voice did then proclaim.
  And straight a hundred thousand eyes
      Were staring at their shame.

  ' "*A hundred thousand piercing eyes,*
      And no disguise was left.
  Their clothes had vanished; they were nude,
      Of every stitch bereft.

  ' "*Judas was branded on their breasts,*
      And Lust *upon their brows.*
  Thus was avenged that hapless maid,
      And eke that poor old spouse." '

I am now thinking about the last scene. After mature consideration I believe it will be best to show nobody in this scene except Henry and Mrs Hackenschmidt. I will put as much intensity as I can into Rivers's description of the accident. (People will listen to such things, if they are well written, and there are good classical examples—e.g. Racine's description of the death of Hippolytus in *Phèdre*.) Then we will go into Rivers's life after the accident and into Henry's old age. After which we open up on Henry in the living room, alone—the others having gone to the funeral, he being too upset to attend. Enter Mrs H through the French window. A very short scene, then Curtain. If we bring the others in, we shall have to find all kinds of talk and business, which won't contribute anything substantial. This solution permits everything to be given by Rivers and reduces the Henry-Hackenschmidt scene to a kind of epigram.

I hope you will like Ruth's poem. This was difficult to do, since it has to be at once rather grotesquely childish and profoundly sinister. I hope the sinisterness will come through and that the comic, childish side won't detract from it.

Yours,
Aldous

704: TO MRS ELISE MURRELL

Care of George Kaufman,
1035 Park Avenue, New York 28, N.Y.
29 May, 1955

Dear friend,

Thank you for your letter and card. I have been in New York for about three weeks now and shall remain here until late in June, when I shall join my son, daughter-in-law and their two children in a house they have taken on the New England coast. There, I suppose, I shall spend the summer, with occasional excursions to Boston and points further north to see friends. Meanwhile life continues in its new, amputated context. Quite apart from everything else, there are certain mechanical difficulties; for, as you probably know, I am pretty blind and depended on Maria for many things requiring sharp eyes, such as driving a car, reading aloud, looking after the practical affairs of life. My old friend Eileen Garrett—Irish like yourself, and a medium, and now the head of the Parapsychology Foundation, which finances research in ESP phenomena and organizes discussions of them by philosophers, psychologists and medical men (we attended two of them this time last year, in France)—told me something very interesting about Maria the other day. M. has appeared to her several times since her death, and particularly vividly on two recent occasions, when she said two things which Eileen didn't understand, but which M told her to pass on to me without fail.

704 *Mrs Murrell, in England, had had an apparently clairvoyant experience at the moment of Maria Huxley's death.*

First, 'I didn't hear the whole of the Bardle' (this was how Eileen heard the message) 'but the effect was to lull me and to carry me through, so that I was still with it on the other side'. The other was, 'I found the Eggart (again Eileen's version) very helpful'. Now I had not told Eileen about M's last days, had not explained how I sat with her telling her again and again to remember the mystical and visionary experiences she had had, while we were living in the deser[t] above all, and describing the light which permeates the desert landscape—the white light of the snow on the mountains, the white light of pure being; the huge sky (the blue light of peace); and then, at sunset, the rosy light of love, the golden light of joy—and telling her that these were but the symbols and outer manifestations of the lights towards which she was advancing and to which she must now open herself up, leaving the body like a bundle of old clothes behind. This reminder of the variously coloured lights resembled in a certain way the ritual for the dying described in the *Bardo Thodol*, or *Tibetan Book of the Dead*—and the word which Eileen interpreted as Bardle was obviously Bardo: for M knew the book well and had a great feeling for it. What she was saying was that she had not heard what I said in detail, but that the repetitions had lulled her and carried her across in a general thought of light towards the fact of Light. As for Eggart— that was obviously Eckhart, whose tremendous phrase, 'The eye with which we see God is the same as the eye with which God sees us', I had repeated. Eileen also said that M had always appeared in the midst of an intense ruby glow (the light of love, I suppose; for she was enormously capable of love); and that she seemed to be less attached to things here, less possessive about those she had loved, than anyone she had ever seen in this posthumous condition. Not interested either in individuals on the further shore; for when Eileen asked, 'Are you seeing old friends and relatives?' M answered in the gayest way, 'Heavens, no!'—which would be entirely typical of her, for she longed above all to be allowed to love the ultimate Love directly and un-interruptedly. Eileen's feeling was that she would not remain in this region for long, but would press onwards in the knowledge that she could do more good that way than by hanging about on the fringes of our poor old world.

And now what about you, dear Elise? I am greatly distressed to hear about your husband's condition. If you will allow me, I will give you some advice[;] and act upon it. Go and see—quite apart from the specialists, whom you should consult anyhow—my friend Mr L. E. Eeman, 24 Baker Street, London W.1. Eeman is a remarkable man who has developed what may be called a scientific method for 'the laying on of hands'. He healed himself after the First World War, when he was smashed up in a plane crash, and has helped a great many people in his unorthodox practice over the last thirty-five years. I don't know whether he can help your husband; but I do feel pretty sure that he can do things himself, and teach you to do things, which will at least heighten his vitality and make him more comfortable. His book *Co-operative Healing* is very interesting, and I recommend it to you. But go and see the man anyhow and take your husband, if he can get to town for treatment.

I don't think, as you say, that we can be really happy until we have nothing to rejoice at—nothing, that is to say, specifically *Ours*. Only then do we begin to have everything, impartially—the entire visible universe and the invisible too—being happy in all the countless reasons for happiness that exist in a world of infinite depth and beauty and significance, and not unhappy in the particular reasons for our own misery, however terrible they may be, nor happy in our particular reasons for rejoicing, however compelling they may seem. But of course this is dreadfully easy to say and dreadfully hard to practise, and if I seem to be smug and preachy, forgive me. Illness (which is death in life) is much harder to cope with than death (which is life in death).

Yours
Aldous Huxley

705: TO DR HUMPHRY OSMOND

1035 *Park, N Y C* 28
18 *June,* 1955

Dear Humphry,

Thank you for your long, good letter. I suppose it was more than could be hoped—that Menninger shd be simultaneously the fountain-head of American psychiatry *and* completely open to new, revolutionary ideas. We *must* have the defects of our virtues—or at least we must have them until such time as we do something pretty heroic and immensely skilful *not* to have them. It is a matter of will plus what the Buddhists call (I think) *upaya,* appropriate means. And the appropriate means, in cases like this, are psychological, or rather psycho-physical, re-education of a kind that will cause the self-educator and self-educatee to realize his absolute existence independent of his conditioning, his virtually infinite potentialities within a world of infinitely varied opportunities and complete impartiality. Which is obviously too much to expect of an elderly gent, however intelligent, at the head of his profession. But I hope all the same that he will end up by giving you the kind of job you want and a free hand to do it.

Play negotiations go forward. I was disappointed with one producer— de Liagre—who got cold feet about the 'unhappy ending' and wanted me to change it—which wd mean, of course, a totally different story. However the other producer I have discussed it with doesn't mind the ending. The problem in his quarter is the director, who, so far, doesn't understand anything and perhaps may never do so—which will mean looking for somebody else.

I enclose a curious letter which may interest and amuse you, and perhaps throw some kind of light on something.

My love to Jane.

Yours
Aldous

Care of George Kaufman,
1035 Park Avenue, New York 28
22 June, 1955

Dearest J,

Many happy and happier returns! Yes, it is hard to feel old—to be quite *sérieux*, as the ageing bourgeois ought to be! We both, I think, belong to that fortunate minority of human beings, who retain the mental openness and elasticity of youth, while being able to enjoy the fruits of an already long experience. Why there should be so few of this sub-species of homo sapiens, or why the majority of men and women, and even adolescents, should develop mental arterio-sclerosis forty or fifty years before they develop physical arterio-sclerosis is a great mystery. And yet the fact is obvious. Most people encapsulate themselves, shut up like oysters, sometimes before they have stopped being undergraduates, and go through life barricaded against every idea, every fresh and unconceptualized perception. It is obvious that education will never give satisfactory results until we learn how to teach children and adults to retain their openness. But the practical problem is as yet hardly even considered by professional educators. I was pleased to learn, however, that the General Semantics people here—Hayakawa and the group which puts out that excellent little review *Etc*—have developed methods for training people to pass at will from conceptualized perception to direct, virgin perception. The exercise keeps the mind fresh and sensitive and teaches a wholesome understanding of the functions of language and its dangers, when taken too seriously, in the way that all pedants, doctrinaires and dogmatists invariably do, with such catastrophic results.

[. . . .]

Your affectionate,
Aldous

1035 Park Avenue,
New York 28, N.Y.
30 June, 1955

Dear Mr Murrell,

Many thanks for your letter. It arrived, curiously enough, a day or so after my return from a conference on 'Unorthodox Healing', attended by a group of psychologists, psychiatrists, neurologists, theologians and two 'sensitives', one who specializes in paranormal diagnosis, the other a 'healer' of the kind who produces his results by the 'laying on of hands'. The discussion of the hypothetical force involved in healing by laying on of hands, as opposed to 'faith healing', suggestive healing, healing at a distance, healing by prayer etc., was most interesting. Some recent evidence tending to confirm von Reichenbach's hypotheses (revived in our day by Dr Wilhelm Reich) was mentioned. My own view is that, while much can be achieved by hypnosis produced by psychological means (e.g. direct suggestion, Fahnestock's technique of making the patient remember an agreeable scene or incident in the past, indirect suggestive methods, such as are employed by very able hypno-therapists, such as Dr [——]), there are effects which follow the use of 'mesmeric passes', without any verbal suggestion, which differ from those induced by suggestive hypnosis. LeCron, a noted authority on hypnosis, is convinced, for example, that the so-called paranormal phenomena reported by the early Animal Magnetists, seldom occur in suggestive hypnosis, but can be made to appear by a therapist who uses the passes. One of the reasons, probably, is that it takes much longer to induce a trance with the passes; hence a closer rapport between patient and operator is established, with possible telepathic relationships. Also I think there is definitely some transmission of some kind of energy, not, in all probability, of the ordinary electro-magnetic kind. It is interesting to note that William James generally induced hypnotic trance by means of passes. I myself have used both methods, and have also used Eeman's 'relaxing circuit', sometimes alone, sometimes in conjunction with suggestion—often with excellent results. (One can get results with animals, on whom, obviously, suggestion cannot work. Also on children below the age when they can understand speech.) Eeman is not a suggestive hypnotist; but the relaxation induced by being in his relaxing circuit tends to induce either sleep or a state of reverie or light trance— which undoubtedly is helpful to many persons, particularly if they make use of the state to give themselves auto-suggestions; for auto-suggestion is the only known method by which we can influence the autonomic nervous system, the only method by which we can hope to implement our good resolutions with any measure of regular success.

Whether release of muscular (and therefore psychological) tension within a relaxing circuit, coupled with suitable suggestions and auto-suggestions can help in any way to control the symptoms of Parkinson's disease, I do not know. I thought that the relaxing circuit technique was at least worth trying, and think that the addition of auto-suggestion and hetero-suggestion would be an excellent thing. No harm could come of it, and perhaps some good might result.

Yours very truly,
Aldous Huxley

707 *L. E. Eeman's relaxing circuit: the method of inducing relaxation by manually 'linking up the positive and negative poles of the body', as described in Huxley's account of Maria's final illness.*

708: TO RALPH ROSE

Newcomb House, Clapboard Hill Rd.,
Guilford, Conn.
8 July, 1955

Dear Ralph,

I was glad to get your letter and to learn that things are going better with you now than they were in the spring. This has been a hard time for me too. There seems to be no remedy except to learn somehow not to identify oneself with the pains and losses one has to suffer, the bewilderments and darknesses one has to go through—to accept them realistically as things that happen, but not to permit oneself to be equated with them, not to forget that they do *not* constitute the entire universe and that we are capable, even in disaster, of being impartially aware of all the other, non-disastrous aspects of the world.

I am returning the script. I have just glanced at it—but frankly don't know enough German to be able to tell if it is good theatre dialogue or not. I am glad that [Joseph] Schildkraut thinks it is and am ready to take his word for it.

I have been busy, while in New York, negotiating for a production of the play which I have written on the same theme as the short novel, *The Genius and the Goddess*, which recently appeared serially in *Harpers Magazine*. Several producers are interested, and I have hopes that I may soon have a definite commitment. In any case it probably won't be till very late this year or early next.

Yours as ever,
Aldous

709: TO MRS GRACE HUBBLE

Newcomb House, Clapboard Hill Road,
Guilford, Conn.
9 July, 1955

My dear Grace,

How are things, I wonder, with you? Here all goes well in a very rustic township, where we live in an eighteenth-century house, under great trees, on the banks of a tidal river. The children flourish, Ellen and a coloured maid, who has a child of her own, like a small goblin with a gigantic voice, run the house; Matthew commutes into New Haven, where he has a job with the Committee on Medical Care of the American Public Health Association, and I work on the appendices to my essay on 'Visionary Experience and Visionary Art', which ought to go to the publisher by the beginning of August. New York was busy. I saw old friends and made some new acquaintances, finished my play and negotiated with interested producers. Nothing is definitely signed or sealed; but it looks as though I may get a production by

751

the end of the year or early next year. I expect to start West early in September and look forward to seeing you some time later in that month. I shall tell you then some very curious and, to me, touching and reassuring things which Eileen Garrett volunteered one day, a few weeks since, in regard to Maria, with whom she had had, as she is convinced, a number of contacts, occurring spontaneously at unexpected moments. Meanwhile keep well, dear Grace.

Yours affectionately,

[Aldous]

710: †TO MADAME JEANNE NEVEUX

Newcomb House, Clapboard Hill Road,
Guilford, Conn.
13 July, 1955

Chère Jeanne,

Mon agent enverra, ou a déjà envoyé à Georges, rue Bonaparte, un exemplaire de la pièce que je viens d'écrire—basée sur le petit roman récemment paru en Angleterre et qui va paraître ici en août. Les arrangements ne sont pas encore définitifs; mais, j'espère que la pièce sera montée à New York cet hiver ou au cours du printemps prochain. J'aimerais avoir l'opinion de

710 TRANSLATION:—'*My agent will send, or has already sent to Georges, rue Bonaparte, a copy of the play I have just written—based on the short novel that recently appeared in England and is going to appear here in August. The arrangements are not yet definite; but I hope that the play will be staged in New York this winter or in the course of next spring. I should like to have Georges's opinion of the play and to know what he thinks of the possibility of a French version, his own, and whether he can spare the necessary time and finds the play worth the trouble; I shall be proud and very happy if he wants to undertake it. If not, he will perhaps know whom to entrust it to. Meanwhile what news of* The Devils? *For my part I have been too busy with too many things to think about this project—which nevertheless is quite interesting.*

'*I spent two months in New York, and am now with Matthew and Ellen in a beautiful eighteenth-century house close to the sea, in a country as green as England and astonishingly rural. I plan to return to Los Angeles in September. If the play is accepted, I shall return to New York for the rehearsals—on what date I don't yet know. All my schemes for next year are consequently very vague. On this date last year, we were all at Dieulefit. A few weeks ago I had a letter from [Henri] Mondeur, who told me that he knew, at first sight, what had to happen, but that he did not say so, in order not to disturb the serenity of that last summer. He was right. Eileen Garrett finds herself fairly often in contact, spontaneously, with Maria—finds her happy, light, gay, young and extraordinarily free. I had not shown Eileen what I had written about the last days; yet she has reported to me a communication having a very precise and specific relation to the incidents of those days.*

'*How are you? And Noële? And Georges? Love from everybody. Very affectionately, dear Jeanne. . . .*'

Mondeur: an eminent French cancer specialist.

Georges sur la pièce et de savoir ce qu'il pense de la possibilité d'une version française, la sienne, et s'il dispose du temps nécessaire et s'il trouve que la pièce en vaut la peine; je serai fier et très content s'il veut l'entreprendre. Si non, il saura peut-être à qui la confier. En attendant quelles nouvelles des *Diables?* Pour moi, j'ai été trop occupé de trop de choses pour penser à ce projet—qui pourtant est bien intéressant.

J'ai passé deux mois à New York, et suis maintenant chez Mathieu et Ellen dans une belle maison du dix-huitième près de la mer, dans un paysage vert comme l'Angleterre et étonnamment rustique. Je compte rentrer à Los Angeles en septembre. Si la pièce est acceptée, je reviendrai à New York pour les répétitions—à quelle date, je ne sais pas encore. Tous mes projets pour l'année prochaine sont en conséquence, très vagues. A cette date l'année dernière, nous étions tous à Dieulefit. J'ai reçu une lettre il y a quelques semaines de [Henri] Mondeur, qui m'a dit qu'il a su, à première vue, ce qui devait arriver, mais qu'il ne l'a pas dit pour ne pas troubler le sérénité de ce dernier été. Il a eu raison. Eileen Garrett se trouve assez souvent en contact, spontanément, avec Maria—la trouve heureuse, légère, gaie, jeune et extra-ordinairement *libre.* Je n'avais pas montré à Eileen ce que j'avais écrit sur les dernières journées; pourtant elle m'a rapporté une communication ayant un rapport très précis et spécifique aux événements de ces journées.

Comment vas-tu? Et Noële? Et Georges? Tendresses de tout le monde.

Bien affectueusement, chère Jeanne,
Aldous

711: TO SIMON MICHAEL BESSIE

Newcomb House, Clapboard Hill Road,
Guilford, Conn.
21 *July,* 1955

Dear Mike,

First of all, I am getting on pretty well with the appendices to *Heaven and Hell* and hope to let you have the material by the end of the month.

Second, I met the other day in New York a man whom I had not seen for years—one [———]. He used to live in Paris, was a friend of Cocteau in the early, unacademic days, and wrote himself—rather well, in a rarefied way. He tells me that he is about to submit, within the next week or so, a collection of his poems to Harpers. Would you see that they get read with sympathetic attention? [———] is a very odd fish, but when I knew him, he undoubtedly had a real, small talent—which he could only exploit sporadically, as he lacked the physical and mental stamina to go driving ahead continuously. He now runs one of the Doubleday bookshops in the Grand Central Station—rather a gloomy ending to a career which began with Parisian aestheticism in the age of Dada.

And now a third point. Do you, or does anyone in the Harper office, know of anybody reliable who would drive my car back to California in early September or latest August, in exchange for his, or her, expenses? There will be a lot of luggage in the car and it will be difficult to accommodate more than two or, at a pinch, three people—only the front seat being available. I'd be most grateful if you could make a few enquiries in this direction. My plan would be to fly to Los Angeles and meet the car at my house there.

I hope Connie and Nicholas are flourishing.

Yours,
Aldous

712: TO MRS BARRY STEVENS

Newcomb House, Clapboard Hill Road,
Guilford, Conn.
23 July, 1955

Dear Barry Stevens,

Your two letters reached me here almost simultaneously. I found them extremely interesting and enlightening. What a mystery chronic illness is! My wife died early this year of cancer. She had a mastectomy four [*i.e.*three] years before—a completely successful operation; it looked as though the thing had been caught in a very early stage and eradicated. But the thing came back —nodules that had to be treated with X-rays, then re-treated and re-treated. Finally, after four or five months of seemingly perfect health last summer, when we travelled in the Near East and in Europe, the thing moved on to the spine, the lung and finally the liver, and it was over. I did what I could to influence the soma through the psyche; but it had no effect on the course of the disease. Perhaps someone else could have done more—or perhaps not. Who knows? Who knows anything about the basic problems in this field? Why are some people healers, and why are some people healees—and others not? Some people can, undoubtedly, establish an astonishing degree of control over their autonomic nervous system and over their general health, through auto-suggestion acting on their cellular and organic intelligence— along the lines laid down in Dr Rolf Alexander's book, *Creative Realism.* But I don't think everyone can—even with the best will in the world. To what extent are these differences between people, as healers and healees, due to constitutional factors? And to what extent are they due to environmental factors? We don't know. Psychiatrists like to believe, and always act as though, all human troubles were due to environmental factors. The frequency with which they fail to do any good would seem to prove that they are wrong, and that built-in, hereditary factors play a part at least as important as the environmental ones. The pioneer work of Draper, Dupertuis and Sheldon in constitutional medicine will have to be carried a lot further before we can begin to understand the obscurer problems of mental and physical disturbance. Constitutional medicine will show us how the soma affects the psyche. After which it may be possible to devise ways in which the psyche of a given individual can be taught to cope with the pressures and stresses imposed by his or her particular soma. Reality, needless to say, is a good deal more complicated than the simple system of psycho-somatic notions now fashionable.

I hope that some day you will elaborate and develop the substance of your letter into a full-blown essay, or even into a psycho-somatic, somato-psychic autobiography. It would prove, I believe, to be extremely enlightening and extremely helpful to many people.

In regard to the suggestions made to your doctor—I simply don't have any *a priori* ideas. The scheme may work—after all, why not?—or, for reasons we are not yet in a position to understand, it may not. But I would most certainly try. I am a strong believer in trying everything. Some good always comes of such trials, even though it may not be the good originally intended, but only an increase in understanding.

Next time I am in New Mexico, I will ask if I may come and see you. Meanwhile this brings you my best wishes and most friendly thoughts.

Very sincerely yours,
Aldous Huxley

713: TO DR HUMPHRY OSMOND

Newcomb House, Clapboard Hill Rd.,
Guilford, Conn.
26 July, 1955

Dear Humphry,

I am two long good letters in your debt. No excuse, except that I have been trying to catch up with vast arrears of correspondence and to finish the series of appendices which will be published with the essay on 'Visionary Experience and Visionary Art', when it comes out next January. The publisher's deadline is August the first; so I have to keep very busy. I have done one of the appendices on popular visionary art—e.g. fireworks, pageantry, theatrical spectacle, magic lantern shows (very important in the past) and certain aspects of the cinema. A curious and interesting subject. One of the striking facts is the close dependence of such arts on technology. For example, the progress in artificial lighting since 1750—spermaceti candles, Argand's burners for oil lamps, gaslight, limelight from 1825 onwards, parabolic reflectors from 1790, electric light after the eighties—has immensely heightened the magical power of pageantry and the theatrical spectacle. Elizabeth II's coronation was better than anything of the kind in the past, because of floodlights. It could also be preserved on film—whereas all previous pageants were ephemeral shows and could only hope 'to live in Settle's numbers one day more'. The producers of Jacobean masques were hopelessly handicapped by having no decent lighting. Magic lanterns are very interesting. The fact that Kircher's invention was christened 'magic' and that the name was universally accepted is highly significant. Intense light plus transparent colour equals vision. And did you realize that the word 'phantasmagoria' was coined in 1802 by the inventors of a new and improved magic lantern which moved on wheels back and forth behind a semi-transparent screen and could project images of varying sizes, which were kept in focus by an automatic focussing device? I cannot help believing that many features in the Romantic imagination were derived from the magic lantern show with its 'dissolving views' (produced by two lanterns with convergent images and shutters that could be stopped down and opened up in correspondence with one another), its 'phantasmagorias', its 'chrometropic slides' (producing three dimensional moving patterns, very like those of mescalin). One sees hints of the lantern show in Shelley and, in another aspect, in Keats, in Fuseli and John Martin. And, talking of lanterns—did I tell you that my friend Dr [L. S.] Cholden had found that the stroboscope improved on mescalin effects, just as Al Hubbard did? His own geometrical visions turned, under the flashing lamp, to Japanese landscapes. How the hell this fits in with the notion that stroboscopic effects result from the interference of two rhythms, the lamp's and the brain waves', I cannot imagine. And anyhow what on earth are the neurological correlations of mescalin and LSD experiences? And if neurological patterns are formed, as presumably they must be, can they be reactivated by a probing electrode, as [Wilder] Penfield reactivates trains of memories, evoking complete vivid recall?

I too have had a birthday, this very day.

> How soon hath Time, the subtle thief of age,
> Stol'n on his wing my first and sixtieth year!

How little to show! One ought to have done so much better. But perhaps it's never too late to mend. And what sad, sad, strange experiences since my last birthday, which was in France! Last week, when I was in New York to see the dentist, I had a sitting with Arthur Ford, one of the best mediums now working. He reported, exactly as Eileen had reported, that his impression of Maria was one of lightness, youth, gaiety, freedom. 'I have lost my leaden feet', he reported her as saying. And there was evidential material in this case as in Eileen's. With Eileen, the communicator had talked about the last days and hours, speaking words which Eileen didn't understand and got slightly wrong, e.g. 'the Bardle'—meaning, of course, the *Bardo*, in reference to the things I had talked to her about. And then, 'Tell him I liked that thing from Eggert'—which was evidently a quotation from Eckhart: The eye with which we see God is the same as the eye with which God sees us. With Ford the reference was to an episode last year in Lebanon—the so-called miracle we witnessed at Beirut, in an Armenian church. And there were references to the essay I subsequently wrote about it. Many names were given, correctly, and a lot of odd extraneous information, some of which, referring to one of

713 *Huxley's essay 'Miracle in Lebanon' was published in* Esquire, *August,* 1955.

my cousins, who is still alive, I still have to check on. There is at the least a great deal of very far ranging ESP—so far ranging that the survival hypothesis seems simpler.

Earlyish in August I shall go to Maine to see what Puharich is up to at the Round Table Foundation. Then return here and go back to California in early September. The play is still a subject of negotiation; at least three producers are after it; but I doubt if it can come out before the end of the year.

Affectionately,
Aldous

714: TO MRS BETH WENDEL

The Warwick, New York 19, *N.Y.*
2 *August,* 1955

Dear Betty,

Well, I have seen Joe Anthony and Mrs. Allen, severally and separately. Anthony is an extremely intelligent, sensitive and, I shd say, original man. What he had to say about the play was far more valuable than anything we have heard from anyone else, including de Liagre. To my delight (for I was sorry to have had to sacrifice them on what appeared to be the altar of 'good theatre'), he wants Old Rivers' daughter and Bimbo restored—for he feels, which is true, that, despite its title, the play is really about Rivers. This being so, we *must* have Molly and Bimbo, as in the book. I suggested opening the play with a brief scene with Molly and husband, just going out to their party—from which they return, prematurely, just before Ruth recites her poem. This will enrich the characters—Barr's as well as Rivers'—and permit of the story of the Maartens episode to be brought in with more *emotional* reason than at present. He mentioned some other points, all of which seemed to me to make good sense, and I shall get to work on the script at once. When I return from Maine, about the 18th of the month, I will come to New York and talk over the changes in more detail with him. They are not great in volume, but will add life and significance out of all proportion to their extent. At least so it seems to me, as I think of them in general terms, away from the script. I will send you the changes as I do them. I imagine they will not be all finished before I get back to LA early in Sept, and we can go over them closely then. Definitely, Anthony seems to me a really desirable director.

Now for Mrs A—she is a small determined woman with a rather

714 *Rita Allen, the producer, agreed to put on the play, which was to be directed by Joseph Anthony. The outcome of the arrangement proved highly disappointing to Huxley. Barr: the character corresponding to the first-person narrator to whom, in the novel, Rivers tells his story. Miss Harvey: Helen Harvey, of the William Morris Agency. Jeff: Jeffreys Corner, Beth Wendel's daughter, who was awaiting the birth of a child.*

synthetic manner from which it is hard to divine her essential nature. But she seems pleasant and sensible, seems to understand the play and Anthony's approach. (One of his ideas, let me mention incidentally, is to have the old men leave their places down front and actually come into the past action—unseen, of course, by the protagonists—so that we shd see old Rivers sympathetically patting the shoulder of young Rivers when the latter talks about his mother and his virginity. It is a Pirandelloish device which cd be most effective if well used.) She is also very keen to do the play, and is free to do it at once, envisaging rehearsals in mid-November. This suits me very well, as I shan't be doing anything much this autumn and wd like to go abroad next spring (and also embark on a long project) and wd *not* want to be tied up with the production at that time. Anthony likes her [. . .] and Miss Harvey assures me that her manager, Milton Barron (I think I have the name correct this time) is first rate. So, on the whole, I am pro-Allen. I shall talk with Harvey again tomorrow and hear what she says. Then she will write or phone you.

About G[eraldine] FitzG[erald] Mrs. A was very pleased with the idea. Anthony thought her a good actress, but wanted to find out why she had played so coldly in *The Doctor's Dilemma* last year. He had thought of Uta Hagen (is that the name?) or perhaps Beatrice Straight. [. . . .]

So there we are. Things seem to be crystallizing.

Today is the hottest of the year, but, thank heaven, I am air-conditioned. I hope all is well with Jeff and the Unknown Quantity. On Friday I go to Boston and on Sunday to Maine

> (c/o Dr. Puharich
> Round Table Foundation
> Glen Cove, Maine).

Shall stay there a few days and then, perhaps, go to Woods Hole for a day or two. Then back to Guilford. Love to all.

> Yours
> *Aldous*

715: †TO NOËLE NEVEUX

The Warwick, New York 19, *N.Y.*
16 *August,* 1955

Chère Noële,
Ellen et Mathieu qui sont venus en ville dimanche, pour voir mon frère,

---

715 TRANSLATION:—'*Ellen and Matthew, who came to town on Sunday to see my brother, on his way from Canada to London, brought me your letter. What a nice surprise!*
'*Time, alas, is not found again. It is we who must find ourselves in time—find*

en route du Canada à Londres, m'ont apporté ta lettre. Quelle bonne surprise!

Hélas, le temps ne se retrouve pas. C'est nous qui devons nous trouver dans le temps—nous trouver tels qu'en nous-mêmes enfin l'Eternité (qui est présente à chaque instant du temps) nous change. Après être presque devenue Elle-même dans notre temps, Coccola est en train de devenir, encore plus complètement et intensément, Elle-même dans un autre temps plus près, peut-être, de l'Eternité intemporelle. Rome, Dieulefit, tout le passé—il ne faut pas essayer de les revivre à la manière de Proust, mais de les utiliser dans le présent, avec les autres données du temps, pour devenir le Soi-même intemporel, *maintenant* et *ici*; ce qui nous fait participer [à] la vie, un peu plus proche ou peut-être beaucoup plus proche de l'Eternité intemporelle, de ceux que nous avons aimés et qui sont sortis de notre temps dans la mort.

Ecris-tu des poèmes? Moi, hélas, je n'écris que des essais, des contes et même une pièce.

Rappelle-moi aux bons souvenirs des demoiselles Scarlett.

Bien affectueusement,
Aldous

716: TO MRS MARIANNA SCHAUER

Newcomb House, Clapboard Hill Rd.,
Guilford, Conn.
23 August, 1955

Dear Marianna,

I am not supposed to know (since both Rose and her mother seem to think that I am too frail to take it!), but I actually do know that things are going very badly—Rose being ill etc. They both seem to be exceedingly disturbed about (a) the cleaning of the house, (b) the fact that neither Marie nor Onnie will be on hand when I arrive. Let us deal first with (a). I have my

---

ourselves as Eternity (*which is present in every moment of time*) *finally changes us into ourselves. After almost becoming Herself in our time, Coccola is now becoming, even more completely and intensely, Herself in another time, nearer perhaps to timeless Eternity. Rome and Dieulefit, all of the past—one must not try to relive them in the manner of Proust, but to use them in the present, with the other gifts of time, in order to become the timeless Self here and now; which makes us partake of life, a little closer or perhaps very much closer to timeless Eternity, and to those whom we have loved and who have gone from our time into death.*
'*Are you writing poems? I, alas, am writing only essays, stories and a play, even.*'
'*Remember me to the young Misses Scarlett. Yours affectionately. . . .*'
The Misses Scarlett were practitioners of the Bates method in London.

716 *Huxley delayed his return to Los Angeles by one day, arriving on* 1 *September.*

ticket on the plane leaving NY at noon on the thirty-first (next Wednesday) and reaching LA (Western time) at 5.35. Let nobody bother to meet me at the plane. It is just as easy for me to take the limousine to the Roosevelt Hotel and a taxi from there. Next, if it is inconvenient for Rose or if she isn't well enough, let her by all means stay (I am writing her this direct). The children can double up and if I have my bedroom and study, all will be well for me. About cleaning—will you please arrange for this to be done by one of those firms of professional cleaners, who send a couple of men to do the job. Have it done either before I arrive, or if Rose stays on and she prefers to have it done later, later on. Will you please take responsibility for this as my professional representative, as I do not want Rose, her mother and/or Peggy getting hot and bothered about something which can be handled so simply by a cleaning firm. If any of them start making a fuss, say that these are your instructions and that I prefer to have the matter handled in this way. I know you can handle this with tact and firmness—both of which seem to be needed at the moment!

As for the fact that Marie and Onnie are both away on vacation—this is really of no importance. I can manage alone very easily for breakfast and lunch and go out for dinner either to a restaurant or to friends. So don't let anybody worry about that. Mme Nys suggested that I should stay on here for two or three more weeks. But this isn't practical, as Ellen and Matthew will shortly be moving to their house in New Haven. Moreover I prefer to return to California now, so as to have as much time there as I can put in before having to come East for rehearsals.

I hope you can manage all this without too much trouble.

Yours,
Aldous

717: TO MRS EILEEN J. GARRETT

Guilford, Conn.
27 August, 1955

My dear Eileen,

Forgive me for not having answered your long, good letter before. I have been very busy making revisions of my play and discussing it with the, I think, really excellent director, who is going to put it on—Joseph Anthony. The producer is Rita Allen and I hope we may go into rehearsal in December, when I shall be back in New York, I suppose. So there will be a chance of seeing you this winter. Meanwhile I leave here next Monday, spend three days in New York and fly to Los Angeles on the first of September.

Thank you for telling me about Maria's recent visit. These last days I have been thinking of going with her to your room at Le Piol and laying on hands. I hope the thought may have had at least some tiny influence for the good of your health. When I was in New York ten days ago I went into your office and had a talk with [Martin] Ebon, who gave me the latest news from Le Piol, which seemed fairly good, I thought, and an account of the Conference, which must have had its comic sides, its all too human sides. But let us hope that the setting up of an international committee and the agreement on standards of evidence and validation will prove to be helpful.

I spent some days, earlier this month, at Glen Cove, in the strange household assembled by Puharich—Alice [Bouverie] and Mrs P[uharich], behaving to one another in a conspicuously friendly way; Elinor Bond, doing telepathic guessing remarkably well, but not producing anything of interest or value in the mediumistic sitting she gave me; Frances Farrelly, with her diagnostic machine—which Puharich's tests have shown to be merely an instrument, like a crystal ball, for concentrating ESP faculties; Harry, the Dutch sculptor, who goes into trances in the Faraday cages and produces automatic scripts in Egyptian hieroglyphics; Narodny, the cockroach man, who is preparing experiments to test the effects of human telepathy on insects. It was all very lively and amusing—and, I really think, promising; for whatever may be said against Puharich, he is certainly very intelligent, extremely well-read and highly enterprising. His aim is to reproduce by modern pharmacological, electronic and physical methods the conditions used by the shamans for getting into a state of travelling clairvoyance and then, if he succeeds, to send people to explore systematically 'the Other World'. This seems to be as good a new approach to the survival problem (along with a lot of other problems) as any of the rest, and may yield some interesting results. Meanwhile, to everyone's immense delight, they have found specimens of amanita muscaria actually growing on the estate—having received instructions where to find them via the ouija board, while trying to contact Mr [Gordon] Wasson's *curandero*, who was under mushroom trance at the moment, in Mexico. This is all the more remarkable as the literature of the mycological society of New England records only one previous instance of the discovery of an amanita in Maine. At Glen Cove they have now found eight fine specimens on the same spot. The effects, when a piece as big as a pin's head, is rubbed for a few seconds into the skin of the scalp are quite alarmingly powerful, and it will obviously take a lot of very cautious experimentation to determine the right psi-enhancing dose of the mushroom.

I go to New York on Monday, shall stay with Anita Loos and talk with my director and producer about my play, then fly to Los Angeles on Thursday. Ellen and Matthew send love.

Affectionately,
Aldous

761

[*Guilford, Conn.*]
As from: 740 *North Kings Road,*
Los Angeles 46, Cal.
27 *August,* 1955

My dear Sybille,

How nice to hear from you and what a kind affectionate letter! Thank you indeed. I am glad you liked the little book [*The Genius and the Goddess*]. It was a favourite of Maria's, in its manuscript form. As you say, one could have gone on with it almost indefinitely; but on the whole I think it is better that the rest should be silence. I have a long essay coming out in January—called *Heaven and Hell*, about visionary experience and its relations to art and the traditional conceptions of the Other World. It springs, of course, from the mescalin experience, which has thrown, I find, a great deal of light on all kinds of things. The essay itself appeared this summer in *Tomorrow*, Eileen Garrett's little quarterly magazine on parapsychological subjects. I spent a good part of this summer writing a series of supplements or appendices—on painters such as Géricault and Georges de Latour; on popular visionary art (pageantry, theatrical spectacle, fireworks, the magic lantern, coloured movies in certain of their aspects) and the technology connected with it; on the bio-chemical conditions of visionary experience and the rationale, in terms of modern pharmacological and physiological knowledge, of traditional ascetic practices. It has been interesting to write and, I hope, will prove as interesting to read. I have also been working on a play, based on *The Genius and the Goddess*, which I wrote in conjunction with a woman called Betty Wendel, who is good at construction. A production has now been arranged, and I am doing revisions in the light of suggestions made by the director—a remarkably intelligent and sensitive man called Joseph Anthony. I hope we shall start rehearsals in December. Meanwhile I go to New York for a few days on Monday and fly back to California on Thursday. The summer here has been pleasant, and would have been pleasanter if the weather had not been intolerably hot and humid, so that Connecticut became a kind of New Guinea. How I admire people who can cope with children! Ellen and Matthew do so remarkably well. But, my goodness, how clearly (because they exhibit human nature with the lid off, or rather before the lid has been put on) children illustrate the four Noble Truths of Buddhism. Life is sorrow. The cause of sorrow is the craving for individualized existence—and do they crave, poor little things! The extinction of craving puts an end to sorrow. And the means to that extinction are the prescriptions of the eightfold path. The path, of course, is out of the question for children, and all that can be done for them is to screw some reasonably acceptable persona over the seething mass of craving and aversion, which constitutes the human being in the raw. After the age of reason they may, if they are lucky, or providentially favoured, or have the right kind of karma, be led to considering the problem of putting an end to sorrow.

Yes, I agree with you: Rome is impossible. But where? Hermitages are all right if one is young and strong. But as age creeps on and the machine requires more coaxing along, I find myself reluctant to move too far from adequate medical attention. Let me know what you decide. Perhaps we shall meet next year, if I cross the Atlantic. Give my love to Allanah. I should have written to thank her for her letter last spring, and if I didn't, it wasn't because I wasn't grateful for it, merely a kind of numbness.

Yours affectionately,
Aldous

719: TO CASS CANFIELD

Guilford, Conn.
[27] *August,* 1955

Dear Cass,

Thank you for the sketch. My own feeling is that the pattern should be made to look three dimensional—as though one were looking into a sphere made of strips of coloured metal. The three-dimensional effect will have to be produced, I take it, by shading, and the whole will have to be seen against a plain background—perhaps dark blue, to suggest celestial space. In that case it is the strips which will have to be variously coloured—some white, as at present, others pink, amethyst, green etc. At the centre of the sphere I suggest, not a plain red square, as in the present design, but a faceted gem, e.g. a ruby. The general design may remain much as it is—or perhaps one might find more complicated and beautiful designs in a text book of projective geometry, or of solid geometry. I would like the thing to be as rich in form and colour, and as intensely three-dimensional, as it is possible to make it. For this reason the blue of the background should be very dark and strong, the colours of the strips composing the spheroid very pale and luminous, the shading, which indicates the depth, unequivocal.

I am glad to hear that the book [*The Genius and the Goddess*] has had such a good start. Parsons tells me that it is doing very well in England and that they have sold about twenty thousand copies to date and are ordering a second printing. So let us hope it will do the same here. Yes, I was puzzled by [——]'s review. It was mainly irrelevant to the book and was couched in the tones of a man who feels himself wronged and affronted, and is bent on getting some of his own back—all, of course, in the name of righteousness.

718 *Allanah: Allanah Harper (Statlender). Huxley had in fact acknowledged her letter on 4 April.*
719 *Suggestions for the jacket of* Heaven and Hell.

I shall be in town from Monday until Thursday morning, when I take the plane to Los Angeles. I will get in touch with you at the office and see what can be arranged to suit your schedule and mine—which may be a bit overcrowded with interviews with producer and director. I shall be staying care of Anita Loos [. . . .]

Yours,
Aldous

720: TO MRS BETH WENDEL

Santa Barbara
Thursday [8 *September,* 1955]

My dear Betty,

I have been thinking over what you said yesterday. The points about telling, or not telling the audience about Katy's death and John's amour—in advance—are small enough to be remedied in five minutes during rehearsal. The big point is, of course, the re-introduction of Molly and Bimbo. My own feeling is that this is good. (a) It gives added solidity to Rivers (who, as you said long ago, is really the hero of the play). (b) It takes away the curse of the old men being *merely* devices for producing a flashback, one by asking leading questions, the other by telling the story. (c) It gives us 3 intrinsically excellent stories. The Bimbo scene at the end of Act II is particularly rich—and my own view is that this makes a much better ending than the amusing but essentially trivial conclusion of Henry's reaction to the French Academy (we get this anyhow—plus a first-rate scene). (d) I don't feel that the new scenes interrupt the action—which is interrupted anyhow by the old men—but serve to diversify the story (this was the purpose, among others, in the novel) and to give reality and a reason for existing to the two interrupters. (e) I prefer these interruptions to what has been taken out—the second scene with Mrs. H (now much shorter and more to the point) and a great deal of non-essential material about Beulah, who has been reduced to what she was in the novel—a subsidiary character, necessary but in the background.

As for Rivers being left without hope by the existence of Molly—my own view is that this is absolutely right. He is a man who is beyond hope as beyond fear, living in the moment and in a state of acceptance of destiny. This was always implicit, and has now been made thoroughly explicit—which I like, and which I think the public will like, if the dialogue is good enough and the actor knows his business. I see nothing depressing in this attitude. On the contrary, it seems to me to be very cheering, since it demonstrates that life can be lived satisfactorily—in spite of everything.

About the sets. I confess stage sets have always left me profoundly indifferent. As long as they are not monstrously ugly or monstrously silly (as in *Cat*), I don't care what they are like, provided they permit the story to be told and the characters to unfold themselves. I wd certainly be opposed to using lights throughout. There must be a solid living room and a solid downstage library—but the passage from one to the other and certain incidents occurring in one or another may most easily and rapidly be accomplished (in many cases) by means of lights. I had the hideous experience, in Traube's sets for *Gioconda Smile* (immensely realistic) of what happens when you try to change a scene very rapidly by mechanical rather than optical methods. Lights can go on and off in 1/100th of a second. Curtains take 5 seconds at least, and the setting up of realistic scenes may take long minutes. Hence I approve of the idea of doing the farm (which gives Katy a most *necessary* farewell scene, which was sadly lacking, as I now see, in the original script) and the love-scene in the den (where the bed is the *only* significant fact) with a minimum of machinery and a maximum of lighting effects. My own conviction is that no play (I am not speaking of a spectacle——ballet, musical comedy etc) was ever made or marred by its setting—at least this is true within very wide limits. All that is required is efficiency—and in this kind of play, where scenes must alternate with maximum rapidity, efficiency is best achieved by lighting (within, of course, a reasonably realistic and good-looking set).

Santa Barbara is surrounded by flames. Last night *all* roads going north were closed. Today one at least is said to be open.

I will call you Sunday night or Monday.

Love
Aldous

721: TO MRS BARRY STEVENS

740 *North Kings Road,*
Los Angeles 46, Cal.
19 *September,* 1955

Dear Barry Stevens,
Deadlines are confronting me from every side and I have been, and am, indecently busy. Hence the delay in replying to your interesting letters and the inadequacy of this note to all but your remarks on the pseudo-sobbing, shaking and twitching, resulting in a sense of liberation and openness to healing. This is a phenomenon I have observed in others and experienced in myself, and seems to be one of the ways in which the entelechy, or physiological intelligence, or deeper self, rids itself of the impediments which the conscious, superficial ego puts in its way. Sometimes there is a recall of buried material, with abreactions. But by no means always. And when there is no such recall, many of its beneficent results seem to be obtained when the deeper self sets up this disturbance in the organism—a disturbance which evidently loosens many of the visceral and muscular knots, which are the results and counterparts of psychological knots. Disturbances of this kind were common among the early Friends—and led to their being called Quakers. 'Quaking' is evidently a kind of somatic equivalent of confession

765

and absolution, of recall of buried memories and abreaction to them, with dissipation of their power to go on doing harm. We should be grateful for the smallest and oddest mercies—and this quaking is evidently one of them, and by no means the smallest.

Sincerely,
Aldous Huxley

722: TO DR HUMPHRY OSMOND

740 *North Kings Rd.,*
Los Angeles 46, Cal.
25 *September,* 1955

Dear Humphry,

It was good to get news of you, all the more good since I had failed for so long to give you any account of myself. I got back here early in September —to find, after the hottest, humidest summer in the history of Connecticut, a heat-wave in full swing with temperatures all over southern California of 110 and up. However, in spite of it all, I have managed to keep pretty well. My doctor, to whom I went for a check-up, pronounces me healthy, and I manage to do a good deal of work—mostly of a very exasperating kind; for I have been revising and re-revising my play, first putting in the subsidiary characters who were in the novel (Rivers' daughter and grandchild) then taking them out, as I instinctively felt they should be out and as everybody, except my over-enthusiastic director, considers best. But I am keeping most of the other suggestions made by the director and incorporated into the script, and hope to be finished with the whole wearisome proceeding, at least until rehearsals begin, in another week or so. All this jigsaw work entailed in shaping a play for stage production is extremely boring. But unfortunately it is necessary, since the neatness of the constructional carpentry may make all the difference between a good acting play and a hopeless stage failure.

[. . . .]

Before I forget, the book you refer to is *not* by Lévy-Bruhl. Its title is *Poisons Sacrés, Ivresses Divines* by Philippe de Félice. Paris, 1936.

While in Guilford I read, or rather nosed about in, [Wilder] Penfield's book on Epilepsy and the brain in general. I wanted to find out whether there was any place on the temporal cortex where an electrode would evoke anything like a mescalin vision. But so far as I could make out (and I followed up every reference in the index to hallucinations) the hallucinations produced by the probing electrode are always characterized by a sense of unreality—the antipodes of the mescalin vision, which is characterized by super-reality. Also I noticed that (in his accounts of spontaneous cases) epileptics seemed to speak of a similar unreality attending their visionary experiences. So there would seem to be little or no relation between the visions of a Blake or an AE, or the visions of a mescalin taker, on the one hand, and the electrically induced vision or the epileptic's visions on the other. Of course, as Penfield says, absence of evidence, in the present state of neuro-surgical knowledge, proves nothing. But at least it is curious and interesting to find that, as yet, no direct stimulation of the cortex can open the door.

I have undertaken, rather rashly, to talk at one of the Monday evening concerts on the madrigals of Gesualdo (the psychotic prince of Venosa, who murdered his wife and could never go to the bathroom unless he had been previously flagellated) and on the Court of Ferrara, where he developed his utterly amazing musical style. This has required a lot of reading—Einstein's history of the Italian Madrigal, books on Tasso (who was a good friend of Gesualdo), histories of the post-renaissance Italy. Very strange stuff that makes one marvel at the extraordinary versatility of the human species, capable of practically anything and able to flourish in the most improbable social environment. I always have the feeling, when I read history, or see or listen to or read the greatest works of art, that, if we knew the right way to set about it, we could do things far more strange and lovely than even the strangest and the loveliest of past history.

My love to you all.

Yours affectionately,
Aldous

723: TO MATTHEW AND ELLEN HUXLEY

740 *North Kings Road,*
Los Angeles 46, Cal.
3 *October,* 1955

Dearest Ellen and Matthew,

Finally I have finished—I hope definitively, or at least until the rehearsals begin—the revisions to the play. It seems to run very smoothly now, with sufficient human element introduced into the parts of the two old men to compensate for the removal of Bimbo and his parents, who turned out to be too distracting. (Also Rita Allen was appalled by the prospect of yet another child actor, particularly of one so young—involving as it does a mother, a social worker, several understudies in case of belly-aches etc.)

They are now trying to get a Swedish actress called Anita Bjork, said to be very good indeed. The only trouble is that she wants to come with her Swedish director, who would be in the way. Old Rivers and young Rivers seem to be pretty well decided upon—a man called John Lund for the former and a new, young TV actor (name forgotten), who is reported to be first rate.

Now I have to catch up on vast arrears of correspondence and at the

722 *Concerts: sponsored by the Southern California Chamber Music Society. The invitation to speak had come from Robert Craft. Huxley's talk became 'Gesualdo: Variations on a Musical Theme', published in* Esquire, *January,* 1956.

same time prepare the talk I somewhat rashly promised to give at Bob Craft's concert of madrigals by Gesualdo—on that mad composer and on music at the court of Ferrara. I knew nothing, of course, about the subject, but have read several books, including Alfred Einstein's monumental history of the Italian madrigal, and now know a great deal and find the subject quite fascinating. The court of Ferrara is really a dream. Jollifications practically every day of the week. The best musicians in the world in residence or passing through—all the great Flemings and Burgundians and most of the great English composers visited or stayed for more or less long periods. First-rate poets in the employ of the Duke, turning out verses for every occasion. The greatest virtuosos on hand. Political intrigue carried on with consummate skill, so that this tiny state in the midst of much more powerful neighbours and on the invasion route from the north, survived triumphantly for two hundred years at the peak of its splendour. Not too many family murders—though there was a good one at this particular period: the strangling of the lover of the duke's sister, who had been married to the Duke of Urbino, fifteen years her junior, came home because her husband neglected her, found a nice man, who had to be murdered because he was only of noble, not of princely blood. After that she returned for a time to her husband who deliberately infected her with syphilis. And then there is a delightful episode at the neighbouring court of Mantua. The young duke marries a Farnese girl. The marriage is annulled on the ground that the lady is malformed and cannot have children. The Farneses are much offended and, when the duke asks for the hand of a Medici princess, spread the rumour that he is impotent. The Grand Duke of Florence is canny, won't invest a large sum in the dowry unless he feels sure that the Duke of Mantua is potent and can produce an heir. A test is arranged at Venice, where the duke deflowers a virgin in the presence of witnesses—and with the approval of the ecclesiastical authorities, who say that, since it is a matter of high politics, it is entirely OK, provided always that the test does not take place on a Friday.

[. . . .]

I hope things are running smoothly now—the house, the school, the baby-sitting. By the way, what are the dates of the children's birthdays? I have completely forgotten. Somewhere around the twentieth of this month —isn't that right?

Much love.

Aldous

724: TO DR HUMPHRY OSMOND

740 *North Kings Road,*
Los Angeles 46, Cal.
24 *October,* 1955

Dear Humphry,

I fear we shall not meet in New York, unless perhaps on your return

768

from Europe. I do not expect to be in the East until the last days of December—and perhaps later: one never knows, where the theatre is concerned. How long do you propose to stay in Switzerland and England? It would be a happy thing if our trajectories were to intersect on your way home.

I had another most extraordinary experience with mescalin the other day. After reading an account by one of Al's patients—a young Canadian engineer, who had recovered all kinds of buried and chronically debilitating traumatic material under LSD, worked it off with appropriate abreactions and had a beatific vision thrown in as a bonus, so that his whole life was transformed overnight—after reading this, I decided it might be interesting to find out why so much of my childhood is hidden from me, so that I cannot remember large areas of early life. So I sat down to a session with a woman who has had a good deal of experience with eliciting recalls and working off abreactions by the methods of dianetics—which do in many cases produce beneficial results, in spite of all that can and must be said against the theorists of dianetics and many of its practitioners. I took half the contents of a 400 mg capsule at ten and the other half about forty minutes later, and the effects began to be strong about an hour and a half after the first dose. There was little vision with the eyes closed, as was the case during my experiment under your auspices, but much transfiguration of the outer world. Dianetic procedures were tried, along the lines described in the account given by Al's patient; but there was absolutely no recall. Instead there was something of incomparably greater importance; for what came through the closed door was the realization—not the knowledge, for this wasn't verbal or abstract—but the direct, total awareness, from the inside, so to say, of Love as the primary and fundamental cosmic fact. The words, of course, have a kind of indecency and must necessarily ring false, seem like twaddle. But the fact remains. (It was the same fact, evidently, as that which the Indians discover in their peyote ceremonies.) I *was* this fact; or perhaps it would be more accurate to say that this fact occupied the place where I had been. The result was that I did not, as in the first experiment, feel cut off from the human world. I was intensely aware of it, but from the standpoint of the living, primordial cosmic fact of Love. And the things which had entirely occupied my attention on that first occasion I now perceived to be temptations—temptations to escape from the central reality into false, or at least imperfect and partial Nirvanas of beauty and mere knowledge. I talked a good deal about these temptations; commented on the light this realization threw on the legend of St Anthony, on the Zen statement that, for a Bodhisattva, the Samadhi of Emptiness, Nirvana apart from the world, apart from love, compassion and sentient beings, is as terrible as the pains of hell. And I remember that I quoted the remark of Pascal, that the worship of truth without charity is idolatry, for truth is merely God's idol, which we have no right to worship. And of course the same is true in regard to beauty. (Actually the Platonic trinity of the good, the true and the beautiful is a faulty expression of the facts. Good implies bad and so perpetuates dualism. Love reconciles all the opposites and is the One.)

I also spoke a good deal, to my own subsequent enlightenment, about objects and subjects. How easy, I kept saying, to turn whatever one looked at, even a human face, into a pure object—an object of the most magical beauty, strangeness, intensity of thereness, of pure existence! Do you remember that account given by Blake of seeing a fold of lambs in the corner of a field, and how he approached and suddenly saw that the lambs were pieces of the most exquisite sculpture? This is a good description of the process of objectification. It is a kind of Gorgon's-head effect—you look at a thing solely with a view to seeing truth and beauty, and it turns into stone— living, changing, self-luminous stone, but still stone, still sculpture. Love de-objectifies the perceived thing or person. At the same time it de-subjectifies the perceiver, who no longer views the outside world with desire or aversion, no longer judges automatically and irrevocably, is no longer an emotionally charged ego, but finds himself an element in the given reality, which is not an affair of objects and subjects, but a cosmic unity of love. The thought of my own and other people's constant effort to impose objectivity and subjectivity on the cosmic fact, thereby creating untold miseries for all concerned, filled me for a moment with intense sadness. But that too, I saw, was a temptation to subjectivity on a higher level, a larger scale.

I looked at some picture books, and was struck especially by a full length portrait by Boucher, of a lady in court dress of the time of Louis XV. It seemed the most perfect example of objectification. The couturier's function is to turn women into objects—objects for men and objects for themselves. Looking at the object they have been turned into by the fashion designer and by their own bovaristic craving to be something other than what in fact they are, the women become self-satisfied and self-dissatisfied subjects, purring with quiet glee or caterwauling with self-pity or spitting and scratching because somebody has blasphemed against the object which is their idol and so has offended the subject which worships the object. And of course the same is true of men—only there didn't happen to be any pictures of masculine fancy dress to remind me of the fact.

I also looked at a volume of photographs of nudes—a lot of them very tricky, bits of bodies taken from odd angles and under queer conditions of light. Objects again. Lust is sexual relations with an object for the benefit of a subject—who may also enjoy, as a kind of bonus, the manifestations of subjective enjoyment proceeding from the object. Love de-objectifies and de-subjectifies, substitutes the primordial fact of unity and the awareness of mutual immanence for a frenzy heightened to despair by the impossibility of that total possession of the object, at which the subject mistakenly aims.

Among the by-products of this state of being the given fact of love was a kind of intuitive understanding of other people, a 'discernment of spirits', in the language of Christian spirituality. I found myself saying things about my dianetic operator, which I didn't know but which, when I said them, turned out to be true. Which, I suppose, is what one would expect if one happens to be manifesting the primordial fact of unity through love and the knowledge of mutual immanence.

Another thing I remember saying was that I now understood such previously incomprehensible events as St Francis's kissing of the leper. Explanations in terms of masochistic perversion etc are ridiculous. This sort of thing is merely the overflow of a cosmic fact too large, so to speak, for the receptacle, fashioned by the subjective ego in its life-long relations with objects and not yet completely melted away, so that the new fact finds itself constricted by the old confining habits, with the result that it boils over, so to speak, under pressure and has to express itself in ways which, though not particularly desirable, are completely understandable and even, in the particular context, logical.

Another thing I remember saying and feeling was that I didn't think I should mind dying; for dying must be like this passage from the known (constituted by life-long habits of subject-object existence) to the unknown cosmic fact.

I have not retained the intensity of my experience of the state of love; but something certainly remains and I hope I shall not allow myself to eclipse it by succumbing to old bad habits. I hope and think that by awareness of what one is doing from moment to moment, one may be able to remain out of one's own light.

What emerges as a general conclusion is the confirmation of the fact that mescalin does genuinely open the door, and that everything including the Unknown in its purest, most comprehensive form can come through. After the theophany it is up to the momentarily enlightened individual to 'co-operate with grace'—not so much by will as by awareness.

Yours affectionately,
Aldous

725: TO DR HUMPHRY OSMOND

740 *North Kings Road,*
Los Angeles 46, Cal.
29 *October,* 1955

Dear Humphry,

How strange that our letters should have crossed! I shall be much interested to hear the details of your joint experiment and to repeat the procedure with Gerald and Al, when the latter comes to Los Angeles. From my own experience I cannot see that it is necessary for anyone to do anything to keep the mescalin consciousness on a high level—it stays there by itself, all the time, so far as I'm concerned. A director or master of ceremonies would be useful, as far as I can see, only if you want to keep the conscious-ness away from the highest level, only if you want to have it directed into other channels on the side, so to speak, to lead it into such 'psychic' areas as telepathy etc., or into an awareness of archetypes (if they exist, which I sometimes wonder!) of shadows, animas or animuses as the case may be (all of them, so far as I personally am concerned, entirely hypothetical and Pickwickian entities). It is, of course, perfectly legitimate and desirable to make such experiments, provided of course that one remembers the warnings of the mystics, the only people who know anything about the subject. First, that though miracles take place, of course, they are gratuitous graces, not saving graces, and have ultimately no importance, or anyhow no more importance than anything else—everything being, naturally, infinitely im-portant if you approach it in the right way. Second, that *siddhis* or odd powers, are fascinating and, being fascinating, dangerous to anyone who is interested in liberation, since they are apt to become, if too much attention is paid to them, distracting impediments. However rich and rewarding, an expedition into the areas on the side of the direct route to the Clear Light, must never be treated idolatrously, as though it had reached the final goal. My own view is that it would be important to break off experimentation from time to time and permit the participants to go, on their own, towards the Clear Light. But perhaps alternation of experimentation and mystical vision would be psychologically impossible; for who, having once come to the realization of the primordial fact of unity in Love, would ever want to return to experimentation on the psychic level? So it will be better to close the proceedings with undirected ascent towards the unknown highest awareness. In this way there will be no need to interrupt the experience of what is supremely important to each participant, in order to bring him back to experiences of lower, ambiguous value. My point is that the opening of the door by mescalin or LSD is too precious an opportunity, too high a privilege to be neglected for the sake of experimentation. There must be experimentation, of course; but it would be wrong if there were nothing else. There is a point where the director must stop directing and leave himself and the other participants to do what they want, or rather what the Unknown Quantity which has taken their place wants to do. Direction can come only, or mainly, from accumulated notional memories of past experience, from the conceptually known; but the highest mystical awareness comes only when there is freedom from the known, when there is no purpose in view, however intrinsically excellent, but pure openness. God's service is perfect freedom and, conversely, perfect freedom is God's service—and where there is a director with a scientific or even an ethical purpose, perfect freedom cannot exist. In practice, I would say, this means that, for at least the last hour of mescalin-induced openness, the director should step aside and leave the unknown quantities of the participants to do what they want. If they want to say things to one another, well and good. If they don't, well and good too.

François de Sales's advice to Mme de Chantal, in regard to 'spiritual exercises', was not to do anything at all, but simply to wait. Every experiment, I feel very strongly, should terminate or (if this should be felt to be better) should be interrupted, by a period of simple waiting, with no direction either from the outside or from within. If we don't do this, we shall be, I feel, committing a kind of sin against the Holy Ghost. Direction necessarily excludes the Holy Ghost. Let us give the Unknownest Quantity at least one hour of our openness. The remaining three or four can go to directed experimentation.

And now let me ask you a favour. There is an unfortunate man in this town (I don't know him personally, but he is a friend of a friend), who has been using peyote on himself and other people who want to explore the remoter regions of their consciousness, get rid of traumas and understand the meaning of Christian charity. He is, apparently, a very worthy, earnest fellow; but, unwittingly, he has committed a felony. For in the state of California it is a felony to be in possession of the peyote cactus, and this man had a consignment of the plants sent to him from a nursery gardener in Texas, where peyote is legal. He will have to plead guilty, for he has undoubtedly broken the law. But meanwhile he can make a statement about peyote not being a dangerous drug. He has some of the references and I have given some others. Can you, without too much trouble, supply other references, medical, anthropological and psychological? I'd be most grateful if you would send me any references you know, so that I can pass them on to this poor fellow who is liable, under this law, to be sent to San Quentin for five years, but who may, if character witnesses are good (which they are) and if expert evidence can be marshalled to show that the stuff is not a dangerous drug, get off with a fine and probation.

My love to the family.

Affectionately
Aldous

726: TO MRS ELLEN HUXLEY

740 North Kings Road,
Los Angeles 46, Cal.
23 November, 1955

Dearest Ellen,

I was very sorry to hear of Trev's tonsilitis. Maybe you will have to resign yourselves to the operation. If he has to have it, try the effect of talking to him in his sleep, before the event. Don't tell him that he is going to have an operation—merely that he is going to the hospital to have his throat looked at, that it is really rather an exciting adventure, that the hospital is an interesting place, that he won't be scared by it, that the nurses love him and the doctors are very kind. I imagine that this might take a good deal of the emotional charge off the experience.

As for Sunday School etc—what a difficult problem! I don't myself get much out of orthodox Christianity, whose theology seems to me to be slightly insane. (How *can* anyone seriously believe in the doctrine of the atonement—a doctrine which asserts that God is *infinitely* offended by human sin and that, as a *quid pro quo* for not damning everybody out of hand, for ever, there must be an *infinite* sacrifice—the only infinite sacrifice being the Son of God. And how *can* anybody seriously believe that the divine is unapproachable except through a mediator? I don't know.) On the other hand, plenty of good ethical advice is given at Sunday School, and there is certainly no harm in being familiar with the Bible, if only because it happens to be written in a particularly fine style of English. To my mind, the most important thing to teach children is a realization that they are more than their own horrid little egos; that there is a greater not-self which underlies the self and makes its existence possible, which looks after the functioning of the body and which provides the conscious mind with its good ideas, its hunches and inspirations. If you care to call this not-self God, you are at liberty to do so—always, however, taking good care not to get involved in a lot of conceptual theology, a set of words which are mistaken for realities and idolatrously worshipped as though they were divine facts.

I am sending you a book by Margaret Isherwood, which deals with this problem. I read part of it in MS and wrote a little note about it; and so far as I remember, it is rather good. With it I enclose another book on *Imagination Games for Children*—games which, so far as I can judge and so far as I can learn from people who have tried them out on children, help the players to get the best out of their imagination and to enrich and organize their personalities.

I have been frightfully busy, finishing off a long essay which I am to deliver as a lecture at the Swami's Tiny Taj Mahal next Sunday. After that I hope to be a bit more free for a time.

No further news except that poor Zoltan Korda is back and desperately ill [. . . .] Bad news too from Matthew's old boss at Warner Bros, Jim Geller, who played golf, got an infected foot and remained four weeks in hospital in imminent danger of amputation. However, he is out of danger now, but having to go very easy.

Much love to both of you and to the children.

Your affectionate
Aldous

P.S. The insurance man wants to know if you wear your ring or have it in a bank vault. If the former, the insurance policy has to be renewed early in December. Please let me know by return if I am to do this.

726 *Matthew and Ellen Huxley had taken a house at Woodbridge, Connecticut, a suburb of New Haven. Margaret Isherwood: a writer on education and religion; the book was* The Root of the Matter (1954).

774

740 *North Kings Road,*
Los Angeles 46, Cal.
11 *December,* 1955

My dear Rita,

I had hoped to hear from you directly, but have only received a second letter from Helen Harvey, advising postponement and stating that you and Joe were of opinion that further changes should be made in the script, particularly in the part of Katy. Also she writes that you would like us both to come to New York in January.

Since I find winter weather unwholesome, I would much rather not go East at this season, and would do so only if it were urgently necessary—as it would have been if rehearsals had started at the date originally fixed. So I hope very much that everything can be settled by correspondence. What I should like is that you and Joe should set down point by point the changes which you think should be made. Looking over these suggestions at our leisure, Betty and I can decide on their desirability and feasibility, and can then go to work accordingly. This is a far more efficient and expeditious method of getting things done than the method of conversational discussion. Conferences, as I have found only too often, when working in the movies, are apt to be an enormous waste of time and energy. In the warmth of conversation and argument, ideas often seem much better (or worse) than they actually are. Consequently ambitious projects often have to be dropped later on, when they come to be considered in cold blood, pen in hand. So let us waste no time, but start by doing all our thinking about the problem, pen in hand and in cold blood—you and Joe making cold-blooded suggestions in black and white, Betty and I subjecting them to cold-blooded scrutiny.

At this point I think it would be well if I gave a brief history of the suggestions made to date, and of what has been done with them. Joe began by making a series of admirable suggestions in regard to construction, all of which were acted upon, with the result that the shape of the play is now much better than it was in its original form. Next there was his suggestion that Rivers's daughter and grandchild should be introduced. I liked the idea very much at first, since I had regretted the loss of these characters from the original story. However, when all the necessary alterations had been made, you, Betty and various other people who read the script felt that the new characters were distracting; and when I re-read the scenes, I came to the conclusion that my original decision to leave them out had been sound. Then came the suggestion for a scene at the farm, which was duly written and is, I think, most valuable. Another suggestion was that the old and

727 *Text from Huxley's hand-corrected carbon copy.*

young Rivers should be played by the same actor. As this would have entailed the scrapping of the present play and the writing of a new one in an entirely different spirit, it was turned down. I also turned down the suggestion made by Joe that Katy should be shown at the beginning of the second act in a scene with John. This, as I pointed out, would be untrue to life—for in real life Katy would obviously have set out for Chicago immediately on receipt of the news of her mother's illness—, and would also be bad literature, since the whole point of the first half of the second act is to show what happens when Katy is away—in contrast with the first act, whose whole point is to show what happens when she is present. Joe's concern that actresses don't like being out of sight for half an act was responsible for his suggestion that Katy should be made to appear, in dumb show, through transparent openings in the backdrop—e.g. at her mother's bedside during the scene between John and Henry in the den, at the telephone during Henry's call to Chicago. But this play, as I pointed out, is essentially realistic, in spite of the appearance of Rivers at two periods of his life, and such stage tricks, which may be justifiable in certain productions, would be out of harmony with its general tone and style. I myself feel strongly that we cannot and should not bring Katy into the first half of the second act, since the dramatic value of that part of the play consists precisely in the fact that Katy is absent. If female stars are unable to grasp this fact, then we shall have to do without them. This play, as I have said repeatedly, is not a starring vehicle. No part is more important than any other part. It is a play for good actors interested in good acting, not a play for stars interested in their own personalities. If there is to be a star, let it be for the part of the Genius or for old Rivers. The part of Katy should go to a woman of less than stellar proportions, who wants to do a good job in an interesting role, not to inflate her own ego.

I have set forth this history of past suggestions in order to make clear in advance what I feel about hypothetical changes in the future. There are many changes which leading ladies might wish to have made, but which simply cannot be made without seriously damaging the play or introducing elements out of harmony with its style. On the other hand there may be changes which will definitely improve it. If you and Joe can suggest how such changes should be made, I shall consider them carefully and, if they seem feasible and desirable, shall gratefully accept your suggestions. And the sooner you send them, the better. Meanwhile I would like to hear from you direct, and not from the representatives of the Morris Agency, whether you feel that it would be possible to cast the play now and take the risk of a delayed opening. If you do, I will of course come east without hesitation; but I have no particular desire to come to New York in order to accomplish work which can be done as well, or better, by correspondence.

Yours as ever,
Aldous Huxley

776

740 North Kings Rd.,
Los Angeles 46, Cal.
11 December, 1955

Dear Miss Harvey,

Thank you for your letter. I have not heard from Rita for several weeks and have therefore no idea what her wishes and intentions are. Should she decide to risk a production this season, I should not, of course, attempt to dissuade her.

In regard to stars, I have said repeatedly that this play is not a starring vehicle, since each part is just as important as every other. If there is to be a star, it had better be a male. The role of Katy should be given to a competent actress of less than stellar proportions—one who is interested in acting a good part well, not in exhibiting her own personality.

In regard to possible changes, I have written to Rita asking her to get together with Joe and send me in black and white a list of suggestions. This is a far more efficient way of tackling the job than is the conference method, when one wastes endless amounts of time and energy merely chatting without a definite and specific point in view.

Yours very sincerely,
Aldous Huxley

P.S. Of course I want Joe as director. All I said in my previous letter was that, if I had realized how much the absence of the director would interfere with the producer's power to make decisions, I would have preferred to sacrifice Anthony's direction in favour of someone else's, so as to guarantee an early production.

729: TO MRS ELLEN HUXLEY

740 North Kings Road,
Los Angeles 46, Cal.
16 December, 1955

Dearest Ellen,

Thank you for your letter and the records, which I have not yet had time to play, as I seem, for no very good reason, to be horribly busy. However, I have finally, or almost finally, polished off the essays which will constitute my next book, and hope to have a bit of a respite thereafter.

I am happy to hear such good news of Trev. Bill Sheldon is a great

728 *Text from Huxley's carbon copy. Joseph Anthony was currently directing* The Lark.

729 *On 17 December, Huxley received from Mrs Allen a letter which, far from setting a date for production, favoured new script revisions. A list of these came later from Anthony.*

believer in treating the over-sensitiveness and nervousness of high-degree ectomorphs by giving them bananas and cream in sufficient quantities to put at least a thin layer of fat between their nerve endings and the external universe. So perhaps, if eating is less of a problem now, you might try some such therapy.

I am ashamed to say that I have done nothing about Christmas—can't face the shops or the post offices. So I am sending a check for you to divvy up between the four of you in whichever ways seem to you best. At least you won't have the bore of sending back unwanted objects for exchange.

The play is in a state of suspended animation—in this sense, that I haven't heard a word from Allen or Anthony for at least three weeks and don't know whether they want to postpone the play until next autumn (which is what the Morris Agency is advising) [. . . .] or push hard to get it on this spring, with a bit of delay. It is all a muddle and a mess, and I have no idea what is going to happen. Betty is in San Francisco, where her mother is very ill, but contrives to send out admirably pointful and forceful letters to all concerned. Without, however, eliciting any response, as I have indicated, from the producer or the director. Such is the theatre, I suppose. No place for anyone who values a quiet life. But then, if one writes a play, this is what one asks for.

Not much news in these parts. The local flu has many victims—Marianna, her child, her mother; Peggy and *her* child. I have escaped so far, thank heaven. Bonne Maman seems to be well. Rose goes to Mexico with her brother in law for Christmas, and I haven't seen her for some time—have had only a postcard from her, in which she seems to say that she doesn't want, after all, to take Mrs. Corbett's course. [. . . .]

Meanwhile [———] is disturbed because her daughter is going to have a baby—husband twenty-one and still at college, daughter supporting the household for the moment. Which is one of those things. Babes rush in where condoms fear to tread.

Much love to you all.

Ever your affectionate,
Aldous

730: TO DR HUMPHRY OSMOND

740 *North Kings Rd.,*
Los Angeles 46, Cal.
23 *December,* 1955

My dear Humphry,

I was very glad to get your long, good, most interesting letter. You certainly succeeded in doing an astonishing number of things in a very short time.

We had our LSD experiment last week, with Al, Gerald and myself taking 75 micrograms and [———] taking about thirty. I found the stuff more potent from a physical point of view than mescalin—e.g. it produced the feelings of intense cold, as though one were in shock, which Maria had with the full dose of mescalin. The psychological effects, in my case, were identical with those of mescalin, and I had the same kind of experience as I had on the previous occasion—transfiguration of the external world, and the understanding, through a realization involving the whole man, that Love is the One, and that this is why Atman is identical with Brahman, and why, in spite of everything, the universe is all right. I had no visions with my eyes shut—even less than I had on the first occasion with mescalin, when the moving geometries were highly organized and, at moments, very beautiful and significant (though at others, very trivial). This time even the patterns were poorly organized, and there was nothing corresponding to what Al and [——] and his pilot friend [——] (isn't that the name?) have described. Evidently, if you are not a congenital or habitual visualizer, you do not get internal visions under mescalin or LSD—only external transfiguration. (Gerald had no visions either. I have not had an opportunity to discuss with him in detail the nature of his experience; but certainly visions with the eyes closed were not part of it.) Time was very different. We played the Bach B-minor suite and the 'Musical Offering', and the experience was overpowering. Other music (e.g. Palestrina and Byrd) seemed unsatisfactory by comparison. Bach was a revelation. The tempo of the pieces did not change; nevertheless they went on for centuries, and they were a manifestation, on the plane of art, of perpetual creation, a demonstration of the necessity of death and the self-evidence of immortality, an expression of the essential all-rightness of the universe—for the music was far beyond tragedy, but included death and suffering with everything else in the divine impartiality which is the One, which is Love, which is Being or Istigkeit. Who on earth was John Sebastian? Certainly not the old gent with sixteen children in a stuffy Protestant environment. Rather, an enormous manifestation of the Other—but the Other canalized, controlled, made available through the intervention of the intellect and the senses and the emotions. All of us, I think, experienced Bach in the same way. One can imagine a ritual of initiation, in which a whole group of people transported to the Other World by one of the elixirs, would sit together listening to, say, the B-minor Suite and so being brought to a direct, unmediated understanding of the divine nature. (One of the other records we tried was one of traditional Byzantine music— the Greek version of Gregorian. To me at least, this seemed merely grotesque. The single voice bawling away its Alleluias and Kyries seemed like the voice of a gigantic flunkey kowtowing before a considerably magnified Louis XIV. Only polyphony, and only the highly organized polyphony (structurally organized and not merely texturally organized, as with Palestrina) can convey the nature of reality, which is multiplicity in unity, the reconciliation of opposites, the not-twoness of diversity, the Nirvana-nature of Samsara, the Love which is the bridge between objective and subjective, good and evil, death and life.) On this occasion I did not have any spontaneous psi awarenesses, and our attempt to induce psi deliberately seemed after a few minutes so artificial and bogus that we gave it up. Al reported psi awareness of the others in the group, and Gerald exhibited the same kind of prophetic discernment of spirits, which characterized his first mescalin experience. Whether I personally shall ever be able to do psi experiments under LSD or mescalin, I don't know. Certainly, if future experiments should turn out to be like these last two, I should feel that such experiments were merely childish and pointless. Which I suppose they are, for purposes of Understanding —though not at all so, for purposes of Knowledge. Meanwhile let me advise you, if ever you use mescalin or LSD in therapy, to try the effect of the B-minor suite. More than anything, I believe, it will serve to lead the patient's mind (wordlessly, without any suggestion or covert bullying by doctor or parson) to the central, primordial Fact, the understanding of which is perfect health during the time of the experience, and the memory of the understanding of which may serve as an antidote to mental sickness in the future. I feel sure, however, that it would be most unwise to subject a patient to sentimental religious music or even good religious music, if it were tragic (e.g., the Mozart or Verdi 'Requiems', or Beethoven's 'Missa Solemnis'). John Sebastian is safer because, ultimately, truer to reality.

To return to your letter. Of course the stroboscope effect is not retinal. One of the stroboscopic effects, as experienced by my friend Dr Cholden, was that the patterns he was seeing under LSD turned, when he sat under the stroboscope, into ineffably beautiful Japanese landscapes.

I wish old Jung were not so hipped on symbols. The trouble with Germans is that they always remember the silliest line in Goethe—'alles Vergaengliche is nur ein Gleichnis'. A bigger lie was never uttered. All transiences are timelessly themselves and, being themselves, are manifestations of the One, which is totally present in any particular—if we could only see it. The symbol business has been a very smelly red herring, leading him off the trail of Given Realities 'out there' in the mind (just as they are out there in the material world, in spite of Berkeley etc), and leading it into the jungle, about which he and his followers write in that inimitably turgid and copious style, which is the Jungian hallmark.

The play seems to be in process of being postponed—the producer having made such a muddle that production at the date contracted for seems now out of the question. As the postponement will be to an election season, which is notoriously the worst possible theatrical season, I am not too happy. But this is what happens when one gets into the clutches of theatrical people. One asks for trouble and, by heaven, one gets what one asks for.

Give my love to Jane and the poetess. I hope the coming year will bring you all contentment, happiness, growth, understanding.

Yours affectionately,
Aldous

740 *N. Kings Rd.,*
L. A. 46, Cal,
24 *December,* 1955

Dear Mr. Atkins,

The thing about Joyce—a page or two only—was written as a preface to a catalogue of Joyce MSS prepared by a dealer called Schwartz. I don't believe I have a copy.

In regard to your questions. I was semi-blind during the first world war. I don't think that the pacifist position will ever be generally accepted on religious or ethical grounds—but it may be forced on the world by the logic of technological advance. Meanwhile the best way to further peace is (for a writer) to call attention to the psychological and demographic factors making for war. I do not feel impelled—nor am I financially able—to give up writing, nor do I think that writing is in any way incompatible with understanding. 'Knowledge', says Lao-tsu, 'is adding to your stock day by day; the practice of the Tao is subtracting.' The secret life is to do both—add and subtract—to the limit. I settled in California mainly on account of my wife's health and my own eyesight. The desert (where we lived for some years) was good for her, and the sunshine (and the presence of excellent teachers of the Bates Method) was good for me. I now live in town, have a telephone, see a few friends and do a good deal of work—with increased difficulty, I may add, since my wife's death deprived me of a pair of vicarious eyes.

Sincerely
Aldous Huxley

732: TO JOSEPH ANTHONY

740 *North Kings Road,*
Los Angeles 46, Cal.
1 *January,* 1956

Dear Joe,

I have read your suggestions and talked them over with Betty Wendel. Some of the cuts you propose are doubtless desirable, and can be made at a moment's notice. But all these are minor matters in comparison with the basic changes you suggest. What you are asking, in effect, is that we should write a new play, different in spirit and style from the present play as well

---

731 *Atkins was at work on a study published under the title* Aldous Huxley: A Literary Study (1956). *The Joyce item was* Joyce, the Artificer: Two Studies of Joyce's Method, *by Huxley and Stuart Gilbert* (1952).

732 *Text from Huxley's hand-corrected second carbon copy.*

as from the book, upon which that play is based. But I happen to like the book and the present play, and had compelling reasons, literary, psychological and philosophical, for writing them as I did. Your assumption seems to be that the author should change his fundamental ideas and his style of writing, in order to accommodate his work to the director's taste in staging. But the Sabbath was made for man, not man for the Sabbath. Stage devices are made to fit plays, and the notion that plays should be tailored to fit preconceived stage devices is merely preposterous.

Let me list a few of the fundamental changes which you want me to make. First, you want me to transform Rivers from a man who has found his way to the realistic acceptance of life and death into a sloppy neurotic, to change him from an integrated man living in present time to a sentimentalist who spends his old age as a ghost, haunting the past. This role of the neurotic wallower in memory is repeatedly rejected by the Rivers of the play and of the book—as, of course, it must be rejected by anyone who has come to terms with reality. But you want me to turn this character, who is almost the hero of the play, into a reality-denying weakling. You want me to insist that his present life is pointless, whereas the life of my Rivers has the rich significance and is marked by the dry, lucid, slightly bitter contentment, which come when good and evil, old age and death are accepted, realistically and impartially, as unavoidable facts. You would like me to paint him as so hopelessly neurotic that, at the end of the play, he has to be hauled back to present time by his friend. Do you seriously expect me to repudiate my whole intention in writing the book and the play—and to do so for the sake of making it easy for you to perform the theatrical stunt of treating the past and present scenes as though they were synchronous? And this brings me to the second basic change you want made—the fusing of then and now. This kind of stunt is appropriate to a Pirandello phantasy, but is wholly inappropriate to this play—which is the reason, of course, why you want me to alter the play. Given Rivers' character and given everything that he and Barr say, your idea of fusing past and present into a single unit is absolutely unsound. The whole point of the play is that past and present are separate. The past is a stage in the education of a man who has learnt to be something other and, in some ways, much better than his old self. The artistic logic of the play demands that John should go through his agonies, while Rivers and Barr look on, through the wrong end of the opera glasses, and comment upon him from their different, mature, totally realistic viewpoint. To telescope the two periods into one, by means of stage tricks and artful settings, would be to destroy the fundamental meaning of the play. I had rather the play were not produced at all than that it should be produced with changes in the text and in a theatrical style calculated to make nonsense of its major premiss. If, as you state in your letter, you don't want to direct the play, unless it can be altered to fit your preconceived notions of staging, then, I am afraid, we must part company; for in no circumstances will I consent to ruin my work for the sake of theatrical devices which, however ingenious in themselves, are completely out of harmony with the characters I have created and the dialogue I have written. In these circumstances I see no point in your flying out to California for discussions; for, if you are wedded to your ideas of direction and settings, there is, so far as I am concerned, no basis for discussion. I speak very frankly and emphatically; for it is imperative that there should be no room for misunderstanding. You want one kind of play; but Betty and I have written quite another kind of play, based upon quite another kind of book. I do not propose to re-write our play in what is, to me, a much worse, more conventional and less interesting way.

Yours very sincerely,
Aldous Huxley

733: TO MRS RITA ALLEN

740 *North Kings Road,*
Los Angeles 46, Cal.
1 *January,* 1956

Dear Rita,

I am enclosing the letter which, after talking it over with Betty, I have written to Joe about his suggestions for major changes in the play. It is self-explanatory and does not have to be enlarged upon here.

Betty told me that, in the course of your last week's phone talk, you had said that you thought I 'was cross with you'. This, I am sorry to say, is perfectly true. And if you reflect on the matter, you must admit that I have very good reasons. Last August you signed a contract in which the production date was fixed, unconditionally, as January nineteenth, 1956. After three months, during which nothing was accomplished, I wrote to Helen Harvey, expressing my concern, and was told in reply that she had advised postponement, although you had not mentioned the possibility. I then wrote to you at length, expressing my feelings in regard to postponement and also in regard to the kind of changes I would be prepared to make in the play. To these letters I received no reply, and at no time have you given me a word of explanation for your failure to live up to your side of the bargain—a bargain which was made solely because you agreed to produce the play in January. Instead of answering my questions or discussing my objections, you merely announced the coming of wonderful suggestions for changes. Well, now the list of suggestions has arrived, and it contains all the items I had told you in advance I would reject, together with many more which betray Joe's unwillingness to understand the play as it stands and his determination to get me to write a new play more in line with his preconceived

733 *Text from Huxley's carbon copy.*

notions of good staging. The only important fact—your failure to live up to your side of the bargain—remains to this day unexplained by you and unregretted. This is a way of conducting business to which I am not accustomed. So it is no wonder, my dear Rita, that I am a little cross with you.

A happy New Year.

Yours,
Aldous Huxley

734: TO JOSEPH ANTHONY

740 *North Kings Road,*
Los Angeles 46, Cal.
10 *January,* 1956

Dear Joe,

Thank you for your letter. You accuse me of being unwilling to co-operate with my director. But let us set the record straight. Last summer, when we worked together so enjoyably, you persuaded me (against my earlier, better judgment—and, as it turned out, against the judgment of all those who saw the changes) to emphasize the richness of old Rivers' present life by introducing his daughter and grandchild. Today you are equally enthusiastic for a revamping of the Rivers scenes, which would entail his having no life in the present at all and, preferably, no wife as a successor to Katy. Moreover, according to Rita, you had at one time sponsored the notion of having the parts of John and Rivers played by one actor—an idea which was soon dropped as being grotesque. This fertility in [. . .] and mutually inconsistent notions was not calculated, as you can imagine, to inspire much confidence in your latest proposals. And in fact you yourself have made it clear that your proposals would be workable only if I consented to change the character of Rivers out of all recognition and to alter the tempo of the dialogue to fit the rhythm demanded by your 'fluid staging'. Fluid staging, as I remember, used to be all the rage in Germany and Belgium thirty-five years ago, and I can see no reason why we should return to this fad—particularly in the case of a play conceived and written in an essentially solid style. There is nothing unreasonable or uncooperative in my attitude, nor anything subversive in my belief that the play's the thing and that the business of a director is to stage the play as it was intended to be staged by the author.

Yours,
Aldous Huxley

734 *Text from Huxley's hand-corrected carbon copy. In a letter of 5 January, Anthony had in effect resigned as director of the play. He protested Huxley's interpretation of the suggested changes.*

784

736: TO DR HOWARD FABING

740 *North Kings Rd.,*
Los Angeles 46, Cal.
16 *January,* 1956

Dear Mr. Hepburn,

That A[rnold] B[ennett] played a part was obvious. He was his own favourite character. And the motives for playing it were partly, I suppose, the desire to compensate for the fact of his provincial middle-class origins—very important in the caste-ridden society of his time—by being a 'Card', partly, as you suppose, a fear of being carried away by his feelings. He was always very kind to me, when I was young, and I felt a great affection for him. His relations with women—or rather the women with whom he elected to have relations—require a good deal of explanation. But this is a mystery beyond my competence to solve! Don't ever quote me as having mentioned it.

Sincerely
Aldous Huxley

736: TO DR HOWARD FABING

740 *North Kings Road,*
Los Angeles 46, Cal.
20 *January,* 1956

Dear Howard,

I hope you had a pleasant and fruitful stay at Monterey and that you are now safely home again. Your visit here was a memorable event, and I am most grateful—and so, I know, is Gerald—for the experiences you made possible and for the opportunities of discussing and evaluating them. If and when I take my eastward trip, I look forward to repeating the experiment and renewing the discussions.

Meanwhile I have been thinking over one of the subjects we raised in our conversation on Sunday morning—the use of hypnosis in conjunction with mescaline or LSD. It seems to me that hypnosis might prove very useful in three ways. First, to prepare the subject for the taking of the drug. Put him into a light trance and talk to him about what he is likely to experience—pointing out that there is nothing to be frightened of. What we ordinarily call 'reality' is merely that slice of total fact which our biological equipment, our linguistic heritage (see Benjamin Whorf) and our social conventions of thought and feeling make it possible for us to apprehend. (The ideas contained in [J. J.] Von Uexküll's classical book on Umweltlehre or

735 *Hepburn is an authority on the life and writings of Bennett and is the editor of the Bennett letters.*
736 *Text from the hand-corrected carbon copy sent by Huxley to Osmond.*

785

'environmentology' are fundamental in this context. The paramecium, the sea urchin and the dog—each has its universe, and each of the universes is very different from the others. Man's biologically, socially and linguistically conditioned universe is much richer than that of the other animals; but it is still only a small slice of the melon. Mescalin and LSD permit us to cut another kind of slice—a slice which is not much good to us as creatures who have to survive and compete, but may be extremely helpful to us in so far as we are creatures capable and desirous of understanding. In simple terms, ideas of this kind could be conveyed to the subject under hypnosis, before the drug is taken. This should prevent him from going into a panic on account of the mere strangeness of the experience.

In the second place, it would be interesting to see what could be done with hypnosis while the subject is under the drug's influence. To start with, is a mescalinized person hypnotizable? If so, can hypnotic suggestion direct his new found visionary capacities into specific channels—e.g. into the realm of buried memories of childhood, or into specific areas of thought and imagery. Can we suggest to him, for example, that he should see an episode from the *Arabian Nights*, or from the Gospel, or in the realm of archetypal symbols or mythology?

Finally, it would be interesting to hypnotize the person after he came back from mescalin, trying to make him re-experience what he lived through under mescalin, but without the aid of the drug. This, it seems to me, should be started while the effects of the drug are wearing off. Try to prolong and re-enhance the experience by suggestion. At the same time give a post-hypnotic suggestion to the effect that there will be no difficulty in recapturing the full experience at later dates. Repeat the experiment on the following days and see if hypnosis can establish not merely a memory of the mescalin experience, but a total recall or even a new experience of the same kind. If this seems to work, give post-hypnotic suggestions to the effect that the person will be able to enter the visionary state at will under auto-suggestion. This vivid recall and re-activation of visionary experience may turn out to be impossible. On the other hand it may not. But I am sure the experiment is worth trying—and trying on a number of subjects, since there is such an enormous difference in these matters between the capacities of one person and another. That some people enter the visionary world under hypnosis, I know experimentally. My wife, for example, would enter a world having the same sort of luminosity and significance as the mescalin world, where there were vast landscapes, mostly of the desert, and a variety of personages. It would be interesting to discover whether, as the result of the door having once been opened by chemical means, persons ordinarily incapable of entering the 'other world' spontaneously or through hypnosis would find it possible to dispense with the chemical key and reach the mescalin destination by purely psychological means (whatever *that* phrase may mean!).

786

Please remember me to Dr P and to Bobby Brown, whom I think of with much affection.

Yours,
Aldous Huxley

737: TO DR HUMPHRY OSMOND

740 *North Kings Road,*
Los Angeles 46, Cal.
21 *January*, 1956

My dear Humphry,

Many thanks for your letter. I hope that the Saskatchewan winter is becoming slightly less bleak. Certainly it seems to be a pretty bad winter everywhere—intense drought here, disastrous rains in the Pacific Northwest, appalling cold in the Mid West and the Eastern states, also in Europe. Perhaps our H-bomb fooleries have something to do with it—inopportune dust clouds triggering precipitation and cloud formation in unexpected ways. Most ignorant of what we are most assured (our glassy essence), like angry apes we play our fantastic tricks not only before high heaven, but *in* it.

And talking of glassy essences, Gerald and I went through another mescalin experience last week. This time with Dr Howard Fabing of Cincinnati —a very nice, open-minded and intelligent man—together with another MD and a young woman pharmacologist, Dr Barbara Brown, mainly responsible for developing Frenquel. Fabing wanted to try the effect of Frenquel on us, so as to get our impressions of the cutting short of the mescalin experience by this new tranquillizer. He gave us 500 mgs of a particularly pure brand of mescalin, specially made up for him by a chemist at Antioch College. The effects were powerful. A good deal of vision with the eyes closed—though never consistent or long-drawn, just moving geometries modulating or on the verge of modulating into architectures. The time sense was altered most profoundly, and there was literally a long life time of experience of beauty, being and love. Fabing gave us a massive intravenous dose of Frenquel about two hours after the ingestion of the mescalin. The effects were noticeable within a quarter of an hour. It was a distressing experience, like that described by Emily Brontë.

> O dreadful is the check—intense the agony—
> When the ear begins to hear and the eye begins to see,

(to see and hear in the manner of a separate, encapsulated ego)

> When the pulse begins to throb, the brain to think again,

(to think discursively and biologically, utilitarianly)

> The soul to feel the flesh, and the flesh to feel the chain.

It was an experience of the Fall, made the more distressing by the fact that returning selfhood was accompanied by dizziness and general physical derangement akin to those experienced when one is drunk. (How curious, it suddenly occurs to me, that Milton's Adam and Eve should feel tight after eating the fruit! I must look up the passage in *Paradise Lost*.) This tipsy experience of the Fall lasted about forty-five minutes, then we both returned to the mescalin condition. Evidently intravenous Frenquel is rapidly excreted. Once it is safely out of the way, the mescalin re-emerges from its hiding place in the liver. Fabing is now convinced that, to be effective, the Frenquel should be given in small doses repeated at short intervals, not in a single large dose. Both Gerald and I continued to feel the effects until far into the night (we took the thing at three in the afternoon). At about six or six-thirty I got up and walked out onto the veranda outside the front door. On the wall of the house, between the windows of the large living room, are two charcoal outlines, still faintly visible, made by my brother-in-law, Joep Nicolas, four or five years ago, of Maria's and my profile—outlines traced round the shadows cast by the setting sun. I did not actually see these outlines, as there was very little light. But suddenly I thought of them and was overwhelmed by intense grief. I don't know how long the weeping lasted, but I must have discharged a great accumulation of unshed tears. It was something very painful but very necessary.

I am enclosing the copy of a letter I am sending to Fabing on the subject of possible experiments with hypnosis, before, during and after the administration of mescalin. I hope he will try them—and I hope you will do so too; for there may be significant possibilities along this line.

My love to Jane.

Yours affectionately,
Aldous

738: TO MATTHEW AND ELLEN HUXLEY

740 *North Kings Road,*
Los Angeles 46, Cal.
30 *January,* 1956

Dearest Ellen and Matthew,

Thank you, Ellen, for a most welcome letter. I am most happy to hear that the news is predominately good, with Trev making such progress in the task of acclimatizing himself to this Vale of Tears, and Tessa already capable of giving ironical good advice to all concerned.

Things have been going pretty well at this end too. Health good, no damage to the house from the phenomenal rainstorm last week—seven inches in a single day; work at a standstill after finishing off my volume of essays [*Adonis and the Alphabet*]—but, I hope and think, fruitfully so, since I begin to have insights into the problem of realizing in practice the notions for a phantasy, which have been haunting me, abstractly, for several years past. The play situation seems finally to be clearing up. The last word from Betty is that, after a fearful, feline war between [——] and [—— . . .], things will be settled definitively this afternoon. (But don't let us rejoice before everything is signed and sealed.) Meanwhile Betty approves of the new director, Arthur Penn (of whom I hear very good accounts from various sources), and likes the suggestions he has made—constructive ones, this time, and not of the Procrustean variety proposed by Anthony, who wanted us to lop and stretch the play in order to fit the kind of staging he has applied to his current success about Joan of Arc. So let us hope that all will end well, in spite of everything. [——], meanwhile, is at the beginning of Love's Young Dream, being now engaged to a gentleman called Mr Gazelle (I suppose it is really Gesell), whom she describes as 'an artist who used to play a wind instrument until he had an accident'. Let us hope that this will calm her down a bit and make her less erratic. Evidently we owe a debt of gratitude to Mr Gazelle, since he is reported to have said that he thought my opinion about the way to stage the play was likely to be sounder than Joe Anthony's. Let us hope that this Gazelle won't be like the one described in Moore's poem.

> I never had a dear Gazelle
>   To glad me with its soft black eye,
> But when it came to know me well
>   And love me, it was sure to die.

Meanwhile other play prospects have suddenly opened up. When shopping in the Largest Drug Store in the World a couple of weeks ago, I was accosted by a young man, who wanted to know if I were me. He turned out to be a rising TV director and incipient movie director at Twentieth-Century Fox —an ex-teacher of dramatics, incidentally, at the New School in New York. His name is T[—] P[—] and he seems to be bright, enterprising and possessed of a good theatrical flair. He has set up a group here including actors (good ones), directors and writers for the purpose of learning about the drama and also of producing plays, first at the Huntington Hartford Theatre in Hollywood and then, since they have connections with the Theatre Guild, in New York. He has become interested in Ralph Rose's version of *After Many a Summer*, and we spent an hour or so last Sunday discussing ideas for strengthening the dramatic power of the play—suggestions which were all sound and for which, I think, we found satisfactory practical expressions. Rose is going to New York in a day or so and will work on the changes there, so that within a couple of months we should have a finished, improved script. Rose is also working on the dramatization I did of *Ape and Essence* —a dramatization which was much too short for practical purposes and which he is re-shaping in the form of a music drama with ballets. Quite a good idea, I think. I count no chickens, but hope none the less that some of these eggs

---

738 *Mr Gazelle or Gesell was a figment; Huxley's ear had not caught the name correctly.*

may hatch out. It would be very nice to get something without having to do any work, for a change!

[. . . .]

Have just finished a lively and interesting book called *Sex in History*, by Rattray Taylor. The item I like best in it is the description of a Victorian chastity belt for boys—a little wire cage to prevent masturbation, so devised that an erection would close a contact and ring an electric bell in the parents' bedroom.

Much love to you all.

Ever your affectionate,
Aldous

739: TO MRS EILEEN J. GARRETT

740 North Kings Road,
Los Angeles 46, Cal.
11 March, 1956

My dear Eileen,

Your letter reached me simultaneously with some information which may perhaps prove useful for all of us. There is a doctor in Mexico, by name Dr Rosete, who has developed a treatment through extracts from the tissues of mammalian embryos—nerve tissues, lung tissues, vascular tissues etc. The results in many instances have been spectacular—a kind of re-creation of impaired tissues, resulting in a new lease of mental and physical life. The Mexican has been granted permission by the Food and Drug Administration to manufacture his cellular extracts in this country and to distribute them, for experimental and clinical use, to doctors. A few medical men in various parts of the country are using them, and from one of the men using them here, I hear glowing accounts of results in cases which did not respond to other forms of treatment. In New York I have heard of one doctor who uses Rosete's products—a Dr Max Jacobson. I don't know his address, but presume it can easily be found. There are apparently no regrettable side effects and no counter-indications to the use of the extracts, so please get hold of Dr Max Jacobson and try the effects of this new and seemingly very promising treatment. I see no point in prolonging life to extreme old age—but a great deal of point in living out one's allotted span with the greatest possible efficiency, physical and mental. If Rosete's extracts help one to do this, then Viva Rosete. So tell Miss Davidson to bully you into going to Dr Jacobson.

I expect to be in New York in the last days of April or the first of May, and shall look forward, dear Eileen, to seeing you then—greatly improved, let us hope, by the new treatment! Meanwhile this brings you all my love.

Affectionately,
Aldous

740 *North Kings Road,*
Los Angeles 46, Cal.
14 *March,* 1956

My dear Humphry,

Thank you for your good and most interesting letter. I think you are right about the Indians. Soma, in India, was taken only by the priests—and it was a dangerous drug, from which many people died. The votaries of Dionysus got drunk together—but alcohol is hardly an elixir, just booze. I dare say some of the tropical takers of mind-changing stuff may have hit upon the Indian device independently—but where can one find out? And anyhow they are too remote and too primitive to be of much significance to us. Gordon Wasson's mushroom eaters in southern Mexico evidently used an elixir in small groups, directed by a priest or priestess. His account of his own experience with the mushrooms in such a group is very interesting. The symptoms seem to have been almost identical with those of peyote —including the vomiting. He was immensely impressed by the whole procedure—and when a partner in J P Morgan is impressed by this sort of thing, it must be pretty impressive! I hope you will find out more about your Native American Church in Saskatchewan. I have a standing invitation from some Indian peyotists in Ponca City, Oklahoma, to attend one of their meetings, but have been unable to accept so far owing to the tyranny of space and time.

I have done three articles for the *Sunday Times* on 'Brave New World Revisited'—one on the future from the demographer's point of view, one on the relevance of the *BNW* political set-up to the immediate future, and the third on soma (*BNW* variety), its relevance to the present mass consumption of 'Happy Pills', (Miltown-Equanil) and its social, ethical and psychological significance. I hope to go further into this problem when I embark on my projected phantasy about an imaginary society, whose purpose is to get its members to realize their highest potentialities. I shall place the fable, not in the future, but on an island, hypothetical, in the Indian ocean, not far from the Andamans, and inhabited by people who are descended from Buddhist colonists from the mainland, and so know all about Tantra (which is more than I do—but one can do some learning and some pretending!). To build a bridge between them and us, I postulate an English-

<hr>

740 *Indians: Osmond had noted that the Native Church of North America (known to him at Red Pheasant, Sask.) had a remarkable and possibly unique religion inasmuch as its rites were performed as a small group activity, dispensing with a formal priesthood, using an elixir, and achieving an experience shared by the whole congregation.* 'Brave New World Revisited': *not to be confused with the book so named; see letters* 784, 786. Twentieth Century: *an editor of the magazine had hoped that Huxley would write a special article on Magic, Mysticism and Psychotherapy.*

man who made a fortune in the most cynical way in the later days of the East India Company, who came to explore the island and stayed because he saw, in a kind of psychological conversion, that its people knew most of the answers. He stays, organizes a kind of East-West school of wisdom and is on hand, as an old man, when another Englishman comes ashore. His history is that of a youth brought up in an Evangelical household, breaking down into madness as a consequence, going to an asylum (I have been reading Zilboorg and other books to get the full flavour of the horror of Early Victorian madhouses), gets cured owing to the arrival at the asylum of a reasonable and human superintendent, like Dr Conolly, is sent on a voyage for his health and winds up on the island, where the older man takes him in hand, re-educates him to a sacramental view of sex and other natural functions, puts him through an initiation, with a local elixir playing an important part in the proceedings etc etc. When he finally returns to England, he is a really sane and fully developed human being—so much so that he very soon finds himself confined, once again, to an asylum by his undeveloped and deranged relatives. Meanwhile of course, the island gets overrun by one of the colonial powers, and all its wisdom is systematically stamped out—as was the case, on a lower level of achievement, when Britain ruined the traditional social order in Burma—largely by introducing, with the best possible intentions, a coherent system of law in place of the logically indefensible, but psychologically successful, no-system of local arbitration by headmen-wthout-authority. This framework should permit a full exposition of what ought to be, what could be perhaps, and what has been and what actually is. (The capitals are an error [of typewriting], not a literary device.) I have not yet started on the book, but keep the idea simmering on the mental hob, while I do other things. I hope to get down to serious work quite soon—which is why I really cannot undertake the article for the 20th Century. These things take me a long time, and I am already far behind-hand owing to my *Esquire* articles and these pieces for the *Sunday Times*. I'm sorry, but there it is.

When do you propose to be in New York? I shall be in the East in the second half of April and early May—lecturing first at Lexington, Kentucky, then at Washington and Baltimore, then in New York, where I should be from April 29th onwards. It would be wonderful if our trajectories could intersect. Please give my love to Jane.

Yours affectionately,
Aldous

P.S I like my architecture to be moderately socio-fugal—not as in most contemporary Californian houses—with no dining room separate from living room, the kitchen absolutely central, the WC and bedrooms hardly isolated. It was Le Corbusier, so far as I know, who started the current campaign against privacy.

740 *N. Kings Rd.,*
Los Angeles 46, Cal.
18 *March,* 1956

My dear Betty,

I have just finished my talk with Arthur Penn, and I think we have hit on some good ideas. He started out with the general idea that Katy's part must somehow be strengthened and that we should see more of the process by which John falls under her spell—and more of the resistance to falling built into him by his upbringing. The problem then arose—how should this be given concrete shape? After some futile pondering, I suddenly had what seems to me an excellent idea. Here it is.

In the present version old Rivers speaks about his mother's plans for his career—a professorship and a marriage to a lovely Lutheran girl. Well, my idea now is that John should arrive at the Maartenses already engaged to precisely this lovely Lutheran girl—a few years older than himself, the beauty of her soul making up for any lack of merely physical good looks (all this comes out under Katy's cross questioning in the first scene in which she and John talk about his background). This lovely Lutheran has been chosen, of course, by his mother, and John has got himself engaged out of filial duty rather than love. Katy tries, during the first act, to get him to admit the lovelessness of the engagement and to interest John in somebody more attractive. He resists—genuinely horrified by the idea that he should get out of this imposed marriage, trying to pretend to himself that it has not been imposed. Meanwhile he is falling in love with Katy, and the first act should end with some scene (which I can't yet quite see) in which he knows, with ecstasy and horror, that he *is* in love with her. But he feels that this is so wrong that he won't admit the truth to himself and forces himself to pretend that he really loves the L.L.G. (The L.L.G. writes to him regularly, and these bi-weekly letters are a standing joke in the Maartens family. To give the audience an impression of the L.L.G, John may read passages of the letters aloud to Katy. Maybe this is how the scene, in which he realizes that he is in love with Katy, begins.)

Act II begins with Katy's departure. At this stage in the game, Ruth is perhaps more jealous of the L.L.G. than of her mother? No, perhaps this is wrong—for I don't see at what point her eyes would be opened. But this is something to be considered. In any case the love scene at the end of Act II seems all the more reprehensible to John because he is still nominally engaged to the L.L.G. (An idea—does Ruth secretly read the letters sent to John by the L.L.G? Their singularly unpassionate tone reassures her in that quarter, and makes her look for her rival elsewhere, nearer home.)

I believe that this new device will add something interesting to John's character and permit him to display his puritanical side more effectively. It will also do a lot for Katy, giving her opportunities in the first act to express her life- and love-affirming attitude, which will contrast all the more strongly with the scene in the second act, where she is depleted and thinks only of death. The repercussions of all this on Ruth require to be worked out.

Will you please think about this new notion. If, as I think you will, you find it an improvement (Arthur was delighted with it), you might start a close examination of the script to see where the changes should be made and the new material introduced. The departure in the second act will provide Katy with more time on the stage, and so will the new material connected with the L.L.G. This extra time will be at the expense of Beulah, the old men and probably Ruth, all of whom can be profitably diminished, if we enlarge Katy.

Affectionately,
Aldous

742: TO MATTHEW AND ELLEN HUXLEY

Yuma, Arizona
19 March, 1956

Dearest Matthew and Ellen,

As you have probably read already in the papers—for the press was on hand within two minutes of our signing the licence—Laura Archera and I got married today, at Yuma in a naive hope of privacy that has turned into publicity all the same. You remember her, I am sure—a young woman who used to be a concert violinist, then turned movie cutter and worked for Pascal. I have come to be very much attached to her in recent months and since it seemed to be reciprocal, we decided to cross the Arizona border and call at the Drive-in Wedding Chapel (actual name). She is twenty years younger than I am, but doesn't seem to mind. Coccola was fond of her and we saw her a lot in Rome, that last summer abroad. I had a sense for a time that I was being unfaithful to that memory. But tenderness, I discover, is the best memorial to tenderness.

You will be seeing her in April, when we come East.

Ever your affectionate,
Aldous

743: TO ANITA LOOS

740 N. Kings Road,
Los Angeles 46, Calif.
25 March, 1956

Dearest Anita,

Thank you for your sweet message, which greeted us on our return from

742 *Huxley wrote several other letters on the same day—to Julian and Juliette Huxley, Rose Wessberg, Margaret Kiskadden, and Beth Wendel—announcing his marriage.*

the local Gretna Green—to which I had resorted in the naive hope of conducting my private affairs in privacy, but instead had the press swooping down like turkey buzzards within (literally) five minutes of signing the application for a licence. We wd have done better to have had a slap-up affair at St. Patrick's with Cardinal Spellman officiating and Clare Luce as bridesmaid.

You asked me most kindly when you were here if I wd like the loan of your apartment in April. Well, I wd very much if it is still available and it is convenient for you. Plans have been altered a little, as I want to be in New York for a few days before going to Lexington and Washington. The idea now is to fly to NY on the 10th or 11th, stay there (with absences of a night or two) till the 22nd and then return for a few more days on the 28th. Wd this be possible? If it is at all inconvenient, please say so. If it is OK, it will be a real delight to be in your spacious place instead of living cooped up in a hotel.

I think some day we shd write a farce called 'The Drive-in Wedding Chapel' (the actual title of the scene of our marriage), with Jimmy Durante starring as the Minister and various lesser lights driving up, and honking, for a quick nuptial. It wd be a rich subject. But tho' I deplore the circumstances, I don't regret the event. Laura is very much all right.

Best love from

Yours affectionately,
Aldous

744: TO DR HUMPHRY OSMOND

740 North Kings Road,
Los Angeles 46, Cal.
30 March, 1956

Dear Humphry,

Thank you for your letter, which I shall answer only briefly, since I look forward to talking to you at length in New York before very long. About a name for these drugs—what a problem! I have looked into Liddell and Scott and find that there is a verb phaneroein, 'to make visible or manifest', and an adjective phaneros, meaning 'manifest, open to sight, evident'. The word is used in botany—phanerogam as opposed to cryptogam. Psychodetic is something I don't quite get the hang of. Is it an analogue of geodetic, geodesy? If so, it would mean mind-dividing, as geodesy means

744 Osmond had mentioned psychedelics, as a new name for mind-changing drugs to replace the term psychotomimetics. Huxley apparently misread the word as 'psychodetics', hence his mystification. Osmond replied:

'To fathom Hell or soar angelic,
Just take a pinch of psychedelic

(Delos to manifest).' Huxley still did not get the spelling, which he made psychodelic.

earth-dividing, from gē and daiein. Could you call these drugs psychophans? or phaneropsychic drugs? Or what about phanerothymes? Thumos means soul, in its primary usage, and is the equivalent of Latin animus. The word is euphonious and easy to pronounce; besides it has relatives in the jargon of psychology—e.g. cyclothyme. On the whole I think this is better than psychophan or phaneropsychic.

I expect to be flying east on the tenth, or eleventh, and will let you know before then where we shall be staying—possibly not in a hotel at all, but in a borrowed apartment.

Yours,
Aldous

Phanerothyme—substantive. Phanerothymic—adjective.

To make this trivial world sublime,
Take half a gramme of phanerothyme.

745: TO JULIAN HUXLEY

740 *North Kings Road,*
Los Angeles 46, *Cal.*
23 *June,* 1956

Dearest J,

Thank you for your letter. I hope your wanderings and knockings upon doors are producing results and that somebody on the Foundations shows some sign of attacking the problem of human faculty and its development. I am enclosing the proofs (uncorrected, so that there are probably a number of printer's errors and omissions) of two essays, which will appear in book form this autumn, connected with this subject. I think you may find them interesting in the context of your project.

So far as I can foresee at present, we shall be here all through the summer —with perhaps a brief excursus in August towards the north, where I may be doing something for the Canadian TV. We shall be happy to see you both in September. Meanwhile I hope Woods Hole will prove to be simultaneously restful and stimulating.

We are expecting Francis from hour to hour; but, like God, he moves in a mysterious way. The last we heard of him was from Chicago, to the effect that he would probably be in Southern California about the twentieth. Since then, only silence. But no doubt he will suddenly manifest himself one fine morning.

I am enclosing, along with the proofs, the copy of a memorandum drawn up by my friend Dr William Kiskadden. Kiskadden has been twice in India and Indonesia within the last three years, and has returned with a very urgent feeling that something more should be done about the population problem than the writing of yet another report. He has established friendly contacts with The Indian Ministry of Health and with all the voluntary, non-governmental birth-control organizations in the country; at the same time he has made good contacts with various Foundations in the US and with capable film makers in Hollywood. This means that he could probably go ahead within a very short time making a few pilot films for exhibition, by mobile projectors carried in specially equipped vans, in Indian villages—the money for which would almost certainly be forthcoming when he has set up the necessary non-profit organization, in whose name the work would be done. I have agreed to have my name appear as one of the sponsoring committee, and Kiskadden has asked me to ask you if you would also give your name, so as to lend weight to the organization. There would be nothing to do, except to agree in principle that it would be a good thing to see if something could be done, by means of audio-visual propaganda, to further the efforts of voluntary and governmental organizations to reduce the Indian birth-rate. The experiment would start in one restricted area and, if it worked, would be expanded, with other languages dubbed into the films, to cover wider areas. I hope you will consent to give your sponsorship. Kiskadden is extremely *sérieux*, a great virtuoso surgeon, who has now, in his early sixties, turned to population control as the work of the rest of his life. He is a man of great determination and has very good contacts—which means that something concrete and practical will certainly get done.

Give my best love to Juliette.

Yours,
Aldous

746: TO MATTHEW HUXLEY

740 *North Kings Road,*
Los Angeles 46, Cal.
23 *June,* 1956

Dearest Matthew,

Yes, I think your scheme for re-organizing your insurance is excellent. I suppose you will need the policy, which I believe is in the safe deposit box at the bank, or at Dick's. I will go and have a look next week, get it out if it is there and send it you. I will continue paying for that part of the whole which corresponds to what I've been paying for to date.

I hope your house hunting is at last proving successful. We shall start moving in the course of the next few days. The house is in the Hollywood hills, above Beechwood Drive, has an incredible view and wild country all about it, with firebreaks to walk on and is within a hundred yards of the house of Laura's friend, Virginia Pfeiffer, where she has been living for the past few years and where there is a swimming pool, along with Virginia's two adopted children, to whom Laura is much attached. We shall keep this

---

746 *Dick: this was Dick Smith, proprietor of a filling station on Sunset Boulevard, who as a favour kept some of Huxley's valuables in his safe.*

house till autumn, so that it will be available for Rose and family during the summer and for Ellen and the children, if it seems too much of a tight fit at the other house.

I saw Harrison Brown the other evening at a cocktail party given by Bob Hutchins, who is leaving Pasadena for good and settling down in or near New York. He (Brown) asked after you and sent his love. He too had been much impressed by the Academy of Science report on the genetic effects of radiation. How wonderfully close modern history is coming to the phantasies of the *Arabian Nights* and *Grimm's Fairy Tales*—the stories of the fisherman who let the djinn out of the bottle and couldn't put it back, and the story of the couple who got the right to have three wishes answered and ended up with the wife losing her temper and wishing that the husband might have a sausage at the end of his nose. With the more philosophical variant on the three-wishes theme, W. W. Jacobs' 'The Monkey's Paw', where the old people wish for a hundred pounds and get it, thanks to the magic paw, as compensation for the death of their son. Atoms will give us all the power we want, but at the price of multiplying the number of monsters and, perhaps, bitching up the whole human species.

Love to you all.

Your affectionate,
Aldous

747: TO DR HUMPHRY OSMOND

740 *North Kings Road,*
Los Angeles 46, Cal.
29 *June,* 1956

Dear Humphry,

We missed you very much at our little conference, and on your side I think, if you had been there, you would have been greatly stimulated and interested by Puharich's report on the effects of the cages and of the release into their atmosphere of positively or negatively charged ions. If his work is confirmed, there will be from now on a method by which (so far only in sensitives) psi faculties can be turned on to their most improbable maximum by the simple pressing of a switch. Having established a standard electronic environment, Puharich is now going to try, systematically, the effect upon psi of various drugs, odours, sound stimuli and the like. It should be a most profitable exploration.

Al [Hubbard] too was in great form. His methods of exposition are a bit muddled; but I suppose he and his group have by now a mass of written material on their cases—material which will show how the other line of experimentation works. For obviously one must proceed on both lines—the pure-scientific, analytical line of Puharich, trying out factor after factor in a standardized environment, and the line of the naturalist, psychologist and therapist, who uses the drug for healing and enlightening, and in the process, if he is a good observer and clear thinker, discovers new facts about the psycho-physical organism.

Here, in Los Angeles, neither line of research is now being pursued. We have one or two doctors giving the stuff and compiling case histories of particular experiments, one or two working with neurotics or psychotics with the aid of the drug, and no analytical researchers. Moreover I hardly see the possibility of setting up such a group as Al now has in Vancouver —because we have no Al, nobody, that is to say, with the necessary business standing (the business man, by definition, can do nothing un-American), the necessary contacts with church and state, and the relationship with a sensitive area of science that permits him to command supplies of the drug. Again, neither Gerald nor I can claim to be a good experimental subject. For we don't have visions with the eyes closed, show no signs of psi and seem to be too much interested in the 'obscure knowledge' of Suchness to want to be bothered with anything else. So it looks as though the scientific work and the therapeutic work will have to be carried on elsewhere.

Now, as to times and seasons. When does it suit you to come to Vancouver during the month of August? I can conform my plans to yours. So please let me know which date suits you best, and I will aim for that. I don't exactly know what my role in this performance will be—presumably the more or less intelligent questioner, asking the expert what it is all about.

Affectionately,

Aldous

748: TO LAWRENCE C. POWELL

740 *North Kings Road,*
Los Angeles 46, Cal.
[*July*, 1956]

Dear Larry,

I would be most grateful if you could help me in a bookish matter. I am trying to get hold of two books by William Barnes, the 'Dorsetshire Poet', who, as well as being the author of charming verses, wrote two fantastic works to illustrate his theory that words of Latin or Greek origin were wicked and that everything in English could be expressed in words of Teutonic origin. (E.g. 'adjective' should be 'mark-word of suchness'; 'Omnibus' becomes 'folkwain'.) The books in question are *An Outline of English Speechcraft* (1878) and a treatise on Logic called *An Outline of English Rede-craft* (1879). The books are not in your library, nor in the Public Library, nor in the Huntington, nor (so Mackenzie of the Public Library tells me) in the catalogue of the Library of Congress. Do you have any way of finding out if they are in the 1[9]th century collections at Harvard or Yale? I would like very much to get hold of one or both of these books, as they would help me in a literary project which I have just begun.

Next time I am in the Library, I will look in at your office in the hope of finding you. Meanwhile this brings all my best wishes.

Yours,
Aldous H.

749: TO DR HUMPHRY OSMOND

3276 *Deronda Drive,*
Los Angeles 28, *Cal.*
17 *July,* 1956

Dear Humphry,

Above is our new address, to which we moved yesterday. It is a house high up in the Hollywood hills, and yet only five or six minutes from the thick of things—with virtually no smog and an incredible view over the city to the south and over completely savage hills in every other direction, hills which remind me a little of Greece by their barrenness, their steep-sided narrow valleys and the unsullied sky overhead. Moving has been a job, and it will be a while before things are in order. Meanwhile we are keeping on the other house for a month or two, so that Ellen and the children will have somewhere to live when they come out for a few weeks' stay—which they do tomorrow. Matthew, poor wretch, has to remain in New Haven, where his boss's unexpected retirement leaves him in charge of the office.

I had a wire yesterday from the Vancouver TV man asking if I could come on the 27th of this month, while you are staying with Al. But, alas, I can't; for I have commitments here during the last days of the month. Moreover, I was on the point of writing to him and you that I shall have to call the whole thing off. *Esquire* requires three long articles within a month —owing to editorial problems connected with deadlines for the Christmas number. And there is more to be done on the play, plus the book, which is falling behind hand and will require undistracted attention as soon as I can get down to it. All of which adds up to only one thing—that I simply cannot get away, not merely this month, but next and for some time thereafter. Moreover, the more I think about the project—I really hadn't given it any thought at all when I light-heartedly said yes to Kelly's invitation—the less I like it. I have no idea what we are supposed to say, or how it should be said, or by what miracle we can improvise a half-hour scenario for a movie, as well as perform in the same, within three days. The same problem has come up recently in relation to CBS, which asked me to participate in a series of

---

748 *Literary project: the novel* Island *in its early stages. Huxley intended to portray a character who shared Barnes's obsession. This part of the manuscript was eliminated before the novel was published, but extracts from it or from a later adaptation of it may be read in Laura Huxley's* This Timeless Moment.

749 *TV man: Ronald Kelly, who had written to Huxley about making a television film with Osmond.*

half hour shows where we would talk about anything. But when one came to look into the problem of constructing a scenario for even the most spontaneous chat, it became clear that each programme would require days of preliminary work, plus a full day of rehearsal and performance. And when it's done, the thing may be entirely unsatisfactory and there is no chance, because of the expense, of revising or re-doing. And, to add injury to artistic insult, one gets a great deal of most unwelcome publicity, with people stopping one in the street, to say how much they liked, or disliked, what you said. This unwelcome publicity would be particularly annoying after a TV show on mescalin. Even if I had boundless leisure, I would be inclined, on second and maturer thought, to give up the project. Mescalin, it seems to me, and the odder aspects of mind are matters to be written about for a small public, not discussed on TV in the presence of a vast audience of baptists, methodists and nothing-but-men plus an immense lunatic fringe, eager to tell you about *my* revelation and to get hold of the dope on its own account. One gets plenty of lunatic fringe even after the publication of a two and a half dollar book; after a gratuitous broadcast, it would be overwhelming.

Meanwhile I'm sorry indeed that I shall miss you. I hope our trajectories may intersect at some later date, either here or in the East. My love to Jane.

Yours affectionately
Aldous

750: TO VICTORIA OCAMPO

3276 Deronda Drive,
Los Angeles 28, Cal.
19 July, 1956

Dear Victoria,

Your letter gave me real pleasure. I don't know if you received a letter of mine—sent I forget in which month of this year (for one loses count of dates). Probably you didn't. But I had some indirect news through the Stravinskys and knew that you were as well as could be expected, malgré tout. I too am well. Last March I married a young Italian woman, in her early forties, whom Maria and I had known, here and in Italy, for the last ten years. As a young girl, she was a musical prodigy on the violin, gave concerts, studied *avec rage*—then gave the whole thing up, feeling that the career of a virtuoso was too life-devouring. Her principal interest now is psychology and its applications. She gets on very well with my friends, and they with her. I am very sure that you will like her. The terrible sadness of Maria's last months and the sense of amputation which followed her death have retreated, and my memories of her are now happy, grateful and tender memories. And that she survives and develops, I feel sure. I myself am very opaque to these influences; but several persons who are not opaque have volunteered to me, on the basis of what they felt were contacts with Maria, that she has achieved an extraordinary degree of liberation—that she gives an overwhelming impression of youthfulness and happiness.

I am glad you liked my little book [*Heaven and Hell*]. How strange that we should all carry about with us this enormous universe of vision and that which lies beyond vision, and yet be mainly unconscious of the fact! How can we learn to pass at will from one world of consciousness to the others? Mescalin and lysergic acid will open the door; but one doesn't like to depend exclusively on these chemicals, even though they seem to be more or less completely harmless. I have taken mescalin about six times now and have been taken beyond the realm of vision to the realm of what the mystics call 'obscure knowledge'—insight into the nature of things accompanied by the realization that, in spite of pain and tragedy, the universe is all right, in other words that God is Love. The words are embarrassingly silly and, on the level of average consciousness, untrue. But when we are on the higher level, they are seen to stand for the primordial Fact, of which the consciousness is now a part. The supreme art of life would be the art of passing at will from obscure knowledge to conceptualized, utilitarian knowledge, from the aesthetic to the mystical; and all the time to be able, in the words of the Zen master, to grasp the non-particular that exists in particulars, to be aware of the not-thought which lies in thought—the absolute in relationships, the infinite in finite things, the eternal in time. The problem is how to learn that supreme art of life?

We have moved to a new house, high up in the hills and all is still confusion. Keep well, dear Victoria.

Ever yours affectionately,
Aldous

751: TO DR HUMPHRY OSMOND

3276 *Deronda Drive,*
Los Angeles 28, *Cal.*
22 *July,* 1965

Dear Humphry,

Our letters crossed, yours being delayed at this end by the fact that we were between two houses, living in one and getting mail at the other. I wish that our leisures might have coincided. I have none at the moment, and along with no leisure a very bad feeling about TV, particularly in relation to this field. My lunatic-fringe mail is already much more copious than I like—I had a letter a few days ago from Mauritius, from a gentleman who went out there twenty years ago to achieve enlightenment and, according to himself, has now written the most extraordinary book in the world's history, and will I please write an introduction and secure him a fellowship at the Ford Foundation's Institute for Advanced Studies in the Social Sciences, or failing that a job on an American newspaper! And I say nothing of the gentleman in Chicago who has discovered the Absolute Truth and sends letters and telegrams about it to President Eisenhower and Bertrand Russell; nor the Mexican dermatologist who thinks that mescalin may be good for eczema, and will I tell him where he can procure the drug, nor the young man from Yorkshire who ate a peyote button supplied by a cactus-growing friend and for three days heard all music one tone higher than it should have been (quite an interesting phenomenon, incidentally, and one which might be worth testing with musical subjects. Laura thinks that it doesn't actually raise the pitch so far as she is concerned; merely makes it sound like music played with more than ordinary verve and perfection and energy—something which tends to make one think that the piece is being played a little sharp).

As you say in your letter, we still know very little about the psychodelics, and, until we know a good deal more, I think the matter should be discussed, and the investigations described, in the relative privacy of learned journals, the decent obscurity of moderately high-brow books and articles. Whatever one says on the air is bound to be misunderstood; for people take from the heard or printed discourse that which they are predisposed to hear or read, not what is there. All that TV can do is to increase the number of misunderstanders by many thousandfold—and at the same time to increase the range of misunderstanding by providing no objective text to which the voluntarily ignorant can be made to refer. Littera scripta manet, volat irrevocabile verbum.

In the intervals of writing articles for *Esquire* and making corrections in the play, I am doing a little work on my phantasy—writing the first chapters of the hero's childhood in an earliest Victorian setting, and ruminating the problems that will arise when he gets out to the hypothetical island in the Indian ocean, where his uncle has gone as surgeon to the local rajah (I shall make him emulate Dr [James] Esdaile and cut off elephantiasis tumours in the mesmeric trance) and has taken to a kind of tantric philosophy and praxis, aimed at helping people to realize their potential capacities and at giving them a certain control of their destiny, primarily through control of the autonomic nervous system and the vegetative soul, plus access to the Atman-Brahman. I do hope I can bring this off with some measure of success.

Give my love to Jane and the Hubbards.

Ever yours affectionately,
Aldous

752: TO HENRY MILLER

3276 *Deronda Drive,*
L.A. 28, Cal.
12 *August,* 1956

Dear Henry Miller,

Thank you for your most friendly letter. I am very glad you liked 'Knowledge and Understanding'. It seems to me to raise at least (tho' of course it doesn't profess to solve except abstractly and by suggestion) the most important of all personal problems: How to make the best of both worlds—of all the both worlds in which we have to live. At present most people seem content to make the worst of one—the verbal-analytical with its practical corollaries in organization and technology.

I have just read a book which I think you will find very interesting— *The Greeks and the Irrational* by E. R. Dodds (who succeeded Gilbert Murray in the chair of Greek at Oxford). It is published by Cal. University Press and, despite i[t]s massive learning, is lively and well-written. And full of instruction and enlightenment and food for disquieting as well as cheering thought.

I hope you will let me know when you are next in these parts. I wd like very much to see you again.

Sincerely
Aldous Huxley

753: TO DR HUMPHRY OSMOND

3276 *Deronda Drive,*
Los Angeles 28, *Cal.*
13 *August,* 1956

Dear Humphry,

I presume you are back now in the prairies and hard at work. Here too hard work is the order of the day. I have finished my three articles for *Esquire*—including one which I think will interest you, on the history of hypnotism; an article based on two texts, one a paper by a local anesth[es]iologist, Dr [M. J.] Marmer, who says that every anesthetist should be a hypnotist; the other, Esdaile's *Mesmerism in India* (1846), with reference to Neilson's *Mesmerism in relation to medical practice* (1855). How odd that it should have taken one hundred and ten years for the medical profession (or at least one small segment of it) to reach the position occupied by Esdaile in 'forty-six and by Dr Elliotson ten or fifteen years earlier! Incidentally, Neilson's book contains some exceedingly significant statistics. Did you know that, before the introduction of chloroform, the average mortality after surgery was twenty-nine per cent, with peaks, during epidemics of streps and staphs, of over fifty per cent? That between chloroform in 1847 and Lister in the sixties, the mortality was still twenty-three per cent? And that Esdaile's mortality, under even more septic conditions in India, but with the 'magnetic sleep' for anaesthetic, was five per cent? Which shows what can be done by psychological means to minimize shock and increase resistance to infection. These facts have been known for more than a century. But nobody seems to have drawn the obvious conclusions or done anything about them either in the field of prevention or in that of cure. And all because 'scientific' people find it so hard to believe in the reality of the mind, or to regard belief in the mind as anything more than a low piece of superstition.

I am now starting work on the play revisions as well as on my phantasy, which begins, as I make notes, to take the rudiments of shape. I can't decide whether to go on with it, full blast, or to go back to a problem, thrown into my lap by the man who made a dramatic version of *Brave New World* many years ago, and who still (thanks to the [. . .] of my then agent) still [*sic*] controls the dramatic rights—the problem of doing something for the stage with *BNW*. It might be very profitable. Or it might not. It might be done quickly, or it might take a long time. Maybe I had better make the plunge and see how the thing works out. But then I shall probably be sorry I didn't get on with the phantasy!

Gerald has been away, lecturing to seminars, and I have spoken to him only on the phone, between two absences. He told me that he thought I had been wise to think twice about talking on TV about mescalin. His own experience, as a lecturer, of the almost infinite capacity of audiences to mis-understand what is said, especially if what is said is novel or outside the customary pale, makes him very chary of using one of the mass media for the exposition of unfamiliar ideas or the tentative discussion of odd, anomalous phenomena.

Ellen and the children have been here for a month, but return to NH the day after tomorrow. Which is sad. But she has to move house before the beginning of September, and Matthew is impatient to see his family again.

Love to you all.

Aldous

754: TO JULIAN HUXLEY

3276 *Deronda Drive,*
Los Angeles 28, Cal.
30 *August,* 1956

Dearest J,

Thank you for your letter. We will expect you, then, on the ninth. The airport is immensely far off, and it is actually quicker for you to take the regular limousine, or bus, to the Hollywood Roosevelt Hotel, where we will pick you up. Let us know the airline and number of the flight. In case of any hitch, our number is Hollywood 7 0152. But I see no reason why there should be a hitch.

About La Jolla—I think the best would be for us to drive down there on the afternoon of the tenth, stay the night and return the following day. You can practise with the car en route. Tentatively I am making an appointment for lunch on Saturday the fifteenth, to meet Harrison Brown of Caltech (the man who wrote *The Challenge of Man's Future*), my friend Dr Kiskadden (whose interest in Indian population I wrote you about) and Fred Zinnerman [Zinnemann], the movie director. There seems to be a good chance of getting a big film on population done by the Ford people on their 'Omnibus' TV Programme. Zinnermann would do the directing, the necessary research into documentaries would be carried out probably by students in the Motion Picture school at the University of California; meanwhile I have written a very brief synopsis, suggesting ways in which the thing might be handled photographically. (This would be a general world population film, not a film for India alone; that will, I hope, come later. But meanwhile, if we can get Ford to do this, it will be a fine thing.) The luncheon would be for the purpose of discussing the project from its various angles—biological and sociological on the part of Brown and yourself, and literary and cinematographical on the part of the rest of us.

Much love to you both. *A bientôt.*

Yours most affectionately,
Aldous

755: TO HEINZ KUSEL

3276 *Deronda Drive,*
Los Angeles 28, Cal.
23 *September,* 1956

Dear Mr Kusel,

Thank you for your letter and most interesting article, which I return herewith. May I suggest that you send a copy of it to my friend Dr Humphry Osmond, Box 1056, Weyburn, Saskatchewan, Canada. Dr Osmond and his co-workers are doing research primarily directed towards uncovering the chemical factor in schizophrenia, and more generally concerning itself with the human mind at large. If you can furnish him with any botanical details regarding Ayahuasca, I know that he will be grateful.

The chances are, of course, that ayahuasca is quite different, chemically speaking, from peyote or the many other natural drugs used by primitive people. The interesting fact is that it too is effective in opening the door which gives access to the Other World of the mind—and to a region of that Other World which seems to be, from your description, very like that to which we are introduced by peyote, mescalin and lysergic acid, not to mention the fungi used in Mexico to induce visions and the numerous beans, seeds, leaves and roots employed for the same purpose elsewhere. If you still have contacts with people in the jungle area where you once lived, it would be very interesting to have them send samples of the vines from which ayahuasca is extracted to some good bio-chemist or pharmacologist for analysis. But I suppose the curanderos are not too anxious to reveal their professional secrets.

Sincerely,
Aldous Huxley

755 *Article:* '*Ayahuasca Drinkers among the Chama Indians of Northeast Peru*', *published in* The Psychedelic Review, *No.* 6 (1965), *pp.* 58-66.

3276 *Deronda Drive,*
Los Angeles 28, *Cal.*
23 *September,* 1956

My dear Humphry,

Your good letter of two days ago heaped coals of fire on my head; for I have been gravely neglectful in the matter of writing. My brother has just left, after having been here, with his wife, for a fortnight; and doing things with him, along with a mass of work, kept me exceedingly busy, so that correspondence has banked up to an alarming height and threatens to engulf me completely.

While Julian was here we went to see, at UCLA, the rats and cats and monkeys with electrodes stuck into various areas of their brains. They press a little lever which gives them a short, mild electric shock—and the experience, in certain positions of the electrode, is evidently so ecstatically wonderful, that they will go on at the rate of eight thousand self-stimuli per hour until they collapse from exhaustion, lack of food and sleep. We are obviously getting very close to reproducing the Moslem paradise, where every orgasm lasts six hundred years.

Our last experiment with LSD in conjunction with hypnosis—the idea being to hypnotize the participants and give them post-hypnotic suggestions to the effect that they wd be able to reproduce the LSD experience at a given word of command—was not very successful, so far as the hypnotic procedure was concerned. It may be that the suggestions, in order to be successful, have to be repeated on several occasions. Or it may be, of course, that the effects of the chemical are not reproducible by psychological means, at any rate in the majority of cases. What was interesting to me in the experiment was the fact that fifty gamma of LSD were sufficient to produce in me virtually the full effect of the standard dose, while with Laura twenty-five gamma proved to be very efficacious. It may be that preliminary hypnotism was a help in maximizing the effect of the chemical.

I had an interesting communication a few days ago from a man who used to be a trader in the jungles of the upper Amazon, at the foot of the Andes, and is now teaching art in a Californian high school. He gave a full account of a drug which the Indians call Ayahuasca, derived from a mixture of local plants and effective only in large doses—you have to swallow a quart of an ill-tasting liquid. The result is something quite close to the peyote experience, with the visions taking predominantly vegetable, or vegetable-like forms, so that the natives use it in a kind of nature worship, combined with paranormal diagnosis and insight into curative simples. The man has asked for his paper to be returned; but I have asked him to send a copy to you, along with any botanical information he may have.

It is good news that you may be coming to California later this autumn. Laura and I will be in New York from about October 16th to November 1st (with possible absences for two or three days). I have to give a talk at the banquet of the NY Academy of Sciences, who are having a meeting about tranquillizers. I shall chat about the history of tension and the methods of release devised by different cultures in the past. Is there any chance that you may be in NY at that time?

The play situation is still in statu quo—de Liagre, the producer, waiting to hear from Deborah Kerr. [. . . .] Meanwhile I have postponed work on my phantasy to embark upon an adaptation for musical comedy of *Brave New World*. The first act is finished and seems to be very lively. After I have finished with my NY Academy of Science thing, I will move on to the Savage Reservation. If all goes well and I can get somebody good to do the music—such as Leonard Bernstein—the results might be remarkable.

Love to you both.

Affectionately,
Aldous

757: TO MATTHEW AND ELLEN HUXLEY

3276 *Deronda Drive,*
Los Angeles 28, *Cal.*
30 *September,* 1956

Dearest Matthew and Ellen,

Life seems to become busier and busier, and correspondence more and more hopelessly in arrears. First of all, let me thank you for the paper on Japanese abortions (of which I had heard a good deal from Harrison Brown). There is some hope that 'Omnibus' may do a TV film on the population problem. I have written a brief outline, Julian and Harrison Brown have made corrective comments, Fred Zinnermann has agreed to direct it, if it should be made. Let us hope that Ford will put up the cash to get the thing done.

Julian and Juliette were here for two weeks and we saw the scientific sights, here, at Caltech, at La Jolla and the San Diego Zoo. In the intervals I have been working on three projects—my usual article for *Esquire*, my speech on the History of Tension for the NY Academy of Sciences, and a musical comedy version of *Brave New World*—for everyone tells me that science fiction can never succeed on the stage as a straight play, but that it will be accepted when the medium ceases to be realistic and makes use of music and lyrics. I have finished the first act—completely re-writing the material produced by Mr [———], the original adapter and still half-owner of the rights. But better half a loaf than no bread, and I hope that, if the other acts work out as satisfactorily as the first, I may have something that will get put on. I am having to depart from the book, since the story must be put over in such an abbreviated form—sixty pages of script as opposed to the standard hundred and twenty for a straight play. But the streamlining will be a dramatic improvement.

We expect to fly to New York on October fifteenth or sixteenth and to stay at the Buckingham. I am asking the Academy to send you an invitation to the banquet on the eighteenth.

I hope all goes well with the children. Here we have been suffering from an intense heat wave and smog wave. Most unpleasant. Love from us both.

Ever your affectionate,

Aldous

Here it is!

Epsilons (singing)

No more Mammy, no more Pappy:
Ain't we lucky, ain't we happy?
Everybody's oh so happy,
Everybody's happy now!

Sex galore, but no more marriages;
No more pushing baby carriages;
No one has to change a nappy—
Ain't we lucky, ain't we happy:
Everybody's happy now.

Dope for tea and dope for dinner,
Fun all night, and love and laughter;
No remorse, no morning after.
Where's the sin, and who's the sinner?
Everybody's happy now.

Girls pneumatic, girls exotic,
Girls ecstatic, girls erotic—
Hug me, Baby; make it snappy.
Everybody's oh so happy,
Everybody's happy now.

Lots to eat and hours for drinking
Soma cocktails—no more thinking.
NO MORE THINKING, NO MORE THINKING!
Everybody's happy now.

758: TO DR HUMPHRY OSMOND

3276 *Deronda Drive,*
Los Angeles 28, *Cal.*
20 *October,* 1956

Dear Humphry,

Thank you for your most interesting letter about the Native American churchmen. I hope the poor devils will be left in peace to worship God in their own, unusually sensible way. But I suppose a combination of Protestan puritanism, hatred of pleasure, dread of ecstasy, and of Catholic disapproval of direct communication with the Transcendent, unmediated by priests,

809

will be too much for them. Why do people have to be so damned stupid and so diabolically bossy and interfering? And (this is a more searching question) could societies retain their stability without a lot of prejudice and stupidity, or their energy without a lot of bumptiousness and bullying? Can we, in a word, make the best of both worlds—of all the worlds?

Our time in New York was a bit strenuous. The NY Academy, for which I was talking, have a publicity man so marvellously active that, on my arrival, I found no less than seven radio and TV appearances lined up for me, at hours ranging from six thirty in the morning to eleven fifteen at night. The conference on meprobamate was quite interesting and I made some pleasant acquaintances—Dr [F. M.] Berger, the inventor of Miltown, and Dr James Miller, who heads an inter-disciplinary group at Ann Arbor, investigating human behaviour and trying to establish some sort of common language among psychologists, chemists, economists, sociologists and ministers. A commendable project. And the man (do you know him?) is obviously very intelligent. [. . . .]

We saw Eileen several times. Lazarus-like, she has popped up from the grave and seems to be more alive, if possible, than ever. I had hoped to see Puharich [. . . .] The whole situation there seems, since Alice Bouverie's death (and before it), both sad and bad—with the Round Table Foundation padlocked by the Treasury Department for back taxes, a first-rate internecine quarrel going on [. . .], fantastic tales [. . . .] In a word, we are such stuff as messes are made on—and in the biggest way.

I leave for St Louis on Wednesday, to attend a kind of seminar on human potentialities. Back here on Saturday, to do a TV show with Gerald on Sunday. In the intervals I am working on the script for my musical version of *Brave New World*. So far, so good. But the most difficult part, I fear, is yet to come.

This house is still in the making, and I think it would be best if you were to go, this time, to Margaret Gage's. But we will have plenty of opportunity, I hope, for talking and planning.

My love to Jane.

Ever yours,
Aldous

759: TO JOHN YALE

3276 *Deronda Drive,*
Los Angeles 28, Cal.
20 *October,* 1956

Dear John,

Your letter finds me on the eve of departure for St Louis, and I must answer briefly and in haste. I would like to do something to help the Swami;

759 *Acknowledgment of an invitation from the Vedanta Society.*

but the trouble is, first, that I am not a religious person—in the sense that I am not a believer in metaphysical propositions, not a worshipper or per-former of rituals, and not a joiner of churches—and therefore I don't feel qualified or inclined to tell people in general what to think or do. The only general advice I can give (apart from exploring individual cases on an ad hoc basis) is that people should use their common sense, act with common decency, cultivate love and extend and intensify their awareness—then ask themselves if they know a little more than they did about the Unknown God. There are, of course, other kinds of discourse—non-homiletic talks about matters of general interest. But the trouble in this case is that the preparations for making such talks cost me a great deal of time, and time is something of which I seem to have less and less, while deadlines tend to grow more and more numerous and more and more urgent. I don't like to say no; but, alas, I simply don't see how I can say anything else.

Sincerely,
Aldous H.

760: TO EDITH A. STANDEN

3276 Deronda Drive,
L.A. 28, Cal.
17 November, 1956

Dear Miss Standen,

Thank you for your reference to the *Ciba Review*. I understand that the *Unesco Courier* has recently returned to the subject. Apparently silk coats etc in the 18th cent were made of small pieces, which cd be unsewn, washed and resewn—a procedure possible only when labour was virtually costless. And imagine the ruffs in Dutch portraits being worn today with household help at $1.00 per hour. But it is interesting to find ruffles coming back—in orlon and nylon, no ironing, no starch.

All the literary evidence points to the dirtiness of the clothes of the poor. They had so few possessions and cd not afford any changes of clothes. And then in winter everybody was so cold and therefore so reluctant to quit any garment. We hear of the vermin which abandoned the corpse of Thomas à Becket when it began to grow cold. And even as late as Pepys, wigs were apt to be full of lice. And one of the old women condemned by Sir Matthew Hales in the 1660's as a witch was accused, among other things, of having implanted lice of supernatural size and strength in her neighbour's best Sunday suit—which had to be burned, since no cleansing agent then known cd get rid of them.

A complicating factor was the dread of public bathing establishments after the introduction of syphilis—a period which also coincided with the

760 *Reference to the* Ciba Review: *No. 56 (April, 1947), 'Soap'. Miss Standen: of the Metropolitan Museum of Art, New York.*

growing disreputableness of such institutions. (Bagnio = brothel.) The fear
was rationalized in medical theory, which regarded baths as dangerous
unless used under medical supervision. Traces of this attitude can be seen
in Father Kneipp's book, *My Water Cure*, published in the 1870's.

Sincerely
Aldous Huxley

761: TO MRS ELLEN HUXLEY

3276 Deronda Drive,
Los Angeles 28, Cal.
20 November, 1956

Dearest Ellen,

Thank you for your fascinating account of the mescalin experience.
Humphry was here and talked a little about the event—but, I felt, with a
certain reticence, as though something had happened, so far as he was
concerned, which he didn't want to discuss too freely. Did you get what I
have got so strongly on the recent occasions when I have taken the stuff—
an overpowering sense of gratitude, a desire to give thanks to the Order of
Things for the privilege of this particular experience, and also for the privilege—for that one feels it to be, in spite of everything—of living in a human
body on this particular planet? And then there is the intense feeling of compassion for those who, for whatever reason, make it impossible for themselves
to get anywhere near the reality revealed by the drug—the reality which is
always there for those who are in the right state of mind to perceive it. Compassion for the people who are too rigidly good or too rigidly intellectual,
who live in the home-made world of their own ethical and social system,
their own favourite notions of what's what; and compassion at the other
end of the scale for those who blind themselves by excessive egotism, by
alcohol and parties and TV. Some of the compassion and some of the
gratitude remain, even after the experience is over. One can never be quite
the same again.

All goes well here. I am sorry I was such a skeleton at the feast, when I
came down that Sunday to Woodbridge. Two successive meals of the
[——] had left me perfectly miserable, and I didn't really recover till we
were on the plane, the following Tuesday.

My brief excursion to St Louis was interesting. Good discussions and
good TV interviews about 'The Actualization of Human Potentialities'.
Then back here for another TV appearance, this time with Gerald, when we
ad libbed for half an hour and had a lot of fun. Since then I have been very
busy—working on the musical *Brave New World*, on an article for *Esquire*
and, for the last two days, on arrears of correspondence. I wrote over forty
letters during the weekend.

Love to you all.

Your affectionate
Aldous

762: TO VICTOR F. WHITE

3276 Deronda Drive,
Los Angeles 28, Calif.
20 November, 1956

Dear Mr. White,

Thank you for your letter and the article on Frieda's funeral. How strange their careers were! The coalminer's son escaping, via Frieda, into the larger world, beyond his social conditioning. And the Richthofen, who had somehow blundered into marriage with possibly the dullest Professor in the Western hemisphere, escaping, via Lawrence into that same world and into an old age in that New Mexico desert which was, in some sort, a projection of her own deep nature. How improbable! But that is the charm and the horror of human history: the impossible actually happens—all in time.

Sincerely,
Aldous Huxley

763: TO MRS ELLEN HUXLEY

3276 Deronda Drive,
Hollywood 28, California
6 December, 1956

Dearest Ellen,

Thank you for your letter. Yes, how strange too is that sense of the unimportance of death, combined with the sense of the supreme importance of life. The only people who *don't* get anything from LSD or mescalin are psycho-analysts. There are 2 experimenters here who have given it to several Freudians. None of them got anything positive—except for one, who said that, when he went to the bathroom, he noticed that 'his excreta smelled stronger and sweeter'. Sig Freud's body lies a-mouldering in the grave, but his soul, or his anus, goes marching along.

I am enclosing a cheque for you to get Xmas presents for all and sundry according to taste. It is much easier than sending parcels and, I hope, will work out more to everyone's satisfaction.

Much love to you all.

Your affectionate
Aldous

764: TO DR HUMPHRY OSMOND

3276 Deronda Drive,
Los Angeles 28, Cal.
Christmas Day [1956]

My dear Humphry,

Thank you for your letter and good wishes, which we return to all of you. May 1957 be as happy as the lunatics in the world's chanceries will

762 *Frieda Lawrence Ravagli had died on* 11 *August.*

permit, and as fruitful as the fund-giving idiots in the Foundations will allow. What a shame that Ford should have dumped all that dough into [——]'s lap! Julian saw him when he was here this summer and came back from the interview appalled by the woolliness of the great man's biological thinking. And talking of woolly thinking—have you read this book by Dr [Ira] Progoff, called *The Death and Rebirth of Psychology*? It is actually a history of the ideas of Freud, Adler, Jung and Otto Rank. And, heavens, how odd these ideas look, when set forth clearly! I was so exasperated by the solemn nonsense that I used the book as a peg to hang one of my *Esquire* articles on. I enclose a copy of it, in the hope that it may amuse you. I look forward to the time when you and Hoffer and the rest can implement the criticism of the current nonsense by means of a brand new psycho-pharmaco-spiritual approach to the problem of man's activities, in health and in sickness. The transcendental operationally verified and pragmatically confirmed, because it works in the field of therapy, as in the field of normal behaviour.

Are there any published papers on the use of niacin in the treatment of high cholesterol conditions? If so, I would be grateful if you would give me the references. I know a number of people, lay and medical, who would be interested to read about the matter in detail. Also, did you try LSD through the lungs? And, if so, what happened?

Not much news here. I stupidly went and got a virus two weeks ago, was in bed for four or five days with a temperature. (I made an interesting observation on mental imagery. Some kind of vague imagery starts, with me, at about a hundred and two. This was as high as I went on this occasion; but I remember from past experiences that the images become progressively more vivid as the fever mounts above that point. I was put on to acromycin, after terramycin had failed to do much good, and the fever dropped rapidly from 102 to 101 within an hour. My first intimation that it was going down came from the almost abrupt passage from mental imagery to my normal state of no mental imagery.)

One feels a bit low and mouldy after these bouts of flu, and I am only just beginning to re-emerge. Meanwhile I have finished *Brave New World* and am awaiting advice from expert friends in New York on what step to take next. People who have read the script all seem to find it amusing, and I hope that, sooner or later, it may find its way on to the stage.

I have just heard from Matthew that he has a new job, to start some time this spring, with the Millbank Foundation [Milbank Memorial Fund] mainly, I gather, in the field of mental health studies. He is pleased about this —though sorry to have to move away from the house at Woodbridge, the job being in New York.

My love to Jane and the poetess.

Yours affectionately,
Aldous

764 *Huxley's article, "The Oddest Science", appeared in March, 1957.*

3276 *Deronda Drive*,
Los Angeles 28, *Cal.*
12 *January*, 1957

Dear Ian,

Thank you for your letters. I saw the Golden Cockerel announcement of the *Après Midi*, which contained a specimen illustration of the most deplorable nature. What a pity!

As for the article in the *People*—I think it is best to do nothing about it. This man [Philip] Pollack has been writing articles in various newspapers here, and there have been counter-articles by people who have benefited by functional training in seeing. What is happening in the US is that optometrists —a breed superior to opticians, inasmuch as they get a long training, but not fool [*sic*] blown oculists (they may prescribe glasses, but not medication for eyes and may not perform surgery)—are steadily adopting more and more the Batesian procedures into their system of 'orthoptics' (eye exercises with various optical machines, mostly rather harmful). A group of these optometrists even publishes a journal of *Psychological Optics*, in which the mental side of seeing is stressed. Pollack obviously belongs to the old school of Helmholtzian oculists, who regard the eye as an optical instrument and take no account of the mind-body with which it is associated. *The Art of Seeing* is about the mental side of seeing and the improvement of function—not by 'exercises', as Pollack likes to call them, but by training in relaxed activity. Even if there are no physical changes in the eye, seeing can be improved by proper function. This is something which someone who has never thought in terms of psycho–somatic medicine cannot understand.

As for the magnifying glasses—I often do use magnifying glasses where conditions of light are bad, and have never claimed to be able to read except under very good conditions.

Incidentally, it looks as though the Bates system were doomed in this country. The medical and optometrical lobby has gone to work in the various state legislatures and laws are being passed in state after state, making it illegal for anyone without a medical or an optometrical degree to tell anyone else how to see better. It is even illegal to teach anyone to relax his eyes! These laws are probably unconstitutional; but it would take a vast amount of money to take a case to the Supreme Court, and the money is not available.

I have just embarked on a new treatment aimed at getting rid of some of the scar tissue on my corneas. It is a combination of diet, of administration,

765 L'Après-midi d'un Faune, *in Huxley's translation, had been reprinted as a limited edition by the Golden Cockerel Press, London*, 1956.

externally and internally, of a sulphur compound (eyes with cataract and, in general, most sick and ageing eyes, have been shown to be short of sulphur, which is normally in rather high concentration in the eye tissues) and of physio-therapy aimed at increasing circulation. The man who has developed this treatment is a very experienced old ophthalmologist, who has had many successes, both with cataracts and corneal opacities. It would be wonderful if the treatment had even a very small effect. However, it will take several months before anything appreciable can be expected.

Yours,
Aldous

766: TO ANITA LOOS

3276 *Deronda Drive,*
Los Angeles 28, *Cal.*
18 *January,* 1957

Dearest Anita,

Your letter arrived at cock crow this morning. Thank you very much for sending the script to [D. R.] Levine. I shall be most interested to hear what his reactions to it will be. Meanwhile, at this end, the play is being read by David Selznick and by Charlie Lederer. Selznick is up to his neck in his forthcoming *Farewell to Arms* film and probably won't be able to read the piece for some days. Charlie has only just received his copy. So I am still in the dark regarding their views. I expect to be seeing S. J. Perelman early next week, who promises to give me advice as to the pitfalls of musical comedy—advice which, I am sure, is very necessary!

Not much news about the *Genius and the Goddess*, except that Binkie [Hugh] Beaumont wants to do the play in London—but also wants the thing modified in such a way that a single actor can play the young and the old Rivers. This, of course, is what all the actors and theatre people who have read the play desire—for it is a good theatrical stunt. Betty and I have resisted hitherto, on the grounds that, though a good stunt, the change would be artistically for the worse. However, if this is the condition of getting a production, I am now resigned to making the necessary changes, in spite of the damage they will inflict, some damage, especially in the second act.

You will probably be seeing Betty very soon, as she plans to go shortly to New York on Sandy's annual business trip.

What news of your projects? I hope some at least are maturing. This theatrical world is dreadfully exasperating; and if I didn't have other things to do, I should find my present, small involvement in it very nerve-racking. To write a play is certainly to ask for trouble.

Laura sends her love, as do I.

Ever yours affectionately,
Aldous

3276 *Deronda Drive,*
Los Angeles 28, *Cal.*
27 *January,* 1957

Dearest Juliette and Julian,

Thank you for your letter, with the news about the Godels—bad as regards the past, but good to the extent that they are now out of the inferno. I wonder what they will do now? I imagine their one-time scheme of retiring to Lebanon—where they have a huge and very beautiful house, completely furnished and super-American in comfort—will not be carried out; for even Lebanon must now be pretty uncomfortable for the French, or indeed for any representative of the Western race. What we are paying for four hundred years of white imperialism—and how long, to all appearances, we shall go on paying! Asians and Africans do not forget and are so far from forgiving that, if they can thereby do some harm to the ex-imperialists, they will blithely damage themselves, even commit suicide. If I can spite *your* face, I will cut off *my* nose. There is no appeal from these passions even to self-interest. Indeed, if people would only act according to their self–interest, this world would be almost a paradise. And the trouble is that these deeprooted passions can now be implemented in violent practice. The great truth enunciated by Hilaire Belloc in *The Modern Traveller*—

Whatever happens, we have got
The Maxim gun, and they have not—

has unhappily ceased to be true. *They* now have the Maxim gun—and unless the West is prepared to out-trump the gun with atomic missiles, *they* will soon be in a position, through their numbers and their guns, to win all the 'little wars'. If I remember rightly, Nostradamus prophesied that in the year two thousand or thereabouts, yellow men would be flying over Paris. It may easily turn out that he was right.

Meanwhile we have just received the beautiful book on the Nude. Thank you very much. It is very handsome from the pictorial point of view and makes, so far as I have gone, excellent reading.

There is not much to report here. I still find myself involved, goodness knows why, in theatrical projects—this time with a version of *After Many a Summer Dies the Swan*, which was unsatisfactory, when made by someone in the business, and which I meant to revise, but am now rewriting—probably in vain, as most writing for the theatre is apt to be. I have embarked recently on a new treatment for the eyes [. . . .]

Love from us both.

Ever your affectionate,
Aldous

767 *Book on the Nude: evidently* The Nude, *by Sir Kenneth Clark, which was first published in* 1956.

3276 *Deronda Drive,*
Los Angeles 28, *Cal.*
22 *February,* 1957

My dear Humphry,

Thank you for your good letter and for the paper, which I found extremely interesting and enlightening. How fantastic it is that the problem of building a hospital that shall do no harm to the patients should not even have been envisaged in recent years, much less tackled and solved! And yet most people have had experience of the unpleasantness of living under the conditions prevalent in hospitals—at school, in barracks. But this has not prevented the architects and psychiatrists from reproducing for others the very state of things which they themselves have found disagreeable. One wonders whether there may not be in this strange behaviour something of that attitude described by Sydney Smith in his essay on 'English Public Schools'. Why did fathers persist in sending their sons to the same, unregenerate schools from which they themselves suffered? And why didn't these fathers do anything to get the schools reformed? Because what was good enough for me is good enough for Johnny, and it's salutary for the boy to undergo a little hardship.

Piranesi's etchings of the *Prisons* give one a very vivid idea of what an institution looks like to a schizophrenic—enormous, inhuman, full of vaguely sinister and perfectly incomprehensible features. It might be useful, if you have to convince legislators and suchlike, of the soundness of your views, to have photographs taken of your hospital—or, better, of some brand-new monstrosity—but taken with a distorting lens, or as mirrored in a curved surface, so that distances would seem exaggerated, surfaces un-flat, right angles obtuse or acute. Better still, do this on a motion picture film, so that the viewer would experience the horror of actually living and moving through such a world. Ellen has a friend, Francis Thompson, who has made a fascinating film of New York, as seen in the backs of spoons and through funny lenses. He could make an absolutely hair-raising documentary of an asylum, as it must appear to its schizophrenic inmates.

Have you read [Jiddu] Krishnamurti's new book, *Commentaries on Living?* Together with the previous volume of selections from his talks, *The First and Last Freedom,* it offers an amazingly subtle diagnosis of our psychological delinquencies and an amazingly practical, though difficult, self-treatment. My own feeling is that, if we could combine Krishnamurti with old Dr Vittoz's brand of psychotherapy and F M Alexander's method of 'creative conscious control' of posture and bodily function, with a bit of general semantics thrown in to help us steer clear of verbal and conceptual pitfalls, and a sensible diet, we would have solved the problem of preventive medicine and, along with it, at least half the problem of education. But, needless to say, people will prefer to go in for vaccines, popery and meprobamate.

To my great regret, my essays in *Esquire* are to come to an end. The magazine is about to change its format. No article may go over into the back of the book and every page is to consist of text and pictures in a fifty-fifty ratio. Evidently the majority of the public don't want to read, and now that so many cents in the advertising dollar go to TV, the magazine publishers (with the resounding crash of *Collier's* and Ladies' [*i.e. Woman's*] *Home Companion* still ringing in their ears) must do everything in their power to increase circulation and please potential advertisers. It is a pity; for I don't imagine I shall ever have such a convenient or well paying pulpit again. Meanwhile I have been busy making what I hope are final revisions on *The Genius and the Goddess*, and rewriting a version which somebody did, three years ago, of *After Many a Summer*. With time out to work in the UPA studios on an outline for an animated cartoon of *Don Quixote*, to be played by the engaging UPA character, Mr Magoo.

Laura sends her love, as do I. I hope all goes well with Jane and the little girl.

Ever yours,
Aldous

769: TO MATTHEW AND ELLEN HUXLEY

3276 *Deronda Drive, Los Angeles* 28, *Cal.*
24 *March,* 1957

Dearest Matthew and Ellen,

Forgive the long silence. I have been so busy that all correspondence has gone by the board and, as well as all the letters I want to write, there are hundreds of accumulated letters which I have to write, and which I doubt if I shall ever be able to cope with at the present rate.

I was interested to hear of the Darwin film. Will it be in the nature of a biography? Or of a documentary about Natural Selection? Or a mixture of both? Darwin himself is a richly comic character, with his mixture of enormous daring and timidity, his calculated use of psycho-somatic illness in the service of his vocation. I hope you will be able to bring him in as a person as well as a man of science and revolutionary thinker.

News of the play seems to be relatively hopeful. After nine months of dilly-dallying de Liagre has bowed himself out, and there seems to be a good prospect of our coming to an agreement very shortly with Courtney Burr— *Seven Year Itch* and *Bad Seed*—who expresses enthusiasm for the play and a desire to produce it in the autumn. The William Morris people are negotiating with him at this moment, and I hope we may really get some action at last. Meanwhile Betty and I have done a lot of streamlining of the play— taking the best part of twenty minutes out of it and thereby, I think, greatly

---

769 *Darwin film: planned by Francis Huxley and Ellen Huxley for National Educational Television, but never made.*

improving it from a theatrical point of view. Now—since plays, for some reason, seem to be my fate at the moment—I am re-writing Ralph Rose's version of *After Many a Summer*. Two acts already done. I have hopes that, when the whole is completed, we may have something at once curious, lively and disquieting. Garson Kanan [Kanin] (is that how you spell him?) has expressed interest in the play, of which he saw one of the earlier unsatisfactory versions; so perhaps we may be able to get some action in that quarter. Meanwhile *Brave New World* remains in abeyance, while Jim Geller attempts to persuade RKO to sell back the rights they acquired twenty-five years ago and never did anything with. Hitherto with no success. RKO are asking fifty thousand dollars for the rights. However we may be able to haggle and connive our way into a more favourable situation—though I am not too optimistic. If the rights were free, it would make everything much easier —for RKO control TV rights as well as movie rights.

Did I tell you that the *Esquire* arrangement has come to an end? They are changing the format of the magazine. More pictures, less reading matter. So this convenient and well paid pulpit has been pulled out from under me. I regret it very much; for there is not the slightest prospect of its place being taken by any other periodical.

We go north in mid April, when I am booked to spend three days at Stanford, talking to students of Creative Writing, whatever that is. Then in May I shall be coming East. (Laura will probably stay here.) I have a lecture at the University of New Hampshire, on May 10th, and shall probably be in New York for a day or two before and a day or two after. *And*, I hope, at N[ew] H[aven], with you.

Much love.

Aldous

770: TO ROBERT CRAFT

3276 *Deronda Drive,*
Los Angeles 28, *Cal.*
26 *March*, 1957

Dear Bob,

Will you please give me some advice. I have made a dramatic adaptation of *Brave New World* in the form, not so much of a conventional musical, as of a play with music—a ballet or two and some songs. Who would you advise me to approach for the score? Bernstein has been suggested, of course, and now someone of my acquaintance wants me to send it to Rodgers and Hammerstein. What would be your suggestion?

Needless to say, if the maestro felt inclined to take some time off to do something light—a little ballet music for brave new worlders and another piece for the Indians on the reservation, plus half a dozen vocal numbers, I

770 *Maestro: Igor Stravinsky.*

would be only too happy. But I hesitate to ask him—wouldn't want to do so before finding out what you think.

I hope all goes well with the family and with you.

Yours,
Aldous

771: TO LEONARD BERNSTEIN

3276 *Deronda Drive,*
Los Angeles 28, *Cal.*
4 *April,* 1957

Dear Mr Bernstein,

As a very busy man with a large correspondence, I can well understand your annoyance at receiving yet another letter from a perfect stranger. But, at the risk of being a bore, I am writing to ask if you would be at all interested in reading a dramatic version of my novel *Brave New World*, which I have recently made, with a view to a musical setting. (I envisage the piece as a play with music and dancing, rather than as a conventional 'musical'.) The story calls for a very resourceful composer, who can run the gamut from the primitive dances of the Indian Reservation to the music of the hypothetical future. So I naturally thought of you and am hopefully writing this on the off chance that you may have the time and the inclination to consider such a project.

Yours sincerely
Aldous Huxley

772: TO DR HUMPHRY OSMOND

3276 *Deronda Drive,*
Los Angeles 28, *Cal.*
8 *April,* 1957

Dear Humphry,

I have been I fear, very remiss in the matter of writing. It has been a case of deadlines—working to finish off a completely new version of a play which a man [Ralph Rose] did, two or three years ago, from my novel, *After Many a Summer*. He made two versions, the first fair, the second less good. So I decided to start from scratch, and have just finished what I hope may turn out to be quite a good, if very disquieting, horror-comedy-parable. Now I can get back to my neglected correspondence.

I hope all goes well with you and the family. Will there be any chance of seeing you in New York in early May? I go east to give a lecture at the University of New Hampshire, see Matthew and Ellen and talk about my play with the new producer, Courtney Burr, who seems really determined to do

771 *The problem of a composer for the dramatic* Brave New World *was not solved, and Huxley laid the project aside.*

821

the thing this autumn. (But I shan't believe it until it actually happens.) I shall also try to see some people in various Foundations, in the hope of getting someone to sponsor a documentary film for TV on population. (We have a little Foundation of our own, called Population Limited, rich in talent—my brother Julian, Harrison Brown, Kingsley Davis, the sociologist, Fred Zinnemann, the film director, and Bill Kiskadden, the surgeon—but poor in money.) I hope we may finally persuade someone to put up the necessary funds for doing a film to educate the American public—after which we shall try to see what can be done in such areas of dire need as India. I have written a synopsis of a film on Egypt—because it is better to attack the general through the particular, and because Egypt is a particularly painful case of overpopulation, and is in a position to make the economic, sociological and political consequences of overpopulation extremely unpleasant to the rest of the world. Whether anyone will put up the money, I don't know. Everyone agrees that the population problem is the most important problem of the present century; but nobody wants to get in trouble with the Papists. Well, as I say, I shall be in New York during the first week in May and perhaps again after the tenth, the day when I am to lecture in New Hampshire. So let me know if you will be in that part of the world.

I have just read a very remarkable book, which was sent me by the publishers. It is Dr William Sargant's *Struggle for the Mind*, which explains the relevance of Pavlov's findings to religious and political conversion, brain washing, confession-extraction and indoctrination. Now that the dictators are equipped with systematic knowledge of the ways in which brain functions can be disturbed, so as to facilitate deconditioning and reconditioning, I really see very little hope for our unfortunate species. And now there is a new horror, just developed by a man called Eagles [M. N. Eagle] at NY University. It makes use of the tachystoscope in a most ingenious way. For example, the image of a perfectly commonplace, neutral man or woman on the screen is preceded by a tachystoscopic flash of a thousandth of a second's duration. This flash is of some strongly charged image—something good or delightful (Abraham Lincoln or Marilyn Monroe) or something horrible (Stalin or Jack the Ripper). The viewer does not consciously see the image flashed before his eyes; but his optic nerves and unconscious mind have taken it in. (This is a familiar feature of the Bates Method—unconscious seeing of things which one has not had the time or the eyesight to see consciously.) The result of this unconscious seeing of the emotionally charged flash is that the consciously seen image of the neutral person, which follows it, becomes charged with the emotion appropriate to the flashed image—admirable if the flashed image is of Lincoln or Monroe, loathsome if of Stalin or Jack the Ripper. I understand from Robert Hutchins that the advertising boys are already on Dr Eagle's trail. Given a skilful use of this technique, it will become impossible *not* to buy Camel Cigarettes or Coca Cola, or to vote Republican. The trouble will come, of course, when *every* brand of cigarettes and *every* political candidate is given the flash treatment. Confronted by equal and opposite categorical imperatives, the victim will break down, like a Pavlovian dog in an ambiguous situation. But what an appallingly effective tool for the dictators! Combined with drugs, brainwashing and straight conditioning, it will rob the individual of the last shred of free will. The ultimate revolution—the physiological and psychological revolution—which, in *Brave New World*, I envisaged as taking place six hundred years hence is here on our doorstep, and I see no way in which it can be arrested.

> *Yours affectionately,*
> *Aldous*

773: TO DR HUMPHRY OSMOND

> 3276 *Deronda Drive,*
> *Los Angeles 28, Cal.*
> 21 *April,* 1957

Dear Humphry,

I returned yesterday from a week at Stanford and San Francisco, to find your letter awaiting me. I fear I can give you no reference to Eagle, since I had the information by word of mouth from Robert Hutchins, who had had it, I think, by word of mouth straight from the Eagle's bill. I will try to find out from Hutchins, when I see him in New York, if the stuff has been published. If the method really works, our only hope under capitalism will lie in multiple and mutually incompatible conditionings by stroboscope, resulting in nervous collapse, in the manner of Pavlov's dogs. Under the totalitarians—as under cartellized business—the conditioning will all be of one kind and there won't be disturbing inconsistencies—so another nail will be hammered into the coffin of free will and individualism.

I should very much like to meet your automation-expert friend. I expect to fly east on the second or third of May, spend a weekend with Matthew and Ellen, then go down to Washington for a lecture on the night of the sixth, stay there a couple of days, then fly up to New Hampshire to lecture there on the ninth, or is it perhaps the tenth? After which I expect to be in New York for a few days, seeing friends and, I trust, influencing people in regard to the play. So far as I know, I shall be staying at the Warwick Hotel, Sixth Avenue and 54th Street.

I had a pleasant time at Stanford—though they kept me talking for more time and to more different kinds of people—members of the 'creative writing' classes, of the Comparative Religion class, of the post-graduate English classes and even of the Ford Foundation's Institute for Advanced Studies in the Behavioral Sciences—than I had bargained for. However the young people were nice and some of their elders were very interesting—e.g.

---

773 *Automation expert: Stanford Ovshinsky, of General Automation in Detroit, a pioneer in the application of theory of neuronal mechanisms to machine design.*

[Frederic] Spiegelberg, the expert on Indian religions, who has a magnificent Tibetan ghost-trap hanging in his office. (This is a contraption made of wood and taut strings, which outline the form of a rather complicated crystal. The ghosts get entangled in the strings and can't get out. The machine is equipped with numerous balls of wool, which become wet when a ghost is caught—for ghosts are somewhat liquid. After giving the captured ghost a stern lecture, one throws the whole contraption down a precipice.) I also saw Gregory Bateson, who does psychiatry from the point of view of an anthropologist at the local Veterans' Hospital. Also Alan Watts, the Zen man, who is dean of the Academy of Asian Studies. In San Francisco we became involved, for some reason, with the Rich. They are apt, I find, to be a bit depressing.

Love to Jane.

Aldous

774: TO DR HUMPHRY OSMOND

> 3276 *Deronda Drive,*
> *Los Angeles 28, Cal.*
> 1 *June,* 1957

Dear Humphry,

I was on the point of writing, when your letter, with the good news of your award, arrived and spurred me into instant action. I am delighted that you should have won recognition, and hope that one thing may lead to another—the hospital award to a bigger grant for research.

Meanwhile what do you say to Eileen's plan (about which she said she was writing to you) for a quiet series of experiments in Mrs Bolton's house in Florida next winter? It sounds to me very good, and if you could get away for at least some of the duration of the experiments, it should be possible to achieve something significant. Using the same subjects in a regular series of tests should make possible a really systematic exploration of their other world. It will also be possible to see what can be done by combining hypnosis with LSD or mescalin. Dr L. J. West, of the Medical School of the University of Oklahoma, was here a few weeks ago—an extremely able young man, I think. His findings are that mescalinized subjects are almost unhypnotizable. I suggested to him that he should hypnotize his people before they took LSD and should give them post-hypnotic suggestions aimed at orientating the drug-induced experience in some desired direction, and also at the very desirable goal of enabling subjects to recapture the LSD experience by purely psychological means, after their return to normal consciousness, and whenever they so desired. The fact that this kind of experience occurs in some persons spontaneously indicates that chemicals are not indispensable, and it may be that the

---

774 *Award: the Mental Hospital Merit Award of the American Psychiatric Association.*

824

unconscious can be persuaded, by means of post-hypnotic suggestions, repeated if necessary again and again, to open the door without the aid of chemical keys. Such a set-up as Eileen envisages would be ideal for this kind of experiment. It would be a great thing if you could get down to Florida to supervise at least the initial phases of the work.

I had a letter a few days since from another doctor in Oklahoma, Dr Philip Smith, who has been experimenting with anaesthetics such as ether, laughing gas etc—testing the psychological effects of light doses. He has evidently had good results himself and he wrote to me asking if I knew any literary references to the matter. I know very few, and he said there were remarkably few in the medical literature. It is evident from the little there is that here is yet another key to the door into the other world.

While I was in New York, I lunched with Wasson at his Temple of Mammon. [. . . .] he has put an immense amount of work into his subject, and the material brought together in his vast tomes is very curious and suggestive. However, he does, as you say, like to think that his mushrooms are somehow unique and infinitely superior to everything else. I tried to disabuse him. But he likes to feel that he had got hold of the One and Only psychodelic—accept no substitutes, none genuine unless sold with the signature of the inventor.

I also saw dear old Suzuki in New York. What a really wonderful old man! Have you read his most recent book on *Mysticism, Christian and Buddhist?* It is very good. And even better is a little pamphlet published by the London Buddhist Society, called the *Essence of Buddhism.* This last is really admirable. It makes one realize how much subtler these Far Eastern Buddhists were, in matters of psychology, than anyone in the West. They know all about 'existential experiences' and the horrors of the human situation as described by Sartre, Camus and the rest—and they know how to come through to the other side, where every relative manifests absolute Suchness, and where Suchness is identical with mahakaruna, the Great Compassion.

The play seems to be going forward satisfactorily. We have an excellent leading lady, Nancy Kelly, but not yet a leading man—though there are several good possibilities. In New York I listened to a number of young girls reading for the part of Ruth, and think we have a good one. Also I saw and heard several very capable young men for the part of young Rivers. The director is to be Cedric Hardwicke and I expect to spend a good deal of time in the next few weeks discussing things with him and Miss Kelly, and making final (but they are never final) cuts and little alterations.

Meanwhile there has been some interest in the musical version of *Brave New World*—but nothing as yet is definite; and in any case nothing can possibly be done about it for another year.

Our love to you all.

Yours affectionately,
Aldo

The Shoreham,
New York 19, *N.Y.*
17 *August,* [1957]

Dear Humphry,

I should have answered your letter before, but have been kept too frantically busy revising the play—which has had to be practically reconstructed
to meet the demands of backers who don't want to invest in anything experimental, of scene designers who don't want to undertake a difficult job and of
producers who pine for economy and a small cast. Now at last the job is
finished—at least for the time being, and it remains to be seen if the producer
and his associates can achieve what they have always said they wanted to
achieve—rehearsals beginning on the tenth of September. It will be a bit of
a miracle if that deadline is met. But perhaps the depths of confusion and
muddle which characterize the theatre may sometimes be compensated for
by heights of one-pointed efficiency. In any case I look forward to seeing
you while you are in the East. Let me know exactly when you are coming,
where staying etc.

New York is not too bad. I have had only four or five days of really
equatorial heat in the four weeks I have been here. And there is always air
conditioning even on the worst days. There has been little time to see things
or people—most of whom are on holiday anyhow—and my extra-curricular
activities have included only the big Picasso show at the Modern Museum
(what a lot of slapdash shoddy stuff surrounding the twenty or thirty masterpieces!), the Metropolitan, where there is a beautiful loan exhibition of French
19th century painting, an evening with Joseph Campbell, (the man who edited
and in part re-wrote Heinrich Zimmier's [Zimmer's] posthumous books and
who is very knowledgeable in oriental matters and comparative mythology)
and a morning with Dr [Karlis] Osis (who has come from Duke to Eileen's
parapsychology foundation and is working on the problem of survival).

Ever yours
Aldous

776: TO JULIAN HUXLEY

[*Hotel Shoreham*]
33 *West* 55*th St., N.Y.C.* 19
10 *September,* 1957

Dearest Julian,

I was happy to get your letter and to know that you are feeling better
and getting back to work again. Don't get back too strenuously, however,
until you feel completely consolidated.

775 *Misdated* 1955 *through a typing error.*

To my mind the problem of religion is one which has to be approached operationally. If you do A, then B is likely to happen; if you do X, then you will probably get Y. The great merit of the oriental systems of philosophy is that they are all of them forms of transcendental pragmatism. Pure speculation is not their primary concern. Their metaphysics and their theology are devised in order to explain certain types of immediate experience. What matters is the experience, not the conceptual system in terms of which the experience is explained—the moon and not the finger which points at the moon. Christianity, Judaism and Islam have been unduly preoccupied with concepts and symbols. They have spent too much time and energy manipulating symbols—in ritual and sacrament, in creeds and theologies. Religion in the West is largely a matter of the intellectual and emotional responses to symbols—belief (credo quia absurdum); faith (it moves mountains and motivates and justifies persecutions and bigotry); conviction of sin (based on beliefs which, in many respects, do not correspond with reality); sense of conversion and being saved (also based on inadequate beliefs). A sensible and realistic religion should be one which is based upon a set of psycho-physiological operations, designed to help individuals to realize their potentialities to the greatest possible extent (we normally live at about twenty per cent of capacity), to heighten their awareness, so that they become conscious of the Unconscious (this is Suzuki's definition of enlightenment) and at the same time fully conscious of other human beings ('mutual forgiveness of each vice', in Blake's words), and fully capable of distinguishing between the moon and the pointing finger, the given fact in all its staggering profundity and beauty and the conventional symbols in terms of which we try to understand, arrange and manipulate the facts. The theology which naturally stems from this kind of religion is a theology of immanence—for only an indwelling God can be experienced, a transcendent deity is always inferred or accepted on authority. And of course even a theology of immanence can get you in trouble if you take it too seriously and become ensnared in the game of manipulating symbols. The Buddha was never tired of telling his hearers that theology and metaphysics were obstacles to enlightenment as grave, very nearly, as malice and insensitiveness. And how refreshing it is to find in the Far Eastern literature those delightful anecdotes about Zen monks who burn images of Buddha in order to keep warm in winter, or who say that anyone who talks too much about Buddha or Buddhism ought to have his mouth washed out—like a child who has used a dirty word. Imagine anyone in the Christian or Hebrew tradition saying anything of the kind about the names of God or Christ.

After weeks of irritation, re-writing and ineptitude [. . .], the play situation seems to be brighter, and it looks as if we should definitely start rehearsals by the fifth of October. We have an excellent feminine lead, Nancy Kelly, and for the man, Alan Webb, an English actor whom I have never seen, but who, according to all accounts, is very good. We have, too, a director

[Richard Whorf] who is said to be very competent. I haven't yet seen him as he is now out of New York, but should be back here in a few days. But, goodness, what a confusion this whole theatre business is! And what trouble one asks for, when one writes a play! I only hope the reward may be commensurate with the bother and the waste of time.

I hope to see Francis before too long, as he will be in these parts, I understand, for a few days or weeks before setting out for Saskatchewan. Humphry Osmond is currently in Switzerland, attending a conference on psycho-chemo-therapeutics, and won't be back till late in October.

Laura is off tomorrow to Italy, where she will stay for a month or so with her father, but will return here for the opening of the play. Our love to you both. Please thank Juliette for her good letter.

Ever your affectionate,
Aldous

777: TO J. B. RHINE

The Shoreham,
New York 19, N.Y.
19 September, 1957

Dear JB,

Thank you for your letter of August 15th, which finds me in New York, wrestling with the preliminaries to the production of a play.

The only information about the effects of LSD on ESP comes from my friend Dr Humphry Osmond, who found that there seemed to be telepathic rapports between himself and another man, while both were under the influence of the drug. They didn't do any systematic tests, however. And the trouble here is that people under LSD or mescalin are generally in a state of intenser, more significant experience—a state in which they are apt to become extremely impatient with the learned foolery of statistics, repeated experiments, scientific precautions, questions by investigators etc. It is rather like asking somebody who is listening with rapt attention to a Bach Prelude and Fugue, or is in the midst of making love, to answer a questionnaire. Human beings, as you have certainly found, are not very good guinea pigs, except on the more rudimentary levels of their vital activity.

Yours sincerely,
Aldous H

778: TO JULIAN HUXLEY

Hotel Shoreham,
33 W. 55th St., N.Y.C. 19
27 September, 1957

Dearest J,

Thank you for your letter. Of course you are right in saying that there must be a general weltanschauung or theology, conformable with the facts as we progressively come to know them. I was thinking, when I wrote, primarily of that part of human destiny which is more or less directly within the control of the individual—what he himself can do to realize his potentialities and come to a state where he enjoys a measure of psychological freedom, whatever the nature of the environment, and where he is functioning, as a mind-body, at, say, fifty per cent of capacity instead of the average fifteen or twenty per cent. Personal religion of this kind is a form of psycho-therapy for the normal, of self-help for people who are bored with their customary, conditioned selves and would like to be something a bit more satisfactory. It is in relation to this kind of personal religion that an excessive preoccupation with theology is deplored by the Buddha and the Zen masters. Not, of course, that we can do without some kind of conceptual compass to guide one. What is being pointed out by the anti-theologians is that it is not much use having a compass if one doesn't possess a ship in which to cross the sea. Among the transcendental pragmatists of the Orient the stress is laid on the ship—the method of self-transcendence, by means of which the individual makes his own destiny and, to some extent, that of the people with whom he comes in contact.

There are, of course, plenty of historical instances that demonstrate how important it is not to entertain wildly inaccurate views about the cosmos. The Aztecs, for example, believed that the sun would stop shining unless plentifully supplied with the hearts of human victims. Hence their curious kind of imperialism—conquest in search of prisoner-victims; hence the hatred for them of all the other Indian peoples, who allied themselves with the Spaniards and helped to destroy the Aztec (and in general the indigenous) civilization. Or take the Athenians before Syracuse. The fleet and army could have got away in safety, but the soothsayers had looked at the moon and *knew* that there should be a month's delay—which, as it turned out, was absolutely fatal. And we have the Byzantines thronging Santa Sophia and the other churches on the day that the Turks stormed the walls of Constantinople—convinced that the Virgin would save them.

Love to you both.

Ever your affectionate,
Aldous

779: TO MRS MARIAN ELIZABETH BREMER

The Warwick,
Philadelphia 3, Pa.
[18 *November,* 1957]

Dear Mrs. Brenner [sic],

Your letter has reached me here. If I were in your situation, I would (if I felt myself able to do so) supplement psychiatric treatment by the kind of self-education in increased awareness described in the volume (by three psychiatrists, whose names I cannot now remember) entitled *Gestalt-Therapy*. As the Swiss psychiatrist, Dr. Vittoz, demonstrated 40 years ago, there is something intrinsically therapeutic in the act, constantly repeated, of becoming fully aware of oneself (muscular movements, sensations etc) and of one's environment (perceptions). Nor wd I neglect such methods as are described by Dr. Hornell Hart in his *Auto-Conditioning*. Still less wd I neglect such bio-chemical aids as are now proving their value—e.g massive doses of niacin (nicotinic acid, part of the B complex). Dr. Abram Hoffer of the University of Saskatchewan at Saskatoon in Canada has treated several hundred patients under his care with 3 to 4 grammes a day of niacin—with striking success in many cases of schizoid neurosis or schizophrenia in its early stages (after many years of illness the treatment doesn't work). These, together with group therapy (a necessary supplement to individual therapy) are what I personally wd try, if I got into a state of psychological distress. Whether these suggestions have any validity in your case is for you and your doctor to decide. I merely tell you what *I* should do in comparable circumstances. In any case, the problem is a purely practical one—to get out of the distressful state by any means whatsoever. Only when the bio-chemical and psychological problems have been solved will it be possible to solve the other problems of social and personal relationships.

Indiana is off my beat; but if ever I find myself in your neighbourhood, I will ring your doorbell and ask for a cup of tea in your marine living room.

Sincerely,
Aldous Huxley

780: TO NANCY KELLY

[*Philadelphia*]
Thursday evening [21 *November*, 1957]

Dear Nancy,

I am distressed to think that I seem to have failed, in the play, to make my conception of the goddess clear to you. It is very clear to me, because

779 Gestalt Therapy *is the work of F. F. Perls, R. F. Hefferline and Paul Goodman.*

780 *Text from Huxley's hand-corrected carbon copy.* The Genius and the Goddess, *the play as written by Huxley and Mrs Wendel in 1955 and subsequently revised by them into its final, authorized version, has never had a stage production. This is regrettable in view of its success in H. E. Herlitschka's translation (1959), which has been televised in Germany and Switzerland. The complete play has also been televised in Australia. But for American and English stage productions, neither of which proved successful, the producers, Courtney Burr and Frank Hauser respectively, used mangled scripts. In the case of Burr's production, in 1957, the authors let themselves be pressured into rewriting the play in accordance with Burr's ideas and even into working with a collaborator, Alec Coppel, chosen by him. What emerged was a weak,*

830

I used to know very well a specimen of the breed. This was Frieda Lawrence, the wife of D. H. Lawrence. I think I told you the other day about the miraculous way in which she raised Lawrence almost from death when he was ill with influenza (superimposed upon chronic and deepening TB) in my house. Katy's miracle with Henry is merely a transcription of what I myself saw, thirty years ago. (Incidentally, the miracle was chronic. Thanks to Frieda, Lawrence remained alive for at least five years after he ought, by all the rules of medicine, to have been in the grave.) Frieda (and Katy is a non-German and less Rabelaisian version of Frieda) was a woman of enormous strength and vitality, completely untouched by the neuroses of the Age of Anxiety. Everything that Katy-Frieda does, she does with her whole heart. With a whole heart she loves and admires her genius and with a whole heart she quarrels with him. (Frieda used to throw plates at Lawrence, and Lawrence threw them back at her. I have spared you this!) Again, it is with a whole heart that Katy-Frieda looks after her man when he is sick, and it is with a whole heart that she makes fun of him when he is being peevish or ridiculous. Frieda and Lawrence had, undoubtedly, a profound and passionate love-life. But this did not prevent Frieda from having, every now and then, affairs with Prussian cavalry officers and Italian peasants, whom she loved for a season without in any way detracting from her love for Lawrence or from her intense devotion to his genius. Lawrence, for his part, was aware of these erotic excursions, got angry about them sometimes, but never made the least effort to break away from her; for he realized his own organic dependence upon her. He felt towards her as a man might feel towards his own liver: the liver may give trouble from time to time, but it remains one of the vital organs, absolutely necessary to survival.

Frieda's attitude towards life was much the same as Katy's. She was profoundly matter-of-fact, accepting events as they were given, in all their painful or delightful confusion. She had little patience with idealism or exalted ethical systems. Her essentially realistic view of life was expressed in Shakespeare's words in *King Lear*—'Ripeness is all'. This ripeness of realism made some people feel, at a first meeting, that she was rather rough and even

conventional domestic comedy. This opened in New Haven on 13 November, with Alan Webb as Maartens, Nancy Kelly as Katy, and Michael Tolan as the young John Rivers. At Philadelphia the following week, Burr engineered secret rehearsals of new lines unknown to the authors, reputedly written by a special adviser of Burr's who had been mysteriously engaged in 'observing'. The new material was introduced in the final performance at Philadelphia, on the 23rd. Huxley was not present, but Mrs Wendel, thwarting a manœuvre by Burr to keep her away from the performance, attended it with Laura Huxley. When Huxley learned what Burr had done, he decided to take legal advice and left for New York. For contractual reasons and in the hope of forestalling unilateral script changes by Burr, Mrs Wendel remained with the company for the Boston run, which began on the 25th. See letters 781-783.

a little heartless. But her teasing and her pricking of idealistic bubbles were always profoundly good-natured. She would speak ironical words, but speak them out of a depth of human kindness and sympathy. Another characteristic trait was her child-likeness. This was a product of her capacity for doing everything with all her heart—for living fully in each successive moment, as a child does. And this gave her a certain superficial air of inconsistency. She identified herself wholly with each mood as it turned up, so that her personality was many-faceted. Finally, she had the most sovereign disregard for what people might think or say about her—a disregard based upon a certain native aristocracy, on the confidence of a very rich personality in its own essential rightness and excellence. This meant that she was never anxious, never apologetic, never tense or nervous. She did everything—baking bread, scrubbing floors, making her own clothes, tending the sick genius—with the unhurried, easy serenity of the heroines and goddesses of the Homeric myths. Her speech reflected the same spirit. She spoke slowly, deliberately, relishing the words she used (for she had a great command of language, even in a tongue which was not her own).

This is the person who, as a young girl, fascinated Henry when he saw her in California, and who, as a mature woman, fascinates John Rivers from the first moment he enters the Maartens household. I have done my best in the play to make my character of Katy do and say nothing incompatible with this person. There are details which might, perhaps, be improved; but I feel that, in essence, this person I knew and then re-imagined in another context is solidly there.

Yours affectionately,
[*Aldous*]

781: TO MRS BETH WENDEL

New York, N.Y.
25 November, 1957

Have just sent the following to Burr in Boston and New York:
'You have flagrantly breached your minimum basic production contract with us by inserting material and making changes in the play without our consent and without consulting us and by having rehearsals for such purposes without our knowledge or consent and have further and in various ways conducted yourself arbitrarily without regard to our rights as authors. You have also failed and refused to make payment of our living expenses as set forth in our letter to you dated October 24, 1957. For the foregoing reasons, despite our lack of confidence in your intention not to continue such conduct, we hereby demand that you correct the foregoing breaches

781 *Telegram, sent to Mrs Wendel in Boston. The message to Burr appears to have been drafted in consultation with a legal adviser.*

within three (3) days after the telegraphing of this notice. If you fail to make such corrections within that period, all your rights in the play shall automatically terminate upon the expiration of that period. To give you opportunity to make such corrections respecting the play, Beth Wendel will remain in Boston during the three (3) day period with authority of both of us to attend rehearsals and grant script approvals.'

Aldous Huxley [,] *Beth Wendel*'

782: TO MRS BETH WENDEL

The Gotham,
Fifth Avenue at 55th St., New York 19
25 November, 1957

Dear Betty,

I am writing to emphasize what Helen Harvey said this morning on the phone—namely, that the one essential thing is to get the management to give you a script of the play in the form in which they propose to present it. If you can get this by Wednesday or Thursday, you could send it me by airmail and special delivery, I could go through it page by page, okaying what is all right and marking what is objectionable. I could then return it to you for the same treatment and, when you are done, you could return it by the end of the week to the producers as the final text of the play. In this way we may be able to exercise some slight control over the actions of these [. . .] people. If, however, the matter is left on the level where it has rested for the past two weeks—the level of snap judgments, talk and successive improvisations—we shall have no control whatsoever. The only hope—and in view of what these people are it is rather a slim hope—lies in having a script, of which the more important parts can, if necessary, be photostated, so that we can produce them as evidence of what we have agreed to. They will, of course, want you to discuss things; but my advice, and the advice of Helen and the lawyer, is, Don't. Just ask for the script.

Meanwhile please rest assured that I am not washing my hands of the matter and thrusting all responsibility on to you. The lawyer thinks it best that I should stay here and that you should remain for the time being in Boston representing our interests. But I don't want you to feel that you are isolated. Thanks to the phone, you are very close to legal and professional advice at the Morris office, as well as to whatever advice I can furnish. Meanwhile I am happy to think that you have Sandy to support and counsel you in this very unpleasant and ticklish situation.

Yours,
Aldous

782 *Sandy: Sanford Wendel.*

3276 *Deronda Drive,*
Los Angeles 28, *Cal.*
4 *December,* 1957

Dear Helen,

Here, for the record, is a brief account of my misadventures with *The Genius and the Goddess*. The play, as it was originally written, followed the novel pretty closely. The story of young Rivers and his adventures in the Maartens household was treated as a play within the framework of the story of Rivers as an old man, talking with his friend Barr on the night of Christmas Eve in the present year of grace. Like the novel, the original play dealt with the love affair between young Rivers and Katy Maartens, and with Ruth Maartens' adolescent passion for young Rivers and her jealousy of her mother. As in the novel, Katy's goddess-like equanimity is shattered by the child's hostile attitude, and the result of this psychological disturbance is that she drives carelessly, has an accident and gets killed. The play ends ironically and realistically with Henry Maartens turning without a moment's delay to another woman, the impossible Mrs Hackenschmidt, for consolation. He needs some woman to be dependent upon and it really makes very little difference to him whether that woman is a goddess or the antithesis of a goddess. He is possessed by his genius, and all this genius requires is some kind of strong female influence to inspire and sustain it.

This play within a play, with its three interwoven stories—the story of the two old men, the story of young Rivers and Katy, and the story of Ruth in relation to John and Katy—was full of dramatic and psychological material and possessed an interesting and original form. It was for this play that Courtney Burr expressed enthusiasm and it was this play that he bought last spring. By July, however, he had changed his mind, insisted that the play in its

783 *Text from a copy sent to Matthew Huxley. On* 1 *December, Burr and his associate producer, Liska March, had telephoned Huxley, who by then was in Los Angeles, and asked him to come to Boston and to put his name back on the play. Burr told him that the new material had been taken out. The next day Huxley wrote to Beth Wendel:* 'I wired them later saying that I still took the position set forth in [*Arnold*] Weissberger's letter and have followed up the wire by a letter, setting forth all that has happened since July and the reasons why I can no longer collaborate with [the] group'. *Burr had not yet in fact purged the inserted material from the play. He finally did so on* 4 *December, before the Boston run ended, and thereupon Beth Wendel left Boston for New York. Contending that he had now fulfilled his obligations, Burr restored the adapters' names to the billing, from which he had been induced to remove them. Huxley's lawyer, Weissberger, protested the resumed use of his clients' names, on grounds that, with the inserted material gone, Burr was staging scenes which, though written by Huxley, had been discarded from the acting script during rehearsals in September; but Burr continued to advertise the names throughout the New York run, which lasted five days* (10-14 *December*).

original form was un-producible and asked for the elimination of the two old men and for an ending which kept Katy Maartens alive and reunited the family.

At this point I made the enormous mistake of supposing that, since I had had but little experience with playwriting, I knew less about the matter than those who had been connected with the theatre for years. Being diffident of my dramatic abilities, I reluctantly gave consent for the play to be changed. The work was carried out, at the producer's request, by Alec Coppel, who did an ingenious job of retailoring the play into a conventional form, with a single plot line—the story of young Rivers and Katy Maartens and Henry. The old men were cut out, and so was the daughter's jealousy of her mother. The new play was a fairly slick piece of conventional craftsmanship with none of the depth imparted to the characters by the comments of the two old men and with a serious paucity of dramatic substance, due to the elimination of the child's passion for young Rivers and jealousy of Katy. The new ending was also essentially weak and somewhat phony. I pointed out these defects; but those who, as I supposed, knew their theatrical business, assured me that the new play was a better piece of dramatic writing than the old and much more likely to be commercially successful. Once again I made the enormous mistake of believing them.

From mid July until late November I remained in New York, at the producer's request, writing and re-writing scenes in an effort to restore to the new play some of the depth and dramatic substance which had distinguished the original. It was a pretty hopeless task; but I did my best. I listened to the suggestions of those whom I mistakenly believed to be more competent in the dramatic field than I was, and I translated these suggestions into scenes and passages of dialogue. All the thanks I got for this long labour of con-scientious co-operation was the producer's repeated refusal to pay the money for living expenses, which was due to myself and my collaborator under the terms of our contract with the management.

With the arrival of the director, new changes were suggested and sum-marily made—mainly consisting of cuts, which reduced many scenes to a kind of digest of themselves. At the director's request a new hilarious scene was written, amusing enough in itself, but embarrassing (as it turned out in performance), inasmuch as it immediately preceded a powerfully emotional scene, which it is hard for an audience to take (in its present context) at its face value. In earlier versions of the play the transition between comic and serious had been carefully worked out. Bowing to what I supposed to be expert opinion, I consented to the removal of this bridge. Today everyone is complaining because, thanks to the change demanded by the expert, the bridge is no longer there.

The breaking point was reached in Philadelphia. The week in that city should have been spent in making a strenuous effort to patch up the feeble last scene and to conceal, as far as that was possible, the phony sentimentality which had been injected into it when, at the producer's request, my original story line was changed. I had written a new version of the last scene at New Haven, and I was anxious to discuss it with [. . .]; but he broke every appointment he made with me and, instead of working on the final scene, concentrated all his and the actors' energies on rehearsing a scene written by Professor [——], which was inserted into the first act. This was done behind my back and in the most flagrant violation of the basic production contract and of a gentleman's agreement entered into at New Haven, where Professor [——] joined the troupe. This final outrage was too much even for my long-suffering nature. I left Philadelphia for New York and immediately got in touch with you, as my agent, and with my attorney. Through the latter I demanded that my name be taken off the play. This the management agreed to in writing. However, I now understand that they propose to violate this agreement too, and that my name will appear on the playbills as though nothing had happened.

Well, I have wasted more than four months, which might have been profitably employed in doing my own work. The experience has been unpleasant and ex[. . .] boring. It has also been highly educational. We live and learn.

Yours very sincerely,

A H

784: TO JULIAN HUXLEY

3276 Deronda Drive,
Los Angeles 28, Cal.
12 December, 1957

Dearest Julian,

I have been meaning to write for some time; but this damned play and all the tiresome unpleasant business connected with it prevented me. I got out, when the producer broke his word and his written contract by inserting unauthorized material. Now the thing has opened in New York, and will doubtless close very soon. All this is in part my fault; for I permitted myself to be persuaded to allow a radical change in the play's structure to be made— in the interest of making the thing more 'commercial'. The result was that most of the psychological depth and much of the dramatic substance of the drama were cut out, while a number of new problems were created—problems which I have been trying to solve for the last four months, without any success; for they are, so far as I can see, insoluble. So there we are. One lives and learns. I wasted several months and made a considerable fool of myself. Now, thank heaven, I can get back to serious work in an atmosphere refreshingly unlike the nightmare world of the theatre.

[. . . .] I took large doses of it [nicotinic acid] for some weeks this autumn, as it helps in reducing cholesterol in the blood and Hoffer thought it might conceivably help in routing cholesterol out of the lens of my right eye, which has had a heavy cataract on it (as well as the old corneal opacities) since the attack of iritis from which I suffered several years ago. Combined with a sulphur preparation (hydrosulphasol) used internally and locally, it seems to have made a faintly perceptible difference, and I shall probably resume the treatment again later on. Meanwhile I was interested to hear from Laura, who was with her family in Turin in the early autumn, that the Italians have been using massive doses of Nicotinamide (a variant on nicotinic acid) in psychological cases for some time. (It is also effective, they say, in many skin troubles—skin and nerves being, of course, closely related.) Perhaps the greatest merit of the nicotinic acid treatment is that it can apparently do no harm. Hoffer tells me that he has had patients on massive doses of it for four years without any ill effects. In view of the growing number of iatrogenic diseases, this harmlessness is something to be thankful for.

Francis, I gather, is now in New York with Matthew and Ellen. As I understand it, he is making a study of environment in relation to mental patients—with a view to the designing of a more satisfactory kind of mental hospital. (Osmond told me, when I saw him briefly in New York last month, that they have made quantitative tests on the changes induced by illness in the perceptual experiences of schizophrenics. Distant objects apparently seem to them much closer than they seem to normal people, so that the outside world is felt to be pressing in on them in a sinister and menacing way. It is typical of Freud that, in his theory of schizophrenia, which was based upon the diary of a German judge of his acquaintance, he completely ignored the frequent references to disquieting perceptual changes and concentrated exclusively on some vague hints that the judge may have had certain homosexual tendencies. How incredibly unscientific the old man could be!)

I have been asked to write a series of articles on methods for altering thoughts and behaviour by by-passing the conscious and rational self and working on human weaknesses and the psycho-physical machine, out of which the developed personality emerges and by which it is conditioned. It is a curious and depressing subject; for it is quite clear that a dictator who systematically made use of existing methods and subsidized research in their refinement could, by the use of drugs, sleep-teaching, hypnosis, subliminal projection and the latest advertising techniques based upon motivational research, establish a high degree of control over his subjects and made them positively enjoy their slavery (provided of course that the slavery could be combined with a standard of living high enough to satisfy physical needs).

I'm delighted to hear about the knighthood and hope that, by the time it comes, you will be able to feel as happy about it as I do.

Our love to you both.

Ever your affectionate,
Aldous

784 *Series of articles: published as a supplement to the paper* Newsday *and in book form as* Brave New World Revisited.

3276 Deronda Drive,
Los Angeles 28, Cal.
15 December, 1957

My dear Betty

Thank you for your letter. It looks as though the only thing one can say, in the circumstances, is that all's well, or at least can be made fairly well, that

---

785 *Huxley's article was called 'Postscript to a Misadventure'; the text follows, from a copy sent to Matthew Huxley.*

'When should one believe the experts? And anyhow who are the experts? And in what fields can experts be genuinely expert? In the field of scholarship, in the fields of technology and science, the answers to these questions are clear enough. All those persons who have systematically studied a subject are experts on that subject. Some of these experts are, of course, better than others. Not every doctor is a good doctor. There are chemists and physicists of average competence, and there are chemists and physicists of less than average and of much more than average competence. It is a matter of native ability, or the lack of it. All this is obvious enough. But when we pass from scholarship and science to the arts, the case is altered. Who are the experts here? And how reliable are those who claim to be experts?

'In the arts, it is obvious, there are two kinds of expert—the expert who knows how to practise an art, more or less effectively, and the expert who lacks the talent to practise an art himself, but who knows enough about the past and present practice of others to be able to pass judgments and give advice. In the first category we find the creators, good, bad and indifferent; in the second, the critics, the editors and the Professors of Dramatics and Creative Writing. Expertness in the second sense has never prevented the experts from making enormous mistakes about their own or other people's artistic productions. Coleridge, for example, was at moments a great poet and at all times a great critic; but his expertness in criticism did not prevent him from writing and (what is even more surprising) publishing some of the silliest verses ever composed in the English language.

> *"Why need I say, Louisa dear,*
> *How glad I am to see you here,*
> *A lovely convalescent,*
> *Risen from the bed of pain and fear*
> *And feverish heat incessant." Etc. etc.*

Or consider the case of another great poet and fine critic, Franz Grillparzer. Grillparzer declared that Weber's music ought to be banned by the police on the grounds that (of all things!) it was completely lacking in melody. It is clear, then, that in the field of the arts even the greatest experts are not to be believed unquestioningly.

'All this, I need hardly say, I have known for a very long time, and the knowledge should have preserved me from accepting at their face value the claims of the dramatic experts with whom, in my latest excursion into the world of the theatre, I have had to deal. Alas, in this case, as in so many others, mere knowledge was not enough. As St Paul so realistically pointed out, one generally knows quite well what one ought to do—and one then goes and does something else. Experts in the field of the drama are probably rather more fallible than experts in other artistic fields. This being so, one should never take

what they say too seriously, nor act too trustfully on their advice. In this particular case, a number of experts assured me that the fairly close adaptation which my collaborator and I had made of my novel, The Genius and the Goddess, *was too unlike a conventional play to be produced and should therefore be radically changed. Wisely, as I now see, I refused to take the advice of expert A, or the different and incompatible advice of expert B. Then, very unwisely, I allowed myself to be persuaded by expert C. I knew better, of course; but, not being a man of the theatre, I had begun to doubt my own judgment and to overestimate the competence of those who were supposed to know the ropes. Besides, the play was moving towards production, and the atmosphere was charged with that near-panic which play-production in an age of rising costs is always apt to generate. Weakening, I let myself be convinced. Expert C called in expert D and, hey presto, the play was reconstructed. Like the novel, the original adaptation was a story of the past set within the framework of a story of the present. Two old men re-evoked an adventure, at once ecstatic, tragical and grotesque, in which one of them had been involved half a lifetime earlier. Experts C and D assured me that the old men were against the rules of play-writing and would have to be eliminated; equally objectionable in their eyes were the more painful, grotesque and life-like elements of the main story. The operation was performed and everyone assured me that it had been wonderfully successful. The only trouble was that most of the psychological depth and half of its dramatic substance had been cut out of the play. For the next four months I wrote and re-wrote scenes in the vain hope of restoring to the emasculated play a little of the vitality which had been so skilfully drained out of it. It was one of those futile tasks which, like drawing water in a sieve, might have gone on forever. Actually, after four months, it was ended, very abruptly, by a disagreeable incident, which it is unnecessary for me to describe in detail. Suffice it to say that it involved the breach of two agreements, one written and one oral, and it ended in my dissociating myself from the management and from a play which, except for the dialogue and a part of the story, was no longer mine, but the experts'. It may turn out, of course, that the experts are right and that their play is better, or at least more commercial, than the original. Time will show. But, whatever may happen, I shall go on preferring my creation to theirs.*

'This story—a very commonplace one, as I am assured by those who know their Broadway—has several morals. First, even during the frenzies of production, the writer should keep his artistic head and retain what I may call (since "the courage of his convictions" is not the right phrase) the obstinacy of his intuitions. Second, he should be extremely sceptical of any claim to superior wisdom on the part of those who call themselves experts. So far as his own play is concerned, the writer's opinion is likely to be as good as, or better than, theirs. Third, if he wants to go on writing plays, let him have them produced in some place where costs are less exorbitantly high than they are on Broadway. There are two kinds of censorship today—the political censorship of heretical ideas imposed by totalitarian governments, and the economic censorship of anything that seems unlikely to appeal to a very large audience imposed by exorbitantly high costs. And exorbitantly high costs have another disadvantage. They create, in the minds of all concerned, the anxious sense of being embarked upon a very dangerous and deadly serious adventure, where humour and light-heartedness are as much out of place as they would be on a burning ship in the middle of the Pacific Ocean. A play should have something playful about it. But how can anyone feel playful about a hundred-thousand-dollar investment? In the grimness of these desperate theatrical gambles the amenities of life and even its common decencies are apt to go by the board.'

ends badly. Weissberger has advised strongly against sueing for damages, and I shall follow his advice. If the expense money can be extracted from these people, it will be a small triumph. If not, then it will be another loss that has to be written off. I have already had to write off four months of time, during which I might have earned several thousand dollars, but which was totally lost in the task of trying to repair the irreparable. As for an article— I wrote one and sent it East to be placed in some paper; but then, on second thoughts and after asking advice, decided against having it printed. I feel that silence and quick oblivion are to be preferred to publicity, controversy and the scoring of debating points. My motive for leaving the play at Philadelphia was disgust—the feeling that I didn't want to be associated any further with people who had broken their word and violated their written agreement. Writing articles and sueing for damages would be a kind of continuance of that association in negative terms, and I don't want to get involved even in that.

Meanwhile what a comfort it is to be doing some kind of useful and interesting work once more!

Hasta la vista.

Yours,
Aldous

786: TO DR HUMPHRY OSMOND

3276 Deronda Drive,
Los Angeles 28, Cal.
4 January, [1958]

Dear Humphry,
I should have answered your good letter long since, but have been horribly busy with accumulations of mail and a series of articles which I have engaged to do. The original idea was to write a series on the newer methods of mind control—through drugs, sleep teaching, Pavlovian brain washing and subliminal projection. But this seems too narrow, and I am reviewing all the methods of mind-changing and mind-moulding, including the conventional techniques of propaganda. Only in this way can one intelligently assess the potential dangers to individual liberty. I shall begin by discussing the impersonal forces pushing us towards increasing central control—the rise in population which renders the economic life of so many nations insecure and calls for increasing centralization and governmental interference, the elaboration of technology that calls for ever more elaborate organization and ever completer subordination of the individual to the group, the chronic threat of war that results in increasing regimentation. After which I shall discuss the available methods for influencing people, for 'engineering their

786 *Misdated 'January fourth* 1957'.

consent', which might be used by rulers for keeping their subjects in order and even loving their servitude. If you have any ideas on this theme, I shall be grateful for comments and suggestions. Meanwhile I have been reading a number of interesting, but depressing books—*The Hidden Persuaders*, *The Organization Man*, various accounts of Hitler's propaganda methods, Sargant on brainwashing and the summary of the Army's report on the indoctrination of American prisoners in Korea etc etc. If we refrain from blowing ourselves up, I suspect that these developments in chemical and psychological control of minds will turn out to be more important than techniques for harnessing atomic energy. Similarly, from the point of view of human well being, the so-called 'conquest of space' will mean much less to mankind than what may be termed its 'conquest by numbers'. By the time your Helen is fifty there will be five and a half billions of us.

I was recently looking through a new edition of Milne Bramwell's big book on hypnosis, just published by the Julian Press. Very interesting— particularly the descriptions of Wetterstrand's and Voisin's techniques of 'prolonged sleep'. These men would keep patients suffering from various kinds of mental and physical illnesses in hypnotic trance for days and even weeks at a time—feeding them while in trance and having them excrete at regular intervals under hypnotic suggestion. They obtained in this way some very remarkable cures. If you don't know the book or have not read Wetterstrand's original publications (of which I had only vaguely heard), do look into Bramwell's. The references to the subject in question can easily be found by consulting the index under 'Sleep, prolonged'. You might find useful hints for the treatment of some of your patients. My strange oriental friend, [Dr ——], used essentially similar methods; for he would put people with various types of mental trouble into his own kind of hypnotic sleep, induced by pressing on hypnogenic points, and leave them in that state for a day or two at a time. Meanwhile I saw in Philadelphia a young doctor, whom I had met two or three years ago in California. He has been experimenting with what in his hospital is called 'The French Cocktail'—a mixture of aspirin, chlorpromazine and phenergen compounded a year or so ago by some French physicians and used for producing a form of hibernation. Administered in large doses, the French cocktail reduces temperature to ninety-two and lowers metabolism. People are not unconscious, but very remote and unconcerned. Dr [Robert] Lynch (that is my young friend's name) had himself dosed with French cocktail during an attack of polio a year ago, and came out with flying colours. On Laura's and my suggestion he is trying the cocktail on a young doctor friend of his who has a horrible case of cancer of the lymphatic system and was given only six months to live by the experts. I argued that, since the cocktail greatly reduces the metabolic rate and since cancer cells require a great deal of nourishment and probably don't like cold, there might be a chance of the malignant cells dying or being checked in their growth, while the healthy cells survived the hibernation process. We also suggested that then he might try the effect of accompanying the chemical hibernation by constant hypnotic suggestions and sleep-teaching. It is all very unorthodox; but conceivably it might work. I heard from Lynch a week or two ago, and he was encouraged by the results obtained in the first two weeks of treatment. I shall be interested to hear how things go on. Meanwhile I wonder very much what effects the hibernation process would have on mental cases. I asked Lynch if there were any French reports on such cases, but he said he thought not. It might well be worth trying.

Love to Jane and the poetess, and all good wishes for 1958.

Yours,
Aldous

787: TO DR HUMPHRY OSMOND

3276 *Deronda Drive,*
Los Angeles 28, *Cal.*
11 *January,* [1958]

Dear Humphry,

Thank you for your long and very interesting letter—written, too, in the most wonderfully black ink, for which I was particularly thankful. Keep it up! What you say of [T.T.] Paterson's work on different kinds of authority interests me very much—more especially in relation to the articles I am now writing about the Enemies of Freedom. One of those enemies, quite clearly, is the over-organization made inevitable and indeed necessary by the complexities of modern production and modern government in very large societies, whose numbers are rapidly growing (with the result that conditions are never stable and that all plans have to be overhauled and replaced by other plans as the population rises). Is it possible to make the best of both worlds—the world of individual freedom and the world of high organization? Under existing conditions, it would seem to be impossible. But perhaps these more realistic conceptions of the nature of authority might somehow permit us to make the best of both worlds. If Paterson has published papers or books, I would be grateful to learn their titles. I can get the books—but the papers are harder to track down, so I'd be very grateful for copies, if he has any spares.

Your letter arrived almost simultaneously with one from D[uncan] Blewett of Regina, written on Commission for Study of Creative Imagination paper, and stating that Drs Osmond, [——] and Hoffer had suggested a meeting of the Commission in Los Angeles at some time in late February. Gerald had a duplicate of the same letter. This has taken both of us by surprise. Who is D. Blewett and what relation has he to the Commission? And,

787 *Misdated* '11 *January,* 1957'. *Paterson was the author of* Morale in War and Work (*London,* 1955). *Blewett, whom Huxley had not met, was acting as consulting psychologist to the Commission.*

secondly, is the Commission still in existence? I thought it had been decided last summer to dissolve the thing, as being practically non existent, or existent only in a Pickwickian sense. And finally what about [——]? [. . . .] A week or two ago, [——] sent a report on an attempted anti-alcoholism project to be set up under R[oman] C[atholic] auspices, together with notes on a session with an RC psychiatrist, who had reluctantly submitted to taking LSD25. Both of them seemed to me to be distressingly absurd, and the report on the session with the psychiatrist was uninhibitedly sectarian. Would it not be best to let [——] go his way within the Church? It is evidently there that he feels increasingly at home. It is evident, too, that his loyalty to the church makes him increasingly anxious to use LSD25 as an instrument for validating Catholic doctrines and for giving new life to Catholic symbols. Of such, perhaps, is the Kingdom of Heaven—but of such is *not* the kingdom of Scientific Research. My own feeling—and I think it is shared by Gerald—is that the commission in its present form should be allowed to die officially— it has been unofficially dead ever since its birth. Those of its members who are interested in scientific research, rather than in the validation of dogma, should try to meet from time to time and, in the intervals, should exchange information and views by letter. I will not answer Mr Blewett's letter until I hear your views on the subject. In any case I know that Gerald will be away from home in the month of February, so won't be able to attend any projected meetings.

Now, to return to your letter. Our summer plans call for an expedition far removed from Glacier National Park; for we have been invited by the Brazilian Government to spend some weeks down under. After which we might go on to Europe via Africa. I do hope that there will be a chance of seeing you before then. We expect to leave in May or June. Everything is still very vague.

As for the guide line for persons taking mescaline or LSD25—I have been too busy to work this out, but will try to do so before too long. I think the best way of doing the job would be to ask a series of questions. For example, 'Do you now understand what Blake meant when he said, "Gratitude is heaven itself"?' 'Eckhart defined God in operational terms as, "The denial of all denials". What is your feeling about this?' 'What does the word "isness" mean to you as you look at the world around you?' 'Samsara and Nirvana are one—the Absolute is present in every relative and particular event. Eternity manifests itself in every moment of time. How do you feel about these paradoxes?' 'In spite of all appearances to the contrary, God is love and things are somehow all right. What about it?' 'Cleave the wood and you will find me, lift the stone and I am there.' 'What a miracle this is! Drawing water and chopping wood.' 'The meanest flea as it is in God is superior to the highest angel as he is in himself.' It would be possible to put together several dozens of such short questions and statements, to be submitted to the subject in the course of his experience. If he set his mind to them, they might act as Zen koans and cause sudden openings into hitherto unglimpsed regions. It is certainly worth trying. If you think this approach is sound, I will go ahead with the plan.

Let me hear what you feel about the Commission and the advisability of a change in the present set up.

Yours,
Aldous

PS How well I understand what you say about writing! It seems so easy and it is so difficult. And, over and above the normal difficulties, I have to wrestle with the problem of not seeing properly—which makes all research and consulting of notes an enormous burden. Which is all, no doubt, ultimately All Right—but proximately pretty fatiguing!

788: TO DR HUMPHRY OSMOND

3276 *Deronda Dr.,*
Los Angeles 28, *Cal.*
2 *February,* 1958

Dear Humphry,

We had dinner yesterday evening with [——], and I found him, I must say, extremely genial and less extravagant than formerly; so please ignore what I wrote in my last letter about him. At the same time I still have doubts about the general validity of his methods. The specifically ritual approach may be all right in some cases, but it certainly won't do in all cases. Moreover both Laura and I felt, while we listened to [——]'s account of what he does, that he gives, knowingly or unknowingly, altogether too much suggestion. Again, this may be all right in some cases—but decidedly not in all. Something more permissive should be the general rule, I feel. As for the projected meeting—[——] tells me that he doesn't see much point in it. Gerald won't be available during February. Sidney Cohen doesn't object, but feels no very great enthusiasm. As for myself, I don't really know. I am anyhow merely a spectator, not a worker in the field, and can only make suggestions from the outside and on theoretical grounds—as I did in regard to giving post-hypnotic suggestions to the effect that LSD experiences be revived by purely psychological means and at will (a suggestion, incidentally, which I have been making to all and sundry for the last three years, and which nobody, to my knowledge, has yet acted upon—though everyone says, 'How interesting!') If we have a meeting of this highly Pickwickian organization, what (outside the pleasure and interest of meeting a number of intelligent people interested in the same sort of thing) will be gained? Probably it would be worth meeting for the meeting's sake. Would there be ulterior advantages? [——] tells me you think of setting up a Headquarters somewhere. But this means money, a secretary, a director. Couldn't the same results be attained more simply and cheaply by discussing matters at a meeting, or by corres-

pondence, and dividing up the work among the various experimenters? Sid
Cohen has an interesting project which he hopes to get financed—a project
that would test the efficacy of graded doses of LSD in affecting the performance of a group of professional artists. Another important project would
be to give the drug to a group carefully selected to include representatives of
the Sheldonian extremes and of the commoner specimens in the middle.
Yet another project should be to find out whether people belonging to
Galton's non-visualizing variety of human beings ever see visions under
average doses of LSD, whether they can be made to see visions by large
doses, and whether (as [——] insists they can) be made to see visions by suitable suggestions. Yet another project—the administration of LSD to terminal cancer cases, in the hope that it would make dying a more spiritual,
less strictly physiological process. I have been asked by the *Saturday
Evening Post* to do a piece on the ethical, religious and social implications
of psychopharmacology and I shall certainly make these suggestions in the
article, and any others you and anyone else in the field think should be made.
If you decide to come here, we can talk about this. Otherwise I'd be grateful
for any epistolary suggestions.

Let me know what you and Abe think about the advisability of a meeting.
I have no strong feelings one way or another—except that I should certainly
like to see you.

Meanwhile I am very busy on my articles on the fate of liberty in the
modern world. The problem is to keep it snappy, but not to oversimplify or
leave out too much.

Ever yours,
Aldous

789: TO SIR JULIAN HUXLEY

3276 Deronda Drive,
Los Angeles 28, Cal.
15 February, [1958]

Dearest J,

I was very happy to have your letter and to know that you were well again
and busy—too busy, as we all are. Why does one have to be? It seems absurd
and unnecessary; but there it is—one always is too busy. My own too-busy-
ness consists, at the moment, in work on a series of articles, to be published
later on, I suppose, in a book, on the problem of freedom in an age of overpopulation (leading to increased economic precariousness and increased
governmental intervention in all the affairs of life), of over-organization
(made necessary by technological progress and leading to increasing centralization of power and an increased demand for the kind of uniformity and tidiness that are so admirable in a work of art or a scientific theory but which,

789 *Misdated* 1956 *through a typing error.*

845

in human life, spell regimentation). To these impersonal forces to the prejudice of individual freedom must be added the new technologies for imposing the will of minorities—the improved techniques of propaganda (I am discussing Hitler's methods, Russian and Chinese brainwashing along Pavlovian lines, American advertising techniques as perfected by the Motivation Analysts, increase of suggestibility by drugs and the production, as in *Brave New World*, of contentment in a state of servitude, by means of chemically induced euphoria—all just round the corner, for pharmacology is now really getting into its stride and we are going to be deluged with tranquillizers, euphorics, hallucinogens, reducers of psychological resistance, all non-addictive and physiologically almost costless). And then there is sleep-teaching—a growing industry of clock-controlled phonographs and mind-changing records has sprung up here, based, as one of the manufacturers of these gadgets told me the other day, on the hypnopaedia of *Brave New World*. There is also subliminal projection—the giving of messages by means of visual or auditory stimuli too faint or too fast to be consciously recorded. It should be possible within a few years to abolish free will almost completely. The technical advances in these psychological, physiological and bio-chemical fields are probably far more important, from a human point of view, than the physical and engineering advances which have put sputniks into the heavens and will soon make possible a trip to the moon or even to Mars.

Our Brazilian trip is to begin in June. The Brazilian government has issued an invitation. (I hope it won't be too bankrupt by next summer to implement its good intentions! Its financial situation seems to be extraordinarily wobbly.) We are to be shown the sights in various parts of the country, and I suppose I will have to give some lectures. After which I expect we shall go to the Argentine for a brief stay with Victoria Ocampo, and then to Europe—the whole, I trust, at someone else's expense.

I hear of Francis from time to time (though not from him) through Humphry Osmond. He seems to be doing two things—an anthropological study of the asylum and a special study, in conjunction with an architect and the resident psychiatrists and psychologists, to determine what kind of buildings are most suitable for mentally ill patients. The standard mental hospital, with its big wards and endless corridors, is calculated to make any schizophrenic (with his grave distortions of perception) much worse. The corridors look to him like those nightmarish tunnels described in 'The Fall of the House of Usher', the wards seem like the Grand Central Station. Exactly what the mentally ill person needs in the way of a physical environment has yet to be determined. Humphry tells me that the hospitals designed by Dr Kilbride in the eighteen-fifties, at the height of what used to be called 'the moral treatment of the insane', were much superior to anything that has been built since. But, obviously, they can now be improved upon. It is a question of a collaboration between architect, psychiatrist, anthropologist, organizer and administrator.

Laura has gone away for the weekend with Ginny Pfeiffer and her two adopted children to do a little ski-ing in the San Bernardino Mountains. But if she were here, she would send her love to you both, as do I. Keep well.

Ever your affectionate

Aldous

PS. Poor Bill Kiskadden, at whose house we met to discuss population, has just been through the most frightful operation for an aneurysm of the aorta. They cut out four or five inches of the broken down aorta and replaced it with a plastic pipe. He has 'recovered'—but is still in a sadly diminished state, a mere ghost of himself. I hope he can return in time to something like normal, but confess I don't feel too confident.

790: TO DR HUMPHRY OSMOND

3276 *Deronda Drive,*
Los Angeles 28, *Cal.*
16 *February,* 1958

Dear Humphry,

Many thanks for your letter. We have not heard from [——] again, after our one meeting, and I don't know how to contact him—for he gave no address or phone number in [....] Perhaps he has now vanished. Who knows?

What you say about the applicability of his method to north-westerners is, I am sure, correct. I am just reaching the point in my articles, where I have to write about what might be done on behalf of liberty by educational methods—and I start with the need for telling people that every human individual is biologically unique and unlike all other individuals, and by pointing out that this fact has been systematically denied by many Behaviourists, sociologists etc. There are preposterous utterances in J. B. Watson's earlier writings, and even today you will find eminent psychologists, like B. F. Skinner of Harvard, solemnly coming out with statements that 'modern science' makes it clear that the achievement of the individual (as opposed to the group and the culture) approximates zero. How can people talk such rot? The reason, I suppose, is that they are inspired by a Will to Order, an urge for tidiness, which revolts against the wild and maddening diversity of men and likes to concentrate instead on the uniformities of culture. But the result, of course, is fatal—for it justifies the Organization Men and the dictators in satisfying their urge for tidiness by means of regimentation. (Regimentation in society is the equivalent of logic in a scientific paper or composition in a work of art. The Will to Order is admirable in matters involving the handling of symbols; in dealing with human beings,

---

790 *North-westerners: i.e., somatotonic and viscerotonic types (in the human-classification system of W. H. Sheldon); the method in question was considered unsuitable for cerebrotonics. The proposed meeting of the Commission for Study of Creative Imagination was not held.*

it can, when pushed too far, become tyranny. As usual, we have to find the happy mean, and as usual this is much easier said than done.)

One of the things that should be read to a person under LSD is Blake's *Marriage of Heaven and Hell,* including the extraordinary 'Memorable Fancies' that precede and follow the 'Proverbs of Hell'. Read the thing through and see if you don't agree. I'm sure that if this were put on a tape it would be found extremely enlightening by the subject. Incidentally, I found on one of the occasions I took LSD that listening to records of poetry or of religious utterances is valuable in many ways. There is first of all the same strange experience which one gets from listening to music—the sense that, though the tempo remains unaltered, the piece endures for ages. The poetry or the religious utterances take on this same quasi-eternal quality. Another interesting point—one seems to penetrate the inner significance of what is being read, the meaning for oneself, more completely than in ordinary circumstances. Thus, the cultured melancholy resignation of Matthew Arnold, which I ordinarily like and feel at home with, is felt under LSD to be far too negative—unrealistically so.

I have just had a letter from Blewett suggesting a date in early May for a meeting. Alternately one in October. I don't expect to be here in October, but shall almost certainly be here in May.

My love to the family.

Yours,
Aldous

PS You mention GAP reports on indoctrination. Could you lend me these for a week or two—or tell me where to get them and their exact titles.

791: TO MRS ELLEN HUXLEY

3276 Deronda Dr.,
Los Angeles 28, California
29 March, 1958

My dear Ellen,

Thank you for your long good letter. I won't answer as fully as you wrote; for I hope to see you all quite soon, as I have been asked by the Fund for the Republic to fly East for a meeting on April 22nd. (I may also hang around for my arbitration proceedings in relation to Courtney Burr's failure to pay expenses last year.) Anyhow, expect me then.

I have been horribly busy on articles—I hope to some effect—and am sick and tired of this kind of writing; but at the same time find it frustratingly difficult to find the right story line for my projected Utopian novel. Let's hope it will present itself soon, so that I can really get to work. We saw Francis Thompson yesterday and the film the day before. It goes very well now, I think. I suggested a film of Old Masters—seen first with a normal lens, then treated to the whole bag of tricks. 'Mona Lisa', 'Philip IV' on horseback, 'La

Grande Jatte', Ingres' 'Odalisques'. The stunt could be very amusing and at the same time instructive, as illustrating the passage from representational to non-representational.

What a bore about Trev's reading! What *is* one to do about these teachers who won't teach and ignore the claims of the brighter children on whom the nation's future depends, in favour of the claims of the sub-normal? The danger, of course, is that in panic we shall start to copy the Russians in their worst aspects as well as their best. I suppose you can't do anything for Trev now, while he is still at public school. He wd be a freak if he cd read better than the others. Let's hope he can catch up during the summer.

Laura thinks she knows where more of those books on imagination games can be found. We will send them when we get hold of them.

My love to you all. A bientôt.

> *Your affectionate,*
> *Aldous*

792: TO ROBERT CRAFT

> *3276 Deronda Dr.,*
> *L.A. 28, Cal.*
> *10 June, 1958*

Dear Bob,

Laura and I spent a whole evening trying to translate Gesualdo's nonsense—but were finally frustrated. This stuff is beyond translation and beneath contempt. I have written a little note which may serve in lieu of translations and as an explanation for their absence. I hope this will do. My own view is that there is really no point in translating this sort of stuff, inasmuch as Gesualdo never set a poem, only the individual words and phrases.

Give our love to Vera and Igor and try to prevent the latter from doing too much too soon. I will send you a copy of the articles on liberty as soon as I receive a supply of them from the East.

> *Yours,*
> *Aldous*

793: TO DR HUMPHRY OSMOND

> *3276 Deronda Dr.,*
> *Los Angeles 28, Cal.*
> *22 June, 1958*

My dear Humphry,

What a long time since I heard from you—or you, alas, from me! Time,

---

792 *Huxley enclosed a note on Gesualdo and specimens of the discarded translations.*
793 *Laura Huxley's production of* The Gioconda Smile *was staged at the Beverly Hills Playhouse. The theatre programme bore the legend* 'BEWARE! *Subliminal Projection Is Used on This Program'—the latter part of the warning being in very small print.*

as one advances in life, seems to become jet propelled and the number of things that have to be done in these abbreviated minutes and hours remains constant or even increases.

For the past weeks Laura has been engaged in producing my play, *The Gioconda Smile*—producing it through thick and thin, and in spite of a succession of catastrophes. Like the Generals of earlier days who used to have horses shot under them in their decisive battles, she has had about six complete casts shot under her in the course of her campaign—only to come up with better replacements, so that now we have a first-rate collection of English actors, highly competent and thoroughly trained in provincial repertory, West End and Broadway productions and now in movies and TV. So that I hope and think we shall have an excellent performance when the play opens next Friday. I wish you could be here to see it.

Meanwhile I have been very busy. After finishing off the articles on the enemies of freedom (of which I am sending you, rather belatedly as I myself was very late in receiving the printed version, a copy), I have been working at my phantasy about a society in which serious efforts are made to realize human potentialities. I don't know yet if I have a satisfactory fable, or how much of a fable will be necessary, or, on the other hand, how reluctant people will be to read material which isn't straight story telling, but is yet (I hope) rather interesting. The locale of the story is a hypothetical island between Ceylon and Sumatra—independent in spite of colonialism, where the process of turning an old Shivaite-cum-Mahayana-Buddhist society into something combining the best features of East and West was inaugurated in the eighteen-forties by a Scottish surgeon, (modelled on James Esdaile) who operates on the then Raja under 'magnetic anaesthesia', becomes his friend and acts as his collaborator in initiating the necessary changes, which are carried on by successors of the Scotchman and the king, during the succeeding three generations. It is interesting to try to imagine what could be done to create a good society, dedicated to eliciting all the latent powers and gifts of individuals, by consciously and deliberately adopting and combining desirable features from different cultures, Indian, modern Western, Polynesian, Chinese—interesting but, as you can guess, exceedingly difficult.

We are supposed to leave for Brazil on July 21st, and I shall really have to start thinking in a practical way about our plans. Hitherto neither of us has done anything—we merely wait for things to happen. And perhaps that is the best policy; for it generally seems to turn out (in Samuel Butler's words) that 'as luck would have it, Providence is on our side'. I am writing to Francis asking him to give me a few introductions.

I met an interesting young Texan MD the other day, who has been using hypnosis to supplement his conventional doctoring—with striking results, he told me, in many serious heart conditions, also in Bergers Disease, in which hypnotic suggestion will often make possible a restoration of circulation to the blood-starved extremities. He has also used Wetterstrand's technique of simply keeping people under hypnosis for considerable periods at a stretch, thus giving the vis medicatrix naturae a chance to do its work without interference from the agitated Ego. This same young man also described the results of having inadvertently taken nearly two grams of mescaline—inability to breathe, internal hemorrhages. A very unpleasant situation indeed. He is reading a paper on LSD at the AMA meeting in San Francisco—his name, T. T. Peck.

Our love to you both.

Yours,
Aldous

794: TO MATTHEW AND ELLEN HUXLEY

3276 Deronda Drive,
Los Angeles 28, Cal.
22 June, 1958

Dearest Ellen and Matthew,

No news from you for a long time. I hope all goes well. Here Laura's production is in its final lap, with the opening next Friday. There have been endless contretemps, including, as a last straw, the collapse of the publicity woman with, of all things, chickenpox. But the performance promises to be good and I hope and think all will turn out satisfactorily.

Meanwhile I have been very busy, feeling my way into the fantasy about a society in which a serious effort is made to realize human potentialities. I can't yet tell how it will turn out, but the only thing is to go ahead, one step at a time, and then see what happens, and how, on the basis of what has happened, to go further.

Brazilian plans have changed to this extent, that we are to fly directly from here to Mexico City and from Mexico City to Lima and so across the Andes to Rio. This means that we shall not be passing through New York and so shan't, alas, have a chance of seeing you before our departure. This being so, I think that you, Matthew, should work out some scheme for the children's educational endowment within the next couple of weeks. I wish one could form the remotest notion of what is likely to happen economically. Are the prophets of doom correct in saying that there is going to be a serious slump—more serious than any previous slump owing to the fantastic scale of the national, local, industrial and personal indebtedness of the USA? Or are the prophets of bigger and better booms in the right? The first alternative would mean deflation, the second continuing inflation. An acquaintance of ours who is an economic analyst reported the consensus of a recent meeting of economic analysts in LA. The general opinion was that the stockmarket was in a very precarious position and everybody should get out of it as quickly as possible. Since when the market has been steadily rising! Rising in the teeth of facts, logic and commonsense. But maybe facts, logic and commonsense have nothing to do with these mysterious matters. I confess myself completely unable to understand economics as they exist today. So if you have a better idea than the insurance plan, let me have it.

I met an interesting young Texan doctor the other day, who has been using hypnosis in conjunction with conventional medicine—straight suggestion combined with probing into the psychological antecedents and concomitants of illnesses. He told me that he has had some spectacular successes with heart cases. Also with Berger's disease, in which suggestion under hypnosis permits the re-establishment of circulation in the areas blocked off by chronic spasm of the vessels. Another interesting man in the same field is Dr Marmer, the chief anaesth[es]iologist of the Cedars of Lebanon Hospital here. He is now using hypnosis regularly, either alone or in conjunction with chemicals—which can be administered in much smaller and less toxic doses. He has used straight hypnosis successfully in operations on lung cancers and on the heart—neither of which, I gather, had been attempted before under hypnoanaesthesia. I asked him if the orthodox MD's objected to his heretical methods, and he told me that his position was secure, because he was a first-rate conventional anaesth[es]iologist, and his use of unconventional methods could not therefore be put down to ignorance or incompetence in the accepted field. I gather, incidentally, that the AMA is to recommend that, henceforward, all students should be told something about hypnosis in their medical courses.

And talking of heart trouble—poor Bill Kiskadden has had another coronary and is in hospital again. One doesn't know what to wish or hope. Recovery and a diminished life of advancing blindness and increasing dependence on Peggy [. . .]? or death? What a misery!

Are you giving Trev special reading lessons? I hope so—and that it may be possible for him, in consequence, to get into the Quaker School.

Our love to you all.

Ever your affectionate,
Aldous

795: TO DR HUMPHRY OSMOND

3276 *Deronda Dr.,*
L.A. 28, *Cal.*
6 *July,* 1958

Dear Humphry,
Many thanks for your note and earlier letter. I am glad you liked the articles—which will come out, with some additions and changes, in the autumn, in book form—and gladder still to learn that you are all glad about the blessed event on the horizon. It is sad that poor Helen will have to be disappointed about the horsey; but no doubt she will be reconciled in due course to the biological facts, whatever they may be.

[Elsa Hall's] address is

> 1129 1/2 N. Genesee
> Los Angeles
> Cal.

She was never much good for me; but perhaps I am a 'bad station', so far as mediums are concerned. I remember how well she did for you.

We have been seeing again a young MD whom we last met in Philadelphia in November 1957, when we urged him to try something wildly unorthodox on a fellow intern at the hospital who had been given 3 months to live, because of a cancer of the lymphatic system (resistant to radiation) which had grown to the size of a football in his chest. We suggested combining semi-hibernation (with the 'French Cocktail'—chlorpromazine, phenacetin, aspirin and demarol) with intensive hypnosis, talking to the cells. The results have been extraordinary—complete disappearance of the tumour, acceptance of the young man as a full-time intern at the U of C hospital at Berkeley, complete recovery of weight, strength, vitality. Our young friend, Dr. Lynch, has got a number of older MD's (*très sérieux*) at Columbia, Phila and Rochester to take an interest and try to duplicate the procedure. I wonder very much if a similar combination of part-hibernation (the young man was alert enough to work during the treatment—albeit slowly, as tho' with thyroid deficiency) with intensive hypnosis might not be useful in certain mental diseases and also in infections, perhaps even in some chronic degenerative diseases.

My love to Jane and the poetess.

> *Yours,*
> *Aldous*

796: TO DR ALBERT HOFMANN

> *Gran Hotel Bolivar, Lima*
> *3 August, 1958*

Dear Dr. Hofmann,

Your letter of July 16th reached me just as I was setting out for South America, and I am writing now from Peru (the land of a most unsatisfactory and dangerous mind-changing drug—coca—still consumed in great quantities by the Indians, mainly, I am told, to suppress the pains of hunger, only too common in the high Andes).

What you say about psillocybin [psilocybin] interests me very much, and I hope that I may have an opportunity of learning more about this new door into the Other World of the mind while I am in Europe this autumn.

---

796 *Huxley did not attend the Psychopharmacological Congress, and his first meeting with Hofmann occurred only in 1961. It was Hofmann who had first synthesized lysergic acid.*

Do you intend to be present at the pharmacological Congress in Rome in September? It is possible that I may be there as an interested observer and learner—but I am not yet certain if I can manage it. The address in Italy which will always find me (after August 25th or thereabouts) is

c/o Felice Archera
31 Corso Abruzzi
Torino.

If we do not meet in Rome, I will try to visit you in Switzerland.

Yours very truly,
Aldous Huxley

797: TO SIR JULIAN AND LADY HUXLEY

Copacabana Palace Hotel,
Rio de Janeiro
11 *August,* 1958

Dearest J. and J.

Here we are in this very odd country, which wd be altogether delightful if it weren't for the fact that I have to give so many interviews and attend official lunches etc—talking when I wd like to be listening. After a lecture at the Foreign Office on Wednesday we are being taken on a trip to the new Capital, Brasilia, and to the picturesque towns of Minas Gerais, thence to S. Paulo—after which we shall fly (about the 23rd or so) to Lisbon and thence to Italy where c/o F. Archera, 31 Corso Abruzzi, Torino, will always find us. What are your plans? I will adapt mine to yours, as I don't want to be in London when you're not there.

Peru was very extraordinary and I had a chance to see Cuzco, Machu Picchu and various other Inca ruins—wonderful, but the altitude is trying when one comes up suddenly from the coast; and oh, how cold it is at 12,000 feet with no heating anywhere.

These are very amiable people—gentle and good-humoured. Temperate pagans as opposed to intemperate puritans—the Americans. Very little drinking or smoking here—but evidently plenty of fun in bed and little tension or frustration.

Love from us both.

Affectionately,
Aldous

798: TO SIR JULIAN AND LADY HUXLEY

Care of F. Archera,
31 Corso Abruzzi, Torino
[9] *September,* 1958

Dearest Julian and Juliette,

I received your letter and telegram almost simultaneously. I wish I could be present at Mr Eaton's luncheon and the Humanist meeting, but unfortunately we are already involved here—first a brief flight to Sicily with some friends and then, at the beginning of October, the celebration here in Torino of Laura's father's eightieth birthday, which is too important an event to be ignored. On October third there is to be this three-way conversation, under Ed Murrow's guidance, between Nehru, Thomas Dewey and myself —why, or what about I cannot imagine. But since the thing is technically feasible, it has to be done, I suppose, and will be done, so far as I am concerned, at a studio here in Torino. After which I hope to come directly to London, if that suits you. Laura has some things to do and people to see in this neighbourhood, and will follow later, at some date not yet fixed. I wish I could have conformed my plans to yours—but unfortunately I didn't know yours until too late.

The Italian papers are full of Gronchi's visit to Brazil, and I am amused to read of his trip with the fanatically enthusiastic Kubitschek into the red dust of Brasilia's present—the golden dream of its hypothetical future. And meanwhile, on the other side of the world—what? Are they going to blow us all up?

Our love to you both.

Ever your affectionate,
Aldous

799: TO MATTHEW AND ELLEN HUXLEY

Rembrandt Hotel,
London, S.W.7
20 October, 1958

Dearest Ellen and Matthew,

It was good to get your news in Ellen's most welcome letter. I'm so glad the children are getting on well at school—and you too, Ellen. Maybe one of these days I may go back to school for a little—but only to a school where there are no examinations and no mathematics! I think it might be rather fun.

Laura arrives tomorrow, and we shall be at the Rembrandt until, I suppose, the end of the month. Meanwhile I have been revolving in the social whirl—seeing everybody from Bertie Russell and E M Forster to Noële Neveux and Yvonne Hamilton (ex-Franchetti), and doing everything from visiting the Zoo to visiting Windsor Castle and the Provost of Eton. London looks curiously old-fashioned after São Paulo and Rio—not a skyscraper to be seen and amazingly little re-building, (and such rebuilding as there is very staid and unpretentious). [Other] old friends live up to form —[——] is infatuated with a Japanese boy; [——] is being cited as a co-respondent by the man whom he cited as a co-respondent last year, the lady having (by force of habit, I suppose) injudiciously slept with her former husband after her second marriage; [——] has just gone round the world with a Greek painter (married, with 5 children) and her husband, [——], has become an alcoholic etc. etc.

I am on a diet and taking mysterious German drops 3 times a day—with good results, I think. Let us hope that the gall stone will melt away, without resort to surgery.

Eileen's conference is too early for me. I shall be lecturing in Italy in mid-November. Alas.

My love to you all.

Ever your affectionate,
Aldous

800: TO OLIVIA DE HAULLEVILLE

C/o F. Archera,
31 Corso Abruzzi, Torino
22 November, 1958

My dear Olivia,

Laura, who is up to her eyes in packing and last-minute business, has asked me to write and ask if you ever picked up the package left for you with the porter of the Hotel Lutétia [in Paris]. It contained a box of chocolates and some money—24,500 francs, I think. I hope very much that you claimed it. We leave Torino tomorrow for Milano, and on Monday night for Rome. Please send a line to Laura at the Hotel Flora in Rome to let her know if all is in order.

We spent a week in Venice—in my case in bed with influenza—and have been a few days here in Turin where I gave a lecture last night. Meanwhile I hope all goes well with you and the pornographic book trade and oriental music. Love from us both.

Ever yours affectionately,
Aldous

801: TO SIR JULIAN AND LADY HUXLEY

3276 Deronda Dr.,
L.A. 28, Cal.
14 December, 1958

Dearest Juliette and Julian,

A brief report on recent happenings. We didn't stop in New York, as I was reluctant to face the cold there after 2 bouts of flu. Felt very low on arrival and decided to have some tests made, so went to hospital for 3 days where they gave me the works. The main trouble seems to be the chronic

800 *Olivia de Haulleville was employed as secretary at the Olympia Press and as a theatrical impresario—hence the allusions in Huxley's last paragraph.*
801 *The sputum test proved negative for tuberculosis.*

emphysema in the right lung, aggravated by the flu. I am taking the pressure breathing treatments which helped me so much in the past. Careful X-rays, taken from many angles with the aid of dyes and barium, made it clear that Rau's diagnosis was wrong. There is no stone in the bile duct, and the shadow he saw is a calcified cyst in the liver—quite harmless. If there are stones, they are in the gall bladder which is 'non-visualizing'—one can't get dye into it, however hard one tries. As the gall bladder was non-visualizing ten years ago, when I had it X-rayed with a dye, it is clear that the stones must have been there for a very long time and that they aren't giving trouble. Anyhow liver function tests show the organ to be virtually 100% perfect. The weight loss is probably due to the emphysema—tho' conceivably there might be TB, (which won't be known for 6 weeks, when the guinea pig infected with my sputum is sacrificed). No indication of cancer, I'm glad to say, and all well with heart, kidneys and pancreas.

[. . . .]

Best love from us both and, a little prematurely, a very happy Christmas and New Year.

Ever your affectionate,
Aldous

802: TO DR HUMPHRY OSMOND

3276 Deronda Dr.,
L.A. 28, Cal.
16 December, 1958

Dear Humphry,

Many thanks for your good letter. I wish I had been able to be present at the parapsychology conference; but unfortunately I had to give four lectures in Italy in the last ten days of November and couldn't get away in time. The lectures were preceded and interrupted by two attacks of flu, the first of which kept me in bed for a week in Venice and the second, which came on after my third lecture, kept me in bed for four days in Rome—after which I had to creep down to Naples and there, hardly able to stand, deliver my final lecture—in Italian, to make matters a little worse. We got back here ten days ago, much delayed by head winds over the Atlantic and the US, and I am only now beginning to emerge from my state of weakness. In the meanwhile I spent three days in hospital having tests and X-rays to determine whether the diagnosis made in London by Julian's pet [German] doctor, Leo Rau, to the effect that I had a large stone in the bile duct, was correct. Careful examination, I'm glad to say, revealed that it was not [. . . .]

It is pleasant to be back here in the sun, able to do some honest work for a change, and free from the swarms of interviewers who plagued me during all our journey, both in South America and Europe. I was simultaneously touched and appalled to discover that I am now, as the result of having been around for so many years, a kind of historical monument, which sightseers will come quite a long way to inspect, and which radio and press reporters find newsworthy. In Brazil it was as though the Leaning Tower of Pisa had just come to town, wherever I blew in; and even in Italy I found myself talking to full houses in large theatres. It was really very odd and embarrassing.

London was very agreeable, and I saw vast numbers of people from Bertie Russell to Rose Macaulay (who expired two days later, poor thing), and from Tom Eliot (who is now curiously dull—as a result, perhaps, of being, at last, happy in his second marriage) to Grey Walter, who told of fascinating experiments with hopeless lunatics, in whose brains electrodes had been stuck, and who can turn on the battery in their pocket and pass, in the twinkling of an eye, from deepest depression to a broad grin. How unimaginative I was in *Brave New World*!

I'm glad to hear that your schizo research goes forward satisfactorily. How widely is it being accepted now? I was disturbed to hear our curious friend, Dr Barbara Brown, the pharmacologist, airily tell us that the whole adrenolutin-adrenochrome idea had been disproved two years ago and that some group at the National Institute of Health had now disposed of all the claims that schizophrenia might have a chemical factor in it.

There is to be a psycho-pharmacological meeting at San Francisco from Jan 25th to 27th, and they have asked me to speak at the dinner meeting on the twenty-sixth. The programme sounds as though it might be interesting. Will you be there? I hope so. It would be good to have a glimpse of you. Meanwhile I hope all goes well with Jane, in spite of the prairie winter.

Best wishes to you all for Christmas and the New Year.

Yours,
Aldous

803: TO CASS CANFIELD

3276 *Deronda, L.A. 28, Cal.*
4 *January,* 1959

Dear Cass,

Many thanks for the *New Yorker* album, which certainly manages to keep up a very high standard of funniness. I always admire the consistency of their achievement in a very difficult field—the comic.

I note what you say about a combined edition of the *Doors of P.* and *Heaven and Hell*. Let us wait then until the moment seems ripe.

Meanwhile wd you please send the statement of my 1958 earnings to Langton and Schorner, 33 West 42nd St. NYC, so that they may start work on my income tax. (How lovely it wd be if, as in Russia, the high-earners paid only 13% in income tax and the masses footed all the bills with the equivalent, in high prices for cheaply produced food and necessities, of an enormous sales tax! No nonsense, there, about social justice. An aristocratic society with plenty of incentive for those at the top. In time, I suspect, all fully technified societies will adopt the Russian solution. Meanwhile, however, please send the figures to my accountants!)

I work on my novel and on the lectures I am to give at the U of C., starting next month. Two whole-time jobs.

All good wishes for 1959.

Yours
Aldous

804: TO SIR JULIAN HUXLEY

3276 *Deronda Drive,*
Los Angeles 28, *Cal.*
5 *January,* 1959

Dearest J.,

Many thanks for your letter. I have written to [Robert] Richman that I can't take part in the symposium, as I shall be too busy with my book and my lectures at the University of California. The trouble with all these talks about culture is that they distract one from doing the things that make a culture worth having and eat up the time and energy that should go into one's work. As for what should be done about science (above all in the form of technology) and the humanities, I don't know. I am now reading Professor Jacques Ellul's book, published in 54, *La Technique*—the best thing, in spite of a rather obscure style, that I have ever read on the subject. The picture he draws of Technique developing, in every field of human activity—techniques of production, techniques of economics, techniques of politics, techniques of mind-manipulation—according to the laws of their own nature and not at all according to the laws of human nature, is extremely depressing. It may be that the only satisfactory solution (from the human point of view) is to accept the inevitability of the technification of everything, with its consequent impoverishment of social relations, and to impart to children and young people, along with their technical education, a psychological education in the art of being spontaneous, of becoming de-conditioned, of passing at will from the cultural world of concepts and the technical world of the cult of efficiency in all things, into the personal world of direct experience of events outside us and events within. It would be a question of tempering technique, ever more perfect, and ever more all-embracing and totalitarian, with a kind of Zen training in spontaneity, in de-conditioning, in becoming open. In any case, do read Ellul's book. He covers the whole field much more thoroughly, I feel, than Mumford does.

Here, meanwhile, all goes well, except that Laura has a bit of a cold, but nothing to worry about. I was hideously tired after my flu, but am now fully recovered, working hard and eating normally—no dietary restrictions except the ones imposed by simple nutritional rules—and regaining weight. I have a notion that all my troubles last autumn were the consequences partly of extreme fatigue due to travelling and too much talking, and partly to a smouldering recrudescence of my old chronic bronchitis. This last came to a head in Italy with influenza, whose symptoms were localized in a congestion of the right lung. Convalescence was delayed by the fact that I had to lecture, and after the third lecture I had another brief flare up of temperature and lung congestion. Now, thanks to the admirable Bennett Valve, which clears up chronic bronchial trouble by making the patient breathe oxygen under slight positive pressure, I am back to normal. The tests for liver function were quite specific. [. . . .]

Our best love to you both.

Ever your affectionate,
Aldous

805: TO MATTHEW HUXLEY

3276 Deronda Dr.,
Los Angeles 28, California
8 January, 1959

Dearest M.,

Many thanks for the tea, which is excellent—tho' I still think that the Jackson blend has a richer taste. (It certainly surpasses the other English Earl Greys, such as Fortnum's, and Ridgeways.) But very good in its own right.

I hope our parcel for the family arrived safely. It was sent off rather belatedly, so I suppose can't have reached you in time for Christmas—but I trust it has got to you by now.

I am working on my lectures for Santa Barbara. My modest theme is 'The Human Situation' and I shall begin with the biological foundations— the state of the planet, population, heredity in relation to environment. Then go on to the great determiner of modern civilization—technique in every field of human activity and its effects on the social and political order. Then pass to the individual and his potentialities, and what he might perhaps do about their realization. It is an impossibly large project—but worth undertaking, even inadequately, as an antidote to academic specialization and fragmentation.

Our love to you all.

Your affectionate,
A.

805 *In a note to Ian Parsons on 4 January, Huxley said of the Santa Barbara lectures, 'I am not attempting to write them out, but am feverishly collecting and organizing materials, so that I may be able to deliver them* extempore, *but with some measure of sense'.*

3276 Deronda Drive,
Los Angeles 28, *Cal.*
9 *January,* 1959

Dearest M,

Your letter and Ellen's made me very sad. But probably what you have decided is the best course that can be taken in this unhappy situation. I know very well what you mean when you talk about dust and aridity and a hard shell that makes communication in or out extremely difficult. It was something that made the first part of our marriage difficult at times; but Coccola was very patient and in the long run I learned to get through the shell and let the dust be irrigated. Unfortunately, when you were a child, I was predominantly in the dust-crust stage, and so, I am afraid, must have been—indeed, know that I was—a pretty bad father.

And now what is to be done? [. . . .]

Meanwhile would it be possible for you to get away from the office for a few days and fly out here? The tourist flights are relatively cheap and I will treat you to the ticket. So do come here if you can. We shall be away for three days in San Francisco from Jan 25th. Otherwise expect to be here permanently—except that after Feb 9th I shall have to go for a couple of nights each week to Santa Barbara for my lectures at the new U of C there. We would love to see you—and Ellen too, if she can come later on, when you or someone else can be with the children. It is quiet on the hill here and, in spite of smog, the sun still shines—a statement that carries more than a merely meteorological meaning.

I shall say nothing to Mère or Rose about all this, unless and until you want me to do so.

Laura sends her love, as do I.

Ever your affectionate,
Aldous

3276 Deronda Drive,
Los Angeles 28, *Cal.*
9 *January,* 1959

My dear Eileen,

Very belatedly let me wish you a happy New Year, with health for yourself and successes for parapsychological research. I had hoped to see you in New York on our way back from Europe; but I was feeling so decrepit as the result of influenza, complicated by the necessity of giving four lectures in French and Italian, that we decided to fly straight through to California without risking the New York winter and another week or two of life in hotels. It was a wise decision; for I am now over my troubles and functioning normally. But still I was very sorry to have missed the chance to seeing you and my grandchildren, and Matthew and Ellen.

And now about Matthew and Ellen—I have just heard the saddening news that they are parting, at least for the time being. Each of them has written; so I understand the story in its main outlines—the friction of dissimilar temperaments—Ellen spontaneous and adventurous, Matthew with his tendency to be rigid, rather censorious, a bit pedantic [. . . .] But the details and the nature of the crisis which brought the trouble to a head are obscure to me. And obscurer still are the prognosis of the case and the treatment, if there is any useful treatment, that should be advised. Ellen tells me that you discussed the whole thing with her and that you had been in touch with Maria in regard to what was happening. I should be grateful for any help you can give me, any advice you can offer as to the best way of helping them. I have written to Matthew (his letter came yesterday), suggesting that he get leave from his office and fly out here for a brief holiday. And perhaps, later on, Ellen can come out too, provided someone can be found to look after the children in her absence. [. . . .]

I shall be most grateful, dear Eileen, for any information you can give me and for any advice as to what should be done, and what can be done, in this predicament. The news of the rupture has left me very sad; but sadness does no good and the problem now is to discover the best way of mending or ending, of changing circumstances within the marriage or outside it.

Yours affectionately,
Aldous

808: TO FR THOMAS MERTON

3276 *Deronda Drive,*
Los Angeles 28, *Cal.*
10 *January,* 1959

Dear Father Merton,

Thank you for your letter. The problems you raise are interesting and difficult, and their solution must be sought on the practical and factual level. A great deal of work has now been done on mescaline and lysergic acid, both by researchers and clinicians using the drugs therapeutically in such conditions as alcoholism and assorted neuroses. (One group now working on alcoholism in British Columbia, incidentally, is using lysergic acid within a religious, specifically Catholic, frame of reference, and achieving remarkable results, largely by getting patients to realize that the universe is profoundly different

808 *Fr Merton had written to Huxley on* 27 *November,* 1958, *raising questions about the validity of drug-induced mystical experience and about the distinction between the mystical and the aesthetic, his letter having been prompted by Huxley's article* 'Drugs That Shape Men's Minds' *in the* Saturday Evening Post.

from what, on their ordinary, conditioned level of experience, it had seemed to be.) Statistically the results of all this experimentation are roughly as follows. About seventy per cent of those who take the drug have a positive experience; the others have a negative experience, which may be really infernal. (A great many of the states experienced by the desert fathers were negative. See the thousands of pictures of the Temptations of St Anthony.) All agree that the experience is profoundly significant. One finds again and again, in the reports written by subjects after the event, the statement that 'this is the most wonderful experience I have ever had' and 'I feel that my life will never be quite the same again'. Among the positive experiences a certain proportion, on the first occasion of taking the drug, are purely aesthetic—transfiguration of the outer world so that it is seen as the young Wordsworth saw it and later described it in the 'Ode on the Intimations of Immortality in Childhood': a universe of inconceivable beauty in which all things are full of life and charged with an obscure but immensely important meaning. Those who are congenitally good visualizers tend to see visions with the eyes closed, or even, projected upon the screen of the external world, with the eyes open. The nature of these visions is often paradisal and the descriptions of them remind one irresistibly of the description of the New Jerusalem in the Apocalypse or the Eden of Ezekiel, or the various paradises of other religions. Finally there are those whose experience seems to be much more than aesthetic and may be labeled as pre-mystical or even, I believe, mystical. In the course of the last five years I have taken mescalin twice and lysergic acid three or four times. My first experience was mainly aesthetic. Later experiences were of another nature and helped me to understand many of the obscure utterances to be found in the writings of the mystics, Christian and Oriental. An unspeakable sense of gratitude for the privilege of being born into this universe. ('Gratitude is heaven itself', says Blake—and I know now exactly what he was talking about.) A transcendence of the ordinary subject-object relationship. A transcendence of the fear of death. A sense of solidarity with the world and its spiritual principle and the conviction that, in spite of pain, evil and all the rest, everything is somehow all right. (One understands such phrases as, 'Yea, though He slay me, yet will I trust in Him' and the great utterance, I can't quote it exactly, of Julian of Norwich.) Finally, an understanding, not intellectual, but in some sort total, an understanding with the entire organism, of the affirmation that God is Love. The experiences are transient, of course; but the memory of them, and the inchoate revivals of them which tend to recur spontaneously or during meditation, continue to exercise a profound effect upon one's mind. There seems to be no evidence in the published literature that the drug is habit forming or that it creates a craving for repetition. There is a feeling—I speak from personal experience and from word-of-mouth reports given me by others—that the experience is so transcendently important that it is in no circumstances a thing to be entered upon light-heartedly or for enjoyment. (In some respects, it is not enjoyable; for it entails a temporary death of the ego, a going-beyond.) Those who desire to make use of this 'gratuitous grace', to co-operate with it, tend to do so, not by repeating the experiment at frequent intervals, but by trying to open themselves up, in a state of alert passivity, to the transcendent 'isness', to use Eckhart's phrase, which they have known and, in some sort, *been*. Theoretically, there exists a danger that subjects would have a craving for constant repetition of the chemically induced experience. In practice this craving doesn't seem to manifest itself. A repetition every year, or every six months, is felt, most often, to be the desirable regimen.

A friend of mine, saved from alcoholism, during the last fatal phases of the disease, by a spontaneous theophany, which changed his life as completely as St Paul's was changed by his theophany on the road to Damascus, has taken lysergic acid two or three times and affirms that his experience under the drug is identical with the spontaneous experience which changed his life—the only difference being that the spontaneous experience did not last so long as the chemically induced one. There is, obviously, a field here for serious and reverent experimentation.

With all good wishes, I am

Yours very sincerely,
Aldous Huxley

809: TO MRS EILEEN J. GARRETT

3276 Deronda Dr.,
L.A. 28, Cal.
8 February, 1959

Dear Eileen,

I have written to Matthew urging him again to come out here, meeting me at Santa Barbara—but have not yet heard from him. From what Ellen has written and said on the phone, I doubt very much if she will go back to the *status quo ante*. Probably the best that can be done is to salvage a friendly relationship between E and M, and to see that the children get as good a psychological break as possible. It is a sad business. I will write you again after I see Matthew—that is if he comes out to California, which I hope he will. Meanwhile look after yourself, dear Eileen, and get well. Laura sends her love.

Ever yours affectionately,
Aldous

PS We witnessed an interesting demonstration yesterday by a man called [———], who has trained his daughter and niece to see without their eyes. If the phenomenon is genuine—and there seems to be no obvious trickery (tho' one never knows, of course)—he has done something very remarkable. He is going to be given an opportunity this spring to train some blind children. It will be interesting to see how far he succeeds.

3276 Deronda Dr.,
Los Angeles 28, Cal.
8 February, 1959

Chère Victoria,

Je viens de lire votre texte qui me semble très bien adapté pour un spectacle de sons et lumières, mais bien difficilement réalisable au cinéma. Un film doit être ou une histoire dramatique où prennent part un nombre limité de personnages—une histoire qui se déroule selon sa propre logique passionnelle. Ou bien il doit être un documentaire c'est à dire une compte rendu cinématographique de faits où les passions et les personnalités humaines n'entrent pas. Votre texte deviendrait au cinéma un documentaire plein de personnages qui paraissent et disparaissent—ou bien un drame trop diffus, sans cette logique des passions qui fait que la fin dérive inévitablement du commencement. Il me semble que la chose à faire serait d'isoler un épisode de la vie de San Martin (vies-biographies cinématographiques sont terriblement difficiles à faire) et d'en tirer une histoire avec commencement, milieu et fin. La biographie et le rôle historique de San Martin seraient suggérés ou très brièvement décrits dans quelque scène préliminaire qui a lieu vers la fin de la carrière du grand homme. L'histoire dramatique et passionnelle se raconterait ensuite—en forme de 'flash-back'. De cette façon on pourrait éviter les inconvénients de la biographie filmée, tout en donnant quelques indications (nécessaires pour un public non-Argentin) sur le rôle historique du personnage—pour se concentrer sur un épisode dramatique susceptible

810 TRANSLATION:—'*I have just read your script, which seems to me very well adapted for a* son et lumière *spectacle, but pretty difficult to achieve in terms of cinema. A film should either be a dramatic story in which a limited number of personages take part—a story which develops in accordance with its own passional logic—or else it should be a documentary, that is to say a filmed record of events, where human passions and personalities do not enter. Your script would become, in motion pictures, a documentary full of personages who appear and disappear—or even a too diffuse drama, without that logic of the passions which makes the end derive inevitably from the beginning. It seems to me that the thing to do would be to isolate an episode from the life of San Martin (life biographies in the movies are terribly hard to do) and to extract from it a story with a beginning, middle and end. The biography and the historic role of San Martin would be suggested or very briefly described in some preliminary scene which takes place near the end of the great man's career. The dramatic and passional story would be told next—in the form of a flashback. In this way one could avoid the inconveniences of the filmed biography while giving some indications (necessary for a non-Argentinian public) about the historical role of the character—in order to concentrate on a dramatic episode susceptible of becoming a good subject of drama. If this drama occurs in the neighbourhood of the house of the Carob-tree, so much the better!*

'*I saw the Stravinskys the other evening and find them in good form. Affectionately. . . .*'

de devenir un bon sujet de drame. Si ce drame se passe aux alentours de la maison du Caroubier, tant mieux!

J'ai vu les Stravinsky l'autre soir et les trouve en bonne forme.

Affectueusement,

Aldous

811: †TO GEORGE SELDES

3276 *Deronda Drive,*
L.A. 28, Cal.
13 *February,* 1959

Dear Mr. Seldes,

Thank you for your letter and for the honour you have done me by including so many quotations from my books. Unfortunately I have written such an unconscionable number of books in the course of a long literary life that I can't remember where the two quotations without a source actually come from. I'm sorry to be so unhelpful.

It might be interesting to have a short section in your book devoted to what may be called negative quotations—utterances of pure nonsense, pollyanna uplift, anti-intelligence and anti-liberty—all drawn from the speeches or writings of the eminent. E.g. passages in praise of the executioner as the main pillar of civilized society from Joseph de Maistre's *Soirées de St. Petersbourg.* Passages from Louis Veuillot's *Parfums de Rome,* holding up the pre-1870 papal government as the best in the world. Passages on infant damnation from St. Augustine and the Calvinists. Passages on Jesus as a salesman from Bruce Barton. And so forth. A few pages of these wd constitute a stimulating Chamber of Horrors—or, divided up, might serve as preface to the various sections of your book.

Sincerely
Aldous Huxley

812: TO MATTHEW HUXLEY

3276 *Deronda Drive,*
Los Angeles 28, Cal.
15 *April,* 1959

Dearest Matthew,

I returned from Santa Barbara today to find your letter awaiting me. What you say in it and the way you say it make me feel that you are indeed,

811 *Seldes, who was editing* The Great Quotations, *had sent Huxley proof-sheets of his section in the book. He had met Huxley in the Sanary period, but Huxley's letter, surprisingly, does not refer to this.*

812 *Prize: the Award of Merit Medal for the Novel, presented to Huxley at the Ceremonial of the American Academy and the National Institute of Arts and Letters.*

866

as you say, making progress, and that something better is beginning to emerge from the sad confusion of the situation. To become capable of love —this is, of course, about two thirds of the battle; the other third is becoming capable of the intelligence that endows the love with effectiveness in an obscure and complicated and largely loveless world. It is not enough merely to know, and it is not enough merely to love; there must be knowledge-love and charity-understanding or prajna-karuna, in the language of Buddhism— wisdom-compassion. People have been saying this for the last several thousand years; but one has to make the discovery oneself, starting from scratch, and to find what old F M Alexander called 'the means whereby', without which good intentions merely pave hell and the idealist remains an ineffectual, self-destructive and other-destructive 'end-gainer'. It has taken me the greater part of a lifetime to begin to discover the immemorially obvious and to try, at least, to act upon the discovery. I hope it will take you only half a lifetime and that you will emerge from this excruciatingly educative ordeal with enough love and understanding to transfigure the second half.

I have Progoff's book on the *Cloud*, but have not yet had time to read it. I will make the time now; for I am most interested to see what psychiatric use he makes of this most extraordinary document. The *Cloud* and some of the Sermons of Eckhart are the most valuable things, I would say, that have come down to us from the Middle Ages—blessedly free from the rigmaroles of dogma, superstition, absurd allegorizing and pedantic rationalizing which make most mediaeval literature so unprofitable and indeed so utterly unreadable. The thirteenth-century German and the fourteenth-century Englishman contrive, in some almost miraculous way, to be all but timeless.

Not much news here. I have been very busy. These Santa Barbara lectures entail a lot of work, and I have had to do a good deal of gibbering on the side—so much, indeed, that, last week, I almost lost my voice. However, everybody seems to like it, and if I were to accept all the invitations that come pouring in, I should be talking non-stop for the next two years. I shall be glad when the talking is over for the summer and I can get down to work on my novel. Meanwhile I hope we shall get through these next months without serious international trouble. I see from an article in the *Bulletin of the Atomic Scientists* that there are now at least twelve countries capable of producing H bombs within five years or even sooner, if they put on a crash programme. Seeing that the last thing that any of the three nuclear powers wants is to have little countries undermining their position by having H bombs, this may mean that there will be a chance for an agreement on the stopping of nuclear tests—which in turn may be an opening wedge for dis- armament. Or is this too optimistic? Meanwhile, have you read Professor Wright Mills's *The Causes of World War Three?* It is excellent. At any rate it seems so to me, inasmuch as it develops in greater detail the fundamental notions which I set forth, thirteen years ago, in *Science, Liberty and Peace.*

We expect to come to New York somewhere about the middle of May (the presentation of my prize takes place on the twentieth) and look forward to seeing you then. Laura sends her love.

Ever your affectionate,

Aldous

813: TO DR HUMPHRY OSMOND

3276 *Deronda Drive,*
Los Angeles 28, *Cal.*
6 *May,* 1959

Dear Humphry,

Many thanks for your letter, which sums up only too correctly the problem that confronts Matthew and Ellen. Inhabitants of different and largely incommensurable worlds *can* live happily together—but only on condition that each recognizes the fact that the other's world is different and has just as much right to exist and be lived in as his own. Once the other's right to live where he or she is temperamentally and, no doubt, physiologically predestined to live is recognized, there can be something very stimulating and liberating about the experience of being joined in a loving relationship with somebody whose universe is radically unlike one's own. It becomes possible for each of the partners to enlarge his own private universe by taking this stand vicariously, through empathy and intelligence, within the other's territory and trying to see what reality looks like from that other vantage point. I remember a very touching passage in one of my grandfather's letters about his own obtuseness—the obtuseness of an immensely intelligent man of the highest integrity—in relation to his wife's insights, immediate, non-rational and almost infallible, into human character. Jack Sprat could eat no fat, his wife could eat no lean—which is precisely why it is possible for them to constitute a symbiotic organism superior to each of its components. But, alas, what is possible goes all too often unrealized and, instead of federating their two worlds, the temperamental aliens settle down to a cold war.

I am glad that work goes forward so well and look forward to reading your next official report on it. Meanwhile what are the drugs you mention? Are they these psychic energizers of which there was much talk at the psycho-pharmacological conference at San Francisco two months ago, and of which I have been hearing more recently from Howard Fabing and our brilliant pharmacological friend, Dr Barbara Brown? There must be something rather disturbing, to people brought up in the traditional Christian fold, in the spectacle of an overwhelming conviction of sin being completely dissipated in a few days by a course of pills. The spiritual problems of the

813 *Drugs: Osmond's latest letter had contained a reference to the leuco compounds as a subject of current study.*

future will revolve around the question: how are we to prevent the intense healthy-mindedness which is now within reach of all from turning into complacency, bumptiousness and philistinism? It may be found necessary to alternate euphorics and energizers with depressants and sense-of-sin-producers.

I have finished the first half of my course of lectures at the U of C at Santa Barbara. It dealt with 'The Human Situation' in its large-scale manifestations—as influenced by destruction of natural resources, population growth, advancing technicization of everything, the suicidal traditions of nationalism etc. Next semester I shall talk about the Human Situation as manifested on the small-scale level—shall talk about the make-up of the individual, the relations between datum and concept, the nature of art, the actualization of latent potentialities etc. In the interval, during the coming summer, I hope to do some work on my Utopian novel, which keeps opening up as I work upon it, so that it threatens to expand into something indefinitely vast—a prospect all the more serious since I don't yet have a very satisfactory story line to support the necessary exposition. However, like Mr Micawber, I confidently expect that Something will Turn Up.

We go to New York on the seventeenth of this month for ten days or two weeks, then shall be back here more or less indefinitely—unless, maybe, we slip away for a little to some mountain or seaside retreat for a little while. I wish there were a chance of seeing you.

Give my love to Jane and the young ladies.

Ever yours,
Aldous

Yes—6 years since we made that first experiment. 'O Death in Life, the days that are no more'—and yet also O life in death.

814: TO MATTHEW HUXLEY

3276 *Deronda Drive,*
Los Angeles 28, Cal.
1 *June,* 1959

Dearest M.,

Not much to report from this end, beyond a safe arrival, the answering of a mass of accumulated mail, two days work on my book and now another two days making notes for tomorrow's lecture—my last, thank goodness, for the time being. After which I hope to get down seriously and continuously to the book, for the fable of which I seem at last to have had some ideas that seem workable—I hope they will turn out to be that way in practice.

I wish our last evening had been less sad; but sad it was. All that can be done is to try to make the best of a bad job. I think the idea of calling in a lawyer to draw up some kind of a written agreement is good. Once it has been drawn up, you will both know where you stand. Ellen will know where she stands in relation to the future, to the over-all situation. And you will have the knowledge that she knows, will have a framework within which you both can function, and will be able within that framework to play the day-to-day situations by ear, so to speak, without having to spend energy, and create friction, by having to insist on the over-all situation and future contingencies. It will mean, I hope, that you will be able to meet with one another on the same level and with the same preoccupation—the day-to-day well being of the children within a long-range scheme which has been worked out by a third party and which both of you accept.

This will mean, I hope, that both of you will be able to follow the gospel injunction, 'Judge not that ye be not judged'—one of the most important and significant sayings in the whole corpus of Jesus' teaching. You will not have to judge Ellen for her reluctance to think of the future and the over-all picture, and she will not have to judge you for what she regards as an undue preoccupation with things which, to a person of her temperament, seem merely mechanical, organizational, abstract. Because of a lack of an objectively determined framework within which to function, both of you have been judging one another (each on the basis of his or her temperamental postulates) and both have been judged in return. Each of you judges in a different way; but in both cases the judging has been there and has been the cause of continuing and increasing misunderstanding and unhappiness. As in all human situations, there is a paradox here. 'Judge not'—they have all insisted upon it, from Gautama and Jesus to Blake and his 'mutual forgiveness of each vice'. And yet, at the same time, choose what seems to be right, reasonable, decent. In other words, judge but don't judge—judge in the sense of discriminating, but don't judge in the sense of condemning. Even where there seems to be a moral evil, don't judge in a condemnatory way. This is stressed in a remarkable passage from the testament of St Catherine of Siena, taken down by someone who was present at her deathbed. 'If one would attain to purity of mind' (the state aimed at by the author of the *Cloud of Unknowing*) 'it is necessary to abstain altogether from any judgment on one's neighbour. With great force she said, "For no reason whatever should one judge the actions of creatures or their motives. Even when we see that it is an actual sin, we ought not to pass judgment on it, but have holy and sincere compassion."' This applies, *a fortiori*, to matters which are not moral evils. Huxleys especially have a tendency not to suffer fools gladly—and also to regard as fools people who are merely different from themselves in temperament and habits. It is difficult for Huxleys to remember that other people have as much right to their habits and temperament as Huxleys have to theirs, and that democracy, the right of self-determination, begins on the level of personal relations, and that co-operation, based upon mutual discrimination and mutual not-judging, is the only satisfactory solution to the problem of hereditary and acquired differences. So do remember this family vice of too much judging. Remem-

870

bering it, you may catch yourself in the act of succumbing and realize the dangers you are running into—the danger of being judged in return, the danger of building up a habit of intolerance, of over-criticism, of proselytism about matters for which there is no reason, ethical, utilitarian or intellectual, to be a crusader. And realizing these dangers, you will be able to enter into more satisfactory relationships.

Write to me from time to time to let me know how you are faring.

Ever your affectionate,
Aldous

15: †TO GEORGES NEVEUX

3276 Deronda Drive,
Los Angeles 28, California
8 June, 1959

Cher Georges,

Betty Wendel m'a rapporté de vos nouvelles—entre autres la bonne nouvelle que vous repensez à ma malheureuse pièce. Il y a deux ou trois semaines j'ai fait lire la pièce à haute voix par de bons acteurs—la pièce, c'est à dire, dans sa forme primitive, telle que vous l'avez. L'effet était assez bon—mais il y avait des longueurs. Je viens de couper l'équivalent d'à peu près 15 pages—dont 5 ou 6 sont tirées des scènes où figurent les deux vieillards. Si cela n'allège pas assez, on pourrait sans doute faire d'autres opérations çà et là sur le texte.

815 TRANSLATION:—'*Betty Wendel has conveyed your news—including the good news that you are reconsidering my unlucky play. Two or three weeks ago I had the play read aloud by some good actors—the play, I mean, in its early form, as you have it. The effect was rather good—but there are dull stretches. I have just cut out the equivalent of about fifteen pages—of which five or six are extracted from scenes in which the two old men take part. If that does not lighten it enough, one could no doubt perform other operations here and there on the text.*

'*As for the old men—I notice that in the play they do not give the effect which they gave in the novel, where they gave weight to the characters of the central drama and revealed certain profundities. I do not really know how to remedy this. A thought came to me yesterday. Instead of two old men, one could have only one—old Rivers—who would be telling the story to a young girl (perhaps a student at his university—a blue-stocking but, beneath a too-serious or even cynical exterior, a romantic). This young girl either could be some student interested in the dead Maartens, about whom she has some false notions that Rivers wants to correct, or else, if you like, she could be the daughter of Ruth—who does not die in the final accident. This daughter comes to Rivers to learn the truth about her grandmother and grandfather. I don't know whether these ideas are good, and in any case I haven't the time to play with. What do you think of them? Love to Jeanne and Noële. . . .*'

Neveux's projected French adaptation of The Genius and the Goddess *was still in the planning stages when Huxley died in 1963.*

Quant aux vieillards—je me rends compte qu'ils ne donnent pas dans la pièce l'effet qu'ils ont donné dans le roman, où ils donnaient du poids aux personnages du drame central et faisaient apparaître des profondeurs. Je ne sais pas trop bien comment y remédier. Une idée m'est venue hier. Au lieu de deux vieillards, on pourrait en n'avoir qu'un—le vieux Rivers—qui raconterait l'histoire à une jeune fille (étudiante peut-être à son université— bas-bleu mais romanesque sous un extérieur trop 'sérieux' ou même cynique). Cette jeune fille pourrait être ou une étudiante quelconque qui s'intéresse au feu Maartens, sur qui elle a des notions fausses que Rivers veut corriger. Ou, si l'on veut, elle pourrait être la fille de Ruth—qui ne meurt pas dans l'acci- dent final. Cette fille vient à Rivers pour apprendre la vérité sur sa grand- mère et son grand-père. Je ne sais pas si ces idées sont bonnes et en tout cas n'ai pas le temps de jouer avec. Qu'en pensez-vous?

Love à Jeanne et Noële.

Aldous

816: TO DR HUMPHRY OSMOND

3276 *Deronda Drive,*
Los Angeles, Cal.
20 *June,* 1959

Dear Humphry,

Thank you for your letter. I hope you and the family have by this time arrived safely in my native town. (I was born in Godalming at a house called 'Laleham' now used, I believe, as a sort of overflow for boys, for whom there is no room in the regular Charterhouse boarding houses. One of my early recollections is being taken to church in Godalming and disgracing myself by vomiting during the sermon—a precocious expression, no doubt, of anti-clericalism. In those days what is now the Headmaster's house belonged to a rich widow, Mrs. Ewart, who had a semi-imbecile son who was a King's Messenger, and who wore a gold bangle from which depended several dozen teeth—the early sheddings of her nieces and nephews. Every Thursday, if I remember rightly, the Muffin Man came round, ringing a dinner bell, like the character in *The Hunting of the Snark.* He had a long white beard and wore a flat topped military cap, on which he carried a large tray, on which, under a white cloth, were the freshly made muffins and crumpets. And of course the meat was delivered in an elegant little box on wheels with the butcher's boy perched on a high seat at the front end of the box, driving a very high-spirited horse. And once a steam roller came and rolled the road outside our gate—a truly glorious object with a spinning fly-wheel and a tall chimney. It exhaled a deliciously thrilling smell of hot oil, and on the front end of the boiler was a golden unicorn.)

You are quite right to be interested in the potentialities of 'straight' perception. The Bates Method people have records of extraordinary feats when eyes and minds are thoroughly relaxed—seeing the moons of Jupiter, reading microscopic type at a distance at which the apparent height of a letter would be less than the diameter of a single retinal rod. The academic testers of perceptual power have consistently neglected to prepare the sense organs and the mind for their best performance by getting them first into a suitable state of relaxation. I think it would be worth your while to do some work with a well trained Bates teacher. If you ever come here, you should have a talk with Mrs Corbett, my teacher, who has had an enormous experience and probably knows more about eyes-and-mind in their functioning than any ophthalmologist or professional psychologist.

I wrote to Julian that you were coming to England. He has been in Wales, but I think must be due back in London about now. His address there is 31 Pond St, London N.W.3.

I have just had a week in bed with the flu, but am on the way up now and hope to be clothed and in my right mind in another day or two. Love to Jane.

Ever yours,
Aldous

PS I suspect that one might pass from ordinary SP to ESP by steadily pushing the Bates procedure to the point where it wd be physically impossible to see in the ordinary way—always suggesting confidence in the subject that he wd go on succeeding.

817: TO MRS ANNE STRICK

3276 Deronda, L.A. 28, Cal.
6 August, 1959

Dear Mrs. Strick,

Thank you for your letter. I don't have much to add to what I said after the film was over—namely that the sequences, tho' individually good, add up to something one-sided and that the 'change of heart' at the end seemed inadequate because in no way prepared for in the earlier sequences, where no alternative to mindless horror was ever shown. Mindlessness and horror are all right provided that they be shown in relationship with the mind and the good will which keep the world from collapsing. Consistent mindlessness, such as one gets in Tennessee Williams' plays, becomes a great bore and is also completely untrue to life. (A Williams play about mindlessness cd not be put on the stage except by a lot of highly intelligent people, displaying all the qualities of perseverance, conscientiousness and collaboration so totally absent in Williams's picture of the world.) Why intensely mindful people shd choose to portray only mindlessness is a psychological enigma, which I have never been able to unriddle to my satisfaction. In

817 *Film: Joseph Strick's* Savage Eye, *narrated by Ben Maddow.*

doing so, they deny themselves, make the survival of humanity as a species completely incomprehensible (we survive solely because many of us are not mindless), and narrow the scope of art as a commentary on life.

Sincerely,
Aldous Huxley

818: TO MARGARET ISHERWOOD

3276 Deronda, L.A. 28, Cal.
12 August, 1959

Dear Margaret,

Thank you for your letter. I am now more or less as good as new, thank goodness—had a really providential escape. As for visionary and mystical experience—I think they are different, but that the first is apt to lead into the second. In my first experiment with mescalin I had a merely aesthetic visionary experience: but since then, with LSD and again with mescalin, I have gone *beyond vision* into many of the experiences described in Eastern and Western literature—the transcendence of the subject-object relationship, the sense of solidarity with all the world so that one actually knows by experience what 'God is love' means: the sense that, in spite of death and suffering, everything is somehow and ultimately All Right (tho' he slay me, yet will I trust in him); the sense of boundless gratitude at being privileged to inhabit this universe. (Blake says, 'Gratitude is heaven itself'— it used to be an incomprehensible phrase: now I know precisely what he was talking about.)

[Hugh] Fausset is quite wrong—speaking on *a priori* moralistic grounds and not out of direct experience. This matter of drugs and mystical experience was discussed years ago by Bergson in *The Two Sources* . . . apropos of Wm James and laughing gas. That a chemical can help people to get out of their own light is distressing to many people; but it happens to be a fact. That the experience is a 'gratuitous grace', neither necessary nor sufficient for salvation, is certain. Ethical and cognitive effort is needed if the experiencer is to go forward from his one-shot experience to permanent enlightenment.

Yours
Aldous

PS Gratuitous graces are not necessary or sufficient—but they can be very helpful if we choose to let them help us.
PPS Subud is simply a technique for reproducing the quaking of the early Quakers—a release via the muscles. Very good in many cases.

818 *Providential escape: despite his limited eyesight, Huxley sometimes took solitary night walks. On one of these he stumbled from the path and fell down an embankment. He was painfully but not seriously injured.*

3276 *Deronda Drive,*
L.A. 28, Cal.
20 *August,* 1959

Dearest M,

I was happy to get your letter and to know that all goes reasonably well with you. The new apartment sounds interesting. When will you be able to move into it? We had a brief note from Ellen, from Woods Hole, not very informative. I take it that the children are well and presume that they will soon be returning to the shades of Brooklyn and school. [. . . .] Julian and Juliette will be coming to the US in late September; you will probably see them in NY as they pause on their way to Chicago.

Not much news here. I am more or less completely over the effects of my fall. It gave my back a bad shaking up and caused a good deal of pain for two or three weeks. But this was so trifling in comparison to what I might have suffered, if I hadn't fallen in the most perfect way imaginable and at the most perfect place, that I can only think of the accident with the most profound thankfulness. If ever guardian angels were on hand, it was on that night.

I am working away on my Utopian novel [*Island*], wrestling with the problem of getting an enormous amount of diversified material into the book without becoming merely expository or didactic. It may be that the job is one which cannot be accomplished with complete success. In point of fact, it hasn't been accomplished in the past. For most Utopian books have been exceedingly didactic and expository. I am trying to lighten up the exposition by putting it into dialogue form, which I make as lively as possible. But meanwhile I am always haunted by the feeling that, if only I had enough talent, I could somehow poetize and dramatize all the intellectual material

---

819 *Utopian novel: in a letter of 4 January to Victoria Ocampo, Huxley had quoted Gide's remark, 'C'est avec les mauvais sentiments qu'on fait de bons romans' (Out of one's wrong opinions good novels are made), and had observed that his own problem at the moment was to write a good novel on a potentially practical theme. Chatterley business: the alleged non-payment to the Lawrence estate of American royalties on certain unexpurgated editions of the novel* Lady Chatterley's Lover. *But it appears that the New American Library, which held rights to an expurgated edition, was paying royalties on its unexpurgated one as well; and on 6 August, the Grove Press, which had waged a legal battle against suppression of the book, had issued a statement saying that it had paid an advance royalty on the first 4,166 copies of its own edition (size unspecified). Various other publishers seem to have been paying nothing. Actually the unexpurgated work was not protected by American copyright. Huxley, hoping that it might be, dispatched a letter of enquiry on 25 August to Laurence Pollinger, the representative of the estate. That letter is not extant, but Pollinger's reply of 3 September indicates that steps were being taken, in the absence of copyright, to apply moral pressure for a guarantee of royalties. The matter was eventually settled to the satisfaction of the estate through an agreement between the New American Library and the Grove Press.*

and create a work which would be simultaneously funny, tragic, lyrical and profound. Alas, I don't possess the necessary talent, and so shall have to be content with something that falls considerably short of the impossible ideal. And in a few days I shall have to turn my attention from the novel to next autumn's lectures at Santa Barbara. The course will deal with the human situation on the individual level, rather than on the macroscopic socio-biological level of last spring. I haven't yet worked out the precise subject matter of each lecture—in fact the whole project is still exceedingly vague in my mind. But I hope that in two or three weeks of intensive work I may be able to lay out an orderly plan and marshal the relevant information.

The *Chatterley* business is certainly pretty stinking. I will write to Pollinger and find out what he is doing and intends to do. The case, it seems to me, is one for the Society of Authors in conjunction with the Writers Guild in this country. Authors in their corporate and professional capacity should intervene in this sort of case, which concerns them all. This would be much better than a suit brought by a single individual or firm. Whether the Guild or the Society will act, I don't know. As organizations, they are apt to be a bit supine. But I will write to Hersey, as you suggest.

As for the number of copies sent to the US when the book was pub-lished—I can say nothing. All the business part of the operation was per-formed by Pino Orioli in Florence. Pino is long since dead and I would guess that his books and records have been destroyed—though perhaps they still exist somewhere in Italy. But how to discover if they do?

[. . . .]

Ever your affectionate,

A.

820: TO JOHN HERSEY

3276 *Deronda Drive,*
Los Angeles 28, Cal.
25 *August,* 1959

Dear Mr Hersey,

I have taken the liberty of writing to you directly in regard to a matter, about which, both as an old friend of D. H. Lawrence and as a practising writer, I feel very strongly. I refer to the recent publication in this country of the unexpurgated edition of *Lady Chatterley's Lover* by the Grove Press. From documents recently sent me I have learned the following facts:

a) The unexpurgated version of *Lady Chatterley* was issued by the Grove

820 *This letter tacitly and mistakenly assumed that* Lady Chatterley's Lover *(unexpurgated version) was in copyright in the United States. The novel being in the public domain, the alleged piracy had not occurred. The position of the Lawrence estate was that, since the novel ought to be in copyright, because it ought never to have been banned, the publishers ought to act* as if *the novel were in copyright.*

Press against the express wishes of the legal representative of the Lawrence estate (Laurence Pollinger, 18 Maddox Street, London W1).

b) Grove Press entered into no preliminary contract with the estate.

c) After the book had been out for some little time, Grove Press submitted a form of contract to the estate in the hope, evidently, of legitimizing a flagrant act of literary piracy. This contract was completely unacceptable to the estate, its royalty scale being absurdly inadequate.

In these circumstances, would it not be a proper thing for the Authors' League to take official cognizance of the affair, determine the facts and (if they are as damning as the documents seem to prove) officially and publicly censure Grove Press and perhaps warn all its members against having dealings with so unscrupulous a firm (as members of the Screen Writers' Guild are periodically warned against TV and motion picture producers who try to break the established rules).

> *Yours sincerely,*
> *Aldous Huxley*

821: TO SIR JULIAN HUXLEY

> 3276 *Deronda Drive,*
> *L.A.* 28, *Cal.*
> 3 *September,* 1959

Dearest J,

Forgive me for having left your previous letter so long unanswered, and thank you at the same time for your second letter which arrived today. I had a nasty fall about five weeks ago, escaped without any serious injury —only a badly jolted back which was very painful for some time, but is now virtually normal again. I was incredibly lucky to have got off so lightly; but the result has been a considerable delay in my work and a neglect of even important correspondence. Hence my unconscionably long silence.

Laura has just written to Juliette (seeing that I had neglected for so long to write to you) about December plans. There had been vague talk of our going to Santa Fe; but I have appointments coming up here which will make this impossible. So we shall be on the spot at the time you specify, which is Christmas week. So we will buy some artificial snow and make Deronda Drive look as much as possible like Dingley Dell. But there is a problem of space. The house, as you will remember, is too small to accommodate you both. But this time Laura will not be able to move down to Ginny Pfeiffer's studio, as that will be in use for some or all of the time. There is, however, a good and fairly reasonable hotel within a short distance, at the foot of the hill. So shall we reserve you a room there from the nineteenth onwards? I'm sorry we can't arrange matters so that you can be in the house, even under the rather uncomfortable conditions of your previous visit; but it just can't be worked out this time. But I think you will be comfortable and quiet at the hotel, and within easy range of us—which is more than can be said of most places in this strange town, whose geometry is governed by the non-Euclidean axiom that no point is less than ten miles from any other point.

I don't know anything about Monterey College, except that, if I remember rightly, they once asked me to speak there, and I couldn't do it. It's a nice part of the world, with Carmel very close, Big Sur not far and the groves of coastal redwoods within a couple of hours' drive.

I am working like mad, partly on my book and mainly, now, on my lectures for the upcoming semester at Santa Barbara—lectures which will continue, each week, until about the time you get to California. A new feature of the Santa Barbara landscape this autumn will be Robert Hutchins, who has moved the entire Fund for the Republic out to SB and is planning to set up his Platonic Academy among the gardens of Montecito—that is, if the local tycoons will provide the necessary dough. We are also to have a new Chancellor—Samuel Gould, lately President of Antioch, a very capable man, I would judge from a couple of brief encounters.

Best love to you both.

Ever your affectionate,

A.

822: TO E. W. TEDLOCK, JR

3276 *Deronda Drive,*
L.A. 28, Cal.
24 *September,* 1959

Dear Mr. Tedlock,

I don't remember much of significance in regard to Frieda's Californian visits—merely that she and Angie used to come to dine with my first wife and myself, and we used to spend pleasant evenings with them in their rented houses or apartments.

I have recently received from Mrs. Gordon Crotch (the 'Auntie' who lived at Vence, where Lawrence died) a typescript in which she records her memories of Frieda in the period immediately after DHL's death. It is quite an interesting little piece, and I am wondering if you could use it in some way which wd be of some profit to poor old Auntie who is over 80, infirm and almost penniless in England. I have provided some financial help in the past—she was living out here until last year—but can't do much more at present. If she cd earn something by her memoirs it wd be good both for the old woman's morale and her economic situation. (The Frieda piece is a chapter from a book of memoirs, unread by me but containing, I gather, a great deal of material on Norman Douglas, who knew her well and confided

822 *To the editor of Frieda Lawrence's* Memoirs and Correspondence (*New York*, 1964); *q.v., p.* 335*n*.

878

in her extensively—and Norman's confidences must have constituted an ear-full!)

If you know of any literary journal which might print some of these things and pay her even a little for them, it would be a charity towards Auntie—and maybe a mild scoop for the magazine.

Auntie's address is

Mrs. Gordon Crotch
Percy House
Isleworth
Middlesex, England.

Meanwhile let me know if you wd like to see the piece on Frieda.

Yours sincerely,
Aldous Huxley

PS One of the most curious facts about Frieda was her extreme helplessness when left alone to cope with a practical situation. She seemed such a powerful Valkyrie—but, as I found out when she came to London after L's death and had to deal with business and stay by herself in a hotel, she was amazingly incapable and, under her emphatic and sometimes truculent façade, deeply afraid. She had relied *totally* on Lawrence, and felt completely lost until she found another man to support her.

823: TO DR HUMPHRY OSMOND

3276 Deronda Dr.,
L.A. 28, Cal.
15 October, 1959

My dear Humphry,

Many thanks for your letter of I don't like to think how many weeks ago. I shall be interested to see the paper when it comes out, and to hear meanwhile of any further advances.

The radio announced blizzards in Sask[atchewan], the other day—hard to believe here, where we have a heat-wave with 94° temperatures and a continuing drought of the most alarming nature.

I am kept very busy with lectures at Santa Barbara, reading for same and spasmodic work on my book. Too much to do and too little time to do it. And my subliminal self always tends to work rather sluggishly—creating not in first fine careless raptures, but in a series of second and third thoughts, which compel me to go back and change or add to or cut out from the material provided by my first thoughts.

Can you recommend a good book that sums up the most advanced treatment of the mentally ill, not merely on the pharmacological level, but all round—in relation to diet, occupational therapy, group therapy, sleep therapy etc? I don't want to have to look up dozens of separate papers, and hope you can supply me with the titles of one or more comprehensive summings-up. And meanwhile have you found in your hospital work that somatotyping along Sheldonian lines has helped in diagnosis and, more important, in programming treatment and general handling?

My love to Jane and blessings to the children.

Ever yours,
Aldous

824: TO MATTHEW HUXLEY

3276 Deronda Dr.,
L.A. 28, Cal.
26 November, 1959

Dearest M,

Many thanks for your letter. I'm glad that you manage to bear up under your enormous weight of work, and I hope that you will finally get some relief and a well-earned holiday.

Work is the order of the day here too. These lectures at UCSB keep me very busy, and I am trying to get on with my book at the same time. It will be easier when my stint at SB is over—which will be in mid-December. Julian and Juliette will be coming here for Christmas; but after the jollifications I shd be able to get down to the book in good earnest.

The Indian project had been vaguely proposed when Radhakrishnan was here last summer. Nothing happened till October, when I received a cable saying that I had been appointed Stefanos Ghose Lecturer for 1960, and wd I cable acceptance and date of arrival. No hint as to nature or number of lectures—and no letter followed, as promised in the wire. I wrote after a couple of weeks asking for details and finally received the news that I was required to give 8 lectures on Comparative Religion in Jan-Feb 1960—still with no hint as to pay etc. So of course I said no—and did they really expect me to prepare 8 lectures in six weeks? The whole thing was all too typically Indian—the Old Man of Thermopylae, who *never* did anything properly. It's comic in this case—but it may turn out to be hideously tragic when their efforts to modernize the country break down under the combined pressures of inefficiency and over-population.

I have been invited tentatively to spend a month or two next spring as visiting Professor at the Menninger Foundation at Topeka. No special duties—just hanging around and occasionally talking. I think it will be interesting. There are some good men at Menninger—Gardner Murphy and Bertalannfy [Bertalanffy], for example. And I shall be curious to see what the Faithful are now doing about Freudian Fundamentalism. I was interested to see in *Time* the report by Nathan Kline on the superiority of Soviet psychiatry. This should do some good in shattering complacency—a kind of mental Sputnik.

May I ask you to do something? Wd you please phone the *Orion Press*, which publishes the American edition of Danilo Dolci's book, with my preface, and ask them to send me 15 copies (they will make good Xmas presents), for which I will pay—at the usual author's discount. I have mislaid Orion's address, or wd write myself. But I hope this won't be too much of a bother for you.

Ever your affectionate,

Aldous

PS If you prefer, just address the enclosed and drop it in the mail. Meanwhile here is another contribution to the children's education fund.

825: TO DR HUMPHRY OSMOND

3276 *Deronda Dr.,*
L.A. 28, Cal.
29 *November,* 1959

Dear Humphry,

What news of you? I keep reading of frightful blizzards blowing down out of Canada, and imagine that you must be having a rather bad time, meteorologically speaking. Here our bad time is of a very different kind—a drought which has lasted for 10 months, and only 5 inches of rain in the preceding year. Temperatures are in the eighties—which is very pleasant, until one starts looking at the vegetation, outside the irrigated areas, which is burnt to a crisp.

I am near the end of my lecturing at Santa Barbara—one more panel discussion of a Darwin Centenary lecture by Prof John Randall, and two more lectures of my own. After which I shall be free to work whole-time on my book. As for plans—I am invited to go in late March or April to Topeka, to be a visiting professor for a few weeks at the Menninger Foundation. It will be interesting, I think, to penetrate the holy of holies of American psychiatry and to take a searching look. Nathan Kline's report on Soviet psychiatry, as summarized in *Time,* was interesting and no doubt, to Menninger et al, disturbing. Have you read the full report? I think I will write and ask him to send it me. Laura, meanwhile, works away at her psychotherapy—with remarkable results in many cases: for she seems to have an intuitive knowledge of what to do at any given moment, what technique to use in each successive phase of the patient's mood and feeling. She has had some very good results with therapy under LSD in a few cases where the method seemed to be justifiable. (Incidentally, what frightful people there are in your profession! We met two Beverly Hills psychiatrists the other day, who specialize in LSD therapy at $100 a shot—and, really, I [have] seldom met people of lower sensitivity, more vulgar mind! To think of people made vulnerable by LSD being exposed to such people is profoundly disturbing. But what can one do about the problem? Psychiatry is an art

824 *Dolci's book:* Report from Palermo (1959), *containing a Preface by Huxley.*

based on a still imperfect science—and as in all the arts there are more bad and indifferent practitioners than good ones. How can one keep the bad artists out? Bad artists don't matter in painting or literature—but they matter enormously in therapy and education; for whole lives and destinies may be affected by their shortcomings. But one doesn't see any practical way in which the ungifted and the unpleasant can be filtered out and only the gifted and good let through.) And talking of LSD—would it be possible for you to send me half a dozen doses of it? I want to try some experiments myself and Laura wd like to give it to a couple of people, to round off their therapy. I don't want to bother Sid Cohen too often—and don't want to have to ask people like [——] or [——] or [——], who have the stuff, use it badly and of whom I disapprove. If this is feasible, I'd be most grateful. And if it isn't feasible, who should I apply to in the Sandoz set-up?

Give my love to Jane and the children.

Yours affectionately,
Aldous

826: TO DR HERBERT KLEMMER

3276 Deronda Dr.,
L.A. 28, Cal.
29 December, 1959

Dear Dr. Klemmer,

Thank you for your letter. I am much looking forward to my stay at the Foundation, where I hope to be able to contribute something as well as to increase my own knowledge and understanding.

In regard to lectures etc. The subject you mention—the art of writing case histories—is one which might be discussed at a seminar. In regard to lectures, I had thought of delivering a few on subjects connected with psychology.

E.g. a talk on earlier conceptions of human nature (in Homer, in the Old Testament etc).

A talk on the relationship between symbols and immediate experience.

A talk on religion as a symbol-system and religion as spiritual experience.

A talk on the nature of visionary experience and its relation to art, religion and folklore.

A talk on human potentialities and the possibility of actualizing more of them than are at present actualized.

As to practical matters—I shall be coming alone; but it is possible that

826 *To the chairman of the Sloan Professorship awards committee at the Menninger Foundation. In a follow-up letter of 28 February, 1960, Huxley added to his list a talk on contemporary ideas of human nature and substituted, for the talk on religion, one on the relation of the individual to history and culture.*

my wife might come for a short time during my stay at Topeka—in which case she wd probably go to a hotel.

What I would like is a small apartment or motel room with a kitchenette. (One gets very tired of restaurant food, and I wd like to be able to make my own culinary mess when I feel like it. So a little kitchen wd be a *sine qua non*.)

Yours very sincerely,
Aldous Huxley

827: †TO HOWARD NELSON

3276 Deronda Drive,
Los Angeles 28, Calif.
10 January, 1960

Dear Mr. Nelson,

Thank you for your letter. I was born at 'Laleham', Godalming, Surrey. At the time of my birth my father was an assistant master at Charterhouse (the school moved from London to Godalming in the 70's, I think, of last century). Then we left the house in 1901, for another 2 miles away called 'Prior's Field' where my mother founded a girls' school which became very large and is still flourishing. 'Laleham' (named after a village on the Thames where my mother's grandfather, Dr. Arnold [of] Rugby, lived as a young man) was a pleasant middle-sized house with about half an acre of garden. It was built shortly before our occupancy of it. Today it is being used—or it was used until recently—as a kind of overflow house for Charterhouse boys for whom no room is to be found in the regular houses. I remember the nursery with a fine rocking horse and a screen covered with coloured pictures or fragments of pictures cut from magazines and catalogues—a fascinating mosaic of unrelated faces, scenes, objects, co-existing in a *surréaliste* confusion.

Sylvia Nicolas is still in Holland, working on stained glass and mosaics with considerable success.

Yours sincerely,
Aldous Huxley

828: TO SIR JULIAN HUXLEY

3276 Deronda Drive,
Los Angeles 28, Cal.
18 January, 1960

Dearest J,

Herewith the script of the chapter on 'Human Potentialities'. It has run rather long, I fear—more than 6000 words, it would seem. But there was so

828 *'Human Potentialities' was published in Sir Julian Huxley's* The Humanist Frame (*New York, 1961*).

much to say, so many different points to make. And even so it is only a scratching of the surface.

I didn't bring in the point you mentioned in your letter from New York —that dynamic psychology had to be thought of in the past in terms of supernatural invasions and possessions. It is a point I discussed in *The Devils of Loudun,* in a context where it was completely relevant. Here it would have been difficult to bring in. In fact it could only have been brought in if I had embarked upon a discussion of psycho-therapy, which would have taken us too far afield.

As to the title of the proposed volume—*Omnibus,* as you say, is pretty boring and undescriptive. Some years ago a comparable volume of selections from Cardinal Newman came out under the title, *A Newman Synthesis.* Why not a *Julian Huxley Synthesis?* It says what it means and describes what it is. Alternatively you might take a hint from St Thomas Aquinas and his *Summa contra Gentiles.* Why not *Summa contra Credentes?*

It was wonderful having you here and I wish the stay could have been longer and the virus avoided. Since you left we have had some desperately needed rain—not enough to bring the precipitation up to average. But something is better than nothing. It has also turned surprisingly cold with snow down to 2500 feet and frost among the oranges. Now that I have your chapter off my mind, I must get to work intensively on my Utopian fantasy, the writing of which presents extraordinary difficulties. Then, in mid March, I go to Topeka for a sojourn with the psychiatrists. It should be educative.

Our love to you both.

Ever your affectionate,
Aldous

829: TO MATTHEW HUXLEY

3276 Deronda Drive,
L.A. 28, Cal.
24 January, 1960

Dearest M,

Many thanks for your letter, which had a good ring in it despite the news that you had been down with one of those damned viruses. I hope you will soon be able to get away for a well-earned rest.

The tea was excellent—*is* excellent, for I have only just scratched the surface of it. We were very remiss about Xmas, I fear—but I hope that my cheque provided a little something for children and adults. Also I sent on to you a lighter presented to me by a Club at SB which I addressed last spring. I have no use for it, but imagine that you will. It will have arrived very late as somebody put it into our mailbox, to be collected by the postman, before L. had written the address, and it came back to us only after about 3 weeks, when it was sent once more on its way. I hope you got it finally.

I have been approached indirectly (through Angelino who has been selling him Lawrence MSS) by Prof W[arren] Roberts of the U of Texas, asking if I wd like to dispose to the U of T of manuscripts and correspondence. This might be a good idea—sell some MSS now and put the money into the children's trust fund. What do you think? I won't make any move until I hear what you feel about the matter. I've no idea what sort of price the U of T will pay: but if they offer a fair sum it might be a good idea to dispose of some MSS now rather than await my demise and a possible slump in the value of such material.

I am working away at my book, which already runs to more than 200 pages and shows no sign of coming to an end—indeed, I don't yet know how the damned thing is going to end.

Rose has retreated again to the desert—waiting for a very hypothetical job as a member of an archeological expedition to Yucatan with 2 gentlemen from Texas. Bonne Maman flourishes under the stimulation of successive disasters in France—the death of Camus and now, very belatedly, the Fréjus dam break, the news of which in the *Figaro Littéraire* and the *Express* excites her and keeps up her morale like a shot of adrenalin or a course of Nardil. What a strange creature! But what a blessing that it takes so little —the account in a newspaper of a French catastrophe (it has to be French: nobody else's catastrophes cut much ice)—to keep her in good shape.

Ever your affectionate

A.

PS I enclose a small contribution to your holiday fund. Don't spend it all on Planter's Punch which is so delicious that, in the Caribbean, one drinks it as tho' it were lemonade, which it very definitely is *not*.

830: TO IAN PARSONS

3276 *Deronda Dr.*,
L.A. 28, *Cal.*
7 *February*, 1960

Dear Ian,

Thank you for your letter and the accounts which make a most surprisingly good showing. I am very sorry about the contract. I must have put it aside somewhere, waiting for someone to be on hand to witness it—and then forgotten all about it. Some future hurricane among my papers will doubtless bring it to the surface again. But meanwhile will you please send me another copy which I will do my best to sign at once.

I am working very hard on my book and have already had nearly 300

829 *Nothing was done about the manuscripts, either Huxley's own or those of D. H. Lawrence stored with them, and all were burned in May,* 1961, *in the fire that destroyed the Huxleys' house.*

pages of it typed. Heaven knows how much more there will be or when I shall get it done—all the more so as I now see that there are things to be altered and added to at the beginning. (The problem in this sort of Utopian phantasy is to find a fable strong enough to support the, necessarily, enormous weight of exposition—a weight considerably lightened by the fact that it is mostly in dialogue form, but still requiring all the drama, variety of character and conflict that can possibly be brought in. I became disturbed by the low ratio of story to exposition and am now, after discussing the problem with Christopher Isherwood, trying to remedy this defect by the introduction of a brand new personage.) I will report progress from time to time.

I hope all goes well with you. So far, thank the Lord, we have both escaped the flu, which afflicted a million people in this area. I see in the papers that it has now struck in Europe. So beware.

Yours,
Aldous

831: TO MRS ELLEN HUXLEY

3276 Deronda Dr.,
L.A. 28, Cal.
8 February, 1960

My dear Ellen,
   A recent letter from Rose has set me wondering about the current situation between Matthew and yourself. I had imagined that by this time you would have come to some definite decision—either to make a reconciliation or a definite break with the past and a new beginning—and I am disturbed to hear that everything remains indefinite with the basic problem unresolved, perhaps not even clearly faced up to: break and all that break entails, or reconciliation and all that reconciliation entails. This half way position with one foot in a marriage and one foot out strikes me as profoundly unsatisfactory—especially for Matthew who is essentially a family man with a deep wish for roots and stability and on whom the present arrangement imposes a rootlessness and a homelessness that for him are peculiarly distressing. That he would still prefer a reconciliation I am sure: but if that is something you can't envisage, I am equally sure that he would like some definite decision that would permit him to cut his emotional losses and his ties with the past, and start afresh.

   [. . . .] Rose evidently feels very strongly that you should decide in favour of reconciliation. If you find it emotionally possible, I would also be for it—but I don't think it should be forced, if you find it emotionally impossible. The important thing, however, is to decide. If there is anything I can do to help you to come to a decision, let me know.

Yours affectionately,
Aldous

3276 *Deronda Dr.,*
L.A. 28, *Cal.*
16 *February,* 1960

Dearest M,

I imagine that by this time you have seen Ellen and come to some definite decision—presumably, to judge from the letter Ellen has written in response to mine, the decision to make the break definitive. This is a sad, sad thing; and there is no consolation—only the reflection that a mending of the break on any basis short of a heartfelt 'marriage of true minds' might be an even sadder thing for all concerned. The problem now is to make the best of the situation. I am quite sure you will be able to preserve a good and helpful relationship with Trev and Tessa and can only hope that you will soon be able to create for yourself a new home base, with its own internal relationships of love and affection, from which you can relate yourself to the children. *Their* well-being will be enhanced by *your* well-being: so it is as much for the children's sake as for yours that I wish and hope for your future happiness.

And for the same reasons I hope for Ellen's future happiness. Her letter to me was full of sadness, and she seems rather lost. So I think it will be a good thing if she comes out here in March, so that we can talk about ways of getting unlost.

Nel mezzo del cammin di nostra vita
mi ritrovai per una selva oscura
chè la diritta via era smarrita.

Each of you must find a way out of the dark wood, for your own sakes and for the children's. And if I can help in any way, that is what I'm there for. Whatever may have happened on the level of the previous generation, the family still persists in Trev and Tessa; and for them the important thing is that they should grow up in an atmosphere uncontaminated, as far as humanly possible, with bitterness.

Meanwhile I hope you can soon get your holiday. Don't let them push you too hard for too long. It isn't right.

Ever your affectionate,
Aldous

3276 *Deronda Drive,*
Los Angeles 28, *Cal.*
6 *March,* 1960

Dear Mrs. Murry,

Thank you for your letter. I have not read the biography of J[ohn] M[iddleton] M[urry], nor any of the reviews of the book. The last time I heard from John was in the late thirties, I think, when we exchanged several letters on the subject of war and pacifism.

Looking back with (I hope) more understanding and less censoriousness and bumptiousness than I had thirty-five years ago, I see John as at once the beneficiary and victim of a great gift. He was an excellent critic and handler of ideas. But his very power of appreciating other men's works of art and philosophies often resulted, it seems to me, in his becoming involved, under their influence, in real-life situations which he was temperamentally un-equipped to cope with. It was as though one part of his mind—the part con-cerned with concepts—were trying to make him feel and believe and do things which the rest of his organism was not inclined to feel or believe or do. It was this gap between the conceptual and constitutional in JMM that so angered Lawrence, who was never thus divided against himself (as so many intellectuals are) and who exhibited the intolerance of his own temper-ament towards men with a different make-up.

Yours sincerely,
Aldous Huxley

834: TO LADY HUXLEY

c/o The Menninger Foundation,
Topeka, Kansas
20 March, 1960

Dearest Juliette,

I was most distressed to hear of your accident—and also of Francis's unpleasant reminder of the Tropics, and hope you are both in your various ways on the mend. From my own experience with a fall last summer I know that it takes some time to get over the shock, which leaves one curiously diminished for two or three months.

Here I am, for 6 weeks, in the Holy of Holies of Psycho-Analysis, finding much of interest, much to admire and also not a little to shake my head over in incomprehension. E.g. they treat hospital patients in a rational way, attacking their problems on all the fronts from the nutritional and gymnastic to the psychological: but their private patients they treat in the grand old Freudian way, as tho' they had no bodies—only mouths and anuses—and as tho' a multiple amphibian cd be cured of his troubles by psychology alone, and psychology of only one, not too realistic brand. Very odd. But there are a lot of very able people here and a vast psychotic popu-lation at large and in a dozen hospitals. The chief disadvantage is that the whole of the Middle West is under 18 inches of snow, which is now melting —so one wades about in rubber boots like a salmon fisher. My love to you all. Get well soon.

Your affectionate
Aldous

The Menninger Foundation,
Topeka, Kansas
16 April, 1960

Dear Dr. Janiger,

Thank you for your letter and the enclosures. *Time* has been its usual unpleasant self—knowing, but inaccurate, Olympian but pettily malicious. And of course there is never any redress.

Sincerely,
Aldous Huxley

836: TO MATTHEW HUXLEY

3276 Deronda Dr., L.A. 28
18 May, 1960

Dearest M,

Many thanks for your letter. I am delighted to hear of your Brazilian projects—vegetable jungle as a change from asphalt jungle, plus an opportunity to do some writing in a completely different field. Very good indeed.

I am now through with all my talking—after a side trip to Berkeley (where I had an overflow audience even more enthusiastic than at Lake Forest) and to Pocatello, Idaho (State College, with occasion to meet several interesting people, including a Swedish anthropologist who has spent 20 years studying the local Indian languages and the peyote cult). Now I have to get down to work on my book. Shall try to finish it by September (when I go to Dartmouth for a symposium on Medicine and Ethics, before proceeding to MIT)—but am doubtful if I shall succeed.

I will keep the reference you gave me in mind—but can't at the moment embark on the reading of so vast a book. On second thoughts why don't you buy it for me and have it sent out here—I enclose 20 dollars for this and for any other book on kindred themes which you think might be useful.

[. . . .]

We talked with Ellen on the phone the other night and the final arrangement is that she won't be coming out now, but that we shall be seeing her when we come East in September.

If you ever have a moment to spare, do write a line to Bonne Maman. She has been having dizzy spells recently and daren't go out for fear of falling in the street—so is feeling very lonely and sorry for herself. Anything you can send in the way of a personal note or a bunch of cuttings from newspapers will help to keep her cheerful and mentally occupied.

Ever your affectionate
Aldous

835 *A reference apparently to an article about lysergic acid therapy, in* Time, *28 March, 1960, which mentioned Huxley (p. 85).*

On the plane from S[an] F[rancisco]
20 May, 1960

Dear Bill and Peggy,

Herewith a brief report. We flew up to S.F this morning and drove to Moff[i]tt Hospital. There I was examined first by Dr. [Franz] Buschke, who is Professor of Radiology; later by Dr. Gallanti [Maurice Galante] (prof. of surgery). After consultation and examination of the slides, they advised me to take the radium needle treatment with Dr. [Max] Cutler. For cases like mine, radium needles are now standard procedure at the University of California. Gallanti [Galante] said that he used to be all for immediate surgery—but now, having seen what radium needles can do he has changed his mind and prefers to reserve surgery for those cases which the radium fails to control. He pointed out that surgery (entailing removal of nearly half the tongue) wd possibly entail some impairment of speech, and that radium wd leave speech unaffected. So I have definitely decided to go ahead with Dr. Cutler.

Meanwhile let me repeat what I said to Peggy last night—that I don't want to worry anybody unnecessarily (including Matthew) and so prefer to keep this business *strictly* private. I wd be grateful if you wd emphasize this to Dr. [Eugene] Ellis.

Ever yours,
Aldous

838: ALDOUS AND LAURA HUXLEY TO MRS JEFFREYS CORNER

3276 Deronda Drive,
L.A. 28, Cal.
17 June, 1960

My dear Jeff,

What can one say? There are no consolations; there is only the bearing of the unbearable for the sake of the life—your own and the children's—that has to go on and be made the best of.

I never knew Doug well—but always felt, whenever I met him, a renewal of the liking and respect that my first meeting had inspired. One had a sense when one was with him that here was an intrinsically good human being, decent, fair, kind, strong but never bumptious or overweening, with that blessed capacity for seeing himself with a humorous eye which is a true

---

837 *Huxley had cancer of the tongue. The radium-needle treatment produced complete local healing, but metastasis took place, leading to his death three and a half years later.*

838 *On the death of Douglas Corner. Mrs Corner is the daughter of Beth Wendel.*

manifestation of the Christian virtue of humility. And now this dreadful, senseless thing has happened—and you are left to cope with the consequences. As I said, there are no consolations; but out of my own experience I can tell you certain things which may be of some practical help. It is profoundly important to remember that, over and above the grief and the loneliness and the near-despair, there will be an organic reaction, closely resembling surgical shock. A bereavement such as yours is an amputation, and like every other amputation it produces a state of psychic and physical shock—a state which may last for weeks or months. For so long as this state of shock persists, the mind-body requires appropriate supportive treatment in the form of adequate rest, a good diet etc. The bereaved person's tendency is to resent this—to feel that it is an ignoble kind of escape from the situation. But neglecting the amputated organism will do nothing to spiritualize the bereavement. On the contrary, it may physiologize it, transform it into a sickness that leaves the sufferer no power to think with love about the past or act constructively in the present, and in relation to the children. God bless you.

Yours affectionately
Aldous

My dear Jeff,

I would like to call you and see you, but maybe it is better I let you call. Please do, soon. I think of you, and feel with you, intensely.

Until soon,
Laura

HO7-0152

839: TO MRS EILEEN J. GARRETT

[From hospital, as from]
3276 Deronda Drive, L.A. 28, Cal.
22 June, 1960

Dear Eileen,

Thank you for your letters, to which at the moment I can reply only telegraphically. About the preface to Myers—I don't think I can undertake a full-blown introduction at this time; for I have *too* much to do. But use whatever suits you from the Psychology Essay. Also, why not find some good quotes from Wm James's Review of the book—in *The Will to Believe?*

About the ectoplasm—I was told of this years ago by a Swiss graphologist (name forgotten). It is preserved, so it seems, like a piece of the True

839 *As Huxley suggested, a foreword based on 'The Oddest Science' was drafted for the new edition of F. W. H. Myers'* Human Personality and Its Survival of Bodily Death (*University Books,* 1961), *but he was not satisfied with the text, and in November he submitted a substitute, which was published in the book.*

Cross at the Zurich S[ociety for] P[sychical R[esearch]. Surely the London SPR will know about it.

Hope you will have a good and fruitful summer.

Love,
Aldous

840: TO MATTHEW HUXLEY

[*From Hospital*] *As from:*
3276 Deronda Dr., L.A. 28, Cal.
23 June, 1960

Dearest M,

A brief word, in case Bonne Maman shd write you an alarmist letter, to tell you that I have been in hospital for the last few days with a laryngitis that has made eating and talking very hard. I leave tomorrow or the next day and shall go down to Tecate, where we had a symposium scheduled on Human Potentialities—quite an interesting panel drawn from many fields. I was to have presided—but doubt if I can participate before the 3rd day of the symposium—so shall remain in the background while the others do their talking. I didn't want Bonne Maman to know, as she gets so agitated— but as bad luck wd have it she met, at Vera Stravinsky's exhibition, Edward James, who knew I was in hospital because he had rung up the house and talked to the coloured maid, who for some strange reason volunteered the fact that she was washing 3 pairs of pyjamas for me to wear in hospital. Edward recognized B.M (who thought he was Gerald, because they both have beards!) and—inveterate gossip that he is blurted out the news. Where-upon she rang up Peggy in a great state. I talked to her by phone this morn-ing and I think all is now in order—all the more so as she is doing very well on the B12 + Folic Acid which I prescribed (after the doctors did nothing but give her tranquillizers) as a cure for her dizzy spells, which were evidently due to a combination of anemia and chlorpromazine. Isn't medicine wonderful!

I hope all goes well with you and the children.

Ever your affectionate,
Aldous

PS Thank you for the paper, which I am looking forward to reading as soon as I am out of here.

841: TO MATTHEW HUXLEY

3276 Deronda Dr.,
L.A. 28, Cal.,
17 July, 1960

Dearest M,

No news of you for a long time. How are things going and what are your plans?

Not much news here. I am working hard on my book, and wish to goodness it were finished. But the end is still a long way off. I expect to be busy here—with perhaps occasional flights to the sea—through August and the first week of September. Then I am invited to Dartmouth College, for a 'Convocation on the Great Issues of Conscience in Modern Medicine', from Sept 8th to 10th. I don't think Laura will come East, and I shall fly directly to Boston—after which I have to get to Hanover, N.H. I was wondering if you wd be able and interested to meet me in Boston with the Microbus and drive me (3 hours) to Hanover, where you might stay for all or part of the Jamboree (at which I am to receive an honorary degree). It wd be very nice if you could. If not, I shall see you after the 10th in New York, where I shall stay until the 20th when I go to Pittsburgh to talk at the U. of Pittsburgh. After which to MIT on the 23rd. Incidentally I have an apartment in Cambridge (100 Memorial Drive), which will be mine from August onwards. If for any reason you want to use it, I am sure it will be easy to arrange with the superintendent of the building. But in any case do try to come up to Dartmouth—if not by Microbus, then by train or a Hertz car from Boston (which might be simpler).

I wish one cd feel much enthusiasm for Messrs Kennedy and Johnson. The thought of old Joe Kennedy, with $200 millions amassed [. . .] on the stockmarket, lurking in the background of the young crusader is very distasteful. But perhaps the man may turn out to be a winner and a good president—Quien sabe? And do we need a good president! Tho' even if we had one, it is hard to see that he cd do very much in the kind of world we now find ourselves in.

Laura sends her love.

Ever your affectionate,
Aldous

842: TO DR HUMPHRY OSMOND

3276 *Deronda Dr.,*
L.A. 28, Cal.
17 *July,* 1960

My dear Humphry,

Thank you for your good letter. [. . . .]

Your work with imagers sounds very interesting. Have you any idea why some people visualize and others don't? I don't, except when my temperature touches 103°. Even LSD—at least in 100 μ doses—doesn't make me see things with my eyes shut. I took some LSD 3 or 4 weeks ago and had some interesting experiences of the way in which, as the Indians say, the thought and the thinker and the thing thought about are one—and then of the way in which this unowned experience becomes something belonging to *me*; then no me any more and a kind of *sat chit ananda*, at one moment without *karuna* or charity (how odd that the Vedantists say nothing about

Love, whereas the Mahayana Buddhists insist that unless *prajnaparamita* (the wisdom of the other shore) has *karuna* as the reverse of the medal, *nirvana* is, for the Bodhisattva, no better than hell). And in this experience with LSD, I had an inkling of both kinds of *nirvana*—the loveless being-consciousness-bliss, and the one with love and, above all, a sense that one can never love enough.

I liked the things you said for Dr. Raynor Johnson's chapter on drugs and spiritual experience in his latest book. An interesting book—tho' perhaps he multiplies spiritual entities beyond what is strictly necessary. But perhaps Ockham's razor isn't a valid scientific principle. Perhaps entities sometimes ought to be multiplied beyond the point of the simplest possible explanation. For the world is doubtless far odder and more complex than we ordinarily think.

I hope your administrative difficulties have been resolved and that you are now free to get on with something more interesting. I'm glad to hear that the Russians have picked up your [adrenochrome] work.

Ever yours,
Aldous

843: TO DR HUMPHRY OSMOND

3276 Deronda Dr.,
L.A. 28, Cal.
28 July 1960

Dear Humphry,

Thank you for your letter. Alas, poor [——]! What an ass—and the worst kind of ass, a clever one! It wd be interesting, apropos of what you say about so many symptoms of schizophrenia being due to altered perception, to test experimentally what people do or don't do when their perceptions are changed artificially. There must be drugs which do yet odder things to perception than LSD: and then there are the mechanical perception-changers—funny spectacles, continuous noises. To these, people evidently soon become accustomed—but in the first few hours they must show many abnormal symptoms. These no doubt have been recorded—but have they been compared with schizophrenic symptoms? I imagine you cd find out a great deal—given your special knowledge of schiz symptoms—by looking into the literature.

An interesting procedure in regard to twins wd be as follows. Give each twin an identical object—say a china figure of a human or an animal. Let them look at these and then learn to visualize them accurately. You can

843 *Twins: Osmond and some of his colleagues had just completed, for the Para-psychology Foundation, a study of twins and ESP, along lines suggested by Galton's work in the* 1880's. *In November, while Huxley was staying in Cambridge, Osmond visited him at MIT.*

then be pretty sure of having 2 minds with but a single thought. Now place an ESP card, (or a picture, or a word) near or on the china figure belonging to one twin, and have the other twin (at a distance) try to see it. The fact that 50% of the image is already perfect in his mind might help him to visualize the unknown 50% represented by the card or picture. It might be interesting, too, to do something similar in relation to the survival hypothesis. Give identical twins identical photos of a recently dead person and see if they get the same reactions, and if these reactions have any kind of evidential value. Have twin mediums ever existed? If so they might reinforce one another and be doubly effective in establishing contact with whatever mediums do establish contact with.

I hope you will be able to come East while I am there. It wd be good to see you.

Yours ever
Aldous

844: TO DR HUMPHRY OSMOND

Hotel Shoreham, 33 W. 55th, NYC
16 September, 1960

Dear Humphry,

Here I am in NYC, preparing to go on to Cambridge next week—where I hope I may be seeing you before too long. The conference on the 'Great Issues of Conscience in Modern Medicine', which was held at Dartmouth last week turned out to be rather disappointing—as most conferences do. We never got down to discussing one of the basic issues—the manipulation of minds—tho' a whole session was devoted to the subject. Wilder Penfield read a long paper wholly about the mind-brain problem, Rado another on the Control of Rage, Weaver talked about ESP—and then time was up, with no mention of hypnosis, brain-washing, mind-changing drugs or hypnopaedia.

Yesterday I lunched with Bill Wilson who spoke enthusiastically of his own experiences with leuko-adrenochrome and of the successful use of it on his ex-alcoholic neurotics. This really sounds like a break-through and I hope you are going ahead with clinical testing. Do you have any of the stuff to spare? If so, I'd be most grateful for a sample. It might relieve my tension-pains in the lower back, as it relieved Bill's aches and those of some of his friends. I wd like too to be able to send a few pills to Laura, who has some of Bill's symptoms—tension, then exhaustion, and then tremendous drive to overcome the exhaustion.

If you and Abram have really found something that will normalize, say, 50% or even more of neurotics, you will be among the great benefactors of humanity. But of course you will be attacked by all the Freudians. They will

844 *Bill Wilson: the founder of Alcoholics Anonymous.*

be fighting, not only for the Master, but for their livelihood. No more ten-year analyses, no more couch-addicts. What will become of the poor fellows?

My address in Cambridge will be

> 100 Memorial Drive
> Cambridge 38
> Mass.

Ever yours,
Aldous

845: TO JOHN WHITING

> 100 *Memorial Drive,*
> *Cambridge, Mass.*
> *29 September,* 1960

Dear Mr Whiting,

I have just finished your script of the *Devils*, and find most of it poetical and powerfully dramatic. Indeed, I wonder if some of the scenes in the last two acts may not prove almost too powerful. The possession, exorcism and torture episodes were hair-raising enough in the narrative (incidentally, I exaggerated nothing; everything in the book is drawn from the original sources). Dramatized and well directed and acted, they may be almost more than many people can take. In any case it will be very interesting to see how an audience reacts to the horror and strangeness of the story. You have done a great deal to make it acceptable by presenting the horrors within a framework of poetical reflection. And a great deal, obviously, will depend on direction, which will have to be particularly skilful and sensitive. My own ignorance of the theatre doesn't permit me to make any suggestions in regard to stage sets and direction. But I feel sure that directors and producers who have worked in the Shakespearean field will be able to cope with the problems raised by a play of many characters, many scenes and gruesome content.

Peters' covering letter speaks of your dissatisfaction with the opening and your desire to change it. I agree that the first few pages are the weakest in the play. An idea for the actual opening has occurred to me. It is this. Cut

845 *An early script of John Whiting's dramatic adaptation of* The Devils of Loudun *had been sent to Huxley by A. D. Peters, Whiting's agent. Whiting was greatly pleased by Huxley's reactions and suggestions. In replying, he predicted that in actual performance the impact of the horror episodes would be softened—'not a generally accepted view' in such cases. He added that a revised script would be ready towards the end of the year. See letter 850. Huxley's description of the torture of Grandier, which is very explicit in the American edition of* The Devils of Loudun, *had been moderated, with his permission, by the English publishers; possibly he had this fact in mind when he wrote to Whiting about the play.*

out the first speech by Grandier altogether. Open with the scene at the city gate. Have the Sewerman (who is a fine Shakespearean character) doing his work. (Incidentally, he wouldn't be doing anything with drains, which were virtually non-existent; he would rather be emptying cess-pools—hauling up muck from an open manhole and pouring it into a barrel on wheels, which he will finally trundle away for sale to farmers outside the town—or for emptying into some pit. Such a pit existed in Oxford during my mother's childhood there, and I remember her telling me that it was known as The Slipe.) I think you could make a very interesting opening with the aid of the corpses hanging from the municipal gibbet. Have Adam and Mannoury casting greedy eyes on the corpses, which they hope to dissect. (This fits in with the later scene, where they have the head of one of the criminals.) Have Philippe Trincant asking her father what they were hanged for, and Trincant telling her that they (or he—for it will be best to have only *one* malefactor) was hanged for debauching a young girl and stealing her jewels. Then have Grandier come in, get into conversation with the sewerman and begin by informing him that he officiated at the criminal's execution and gave the man absolution and a benediction as he was turned off. He should speak of this in a humane and forgiving way and should comment on the monstrous injustice of hanging a man for an offence motivated by irresistible sexual desire and irresistible hunger. (Perhaps the criminal did not take the girl's jewels—merely stole half a crown after sleeping with her, to buy himself a good meal at the local inn.) This opening will give a certain symmetry to the play—an execution with Grandier at the forgiving end in the first scene and an execution with Grandier as the victim of unforgiving friends at the end—and can be made to enrich the conversation with the sewerman, emphasize Philippe's innocence and purity, and provide a good introduction to two minor, but important characters, Adam and Mannoury.

Here are some other points which struck me as I read. Page 4. Have Trincant read a brief specimen of his poetry to d'Armagnac and Cerisay. Its pretentious badness will give added point to the scene where Grandier changes his mind about criticizing it, when he sees Philippe. (There is good precedent for the reading of bad poetry in Molière's *Misanthrope*. Perhaps Trincant writes in the same alembicated style.)

Page 7. It might be a good thing if Grandier followed up his remark about Ninon having been a good little animal, by telling her to become fully human and religious again. During their love making they have drawn a curtain across the niche in which Ninon keeps an image of the Virgin. As Grandier takes his leave, he draws back the curtain and commends Ninon to the life of reason, virtue and devotion.

Page 12. Grandier's scented handkerchief should be seen as well as talked about. He uses it when talking to the sewerman—holding it repeatedly to his nose. Again in the scene with Adam and Mannoury, with the criminal's head. (It and they smell bad.) Finally, in Ninon's room he pours some of her perfume on the handkerchief.

Page 18. The Prioress might have a few remarks to make on the 'discipline'—the wire cat o' ninetails with which nuns were expected to beat themselves. This would help to create the convent atmosphere. Has she actually flagellated herself? Is she going to? Does she think her nuns should beat themselves more than they do?

Page 20. Philippe's speech, 'I know there are forces inside me etc' seems too bald. Wouldn't it be better if she said the same thing indirectly, in relationship to the poem they have just been reading? She won't tell him what troubles her. Then at last, under her breath, brings out *Foeda Voluptas*.

Also on page 20, in the scene with d'Armagnac. Would it not be good to have a large sheet of paper on which we can see both the plan and the elevation of the castle. This will permit the audience to have a direct apprehension of what it is that Richelieu wants to pull down.

Page 34. I would suggest that Mannoury should ask the prioress for details regarding the indecencies spoken by the vision. Soeur Jeanne refuses to utter them. But finally whispers a few of them in the old man's ear. The audience will see Mannoury reacting to the shock of hearing a nun pronounce four-letter words.

In the remainder of the play I saw nothing that needed changing. The problem, as I said at the beginning of this letter, will be to prevent the piece from becoming too frightful or too extravagantly indecent and blasphemous. The director and the actors will have to preserve the horror, but avoid Grand Guignol on the one hand and the outrageousness that turns to farce on the other. It will take a great deal of tact and skill. But if the tact and skill are forthcoming, I think the play ought to reveal itself as something very powerful, strange and moving.

Yours very sincerely,
Aldous Huxley

846: TO CYRIL BIBBY

100 *Memorial Drive,*
Cambridge, Mass.
12 *November,* 1960

Dear Cyril,

Your query leaves me stumped—for tho' I do vaguely remember that I was once elected to the I[nternational] I[nstitute of] A[rts] and L[etters], I have never to my knowledge received any further communication from the organization, and don't know what it does or why it exists.

I am here for the moment working as a Visiting Professor at MIT—an interesting job in an interesting place. Nevertheless I shall be glad when my term of office is over and I can get back to writing.

I was advising some educators the other day to read your book and find out how all their problems were in full bloom in THH's day, from excessive specialization to science-vs-humanities.

Sincerely,
Aldous Huxley

847: TO MATTHEW HUXLEY

3276 Deronda Dr.,
L.A. 28, Cal.
4 December, 1960

Dearest M,

How did you get on with the mushrooms? I shall be most interested to hear. Oh, and before I forget—did you find a mask, with a slit in it for reading, in the apartment? If so, please put it in an envelope and send it me.

All goes well here, I'm glad to say—except that everybody is too busy, Laura with her disturbed and unhappy people (what a lot there are, my God, and how right Thoreau was when he said that most men and women lived in a state of quiet desperation!), and I with my book and arrears of correspondence.

I had a note the other day from Jake Zeitlin, saying that he had a customer who wd like to buy the DHL MS of *St Mawr*, which I have—somewhere or other. Now what do you think? Wd you like me to hang on to it and bequeath it to you or the children in my will? Or shall I sell it and put the cash in the children's fund? I myself incline to the second alternative, as I have no collector's itch and don't feel sentimental about objects and mementos. But if you prefer, I will keep it.

There has also been an enquiry from the U of Texas about my MSS. I have asked Zeitlin what I can expect to get for them, and when I know we can decide what to do. What is your feeling in this matter—and your practical estimate of pros and cons? Laura sends love.

Ever your affectionate,
Aldous

848: TO DR HUMPHRY OSMOND

3276 Deronda Dr.,
L.A. 28, Cal.
14 December, 1960

My dear Humphry,

Thank you for your letter and the two papers, both of which are excellent. This matter of death—how badly we handle it! I have a whole chapter illustrating the art of dying, as practised by my hypothetical islanders—

846 Book: Bibby's T. H. Huxley (*London*, 1959).

plus other passages concerning the fear of death and the training for its acceptance. My own experience with Maria convinced me that the living can do a great deal to make the passage easier for the dying, to raise the most purely physiological act of human existence to the level of consciousness and perhaps even of spirituality. The last rites of Catholicism are good, but too much preoccupied with morality and the past. The emphasis has to be on the present and the posthumous future, which one must assume—and I think with justification—to be a reality. Eileen told me that, in one of her contacts with what she was convinced was Maria, there was a message for me to the effect that what I had said had helped to float the soul across the chasm. (This message, incidentally, contained two items which I felt to be evidential—one a reference to something which Eileen cd not understand, something she heard as 'the Bardle', (which was obviously the *Bardo*, which M knew well and from whose spirit and whose techniques I had borrowed when talking to her in the last hours); the other word which Eileen heard as 'Ecker' which referred to a quotation from Meister Eckhart which I used once or twice.)

All goes well here. Dr. Cutler, the surgeon who treated me last summer, has given me a clean bill of health. I am working very hard on my book, trying to write a brief but satisfactory ending—the near-end is the chapter on the LSD state of which I read you a small piece and which I am completing now. After which I must go back and try to improve some passages in the earlier chapters. I shall be thankful when I finally get through. It won't be as good as I wd like it to be, I fear: but still I think it will have been worth attempting.

Give my love and seasonable greetings to Jane and the family.

Yours affectionately
Aldous

849: TO SIR JULIAN AND LADY HUXLEY

3276 Deronda Dr.,
L.A. 28, Cal.
27 December, 1960

Dearest J. and J.,

Too late for Christmas, but still in time, I hope, to wish you happiness and health for 1961. It can't be said that the public prospects look very rosy: but perhaps young Mr. Kennedy will be able to do something about them —tho' it seems doubtful.

I have been working like mad on my book since returning from MIT, and hope and pray that I may get the damned thing finished by the spring. Meanwhile I am very happy to know that you, Julian, liked the collection

849 *Collection: Huxley's* On Art and Artists *(New York, 1960). Sir Julian had suggested that his brother's observations on art might be made into an illustrated book.*

of pieces on art. Cass has written me about your suggestion, and perhaps later on, when there is world enough and time, I may do something about it. I wd like to: but heaven knows if all the other things I have to do will permit me to make the necessary changes and additions.

We go to Hawaii for a week in January—the excuse being some lectures, the motive a wish to look at the islands which I haven't seen for many years. After that a conference on Control of the Mind at San Francisco, with a lot of very various and interesting participants—preceded by a brief trip to New York, where NBC wants me to prepare the way for their broadcasting of the conference. Then a day or two in Oregon where Maxwell Jones, who pioneered the Open Ward system in English mental hospitals, is introducing his methods at the State Hospital at Salem. After which, back to work on the book.

How good it was to see you for those 3 days in Cambridge! I hope there will be more leisurely meetings next spring or summer. Plans are still vague and must depend on what happens with my book. But it will be finished some time. At least I hope so.

Love to you both from both of us.

Ever your
Aldous

850: TO JOHN WHITING

3276 Deronda, L.A. 28, Cal.
1 January, 1961

Dear John Whiting,
I have just finished reading the revised version of *The Devils*, and want to tell you how excellent I think it is. Your revisions have deepened and enriched the play in an extraordinary way, and I feel that it has now become a fully integrated work of dramatic art. I am glad you brought in the marriage ceremony. It adds another dimension to Grandier's character. But it might be a good thing to introduce—either before or during the ceremony, preferably, I think before and in conversation with someone who is not Philippe—a few lines in which G's arguments in favour of priestly marriage and against celibacy (as set forth in his book and summarized somewhere in the *Devils of L*) are expressed. It will be a good thing, I feel, to let the audience know that he has an intellectual justification for what he is doing as well as an emotional and spiritual motive. As it is, you merely mention a book on priestly celibacy and pass on. Two lines will be enough to convey the contents of the treatise.

At the end of the play, where we see the townspeople fighting over Grandier's relics—might it not be a good thing to show someone actually applying a piece of bone for the cure of lumbago or dysmenorrhea? This wd give added force to the Sewerman's comments—which might be made to arise from the spectacle of the relics being put to magical use. (Perhaps Philippe's aged husband might be using one to enhance his potency?)

I don't yet know if I shall be able to get over for the opening performance. I am wrestling with a book, which I am desperately trying to finish (after altogether too much work on the damned thing), and my movements must depend to a considerable extent on the degree of my success in solving the problems that confront me.

Thank you for writing such a good play and all good wishes for it and you during this New Year.

Yours very sincerely,
Aldous Huxley

851: TO DR HUMPHRY OSMOND

3276 *Deronda Drive,*
Los Angeles 28, *California*
8 *January,* 1961

Dear Humphry,

Thank you for your letter and New Year wishes—herewith returned with interest.

What you say of Hoffer's work with hypnosis is very interesting. How remarkable that these artificially induced perceptual changes shd evoke precisely those gestures which are so characteristic of the mentally sick! One sees that Freud's notions about the cause of schizophrenia being Homosexuality are pretty wide of the mark. Do I understand that Abram has been successful in hypnotizing far-out psychotics? I always thought this was all but impossible. (But then one so often finds that 'impossible' merely means 'incapable' or 'incompetent'.)

I have been reading Groddeck's paper on massage and psychotherapy. It is full of interesting hints—tho' he doesn't tell one in any detail precisely how he achieved his therapeutic results,—results which everyone agrees were remarkably much better than those obtained by his psychiatric contemporaries.

In your re-education of schizophrenics, are you making use of the techniques of teaching pure receptive awareness of internal and external events, here and now—along the lines described by Dr. Roger Vittoz (another immensely successful therapist whose work was ignored) and revived recently by Perls, Hefferline and Goodman in their *Gestalt Therapy*? I feel sure that this sort of thing can be extremely therapeutic. Pure perceptual receptivity is the basis, incidentally, of many Tantrik exercises aimed at preparing people for self-transcendence into cosmic consciousness. (And something of the kind is at the root of all Krishnamurti's teaching.) One can imagine a genuinely realistic treatment of the mentally ill, in which the problem is attacked on all the fronts—by diet, by hypnosis, by massage, by teaching of various kinds (pure receptivity, devices for coping with odd psychological happenings etc), by pharmacological methods, by work and play therapy, by the provision of harmless or positively helpful ways of blowing off steam—corybantic dancing, going out and hacking at trees (as some of Margaret Mead's savages do when they feel that adrenalin is piling up inside them), and by other yet undiscovered 'moral equivalents of war' and personal violence. And of course these attacks on all the fronts can be used in prevention of mental illness even more effectively than in its cure. A rational system of child- and adult-education wd include them all in its curriculum.

Another interesting book I have just read is Dr. Bernard Aschner's *Arthritis Can be Cured*. It contains a long section on pre-modern medicine, in which Aschner points out that the moderns have turned their back on numerous methods of cure which worked much better than the 'scientific' methods now in vogue. If you don't know this book, do read it—especially the historical part.

Yours
Aldous

852: TO CLAIRE JOHN ESCHELBACH

3276 *Deronda Drive,*
L.A. 28, Cal.
13 *January,* 1961

Dear Mr. Eschelbach,
Excuse the long delay in answering your letter, which came and went, from one coast to the other, before reaching me. And when it did finally reach me, I was so busy with trying to finish a book that all correspondence suffered.

I have no suggestions to make in regard to the bibliography, before which I stand appalled at the thought of all I have written over the years. 'What, Mr. Gibbon! Nothing but scribble, scribble, scribble'—as the Duke of Kent remarked on receiving the fourth volume of the *Decline and Fall* from the hands of its author. 'Another thick, damned, square book.' Even the bibliography will be thick, damned and square—and it is merely the logarithm of the millions of scribbled words to which it refers.

When and if the time for publication comes, I will gladly write a fore-word. Meanwhile let me express my thanks to Miss Shober and yourself for having carried through what I fear must have been an enormous and often not very rewarding project.

Sincerely
Aldous Huxley

852 *To the editor, along with Joyce Lee Shober, of* Aldous Huxley: A Biblio-graphy 1916-1959, *which was published with a foreword by Huxley in* 1961.

Waiaka Lodge, Kailua,
Kona, Hawaii
17 January, 1961

Dearest M,

We have been driving round the large island, Hawaii, before going to Honolulu for my lectures. The volcano is spectacular and so are the forests on the rainy side of the island (150-200 inches of rain P.A. as against 20 on the other side). Beautiful, except for the frightful Hawaiian music which is ubiquitous, and the tourists—who all look like Grant Wood's 'American Gothic', but with garlands of flowers and cameras round their necks and all in costume, the men in flowered shirts and shorts, the women in native garments that look like nightgowns made of upholstery material.

We leave for Oahu tomorrow, back to LA on Friday night. Incidentally I shall *not* be coming to NY, as NBC now wants to interview me in SF 2 days before the conference.

I found a miniature canoe for Trev and a bracelet for Tessa, which are being mailed direct from the Gifte Shoppe at Hilo.

Love from us both.

Ever your affectionate,

A.

854: TO CHRISTOPHER ISHERWOOD

[Los Angeles]
[21 February, 1961]

DHL's *ipsissima verba* are: 'The hot stinging centrality of the goose on the cold shifting flux of mud and waters'. I enjoyed your lecture very much. Apropos of Melville there is a fine hexameter by DHL
'Melville
'Hunts the remote white whale of the deepest passional body.'

Ever yours,
Aldous

855: TO SIR JULIAN AND LADY HUXLEY

3276 Deronda Dr.,
L.A. 28, Cal.
26 February, 1961

Dearest Juliette and Julian,

Thank you for the report on *The Devils*. I understand from my agent,

---

854 *Lecture: Isherwood had succeeded Huxley in the Santa Barbara lectureship. The reference is probably to a broadcast, perhaps of Isherwood's concluding address, called 'A Last Lecture', in which he spoke for political liberalism.*

855 *Huxley's letter to Mme Godel, dated 10 February, is comparable to letter 838.*

whose letter came by the same mail, that the leading man had the flu and was playing with a temperature of 104°, which can hardly have [been] compatible with a good performance. But why do these idiots of producers and directors always make the mistake of putting on plays that are half an hour too long? They know how long the play ought to be and they have had plenty of time during rehearsals to cut. So why don't they do it? Mystery.

I was very sorry to hear of Roger Godel's death. I wrote to Alice and have had a letter from her [. . . .] I shall miss Roger; for he was a genuinely good man with a most remarkable width of vision and also of detailed knowledge. A man whom it was always profitable as well as pleasant and somehow therapeutic to be with.

I was sorry to hear of your troubles, Juliette, and thankful that you are better. All is pretty well here—tho' I am much too busy with this damned book as Laura is with her therapy. I go to MIT for a brief spell at the beginning of April, then back here to polish off the book, I hope definitively—then, as soon as that's done, shall fly in your direction. What are your plans for late spring and early summer?

Ever your affectionate,
Aldous

856: TO DR HUMPHRY OSMOND

3276 Deronda, L.A. 28, Cal.
26 February, 1961

Dear Humphry,

Thank you for your letter which I am answering very briefly, at the moment, just to say that all goes well here, deo gratias, and to forewarn you that a young man called [——], who took LSD with Al and who is now a white-hot enthusiast, is about to visit you on his way back to Toronto. He wants, he says, to write a book 'dramatizing' LSD. I told him that, given the present climate of public opinion, dramatization was about the last thing that shd be attempted. So please cool him off when you see him. (He also naively imagines that his book's royalties will contribute substantially to the treasury of the new organization that is to sponsor LSD work in the West.)

I saw John Spiegel a few days ago, who reported on [——]'s latest activities. [——], it seems, is a little less disorganized than he was last autumn—but still in too much of a mess for his own (or his subjects', I would think) good. It is all a great pity.

The Devils of Loudun had their first night last Monday in London. The play was too long and the leading man had influenza and a temperature of 104°. But otherwise it seems to have gone off fairly well. I hope the author and director can put it into better shape before it is too late. Love to the family.

Yours
Aldous

857: TO JOHN WHITING

3276 *Deronda Drive*,
Los Angeles 28, *Cal.*
6 *March*, [1961]

Dear John Whiting,

Unfortunately I couldn't get away for the opening of *The Devils* and must continue to keep my nose to the grindstone for some weeks to come. From my brother and sister-in-law and from others who were present at the first night I have had reports by letter, and a number of reviews by the dramatic critics have since come in. Apart from the misfortune of having a leading man with the flu, I gather that the chief troubles were excessive length, too farcical a playing of Barré (who was in fact the most dangerous and ruthless kind of fanatic) and a sense of uncertainty experienced by the audience regarding the character of Grandier himself. Historically, as I tried to make clear in my book, Grandier was an example of the Hubris generated by self-conscious cleverness, early professional and social success, and an almost irresistible sexual attractiveness. His tragedy is the tragedy of pride riding for a fall, and his final conversion is the transformation of pride into heroic acceptance. The Grandier of your play—whom I found very interesting as I read the script—is already weary of the world he is so successfully making the best of, and at the same time, in spite of his worldliness, or because of the worldliness and his disgust with the world, secretly God-drunk, subterraneously dedicated to the Manichean proposition that suicide into purity and heaven is better than the essentially impure struggle of life here on earth. When I read the script, as I say, I found this version of Grandier very interesting. But from the reactions to the acted play I get the impression that this obscurely Gnostic or Albigensian Grandier seems insufficiently dramatic, and that it might have been better, theatrically speaking, to stick to the historic figure, insolent in success and so bumptiously certain of his native superiority and his good luck that, until a very late stage in the proceedings, the idea of defeat was simply unthinkable. When it becomes thinkable and then only too manifestly a physical certainty, he begins by reacting with anger and despair, and then almost suddenly, as the result of experiencing the God he had merely talked about and swung censers to, with heroism. I am wondering now whether it would somehow be possible to make the best of both these Grandiers—the insolent, hubristic, cock-sure in every sense of the word cock priest and the obscurely world-weary God-intoxicated Albigensian-with-a-death-wish. The two are not incompatible. The world-hater can wallow in the world and hate it precisely because he wallows, long to get out of it because he loathes and despises the bumptiousness which it is so fatally natural and easy for him to display.

857 *Misdated* 1951 *through a typing error. Huxley wrote to Jeanne Neveux on* 16 *March in some of the same terms. See, however, letter* 870.

Such a man could be a kind of cosmic gambler—life, success, women and hell if he wins (or loses, whichever you prefer), or failure, humiliation, torture, death and heaven if he loses (or wins). I have a feeling—which may of course be sadly mistaken—that it would be possible by making quite small changes and additions and by re-directing the playing of the part and the key in which the lines are spoken, to add this other, classically hubristic dimension to your Albigensian Grandier and in this way make him more dramatic, more all-too-human, more exciting in terms of the theatre than he is at present.

All this may be quite impracticable; but I can't help feeling that if changes along these lines could be made, the play would gain in theatrical power without losing anything (on the contrary, while actually gaining) in psychological and metaphysical depth.

The play only needs a very little something to become a classic of the theatre—and that something has to be *theatrical*, an added quota of conflict rooted in personality. Let me know how you feel about these suggestions and forgive me if they seem impertinent.

Yours very sincerely
Aldous Huxley

PS. Would it be possible, I wonder—this idea has just occurred to me—to have Philippe retiring, after her pregnancy, to the Ursuline Convent (where she will have her baby in privacy). This would provide a bridge between Grandier and the nuns (theatrically useful); and the impending bastard would add fuel to the nuns' hysteria, while the seduced and abandoned girl could be made to build up the image of Grandier into a diabolic-angelic-priapic figure of supernatural proportions.

858: TO T. W. H. ECKERSLEY

3276 Deronda Dr.,
Los Angeles 28, Cal.
12 March, 1961

Dear Cousin Tobias,

Thank you for your letter with its reminder of Roger and poor Tom and my aunt Rachel and the days before the Flood—before the succession of Floods, all without Noahs, doves or rainbows.

I wd advise you, when you get back to England, to consult Miss Scarlett, 46 Portland Place, London W1. She and her sister are excellent teachers of the Bates Method and can give you much better advice than I can do at this distance—and with no teaching experience, merely the experience of a patient with a certain kind of problem. Myopia is sometimes easy to over-

858 *Tobias Eckersley, who was then teaching in Pakistan, is a grandson of Huxley's cousin Roger Eckersley.*

come by Batesian methods, sometimes difficult. One never knows in advance.

Meanwhile I wd advise you to palm, take the sun on the closed lids and, after preparation in this way, directly on the eyes, swinging the head and blinking, for a few seconds at a time. 'Whipping' is also good—moving a printed page back and forth fairly rapidly from just in front of the nose to arm's length—not trying to read (turn the page upside down in order to resist that temptation), merely watching the print enlarge and diminish. Swinging, juggling with balls and remembering to blink are also good. Pakistanian sun may be a bit excessive—so don't work in it if it bothers you. Poor artificial light is a handicap—but if one pauses from time to time to palm, swing, make the eyes shift, it shd not be too troublesome.

Yours,
Aldous Huxley

859: TO SIR JULIAN HUXLEY

3276 Deronda Dr.,
L.A. 28, Cal.
27 March, 1961

Dearest J,

Thank you for your letter. By all means have my chapter printed in the *Observer*, if they want it and it isn't too long.

Yes, I think you wd be well advised to come to UCLA only for a short time. I shall probably be spending some time at Berkeley in early 1962 as visiting Ford Research Professor. I am thinking of using the salary to finance the writing of a reflective travel book on the West Coast—a very extraordinary region, if you take the whole strip, including sea, mountain and desert, from Canada to Mexico. In the intervals I wd give a regular seminar at Berkeley. Details are still vague, but will be made definite, I hope, fairly soon.

Meanwhile I go next week to MIT for a week's celebration of their Centennial. Then back here to finish my book. Then I hope to Europe. What are your plans for the summer? I have to be in Copenhagen in mid August for a psychology conference. Then go to India for a few weeks in late October. I'd thought of spending the first part of the summer in England. Laura will probably come over later—then we wd go down to Italy, after Copenhagen.

All my love to you both. Tell Juliette to be careful. These post-flu periods are trying and one has to work hard at resting and, in Burton's words, 'refocillating the wasted spirits'.

Ever your affectionate,
Aldous

859 *The title of the address at M.I.T. was 'Education on the Non-Verbal Level'. The text was published in* Daedalus, *Spring,* 1962.

860: TO DR FELIX MANN

3276 *Deronda Drive,*
L.A. 28, Cal.
4 *April,* 1961

Dear Dr. Felix Mann,

Thank you for your letter. I hope to be in England in the course of the summer and will get in touch with you then—to talk acupuncture and, professionally, be practised on. At that time I will, if I may, look at the script of your book. At the moment I am trying to finish one of my own and have no time or eye-power for anything else, either in the way of reading or writing.

I was glad to get your description of yourself. Long acquaintance with your namesake, Thomas, had led me to visualize you as an eccentric German of about 65. It is very gratifying to find that I was mistaken!

Yours sincerely,
Aldous Huxley

861: TO TIMOTHY LEARY

The Plaza,
Fifth Avenue at 59*th Street, New York*
13 *April,* 1961

Dear Tim,

Next time you are in New York, go and see the Max Ernst show at the Museum of Modern Art. Some of the pictures are wonderful examples of the world as seen from the vantage point of LSD or mushrooms. Ernst sees in a visionary way and is also a first-rate artist capable of expressing what he sees in paintings which are about as adequate to the visionary facts as any I know. It might be interesting to get in touch with him, find out what his normal state is, and then give him mushrooms or LSD and get him to compare his normal experiences with his drug-induced ones. His combination of psychological idiosyncrasy and enormous talent makes him a uniquely valuable case.

Yours,
Aldous

862: TO MRS FLORENCE A. LEONARD

3276 *Deronda Drive,*
L.A. 28, Cal.
16 *April,* 1961

Dear Mrs. Leonard,

Thank you for your letter. I feel that we have to think of the world as

860 *Huxley, in September, wrote a foreword to Mann's book* Acupuncture: the Ancient Chinese Art of Healing (*London,* 1962).

862 *An elaboration of a point made by Huxley in a broadcast discussion with Harold Urey.*

909

being inhabited by people who are synchronous without being contemporaries. Nuclear physicists rub shoulders with Neanderthalers and 13th century peasants; Behaviorists and advertising agents with medieval saints; logical positivists with mystics; TV-watchers with lyric poets. As always, the destinies of the race are largely in the hands of a ruling minority. How intelligently and benevolently will that minority behave? There are no guarantees that it won't be dominated by madmen (Hitler and Stalin are a sobering reminder of this). On the other hand, the fact that the human race is still here, going strong in spite of all its collective insanities and crimes, suggests that on the whole ruling minorities have been a little better than one had any reason (after observing the behaviour of the majority) to expect. For a number of reasons, the situation is more ticklish now than ever before. Consequently the ruling minority will have to be better than earlier minorities. Will it live up to the demands now being made upon it? That is the question.

Sincerely,
Aldous Huxley

863: TO DR HUMPHRY OSMOND

3276 Deronda Dr.,
L.A. 28, Cal.
5 May, 1961

Dear Humphry,

I am all for the Eileen biography. But it must be more than a straight biography. You can use it (as I used Father Joseph and the Grandier-Surin stories) as a device for expounding, in concrete terms and therefore all the more penetratingly, a great variety of general ideas. My own feeling is that philosophy is best expounded through a biography, real or fictional, or a historical narrative. The narrative doesn't suffer from being made the centre out of which the philosophy radiates—indeed, it is actually enriched by its association with the general ideas. And the general ideas take on greater force through being concretized in, and illustrated by, a particular case history. Eileen's life will permit you to ramify out into all kinds of interesting fields about which you are uniquely qualified to talk—the nature of ESP, the temperamental, bio-chemical, neuro-physiological conditions of mediumship, the relationship between imaging and ESP, the history and sociology of parapsychology and spiritualism, mediumistic possession and its relationship to states observable in mental illness, the nature of the mind. All this can be woven into a biography of Eileen so as to make an extraordinary and unique kind of book. You certainly know enough and are skilful enough as a writer to be able to undertake the job and carry it out successfully. So I would say, don't hesitate to take on the job if the Foundation will support you while you are doing it. And come and live somewhere in this neighbourhood while you are writing.

My work goes forward, and I hope I am finally near the end of it. I want to get away by mid-June, so must finish well before that. But goodness, how difficult this last chapter—the mushroom experience, its philosophical implications and psychological consequences—is turning out to be!

Did you read Grey Walter's lecture to the SPR on the neurological basis of hallucinations? It was interesting, I thought.

Max Cutler, whom I saw last week, gave me a clean bill of health and pronounced me one of his most successful cases. So I'm very thankful I didn't let myself be railroaded (as the other surgeons wanted to do) into having half my tongue and a quarter of my neck cut out. It's just a year now since I went to hospital: and tho' the subsequent 10 weeks were unpleasant, what I had to put up with was incomparably less than I should have had to suffer (and still be handicapped by) as the result of radical surgery instead of radium needles.

Give my love to Jane and tell her that Southern California is a good place for children—both those already extant and those (congratulations) to be.

Yours
Aldous

864: TO IAN PARSONS

[As from]
3276 Deronda Dr., L.A. 28, Cal.
15 May, 1961

Dear Ian,

This address will continue to find me, altho' (as you have probably heard or seen in the papers) my house is no more. It went last Friday night in a raging brush fire fanned by a gale, and with it went books, papers, MSS, old letters, etc etc—all the accumulations. So now I am preparing to start again from scratch. I saved the MS of *Island* and hope to finish it in the next two or three weeks—tho' at the moment writing seems difficult. Thank you for trying to get me an apartment. If nothing startlingly better presents itself, close a deal with Dalmeny Court, which at least is very near the London Library and the Athenaeum.

Thank you too for the pamphlet by Dr. [Neville] Leyton. Please order his two books and have them sent to my wife, who will probably be staying here for a time after my departure. (But all plans are vague—particularly those of the remoter future. I'm supposed to go to India in the autumn and

---

864 *Leyton was a well-known migraine therapist.*

after that to be a visiting professor of nothing at Berkeley—where I plan to write a travel book about the West. After that, what?)

Yours
Aldous

865: TO ROBERT M. HUTCHINS

[*As from*]
3276 Deronda Dr, L.A. 28, Cal.
15 *May*, 1961

Dear Bob,

Laura and I were touched by Vesta's and your very kind offer which we would very gratefully have accepted, if it were not for the fact that there is a lot of business to attend to and, for me, a series of dental appointments. So I shall probably move down to Santa Monica, to stay with Gerald Heard, while Laura moves in with Virginia Pfeiffer and her children, (who also lost their house) in a rented apartment or house.

I am trying to finish a book before leaving for England about June 15th. The circumstances are not too propitious for writing; but perhaps I shall get the job done in time.

It is odd to be starting from scratch at my age—with literally nothing in the way of possessions, books, mementos, letters, diaries. I am evidently intended to learn, a little in advance of the final denudation, that you can't take it with you.

Our love to you both.

Yours,
Aldous

866: TO MRS EILEEN J. GARRETT

[*Santa Monica, as from*]
3276 Deronda Dr., L.A. 28, Cal.
19 *May*, 1961

Dear Eileen,

Thank you for your letter. Yes, all the MSS were burned and all my letters from others and in the case of Maria, my letters to her. So there is no more any tangible link with the past. It is an interesting challenge and I hope I shall be able to cope with it properly.

About books—don't do anything officially. (I think it wd be best not.) But if, when I again have a place to put them, people wd send me a few useful volumes, I shall be grateful.

I still hope to get away to England by June 15th. Perhaps we shall meet over there.

Love,
Aldous

[Santa Monica, as from]
3276 Deronda Dr., L.A. 28, Cal.
28 May, 1961

Dear Mr. Kennedy,

Had I read *Herbert Spencer: by Two* at the time I wrote 'Uncle Spencer'? I can't remember; but if there are traits in my story drawn from that book, I must have. (I haven't read the story since I wrote it.)

The name Uncle Spencer had nothing to do with Herbert Spencer, and was suggested by a tiresome relative of a relative by marriage.

I never talked to A[rnold] B[ennett] about Herbert Spencer and don't recall what was said when he talked of my story.

I have no idea when the story was begun or ended. Its scene was Saint-Trond in Belgium, the home town of my first wife's grandparents.

I read *Du Côté de Chez Swann* in 1915, in the original Mercure de France edition. I never met Proust and have no idea how he came to know about me—as it was far from being true that (to quote his words) I occupied a preponderant position in English literature at that time.

Sincerely,
Aldous Huxley

[Santa Monica, as from]
3276 Deronda Dr., L.A. 28, Cal.
29 May, 1961

My dear Gervas,

Thank you for your letter which finds us both intact, tho' without possessions or a tangible link with the past. By the time you get this I hope you will be well on your way to convalescence and that you will be fully recovered when I get to England in the second half of June, I hope.

Africa must indeed be grisly. But what isn't grisly at the moment? Those whom the gods wish to destroy they first make mad—either raving mad or else absurdly mad, as when we rush to spend the billions that ought to be going into basic research and contraceptive techniques on putting a man on the moon.

A bientôt, I hope. Love to you both.

Aldous

867 *Arnold Bennett, in his* Journals, *mentions a conversation with Huxley, in* 1923, *referring to* 'Uncle Spencer'. *Proust:* Sodome et Gomorrhe, *Chapter* I (1920).

[*Santa Monica, as from*]
3276 Deronda Dr., L.A. 28, Cal.
5 June, 1961

Dear Professor Estabrooks,

Thank you for your letter and the papers which will take their place in the as yet non-existent library by which I hope to replace the one I lost in the fire.

Your book, *The Future of the Human Mind,* disappeared in the flames, but not before my wife and I had read it—with the greatest interest. I have just concluded a Utopian phantasy about a society which makes a serious attempt to help its members to realize their desirable potentialities and in which education [*sic, i.e.* hypnotism] plays a significant part in education and therapy—as also in the history of the hypothetical island, where a fictional counterpart of James Esdaile operated on the Raja (under mesmeric anesthesia) in the 1840's, and thereafter became his chief adviser.

I had a good collection of books on hypnosis and greatly regret their loss. When I am next in the East, I will try to contact you; for I wd like very much to discuss this fascinating and important subject.

Sincerely,
Aldous Huxley

870: TO JOHN WHITING

*4 Ennismore Gdns, S.W.*7
(*Knightsbridge* 0357)
21 June, 1961

Dear Mr. Whiting,

I saw *The Devils* last night and found the play, the production and the performances excellent. I see I was wrong in my reservations about Grandier's character. On the stage, your personage comes through clearly and interestingly.

If you are in town during the next 3 weeks, I hope you will let me know so that we may arrange to meet.

Yours very sincerely
Aldous Huxley

869 *Estabrooks, then Professor of Psychology at Colgate University, is an authority on hypnosis, much of whose work has been in the field of discovering new practical uses for hypnotic techniques.*

4 *Ennismore Gdns,*
*London, S.W.*7
2 *July,* 1961

Dear Cass,

Since coming to London, where we are in the midst of a heat wave, I have been looking at the script of *Island* and, in the light of some of Ian Parsons's comments, making some cuts of passages that seemed redundant and, for fictional purposes, unnecessarily long. I shall have the whole thing re-typed, and you will be receiving a copy within the next 2 or 3 weeks, I imagine.

I expect to be here until July 15th, then a week in the Midi for a conference, then a few days in Paris—after which I may come back to England until we go to Copenhagen for the Psychology Congress on August 13th. But these plans are still a bit uncertain and may be changed if Laura can get over earlier than at present seems practicable. (She is still in LA, coping with insurance matters, and helping out a friend who has broken her collar bone and can't cope with her children or the car.) In any case this address will find me until July 15; then Le Piol, Saint Paul de Vence, A.M., France until the 20th. Will let you know thereafter.

Yours,
Aldous

872: TO MRS SYBILLE BEDFORD

The Athenaeum,
*Pall Mall, S.W.*1
3 *July,* 1961

My dear Sybille,

Thank you for your letter. Yes, how good it was to meet again after all this time. There is too much of space in this world and, for our human purposes, too little time moving forward too precipitately. I leave for Eileen Garrett's congress at St. Paul de Vence on July 15th, shall spend five days there and perhaps a few days with Jeanne and Georges Neveux at Vaison-la-Romaine. What is to happen after that depends on what Laura decides to do—at present she doesn't seem to be free, because of all kinds of involvements, to decide anything. It may be that, if she doesn't come to Europe until later on, I shall return to England until mid-August. In which case I wd like to accept your invitation—and also to suggest that, if you have the time and the inclination we might take a motor trip together. If you can provide the car and the driving, I will provide the petrol and the living

871 *The cuts in* Island *involved the elimination of lengthy passages from the Old Raja's* Notes on What's What.

expenses. It might, I think, be fun; and if we avoided the obvious resorts we ought to be able to find accommodations even in early August. Let me know if this idea appeals to you. At present it is only an idea—to be made concrete and definite in due course, as and when I hear what Laura means to do.

Ever yours
Aldous

873: TO MARK TREVENEN HUXLEY

[London]
[5 July, 1961]

Dearest Trev,

This is a famous bridge across the River Thames. It is a drawbridge, and the middle section can be lifted up so as to let big ships go through. When the ships have passed, the roadway is lowered and the cars go across. I hope you like your camp.

Love
Aldous

874: TO TERESA HUXLEY

[London]
[5 July, 1961]

Dearest Tessa,

This is a picture of the Queen standing on the balcony, looking at some of her soldiers in their best clothes. They wear hats made of the fur of black bears which must be terribly hot in summer.

Much love from
Aldous

875: TO MATTHEW HUXLEY

Woodfolds, Oaksey,
Nr. Malmesbury, Wilts.
9 July, 1961

Dearest M,

Thank you for your letter and anticipatory birthday wishes. And all good wishes for your Peruvian venture. I can't remember his name; but

873 *On a picture postcard of Tower Bridge.*

874 *On a picture postcard depicting the Queen at the ceremony of Trooping the Colour* (not *standing on the balcony*).

875 *Matthew Huxley was going to Peru to do sociological research among the Indians; his book* Back to Eden, *illustrated with photographs by Cornell Capa, was published in 1964. In London, Huxley had been interviewed by John Morgan for BBC-TV and by Walter Allen for radio.*

there was a very helpful and quite pleasant man in charge of the British Council branch at Lima. It might be worth your while to look in there and say hullo to whoever may be there on my behalf. I talked there in 58, and they might be of some use to you. By all means try to get up to Cuzco and Machu Picchu. The Inca remains are among the most extraordinary of all archaeological monuments.

Life here is busy—seeing lots of people, making recordings for BBC radio and TV, writing up my notes for the meeting in Copenhagen. England is prosperous and complacent—too complacent, for the prosperity is menaced by the unfavourable balance of payments and the seeming inability of British industry to increase its productivity and competitiveness. Prices enormously higher than they were in 58. A meal at a not very smart restaurant costs the equivalent of three dollars, and clothes are as expensive as in the US.

I leave for the south of France next Saturday to attend Eileen's parapsychology congress at Le Piol, Saint-Paul de Vence, A.M. After that shall spend a few days at Vaison, where Georges Neveux is producing one of his plays in the Roman theatre. Then, I think, back to England until the Copenhagen congress on August 13th.

Gervas, with whom I am staying this weekend, sends his love. He had a bad operation [. . .] but seems well now and normally energetic. (The whole thing completely free of charge in the public hospital at Bristol, where the nursing was first rate, tho' the ward was a bit noisy!) All [my love.]

Yours
Aldous

876: TO DR HUMPHRY OSMOND

Palace Hotel,
Gstaad, Switzerland
4 August, 1961

My dear Humphry,

I owe you several letters—but have been so rushed these last weeks that correspondence has gone by the board. I was in London for a month, seeing old friends and making new acquaintances. Then spent a week at Le Piol, where we had a good meeting, greatly enlivened by Grey Walter, who is as intelligent and open-minded as he is knowledgeable. Thence to Vaison in Provence, where my French brother-in-law, Georges Neveux, was having one of his plays put on in the Roman theatre. And thence to Gstaad, where Laura has rejoined me, and we breathe good air, eat large meals and listen to Krishnamurti, who is giving a series of talks here—the most recent of them among the most impressive things I ever listened to. It was like listening to a discourse of the Buddha—such power, such intrinsic authority, such an uncompromising refusal to allow the poor *homme moyen sensuel* any escapes or surrogates, any *gurus*, saviours, *führers*, churches. 'I show you sorrow and the ending of sorrow'—and if you don't choose to fulfil the conditions for ending sorrow, be prepared, whatever gurus, churches etc you may believe in, for the indefinite continuance of sorrow.

We leave for Italy on Monday, see Laura's family for a few days, then fly to Copenhagen for the Congress on Applied Psychology, then back to Italy. For how long? I don't yet know. I might go back to England for a bit —in which case I look forward to seeing you. When you're there, incidentally, do try to do something for [——]. He is in a bad way, psychologically —can't work, can't commit himself to a job or to marriage or even to a love affair. There are, of course, early traumas involved. Can you dig them out and abreact them?

Love to the family.

Aldous

877: TO MRS LUCILLE KAHN

Apt. 12, Fabbricato D,
Torre del Mare [Bergeggi, Savona]
8 August, 1961

Dear Lucille,

Thank you very much for your kind letter. I shall be very happy, of course, to receive some books. The poets, first of all. A compendious Shakespeare and Chaucer. Then Wordsworth, Keats (and the letters as well as the poetry), Browning, Arnold, Hopkins, Yeats, Eliot—and Auden's anthology of English verse, plus the *Oxford Books* of 17th cent verse, French verse, German verse, Latin and medieval Latin verse.

Then I'd like, if it isn't asking too much, some of the books on oriental philosophy and religion which I valued. Conze's *Buddhism* and his anthology of Buddhist texts. Suzuki's *Zen Essays* and *Zen Doctrine of No-Mind*, Evans-Wentz's 3 books published by Oxford U. Press, *Tibetan Book of the Dead, Milarepa* and *Great Wisdom* (I think that's the title). Also Zimmer's *Philosophies of India* and *Myths and Symbols of India.* Krishnamurti's *Commentaries on Living.* Benoit's *Supreme Doctrine.* And, from the West, Eckhart—the 1 vol selection by Blakney. William Law—selected by Hobhouse. Wm James, *Varieties of Religious Experience.* Russell's *History of Western Philosophy.*

And if anyone has a spare Dostoevski or two, a spare *War and Peace* and *Karenina* and short stories of Tolstoy, a spare odd volume of Dickens, I shall be grateful for them.

Yours
Aldous H.

877 *A number of the books which Huxley had lost by fire were replaced, during the next months, through the zealous efforts of Lucille Kahn.*

Apt. 12, *Fabbricato D,*
Torre del Mare [*Bergeggi, Savona*]
8 *August,* 1961

My dear Eileen,

Thank you for your good letter. It occurs to me that while you are working with Grey Walter, it wd be interesting to repeat and extend the experiments which Laura did with passes, under the auspices of Dr. Barbara Brown and Andrija Puharich. A woman whom L[aura] had previously helped a great deal with the passes, was hooked up to an EEG and electrocardiograph machine. When the hands (never touching the body) passed over a certain point on the spine, there were immediate changes in the EEG and heart recordings. It might be worth while to check these results with (a) you giving passes to someone else (b) you receiving passes.

We are here for 2 or 3 days—then fly up to Copenhagen for a week.

Love,
Aldous

879: TO LADY HUXLEY

The Plaza,
Fifth Avenue at 59th *Street, New York*
3 *October,* 1961

Dearest Juliette,

I was just sitting down to write to you about my idiocy in forgetting to pack the Danish bowls, when your letter was brought to my door. I realized what I had done at the Customs—for I had conscientiously made a declaration on the form provided on the plane—only to discover that the objects listed weren't there. There's no hurry for them. Slow parcel post may be the simplest course. The blessed word 'Gift' may pacify the *douaniers.* Meanwhile, if you have to state a value, you can say that the large bowl is worth $15.00 and the small ones $6.00 each.

I had an uneventful trip, followed by a busy weekend—a night in Cambridge with MIT friends, the [Roy] Lamsons; thence to Syracuse (NY not Sicily) and a night at Colgate University where I had long talks with Prof. Estabrooks, who teaches psychology and is an expert in hypnotism.

---

878 *From Vaison, Huxley had gone to Gstaad, about 26 July, to meet his wife.*
They both left for Italy on 7 August and went to Copenhagen a week later, to attend a
Congress on Applied Psychology, for which Huxley had prepared an address on
visionary experience. On the 22nd they were in Zürich, where Huxley had arranged to
meet, for the first time, Albert Hofmann, the discoverer of LSD. They spent most of the
next three weeks at Bergeggi and at Turin and arrived in London on 12 September.
Laura then flew to California, but Aldous prolonged his trip by three weeks.

Incidentally, he is organizing a symposium for next April 7th, to discuss hypnotism in its possible applications to education, delinquency, unburying of hidden talents, actualization of potentialities etc. I think I shall be going. He wd very much like Julian to come too. If it fits your dates, it might be interesting. The country is very pretty—250 miles from New York and 40 from Syracuse, which has a good plane service. He will write to Julian about this.

I leave for LA this afternoon. Much love to you both.

Aldous

PS What a blessed relief to find that I have written something about Roger Godel that can be published—and that even makes sense!

880: TO MRS PEGGY LAMSON

6233 *Mulholland Highway,*
Los Angeles 28, Cal.
7 October, 1961

Dear Peggy,

I should have written before to thank you for your warm welcome and the pleasant hours passed with you both. Accumulated mail and miscellaneous business have kept me monstrously busy since my arrival here. But now I have been able to consider the play ['Voices'] and am able to find time for a letter.

I have been working on the end of the third act and discover that, while it is fairly easy to get a potentially powerful and eerie scene out of Pamela (after the scene with Alec) being egged on by the Voices to commit suicide, it is very difficult, perhaps artistically impossible, to follow this up with a scene between the girl and Miss Dillon. Dramatically such a scene would be an anti-climax, and the play ought to end with Pamela being rescued from self-slaughter in the nick of time. (Incidentally, she contemplates suicide not by hanging, which raises all kinds of practical difficulties, but by slashing her wrist with the same knife (a pruning knife stored in the summerhouse closet along with other gardening implements) as she has just

879 *The postscript refers to a contribution to the Godel memorial volume,* Roger Godel: de l'humanisme à l'humain, *published by Belles Lettres, Paris.*

880 *From March, 1961, to April, 1962, Huxley collaborated on a dramatic version of his short story 'Voices' with Peggy Lamson, the wife of Roy Lamson, of the Massachusetts Institute of Technology. This letter is part of their detailed correspondence while the play was being constructed. Huxley finally ended the collaboration when he became dissatisfied with their progress on the script and experienced doubts whether the story was suited to three-act treatment. A leitmotif of the play was to be expressed through a repeated quotation from J. P. de Caussade: 'Do what you are doing now, suffer what you are suffering now. Nothing need be changed but your heart'.*

used to decapitate the talking dummy.) And dialectically the final scene with Miss Dillon is bad—for it means that there is no conflict between the forces of destruction and the forces of health and goodness, only a case for the negative, followed by, but not combatted by, a case for the positive side. Actual work on these two scenes—the scene with the voices and the scene with Miss Dillon—has convinced me that the structure of the last act must be altered. I suggest the following. Open with Pamela alone, haunted by her memories of Eleanor's death and by remorse in regard to her own part in it. (We can link this up with the preceding scene by sound effects. I have introduced into the scene between Pamela and the Voices the tolling of a funeral bell, now distant, now terrifyingly loud. This supernatural bell can sound while Pamela is playing her dreadful practical joke on Eleanor. It is sounding when the third act opens, indicating the fact that Pamela cannot escape from the memory of what she has done.) Miss Dillon enters, and there is a scene in which she tells Pamela that remorse is not the antidote to wrong-doing. The only antidote is love and better doing in the future. Sickness cannot be cured by thinking about sickness, only by using the means that lead to health. And so forth. Alec enters. He has a number of checks for Pamela to sign. (The executors have placed some cash at her disposal for running the household until the will goes through probate.) Conversation about Pamela's new financial status. Miss Dillon takes her leave. (Some-where in the course of her scene with Pamela, she should talk about Rose and Bert, emphasizing the admirable aspects of their characters and the fundamental decency of their relationship. This is necessary as it will be the entry of Rose and Bert at the last moment that saves Pamela from suicide.)

Scene between Pamela and Alec. He scoffs at her protestation that she didn't know she was going to inherit Eleanor's fortune, insists that, half consciously or quite consciously, she was trying to get rid of the old woman. He threatens to blackmail her. Legally she might be safe; but morally, in the eyes of decent human beings, she could be made to seem a monster. The alternative to exposure is marriage to himself. Telling her to think it over, he goes out. There follows the scene with the Voices. The dummy starts talking. Pamela takes as much as she can stand, then cuts off its head with the knife which, later, is to be the instrument of her proposed suicide. The voices are not stilled, but issue from all over the summer house and outside it. (I have written the greater part of this scene, and it seems to work very well.) Interspersed with the diabolic reminders of her guilt, of the disgusting prospects of a marriage with Alec, of incitements to suicide, are memories of things which Miss Dillon has said. There is a kind of argument between the forces of good and evil, with Pamela distraught in the middle. (In this context, let me quote something I have just read in Erich Heller's book, *The Disinherited Mind*. It comes from a letter written by Schiller to Goethe, criticizing the latter's *Iphigenie*. 'Your Orestes is the most doubtful figure of the drama. *There is no Orestes without Furies*; and when the cause of his condition does not strike the senses but lies hidden in his mind and emotions, his is too long and monotonous an agony—without an object. Here we are up against one of the limitations of modern drama as compared with ancient tragedy. I wish you could think of a remedy; but bearing in mind the economy of the play, I do not think that you will; for you have indeed done everything that is possible without gods and spirits.') No Orestes without Furies, gods and spirits. This is the justification for the Voices, both pro and con. And I think that, if the thing is properly handled, it could be extremely powerful and convincing. It means, however, that the central theme of the conflict between good and evil, love and hate, health and madness, must be treated with the utmost seriousness. The final supernatural struggle for Pamela's soul will have to be prepared for in the earlier part of the play—in Miss Dillon's speech about love, in Act I; in Rose's apprehensive remarks about Pamela being up to no good, and in her talk about her fears to Eleanor in Act II.

Tell me what you think about this proposed construction for Act III. It may not yet be quite right. But I *know* that the anti-climactic presentation of the case for Life given by Miss D *after* the scene with the Voices (as in our present plan) is unwritable.

Give my love to Roy, and ask him what he thinks about all this.

Yours,
Aldous

881: TO CASS CANFIELD

6233 *Mulholland Highway,*
Los Angeles 28, *Cal.*
25 *October,* 1961

Dear Cass,

Thank you for your letter and the catalogue, which I am returning separately—marked. If you will send me any of the marked items, I shall be most grateful. I wd also be very glad to have some of my own books—particularly *Grey Eminence, The Devils of Loudun, The Perennial Philosophy, After Many a Summer* and *Time Must Have a Stop.* If *Texts and Pretexts* is still available, I wd very much like to have that too.

Thank you again.

Yours,
Aldous

881 *In a letter of 29 June, posted to London and apparently never received, Canfield had invited Huxley to accept from Harper & Brothers a set of his own works and to choose as a gift additional books from the Harper trade list. Eventually the firm sent him all of his books which were in stock, supplementing these with purchases of out-of-print items. The list of books checked by Huxley in the catalogue is as follows: Alexander,*

[*6233 Mulholland Highway,*
Los Angeles 28]
29 *October,* 1961

Dear Mr. Brooke,

It seems to me that any movement in favour of non-violence needs first, a realistic appraisal of the nature of human beings, and, second, a repertory of psycho-physical procedures designed, in the light of that appraisal, to render feasible the implementation of non-violent ideals.

First, human beings are, amongst other things, animals descended from a primate stock that branched off from a yet older mammalian stock which in its turn branched off from a yet older vertebrate stock. Most vertebrates, including the primates, exhibit (as recent studies of animal behaviour have clearly shown) certain instinctive drives which are the evolutionary basis of many of our least desirable social and political arrangements. Most vertebrates and, except for gorillas, all primates exhibit a passionate concern with territory. (This fact was first observed and clearly described by Eliot Howard in the 1920s. It is incredible how recent anything like a complete and accurate knowledge of animal behaviour is.) Non-social animals such as most birds, will claim a piece of territory as their private property, warn off other members of their species and defend it forcefully if encroachments are made upon it. Among social species, groups of animals will claim a communal territory and will defend it collectively against trespassers of their own kind. Their ethics, if one may apply the word to animals, are completely ambivalent—co-operation, devotion and self-sacrifice in relation to 'our' group,—xenophobia and intense hostility towards members of other groups. Tribalism, and later nationalism, wd seem quite clearly to be derived from

---

The History of Psychiatry; *Ancelot-Hustache*, Master Eckhart and the Rhineland Mystics; The Cloud of Unknowing; *Anshen, ed.*, Alfred North Whitehead; *Bergson*, Time and Free Will; *Bronowski*, Science and Human Values; *Burckhardt*, The Civilization of the Renaissance in Italy; *Butler*, The Way of All Flesh; *Chen-Chi*, The Practice of Zen; *Coulton*, Medieval Faith and Symbolism, Medieval Village, Manor and Monastery, *and* The Fate of Medieval Art in the Renaissance and Reformation; *Dick Read*, Childbirth Without Fear; *Fénelon, Molinos and Guyon*, A Guide to True Peace; *Goldsmith*, The Thunder of Silence; *Baker*, The Image of Man; *Bate*, From Classic to Romantic; *Blackham*, Six Existentialist Thinkers; *Bromberg*, The Mind of Man; *Nef*, Cultural Foundations of Industrial Civilization; *Payne*, Hubris; *Poulet*, Studies in Human Time; *Jacobi*, Psychological Reflections; *Eckhart*, Meister Eckhart; *Eliade*, The Sacred and the Profane; *Haller*, The Rise of Puritanism; *Koyré*, From the Closed World to the Infinite Universe; *Mâle*, The Gothic Image; *Richards*, The Social Insects; *Sinnott*, Cell and Psyche; *Marrou*, Saint Augustine and His Influence Through the Ages; *Van Etten*, George Fox and the Quakers; *Traherne*, Centuries of Meditation.

very ancient tendencies built into almost all species of social vertebrates, including most of the social primates.

Second. As well as a drive for territoriality, most vertebrates exhibit drives for individual dominance and, in animal societies, drives for imposing and maintaining a hierarchy or, in barnyard terms, a pecking order. The drives for territory and dominance often take precedence of the sexual drive and even of the drive for self-preservation. Here again it is pretty obvious that some of the least endearing aspects of man's social and political life have deep evolutionary roots. Most animals have a built-in tendency to fight for territory, either their private property or the property of the local group, and for their status, their position within the group. All social animals practise mutual aid within the group, but hate all 'foreigners' 'on principle' and forcefully drive them away if they come trespassing. Mutatis mutandis, the members of all human groups, from the tiniest tribes to the hugest empires have always done the same. The great mistake that vitiated all earlier studies of animal behaviour was the assumption that most conflicts between sub-human creatures were fights about food or about sex. This assumption is simply not true. The ethologists of the last 30 years have accumulated a mass of material from which it is quite clear that most animal conflicts are about *status* and about *property*, private or collective. Animals behave instinctively much more like power politicians and ambitious status-seekers, than like heroes of romance doing battle for the love of a fair lady.

Any realistic appraisal of human beings must take into consideration the findings of modern studies of animal behaviour. The superstructures of nationalism, social climbing and hierarchical order are obviously conventional and strictly home-made; but their foundations are instinctive and inherited coming to us from a remote evolutionary past. This means surely, that we are merely foolish if we suppose that these tendencies can be eliminated by an appeal to reason through argument, or to 'better feeling' and a 'higher self' through ethical exhortations or religious preaching.

Preaching, exhortation and argument are verbal activities: but the drives for territory, dominance and status in a hierarchy are sub-verbal and can be controlled by words to about the same extent as the functioning of the liver or the adrenals can be affected through suggestion—that is to say to a slight extent but not very much.

What then must be done if the ideals of non-violence and of human brotherhood beyond the confines of 'our' group are to be realised? The clue to a solution of this problem—though not as yet a solution—is to be found in Wm. James' essay: 'The Moral Equivalent of War'. James' suggestions are good as far as they go, but they do not go very far. Conscription for the performance of useful and constructive work in place of conscription for military training—this is all right but by no means enough. The moral equivalent of war, if it is ever to be found, will have to comprise a consider-

924

able number of social arrangements, educational procedures, psycho-physical exercises and activities, all contrived for the express purpose of giving satisfaction to those instinctive or quasi-instinctive drives which we have inherited from xenophobic, territory-claiming and status seeking animal ancestors and which, in the human context, inevitably make for war, —and give satisfaction to those drives in ways that individuals and groups will find rewarding, but which will be harmless or beneficial to all concerned. One of the most important functions of reason is to discover the means whereby the irrationality with which it is always associated may find expression (it is fruitless to attempt to repress it) in an innocuous way. This problem has been obscurely recognized and partially solved by many primitive peoples and by a number of highly civilized peoples of the past. (See Prof. Dodds' book *The Greeks and the Irrational*.) Maenadism, the Dionysian orgies, the maxumba and candomblé of Brazil, the dances, the chantings, the religious rites, the ordeals of many primitive peoples—all these represent methods for harmlessly expressing the dangerous feelings engendered by instinctive drives and the frustrations of social life. Any positive programme for non-violence should be based upon a sympathetic study of practises current in earlier civilizations and among contemporary primitives. In most cases, these practises cannot be borrowed as they stand. They can, however, be adapted to present needs under present cultural circumstances.

At the same time new procedures will have to be invented—procedures capable of giving some kind of harmless satisfactions to the territorial, xenophobic and dominance-directed drives, present in all descendants from the primate stock, and in some individuals very strong. What these procedures should be, I do not know. All I know is that the problem needs to be studied and a great deal of thought devoted to finding some kind of satisfactory solution. If these equivalent outlets for the war-producing drives are now discovered and made widely available, a campaign in favour of peace and non-violence has a chance of succeeding. Otherwise, so it seems to me, it has little or no chance of being successful. Needless to say, work in favour of peace and non-violence shd continue to be performed on the verbal and rational level. But the convincing arguments and the moral categorical imperatives will be ignored, if nothing is done at the same time, about the instinctual and emotional factors involved in individual and collective violence. It is in the combination of verbal and non-verbal, rational and emotional-physical procedures that any positive and constructive campaign for non-violence must consist.

With apologies for the length of this letter and with all good wishes for yourself and for the cause for which you are working,

I am, yours very sincerely
Aldous Huxley

6233 *Mulholland Highway,*
L.A. 28, *Cal.*
[7 *November,* 1961]

Dearest Matthew,

The above is my address until further notice (HO. 4-8024)—tho' the Deronda address will always find us.

Off in an hour for Hong Kong; then Delhi (11-16 Nov., Asoka Hotel); then c/o Krishnamurti, Vasanta Vihara, Greenways Rd, Madras 28; then to Ceylon and perhaps for a few days to Japan. But I have no addresses there. We plan to be back here by Dec 2nd or 3rd.

I was very happy to hear your voice and to get such a good report of your health—in spite of the jungle.

We are in the midst here of the most ghastly fire, compared to which what happened last May was no more than a Guy Fawkes day display. If this drought continues, Los Angeles is really done for—or at least so it seems under existing circumstances. One may be forced to move somewhere a little damper.

Ever your affectionate,
Aldous

884: TO DR HUMPHRY OSMOND

6233 *Mulholland Highway,*
Los Angeles 28, *Cal.*
2 *January,* 1962

My dear Humphry,

A happy New Year to you and the family. How are things going with you, and what is afoot? Here all is pretty well. We made a headlong trip to India in November—a congress to celebrate Tagore's centenary at New Delhi, then a few days at Madras staying with Krishnamurti, then back via Colombo, Hong Kong and Tokyo. India is almost infinitely depressing; for there seems to be no solution to its problems in any way that any of us wd regard as acceptable, the prospect of overpopulation, underemployment, growing unrest, social breakdown, followed, I suppose, by the imposition of a military or communistic dictatorship. And of course, so long as the more prosperous countries spend 40% of their revenues on armaments, nothing effective can be done about India and all the other places in the same fix. *Quos Deus vult perdere, prius dementat.*

At the end of this month I go to Berkeley as a visiting Ford Professor, with no functions—so that I hope to be free to use the resources of the post

883 *Address: the Huxleys had moved in with Mrs Virginia Pfeiffer, their neighbour from Deronda Drive.*

to travel about and write a reflective book of notes and essays on the West Coast—in the manner of *Beyond the Mexique Bay*. I am hoping that this may turn out to be an interesting project, and an educational one—for how little one knows, really, about anything! and how grossly incurious one remains about so many things, what an enormous number of intrinsically astonishing achievements one merely takes for granted! Meanwhile I have just finished the weary chore of correcting two sets of proofs of *Island*, and find myself wondering if the book is any good, or at least more than spottily good. Heaven knows. I will ask Chattos to send you a set of proofs.

Did you ever contact Dr. Volf? We have had no word from him for months and I am wondering what has happened to him. [. . . .]

Ever yours,
Aldous

885: TO SIR JULIAN AND LADY HUXLEY

6233 Mulholland,
L.A. 28, Cal.
7 January, 1962

Dearest Julian and Juliette,

Thank the Lord for quinine, and let's hope it will scotch the possibility of future recurrences of the malaria. I am happy to say that we did all our travelling without so much as a collywobble.

I met no high-up Indians who were not pretty gloomy about the country's prospects—the impossibility of keeping up with the population increase, of achieving any improvement in the condition of the masses in the short time that remains between the present uneasiness and the deeper wider social unrest that the non-fulfilment of high expectations is likely to engender. My guess is that, when Nehru goes, the government will become a military dictatorship—as in so many of the newly independent states, for the army seems to be the only highly organized centre of power. Nehru was being harshly criticized while we were there for being so apathetic about the Chinese, and I was not too surprised by his Goan adventure. He had to prove that he could DO SOMETHING and win a victory, if not over China at least over Portugal.

The Tagore Centenary gave one a very vivid sense of the enormous difficulties in communication that compound the other problems—14 major languages and 3 or 4 alphabets, and everywhere intense linguistic patriotism for which, as was shown 18 months ago in Bombay, people are ready to kill and die. Tagore's Bengali is as alien to a Tamil as Magyar is to us.

I expect to go to Berkeley at the beginning of Feb and shall be there, and travelling about, through the spring. We might do some trips together while you are at Reed [College]. Love to you both from both of us.

Aldous

886: TO IAN PARSONS

6233 Mulholland,
L.A. 28, Cal.
16 January, 1962

Dear Ian,

In reply to your cable—the quotations from Sears Roebuck are taken from an actual S-R catalogue, either of 1959 or 1960.

Roosevelt is said to have advocated free distributions of S-R catalogues in Communist countries, to convert the inhabitants, not to Christianity, but Consumerism.

Yours,
Aldous

887: TO IAN PARSONS

6233 Mulholland,
L.A. 28, Cal.
19 January, 1962

Dear Ian,

After sending off my letter and the sketch for the cover, a wild idea occurred to me. Would it be possible to reproduce on the jacket a picture by some good artist that is suggestive of the book's subject. I enclose a postcard of Van Gogh's 'Fields under Storm-clouds' (his last painting, I believe), which symbolizes very forcibly the precariousness of happiness, the perilous position of any Utopian island in the context of the modern world. If this picture cd be reproduced on the jacket, the effect wd be very striking. Or perhaps one cd find a good black-and-white drawing (if colour reproduction is too expensive)—some Chinese or Japanese rendering of rocks in water, suggestive of an island.

Perhaps all this is wildly out of the question; but Laura brought up the idea suddenly and it fired my imagination. So here, for what it's worth, it is.

Yours,
Aldous

888: TO TIMOTHY LEARY

2533 Hillegass,
Berkeley 4, Cal.
11 February, 1962

Dear Tim,

I forgot, in my last letter, to answer your question about Tantra. There

887 *The jacket of* Island, *as in the sketch, was decorated with a white spot on a background of red, enclosed within the horns of a crescent earth.*

are enormous books on the subject by 'Arthur Avalon' (Sir John Woodroffe), which one can dip into with some profit. Then there is a chapter on it in Heinrich Zimmer's *Philosophies of India*. The fullest scholarly treatment, on a manageable scale, is in Mircea Eliade's various books on Yoga. See also Conze's *Buddhist Texts*. As far as one can understand it, Tantra seems to be a strange mixture of superstition and magic with sublime philosophy and acute philosophical insights. There is an endless amount of ritual and word-magic. But the basic ideal seems to me the highest possible ideal—enlightenment, not apart from the world (as with the Vedantists and the Nirvana-addicts of the Hinayana School of Buddhists) but within the world, through the world, by means of the ordinary processes of living. Tantra teaches a yoga of sex, a yoga of eating (even eating forbidden foods and drinking forbidden drinks). The sacramentalizing of common life, so that every event may become a means whereby enlightenment can be realized, is achieved, essentially, through constant awareness. This is the ultimate yoga—being aware, conscious even of the unconscious—on every level from the physiological to the spiritual. In this context see the list of 112 exercises in awareness, extracted from a Tantrik text and printed at the end of *Zen Flesh, Zen Bones* [by Paul Reps] (now in paperback). The whole of 'Gestalt Therapy' is anticipated in these exercises—and the therapy is not merely for the abnormal, it is above all a therapy for the much graver sickness of insensitiveness and ignorance which we call 'normality' or 'mental health'. LSD and the mushrooms shd be used, it seems to me, in the context of this basic Tantrik idea of the yoga of total awareness, leading to enlightenment within the world of everyday experience—which of course becomes the world of miracle and beauty and divine mystery when experience is what it always ought to be.

Yours,
Aldous

889: TO MYRICK LAND

[*As from*] 6233 *Mulholland,*
Los Angeles 28, *Cal.*
1 *March,* 1962

Dear Mr. Land,

Murry's was an acute and subtle mind, and there was something curiously fascinating about his conversation. Moreover he would radiate a kind of religious enthusiasm—about Dostoevsky and his ideas, about 'metabiology', about Lawrence as 'The Son of Man', the 20th-century Messiah.

889 *Land, who was then writing* The Fine Art of Literary Mayhem, *had asked Huxley what qualities of John Middleton Murry attracted Lawrence and finally repelled him.*

At first, people tended to catch fire from this enthusiasm, this flame of earnestness. But after a while they began to discover that the flame was only a stage effect, that the enthusiasm and the earnestness were not spontaneous—for Murry (and Catherine [Katherine Mansfield] too) had a strange way of churning themselves, violently and indefatigably, in the hope of transforming a native inability to feel very strongly or continuously into a butter-pat of genuine emotion, true passion, unquestioning faith. (Read in this context Murry's novel, *The Things We Are*. It contains the most extraordinary passages, in which the hero (Murry) works up bogus Dostoevskyan passions out of nothing at all.) Lawrence, like most other people, was fascinated by Murry at first, was convinced by his show of passionate enthusiasm—and also flattered, I'm afraid, by the ascription to himself of messianic qualities. Then, as the letters show, he discovered that 'the things we are' were in fact merely the product of an emotionally underendowed (but intellectually highly gifted) play actor who had set out half unconsciously, half deliberately, to churn his vacuum into the semblance of substance —to transform 'the things we are not' into something which the unwary might mistake for the genuine article, the 'high-priced spread', as the margarine advertisers put it.

Hypocrisy, says La Rochefoucauld, is the tribute that vice pays to virtue. Murry's brand of hypocrisy was rather different—it was the tribute that emotional impotence pays to faith and passion. Lawrence was at first taken in by the hypocrisy—and the genuine charm; then, when he saw through it, he was appalled and indignant, all the more indignant for having been taken in.

Sincerely,

Aldous Huxley

PS I'm glad you liked *Island*. The weakness of the book consists in a disbalance between fable and exposition. The story has too much weight, in the way of ideas and reflections, to carry. Alas, I didn't know how to remedy this defect.

890: TO MATTHEW HUXLEY

Santa Barbara Biltmore, Montecito,
Santa Barbara, California
17 March, 1962

Dearest Matthew,

I should have written long since to thank you for your letter and to keep you posted as to what is happening here in the Far West. My only excuse is that I arrived in Berkeley, early in Feb. with a cold on the chest which lingered on and on, and turned out in the end to be what they call pneumonitis. So I flew back to LA, went to bed and took antibiotics which cleared the thing up in a week. After which I returned to Berkeley, performed my visiting professor act for a little, then came down here for a Conference on Technology in the Modern World, under the auspices of Bob Hutchins's Centre for the Study of Democratic Institutions. Some of it was quite interesting, some of it very boring; but I enjoyed it on the whole—for there were a number of very able and well-informed participants with whom it was a pleasure to talk. Needless to say, we came to no conclusions—merely succeeded in posing the problems and establishing the fact that nobody is coming up with satisfactory solutions. Today it is all over and tomorrow I return to Berkeley (where my address is 2533 Hillegass Ave, Berkeley 4—Tel. Thornwall 5-4570). I expect to come and go a good deal—looking at the kind of things (agri-business, new factories, lunatic asylums, scenery) which can be written about in the reflective travel book that I have in mind. I expect to come East quite soon—March 29th at the U. of Alabama, 31st at Phila, 1st at the Poetry Center N.Y.C. Stay in NYC for a day or two. Then perhaps Boston for a few hours, then Syracuse for a 2-day conference on Hypnosis at Colgate U. Then back to Berkeley. I will try to get to New York on Sunday morning, April 1st, and shall stay at the Plaza. Let's make a date for lunch that day and an afternoon together. I want to hear about the book and how you are getting along with what must be a difficult job.

Just before I came down here, I spent a couple of days with Frank Hauser, a very bright producer-director who is putting on *The Genius and the Goddess* at the end of April—first at Oxford, then, if all goes well, in London. An intelligent, sensitive and very professional man, all of whose suggestions were to the point. The play remains what it was in its original form—but with his aid I have streamlined the 3rd act so that if flows easily and uninterruptedly towards the conclusion, and have made the outer play of old Rivers and Barr more interesting and more relevant to the main play. I think now that the piece will work well and perhaps be successful. What fun if it were! Meanwhile there is to be a film of the *Devils of Loudun*. What on earth will they make out of it? I feel a great deal of curiosity—and some apprehension!

I hope you have had your copy of *Island*.

A bientôt, dearest M. There will be long arrears to be made good when we meet, and I am looking forward to our time together in New York.

Ever your affectionate,
Aldous

> 2533 *Hillegass,*
> *Berkeley 4, Cal.*
> 20 *March,* 1962

Dear Professor Dubin,

My last line was, 'And she finds him decidedly firmer'. Yours is perhaps more musical—with a touch of Edgar Allan Poe in it. And the Cell piece is delightful. In a very amusing way, it brings home one of our toughest philosophical problems—how to express within a single frame of reference and in terms of an inclusive, monistic vocabulary, the seemingly incommensurable data of immediate subjective experience and objective bio-chemistry and cytology.

> The man who puts all that into a single bottle
> Will rank as forty times as great as Aristotle.
>> *Sincerely,*
>> *Aldous Huxley*

892: TO ROBERT M. HUTCHINS

> [? *Tuscaloosa, Alabama*]
> *As from:* 2533 *Hillegass,*
> *Berkeley 4, Cal.*
> 28 *March,* 1962

Dear Bob,

It was a real delight to see you again—even tho' I felt you were depressed by the prospect of having to make forays into the world of the Post-Prostate Rich, by the spectacle of Education in particular and, in general, of the immense Organized Insanity within which we must all live and move and have our being, and from which there seems to be no escape except subjectively, in Stoicism, mysticism or alcohol.

The young man who collaborated with me in collecting materials for the

---

891 *Last line: to an incomplete limerick in* Eyeless in Gaza, *Chapter X:*
> '*There was a Young Fellow of Burma*
> *Whose betrothed had good reasons to murmur,*
> *But now that they're married he's*
> *Been using cantharides*
> . . . . '

Dubin's last line was 'And now she don't murmur, he's firmer'. The cell piece: his poem '*The Cell Theory', published in* Perspectives in Biology and Medicine, *VI (Autumn, 1962), two lines of which Huxley echoed in his own couplet. Dubin is Professor of Pathology at the Woman's Medical College of Pennsylvania, in Philadelphia.*

892 *The collaborator on the anthology, which remains unpublished, was William Geoffrey. Huxley had written to Lawrence C. Powell of the U.C.L.A. library, 16 May, 1945, asking him to provide Geoffrey with a reader's card so that he might work on the compilation.*

project has just sent back to me the MS of all the essays I wrote for an anthology of World Essays (with commentaries) for the *Britannica*—in 1946 or 1947, I believe. The *EB* never published this anthology, but wrote me about a year or so ago asking if I wd make some revisions and additions to the biographical notes. To which I said, No. I did a great deal of work for very little money, and have no wish to do more now. Can you find out what the *EB* intends to do with the anthologized essays and my material? If nothing, would they have any objection to my making use of my material in serial form, or possibly in a volume of essays?

Ever yours,
Aldous

893: TO MRS EILEEN J. GARRETT

2533 Hillegass Ave.,
Berkeley 4, Cal.
14 April, 1962

Dear Eileen,

Thank you for your letter. Yes, I was sorry to miss you in NY, but hope I may catch you when I come through for my talk at the American Academy on May 24th.

About [——]—I hear from [——] that he is a bit better, but still very neurotic and inhibited from effective action. What is to be done? If only he cd commit himself—to a woman first of all, and then to a job, a cause, a literary project. But he lives in terror of being committed—feels that any form of commitment is a trap and a prison. I told him last summer that the art of life consists precisely in getting into a trap and transforming it into a vehicle for getting to the ends of the earth, into a machine for self-development. He knows it—but can't act on his knowledge.

[. . . .]

Affectionately,
Aldous

894: TO MRS MARGARET KISKADDEN

The Plaza,
Fifth Avenue at 59th Street, New York
23 May, 1962

My dear Peggy,

Opening today's *N.Y. Times*, I was distressed to read the news of Curtis's death. These vital threads that link the present to the past—how many of them have already been broken, and how increasingly often, as one grows older, does one receive the news of yet another break! And the questions keep multiplying. How are we related to what we were? Who are we now and what were we then? And who were the others—in our minds,

894 *Curtis: W. Curtis Bok, author and Pennsylvania jurist.*

in their minds, in the mind of omniscience? There are no answers, of course
—only the facts of living, changing, remembering and at last dying.

Affectionately,
Aldous

895: TO MRS BETH WENDEL

6233 *Mulholland,*
L.A. 28, Cal.
13 *June,* 1962

Dear Betty,

Thank you for your letter, which was followed today by one from [Max]
Kester. It is melancholy that the play shd have had to be closed on the threshold of London, and I hope most fervently that a theatre will open up before
the cast grows tired of waiting and disperses. Meanwhile, if you see ways in
which the play can be improved (e.g. Mrs Hack[enschmidt] at the end, old
and young Rivers played by one actor), please go ahead and make the
necessary changes in conjunction with Frank or any other director. It will be
much better that way than for me to try to do anything out here at a distance
and without first hand knowledge of personalities and events in and around
the theatre.

I am rather surprised that Hauser has not taken the play to a few other
provincial centres—e.g. Birmingham, Liverpool, Edinburgh, Brighton. I
wd have thought that he wd have found good audiences there while waiting
for a West End outlet.

I am back now from Berkeley, but find myself with a lot to do down here.
Let me know how things go at your end. Love from us both.

Yours ever,
Aldous

896: TO MRS CAROLYN HAWLEY

6233 *Mulholland,*
Los Angeles 28, Cal.
17 *June,* 1962

Dear Mrs. Hawley,

Thank you for your letter. What I said about a psycho-analytic ballet
was uttered on the spur of the moment—but perhaps, as you seem to think,
there is something in it. I envisage something along the following lines.

At the back of the stage, or to one side, the patient on a couch with the
analyst behind him or her. They remain more or less motionless throughout
the performance. The ballet is the projection into dance-forms of what hap-

---

895 *Max Kester, of the Fosters' Agency in London, was Huxley's agent outside of
the United States.*

896 *Carolyn Hawley teaches music at Laney College, Oakland, California. She
had met Huxley at the University of California, Berkeley.*

pens as fragments of buried memories come to the surface. Memories of ecstatic adolescent happiness and of adolescent despair. Memories of traumatic events in childhood—punishments, humiliations, an attempted rape. Archetypal visions—solemn, beautiful, prophetic. And so forth. Probably you wd have to have a narrator, who wd give verbal continuity to the successive episodes. Anyhow there are endless possibilities to play with. Good luck to you!

Sincerely,
Aldous Huxley

897: TO REID GARDNER

6233 Mulholland,
L.A. 28, Cal.
25 June, 1962

Dear Mr. Gardner,

Your very interesting letter of May 7th got mislaid during my comings and goings between LA and Berkeley, where I spent the spring semester as a Full Professor of Nothing-in-Particular, and has only just now come up to the surface. Hence the long delay in thanking you for the kind things you say about *Island* and for the useful criticisms of the book's deficiencies and for the valuable and illuminating comments on 'superstitions' and myth. It is, of course, quite true that I undervalue myth and indeed have a certain prejudice against it—the product, I suppose, of a rationalist upbringing. I remain an agnostic who aspires to be a gnostic—but a gnostic only on the mystical level, a gnostic without symbols, cosmologies or a pantheon. Perhaps, as you say, one should—experimentally and with proper scepticism —cultivate a traditional superstition for the sake of its psychological results. I am an old dog, but perhaps not too old to learn a new trick or two.

Perhaps we might meet one day? I wd like to hear more about the Wakers Circle, how you work and what you experience.

Sincerely,
Aldous Huxley

898: TO GEORGE WICKES

6233 Mulholland,
L.A. 28, Cal.
10 July, 1962

Dear Mr. Wickes,

Alas, I cant expatiate on Henry Miller, for, except for one or two items,

897 *Wakers Circle: a Tantric Buddhist group.*

898 *Declining a request that he write an article on Miller for a symposium to be called* Henry Miller and the Critics (*published* 1963). *Wickes included instead a brief statement on Miller which Huxley had made for the Los Angeles* Times.

I have not read him—and when I have tried to read him, have found him a bit too cosmic for my taste.

Sincerely,
Aldous Huxley

899: TO DR HUMPHRY OSMOND

6233 Mulholland,
Los Angeles 28, Cal.
19 August, 1962

Dear Humphry,

Your welcome letter has crossed a postcard of my own—sent off, I now suspect, without a sufficiency of stamps, so that it will reach you very belatedly by ship. In that pc I announced that I expect to be in Europe during September and hope to see you. I hadn't meant to take in Europe en route to Argentina (where we are expected in early October); but have just been asked to attend a meeting at Brussels of a new World Academy of Arts and Sciences, started by a lot of Nobel Prizemen who would like to see that their science is used in a relatively sane manner. ('Ends are ape-chosen; only the means are man's', as I remarked in *Ape and Essence*. Maybe we could do something to humanize the ends.) I think the Brussels conference may be interesting; anyhow it seems worth trying at least to do something to mitigate the current organized insanity. How fabulously well-organized the insanity is was borne in upon me the other day at the local North American Aviation plant, where I went to have a look at the Apollo moon-shot capsule and the latest plane-to-ground missiles, which can turn at right angles, skim along the ground, shoot perpendicularly up into the air to avoid interception and finally be guided, warhead and all, to whatever orphanage or old people's home may have been selected as the target. All this concentrated knowledge, genius, hard work and devotion, not to mention all those incalculable billions of dollars, poured forth in the service of vast collective paranoias—and meanwhile our three billions of mainly hungry people are to become six billions in less than forty years and, like parasites, are threatening to destroy their planetary host and, with their host, themselves.

I was most interested to hear of [Mark] Altschule's work and of the possibilities in New Jersey. I hope you will take the NJ job; for the most import-

899 *Altschule, of the Harvard Medical School, had been working with amino-chromes (adrenochrome and similar substances). Osmond was considering a post (which he accepted) as Director of the Bureau of Research in Neurology and Psychiatry at the New Jersey Neuro-Psychiatric Institute. Huxley flew to Brussels to attend the meeting of the new World Academy. The trip to Argentina was cancelled. Laura Huxley's book was published in 1963 as* You Are Not the Target, *with a foreword by Aldous.*

ant research is that which is aimed at the cracks in the armour between two solid scientific disciplines. We need the most intelligent and freely operating people, like yourself, to do the probing through those vulnerable joints in the conceptual carapace that encases reality.

My plans call for a short stay in Brussels, August 30th to Sept. 3rd. I may remain a few days more in the region, then shall go to London. Will you be around? I hope so.

Laura is fearfully busy, trying to meet the deadline on her book of *Recipes for Living*, so will not be coming to Brussels. We are to meet later on in Argentina. My love to Jane and the children.

Yours,
Aldous

900: TO MATTHEW HUXLEY

The Athenaeum,
*Pall Mall, S.W.*1
12 *September,* 1962

Dearest Matthew,

I have taken the first steps towards setting up a trust fund, here in London, for the benefit of Trev and Tessa. My idea is this: to make over to the trust a certain number of English copyrights, the income from which wd accumulate until required for educational (or other) purposes later on. I would start with copyrights of books up to a certain date—say 1928. Other copyrights might be added at subsequent dates. If I live for five years after the date of the gift, there will be that much less to pay in death duties. Additions to the trust will be contingent, I suppose, on my own earning powers in the future. If I find I can dispense with the income from earlier books, I will hand over more copyrights. If I don't do so well currently, I shall have to cling to the older sources of supply.

You will be one of the trustees, and there will have to be another on this side. Do you have anyone you wd like to take on the job? It had better be someone relatively young. Perhaps Andrew Huxley? Or Humphry Osmond?

Meanwhile please send me the birth dates of the 2 children, and their full names. (Does Tessa have a second name? And what about Trev?)

Please answer as soon as may be, as I shd like to get the legal arrangements set up before I leave London.

I caught an unpleasant chest cold in Holland, and am still on the feeble side. But I hope all goes well with you.

Ever your affectionate
Aldous

31 Pond Street, N. W. 3
17 September, 1962

Dearest M,

Thank you for your letter, which must have crossed my second communication saying that the lawyer now advised against an English trust, but for an American one. This being so, can you unofficially ask David's advice in this matter? When I have to be in the East for lectures at the end of Oct: and beginning of November, we can make the thing official.

Have just returned from a pleasant, but *cold*, weekend with Gervas. What a climate!

Ever your affectionate,
Aldous

902: TO REID GARDNER

At 31 Pond Street,
Hampstead, N.W.3
18 September, 1962

Dear Mr. Gardner,

Thank you for your very interesting letter. Needless to say, I am not a thorough-going anti-conceptualist. I am only concerned with not taking words too seriously; with understanding the nature and limitations of language, and its relations with what it stands for; with making the best of both worlds—the experiential and the symbolic. I have tried to set forth my position in such essays as 'The Education of an Amphibian', 'Knowledge and Understanding' and (in a recent issue of *Daedalus*) 'Non-Verbal Education'—not to mention *Island*, passim. Krishnamurti (for whom I have a great affection and respect) never deals with the constructive use of 'mind' —tho' he does say, perfunctorily, that of course it has its uses and is necessary. He is too much preoccupied with its wrong use to be able to give attention to the problems of its right use. This is his weakness—a weakness which one must always bear in mind as one reads his analyses of the various delinquencies engendered by an excessive addiction to concepts.

I did not know that [Robert] Graves had written on psilocybin, and must read his article. In experiments with LSD and psilocybin subsequent to the mescalin experience described in *Doors of Perception*, I have known that sense of affectionate solidarity with the people around me, and with the universe at large—also the sense of the world's fundamental All Rightness,

901 *Huxley had written on the 14th to say that, for tax reasons, an American trust would be more advantageous than an English one.*
902 *Graves has written on hallucinatory mushrooms; see his book* Food for Centaurs (1960).

in spite of pain, death and bereavement. This All Rightness can be expressed in words or other symbols—but its nature cannot be conveyed to anyone who had not gone through the unmediated experience. And can the experience be induced by even the most transportingly poetical words? I have never found that it could be so induced—at the most, only prepared for. (Incidentally, mescalin, LSD and psilocybin all produce a state of affairs in which verbalizing and conceptualizing are in some sort by-passed. One can talk about the experience—but always with the knowledge that 'the rest is silence'.)

When I am back in California, I hope you will come and see me.

Sincerely,
Aldous Huxley

903: TO MRS BETH WENDEL

6233 Mulholland,
L.A. 28, Cal.
14 October, 1962

Dear Betty,

Herewith the revised pages. After long hesitation, I decided that it wd be best to omit the confession by Rivers that he was in love with Katy. It is all going to come out in the main play, and the mention of it at this point may blunt the impact later on.

I rather regret the 'every one you meet will be drunk' line as an ending to the play. But perhaps something of the kind I have written here will be better.

Yours ever,
Aldous

PS The pages you sent me c/o Jeanne arrived by yesterday's mail!

904: †TO GEORGES NEVEUX

En avion
30 October, 1962

Cher Georges,

Je viens de recevoir votre lettre, qui m'a suivi de Los Angeles jusqu'à Memphis, Tennessee, où je viens de donner une conférence. Les droits de

---

903 *After its failure in London, where it had been produced from a script disastrously altered from the version used at Oxford,* The Genius and the Goddess *was undergoing further revisions so that a proper script might be available to foreign producers.*

904 TRANSLATION:—*'I have just received your letter, which followed me from Los Angeles to Memphis, Tennessee, where I have just given a lecture. The rights to* Brave New World *are not free—having been sold, thirty years ago, to the RKO people, who*

[*Continued on next page*

939

Brave New World ne sont pas libres—ayant été vendus, il y a 30 ans, à la compagnie RKO, qui n'a jamais fait quoique ce soit, mais qui reste pourtant propriétaire. En attendant une adaptation dramatique-musicale a été faite et j'espère que la pièce sera bientôt mise en scène. Nous verrons. En attendant je suis heureux d'apprendre le succès d' *Arsène Lupin contre Arsène Lupin.*

Je regrette énormément que j'aie dû renoncer à vous voir cet été; mais cette petite grippe que j'ai attrapée en Belgique ne faisait qu'emparer et j'ai cru plus sage de prendre vol directement pour la Californie et une semaine de repos et d'antibiotiques. Tout va bien maintenant, et je travaille—un long essai *Littérature et Science* et d'autres morceaux plus courts. Mon roman Utopique *Island* a eu un certain succès en Angleterre et aux Etats-Unis, et je crois que Plon prépare une traduction française.

Quant aux projets—tout reste assez vague. Mais j'espère—si la folie organisée de la politique internationale ne devient pas furieuse—que nous nous trouverons en votre voisinage au cours de l'année prochaine.

Love to Jeane and Noële. Bien amicalement, cher Georges.

Aldous

905: TO MRS CLAIRE WHITE

6233 *Mulholland,*
Los Angeles 28, Cal.
17 *November,* 1962

Dear Claire,

Thank you for your very sweet letter. It is always a great delight to see you and Bobby and the children—and an enduring satisfaction to know that

---

have never done anything with it but who nevertheless retain ownership. Meanwhile a musical adaptation has been made and I hope that the play will soon be produced. We shall see. Meanwhile I am happy to learn of the success of Arsène Lupin *versus* Arsène Lupin.

'*I regret enormously that I had to renounce seeing you this summer; but that minor 'flu I got in Belgium hung on and I thought it wiser to take flight directly for California and a week of rest and antibiotics. All goes well now, and I am working—a long essay* Literature and Science *and some other, shorter pieces. My Utopian novel* Island *has had a certain success in England and the United States, and I believe that Plon is preparing a French translation.*

'*As for plans—all remains rather vague. But I hope—if the organized madness of international politics doesn't grow furious—that we shall find ourselves in your neighbourhood in the course of next year.*

'*Love to Jeanne and Noële. With very friendly wishes, dear George.*'

This musical adaptation of Brave New World *had been made by Franklin Lacey. Like the one written by Huxley himself in 1956, it has not been produced.*

905 *St James: Matthew Huxley lived for a time on the White estate at St James, New York.*

Matthew and his children have put down a set of subsidiary roots at St. James.

Alas for Erasmus! How I shd like to be like him! And how sadly I realize that his sweet reasonableness made him abhorrent to both parties, who went on with their wars and agreed only in denouncing the apostle of good will, intelligence and compromise.

Yours affectionately,
Aldous

906: TO MRS ELLEN FITCH

6233 Mulholland,
Los Angeles 28, Cal.
27 November, 1962

Dear Mrs. Fitch,

Thank you for your most interesting letter. These spontaneous experiences of light are very wonderful. They are certainly not manufactured; they are 'given'—by what or whom? One is impressed, in reading such books as Dr. Bucke's *Cosmic Consciousness* or Dr Raynor Johnson's *The Watcher on the Hills*, to discover how often they are given. One hears about them only when they happen to people who have a gift of artistic expression, or the power and wish to influence others. One does not hear of the many who don't possess these qualifications, but to whom the light presents itself just as strongly and *effectively*.

Yours sincerely,
Aldous Huxley

907: TO MATTHEW HUXLEY

6233 Mulholland,
L.A. 28, Cal.
9 December, 1962

Dearest M,

Thank you for your letter. No word from Dr. Kessel yet—but I look forward to seeing him whenever he reaches these parts.

You sound just too busy—and so am I. It is a curse and an addiction, this being busy overmuch and one shd do something about it—a course of Antabuse-iness and membership in Busy-bodies Anonymous. My current busy-ness, after writing a paper for last week's Conference at the Centre for the Study of Democratic Institutions is with a long piece on *Literature and Science*, which keeps on developing as I write but which I hope to finish off within the next month or so. All the essays on the subject—from T. H. Huxley's and Matthew Arnold's in the 1880's (still the best in the field) to [Sir Charles] Snow's, [F.R.] Leavis's, [Lionel] Trilling's and [J.R.]

941

Oppenheimer's—are too abstract and generalized. I am trying to approach the subject in more concrete terms, thinking about what might be done by men of letters in our age of science and reflecting on what in fact has been done by earlier men of letters in relation to the science of their day.

Ellen mentioned in a recent letter that the children need an encyclopaedia—so I am sending her a cheque with which to buy a set of *World Book Children's Encyclopaedia* (which educators assure me is the best). I got a set for Ginny Pfeiffer's children (for Xmas) and paid $130.00 (instead of $189—advertised price): so presume one can get the same sort of discounts in New York.

Meanwhile here is a little something to buy some good cheer with over the holidays.

Love to Judy, and to Claire and Bobby, if you see them.

Ever your affectionate,

A.

908: TO GEORGE H. ESTABROOKS

6233 Mulholland,
Los Angeles 28, Cal.
10 December, 1962

Dear George,

Thank you for your two letters. For various reasons—among others, because my wife has to remain in this neighbourhood on account of her work and because I don't want to take so much time away from my own, literary work—I must say no to your very kind invitation. But when I next go East for a visit, I will certainly let you know and come and see what you are doing—maybe ask you to improve my creativity.

You speak of the abominable snowman—do you know Prince [——]'s favourite riddle? 'What is the difference between the abominable snowman and the abominable snowwoman?' Answer: 'Abominable snowballs'.

All good Christmas wishes,

Yours,
Aldous

909: TO DR HUMPHRY OSMOND

6233 Mulholland,
L.A. 28, Cal.
15 December, 1962

Dear Humphry,

A merry Christmas to you all and a happy new year! Meanwhile what are

907 *Judy: Judith Wallet Bordage, to whom Matthew Huxley was married in March, 1963.*

you up to? When are you taking up your job in New Jersey? Let me have some news.

Here all goes pretty well. Laura is putting the final touches to her book, and I am hard at work on a long essay on *Literature and Science*, which I hope to finish in another month or so. After that—who knows? I don't, at the moment.

I spent a couple of interesting days this autumn with Roger Williams at the Univ. of Texas, looking at his collection of pictures and statistics of human differences. One wonders, sometimes, how creatures so dissimilar manage to interbreed. Meanwhile what an immense amount of enlightening research remains to be done in this region. How are these anatomical and biochemical differences related to resistance or proneness to mental disease or the milder neuroses and hysterias? How can [Hans] Eysenck's theory of innate differences in conditionability be related to these anatomical and biochemical differences? Etcetera, etcetera. I am sure you will have a lot of fun with this sort of thing when you get to N.J. My love to Jane and the children.

Yours affectionately
Aldous

910: TO IAN PARSONS

6233 Mulholland,
Los Angeles 28, Cal.
16 December, 1962

Dear Ian,

The news of Phil Nichols' death is very saddening. He was at Balliol with me and we have been good friends—tho' meeting only off and on, now in England, now in Rome, now somewhere else, ever since. One was very fond of Robert, despite the fact that he was impossible: and one was very fond of Phil, because he had all the engaging qualities which dear Bob so theatrically lacked. Soon one will have no contemporaries.

About the Santa Barbara paper—I have looked at it again and have decided that there really isn't much point in having it published. The same sort of things have been said so often before—by me and by other people—that it seems hardly worth while to say them again, except in the relative privacy of an *ad hoc* conference. So I'm not bothering to make the revisions, but am pressing on as fast as I can with the *Literature and Science* piece.

May I ask you to send me copies of *Time Must Have a Stop, Adonis and the Alphabet* and *Brief Candles* (if that is the volume in which 'After the Fireworks' is printed). Also *The Olive Tree*—hard cover or paperback in every case, whichever is simplest. All good Christmas wishes.

Yours,
Aldous

911: †TO H. H. MAHARAJA DR KARAN SINGH, OF JAMMU AND
KASHMIR

> 6233 *Mulholland Highway,*
> *Los Angeles* 28, *California*
> 22 *December,* 1962

Your Highness,

Thank you for your kind letter. *Island* is a kind of pragmatic dream—a fantasy with detailed and (conceivably) practical instructions for making the imagined and desirable harmonization of European and Indian insights become a fact. But alas, in spite of these pragmatic aspects, the book still remains a dream—far removed (as I sadly made clear in the final paragraphs of the story) from our present reality. And yet, if we weren't all so busy trying to do something else, we *could*, I believe, make this world a place fit for fully human beings to live in.

As for the 'psychodelic' drugs, LSD, mescalin, psylocybin—these are in short supply and available only to research workers. I have no idea whether any research in this area is being carried on in one of the Indian Universities. You could find out by writing to the Sandoz Company, Basel, Switzerland (the manufacturers of LSD and psylocybin).

Another possibility:—my friend Dr. Timothy Leary, Department of Psychology, Harvard University, Cambridge, Mass., U.S.A. is conducting research on a large scale. It is possible that he might like to have an opportunity of working with the psychodelics in relation to subjects brought up within another culture than his own. If you could put a house at his disposal for a few weeks he might like to come to India and make this socio-psychological experiment. And if and when I come again to your country I will certainly remember your kind invitation.

> *Aldous Huxley*

912: TO MADAME SUZANNE NICOLAS

> 6233 *Mulholland,*
> *L.A.* 28, *Cal.*
> 22 *December,* 1962

Chère Suzanne,

Merci de ta letter et du chèque, que je garderai pour des crises dans la

912 TRANSLATION:—'*Thank you for your letter and the cheque, which I will keep for crises in the life of Mère. Fortunately she is always well and takes an interest in everything.*

'*I often think of my stay at Tegelen and of our tour, of which I have a very happy memory in spite of the insidious virus.*

'*All goes well here. Laura has at length completed her book, and I have just done the same thing—a long essay on* Literature and Science, *of which I read you, I believe, the first draft—too brief and inadequate for the subject.*

'*Merry Christmas to all of you, and a happy New Year, dear Suzanne—good health, good work and, let us hope, a good reunion somewhere. . . .*'

vie de Mère. Heureusement elle se porte toujours bien et s'intéresse à tout.

Je pense souvent à mon séjour à Tegelen et à notre tournée, dont je garde, malgré le virus insidieux, un souvenir très heureux.

Tout va bien ici. Laura a enfin terminé son livre, et je viens de faire la même chose—un long essai sur *Littérature et Science*, dont je vous ai lu, je crois, la première esquisse—trop brève et inadéquate au sujet.

Heureux Noël à vous tous, et bonne année, chère Suzanne—bonne santé, bon travail et (espérons-le) bonne réunion quelque part. Love to Joep and Sylvia.

> *Affectueusement,*
> *Aldous*

913: TO DR HUMPHRY OSMOND

> *6233 Mulholland,*
> *Los Angeles 28, Cal.*
> *26 December,* 1962

Dear Humphry,

Thank you for your good and most interesting letter. Yes, what about [——]? I spent an evening with him here a few weeks ago—and he talked such nonsense (about the conscious mind being merely a robot, about true intelligence residing only in the D[eoxyribo] N[ucleic] A[cid] molecule, about some kind of Providence looking after the population problem, which therefore wasn't any problem at all) that I became quite concerned. Not about his sanity—because he is perfectly sane—but about his prospects in the world; for this nonsense-talking is just another device for annoying people in authority, flouting convention, cocking snooks at the academic world. It is the reaction of a mischievous Irish boy to the headmaster of his school. One of these days the headmaster will lose patience—and then good-bye to [——]'s psilocybin research. I am very fond of [——]—but why, oh why, does he *have* to be such an ass? I have told him repeatedly that the only attitude for a researcher in this ticklish field is that of an anthropologist living in the midst of a tribe of potentially dangerous savages. Go about your business quietly, don't break the taboos or criticize the locally accepted dogmas. Be polite and friendly—and get on with the job. If you leave them alone, they will probably leave you alone. But evidently the temptation to cock snooks is quite irresistible—so there he goes again!

Give my love to Jane and the children. It's unfortunate that they must

913 *Osmond in a letter of* 18 *December had commented on the rashness of a certain conspicuous researcher in the psychedelics field who was apparently* 'impervious to the idea that psychedelic substances may be both valuable and dangerous if misused', *not having* 'grasped that because one dose of psylocybin is safe this does not mean that regular and repeated doses are safe'.

945

remain in one hemisphere while you are in another—but no doubt it's the best solution for the time being.

Yours,
Aldous

914: TO MRS MARIA PETRIE

6233 Mulholland,
L.A. 28, Cal.
31 December, 1962

Dear Maria,

Thank you for your good wishes and the photograph—oddly different, at the angle from which it is taken, from my memory of the original, which I always looked at from straight in front.

They kept us so busy at the Centre for the Study of Democratic Institutions that I had no time for any extra-curricular activities. But I hope there will be an opportunity to see you both on my next visit.

Not much news to report from this end. I was in Belgium, Holland and England this summer, and had a month of lecturing, during the fall, in the East and Middle West. Since when I have been busy on a long essay on *Literature and Science,* now completed, thank goodness. And tomorrow we start a new year. Will the few scores of people who decide the world's immediate fate permit it to be a tolerably good year? And will the impersonal forces which determine our long-range destiny permit themselves to be controlled for man's benefit—and shall we even attempt to control them? It remains to be seen. Meanwhile this brings you and Eric my warmest wishes for good health, good work and, *malgré tout,* inner peace.

Yours
Aldous

915: TO DR HUMPHRY OSMOND

6233 Mulholland,
L.A. 28, Cal.
7 January, 1963

Dear Humphry,

Thank you for your letter. A good example of what happens to a man when he gets too much inspiration is provided by Christopher Smart. 'Jubilate Agno' is the product of an acute phase of his mental illness, when he had no control over his pre-conscious mind and its torrent of images, notions, words and rhythms. *David* and the 'Nativity' poem were written when he was crazy enough to forget that he was a product of 18th century

914 *The subject of the photograph was Mrs Petrie's bronze portrait bust of Huxley, now in the collection of the University of California at Los Angeles.*

conditioning, but not so crazy as to be unable to organize his automatic writing artistically. And then there are the boring, conventional poems that he produced when he was too sane, too well adjusted to the 18th century. Too much and too frequent LSD wd probably be fatal to art—as fatal as no LSD or none of its spontaneously occurring equivalent.

Let me have your address in Princeton so that I may contact you there if and when I go to the not-so-gorgeous East.

My love to Jane and the children.

Yours affectionately,
Aldous

916: TO MATTHEW HUXLEY

6233 *Mulholland,*
L.A. 28, Cal.
8 *January,* 1963

Dearest Matthew,

I shd have written before to thank you for the good tea. 'The cup that cheers but not inebriates' remains, after all, one of the greatest of our blessings.

The festive season passed off, I am happy to say, without too much stress or hullaballoo and now we are launched on yet another year. I hope it will be a good one for you and for the rest of us. For me, it opens with the completion of my essay on *Literature and Science*—101 pages of it, which I am just starting to correct for publication. After which—what? I have vague projects for a rather long and complicated novel, but have no idea as yet about the way in which I shall carry them out in practice.

Last autumn, rather rashly as I now find, I said yes to a request from *Harper's Bazaar* to take photographs of me in the company of one of their models. The picture, which has just appeared, is good—but the caption on my towering mind and the model's towering hat is like something out of an early novel by Evelyn Waugh. And now it's got into *Time*, with the usual stinking commentary. It is doubtless salutary to be made a fool of from time to time—but I now wish I had taken Laura's advice and turned the whole thing down.

Ever your affectionate,
Aldous

917: TO GEORGE H. ESTABROOKS

6233 *Mulholland,*
L.A. 28, Cal.
20 *January,* 1963

Dear George,

Thank you for your letter. I will certainly take advantage of your invitation if I find myself in the New York region at the time you mention. Will let you know when I know myself.

Meanwhile I keep wondering whether (in the context of your genius-via-hypnosis projects) something might be done by acting directly, through hypnosis, on the brain. In cases of paralysis one can do quite a lot, I believe, to re-activate brain and nervous system by hypnosis. Could one do something comparable for normal individuals? E.g. suggest them into making greater use of the largely unused right side of the cortex? If one could open up more pathways of association in this way one might increase available intelligence. Is this possible, I wonder? And have experiments been made along these lines?

Yours
Aldous H.

918: †TO ALLAN J. CRANE

6233 Mulholland,
Los Angeles 28, Cal.
27 January, 1963

Dear Mr. Crane,
    Yes I knew Katherine Mansfield fairly well, and liked her stories. She was an unhappy woman, capable of acting any number of parts but uncertain of who, essentially, she was—a series of points and arcs on the circumference of a circle that was uncertain of the location of its centre.
    Since *The Doors of Perception* I have written a short novel, *The Genius and the Goddess* (Edwin Muir thought it the best thing I ever did—but I don't know if he is right) and a long Utopian phantasy published last spring called *Island*, a book which I regard as important and which has aroused enthusiasm and annoyance on the part of its readers. I have also written a volume of Essays, *Adonis and the Alphabet*, and a short volume (to be published this year) on *Literature and Science*.

Yours truly
Aldous Huxley

919: TO LADY HUXLEY

6233 Mulholland,
Los Angeles 28, Cal.
17 February, 1963

Dearest Juliette,
    Julian tells me that your book is now definitely on the launching pad and about to go into orbit. The news has inspired me to write a little blurb, puff, prolegomenon or whatever you like to call it. Use it or don't use it, as you and the publishers see fit. In any event, it comes to you with my love and in memory of forty-seven years (is it possible?) of Old Acquaintance. Do you

919 Book: Juliette Huxley's Wild Lives of Africa (*London*, 1963).

find, as I do, that the older one gets, the more unutterably mysterious, unlikely and totally implausible one's own life and the universe at large steadily become? For practical purposes, one tries to make a little scientific and ethical sense of it all; for non-practical purposes—aesthetic and 'spiritual' —one cultivates Wordsworth's 'wise passiveness' and opens oneself up receptively to the *Mysterium tremendum et fascinans* within and without.

Our love to you both.

Ever your affectionate,
Aldous

920: TO MRS MARIANNA NEWTON

6233 Mulholland,
Los Angeles 28, Cal.
24 February, 1963

Dear Marianna,

Since I have not the faintest idea who Dr. Spock is, where he comes from, or what he has done or written, I cannot enrol myself among his sponsors. He may be very good—or he may not. I don't know; and it would be a piece of intellectual dishonesty on my part if I pretended to know, which I would be doing if I became a signatory to the circular letter which you have sent me.

Yours
Aldous

PS I'm glad all goes relatively well at Ojai. I expect to be going to Rome for a meeting of the [United Nations] F[ood and] A[griculture] O[rganization] in March. After which, in April, a foray into Oregon with stopovers at Stanford and Berkeley.

921: TO MRS SYBILLE BEDFORD

On the plane—
L[os] A[ngeles] to Rome
9 March, 1963

My dear Sybille,

Thank you so much for *The Favourite of the Gods*, which I finished just before setting out on this whirlwind trip to Rome, where I am to attend a Congress in connection with FAO's Campaign against Hunger. I have to be back in New York by March 22nd, when Matthew is getting married—to a pleasant young woman with whom he seems to get on very well and who gets on very well with his children. So all seems to be for the best, in that quarter. Meanwhile I hope you got through the winter without too much misery or sickness, and that you are hard at work again on something else.

920 *Mrs Newton was formerly Marianna Schauer, Huxley's secretary and business assistant in 1955. Dr Spock: Benjamin Spock, pediatrician and psychiatrist.*

I liked your book very much. My only criticism of it is that, in a certain sense, it is too consistently perfect—of a stylistic elegance and homogeneity which seem on occasion to exclude some of the wilder, more schizophrenic, more rapturous and appalling aspects of subjective experience and social life, even at its most civilized. For example, it seems to me that you have sacrificed to your consistently elegant writing two important aspects of Constanza's character—her sexuality and her courage. In Fascist Italy she runs risks—but you don't permit yourself to describe her feelings in dangerous situations or the oppressive circumstances surrounding her; again she has affairs in which she gives and receives sensuality—but the sensuality should have been important enough to deserve, if not a Chatterleyan description, at least something more subjective than the brief, *dix-huitième* account of the matter from the outside. But the book remains a fine piece of work and I congratulate you most heartily.

Laura is correcting the proofs of her book and I gather that the publishers will soon be sending you a set. Meanwhile I have finished a long essay—100 pages or so—on *Literature and Science*, and am now feeling my way into a kind of novel. I don't yet know what it will really be like and proceed by a process of trial and error, guided by whatever turns up, from paragraph to paragraph.

I expect to be in England in June and hope I may see you then. So *à bientôt*, dear Sybille.

Ever yours,
Aldous

922: TO MRS CLAIRE WHITE

On the plane—
L[os] A[ngeles] to Rome
9 March, 1963

My dear Claire,

I take the opportunity provided by a flight to Rome (where I am attending a conference in connection with FAO's Campaign against Hunger) to write you about *The Death of the Orange Trees*. I read it with a great deal of pleasure—for it is full of good things, well said—but also with twinges every now and then of disappointment—for there were things, I thought, which might have been better. What was good was the over-all picture—of the house, and of the family which is the beneficiary and victim of the house. The things which might have been better were the relations between Maria and her painter-husband, which were never made very clear. (E.g were they sexually compatible? How much did she care about his professional preoccupations with art? And if she didn't take an interest in these, what was the basis of their happy symbiosis?) The character of Steven was another thing that might have been better. I found it difficult to believe in him as a small boy. His conversation, thoughts and actions didn't strike me as charac-

teristic of his age—an age when children feel deeply, but feel deeply intermittently and also, equally deeply, about many (often incompatible) things.
To me, Steven was too much of one piece to be wholly credible. He migh[t]
very well have done what you have him do—but surely he would have done
a lot of other irrelevant and even incompatible things on the way to the final
act of arson. And didn't you perhaps miss a rich dramatic opportunity by not
having the authorities investigate the arson and confront him with his share
in the crime and his family with the reasons, in him and in them, for his
delinquent behaviour? As the book now stands, the extrication of Steven
and his parents from the mess they have got into is accomplished too easily.

Dear Claire, if I make these criticisms, it is not for the sake of carping,
but simply because the rest of the book is so good that I feel you could do
still better next time.

Love to you all. I hope to be in New York by March 22nd—in time for
Matthew's wedding. Shall I see you then? I hope so.

Ever yours affectionately
Aldous

PS Excuse the horrible writing. I hate these ball points, and there is a slight
vibration all the time.

923: TO MRS EILEEN J. GARRETT

6233 Mulholland,
Los Angeles 28, Cal.
27 March, 1963

Dear Eileen,

George Cukor (the movie director) is interested in the possibility of
filming Trevor Hall's book about Sir Wm Crookes and the Cook family.
(What a marvellous story it is!) He has asked me to find out from you
whether (a) you or the Parapsy. Foundation has the documentation upon
which Hall based his book and (b) whether there is anything of significance
in that documentation which did not find a place in the book. Meanwhile
George (through intermediaries, for he doesn't want his name to appear at
this stage) is making enquiries about film rights, the legal situation in respect
to possible action by the descendants of Crookes or the Cooks, etc. I
would be most grateful if you will let me know whatever you feel to be
relevant in regard to documents, book and possible film.

I was in New York for 2 days on my way back from a brief trip to Rome,
and was very sorry to find that you weren't there. How are you? Well, I
hope. Here we modestly flourish. I have finished a short book on *Literature
and Science*, and Laura is about to burst into authorship with a volume of

---

923 *Hall's book:* The Spiritualists: The Story of Florence Cook and William
Crookes (*London*, 1962).

Recipes for Living, based on her psycho-therapeutic methods. Meanwhile Matthew got married again last Saturday and is very happy. The new wife seems to be just what he needed, warm, intelligent and good with his two children. So that is a great comfort.

I had a long day with Humphry Osmond, who is in very good form, and also made contact with Dr. John Beresford and heard of his plans for an LSD Institute. As he is more prudent than [———], he may be more successful in setting up shop within the US—whereas [———], with his mania for cocking snooks at those in authority, may well find himself compelled to operate exclusively across the border.

Ever yours, dear Eileen,
Aldous

924: TO SIR JULIAN HUXLEY

6233 Mulholland,
L.A. 28, Cal.
2 June, 1963

Dearest J,

Thank you for your good letter. Your Jordanian trip must have been extraordina[r]y. When Maria and I were there in 54 we saw only Jerusalem, Jericho and the Dead Sea—nothing, alas, of the desert.

You ask about plans. They were so straightforward up to a couple of weeks ago. Now all is in confusion, owing to the fact that we lent some money to a young man who has got himself into legal trouble which will entail our staying on here until the case comes up for trial in late June—which in its turn has made it necessary for me to cancel a lecture in Munich on June 14th, and a lecture and banquet in London on the 20th and 25th—to the vast inconvenience, I am sure, of all concerned. So I don't exactly know when we shall be coming over. Probably early in July. Where will you be staying in Switzerland at that time? We may go to Switzerland at that time to be with Laura's sister, whose children are going to a summer camp at Leysin.

I'm still uncertain whether or not to go to the World Academy meeting at Stockholm early in August. Probably yes—if only for tax purposes! (My trip wd then be a professional expense. Faith, Hope, Charity—these three, and the greatest of these is Income Tax.) So it may be that I shall not get to London until late August or early September. What are your plans for that time?

L. is just back from New York, where she spent a week giving interviews and making TV and radio appearances in connection with her book. This last is turning into a rampaging best seller. A second printing after a week—and the computers predict a sale of 107,000 by August! As these are the same computers that correctly predict the outcome of elections on the basis of the first hour's returns, I presume that this is what in fact will happen. The publisher is out of his mind with joy and we are feeling elatedly flabbergasted.

Otherwise there isn't much to report. I have just finished an essay on the ambivalence of culture—(every individual is at once the beneficiary and the victim of culture: how can he reap the benefits without paying the price of being the heir to a tradition which transmits outdated nonsense as well as indispensable knowledge and the techniques of logical thinking?) And now I am feeling my way into a kind of reflective novel.

Matthew's new marriage seems to be a great success, and he is happier now than he has ever been. Ellen also is getting married, and the children are thoroughly enjoying the experience of having a father and a deputy father whom they like, and a mother and a deputy mother with whom they get on extremely well. Matthew moves down to Washington in Sept and will be working henceforth at the National Institute of Mental Health, on a committee that plans federal policy in the mental health field and advises states and municipalities what to do. He is delighted at the prospect.

Our best love to you both.

Ever your affectionate,
Aldous

925: TO DR HUMPHRY OSMOND

6233 Mulholland,
L.A. 28, Cal.
2 June, 1963

Dear Humphry,

Thank you for your letter. I have passed on the gist of your remarks about green LSD to [——] at [. . . .] I don't know if he bought any of the [boot-legged] stuff [. . . .] I hope not—but fear that he may have. A single untoward reaction to the green stuff cd imperil his whole grandiose scheme for the reformation of society through psychodelics.

[. . . .]

I hope we may have a few days together in Scandinavia this August. If not there, then in October when I expect to be in the East for some lectures and will look you up at Princeton.

Ever yours,
Aldous

926: TO TIMOTHY LEARY

6233 Mulholland,
L.A. 28, Cal.
3 June, 1963

Dear Tim,

Herewith a script of my essay-in-introduction, which I have deliberately

926 *Huxley's essay appeared as a* chapter *in* LSD: The Consciousness Expanding Drug, *ed. David Solomon (New York,* 1964).

not confined to a discussion of psychodelics, but have treated in more general terms the whole problem of the individual's relation to his culture—a problem in whose solution the psychodelics can undoubtedly play their part. In haste

Ever yours,
Aldous

927: TO IAN PARSONS

6233 Mulholland,
Los Angeles 28, Cal.
5 June, 1963

Dear Ian,

I discovered to-day that I made a gross blunder in *Literature and Science*, attributing the phrase 'Whom not to know argues yourself unknown' to Shakespeare. It is by Milton—and the correct quotation is 'Not to know me argues yourselves unknown'. If this is still correctable, I'd be grateful if you'd have it changed. I don't have galley proofs, so can't pinpoint it. The quotation accompanies a line from Mallarmé in the section dealing with unusual syntax.

Owing to a tiresome concatenation of circumstances, I have had to delay my trip and shan't be in Europe before July—thus causing a lot of inconvenience, I fear, to the British Council, on whose behalf I was to speak in Munich, and to the R[oyal] Soc[iety] of Lit[erature], for whom I was to lecture in London. It is a great nuisance, and I wish there was something I cd do about it. But I can't.

Yours,
Aldous

928: TO MRS ELLEN HUXLEY

6233 Mulholland,
L.A. 28, Cal.
5 July, 1963

Dearest Ellen,

Business first. We don't at the moment have any large amount available for investment—and anyhow would feel uncomfortable about collecting interest from you. So what about this? A loan of $2000 which you and Adam can repay at your convenience. With 50 % of the price of the land paid for in cash, it shd be easy to get a mortgage for the remainder.

All goes pretty well here. Laura is very busy signing books and giving interviews—and *You are not the Target* continues to act like a best seller. For myself, I have been writing odds and ends of things—including a piece on 'The Individual and his Culture' which is supposed to serve as an introduction to Tim Leary's anthology on Psychodelics—tho' what is happening

928 *Adam: Adam Giffard, to whom Ellen Huxley was married in August.*

to that project or to Tim himself, I don't know. He answers no letters of mine, so I have no idea where he is or what he is doing. [. . . .]

We hope to fly to Stockholm at the end of the month for a meeting of the World Academy. Thence I wd go to London, Laura to stay with her sister in Italy.

Our love to you and the children.

Affectionately,
Aldous

929: †TO TIMOTHY LEARY

6233 *Mulholland,*
L.A. 28, *Cal.*
20 *July,* 1963

Dear Tim,

Thank you for your letters. I think the idea of a school is excellent, for what needs exploring, more than anything else, is the problem of fruitfully relating what Wordsworth calls 'wise passiveness' to wise activity—receptivity and immediate experience to concept-making and the projection upon experience of intelligible order. How do we make the best of *both* the worlds described in Wordsworth's 'Expostulation and Reply' and 'The Tables Turned'? That is what has to be discovered. And one should make use of all the available resources—the best methods of formal teaching and also LSD, hypnosis (used, among other things, to help people to re-enter the LSD state without having recourse to a chemical), time distortion (to speed up the learning process), auto-conditioning for control of autonomic processes and heightening of physical and psychological resistance to disease and trauma etc etc. [. . . .]

Ever yours
Aldous

930: TO MATTHEW AND JUDITH HUXLEY

Hotel Continental,
Stockholm, Sweden
28 *July,* 1963

Dearest Matthew and Judy,

Well, here we are—still a little uncertain whether we are on our heads or our heels after 12 hours in the plane with 8 hours time change, a stop in Greenland and a sun that went down for 19 minutes and then popped up again, glaring in for the rest of the night. Business doesn't start until tomorrow; meanwhile we're trying to catch up on lost sleep and taking strolls about this pleasant town with its mixture of rather solemn and respectably old-fashioned architecture and brand new skyscrapers.

929 *School: established as the Castalia Foundation, at Millbrook, New York, for training in methods of consciousness-expansion.*

I hope the Washington muddle described by Judy in her letter will soon get straightened out and that you will be able to make your move on time and not too painfully. Laura goes down to stay with her sister in 2 or 3 days —I stay on for another brief spell, then fly to London c/o Julian at 31 Pond St NW3. Shall return to LA some time in Sept—after which I expect to be in the East, lecturing here and there, between Oct 9th and 20th, when I hope to see you.

Love from us both.

Ever your affectionate
Aldous

931: TO GERVAS HUXLEY

108 *Corso Galileo Ferraris,*
Torino
24 *August,* 1963

Dear Ger,

I was so sorry to have missed you on this visit—and yet sorrier to hear of the reasons why our meeting was impossible. I do hope you are making satisfactory progress towards complete health. 'Growing old gracefully'—it isn't easy when the physiological machine starts to break down, or even just slowly to wear out, creeping almost imperceptibly from decrepitude to decrepitude. One learns the Second Law of Thermodynamics by direct experience.

Give my love to Elspeth.

Yours affectionately,
Aldous

932: †TO KRISHNA KRIPALANI

6233 *Mulholland,*
Los Angeles 28, *Cal.*
30 *August,* 1963

Dear Mr Kripalani,

I returned yesterday from Europe to find your letter and enclosure awaiting me. I feel guilty about my failure to correct the record of my speech; but the truth is that, owing to my visual handicap, I find this kind of job intolerably trying. The spirit is willing, but the flesh is weak. I should be most grateful if you could have the necessary editing done by someone with normal vision and so sparing me a task from which I shrink. In general I don't like to see extempore speeches translated into print. And when people insist on turning talk into letter [press] I always ask them to do the job themselves and leave me out of it. So can you please do this for me.

932 *To Tagore's biographer, whom Huxley had met at the time of the Tagore centenary conference in New Delhi, November,* 1961.

Three weeks ago I was spending the week-end at Dartington, and talked much with Leonard Elmhirst about his experiences with Tagore at Shantini-ketan and elsewhere. He himself has done wonderful things at Dartington, which is one of the few places in the world where one can feel an almost unqualified optimism.

My wife joins me in sending kindest regards to both of you.

Yours sincerely,
Aldous Huxley

933: TO DR HUMPHRY OSMOND

6233 Mulholland,
L.A. 28, Cal.
4 September, 1963

My dear Humphry,

Herewith a suggested skeleton outline for the Human Resources volume, which we so unwisely got ourselves involved in. Let me have your comments and suggestions for changes and additions. I hope to come East early in October—exact date to be fixed later—and hope to spend a day or two at Princeton discussing the book with you. After which we might slip down to Philadelphia to show the results of our confabulations to Stuart Mudd and to get his opinion.

I had three weeks in London, with weekends in the country—at Lawford, at Kenneth Clark's fantastic Saltwood Castle, near Hythe, and under another mediaeval roof at Dartington—all very pleasant, except for the preposter-ously cold and rainy weather.

After London a week in Turin, with trips into the mountains—to Courmayeur and a funicular ride half way up Mont Blanc, then up the Val di Susa to Salice d'Oulx, where an Alpine village is in process of being trans-formed into a town of 10 and 15-story apartment houses for vacationing Italians from Torino. We've come a long way from the Swiss chalet!

Ever yours,
Aldous

934: TO DANIEL T. O'SHEA

6233 Mulholland Highway,
Los Angeles 28, California
5 September, 1963

Dear Mr O'Shea,

On my return from Europe a few days ago, I learned from newspaper

933 *Human Resources volume: a proposed publication of the* World Academy of Art and Science.

934 *The film rights to* Brave New World *had been bought by Samuel Bronston. O'Shea, representing R.K.O., seems to have answered this letter disappointingly.*

957

reports that RKO had just sold the motion picture rights of my novel, *Brave New World*. Before his death, my old friend and agent, Jim Geller, had told me that this sale was being considered; he also informed me that he had come to an agreement with you that, in the event of the sale taking place, RKO would pay me a certain percentage of the sums received from the purchaser.

Unfortunately Jim Geller is no longer with us, and I am therefore writing to you directly with a request for further information on this subject.

With all good wishes, I am

Yours sincerely,
Aldous Huxley

935: TO RALPH ROSE

6233 Mulholland,
L.A. 28, Cal.
6 September, 1963

Dear Ralph,

Further to my wire—the book is still available for a movie. Meanwhile what of the play? Who is taking an interest?

I got back from Europe a week ago and am getting ready to embark on a lecture tour in the East, in early October. Shall be here for the rest of this month.

I hope all goes well with you. As for me—I am growing old, but otherwise don't have too much to complain of.

Yours,
Aldous

936: TO DR HUMPHRY OSMOND

6233 Mulholland,
L.A. 28, Cal.
14 September, 1963

Dear Humphry,

Thank you for your letter of Sept 3rd which has followed me here, where we have been for about 2 weeks. Did you, by the way, receive an outline of the projected vol on human resources which I sent you about 10 days ago? I hope it didn't go astray.

Meanwhile my plans have had to undergo some drastic modifications. I had a recurrence of trouble this spring—a neoplasm in the neck, centring on a gland, I suppose, which was treated with cobalt-radiation. This left me in an extremely low state, from which I was only just emerging when I saw you in Stockholm. Since returning to LA there has been a flare-up of what the doctor thinks is a secondary inflammation of the radiation-weakened tissues, and I'm feeling pretty low again. This—plus the fact that my voice

935 *Book:* After Many a Summer.

has been affected (the nerve leading to the right vocal cord having been knocked out, temporarily I hope, permanently I rather fear)—I have cancelled my lecture tour in the East and shall not, as I wrote in my letter, be visiting you in early October. Alas! But I think the sensible thing is to lie low and try to build up resistance and general health. It remains to be seen whether I can undertake the job of editing the human resources volume. At present I have my doubts—but perhaps I may get back the necessary energy later.

Thank you for writing to [——]. I hope the poor boy will emerge from his present darkness. The genetic background isn't too encouraging. His grandmother died insane, his uncle, [——], was constantly on the verge of paranoia, and his elder sister had a psychotic break a year or two ago, but happily got better.

Ever yours,
Aldous

PS. I send you my news in confidence—so please dont mention it to Ellen or Matthew.

937: TO SIR JULIAN AND LADY HUXLEY

6233 Mulholland,
Los Angeles 28, Cal.
29 September, 1963

Dearest Julian and Juliette,

You must be back from Africa, I imagine, by now—but meanwhile Africa has come to us, with a vengeance, in a frightful heat wave with temperatures day after day of 105 and 80 degree nights. In my own case meteorology has been compounded by a spell of ill health, due to the after effects of a long course of radiation which I had to take this spring. I hadn't told you of this trouble before, since it hadn't seriously interfered with my activities and there seemed to be no point in spreading unnecessary apprehensions. It started in 1960, with a malignant tumour on the tongue. The first surgeon I was sent to wanted to cut out half the tongue and leave me more or less speechless. I went from him to my old friend, Max Cutler (who was trained at Johns Hopkins and the Curie Institute in Paris, and is the co-author with the late Sir Lenthal Cheatle of a medical classic, *Tumours of the Breast*. He headed the Chicago Tumour Institute for a good many years, then came out here ten years ago and is now in private practice. I find that both here and in Europe he is regarded as among the greatest of living surgeons and radiologists). Cutler recommended treatment with radium needles and so did the Professors of Radiology and Surgery at the U of Cal Medical Centre at San Francisco, whom I consulted. I took the treatment in the early summer

937 *Huxley had already broken the news of his illness to his son in a similar letter of 24 September.*

of sixty, and it was remarkably successful. The tumour on the tongue was knocked out and has shown no signs of returning. However, as generally happens in these cases, the lymph glands of the neck became involved. I had one taken out in sixty-two, and this spring another mass appeared. This was subjected to twenty-five exposures to radioactive cobalt, an extremely exhausting treatment from which I was just recovering when at last I was able to make the trip to Stockholm and London. Since my return there was [has] been a flare-up of secondary inflammation, to which tissues weakened by radiation are peculiarly liable, often after considerable intervals. Result: I have had to cancel my lecture tour, much to Mr Harry Walker's distress. (Incidentally, he hoped that you, Julian, might take over some of my cancelled engagements; but I told him I thought this wouldn't be feasible for you at this time. However he still may ask you.) Another handicap is my persistent hoarseness, due to the nerve that supplies the right-hand vocal cord having been knocked out either by an infiltration of the malignancy, or by the radiation. I hope this hoarseness may be only temporary, but rather fear that I may carry it to the grave.

What the future holds, one doesn't know. In general these malignancies in the neck and head don't do much metastasizing. Meanwhile I am trying to build up resistance with the combination of a treatment which has proved rather successful at the University of Montreal and the U[niversity] of Manila —the only institutions where it has been tried out over a period [of] years— and which has been elaborated upon by Professor Guidetti, of the University of Turin, who has read papers on his work at the two last International Cancer Congresses, at Buenos Aires and Moscow. I saw Guidetti while in Turin and was impressed by some of his case histories, and with Cutler's approval we are carrying out his treatment here. When this damned inflammation dies down, which it may be expected to do in a few weeks, I hope to get back to regular work. For the present I am functioning at only a fraction of normal capacity.

Much love to you both from both of us.

Ever your affectionate,
Aldous

938: TO GEORGE H. ESTABROOKS

6233 Mulholland,
Los Angeles 28, Cal.
30 September, 1963

Dear George,

Thank you for your letter and enclosed article, my only criticism of which is that it does not go into the means whereby we can teach people to want to implement their good intentions.

It might be that a good place for you to come next year when you retire and are free to do the kind of work you want to do, wd be La Jolla, Cal.

There is an institute there—I forget the exact title, but it is something like 'Western Inst. for Advanced Studies in the behavioral sciences'. They have a permanent staff and invite fellows to come and spend time there. (Abra[ha]m Maslow was with them last year.) There are bright psychologists and social scientists there—plus the new branch of the U of C, the Salk Institute, the Scripps Oceanographic Institute and numerous industrial research centres— so the Scientific Company wd be good. And the place is charming.

Alas, I shan't be seeing you this fall. I have not been well and have had to cancel my lecture tour in the east. So the visit to Colgate, to which I was eagerly looking forward, is for the time being out.

All good wishes,

Yours,
Aldous H.

939: TO MRS GRACE HUBBLE

6233 Mulholland,
L.A. 28, Cal.
2 October, 1963

Dear Grace,

Thank you for your letter. I think Edwin wd have approved of *Literature and Science*, and hope that you will like it.

We were in Europe this summer; but since returning, I have been under the weather and have had to cancel all my speaking engagements to confine myself to the house and a regimen of not too *dolce far niente*. When things go better I hope we can make the Pasadena trip and drink a cup of tea with you. I shall miss Nicolas.

Yours affectionately,
Aldous

940: TO MRS ELLEN GIFFARD

6233 Mulholland
L.A. 28, Cal.
9 October, 1963

Dearest Ellen,

Herewith goes a check for $1000 to start the children off. I shd have

939 *Nicolas: Edwin Hubble's cat, which had died. Apart from letter 274 this remark about Nicolas is the only indication in the correspondence of Huxley's interest in cats. But at one time Aldous and Maria had owned several rare and beautiful Siamese, whose personalities suggested his essay 'Sermons in Cats' (1930). The charm of these, when the Huxleys were taking their luggage across frontiers, would sometimes lead to generous oversights by customs agents.*

940 *Mrs Giffard was preparing to make and send to Huxley some taped readings, and had suggested as material Elizabeth Thomas's* The Harmless People, *a book about the Kalahari desert and its inhabitants.*

sent it before, but have been in bed with some damned low infection, which keeps me incapable of doing anything. I hope I am now beginning to emerge.

About reading—what I wd do is to transfer the material from your tape to my Gray Audigraph records (I have a home-made library of many hours of poetry, and keep the machine at my bedside). Laura has an excellent tape machine which will permit me to do this. As for books, that's a problem. I like material that I can take in small doses and that provides food for thought. There is an excellent anthology called *The Practical Cogitator* by Curtis and Greenslet (Houghton Mifflin). Maybe you cd start on that. Anyhow, not the Kalahari Desert. There are too many historically more important deserts to be thought about; the Kalahari is just too irrelevantly remote.

Love to the children.

Your affectionate,
Aldous

941: †TO MADAME JEANNE NEVEUX

6233 *Mulholland,*
L.A. 28, Cal.
10 *October,* 1963

Chère Jeanne,

Merci de ta lettre et du second chèque, qui rejoindra le premier dans un fond contre une crise éventuelle dans la vie de Mère—qui présidera—telle est mon impression—à l'enterrement de nous tous, filles, gendres, peut-être quelques petits enfants.

Rose m'a chuchoté la nouvelle que tu devais venir, mais qu'à cause d'une lettre où ta Mère a prôné les avantages des échanges epistolaires à longue distance, tu as renoncé au voyage. Je le regrette. Mon séjour en Europe cet

941 TRANSLATION:—'*Thank you for your letter and for the second cheque, which will rejoin the first in a stock against some future crisis in the life of Mère—who will preside—such is my impression—at the burial of us all, daughters, sons-in-law and maybe a few grandchildren.*

'*Rose whispered the news to me that you intended to come, but that because of a letter in which Mère preached the advantages of long-distance correspondence, you have given up the trip. I am sorry. My stay in Europe this summer was too short to allow me a stop-over in France, and I should have loved to see you here.*

'*I hope that the play will finally be produced. A German company holds an option to make it into a film. For all the rest, genius and goddess are dead. We were massacred in London as in New York. Those idiots at Plon have given* Island *the title of* L'Île. *But* Île *was indicated. In Italy the book is called* Isola, *in Sweden* Ön *and in Denmark (miracle of brevity)* Ø.

'*Love to Noële and to yourself. . . .*'

962

été a été trop court pour me permettre un arrêt en France, et j'aurais ai[mé]
te voir ici.

J'espère que la pièce se jouera enfin. Une Cie. Allemande tient une option
pour en faire un film. Pour le reste, génie et déesse sont morts. On nous a
massacrés à Londres comme à New York. Ces idiots chez Plon ont donné à
Island le titre *L'Île*. Mais *Île* était indiqué. En Italie le livre s'appelle *Isola*,
en Suède *Ön* et en Danemark (miracle de brièveté) *Ø*.

Tendresses à Noële et à toi.

Affectueusement,
Aldous

942: TO DR HUMPHRY OSMOND

6233 Mulholland,
Los Angeles 28, Cal.
15 October, 1963

Dear Humphry,

Thank you for your letter and also for the paper, which I was in no state
to go and hear Bob Lynch read. In our hypothetical volume on human
resources there will obviously have to be a chapter—by you, no doubt—
on the best emotional contexts in which the learning of new ways to use the
mind should be placed. The Indians tried to solve the problem by means of
the guru system. But this lends itself to all kinds of psychological and social
abuses (you should hear Krishnamurti on the subject of gurus!), and something less dangerous will have to be worked out.

Stuart Mudd has asked me to send him a copy of my projected outline for
the book—but being an Old Man of Thermopylae who never does anything
properly, I can't lay my hands on the carbon I made of it. If you have
secretaries or mechanical facsimile makers available in your office, would
you have a few copies made and send one to Dr Mudd (VA Hospital,
University and Woodland Aves, Philadelphia 4, Pa), together, if possible,
with your own emendations and suggestions. Also a copy or two to me. I
still don't know if I shall be able to undertake the work. At the moment I
am so low with this secondary inflammation of the radiation-weakened tissues
that I feel I shall never again be good for anything. But I hope and think
this state of affairs will pass in due course. ('It will pass'—the only motto
appropriate to every human situation, whether good or bad.)

Ever yours,
Aldous

942 *In his last letter to Huxley, on* 31 *October, Osmond wrote, 'I hope that the*
Road is not too hard'.

963

[6233 *Mulholland,*
Los Angeles 28, California]
17 *November,* 1963

Fosters' Agency
London, England

Dear Max,

Talk about the long arm of coincidence! The mail which brought your note about 'The Tillotson Banquet' brought also at the same time a letter from Betty Wendel, who is now in New York, who has been talking to Alan Webb about 'The Tillotson Banquet' as a subject she could do very well for a TV show. Webb, it appears, is enthusiastic about it, and there probably would be no difficulty at all with a man of his stature securing a production. Would it not be wiser to hold up any definite commitment until we hear more what is happening in New York?

A new interest in a theatrical production of *After Many a Summer* has recently manifested itself. I will let you know whatever progress is made over here.

I am much surprised to learn that *The Devils* is being performed by a repertory company in Washington, D.C. I had no news of this either from you or Harvey. Under what conditions is this being done and where do I come into the picture? Is there any prospect of the work being produced by another company outside Washington?

All good wishes.

Very sincerely,
Aldous Huxley

943 *Dictated; text from Laura Huxley's transcription of the sound tape.*

INDEX

The Preface, Acknowledgments and Chronology are not indexed. Personal names, in general, are cited each time they appear except in valedictions of the 'love to' and 'love from' variety. Titles of works by Huxley are grouped together under his name. The abbreviation 'A. H.' refers of course to him.

Bagehot, Walter, *quoted*, 360
Bagenal, Barbara Hiles, 42n., 43, 45, 90, 91, 97
Bailey, F. M., 431
Baillot, Marie Juliette: *see* Huxley, Lady
Baker, Herschel, 923n.
Baker, Ida, 140n.
Baldwin, 1st Earl, 222
Baltus, Madame, 176, 189, 286, 303, 913
Baltus, Monsieur, 176, 286, 913
Baltus, Ado, 288n. 289, 522
Baltus, Georges, 176, 288n., 289, 360, 522, 579
Baltus, Raymond, 176
Baltus, Sylvia, 176, 288n.
Balzac, Honoré de, 170, 178, 190, 221, 224, 225-26, 225n., 226-27, 228, 286, 516; *allusions to*, 432, 498
Baptism, infant, 191-92, 191n.
Barbusse, Henri, 395-96
Bardo Thodol (*The Tibetan Book of the Dead*), 431, 484, 733, 747, 756, 900
Barker, H. Granville, 66
Barker, Valerie, 311, 311n.
Barnes, William, 799-800, 800n.
Baronne, the, 113, 115, 116, 122, 148, 159
Barr, Barbara Weekley, 331, 334n., 335, 347
Barrès, Maurice, 129
Barrie, Sir James, 68-69, 290, 338
Barron, Mr and Mrs, 610
Barron, Milton, 758
Barton, Bruce, 866
Bate, W. J., 923n.
Bates, W. H., and the Bates Method, 445, 450, 451, 462, 468-69, 473, 477, 482-483, 526-27, 550, 591, 595, 605-6, 641, 649, 695, 759n., 781, 815, 822, 872-73, 907-8
Bateson, Gregory, 824
Batuta, Ibn, 44
Baudelaire, 282, 301, 303, 308-9, 308n., 533; *quoted*, 64
Baudouin, Charles, 658
Bax, Clifford, *letter to*, 703
Beach, Sylvia, 304, 304n.
Beaumont and Fletcher, 101
Beaumont, Hugh, 816
Beaverbrook, 1st Baron, 146, 168, 307
Becket, Thomas à, 811
Beckett, Samuel, 457
Bedford, Sybille von Schönebeck, 377, 377n., 445, 711
  Letters to, 476, 762-63, 915-16, 949-50
Beerbohm, Marie, 130, 130n., 131, 148, 149-50
Beerbohm, Sir Max, 130n., 150
  Letter to, 206-7
Beethoven, 43, 45, 46, 288, 308n., 309, 323, 323n., 324, 325, 328, 329, 375, 779, 780
Béhague, Madame de, 395, 472
Behmen, Jacob: *see* Boehme, Jacob
Bell, Clive, 140
  Letter to, 344-45
Bell, Vanessa, 172

Bella: *see* Salkowski, Ella
Belloc, Hilaire, 701: *quoted*, 724, 817
Benda, Julien, 281
Bender, Hans, 705
Benét, William R., 278
Benet of Canfield (William Fitch), 461, 466, 467, 504
Bennett, Arnold, 181n., 211n., 228, 279, 282-83, 284, 307, 352, 352n., 516, 785, 785n., 913, 913n.
  Letters to, 181, 183-84, 193, 211, 212
Bennett, Dorothy Cheston, 352
Benoit, Hubert, 603n., 608n., 639, 730, 918
  Letters to, 603-4, 607-9, 612-14, 617-18, 619-21
Benson, A. C., 53, 98, 110
Benson, E. F., 49
Benthall, E. C. 42
Bentinck, Lord Henry, 136, 143
Beowulf, 81
Beresford, John, 952
Berg, Alban, 682
Berger, F. M., 810
Bergson, 79, 668, 874, 923n.
Berkeley, Bishop, 780
Berl, Emmanuel, 333-34
Bernardino, 615
Bernini, Giovanni, 201-2
Bernstein, Leonard, 808, 820
  Letter to, 821
Bertalanffy, Ludwig von, 602n., 612, 659, 664, 693, 880
  Letters to, 602-3, 654-55, 694-95
Bérulle, Cardinal, 524
Besant, Annie, 136-37
Besse, Antonin, 635
Bessie, S. M., *letter to*, 753-54
Betty: *see* Wendel, Beth
Bevan, C. O., 131, 132-33, 134, 145, 149, 157, 157n., 159, 167, 173, 174
Bhagavad-Gita, 510n., 511, 513
Bhagavatam, 511
Bibby, Cyril, 899n.
  Letter to, 898-99
Bibesco, Prince, 156
Bible, 436, 438, 529, 577, 577n., 633, 705, 774, 786, 863, 874, 882
Biddle, Francis, 551
Bill: *see* Kiskadden, William; Wright, William
Billing, N. P., 156, 156n.
Billy: *see* Wessberg, William
The Bing Boys Are Here (*musical comedy*), 120, 120n.
Biography, expository use of, 601-2, 607n., 608, 608n., 910
Birrell, Augustine, 117, 150
Birth control, 290; *see also* Abortion, Population problem
The Birth of a Nation (*film*), 94n., 95
Bismarck, 33, 44, 46
Bjork, Anita, 767
Blackham, H. J., 923n.
Blackie, J. S., *quoted*, 139
Blackwell, Sir Basil, 108, 115, 137, 138, 185

966

Blair, E. H.: *see* Orwell, George
Blake, William, 96, 323n., 324, 766, 770, 848; *quoted*, 678, 827, 843, 863, 870, 874
Blakiston, C. H., 147
Blakney, R. B., 475, 918
Blewett, Duncan, 842, 842n., 843, 848
Bliss, R. W., family of, 741
Bloomfield, Leonard, 453, 491
Blum, Léon, 407, 585
Blyth, Ann, 572, 576n., 577, 616
Blyth, R. H., 638-39
Bob: *see* Nichols, Robert
Boccaccio, 322, 548, 567
Bodkin, Aileen Cox, 85, 85n., 106, 109, 111, 142
Bodkin, Thomas, 85n.
Boehme (Behmen), Jacob, 96, 248
Boillot, Claude, 708
Boito, Arrigo, 682
Bok, W. Curtis, 933, 933n.
Bolshevism, 169-70, 697; *see also* Communism
Bolton, Frances P., 824
Bond, Elinor, 761
Bonham-Carter, Lady Violet, 99, 122
Bonnoli, Alberto, 586n.
Letter to, 586-88
Bonpensiere, Luigi, 695, 695n.
The Bookman (magazine), 235n., 252n.
Booth, William, 25
Bordage, Judith: *see* Huxley, Judith Wallet Bordage
Borgese, G. A., 342
Borgia, Cesare, 44
Borsodi, Ralph, 434, 434n.
Bosco, John, 545, 562
Bose, Sir J. C., 267
Boswell, Ronald, 65
Bottomley, Horatio, 99, 158
Boucher, François, 770
Boult, Sir Adrian, 166
Bouverie, Alice, 738, 761, 810
Boyd, Phyllis, 130, 130n.
Boyer, Charles, 571, 573, 576n., 577
Brahms, 54, 67
Braid, James, 604, 634
Braille system, 39n., 44n., 344-45
Bramwell, Milne, 841
Bremer, Marian Elizabeth, *letter to*, 829-30
Brémond, Henri, 438, 468, 504, 651
Breton, André, 184
Brett, Hon. Dorothy, 118, 140n., 143, 163, 166, 171, 174, 177, 422, 422n.
Letters to, 164, 172-73, 338-39, 346-47
Brewster, Earl and Achsah, 304n., 305, 355, 355n.
Bridges, Robert, 79
Bridgman, P. W., 447, 448
Broad, C. D., 347, 415, 489, 546-47
Broadbent, Henry, 134
Broch, Hermann, 364-65, 519n.
Letters to, 519-20, 523-25
Brockway, Wallace, 637
Bromberg, Walter, 923n.

Bronowski, Jacob, 923n.
Bronston, Samuel, 957n.
Brontë, Charlotte, 94-95, 94n., 469, 469n., 471, 477, 640
Brontë, Emily, *quoted*, 787
Bronzino, Il, 290
Brook, Clive, 628
Brooke, Anthony, *letter to*, 923-25
Brooke, Fulke Greville, Lord, 82; his 'Mustapha' *quoted*, 296
Brooke, Rupert, 76, 82n., 110
Brooke, Hon. Sylvia, Ranee of Sarawak, 137, 139, 140n., 151n., 265
Brooks, B. G., 189n.
Letters to, 184-85, 189, 230-31, 287
Brooks, Mrs B. G., 189n.
Brown, Barbara, 787, 858, 868, 919
Brown, Harrison, 798, 805, 806, 808, 822
Brown, Pamela, 585
Browning, Elizabeth Barrett, 53
Browning, Robert, 33, 34, 81, 357, 918
Bruce, Brenda, 616n.
Bruce, Marjorie, 179
Brunelleschi, Filippo, 201
Brunschvicg, Léon, 390
Bucke, R. M., 941
Buckle, H. T., 241
Buday, György, 404n.
Letter to, 404-5
Buddha: *see* Gautama Buddha
Buddhism, 162, 162n., 405n., 438, 489, 520, 554, 564n., 693, 720, 748, 762-63, 867; Hinayana, 648, 650, 699, 929; Mahayana and Tibetan, 428, 431, 484-85, 526, 533, 550-51, 597, 620, 894; Tantric, 791, 803, 902, 928-29, 935n.; Zen, 406, 533, 534, 608n., 609, 612-14, 612n.-613n., 618, 638-39, 730, 769, 802, 827, 829, 843, 844, 929; *see also Bardo Thodol*, Gautama Buddha
Buddhism, Pali Canon of, 406n., 526, 530, 648, 650, 699
Bulletin of the Atomic Scientists, 578, 867
Burckhardt, Jacob, 923n.
Burke, 244, 254, 438
Burnham, James, 471
Burns, 301
Burr, Courtney, 819, 821-22, 826, 830n., 831n., 832, 832n., 834-35, 834n., 836, 848
Burt, Sir Cyril, 582, 588
Burton, Robert, *quoted*, 908
Burton-Brown, Mrs, 37n., 68n., 69
Burton-Brown, Bice, 68n., 69
Burtt, E. A., 253, 276
Buschke, Franz, 890, 959
Bussweiler, Reuben, 65
Butler, Samuel (*novelist*), 231, 850, 923n.
Buzzard, Frank Anstie, 39n., 441n.
Buzzard, Joan Collier (*daughter of the Hon John and Ethel Collier*), 30, 30n., 36, 39n., 40n., 62n., 441n.
Letters to, 39, 441, 467, 479-80
Byles, Sir William, 95, 95n.
Byrd, William, 779

Byron, 81, 96, 230, 555

Caesar, 422
Cairns, Huntington, 741
Callot, Jacques, 466, 467, 509
Calvin, 730, 866
Campbell, Joseph, 826
Campbell, Lewis, 234
Campbell, Roy, 192n.
Camus, Albert, 543, 825, 885
Camus, Pierre, 495, 610
Canby, Henry S., 312n., 322
    Letter to, 312
Cane, Florence, 656
Canfield, Cass, 498n., 505, 645n., 646,
    653, 692, 715n., 901, 922n.
    Letters to, 498-99, 501-2, 548, 581,
    609-10, 637, 763-64, 858-59, 915, 922
Canning, George, 344
Cannon, Sir Alexander, 684
Capa, Cornell, 916n.
Caravaggio, M. M. da, 202, 724n.
Carlyle, 491
Carnap, Rudolf, 437-38, 453
Carrà, C. D., 363
Carrell, Alexis, 400
Carrington, Dorothy, 108n., 109, 118,
    140, 166, 172, 478
    Letters to, 121, 129
Carrington, Hereward, 489
Carroll, Lewis, 535, 537, 609n., 872
Carruthers (*schoolboy*), 28
Carson, Sir Edward, 100, 104
Carswell, Catherine, 355n.
    Letter to, 355
Carter, Frederick, 107
Casanova, 151, 171
Cassapidis, Olivia de Haulleville (*Mrs
    Yorgo Cassapidis, daughter of Eric
    and Rose de Haulleville*), 455, 459,
    479, 486, 503, 856n.
    Letter to, 856
Cassell's Weekly (*paper*), 216
'Casuistical' writing: *see* Biography,
    expository use of
Catherine of Siena, 548, 548n., 561, 562,
    565, 567; *quoted*, 870
Catholicism, Roman, 191n., 326, 372,
    763, 774, 809-10, 843, 862-63, 900
Caussade, J. P. de, *quoted*, 920n.
Cavell, Edith, 121, 371
Caxton, William, 101
Cecil, Lord David, 146
Cendrars, Blaise, 184, 185
Censorship, 85, 95, 304, 330, 373, 416n.,
    417, 535, 535n., 571, 572, 876n.
Cervantes, 321, 819
Cézanne, 156, 164
Chaffin, Lawrence, 730
Chagall, Marc, 640
Chaliapin, F. I., 375
Chambers, Mr, 493
Chambrun, Jacques, 653, 676, 690
Champagne, P. de, 466
Chantal, Baronne de, 773
The Chapbook (*magazine*), 187n.

Chapelain, Yvette, 64, 133
Chaplin, Charles, 427, 458-59
Chapman, D. A. J., 36, 36n.
Chapman, Abbot John, 481
Charles Edward, Prince, 156
Charterhouse School, 28n., 75n., 118, 119,
    872, 883
Chase, Eugene, 138
Chase, Stuart, 453
Chatto and Windus, Ltd., 199, 216, 217,
    225, 225n., 227, 228n., 332, 334, 356,
    392, 400, 403n., 463, 466, 482, 501,
    502, 531, 546, 689, 716, 728
    For letters to, see Parsons, Ian; Prentice,
    C. H. C.; Raymond, Harold;
    Raymond, Piers
Chaucer, 54, 100, 101, 301, 322, 436, 548, 918
Chavasse (*Irish patriot*), 98
Cheatle, Sir Lenthal, 959
Chelsea Book Club, 186, 186n., 190, 190n.
Chen-Chi, 923n.
Chesterton, G. K., 516, 701
Childe, W. R., 104, 138
Cholden, Louis S., 741, 743, 756, 780
Chopin, 43, 45, 46, 308n., 309
Christ: *see* Jesus Christ
The Christian Century (*magazine*), 528
Ciba Review, 811, 811n.
Circle (*magazine*), 529
Claire: *see* White, Claire Nicolas
Clark, Mr (*schoolmaster*), 28
Clark, Sir George, 44n., 82n., 83, 91, 102-3
Clark, Sir Kenneth, 817n., 957
Clarke, Ernest, 44, 44n., 103, 104, 116, 117
Cleiveland, John, 161
Clergy, Anglican, 25n., 31, 57, 78, 87, 106,
    109, 110, 112, 132, 139, 158
Climbers' Club Journal, 56n.
Closs, Hannah, 561n.
    Letter to, 561-62
The Cloud of Unknowing, 613, 613n., 867,
    870, 923
'Coccola' (*nick-name of Maria Huxley*),
    origin of, 194n.
Cocteau, Jean, 182-83, 185, 344, 753
Cohen, Sidney, 844, 845, 882
Colefax, Sir Arthur, 138n., 224
Colefax, Lady, 138, 138n., 224, 270, 275,
    629
Coleridge, 110; *quoted*, 838n.
Colet, John, 153
Collier, Constance, 442, 549, 593, 622,
    623, 741, 742, 742n.
    Letter to, 686
Collier, Ethel Huxley (*aunt of A.H.;
    second wife of the Hon. John Collier*),
    30n., 52, 208, 269n., 270, 270n., 467
    Letters to, 51, 231
Collier, Joan: *see* Buzzard, Joan Collier
Collier, Hon. John, 30n., 68n., 208, 232,
    269n.
Collier, Sir Laurence (*son of the Hon.
    John and Ethel Collier*), 62, 62n., 69
Collier, Marian Huxley (*aunt of A.H.;
    first wife of the Hon. John Collier*),
    177n.

968

Dickinson, Eric, 111
Dill, Sir Samuel, 318
Diogenes, 30n.
Dionysius the Areopagite (the Pseudo-Dionysius), 481, 504, 545
Disney, Walt, 535, 537
Dixon, Campbell, *This Way to Paradise*, 327, 327n., 328, 329
Dobrée, Bonamy, 378n.
The Doddite (*paper*), 29, 29n., 32, 32n.
Dodds, E. R., 138, 804, 925
Dodgson, C. L.,: *see* Carroll, Lewis
Dohrn, Anton, and family of, 246n., 247
Dolci, Danilo, 880, 881n.
Donne, 70n., 81, 101, 112, 152; *quoted*, 70
Doran, George H., 210n., 341n.
  Letter to, 210
Doran, George H., Company (*publishers*), 210n., 224, 235n., 292
Doriot, Jacques, 472, 518
Dorn, Marion V.,: *see* Kauffer, Marion Dorn
Dostoevsky, 131, 226, 281, 409, 516, 600, 918, 929, 930
Doubleday, Doran and Company (*publishers*), 210n., 292, 296n., 332, 334, 341n.
Douglas, Lord Alfred, 156
Douglas, C. H., 378
Douglas, James (*journalist*), 373
Douglas, Norman, 220, 223, 331, 878-79
  Letters to, 206, 239, 250-51, 312, 326, 385
Douglas, Robin, 250
Dowson, Ernest, 120n.
Doyle, Sir Arthur Conan, 39n., 242, 516
Draper, 513, 754
Drayton, Michael, 116
Driesch, Hans, 449, 654
Drieu la Rochelle, Pierre, 181-82, 184, 185, 349n., 397, 472, 517-18, 536, 543
Drinkwater, John, 205
Dryden, 55-56, 81, 594n., *quoted*, 595
Du Bos, Charles, 334
Dubin, Nathan, 932n.
  Letter to, 932
Dubreuil, Hyacinthe, 541
Ducasse, C. J., 705
Duckworth and Company (*publishers*), 86n.
Dürer, Albrecht, 298
Dumaine, Philippe, 521n.
  Letters to, 521, 533-34, 563
Dumas, Alexandre (*père*), 352, 516
Dumas, Alexandre (*? fils*), 113
Duncan, Isadora, 130n.
Dupertuis, C. W., 513, 754
Durante, Jimmy, 795

Eagle, M. N., 822, 823
Earp, T. W., 87, 94, 97, 97n., 107, 110, 126, 128, 138, 144, 171, 173, 192n., 193, 250
Easter Rising, 98
Eaton, Cyrus, 855
Ebon, Martin, 761

Eccles, Mr. 168
Échanges (*magazine*), 476n.
Eckersley, Alfred, 35n.
Eckersley, Rachel (*wife of Alfred Eckersley*): *see* Shawcross, Rachel Huxley Eckersley
Eckersley, Roger (*son of Alfred Eckersley and Rachel Eckersley Shawcross*), 35, 35n., 102n., 907
Eckersley, Thomas (*son of Alfred Eckersley and Rachel Eckersley Shawcross*), 35n., 102n., 907
Eckersley, Tobias W. H., 907
  Letter to, 907-8
Eckhart, Meister, 475, 603-4, 603n., 867, 900, 918, 932n.; *quoted*, 747, 756, 843, 864
Eddington, Sir Arthur, 357
Eddy, Mary Baker, 525
Education: how to solve the problem of, 818; the arts no basis for, 431; in awareness, 827, 830; through drugs, 668-69; of human potentialities, 445, 473-74, 796, 812, 827, 829, 860; through hypnosis 920; for liberty, 847; and literary studies, 70-71; for mental health, 902-3; within militaristic societies, 413-14; politics no basis for, 159; psycho-physical, 525ff., 617-18, 658-59, 695, 748; religious, 774; rôle of sexual continence in, 430-31; in spontaneity, 859; through the subconscious, 656-57, 657-58, 684; visual, and archery, 495-96; *see also* Bates, W. H., and the Bates Method; Sleep-teaching
Edward VII, King, 36n., 360
Edwin: *see* Hubble, Edwin
Eeman, L. E., 683, 683n., 747-48, 750, 750n.
The Egoist (*magazine*), 132, 132n.
Einfeld, Charles, 549
Einstein, Albert, 227, 277, 490
Einstein, Alfred, 767, 768
Eisenhower, 803
El Greco, 319
Elgar, Sir Edward, 80, 166
Eliade, Mircea, 923n., 929
Eliot, T. S., 117, 123, 132, 140, 141, 149, 156, 162, 170, 189, 189n., 192n., 378n., 565, 627, 640, 640n., 858
  Letters to, 232-33, 333-34, 378-79, 379-80, 403-4, 405-6
Eliot, Vivienne, 156, 189n., 232n., 233, 334
Elisabeth, Queen of the Belgians, 360
Elizabeth II, Queen, 755, 916, 916n.
Ella, Miss: *see* Salkowski, Ella
Ellen: *see* Giffard, Ellen Hovde Huxley
Elliotson, John, 634, 804
Ellis, Eugene, 890
Ellis, Havelock, 385, 678
Ellul, Jacques, 859
Elmhirst, Leonard, 957
Elspeth: *see* Huxley, Elspeth Grant

Eluard, Paul, 184
Encyclopaedia Britannica, 539, 554, 637, 933; *quoted*, 290
Encyclopedia Americana, 468
English, Miss (*schoolmistress*), 24, 24n.
The English Review, 202
'Entelechy', Driesch's: *see* Subconscious
Epistolae Virorum Obscurorum, 156
Erasmus, 153, 941
Erigena, Scotus, 523
Erlanger, Baroness d', 156
Erlanger, Gustav, 591, 605
Ernst, Max, 909
Ernst, Morris, 692
Erosion: *see* Food problem.
Eschelbach, Claire John, 903n.
  Letter to, 903
Esdaile, James, 604, 634, 803, 804, 850, 914
Esher, 2nd Viscount, 140n., 422
Esmonde, Osmond Grattan, 85, 89
Esquire (magazine), 683, 684, 724-25, 739, 756n., 767n., 792, 800, 803, 804, 808, 812, 814, 819, 820
Estabrooks, George H., 914n., 919-20
  Letters to, 914, 942, 947-48, 960-61
Etc (journal), 655, 749
Eton College, 23n., 24, 29ff., 118, 119, 131, 132ff., 143, 145, 146, 147, 152, 158, 168ff., 174
Etten, Henry van, 923n.
Euclid, 344
Eugénie, Empress, 706
Evans, Margiad, 695n.
Evans, S. T. G., 33
Evans-Wentz, W. Y., 431, 484, 918
The Evening Standard, 585
Ewart, Mrs, 872
Extra-sensory perception (ESP), 86-87, 86n., 383, 415, 485, 485n., 489-90, 546-47, 551, 643, 674, 679, 680-81, 693, 693n., 696, 699, 713, 714, 718, 729, 738, 746, 750, 757, 761, 772, 798, 799, 828, 895, 910; *see also* Parapsychology
Eysenck, Hans, 943

Fabing, Howard, 787, 788, 868
  Letter to, 785-87
Fachiri, Adila d'Aranyi, 83, 83n.
Fachiri, Alexander, 83n.
Fagniez, G., 466
Fahnestock, W. B., 634, 649, 750
Fairbanks, Douglas, 270
Fairlees, Michael, 187
Fairtlough, F. H., 82n., 83
Famine: *see* Food problem
Farrelly, Frances, 761
Fascisti and Fascism, 199, 200, 249, 273, 289, 361, 363, 378, 380, 434, 462, 505, 518, 536, 553
Fasola family, 194, 194n., 219
Fasola, Signora, 221
Fasola, Costanza: *see* Petterich, Costanza Fasola
Fausset, Hugh I'Anson, 874

Fausset, Robin, 85
Félice, Philippe de, 708, 725, 766
Fellowes, R. C. B., 115
Fénelon, 610, 923n.
Fenollosa, Ernest, 120n.
Fenton, Roy, 371n., 410n.
  Letters to, 371-72, 392-93, 424-27
Fernandel, 630
Feuchtwanger, Lion, 375, 378, 381, 381n.
Figaro Littéraire, 652, 885
Fink, D. H., 657
Firth, C. H., 100
Fishbein, Morris, 510
Fisher of Lambeth, Baron, 105n., 106
Fitch, Ellen, *letter to*, 941
Fitch, William: *see* Benet of Canfield
Flaubert, 170, 171, 291, 335, 343
Flechtheim, Ossip K., 542n.
  Letter to, 542-43
Flecker, J. E., 76
Fletcher, John: *see* Beaumont and Fletcher
Food problem, 465, 486, 492, 494, 528, 531, 555, 562-63, 578, 579-80, 582, 587, 606, 636, 691, 936; *see also* Population problem
Foot, Lindsey: *see* Huxley, Lindsey Foot
Forbes, W. H., 233
Ford, Arthur, 756
Ford Foundation, 653-54, 657, 663, 668, 677, 684, 694-95, 696, 802, 814, 823
Ford Times (magazine), 653
Fordham, Kathleen: *see* Watt, Kathleen Fordham
Form (magazine), 94
Forster, E. M., 343, 855
  Letter to, 391
Forster, Flora, 138, 141
Fort, Charles, 510
Fortune (magazine), 666
Foucauld, Charles de, 559
Fox, George, 464-65
Frampton, Sir George, 104
France, Anatole, 124
Frances: *see* Zuccaro, Frances Petersen
Franchetti, Luigino, 275-76, 288, 291-92
Franchetti, Yvonne: *see* Hamilton, Yvonne Franchetti
Francis: *see* Huxley, Francis John Heathorn
Francis of Assisi, 303, 771
Franco, Francisco, 423n.
François de Sales, 495, 773
Frank, Anne, 574n.
Franklin, Sidney, 435n.
Frederick the Great, 372
Freud, 290, 351, 382, 395, 567-68, 605, 647, 698, 813, 814, 837, 880, 888, 895-96, 902; *see also* Psychoanalysis
Frieda: *see* Ravagli, Frieda von Richthofen Weekley Lawrence
Froissart, Jean, 548
Frost, Bede, 406
Fry, Roger, 167; *quoted*, 527
Fülöp-Miller, René, 294

Green, Mr, 473n.
Letter to, 473-74
Green, J. R. 71
Green, Russell, 111, 192n. 383n.
Letter to, 383-84
Greene, Graham, 330
Greenslet, Ferris, 962
Greenwood, Harold, 202, 202n., 566
Gregory, Eric, 403
Gresham, Sir Thomas: Gresham's Law, 438
Grillparzer, Franz, 838n.
Grimm, Jacob and Wilhelm, 798
Gris, Juan, 716
Groddeck, G. W., 390, 902
Gronchi, Givanni, 855
Grove, E. T. N., 29
Grove Press (*publishers*), 875n., 876-77
Grunne, Willie de, 360
Guedalla, Philip, 69
Guidetti, Professor, 960
Guillemard, Sir Laurence and Lady, 256n., 260, 268
Guitry, Sacha, 186
Gumilyov, N. S., 126
Gurney, Edmund, 634
Guyon, Jeanne Marie, 282, 291, 923n.
Guyon, René, 385
Gwynn, Nell, 129

Hagen, Uta, 758
Haire, Norman, 385
Haldane family, 47, 55, 57n., 63, 64, 76, 82, 89, 116, 122, 130, 150-51, 189
Haldane, J. B. S., 46n., 55, 64, 65, 66, 69, 122, 202-3, 655
Haldane, John Scott, 46n., 47, 64n., 66, 69, 71, 116, 655
Haldane, Louisa, 46n., 47, 64, 64n., 66, 85, 131, 133, 138, 151, 189-90
Haldane, Naomi: *see* Mitchison, Naomi Haldane
Haldane of Cloan, Richard Burdon, Viscount, 43, 46n., 138, 146
Hales, Sir Matthew, 811
Hall, Elsa, 674, 674n., 853
Hall, Manley, 681
Hall, Trevor, 951, 951n.
Haller, William, 923n.
Halliday, James, 583, 659
Halsberg, Helen, 732, 735n.
Hamann, Paul, 336
Hamilton, Emma, Lady, 167, 167n.
Hamilton, Hamish, 412
Hamilton, Yvonne Franchetti, 292, 855
Hammerstein, Oscar (2nd), 820
Hamnett, Nina, 130, 130n.
Handley, Leonard, 387, 388
Handley, Sally, 387n.
Letter to, 387-88
Hardcastle family, 75
Harding, Marjorie, Lady (*daughter of Henry and Sophy Huxley*), 177, 177n.
Harding, Warren G., 522
Hardwicke, Sir Cedric, 572, 573, 576n., 585, 616, 825

Hardy, Sir Alister, 678n., 679
Hardy, Thomas, 66
Hare, Jean E.: *see* Heywood, Jean Hare
Harmsworth, Alfred: *see* Northcliffe, Alfred Harmsworth, Viscount
Harper, Allanah (Mme Statlender), 476, 476n., 763, 763n.
Letter to, 710-11
Harper & Row, Inc. (formerly Harper & Brothers), 235n., 366, 370, 410, 466, 482, 487, 498n., 502, 505, 508, 532, 532n., 534, 543, 581, 609, 610, 616, 637, 646, 689, 692, 715n., 716, 728, 753, 922n.
For letters to, see Aswell, Edward C.; Bessie, S. M.; Canfield, Cass; Saxton, Eugene F.
Harper's (*magazine*), 225, 508n., 587, 589, 666, 727, 728, 734, 737, 751
Harper's Bazaar (*magazine*), 549, 947
Harry (*sculptor*), 761
Hart, Hornell, 830
Hartmann, K. R. E. von, 75, 81
Harvey, Helen, 757n., 758, 775, 783, 833, 964
Letters to, 777, 834-36
Harwood, H. C., 110, 144, 149
Hassall, Christopher, 82n.
Hatry, Clarence, 327
Hattersley, Marshall, 378
Haulleville, Baron Eric de, 398n., 459, 479n.
Haulleville, Olivia de: *see* Cassapidis, Olivia de Haulleville
Haulleville, Rose Nys de (*sister of Maria Nys Huxley*), 211n., 279, 280, 315, 398, 398n., 455, 459, 468, 472, 479, 479n., 486, 496n., 502-3, 517, 590, 614, 652, 653, 675, 731, 733, 738, 740n., 741, 759, 760, 778, 794n., 798, 861, 885, 886, 962, 962n.
Letter to, 739-40
Hauser, Frank, 830n., 931
Hawkins, Leland, 605, 726, 730, 731
Hawley, Carolyn, 934n.
Letter to, 934-35
Hay, Dr, 370
Hayakawa, S. I., 749
Haydon, B. R., 311
Hayes, Helen, 549, 549n.
Haynes, E. S. P., 16, 33, 33n., 98, 110, 212n., 463, 596, 596n.
Letters to, 212, 233, 293-94, 450-51, 516-17
Haynes, Oriana (Ria) Waller (*daughter of F. W. and Jessie Waller*), 33, 33n., 516
Hayward, Leland, 463
Head, Henry, 316, 316n.
Heard, Gerald, 302n., 322, 322n., 347, 353, 358n., 374, 375, 389, 398, 408, 410n., 412, 413, 415, 421n., 422, 424-25, 426, 427-28, 432, 443-44, 443n., 448, 475, 484, 495, 556, 569, 601, 622, 636, 653, 717, 722, 723, 729, 737, 741, 771, 778, 779, 780, 785, 787, 788, 799, 805, 810, 812, 842, 843, 844, 892, 912

Kierkegaard, S., 356, 541
Kilbride, Dr, 846
Kilburn, Joyce Collier (*daughter of the Hon. John and Marian Collier*), 177n.
King, Carlyle, 723n.
 Letter to, 723-24
Kinglake, A. W., 559
Kircher, Athanasius, 755-56
Kirchner, Raphael, 174
Kiskadden, 'Bull', 628, 629, 778
Kiskadden, Margaret, 590n., 591, 731n., 741, 760, 778, 794n., 852, 892
 Letters to, 628-29, 731, 890, 933-34
Kiskadden, William, 590n., 690, 731n., 741, 796-97, 805, 822, 847, 852
 Letter to, 890
Kissack (*photographer*), 29
Kitchener, 1st Earl, 69, 72, 79
Kitselman, A. L., 648, 650, 699
Klemmer, Herbert, 882n.
 Letter to, 882-83
Klepa, Mr (*decorator*), 598
Kley, Heinrich, 80
Kline, Nathan, 880, 881
Klinger, Max, 80
Klyce, Scudder, 324n.
 Letter to, 324-25
Kneipp, Sebastian, 812
Knight, G. Wilson, 329
 Letter to, 353-54
Knopf, Alfred A., Inc. (*publishers*), 332
Kolisch, Joseph, 493, 496-97, 498, 573
Kopeloff, Dr, 250
Korda, Sir Alexander, 395, 549, 554, 565, 572, 580
Korda, Zoltan, 549-50, 554, 565, 570n., 572, 573, 576, 580, 582, 583n., 584, 584n., 618, 774
Korzybski, Alfred, 436, 438, 453, 491
Koteliansky, S. S., 387, 665-66, 666n.
Kouyoumdjian, Dikran: *see* Arlen, Michael
Koyré, Alexandre, 923n.
Krafft-Ebing, Baron R. von, 385
Kretschmer, Ernst, 390, 428, 487, 655
Kreuger, Ivar, 364n.
Kripalani, Krishna, 956n.
 Letter to, 956-57
Krishnamurti, Jiddu, 475, 569, 608n., 609, 612n., 613, 818, 902, 917-18, 938, 963
Kubitschek de Oliveira, J., 855
Kuentz, Charles, 708
Kunz, F. L., 488, 490
Kusel, Heinz, 806n., 807
 Letter to, 806

La Fontaine, Jean de, 49, 308n., 309
La Ramée, Marie Louise de: *see* Ouida
La Rochefoucauld, 156, 930
La Tour du Pin, Patrice de, 541
La Vallée Poussin, Louis de, 449
Lacey, Franklin, musical version of *Brave New World*, 940, 940n.,; *see also* Huxley, Aldous (*Plays and Scripts*)

Laforgue, Jules, 72n., 75, 75n., 78n., 96, 127-28, 377; *quoted*, 73, 76, 81
Lagerlöf, Selma, 162n., 179
Lall, Chaman, 251, 252, 255-56
Lamartine, de, 185
Lamson, Peggy, 919n., 920n.
 Letter to, 920-22
Lamson, Roy, 919n., 920n., 922
Land, Myrick, 929n.
 Letter to, 929-30
Langevin, Paul, 396
Lansbury, George, 136, 139
Lao Tzu, 242-43, 245, 542; *quoted*, 781; *see also* Taoism
Lape, Esther, 591
LaPorte, 'Zezelle', 272n., 273, 274, 278n., 283, 291, 292, 293
Lasne, Michel, 466
Lasson, Adolf, 79
Latour, Georges de, 762
Laura: *see* Huxley, Laura Archera
Law, William, 504, 574, 918
Lawrence, D. H., 85-86, 88, 88n., 95, 187, 248, 275, 275n., 288, 294, 295, 300, 304n., 313-14, 315, 327, 329, 330-33, 331n., 334, 335-37, 335n., 338-40, 339n., 340n., 342, 343, 346-47, 346n., 347, 349n., 350, 352-53, 355, 357-58, 362, 364, 365, 409, 422, 422n., 432, 455ff., 502, 544n., 559, 620, 665-66, 666n., 715, 715n., 813, 831, 875n., 876-77, 876n., 879, 884n., 885, 888, 899, 929-30, 929n.; *quoted*, 683, 904
 Letters to, 304-5, 327-28
Lawrence, Frieda: *see* Ravagli, Frieda von Richthofen Weekley Lawrence
Lawrence, George, 337, 338, 355, 364
Lawrence, T. E., 547, 548, 558-59, 583n., 584
Le Corbusier, 792
Le Gouvello, Vicomte, 651
Le Grand, Louis, 80
Le Roy, Mervyn, 435n.
Le Sage, A. R., 343
Lea, H. C., 318
Lear, Edward, 610
Lear, H. S., 610
Leary, Timothy, 944, 954-55
 Letters to, 909, 928-29, 953-54, 955
Leavis, F. R., 941
Lebrun, Albert, 375
LeCron, Leslie, 646, 647, 650, 699, 730, 735n., 741, 750
Lederer, Charles, 816
Lee, I. J., 491
Lee, Sir Sidney, 86
Lee, Vernon: *see* Paget, Violet
The Left Review, 411n., 423n.
 Letter to, 423
Leigh, Vivien, 653
Leighton, Baron, 80
Lenclos, Ninon de, 225n.
Léner String Quartet, 288
Lengyel, Melchior, 455-58
Leno, Dan, 31, 31n.
Leonard, Florence A., *letter to*, 909-10

Leonard, Robert Z., 447n.
Leonardo da Vinci, 298, 323, 323n., 324, 700; 'Mona Lisa', 848
Leopold II, King of the Belgians, 360
LePut, Marie, 734, 759
Leslie, Seymour, 186n.
  Letter to, 190
Leuba, J. H., 291, 347
Levine, D. R., 816
Lévy-Bruhl, Lucien, 766
Lewis: *see* Gielgud, Lewis Evelyn
Lewis, P. Wyndham, 220
Lewis, Sinclair, 370n., 371
Leyton, Neville, 911, 911n.
Liberty: decline of, 96, 212, 522; of the mind, 173-74; and private property, 362-63, 464, 500; psychological freedom, 829; and solitude, 473; of the subject, 95, 95n.,; threatened by applied psychology, 539, 542, 604-5, 823; threatened by bureaucracy, 451; threatened by conditioning to enjoy slavery, 837, 840-41; threatened by efficiency, 515; threatened by leftist programmes, 504, 531; threatened by technology, 438, 455, 611, 859; threatened by the wish for 'tidiness', 847-48; and the uniqueness of the individual, 847; use of, 461-62; *see also* Decentralization, Utopianism
Life (*magazine*), 582, 593, 614, 636, 666, 678, 693n., 696, 697
Ligt, Barthélemy de, 411
Lincelon, Abbé, 49
Lincoln, Abraham, 822
Lindbergh, C. A., 407
Lindley, Denver, 508n.
Lion, Leon M., 327n., 334n., 506n.
  Letters to, 506-7, 565-67
Lissauer, Mr, 432
Lister, 1st Baron, 804
Liszt, Franz, 282, 292
The Little Review, 168, 170
Livesay, Florence, 120n.
Livingston, Arthur, 379
Lobatchevsky, N. I., 344
Lodge, Henry Cabot (*the elder*), 168
Loeser, Charles, and Mrs Loeser, 288
The London Mercury (*magazine*), 179n.
Long, Haniel, 529
Loos, Anita, 269n., 272, 427, 446, 549n. 567n., 601, 614n., 653, 742, 761, 764
  Letters to, 269-70, 270-71, 534-36, 549-50, 567-69, 572-73, 614-15, 631-632, 674, 733, 794-95, 816
Loos, Clifford, 614, 614n., 615
Lopokova, Lydia (Baroness Keynes), 163
Lorenz, Konrad, 644n., 645
Louis XIV, 464, 779
Louis XV, 770
Low, David, 385
Low, Sir Sidney, 148
Lucas, 8th Baron, 150
Luce, Clare, 795
Luce, Henry, 582
Lucretius, 284

Luftig, Wilhelm, 626
Luhan, Mabel Dodge, 331, 338n., 339, 340n., 355, 355n., 422, 422n.
  Letter to, 340
Lund, John, 767
Lutz, Dr, 722
Lydgate, John, 65
Lynch, Robert, 841-42, 853, 963
Lynd, Robert, 290
Lysenko, T. D., 611, 611n.

Mabuse, Jan, 172
MacArthur, Douglas, 633
Macaulay, Rose, 858
Macaulay, Thomas Babington, 1st Baron, 47, 70, 254
MacCarthy, Sir Desmond, 156, 220, 348
MacColl, Andrée, 167, 167n.
MacColl, D. S., 167n.
McCormack, Thomas H., Jr., *letter to*, 545-46
McDonagh, J. E. R., 408, 435, 525-26
MacDonagh, James, 98
McDougall, William, 276, 318
McDowall, Arthur, 170
McEldowney, Mary: *see* Hupfel, Mary McEldowney
McEvoy, Ambrose, 130, 130n.
Machiavelli, 153, 553
Mackenzie, Sir Compton, 87
Maclean's (*magazine*), 686, 686n., 701
McLeod, A. W., 331, 141n.
McLeod, Irene Rutherford, 141, 141n.
Macmillan, Sir Harold, 379
Macnaghten, H. V., 35
MacPhail, Dr, 367
McQuilland, Louis J., 188, 188n.
Madach, Emeric, 404n., 405
Madan, Falconer, 47, 56n.
Madan, Geoffrey, 56, 56n.
Maddow, Ben, 873n.
Maeterlinck, Maurice, 77
Magnelli (*painter*), 363
Magnetism, animal: *see* Hypnosis and Hypnotism
Maillol, Aristide, 322
Main Currents in Modern Thought (*magazine*), 488, 490
Maine de Biran, P., 354, 589, 597, 598, 601-2, 607n., 608, 608n., 611, 612n. 613, 620
Maison, G. L., 688
Maistre, Joseph de, 866
Malamud, William, 688
Malcolm, Pulteney, 36, 36n.
Mâle, Émile, 923n.
Malebranche, Nicolas de, 414n.; *quoted*, 414
Malinowski, Bronislaw, 314, 318, 326, 343
Mallarmé, André, 388, 388n.
Mallarmé, Stéphane, 67, 78, 308n., 309, 954; *quoted*, 620
Malraux, André, 342, 692, 692n.
Malthus, 531, 562-63
The Manchester Guardian, 168
Manichaeism, 79

Mosley, Lady Cynthia, 352
Mosley, Sir Oswald, Bt, 375
Motteux, Peter, 215
Moulaert, René, 250
Moulaert, Sophie: *see* Welling, Sophie Moulaert
Moussorgsky, M. P., 375
Mozart, 205, 208, 308n., 309, 375, 445, 682, 780
Mudd, Stuart, 957, 963
Mügge, Maximilian, 282
Muhl, Anita, 635, 635n., 679
Muhlfeld, Jeanne, 308n., 309
Muir, Edwin, 345, 378n., 948
Muir, Ramsay, 212n.
Mumford, Lewis, 859
Mundle, C. W. K., 705
Murasaki Shikibu, 433
Murfin, Jane, 447n.
Murphy, Gardner, 729, 880
Murray, Agnes, 106, 106n.
Murray, Gilbert, 56, 67, 86-87, 86n., 96, 106n., 804
Murray, John, 122
Murray, John (*publishers*), 131, 186n.
Murray, Rosalind: *see* Toynbee, Rosalind
Murrell, A. W., 747-48
  Letter to, 749-50
Murrell, Elise, 638n., 643n., 746n.
  Letters to, 638-39, 642-44, 685-86, 746-48
Murrow, E. R., 855
Murry, John Middleton, 118, 141, 179n., 243n., 331, 352-53, 352n., 355, 544n., 733n., 887, 888, 929-30, 929n.
  Letters to, 243-44, 544-45, 546-47, 556
Murry, Mary Middleton, *letter to*, 887-88
Musset, Alfred de, 49, 155, 162
Mussolini, Arnaldo, 342n.
Mussolini, Benito, 222-23, 245, 291, 361, 363, 378, 379, 385, 398, 427, 459
Myers, F. W. H., 634, 647, 649, 656, 891, 891n.
Mysticism, 88, 234, 235, 245, 430, 431-32, 473, 474, 494-95, 538, 545, 651, 659, 668-69, 681, 698, 725-26, 735n., 772, 863, 874, 932, 935; *see also* Visionary experience

Naidu, Miss, 254, 255
Naidu, Sarojini, 253-54, 255, 264
Naomi: *see* Mitchison, Naomi Haldane
Napier, L. R. M., 30
Napoleon, 155, 363, 464, 515, 518
Narodny (*researcher in telepathy*), 761
Nash's Pall Mall Magazine, 340n., 383
Nast, Condé, 206, 216
The Nation (London), 92, 94, 110, 115, 162n., 216, 217, 252n.
Nature (*magazine*), 488, 583, 606
Natwick, Mildred, 616, 616n.
Nazism and the Nazi régime, 371, 375, 383, 439, 453, 470, 483, 553
Nef, J. U., 923n.
Nefertiti, 211
Nehru, Jawaharlal, 264, 855, 927

Nehru, Pandit Motilal, 254, 264, 267
Neilson, William, 804
Nelson, Horatio, Viscount, 167, 167n.
Nelson, Howard, *letter to*, 883
Neri, Philip, 562
Nero, 545, 587
Neroutsos, Miss (*schoolmistress*), 24, 24n.
Neurath, Otto, 437-38
Neveux, Georges, 459, 460, 522, 539, 574n., 580, 585, 598, 624, 624n., 672n., 705, 710n., 752-53, 752n., 871n., 915, 917
  Letters to, 574-75, 576-78, 598-600, 672-73, 871-72, 939-40
Neveux, Jeanne (Jehanne) Nys Moulaert (*sister of Maria Nys Huxley*), 176, 211n., 250, 286, 295, 371, 424n., 426, 446, 455, 459, 460, 465, 487, 517, 522, 574n., 594-95, 621, 624, 624n., 626, 705, 710, 710n., 737, 906n., 915, 939
  Letters to, 574-75, 752-53, 962-63
Neveux, Noële (*daughter of Georges and Jeanne Neveux*), 465, 517, 522, 752n., 753, 855
  Letter to, 758-59
Nevinson, C. R. W., 144, 144n.
The New American Library (*publishers*), 875n.
The New Republic, 219-20
The New Statesman, 120, 120n., 162n., 216, 585
The New York Herald Tribune, 379n., 397, 519, 519n., 632
The New York Times, 632
The New Yorker, 858
Newsday (*newspaper*), 837n.
Newton, Sir Isaac, 235
Newton, Marianna Schauer, 734, 778
  Letters to, 741, 759-60, 949
Nicholas of Cusa: *see* Nicolas of Cusa
Nichols family, 141n., 147n., 159n.
Nichols, Irene: *see* Gater, Irene Nichols
Nichols, John Bowyer, 147, 147n., 208, 234
Nichols, Norah, 297, 373
Nichols, Sir Philip, 147n., 208, 943
Nichols, Robert, 98, 98n., 138, 141, 147n., 154, 155, 159, 207, 296n., 316n., 943
  Letters to, 107, 215-17, 233-35, 245-46, 266, 268-69, 276-77, 281-82, 296-97, 301-2, 315-16, 322-23, 329-30, 335, 342-43, 346, 373-74, 389-90, 397-98, 414-15
Nicolas, Armelle, 651
Nicolas, Claire: *see* White, Claire Nicolas
Nicolas, Joep, 229, 365, 581, 788
  Letter to, 540
Nicolas, Suzanne Nys (*sister of Maria Nys Huxley*), 211n., 229, 302-3, 365, 459, 549, 558, 574n., 596, 611, 733, 735n., 741
  Letters to, 211, 944-45
Nicolas, Sylvia: *see* Semprun, Sylvia Nicolas de
Nicolas of Cusa, 603, 612, 659
Nietzsche, 282

Niven, M. D., 103n.
Noailles, Charles, Vicomte de, 344, 344n., 395, 435n., 472, 682
Letter to, 365
Noailles, Marie Laure, Vicomtesse de, 344n., 395, 682, 682n.
Noële: *see* Neveux, Noële
Noon, Miss (*schoolmistress*), 23n., 274
Letter to, 23
Norris, E. E. A., 596n.
Letter to, 596
Northcliffe, Alfred Harmsworth, Viscount, 79, 119, 146, 168, 242
Norton, Robert, 472
Nostradamus, 817
Not-self: *see* Subconscious
Novel of ideas, 312, 600
Noyes, Alfred, 33
Nys family, 146, 166, 169, 174, 175-76
Nys, Jeanne (Jehanne): *see* Neveux, Jeanne (Jehanne) Nys Moulaert
Nys, Marguerite Baltus (*mother of Maria Nys Huxley*), 119, 176, 219, 249, 252, 263, 313, 455, 459, 460, 468, 472, 479, 481, 517, 540, 599n., 600, 652-53, 652n., 665, 675, 759, 760, 778, 861, 885, 889, 892, 944n., 945, 962, 962n.
Nys, Maria: *see* Huxley, Maria Nys
Nys, Norbert (*father of Maria Nys Huxley*), 169, 174, 176
Nys, Rose: *see* Haulleville, Rose Nys de
Nys, Suzanne: *see* Nicolas, Suzanne Nys

The Observer, 908
Ocampo, Victoria, 349n., 846, 875n.
Letters to, 349-50, 396-97, 398, 401-2, 408, 494-95, 517-19, 531-32, 536-38, 541-42, 543, 547-48, 558-59, 583-85, 640-41, 801-2, 865-66
Occleve, Thomas, 65
Ockham, William of, 894
O'Connor, Hubert, 136
Ogden, C. K., 453, 491
O'Keefe, Georgia, 445
Olivia: *see* Cassapidis, Olivia de Haulleville
Olivier, Sir Laurence, 653
Olympia Press, 856n.
Oman, C. W. C., 71
O'Neill, Eugene, 568
Operational philosophy, 447, 448, 554, 827, 829, 843, 938
Oppenheimer, J. Robert, 941-42
Orioli, Giuseppi (Pino), 239, 239n., 304, 304n., 316-17, 385, 876; *quoted*, 316n.
Orr, Sir John, 587
Ortega y Gasset, José, 725
Orwell, George, 715
Letter to, 604-5
Osborn, Fairfield, 587, 592, 691n.
Letters to, 578-79, 691
O'Shea, Daniel T., 957n.
Letter to, 957-58
Osis, Karlis, 826
Osmond, Helen, 687n., 717, 734, 841, 852

Osmond, Humphry, 669n., 676n., 677, 677n., 679, 687n., 692, 700, 701, 703, 715, 716-17, 718, 722n., 723n., 729, 733n., 734n., 738n., 791n., 795n., 800n., 806, 812, 828, 837, 846, 868n., 894n., 936n., 937, 945n., 952, 963n.
Letters to, 668-70, 676-77, 682-85, 686-89, 690-91, 695-96, 698-700, 701-2, 704-5, 711-12, 713-14, 722-23, 725-26, 729-30, 732-33, 734-38, 742-743, 748, 755-57, 768-73, 778-80, 791-92, 795-96, 798-99, 800-801, 802-3, 804-5, 807-8, 809-10, 813-14, 818-19, 821-26, 840-45, 847-48, 849-851, 852-53, 857-58, 868-69, 872-73, 879-80, 881-82, 893-96, 899-900, 902-3, 905, 910-11, 917-18, 926-27, 936-37, 942-43, 945-46, 946-47, 953, 957, 958-59, 963
Osmond, Jane, 702, 732, 733, 858, 911, 945-46
Osty, Eugène, 241-42
Otto, Rudolf, 333
Ouida, 160
Ovid, *quoted*, 488
Ovshinsky, Stanford, 823, 823n.
Owen, David, 663, 665
Owen, Janet C., 370n.
Oxford and Asquith, 1st Earl of: *see* Asquith, Herbert Henry
Oxford Poetry 1916, 85n., 102, 104, 108, 118, 119
Oxford Poetry 1917, 128, 138, 138n.
Oxford Poetry 1918, 148n., 167

Pacifism, 146, 395-96, 398, 399n., 400-401, 403n., 408, 423, 426, 469-70, 781, 923-25; *see also* Conscientious objection to war
Packard, Vance, 841
Paganini, 202
Paget, Violet (Vernon Lee), 180, 197, 221, 275
Letter to, 248
Pagnol, Marcel, 630
Painter and draughtsman, A. H.'s work as a, 33, 37, 59, 164, 315, 358, 361, 373-74, 385, 393-94, 414, 445
The Palatine Review, 78n., 87-88, 88-89, 90, 94, 104
Palestrina, 779
Palgrave, F. T., 357
Panini, 491
Papini, Giovanni, 204
Parapsychology, 410n., 415, 484-85, 485n., 489-90, 550, 561, 634, 678, 713, 723, 762, 828, 856, 857, 861, 901; *see also* Extra-sensory perception (ESP)
Parapsychology Foundation, 687, 691n., 746, 826, 894n., 910-11, 951
Pareto, Vilfredo, 276, 365n., 376, 379-80, 379n., 397
Parker, Mrs, 53, 60
Parmentier, Mr, 280
Parr, H. W. M., 32, 32n.
Parry, C. H., 98n., 99

Psychedelic drugs—*contd.*
814, 824-25, 828, 843, 844-45, 848, 851, 853, 862-64, 874, 881-82, 889, 889n., 893-94, 895, 899, 900, 909, 911, 929, 938-39, 944, 945, 945n., 947, 952, 953-54, 953n., 954, 955
The Psychedelic Review, 806n.
Psycho-analysis, 243-44, 245, 355, 382, 605, 635, 813, 934-35; *see also* Freud
Psychological types; *see* Temperament and physique
Psychology: comparative, 243; and crowds, 725; and eternity, 603-4, 603n.; in medical practice, 706; and physics, 702; and physiology, 372-73; religious, 438; and spirituality, 633; as an instrument of tyranny, 539, 542, 604-5, 823; *see also* Parapsychology, Psycho-analysis, Subconscious
Puharich, Henry, 688, 702, 714, 738, 739, 757, 758, 798, 810, 919
Puharich, Virginia, 761
Putnam, G. P. (*publishers*), 115
Puységur, Marquis de, 634

Quakers, 464-65, 470-71, 472, 474n., 503, 528, 765-66, 852, 874
Queen's Quarterly, 723n.
Queval, Jean, *letter to*, 692

Rabelais, 124-25, 215, 358n., 600; *allusions to*, 160, 161
Rabia (Rabiah of Basra), 594
Racine, 308n., 309, 746
Radhakrishnan, S. S., 880
Radin, Paul, 530
Rado, Sandor, 895
Raglan, 1st Baron, 515
Rai, Lala Lajpat, 264
Raimu, 630
Raines, Claude, 571, 572
Rajagopal, Rosalind, 496, 496n., 596
Raleigh, Sir Walter (*professor*), 48, 54, 55-56, 65, 82, 85, 87, 101, 117, 169, 173
Ramakrishna, 545, 608n., 609
Ramuz, C. F., 599, 599n.
Randall (*schoolboy*), 28
Randall, John H., 881
Rank, Otto, 814
Rao, Sharna, 171, 173
Raphael, 201
Rathbone, Basil, 623, 630
Rau, Leo, 857
Ravagli, Angelo, 422, 422n., 425, 500, 501, 734, 740n., 878, 885
Ravagli, Frieda von Richthofen Weekley Lawrence, 88, 88n., 294, 300, 305, 313-14, 331-32, 334n., 335, 337, 338, 347, 352-53, 355, 364, 409, 421-22, 421n., 423n., 425, 429n., 432, 455, 631, 665, 733n., 739-40, 740n., 742, 813, 813n., 831-32, 878, 878n., 879

Letters to, 334-35, 455-59, 500-501, 502-4, 733-34
Rawlley, Mr, 256
Raymond, Harold, 228n., 294, 296n., 403n., 488, 548n., 591, 608n., 732
Letters to, 358-59, 391-92, 403, 416-17, 429, 440, 446, 451-52, 460-61, 466-67, 480-81, 493-94, 507-8, 511-12, 531, 580, 585-86, 588, 596-97, 630-31, 664, 677-78, 689-90, 700-701
Raymond, Piers, 466, 481, 512
Letter to, 731-32
Raymond, Tony, 466, 481, 494, 512
Raymond, Vera, 429, 460, 466, 588
Read, G. Dick, 923n.
Read, Sir Herbert, 378n.
The Reader's Digest, 696, 697-98
The Realist (*magazine*), 302n. 303
Reeves, Frere, 355, 400
Reger, Max, 80
Reich, Wilhelm, 750
Reichenbach, Baron Karl von, 750
Reiser, Oliver Leslie, 485
Religion, feelings of A. H. about, 810-11, 935
Religions, Oriental, 162, 162n., 242-43, 245, 335, 382, 389, 405n., 406, 428, 431, 438, 484-85, 489-90, 506, 510n., 511, 520, 523, 526-27, 530, 533-34, 537, 542, 550-51, 554, 559, 561, 564n., 569-70, 579, 585, 597, 608n., 609, 612-14, 612n.-613n., 618, 620, 635, 638-39, 648; 650, 654-55, 679, 681, 693, 699, 709, 710-11, 720, 730, 748, 762-63, 769, 779-80, 791, 802, 803, 827, 829, 843-44, 867, 893-94, 902, 928-29, 935n.; *see also* Buddhism, Taoism, Vedanta
Relph, George, 631
Rembrandt, 298, 509, 716
Renan, J. E., 282
Renshaw, Samuel, 656-57, 684, 686, 695
Reps, Paul, 929
Repton School, 105-8, 114, 158-59
Reti, Ladislao, 700, 701
Rhine, Joseph Banks, 410n., 415n., 678n., 700, 713
Letters to, 415, 484-85, 489-90, 550-51, 561, 634, 678-79, 680-81, 693-94, 697-98, 712-13, 718-19, 828
Rhine, Louisa, 679, 713
Richards, I. A., 378n., 453, 491
Richards, O. W., 923n.
Richardson, Sir Ralph, 616
Richelieu, 460, 462, 466, 467
Richman, Robert, 741, 859
Richmond, B. L., 117, 117n.
Rimbaud, Arthur, 282, 531n.; *quoted*, 521
Rimsky-Korsakov, N. A., 80, 165, 167
Ritchie, Andrew, 84
Roberts, 1st Earl, 31, 88
Roberts, Kethevan, 342n., 359n., 406n.
Letters to, 342, 343-44, 356, 359, 363, 375-76, 390-91, 433, 461-62
Roberts, Warren, 885
Robertson, Grant, 96

Robespierre, 604
Robinson, G. Gidley, 70n.
    Letters to, 70-71, 179-80
Robinson, Percy, 336-37
Rockefeller, Nelson, 722
Rockefeller Foundation, 636, 655, 696
Rodgers, Richard, 820
Rodin, Auguste, 80
Roller, Henrietta (Nettie) Huxley (*aunt of A. H.; wife of John Harold Roller*), 208, 209-10, 270, 270n.
Rollier, Auguste, 246
Romains, Jules, 77, 96, 241
Romanov, P. S., 352
Roosevelt, Franklin D., 374, 511, 928
Roosevelt, Theodore, 168, 170
Rops, Félicien, 80
Rorem, Ned, *letter to*, 682
Rosa, Salvator, 43
Rosalind: *see* Huxley, Rosalind Bruce
Rose: *see* Haulleville, Rose Nys de
Rose, Ralph: play, *After Many a Summer*, 637, 702n., 789, 820, 821; *see also* Huxley, Aldous (*Plays and Scripts*)
    Letters to, 702, 703-4, 751, 958
Rosebery, 5th Earl of, 31
Roser, W. F., 43, 43n.
Rosete, Dr, 790
Ross, Nancy, 744
Ross, Robert, 141, 141n., 156, 168
Ross Johnstone, Miss (*shop assistant*), 190, 190n.
Roth, Sanford, 640, 645n., 705, 707
    Letter to, 645-46
Rothenstein, Sir William, 210n., 232
    Letter to, 210
Roy, Dilip Kumar, *letter to*, 585
Roy, Pierre, 445
Royde-Smith, Naomi, *letter to*, 205
Rozanov, V. V., *quoted*, 552
Rubinstein, Artur, 601
Rugby School, 28-29, 28n., 32, 36, 70, 108, 108n., 109
Rumi, Jalall-uddin, 594
Ruskin, John, 559
Russell, Bertrand (3rd Earl), 118, 146, 150, 166, 325, 331, 390, 391, 411, 413, 438, 454, 475, 491, 803, 855, 858, 918
Russell, George William (AE), 766
Russell, Sir John, 606
Russell, Patricia, Countess, 739, 739n.
Russell, Rachel, 99, 197, 232n.
Ruysbroeck, Jan van, 603-4, 603n.
Ryland, Henry E., *letter to*, 377
Rypins, 111

Sackville-West, Hon. Edward (5th Baron Sackville), 182n.
    Letters to, 182-83, 275-76, 356-57, 377-78
Sade, Marquis de, 604, 682, 682n.
Sagar, N., 383n.
    Letter to, 383
Sainsbury, Philip, 233
Salandra, Antonio, 83
Sale, Mary Anita, 549, 549n.

Salisbury, 3rd Marquis, 146
Salkowski, Ella (Bella), 29, 30n., 32, 52, 194, 195, 208, 209, 219
Salvemini, Gaetano, 249
Samkara, 511
Die Sammlung (*magazine*), 381, 381n.
Samuel, Sir Herbert (1st Viscount), 417
Samuel, Lesser, 606
San Martin, José, 865, 865n.
Sand, George, 140, 155, 162
Santayana, George, 251, 449
Sappho, 96
Sarah (*parlourmaid*), 52, 52n., 101, 103
Sarawak, Ranee of: *see* Brooke, Hon. Sylvia
Sargant, William, 822
Sartre, Jean-Paul, 825
Sassoon, Sir Philip, 387
Sassoon, Siegfried, 181
Saturday Evening Post (*magazine*), 845, 862n.
Saunders, Carr, 264
Saurat, Denis, 347
Saxton family, 279, 280, 333, 366
Saxton, Eugene F., 235n., 492-93, 492n., 498n., 505
    Letters to, 235-36, 279-81, 332-33, 354, 365-66, 399-400, 410-11, 412-13, 467-69, 477
Saxton, Mark, 366
Saxton, Martha, 279, 280, 333, 400, 447
    Letter to, 492-93
Saxton, 'Sandy', 400
Sayers, Dorothy L., 138, 138n.
Sayre, Nevin, 546
Scarlett, the Misses, 759, 759n., 907
Schauer, Marianna: *see* Newton, Marianna Schauer
Schickele, René, 378
Schiff, Sydney, 387
Schildkraut, Joseph, 751
Schiller, 43, 45, 46; *quoted*, 921-22
Schönebeck, Sybille von: *see* Bedford, Sybille von Schönebeck
Scholem, G. G., 659
Schopenhauer, 75
Schroedinger, Erwin, 561
Schumann, Robert, 54
Schuster, Adela, 154n.
Schuster, Frank, 153, 154n., 166
Schwartz, Jacob, 598, 781
Schweitzer, Albert, 601
The Scientific Monthly, 693
Scott, Geoffrey, 197, 221, 224, 251
Scott, Robert Falcon, 44
Scott, Lady Sybil, 197, 221
Scott, Sir Walter, Bt, 56, 516
Scriabin, Alexander, 80
Seabrook, Marjorie Worthington: *see* Worthington, Marjorie
Seabrook, William, 365, 365n., 425, 429n.
Secker, Martin, *letter to*, 364-65
Secker, Martin (*publishers*), 86, 86n., 332
Seldes, George, 866n.
    Letter to, 866
Seldon, Albert, 742, 742n., 744

Thurber, James, 508n.
Tibetan Book of the Dead: see Bardo Thodol
Tich, Little (*comedian*), 121, 206
Tickell, Renée (*daughter of E. S. P. Haynes and Oriana Haynes*), 670n.
  Letter to, 670
Tiddy, R. J. E., 54, 54n., 66, 168
Time (*magazine*), 511, 517, 582, 666, 880, 881, 889, 889n., 947
Time and Tide, 401
The Times, 79, 122, 251, 253, 305, 311, 378, 417, 585; *Literary Supplement*, 77, 77n., 86, 116, 116n., 117, 117n.
Tintoretto, 172
Titian, 172
Titus, Edward, 304n.
  Letter to, 331-32
Todd, Miss (*journalist*), 216
Togliatti, Palmiro, 586
Tolan, Michael, 831n.
Tolstoy, 115-16, 226, 363, 395, 476, 516, 552, 918
Tomorrow (*magazine*), 674, 692, 700, 727, 762
Toynbee, Arnold, 96, 594
Toynbee, Rosalind Murray, 86n , 8,
Trabuco College, 443n., 475, 495
Traherne, Thomas, 533-34, 542, 923n.
Traube, Shepard, 622, 622n., 630, 632, 765
  Letters to, 615-16, 618-19, 622-23, 627-28
Tredegar, Evan Morgan, 2nd Viscount, 128, 128n., 129, 130, 131, 139, 140, 149, 191n., 192, 322, 322n., 399n.
Tredegar, Katharine, Viscountess, 139, 140
Tree, Iris, 132, 188n.
Tree, Viola, 141
Trev: see Huxley, Mark Trevenen; Huxley, Noel Trevenen
Trevelyan, George Macaulay, 145, 168, 191n.
Trevelyan, Humphry (*son of George and Janet Trevelyan*), 191n.
Trevelyan, Janet Ward (*daughter of Thomas Humphry and Mary Augusta Ward*), 191n.
Trevelyan, Mary: see Moorman, Mary Trevelyan
Trilling, Lionel, 941
Truman, Harry S., 639
Tully, J., 296n.
Turner, J. M. W., 300
Turner, W. J., 220
Twentieth Century (*magazine*), 791, 792
Tyranny: see Liberty
Tyrrell, Frank, 67
Tzara, Tristan, 184, 185

Uexküll, Baron J. J. von, 785-86
Unconscious, the, 75-76, 81, 449, 621
Underhill, Evelyn, 504
Unesco Courier (*magazine*), 811
Unwin, J. D., 430

Urey, Harold, 909n.
Urquhart, F. F., 65, 67, 99, 168
Utopianism, 348, 351, 353, 444, 460, 462, 466, 483, 553; *see also* Communism, Liberty, Socialism
Utrillo, Maurice, 640

Vaca, Cabeza de, 529, 530
Vaihinger, Hans, 245, 299
Valéry, Paul, 184, 308n., 323n., 375, 472, 531-32, 548, 607n., 608
  Letters to, 308-9, 323-24, 388
van Druten, John, 458, 532n., 560n., 738
  Letters to, 532-33, 560
Vandervelde, Émile, 141n., 208
Vandervelde, Lalla, 141, 141n., 166, 205, 208, 209-10, 280-81
Vanity Fair (New York) (*magazine*), 206, 216, 593
Vassall, Mr (*schoolmaster*), 105
Vedanta, 485n., 569-70, 569n., 608n., 609, 613n., 614, 620, 635, 810n., 893-94, 929; *see also* Bhagavad-Gita, Upanishads
Vedanta and the West (*magazine*), 613n., 614
Velasquez, 319; 'Philip IV', 848
Venturi, Lauro, 640n.
'Venus de Milo', 59
Verdi, Giuseppi, 780
Verga, Giovanni, 342
Verhaeren, Emile, 120n.
Verlaine, Paul, 511; *quoted*, 711
Verne, Jules, *quoted*, 317
Vesey, Mr (*schoolmaster*), 28
Vessey, G. P. D., 137-38
Veuillot, Louis, 866
Victoria, Queen, 36, 535, 640
Villiers de l'Isle Adam, Philippe, 96
Vines, Sherard, 132
Vinogradoff, Julian Morrell, 125n., 127, 163
Viola, Dr, 487
Virgil, 84, 520, 524
Visionary   experience,   643-44,   643n., 668-69, 678, 679, 681, 687, 688, 693-94, 698, 699, 712, 714, 732-33, 735n., 762, 766-67, 769-73, 786, 802, 806, 863-64, 874, 909; *see also* Mysticism, Psychedelic drugs
Vittoz, Roger, 526, 527, 617, 818, 830, 902
Les Vivants (*magazine*), 533, 541, 563n.
Vlaminck, Maurice de, 640
Vogt, William, 587
Vogue (London), 191, 204, 216
Vogue (New York), 569n., 570, 646
Voisin, Auguste, 841
Volf, Christian, 626, 927
Voltaire, 103
Voss, May, 402

Wadham, J. W., 28, 28n.
Wadham, Nicholas, 28n., 32
Wagner, Richard, 47, 570
Waley, Arthur, 544, 699
Walker, Ernest, 54, 54n.